Encyclopedia of
ASIAN FOOD

Charmaine Solomon has written many books, some of which have been translated into German, French, Dutch and Norwegian. Her best known book, *The Complete Asian Cookbook*, is sold throughout the world and has become a classic over the past 20 years. It is used as a text book in teaching young chefs, as well as being a foolproof guide to great home cooking.

Other titles include:

Indian Cooking for Pleasure
Wok Cookbook
The Chinese Diet Cookbook
The Curry Cookbook
The Best of Belle International Cookbook
Love and a Wooden Spoon
Best Loved Recipes from Charmaine Solomon
Mastering the Art of Chinese Cooking
Gourmet Barbecue Cookbook
Charmaine Solomon's Thai Cookbook
The Complete Vegetarian Cookbook
Hot and Spicy Cookbook
South East Asian Cookbook
Chinese Cooking for Pleasure
The Asian Cooking Library
The Wok Book
The Hot and Spicy Book
The Vegetarian Book
The Rice and Noodle Book

CHARMAINE SOLOMON'S

Encyclopedia of
ASIAN FOOD

with Nina Solomon

NEW
HOLLAND

To my family,
and all those who share
a consuming curiosity
about comestibles

This edition published in 1998 by New Holland
Publishers (UK) Ltd
24 Nutford Place, London W1H 6DQ
London • Cape Town • Sydney • Singapore

First published in 1996 by William Heinemann Australia
Reprinted in 1997 by Hamlyn Australia,
a part of Reed Books Australia

ISBN 1 86436 378 9

Illustrations by Peter Schouten
Cover design by Mary Callahan
Text design by Brash Design Pty Ltd
Edited by Neil Conning and Associates
Typeset by Melbourne Media Services
Produced by Mandarin Book Production

Printed by Times Offset, Malaysia

Photography Credits
Photographs by Richard l'Anson, Tom Cockrem,
Greg Elms and Brian Gilkes were supplied by Great
Southern Stock.

Opposite page xvi Richard l'Anson; Opposite page 1
Brian Gilkes; Opposite page 16 Richard l'Anson;
Opposite page 17 Tom Cockrem; Opposite page 64 Brian
Gilkes; Opposite page 65 Simon Griffiths Photography;
Opposite page 80 Richard l'Anson; Opposite page 81
Brian Gilkes; Opposite page 128 Brian Gilkes; Opposite
page 129 Tom Cockrem; Opposite page 144 Simon
Griffiths Photography; Opposite page 145 Tom Cockrem;
Opposite page 192 Simon Griffiths Photography;
Opposite page 193 Richard l'Anson; Opposite page 208
Richard l'Anson; Opposite page 209 Greg Elms; Opposite
page 256 Greg Elms; Opposite page 257 Greg Elms;
Opposite page 272 Richard l'Anson; Opposite page 273
Lindsay Cox; Opposite page 320 Richard l'Anson;
Opposite page 321 Simon Griffiths Photography;
Opposite page 336 Greg Elms; Opposite page 337 Greg
Elms; Opposite page 384 Greg Elms; Opposite page 385
Brian Gilkes; Opposite page 400 Greg Elms; Opposite
page 401 Richard l'Anson

Contents

List of Illustrations   vii

Introduction   ix

How to Use the *Encyclopedia of Asian Food*   xi

Acknowledgements   xiii

A–Z of Asian Food   1

Bibliography   419

Illustrated Index of Selected Ingredients   423

Index of Recipes   457

Index of Alternative Words and Main Entries   465

List of Illustrations

Flowers 425

Banana flower
Ginger flower

Fruits 426–31

Breadfruit
Custard apple
Durian
Guava
Jakfruit
Kaffir lime
Longans
Lychee
Mangosteen
Passionfruit
Pomelo
Rambutan
Sapodilla
Soursop
Star apple
Star fruit
Tamarind, sour
Tamarind, sweet

Nuts 432–3

Betel (Areca) nuts
Candle nuts
Cashew fruit and nut
Macadamia nut and kernel
Pine nuts
Pistachio nuts

Pods and Legumes 434–6

Broad bean
Drumstick pod and leaves
Okra
Parkia
Snow pea and shoots
Soy bean
Winged beans
Yard-long bean

Gourds and other Vegetables 437–40

Bitter gourd
Chilli varieties
Eggplant (Aubergine) varieties
Fuzzy melon
Ridged gourd
Sponge gourd

Leaf Vegetables 441–3

Amaranth
Boxthorn leaves and wolfberries
Ceylon spinach
Cha plu
Chinese cabbage
   (Wong nga bak)
Chinese chard
   (Bok choy)
Chrysanthemum leaves
Mustard cabbage
   (Gai choy)
Pennywort
Purslane
Rosette bok choy
Warrigal greens

Flavourings 444–7

Basil leaves
Betel leaves
Cassia leaves
Chinese chives
Curry leaves
Eryngo leaves
Fenugreek leaves
Flowering chives
Kaffir lime leaves
Pandanus leaf
Perilla leaves
Rice paddy herb
Salam leaves
Shallots
Spring onion (Scallion)
Vietnamese mint leaves

Roots, Tubers and Rhizomes 448–9

Cassava
Greater galangal
Krachai (Chinese keys)
Taro
Turmeric
White radish (Daikon)
Yam bean

Water Plants 450–1

Lotus rhizome
Water chestnuts
Water lily
Water spinach

Mushrooms and Fungi 452–3

Black fungus (Cloud ears)
Enokitake mushrooms
Oyster mushrooms
Shiitake mushrooms
Shimeji mushrooms
Straw mushroom
White fungus

Spices 454–5

Ajowan seeds
Black cumin seeds
Cardamom pods
Cinnamon quill
Clove flowers
Cumin seeds
Fenugreek seeds
Nigella seeds
Nutmeg
Pepper
Saffron crocus flower
Star anise
Szechwan pepper

Stems 456

Bamboo shoot
Banana stem
Lemon grass

Introduction

How many times have you stood in markets in faraway places and wondered what things were and how they might be used? How often have you been shopping and, even in supermarkets, seen unfamiliar produce and felt you were missing out? In today's global market place, it is possible to buy just about anything, especially in major cities, but first you have to know what's what.

There are times, too, when eating overseas or in a restaurant, your taste buds are captivated by a dish. You remember the name, want to recreate the flavours but don't know where to start. Have you embarked on shopping expeditions for unfamiliar ingredients, only to encounter puzzled looks from shopkeepers? Perhaps you know the name of an ingredient in a foreign language but cannot be sure of its English name, the term used on the label or in a particular shop.

Having lived and shopped in the cosmopolitan city of Sydney for over thirty years and visited markets the world over, I have learned that it helps to know the names by which shopkeepers from different countries know identical items. When seeking the foods of a particular cuisine, it makes sense to shop in areas where people from that country live and purchase their needs.

The *Encyclopedia of Asian Food* aims to take the mystery out of exotic foods by describing fresh, dried and processed ingredients commonly used in Asia and the Pacific and telling you something about their purchase, preparation and storage. It explains local and traditional foods, provides recipes and discusses techniques which make it possible to create authentic dishes in your own kitchen. Coloured illustrations of selected ingredients are included for easy and accurate identification. There are translations and cross references provided in the entries as well as the Index of Alternative Words and Main Entries to help you understand non-English terms. The Index of Recipes lets you use the Encyclopedia as a cookery book, with headings leading you to recipes using the ingredients.

In the Orient, it is a strongly held belief that one's food is one's medicine and some ingredients are not only eaten as food but also have medicinal value or special social significance. Many recipes in the book are prepared from ingredients which are claimed to have healing properties. It seems a good thing if a meal you enjoy is also doing you a power of good.

Where certain foods have proven health benefits, it would be wise to take note and make use of them, always bearing in mind your own sensitivities. If a particular food does not agree with you and never has, please omit it from any recipe in which it appears. I have also provided information about a few potentially dangerous foods, as well as rules about their preparation.

I have conveyed all the useful facts I could garner, up-to-date nutritional information and some folklore about herbs, spices and other foodstuffs promising to fix everything from failing eyesight to impotence. These intriguing tidbits make entertaining reading but I would urge readers not to try self-treatment. The medicinal value of plants must be understood and prescribed by those who have studied herbal medicine and can apply their knowledge to each individual case.

The driving force behind this Encyclopedia has been collective curiosity — mine and those whose help I have sought in collating the information between these covers. Toss a question at us and we cannot rest until we find the answer. In addition to the lively minds that sought answers and the willing hands that tried out recipes, I acknowledge those who have followed some of these paths before and documented their findings. In the Bibliography I have listed publications consulted and am grateful to those who lent me precious books.

In compiling the *Encyclopedia of Asian Food* the skills acquired in my early career as a newspaper reporter were brought into play. Once more I became the news gatherer, the fact finder I was in my first job. Approaching strangers in markets and agri-scientists in botanical gardens in more than one country, following willing chefs into restaurant kitchens, watching their every move at outdoor food stalls, being invited into home kitchens on my travels to experiment with newly found ingredients I simply had to try. This book has led me on a journey of discovery, stimulating and informative.

I left Asia half a lifetime ago, settled in Australia and watched as the cuisine changed in ways I could not have imagined. With regard to 'Australian Cuisine', I found that in the 1960s anything not stamped with the 'British colonial' identity was unmistakably Continental — the continent in question being Europe. Over the years, there has been a gradual but inevitable leaning towards the cuisines of Asia. The Asian influence is also evident in many other parts of the world due to migration and the transfer of knowledge by chefs and the media. Because of the rich mix of cultures in most major cities, it is now possible to buy just about every ingredient. Having experienced Asian and Pacific foods both in the lands of origin and abroad, where substitutes are sometimes necessary, it is a special bonus to have the opportunity to share my experience of these cuisines.

COVERING HALF THE WORLD AND MORE

In terms of population and area (if one includes ocean as well as land), the *Encyclopedia of Asian Food* covers the cuisines of more than half the world. With climates as different as Kashmir and Kuala Lumpur, and people as diverse as Solomon Islanders and Sri Lankans, where is the commonality in the vast Asia Pacific region? Where, indeed, does Asia begin?

In this volume, we range as far west as Pakistan, and include India, all of North Asia (Japan, Korea and China), and South East Asia (Sri Lanka, Burma, Malaysia, Singapore, Thailand, Indonesia and the Philippines). We look at Vietnam, Laos, Cambodia. We cross the Pacific and visit its beautiful islands.

Despite differences in geography and climate, the peoples of Asia have much in common when it comes to food. Rice is almost the universal staple, and spices are cleverly used to enhance flavours from the Indian subcontinent right through South East Asia.

Indochina (Vietnam, Laos and Cambodia) acts as a culinary stepping stone between the herbs and spices of South East Asia and the distinctly different repertoire of China's cuisine.

Japanese cuisine holds itself proudly apart from China, yet uses many ingredients which originated in China. The same holds true for Korea, which surprises palates with its lavish use of chillies and garlic. Soy sauce, noodles, bean curd and bean sprouts have travelled widely over the centuries, and continue to do so.

The cuisines of the Pacific islands are relatively simple, innocent of spice, and based on the freshest of fish and fruit, with staples such as taro, sweet potato, cassava and yam. However, a Gallic touch transforms the food in French Polynesia; both the Indians and Chinese have brought changes in Fiji; across the Pacific in Hawaii, the basically Polynesian cuisine of native Hawaiians has happily blended with Japanese, Chinese, Korean and Filipino.

Although Australia and New Zealand are part of the Pacific region, the population in both countries (apart from the indigenous peoples) are recent arrivals who have brought cuisines from Europe and Britain. These are outside the scope of this book except in that phenomenon known as 'East meets West'.

Just as Westerners are discovering Asian ingredients and cooking styles, so too have people of this vast region learned and adapted from traders and conquerors in the past. Many of the fruits and vegetables — including the ubiquitous chilli pepper — came originally from South or central America, courtesy of the seafaring Spanish and Portuguese. Some spices that are such an indispensable part of South East Asian cuisine came from the Mediterranean region, North Africa and Southern Russia, via the Arab traders and the Silk Road.

I hope you feel some of the sense of discovery I have experienced researching and writing this book — a project which I feel is never going to be finished. There will always be other ingredients which will become more widely available in the future, and I will wish I could have included them in this body of work. However, as my publisher gently reminds me, there has to be a cut-off point. Even as she coaxes the manuscript from my reluctant fingers, I realise she is right and all I can do is share the road with you up to this point. I hope that reading and cooking from this book leads you to your own joyous journey of discovery.

How to Use the
Encyclopedia of Asian Food

This is an encyclopedia of ingredients more than regions or recipes, although you will also come across entries discussing places, dishes, techniques and utensils. The Index of Alternative Words and Main Entries is your complete reference. Here you'll find items not listed as main entries, including non-English names. Some foreign terms do appear as main entries, where the English translations are not known or used.

For ease of use, every entry in this book, head word or not, foreign or English, is listed in the Index of Alternative Words and Main Entries. If the word happens to be a dish, the index may refer to an entry on the country of its origin or the special ingredient which characterises that dish. Head words for main entries are featured in capital letters in the Index.

The Index of Recipes includes references to the ingredients explained in the Encyclopedia as well as local names for recipes.

To assist with identification, botanical names are given for fruits, herbs, spices and vegetables. Even these names are not immune to change, so in some instances you will find more than one Latin name; this gives you the best chance of finding the right plant in a nursery, whether or not the plant tags and nursery staff are up-to-date with botanical information. At markets, it would be best to use the local name or a foreign name that might be familiar to the vendor.

To help with the identification of unfamiliar ingredients, many of them are shown in detail in the Illustrated Index of Selected Ingredients. Each illustration has an approximate indication of size and a reference to the page of the Encyclopedia on which it is described. I hope that seeing the real thing may encourage you to try some new ingredients, and find out more about those that still mystify you. Your curiosity will determine how deeply you delve.

The entries in the Encyclopedia are in alphabetical order under the most common English name where one exists. The most widely used non-English names are listed at the end of most entries.

MEASUREMENTS FOR RECIPES

Anyone who has watched an Asian cook in action knows that all of the measurements used are 'by eye' and 'by hand'. It would be considered an affectation to use standard measuring spoons and cups. That's fine for someone who knows what they are doing and also knows how to adapt the amount of a certain ingredient used (such as chillies or ginger) according to the variety and heat of the chilli, or the age and strength of the ginger. But for the average Westerner venturing into the exciting world of Asian cooking, guidelines are required. All of the recipes in this book have been carefully tested using scales and standard 250 ml (8 fl oz) cups. Metric, imperial, and cup measurements are given.

Spoon measures are fine when it comes to teaspoons and half or quarter teaspoons. But talk about tablespoons and we are in troubled waters. In most Western countries the tablespoon measure is equivalent to 15 ml or three 5 ml teaspoons. In Australia the standard tablespoon is equal to 20 ml or four 5 ml teaspoons. When it comes right down to it, the home cook usually reaches for the home cutlery set and uses that. Those tablespoons can vary. In most recipes, and measuring most ingredients the difference is not crucial. However, when measuring gelatine, yeast, baking powder or bicarbonate of soda, a difference of 5 ml could make a dramatic difference to the result. I have given measurements in standard 5 ml teaspoons when dealing with such ingredients.

All measurements are level. A heaped spoonful has not been used because my 'heaped' could be different to yours.

When measuring dry ingredients such as flour, do not press down into the cup. Do not shake or tap the cup on the bench as that will cause the dry ingredient to settle and result in more than is intended for the recipe. Spoon in, and level off with the back of a knife so that it is just to the rim.

PRONUNCIATION

Many of the non-English words are pronounced just the way they are written, but some languages have adopted a spelling in Roman characters that reads nothing like the way it should sound.

In general, the following rules apply to vowel sounds: A as in 'father', not as in 'fat' (final 'a' is usually short); E as in 'pet', but sometimes as the a in 'fate'; I as in 'pit', but sometimes as in 'machine' (not as in pint); O as in 'potion', but sometimes as in 'pot'; U as in 'put', or 'flute' but sometimes as in 'putt'.

In the new unified system of spelling introduced some years ago in Malaysia and Indonesia, the pronunciation of the letter C can be confusing. C replaces CH (blachan is now written as blacan), or, if you're used to the Dutch-Indonesian spelling, C replaces TJ (ketjap is now written as kecap). However, the sound is still that of CH as in chump.

In Hindi, Sri Lankan, Thai, Malay and Indonesian: D is soft and sounded like 'th' in 'thus' or 'the'. I have tried to convey this by using DH; PH does not give the sound of 'f' as in English, but is a slightly aspirated P — the way it might sound if a radio announcer is too close to the microphone.

In Japanese and Chinese words double consonants are used as follows: hs as in she; sze as in see; tsi as in see; tso as in so; tsu as in sue; nga as in nah.

In most of the Asian languages, you have a choice whether you pronounce on the in-breath or the out-breath, which means that B could be P, G could be K, D could be T, J could be CH. Take for instance Chinese cabbage which some call bok choi and others call pak tsai. Or Thai crisp noodles which can be mee krob or mee grob. Or chicken which could be gai or kai. Even more puzzling in the changing L or R. Klong or krong — its all the same to the Thais, but very puzzling for foreigners, those poor befuddled people known as 'farang' or 'falang'!

In Polynesian languages where consonants seem to be in short supply, each vowel is given its full value and pronounced separately, as in luau, though sometimes they are run together as a diphthong. AI rhymes with 'why'; AU rhymes with 'wow'; EI rhymes with 'way'; OI rhymes with 'toy'.

The exception to the general rules comes in the Filipino language which borrows much from the Spanish and Portuguese. Thus: A as in grand; A as in father; O as in home; J is pronounced as H; H at the start of a word is silent; Z at the end of a word as S.

Acknowledgements

A task such as this needs many heads, many hands. I would like to thank the owners of the other heads and hands, without whose help I would still be struggling to complete it.

Chief among these is my daughter Nina, who wrote along with me, sat across the room in which piles of reference books threatened to engulf us, and tirelessly consulted volume after volume for particular pieces of information, proving herself as compulsive a researcher as her mother. With my other daughter, Deborah, we worked long and hard on reading and correcting proofs.

Anyone who has tackled the task of writing a book knows there has to be someone who takes on the day-to-day duties that do not cease to be necessary just because the word processor is running hot. That someone has been, as always, my husband Reuben who has cooked meals, gone shopping, tested recipes, rushed numerous documents to catch overnight express mail and kept the place in working order. He made innumerable cups of really good coffee when we needed them.

Wendy Hutton, friend, writer, editor and food expert has lived in Asia for 25 years and has always been a delight to bounce ideas off. Her willingness to help, her determination to get to the bottom of the trickiest problems, has sustained me during our long association.

Shirley Stackhouse, whose knowledge of things botanical is truly encyclopaedic, has come to the rescue time and again and never minds my calling her when my enquiries lead me to a dead end.

Stirling Macoboy, botanical expert and author, has also answered my questions with great patience and care.

Peter Schouten, illustrator extraordinaire, tracked down ingredients with an ardour beyond the call of duty and depicted them with accuracy and detail. It has been a pleasure to work with him.

Dr Alistair Hay, Research Scientist at the Royal Botanic Gardens in Sydney, willingly helped with information. His particular fields of research are those elusive aroids and galangals that were one of my biggest headaches.

I would especially like to thank Mr Alan Davidson in England for his prompt and friendly faxes in reply to mine, despite the fact that he is engaged in a huge project himself; and my good friend Joyce Westrip in Perth, Western Australia, who introduced us. On more than one occasion she has referred to books in her extensive library on the subject of Indian food. She is a researcher who loves the 'thrill of the chase' as much as I do.

Thanks to William Lai, a gentleman and a scholar with a wide knowledge of Chinese food, for patiently answering endless questions and for researching some items by translating Chinese texts.

Tony Tan arranged my visit to the Shah Alam Agricultural Park in Kuala Lumpur and guided me through the markets of Malaysia and was always willing to answer questions; Rachnee Howarth provided answers to my questions about the Thai language; Ida Phay guided me through the intricacies of the Burmese vocabulary; Mr I. C. Khanna, from his wide knowledge, answered my questions about India and masterminded my best research trip through the Indian subcontinent.

Long-time friends Chris and Carmel Raffel, whom I have known most of my life, entrusted me with a book dear to us all, but now out of print, *Tropical Planting and Gardening* by H. F. Macmillan, a truly useful and authoritative publication. (If anyone reading this has a copy they do not use, please contact me through my publisher, as I am going to have withdrawal symptoms when I return their copy!)

Gordon Bootes entrusted me with many of his books on food, food plants and related subjects. He generously allowed me to borrow whichever books I wanted and keep them as long as I needed.

Dr A. H. M. Jayasuriya, Curator of the National Herbarium, National Botanic Gardens, Peradeniya, Sri Lanka, sent information on members of the

Zingiberaceae family (those galangals again) and put me in touch with Dr R. L. Burtt of the Royal Botanic Garden in Edinburgh, who was also very helpful.

Mrs Charmalie Abayasekara, botanist, University of Peradeniya, and Professor M.D. Dassanayake, Emeritus Professor of Botany, Faculty of Science, University of Peradeniya, Sri Lanka also answered questions.

Dr Ismail Idris, Deputy Farm Director of Universiti Pertanian, Malaysia, devoted time to taking me around the plant nursery to identify exotic herbs and spices.

I appreciate the interest from people who knew of the project I was engaged in, who wrote from afar and sent books and snippets of information pertaining to the work, among them Trisha Arbib and Howard Nicholson of Bundanoon Village Nursery and Shirley Fenton-Huie, author and travel writer, a source of information and inspiration. Friends from Sri Lanka answered my questions about everything from jakfruit to drumstick leaves, when my own memory proved wanting.

Thanks to my editor Neil Conning for his concentration and his patience. If you think the book is a big one now, you should have seen the manuscript before he took to it with his blue pencil!

Last but by no means least I would like to thank my publisher, Sue Hines, who cooks my recipes in her own home, and tells me she has done so for many years, long before we met and started a business relationship. Her trust both in my recipes and in my ability to undertake and fulfil this huge project has made the long haul a very pleasant one.

A–Z
of
ASIAN
FOOD

Abalone

The scientific name for abalone is *Haliotis ruber* or *H. laevigata*, depending on whether it has a black lip or green lip. Then again it might be *H. tuberculata* (from the Atlantic) or *H. lamellosa* (from the Mediterranean), or *H. rufescens*, the true abalone or red abalone, fished in southern Californian waters.

The word 'abalone' is in fact the Californian Spanish name for the species known as 'sea ears'. One look at the handsome shells will tell you why. These much-sought-after molluscs with a firm texture and delicate flavour may be purchased fresh, canned or dried.

Assuming you are willing to pay the asking price for fresh abalone, two to three times the cost of premium eye fillet, you must be prepared to tackle it with scouring brush and sharp knife. The sharp knife is necessary to remove the intestines and frilly outer rim and the brush to scrub away the dark coating from the foot (white fleshy portion), which is the edible part. This part is muscle, which the abalone tenses when wrenched from its rock, so it is necessary to cut it into paper-thin slices, against the grain and then beat the slices with a mallet until tender. Next, decide whether you want your abalone short-cooked or long-cooked. The first way is literally a matter of a few seconds, the second requires many hours of gentle simmering.

Canned abalone varies in tenderness depending on the processing, Japanese brands usually being the best but also the most expensive. Slice finely and add to cooked dishes at the last moment, since it needs no further cooking. Or marinate the slices in soy sauce, mirin, a few drops of sesame oil and pinch of sugar and serve as part of a cold hors d'oeuvre. Don't waste the liquid in the can either: add it to soups for a delicious flavour.

Dried abalone needs to be soaked for 4 days, scrubbed clean and trimmed, simmered for at least 4 hours, drained, rinsed, trimmed and sliced before using. The whole thing is rather daunting and canned or fresh abalone produces better results.

Burma: *baun*
China: *bow yu*
Indonesia: *lapar kenyang*
Japan: *awabi*
Malaysia: *siput*
Thailand: *hoy knong thaleh*

Marinated Abalone

Slice the larger pieces of abalone for this and save the frills and trimmings to chop finely and add to the soup which follows.

425 g/14 oz can abalone
2 tablespoons Japanese soy sauce
2 tablespoons mirin
2 teaspoons sugar
1 teaspoon oriental sesame oil
1 teaspoon ginger juice (squeezed from grated fresh ginger)

With a sharp knife cut the abalone into paper-thin slices. Marinate with a mixture of 2 tablespoons each of Japanese soy sauce and mirin, 2 teaspoons each of sesame oil and ginger juice. Cover and leave for 10 minutes, then serve, still in the marinade, among other cold hors d'oeuvres. For a more decorative presentation, arrange abalone slices in a fan pattern, alternately with very thin slices of cucumber. Halve the circular cucumber slices if large so they are more or less the same size as the slices of abalone so the green skin and white centre provide effective contrast.

Abalone and Shiitake Soup

If you want to make a can of this expensive ingredient go further than one dish, use the liquid from the can and the trimmings of abalone for this soup. Serves 5–6.

100 g/3½ oz fresh shiitake mushrooms
1 tablespoon peanut oil
salt and pepper to taste
425 g/14 oz can abalone
1 litre/2 pints de-fatted Chinese chicken stock
1 tablespoon light soy sauce
1 teaspoon sugar
1 tablespoon cornflour (cornstarch)
3 tablespoons cold water
1 egg, lightly beaten
1 tablespoon very finely chopped garlic chives
¼ teaspoon oriental sesame oil

Wipe over mushrooms and slice thinly. Heat peanut oil and on gentle heat sauté mushroom slices until softened, seasoning with salt and pepper. Drain abalone and add the liquid (approximately 1 cup) to the chicken stock. Finely chop trimmings of abalone.

Heat the stock to boiling, add soy sauce and sugar and season to taste, then stir in cornflour mixed with cold water and boil until it becomes clear and thickens slightly. Pour beaten egg into the boiling soup in a thin stream, without stirring. Sprinkle in garlic chives. Remove from heat and stir in abalone and sesame oil. Serve at once.

Acid Fruits

In Asian cooking, acid flavours are achieved by adding fruit juice, pulp or whole fruits with piquant flavours. Some acid fruits, e.g. tamarind, are widely available and well known. Others are only known in the area of origin.

Some common acid fruits are: belimbing or billing (*Averrhoa bilimbi*) which looks like a miniature cucumber with thin, pale green skin and belongs to the same family as star fruit; gamboge (*Garcinia cambogia*) which starts out as a brilliant orange-coloured segmented fruit but is dried for storing, turning black in the process; and asam gelugor (*G. atroviridis*), a sour fruit which is sliced, dried and used instead of tamarind in certain Malay dishes.

What leads to confusion is the free-wheeling labelling of some producers, who refer to gamboge as 'fish tamarind' and gelugor as 'tamarind slices', though they are not even from the same botanical family as tamarind. The fact that they provide acidity is reason enough — for them, at any rate — to justify the mislabelling. See GAMBOGE, GELUGOR.

In India, unripe mangoes are dried and ground into a powder called amchur which is useful when a piquant flavour is required without the liquid element of lime juice or tamarind. See MANGO. Dried pomegranate seeds, anardhana, are used in Indian cooking and added to certain dishes for a sour flavour. See POMEGRANATE.

Limes of many different types are used throughout Asia, with some kinds being favoured in certain countries. In the Philippines, kalamansi (small round citrus fruits also called musk lime) are indispensable. Malaysian cooks use limau nipis (a large lime) and limau kesturi (another name for kalamansi). In Indonesia, Malaysia and Sri Lanka, tamarind and fresh lime juice are as essential as salt. See TAMARIND. In Thailand, cooks cannot do without the highly perfumed rind and leaves of makrut (kaffir lime), a deep green fruit with knobbly skin. See LIME.

Acorn

All species of oak produce edible acorns, but those from the English oak (*Quercus robur*) are very astringent and need to be boiled in water or ground and washed thoroughly to remove the water soluble tannins. Some acorns are so sweet they can be eaten like chestnuts, boiled or roasted.

The acorns eaten in China are *Q. cornea*; in Japan, *Q. cuspidata*. A Japanese food firm recently introduced acorn wheat noodles, donguri udon, made by adding just under 10 per cent of ground acorn to wheat flour. The noodles acquire a nutty flavour and it is said that the presence of tannin helps rid the body of oxides.

In Korea, where acorns have long been eaten, acorn starch (mook) is boiled with water to make a gelatinous 'blancmange'. See FLOURS & STARCHES.

Medicinal uses: Acorns are astringent and are an old remedy for diarrhoea.

Adzuki Bean

See LEGUMES & PULSES.

Agar-Agar

Vegetable 'gelatine' derived from a number of sea-weeds (*Gelidium amansii*) which are processed by boiling and drying. Agar-agar is used as a quick-setting base for many sweets and desserts in Asia. Refrigerators are a luxury many people in Asia do not have, and agar-agar's chief advantage is that it will set without refrigeration and not melt down in tropical heat. It is also used as a finishing glaze.

Agar-agar is more readily available in Asia than gelatine. It also has the advantage of being 'halal', so is acceptable to Moslems while gelatine, derived from animals, is not.

Purchasing and storing: Refined agar-agar is purchased as fine white powder in small packets, or extruded into large square sticks (sometimes coloured) which the Japanese call kanten, or fine, crinkly strands (usually in bundles bound with pink raffia ties) in long cellophane packets. These strands are used, soaked in cold water and softened, as a texture ingredient to supplement the very expensive bird's nest in soups, and also as an addition to cold platters or salads in Chinese cuisine. Dried forms of agar-agar will keep indefinitely in an airtight container.

Preparation: Quantities should be measured carefully, depending on the result required. Each form of agar-agar needs a different approach.

If using powder, sprinkle it over the surface of the measured water in a saucepan, bring to the boil, and it should dissolve in a few minutes of simmering. If using strands or sticks, soak in cold water for an hour, drain, bring to the boil in the measured amount of water and simmer until dissolved.

Sugar, flavouring and colouring are added and it sets as a firm jelly without refrigeration, even in tropical climates. It is the base for the famous Almond Bean Curd, Coconut Jelly, Awayuki and numerous other sweets throughout Asia.

Burma: *kyauk kyaw*
China: *dai choy goh*
Indonesia: *agar-agar*
Malaysia: *agar-agar*
Japan: *kanten*
Philippines: *gulaman*
Sri Lanka: *chun chow*
Thailand: *woon*

Almond Bean Curd

Serves 8

1 litre/2 pints/14 cups water
4 teaspoons agar-agar powder
400ml/14 fl oz can sweetened condensed milk
1½ teaspoons almond essence

Measure water into a saucepan, sprinkle agar-agar powder over surface or add soaked agar-agar strands. One cup of soaked and drained agar-agar strands may be used instead of the agar-agar powder. Bring to the boil, stir until agar-agar is dissolved. Turn off heat and add condensed milk and almond essence, stirring well. Pour into a large shallow dish and leave to set. Cut into diamond shapes and serve on its own, or with a mixture of oriental fruits such as canned lychees or longans, canned mandarin segments, or fresh melon balls.

Japanese Jelly Dessert (Awayuki)

Serves 6

1½ sticks kanten
  or 4 teaspoons agar-agar powder
250 g/8 oz/1 cup sugar
3 tablespoons strained lemon juice
  or fruit flavoured liqueur
2 egg whites
lemon slices or strawberry fans for decoration

If using kanten, break sticks into pieces and soak in 2 cups water for 30 minutes, then bring to boil and simmer until completely dissolved. If using agar-agar powder, sprinkle evenly over surface of 2 cups water in a saucepan and stir until it boils and dissolves. Add sugar and stir to dissolve. Remove from heat and stir in lemon juice.

Whisk egg whites in a clean, dry bowl until stiff. When agar-agar mixture is still slightly warm add it to the egg whites, mixing well. (Do not let it cool too much or it will set before you can mix it into the egg whites.) Pour into a mould or individual dishes and leave to set. Chill and decorate.

Coconut Jelly

A favourite in Burma, where it is called kyauk kyaw (pronounced chow chaw), Burmese for agar-agar, or any jelly made from it. Serves 8.

**7 g/¼ oz agar-agar strands
  or 4 teaspoons agar-agar powder
400 ml/14 fl oz can coconut milk
375 ml/12 fl oz/1½ cups water
125 ml/4 fl oz/½ cup canned coconut cream
125 g/4 oz/½ cup sugar
rose water to flavour**

Soak the strands of agar-agar in cold water overnight or at least 1 hour. Drain and measure. There should be 1½ cups, loosely packed.

Put the strands with coconut milk and water into a saucepan and stir constantly while bringing to the boil. Add sugar and keep stirring and simmering 10–15 minutes or until all the strands are completely dissolved.

If using agar-agar powder, sprinkle over the coconut milk, add sugar and simmer for 10 minutes. Remove from heat and stir in the coconut cream.

Flavour to taste, then pour into a dish rinsed out with cold water and allow to set. Cut into diamond shapes or squares. This firm jelly is meant to be picked up with the fingers.

Agar-Agar Salad

Serves 4

**30 g/1 oz refined agar-agar strands
1 bundle flowering garlic chives
3 eggs
salt and pepper to taste
1 tablespoon peanut oil
250 g/8 oz fresh bean sprouts**

DRESSING

**1 clove garlic
1 teaspoon sugar
3 tablespoons light soy sauce
2 tablespoons oriental sesame oil
2 teaspoons honey**

Soak agar-agar strands in cold water for 30 minutes to one hour while preparing the rest of the salad. Wash the flowering chives and snap off any tough lower ends. Finely chop some of the stalks to yield about

3 tablespoons. Cut the rest of the chives into bite-sized lengths and drop into boiling water for 30 seconds, then drain and immerse in iced water to set the colour. Drain as soon as they are cold.

Beat the eggs, season with salt and pepper and stir in chopped chives. Heat a heavy frying pan and cook just enough egg mixture to coat the pan with a thin layer. When set but not browned turn egg sheet onto a plate and rub pan lightly with oil before making another. Continue until all the egg is used up. When cool, cut into thin strips (to make this easier, stack egg sheets and roll them into a cylindrical shape first).

Wash bean sprouts, pinching off any straggly tails. Drain the agar-agar well and cut into bite-sized strips. Combine all the ingredients, cover and chill.

In a bowl whisk together the dressing, first crushing the garlic to a smooth paste with the sugar. Pour over the salad, toss and serve.

Note: To make this a more substantial dish, cold noodles, strips of cold cooked chicken or slices of smoked bean curd may be added.

Aji-no-moto

See MONOSODIUM GLUTAMATE.

Ajowan

(*Carum ajowan*) SEE ILLUSTRATION. Also spelled ajwain, Hindi name for the tiny, pungent seed of a herb belonging to the same family as cumin and parsley (Umbelliferae). It is also known as bishop's weed, omum and carom seed. It looks like celery seed, but the flavour is more like thyme.

Ajowan is used in Indian lentil dishes, but always used sparingly as the flavour is very strong. A guide is to use 1 teaspoon ajowan seeds for every 2 cups of dhal or lentil flour. It is also recommended that 1 teaspoon is used for every 4 cups of wheat flour when making Indian breads. Ajowan is used more generously in Indian pickles.

Medicinal uses: Ajowan contains thymol which is a germicide and antiseptic and is prescribed for diarrhoea, colic and other bowel problems, helping expel wind and mucus. Sometimes used in the treatment of asthma, the seeds being smoked in a pipe to relieve shortness of breath. Water in which ajowan seeds have been boiled is used to 'cleanse the eyes and cure the ears of deafness.' It is said that if ajowan seeds are soaked in the juice of a lemon and dried 7 times, then ingested, they cure impotence. (No guarantees!)

India: *ajwain, omum*

Deep Fried Crisps (Sev, Murukku)

Ajowan flavours a spicy Indian snack.

250 g/8 oz/2 cups besan (chick pea flour)
125 g/4 oz/1 cup ground rice
2 teaspoons garam masala (recipe page 354)
2 teaspoons salt
1 teaspoon ajowan seeds
1 teaspoon cumin seeds, lightly crushed
1 teaspoon chilli powder (optional)
4 tablespoons melted ghee
approx. 250 ml/8 fl oz/1 cup water

Sift besan and ground rice into a bowl and stir in the garam masala, salt, ajowan and cumin seeds, and the chilli powder if used. Rub in ghee, add water a little at a time and knead to a stiff dough, suitable for pressing through a mould if you have one, or you may use a potato ricer or hand shredder.

Heat sufficient oil for deep frying (it takes less in a wok or karhai) and push dough through mould into the hot oil, not adding too much at a time. Fry on medium heat until golden brown, lift out on slotted spoon and drain on paper towels. Continue frying in batches until all the dough is used up, replenishing the oil as necessary.

Cool completely before storing in an airtight container. More chilli powder and salt may be sprinkled over before serving.

Almond

(*Prunus dulcus*) An edible nut mentioned in the Old Testament, the almond is probably native to the eastern Mediterranean. It is much prized in the Moghul style cooking of northern India with its Persian influence. Almonds are eaten fresh, used as a base for fudge-like candies (Badam Barfi), ground into a nourishing beverage and used to thicken sauces in braised meat dishes like korma. They are also made into rich, creamy desserts such as Creamed Almonds.

Since they do not grow well in the tropics and prefer the cold climate of Kashmir and Afghanistan, their lavish use is confined to northern India. In other parts of Asia, cashews and other nuts take their place.

Purchasing and storing: Make sure almonds are fresh by purchasing from a vendor whose stock moves quickly. If buying more than you will use fairly soon, store in the freezer to keep them sweet and fresh, because nuts, being high in oil content, are likely to go rancid if left at room temperature through summer months.

Almonds are available in their shells, natural (shelled but with the brown inner skin left on), blanched (skin removed) either whole or in halves, slivered, flaked (sliced), chopped or ground. Never has a nut been easier to purchase in whatever form you may wish to use.

Preparation: Natural almonds have more flavour than blanched ones, but when blanching is necessary it is quite easily done by dropping the almonds into a small pan of boiling water for 1 minute, then draining and plunging into cold water. Press firmly on the skins and the almonds will pop out. If not using at once, dry thoroughly, but I recommend blanching almonds only as you need them.

Freshly ground almonds are nicest, but this depends on your having the time and the requisite appliance to grind nuts. High-speed electric blenders are not very successful as they make the almonds oily. There are small, quite inexpensive nut graters which do a good job, and some of the larger appliances have fine graters which work well.

Medicinal: High in protein, almonds are looked upon as nourishment, not merely a treat. During hot weather in India, a cool almond drink is considered as sustaining as a meal, and mothers with school children who are sitting for examinations make it a point to serve this drink to them, for it is supposed to nourish the brain. The traditional way of making it involves much pounding using mortar and pestle, but the modern, quick way is used in the following recipe.

See also recipe for Thandai under DRINKS & BEVERAGES (page 123).

China: *hung yun*
India: *badam*

Almond

Almond Beverage (Thandai)

Serves 4

90 g/3 oz blanched almonds
10 whole peppercorns (optional)
60 g/2 oz raw sunflower seeds or pumpkin seeds
½ teaspoon cardamom seeds
** or ground cardamom**
750 ml/1½ pints/3 cups water
500 ml/1 pint/2 cups milk
125 g/4 oz/½ cup sugar or to taste
rose water (optional)

In an electric blender combine almonds, peppercorns and seeds with half the water and blend at high speed until finely ground. Strain into a jug using double thickness of clean muslin. Press out as much moisture as possible, then return the residue to the blender with the remaining water and repeat.

Mix strained liquid with milk and sugar to taste, and a dash of rose water if liked. Pour over crushed ice and serve.

Note: Save the ground almond meal and use it for thickening curries, particularly northern Indian classics like lamb korma. Or collect in a freezer container and when you have sufficient, make one of the almond sweetmeats below. Leave out the peppercorns for this. See also SWEETMEATS, INDIAN.

Almond Cream Fudge (Badam Barfi)

This is sold in Indian sweet shops in large, flat diamond shapes on which thin sheets of edible silver are sometimes pressed for decoration.

1 litre/2 pints/4 cups milk
185 g/6 oz/¾ cup white sugar
375 g/12 oz blanched ground almonds
½ teaspoon ground cardamom
** or 6 drops cardamom extract**
2 tablespoons blanched pistachio nuts
edible silver leaf (optional)

In a heavy saucepan (preferably one with a non-stick surface) boil the milk, stirring constantly until it has reduced and thickened. Add the sugar and stir over low heat. Add ground almonds and cardamom, and continue cooking and stirring until mixture leaves sides of pan in one mass.

Turn onto a buttered dish and quickly smooth top with the back of a buttered spoon, or press a lightly buttered piece of banana leaf (or aluminium foil) on the surface, and roll lightly with a rolling pin to smooth and flatten the surface. Remove foil and when sweet is almost cold, decorate with pistachio nuts which have been blanched for 30 seconds in boiling water. Remove the skins and split pistachios in two, or cut into slivers. If using silver leaf decoration, handle it very delicately, holding with the interleaved pieces of tissue and gently fluttering the silver leaf (varak) onto the surface.

Creamed Almonds (Badam Kheer)

Serves 4

1 litre/2 pints/4 cups milk
300 ml/10 fl oz cream
1 tablespoon ghee or unsalted butter
100 g/3½ oz/1 cup flaked almonds
125 g/4 oz/½ cup sugar
pinch saffron strands
½ teaspoon ground cardamom
flaked almonds for garnish

In a heavy saucepan combine milk, cream and ghee and bring to the boil, stirring constantly. Turn heat very low, add almonds and sugar and stir till sugar dissolves. Simmer for 20 minutes or until the mixture reduces and is as thick as a custard, during which time only an occasional stir is necessary. In a small pan toast the saffron strands for 1 minute over medium heat, until they just dry out. Make sure they don't blacken. Turn the saffron at once onto a saucer and leave to cool and crisp, then crush with the back of a spoon. Dissolve in a tablespoon of boiling water and stir into the almond mixture together with the ground cardamom. Pour into individual dishes or one serving dish, cool and chill. Garnish with extra flaked almonds before serving.

Amaranth

(*Amaranthus gangeticus*) SEE ILLUSTRATION. There are many members of the amaranth family. They are known as careless weed, pig weed and other uncomplimentary names, but all are eaten in various parts of the world. Some are grown primarily for their seed which is treated as a grain, others are decorative, and some are considered weeds — *A. alba*, *A. lividus*, *A. retroflexus*. All are edible.

We are concerned with those cultivated as a leaf vegetable, among them *A. tricolor*, *A. oleraceus*, *A. dubius* and *A. spinosus*.

The two main types grown as a leafy food crop are loosely termed green amaranth and red amaranth. (Red amaranth also includes ornamental varieties such as 'Joseph's Coat' 'Red Stripe' and 'Early Splendour'.)

Red amaranth is sold as 'Chinese spinach' (though it is not spinach), 'een choy' or 'hsien'.

The plant has dark green leaves splotched and deeply veined in red. It is delicious, cooks quickly and has even more nutritional value than spinach. Recognise it by its pink roots and oval leaves which may have patches of red along the centre vein.

Green amaranth grows to about a metre tall. The leaves are oval with pointed tips and slightly furry undersides, and have a flavour that stands up to spices. Amaranth is higher in protein than many beans and contains vitamin A, calcium and iron

If the weeds in your garden turn out to be the ubiquitous green amaranth, give thanks to Mother Nature and make the best of it. Don't spray with weed killer and don't pull them out by the roots. Pinch out the tender tops of the plants and cook them. Wherever you pick, the plant branches and produces more leaves, providing an inexhaustible source of fresh greens throughout the warmer months. Remove any flowers which develop. These are small and insignificant, forming on small flexible spikes at the crown of the plant.

Some species of Amaranthus, especially *A. leucocarpus* produce seeds in abundance. When mature, these are gathered and ground into meal by native North Americans and Latin Americans.

Purchasing and storing: Like any leafy vegetable, buy fresh and sprightly looking bunches with the roots on. If only leaves are sold, cook and eat them as soon as possible. If you do have to keep them a day or two, wrap them in damp paper, put this in a plastic bag and refrigerate. Whole plants will keep in the same way for about a week, but remember that the fresher it is when consumed, the more food value it will have.

Preparation: Discard roots and tough lower stems. Wash very thoroughly to get rid of sand which is harboured in most leafy vegetables. Cook as spinach, add to soups, or stir-fry with spices.

Medicinal uses: Chinese people eat amaranth during summer, believing it to 'reduce internal heat and dampness'. It is most often added to soups, but also stir-fried with garlic. The roots are used to alleviate colds, and are also considered a diuretic.

China: *een choy, yin choy, in-tsai, hsien tsai, xian cai.*
Japan: *hiyuna*
India: *marsa*
Indonesia: *bayam*
Malaysia: *bayam*
Laos: *pak hom*
Philippines: *kulitis*
Sri Lanka: *thampala*
Thailand: *pak khom hat, pak khom suan*
Vietnam: *yan yang*

Stir-Fried Green Amaranth with Coconut

Serves 4–6

250 g/8 oz/4 cups green amaranth leaves
2 tablespoons oil
1 onion, finely chopped
1 teaspoon crushed garlic
1 teaspoon grated fresh ginger
½ teaspoon ground turmeric
1 teaspoon chilli powder
¼ teaspoon salt or to taste
6 tablespoons grated fresh coconut
  or 3 tablespoons desiccated coconut

Wash the leaves and shake off the water. Roll them in a bundle and shred finely, or chop in food processor. Heat the oil and fry the onion, garlic and ginger over low heat until fragrant, stirring frequently. Add the ground spices, then the leaves. Stir-fry for a minute, then sprinkle with salt and a few tablespoons of water. Mix in coconut. Cover and simmer for 5 minutes or until liquid evaporates. Serve with rice.

Red Amaranth with Garlic and Oyster Sauce

Serves 4–6

1 bunch red amaranth
2 tablespoons oil
1 teaspoon crushed garlic
2 tablespoons oyster sauce
2 teaspoons sugar
2 teaspoons cornflour (cornstarch)

Wash amaranth and shake dry. Discard lower stems which may be tough. Pick leaves and cut tender stems into bite-sized pieces. Heat oil in a wok and fry the garlic on low heat, stirring until it is pale golden. Add the amaranth, increase heat to medium and toss with a spatula until the leaves are wilted. Add oyster sauce and sugar, cover with lid and allow to steam for a minute or two. Meanwhile, combine cornflour with 2 tablespoons of cold water in a small bowl. Stir into liquid in pan until it boils and thickens. Serve at once with steamed rice.

Amaranth with Flowering Chives

Serves 4–6

1 bunch amaranth
1 bunch flowering chives
2 teaspoons oriental sesame oil
1 tablespoon light soy sauce
½ teaspoon sugar

Wash and prepare amaranth as described in preceding recipe, but do not shake off the water. Wash flowering chives, snap or trim off tough lower ends of stalks. Cut into bite-sized lengths and combine with amaranth leaves in a heatproof dish. Steam over boiling water or put into a saucepan with well-fitting lid and steam on very low heat with just the water that remains on the leaves, about 7 minutes or until wilted but still deep green. Remove to a serving dish. Combine sesame oil, soy sauce and sugar, drizzle over the leaves and serve. Or use as a bed for steamed fish fillets, shrimp or prawns.

Amaranth with Red Lentils

Serves 6

125 g/4 oz/2 cups green amaranth leaves
300 g/10 oz/1½ cups red lentils
500 ml/1 pint/2 cups thin coconut milk
1 dried red chilli
1 teaspoon turmeric
2 teaspoons pounded Maldive fish
1 tablespoon oil
sprig of fresh curry leaves
strip of fresh or dried pandan leaf
1 onion, finely sliced
1 small cinnamon quill
lower portion of stem of lemon grass, bruised
salt to taste
3 tablespoons thick coconut milk

Wash amaranth, pick the leaves and put into a saucepan. Pick over red lentils, discarding any small stones. Wash lentils in several changes of water, drain, and add to saucepan with thin coconut milk. This could be canned coconut milk diluted with water if it is thick and rich. Discard stalk and seeds of chilli, break the chilli into pieces and add to pan with turmeric and Maldive fish. Bring to a boil, lower heat and simmer until lentils are soft and like thick soup. Add a little extra water if necessary.

In another pan heat the oil and fry curry leaves, pandan leaf, sliced onion, cinnamon and lemon grass, stirring frequently, until onion starts to colour. Add contents of first saucepan, stir in thick coconut milk and simmer uncovered for 5 minutes. Serve with rice.

Ambarella

(*Spondias cytherea*, *S. dulcis*) Other names for this fruit and close relatives are Otaheite apple, Tahitian quince, Jamaica plum, golden apple and wi. The general consensus is that it is indigenous to Polynesia, but it grows in Asia's tropical zones too. Foreigners living where this fruit grows refer to it by its local name, whatever that happens to be.

The tree grows tall, reaching almost 20 m (60 ft).

The fruit, which is popular in Asia, is plum shaped, sweet-sour and eaten at all stages of ripeness. Its distinguishing feature is a spiny seed. The spines toughen as the fruit matures, so that when eating conserve made from the almost-ripe fruit the sweet flesh should be carefully sucked from the seed to avoid an unsolicited lip-piercing or a tough fibre stuck between the teeth.

In the unripe stages the green skin is peeled with a knife and slices of the firm, pale flesh dipped in chilli powder and salt before being relished by street-side snackers or school children. Unripe fruit is also cooked in chutneys.

As the fruit ripens it becomes yellow to orange in colour and more fragrant and sweet, though still with a good percentage of acidity. It has been described as having a flavour like pineapple. Ambarellas are sometimes simmered in curries, but are more commonly cooked with sugar and a stick of cinnamon and are popular with home cooks for jams, jellies and cordials. Being high in pectin, it is sometimes added to other low-pectin fruit to obtain a good set when making jams and jellies.

A member of the same botanical family, *S. mombin*, is referred to as hog plum or hog apple, but there are differences. Another member of the Spondias clan is *S. pinnata* which is grown in Thailand for its leaves (served raw with nam prik), its fruit (added to green papaya salad) and its bark.

Purchasing and storing: Buy hard, greenish fruit if you wish to make chutneys or eat them as a sour snack. Look for yellowing skin for half-ripe fruit and a deep-yellow skin if you want them ripe. Being a hard fruit, they keep well.

Medicinal uses: The bark of the tree can be used to cure diarrhoea.

Fiji: *wi*
India: *jungli amba*
Indonesia: *kedondong*
Malaysia: *kedondong*
Sri Lanka: *ambarella*
Tahiti: *otaheite apple*
Thailand: *ma-kok farang*
Vietnam: *trai coc*

Ambarella Conserve

500 g/1 lb ripe ambarellas
500 g/1 lb/2 cups white sugar
250 ml/8 fl oz/1 cup water
1 small stick cinnamon
2 tablespoons rose water
  or 4 drops rose essence

Wash the ambarellas well and prick them all over with a fork. Put sugar and water into a

heavy pan and bring to the boil, stirring to dissolve the sugar. Add ambarellas and cinnamon stick and boil over medium heat, stirring frequently, until fruit is translucent and syrup thick. Remove from heat, stir in rose water or essence. Bottle in hot sterile jars.

Ambarella and Raisin Chutney

1 kg/2 lb half-ripe ambarellas
250 g/8 oz sultanas (golden raisins)
125 g/4 oz raisins
1 tablespoon finely crushed garlic
2 tablespoons finely grated fresh ginger
750 ml/1½ pints/3 cups white vinegar
750 g/1½ pounds/3 cups white sugar
2 tablespoons/30 g/1 oz salt
10 dried red chillies
  or fresh hot chillies
5 whole cloves
1 stick cinnamon

Wash and slice the fruit, discarding seeds. Put into a non-aluminium, heavy based saucepan with all the remaining ingredients, first breaking off and discarding stems of chillies and shaking out the seeds. Bring to the boil, stirring, and cook over low heat until thick, about 1½ hours. Use a heat diffuser if necessary to keep chutney from scorching at base of pan. Fill hot sterile jars and cover with non-metal lids.

Anchovy

Billions of these little fish are continually being caught, dried, salted, made into fish sauce and other fish products. They are also cooked freshly caught, the main disadvantage being that there is considerable cleaning and preparation as each fish is no bigger than 12 cm (5 in) and most of them are much smaller. These small fish are sometimes loosely labelled sprats, a name applied to any small fish.

I prefer the very small ones because when they are dipped in seasoned flour and deep fried, even the bones become meltingly crisp. One variety of tiny fish with a silvery stripe running the length of the body is sold dried in packets labelled ikan bilis or ikan teri. They make a delicious snack, deep fried with peanuts and sprinkled with a touch of chilli powder and sugar. See recipe for Fried Anchovies with Peanuts (page 10).

Fresh anchovies have white flesh and it is only after salting and leaving for at least a month that they develop the red colour and special taste that one associates with fermented anchovies in jars or cans.

I am indebted to Alan Davidson for permission to quote from his book *Seafood of South East Asia* how anchovies are preserved at Chanburi, Thailand.

The anchovies should be fresh from the sea and of the most soft tender variety.

2 cupfuls anchovies, well cleaned
with sea water
3 to 4 cups rock salt
2 tablespoonfuls best quality plain vinegar
3 tablespoonfuls brown sugar
½ cup kao koi (uncooked rice which has been
toasted in a dry pan and then pounded to a
powder while still hot)
2 tablespoonfuls galingale which has been
grated and then dried out in the sun to make
it fluffy

Marinate the fish in a mixture of the salt and vinegar for 1 to 2 hours, until they are soft and juicy, then mix well with the brown sugar and add the kao koi and galingale [galangal]. Let the preparation mature in a sterilised glass container for 3 to 4 months, or until the anchovies turn brown, with a clear liquid formed on top and a good aroma arising from the brew.

When you come to eat these preserved anchovies, season them with finely cut lemon grass, young ginger, spring onion, tamarind juice (made by squeezing fully ripe tamarind fruit with warm water until it turns into a brownish liquid), a little sugar and lime juice to taste.

Burma: *nga-nan-gyaung*
Cambodia: *ca cum*
Hong Kong: *lung yue*
Indonesia: *ikan bilis, ikan teri*
Malaysia: *ikan bilis, ikan teri*
Singapore: *ikan bilis, ikan teri*
Philippines: *dilis*
Sri Lanka: *haal masso*
Vietnam: *ca com*

Fresh Anchovy Relish

Serves 6

250 g/8 oz fresh small anchovies,
    about 5–8 cm/2–3 in size
2 pieces dried gamboge
    or small knob dried tamarind or half a lime
3 tablespoons oil
1 large onion, finely chopped
2 teaspoons finely chopped garlic
sprig of fresh curry leaves
2 teaspoons salt
2 teaspoons chilli powder

Wash the fish well, removing heads and intestines. Wash in several changes of water, adding gamboge, tamarind or lime to the washing water. Drain.

Heat oil and add remaining ingredients. Fry for 5 minutes on high heat, then add anchovies, turn heat low and simmer for 10 minutes. Taste and adjust seasoning. Serve as a hot relish with rice.

Fried Anchovies with Peanuts

A delicious crisp nibble served with drinks, the salt, fish, hot and sweet flavours competing for attention.

peanut oil for deep frying
90 g/3 oz/1 cup dried small anchovies (ikan bilis)
150 g/5 oz/1 cup raw peanuts
1 teaspoon caster sugar (superfine sugar)
½ teaspoon salt
½ teaspoon chilli powder

Heat oil in a wok and fry anchovies over medium heat until pale brown. Remember they will continue to darken even after being removed from the heat. Lift out on a slotted spoon and drain on paper towels. Fry the peanuts in the oil until golden brown, lift out and drain. Mix sugar, salt and chilli powder and sprinkle over the combined fish and peanuts, tossing well. Cool and serve. If not serving straight away, cool and store airtight for a day or two.

Anise Pepper

See SZECHWAN PEPPER.

Aniseed

(*Pimpinella anisum*) Not used in Asian cooking though saunf (Hindi for fennel) is frequently wrongly translated as aniseed. Aniseed and fennel both have a licorice flavour which is stronger in aniseed. If a recipe calls for aniseed, fennel seeds can be used instead.

The other spice which provides a sweet licorice flavour is star anise, but this is a different plant and is used mainly in Chinese and Vietnamese food. See STAR ANISE.

Annatto

(*Bixa orellana*) An evergreen flowering tree which grows throughout central and South America and was introduced to the Philippines by the sea-faring Spanish. Heart-shaped scarlet fruits which grow in showy bunches contain numerous small rust-red seeds sold as annatto or achuete. Annatto is also sold in powdered form.

Annatto is widely used in the Philippines. The colour is leeched from the seeds by cooking them in oil or fat, the seeds discarded and the oil used to cook food and give it a bright orange-yellow colour. Perhaps the most famous Filipino dish which counts annatto as an essential ingredient is Beef Stew (Kari-kari). See recipe page 36. In the recipe below annatto is used to colour what would otherwise be a somewhat pallid dish. See also FOOD COLOURINGS.

Philippines: *achuete, atsuete*
Vietnam: *hot dieu mau*

Chicken with Bean Thread Noodles

Serves 6

1 × 1.5 kg/3 lb roasting chicken
3 sprigs celery leaves
1 carrot
1 onion studded with 4 cloves
½ teaspoon whole black peppercorns
2 teaspoons salt
250 g/8 oz bean thread noodles
3 tablespoons oil
2 teaspoons annatto seeds
1 onion, finely sliced
3 teaspoons finely chopped garlic
2 tablespoons fish sauce
8 large dried shiitake mushrooms, soaked and sliced
4 spring onions (scallions), finely sliced

Put the chicken into a pot just large enough to hold it, add cold water to cover and place the celery leaves, carrot and clove-studded onion around it. Add the peppercorns and salt, cover and bring to simmering point. Cook for 45 minutes, turn off heat and leave until cool enough to handle. Remove all bones and cut meat into large pieces. Strain the stock. Soak the noodles in hot water for 10 minutes, then drain and cut into short lengths.

Heat oil, add 1 teaspoon annatto seeds and fry gently until seeds have coloured the oil. Cover pan with a frying screen as the seeds tend to jump. Lift out and discard seeds, and in the coloured oil fry onions and garlic until soft. Add chicken pieces and fish sauce and simmer for a few minutes.

Soak remaining annatto seeds in about 3 tablespoons hot water, stirring until water is coloured. Strain into pan with chicken stock and bring to the boil. Add noodles and mushrooms and simmer for 15 minutes. Stir in the chicken mixture and serve, scattered with the sliced spring onions.

Antigonon

(*Antigonon leptopus*) Also known as Mexican creeper. One may be forgiven for thinking this is purely a decorative flowering climber, its heart-shaped leaves and delicate pink or white flowers being reason enough to allow it to grow riotously over fences and climb any post. In Thailand, however, the leaves and flowers are dipped in flour, fried and served with vermicelli. The flowers are also mixed into omelettes.

Thailand: *chompoo phuang*

Apricot

Grown in the cool climate of northern India and Kashmir, apricots are dried and sold for inclusion in many savoury dishes. Unlike the bright-coloured dried apricots in Western supermarkets, these are small, pale beige-brown, quite leathery and rather fibrous, though the flavour is good. They are soaked until soft, then cooked in the spicy

Apricot Kernel

sauce of a lamb or chicken dish. The word 'jardaloo' in a recipe title means dried apricots are included. If supermarket apricots are used instead of the Indian type, it is not necessary to soak or pre-cook them. See recipe for Lamb with Apricots (page 203).

Apricot Kernel

See CHINESE ALMOND.

Areca Nut

See BETEL NUT.

Aromatic Ginger

See GINGER, AROMATIC.

Arrack

A potent alcoholic drink distilled from toddy, the fermented sap of palm trees. It is a clear, amber-coloured spirit which is aged until it resembles whisky. Connoisseurs appreciate aged arrack much as some appreciate a 12-year-old Scotch. Arrack is an important ingredient in some curries which, for some unfathomable reason, have been labelled 'padre' curries.

Arrowhead

(*Sagittaria sinensis, S. sagittifolia*) Other names are Chinese potato and swamp potato as it grows under water. A tuberous seasonal vegetable used in China, mainly in the Szechwan and Yunnan provinces. The flesh has a crunchy texture like water chestnuts, which grow in similar conditions.

They look rather like small onions in size and shape, but have a dark line or two around their circumference. Used as a starchy foil for rich meats, they must be pre-boiled or pre-fried to remove a natural bitterness.

Purchasing: Look for those with short shoots as they will be sweeter and more tender.

Preparation: Peel outer skin until white flesh is exposed. Remove and discard the shoot. Fry or boil either whole or sliced to remove bitterness. A little sugar may also be added to balance the flavour.

Add to braised meats for final cooking, or boil until tender.

Medicinal uses: Chinese believe anybody who suffers from constipation should not eat too many, but nutritionally they are a well-balanced food.

China: *tsee goo*
Japan: *kuwai*

Arrowroot

See FLOURS & STARCHES.

Artichoke, Chinese

(*Stachys affinis*) Also called Japanese artichoke (a native of both countries). Not related to globe artichokes or Jerusalem artichokes, but a perennial plant of the mint family which produces small, white, edible tubers, rarely more than 5 cm (2 in) long and 2 cm (¾ in) wide.

Only available during winter, they have an intriguing shape which has been described as looking like spiral sea shells, white jade beads, or chubby maggots! It is their pearly sheen which has inspired the best and worst of the descriptions. They are not likely to be found in the marketplace, as once exposed to air they quickly lose their translucence and become dull.

For those determined to try this rare tuber, the solution is to purchase them as a growing kit, plant them and look forward to trying them when the leaves die back. Not every nursery will have heard of them, but gardening magazines sometimes feature advertisements for growers selling unusual vegetables.

China: *gan lu zi, kon loh*
Japan: *choro-gi*

Asafoetida

(*Ferula assafoetida*) The resinous gum of a plant which grows in Afghanistan and Iran. The smell is unpleasant (one of its common names is 'devil's dung') but once incorporated in a dish it gives no hint of its malodorous beginnings. It used to be popular as a condiment in Roman times, and a favourite with Apicius, a Roman gourmet of the first century.

It is used as a seasoning, but its real importance is that it acts as an anti-flatulent and is therefore especially important in Indian lentil dishes. Pure asafoetida resin is sold in small lumps in a tin or box. Sometimes each lump is wrapped tightly in paper. Unwrap, pound using a mortar and pestle and use a piece no larger than a peppercorn. Nowadays, asafoetida is usually sold powdered and mixed with rice flour to keep it free running and to diffuse the strong aroma. Because of this the flavour is milder and in this form asafoetida may be measured and used in quantities from a pinch to a half-teaspoon, depending on how pure and strong it is. Don't over-do it.

Asafoetida comes into its own in Brahman cooking where it is used as a flavour substitute for garlic and onions. The latter are ruled out because they are believed to inflame the baser passions.

Purchasing and preparation: Asafoetida may be purchased in two forms — the pure resin individually wrapped in lumps of approximately 2 g (⅛ oz), or in powdered form mixed with ground rice and sometimes also with powdered turmeric. Powdered is easier to use, but there is not much asafoetida in the formula.

If using pure resin, use a mortar and pestle to pound to a fine powder, mix with twice to four times as much (by volume) of rice flour, and store in a small screw-top glass jar. Use sparingly, as it will be stronger than the ready-mixed version. Another method is to press a peppercorn-sized piece of the resin onto the inside of the lid of the pan in which food is being cooked. The steam then carries the flavour and its carminative properties into the food.

Storing: Store asafoetida in a screw-top glass jar to prevent the odour pervading pantry shelves. In this airtight environment it will last indefinitely. (If the asafoetida is ground, double jar storage is recommended — sort of a high security precaution for containing the odour.)

Medicinal uses: As a carminative and reliever of flatulence it is invaluable in lentil dishes. It is also used to treat nervous conditions, bronchitis and asthma, and is being researched as an anti-coagulant and treatment for blood pressure.

Burma: *sheingho*
India: *hing, perunkaya*

Chick Peas with Vegetables

Serves 6

100 g/3½ oz/1 cup dried chick peas
2 slender eggplants (aubergines),
   about 500 g/1 lb
1 teaspoon salt
1 teaspoon ground turmeric
125 ml/4 fl oz/½ cup light vegetable oil
2 tablespoons ghee
1 tablespoon finely chopped fresh ginger
1 teaspoon brown mustard seeds
2 teaspoons cumin seeds
1 fresh chilli, sliced
½ teaspoon asafoetida mixed with rice powder
   or peppercorn-sized piece pure asafoetida
3 large ripe tomatoes, chopped
1 large red capsicum (bell pepper) diced
salt to taste
1 teaspoon garam masala (recipe page 354)
3 tablespoons chopped fresh mint
   or coriander leaves

Soak chick peas overnight. Drain, cover with fresh water and boil until tender. To avoid overnight soaking bring to the boil in water to cover, turn off heat and leave to soak in covered pan for 2 hours. Change water and cook with half the salt and turmeric until tender, about 1 hour. Drain, reserving cooking liquid.

Wash but do not peel the eggplants. Cut into large dice or slice crossways 1 cm (½ in) thick. Sprinkle lightly with remaining salt and turmeric and set aside for 20 minutes. Blot moisture with paper towels.

Heat oil in a wok and fry the eggplant until brown and soft. Lift out with slotted spoon and put into a bowl. Pour off oil except for 2 tablespoons. Add ghee to the oil remaining in pan and fry the ginger, mustard and cumin seeds until ginger is golden and mustard seeds pop. Add sliced chilli and asafoetida, then the tomatoes. Cover and simmer until tomatoes are pulpy.

Add 1 cup reserved liquid from the chick peas and the peas themselves, the eggplant and diced capsicum. Simmer for 15 minutes or until tender, stirring from time to time, then stir in the garam masala, chopped mint or coriander and serve with rice or flat bread.

Asam

This is a word common to Malaysia, Singapore and Indonesia which simply means 'sour'. It is used to indicate any of the common sour fruits used to supply this flavour, and most often means tamarind which is a popular souring agent and is available all year round in many forms. See ACID FRUITS.

Ash Gourd

See GOURDS.

Asparagus

(*Asparagus officinalis*) A member of the lily family, asparagus is a native of Europe and has been cultivated since the time of the ancient Greeks. However, some of the best asparagus I've seen has been in the markets of Thailand, where it is highly regarded and called nor mai farang (foreign bamboo shoot). I have also been served superb asparagus in a mountain-top Buddhist monastery on one of the outlying islands of Hong Kong. No longer is European style asparagus polonaise or asparagus with hollandaise sauce my preferred method of serving this delightfully flavoured, tender shoot. Instead, I cook it Thai style with garlic, chillies and green peppercorns; or Chinese style, in a sauce delicate enough to let the asparagus flavour shine through.

Purchasing and storing: Make sure the tips of the spears are dry and have no odour. Look at the base of the spears to make sure they are not withered. Freshness is of paramount importance. If these criteria are met, it does not matter if the spears are thin or thick — both can be tender and flavourful. If they have to be kept for a few days, stand them upright in a beaker with 1 cm (½ in) water in the refrigerator. Cover with a plastic bag and fasten with a rubber band around the container.

Medicinal uses: The part of the plant used in herbal medicine is the root. *Potter's New Cyclopaedia of Botanical Drugs and Preparations* says: 'It is a diuretic, laxative, cardiac and sedative, and has been recommended in dropsy, enlargement of heart, etc. The fresh expressed juice is taken in tablespoonful doses. More palatable in the form of a syrup and is used as such in doses of 1–2 tablespoonfuls.'

Thai Style Asparagus

Serves 2

250 g/8 oz fresh green asparagus
1 small red capsicum (bell pepper) (optional)
1 teaspoon finely chopped garlic
2 teaspoons green peppercorns in brine, crushed
1 tablespoon fish sauce
2 tablespoons Maggi seasoning
    (see GOLDEN MOUNTAIN SAUCE)
2 teaspoons sugar
1 teaspoon cornflour (cornstarch)
2 red chillies, sliced
2 tablespoons peanut oil

Wash asparagus and capsicum and dry well. (Wet vegetables make the oil spatter.) Snap tough ends off asparagus and cut spears into bite-sized pieces. Cut capsicum into strips of same size. Combine in a small bowl the garlic, crushed peppercorns, fish sauce, seasoning, sugar, cornflour and chilli, stirring until sugar dissolves.

Heat oil in a wok and stir-fry vegetables on high heat until colours intensify. Add 3 tablespoons water, cover and steam for 2 minutes or until just tender. Add flavouring mixture, stir until sauce boils and thickens slightly and serve immediately.

Chinese Style Asparagus

Serves 4

400 g/14 oz fresh green asparagus
1 tablespoon peanut oil
1 tablespoon oyster sauce
1 teaspoon sugar

Wash asparagus and snap off about 2½ cm (1 in) at the base of the stems if they are not tender right through. (If stems bend instead of snapping crisply at that point, move a little higher up the stalk to where they snap.) Discard tough ends. Bring water to the boil in a wok, deep enough to immerse the asparagus. Add peanut oil and asparagus. When water returns to the boil cook for 2 minutes or until tender but crisp. Lift out asparagus and on a board cut into finger lengths. Arrange on serving dish. Empty the wok, add oyster sauce, sugar and 2 tablespoons water to the wok and bring to boil. Pour over asparagus and serve at once.

Asparagus Pea

See LEGUMES & PULSES.

Atta

See FLOURS & STARCHES.

Aubergine

See EGGPLANT.

Australia

In the early days of European settlement of Australia, sheep and wheat were important food sources. Pioneering chefs managed to create 'colonial goose' and 'baked ham' with a leg of mutton. With potatoes and pumpkin baked in the drippings of the meat, mutton was the staple meal.

'What about kangaroo tail soup?' you ask. This was a curiosity more often canned for export than served on Australian tables.

In the closing decades of the 20th century there has been a change in Australian cuisine which is remarkable even to observers from long-established cuisines in other parts of the world. There has been a transformation, an explosion of creativity, an emerging cuisine which makes Australia a force to be reckoned with.

Australia grows a wide range of foods due to the diversity of its climatic regions. From its tropical north, the riches of exotic fruits from the land and reef fish from its abundant coastline; from the Mediterranean climate which prevails in southern Australia, olives, olive oil and wines which take prizes worldwide; from the cold, unpolluted waters and green pastures of Tasmania and other smaller islands off its southern coast, come ingredients which the rest of the world regards with admiration and a touch of envy. Inspired chefs take pride in this produce and are doing wonderful things with it.

After two hundred years of settlement, there is an interest in bush foods, what indigenous people eat and how some of these little-known foods may be incorporated in today's menus. Wattle seed, lemon myrtle, kakadu plums and other flavours are being used in up-market restaurants and arousing interest in other parts of the world. The range of bush foods is vast and much is still being learned about them.

Chinese labourers brought in to work in the goldfields in the 19th century introduced something different: Chinese food. Not the high-class, genuine Chinese food featured in most restaurants in the cities of Australia today, but a timidly homogeneous kind of oriental cooking which was relentlessly bent to what Chinese cooks thought might appeal to the 'gweilo' (foreign devils).

In the middle of the 20th century, influenced by post-World War II migration, came an awareness of European ingredients. Until the 1960s, the food most admired and aspired to was the rich, extravagant, middle European and French haute cuisine.

Other influences arrived with ships bringing migrants from Europe after the war. Greek and Italian migrants brought the Mediterranean cuisine so well received today, but scorned until the recent awareness of how healthy it is to base a diet around skilfully cooked vegetables, fish, olives and olive oil with herbs and garlic for flavouring.

Lebanese and other Middle Eastern restaurants became popular, and even middle Australia fell under the spell of mezze, including the dips of legumes and vegetables redolent of garlic. Until then, if used at all, in true British fashion garlic was delicately rubbed around a salad bowl and the clove discarded.

Since the 1970s, there have been dramatic changes in the way Australians eat. While the old habit of meat three times a day was dropped much earlier, there have been other changes making the diet more nutritious and varied.

Immigration from Asian countries and travel have increased the appreciation of Asian cuisines within Australia. Two hundred years after the voyages of Captain Cook, those who shape and influence cuisine are opening their minds and palates to such diverse influences as Mediterranean food and diversely flavoured Asian cuisines.

Instead of being a culinary outpost of Britain as it was for so long, Australian cuisine is developing its own personality, one with a distinctly Asian bias. It retains what is most pleasing from the past and uses the best of the imported cuisines as they are suited to the varied climates of this vast continent.

Avocado

(*Persea americana*) An import from the Americas which grows easily in tropical Asia. Also known as avocado pear (it is no relative of the pear, but has a similar shape) and alligator pear (some varieties have a knobbly skin like that of an alligator).

In Asian cuisine, avocado is used in desserts. It makes beautifully smooth ice cream and milk shakes. In its simplest form the ripe fruit is scooped out of its shell, mashed smoothly and mixed with sweetened condensed milk to taste, since fresh cream is not available in many Asian countries. Avocado vinaigrette is a concept foreign to Asia.

Different varieties of avocado are available, and while flavour and texture vary slightly from one to the other, there are not dramatic variations such as one comes across in mangoes where one strain is superb while another is practically inedible.

Purchasing and storing: Avocados are hard when picked and shipped off to market. Like mangoes, they ripen off the tree. A good greengrocer usually knows which avocados are ripe and ready, and these, while firm, will yield to gentle pressure. Avocados that feel soft are too ripe and may have a rancid flavour. Avoid fruit with dark spots, or fruit with bruises. It is easier to spot these on avocados with thin green skin like 'Fuerte' and 'Sharwil' than on those varieties which are all brown bumps, like 'Haas' and 'Hazzard'.

Store avocados at room temperature and if you wish to speed up the ripening, put them in a paper bag with an apple or ripe banana which gives off ethanol gas. Close the bag tightly to keep in the gas. Another method of ripening is to put the avocado in a plastic bag and leave it in a sunny spot for an hour or two. Take care doing this in summer — you don't want to cook the avocado.

Preparation: Always use a stainless steel knife to cut the fruit. Cut avocado in half lengthways and separate halves by gently twisting. To release the seed, hit it gently with the blade of a sharp knife, skew the knife slightly and lift the seed out. If avocado is ripe, the skin may be peeled off quite easily. Prepare avocado shortly before serving as it darkens when exposed to air.

An avocado is not a fruit for cooking. Gentle heating is all it can take without developing a metallic flavour.

Avocado Sashimi

The unctuous, buttery texture of avocado is reminiscent of high quality raw tuna, so is an obvious choice for vegetarian 'sashimi'.

1 firm ripe avocado
4 tablespoons Japanese soy sauce
2 teaspoons wasabi powder

Prepare the avocado as close to serving time as possible so it retains its bright colour. With a stainless steel knife cut in quarters lengthways, then remove each quarter from the seed and carefully peel away the skin. Slice avocado crossways and gently spread the slices so that the dark green just under the skin and the yellowish green of the centre are seen alternately. Arrange 2 of the quarters on each plate and serve with a small sauce dish containing Japanese soy sauce and a small ball of wasabi paste, made by mixing wasabi powder to a stiff paste with cold water.

Avocado Fool

Try not to make this more than a few hours in advance or it will discolour. Serves 4.

2 ripe avocados
2–3 tablespoons caster sugar (superfine sugar)
squeeze of lime juice, optional
125 ml/4 fl oz/½ cup cream

Avocados for desserts should be fully ripe and soft enough to be easily mashed with a fork. Cut fruit in halves, remove stone and scoop out the flesh into a shallow bowl. Mash smoothly, adding sugar, lime juice and finally blending in the cream. Spoon into serving bowl or individual dessert dishes, cover and chill.

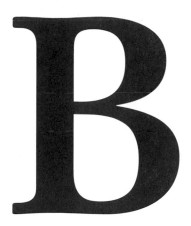

B

Bael Fruit

(*Aegle marmelos*) Also known as beli fruit, bel fruit, Indian bael and Bengal quince. This deciduous tree grows from 6–15 m (20–50 ft) tall and is thorny, with trifoliate leaves and fragrant flowers. It is grown in temple gardens throughout India, the trees dedicated to the deity Siva and the leaves used in religious ceremonies.

In northern Thailand, the young shoots and leaves are eaten raw with larb, a salad featuring either raw or lightly cooked meat which may be beef, pork or chicken. The young leaves may also be added to salads.

A close relative of citrus, the fruit is about the size of an orange and has a pale green, smooth, hard, woody shell. Inside the shell is a pale orange-coloured, floury pulp around numerous seeds, each seed encased in a clear, glutinous substance which is esteemed for its medicinal properties. Dried slices of the fruit are sold. These are soaked and boiled, strained free of fibre and the liquid sweetened and drunk as a tisane (infusion).

Not readily available fresh outside South East Asia, but a canned, sweetened purée of ripe bael fruits is produced in Sri Lanka and exported. It may be diluted with water and ice and a squeeze of lime juice added to make a refreshing drink.

Medicinal uses: The fruit is used as a remedy for stomach upsets. The unripe fruit is a traditional Indian remedy for dysentery and diarrhoea. It does not constipate and is also effective for haemorrhoids. Eating the ripe fruit, on the other hand, has a laxative effect. The juice from the leaves is used as an anti-diabetic.

India: *vilvam*
Sri Lanka: *baeli*

Balachaung

A traditional Burmese fried relish in which the main ingredients are pounded dried shrimp, sliced onions and lots of garlic. Crisp, salty, garlicky, hot, sour, it is just about the most typical accompaniment to a Burmese meal. I have known people to use it as a sandwich filling, or a topping for crackers. Will keep for months in a glass jar, if well hidden. See recipe for Burmese Dried Shrimp Relish (page 342).

Balut

See EGGS.

Bamboo

(*Bambusa vulgaris, Phyllostachys edulis, P. pubescens, Dendrocalamus asper*) SEE ILLUSTRATION. There are many different species of bamboo, not all edible. The inside of the shoots is used as food after the tough outer leaves have been removed. Depending on what season of the year it is dug, bamboo has varying characteristics. Spring bamboo shoots (mo sun) are chunky and pale in colour. Winter shoots (doeng sun) are a daintier, more elongated shape, finer in texture, deeper in colour and have a distinctive flavour. Summer bamboo shoots (jook sun) is a small species that is seldom available outside China.

All fresh bamboo needs to be carefully peeled to remove every trace of the fine, sharp hairs that grow on the outer husk. They are then boiled for anything from 10 minutes to several hours, (depending on variety) to remove the toxic hydrocyanic acid before cooking or eating.

I suspect there are as many ways to cook bamboo as there are cooks. I was advised by a Vietnamese man I met at the markets that bamboo shoots must be boiled until they are easily pierced by the blunt end of a chopstick. While the bamboo shoot I had purchased under his guidance seemed very young and tender, it seemed to boil forever and still a chopstick could hardly make an impression.

As luck would have it, the very next week a leading Western chef with pronounced Asian leanings was quoted in a newspaper interview as saying that fresh bamboo shoots were his favourite ingredient, so I asked how he makes them tender. He generously shared his method which is to peel them, cut the shoots in crosswise slices, cover with cold water, bring to the boil, drain off the water and repeat this 3 times. He assured me the bamboo is then ready to be combined with sauces and other ingredients.

Except to a connoisseur, there is not an appreciable difference between fresh and canned bamboo shoots, so if uncertain, use canned for ease and safety. Of the canned varieties, whole shoots in water are best and winter bamboo shoots are favoured over the larger type. If they have a strong odour or tinny flavour, boil them in fresh water for 5 minutes. Canned bamboo shoots will keep after opening, submerged in fresh water, for more than a week provided you keep them refrigerated and change the water daily.

A specialist grocer may have vacuum-packed bamboo in the refrigerator. They are also sold dried but in this form require long soaking and slow, separate cooking before including in a recipe.

Dried bamboo leaves, soaked in very hot water to soften, can be used for wrapping foods before steaming or grilling to impart a delicate flavour and retain the food's moisture.

Burma: *wah-bho-khmyit*
Cambodia: *tumpeang*
China: *doeng-sun, jook sun, mo sun*
Japan: *takenoko*
Indonesia: *rebung*
Malaysia: *rebong*
Philippines: *labong*
Thailand: *normai*
Vietnam: *mang*

Chicken Curry with Bamboo Shoot

Serves 6–8

1 kg/2 lb chicken pieces
250 g/8 oz canned bamboo shoot
3 tablespoons peanut oil
1 medium onion, finely chopped
2 teaspoons finely chopped garlic
2 teaspoons finely chopped ginger
1 teaspoon dried shrimp paste
2 tablespoons ground coriander
1 teaspoon chilli powder
2 teaspoons salt
400 ml/14 fl oz can coconut milk

Cut chicken joints into curry-sized pieces, through the bone. Wipe bone ends with damp paper towel to remove any bone chips. Cut bamboo shoot in quarters lengthways (if large) or halves if smaller winter bamboo shoots are used. Slice crossways into thick slices.

Heat oil in a heavy saucepan and cook the onion, garlic and ginger on low heat, stirring frequently, until soft and translucent. Stir in the shrimp paste, coriander, chilli powder and salt, and fry for 2 minutes, stirring. Add chicken pieces and stir to coat with spices, then add two thirds of the can of coconut milk diluted with an equal amount of water. Stir while bringing to the boil, add bamboo slices, then lower heat and simmer, uncovered, until chicken is tender. Stir in remaining undiluted coconut milk. Serve with rice.

Thai Beef with Bamboo Shoot

Serves 4

375 g/12 oz lean rump steak
½ teaspoon coarsely ground black pepper
2 teaspoons crushed garlic
3 tablespoons oil
125 g/4 oz sliced canned bamboo shoot
2 small red chillies, sliced
1 tablespoon fish sauce
1 teaspoon palm sugar or brown sugar
2 kaffir lime leaves, cut in threads
20 fresh basil leaves

Cut beef into thin strips and rub with pepper and half the garlic. Leave for 30 minutes. Heat oil in a wok and on high heat stir-fry the beef until colour changes. Add remaining garlic and bamboo, chillies, fish sauce and sugar, and continue to stir-fry until fragrant. Serve sprinkled with the lime leaf shreds and fresh basil leaves. Serve with steamed rice.

Banana

(*Musa × paradisiaca*) This fast-growing species of the genus Musa has more than 400 varieties. A nutritious fruit, technically an angled berry, it grows on what is casually described as a tree but is in fact a giant herb. The stem is composed of overlapping bases of the leaves above and can grow up to 10 m (30 ft) tall.

If you've seen bananas growing, what may appear to be, from a distance, a giant bunch is actually a number of 'hands' of bananas growing around a thick central stalk which can be as long as a metre. For marketing, the 'hands', comprising a number of individual bananas, are detached by cutting them off the stalk.

The banana plant is used for more than just its fruit. Its flowers, leaves and trunk are also important in the cuisine of Asian and Pacific countries. The deep crimson banana flower is used as a vegetable. The heart of the main stem is featured in the national dish of Burma.

Ripe bananas are eaten as a sweet fruit. When green, the fruit is starchy and suitable for cooking like potato chips or in curries where it takes the place of other starchy vegetables. This is, for the most part, confined to the tropics where unripe bananas are an important food source. In some cases cooking bananas are called plantains, but in other countries dessert varieties are also referred to as plantains. Some are grown for roasting, some for steaming.

Some varieties of cooking bananas are made into flour which is more easily digested than cereal starches.

Purchasing and storing: The most widely known varieties are dessert bananas which are exported to temperate countries because their high sugar content (about 17–19 per cent) makes them ideal for eating ripe and raw. Still, only a few varieties are exported, the decisive factor being which varieties are able to be transported. There are many kinds of delicious bananas which can only be enjoyed in the warm climates in which they grow.

When buying bananas for eating, ensure they are firm and unbruised. Bruising shows in dark patches which are soft to the touch, but brown or black streaks on yellow skin indicate that they are ripe. Green tips usually mean they are under-ripe and should be held at room temperature for a few days to ripen, although some varieties of bananas with green skins may be fully ripe and on peeling prove to be soft and sweet.

Do not refrigerate bananas unless they have ripened and have to be held for a few days, in which case they could be refrigerated in a polythene bag. Refrigerating will cause the skin to darken, but the fruit will be all right for 3–4 days.

Preparation: Peel bananas just before eating or slicing. If they have to be kept a while before serving, sprinkle with lime or lemon juice to prevent discolouring.

Some varieties of banana are more suited to cooking, having flesh that firms when subjected to heat. These varieties are good for chips and fritters. Some recipes, on the other hand, require ripe bananas which do not toughen when cooked. It takes a little experience to know which is which.

The sugar or ladies' finger banana firms when cooked and is suitable for cutting into thick slices which are battered and fried.

The common Cavendish banana (soft when cooked) is suited to making banana cake or steamed in a soft blancmange made from mung bean flour and coconut milk and wrapped in little parcels of banana leaf.

Firm ripe bananas of any type may be used in Chinese Toffee Bananas (see recipe page 20). This is a special dessert in which batter-coated slices of banana are dipped into clear caramel and dropped into a bowl of ice to harden the transparent glaze.

Medicinal uses: The ripe fruit is demulcent, unripe fruit astringent. The inflorescences are supposed to be anti-diabetic, the sap astringent. The leaves staunch bleeding and the roots are said to be diuretic.

Burma: *ngapyawthee*
Fiji: *vudi*
Hawaii: *mai'a*
India: *kela*
Indonesia: *pisang, biju*
Malaysia: *pisang*
Philippines: *sageng, pisang*
Samoa: *fa'i, fei*
Tahiti: *fa'i, fei*
Sri Lanka: *kehel*
Thailand: *kluay*
Tonga: *siaine*
Vietnam: *chuoi*

Thai Style Fried Bananas

I tasted these fried bananas at the floating market in Thonburi, Thailand. They have a crisp coating, and are well worth the trouble.

8 firm ripe sugar bananas
1 litre/2 pints/4 cups oil for frying

BATTER
60 g/2 oz/½ cup rice flour
60 g/2 oz/½ cup self-raising flour
½ teaspoon baking soda
250 ml/8 fl oz/1 cup water
3 tablespoons coconut milk
½ teaspoon salt
1 tablespoon sesame seeds (optional)
2 tablespoons shredded coconut (optional)
2 tablespoons sugar

Peel the bananas and cut lengthways into halves or quarters, depending on their size. Pour oil into a wok or other deep frying pan as the fritters must have sufficient depth of oil to float.

Combine all the ingredients for the batter in a bowl, then mix until smooth without beating.

Heat oil to 190°C (375°F). Dip banana slices in batter and deep fry 2–3 at a time until golden brown, splashing hot oil over them as soon as they are dropped into the pan. Lift out on a slotted spoon and drain on paper towels. Serve while still crisp and warm.

Chinese Toffee Bananas

1 egg
185 ml/6 fl oz/¾ cup cold water
125 g/4 oz/1 cup plain (all-purpose) flour
peanut oil for deep frying
4 firm ripe bananas

SUGAR GLAZE
375 g/12 oz/1½ cups sugar
125 ml/4 oz/½ cup cold water
2 teaspoons black sesame seeds

Beat egg, add water and beat again, then add flour all at once and beat until smooth. Let batter stand while making glaze. (To make the glaze, heat sugar and water in a small heavy pan, without stirring, until golden. Add the sesame seeds, remove from heat.) Start heating oil for deep frying, as the success of

this sweet depends on having the glaze ready and the oil hot enough at the same time!

Slice bananas thickly, dip into batter to coat, then take one piece at a time and drop into the oil. Do not crowd the pan or they will stick together. If the temperature of the oil drops too much the batter will be heavy and absorb too much oil.

As soon as each piece of banana in batter is golden, lift out with a slotted spoon and put immediately into the saucepan with the glaze, turning to coat all over. Lift out and drop into a bowl containing cold water and ice cubes. The glaze will harden and become brittle almost at once. Lift out quickly onto a platter which has been lightly oiled to prevent sticking. Serve as soon as possible, while sugar is brittle and batter crisp.

Bananas in Yoghurt (Kela Raita)

One of the favourite accompaniments to an Indian curry meal, it is cooling, spicy and sweet, all at the same time. Serves 4.

1 teaspoon ghee or oil
1 teaspoon black mustard seeds
1 teaspoon cumin seeds
¼ teaspoon chilli powder
¼ teaspoon salt
2 teaspoons sugar
250 ml/8 fl oz/1 cup natural yoghurt
3 tablespoons fresh grated coconut
**   or desiccated coconut**
2 or 3 firm ripe bananas
2 tablespoons lime or lemon juice

Heat ghee or oil in a small saucepan with a lid. Add mustard and cumin seeds, cover to prevent mustard seeds jumping all over the stove and fry on medium-low heat until they pop. Remove from heat and add chilli powder, salt, sugar and yoghurt. Turn into a bowl. If using fresh coconut stir it into the mixture. If desiccated coconut is used, sprinkle it with a tablespoon of water and mix with fingertips until evenly moistened before adding. Peel and slice the bananas, and sprinkle with lime or lemon juice to prevent discolouration. Fold into yoghurt mixture, chill and serve with rice and curries.

Fried Bananas

One of the favourite accompaniments to a curry meal. The sweetness is a contrast to the spiciness of curry. Cavendish style bananas are best.

4 firm ripe bananas (not sugar bananas)
2 tablespoons butter or oil

Peel the bananas and fry in the butter or oil, turning them gently until the natural sugars caramelise and they are golden brown all over. They may be cut across in half to make shorter pieces which are easier to handle. Serve warm.

Banana Flower

(*Musa* spp.) SEE ILLUSTRATION. The deep purplish-crimson-coloured banana flower is used as a vegetable from Sri Lanka to Laos. The flower is borne at the end of the stem. Long, slender, sterile male flowers with a faint sweet fragrance are lined up in tidy rows and protected by large reddish bracts. Higher up the stem are groups of female flowers which develop into fruit without fertilisation.

In Thailand, slices of tender banana flower are eaten raw with the pungent dip known as nam prik, or with fried noodles, or simmered in a hot sour soup with chicken, galangal and coconut milk.

In the Philippines, banana blossom is added to the famous kari-kari, a rich beef stew. 'Banana blossom' or 'banana heart' are the favoured names in the Philippines and 'banana heart' in Indonesia purely because its colour and shape suggest a heart; (nothing to do with the 'heart' of the trunk used in Burma). In Sri Lanka, it is simply 'plantain flower'. In Australia it is known as 'banana bell'.

Purchasing and storing: Buy flowers which look fresh and bright. Often they are wrapped in transparent plastic, which keeps them from drying out too quickly. If they must be kept for a few days leave them in the wrapping and store in the vegetable crisper of the refrigerator.

Preparation: To prepare the flower for cooking, remove and discard outer bracts until the inner, paler portion is revealed. Some recipes advise steaming the whole blossom for 20 minutes or so before cutting into it. This may also be done in the microwave oven in a much shorter time by first putting the blossom on a dish and covering it with microwave-proof plastic wrap. Allow to cool before slicing.

Burma: *ngapyaw phoo*
China: *shang chao fua*
India: *kere kafool*
Japan: *banana no tsubomi*
Indonesia: *jantung pisang*
Philippines: *puso*
Sri Lanka: *kehel mal*
Thailand: *dok kluai*

Banana Blossom Guinatan

Serves 4

500 g/1 lb banana blossom
salt
2 tablespoons oil
1 medium onion, sliced
2 cloves garlic, finely chopped
1 small tomato, diced
2 tablespoons vinegar
salt and pepper to taste
250 ml/8 fl oz/1 cup thick coconut milk

Discard tough outer layers and slice the blossom thinly, first cutting it in two lengthways if it is large. Put the slices in a bowl, sprinkle with a tablespoon of salt, rubbing it well in. Leave for 10–15 minutes, squeeze out juices, rinse under cold water and squeeze dry.

Heat oil in a wok or frying pan and cook onion and garlic until golden brown. Add tomato, stir for 3 minutes, then add banana blossom and vinegar and bring to the boil. Simmer for 5 minutes. Taste and add salt and pepper as required. Cook until blossom is tender, then stir in coconut milk and remove from heat. Serve with rice.

Plantain Flower with Spices

500 g/1 lb plantain flower
1 teaspoon salt
2 teaspoons chilli powder or to taste
3 tablespoons oil
sprig of fresh curry leaves
**   or 6 dried curry leaves**
2 medium onions, finely sliced

Discard tough outer layer and cut the tender portion into bite-sized pieces. Add salt and chilli powder and mix well.

Heat oil and fry the curry leaves and onions, stirring, until onions are golden brown. Add the plantain flower and keep tossing over heat until tender. Serve as a vegetable accompaniment with rice and other dishes.

Thai Soup with Banana Flower

Serves 4–6

1 banana flower
1.5 litres/3 pints/6 cups water
1 teaspoon salt
2 stems fresh lemon grass, thinly sliced
**   or 4 strips lemon zest**
4 kaffir lime leaves
4 slices galangal
3 fresh chillies
2 teaspoons chopped garlic
250 ml/8 fl oz/1 cup thick coconut milk
2 tablespoons fish sauce
3 tablespoons lime juice
3 tablespoons chopped fresh coriander
3 tablespoons chopped spring onions (scallions)

Discard tough outer layers of the banana flower. Steam or boil for 15 minutes (or cover with wrap and microwave on high for 3 minutes). When cool enough to handle, cut in quarters lengthways, then across into fairly thin slices.

Put slices into a saucepan with the water, salt, lemon grass, lime leaves, galangal, chillies and garlic. Bring to the boil, cover and simmer for 20 minutes or until banana flower is tender. Stir in coconut milk, fish sauce, lime juice and remove from heat. Serve sprinkled with chopped coriander and spring onions.

Banana Flower with Petai

Serves 6

220 /7 oz banana flower
2 tablespoons dried shrimps
½ teaspoon crushed garlic
½ teaspoon finely grated fresh ginger
185 g/6 oz can petai, drained
**   or 100 g/3½ oz fresh petai**
2 tablespoons oil
½ teaspoon turmeric
1 teaspoon salt
1 teaspoon chilli powder
1 teaspoon tamarind purée
1 bulb pickled garlic, chopped

Discard tough outer layers of the banana flower. Steam or boil for 15 minutes (or cover with wrap and microwave on high for 3 minutes). Cool to lukewarm, halve lengthways and slice in thin slices crosswise. Meanwhile, soak dried shrimps in ½ cup boiling water until softened, then chop roughly. Save soaking water.

Heat oil and fry garlic and ginger on low heat, stirring until golden. Add sliced banana flower, shrimps, petai and soaking water. Sprinkle with turmeric, salt and chilli powder. Toss well. Cover and cook for about 8 minutes or until tender. Stir in tamarind purée, taste and correct seasoning. Scatter pickled garlic scattered on top and serve with rice.

Banana Plant

(*Musa* spp.) A banana plant is used for more than just its fruit. Its flowers (see BANANA FLOWER), leaves and trunk are also important in the cuisines of some Asian and Pacific countries. In Sri Lanka, the skins of green plantains are also used to make a tasty accompaniment.

The heart of the main stem (SEE ILLUSTRATION) is featured in more than one South East Asian dish and notably the national dish of Burma, a spicy fish soup called Moh Hin Gha (see recipe page 23). It is also used in a Balinese chicken soup with different spicing and stock instead of coconut milk. The tender inner portion of the trunk is eaten in Thailand, either boiled and dipped in nam prik or cooked in curries.

The word 'trunk' implies a tree, but botanically speaking the banana is a giant herb. What makes the upright stem is actually the thick, overlapping bases of the leaves. Although not strictly accurate, the term 'trunk' does help identify which part of the plant provides the ingredient.

In the islands of the Pacific the outer layers of banana trunk are used as dishes. Thick enough to be rigid, the surface smooth and waterproof, and the shape curved so they can hold even a dish with gravy, they make great disposable dinnerware.

Another useful part of the banana plant is the leaves. In southern India they are used as plates, and for this the middle rib is retained. In almost every Asian country, the leaves are used as a wrapping for food to be cooked or deftly shaped into dainty serving cups or cones or square containers. For this purpose the thick mid-rib is discarded after cutting off the flexible leaf. A piece of banana leaf with its naturally smooth surface takes the place of grease-proof paper or foil for smoothing the top of sweet-meats, rice cooked in coconut milk, and other dishes.

The traditional Sri Lankan meal of Lampries (parcels of fragrant rice, curries and accompaniments wrapped in a banana leaf and baked) would lack a vital flavour component were the banana leaf to be omitted. Before using fresh banana leaf as a wrapping, pass over a flame to soften and make flexible. Alternatively, blanch in boiling water for a few seconds. This renders the leaves pliable for easier handling.

Once a banana plant has borne fruit, it has outlived its usefulness. This is the perfect time to harvest it. The rhizome sends up suckers to replace the parent plant and, in this way, a banana can continue to produce for up to 60 years from the original rhizome. Before the heart can be cooked or eaten, the outer layers are discarded and the tender innermost portion sliced and soaked in a basin of salted water for several hours. This procedure draws the sap into strands which can be easily pulled away. When cutting down banana saplings, wear old clothes and gloves as the sap is fiendishly sticky and staining.

Since bananas grow in sub-tropical and temperate zones, my grandmother, who was born in Burma and spent much of her life there, felled one of the banana plants in my suburban garden in Sydney, Australia and taught my husband and me how to cook Moh Hin Gha the genuine Burmese way, something we have done many times since.

Spicy Fish Soup (Moh Hin Gha)

A meal in a bowl, in the city of Rangoon it is mostly bought from itinerant vendors who call their wares through the streets, carrying their portable kitchen on a bamboo pole slung over one shoulder, ingredients at one end, fire and cooking pot at the other. Housewives come out with dishes and buy the family meal which comprises a spicy fish soup with slices of banana heart and freshly made rice noodles. In Asian areas and growers' markets I have seen banana heart for sale, but if this proves unobtainable, slices of canned bamboo shoot may be substituted. Serves 6–8.

about 30 cm/12 in banana heart
500 g/1 lb fillets of strong flavoured fish
    or 2 cans of herrings in tomato sauce
3 medium onions, chopped
1 tablespoon finely chopped garlic
2 teaspoons finely chopped fresh ginger
1 teaspoon ground turmeric
1 teaspoon chilli powder
    or 2 fresh red chillies, seeded
4 tablespoons peanut oil
3 tablespoons oriental sesame oil
250 ml/8 fl oz/1 cup thin coconut milk
1 teaspoon dried shrimp paste
1 tablespoon fish sauce
3 tablespoons chick pea flour (besan)
500 ml/1 pint/2 cups thick coconut milk
2 or 3 tablespoons lime or lemon juice
salt to taste
500 g packet of rice vermicelli
accompaniments (see page 24)

Discard one or two of the outer layers of banana heart. Slice the tender inner portion in crosswise slices about 1 cm (½ in) thick. Soak the slices in a large basin of salted water for about 2 hours. The sticky juice forms strands which should be pulled away and discarded.

If using fresh fish, make sure there are no bones or scales on the fillets. Put into a pan with just enough water to cover and simmer for 5 minutes. Set aside.

In electric blender purée the onion, garlic, ginger, turmeric and chilli. Heat both kinds of oil in a large saucepan until smoking hot, turn in the puréed mixture and cook over low heat, stirring frequently, about 15 minutes or until it smells cooked and the oil separates from the onion mixture. It should be a rich golden brown before going on to the next stage.

Add fish stock (reserve fillets), thin coconut milk and sliced banana heart and bring to the boil, stirring. Reduce heat and simmer until banana heart slices are tender but still crunchy. Dissolve dried shrimp paste in a little boiling water, add fish sauce and stir into the soup. Mix chick pea flour smoothly with a little cold water and add to the pan. Stir as it comes to the boil to prevent lumping. Simmer for 5 minutes, then add the fish fillets broken into bite-sized pieces. If using canned fish add it now, together with liquid from the cans.

Add thick coconut milk, salt and lime or lemon juice, stirring. Immerse rice vermicelli in boiling water for about 90 seconds. Drain.

Put noodles into individual bowls and ladle the fish soup over. Guests choose accompaniments from the array suggested below which can be prepared ahead of time and set out on the table, leaving only the noodles and piping hot soup to be brought to the table just before serving.

ACCOMPANIMENTS FOR MOH HIN GHA

finely sliced spring onions (scallions)
roughly chopped fresh coriander herb
finely sliced white onion
roasted chick peas, finely ground,
  for adding thickness
chilli powder for extra heat
lime or lemon wedges for adding piquancy
fish sauce for extra saltiness
sliced fresh chillies for pungency
dried chillies, fried in oil
fried onion flakes
fried garlic slices
crisp fried noodles, broken small

Barbecue Sauce

Chinese barbecue sauce is a thick, salty-sweet reddish sauce used to marinate meats for barbecuing. Basically, it is hoi sin sauce with a few things added: vinegar, sesame paste, tomato paste, bean sauce. Don't be afraid to combine a few ingredients and make your own. A Japanese barbecue sauce, tonkatsu sauce, is closer in flavour to Western style barbecue sauce with basic flavours of Worcestershire sauce, tomato sauce, mustard and soy. See also SAUCES.

Barley

(*Hordeum vulgare*) Not a common foodstuff in Asia or the Pacific islands, with a few notable exceptions. In Japan, it is used to make barley miso (mugi miso) and in Vietnam the small, soft grains may be found in the iced drinks so popular and looked on as a health food rather than an indulgence. It is always pearl barley which is used, boiled until tender but still holding its shape. Due to British influence, barley water is regarded as a cooling drink to be taken by children and invalids, being demulcent and soothing to the kidneys and bowels in cases of diarrhoea and inflammation. The barley should be washed well, and 60 g (2 oz) of pearl barley boiled in 500 ml (1 pint) water. In

Korea, barley flour is sold as malt flour (see FLOURS & STARCHES) and the soaking water used in some cooking preparations.

Basil

(*Ocimum* spp.) SEE ILLUSTRATION. An herb of the Labiatae family which includes other fragrant herbs such as mint and lemon balm. There are numerous varieties of basil including licorice, cinnamon, clove, camphor, lettuce leaf, lemon, holy and purple basil. Various kinds of basil are used in Thai, Malaysian and Indonesian food, the leaves usually added at the end of cooking to allow their sweet, fresh fragrance to balance the complex underlying spices.

Thai cookery uses three main kinds of basil which have distinctly different flavours from that of European basil. Fresh basil is an indispensable addition in many Thai and Indonesian dishes, one for which there really is no substitute, since dried basil does not have the same flavour. It is better to substitute fresh coriander in cooked dishes, and fresh mint in salads. The three kinds of basil used in Thai cooking are described below.

Horapa: (*O. basilicum*), with medium to large leaves, has a sweet, licorice flavour. This is the closest to sweet basil used in European cookery.

Manglak: (*O. canum, O. citriodorum*), with its smaller, slightly hairy leaves has a lemon scent and can be quite pungent. Its seeds (luk manglak) are used in desserts and drinks. See BASIL SEED.

Krapow, kaprao: (*O. sanctum*), is also known as holy basil because it is planted around temples. Claimed to repel mosquitos, it has a strong odour. The leaves are smaller and darker in colour, the stems and young leaves distinctly reddish-purple. Used only in strong-flavoured dishes such as fish curries or chilli-flavoured stir-fries.

Medicinal uses: The leaves are said to aid digestion, and the leaf wine is regarded as a tonic and aphrodisiac.

India: *sabzah, tulsi, gulal tulsi*
Indonesia: *selasih, kemangi*
Malaysia: *selaseh, kemangi*
Philippines: *belanoi, sulasi*
Sri Lanka: *suwenda-tala, maduru-tala*
Thailand: *horapa, manglak, krapow*
Vietnam: *rau que*

Deep Fried Basil Leaves

1 bunch fresh sweet basil
oil for deep frying

If the leaves are from your own garden or are organically grown and you know they have not been sprayed, there is no need to wash them. If they have been washed, dry them as thoroughly as possible. Strip leaves from stems.

Heat 2 cups oil in a wok until almost smoking and drop in handfuls of leaves so they turn brilliant green and crisp in seconds. Lift onto paper towels with a slotted spoon. Serve quickly, sprinkled over other dishes just before serving so the leaves don't have time to lose their crispness. Or pass a bowl of them around on their own for a new sensation in flavour and texture.

Basil Seed

(*Ocimum canum*) The small (half the size of a sesame seed), black, oval-shaped, seeds of lemon scented basil, when soaked in water, develop a slippery, translucent coat. These are floated in the sweet cold drinks which are popular in hot countries and are claimed to have a very cooling effect on the system. Their texture is slippery (gelatinous coating) and at the same time crunchy (the actual seed) with no appreciable flavour.

Medicinal uses: The seeds are said to relieve stomach ailments. Because of their slippery coating, they are considered soothing to the digestive system.

India: *tucmeria, tookmuria*
Sri Lanka: *khasa-khasa*
Thailand: *luk manglak*

Young Coconut and Basil Seeds

While in most recipes basil seeds are simply an addition, there are some desserts in which they are a major component, as in the following recipe for a cool thirst-quencher featuring basil seeds and young coconut or palm sugar seeds. Serves 6–8.

2 tablespoons basil seeds
125 g/4 oz/½ cup sugar
400 ml/14 fl oz can coconut milk
400 ml/14 fl oz can young coconut in syrup

Soak the basil seeds in plenty of cold water and leave for 10 minutes or until each seed develops a translucent coating. Dissolve sugar in ½ cup water on gentle heat. Combine sugar syrup with coconut milk. Brands vary, and if you know your brands well enough, use one which is fairly light and smooth. If it turns out to be thick and lumpy, warm it gently until smooth and dilute with a little water. Add the drained basil seeds. Stir in syrup from can of young coconut. Cut young coconut flesh into neat pieces or slender strips and stir into the mixture. Serve at room temperature, or ladle it over a couple of ice cubes in each bowl.

Bauhinia

(*Bauhinia malabarica*) The tender young leaves and shoots of this ornamental tree are used in sour soups in the Philippines and blanched and eaten with the ever-present nam prik in Thailand. The popular tree is mainly grown for its white, pinky-red or mauve flowers which look like orchids. They are a popular street plant in cities. The butterfly-shaped leaves are sometimes used in curries instead of lime juice.

India: *amli*
Indonesia: *benculuk*
Japan: *bauhinia*
Philippines: *alibangbang*
Thailand: *chung koo*

Bay Leaf

(*Laurus nobilis*) Also known as bay laurel leaf. Except for the food of the Philippines with its four hundred years of Spanish influence and more recent connection with America, this popular leaf, almost compulsory in European casseroles and stews, has no place in an Asia/Pacific encyclopaedia. The reason it is included is because it is necessary to state unequivocally that it also has no place in Asian dishes as a substitute for other leaves which are used for flavouring.

This view is contrary to that of many cookery writers who suggest substituting bay leaves for curry leaves (*Murraya koenigii*), cassia leaves (*Cinnamomum cassia*), kaffir lime leaves (*Citrus hystrix*) and salam leaves (*Eugenia polyantha*).

I may have fallen into the same trap many years ago when other leaves were unobtainable, but on further reflection, have realised this is not the wisest thing to do. Each of these leaves has a strong and distinctive fragrance and flavour, and in no way resembles any of the others. Just because a certain leaf is readily available to Western cooks does not sanction its use. If unable to procure the one called for, omit it altogether.

Often the confusion is a question of terminology. Cassia leaves are erroneously referred to as 'Indian bay leaves', even though they belong to a totally different botanical family and look nothing like a bay leaf. Cassia leaves can be twice the size (both in width and length) of the European bay leaf and when dried turn a dull brown colour and are inclined to break whereas bay leaves, tough and leathery as they are, are more likely to survive the drying process intact. See CASSIA LEAF.

The confusion is compounded by merchants labelling their cassia leaves 'Indian Bay Leaves' and their salam leaves 'Indonesian Bay Leaves'. Underneath, in small print, some labels state what they really are.

Bean

See LEGUMES & PULSES.

Bean Curd

An easy to digest, high protein food made from soy beans, bean curd is also low in calories. Rich in calcium, iron, phosphorus, potassium and sodium as well as essential B vitamins, choline and fat-soluble vitamin E, it is the low-cost solution to a meatless diet. Available in a number of shapes (blocks, sheets, sticks, pouches) and forms (fresh, dried, freeze-dried, deep-fried, pickled and fermented) with varying textures and flavours, it is a versatile ingredient much used in Asian cookery. Bean curd, in its many guises, is generally marketed under the name tofu.

Known in China as doufu and in Japan as tofu, there are several basic kinds. Silken tofu (kinugoshi, sui-doufu), literally 'strained through silk', is an apt description of the silken smooth, soft white tofu. The Chinese make a soft variety, doufu nao — literally 'bean brain' — from soy milk that has barely coagulated and is therefore softer than, and not as smooth as Japanese kinugoshi. Chinese style tofu (doufu, bean cake) sold as squares in water-packed containers, is creamy-white and firm enough to cut and hold its shape. Pressed tofu

(doufu-kan, doufu gar) is the firmest of all.

Dried-frozen tofu is another concentrated protein package, with over seven times the protein and energy value of regular tofu. Its affordability has helped its popularity to grow. Other benefits are being an 'instant' food (it takes less than 10 minutes to defrost). Light in weight, it is an ideal food for campers and backpackers. Its ability to absorb and carry flavours in a dish is unsurpassed. Rehydrated by a brief soaking in hot or cold water (there is some controversy on this issue) and well squeezed to express the soaking water, dried-frozen tofu is an edible, nutritious 'sponge'.

Technology introduced ammonia gas at the final stages of processing to improve softness and absorbency. Don't be put off by strong ammonia fumes when you open the packet — they will disappear when you reconstitute the tofu in hot water. The stronger the ammonia fumes, the fresher the batch of tofu. Not all manufacturers use ammonia gas in production.

Still another form of bean curd is the dried sheets or wrappers (yuba, doufu-p'i, doufu-i), also called bean curd skins (the skin that forms on soymilk when it is heated, lifted off and dried on bamboo mats). Rarely available, fresh yuba (nama yuba) is highly perishable, with a life of only 2–4 days even if refrigerated. It is more commonly encountered half dried (nama-gawaki, han-gawaki) in airtight plastic in the freezer.

Dried sheets or wrappers (kanso-yuba, hoshi-yuba) and variations are: flat sheets (hira-yuba, taira-yuba); the yellow-coloured version (kiyuba) is a popular topping for sushi; long rolls (komaki); short rolls (kiri-komaki); yuba troughs (toyuba) which are made of multiple layers shaped by the curve of the bamboo rods over which the sheets are hung to dry; large spirals (omaki, futomaki, uzumaki-yuba); flakes and shreds (kuzu-yuba, mimi); knots (musubi yuba); flattened rolls tied with a strip of kombu (oharagi); ginko-leaf yuba — leaf shapes cut from fresh sheets, then dried. Used to garnish soups and sushi.

Unless being added to a broth or sauce, all dried forms of bean curd need to be reconstituted in water before being used as a recipe ingredient unless a crisp result is desired, in which case they are deep fried from the dry state (only possible with thin dried bean curd products).

Another variation on the dried sheets are pressed bean curd wrappers (pai-yeh), noodles (doufu-ssu), shreds (kan-ssu) and knotted dried strips (pai-yeh chieh).

The process for making pressed bean curd sheets, sometimes called Chinese yuba, involves ladling firm curds onto numerous layers of cloth in a wooden frame. These are then compressed and weighted for several hours, resulting in thin, malleable sheets. The sheets can then be cut into very thin strips for bean curd noodles (pressed tofu noodles) or bean curd shreds and knots. The sheets are also made into tightly rolled cylinders which are tied with cloth then simmered until tender. When unwrapped they hold their shape and this firm rolled tofu is sold as a meat substitute called Buddha's chicken (su-chi) or Buddha's ham (suhuo-t'ui). Dried tofu has the highest protein content of any food.

There are also a number of forms of deep-fried tofu which need to be first simmered in boiling water to remove excess oil. In Japan, the thin deep-fried tofu needs to be simmmered twice, first for a couple of minutes and then, in a change of water, for about 10 minutes, discarding the water each time. The thick deep-fried tofu needs to be simmered only once, after which it is pricked all over with a toothpick or sharp fork so that it better absorbs the flavour of the broth it is to be cooked in. Deep-fried tofu adds a rich, 'meaty' taste to vegetarian soups and simmmered dishes.

You will find deep-fried tofu labelled as follows: doufu pok, yu-dofu, cha-dofu (Chinese) and abura-age, usu-age (thin) or atsu-age (thick) from Japan. Tofu may also be salted or pickled. Salted dried tofu is firm and dark brown in colour (doufu-kan) and fermented, preserved or pickled tofu (doufu-ru, furu, rufu, fuyu, funan) is aged tofu with a soft, creamy texture and an aroma not unlike ripe camembert cheese. Mainly used as a seasoning, these most pungent forms of tofu are unique to Chinese cuisine.

There are four main kinds of doufu-ru: white doufu-ru, red doufu-ru, tsao-doufu and chiang-doufu. The white doufu-ru (pai doufu-ru) is the most popular fermented tofu and there are numerous versions of it, seasoned with red pepper, sesame oil, and spices such as anise and cinnamon or ingredients such as lemon juice or rind, minced ham and dried shrimp. Red doufu-ru (hung doufu-ru, nanru, nanyu) is identical in preparation to the white, except that fermented red rice is added to the pickling liquor, imparting a rich red colour, thick

consistency and different flavour and aroma.

Tsao–dofu, those notoriously odiferous tofu, include: chu-tsao, which is aged in rice wine and wine lees, and the green tofu so popular in Taiwan, ch'ou doufu ('foul-smelling tofu'), made from pressed tofu squares aged with rice wine lees to which has been added crushed leaves and a green mould. Despite its overpowering aroma, slimy texture, unappetizing colour and the unfortunate odour it leaves on the breath, those brave enough to partake of it consider it a delicacy.

Chiang-doufu, or firm cubes of tofu fermented for several days in soy sauce (chiang-yu) or Chinese style miso (chiang) is red-brown in colour and salty or salty-sweet depending on whether rice wine or mould was introduced before fermentation. Chiang-doufu sauce (chiang-doufu chih), used to flavour Chinese lamb or beef dishes, is the result of mashing pickled tofu to a smooth paste with its pickling liquor. The Philippines has its own fermented tofu called tahuri made by packing cakes of firm moulded tofu with salt. No alcohol or brine is used in the process. Matured for several months, it becomes a brownish-yellow and acquires a uniquely complex salty flavour. Indonesia has a fermented 'tahu' called ragi.

China: *dow foo, doufu, doufu-ru*
Indonesia: *tahu*
Japan: *tofu, doufu-kan, abura-age, yuba*
Korea: *tubu, du bu, soon du bu*
Malaysia: *taukwa*
Philippines: *tojo, tokua*
Thailand: *tao hu, forng tao hu*
Vietnam: *dau hu*

Rice with Fried Bean Curd

Serves 6

500 g/1 lb short grain rice
750 ml/1½ pints/3 cups cold water
4 sheets fried bean curd (aburage)
500 ml/1 pint/2½ cups dashi or chicken stock
125 ml/4 fl oz/½ cup shoyu (Japanese soy sauce)
125 ml/4 fl oz/½ cup mirin or dry sherry
1 tablespoon sugar
6 spring onions (scallions) finely sliced diagonally

Wash rice and drain. Put into a saucepan with a well-fitting lid and add the water. Bring to the boil over high heat, cover pan and turn heat very low. Cook for 15 minutes without lifting lid.

Remove from heat, do not uncover for a further 10 minutes.

While rice is cooking pour 1 litre boiling water over fried bean curd in a colander to remove some of the oil. Cut each sheet of bean curd in half lengthways, then crossways into strips about 1 cm (½ in) wide.

In a saucepan combine dashi, soy sauce, mirin and sugar, add strips of bean curd and simmer for 10 minutes. Add sliced spring onions, cover and simmer for 1 minute. Ladle over the rice in a serving bowl or individual bowls and serve hot.

Korean Braised Bean Curd

Serves 4

250 g/8 oz Korean style bean curd
salt
3 tablespoons vegetable oil
3 tablespoons Korean soy sauce
 or Japanese soy sauce
3 tablespoons water
1 teaspoon chilli powder
1 teaspoon crushed toasted sesame seeds
1 teaspoon crushed garlic
2 spring onions (scallions), sliced
20 dried chilli threads (silgochu)

Slice bean curd into 2 cm (¾ in) slices and leave on double thickness of paper towels for 5 minutes to drain excess moisture. Sprinkle a little salt on each slice and leave for 10 minutes.

In a heavy frying pan large enough to take the bean curd in one layer heat the oil and brown the slices over moderate heat. Or fry them in 2 batches, about 3 minutes on each side. Drain on paper towels.

Add soy sauce, water, chilli powder, sesame seeds, garlic, spring onions and chilli threads, and if the bean curd has been browned in 2 lots, return all the pieces to the pan.

Bring liquid to the boil, cover the pan and simmer over low heat for 10 minutes or until much of the sauce is absorbed. If all the bean curd is not immersed in the liquid, after a few minutes move those on the bottom to the top and vice versa. Serve with rice.

Bean Curd with Hot Sauce

Because of its blandness, bean curd is relished with hot flavourings. Here is a vegetarian version. Serves 6.

500 g (1 lb) firm bean curd
2 tablespoons peanut oil
3 tablespoons finely chopped spring onions
 (scallions)
2 teaspoons finely chopped garlic
2 teaspoons finely chopped fresh ginger
1 tablespoon ground bean sauce (mor sze jeung)
1 teaspoon chilli bean paste
3 tablespoons sweet chilli sauce
1 tablespoon light soy sauce
2 teaspoons red bean curd, mashed*
2 teaspoons cornflour (cornstarch)
2 tablespoons water
1 teaspoon chilli oil
 or oriental sesame oil

Cut bean curd into 2 cm (¾ in) dice and drop into a pan of boiling water until heated through, about 4 minutes. Drain in a colander.

Heat peanut oil in a wok and on low heat fry spring onion for a few seconds before adding garlic and ginger. Stir and fry over low heat until fragrant and starting to turn golden. Add chilli bean paste, sauces and mashed red bean curd mixed with ⅔ cup stock or water. Stir until boiling, then mix in cornflour stirred with cold water and stir until sauce boils and thickens. Add bean curd and heat gently in the sauce. Sprinkle with sesame oil and serve on steamed rice.

* Red bean curd is the Chinese equivalent of ripe gorgonzola cheese. It is fermented and packed in jars. Use a clean dry spoon to take small amounts. Keeps without refrigeration even after the jar is opened.

Bean Curd with Meat

For variation of the above recipe, add a small amount, say 125 g (4 oz) of minced (ground) pork or beef. In many Asian recipes, meat is treated as a condiment and not as a main ingredient. Simply fry the meat together with the ginger and garlic, and proceed as above.

Bean Paste, Sweet

A sweetened paste made from dried beans is a popular filling for steamed buns and moon cakes. Available in a choice of colours: red (from adzuki beans); yellow (from mung beans, husked and split); or black (from black soy beans). The pastes are usually available ready-made sweetened in cans. It is possible to make your own, starting out with dried beans.

> **China:** *dow sa, tau-sa* (sweet bean paste)
> **Japan:** *an* (smooth red bean paste),
> *tsubushi-an* (chunky red bean paste)

Red Bean Paste (An)

220 g/7 oz/1 cup adzuki beans
250 g/8 oz/1 cup sugar
¼ teaspoon salt

Place beans in a pan with water to cover. Bring to boil. Turn off heat and soak for 1 hour. Drain, cover with fresh water then simmer for 30 minutes or until beans are soft and most of the water has evaporated. Add sugar and stir with a wooden spoon to roughly mash the beans (tsubushi-an). If a smooth paste is required, push cooked beans through sieve, add sugar and cook, stirring, until sugar is dissolved and the paste is thick.

The last stage of cooking, after adding sugar, may be done in a microwave oven without having to stir. Mix sugar into puréed beans and cook on full power for 5 minutes or until mixture no longer looks wet (check it after 3 minutes). Allow to rest for a couple of minutes before mixing. Use as required to flavour sweet soup or jellies. This paste will keep about a week refrigerated.

Chinese red bean paste uses a little less sugar and has ⅓ cup of peanut oil or lard incorporated after sugar is added and mixture has thickened.

Bean Paste, Yellow

Despite what it says on the label, the colour of this thick, salty condiment is not yellow but brown. It is used when a lighter sauce is required.

Bean Sauces

On the shelves of any oriental store you will see so many bean sauces it will make your head spin! Made from fermented soy beans, they vary in colour from yellow to brown to black. Not pourable like tomato ketchup, they are more like thick pastes and must be spooned from the jar, but since they are labelled 'bean sauce' let's continue to refer to them thus. In moderate amounts they add depth and flavour to many dishes.

There are hot bean sauces, sweet bean sauces, oily bean sauces, sauces with whole beans and sauces which are smoothly ground. The most basic among Chinese bean sauces are mor sze jeung, a smooth bean sauce, and min sze jeung, which contains mashed and whole fermented soy beans. Whenever 'bean sauce' is called for in a recipe from China, Singapore or Malaysia, this is the one to use (otherwise it would specify smooth bean sauce or ground bean sauce). If all you have on the shelf is smooth bean sauce, give it a bit of texture by mixing in an equal quantity of rinsed, salted black beans, lightly mashed with a fork.

Probably the most widely known of the sauces is hoi sin jeung, very useful with its balance of sweetness, saltiness, garlic and five-spice powder. Also well known is tim mein jeung, a sweet and salty ground bean sauce.

Among the hot bean sauces are chilli bean sauce (to be used with discretion) and soy chilli sauce. All these sauces should keep almost indefinitely even without refrigeration, but be particular to use only a clean, dry spoon.

Bean sauces, in particular those spiked with chilli, are essential in Hunan and Szechwan cuisine, and are the favoured seasoning for meat dishes in northern China.

In the Korean kitchen, there is the indispensable dhwen jang (thick bean sauce) and a tasty variation on smooth bean paste with a healthy dose of chilli, called gochu jang. Chinese smooth bean paste or Japanese aka miso are acceptable substitutes.

See also BARBECUE SAUCE.

Bean Sprouts

Mung beans and soy beans are the beans most commonly used throughout Asia for growing bean sprouts, but in the West mung beans are much better known and more easily obtained. If you intend eating them raw, soy beans aren't the wisest choice. They must be cooked for 10 minutes (see SOY BEAN, FRESH).

Bean sprouts are now available from most supermarkets and greengrocers, usually in plastic tubs or packets. The texture of the sprouts in tubs is very crunchy and nutty with hardly any stringy rootlet. There is more work involved in preparing the long, straight sprouts that come in cellophane packets for cooking: picking off long, straggly brown 'tails'. The straighter sprouts are traditional for Asian cuisine. Either form should be used as soon as possible after purchase, although they may be stored for a brief period under refrigeration.

At the risk of upsetting the purists, I have to say I rather like the sweetness and crunch of short sprouts (not to mention the added convenience of not having to pick over the tails). However, if there are lots of green skins, place the sprouts in a bowl, cover with cold water, agitate and skim off and discard loose skins that float to the surface. They are rather tough and don't enhance the appearance of a dish, although they do increase the fibre content. Drain sprouts well before adding to your wok and keep cooking time short.

Canned bean sprouts have none of the wonderful crisp texture and sweet fresh flavour one expects from bean sprouts. If fresh bean sprouts are unavailable, it is not difficult to sprout your own.

Depending on the methods used for sprouting mung beans, they will be short and curly or long and straight. A commercial sprouting process is responsible for the straight sprouts, and it is not possible to duplicate these conditions under the kitchen sink. Home sprouted seeds are curly. The seed, with its green coat split open but often still clinging, is at one end of the sprout with a small root at the other. When the beans are rinsed many of the seed coats float away, but it is not essential to remove every single one.

In the best circles (and most expensive restaurants) bean sprouts have their 'tails' pinched off during preparation. It is somewhat disconcerting to take a mouthful and find one or two thread-like roots trailing behind the rest of the food, so always take time to pinch them off.

More rarely the seeds are removed also, leaving only the straight white portion of the sprouts which then qualify for the name, 'silver sprouts'. Very refined, but the sprouting seeds are nice to eat and I prefer not to remove them.

The procedure for sprouting is quite simple. First, soak 3 tablespoons of mung beans overnight in water to cover. Drain and put the beans in a large glass jar, at least 3 cups capacity, as the beans will expand to many times their original volume. Cover with a piece of muslin held on with a rubber band and leave in a warm, dark place such as under the sink or in a cupboard. Morning and evening (and a couple of times in between if you can manage it), fill the jar with barely tepid water and pour the water off, and in 5 or 6 days the jar will be filled with fresh, crisp bean sprouts. Transfer to a plastic bag and refrigerate. Use within a week.

See also SOY BEAN SPROUTS.

Burma: *pepinauk*
China: *nga choi*
Indonesia: *taoge*
Korea: *suk ju*
Japan: *moyashi*
Malaysia: *taugeh*
Singapore: *taugeh*
Thailand: *tau ngork*
Vietnam: *gia*

Bean Starch Noodles

See NOODLES.

Bean Starch Sheets

Made from the starch of green mung beans, these translucent, round sheets bear the imprint of the bamboo mats they are dried on. Brittle when dry, they need to be soaked in hot water for about 20 minutes and then boiled for 5 minutes before being refreshed under cold water. Drained and cut into strips, they make an attractive addition to a dish and add unique texture.

Bean Starch Sheets with Prawns (Shrimp)

Serves 4

6 bean starch sheets
500 g/1 lb raw prawns (shrimp)
2 teaspoons salt
¼ teaspoon white pepper
2 tablespoons peanut oil
1 teaspoon finely chopped fresh ginger
1 tablespoon oyster sauce

Soak bean starch sheets in a large dish of hot water for 20 minutes. Bring a pan of lightly salted water to the boil, take the sheets from the soaking water and drop them into the pan. Boil for 5 minutes, drain and when cool enough cut into bite-sized strips.

Shell and devein the prawns, rub well with half the salt and rinse thoroughly. Repeat. Blot prawns dry on paper towels and sprinkle with white pepper.

Heat peanut oil and stir-fry ginger and prawns together just until prawns become opaque and are cooked. Turn off heat. Add oyster sauce and strips of bean starch. Serve at once.

Beans, Salted Yellow

Yellow soy beans which have been salted and fermented are sold in small cans. They give good flavour to Chinese sauces and are especially useful when you do not wish to darken a sauce by using salted black beans. Use sparingly. They will keep indefinitely in the refrigerator and do not need rinsing before use.

Beef

Beef is eaten in most Asian countries where religious restrictions don't confine the eating of beef to the minorities.

The Japanese have raised cattle from as early as the third century. Though not well documented, enough must have found its way onto tables for the Emperor Temmu to decree, in 676, that the eating of cows (chickens, horses and monkeys too) be stopped to obey the Buddhist prohibitions against eating flesh. The influx of Portuguese in the 16th century probably put the focus back on meat, and some assert that this is when the world-famous Japanese meat dish sukiyaki came into being. If not then, beef probably increased in popularity in the 1860s, in the reign of the new Meiji emperor, when Japan opened its shores to foreigners.

At first the Japanese were aghast to observe the foreigners' diet: not only did they eat the cow, they drank its milk as well! However, after the establishment of the first official abattoir (on premises purified by Shinto priests) the barriers slowly came down.

In 1873 the emperor called the taboo against meat 'an unreasonable tradition' and a popular saying of the day was: 'A man who does not eat beef is an uncivilised man'. Oh, the lure of the West!

There are many variations on Japan's most popular beef dish, sukiyaki (also called gyu-nabe). Kanto in the Tokyo area has the sauce made in the pan before adding meat and other ingredients.

It is traditionally cooked in a heavy iron pan over a gas flame at the table, quickly frying thinly sliced beef in melted suet and then arranging on top the grilled tofu, diagonal slices of green spring onion (scallion), shiitake mushrooms and threads of konnyaku before pouring over the stock (shoyu, sugar, mirin and water). This is Kansai (Osaka–Kyoto) style. Simmered briefly then served, each diner is given an individual bowl containing a raw egg, lightly beaten, flavoured with a little soy if desired. The hot morsels are picked out of the broth with chopsticks, a piece at a time, and dipped in the egg to form a delicate, light coating. Other regional variations on the theme include using ground beef (Nagasaki), substituting venison or wild boar for the beef (Honshu) or omitting the suet and simmering the dish right from the start.

The best beef in Japan is undoubtedly the world-famous and expensive Kobe beef. Produced from pampered cattle fed on beer and grain and hand-massaged daily, it results in beef evenly marbled with fat (shimofuri niku). Kobe beef literally melts in the mouth. For dishes like shabu-shabu, the meat may be partially frozen to facilitate slicing it paper-thin against the grain and it is usually sold ready sliced. Now it requires only the briefest cooking. Or don't cook it at all! Niku-no-sashimi (sliced beef) and niku-no-tataki (chopped, marinated beef) are two uncooked dishes. Another uncooked dish is beef sushi, in which thin slices of raw beef are rubbed with garlic then served on sushi rice.

Another delicious way to eat beef is to marinate it before cooking, a method used for the famous Korean barbecued dish bulgogi. A variation on this theme is barbecued short ribs of beef, bulgalbi. Add to this a large repertoire of Korean stewed, fried and braised beef dishes.

Due to its largely Hindu population, to which the cow is considered sacred, beef is not a popular meat in India except among Parsis, Christians and other minorities. When available it is of variable quality and needs long, slow cooking and plenty of spicing to help make it palatable.

Beef, appreciated in Chinese cuisine for its

distinctive flavour, is usually served as a tasty side dish for rice. (The proportion of meat at an Asian meal is quite the opposite to the West.) It is believed to be 'heating' which is bad for the health. Expense aside, when meat is eaten, pork or chicken usually gets preference (except in the north, where lamb is more popular).

Beef is often marinated to both boost its flavour and tenderise it. A very small amount of bicarbonate of soda (baking soda) dissolved in water may be used for maximum effect (see recipe for Chinese Stir-fried Beef, page 34). This does, indeed, make even the cheapest cut quite easy to chew, but there is a subtle change in the texture and flavour which may not be to everyone's liking.

Corned beef, or old-fashioned canned 'bully beef' well known in wartime rations, is found on the shelves of every country colonised by the British. It is a great favourite among Pacific peoples. If the feast is really important and a VIP is present, the prized can of corned beef will be opened.

Korean Barbecued Beef (Bulgogi)

Serves 6–8

1 kg/2 lb lean rump or fillet
3 tablespoons light soy sauce
3 tablespoons water
2 tablespoons finely chopped spring onions
  (scallions)
1 teaspoon crushed garlic
2 teaspoons sugar
1 teaspoon finely grated fresh ginger
¼ teaspoon ground black pepper
1 tablespoon toasted, crushed sesame seeds

BULGOGI SAUCE

3 tablespoons soy sauce
2 teaspoons oriental sesame oil
1 teaspoon Korean bean paste
2 tablespoons water
2 tablespoons rice wine
2 teaspoons toasted, ground sesame seeds
1 tablespoon finely chopped spring onions
  (scallions)
1 teaspoon chilli sauce
1 teaspoon finely chopped garlic
2 teaspoons sugar
salt to taste

Cut beef into thin slices and beat them out flat, then cut into squares. Combine remaining ingredients, using some of the sugar to crush the garlic to a smooth paste. Mix with the beef, cover and marinate for 3 hours or longer. Grill briefly over glowing coals and serve with white rice and bulgogi sauce.

To make the bulgogi sauce: Combine soy sauce and sesame oil and stir in next 6 ingredients. Crush garlic to a smooth paste with sugar and mix well, adding salt if necessary. Serve in small individual sauce dishes.

Teriyaki Steak

Serves 6

6 small slices fillet steak
½ teaspoon chopped garlic
½ teaspoon sugar
1 teaspoon ginger juice
125 ml/4 fl oz/½ cup Japanese soy sauce
125 ml/4 fl oz/½ cup mirin or sherry
2 tablespoons oil
2 teaspoons sugar
4 tablespoons water or dashi
1 teaspoon cornflour (cornstarch)
cold water

Trim beef of any excess fat. Sprinkle garlic with sugar on a wooden chopping board and purée with the flat of a knife. Mix with ginger juice (squeezed from grated fresh ginger), soy sauce and mirin. Dip each steak into marinade on both sides and leave for about 30 minutes.

Heat a heavy griddle plate or frying pan. Spread oil over cooking surface and when very hot put steaks on the griddle for 1 minute. Turn over with tongs to brown other side. Turn heat low and continue to cook until done, depending both on the thickness of the meat and the way it is preferred: rare or medium.

Heat remaining marinade in a small pan with sugar, water or dashi and cornflour mixed smoothly with very little cold water. Stir until it boils and becomes clear, then spoon this glaze over the steaks and serve immediately. For easy eating with chopsticks the steaks may be sliced and reassembled in their original shape.

Sukiyaki

Serves 6

**1 kg/2 lb well-marbled tender beef in one piece
  (or ready-sliced from a Japanese store)**
oil or beef suet for greasing pan
125 ml/4 fl oz/½ cup Japanese soy sauce
1 tablespoon sugar
3 tablespoons sake
250 ml/8 fl oz/1 cup beef stock
**1 small can winter bamboo shoots,
  drained and sliced**
6 spring onions (scallions) in bite-sized lengths
**250 g/8 oz fresh mushrooms, wiped with damp
  paper and thickly sliced**
2 white onions, each cut in 8 wedges
2 cups fresh bean sprouts, tails removed
½ small Chinese white cabbage, sliced
2 squares bean curd, sliced
**1 packet shirataki
  or 60 g/2 oz bean starch vermicelli**
6 eggs, optional

Freeze the steak for an hour or until firm
enough to cut into very thin slices. Combine
soy sauce, sugar, sake and beef stock in a jug.
Prepare the vegetables and bean curd, and lay
them out on a tray. Cook and drain the
noodles.

Heat a heavy iron frying pan and add just
enough oil to grease base lightly, or rub pan
with beef suet until well greased. Add half of
each vegetable to pan and fry on high heat for
2 minutes or until half cooked. Push to side of
pan and add slices of meat in one layer. Turn
each piece over almost immediately. Sprinkle
with some of the liquid, adding enough to
moisten all the food in the pan.

Break an egg in each bowl and beat lightly
with chopsticks. Each diner takes food from
the pan, dips it into the beaten egg to coat
lightly and eats it with steaming hot rice. This
step may be omitted if preferred. When the pan
is empty, start cooking the rest of the
ingredients, adding more sauce as required.
An electric frypan is ideal for cooking this dish
at the table.

Beef and Vegetable Rolls

A Japanese style dish which is as colourful as
it is delicious. Serves 4.

375 g/12 oz lean beef, in thin slices
2 carrots
3 spring onions (scallions)
125 g/4 oz green beans
cornflour (cornstarch)
1 piece pickled radish (takuan)
1–2 tablespoons vegetable oil
iced water

SAUCE

2 tablespoons sake or mirin
3 tablespoons Japanese soy sauce
1 tablespoon sugar
3 tablespoons water

Ask the butcher to cut the beef into thin slices,
and if they are not very thin, take them home
and pound them lightly with a meat mallet on a
wooden board until no more than 6 mm (¼ in)
thick. Then cut them into strips about 5 cm
(2 in) wide.

Peel carrots and trim into sticks the same
length as the green beans — about 15 cm (6 in)
long and 6 mm (¼ in) square. Trim spring
onions to the same length. Top and tail the
beans, and cut the pickled radish into narrow
strips.

Bring a pan of water to the boil, add the
carrots and boil for about 4 minutes or until
almost tender. Lift out. Add the beans. Cook
uncovered for about 3 minutes, drain and drop
into iced water to stop cooking.

Sift a little cornflour over each strip of beef,
and place a bundle consisting of 2 carrot
sticks, 2 or 3 beans, a couple of lengths of
spring onion and pickled radish on each of the
beef strips. Roll up, starting at one end of the
vegetables and completely enclosing them in
the beef. Fasten with a wooden toothpick. Dust
outside of rolls lightly with cornflour.

Heat a large, heavy frypan with oil and
brown the beef rolls on all sides, turning them
over with tongs. Combine ingredients for sauce
and add to the pan. Simmer for about 5
minutes until they are evenly coloured and
flavoured with the sauce. Turn off heat and
allow to cool slightly before cutting crossways
into 5 cm (2 in) slices. Serve with steamed rice.

Curried Beef Satays

Serves 6

750 g/1½ lb rump steak
½ teaspoon salt
½ teaspoon ground black pepper
½ teaspoon ground turmeric
thin slices peeled garlic
thin slices fresh ginger
3 tablespoons ghee or oil
sprig of fresh curry leaves
**   or 10 dried curry leaves**
¼ teaspoon dried fenugreek seeds
2 medium onions, finely chopped
2 teaspoons finely chopped garlic
1 teaspoon finely grated ginger
1 tablespoon ground coriander
2 teaspoons ground cumin
½ teaspoon ground fennel
½ teaspoon ground aromatic ginger
½ teaspoon ground cardamom
½ teaspoon chilli powder
1 teaspoon salt
400 ml/14 fl oz can coconut milk

Cut steak into cubes, sprinkle with salt, pepper and turmeric and mix well. Thread cubes of beef on short bamboo skewers, putting a slice of ginger and one of garlic between them. Allow 3 or 4 cubes of beef for each skewer.

In a heavy frying pan heat ghee or oil and fry skewers on high heat, turning, to brown the beef. Do not add too many to the pan at a time, and remove them to a plate as they brown. Add curry leaves, fenugreek, onion, garlic, ginger and cook over low heat until onions are soft and golden. Stir frequently to prevent scorching.

As ghee or oil starts to separate from the mass, add the ground spices and stir for a minute longer. Add salt and coconut milk and cook, uncovered, until gravy is thick. Return skewered beef to the gravy and simmer for 15 minutes or until beef is tender. Serve with rice and accompaniments.

Chinese Stir-Fried Beef

Here is a recipe using budget-priced cuts of beef, but allow sufficient time for tenderising. Use lean round, blade or skirt steak and freeze just long enough to firm the meat, since this makes it possible to cut very thin slices. Put the sliced beef into a bowl and for each 500 g (1 lb) of beef, dissolve ½ teaspoon of bicarbonate of soda (baking soda) in 3 tablespoons warm water. Pour over the beef and knead well until evenly distributed and absorbed. Cover and refrigerate at least 3 hours, overnight if possible. Proceed with the recipe. If time is short, you have to buy the more expensive tender cuts. Serves 3–4.

375 g/12 oz tender, lean grilling steak
½ teaspoon crushed garlic
½ teaspoon salt
½ teaspoon finely grated fresh ginger
2 teaspoons cornflour (cornstarch)
4 tablespoons cold water
2 tablespoons dark soy sauce
1 teaspoon oriental sesame oil
2 tablespoons peanut oil
4 spring onions (scallions), chopped

Freeze beef to firm it, then cut in thin, bite-sized slices across the grain. Combine garlic, salt and ginger and rub into beef, mixing well. Set aside for 10 minutes. Mix cornflour with water, soy sauce and sesame oil.

Heat a wok, add peanut oil and swirl to coat. Add beef and stir-fry over high heat until colour changes. Add spring onions and fry for 1 minute longer. Add cornflour mixture and stir until it boils and thickens. Serve immediately with rice.

Chinese Clay-Pot Beef

Simmered in a heavy casserole which takes the place of a Chinese clay pot, this makes a succulent, warming winter dish. Serves 8–10.

1.5 kg/3 lb brisket of beef
3 tablespoons oil
1 teaspoon salt
1 teaspoon Szechwan peppercorns
2 teaspoons sugar
6 slices fresh ginger
4 unpeeled garlic cloves
2 tablespoons Chinese rose wine

2 whole star anise
2 pieces dried tangerine peel
8 dried shiitake mushrooms
6 spring onions (scallions)
2 tablespoons dark soy sauce

Bring to the boil some water in a pan large enough to hold the piece of beef. Lower the beef into the boiling water, return to the boil and simmer for 5 minutes. Remove and rinse under cold water and trim off any fat and gristle. Place on a board and with a sharp knife cut the meat into 1.5 cm (1 in) slices. Heat half the oil in a wok and fry slices of beef to brown both sides. Transfer to casserole or clay pot. Add roasted and ground peppercorns, sugar, ginger, garlic, wine, star anise and tangerine peel. Cover with lid or foil and place in a large steamer with about 5 cm (2 in) water. Simmer for 2 hours, replenishing water as required.

Soak mushrooms in 2 cups very hot water for 30 minutes. Squeeze out water. Cut off and discard the mushroom stems and cut caps into quarters. Cut spring onions into short lengths.

Heat a wok and add remaining oil. Fry the spring onions and mushroom caps for 2 minutes. Then add meat together with any liquid in the bowl. Remove star anise and tangerine peel. Add wine and soy sauce, cover wok and simmer for 10 minutes. Serve with steamed rice.

Beef with Black Bean Sauce

Serves 4–6

500 g/1 lb lean rump or fillet steak
2 tablespoons canned salted black beans
1 tablespoon dark soy sauce
3 tablespoons water or stock
1 teaspoon finely chopped garlic
1 teaspoon sugar
2 tablespoons peanut oil
1 teaspoon cornflour (cornstarch)
1 teaspoon oriental sesame oil

Freeze beef for 1 hour or until firm enough to slice paper thin. Put black beans into a small strainer and rinse under cold tap for a few seconds. Drain, then mash roughly with a fork. Combine with the soy sauce and water. Put chopped garlic on a board and crush with the sugar to a smooth paste.

Heat a wok, add peanut oil and swirl to coat the wok. Add beef and fry over high heat, tossing and stirring until beef is no longer red. Add garlic and fry for 30 seconds, then add bean mixture. Bring to the boil. Lower heat, cover and simmer for 2 minutes, then stir in cornflour mixed with a tablespoon of cold water and let sauce boil and thicken. Stir in sesame oil and serve with steamed rice.

Beef Balls with Tangerine Peel

Serves 4

2 pieces dried tangerine peel
2 tablespoons boiling water
500 g/1 lb minced (ground) beef
1 teaspoon salt
½ teaspoon crushed garlic
½ teaspoon sugar
½ teaspoon finely grated fresh ginger
2 tablespoons finely chopped spring onions
  (scallions), green leaves included
1 tablespoon Chinese rose wine, optional
1 tablespoon cornflour (cornstarch)
2 tablespoons cold water
1 egg white, beaten

SAUCE

1 tablespoon oil
1 small red capsicum (sweet pepper), diced
125 ml/4 fl oz/½ cup stock
1 tablespoon oyster sauce
½ teaspoon sugar
1 teaspoon cornflour (cornstarch)

Soak tangerine peel in water until soft, or hurry the process by placing over low heat or in microwave for 1 minute. Mince the peel very finely. Add to the beef together with the rest of the main ingredients.

Mix together well, folding in egg white last. Cover and chill for 30 minutes or longer, then form into 16 meatballs.

Heat half the oil in a wok or heavy non-stick frying pan. On high heat stir-fry the diced capsicum for 1 minute. Remove from pan, heat remaining oil and lightly brown the beef balls. Add stock, oyster sauce and sugar, cover and simmer for 10 minutes. Add cornflour mixed with a little cold water and stir until sauce thickens. Return red capsicum to pan, toss to mix and serve with steamed rice.

Beef Rendang

This Indonesian/Malaysian dish with its complex seasoning is easy to make. Everything goes in the pot at once and simmers until rich and thick. Serves 8.

1.5 kg/3 lb lean stewing beef
2 medium onions, chopped
2 tablespoons finely chopped garlic
1 tablespoon finely chopped ginger
1 tablespoon chopped galangal, fresh or bottled
6 fresh red chillies, seeded
400 ml/14 fl oz can coconut milk
1½ teaspoons salt
1 teaspoon ground turmeric
2 teaspoons chilli powder or to taste
3 teaspoons ground coriander
1 teaspoon ground cumin
½ teaspoon ground aromatic ginger
1 stalk fresh lemon grass, bruised
125 ml/4 fl oz/½ cup tamarind liquid
2 teaspoons sugar

Cut beef into strips and put into a large, heavy saucepan. Put onion, garlic, ginger, galangal, chillies and ½ cup water into a blender, cover and blend until smooth. Pour over meat and add all remaining ingredients except tamarind liquid and sugar. Mix well and bring to the boil, uncovered.

Reduce heat to low, add tamarind liquid and simmer uncovered until gravy is thick, stirring occasionally. Simmer for about 2 hours, stirring from time to time, until oil separates from the gravy. Add sugar and stir constantly. Serve with steamed white rice and vegetable dishes and sambals.

Beef Stew (Kari-Kari)

Every good cook in the Philippines has his or her own version of this stew. One thing remains constant, and that is the fact that this is a big, heavy meal usually served for lunch on Sundays or holidays, so that it may be followed by a siesta. Serves 8.

3 tablespoons oil
2.5 kg/5 lb oxtail
**   or 2 kg/4 lb shin of beef**
3 teaspoons salt
2 tablespoons annatto seeds
2 large onions, finely sliced
1 tablespoon finely chopped garlic

2 litres/4 pints/8 cups water
½ teaspoon ground black pepper
4 tablespoons roasted and ground rice
4 tablespoons crushed roasted peanuts
1 banana blossom
250 g/8 oz green beans
250 g/8 oz slender eggplants (aubergines)
3 spring onions (scallions), sliced
3 tablespoons chopped Asian celery leaves
fish sauce to taste

Ask the butcher to trim the oxtail of excess fat and cut it into joints. If using shin of beef, ask him to saw it into thick slices. Season meat with salt on all sides.

In a large, heavy pan heat the oil and brown the meat in batches. Transfer to a plate on a slotted spoon and in the fat remaining in pan fry the annatto seeds, keeping a lid on the pan to prevent seeds jumping out. The oil should become a bright orange colour. Remove pan from heat, remove seeds with perforated spoon and discard. In the same oil cook the onions and garlic, stirring occasionally, until soft. Return meat to pan and add water and pepper. Bring to the boil, then cover pan and simmer on low heat until meat is tender — about 2 hours. If time permits, pour off liquid and refrigerate it long enough to be able to remove fat from surface, otherwise skim off as much fat as possible before proceeding with last stage of recipe.

Combine roasted ground rice and crushed peanuts. Discard outer bracts of banana blossom until the inner, tender portion is reached. Steam for 10 minutes, then cut in halves lengthways and across into slices. Top and tail beans, string if necessary and cut into bite-sized pieces. Wash but do not peel eggplants, and cut into thick diagonal slices. If only large eggplants are available, cut into lengthways wedges.

Add vegetables and the rice and peanut combination to the pan, stirring gently. Simmer until vegetables are tender and gravy thick. Add 2 tablespoons fish sauce and taste to see if more is needed. Sprinkle with chopped spring onions and celery. Serve with rice, and sauces such as soy sauce, fish sauce, chilli sauce, or the Filipino favourite made from equal amounts of bagoong (shrimp paste) and lime juice.

It is possible to buy roasted ground rice powder in small packets. If not available, it is simple enough to make. Roast rice in a heavy frying pan without oil and stir constantly or shake pan to let grains gradually become a deep golden colour. Pulverise in a blender or pound with a mortar and pestle. Sift through a strainer and discard coarse pieces.

Thai Masaman Beef Curry

One of the favourite dishes of Thai cuisine, this dish shows the influence of Indian traders since it combines fragrant Moslem spices with the flavours of a typical Thai curry. Economy cuts such as shin beef or blade are really best for this dish. Serves 6–8.

1.5 kg/3 lb stewing beef
8 cardamom pods, bruised
1 teaspoon salt
500 ml/1 pint/2 cups coconut milk
6 tablespoons Thai Masaman curry paste
  (recipe page 115)
8 small new potatoes
10 small pickling onions, peeled
2 tablespoons fish sauce
3 tablespoons lime or lemon juice
2 tablespoons palm sugar
  or brown sugar
20 fresh basil leaves
90 g/3 oz/½ cup whole roasted peanuts

Cut beef into 5 cm (2 in) cubes and put into a pan with the cardamom pods, salt and 1½ cups of the coconut milk diluted with an equal amount of water. Bring to the boil, then lower heat, cover and simmer until meat is almost tender.

In a wok heat the remaining undiluted coconut milk and stir over medium heat until thick and oily. Add Masaman curry paste and fry until fragrant. Add meat, potatoes, onions, fish sauce, lime juice and palm sugar. Simmer uncovered until potatoes are done, adding stock from meat as required. When almost ready stir in basil leaves and peanuts and simmer for a few minutes longer. Serve with steamed rice.

Thai Beef Salad

One of the most popular restaurant dishes, and easy to make at home. Serves 6.

500 g/1 lb fillet, lean rump or other tender steak
1 teaspoon crushed garlic
1 tablespoon pounded coriander roots and stems
¼ teaspoon ground black pepper
1 tablespoon palm sugar or brown sugar
3 teaspoons Maggi seasoning
  or Golden Mountain sauce*
1 tablespoon lime juice
2 teaspoons fish sauce
3 fresh red chillies
3 tablespoons sliced purple shallots
3 tablespoons finely sliced lemon grass
  (tender white portion only)
1 seedless cucumber, finely sliced
20 fresh mint leaves

Grill the steak over coals or under a preheated grill until medium-rare. Allow to cool. (Or use thin slices of rare roast beef.)

Combine crushed garlic with pounded coriander and stir in the pepper, palm sugar, Maggi seasoning, lime juice and fish sauce. Stir to dissolve sugar. Slice the chillies finely, removing seeds if preferred. Combine seasonings with the sliced shallots, lemon grass, cucumber, mint and the thinly sliced steak. Toss lightly and serve.

* Golden Mountain sauce is a Thai product which contains monosodium glutamate (MSG). It is very similar in flavour to Maggi seasoning which is Swiss made with no added MSG.

Beefsteak Plant

See PERILLA.

Bele

(*Hibiscus manihot*) A vegetable similar to spinach used in the Pacific. Bele is the Tongan name for this large leaf with 7 points. Young leaves near the top of the stems are the most tender, and are usually blanched in lightly salted water for about 5 minutes, drained and served with coconut cream.

Besan

See FLOURS & STARCHES.

Betel Leaf

(*Piper betel*) SEE ILLUSTRATION. A thick, smooth, dark green leaf, broad at one end and pointed at the other. This is the leaf known as paan in India, a word indicating not only the leaf but also the whole package called a chew or quid of betel. This is a little parcel of betel leaf wrapped around fragrant spices, tobacco leaf, slaked lime paste, coloured shreds of coconut and fine shreds of areca nut (often called betel nut through association, though it belongs to a different species).

Chosen according to the taste and the purchasing power of the customer, the betel leaf may be covered with tissue-thin beaten silver. For those who can afford it, gold leaf is included for its supposed aphrodisiac qualities. In little shops tucked away in the suburbs of London or any other large city where Indians have settled, one sees paan being sold.

However, in most Burmese, Sri Lankan or Indian homes they prefer to put together the paan themselves. The ingredients are displayed in a decorative silver or lacquered container with different compartments for the various ingredients, which is placed in the middle of the table or, in traditional homes, in the middle of the carpet on which family and guests sit cross-legged. During the long gossip session which is par for the course when families and friends get together, each adult will make their own selection to enclose in the paan or betel leaf. In families where betel chewing is the custom, there are always discreetly placed brass spittoons, burnished and gleaming.

The betel chew is a masticatory often served after a meal, which acts as breath-freshener, digestive, antacid and carminative.

A very basic paan consists of 2 betel leaves, a smear of slaked lime, and shreds or a fine slice of areca nut (betel nut). A few strands of tobacco may also be added. On festive occasions cloves, cardamom seeds, aromatic ginger, fennel seeds and coloured shredded coconut are included and the leaf is covered with varak (silver leaf).

A related leaf sometimes referred to as wild betel leaf but used in different ways is *P. sarmentosum*. It is used in cooking and wrapping little snacks to be consumed, unlike *P. betel* which is only used as a masticatory. See CHA PLU.

Medicinal uses: Betel leaves are considered a cough cure and decongestant and are crushed and included in small pastilles. They are also steeped in boiling water and the hot liquid drunk to bring down fever.

India: *paan*
Sri Lanka: *bulath*
Thailand: *phluu, see keh*

Betel Nut

(*Areca catechu*) SEE ILLUSTRATION. Such is the power of common usage, the areca nut is better known as betel nut because it is an essential part of the betel chew. Botanically, that which is called a nut is actually a seed. The fruits grow on tall palms (up to 30 m/100 ft) in bunches of a hundred or more, turning an attractive bright orange colour when ripe. After drying in the sun the outer husk is removed and the large round seeds sold whole or cracked. Special cutters are required to slice the hard seed thinly before using.

I am told that the betel nut is a stimulant, and that chewing it produces a 'high', but most users will only admit to using it as a digestive. It has an astringent effect, which I can vouch for. The one and only time I tried a chew of betel (to refuse would have been impolite to my host), the inside of my cheek felt puckered for hours afterwards. I cannot truthfully say that it had any other effect, in spite of the claims made on its behalf.

Medicinal uses: Betel nut is used in certain Chinese medicinal preparations and thin slices of the dried nuts fill glass jars in medicine shops. They are very decorative with their intricate patterns of brown and white. Regarded as an aphrodisiac. Used by the Chinese in the treatment of tapeworms and roundworms, and for diarrhoea, indigestion, lumbago, urinary and menstrual problems. The nut is supposed to show anti-cancer activity.

Thanks to William Lai for his help in translating Chinese texts. I pass on what his book on Eastern medicine has to say about the betel nut. 'It makes a drunken person sober, a sober person drunk. It makes a hungry person feel satisfied and a person who has eaten too well, feel ready for his next meal.'

China: *pin lung*
India: *supari, pak-ku*
Malaysia: *pinang*
Sri Lanka: *puwak*

Bilimbi

(*Averrhoa bilimbi*) Also known as belimbing or billing. Native of the Moluccas sometimes called cucumber tree because of the shape of its fruits. The pale green fruit is mostly water and sharp acid flavour. As children we would eat it but it is mainly used for providing an acid flavour in curries. The fruit looks like a miniature cucumber and grows in clusters on the trunk and older branches of small trees. Like other acid fruit, it is used, dipped in salt, for removing tarnish and burnishing brass.

It is frequently salted and dried for storing, and added to curries when a sour flavour is required. This salting may be undertaken at home, because the fruit grows in many kitchen gardens. It is first pricked well with a fork, then arranged in a stone jar, each layer sprinkled liberally with salt. Dried in the sun for a few days it becomes brownish and leathery. The fresh fruit is also made into jams or chutneys — any fruit with acid content ends up in the preserving pot.

Indonesia: *belimbing wuluh*
Malaysia: *belimbing asam*
India: *bilimbikai*
Philippines: *camias, kamias*
Sri Lanka: *billing*
Thailand: *ka-ling-pring, ta-ling-pring*

Bilimbi Curry

500 g/1 lb bilimbi fruit
2 teaspoons salt
2 tablespoons oil
sprig of fresh curry leaves
1 medium onion, finely chopped
2 fresh green chillies, seeded and sliced
½ teaspoon turmeric
2 teaspoons roasted ground coriander
1 teaspoon chilli powder or to taste
125 ml/4 fl oz/½ cup coconut milk
1 teaspoon salt or to taste

Slice the bilimbi, put into a bowl and pour over just enough water to cover. Stir in 2 teaspoons salt and leave for 30 minutes or longer, then rinse and squeeze out as much moisture as possible from the bilimbi.

Heat the oil in a pan and fry the curry leaves and onion until the onion is soft and starts turning golden. Add the chillies, turmeric, coriander and chilli powder and fry for 1 minute, then add the bilimbi and fry, stirring, for 5 minutes.

Add coconut milk and salt. Simmer uncovered until the mixture is thick and oily. Serve with rice.

Bilimbi Pickle

1 kg/2 lb bilimbi
2 teaspoons salt
8 dried red chillies
2 tablespoons pounded Maldive fish
1 onion, finely chopped
1 tablespoon finely chopped garlic
1 tablespoon finely grated ginger
1 teaspoon ground turmeric
3 tablespoons oil
small stick cinnamon
1 stem lemon grass
1 fresh or dried pandan leaf
salt to taste

Slice and soak the bilimbi in salt as for the previous recipe, leave for 1 hour, then rinse in cold water and squeeze out as much moisture as possible.

Remove stems of dried chillies and soak in hot water for 10 minutes. Put the chillies into a blender jar with a little of the soaking water, the Maldive fish, onion, garlic, ginger and turmeric. Blend to a purée, adding just enough water to facilitate blending.

Heat the oil, add the blended mixture and fry, stirring, until it smells fragrant and the oil separates from the mass. Add cinnamon, lemon grass, pandan leaf and salt. Cover and simmer until bilimbi is cooked. Put into clean dry jars and store.

Bird's Nest

A luxury ingredient reserved for special occasions, bird's nests may be served in a clear consommé savoury soup with minced chicken or ham and quail eggs, or a sweet soup with rock sugar.

These bird's nests are not made from twigs and straw but are the dried spittle of cave-dwelling swifts, a breed of swallows found mainly along the coast of southern China and South East Asia, and inland where nature provides the requisite caves. Their gelatinous saliva contains predigested seaweed and adheres the nests to the cave walls. The collecting of these nests is a precarious business and, in addition to the rarity of the commodity, must contribute to its great expense.

'Black' nests and 'white' nests are made by different species of swift, which usually occupy different caves. In managed wildlife areas there are strict rules about when collection of nests should take place. A first collection is when the swifts have made their nests and before they have laid their eggs. This means they have to set about making more nests. The second collection is allowed after the swiftlets have hatched and flown away. Twice a year over a period of two weeks each time, workers risk life and limb, climbing flexible rattan ladders dangling from the ceiling of the caves, then inch along bamboo ladders to gather nests adhering to the roof which can be as much as 60 m (200 ft) above the floor.

The 'white' nests, cleanest and most entire (cup shaped), are most sought after; 'black' nests (peppered with twigs, feathers, grass and moss), are considered inferior, and require lots of cleaning. Steer clear of precleaned nests that have a granular look. These are considered quite inferior by serious cooks. Expect to pay a premium price (hundreds of dollars) for clean, whole nests. You may also come across bird's nests in clean, curved fragments (pieces of nesting) called 'dragon's teeth' (loong nga).

If you're determined to make your own bird's nest soup, you'll want to know how to clean it. Even though the nests may look relatively clean, there is a bit of bother involved in preparing them for cooking. Here is one method. First, soak the dried nest in 2 litres (4 pints) of cold water overnight. Drain and rub a teaspoon of peanut oil over nest. Cover with more water, and loosened feathers should float to the top. Repeat as necessary until no more feathers float free.

The attraction of bird's nest is its reputed tonic value (which is why it is part of any traditional Chinese banquet) and, I feel certain, the knowledge that it is an honour to serve your guests such a rare and expensive commodity.

If you're not hell-bent on eating actual bird's nests, a less costly version is mock bird's nest soup. This uses fish maw and strands of agar-agar or white fungus as a substitute, as the textures are similar.

Start with a rich, well-flavoured chicken stock and add soaked and shredded fish maw or soaked agar-agar strips or soaked white fungus, with the tough portions trimmed away. Bring to a simmer, then stir in finely minced chicken breast meat and a small amount of finely chopped ham. Remove from heat as soon as it is heated through and serve garnished with boiled and halved pigeon or quail eggs.

China: *yin waw, yen wuo*

Bitter Almond

See CHINESE ALMOND.

Bitter Gourd

(*Momordica charantia*) SEE ILLUSTRATION. Also known as bitter melon, bitter cucumber or balsam pear. Found in the cuisine of tropical south China and most of South East Asia. Green and attractively warty (if that is possible), they remind me of those horny-skinned dinosaurs in picture books. Truly bitter, due to the presence of quinine (an anti-malarial substance), bitter gourd may take the Western palate some getting used to. The deeper green and younger they are the better, as they toughen with age. When young, it is possible to eat the melon in its entirety, seeds and pith included.

Bitter gourd may be eaten raw, as a salad, or fried and made into a sambal with onion and chilli. In either case, it is advisable to first degorge them by slicing thinly, sprinkling with salt (or a mixture of salt and turmeric) to draw out the liquid and some of the bitterness, then drying them on paper towels before proceeding with the recipe. If your melons aren't as young as they should be the seeds will be hard and need to be removed.

Although it is an acquired taste, the bitter flavour can be very attractive in combination with spices. It makes a popular pickle in India. In Sri Lanka it is much sought after as a sambal when sliced and fried crisply before being dressed with coconut milk, sliced chillies and shallots. It is also cooked into a curry. In Burma, it is eaten raw, finely sliced and salted to draw out some of the bitterness, then mixed with sliced onions and garlic. In Chinese cuisine it is usually stuffed with minced pork and served in a strong-flavoured black bean sauce that can stand up to the bitter flavour. Sometimes it is blanched to remove some of the bitterness, then fried with egg.

The tender shoots and leaves, rich in vitamin A, are blanched and served with a savoury dip made from chilli and shrimp. The leaves may also be lightly fried with chilli and salt, or cooked as a 'white vegetable', meaning simmered in coconut milk.

A cousin of the bitter gourd is the spiny bitter gourd (*Momordica cochinchinesis*) which looks like a prickly, yellow-green kiwifruit on a long green stem. Known in India as kantola or kakrol, tumba-karavila in Sri Lanka, teruah in Malaysia, fak-khaao in Thailand, mokube-tsushi in Japan and buyok-buyok in the Philippines, it is not quite as bitter but used in the same way as bitter gourd. In the same family there is also a balsam apple (*M. muricata*) and another species (*M. subangulata*).

Purchasing and storing: Buy shiny, fresh look-ing bitter gourds which are green without any trace of yellow, a sign of age. Store in a plastic bag in the refrigerator, but not for more than a day or two, as gourds will continue to ripen and instead of a ten-der centre the seeds will develop and become hard.

Preparation: Slice crossways — thinly for salads and frying, thick so it can hold a filling if it is to be stuffed. Rub over with salt and turmeric, leave for 20 minutes, then fry until golden. For a milder flavour the pieces should be blanched to remove some of the bitterness.

Medicinal uses: Like so many Asian foods, bit-ter gourd started out as a medicine: to purify the blood, counter diabetes and replenish the milk of nursing mothers. The leaves were used to treat sore eyes in elephants. It is one of the few ingredients stocked by Chinese herbalists that is sold fresh as opposed to dried. Bitter gourd tops the list of bioactive 'herbs' according to scientists in the Philippines, and other spin-offs of eating it include increased energy and stamina.

The latest studies indicate bitter gourd is an invaluable dietary supplement for those with immune system damage. As such, it is being inves-tigated as a possible cure for AIDS.

Burma: *kyethinkhathee*
China: *fu gwa, foo kwa*
India: *karela*
Indonesia: *pare, peria*
Japan: *niga-uri*
Laos: *bai maha*
Malaysia: *peria*
Philippines: *ampalaya*
Sri Lanka: *karavila*
Thailand: *mara*
Vietnam: *kho qua*

Bitter Gourd Curry

Serves 4

2 medium-sized bitter gourds
salt
turmeric
oil for frying
1 onion, finely chopped
1 teaspoon chopped garlic
2 teaspoons chopped ginger
2 tablespoons Ceylon curry powder
125 ml/4 fl oz/½ cup coconut milk
1 stick cinnamon
lime juice to taste

Cut the gourds across into 1 cm (½ in) rounds. Rub with salt and turmeric and set aside for at least 20 minutes. Dry well on paper towels, then fry the slices in hot oil until golden brown. Lift out and drain.

In a saucepan fry the onion in 2 tablespoons of oil until soft and translucent. Add garlic and ginger and continue to cook, stirring, until they are fragrant and start to turn golden. Add curry powder and fry, stirring. Add coconut milk with an equal amount of water and a stick of cinnamon, bring to the boil and simmer for 10 minutes. Add bitter gourd slices, simmer for 10 minutes longer. Serve with rice.

Bitter Gourd Curry, Bengal Style

Try this zingy dish and you will never again think that vegetables are dull. On a cold winter day, it could be the main dish of a meal, either on its own, or with rice or chapatis. The heat of the mustard (don't overdo it) is toned down by the slight sweetness of the vegetables and a touch of sugar. While it does not include ground spices, the seeds of the panch phora flavour the dish beautifully. I have not given precise weights for the vegetables. Use what you can to get in total about 750 g (1½ lb), but proportions are not vital. Serves 4.

1 or 2 small bitter gourds
½ teaspoon salt
½ teaspoon ground turmeric
1 medium-sized sweet potato
1 large potato
handful of green or yellow runner beans
medium-sized head of broccoli
  (about 2 cups florets)
3 tablespoons ghee or vegetable oil, or a mixture
1 teaspoon panch phora
1 tablespoon finely grated ginger
1 tablespoon sliced fresh chilli (optional)
1 cassia leaf (tej pattar) (optional)
2 teaspoons salt or to taste
2 teaspoons jaggery or brown sugar
1 teaspoon hot English mustard

Slice gourds crossways into slices about 6 mm (¼ in) thick. Rub ½ teaspoon salt and turmeric over the cut surfaces. Peel and dice potatoes. String beans if necessary before cutting into bite-sized pieces. Peel broccoli stem and cut into thick slices. Divide florets, keeping a small stem on each.

In a wok or karahi heat the ghee or oil, then fry bitter gourd slices, turning them from time to time until golden brown on both sides. Remove and drain on paper towels. To oil remaining in wok add panch phora until mustard seeds pop, then add ginger, chilli and cassia leaf and fry, stirring, until ginger is soft. Add the vegetables and fry, stirring, for 5–8 minutes. Add salt, sugar and 1 cup hot water. Cover and cook over low heat until vegetables are tender, about 15 minutes. Softer vegetables that need less time to cook may be added half way through cooking together with the fried bitter gourd. Turn off heat and stir the mustard into the liquid to disperse it evenly, then toss all the vegetables through the sauce. This dish may be prepared ahead and gently reheated for serving.

Bitter Gourd with Pork and Fermented Beans

2 tender bitter gourds, about 155 g/5 oz
1 teaspoon crushed garlic
1 teaspoon finely grated ginger
2 tablespoons peanut oil
155 g/5 oz minced (ground) pork
1 tablespoon chilli with fermented beans
4 tablespoons water

Cut the bitter gourds in two lengthways, scoop out seeds and centre membrane and cut across into thick slices. Put into a pan of salted cold water and bring to the boil. Boil for 3 minutes then drain and refresh in cold water.

Heat oil in a wok and fry the garlic and ginger, stirring, for a few seconds. Add the minced pork and fry, breaking up the meat into small pieces, until it is no longer pink. Add the chilli with fermented beans (from a shop selling Korean or other Far Eastern ingredients). Add water, cover and simmer for 10 minutes or until tender. Serve with rice.

Burmese Bitter Gourd Salad

1 tender bitter gourd
1 teaspoon salt
1 teaspoon finely chopped garlic
1 teaspoon finely chopped ginger
lime juice to taste

Wash the bitter gourd, then slice it as thinly as possible, sprinkle with salt and mix well. Leave for 30 minutes, then rinse under cold water and squeeze dry. Put it into a bowl with the garlic and ginger and squeeze all together to mix well. Add lime juice and mix again. Serve as an accompaniment to rice and curry.

Fried Bitter Gourd Salad

Serves 4

2 tender bitter gourds
salt and ground turmeric
peanut oil
3 golden shallots, sliced finely
2 fresh green chillies, seeded and sliced
2 tablespoons lime juice
½ teaspoon sugar
3 tablespoons coconut cream

Wash and dry bitter gourds. Cut crossways into slices about 6 mm (¼ in) thick. Lay them out on a platter and sprinkle with salt and turmeric on one side, turn the slices over and sprinkle on reverse side. Leave for 20 minutes, then blot dry on paper towels.

Heat sufficient oil to cover base of a heavy frying pan and lay the slices of bitter gourd in the oil in one layer. Cook on medium heat until golden underneath, then turn slices over and cook second side. Transfer to paper towels with a slotted spoon. Lightly mix with shallots and chillies. Dissolve sugar in lime juice and pour over. Just before serving spoon coconut cream over the salad.

Bitter Gourd Stuffed with Seafood

3 medium-sized bitter gourds
375 g/12 oz fillet of firm white fish
125 g/4 oz raw prawns (shrimp)
½ teaspoon salt
1 teaspoon finely grated fresh ginger
1 tablespoon egg white
1 teaspoon cornflour (cornstarch)
125 ml/4 fl oz/½ cup peanut oil

SAUCE
2 tablespoons canned salted black beans
½ teaspoon crushed garlic
1 teaspoon sugar
½ cup stock or water
1 teaspoon cornflour (cornstarch)

Slice off pointed ends of melon and discard, then cut into straight sections about 5 cm (2 in) long. With a small, sharp knife remove spongy centre and seeds, leaving small tubes of melon.

Remove any skin and bones from fish. Shell and devein the prawns. Put both into food processor and chop finely. Mix with salt, ginger, egg white and cornflour and fill sections of melon with the mixture, rounding filling on one end.

Heat oil and fry the melon rounded end down, until fish is firm and just turning golden. Transfer to plate.

Sauce: Rinse salted beans in a strainer under cold water for a few seconds, drain, mash with a fork. Mix with garlic and fry in remaining oil, stirring. Add sugar and stock or water and when simmering return pieces of melon to pan, rounded end upwards. Cover and simmer over very low heat for 20 minutes.

Place melon on a plate, add cornflour mixed with a little cold water and stir until it boils and thickens. Spoon over melon and serve with rice.

Bitter Gourd Pickle

750 g/1½ lb bitter gourds
2 teaspoons salt
2 teaspoons ground turmeric
100 g/3½ oz fresh red or green chillies
375 ml/12 fl oz/1½ cups vinegar
2 tablespoons black mustard seeds
3 tablespoons peeled garlic
3 tablespoons sliced fresh ginger
3 tablespoons ground coriander
3 tablespoons ground cumin
500 ml/1 pint/2 cups mustard oil
1 tablespoon fennel seeds
2 teaspoons nigella seeds
3 tablespoons sugar

Slice the bitter gourds in lengthways strips and cut the strips into short lengths, about 5 cm (2 in). Sprinkle with salt and turmeric, mix well with gloved hand (turmeric stains badly) and set aside for 1 hour. Dry on paper towels. Cut chillies across into thick slices.
Put ½ cup vinegar and 1 tablespoon mustard seeds into blender and grind, then add garlic and ginger and blend to a purée. Mix in coriander and cumin.

In a deep frying pan heat the oil and fry the bitter gourd pieces until golden. Remove to a plate. In the same oil fry the remaining tablespoon of mustard seeds until they pop. Add the blended mixture and cook on low heat, stirring, until fragrant. Add fennel and nigella seeds and fry for a minute longer. Then pour in the remaining vinegar, add sugar and stir in fried bitter gourd. Taste and add more salt and sugar if desired. Bring to the boil, fill into hot sterile jars and if oil does not cover top of pickle, heat more oil and add. Cover and store in an airtight container. Keep this pickle for at least 2 weeks and always use a clean, dry spoon.

Blachan

See SHRIMP PASTE, DRIED.

Black Bean

(*Glycine max*) Black soy beans which are fermented and heavily salted. Some are sold in cans in a salty liquid, others in plastic bags, covered with salt crystals. Some brands are labelled 'preserved black beans'. They are ready to use, needing only a brief rinse under the cold tap before being added to a dish as described in the recipe. One of the most popular of all Chinese dishes using this ingredient is probably Beef in Black Bean Sauce. If you wonder why I don't recommend using the ready-made black bean sauce sometimes sold in jars, it's because with very little extra effort you can get a much better tasting result making your own. Instructions are given with individual recipes, such as Crab in Black Bean Sauce (see page 109) and Beef with Black Bean Sauce (see page 35).

For dried black beans see LEGUMES & PULSES.

Black Cumin

See CUMIN, BLACK.

Black-Eyed Pea

See LEGUMES & PULSES.

Black Fungus

See MUSHROOMS & FUNGI.

Black Gram

See LEGUMES & PULSES.

Black Moss

(*Nostoc commune*) This hair-like ingredient is always served at Chinese New Year. Its name is fat tsai ('hair vegetable') pronounced 'fat choy', as in the Cantonese words which denote prosperity in the new-year greeting '*Kung hei fat choy*'. The common belief is that it is a seaweed, which is why it is often referred to as black seaweed. I am indebted to *Bruce Cost's Asian Ingredients* for the surprising revelation that it is not in fact a seaweed, but an algae that grows in the Mongolian desert in water from mountain springs!

It is considered very cooling, and is prized in Chinese medicine for both its cooling and cleansing properties. It is expensive. It needs soaking and rinsing, and is simmered for 10 minutes in a light stock with a little salt, sugar and Chinese wine. Most often encountered in New Year specialities or in the vegetarian dish, lo han chai.

Black Nut

(*Pangium edule*) The English name is a literal translation of the Malay name, buah keluak. As far as I can ascertain it is used only in Nonya and Indonesian cuisine. Seasonal and not plentiful, therefore highly prized, it requires much preparation. The fresh kernel can be poisonous, necessitating thorough cooking. It has a peculiar, slightly bitter flavour but one gets used to it. The preparation of a classic dish in which the large shells are stuffed with a mixture of the kernels mashed with minced pork, was demonstrated to me by a fifth-generation Nonya, and it was fascinating to see the trouble she went to, vigorously scrubbing the rather dirty shells in a sink of water, digging out the kernel, pounding it and mixing it with pork, stuffing the pork mixture back inside the shell, then simmering the filled nuts in a sour curry of chicken. Definitely a dish for connoisseurs.

Indonesia: *kluwek*
Malaysia: *buah keluak*

Blood

The blood of pigs and chickens is often seen for sale in Asian butchers. It is considered a nourishing, warming food so is added to soups and braised dishes for winter eating. It is also used in the filling of a special Korean sausage. In the Philippines and Macao it is added to certain dishes during long simmering periods.

Bok Choy

See CABBAGE.

Bombay Duck

(*Harpodon neherius*) Not a fowl at all. A variety of small, translucent fish caught off the west coast of India and dried. Sold in packets. Store airtight. Also known as bummalo.

Fried Bombay Duck

Deep fried or grilled, this is a pungent yet popular accompaniment to a meal of rice and curry, its crisp texture and salty flavour making it one of the easy to prepare 'rice-pullers'.

**4 strips of dried Bombay duck
oil for deep frying**

Cut the dried fish into 5 cm (2 in) lengths. Heat oil in a small pan for deep frying and drop in a few pieces of Bombay duck at a time. It will fry in a very short time, so be ready to lift it out on a slotted spoon and drain on paper towels. It is nibbled with mouthfuls of rice and curry.

Bombay Duck Sambal

**6 strips of Bombay duck
4 tablespoons oil
4 dried red chillies
2 onions, finely sliced
2 teaspoons garlic, finely chopped
lime juice to taste
salt to taste**

Cut Bombay duck into 5 cm (2 in) pieces. Heat the oil in a small, curved pan and fry the Bombay duck briefly. Lift out and drain on paper towels. In the same pan fry the chillies for a minute or so, until they puff and turn almost black. This does not take long. Lift out and drain together with the Bombay duck. Put sliced onions into the pan and fry slowly until they become soft and translucent. Add the garlic and fry a few minutes longer until onions and garlic are golden. Return Bombay duck and the chillies broken into pieces and the seeds shaken out. Stir-fry for a minute, then add lime juice and salt and serve with rice.

Bonito

(*Auxis thazard*, *Sarda orientalis*) While not a great fish for eating fresh, it is indispensable for drying and storing, to add flavour and protein to otherwise protein-deficient diets. In Sri Lanka, almost everything which is cooked in the local style includes a small amount of Maldive fish (which is what it is called after drying, since the Maldive Islands' main industry, apart from tourism, is the catching and preserving of bonito). Dried bonito resembles a piece of hard wood, but when pounded with a mortar and pestle to small chips, a little added to a dish gives flavour to the blandest of main ingredients.

Bonito is also the only raw ingredient for that Japanese staple, katsuobushi, which is made by a complex method of drying, smoking and mould fermentation. It will keep indefinitely without refrigeration. Quite expensive, katsuobushi used to be given as a wedding gift. It is a vital flavouring in one of the basics of Japanese cookery, dashi (stock). Dried bonito is so hard that there is a special sharp tool for shaving it into flakes. These days it is usually purchased in packets already flaked.

See also MALDIVE FISH.

Burma: *nga-kyi-kan*
Indonesia: *balaki, tongkol*
Japan: *katsuo*
Malaysia: *kayau*
Philippines: *bonito, rayado*
Sri Lanka: *balaya*
Thailand: *pla o*
Vietnam: *ca bo*

Bottle Gourd

See GOURDS.

Boxthorn

(*Lycium chinense*) SEE ILLUSTRATION. Also known as Chinese boxthorn. Native to China and Japan, the boxthorn is sold only during its season, and in warm tropical countries it has to be grown in the highlands. The branches, stiff, straight and unbranched, are called 'the walking stick of the immortals'. The shrub's long, thorny branches bear dark green oval leaves of varied sizes, 2–6 cm (1–2½ in) in length. When stripping the leaves for cooking, beware of the thorns. The top few tender leaves are usually not thorny, but as you descend further, you will find they lurk where leaves sprout from the stem. There will be the occasional stem without a thorn in sight, but don't be lulled into a false sense of security: assume there are some at each juncture as you strip the stems. Chinese boxthorn also bears purplish flowers and reddish-orange berries which are sold dried in packets. Besides being pleasantly sweet-sour, these berries are very high in carotene which would support the claim that they are good for the eyes. The berries are commonly called wolfberries and make a delicately sweet addition to many dishes (see WOLFBERRY), while the leaves are cooked with pork and added to soups. When cooking these leaves in soup, counter the slightly bitter flavour by adding ginger, pepper and a little sugar.

China: *kou-kay-choi, gau gei choi*

Boxthorn Soup

2 tablespoons oil
250 g/8 oz tender pork, sliced thinly
3 cups boxthorn leaves, washed and dried
6 slices fresh ginger
1 tablespoon finely grated ginger
1.5 litres/3 pints/6 cups chicken or pork stock
2 teaspoons sugar
salt and pepper to taste
few drops sesame oil

Heat oil and stir-fry the pork slices until they lose just their pinkness. Add leaves and stir-fry until wilted. Add ginger slices and juice squeezed from the tablespoon of grated ginger. Pour in the stock and bring to a simmer. Add sugar, salt and pepper to taste and just before serving stir in the sesame oil.

Breadcrumbs, Japanese

Japanese breadcrumbs, or panko are not like Western style breadcrumbs at all, and if a recipe requires them don't try to substitute any other. They are large, light and give a crispness which cannot be duplicated. Sold in packets in Japanese stores.

Breadfruit

(*Artocarpus communis*) SEE ILLUSTRATION. Notable for its size and knobbly skin which starts out green and ripens to browny-yellow, this prolific fruit native to the Pacific islands and South East Asia was aptly named. Its main nutritional constituent is starch.

The tree can be up to 20 m (65 ft) tall given the right conditions. The leaves with their distinctive fingerlike splits, range from 30 cm (12 in) to 100 cm (40 in) in length. Ideal for wrapping food to be baked in underground ovens in the Pacific islands. The fruits weigh from 1–5 kg (2–10 lb). In its unripe state it is prepared like yam or potato and eaten roasted, boiled or fried as a staple food. In the Pacific it is wrapped in leaves and roasted in an underground oven. In Sri Lanka the common practice is to slice off the skin and cut the fruit into large wedges which are boiled with salt and turmeric so it is yellow and lightly spiced, giving it more flavour than its Pacific counterpart, its simple accompaniments being a sambal of ground chillies and onions. Fresh grated coconut may be served alongside to subdue the heat of the sambal.

Thin, crisp breadfruit chips, fried until deep golden, are much tastier than potato chips.

Vegetarians use the fruit as others would use meat, cooking it with spices and rich coconut milk.

On a visit to an exotic fruit farm in Far North Queensland I encountered, for the very first time, breadfruit presented on a fruit platter as a ripe fruit. Sweet and custardy in texture with a strong, sweet smell, it was a total surprise — in Asia it is strictly a savoury food.

In the Pacific islands the ripe fruit is cooked with coconut milk and sugar and served as a dessert. In Papua New Guinea the ripe fruit is eaten raw or baked and the unripe fruit is boiled like potatoes and served as starch food. The seeds of mature breadfruit are roasted over coals and eaten like roasted chestnuts. In the highlands of Papua New Guinea, people eat the seeds and throw the rest of the fruit away! In Polynesia, breadfruit is fermented in large pits lined with leaves, and preserved for several years.

China: *mian-boo-kuo*
Fiji: *uto, kula*
Guam: *lemai*
Hawaii: *ulu*
Indonesia: *sukun*
Japan: *pan-no-mi*
Malaysia: *sukun*
Philippines: *rimas*
Samoa: *ulu*
Sri Lanka: *dhel*
Tahiti: *uru*
Thailand: *saake*
Tonga: *mei*

Breadfruit Chips

Choose a firm, unripe fruit and remove the skin with a sharp knife. Cut lengthways into 6–8 wedges, then cut each wedge crossways into very thin slices, no more than 2 mm (1/12 in) thick. Sprinkle lightly with ground turmeric and salt, rubbing evenly over the slices. Leave for 15 minutes, then dry on paper towels to absorb as much of the moisture as possible.

Heat oil for deep frying (coconut oil is traditional but peanut oil is more readily available, and healthier) and fry a handful of chips at a time on medium high heat. When golden brown remove on a slotted spoon and drain on paper towels. Continue until all the chips are fried. When quite cold store in an airtight container and use within a week.

Boiled Breadfruit

Peel a mature but unripe breadfruit and cut it into large chunks of even size. Bring to the boil sufficient water to just cover the breadfruit and add a teaspoon of ground turmeric and a teaspoon of salt (or to taste). Add breadfruit, cover and simmer until a piece is easily pierced with a fine skewer. Drain the liquid away, and put the pot back on the heat for a minute or two. Serve hot, accompanied by freshly grated coconut and hot chilli sambal made by mixing ground chillies, onions, salt and lime juice.

Baked Stuffed Breadfruit

1 firm unripe breadfruit, about 1.5 kg/3 lb
salt and pepper
1 tablespoon oil
1 onion, finely chopped
1 teaspoon finely chopped garlic
250 g/8 oz minced (ground) beef
1 fresh chilli, seeded and chopped
2 teaspoons ground coriander
1 teaspoon ground cumin
oil or butter

Wash breadfruit but do not peel it. Cut a small slice off one side so it will sit flat on the baking dish. Cut another slice off the opposite side and scoop out the centre of the breadfruit, leaving a thick shell all around. Season the cavity with salt and pepper, and finely chop the scooped out breadfruit.

Heat oil and over low heat fry onion and garlic until soft and starting to colour. Add beef, chilli, coriander and cumin and stir-fry until beef is brown. Add the chopped breadfruit and a tablespoon or two of stock or water. Cover and simmer for 5 minutes, then spoon the meat mixture into the cavity of the breadfruit. Replace the slice to cover the filling. Brush all over with oil or butter and place in an ovenproof dish. Bake in a moderate oven, 180°C (350°F), for about 1½ hours or until the breadfruit is soft enough to be pierced by a fine skewer. Serve hot.

Breadfruit Coconut Curry

750 g/1½ lb firm, unripe breadfruit
400 ml/14 fl oz can coconut milk
1 onion, finely grated
1 teaspoon finely grated ginger
1 teaspoon crushed garlic
2 fresh green chillies, split
½ teaspoon ground turmeric
3 short strips pandan leaf
1 small stick cinnamon
2 sprigs fresh curry leaves
1 teaspoon salt or to taste

Peel the breadfruit and cut into thick slices. Reserve ½ cup of the canned coconut milk and dilute the rest with water to make 3 cups. Put the diluted coconut milk into a saucepan with the rest of the ingredients except breadfruit, bring to the boil and simmer uncovered for 10 minutes. Add the breadfruit and continue cooking until it is soft. Gently stir in reserved coconut milk and serve with rice.

Breadfruit with Coconut Cream

This Samoan preparation may be served as a vegetable or as dessert. Serves 8.

1 half-ripe breadfruit, about 1.5 kg/3 lb
500 ml/1 pint/2 cups freshly squeezed
    coconut cream
    or 400 ml/14 fl oz can coconut cream
1 teaspoon sea salt or to taste

Bake the breadfruit in a moderate oven for 1 hour or until it is easily pierced with a fork. Remove from oven and cut it in half. Discard core and skin, and put the pulp into a large bowl in which it can be mashed with a potato masher. It is easier if this is done while the breadfruit is hot. Add the salt and coconut cream and with a spoon divide the breadfruit into walnut-sized pieces. Serve hot.

Note: If the breadfruit is perfectly ripe, soft and sweet, it need not be baked. Instead, pull out the stem, cut the fruit in halves lengthways and scoop out pulp with a spoon. Measure the pulp and mix in half the volume of coconut cream, and one sixth the volume of sugar. Add salt to bring out the flavour.

Breads

The breads of Asia are quite different to European types of bread, and well worth trying. Many are unleavened. There are some which use yeast, yet are not baked in large, light loaves which lend themselves to slicing. They are somewhat flat compared to Western bread, but with very special flavour. Asian breads are not usually baked in an oven, since ovens are not a feature of the average Asian kitchen. Instead, they are griddle-baked, shallow fried or deep fried. In the case of Chinese breads, they are steamed in bamboo steamers (or any other kind of steamer available). Most of the breads are found in India and other countries where the Indian influence is strong.

Chapati: The everyday bread of millions in India, made simply with flour, water and salt, baked on a griddle called a tawa and depending only on the way it is kneaded and rested and rolled for its lightness and amazing ability to puff like a balloon.

Chinese bread: Leavened with yeast and usually steamed in individual shapes — flower rolls, silver thread rolls, and round buns either plain or with fillings. Steaming gives the bread a thin, smooth, shiny skin, not a crust which results from the dry heat of baking.

Naan: A yeast-risen bread, flat but with a soft centre and smoky, crisp crust. It is made from white wheat flour enriched with yoghurt, egg and butter. Traditionally baked in a charcoal-fired clay oven called a tandoor, but a hot oven does the job too.

Roti: A general term for bread which can take many forms. If it is made from ground grain — whether wheat, rice, corn or millet — it qualifies for the name roti. Roti can be fine or thick, plain or with freshly grated coconut incorporated in the dough, or chillies and onions, which make it tasty enough to eat on its own. It can enclose a savoury filling of cooked and seasoned vegetables or meat, or a sweet filling of mashed lentils. These breads with fillings are ideal picnic fare served with fresh chutney or yoghurt.

Rumali roti: (Northern India) A very large, very thin bread supposed to be as fine as a silken scarf, is cooked on what looks like an upturned wok — a convex metal pan similar to those used for the large Middle Eastern loaves called 'mountain bread'.

Roti jalah: (Malaysia) Like a French crepe with holes in it. It is named after a fishermen's net and the lacy pattern is formed by drizzling the batter through a cup with many small funnels, into a pan hot enough to set the batter within a minute or so. It is served with curry, into which the pliable roti is dipped.

Paratha: Baked for special occasions, being richly flavoured with ghee (clarified butter). While very thin, it is multi-layered like flaky pastry, achieved by a special method of rolling and folding.

Yeast risen bread: Now popular in Asian countries. Vietnamese bakers make the best French bread outside of France. Sometimes the breads are plain, but often have a savoury filling so they are a complete snack or meal in themselves.

Chapati

375 g/12 oz/3 cups atta flour or roti flour
1½ teaspoons salt
1 tablespoon ghee or oil
250 ml/8 fl oz/1 cup lukewarm water

Put flour in a large mixing bowl, setting aside about half a cup for rolling chapatis. Stir salt through the flour, then add ghee or oil and rub in with fingertips, as though making pastry. Add the measured water all at once, moisten all the flour and mix to a firm dough. Knead dough for at least 10 minutes or until dough is smooth and elastic. Since there is no leavening agent in these breads, kneading is used to develop lightness. Gather dough into a ball, put into a small bowl and cover tightly with plastic food wrap. Leave for 1 hour or longer. This resting period is also vital for making light, tender breads.

   Divide dough into balls of even size, about as big as a large walnut or small egg. Roll each out on a lightly floured board, lightly dusting board and rolling pin with reserved flour and keeping the shape perfectly round if possible. Roll out the chapatis to be cooked, and when starting to cook them, start with those which were rolled first, since the short rest between rolling and cooking makes the chapatis lighter.

   Heat a tawa; griddle or heavy frying pan, put the first chapati on the hot pan and leave for 1 minute on medium heat. Turn it over and place second side down. After a further minute, press lightly around the edges of the chapati with a folded tea towel to encourage the disc of bread to puff up and bubble. Do not overcook or the chapatis will become crisp and dry instead of pliable and tender. Wrap the cooked chapatis in a tea towel. Serve warm with butter, curry or other dishes.

Puri

Puris are made in the same way as chapatis, except that they are slightly smaller, and are deep fried instead of griddle-baked. Heat about 3 cm (1¼ in) oil in a deep frying pan or wok, until a faint haze rises from the surface. Fry the puris one at a time over medium heat, spooning hot oil constantly over the top of the puri until it puffs up like a balloon. Turn it over gently, without piercing, and fry other side until golden. Lift out on slotted frying spoon and drain on paper towels. Serve immediately with curries or other dry vegetable dishes.

Bhel Puri

This is a miniature version, rolled very thinly and cut into small (5 cm, 2 in) rounds. Deep fry until puffed, golden and crisp. They are combined with spicy sev, chopped onions, coriander, fresh chillies and tamarind sauce just before serving as a savoury snack.

half portion of chapati dough
oil for deep frying
2 cups fine sev
2 cups puffed unsweetened rice (phoa)
1 teaspoon garam masala (recipe page 354)
½ teaspoon chilli powder
½ teaspoon salt
1 medium onion, finely chopped
2 or 3 fresh green chillies, chopped
1 cup coarsely chopped fresh coriander
1 cup tamarind chatni (recipe page 73)

On a lightly floured surface roll dough very thinly and cut into 5 cm (2 in) rounds. Put on a tray, cover with a slightly damp tea towel to prevent drying out and let the pastry rest for 10–15 minutes. Heat oil and test by frying one of the rounds. It should puff and swell. If it doesn't, the oil needs to be hotter. Splash oil

over the top with a frying spoon, and fry a few at a time. As they turn golden, lift out with a slotted spoon and drain on paper towels laid over a cake cooler. Allow to cool completely.

Combine puris and sev in a bowl. Heat 3 tablespoons oil in a wok and toss the puffed rice in it very quickly. Lift out on slotted spoon and drain on paper towels. When cool add to bowl, sprinkle with garam masala, chilli powder and salt and toss to distribute.

Just before serving, combine chopped onion, chillies and coriander in a small bowl. For each serving put a large spoonful of the crisp nibbles into a bowl, sprinkle with chopped mixture and a spoonful of tamarind chatni. Mix quickly and eat at once so none of the delightful crunchiness is lost.

Note: Sev is deep-fried vermicelli made from chick pea flour, sold in packets marked to indicate whether the spicing is hot.

Paratha

These rich and flaky discs of bread are the traditional accompaniment to Lamb Kebabs (see page 202) as well as dry vegetable preparations. They may be cooled, wrapped in foil and frozen for future use. Reheat in a moderately hot oven still wrapped in foil. Makes 12.

185 g/6 oz/1½ cups atta flour
185 g/6 oz/1½ cups plain (all-purpose) flour
  or roti flour
1½ teaspoons salt
1 tablespoon ghee at room temperature
250 ml/8 fl oz/1 cup water
185 ml/6 fl oz/¾ cup melted and cooled ghee

Sift both kinds of flour with salt into a large bowl and rub in the tablespoon of ghee. Add water and knead for at least 10 minutes. Form into a smooth ball, cover with food wrap and set aside for at least 1 hour.

Divide dough into 12 equal portions and roll each into a smooth ball without surface cracks. Roll out on a lightly floured board to a circle the size of a dinner plate. Spread with 2 teaspoons of the melted ghee, taking it right to the edges. It is best to spread this with the hand, as a brush would just soak up the ghee. With a knife, cut a straight line from the centre of the circle to the edge. Starting at the cut edge, roll the circle of dough very closely into a cone shape. Pick it up and with the base of the cone sitting on one palm, press the apex down towards the base and flatten slightly. Now roll out this ball of dough again on a floured surface, using a floured rolling pin, but this time roll very gently and not as thinly as before — the aim is not to let the air out at the edges — rather like making flaky pastry. Try to keep the parathas as round as possible. Repeat with the rest of the dough and when all are rolled for the second time, start cooking.

Heat a heavy griddle or frying pan and spread about 2 teaspoons of melted ghee on it. Put the paratha on the hot pan and while the first side is cooking, spread another teaspoonful of ghee on the top side. Turn over with a spatula and cook other side. Serve warm, or cool completely before wrapping in foil for freezing.

Lentil-Filled Paratha

Filled parathas are another popular bread, and are a meal in themselves when served with natural yoghurt and a fresh chutney. Makes 8–10.

1 quantity paratha dough (recipe above)
220 g/7 oz/1 cup red lentils
2 tablespoons oil or ghee
1 medium onion, finely chopped
1 teaspoon finely chopped garlic
1 teaspoon ground cumin
1 teaspoon garam masala
1 teaspoon salt or to taste
1 tablespoon lime or lemon juice

Mix and knead paratha dough, and while it is resting make the lentil filling. Pick over the lentils, discarding small stones. Wash lentils thoroughly. Put into a saucepan with water to cover, bring to the boil and cook until soft and water is absorbed. In another pan heat ghee and fry the onion and garlic until soft and turning golden. Add the lentils, mashing well with a wooden spoon. Stir in ground cumin and garam masala, add salt and lime juice to taste and cook until no liquid remains, stirring constantly and keeping heat low to prevent scorching. Leave to cool.

Divide dough into 8 portions and roll each to a circle the size of a saucer. Put a portion of the cooled lentils into the centre, bring the dough together to enclose the filling, and pinch together to seal the dough firmly. Flatten between the hands to a round shape and on a lightly floured board roll very gently to the size of a bread-and-butter plate, taking care not to press too hard, so that the filling does not break through the dough. If this does happen, patch with an extra piece of dough. Do not start cooking until all the parathas are filled. Heat a heavy frying pan or tawa, spread 2 teaspoons ghee or oil over the surface and place a paratha in it over medium heat. While first side is cooking spread a little more ghee or oil over the top so that when paratha is turned over the second side is also greased. Cook until golden brown on both sides. Pile parathas on a plate and keep warm until all are cooked, then serve as soon as possible.

Paratha with Sweet Lentil Filling

While these flat bread (mithai paratha) have a sweetened filling, they go well with savoury dishes. They are also popular treats for children, served with yoghurt. Makes 10.

220 g/7 oz/1 cup toor or channa dhal
250 g/8 oz/1 cup sugar
2 tablespoons ghee
1 teaspoon ground cardamom
1 quantity paratha dough (recipe page 49)

Wash the dhal well, and soak overnight. Cook in plenty of water until very tender. A pressure cooker may be used to speed things up. Drain away excess moisture and mash the dhal to a purée. For extra smoothness, push it through a sieve. Return mashed dhal to a heavy saucepan, add sugar and 1 tablespoon of the ghee and cook over medium heat, stirring. The sugar will cause the mixture to become wet, but in about 10 minutes the mixture should be thick and dry once more. Stir constantly to ensure it does not burn. Remove to a bowl, stir in cardamom and leave to cool.

Knead the paratha dough until smooth and elastic and set aside, covered, for at least 30 minutes. Divide into 10 portions. Take spoonfuls of lentil filling about the same size.

Flatten the dough to a small circle, place a ball of filling on it and close the dough around it to completely enclose, pressing edges together to seal.

On a lightly floured surface roll out parathas very gently, taking care that the filling does not break through the dough. The loaves should be about the size of a large saucer, and rolled quite thinly.

Cook on a hot griddle or heavy pan, using a little ghee. Drizzle a few drops of melted ghee over the top of each while it cooks, turning over to cook the second side. Continue turning and cooking until golden brown on both sides. Serve warm.

Naan

This yeast-risen bread should be cooked in a clay oven called a tandoor, which is why it is often called tandoori naan. The smoky flavour of the tandoor, the crisp crust where the loaf has been kissed a little too fiercely by the flame, and the soft, slightly sweet centre combine to make this one of the most popular of Indian breads. It is still worth trying in a conventional griller or oven. Makes 8.

**30 g/1 oz fresh compressed yeast
  or 1 sachet dried yeast
3 tablespoons lukewarm water
3 teaspoons white sugar
125 ml/4 fl oz/½ cup natural yoghurt
1 egg, beaten
3 tablespoons melted ghee or butter
2 teaspoons salt
approx. 500 g/1 lb plain (all-purpose) flour
2 tablespoons poppy seeds or nigella seeds**

Sprinkle yeast over 3 tablespoons warm water in a bowl and leave for 5 minutes to soften, then stir to dissolve. Add 1 teaspoon sugar and leave in a warm place for 10 minutes or until it froths. If it doesn't froth, check the expiry date of the yeast and start again with a fresh batch.

In a small bowl beat half the yoghurt until smooth, mix in remaining 2 teaspoons sugar, beaten egg, ghee or butter, salt, and an extra ½ cup lukewarm water. Stir in dissolved yeast.

Put 2 cups flour into a large bowl, pour in liquid and beat hard until a smooth batter

forms. Add remaining flour a little at a time and when it becomes too stiff to stir, knead on a floured board for at least 10 minutes, or until dough is smooth and elastic. Shape dough into a ball and transfer to a warm, greased bowl. Turn dough over once so top is greased. Cover and leave in a warm place until doubled in bulk (time will vary according to room temperature). Test by pushing a finger gently into the dough. If it holds an impression it is ready. If the hole fills up, leave dough longer.

Punch down the dough and divide into 8 equal balls. Leave to rest for 10 minutes. Shape each ball of dough into a circle thinner in the centre than the edges. Pull one side of the circle outwards, forming a teardrop shape about 20 cm (8 in) long and 12 cm (5 in) wide at the base. The size governs how thick the bread will be, which is especially important when grilling.

To grill: Preheat grill on medium heat. Spray loaves lightly with water or brush with some of the remaining yoghurt and sprinkle lightly with seeds. Place on tray as many as will fit without touching and grill, about 12 cm (5 in) away from heat source. Grill for at least 3 minutes on each side or until risen and golden brown. It is important not to have the heat too close or the outside will brown but the inside may be doughy and half raw.

To bake: Preheat oven to very hot, 230°C (450°F). Preheat 2 ungreased baking trays. Brush loaves with remaining yoghurt and sprinkle with seeds. Place 2 or 3 loaves on each baking tray and bake for 10 minutes or until risen and golden.

Garlic Naan

This simple variation is delicious when well done, but harsh and raw tasting when not handled with care. Crush a small clove of garlic with ½ teaspoon salt and mix it into the yoghurt which is brushed over the naan before baking or grilling. Many restaurants take the short cut of simply scattering soaked dried minced garlic heavily over the loaves, giving garlic naan a bad name and a reputation for losing you friends!

Chick Pea Flour Bread

Known as besan roti, these are nutritious because of the protein content of chick peas. Besan is made from the small brown variety of chick peas known as Bengal gram. Makes about 15.

140 g/4½ oz/1 cup besan
250 g/8 oz/2 cups atta or roti flour
2 teaspoons salt
½ teaspoon ground black pepper
½ teaspoon crushed ajowan seeds
1 tablespoon ghee or oil
250 ml/8 fl oz/1 cup water
ghee or oil for shallow frying

Sift besan before measuring it, and in a heavy pan roast it over low heat, stirring constantly all over the base of the pan as it burns very easily. It will turn from pale yellow to gold. Remove from heat and continue stirring until it is cold, or turn it out into a bowl so it doesn't scorch in the hot pan.

Sift both kinds of flour together with salt, pepper and ajowan into a bowl. Rub in ghee or oil. Add water and mix to a dough, kneading firmly until it is smooth and elastic. Cover with food (plastic) wrap and set aside for at least 1 hour.

Take balls of the dough, roll out on a lightly floured surface to the size of a large saucer, and about 3 mm (⅛ in) thick. (Spreading with ghee and rolling twice, as in the recipe for parathas, gives a much softer result.) Heat a griddle or heavy frying pan and cook as for parathas.

Roti with Coconut, Onion and Chilli

These flat breads are best made with freshly grated coconut, which is often sold in Asian shops. If not available, moisten desiccated coconut with a few tablespoons cold water, tossing until evenly moist. If preferred, the onion and chilli may be omitted from the recipe. Makes 12 rotis.

500 g/1 lb/4 cups fine rice flour
1 teaspoon baking powder
75 g/2½ oz/1 cup freshly grated coconut
  or desiccated coconut
2 teaspoons salt

2 teaspoons ghee or butter
2 tablespoons very finely chopped shallots
1 tablespoon finely chopped fresh chilli
1 egg, beaten
500 ml/8 fl oz/2 cups water
ghee or oil for cooking

Mix flour, baking powder, coconut and salt in a large bowl. Rub in the ghee or butter, stir shallots and chilli through, then add egg and sufficient water to form a dough. Leave dough to rest for at least 30 minutes, then take egg-sized pieces of dough and pat between floured hands or roll lightly on floured board to a circle about the size of a saucer. Cook on a hot griddle or heavy frying pan with only a very light coating of ghee or oil. Serve with curries or sambals.

Cornmeal Roti

These discs of flat bread have a warm yellow colour and slightly sweet flavour, and stay moist and pliable after cooking. The type of cornmeal to use is a very finely ground yellow cornmeal usually available in Indian grocers and not the coarser Italian type sold as polenta. Makes 8–10.

250 ml/8 fl oz/1 cup water
¾ teaspoon salt
2 teaspoons sugar
1 tablespoon ghee or butter, melted
½ cup fine-ground yellow cornmeal
1 ear tender fresh corn (optional)*
150 g/5 oz/1¼ cups atta or roti flour

Combine cold water, salt, sugar, butter and cornmeal in a medium saucepan, stirring until there are no lumps in the cornmeal. Place over low heat and stir constantly until mixture boils and thickens. Turn heat as low as possible, cover the pan and leave over heat for 3 minutes. Remove to a bowl and allow to cool to lukewarm. Add corn (if using) and atta or roti flour and mix to a pliable dough. It may be necessary to add a little extra flour or a few drops of water to achieve a consistency which will allow the dough to be kneaded. On a lightly floured surface, knead for 8–10 minutes until smooth. Cover closely with plastic wrap and allow to rest for at least 1 hour.

Divide the dough into egg-sized portions,

rolling each one into a smooth ball with floured hands. On a lightly floured surface, roll each one with a lightly floured rolling pin to as perfect a circle as possible. The rotis should be thinly rolled, and about the size of a bread-and-butter plate. When all are rolled out, start cooking them, starting with those that were rolled first. The brief resting after rolling gives a lighter result.

Heat a tawa or heavy frying pan (non-stick if possible) and cook rotis over medium heat in a dry pan. No fat is used. Allow the first side to cook undisturbed for a minute, then flip the roti over and cook the second side for a minute. Now comes the interesting part. After the first couple of minutes cooking the roti is gently pressed, first around the edges and then in the centre, with a folded tea towel or with a spatula. This encourages rising. Small bubbles make the texture light and delicious and often the roti will puff like a balloon. Turn once and press the other side also. Stop the cooking when there are a few brown spots on the roti. Stack rotis on clean tea towel and fold the towel over them to keep warm while cooking the rest. Serve with dry, spiced dishes or simply spread with butter as a snack.

*If sweet corn is in season, take an ear of very fresh and tender corn and with a sharp knife slice off the tops of the kernels. Save them to use in another dish such as Spinach and Corn Bhaji (see recipe page 106). Scrape the sweet milky juice from the corn into a bowl using a spoon or the back of a knife. Avoid the outer skin of the kernels. A single ear of corn should yield the ¼ cup you need. In case you're wondering why the tops of the kernels are not included in the roti, they make holes in the dough when rolling it thinly. Canned creamed corn may not be used for the same reason.

Chinese Steamed Bread

30 g/1 oz fresh yeast
  or 1 sachet dried yeast
250 ml/8 fl oz/1 cup warm water
3 tablespoons sugar
approx. 625 g/1¼ lb/5 cups plain
  (all-purpose) flour
1 teaspoon baking powder
sesame oil

In a large bowl sprinkle yeast over warm water, leave to soften for 5 minutes, then stir in 2 teaspoons sugar and ½ cup flour and leave in a warm place for 10 minutes or until mixture bubbles. Add 1 more cup warm water and remaining sugar, stirring to dissolve. Beat in 2 cups flour sifted with the baking powder until smooth. Add remaining flour and knead at least 5 minutes or until dough is smooth and elastic.

Wash and dry the bowl, lightly grease with sesame oil and put the ball of dough in it, then turn the dough over so the top surface is oiled. Cover and leave in a warm place to rise until doubled in bulk, about 2 hours, depending on temperature. Turn dough out onto a lightly floured surface and knead lightly, then divide into 2 equal portions.

Plain steamed buns: Divide half the dough into 8–10 even-sized pieces, and mould each one into a smooth ball. Place each one on a square of greaseproof or non-stick baking paper brushed lightly with sesame oil, and put them into a bamboo or other steamer, allowing room for them to rise and spread. Leave in a warm place for 30 minutes, or until doubled in size, then place over boiling water and steam for 10 minutes. Do not uncover immediately the cooking is finished, but allow them to remain covered for a further 5 minutes and cool off slightly, as a sudden rush of cold air can cause the tops to wrinkle.

Flower rolls: Divide remaining half of dough in 2 equal portions. On a lightly floured board, roll out one portion with a floured rolling pin, to make a rectangle 40 × 30 cm (16 × 12 in). Brush surface with sesame oil, and roll up to form a cylinder, starting at the long edge. Cut into 12 equal slices.

Place two slices together, one slice on top of another. Use a chopstick to press firmly in the centre, causing the cut edges to open like the petals of a flower. Repeat with remaining 5 slices, and place in a lightly oiled bamboo or other steamer. Repeat with remaining half of dough. Leave covered in a warm place until about double in size. Steam over boiling water for 10 minutes. When ready to serve, reheat by steaming gently for 3 minutes.

Note: Bamboo steamers are particularly good for steaming breads because of their woven lids. If a bamboo steamer is not available, use a large saucepan and place the buns or rolls on a plate held on a trivet above the water level, but wrap the lid of the saucepan in a tea towel to prevent condensation collecting and dropping on the rolls.

Ensaimada

In the Philippines, these sweet yeast rolls with the salty contrast of cheese, are a favourite with morning coffee or hot chocolate.
Makes 18.

120 ml/4 fl oz/½ cup warm water
7 g/¼ oz sachet active dry yeast
185 g/6 oz/¾ cup caster sugar (superfine sugar)
250 g/8 oz butter
3 eggs
570 g/1⅛ lb/4½ cups plain (all-purpose) flour
125 ml/4 fl oz/½ cup milk
125 g/4 oz sharp cheddar cheese, finely grated

Measure warm water into a bowl, sprinkle yeast over and add 1 teaspoon of the measured sugar. Stir until dissolved and leave in a warm place until frothy.

Cream 185 g (6 oz) of butter with ½ cup caster sugar until light. Add 2 eggs, one at a time, beating well after each. Stir in yeast mixture, then flour and milk alternately, beating until smooth. Dough should be soft but not sticky. Shape into a ball and place in a warm, greased bowl. Cover and leave in a warm place for about 1 hour or until risen to double its original volume.

Divide dough in halves. On a lightly floured surface roll one piece to a rectangle 45 × 38 cm (18 × 15 in). Melt remaining butter and brush over the dough, then sprinkle evenly with half the cheese. Cut rectangle lengthways into 3 equal strips and roll up strips, starting at long end. Cut each into 3.

Roll each between palms and board until the thickness of a pencil, and form into twists or coils on greased baking tray, leaving space for rising. Repeat process using remaining dough, butter and cheese. Brush all the formed rolls with remaining egg, beaten. Cover and leave to prove in a warm place about 30 minutes.

Meanwhile, preheat oven to moderate, 180°C (350°F). Bake 12–15 minutes or until golden brown.

Remove to wire racks and while still hot brush with melted butter and sprinkle with caster sugar. Serve warm or at room temperature.

British–Indian Cuisine

This hybrid cuisine dear to the heart of many for whom the years of British rule in India hold fond memories of household cooks thoughtfully adapting spice levels to suit the master and mistress. It clung to the security of hearty cooked English breakfasts, tiffins and afternoon teas, replete with sandwiches and cakes. However, it will probably be best remembered for its Anglicised adaptations of Indian cookery. See KEDGEREE and recipes for Country Captain (page 86) and Fruit Chutney (page 97).

Broad Bean

See LEGUMES & PULSES.

Buffalo

The water buffalo or carabao is more a working animal than a source of food. While in India it is regarded by Hindus with the same reverence as bulls and cows, its rich milk is valued for making certain milk-based sweets and the cheese called surati panir. In the Philippines, buffalo milk is used for kesong puti, a white, salty cheese. In some South East Asian countries as well as the lands once called Indochina the meat is eaten in satays, stews and curries, and features raw in a Laotian dish called larb. In Sri Lanka the favourite local dessert is 'curd and honey' (kiri pani), based on rich buffalo milk. This local yoghurt or curd, thick and firm with a 6 mm (¼ in) skin of yellow cream on top, is poured into shallow clay pots to set, these being the disposable take-away container of South East Asia. The 'honey' is nectar from various palms, boiled down to concentrate the sweetness into thick, dark brown syrup.

Bummalo

See BOMBAY DUCK.

Burdock Root

(*Arctium lappa*) The long, tapering root of the burdock plant which is part of the European herbalist's armoury. It is cultivated in Japan (gobo) as a food plant and, shredded or peeled and cut into cylinders, included in a variety of dishes from sushi to soup. It does not seem to be used in other Asian countries. Look for it in the refrigerator section of Japanese stores, or among the canned goods. If available fresh, it has a rough dark grey exterior. Only the roots are used for food.

Medicinal uses: Roots, leaves and small fruits are used. Roots and fruits (which are wrongly called seeds since they are wrinkled and tiny) are made into a decoction. Purported to be one of the finest blood purifiers in herbal medicine, it is recommended in all such cases alone or in conjunction with other remedies and is used as an alterative, diuretic and diaphoretic. The leaves, bruised and dipped in the white of an egg, are said to relieve the pain of burns.

Gobo and Hijiki with Brown Rice

2 tablespoons hijiki seaweed
100 g/3½ oz burdock root (gobo)
100 g/3½ oz carrot
1 tablespoon oriental sesame oil
1 cup brown rice
2 tablespoons Japanese soy sauce or tamari
1 tablespoon toasted sesame seeds

Soak the hijiki in warm water to cover. It will expand to many times its original size. Peel burdock and cut into small pieces, and to prevent discolouring soak in water. Peel carrot and cut into matchstick strips. In a heavy saucepan heat the oil and toss the carrot and drained burdock for a minute, then add the rice, soy sauce and 2 cups hot water. Bring to the boil, cover tightly and allow to steam for 35 minutes. Add drained hijiki and continue cooking for a further 10 minutes or until all the liquid is absorbed and rice is tender. Fork the hijiki through the rice and serve sprinkled with sesame seeds.

Burma

Sharing borders with Thailand, Laos, China, India and Bangladesh, Burma is home to Buddhism, glittering gilt pagodas, a handsome and tranquil people and some unique culinary delicacies.

One of the first dishes my grandmother taught me to cook, in preparation for marriage (she found out it was my husband-to-be's favourite dish), was a Burmese Fish Kofta Curry (see recipe page 148).

Vendors stream through the streets calling their wares, and in the bazaar areas, an evening wouldn't feel complete without a glass of freshly crushed sugar cane juice, ice cubes clinking, to sip while sampling some of the delights on offer from the food stalls.

Burma's long sea coast means an abundance of seafood flavours. Other ingredients reflect the culinary influence of her neighbours: from India, chick pea flour and spices like coriander, cumin and turmeric; from China noodles, soy sauce and shiitake mushrooms; from Laos, Vietnam and Thailand the pungent flavours of fish sauce and dried shrimp paste as well as ingredients like coconut milk, glutinous rice, palm sugar and sesame seeds which are common to many Asian cuisines.

The tender heart of the banana tree is a feature of Burma's national dish, a spicy fish soup with noodles, called Moh Hin Gha.

As in so many other South East Asian countries, long-grain rice, served steaming hot, is the cornerstone of the meal. And, surprisingly, in Burma it is not cooked by the absorption method. Instead, it is boiled in plenty of water, the water is poured away, the pot covered and returned to the heat so the rice finishes cooking and dries to fluffy perfection.

Soup, served piping hot, is also frequently part of a meal, its flavour varying from mild to strong to offset the other dishes. There is always a selection of curries (meat, chicken, fish, prawns or eggs) and an array of accompaniments including a chilli condiment, a salad of raw leaves, fruit or vegetables, crisp fried onion and garlic, sliced spring onions, roasted chick pea flour, chopped fresh coriander leaf and a home-made pickle.

Most typical of all is Burma's notoriously pungent ngapi htaung. This is not for the uninitiated or the faint-hearted, being a high-powered combination of roasted shrimp paste, roasted onions and garlic combined with chilli, lime juice and salt. Needless to say, it should be approached with caution and eaten in minute quantities, always with rice.

In Burma it is customary to eat with the fingers, adding accompaniments according to personal taste. This applies to 'dry' dishes such as htamin lethoke which translates as 'rice mixed with fingers'. Of course, where the meal is a soupy one, spoons are used.

Butter, Clarified

See GHEE.

Butterbur

See COLTSFOOT.

Butterfly Pea Flower

(*Clitoria ternatea*) Also known as butterfly pea and pigeon wings. A deep blue flower of the Leguminoseae family which is used to give blue colouring to the many sweets and sticky rice cakes so popular in South East Asia. Or rather, it was used until it became easy to buy bottles of artificial colours of any hue. Among traditional Malaysian and Nonya cooks the blue flowers are prized and are still the source of a vibrant deep blue in the kueh or cakes. To make the colouring, a handful of dried flowers is steeped in boiling water, and the coloured water used to tint sticky rice or tapioca, the basis of many Asian sweets. In Thailand, a popular savoury dumpling filled with pork and prawn has the dough tinted blue with an infusion of 2 tablespoons of the dried flowers steeped in just enough boiling water to cover.

These are not sold commercially, but seeds are available through many nursery catalogues and the plant will do well in a tropical or sub-tropical climate. Seeds take rather a long time to germinate since they have a tough seed coat. Rubbing them with sandpaper or a nail file and soaking the seeds in hot water prior to planting is helpful.

Malaysia: *bunga telang*
Thailand: *anjan*

Cabbage

The Brassica family has many members. Below are descriptions of those which are used in Asian cooking.

In many markets or greengrocers they are mostly lumped together under the blanket term 'Chinese cabbage', which is not much help because they have different characteristics and are used in different ways.

Most of these cabbages need only brief cooking. One in particular, the pale green and white cabbage known as wong nga bak, wong bok or hakusai, is delicious shredded and served raw in a salad.

Chinese broccoli (gai larn): (*Brassica alboglabra*) Also called Chinese kale. May be distinguished by its dark green leaves, stout stems, and small white flowers.

This is one of the most popular vegetables, often appearing as a dish in its own right at banquets and even at yum cha, where it is usually lightly boiled and served with oyster sauce.

Purchasing and storing: Choose fresh looking gai larn with leaves which are not wilted, though the leaves themselves are not the important part: it is the stem which is the choice portion.

Preparation: Since the stems have a tough skin it makes for easier eating if, after washing thoroughly, they are peeled and split. Gai larn may be steamed, boiled, stir-fried or braised. The simplest way to serve them is to discard the large outer leaves, cut the stems into finger lengths, drop them into lightly salted boiling water with a spoonful of peanut oil added, and cook until tender-crisp. Drain well, splash a little oyster sauce over and serve hot.

> **China:** *gai larn, jie lan, kailan*
> **Japan:** *kairan*

Chinese Cabbage (Wong nga bak): (*Brassica pekinensis*) SEE ILLUSTRATION. One of the most popular Asian vegetables. Also known as Chinese cabbage, Tientsin cabbage, Peking cabbage, Shantung cabbage, petsai, Napa cabbage and celery cabbage.

It has a long shape like cos lettuce. Its broad leaves with almost white midrib and pale-green edges are closely packed. There are two types: one narrower and more tapered; the other broad and squat. Both are equally delicate in flavour.

Purchasing and storing: Avoid cabbages that have been nibbled by garden pests. Check among the leaves for house guests. Stored in a plastic bag in the refrigerator it will keep well for a week, provided it is fresh and in good condition to start with.

Preparation: Cut the cabbage in halves or quarters lengthways. Wash thoroughly and shake off water. Shred finely for salad, or cut into chunks for stir-frying, steaming or adding to long-cooked dishes for the last few minutes of simmering. It has the most delicate flavour of all the cabbages and is eaten raw in salads, shredded and added to soups at the last minute, stir-fried or lightly braised. It features in the famous Korean pickle, Kim Chi (see recipe below).

> **China:** *wong nga bak, ta paak tsai*
> **Indonesia:** *sawi*
> **Japan:** *hakusai*
> **Malaysia:** *kobis china*
> **Philippines:** *petsai tsina*
> **Sri Lanka:** *kala gova*
> **Thailand:** *phakkat khaoplee*

Kim Chi

1 large wong nga bak, about 1.5 kg/3 lb
coarse sea salt (not iodised)
2 tablespoons hot chilli powder
6 large cloves garlic, finely chopped
6 spring onions (scallions) finely chopped
3 fresh red chillies, finely sliced
1 tablespoon fine shreds of fresh ginger
4 tablespoons fine shreds of white radish
500 ml/1 pint/2 cups dashi stock (recipe page 118)
2 tablespoons Korean light soy sauce

Trim root end off cabbage. Halve lengthways, then cut each half into three equal strips. Sprinkle with handfuls of salt, put into an earthenware pot, cover with a wooden lid small enough to fit inside the pot and weight it down. Leave for 2 days and rinse with cold water. Press out as much liquid as possible and cut into shorter lengths. Combine with the chilli powder, garlic, spring onions, chillies, ginger and radish mixed together. Pour dashi and soy sauce over, cover with wax paper and replace lid. Refrigerate for at least 4 days before eating. Serve with steamed rice and other dishes. If liked, a good spoonful of gochujang (Korean chilli bean paste) may be mixed with the kim chi before serving.

Chinese chard (bok choy): (*Brassica chinensis*) SEE ILLUSTRATION. Also called Chinese white cabbage because of its thick white leaf ribs which contrast with the dark green leaves. It can vary in size from quite small, 10 cm (4 in) long to very large, 30 cm (12 in) long. The smaller type is called Shanghai bok choy or baby bok choy and is much sought after for banquet dishes in which they are braised whole. Mild in flavour, it should be cooked only a few minutes so it retains colour and texture when served. The white portion, thinly sliced, may be eaten raw.

Preparation: Wash well, separating the leaves so that any sand which is between the leaves is washed away. Small ones may be kept whole. After separating the leaves of the large variety, trim off the dark green leaf, leaving only a narrow border along the white leaf rib. The rather tough green portion of the leaf is used for soup or deep frying. See recipe for Mermaid's Tresses below.

> **China:** *bok choy, baak choy, pak choi, bai cai, pau tsai, ching tsai*
> **Indonesia:** *petsai*
> **Japan:** *taisai, shakushina*
> **Malaysia:** *sawi puteh*
> **Philippines:** *petsai*
> **Sri Lanka:** *kala gova*
> **Thailand:** *phakket bai*

Vietnamese Chicken and Cabbage Salad

Serves 6

500 g/1 lb chicken thigh fillets
salt and pepper
1 small wong nga bak
2 medium onions
1 teaspoon salt
3 tablespoons sugar
3 tablespoons fish sauce
4 tablespoons lime juice
1 tablespoon white vinegar
30 g/1 oz chopped mint or Vietnamese mint
30 g/1 oz chopped fresh coriander

Remove fat from chicken fillets. Put fillets in a saucepan with sufficient water to cover, add a little salt and pepper and bring to a slow simmer. Cover and cook until done, taking care not to overcook. Allow chicken to cool in liquid.

Halve the cabbage lengthways, and cut each half again lengthways. Wash in cold water, shake out all the water and place sections on a wooden board, cut surface down. Placing two halves together to make slicing quicker and, with a sharp knife, shred very finely. Put into a large bowl, cover and chill.

Peel onions, halve lengthways and slice very thinly crosswise. Sprinkle with salt in a bowl, working the salt well into the onion with fingers. Leave for 30 minutes before rinsing with water and squeezing out juices. Add half the sugar and mix.

In another bowl combine remaining sugar, fish sauce, lime juice and vinegar. Slice the cooled chicken into thin strips. Just before serving toss and mix chicken, cabbage, onion, dressing, mint and coriander.

Mermaid's Tresses

The addition of a sprinkling of crisply fried, tiny dried shrimp over the finely shredded cabbage adds flavour and extra texture. Make sure the leaves are quite dry or they will spatter when dropped into hot oil.

1 bunch bok choy
oil for deep frying
½ teaspoon salt
2 pinches caster sugar (superfine sugar)
2 tablespoons very tiny dried shrimp (optional)

With a sharp knife cut away the white central rib of the leaves and set aside for braised bok choy (recipe below). Place 3 or 4 green leaves together and roll up tightly. Shred in very fine even slices, and separate the shreds.

Heat at least 2 cups oil in a wok or other deep pan, and drop in a large handful of the shredded leaves at a time. Stir-fry for about 60 to 80 seconds, scoop them out on a large perforated spoon and drain on paper towels. The colour should be brilliant green. If cooked for even a few seconds too long they will turn brown.

In a few minutes, when the leaves have cooled and crisped, sprinkle lightly with the merest pinch of salt and caster sugar. If using the dried shrimp, deep fry in the same oil, drain, and sprinkle over the fried cabbage. Serve while crisp, as an hors d'oeuvre or as a background for fried scallops or other delicate, unsauced foods.

Braised Bok Choy

1 bunch bok choy
3 tablespoons peanut oil
1 large clove garlic, bruised
3 thin slices fresh ginger
1 teaspoon sugar
salt to taste
1 teaspoon oriental sesame oil

Separate leaves, wash thoroughly and shake dry. Trim base of stem if necessary and remove tough portions of large leaves with sharp knife, leaving a narrow green border on the white. Cut into 5–8 cm (2–3 in) lengths.

Heat a wok, add the oil and swirl to coat surface, then fry garlic and ginger for a few seconds. Add bok choy and stir-fry for 1 minute on high heat, then add 3 tablespoons water or stock, sugar and salt. Cover and simmer for 3 minutes or until stems are tender-crisp. Add sesame oil and toss to distribute. Serve at once.

Flowering cabbage (choy sum): (*Brassica chinensis* var. *parachinensis*) This member of the family has small yellow flowers and mid-green leaves and stems which are tender enough not to need peeling. Steam, stir-fry or boil. Season with salt, a pinch of sugar and a few drops of sesame oil. Serve it with other vegetables or as a side dish on its own with oyster sauce mixed with a pinch of sugar.

China: *cai xin, choy sum, chye sim*
Japan: *saishin*
Malaysia: *sawi*

Stir-Fried Choy Sum with Barbecued Pork

Slices of barbecued pork make a tasty addition to a dish of simple greens.

2 tablespoons peanut oil
2 cloves garlic, finely chopped
1 teaspoon chopped ginger
125 g/4 oz barbecued pork slices
500 g/1 lb choy sum, washed and dried and cut into bite-sized lengths
125 g/4 oz/½ cup chicken stock
1 tablespoon soy sauce
½ teaspoon sugar
few drops oriental sesame oil

Heat wok, add oil and stir-fry the garlic and ginger for 30 seconds. Add pork and stir-fry for a minute or so longer, then add the choy sum and stir-fry until all the greens have come into contact with the hot oil. Add chicken stock, cover and steam for 3 minutes. Turn off heat, sprinkle with soy sauce and sugar and toss to distribute flavours. Serve at once with steamed rice.

Mustard cabbage (gai choy): (*Brassica juncea*). SEE ILLUSTRATION. There are two varieties commonly available, although four are listed as members of the mustard cabbage group. The most common is Swatow mustard cabbage which has thick, curving leaf ribs springing from a thick central stalk (*Brassica alba*). The ribs are the main part of the leaf with prominent veins extending almost the width of the leaf. The thick ribs are most suited to pickling and it is this variety which is used in Szechwan pickled cabbage.

The other variety, commonly known as bamboo mustard cabbage (jook gai choy), has longer, thinner leaves. Used in soups and stir-fries. Because of its strong flavour, some recipes advise blanching it before use in stir-fried dishes, but for those who like its mustardy tang this is not necessary.

Purchasing and storing: As in any green leafy vegetable, look for mustard cabbage that is fresh and bright, not dark and limp. The leaf ribs are the important part, so choose specimens in which these are well developed. This vegetable keeps well for a few days if refrigerated.

Preparation: I have often found sand lurking where the leaves join the stem, so would advise that just prior to preparation the leaves are detached from the stem and the whole lot given a good wash. Cut crossways into bite-sized pieces or, for pickling, into chunks.

Medicinal uses: If not pickled, Swatow mustard cabbage is considered a challenge to the digestion, and better avoided for other reasons. When pressed, one old Chinese said I should not let my husband eat it as it is believed to affect virility. Cantonese only use it in soup which has a reputation as an anti-flu beverage: add chopped cabbage to boiling water, simmer for 15 minutes, season to taste and serve immediately.

China: *dai gai choy, jook gai choy*
India: *sarson*
Indonesia: *sawi hijau*
Japan: *takana, karashi-na*
Philippines: *mustasa*
Sri Lanka: *abba kolle*
Thailand: *phakkat khieo*
Vietnam: *rau cai*

Mustard Cabbage Relish

250 g/8 oz/1 cup white sugar
750 ml/1½ pints/3 cups water
1 tablespoon salt
125 ml/4 fl oz/½ cup cider vinegar
1 bunch gai choy
iced water
few slices fresh ginger

In a stainless steel saucepan bring sugar, water, salt and vinegar to the boil, stirring until sugar dissolves. Simmer for 5 minutes then leave to cool completely.

Wash the gai choy and trim off the leaves, saving them to use in soup. Only the thick leaf ribs and tender stems are used for this relish. Cut into chunks and weigh 250 g (8 oz). Blanch in boiling water for 1 minute, drain and plunge

into iced water to stop the cooking and set the colour. Put cabbage and ginger in a glass jar which has been rinsed in very hot water. Pour in the cold vinegar mixture, cover and refrigerate for about 4 days before using. Serve as a relish with meals, sprinkling a few drops of sesame oil over if liked.

Rosette bok choy: (*Brassica chinensis* var. *rosularis*) SEE ILLUSTRATION. A variety of bok choy which also has white leaf ribs and dark leaf edges but a different growth habit: it fans out in a circle, low and flat to the ground. It has the same flavour and food value (vitamins A and C) but is tougher and requires longer cooking. Wash well, cut it in sections rather than separate the leaves, and use it, like its taller cousin, in soups, braised or stir-fried dishes.

China: *tai gu choy, wu ta cai*
Japan: *tasai*

Cakes

Cakes are a comparatively recent innovation because ovens were not originally part of an Asian kitchen. The confections known as kueh, or kavum, or rasa kavili, are examples of the true cakes of Asia. These local cakes are fried or steamed, and usually wrapped in leaves which are not eaten with the cake, but give a good flavour or attractive shape. Sometimes the mixture is boiled and moulded; in other recipes, ingenious clay or metal trays with plain or fancy depressions are filled with batter and cooked over hot coals.

Until fairly recently, if there was an oven in an Asian kitchen it was usually made from a converted kerosene tin. Anything requiring a proper oven would be sent to the local bread oven to be cooked, or purchased from the bakery. With the increased availability of gas and electric ovens, home cooks are finding new outlets for their creativity.

What follows are the deliciously spicy cakes which are more closely related to rich continental cakes than to the airy sponges and butter cakes enjoyed by the British. The influence of Portuguese, Dutch, French and British colonisers is apparent in these, and yet they have a character of their own: spicier and sweeter than what originally inspired them, and adapted to use the ingredients more readily available. Rich, with good keeping qualities, they are well worth making for special occasions.

Indonesian Spice Layer Cake

This is no ordinary cake. The baking process requires time and patience since the many layers (usually 18–20) are baked and grilled one at a time! Makes 1 × 20 cm (8 in) round or square cake.

10 egg yolks
375 g/12 oz/1½ cups caster sugar (superfine sugar)
250 g/8 oz butter
2 teaspoons vanilla essence
8 egg whites
185 g/6 oz/1½ cups plain (all-purpose) flour, sifted
1 teaspoon ground cinnamon
1 teaspoon freshly grated nutmeg
1 teaspoon ground cardamom
½ teaspoon ground cloves
extra melted butter (optional)

In electric mixer whisk egg yolks with ½ cup sugar until thick and light. Cream butter with ¾ cup sugar and the vanilla essence until light and smooth. In a clean, dry bowl whisk egg whites until stiff, add the remaining ¼ cup sugar and whisk again until thick and glossy.

Mix egg yolk and butter mixtures together well. Fold in the flour, then the egg whites. Divide mixture into two almost equal portions and mix the ground spices into the slightly larger portion.

Preheat oven to 160°C (325°F). Generously butter a 20 cm (8 in) springform cake pan with softened butter. Line the base with baking paper and brush with melted butter. Dust with flour and tip out excess.

Put a measured amount of spice batter into the tin, approximately ⅓ cup. Spread the batter thinly with a spatula and tap the tin very firmly on the bench top to help the batter spread thinly and evenly. Bake in the centre of the oven until firm, about 10 minutes. Meanwhile, preheat grill and place the tin under the grill about 15 cm (6 in) from the heat for 30–40 seconds until top is evenly browned. Watch carefully to ensure it doesn't burn but achieves a coffee colour.

Spread the same amount of plain batter over the spicy layer, tapping the tin to ensure a thin, even layer. Return to oven and cook for 10 minutes, then grill as before. Continue with alternate layers of spiced and plain mixture until the batter has been used.

For those who enjoy a really buttery cake, the extra melted butter may be used to brush lightly over each layer after grilling and before the next layer of batter is spread over.

When the last layer has been baked, test by inserting a skewer into the centre. It should emerge slightly buttery. If there is any uncooked batter clinging to it, bake the whole cake for a few minutes longer. Cool completely, then remove the side of the springform pan and cut the cake into thin, small slices as it is very rich.

Sri Lankan Love Cake

A legacy from the Portuguese who once ruled the island of Ceylon as it was then called. There are as many recipes for Love Cake as there are cooks, and as many strong opinions on just how to achieve a soft texture in the centre while having a firm and chewy exterior. The secret is in slow baking and correct size of cake tin.

6 large eggs
500 g/1 lb/2 cups caster sugar (superfine sugar)
150 g/5 oz unsalted butter
3 tablespoons honey
2 tablespoons rose water
 or ¼ teaspoon rose essence
finely chopped zest of 1 lime or lemon
1 teaspoon freshly grated nutmeg
1 teaspoon ground cardamom
250 g/8 oz raw cashews
250 g/8 oz coarse semolina
125 g/4 oz crystallised winter melon
 or pineapple (optional)

Line a 25 × 30 cm (10 × 12 in) cake tin with baking paper. Preheat oven to 150°C (300°F).

Beat eggs and sugar until thick and light. Add softened butter and honey, rose water, lime zest, nutmeg and cardamom. Beat well. Chop cashews coarsely and stir in together with the semolina and crystallised fruit. Turn into prepared tin and bake in a slow oven for 1 hour or until pale golden on top. If the cake starts to brown too quickly, cover loosely with foil. Do not use the skewer test, because if a skewer comes out clean it means the cake is overcooked by Sri Lankan standards. It will taste good, but there won't be the moist centre which is typical of this confection. Leave cake in tin to cool. Cut into small squares to serve.

Goan Bibingka

500 g/1 lb/2 cups sugar
125 ml/4 fl oz/½ cup water
½ teaspoon cardamom seeds, crushed
5 egg yolks
250 ml/8 fl oz/1 cup thick coconut milk
60 g/2 oz/½ cup flour
4 tablespoons melted ghee

Put the sugar, water and cardamom into a small heavy pan and simmer for 5 minutes. Cool. Beat egg yolks and add the cooled syrup, coconut milk and flour. Leave to stand for at least an hour.

In a bar or loaf tin, heat enough ghee to cover the base. Pour in sufficient batter to form a thin layer. Bake until set and brown. Brush surface with more ghee and pour in another layer of batter. Cook under a preheated grill until brown. Continue until all the batter has been used. Cool in the tin and leave overnight, then cut across into thin slices.

Filipino Bibingka Especial

3 large eggs, beaten
¾ cup caster sugar (superfine sugar)
300 ml/10 fl oz/1¼ cups coconut milk
2 tablespoons melted butter
250 g/8 oz/2 cups plain (all-purpose) flour
4 teaspoons baking powder
2 tablespoons extra melted butter
3 tablespoons finely grated sharp cheese
1 tablespoon caster sugar (superfine sugar)
fresh grated coconut (optional)

Line a 23 cm (9 in) square baking tin and line with baking paper. Preheat oven to 180°C (350°F).

Beat eggs well, gradually add the caster sugar and beat until thick and light. Stir in coconut milk and 2 tablespoons melted butter.

Sift together flour and baking powder. Fold into egg and coconut and mix thoroughly. Pour into prepared tin and bake for about 20 minutes, until firm and golden, and top should spring back when lightly pressed with fingertip. Remove pan from oven, brush top quickly with extra melted butter and sprinkle with grated cheese and extra sugar. Cut into squares. Serve sprinkled with coconut if desired.

Cambodia

The food of Cambodia resembles closely the food of Laos and Thailand. Even the names of certain ingredients and dishes have similar pronunciations.

There is a reliance on fish and rice, vegetables of the region, green leaves and shoots, flavouring herbs and the ever-present fish sauce which is used to season any dish put on the table. Predominant flavours in most dishes are garlic (kthem), galangal (rom deng), ginger (khnei), kaffir lime leaves (sleuk kroy saach), fresh coriander (wun swee), mint (chee on kham), basil (chee krohom) and eryngo (chee bonla).

Rice is eaten three times a day. At breakfast, rice porridge is eaten with either fried salted fish or pickled mustard cabbage to enliven its blandness. At midday and for the evening meal, long-grain white rice is the foundation of the meal, together with the stir-fried dishes and curries. Rice is always cooked without salt and the curries are somewhat similar to Thai curries, though not as spicily hot. They are rather liquid, and usually combine vegetables with meat, both to extend the dish and because Cambodians like the way pumpkin, squash, beans and other bland vegetables take on flavours of the curry.

For frying, pork fat is the preferred medium, both for its availability and flavour.

When grilling whole fish, it is usually with the scales left on to protect the delicate flesh. The Mekong River flows through this country as it does through Laos, supplying both with an abundance of freshwater fish, but Cambodia has, in addition to this source, access to seafood from the Gulf of Thailand. Fish is the major source of protein, whether as fresh fish, salted and dried fish, or the salty, fermented pastes so essential to the flavours of this region.

Soups are clear, with the refreshing piquancy of tamarind, tomatoes, lime or unripe pineapple. Meat is most often pork or chicken but sometimes beef or buffalo. It is always highly seasoned, so a little goes a long way. Game birds are favoured eating too, some of them smaller than sparrows.

Tea and coffee are not beverages of choice in Cambodia. Orange juice is popular. It is common for cups of steaming water to be sipped during a meal, as it is believed this helps digestion.

Camel's Milk

See KEPHIR.

Candle Nut

(*Aleurites moluccana*) SEE ILLUSTRATION. Native to the Molucca Islands, Malaysia and the South Pacific. Uses include varnish, medicine, fertilizer and lamp oil, which accounts for the common English name. Husks and roots provide tapa cloth dye. A hard, oily nut which, in a culinary context, is ground and used mostly in Indonesian and Malaysian dishes as a thickening agent. Macadamias and Brazil nuts make good substitutes, though both are sweeter than the slightly bitter candle nut.

Purchasing and storing: Buy in small quantities, and because of the high oil content, store in the freezer if not being used quickly, in order to prevent rancidity.

Preparation: Crush, pound or grate finely. The raw nut is mildly toxic, but once cooked is quite safe so always cook with the dishes which they are used to thicken.

> **Burma:** *kyainthee*
> **Fiji:** *lauci, tutui*
> **Hawaii:** *kukui*
> **Indonesia:** *kemiri*
> **Malaysia:** *buah keras*
> **Philippines:** *lumbang bato*
> **Samoa:** *pu'a, lama*
> **Sri Lanka:** *kekuna, tel kekuna*
> **Tahiti:** *tuitui*
> **Marquesas:** *tuitui*
> **Tonga:** *tuitui*

Capsicum (bell peppers)

(*Capsicum annuum*) There are many different shapes, sizes and degrees of heat in capsicums and chillies, which are natives of central America. When the term capsicum is applied, it is generally to denote the large, mild varieties known as sweet peppers, bell peppers or banana peppers. The use of sweet, mild peppers is quite legitimate in Asian cuisines, and the recipes which follow illustrate the fact.

Purchasing and storing: Buy firm, smooth-skinned specimens, and make sure the stalk is fresh and green. They will keep reasonably well in a polythene bag in the refrigerator for a few days but, like all garden produce, are best when freshest. Choose those of even size and regular shape for easy handling: straight ones are much easier to fill than those with a built-in curve or twist.

Preparation: To prepare for stuffing, carefully remove seeds and central membranes, leaving cavity free for filling. Depending on the shape and size of the capsicum, it may be necessary to make one or two slits in order to fill it. With the tip of a small knife, make one slit lengthways from just under the stalk almost to the tip, and a short slit half way around the top, to facilitate filling. Of course, the easy way is to slice off the top, remove the seeds and membrane, fill the capsicum and simply replace the top complete with stem.

> **China:** *tien chiao*
> **India:** *simla mirich, bari mirch*
> **Indonesia:** *cabe besar*
> **Japan:** *piiman*
> **Malaysia:** *lada merah*
> **Philippines:** *sili peaman*
> **Sri Lanka:** *malu miris*
> **Thailand:** *prik yuak*

Banana Peppers in Coconut Milk

Serves 4

500 g/1 lb banana peppers, whole
250 g/8 fl oz/1 cup thin coconut milk
2 teaspoons pounded Maldive fish
1 teaspoon salt
sprig of fresh curry leaves
4 tablespoons finely chopped onions or shallots
3 fresh green chillies
½ teaspoon fenugreek seeds
½ teaspoon ground turmeric
3 tablespoons thick coconut milk

Put all the ingredients except thick coconut milk into a saucepan and simmer until peppers are soft and gravy thickened. Add thick coconut milk and bring back to simmering point. Serve with rice.

Stuffed Banana Peppers, Thai Style

Serves 4

6–8 medium sized banana peppers
250 g/8 oz minced pork
125 g/4 oz raw prawn meat, chopped
1 teaspoon finely chopped garlic
½ teaspoon salt
¼ teaspoon ground black pepper
1 tablespoon finely chopped fresh coriander
2 tablespoons oil
2 tablespoons Thai green or red curry paste
375 ml/12 fl oz/1½ cups coconut milk
1–2 tablespoons fish sauce
2 teaspoons palm sugar or brown sugar
20 fresh basil leaves
sliced red chillies (optional)

Slit the capsicums lengthways and scrape out the seeds and membrane. Mix pork and chopped prawns in a bowl. Crush the garlic with the salt to a smooth paste. Add pepper and coriander, mix into the pork and prawns. With a teaspoon, fill the capsicums with the mixture.

Heat the oil and fry the curry paste over gentle heat, stirring, until it is fragrant. Add coconut milk, fish sauce, sugar and stir while bringing to simmering point. Lay the capsicums in the sauce and simmer for 15 minutes, adding a little extra coconut milk or water if necessary. Turn them over and cook for a further 10 minutes, then scatter with basil leaves and chilli slices and serve with steamed rice.

Carambola

See STAR FRUIT.

Caraway

(*Carum carvi*) Botanically, caraway is from the same family (Umbelliferae) as coriander, cumin, dill and fennel. The herb has fine, feathery leaves and pretty bells of lacy flowers, and the 'seeds' are actually split halves of the fruit. It is native to Europe, Asia and North Africa.

Caraway is very popular in Europe (those fragrant, elongated seeds in rye breads, sauerkraut, seed cake and certain cheeses are caraway), but is not used in Asian cooking. That is, not unless someone takes literally the instruction in some Indian recipes where caraway seed is mentioned when what is actually meant is cumin. The confusion is understandable, for caraway is sometimes referred to as 'foreign cumin' in the orient.

While caraway is more curved and darker in colour than cumin, they are look-alikes to the casual observer. However, the flavour is different and if you come across formulae for curry spices in which caraway is named, please translate to cumin. In North African spice mixes caraway would be correct, but not in Asia.

Medicinal uses: As a home remedy for flatulence and colic, caraway and dill are strongly recommended. In Asian homes a bottle of dill water is always present when there is a baby in the family. In the ubiquitous 'gripe water' (made in England and purchased at chemists) the sweet smell of these seeds is quite easily recognised. It used to be given to colicky infants until relatively recently, when it was discovered that quite a percentage of alcohol was also part of the formula. It was a wonderful cure both for baby's colic and mother's desperation during the years when I needed to soothe colicky infants and it doesn't seem to have done them any harm — in fact, not one of them shows a fondness for alcohol in adulthood. But these days, other means of dispelling infant colic are preferred.

Cardamom

(*Elettaria cardamomum*) (Also spelled cardamum. Often wrongly spelled cardamon.) SEE ILLUSTRATION. A member of the ginger family, indigenous to Sri Lanka and southern India. The pale green oval pods containing from 15–20 brown or black seeds, are the best kind to buy and use. (Sometimes the pods are chemically bleached white to make them more appealing, but I cannot quite see the point and prefer to use them in their naturally dried state.)

There are many pretenders, among them *Amomum subulatum*, called black or brown cardamom or, in Hindi, barra illaichi ('large cardamom'). It is also called 'false cardamom' and its flavour is not as sweetly fragrant. The seeds look similar but have an antiseptic flavour, and are used only in savoury recipes, and never to flavour sweets.

There are also other seeds which look very much

like cardamom seeds to the casual observer, but which come from a different plant, and are actually Melegueta pepper, also known as grains of paradise or Guinea grains. They are related to cardamom, but have a less fragrant, more peppery flavour.

There is quite a lot of flavour in the cardamom pod, and when using cardamoms whole in simmered dishes, the favoured method is to lightly bruise whole pods and drop them in. The fragrance will permeate the dish. The pods may be lifted out before serving or left in as many people quite enjoy finding a cardamom pod and may chew on it after the meal. Cardamom is known and used as a breath freshener.

Cardamom is overtaken only by saffron and vanilla when assessing the world's most valuable spices. Because of its high cost, the temptation to adulterate ground cardamom is frequently yielded to, another reason to buy the whole pods and crush them yourself with a mortar and pestle for the very best results. One of the newer ways of adding cardamom flavour is cardamom extract to be added only a few drops at a time. It is guaranteed 100 per cent pure cardamom, and certainly smells and tastes like it is. Read the label to be sure it is 'extract', not 'essence'.

Purchasing and storing: It is always preferable to buy green cardamom and to buy it in the pod. Reputable spice companies offer ground cardamom in small glass jars which is excellent, particularly the decorticated type (seeds only). It is strong and retains its fresh fragrance very well, but is necessarily expensive and does not move fast off grocery shelves, so is not widely stocked. Ground whole cardamom (pods and all), while not as strong as the decorticated type, is perfectly adequate though you will need to use a bit more than if you peel and grind your own.

Preparation: It is best to lightly toast cardamom pods before removing the seeds for grinding. Do this over medium-low heat in a dry pan. To split the pods, put a few at a time in a mortar and give a few gentle thumps with a pestle. Remove the small dark seeds and pound finely. Store airtight in a cool, dark place. With regard to the cost and trouble taken to make pure ground cardamom, I usually keep the precious spice in the freezer.

Medicinal uses: Cardamom seeds are regarded as a digestive, either on their own or as part of the betel chew (see BETEL LEAF) which is often served after a meal in India. They are considered effective against

flatulence and minor stomach problems and as an anti-spasmodic.

Burma: *phalazee*
India: *elaichi, illaichi*
Indonesia: *kapulaga*
Malaysia: *buah pelaga*
Thailand: *kravan, luk kravan*
Sri Lanka: *enasal*

Carrot

(*Daucus carota* ssp. *sativus*) From a wild plant which grows all over Europe. There are many varieties of carrot, differing in shape, colour and flavour. If young and freshly pulled they are sweet and delicious and rich in vitamin A. They are used in vegetable curries and other spiced preparations in India, and are the basis of a well-known sweetmeat, Carrot Halva (see recipe page 66). The carrot variety grown in India is much deeper in colour than the Western carrot, but carrots of whatever variety can be used in Indian recipes.

In Vietnam they are finely grated and added to nuoc cham, the all-purpose dipping sauce, as well as being used in their adopted French baguette sandwiches. In Japanese, Chinese and Korean cooking they are carved to look like blossoms and dropped into soups or used as garnish. In Thailand they are carved to resemble flowers, leaves, or ears of wheat. For those who have neither the skill nor the time to carve a carrot into a work of art, a small, inexpensive Japanese grater will transform a carrot into fine, long shreds which, crisped in iced water, can decorate a plate in no time at all. For a brief description of how to make simple and quick carrot flowers, see page 167.

Carrot Relish

A friend from India makes this relish which is simple and quite delicious.

500 g/1 lb carrots
3 tablespoons oil or mixture of oil and ghee
2 teaspoons crushed garlic
1 teaspoon ground cumin
½ teaspoon ground turmeric
½ teaspoon chilli powder
½ teaspoon salt or to taste
1 teaspoon jaggery or brown sugar
finely chopped mint or coriander

Wash and peel the carrots, then slice in thin rounds. Heat the oil and gently fry garlic until soft and fragrant. Add cumin, turmeric, chilli powder and salt, mix and add the carrots, tossing to coat with the spice. Add 2 tablespoons water and the jaggery, cover and steam for 10 minutes or until carrots are tender but still slightly crisp. Sprinkle with fresh herbs before serving.

Carrot and Dried Fruit Chutney

90 g/3 oz/½ cup chopped dates
90 g/3 oz/½ cup raisins
90 g/3 oz/½ cup chopped dried apricots
90 g/3 oz/½ cup chopped dried figs
250 ml/8 fl oz/1 cup water
500 g/1 lb carrots, finely grated
1 teaspoon cumin seeds
2 cinnamon sticks
1 teaspoon ground cardamom
¼ teaspoon ground cloves
500 ml/1 pint/2 cups vinegar
500 g/1 lb/2 cups chopped jaggery
  or brown sugar
3 teaspoons salt
2 teaspoons chilli powder
2 teaspoons ground black mustard
1 teaspoon crushed garlic
1 teaspoon grated fresh ginger

Soak dried fruits in water for 1 hour or soften them in the microwave for a few minutes. Put all the ingredients into a non-aluminium pan and bring slowly to the boil, stirring. Simmer until the fruit is very soft and the consistency like that of thick jam. Remove cinnamon sticks, cool and store in sterile bottles.

Carrot Halva (Gajjar Halwa)

500 g/1 lb carrots
60 g/2 oz ghee
½ teaspoon ground cardamom
  or 6 drops cardamom extract
375 g/12 oz/1½ cups sugar
125 ml/4 fl oz/½ cup hot water
250 ml/8 fl oz/1 cup cream
4 tablespoons dried milk powder or khoa
2 tablespoons blanched pistachios or almond
  slivers
edible silver leaf to garnish (optional)

Wash and peel carrots and grate them finely. Heat ghee in a heavy pan and add the carrots. Cook uncovered over medium heat, stirring. Turn heat very low, cover and cook until carrots are soft and almost all the liquid evaporated.

Make a syrup with the sugar and water, add syrup to carrots and stir in the cream and milk powder or khoa, blending well. Stir constantly over medium heat until mixture is thick and comes away from side of pan in one mass. Stir in cardamom. Turn onto a buttered dish, smooth top with buttered foil and allow to cool. Decorate with pistachios or almonds. For a festive occasion, flutter silver leaf onto the surface. Cut into small diamonds or squares for serving.

Cashew

(*Anacardium occidentale*) SEE ILLUSTRATION. Although a native of Brazil, the cashew was taken by the Portuguese to Goa on the south-western coast of India. Its native (South American) name of acaju became caju or cadju or kaju in the Indian sub-continent, Sri Lanka and Malaysia. South India is now one of the world's leading exporters of cashews, growing as many as Brazil.

The cashew fruit, sometimes called cashew apple, has a shiny skin which turns orange-red when ripe. It is eaten, but not in large amounts as its flesh has considerable astringency. It is used to make feni, the local clear spirit made in Goa. See FENI.

A strange fruit, it carries its seed outside, not in. The seed is enclosed in a thick, hard shell which hangs off the end of the somewhat pear-shaped fruit and the cashew as we know it is the kernel of the seed. The shell contains anacordolic acid, a substance which can damage the salivary glands and cause paralysis of the jaw. While it is unlikely anyone would attempt to eat the shells, they have to be cut open in order to get the kernels. The sap is capable of blistering the hands.

Fresh cashews have a sweet, milky and crunchy rather than crisp texture. In Asia they are boiled with turmeric and salt, and small parcels of these boiled nuts wrapped in mango leaves are taken round by street-sellers.

When roasted, cashews are crisp yet softer to bite through than many other nuts. In Goa, they are lightly fried and sprinkled with salt and chilli powder, just enough to add a touch of excitement. These are often served with a drink of fresh coconut juice and feni.

Since cashews are grown in Asia and are much cheaper than imported almonds, they take the place of almonds in many recipes such as cake, marzipan and fudge. See recipe for Sri Lankan Love Cake (page 61) which uses cashews for its texture.

In southern India cashews are added to thicken sauces in much the same way almonds are used in northern India.

Cashews are also used in savoury dishes, and in Sri Lanka, one of the regional specialities is a cashew nut curry. Fresh cashews are not available in countries where they are not grown. Raw cashews, if soaked in water for 30 minutes, are reasonably like fresh cashews, and certainly have a much better texture than canned cashew curry.

China: *yao dou*
India: *kaju*
Indonesia: *kacang mete*
Malaysia: *gaju*
Philippines: *casoy, casuy*
Sri Lanka: *cadju*
Thailand: *mamuang himmaphaan, katae-ka*

Devilled Cashews

Served as a savoury with pre-dinner drinks in the chilli belt of Asia.

500 g/1 lb raw cashews
oil for deep frying
2 teaspoons chilli powder
2 teaspoons salt

Heat oil in a wok or other deep pan and fry the cashews over moderate heat, stirring constantly with a slotted metal spoon so they colour evenly. When pale golden, remove with slotted spoon and drain on paper towels. Don't wait until the colour is as deep as you think it should be, because the nuts will continue to cook in their own heat even after they have been removed from the oil. When all the nuts have been fried and drained, combine chilli powder and salt and sprinkle over, tossing well to distribute the flavours. When cold, dust off excess salt and chilli powder and serve. May be made a week or two before required and stored in an airtight container.

Boiled Cashews

If fresh cashews are not available (even in the countries where they grow, they are mostly earmarked for export), the effect can be successfully duplicated with raw cashews.

185 g/6 oz/1 cup raw cashews
¼ teaspoon ground turmeric
½ teaspoon salt

Soak cashews in hot water, leave for 30 minutes. Drain and put into a saucepan with just enough water to cover. Stir in turmeric and salt, bring to the boil, cover and simmer for 20 minutes. (The cashews will colour more evenly if they are split in half after soaking.) Drain and serve at room temperature.

Cashew Nut Curry

Cashews in a coconut milk sauce are a rare treat. Serves 4–6.

250 g/8 oz raw cashews
750 ml/1½ pints/3 cups thin coconut milk
1 large onion, finely sliced
2 fresh green chillies, seeded
½ teaspoon ground turmeric
2 cloves garlic, sliced
1 teaspoon finely grated fresh ginger
1 cinnamon stick
strip of dried pandan leaf
sprig of fresh curry leaves
2 stems lemon grass
1 teaspoon salt or to taste
250 ml/8 fl oz/1 cup thick coconut milk

Soak cashews in water for 30 minutes while preparing sauce. Put all ingredients except thick coconut milk into a saucepan and simmer uncovered for 10 minutes. Drain the cashews and add to the coconut milk mixture, simmer for a further 30 minutes or until cashews are tender. Stir in thick coconut milk and serve with rice.

Cassava

(*Manihot esculenta*) SEE ILLUSTRATION. Also known as manioc or yuca, a large tuber used as a staple in the Pacific. Native to tropical America, it is thought to have been introduced to the tropics of Asia by the Portuguese in the 17th century. There are different varieties of cassava. The long, fairly even-shaped tubers, 5–10 cm (2–4 in) in diameter, have dark brown rough skin and hard white flesh.

According to the botanist H. F. Macmillan, two distinct kinds of cassava are recognised: 'bitter' (*M. utilissima*) and 'sweet' (*M. palmata*). Both have hydrocyanic acid in the juice of the roots, with the 'bitter' type containing a higher percentage. For safety they should all be cooked thoroughly before eating as hydrocyanic acid is volatile and driven off by cooking. The tubers are relished by people the world over with perfect safety once cooked and drained.

The 'sweet' variety of cassava is used mainly as a source of starch. In order to produce granulated tapioca the roots are grated, thoroughly washed, pressed through fine meshes and heated.

The tuber contains very little in food value apart from starch, which is a source of concern to nutritionists in countries where this is a staple food. It has very low fat and protein content, consequently fat-soluble vitamins A and D are lacking, but does contain vitamin C. A staple in much of the Pacific, its use is supplemented with greens, meat and seafood, fat and legumes.

In countries with a preference for pungent foods, cassava or manioc tubers are well boiled until tender in salted water and drained, and served with fresh grated coconut and an accompaniment made with pounded chillies, onions, lime juice and salt.

Grated fresh cassava is a popular ingredient in the Pacific islands, and is now available in Western markets. It may be already packaged in 1 kg (2 lb) plastic bags, or sold by weight from the pile of snowy white, finely grated cassava. Eagerly awaited by customers, it never lasts long. It is made into cakes and dumplings dear to the hearts and taste-buds of those brought up with them, though the texture is not fluffy and light as are Western cakes, but rather glutinous and solid.

Purchasing and storing: Look over the tubers and make sure the skin is unbroken, that there are no mouldy spots and that the smell is fresh. The tubers will keep, in a basket or cupboard protected from light, for up to 10 days. Frozen cassava, peeled and cut into convenient lengths, is sold in plastic packets. Grated cassava will keep in the refrigerator for 5 or 6 days.

Preparation: If you purchase the whole fresh tuber, don't try to peel it with a vegetable peeler as you might a potato. The skin is too tough for that. Scrub the tubers, then cut into short sections about 5 cm (2 in) long. With a sharp knife slit the skin and its underlying layer along the length of the section, slip the blade underneath, lift up one end and pull both layers away from the flesh. The outer skin is like the rough bark of a tree. The under layer is smooth and leathery, pink on the outer surface and creamy white on the inside next to the yam. Any tubers which smell strongly of almonds should be avoided as they may be poisonous.

China: *muk-shu*
India: *tikhoor*
Indonesia: *katera pohon*
Japan: *tapioka*
Malaysia: *ubi kayu*
Philippines: *kamoteng kahoy*
Sri Lanka: *manioc, maniokka*
Thailand: *sampalang*

Boiled Cassava

Put short lengths of peeled cassava into a pan of boiling water with salt and a teaspoon of turmeric. Cook, uncovered, until tender, about 20 minutes. Test by piercing with a fine skewer after 15 minutes, and lift out those pieces which pierce easily. Lift each piece as it is done and put into a colander to drain. Strangely, every piece of cassava will not cook in the same length of time, and when almost ready they all develop a split down the centre, lengthways. In the very middle you will come across a tough, wiry, stringy core, not very thick, but very strong. Lift this out and discard it. Serve cassava hot with freshly grated coconut and a hot chilli sambal.

Fried Cassava

Boil peeled cassava until tender but firm. Drain well, then break into lengthways finger strips. Since the cassava has natural divisions running the length of the tuber anyway, it is best to use these rather than try to cut them into precise pieces. Don't forget to find and lift out the core, which is totally inedible. Shallow fry in hot oil until golden and crisp on all sides, turning pieces with tongs. Sprinkle with salt (and a pinch of chilli powder if liked). They have the texture of the most perfectly oven-roasted potatoes, but crisper than potatoes can ever be, with a thick, crusty shell enclosing fluffy cassava.

Serve these delicious chips as a snack on their own, or as a vegetable accompaniment to a meal.

Cassava Savouries

When you see grated cassava, buy some and try this. Or peel cassava tubers and grate in a food processor.

250 g/8 oz/1 cup grated cassava
¾ teaspoon salt or to taste
¼ teaspoon freshly ground black pepper
1 or 2 fresh chillies, finely chopped
1 tablespoon finely chopped coriander leaves,
**   spring onions (scallions) or snipped fresh dill**
1 onion, finely chopped
1 small egg, beaten
oil for deep frying

Put cassava in a bowl and toss lightly with fingers. Remove any tough fibres.

Combine grated cassava with salt and pepper, chillies, fresh herb and onion. Add beaten egg and mix well. If egg is large, reserve some of it rather than risk the mixture becoming too wet to handle.

Form into small balls no more than 2.5 cm (1 in) in diameter. Heat oil and deep fry the cassava savouries (not too many at one time) in peanut or other vegetable oil until golden, about 5 minutes. Lift out on a slotted spoon to a colander lined with paper towels. Serve warm. Makes about 20.

Bibingka Especial

2 eggs
1 cup sugar
1 tablespoon melted butter
½ teaspoon salt
250 ml/8 fl oz/1 cup coconut milk
**   or full cream milk**
250 g/8 oz/1 cup grated cassava
2 tablespoons grated sharp cheese

Beat eggs, add sugar and beat again until thick and light. Stir in butter and salt, mix in milk, cassava and cheese. Pour the mixture (it is very wet) into a 23 cm (9 in) round or square pan lined with baking paper. Bake at 160°C (325°F) for about 1¼ hours or until risen and golden. Traditional recipes of the Philippines sprinkle the top with grated cheese and return to the oven until the cheese melts and turns golden, but I find that on cooling this forms a tough, chewy crust and it is better to mix the cheese into the batter.

Note: The bottom of the cake will have a jelly-like consistency, but this is a feature inherent in cassava cakes. You can turn the cake upside down when it has cooled and make it a feature, a baked-on glaze.

Cassia Bark

(*Cinnamomum cassia*, *C. aromaticum*). A native of China, particularly the Kweilin province, where there is evidence it grew as long ago as 216 BC. Today it is grown in Indonesia, mainland China, Vietnam and Malaysia. The United States is the chief market for this spice where, instead of bearing its own name, it masquerades as cinnamon.

There are instances where cassia may indeed be more appropriate than cinnamon, for example as a component in five-spice powder. Some countries export pieces of cassia bark labelled 'cinnamon'. They are much thicker and darker in colour than true cinnamon, as the corky outer bark is still attached.

See also CINNAMON.

Cassia Leaf

(*Cinnamomum cassia*) SEE ILLUSTRATION. Cassia leaves (tej pattar) are used in Indian cooking and are erroneously referred to as 'Indian bay leaves'. Often bay leaves are suggested as a substitute though the aroma is not similar. See BAY LEAF.

Medicinal uses: Cassia leaves are used in Eastern medicine as a cure for colic and diarrhoea.

India: *tej pattar*
Thailand: *bai kravan*

Cauliflower

(*Brassica oleracea* var. *botrytis*) While cauliflower is usually considered a Western vegetable, it stands up well to spicy treatments. The Asian cauliflower is small and more strongly flavoured, and does not

Cauliflower

impress by its appearance. The large, whiter, more delicately flavoured cauliflower grown in temperate climates may be used without loss of enjoyment. Depending on how it is cooked, the texture can be butter-soft or crisp and crunchy. In Cauliflower Pilau (recipe below) the texture is meltingly soft.

China: *fa yeh tsoi*
India: *phul gobi*
Indonesia: *bunga kol*
Japan: *hana yasai*
Malaysia: *kobis*
Philippines: *koliplower*
Sri Lanka: *mal gova*
Thailand: *dok galum*

Spiced Cauliflower, Indian Style

half a medium cauliflower
3 tablespoons oil
1 teaspoon brown mustard seeds
1 teaspoon crushed garlic
2 teaspoons finely grated fresh ginger
½ teaspoon ground turmeric
1 teaspoon salt
3 tablespoons water
½ teaspoon garam masala (recipe page 354)

Wash cauliflower and separate into florets. Cut florets into thick slices, making sure each slice has some of the stem attached. Heat oil in a wok or deep pan and fry the mustard seeds until they pop. Add garlic and ginger and fry, stirring, until pale golden and fragrant. Add turmeric and salt and the cauliflower slices, stirring to mix well. Add water, cover and cook for about 6 minutes or until cauliflower is tender-crisp. Sprinkle garam masala over and serve with rice or chapatis.

Cauliflower Pilau

This is such a tasty and satisfying dish it needs only yoghurt and chutney to accompany it. Serves 4–6.

375 g/12 oz/2 cups basmati rice
500 g/1 lb cauliflower
2 tablespoons ghee
2 tablespoons oil
2 tablespoons Indian green masala paste
  (recipe page 115)

125 ml/4 fl oz/½ cup natural yoghurt
3 cardamom pods, bruised
1 cinnamon stick
1 litre/2 pints/4 cups water
2 teaspoons salt
2 tablespoons sultanas (golden raisins)

Wash the rice well and leave to drain in a sieve. Cut the cauliflower into florets and cut each floret in half, keeping some of the stem on each piece. Heat half the ghee and oil in a wok or frying pan until very hot and fry the cauliflower, pressing against the pan with the back of a frying spoon until the cauliflower is tinged with brown. Lower heat, add green masala paste and fry for a minute, then add the yoghurt and mix. Cover and cook for 4 or 5 minutes. Turn off heat.

Heat remaining ghee and oil in a saucepan with a well-fitting lid. Fry the cardamom and cinnamon, then add the rice and fry for 3 minutes. Add the cauliflower and its spice mixture, rinse the wok or frying pan with the measured water and pour it into the rice. Stir in salt and sultanas, bring to the boil, cover with lid and turn heat very low. Steam for 15 minutes without lifting lid. Remove from heat, uncover and allow steam to escape for a few minutes before serving with a bowl of yoghurt and sweet mango chutney.

Braised Cauliflower, Chinese Style

Serves 4

half a small cauliflower
125 g/4 oz snow peas or sugar snap peas
2 tablespoons peanut oil
½ teaspoon finely chopped garlic
1 teaspoon grated ginger
125 ml/4 fl oz/½ cup hot water or stock
1 tablespoon oyster or soy sauce
½ teaspoon salt
2 teaspoons cornflour (cornstarch)

Divide cauliflower into small florets. String the peas if necessary. Heat oil in a wok and fry garlic and ginger, stirring, until fragrant. Add the vegetables and stir-fry for 2 minutes, then pour in water mixed with sauce and add salt. Cover and cook until barely tender, then thicken sauce with the cornflour mixed with a little cold water. Serve with rice.

Caviar

See FISH ROE.

Celery

(*Apium graveolens* var. *dulce*) Asian celery is much smaller, darker green and stronger in flavour than the thick, pale green stems of celery grown for Western needs. It is not used in salads or as a vegetable (too strong) but as a flavouring for soups, a role in which it is perfectly cast. Use less than you would the large, pale leaves of celery.

Large 'white' celery makes a delicious vegetable when stir-fried the Chinese way, combined with seafood or poultry. It should have any tough strings removed. Grooved side up, cut a slice not quite through at one end and then snap backwards and strip along the stem. Then the stem itself can be sliced holding the knife at a 45 degree angle to the board to highlight the curved shape and present a greater surface area for quick cooking.

> **China:** *kan-tsai*
> **Japan:** *serori*
> **Indonesia:** *selderi*
> **Malaysia:** *daun sop*
> **Philippines:** *kintsay, kinchay*
> **Singapore:** *kin chye*
> **Sri Lanka:** *salderi*
> **Thailand:** *kin chai*

Stir-Fried Prawns (Shrimp) and Celery

Serves 4–5

500 g/1 lb raw prawns (shrimp)
½ teaspoon crushed garlic
½ teaspoon salt
2 stalks celery
1 tablespoon peanut oil
1 teaspoon finely chopped ginger
1 tablespoon oyster sauce or soy sauce
1 teaspoon cornflour (cornstarch)

Shell and devein the prawns and rub the garlic and salt over them. Slice celery into thick slices shaped like crescents. Heat peanut oil in a wok and fry the ginger, stirring, until fragrant. Add celery and stir-fry on moderately high heat for 1 minute. Add prawns and continue to stir-fry for a further 2 minutes. Add oyster sauce and then the cornflour mixed smoothly with 2 tablespoons of water. Stir until clear and thickened, and serve with steamed rice.

Cepe

See MUSHROOMS & FUNGI.

Ceylon Curry Powder

See SPICE BLENDS.

Ceylon Olive

(*Elaeocarpus serratus*) Indigenous to Ceylon (now known as Sri Lanka), this dull green fruit about the size and shape of a large olive is eaten both ripe and unripe. It is very popular in pickles of the mustardy variety. The unripe fruit is first boiled, then squashed flat so the flesh cracks open around the seed, but the seed is left in. Whole fruit, together with tiny reddish purple shallots, are immersed in the mixture known as Country Mustard (see page 242). This is a favourite pickle known as veralu acharu. At roadside stalls the fruit is simply boiled, pressed as described above, and sold with a twist of paper containing salt and chilli powder. The ripe fruits are softer and somewhat sweeter, and are eaten with jaggery (palm sugar), making a pleasant snack.

In Asian shops it is possible to buy these fruits in a light pickling liquid of salt, sugar and vinegar. They are labelled 'Thai olives'.

> **India:** *verali pallam*
> **Sri Lanka:** *veralu*
> **Thailand:** *ca na*

Cha Plu

(*Piper sarmentosum*) SEE ILLUSTRATION. There is no common English name for this leaf, though it is sometimes erroneously referred to as 'betel leaf' or 'wild betel leaf'. They are sold in bunches, still on the stems, at Asian shops where they are called by their Thai name, cha plu, or the Vietnamese name, bo la lot. Though of the same family (Piperaceae) as the betel leaf (see BETEL LEAF), cha plu is a finer, tender leaf, brighter green and with distinct veins. It is more delicate in flavour than betel leaf though still slightly pungent, and is eaten raw in Thai cuisine, especially as a leafy wrapping for snacks and appetisers called miang.

In Laos it is used in salad. In Malaysia (where they are called daun kadok) the leaves are shredded for ulam (a mixture of fresh herbs). In one of the top hotels in Kuala Lumpur, the chef used the leaves in a recipe which was not traditional: a cross-culture creation midway between a fish terrine and the local Nonya otak-otak, a highly spiced fish paste. It was formed in a triangular mould lined with daun kadok leaves, turned out on a serving dish, then cut in elegant triangular slices.

Otak-otak (recipe page 151) is usually pressed between coconut leaves or strips of banana leaves and grilled over coals, often at roadside stalls. The coconut or banana leaf wrapper is stripped away and discarded after the layer of fish is eaten. In the hotel presentation, the soft *P. sarmentosum* leaf, no thicker than spinach, was eaten with the fish.

Purchasing and storing: Choose bright green, uncrushed leaves which are not faded or limp. Leaves can be kept wrapped loosely in damp paper and refrigerated for a day or two. If leaves need reviving, try soaking for 2 or 3 hours in cold water to which a spoonful of sugar has been added. This also sweetens the flavour of the leaves.

Laos: *phak i leut*
Malaysia: *daun kadok*
Thailand: *cha plu*
Vietnam: *bo la lot*

Leaf-Wrapped Snacks

1 bunch cha plu leaves

FILLINGS

200 g/7 oz shredded cooked pork, or chicken, or small shelled prawns (shrimp)
90 g/3 oz/½ cup roasted, salted peanuts
60 g/2 oz/½ cup sliced shallots
sliced chillies
3 tablespoons sliced pickled radish (optional)

SAUCE

1 tablespoon palm sugar or brown sugar
1 tablespoon lime juice
1 tablespoon tamarind purée
2 tablespoons fish sauce
2 tablespoons dried shrimp floss (optional)
½ teaspoon crushed garlic

Wash the leaves well and soak in cold, lightly sugared water for a couple of hours. Pat leaves dry. Prepare the fillings and arrange around a platter, with the leaves. Mix sauce ingredients in a small bowl. Each person puts their choice of fillings on a leaf, wraps it and dips the leaf in the sauce before eating.

Note: For special occasions, the leaf snacks may be presented already wrapped, and luxury ingredients such as crab meat included in the filling. The leaf parcel is secured with a cocktail stick.

Chanterelle

See MUSHROOMS & FUNGI.

Chapati

See BREADS.

Char Magaz

A mix of four seed kernels (charoli, sweet melon, watermelon and pumpkin) which is used in Indian sweetmeats. Not often found outside India, and if you do manage to get some, use it fairly quickly or store in the freezer as the high oil content of the kernels makes them prone to rancidity.

Charoli

(*Buchanania latifolia*) Also known as chironji. A small, rounded, lentil-shaped, almond-flavoured seed hardly 6 mm (¼ in) long. It is used in Indian sweets, most often topping Karachi halwa and the simple but delicious yoghurt dessert, shrikhand (see YOGHURT). It is also one of the four seed kernels in the mixture called char magaz.

Chatni

Original Indian word which has become the commonly adopted English word, 'chutney'. While chutney has come to mean a cooked mixture of fruit, vinegar, sugar and spices with good keeping qualities, chatni denotes a fresh, uncooked paste of herbs, coconut and spices ground fine which should be refrigerated and used within a day or two, served as an accompaniment to rice and curries. In order to fulfil expectations of readers who are seeking one or the other type of relish, I have given recipes for cooked, long-lasting, 'Major Grey' type chutneys under CHUTNEY.

Mint or Coriander Chatni

1 bunch fresh mint or coriander
5 spring onions (scallions)
2 or 3 fresh green chillies
½ teaspoon crushed garlic
1 teaspoon salt
2 teaspoons sugar
1 teaspoon garam masala (recipe page 354)
125 ml/4 fl oz/½ cup lime or lemon juice
2 tablespoons water

Wash the fresh herb, shake off excess water and pick the leaves, measuring in a cup to give 1 cup firmly packed leaves. Cut the spring onions into short lengths, using the green leaves as well as the white portions. Discard stems of chillies, seed them and cut into pieces.

The easiest way to make this fresh chatni is to use an electric blender. Put all the ingredients into the blender and start on low speed, stopping now and then to scrape ingredients down onto the blades. It may be necessary to add a spoonful or so more water or lemon juice. Increase speed of blender until you have a smooth purée. Turn into a bowl and cover immediately with plastic wrap to preserve the bright green colour. Chill until required.

If a blender is not available, chop everything finely and pound using a mortar and pestle, adding the liquid after pounding.

Note: For a milder version of this fresh herb chatni, stir in about half its volume of thick natural yoghurt after blending herbs.

Coconut Chatni

half a fresh coconut, grated
  or 1 cup desiccated coconut
1 lime or lemon
3 fresh red or green chillies
1 teaspoon salt
2 teaspoons ghee or oil
1 teaspoon black mustard seeds
½ teaspoon urad dhal
1 teaspoon nigella seeds
small sprig fresh curry leaves
¼ teaspoon ground asafoetida, optional

If desiccated coconut is used, sprinkle it with 3 tablespoons water and moisten evenly with the fingers. Peel the lime or lemon, removing all white pith. Cut in pieces and remove the seeds. In an electric blender combine citrus fruit with chillies and salt. Blend to a purée. Add the coconut and blend to a smooth paste, scraping down sides of blender and adding a little more liquid if necessary.

Heat ghee or oil in a small pan and fry the mustard seeds and dhal until the seeds pop and the dhal is golden, covering the pan with a lid as the mustard seeds will scatter. Add the nigella, curry leaves and asafoetida and turn off heat immediately. Mix with the blended coconut mixture, pat into a flat cake and serve as an accompaniment to dosai (see PANCAKES) or rice and curries.

Tamarind Chatni

3 tablespoons dried tamarind pulp
250 ml/8 fl oz/1 cup hot water
1 teaspoon salt
2 teaspoons jaggery or brown sugar
1 teaspoon ground cumin
½ teaspoon ground fennel
2 teaspoons finely grated fresh ginger
pinch chilli powder (optional)
lime or lemon juice to taste

Put tamarind pulp in a bowl with hot water and soak until water is cool. Knead vigorously, dissolving pulp in the water. Strain through a nylon sieve, pushing all the pulp through and discarding fibres and seeds. If necessary, add a little more water to dissolve any remaining pulp around the seeds. The liquid should be thick. Stir in salt, sugar and other ingredients.

Cheese

Cheese is not an item of food produced and eaten in Asian countries with the notable exceptions of India and the Philippines.

In India, cheese is not the aged and fermented product of Western culture — it is a fresh, usually home-made product called panir or chenna (see recipe page 74).

Depending on the use for which it is required it may be pressed to extract more moisture, or used in a softer form. Soft cheese called chenna is used for making some of the many milk-based sweetmeats which are so popular in India. For cooking in spiced dishes it must be quite firm, so it is further pressed between two plates to make panir or paneer.

A time-saving trick is to use cubes of baked ricotta cheese (available at Italian delicatessens) as a substitute for home-made panir in recipes where the cheese is simply cubed. When the cheese has to be moulded as for koftas, it has to be home-made as described below.

Cheese is also popular in some of the special dishes of the Philippines. There is a local fresh cheese, but also popular is imported Edam in red, wax-covered balls, which is called queso de bola. (There is one such cheese which is made locally.) The sharp cheese is finely grated and included as a savoury component in sweet breads and cakes, for instance in Ensaimada (see page 54) or Filipino Bibingka Especial (see page 62).

The recipes which follow illustrate how fresh cheese is made and used in savoury dishes as well as in that most famous of all Indian sweetmeats, Rasgullas.

Panir

2–3 litres/4–6 pints/8–12 cups
  fresh full-cream milk
juice of 1 lemon or 2 limes,
  or 1 teaspoon tartaric acid dissolved in
  125 ml/4 fl oz/½ cup water

In a large saucepan bring milk to the boil, stirring frequently to prevent a skin forming on the surface. As milk approaches boiling point and rises in the pan, stir in lemon juice or tartaric acid (2 tablespoons per litre [2 pints] of milk) and remove pan from the heat. Stir once and leave to stand for 5 minutes. Firm curds will form. Pour into clean muslin placed over a large, deep bowl, tie the ends together and let it hang for at least 30 minutes, then press to remove as much of the whey as possible. (This whey is valued as a cool drink, and often used in the treatment of stomach upsets.)

Depending on the use of the panir, it may be used right away. Nice to eat on its own, and ideal for those who are looking to reduce salt in their diets.

If a very firm cheese is required, place it between two plates and weight it down for 1–2 hours in a cool place. This should be done for recipes in which it is diced and cooked again.

Cheese Koftas

Only home-made cheese is suitable for this recipe — cottage cheese, farm cheese and ricotta cheese don't work. Serves 4–6.

FOR THE KOFTAS
1 quantity panir (recipe above)
30 g/1 oz/½ cup finely chopped fresh coriander
2 tablespoons chopped sultanas (golden raisins)
2 tablespoons chopped almonds
2 teaspoons seeded and chopped fresh chillies
salt and pepper to taste
oil and ghee for deep frying

FOR THE SAUCE
1 tablespoon ghee or butter
2 teaspoons finely chopped garlic
1 large onion, finely chopped
4 tablespoons tomato paste
1½ teaspoons salt
1 tablespoon sugar
3 thin slices ginger, cut into shreds
125 ml/4 fl oz/½ cup light cream
  or evaporated milk
1 teaspoon garam masala (recipe page 354)
3 tablespoons chopped fresh coriander or mint

Prepare the panir (reserving whey) and leave it to drain for 30 minutes. Press between two plates to remove any excess moisture, then untie the muslin. Break curds into pieces and knead vigorously until smooth and palm of the hand feels greasy. Divide into 8 equal portions and roll each into a smooth ball.

Combine coriander, sultanas, almonds and chillies, adding salt and pepper to taste. Make a depression in each ball and fill with some of the coriander mixture, then mould ball around filling again, making a smooth surface without cracks. Heat about 2 cups oil with 2 table-spoons ghee to flavour it and slip in the cheese koftas, frying them over medium heat until golden brown on all sides. Lift out on slotted spoon and drain on paper towels.

Sauce: To make the sauce, melt ghee in a heavy pan with a tablespoon of the frying oil and cook garlic and onion until soft and translucent. Add tomato paste, salt, sugar and ginger and stir in 1½ cups whey. Cover and simmer for 10 minutes. Stir in cream, add koftas and simmer in sauce for 10 minutes. Sprinkle with garam masala and coriander just before serving with Indian bread or rice.

Spinach and Cheese

Serves 6

2 bunches spinach
1 quantity panir or 250 g/8 oz baked ricotta
1 tablespoon ghee or oil
1 teaspoon panch phora
1 teaspoon ground turmeric
1 teaspoon ground cumin
1 teaspoon finely grated fresh ginger
250 ml/8 oz/1 cup natural yoghurt
salt to taste
1 teaspoon garam masala (recipe page 354)

Wash spinach in several changes of cold water and put leaves into a saucepan with moisture that clings. Cover and steam for 10 minutes or until tender. Drain and chop. Cut cheese into 2.5 cm (1 in) dice.

Heat ghee or oil and fry panch phora until mustard seeds pop. Add turmeric, cumin and ginger and stir for a minute, then add spinach and mix well. Stir in yoghurt, season with salt and when mixture is heated through add cheese and simmer gently for 10 minutes. Sprinkle with garam masala towards end of cooking. Serve with rice or flat bread.

Rasgullas

Fresh cheese balls in syrup. These require skill and patience, but for those who have been introduced to the delights of this Bengali specialty, they are well worth the trouble taken. Makes 12 balls.

2 litres/4 pints/8 cups milk
1 teaspoon tartaric acid
  dissolved in 125 ml/4 fl oz/½ cup hot water
2 teaspoons fine semolina
pinch bicarbonate of soda (baking soda)
750 g/1½ lb/3 cups sugar
1.5 litres/3 pints/6 cups water
10 cardamom pods, bruised
2 tablespoons rose water or few drops rose
  essence
few blanched pistachio kernels

Make the fresh cheese (panir) as described on page 74, allowing curds to firm for 15 minutes before straining through muslin and draining for 30 minutes. (If milk does not curdle readily, add a little more tartaric acid, dissolved in water.) When whey has stopped dripping from the curds and before the curds get too dry, turn them into a bowl (or onto a marble slab or other smooth, cool surface) and knead hard for 5 minutes. Add semolina and bicarbonate of soda and knead again until the palm of your hand feels greasy. Divide into 10 or 12 equal portions and mould each into a ball.

Make a syrup with the sugar, water and cardamom pods, in a saucepan which is about 23 cm (9 in) across. Stir until the sugar dissolves and boil hard for 5 minutes. Pour 1 cup of this syrup into a bowl and reserve. Add enough water to the pan with the syrup to give a depth of about 5 cm (2 in) and bring to a fast boil. Gently put the cheese balls in, leaving enough room for them to expand — they will almost double in size. Boil fast for 15–20 minutes, then lift out on slotted spoon and transfer to the reserved syrup. Repeat with more balls until they are all done. Flavour with rose water and leave to soak overnight for at least 4 hours. Do not serve rasgullas chilled as they will lose their spongy texture. Heat gently, just to slightly warm them. When serving, decorate with slivers of unsalted pistachio nuts.

Chestnut

(*Castanea* sp.) Much as we associate chestnuts with European culture, there is probably not a cuisine which has embraced them as wholeheartedly as that of Japan. Baked, grilled or cooked in rice as well as a central ingredient in many sweets, the humble chestnut has been paid far greater homage there than the simple snack bought from street vendors to warm mittened hands in northern winter months.

As delicious as they can be, chestnuts are the most deceptive of all ingredients. I recently purchased a batch which were large, dark and glossy. After boiling and peeling them I found that most were black inside. A good chestnut should be a creamy off-white inside and without signs of mould or mildew on the skin. Some varieties seem to defy skinning. It is easy enough to remove the outer shell — it is removing the inside, downy membrane which can drive you to the point of distraction, especially if you are trying to keep the chestnuts whole. Often it is necessary to boil for an extra 10 minutes, particularly if the skin is still brittle or if the chestnut 'meat' does not yield to gentle pressure. As well as cooking the chestnut, it will help loosen stubborn skins — there are few things worse than a fragment under a fingernail.

Anyone who has ever roasted or grilled chestnuts without first slitting the shells will have learned the hard way that they explode without a 'release valve', and are extremely messy to clean up. If boiling, it's not strictly necessary to slit the skins (they won't explode), but a shallow horizontal slit on the curved surface across the widest part will facilitate peeling. Boil for 20–30 minutes, or until the meat gives when squeezed gently. (Don't panic when the water turns deep brown. This is normal.)

Peeling off the inner skins seems easier while they are still warm, so get to it as soon as they are cool enough to handle and, with a small, sharp knife to help you, prise every last vestige of skin out of cracks and crevices. It only needs the tiniest bit of this inner skin to pucker the mouth worse than the unripest persimmon. If the chestnuts are very difficult to skin, there is a method to remove the pulp (only suitable for recipes that require chestnut purée) by taking a slice off the flat end, enough to get past the inner skin, and squeezing out the pulp. It is a little wasteful but much quicker. The chestnuts will need to be quite soft for this method to work — usually 25–30 minutes will soften even large chestnuts. The pulp resembles the texture of boiled potatoes, soft and floury. Unsweetened purée is available in cans but, to me, it doesn't taste very 'chestnutty'.

A recent experience peeling chestnuts made me swear off ever doing it again — it really is fiddly work, and so slow! If you're making them into a sweet purée, save yourself the aggravation and buy the sweetened purée that comes in small cans. It's not cheap, but will work out cheaper in hours and frustration, unless you are a very patient person with few demands on your time. Having said all that, the next batch of chestnuts I bought were remarkably easy to peel — I guess there is more than one kind of chestnut, but I cannot say they looked any different from those which had taken so much time.

Dried chestnuts: When whole chestnuts are called for, don't overlook the prospect of dried chestnuts, which can be reconstituted by soaking in boiling water for 1 hour, draining and replacing with freshly boiled water half way through. I would only use these in savoury dishes, however, as the flavour of dried chestnuts is not as suitable for sweets.

In Chinese cooking mostly dried chestnuts are used. It does save time and trouble getting the shell and skin off, but requires time and effort to soak and soften. Chestnuts make a good addition to braised dishes featuring rich meats such as duck and pork, as their mealy texture balances the fat.

If time permits, soak dried chestnuts overnight. If you don't have the time, soak chestnuts in boiling water with a pinch of bicarbonate of soda for 1 hour. Rinse them well and cover again with boiling water and leave until water is cool. They may then be added to a dish which is going to be simmered for a minimum of 1 hour, by which time they should be tender. If the dish does not require long cooking, cook the chestnuts first until tender before adding.

Chinese cuisine does not include numerous desserts, but there is one which is quite famous, called Peking Dust (see recipe page 77). It features boiled and peeled fresh chestnuts, finely grated, and whipped cream. It is remarkably similar to that French classic, Mont Blanc.

Pork with Chestnuts

125 g/4 oz dried chestnuts
1 kg/2 lb pork spareribs, not too fatty
1 teaspoon chopped garlic
2 teaspoons sugar
2 tablespoons soy sauce
2 tablespoons peanut oil
500 ml/1 pint/2 cups hot water
2 teaspoons cornflour (cornstarch)

Pour boiling water over dried chestnuts in a bowl, cover and soak for 30 minutes. Pour off water, replace with more boiling water and soak for 30 minutes longer. Or soak overnight in warm water.

Ask the butcher to cut the spareribs into chunky pieces. Crush garlic with sugar to a smooth purée. Mix with soy sauce and use to marinate the ribs for 30 minutes or longer.

Heat a wok, add oil and when hot fry the spareribs, tossing them so they are well browned. Add hot water and drained chestnuts, cover and simmer for 1 hour or until the pork is tender. Blend cornflour with a little cold water and stir into the liquid in the wok until sauce boils and thickens. Serve hot with steamed rice.

Peking Dust

A surprisingly delicious dessert in spite of its extreme simplicity. Serves 8.

500 g/1 lb fresh chestnuts
300ml/10 fl oz/1¼ cups cream
4 tablespoons caster sugar (superfine sugar)
glazed walnuts (optional)

Make small slits in the chestnut shells or take a thin slice off the broad end to make them easier to peel. Bring to the boil in water to cover. Simmer for 20–25 minutes. Drain and when cool enough to handle, peel, taking care to remove all traces of the thin inner skin.

Whip cream with caster sugar until soft peaks form. Put a spoonful of cream in each of 8 dessert dishes. Press warm chestnuts through a coarse wire sieve over a plate to make what really does look like 'dust'. With a spoon, heap a thick layer of the sieved chestnut over the cream. Top with a glazed walnut if liked. The texture of this dessert cannot be achieved using chestnut purée.

Chick Pea

See LEGUMES & PULSES.

Chick Pea Flour

See FLOURS & STARCHES (Besan).

Chicken

The common barnyard fowl is probably the most accessible source of meat in Asia. They are easily raised, cost next to nothing to feed, and require little space to grow and multiply. No wonder many of Asia's most popular dishes have chicken as a main ingredient.

While these scrawny specimens are the same species as the plump-breasted, tidily trussed, impeccably clean birds available in Western supermarkets or specialty poultry shops, there is a world of difference in what goes on in preparation for the table.

There are many complaints that modern methods of raising poultry mean a great loss of flavour and there, I think, is where Asian cooking has the advantage. So much flavour is added in sauces, spices and seasonings that chicken becomes a treat, whether free-range or not.

Poultry in Asia are used as laying birds for as long as possible before being considered candidates for the pot, while in Western countries, chickens are bred for their meat. The main difference as far as the cook is concerned, is in cooking times. All the recipes given below have been tested using chickens bred for the table.

If you are using this book in a country where the chickens available to you have had a long and productive life before retirement, please adjust cooking times until the meat is tender enough, adding more liquid and stirring from time to time as the sauce reduces.

There are cultural differences too in what is considered appropriate to eat. In the West, a chicken is always roasted complete with tail, and family members may argue over who gets the 'bishop's nose'. But in Chinese cooking, this offending member is given the chop, taking care to eliminate the two small glands on either side of it as well. It is considered that leaving these on gives an unpleasant odour to the flesh. On the other hand, one of the specialities of Chinese cuisine is chicken feet, from which most other cultures turn away with a genteel shudder.

Chopping a raw chicken Chinese style: This requires a strong and steady arm, good aim, a sharp, heavy chopper and, equally important, a sturdy wooden chopping board.

It is not merely a matter of jointing the bird, as each joint is also cut through the bone into mouth-sized pieces. First bend the wings and legs away from the body and with a sharp knife detach where they join the body. Do not divide wings at middle joint or thigh from drumstick. Lay them flat on the board and chop each wing into 3 pieces, each leg and thigh into 5, using decisive strokes. Cut on either side of the joints, not through them. Separate breast from back. Divide breast down the middle and chop each half into 3 pieces. It is a good idea to wipe the cut ends of the bone with a wad of damp paper towels to remove any splinters.

Except for the succulent little 'oysters' of dark meat, the bony back does not yield serving pieces but, together with the neck, it can be used for stock. Freeze these portions until you have at least a kilogram (2lbs), then make chicken stock according to the recipe on page 78. Freeze the stock in portions convenient to the quantities you usually cook.

Cutting a cooked chicken Chinese style: Divide in half down the centre with a sharp cleaver. Place each half, cut side down, on a heavy wooden chopping board and chop crossways into strips. It is easier if the wing and leg are detached from the body first and chopped as for the raw chicken — wings into 3 pieces, legs into 5 pieces, cutting either side of the joints. The rest of the chicken is much easier to chop into roughly 2.5 cm (1 in) strips when the legs and wings are done separately. Re-assemble bird on serving plate. It will never look as good as before you took to it with the chopper, but is certainly easier to serve and eat when cut this way. A few sprigs of coriander will cover a multitude of mis-aimed chops!

Cutting a chicken for curry: When the recipe says to cut a chicken into 'curry-sized pieces', it simply means cutting the pieces smaller than joints. This is done so the spices can more readily flavour the meat. The cuts are placed differently to the Chinese method.

First joint the chicken, then cut the breast in halves and cut each half in two again. Chop each thigh in two, but leave the drumsticks whole unless they are very large. Divide the wings at the middle joint, leaving the wing tips attached. Cut back into 4 pieces, and add to curry for flavour, but do not count as serving portions. Neck and giblets are also included.

Chinese Chicken Stock

Some butchers and delicatessens sell the off-cuts as soup pieces, and these are excellent for making stock. Preparing good strong stock and having it ready in the freezer is a great time saver.

**1 large whole chicken
   or 2 kg/4 lb chicken soup pieces
2 spring onions with leaves
6 slices fresh ginger
½ teaspoon whole black peppercorns
3 sprigs celery leaves
2 teaspoons salt**

Wash the chicken well, rinsing inside the cavity to remove any bits of organs and blood, as these will result in a cloudy stock. Chop off the tail of the chicken together with the two small glands positioned on either side of it and discard. Chop chicken through the bones as described on page 77.

In a large pan with a well-fitting lid put the chicken pieces and enough cold water to cover. Add the remaining ingredients and bring slowly to the boil. Skim off any scum on the surface, cover and simmer very gently for 3 hours. If heat cannot be adjusted to maintain a gentle simmer, put a heat diffuser under the pot. Let stock cool for a while, then strain into another large pot and refrigerate until completely cold. Remove congealed fat from surface. Divide stock into freezer containers and freeze for future use.

White-Cut Chicken

Although this is the traditional Chinese name, I always think of this dish as Crystal Chicken, because after finishing cooking in stored heat the chicken is submerged beneath cubes of ice, which look like crystals. Serves 6.

**1 × 1.5 kg/3 lb roasting chicken
2 spring onions with leaves
6 slices fresh ginger
½ teaspoon whole black peppercorns
3 sprigs celery leaves
2 teaspoons salt**

Wash the chicken well, removing any fat from the cavity. Cut off the tail as described in the recipe for Chinese Chicken Stock above. Choose a pot just large enough to hold the chicken, put in the ingredients and enough water to submerge the chicken. Put the chicken in the pot to check that there is enough water, but take it out again and bring the water to the boil with the remaining ingredients.

Put a stainless steel spoon into the cavity of the chicken as this serves to conduct heat. Gently lower the chicken into the pot, breast downwards, and let the water return to a simmer. Skim if necessary. Put lid on pot and simmer for 20 minutes, then turn off heat and leave for a further 40 minutes without uncovering the pot as this would mean loss of heat, and it is the stored heat which is used to finish cooking the chicken.

Have ready a large pan or bowl with cold water and at least 3 trays of ice cubes in it. Remove chicken from the hot liquid, drain liquid from cavity and remove spoon. Place chicken in the container of ice and water, making sure there is enough ice to cover it completely. Leave to soak and chill for 15 minutes. Drain, put into a large bowl, cover and refrigerate for at least 3 hours.

To serve: The chicken meat may be carefully removed from the bones, keeping the skin intact because this method of quick chilling results in a layer of jellied stock between skin and flesh. Arrange on serving plate and keep covered in the refrigerator until serving time. Serve brushed with 3 parts light soy sauce to 1 part sesame oil. Or have a dipping sauce of 3 tablespoons soy sauce mixed with 2 teaspoons ginger juice (press grated fresh ginger against small strainer) and 1 teaspoon sugar. If preferred, the chicken can be chopped through the bones into bite-sized pieces.

Red-Cooked Chicken

When cooked in liquid including a high proportion of dark soy sauce, food acquires a rich brown colour and the term 'red-cooked' is applied to the finished dish. The well-flavoured liquid is called a master sauce in Chinese cuisine, and it may be frozen or refrigerated and used again and again. If re-used once a week at least, it need not be frozen. Serves 6.

1 large roasting chicken, about 1.5 kg/3 lb
375 ml/12 fl oz/1½ cups dark soy sauce
375 ml/12 fl oz/1½ cups water
125 ml/4 fl oz/½ cup Chinese wine or sherry
8 large slices fresh ginger
2 whole star anise (or about 12 sections)
1 large clove garlic
2 tablespoons crushed rock sugar
2 teaspoons oriental sesame oil

Rinse chicken with cold water inside and out, remove any flaps of fat from the cavity and discard. Choose a saucepan just large enough to hold the chicken so it will be almost submerged in the cooking liquid. Put chicken into saucepan breast downwards and add all the ingredients except the sesame oil. Bring slowly to the boil. Turn heat very low, cover and simmer gently for 15 minutes. Use tongs to turn the chicken over without piercing its skin. Replace lid and simmer for 15 minutes more,

basting with liquid every 5 minutes.

Turn off heat and leave chicken submerged in liquid in the covered saucepan for 45 minutes. Lift chicken out, letting any liquid in the cavity drain back into the saucepan. Brush the chicken all over with sesame oil. Carve or chop in the Chinese manner (see directions on page 77) and assemble on serving plate. Serve with some of the cooking liquid as a dipping sauce. Save remaining liquid, refrigerate and use for red-cooking other food. The flavour will become deeper and more intense with each time it is cooked. Add a little of this master sauce to flavour other dishes.

Jasmine Tea Smoked Chicken

Serves 6

1 × 1.5 kg/3 lb roasting chicken
1 tablespoon Chinese rose wine
1 tablespoon light soy sauce
1 teaspoon salt
1 teaspoon sugar
4 slices ginger
1 spring onion (scallion)
6 tablespoons jasmine tea leaves
100 g/3½ oz/½ cup raw rice
3 tablespoons brown sugar
1 whole star anise (or 8 sections)

Remove fat from within cavity and rinse chicken under cold tap. Dry well inside and out with paper towels. Combine wine, soy sauce, salt and sugar and rub well inside the cavity and over the chicken. Put the slices of ginger and the spring onion into the cavity. Cover and marinate for 30 minutes.

Prepare a large pan with a well-fitting lid, pour 5 cm (2 in) water into it and bring to the boil. Place chicken in a heatproof plate and put it on a trivet over the water. Cover and steam for 15–20 minutes. Remove from pan, pour away water and line the base of the pan with heavy-duty foil, taking it a little way up the side of the pan all around to protect the pan from the smoking mixture.

Combine dry tea leaves, rice, brown sugar and star anise, crushed. Sprinkle it evenly over the foil, return trivet to pan and place chicken on it, this time without the dish. Cover pan tightly and place over medium heat. When smoke escapes from under lid, turn heat very low and smoke chicken for 15 minutes or until a fine skewer inserted into the thigh enters easily and the juice that runs out is clear, not pink.

Serve hot, cold or at room temperature, accompanied by Flower Rolls (see Chinese Steamed Bread, page 53 or Mandarin Pancakes, page 266).

Spiced Roast Chicken

Using chicken pieces of one type such as thigh cutlets, drumsticks or wings, makes the recipe easy as they should all cook in the same time. If cutting up a whole chicken, add breast pieces half way through roasting time.

1 kg/2 lb chicken thigh cutlets
3 tablespoons dark soy sauce
2 tablespoons peanut oil
1 tablespoon honey
1 tablespoon Chinese wine or dry sherry
1 clove garlic
½ teaspoon salt
1 teaspoon finely grated fresh ginger
½ teaspoon five-spice powder

Rinse and dry chicken pieces. Combine soy sauce with oil, honey and Chinese wine. Crush garlic with the salt and stir into the mixture with ginger and five-spice powder. Marinate the chicken pieces in this for at least 1 hour.

Put chicken in a roasting dish and roast at 180°C (350°F) for 1 hour, turning the pieces over with tongs when the tops are browned, and brushing chicken with marinade every 15 minutes.

Braised Chicken with Ginger

The ginger for this dish should be young, tender and not too strong. If using mature ginger, halve the amount. Serves 5–6.

1 × 1.5 kg/3 lb roasting chicken
5 cm/2 in piece tender ginger
1 teaspoon Szechwan peppercorns
1 clove garlic
1 teaspoon salt
2 tablespoons peanut oil
3 tablespoons Chinese wine or sherry
3 tablespoons soy sauce
1 star anise
1 tablespoon honey

Rinse and dry chicken, cut off tail, making sure the oil glands on either side are removed with it, as well as any excess fat from within the cavity. Chop chicken into pieces according to instructions on page 77.

Wash ginger and cut into fine slices, then lay the slices on a board and cut them into thin shreds to give about 2 tablespoons. Roast the Szechwan peppercorns (without seeds) in a dry pan for a few minutes until fragrant, then crush with a pestle or place between folded paper and crush with a heavy bottle. Crush garlic to a paste with the salt.

Heat a wok over high heat, add the peanut oil and on low heat fry ginger and garlic until fragrant, without browning. Add crushed chicken, raise heat and fry until the chicken changes colour. Sprinkle with peppercorns, and add wine, soy sauce, star anise and honey. Cover the wok, lower heat and simmer until chicken is tender, 20–30 minutes. If necessary, add a little water to wok. Serve with rice.

Glazed Chicken Wings

Serves 4–6

750 g/1½ lb chicken wings
4 tablespoons dark soy sauce
4 tablespoons Chinese wine or sherry
1 tablespoon crushed rock sugar
  or honey
1 teaspoon crushed garlic
1 teaspoon finely grated ginger
2 teaspoons oriental sesame oil

Rinse the chicken wings and pat dry. With a sharp knife cut off and discard wing tips, and separate the wings at the centre joint.

Put the wings into a saucepan with water to just cover and bring to the boil. Drain immediately. Combine all other ingredients except sesame oil and marinate the wings for 1 hour, or cover and leave overnight in refrigerator.

Return to saucepan and simmer, covered, until wings are tender, about 25 minutes, turning wings from time to time. Transfer wings to serving dish, leaving sauce in the pan and allowing it to cook uncovered and thicken slightly. Stir in sesame oil and spoon over the chicken. Serve at room temperature.

Crisp Skin Chicken

One of the classic dishes in many a Chinese restaurant's repertoire, the succulent chicken is served with a salt and spice mix and wedges of lemon for squeezing over. Serves 6–8.

2 small roasting chickens, about 750 g/1½ lb
2 teaspoons five-spice powder
2 teaspoons salt
2 teaspoons ground cinnamon
2 tablespoons honey

FOR SERVING
1 lemon
salt and five-spice mix*

Rinse and dry the chicken, removing any excess fat from cavity. Rub inside with ½ teaspoon five-spice mixed with 1 teaspoon salt and place in a bowl or saucepan just large enough to hold it. Bring 2 litres (4 pints) water to the boil with the remaining five-spice powder, salt and the ground cinnamon, and pour over the chicken. Cover and leave them in this while bringing 3 more cups of water to the boil with the honey.

Drain chicken and remove to a colander placed over a large bowl. Ladle the honey mixture over, making sure it coats the entire skin. Place chicken on a wire rack in front of an airy window, or tie legs firmly with strong string and hang in a safe place to dry for 4 or 5 hours.

Heat about 6 cups oil in a wok, and when it is hot but not smoking, lower the chickens one at a time into the oil and ladle oil over, turning it so it becomes evenly brown all over. Keep the heat to medium so chicken cooks through before it becomes too brown. It should be cooked in 10–12 minutes. Remove from oil and pierce with a fine skewer where thigh joins body to see if juices that run out are clear, indicating that chicken is done. If juices are pink, it needs further cooking. Drain chicken briefly while repeating the process with the remaining chicken, then place on wooden board and cut in halves lengthways down the centre. Place halves cut side down on board and chop across into strips. Assemble on serving platter and put wedges of lemon and a small dish of salt and spice mix to sprinkle over the pieces of chicken just before eating.

* Combine a tablespoon of fine salt with ½ teaspoon five-spice powder or 2 teaspoons Szechwan pepper husks and roast in a dry pan until very hot and fragrant. Allow to cool and, if using Szechwan pepper, crush using a mortar and pestle.

Hunan Chicken

My favourite chicken recipes are from those areas where the flavourings are pungent and spicy, yet not too hot. Since it is now possible to purchase boned drumsticks and thighs in many poultry shops, preparing this dish is much quicker and easier. Serves 6.

1 kg/2 lb thigh or drumstick fillets
1 teaspoon Szechwan pepper husks (no seeds)
½ teaspoon salt
3 tablespoons dark soy sauce
3 tablespoons Chinese wine or sherry
2 teaspoons sugar
2 tablespoons peanut oil
2 dried red chillies
1 spring onion (scallion), finely chopped
2 teaspoons finely chopped ginger
1 teaspoon finely chopped garlic
1 teaspoon oriental sesame oil
2 tablespoons Chinese black vinegar
½ teaspoon chilli bean sauce or to taste

Flatten the chicken fillets by pounding with the blunt edge of a cleaver, then cut into bite-sized pieces.

Roast pepper in a dry pan, stirring or shaking the pan, until fragrant, then turn onto a board and crush finely or pound using a mortar and pestle. Mix with salt and sprinkle over chicken, mix and leave 5–10 minutes.

Stir together the soy sauce, wine and sugar until sugar dissolves. Pour over chicken, turning the pieces well in the marinade and leave for 30 minutes.

Heat a wok, add the peanut oil and fry the dried chillies for 1 minute. Add spring onion, ginger and garlic and stir-fry for no more than 10 seconds. Add chicken and marinade and stir-fry on high heat until all the chicken has come in contact with the hot wok and changed colour. Turn heat low, cover and simmer until chicken is tender, about 5 minutes.

Combine sesame oil, vinegar and chilli bean

sauce. If there is too much liquid in the wok raise heat and turn pieces of chicken over until the sauce reduces and coats the chicken. Pour the vinegar mixture over and toss to distribute. Discard dry chillies and serve immediately, with steamed rice.

Szechwan Chicken

Similar to Hunan chicken, since these regions are close to each other. The difference is that for this recipe the marinated chicken is tossed in cornflour (cornstarch) and deep fried, and 10–15 large dried red chillies, fried until black and crisp, are used to garnish the dish.

Hainan Chicken

This has become a favourite in places far removed from the area for which it is named. It is a comforting, flavourful meal-in-one dish, equally suitable for children and adults. Just keep the hot dipping sauce away from tender tongues. Serves 6.

1 × 1.5 kg/3 lb roasting chicken
salt
2 or 3 sprigs fresh coriander
2 or 3 sprigs celery leaves
3 spring onions (scallions), chopped
½ teaspoon whole black peppercorns
2 tablespoons salt

FOR THE RICE

500 g/1 lb long grain rice
2 tablespoons peanut oil
2 tablespoons oriental sesame oil
1 tablespoon sliced garlic
1 tablespoon chopped ginger
1 onion, finely sliced

FOR THE DIPPING SAUCES

1 tablespoon finely grated ginger
1 tablespoon ground fresh chilli or sambal ulek
  (recipe page 91)
4 tablespoons dark soy sauce
1 tablespoon sliced hot red chilli

Remove excess fat from cavity of chicken. Cut off and discard the tail including the two fat glands on either side, also the wing tips. Rinse and dry the bird with paper towels, then rub inside and out with salt.

In a saucepan just large enough to hold the chicken put 8–10 cups of water, the coriander, celery, spring onions, peppercorns and salt. Bring to the boil, gently lower chicken into pan with breast downwards. When water returns to the boil, reduce heat so that it just simmers. Cover pan tightly and simmer for 25 minutes. Remove from heat and allow chicken to finish cooking in the stored heat for 40 minutes without uncovering the pan.

Meanwhile, wash rice and leave to drain for 1 hour. In a pan with heavy base and well-fitting lid heat both kinds of oil and fry the garlic, ginger and onion over low heat, stirring and letting them become soft but not brown. Remove a tablespoon of the flavoured oil and set aside for one of the dipping sauces.

Add rice to the pan and fry, stirring, for 2 or 3 minutes until all the grains are coated with oil. Measure 4 cups of the stock from cooking the chicken and add to the pan. Bring quickly to the boil, stir in 2 teaspoons salt and cover pan with lid. Lower heat and cook very gently for 15 minutes. Remove from heat and leave covered for 10 minutes longer.

Take chicken from stock and cut into bite-sized pieces. Serve chicken with the following dipping sauces and the well flavoured rice. Strain the stock and serve as a soup.

Sauces: For one sauce combine the reserved oil, ginger and ground fresh chilli or sambal ulek. For the second sauce, combine soy sauce with sliced chilli.

Tangerine Chicken

Serves 6

1 × 1.5 kg/3 lb roasting chicken
  or 1 kg/2 lb chicken thigh fillets
2 tangerines or mandarins*
1 teaspoon Szechwan pepper
2 tablespoons peanut oil
1 teaspoon finely chopped garlic
2 teaspoons finely chopped ginger
3 tablespoons tangerine juice or orange juice
3 tablespoons Chinese wine or sherry
1 tablespoon dark soy sauce
1 teaspoon oriental sesame oil

Cut chicken in pieces Chinese style (see page 77).

Remove the zest of one of the tangerines and cut into fine strips. Squeeze the juice, strain and reserve. Peel the second tangerine, divide into segments, peel and set aside for garnishing. Roast Szechwan pepper, crush to a powder.

Heat oil in a wok and on low heat fry the garlic and ginger until fragrant. Add the chicken and toss over high heat until the colour changes. Sprinkle with the Szechwan pepper, add tangerine juice, wine or sherry and soy sauce. Cover and cook until chicken is just tender. Just before serving stir in the sesame oil.

* If tangerines are not in season, use 3 or 4 pieces of dried tangerine peel, soaked in a little warm water or Chinese wine until soft. Cut into fine shreds and add while simmering the chicken.

Cantonese Steamed Chicken

This is a beautifully simple, one-step dish ideally suited to family meals — children love it. Serves 4.

750 g/1½ lb assorted chicken pieces on the bone
   or half a roasting chicken
1 tablespoon light soy sauce
1 tablespoon Chinese wine or sherry
1 teaspoon fresh ginger juice*
2 teaspoons cornflour (cornstarch)
¼ teaspoon salt
½ teaspoon sugar
½ teaspoon oriental sesame oil

Place chicken on sturdy wooden chopping board and with a heavy cleaver chop into bite-sized pieces, Chinese style (see page 77). Wipe over pieces with damp paper towels to remove any chips of bone. Put chicken on a heatproof plate, add all the other ingredients and mix well.

Put the plate on a trivet or in a steamer over boiling water. Cover and steam on high heat for 15 minutes. Serve hot with steamed rice. Vegetables may be steamed at the same time as an accompaniment.

* To obtain ginger juice, press grated fresh ginger in a small strainer and discard solids left in strainer.

Velveted Chicken with Snow Peas

Serves 4

500 g/1 lb chicken breast fillets
½ teaspoon salt
1 tablespoon Chinese wine or sherry
1 egg white
1 tablespoon cornflour (cornstarch)
500 ml/1 pint/2 cups peanut oil
1 teaspoon finely chopped ginger
1 teaspoon finely chopped garlic
125 g/4 oz snow peas
125 ml/4 fl oz/½ cup chicken stock
1 tablespoon light soy sauce
½ teaspoon oriental sesame oil

Remove fat and sinew from chicken breast. Cut into 2.5 cm (1 in) dice, and in a bowl mix with the salt and wine and the slightly beaten egg white. Leave for 10 minutes, then sprinkle with the cornflour and 1 tablespoon of the peanut oil. Mix well, cover and refrigerate for at least 30 minutes.

String the snow peas. Combine stock, soy sauce, cornflour and sesame oil ready for the final step.

Heat the peanut oil in a wok and over medium heat fry the chicken pieces, stirring with wooden chopsticks to keep them separate and making sure they don't overcook. When they turn white, pour chicken and oil into a colander over a metal or other heatproof bowl. Return wok to heat with 1 tablespoon of the oil, and on gentle heat fry the ginger and garlic, stirring, until fragrant and pale golden. Add the snow peas, raise heat and stir-fry for 1 minute. Stir the liquid ingredients to disperse the cornflour and pour into the wok, and as soon as the sauce boils and becomes clear, return the chicken and stir through. Serve with rice.

Korean Chicken Stew

Serves 4–6

1 roasting chicken
3 tablespoons Korean soy sauce,
  or Japanese soy sauce
1 tablespoon finely chopped garlic
2 teaspoons Korean bean and chilli paste*
60 g/2 oz finely chopped spring onions
  (scallions)
½ teaspoon salt
1 tablespoon oriental sesame oil

Cut chicken into small serving pieces through the bone, and wipe with paper towel to make sure there are no chips of bone. Combine with all the flavourings except sesame oil. Cover and leave for 2 hours at room temperature except in very hot weather, when it should be refrigerated. Put into a heavy pan, cover with lid and cook on low heat until chicken is very tender. Sprinkle with sesame oil. Serve with steamed rice and side dishes such as Kim Chi (see recipe page 57).

* This deep red paste, full of flavour, is called gochu-jang, and is not as hot as it looks.

Braised Chicken and Mushrooms

Serves 4–5

12 large dried shiitake mushrooms
1 kg/2 lb chicken joints
2 teaspoons finely chopped garlic
3 tablespoons Korean soy sauce
  or Japanese soy sauce
1 tablespoon oriental sesame oil
½ teaspoon freshly ground black pepper
½ teaspoon dried chilli flakes
2 tablespoons peanut oil
2 large onions, cut into 8 wedges
125 g/4 oz of canned winter bamboo shoot
  quartered and sliced thickly
3 spring onions (scallions)
2 tablespoons toasted sesame seeds

Soak the mushrooms in very hot water for 30 minutes to soften. Discard stems, cut the caps into quarters and reserve the soaking liquid.

Chop the chicken joints through the bones with a sharp cleaver. Marinate chicken in a mixture of the garlic, soy, sesame oil, pepper and chilli for 30 minutes, then drain well and reserve marinade.

Heat peanut oil in a wok and stir-fry the chicken over medium heat until lightly browned. Add mushrooms, ½ cup of the soaking water and marinade from chicken. Cover and simmer for 20 minutes or until chicken is tender. Add all the vegetables, cook for a further 3 or 4 minutes. Crush the sesame seeds with mortar and pestle, sprinkle over the chicken and serve hot with steamed rice.

Grilled Teriyaki Chicken

1 roasting chicken
  or 1 kg/2 lb chicken fillets
4 tablespoons Japanese soy sauce
4 tablespoons mirin or sherry
2 tablespoons sugar
1 teaspoon crushed garlic
2 teaspoons finely grated fresh ginger
½ teaspoon oriental sesame oil

Joint chicken and cut each joint in halves, or dice chicken fillets. Combine remaining ingredients and marinate chicken in the mixture. Cover and refrigerate for 1 hour or overnight. If using fillets, thread the dice on small bamboo skewers soaked for at least 1 hour in water to prevent burning.

Preheat grill and place chicken on oiled foil. Grill, turning chicken pieces with tongs and brushing with marinade from time to time. Diced chicken fillets should be done in about 5 minutes. Reduce marinade by cooking in a small uncovered pan and use as a glaze.

Tandoori Style Chicken

There are probably as many recipes for tandoori chicken as there are cooks, but without a tandoor (charcoal-fired earthen oven with intense heat) the best we can hope for is to duplicate the spicing and call it tandoori style. To make it as close to the original as possible, use small roasting chickens. Allow half a small chicken for each serving.

2 small roasting chickens
½ teaspoon saffron strands
125 ml/4 fl oz/½ cup natural yoghurt

1 tablespoon finely grated ginger
2 teaspoons chopped garlic
2 teaspoons salt
pinch chilli powder
2 teaspoons paprika
1½ teaspoons garam masala (recipe page 354)
2 tablespoons melted ghee

Remove the skin to allow flavours to penetrate and make slits in the thickest part of the flesh to assist this further. Toast the saffron strands for a minute in a dry pan, turn onto a saucer and when cool and crisp, crush to a powder with the back of a spoon. Mix with the yoghurt. Combine ginger, garlic crushed to a paste with the salt, chilli powder, paprika and garam masala. Mix into the yoghurt and rub all over the chickens. Leave for 2 hours, or cover and refrigerate overnight.

Preheat oven to 220°C (450°F). Put ghee in a roasting pan and put chickens in the pan breast downwards. Spoon melted ghee over the birds and roast for 15 minutes. Turn the chickens over on one side, roast for 10 minutes then turn on the other side and allow a further 10 minutes. Turn the breasts upwards for a final few minutes, basting well with melted ghee. Serve hot with naan or parathas and onion salad.

Note: A rotisserie oven or grill is useful for cooking the chickens, but basting is still necessary. To cook on a barbecue, light the fire 1 hour beforehand and allow time for it to burn down to glowing coals. Cut chickens in halves down the centre and place on a rack above the coals. Cook until tender, turning so they cook through.

Chicken Tikka

Skewers of bite-sized pieces of chicken barbecued in a tandoor, these may be marinated in a very similar mixture as that used for tandoori style chicken — the saffron may be omitted. Add a tablespoon of ground almonds for thickening, and use chicken fillets rather than joints. Grill over glowing coals or under a preheated griller. Serve with chapatis or naan and onion slices.

Kashmiri Roast Chicken

Serves 6

1 × 1.5 kg/3 lb roasting chicken
2 teaspoons finely grated fresh ginger
2 teaspoons ground dry ginger
2 teaspoons crushed garlic
1 small onion, finely grated
1 teaspoon salt
1 teaspoon Kashmiri garam masala
  (recipe page 355)
2 tablespoons white poppy seeds
  or ground almonds
2 tablespoons natural yoghurt

RICE STUFFING

100 g/3½ oz/½ cup basmati rice
1 tablespoon ghee
2 tablespoons slivered almonds
2 tablespoons pistachio kernels
2 tablespoons sultanas (golden raisins)
½ teaspoon salt
250 ml/8 fl oz/1 cup chicken stock or water

Rinse and dry the chicken, removing any excess fat from cavity. Mix the rest of the ingredients together and rub well inside and outside the chicken. Leave for 1 hour or longer in refrigerator.

To prepare the rice stuffing, wash rice well and soak for 1 hour in cold water, then drain well. Melt ghee and fry the rice for a few minutes, stirring. Add all the remaining ingredients, bring to the boil, then turn heat very low, cover and cook for 15 minutes. Allow to cool.

Fill cavity of chicken, not forcing too much into it. Fasten vent with small poultry skewers and truss the chicken, tying legs together and tucking wings underneath.

Place chicken in a heavy saucepan with 1 tablespoon ghee and ½ cup water. Cover and cook on low heat until tender, about 70 minutes. Turn chicken during cooking so it browns on all sides. Or finish by browning the chicken in a moderately hot oven for the final 15 minutes.

Country Captain

Some say this is what the native cooks called a capon (domestic cockerel castrated and fattened for eating). It does not matter whether a capon or hen is used. The gentle spicing adds interest to a pot roast. Serves 5–6.

**1.5 kg/3 lb roasting chicken
  or chicken joints
2 teaspoons finely grated fresh ginger
2 teaspoons finely chopped garlic
2 teaspoons salt
1 teaspoon ground turmeric
½ teaspoon ground black pepper
¼ teaspoon chilli powder (optional)
1 tablespoon lime or lemon juice
3 tablespoons ghee or oil
4 large onions, thinly sliced
1 or 2 fresh chillies, seeded and sliced**

Mix together the ginger, garlic crushed with salt, turmeric, pepper and chilli powder, blending to a paste with a little lime or lemon juice. Prick the skin of the chicken and rub all over with the mixture. Leave to marinate for at least 30 minutes.

Heat ghee or oil in a heavy pan and fry half the onions, stirring frequently, until deep golden brown. Remove with a slotted spoon and set aside for garnishing the dish. Fry remaining onion and chillies until onion is pale golden, adding a little more ghee or oil if needed. Add chicken and fry until golden, turning it with tongs to brown both sides. Add a few tablespoons water to pan, cover and simmer until chicken is tender. At end of cooking uncover and allow liquid in pan to evaporate. Serve chicken hot, accompanied by fried potatoes or ghee rice, and garnished with the browned onions.

Vietnamese Chicken with Lemon Grass

Serves 4

**1 small roasting chicken
4 stems lemon grass
3 spring onions (scallions)
1 teaspoon salt
¼ teaspoon ground black pepper
2 tablespoons oil
2 fresh red chillies, seeded and chopped**

**2 teaspoons sugar
2 tablespoons fish sauce
4 tablespoons chopped roasted peanuts**

Cut chicken into pieces, Chinese style, chopping through the bones as described on page 77. Remove outer layers of lemon grass, and cut the tender, white portion at the base of the stalks into fine slices. Pound using a mortar and pestle to bruise. Slice spring onions, including green leaves. Mix chicken with salt, pepper, lemon grass and spring onions, cover and leave for 30 minutes.

Heat oil in wok and stir-fry the chicken for a few minutes. Add chillies and stir-fry on medium heat about 10 minutes or until chicken is well cooked. Add sugar and fish sauce, mix well, sprinkle with roasted peanuts and serve with rice.

Indonesian Braised Chicken

Serves 6

**1 × 1.5 kg/3 lb roasting chicken
  or chicken thigh cutlets
2 teaspoons finely grated ginger
2 teaspoons crushed garlic
1 slice galangal, fresh or in brine
1 teaspoon salt
freshly ground black pepper
5 candle nuts, pounded
1 tablespoon ground coriander
1 teaspoon ground cumin
1 teaspoon ground fennel
4 tablespoons peanut oil
2 large onions, sliced finely
400 ml/14 fl oz can coconut milk
2 salam leaves or sprig of curry leaves
1 small stick cinnamon
2 stems lemon grass
juice of 1 lime**

Cut chicken into joints and cut large joints in halves. Combine ginger, garlic, galangal, salt, pepper, nuts, coriander, cumin and fennel and pound to a paste. Rub over the chicken and leave at least 1 hour. Heat oil and fry sliced onion slowly until golden brown. Remove on a slotted spoon, letting oil drain back into the pan.

Fry the chicken pieces in the same oil until they change colour. Add 1 cup of the coconut milk mixed with 1 cup water. Drop in the daun salam or curry leaves, cinnamon stick and the lemon grass stalks, bruised and roughly tied in a knot for easy removal. Stir until it comes to a simmer, then cook uncovered until chicken is almost done, about 30 minutes. Add remaining coconut milk, undiluted, stirring well. Simmer for 10 minutes longer, uncovered. Remove from heat and stir in the lime juice. Taste and correct seasoning if necessary. Remove lemon grass, cinnamon stick and daun salam or curry leaves. Serve with steamed rice.

Thai Style Barbecued Chicken

Serves 6

**1 × 1.5 kg/3 lb roasting chicken
or chicken thigh fillets
3 teaspoons chopped garlic
2 teaspoons salt
2 tablespoons black peppercorns
60 g/2 oz/1 cup chopped fresh coriander
2 tablespoons lime juice**

If using a whole chicken cut in halves lengthways and, if liked, remove bones except for the wing bones. Hold in shape with 2 long skewers which will make it easy to turn on the barbecue.

Crush garlic and salt to a smooth paste. Pound peppercorns with a mortar and pestle, add the coriander and garlic and pound again to a paste. Mix in the lime juice. Rub the mixture into the chicken on all sides, cover and leave at least 1 hour.

Heat barbecue (or grill) and cook the chicken over glowing coals or under gas or electric heat until no longer pink. Keep chicken about 15 cm (6 in) from source of heat so the chicken cooks through and doesn't char on the outside and leave the inside underdone. Cut into pieces and serve with salad.

Thai Stuffed Chicken Wings

Serves 4–6

**1 kg/2 lb medium-sized chicken wings
250 g/8 oz minced (ground) pork
2 tablespoons fish sauce
2 spring onions (scallions), finely chopped
1 tablespoon finely chopped fresh coriander
1 large clove garlic
1 teaspoon sugar
1 teaspoon black pepper**

**1 fresh kaffir lime leaf, very finely shredded
rice flour or plain (all-purpose) flour for coating
oil for frying**

Cut the chicken wings in two pieces and save the top joint of the chicken for another dish. For this recipe you need just the middle joint and the wing tip. With a small, pointed knife remove bones from mid-joint. Run the knife around the top of each bone, push the flesh down to expose the bone and carefully twist each bone out.

Put pork in a food processor with the fish sauce, spring onions and coriander. Crush garlic to a paste with the sugar and add together with the black pepper and shreds of lime leaf. Process until well mixed.

Fill each chicken wing with mixture but do not overfill or they will burst when steamed. Secure tops with small poultry skewers or cocktail sticks. Place the wings on heatproof plates and steam over boiling water for about 7 minutes. Leave to cool. Roll in rice flour or wheat flour and dust off excess. Heat oil in a wok and deep-fry the wings until they are golden brown. Drain on paper towels and serve with a dipping sauce or bottled chilli sauce.

Chicken in Coconut Milk, Malay Style

Serves 6

**1 × 1.5 kg/3 lb roasting chicken
2 medium onions, roughly chopped
1 tablespoon chopped garlic
1 tablespoon chopped fresh ginger
2 stalks fresh lemon grass, finely sliced
2 or 3 fresh red chillies
2 slices galangal, fresh or brined
400 ml/14 fl oz can coconut milk
2 teaspoons ground coriander
½ teaspoon ground turmeric
½ teaspoon ground black pepper
1½ teaspoons salt
2 salam leaves or sprig of fresh curry leaves**

Cut chicken as for curry (see page 78) and put into a heavy saucepan.

In an electric blender put the onions, garlic, ginger, lemon grass, chillies, galangal and ½ cup coconut milk and blend until puréed.

Pour over chicken. Rinse blender jar with some of the remaining coconut milk and pour into saucepan. Add ground spices, salt and daun salam or curry leaves and bring slowly to simmering point, stirring now and then. Simmer uncovered until chicken is tender and sauce thick and reduced.

If chicken is so tender it starts to fall apart, remove from pan with slotted spoon and reduce the sauce on its own, then pour over the chicken and serve with rice and accompaniments.

Sri Lankan Chicken Curry

Serves 6

1 × 1.5 kg/3 lb roasting chicken
3 tablespoons ghee or oil
¼ teaspoon fenugreek seeds
sprig of fresh curry leaves
1 large onion, finely chopped
1 tablespoon chopped garlic
2 teaspoons finely grated fresh ginger
1 teaspoon ground turmeric
1–2 teaspoons chilli powder
1 tablespoon ground coriander
1 teaspoon ground cumin
½ teaspoon ground fennel
2 teaspoons salt
2 tablespoons vinegar
2 tablespoons paprika (optional)
2 ripe tomatoes, peeled and chopped
6 cardamom pods, bruised
1 stick cinnamon
1 stalk lemon grass
250 ml/8 fl oz/1 cup thick coconut milk
lime juice (optional)

Cut chicken into curry pieces as described on page 78. Heat ghee or oil and on low heat fry fenugreek seeds and curry leaves until they start to brown. Add onion, garlic and ginger and fry gently until onions are soft and golden. Add turmeric, chilli, coriander, cumin, fennel, salt and vinegar. If the curry isn't quite red enough, add the paprika because while it isn't used in Sri Lanka, using enough chilli to give the required colour would mean a curry too hot for most people. Stir well, add chicken and turn the pieces in the mixture. Add tomatoes, whole spices and lemon grass. Cover and simmer over low heat for 45 minutes. Add coconut milk, cook uncovered for a further few minutes, then remove from heat and stir in a squeeze of lime juice if desired. Serve with rice and accompaniments.

Yellow Curry of Chicken and Bamboo Shoot

Serves 4

2 tablespoons yellow curry paste
2 tablespoons oil
500 g/1 lb chicken thigh or drumstick fillets, diced
125 ml/4 fl oz/½ cup coconut milk
125 ml/4 fl oz/½ cup water
1 canned bamboo shoot, sliced
1 tablespoon fish sauce
1 teaspoon palm or brown sugar
2 kaffir lime leaves

Fry curry paste over medium-low heat in oil for 3 minutes. Add chicken and fry for a minute longer, stirring. Add coconut milk and water, bamboo shoot, fish sauce, sugar and lime leaves and simmer until chicken is tender and gravy reduced. Serve with steamed rice.

Hawaiian Chicken and Taro Leaves

Serves 4–6

1 kg/2 lb chicken thigh fillets
2 tablespoons lard or oil
1 teaspoon salt
60 taro leaves
**   or 2 bunches spinach if preferred**
250 ml/8 fl oz/1 cup coconut milk
60 g/2 oz butter

Cut chicken fillets into large dice, about 2.5 cm (1 in).

Heat lard or oil in a large, heavy pan and brown the chicken. Sprinkle with salt, cover and cook until chicken is tender.

Wash the taro leaves and remove the stems and tough parts of the ribs. Put into a large saucepan with 2 cups water and ½ teaspoon salt, cover and simmer for 1 hour (much shorter if spinach used) or until leaves are tender and there is no 'sting' when they are tasted. Squeeze out liquid from the leaves. Combine with coconut milk and chicken and heat through just before serving.

Laulau

These ti-leaf packages of pork and chicken are almost always part of a festive Luau in the Pacific islands. In some cases salted pork is used. Makes 8 parcels.

16 ti leaves
250 g/8 oz pork belly, salted or fresh
250 g/8 oz chicken breast fillets
6 spring onions (scallions) including leaves
2 or 3 large bunches taro leaves,
   spinach or silver beet
salt and pepper to taste

If using dried ti leaves, soak in warm water until pliable. Fresh leaves need only to be washed and dried on paper towels.

Cut pork into small dice and fry in a heavy pan until the fat has melted and the pork is crisp and brown. Cut chicken into dice which are larger than the pork pieces but still fairly small, about 1 cm (½ in). Fry the chicken in the same pan until it turns white.

If using taro leaves, they need to have the stems and tough ribs removed and the leaves themselves cooked in 2 cups water, covered, for at least 1 hour or until they no longer sting when tasted. If spinach or silver beet is used, the leaves should be well washed and cooked until limp, then the excess liquid pressed out and the leaves mixed with the cooked meats and the spring onions. Season to taste and divide into 8 portions.

Place 2 ti leaves one on top of the other at right angles and put a portion of the meat and spinach mixture on the top leaf. Fold it over to enclose, then fold the second leaf over in the opposite direction to make the parcel secure. Tie, then place in a steamer and steam for 30 minutes. Serve in the leaf bundles.

Chilli

(*Capsicum frutescens*) (Also spelled chili, chile.) SEE ILLUSTRATION. Fresh, dried, powdered, flaked, in sauces, sambals and pastes, chillies appear in many forms, to be used with discretion. It is well for the uninitiated to be aware that all chillies are not created equal. They range from mild to wild. As a general rule the smaller the chilli, the hotter it is.

It is hard to imagine Asian food without chillies, although they are native to Mexico and were not known in Asia until after the New World was discovered. The many and varied members of the Capsicum family were taken by the Spanish conquistadors to Europe in 1514. In 1611, the seafaring Portuguese introduced chillies to India. This is very recent in comparison with evidence that the natives of Brazil and Peru began eating wild chillies between 6500 and 5000 BC.

The reason chillies are often called chilli-peppers has a connection to why the natives of the Americas were called Red Indians or American Indians. One is no more pepper than the other is Indian; but when Columbus and his crew set sail back in 1492, he was confident he was on course for India. Among the treasures he hoped to bring back from his voyage were spices such as cinnamon, cloves and pepper, as precious as gold in Europe during the Middle Ages.

Instead, he found the Americas and pungent fruits called aji by the natives. The Spanish named the people 'Indians' and the pungent fruit 'red peppers'. In today's enlightened world the people are referred to as Native Americans, but the plant gets called everything from sweet or bell peppers to hot peppers or paprika peppers, though they are not in any way related to pepper.

Capsicum varieties were introduced to Europe and caught on in a big way in Hungary. Can you imagine Hungarian food without paprika? The milder types are more popular in the United States and Europe, but Asians appreciate the hotter varieties.

It seems that the further from the equator, the milder the food. Large, deep-red dried chillies are used in Kashmir to give a glowing red colour to dishes without imparting too much heat. A scene that has vividly fixed itself in my mind is that of a huge basket piled high with these deep-red chillies at a road stall in Kashmir. The morning sun shone through the translucent pods, illuminating them like a pyramid of miniature lanterns.

South India and Sri Lanka, on the other hand, close to the equator, are renowned for their hot food. The heat comes from fresh red or green chillies, dried chillies, or ripe red chillies of different types dried and ground into powder.

In Burma, large dried red chillies are fried in oil until crisp and almost black, and used as an accompaniment to meals — sort of a chilli pappadam which is held by the stem and bitten into. Small bites are recommended. In India, chillies are soaked in yoghurt and salt and dried in the sun for storing. These are called chilli tairu, and are treated like fiery pappadams, being fried in oil until crisp and eaten with rice. In the Philippines, the leaves of chilli plants are added to food in quite generous amounts — a cup of leaves in a dish to serve 4 people — and they are added during the last 3 or 4 minutes of cooking.

Banana chillies (banana capsicums) are used not as a flavouring but as a vegetable. They are ideal for stuffing with savoury mixtures. Smaller, hotter chillies are used extensively in salads, sambals, curries and sometimes just on their own as an offering should it be necessary to add excitement to a meal.

Assessing chillies: Be careful if you are just beginning an acquaintance with chillies. They are to be treated with respect at all times, no matter whether they are fire-engine red or a pale, innocent green.

Even with larger chillies, don't be lulled into a false sense of security if the tip of a chilli is so mild that you wonder what all the fuss is about. As it nears the stem, seeds and placenta, heat ratings rise.

Remember the rule that the smaller the chilli, the hotter it is. Test the truth of this by (cautiously) tasting the tiny bird's eye chilli (prik kee noo suan) so popular in Thai food. No, don't pop it into your mouth and chew on it, just bite the tip and touch it to your tongue. That will do for a start. (Milk or yoghurt is the antidote, and a teaspoonful of sugar helps too.)

Another very hot variety is the habanero, a wonderfully fruity but exceedingly hot chilli prized among West Indians, which belongs to a different species, *Capsicum chinense*.

Handling chillies: If slicing or chopping chillies, it is a wise precaution to wear disposable plastic gloves. Holding a chilli by the stem and snipping it with scissors or a sharp knife can be done without making contact with the pungent capsaicin, a phenolic compound found mostly where the seeds are attached to the central membrane known botanically as the placenta, and the paler-coloured partitions inside the fruit. This doesn't mean, however, that only the seeds are hot: the fleshy walls of a chilli can also provide plenty of heat.

If you have been handling chillies before reading this and your hands are on fire, make a paste of bicarbonate of soda (baking soda) and cool water and apply it to the affected parts. It won't work

miracles, but will help somewhat. Keep your hands out of hot water too — the heat seems to raise the intensity of the chilli burn to a most uncomfortable degree. Whatever you do, don't touch your eyes. Wash the board and knife used for chillies with cold water and kitchen salt.

Medicinal uses: The capsaicin of chillies does have a medical application, in the truest sense of the word. It is used in plasters to be applied externally in cases of severe muscle pain, acting in much the same way as the pleasantly 'hot' menthol creams. Internally, chillies and all members of the capsicum family are rich in vitamin C. They are reputed to help keep capillaries from hardening, thus lessening the risk of cardiovascular disease.

China: *la chiao, lup chew*
India: *mirch*
Indonesia: *lombok*
Japan: *togarashi*
Korea: *gochu*
Malaysia: *cili, lombok, cili padi* (bird's eye)
Philippines: *sili, siling haba* (long),
   siling labuyo (bird's eye)
Sri Lanka: *amu miris* (fresh green chilli),
   rathu miris (red chilli),
   kochchi miris (bird's eye)
Thailand: *prik chee faa,*
   prik kee noo suan (bird's eye)
Vietnam: *ot*

Dried chillies: Even in countries which grow fresh chillies as commercial crops, many recipes specify dried chillies as well as fresh be used in the spicing. It is, I can only guess, a guarantee against seasonal shortages of the fresh product, and the instant availability when there is a packet of dried chillies in your pantry. As with fresh chillies, larger dried chillies are not quite as hot as the small variety. Apart from whole dried chillies one can also purchase crushed dried chillies (seeds and all) and thread-fine strips called silgochu which are much used in Korean food. During summer it may be wise to refrigerate dried chillies, as they are susceptible to weevil attack.

Chilli oil: Buy in small bottles and use sparingly as it is quite hot. Unless you own a restaurant, a large bottle will go rancid before you can use it up. If you need to make it yourself, heat 1 cup oil in a small pan. On low heat stir in 2 tablespoons crushed dried chillies or chilli powder, or 10 whole dried chillies. After a minute turn off heat and leave to cool before straining through muslin or filter paper. Store in a narrow-necked bottle.

Chilli pastes: In Asian stores and now on many supermarket shelves, one may find chilli pastes which take much of the pain out of preparation. Simply spoon out by the half-teaspoonful or whatever your chilli tolerance dictates. Taste before adding to food as some are hotter than others.

Chilli powders: Once again be warned — different chilli powders have different heat ratings. If purchasing from Asian stores, most often spices are bulk-packed in plastic bags and if not clearly marked, ask the shopkeeper.

For Asian recipes never use Mexican chilli powder, as it is already mixed with cumin and will not give the correct flavour. Chilli powders can vary tremendously, depending on the type of chilli from which they are made. While you can use the description on the label as a guide, always test the truth by practical taste tests before adding to your recipe. Touch to the tip of your tongue with a moistened finger, tasting the tiniest bit of each new batch of chilli powder you buy and comparing it with the last lot. If it is more fiery, you know you have to reduce the amounts you have been using. During hot and humid weather store chilli powder in a screwtop jar in the refrigerator or freezer, for it is susceptible to weevil infestation.

I base my recipes on a medium strength chilli powder and the quantities recommended should not cause distress to anyone. They would probably not be sufficient to satisfy real chilli enthusiasts, but I recommend that a main dish is never made searingly hot. For those who must have it, a small dish of fresh chillies or a hot chilli sambal may be provided, but always use a small teaspoon for serving, as a hint that this particular dish is to be approached with caution.

Chilli sauces: There are more kinds of chilli sauce than I can possibly enumerate. Some are sweet and gently pungent, others should come with a warning. Always go easy at first until you know the strength of the product. Remember too that even the same brand may vary according to seasonal variations. Some include garlic and ginger, some are based on vinegar with no oil, others are cooked and preserved in oil. Different sauces suit different cuisines so try to use the appropriate variety.

Purchasing and storing: Read labels carefully, buy small quantities and assess them. As a general rule, sauces that are bright red and have the consistency of ketchup are not savagely hot, but there are always exceptions. Even after opening, they will keep for months without refrigeration.

Sambal Ulek

This is about as basic as sambal can be: crushed chillies, vinegar and salt. With this in the refrigerator, simply spoon out a quantity when fresh chillies are required for a recipe.

250 g/8 oz fresh red chillies
white vinegar
1 tablespoon salt

Wash the chillies and remove the stems. If a smoother sambal is required, split chillies and flip out the seeds with point of knife. Roughly chop the chillies and put into the jar of an electric blender with salt and sufficient vinegar to facilitate blending. Puree and put into a clean, dry jar. Cover and refrigerate.

Note: If storing for any length of time, ensure preservation by adding 1 teaspoon citric acid dissolved in 2 tablespoons hot water.

Sambal Bajak

Not just an accompaniment to a rice meal, this tasty sambal may be spread sparingly on crackers or small squares of toast and served as cocktail savouries.

250 g/8 oz fresh red chillies
125 g/4 oz peeled shallots
2 tablespoons finely chopped garlic
1 tablespoon chopped galangal, fresh or brined
3 tablespoons candle nuts or macadamia nuts
125 ml/4 fl oz/½ cup peanut oil
30 g/1 oz dried shrimp paste
1 teaspoon salt
125 ml/4 fl oz/½ cup tamarind liquid
2 tablespoons palm sugar or brown sugar

Prepare chillies as described for Sambal Ulek and put into a blender container with shallots, garlic, galangal and candle nuts. Blend to a purée. Heat oil in a wok or heavy saucepan and fry the blended mixture over low heat, stirring constantly, until fragrant. Add shrimp paste, salt, tamarind and sugar. Stir and cook until reddish brown and the oil shimmers on the surface. Cool, then store in a clean, dry bottle in the refrigerator.

Indian Chilli Pickle

1 kg/2 lb long, hot, fresh red or green chillies
2 tablespoons salt
1 tablespoon ground turmeric
2 tablespoons black mustard seeds
125 ml/4 fl oz/½ cup vinegar
2 tablespoons chopped garlic
500 ml/1 pint/2 cups mustard oil
1 teaspoon fenugreek seeds
2 teaspoons nigella seeds
2 teaspoons crushed asafoetida

Wash chillies and dry them well. Cut off stalks and slice chillies across into 1 cm (½ in) slices. Sprinkle with salt and turmeric, toss to mix evenly, cover and leave for 2 days in the sun or place in a very low oven for 2 hours each day. Soak mustard seeds in vinegar overnight, and grind in an electric blender with the garlic.

Heat oil in a large pan and add the fenugreek and nigella seeds. Stir and fry until fenugreek is golden brown, then add the asafoetida, stir once, and add the blended mixture and the chillies together with the liquid that will have gathered.

Cook, stirring now and then, until oil rises and chillies are cooked but not too soft. Cool and put into sterilised jars.

Thai Dipping Sauce

3 tablespoons lime juice
3 tablespoons fish sauce
3 tablespoons water
2 tablespoons white or light palm sugar
1 teaspoon crushed garlic
2 tablespoons finely sliced fresh bird's eye
  chillies

Combine all ingredients and stir until sugar dissolves. Serve as a dipping sauce or salad dressing.

Fried Chilli Sambal

This popular sambal is served with any main meal, but is particularly important in the Sri Lankan festive dish known as Lampries (see recipe page 204) — a combination of spiced rice and a number of different curries and accompaniments. It keeps well in the refrigerator.

250 ml/8 fl oz/1 cup oil
sprig of curry leaves
500 g/1 lb finely sliced onions
2 tablespoons chilli powder
125 g/4 oz Maldive fish
2 cardamom pods, bruised
2 whole cloves
1 small stick cinnamon
strip of fresh, frozen or dried pandan leaf
3 tablespoons vinegar
2 teaspoons salt or to taste
1 tablespoon sugar

Heat half the oil in a heavy pan and fry the curry leaves and onions until onions are soft and golden brown. It is important to fry the onions slowly for this sambal to have good keeping qualities. Turn them into a bowl and add chilli powder. Pound the Maldive fish with a mortar and pestle until finely ground. Heat remaining oil in pan and fry the Maldive fish, cardamom pods, cloves, cinnamon and pandan leaf for a few minutes, stirring. Add vinegar, return onions to pan and simmer until the mixture is thick and almost dry. Stir in salt and sugar, allow to cool completely and store in a clean glass jar in the refrigerator.

A quicker method is to use a tin of 'prawns in spices' or 'minced prawns' instead of the Maldive fish. These are sold in most Asian stores, a product of Malaysia.

Sweet Chilli Sauce

The strength of this sauce will depend on the kind of chilli you use. Large, plump chillies are usually milder than small, thin ones. If the sauce turns out to be too hot for your taste, simply add a proportion of tomato ketchup until it feels right.

250 g/8 oz fresh red chillies,
  or ½ cup chilli powder
750 g/1½ lb/3 cups white sugar

750 ml/1½ pints/3 cups white cider vinegar
375 g/12 oz sultanas (golden raisins)
10 cloves garlic, peeled
2 tablespoons finely grated fresh ginger
    (discard fibres)
3 teaspoons salt or to taste

Cut off and discard chilli stems. Cut chillies in halves lengthways and scrape out seeds with a teaspoon.

In a non-aluminium saucepan combine all ingredients and simmer until chillies, garlic and sultanas are very soft. Cool, purée in a food processor or blender, or push through a non-metal sieve. Bring to the boil once more. Pour into sterilised bottles and seal.

China

A vast country where relatively little of the land is arable. Add to that equation world's largest population and the effects of drought and flood on food crops — little wonder the Chinese have learned to make use of everything edible. Boasting one of the oldest cuisines in the world, it must also surely be one of the most diverse. Within its borders are numerous provinces with distinctive climates, produce and cooking styles.

Although no two authorities seem to be in agreement as to which are most important, the diversity is well represented by just five: Canton, Fukien, Honan, Peking (Shantung) and Szechwan. The Cantonese style is characterised by its light, digestible foods which use less fat (e.g. stir-fried dishes, steamed dumplings and dim sum). The Fukien school is famous for its clear soups, seafood dishes and subtle flavours. Honan is spicy, sweet and sour. Peking is famed for delicacy of flavour. And Szechwan food is hot and spicy.

Pivotal to the philosophy of Chinese cooking is an understanding of how the flavours and textures of foods need to be taken into consideration to achieve a perfectly balanced dish. The primary characteristics of flavour are expressed, enigmatically, in almost indefinable terms. I turn to the excellent translations in *Chinese Gastronomy*, by Hsiang Ju Lin and Tsuifeng Lin:

Hsien: sweet, natural flavour. The word is used to describe the taste of fresh fish, prawns, bamboo and fatty pork. Its quality may be imbued to a dish through judicious use of seasonings, particularly sugar.

Hsiang: characteristic flavour, natural aroma. Used to describe foods that tantalise not only the tastebuds but the olfactory sense as well. Into this category fall roasted meats, chicken fat, mushrooms and onions cooking. The carrier of hsiang is oil.

Nung: rich, heady, concentrated. The 'contrived' appeal of complex, aromatic foods such as a well-reduced stock based on a number of meats and the salty-sweet spiciness of glazed duck. Nung can also imply a dish is overly rich.

Yu-er-pu-ni: tasting of fat without oiliness. A most desirable attribute. This should be the taste of properly prepared belly pork, fish roe and caviar.

In addition, there are terms describing texture that give us added insight into the heights of skill to which Chinese cooks aspire. A classic essay on Chinese gastronomy differentiates between crunchy, smooth, elastic, chewy, soft, resilient, spongy, melting, grainy, unctuous, fibrous and gelatinous. Tell me these people aren't serious about their food!

All these qualities are naturally occurring — in certain foods. The challenge comes in creating these qualities in foods that do not naturally possess them.

'Schools' of Regional Cooking

Peking (Northern) School: This is the largest region, comprising many provinces. Although there are some exceptions, the climate is extreme and very harsh. Grains (wheat, millet, soy beans, sorghum, corn) and peanuts replace rice crops, and vegetables are rather limited. Breads and noodles replace rice in the diet, but here noodles are eaten as a seasoned dish, rather than in soup. The influence of Mongolia in the north can be seen in the predominance of lamb, cooked and eaten in a variety of ways including sliced and barbecued on a spit. The flavours of leeks and raw garlic come from Shantung. Nonetheless, the dish that most of the world identifies with Peking cooking is Peking Duck. See PEKING DUCK.

Cantonese (Southern) School: Kwantung and Fukien provinces. A sub-tropical zone that experiences a distinct rainy season and tropical cyclones, its rice crops yield twice a year. Besides rice, which is eaten every day, corn, sweet potato, taro and wheat are grown. Chicken, pigs and fish are farmed. Leafy green vegetables are plentiful and there are tropical as well as temperate fruits, including lychees. In coastal areas there is a wealth of fish, crustacea and shellfish. This rich diversity of produce has helped the cuisine become one of the most eclectic and imaginative of all. This is probably due, in part at least, to the arrival of chefs from Peking's imperial household who fled the overthrow of the Ming Dynasty in 1644. They journeyed south, passing through a great many regions and collecting many excellent recipes. This is considered by many to be the 'haute cuisine' of China. Of all the regions in China, this is the one renowned for consummate stir-fried dishes. Fukien province is also famous for its tea.

This was the cuisine taken overseas by the earliest Chinese migrants to Europe and America. Its earmarks are dim sum, sweet and sour dishes and exotic delicacies (dog, frog's legs, snake, snails, fried sparrows and turtle). Unfortunately, this is the style of cooking that has been most popularised and, as a result, most abased by third-rate Chinese restaurants who try to second-guess what Western palates expect of Chinese cuisine.

Shangai (Eastern) School: Taking in a large section of the eastern seaboard (on which China's biggest city, Shanghai, is situated) and extending as far inland as central China (Hupei province). It includes some of China's most fertile land, so fruit and vegetables grow in variety and abundance. The logical place to find the best of China's vegetarian cuisine. In addition, fish and shellfish play a major part in the diet with the abundance of the ocean at its door and the rice and wheat which grow in the fertile delta of the Yangtze. Highly decorative yet delicately seasoned food (garlic is used sparingly), if a little on the sweet side. The flavours of fresh ingredients shine through. Most popular cooking techniques are blanching, steaming, stir-frying and red-cooking. In spite of these seemingly healthy methods, a fondness for oil gives the food a reputation for being rather rich. Specialities of the area include the unique flavour of the specially cured chinhua or jinhua ham; rich, dark chinkiang vinegar; shao hsing rice wine; and some of the best soy sauce in China. Some regional specialities include delicate fish from the West Lake with sweet and sour sauce, lion's head meatballs, crisp stir-fried shrimp, and eel cooked in oil.

Szechwan (Western) School: Comprising the provinces of Yunnan and Hunan as well, Szechwan exerts the greatest influence. Fresh and dried chillies are used with abandon, but the complexity of flavour is owed to other ingredients: sugar, salt and vinegar. Also renowned for its unique spice, Szechwan pepper. Its effect on the tongue is literally tingling — more anaesthetising than hot. The climate is suitable for year-round cultivation and the region produces rice, wheat, corn, bamboo, mushrooms, citrus fruit and, of course, Szechwan pepper. A feature of its cuisine are dishes requiring more than one cookery technique: smoked duck (which is marinated, smoked, steamed and deep fried); twice-cooked pork; hot, sour soup; and one of my family's favourites, spicy Szechwan eggplant (deep fried, then braised), fragrant with garlic and tangy with soy, sugar and vinegar.

Chinese Almond

(*Prunus armeniaca*) Although these small, blanched kernels may be labelled Chinese almonds or bitter almonds, they are actually apricot kernels. In some cases they are accurately labelled.

Apricots are native to China and the Chinese prefer the strong flavour to the gentle flavour of true almonds. Controversy reigns about the use of apricot kernels, as eating them raw in anything but small quantities can be toxic. However, hydrocyanic acid, the toxic substance that forms when they are eaten raw, is destroyed by heat. For this reason, the apricot kernels sold in Chinese shops have been blanched, but before using they may be boiled, fried or roasted in a low oven. Twenty minutes at 100°C (200°F) is sufficient.

In the recipes which follow, the seeds provide the flavour, so no artificial almond essence is necessary.

Medicinal uses: An extract of these kernels is used in cough and asthma remedies.

China: *hung ngan*

Almond Jelly

Serves 6

This recipes uses blanched apricot kernels sometimes labelled 'Almonds'. They are smaller and rounder than almonds and have a distinctly stronger flavour.

60 g/2 oz blanched apricot kernels
750 ml/1½ pints/3 cups water
3 tablespoons sugar

2 teaspoons agar-agar powder
3 tablespoons sweetened condensed milk

Put apricot kernels and 1 cup water into an electric blender and blend at high speed for 2 minutes or until kernels are very finely ground. Strain through a fine strainer. Measure remaining water into a saucepan, add the sugar and sprinkle agar-agar over the surface. Bring to the boil, stirring, until agar-agar is dissolved. Add the strained kernel liquid and the sweetened condensed milk. Stir, pour into a mould or flat dish and allow to set. Unmould or cut into small squares and serve chilled, either on its own or with diced fresh fruits or canned fruits in syrup.

Almond Tea

Serves 4

3 tablespoons blanched apricot kernels
  or blanched almonds
500 ml/1 pint/2 cups water
4 tablespoons sugar
1½ tablespoons fine ground rice

Grind apricot kernels and water together at high speed in an electric blender until smooth. Strain through a fine sieve or square of muslin. Put into a saucepan with the sugar and bring to the boil. Mix ground rice smoothly with 3 tablespoons cold water and stir into the simmering liquid until it boils and thickens. Pour into small Chinese bowls and serve hot, before a skin forms on the surface.

Chinese Brocolli

See CABBAGE.

Chinese Chard

See CABBAGE.

Chinese Date

See JUJUBE.

Chives, Chinese

(*Allium tuberosum*) SEE ILLUSTRATION. Unlike the slender chives used in Western cooking, these have flat leaves which are much stronger in flavour. Called garlic chives, koo chye or gau choy. Sometimes it is possible to buy a type of these chives which have been blanched by growing them under cover (gau wong). These are highly prized and used as a vegetable, stir-fried.

A particular delicacy are flowering chives, the stems ending in a fat little pointed bud (gau choy fa). They are a very special vegetable if cooked lightly and dressed with oyster sauce or a combination of flavours. SEE ILLUSTRATION.

Purchasing and storing: Look for shiny green stems and smooth, plump buds. Examine the lower ends of the stems too, and try snapping the end of one. If it is not crisp and fresh enough to snap, it is probably old and tough and won't be pleasant to eat. If they have to be kept, let it be for no more than a day, and wrap the bunch in damp paper towels, put into a polythene bag and refrigerate.

Preparation: The stems can be woody so trim tough stems by snapping off the lower ends, as with asparagus. If fresh and tender enough to snap, they should not be tough. And do eat the flower buds.

China: *jiu tsai, gau tsoi, gau choy fa*
Indonesia: *kucai*
Japan: *nira*
Malaysia: *kucai*
Philippines: *kutsay*
Thailand: *kui chaai*
Vietnam: *he*

Stir-Fried Flowering Chives

1 or 2 bunches flowering chives
2 tablespoons peanut oil
2 tablespoons oyster sauce
3 tablespoons water
1 teaspoon cornflour (cornstarch)
1 teaspoon sugar

Wash and dry the chives, snap off ends about 2.5 cm (1 in) or so from the end of the stem, then cut the chives into finger-lengths. Heat the oil in a wok and quickly stir-fry the chives for a minute on medium-high heat. Add oyster sauce, water, cornflour and sugar mixed together, stir until boiling and thickened, and serve at once.

Chives, Garlic

See CHIVES, CHINESE.

Chocolate

See COCOA.

Chocolate Pudding Fruit

See SAPOTE, BLACK.

Choko

(*Sechium edule*) A squash from tropical America, it is known in that part of the world by various names including chayote, christophene, custard marrow, mirliton, pepinella, and vegetable pear. A perennial vine, it adapts well to any sunny climate. There is more than one edible part to the plant: the fruits may be steamed or boiled, or battered and fried, and also make a delicate addition to Asian soups and stir-fries; the tender shoots, boiled, are served like asparagus; the leaves are eaten like spinach and the large, tuberous roots (weighing up to 10 kg/20 lb) are used like yams. A popular vegetable in all the cuisines of Asia.

Shaped like a flattened pear 10–15 cm (4–6 in) long with deep creases at both ends, it has a thin but tough jade-green skin, occasional soft spines and a single seed which is soft and edible, provided the fruit is not too mature.

Purchasing and storing: Choose the smallest (therefore youngest and most tender) chokos from the pile. Even if the fruit are large, those with the softest spines will be the more tender. They keep well at room temperature, but if kept too long will start to sprout from the seed and become stringy. They are easy to grow: simply bury one in the garden. But be warned, they are vigorous growers and will twine their sturdy tendrils around anything that stands still. I have had to discourage them from clothes lines, other trees, and the garage roof.

Preparation: Wash the chokos, halve lengthways and cook them either with or without peeling. The skin, which should be removed before eating, protects the pale, delicate flesh which remains curiously crisp when cooked. If the choko is to be sliced or diced, it is better to peel it before cutting it up. The cut flesh of the raw fruit exudes a strangely slippery sap which is difficult to wash off one's hands, so if sensitive skin is a problem, oil hands lightly or protect hands with thin rubber gloves before peeling. Chokos are delicious simply steamed and buttered with a grinding of black pepper. Added to soups they provide unique texture without adding an obtrusive flavour.

> **Burma:** *goorakathee*
> **China:** *harp jeung kwa, fat shau kwa*
> **Indonesia:** *walu jepan, labu siem*
> **Japan:** *hayato-uri*
> **Malaysia:** *labu siam*
> **Philippines:** *sayote*
> **Thailand:** *fak mao, fak meo*

Chow Chow Preserve

Chow chow preserve is a mixture of fruit and vegetables in a thick, ginger-flavoured sugar syrup. Finely sliced or diced and spooned over ice cream or puddings, it is delicious. It is an important ingredient when making Sri Lankan fruit cake. Chow chow preserve is not to be confused with chow chow pickle which is a mixture of cauliflower and other vegetables in a thick, yellow sauce of mustard and vinegar.

Choy Sum

See CABBAGE (Flowering cabbage).

Chrysanthemum

(*Chrysanthemum coronarium*) SEE ILLUSTRATION. In Western countries, Mother's Day flowers. In China and Japan, a part of the culture. Fresh petals are sprinkled into soups or over steamboat dishes; the dried flowers (not the glorious large chrysanthemums but a small, single daisy type) are sold in packets for making infusions to drink like tea.

The leaves are used as cooked vegetables. There are more than one kind, some deeply lobed, and others with more rounded, softer, succulent leaves. Very tender leaves are eaten raw while older leaves are blanched, then refreshed in iced water to set the colour, and served as a salad. The leaves and flower petals may be added to soups shortly before serving as overcooking makes them bitter.

Purchasing and storing: Choose leaves which look fresh and young, and are not too large or mature. The flavour becomes stronger and borders on the bitter when the plant is past its first flush of youth and starts to bloom. Chrysanthemum greens wilt easily, so buy or harvest from your garden shortly before cooking. Wrapped in paper and stored in the vegetable bin of the refrigerator they will keep for only a day or two.

Preparation: Wash very well, ensuring all sand has been removed. If the stems seem tough, pick off individual leaves. Cook only briefly.

China: *tung hao, chong ho, tong ho choi*
India: *gul chini*
Japan: *shungiku, shingiku, kikuna*
Korea: *sookgat*
Philippines: *tunghao*
Thailand: *khee kwai*
Vietnam: *cay cuc*

Chutney

This is how the English spell 'chatni'. It also implies that what is served under this name is a 'Major Grey' type, long-cooked, sweet and spicy, jam-like in texture and keeping power. Major Grey chutneys are famous the world over. (For real Indian style fresh chatnis, see CHATNI.) But if what you want is a cooked chutney, here are some recipes for fruit chutneys. While not authentically Indian they are delicious as an accompaniment to a curry meal.

Mango Chutney

2 kg/4 lb firm green mangoes
10 large red dried chillies
1 litre/2 pints/4 cups malt vinegar
60 g/2 oz/½ cup peeled,
  chopped fresh ginger
10 cloves garlic, sliced
750 g/1½ lb/3 cups sugar
1 tablespoon salt
2 sticks cinnamon

With a sharp knife peel the mangoes and cut the flesh into dice. Discard seeds. Remove stems and seeds of chillies and soak in 1 cup vinegar for 20 minutes, then purée roughly in food processor or electric blender with the chopped ginger. Put the ingredients into a non-aluminium pan and bring to the boil. Simmer uncovered until thick. Discard cinnamon sticks. Fill sterile bottles and cap while hot. If mangoes are not available, use firm apricots, peaches, nectarines or green apples instead.

Fruit Chutney

2 large unripe mangoes or cooking apples
150 g/5 oz dried apricot halves
100 g/3½ oz sultanas (golden raisins)
1 tablespoon finely chopped fresh ginger
1 tablespoon finely sliced garlic
1–2 tablespoons chopped fresh red chillies
500 g/1 lb/2 cups sugar
500 ml/1 pint/2 cups white vinegar
3 teaspoons salt
1 teaspoon cumin seeds
½ teaspoon nigella seeds
½ teaspoon black mustard seeds
2 teaspoons garam masala (recipe page 354)

Peel and slice mangoes or peel, core and dice apples. Put all ingredients in a non-aluminium pan, add 1 cup water and stir over medium heat until sugar is dissolved. Simmer for 30 minutes or until thick, and bottle in clean, dry, hot jars. Seal airtight.

Cilantro

See CORIANDER HERB.

Cinnamon

(*Cinnamomum zeylanicum*) SEE ILLUSTRATION. A native of Sri Lanka (Ceylon), the 'zeylanicum' in its botanical name is a reminder that the ancient Dutch name for this island was Zeilan — later anglicised to Ceylon.

It is probably the most popular cooking spice in the Western world. There is a chain of shops in the United States where everything — doughnuts, cookies, cakes — is supposedly spiced with cinnamon. However, most of what is sold as cinnamon in the United States is, in fact, *C. aromaticum* syn. *C. cassia*, a close relative, but with a flavour much stronger than the delicate flavour of true cinnamon.

It does not help that some countries export pieces of cassia bark brazenly labelled 'Cinnamon'. They are thick and dark in colour and woody, as the corky outer bark is still attached. Cinnamon quills, by contrast, are paler and are made of 4 or 5 very fine, tan-coloured layers of parchment-thin bark which has been fermented for 24 hours and the corky outer layer carefully removed. The fine bark curls as it dries, and smaller quills are inserted into wider quills, giving true cinnamon its grading of 'five zeroes' or 'four zeroes' for top quality quills. These quills are usually cut into 8 cm (3 in) lengths.

Ground cinnamon is a pale tan colour and has a delicate fragrance while ground cassia is reddish brown and much more pungent. The next time you purchase cinnamon, bear these guidelines in mind and discover for yourself the delicate fragrance of true cinnamon.

In India, Sri Lanka, Indonesia and Malaysia, cinnamon is as much part of savoury spice blends as the more pungent spices (see recipes under SPICE BLENDS). A true Sri Lankan curry, whether mild or hot, always includes a cinnamon stick simmered in the sauce.

It is used in sweet cookery also, but not with the same abandon as in Western countries. For a sweet recipe using cinnamon, see Indonesian Spice Layer Cake (page 61).

Burma: *thit-ja-boh-gauk*
India: *darchini*
Indonesia: *kayu manis*
Malaysia: *kayu manis*
Sri Lanka: *kurundu*
Thailand: *ob chuey*
Vietnam: *que*

Citron

(*Citrus medica*) One of the first citrus fruits to have been introduced from the Far East to the Mediterranean area, around 300 BC. The ancient Greeks discovered them growing in the land of the Medes, which is why it is named *C. medica*. It was cultivated in the Hanging Gardens of Babylon, one of the wonders of the ancient world, and was used in perfumery.

It is long-shaped rather than round or oval, and has a very thick skin and pith, which makes it ideal for candying. In Japan it is called yuzu and is much prized for its unique fragrance. Little slivers of the rind are used to garnish dishes, and the juice is used in dressings.

Indonesia: *jeruk bodong*
Japan: *yuzu*
Malaysia: *limau susu*
Philippines: *cidra*
Sri Lanka: *cidran*
Thailand: *som mu, som saa*

Citrus Fruits

There are many kinds of citrus used in Asian food, and some are so distinctively flavoured that substitution means a loss of character. Each has its own flavour and fragrance. In Asian countries, every effort is made to obtain the variety which provides the correct fragrance for the particular dish. See entries under individual names: CITRON; KAFFIR LIME; KALAMANSI; LEMON; LIME, SWEET; MANDARIN; POMELO.

Clams

When available, clams make a nice addition to seafood soups. They are also delicious with spicy flavours. The main thing to remember is not to overcook them or they will toughen. They are often available frozen in Japanese grocers and added to nabemono dishes or soups.

Like mussels, make sure the shells of fresh clams are firmly closed or that they close when lightly tapped with a finger. Soak clams in fresh water and swish around to encourage them to disgorge sand. If you need to keep them for a few hours, keep in a cool, moist place. Cook them as soon as possible, using recipes given under MUSSELS.

Cloud Ear

See MUSHROOMS & FUNGI (Black fungus).

Cloves

(*Syzygium aromaticum*, also known as *Eugenia caryophyllus* and *E. aromatica*) SEE ILLUSTRATION. The word 'clove' comes from the French 'clou', meaning nail.

Cloves are the unopened flower buds of a tree of the myrtle family, indigenous to the Moluccas, the fabled Spice Islands of old. They grow on strong but slender stems in groups of two, three or four and each bud measures about 1 cm (½ in) from the base of the long calyx to the rounded tip of the bud. When fresh they are deep pink and even as tightly closed buds, give off a spicy, floral fragrance. They are never allowed to bloom because if they do, they become worthless as a spice.

The buds are picked twice a year, separated from the stems and spread on mats to dry in the sun for several days until dark brown. They lose two-thirds of their weight after drying, and it takes from 10,000 to 14,000 of the dried buds to make a kilo of the spice.

The clove plant provides essential oils which are used in perfumes, toothpastes, mouthwashes and breath fresheners. Courtiers in China during the third century BC were required to keep a few cloves in their mouths to sweeten the breath whenever addressing the emperor.

The flavour of cloves, measure for measure, is stronger than most other spices, so the quantity added is generally less than, for instance, cinnamon or nutmeg, so that it doesn't overwhelm. A clove or two simmered with stewed fruit, then removed, adds interest; and for pickling, cloves are as essential as mustard seed. In Western cooking, the Christmas ham wouldn't be the same if not studded with cloves before baking, and a pinch of ground cloves added to the ham glaze of mustard and brown sugar lifts the flavour tremendously.

Cloves are an essential ingredient in many spice blends, but perhaps nowhere more important than in Indian curry powder (see recipe page 356).

Medicinal uses: Oil of clove is an old and reliable toothache reliever, is antiseptic and was used in medicine to aid digestion.

Burma: *ley-nyin-bwint*
India: *laung*
Indonesia: *cingkeh (chinkeh)*
Malaysia: *bunga cengkeh*
Sri Lanka: *karabu*
Thailand: *kaan ploo*

Cocoa

(*Theobroma cacao*) Also spelled cacao. The cocoa bean, from which chocolate is made, grows on trees which are native to tropical America but which are now extensively cultivated in Asia and Africa to satisfy demand for that most seductive of confections. The cocoa beans are packed tightly inside large, yellow-orange pods which grow directly from the trunk and branches of the trees, and have to be processed by fermenting, drying in the sun, roasting and pounding, and followed by fine grinding, refining and conching.

In the Philippines, echoing the influences left by the Spanish, chocolate is a favourite drink and features at breakfast in champurado (also spelled tsampurado), a rice porridge with chocolate.

Coconut

(*Cocos nucifera*) In the Pacific islands and South East Asia, the coconut is the tree of life. It provides more than food and drink: its wood is used to build cottages; its leaves, plaited tightly on either side of the stout mid-rib, form a waterproof roof; the husk is teased into coir which makes ropes and mats; the shells are polished and fashioned into all kinds of ornamental and useful objects, cooking and serving spoons being foremost. However, it is as food and drink that coconuts are of prime importance.

India: *nariyal*
Indonesia: *kelapa*
Malaysia: *kelapa*
Pacific: *niu*
Sri Lanka: *pol*
Thailand: *maprao*
Vietnam: *dua*

Drinking coconuts: A small proportion of the crop is sold during the immature stage as drinking coconuts, the clear, sweet water within being popular as a thirst-quencher. (This is not coconut milk.) The seller normally uses a machete to remove the outer green or orange-coloured skin and cut through the husk, then with one swift slash opens the top of the nut. Some varieties are considered specially fine for drinking. See KING COCONUT.

The clear coconut water, together with a few pieces of tender endosperm, is now sold in just about every Asian shop, or better still, frozen in plastic cylinders. It is lightly sweetened and, in many cases, flavoured with a touch of pandan leaf, the Asian equivalent of vanilla.

The flesh of the coconut (endosperm) at this stage is translucent, jelly-like and quite delicious. If not consumed straight away it can be mixed with the juice, sweetened with sugar and frozen to make refreshing ice blocks. In the Philippines it is called buko and incorporated into desserts.

At the weekend market in Bangkok I encountered drinking nuts which had their thick husks removed. The nuts had been roasted, so the creamy white shells had scorch marks on them and were packed in a large bag of crushed ice. The vendor opened them deftly with a chopper. These were the sweetest coconuts I ever tasted, served in a most civilised way — with a drinking straw.

In Goa, on India's west coast, the coconut, still wearing its green husk, is opened at the top, and to its innocent liquid is added some not-so-innocent feni (a potent alcoholic drink made from cashew fruit), crushed ice and some sweet, fruit-flavoured cordial. Beware. It is a powerful concoction. In Vietnam, the French added Pernod and ice to young coconut.

While the water of young coconuts is appreciated, most Asians avoid drinking the juice of mature nuts, the saying being that it is bad for you. The juice is used in cooking in Vietnam and a few Malay dishes.

Coconut oil: The mature nut with its well-developed endosperm by now white and opaque and at least 1 cm (½ in) thick, is used commercially. The nuts are split open and dried in the sun. The dried meat, called copra, is separated from the shell and pressed to produce coconut oil. This is refined and used for cooking either in liquid form or rendered solid by hydrogenation. Coconut oil is also widely used in making soaps and shampoos. Among the raven-haired women of southern India, Sri Lanka and Malaysia, coconut oil is used as a hair oil to keep their crowning glory shiny and well nourished. Coconut oil is one of the vegetable oils which is saturated and therefore not recommended for use on a daily basis, though in countries where coconut is king it is the accepted cooking medium.

Coconut milk: In some Asian and Pacific countries there are industries producing coconut milk. Factories extract the rich milk from the grated flesh of mature coconuts and package it in cans or cartons for export either as coconut cream, coconut milk or coconut extract. If a recipe requires a rich coconut milk and you are unfamiliar with the brands on offer, it is probably safer to buy a tin marked cocunut cream. There is also a solid block called creamed coconut which I do not recommend since it lacks the smoothness and fresh flavour of good coconut milk.

Other factories freeze-dry the milk to a powder which is reconstituted before use, but this has a heat-treated taste, much as evaporated dairy milk has. Use it if you have to, but fresh coconut milk is best, with canned coconut milk a close second.

Before canned coconut milk, thick coconut milk (first pressing) and thin coconut milk (second or third pressing) was extracted from desiccated (dried, shredded) coconut steeped in hot milk or water.

Coconut milk is the extract of the grated flesh of mature coconuts. It is a mistake to refer to the clear liquid inside the coconut as 'coconut milk'. The liquid inside a coconut is 'coconut water' or 'coconut juice'.

Choosing a good coconut: When coconuts are exported for sale they have the husk removed, revealing the woody shell. The shell of the coconut should be dry with no sign of dampness or mould. If there is any leakage from the 'eyes' at one end of the nut, choose another one. A good coconut should weigh heavy in the hand and when shaken should have liquid sloshing around inside. Absence of water in the nut means that it has leaked out and the flesh will be rancid.

Opening a coconut: Some people recommend piercing two of the round indentations with a skewer and draining the juice into a jug, but I find this more difficult than tapping firmly and repeatedly around the centre of the nut (between the indentations on one end and the slight point on the other). The best implement for this is the back edge of a stout chopper. When a crack appears, insert the point of the blade and lever the crack apart sufficiently to allow the liquid to run out into a jug. Then administer a couple more sharp taps and the nut should fall cleanly into two halves.

Extracting coconut milk: Coconut milk is very important, for it is the magic that smoothes out a fiery sauce and gives richness to many curries. It is also used without spices in the foods of the Pacific, where it takes the place of every velouté, emulsion or sauce you can think of in Western cooking.

Place the grated flesh of one coconut in a bowl with a cup of hot water or milk and squeeze firmly to release the richness. Instead of squeezing and kneading, it is more easily done in a blender. Strain and set aside. The first extract is known as coconut cream or thick milk and is usually added at the end of a recipe. Repeat the procedure using the same coconut with more liquid. Use where thin coconut milk is required, as in long simmering of ingredients.

If using desiccated coconut it is definitely easier with a blender. Soak 2 cups desiccated coconut in 2½ cups hot water or milk and allow to cool before putting into the blender and processing at high speed. Strain, pressing out all the liquid. Repeat using the same coconut and slightly less liquid as the coconut is already moist. Second and even third extracts have flavour and may be used as cooking liquid.

Remember, coconut milk is very perishable, even under refrigeration. It should be used within a day of extracting it or opening a can. If only a small quantity is needed, immediately pour the rest into ice-cube trays and freeze until firm, then store in plastic bags in the freezer. These cubes come in very useful when just a light flavour of coconut is required. If watching intake of fats, a good way to enjoy the flavour of coconut milk without excess richness is to add 3 or 4 cubes to a cup of water or stock and use as the liquid in a soup or curry. Each cube equals approximately a tablespoon.

Coconut milk has a tendency to curdle at high temperatures, and in Asia it is recommended that the pan in which it cooks should not be covered, as this encourages curdling. Also, it is stirred while coming to simmering point. In the Pacific, the rule is that dishes featuring thick coconut milk or cream are only simmered, never boiled, and the addition of a little slaked cornflour (cornstarch) is extra insurance against curdling.

Fiji: *lolo*
Hawaii: *me wai niu*
Indonesia: *santan*
Malaysia: *santan*
Philipinnes: *gata*
Samoa: *pe'epe'e*
Sri Lanka: *mit kiri*
Thailand: *nam katee*

Grating coconut: In the Pacific and throughout Asia, there are special implements for grating the flesh from a coconut, with curved blades which fit into the curved shell, making it easy and safe. If such an implement is not available, heat the halved coconut in a moderate oven for 15–20 minutes which will make the white meat shrink from the shell. Carefully prise the meat out of the shell and remove the dark brown skin on the outer curves using a vegetable peeler. The pieces of coconut can then be grated, processed or blended.

Coconut is used in many ways. Freshly grated, served alongside curries or sambals with the sting of chillies, it serves to cool the tongue and give a touch of sweetness. With chillies, onion, lime juice and salt added, it can do just the opposite and become a hot sambal.

A coconut sambal can be as varied as the cook wants it to be. A red sambal, with chilli powder; a green sambal, with ground fresh curry leaves, coriander or mint; a brown sambal, in which the coconut is toasted until it takes on a completely different flavour; or a piquant dried shrimp sambal. The coconut enriches and balances the other flavours.

Another indispensable use for grated coconut is when it is toasted until deep brown, ground finely and used to thicken and enrich certain dishes. In Asian markets it is possible to purchase small plastic bags containing roasted and ground coconut, looking not unlike ground coffee. In Western kitchens it can be achieved, perhaps not quite so finely ground, using a powerful electric blender, after the coconut has been toasted in a dry frying pan.

Curry with Dark Roasted Coconut

Serves 6

60 g/2 oz/¾ cup freshly grated
** or desiccated coconut**
1 large onion, chopped
1 tablespoon chopped garlic
2.5 cm/1 in square dried shrimp paste
1 tablespoon ground coriander
2 teaspoons ground cumin
1 teaspoon ground turmeric
1–2 teaspoons chilli powder
** or 3 fresh red chillies**
3 tablespoons finely sliced lemon grass
** (tender white portion)**
** or 2 strips lemon rind**
3 tablespoons chopped galangal, fresh or brined
2 teaspoons salt
2 tablespoons peanut oil
400 ml/14 fl oz can thick coconut milk
1 kg/2 lb beef cut in thin slices
** or 1.5 kg/3 lb roasting chicken, jointed**
sprig of fresh curry leaves
** or 2 salam leaves**

In a heavy frying pan stir the coconut over medium heat until it turns a rich, dark brown (like coffee beans). Immediately turn it onto a dish to prevent it burning in the pan.

When cooled, put into an electric blender, grind finely, then add about ½ cup water and blend on high speed to a fine purée. Pour into a bowl, and without washing blender put onions, garlic, shrimp paste, coriander, cumin, turmeric, chillies, lemon grass, galangal and salt into blender and purée, stopping from time to time to scrape down the sides of blender jar.

Heat oil in a heavy saucepan and fry the puréed mixture on low heat, stirring, until fragrant and oil separates from the mass. Add ground coconut, coconut milk and curry leaves or daun salam. Add beef or chicken and stir gently as mixture comes to the simmer. Cook uncovered for 1 hour or until chicken or beef is tender. Serve with rice and accompaniments.

Roasted Coconut Sambal

75 g/2½ oz/1 cup fresh grated
or desiccated coconut
1 small onion, chopped
1 teaspoon salt
2 teaspoons pounded Maldive fish
or dried prawns (shrimp)
3–4 tablespoons lime juice

Roast the coconut as described in previous recipe. Combine all ingredients in electric blender, cover and blend on high speed until smooth. It may be necessary to add a little extra lime juice or water. Shape into a flat cake and mark top in lines with back of knife. Serve with rice and curries.

Red Coconut Sambal

75 g/2½ oz/1 cup fresh grated
or desiccated coconut
1 teaspoon salt
1 teaspoon chilli powder or to taste
2 teaspoons paprika
2 teaspoons pounded Maldive fish
or dried prawns (shrimp)
1 small onion, finely chopped
2 tablespoons lime or lemon juice

If using desiccated coconut, sprinkle with 3 tablespoons hot milk or water and toss to moisten. Combine all ingredients in a bowl and mix well, rubbing ingredients together. Serve in a small bowl, and if liked add a fresh chilli, finely chopped.

Coconut and Dried Shrimp Mallung

Mallung may be translated as 'mixed up' or 'tossed together'. The consistency should be dry and the flavours strong, as their place in the meal is as an accompaniment. Coconut is a favourite main ingredient for these small dishes, with strong-flavoured ingredients added — in this case, the tiny, transparent dried shrimps about the size and shape of a fingernail paring. Serves 6.

150 g/5 oz/2 cups freshly grated
or desiccated coconut
2 medium onions, finely chopped
3 tablespoons sliced fresh chillies
½ teaspoon fenugreek seeds
1½ teaspoons salt
1 teaspoon ground turmeric
5 tablespoons dried shrimps
6 tablespoons water
3 tablespoons lime or lemon juice

If using desiccated coconut, sprinkle with a little extra water and moisten by rubbing lightly with the fingers. Put all the ingredients except lemon juice and coconut into a saucepan and cook, covered, until coconut absorbs all the liquid. Taste and add more salt and lime juice if needed. Serve with rice and curries.

Coconut Milk Soup

This is not served as a soup on its own, but rather as something to make boiled rice moist and flavourful.

2 teaspoons fenugreek seeds
1 onion, finely chopped
1 sprig fresh curry leaves
1 small stick cinnamon
2 fresh green chillies, slit
2 teaspoons pounded Maldive fish
or dried prawns (shrimp)
¼ teaspoon ground turmeric
½ teaspoon salt
400 ml/14 fl oz can coconut milk
squeeze of lime juice

Soak fenugreek seeds in hot water for 1 hour. Drain and put into a saucepan with all the ingredients except lime juice and ½ cup coconut milk. Add 1½ cups water to the pan and simmer very gently until onions and the fenugreek seeds thicken the coconut milk. Add reserved coconut milk and remove from heat. Stir in lime juice, taste and adjust seasoning. If a thicker soup is preferred, add a few thin slices of potato when starting to simmer.

Coconut and Vegetable Curry

Very similar to the coconut soup, except that bite-sized pieces of tender beans, zucchini or other vegetables are simmered in the soup until tender.

Coconut Apple

When a coconut germinates, a spongy mass forms inside the cavity, so there is no longer water and albumen, but a solid white ball with traces of buttery yellow exterior. When bitten into, it tastes deliciously of coconut, but the texture is moist and yielding, nothing like the hard endosperm it replaces.

Coffee

(*Coffea arabica*) As the name indicates, this plant comes from somewhere in Arabia, though there is no clear-cut decision on just where. The small trees with their glossy green leaves and bright orange or red berries are sometimes grown as ornamental plants. Coffee drinking is not widespread in most parts of Asia, but in southern India, Malaysia and Indonesia coffee is a favourite drink. Indonesians will always serve coffee black unless otherwise specified, but in India and Malaysia it is never served black or unsweetened, nor are you given the choice: it will be served to you thick with condensed milk, more a dessert than a beverage.

In India, the roasting of coffee beans is usually done in the home, and 'butter-roasted' coffee is a special boast. The beans are purchased by variety and the roasting is done to the liking of that particular household. Similar to the roasting and blending of spices, the coffee of each home has its own flavour and individuality which the connoisseur recognises.

Coffee may be roasted in a pan or in a special coffee roaster with the beans kept in constant motion so that not one bean gets burnt. It takes about 15 minutes to roast coffee, turning the beans over without stopping until they are done to the desired degree: light, medium or dark. Then they must be spread out and cooled quickly since the heat dissipates the delicious essential oils.

Coffee is seldom prepared any other way than by brewing (pouring boiling water over freshly ground beans, leaving for 5 minutes, then straining through a fine strainer). Most coffee is mixed with almost an equal amount of milk, which has been boiled and made frothy by the simple expedient of pouring it from one vessel to another, stretching the distance between the two vessels as much as one dares. Those who make and sell coffee and tea from the roadside boutiques have this down to a fine art, so much so that it is known as 'long tea', or coffee by the yard. The Malay name is kopi tarek — literally 'pulled coffee'.

Coltsfoot

(*Petasites japonicus*) One of the varieties of coltsfoot is used in Japan, the long leaf stalk being peeled and pickled to make fuki. It is not to be confused with another variety, *P. hybridus*, also known as butterbur.

Strip the stalks of leaves and cook in a large pan of salted, boiling water for 3–7 minutes, depending on thickness of stalks. Lift out and plunge into cold water. Peel fibrous skin off stems from bottom up, slice into short lengths and add to soup. The flavour is said to resemble that of celery.

Congee

Rice gruel. Not liquid, not solid, but rice and water cooked to a spoonable consistency. It is surprising how many conflicting views exist about the correct way to go about cooking it. One says wash the rice, another says don't wash away the starch which surrounds the grains. One says soak the rice for a few hours, another says to drop the rice into boiling water, yet another prefers to put rice and cold water into the pan and bring to the boil, then keep at a quick simmer for 45 minutes to 1 hour. A Chinese friend recommends putting a spoon into the pan (a Chinese porcelain spoon, not a metal spoon) to keep the congee from scorching on the base of the pan. When done, the rice grains should have 'blossomed' and be suspended in the starchy liquid.

There is more than one kind of congee. On the streets of Asian cities in the early morning where Chinese workers are breakfasting after a night's labour, or fortifying themselves for the day's work ahead, there are stalls selling congee accompanied by deep fried Chinese crullers (long sticks of yeast dough) and what the stall-holder euphemistically calls 'pig's spare parts'. These include intestines and other offal.

Conpoy

Another kind of congee is more refined, being simply rice simmered in water to make a thick gruel. Served at the breakfast buffet in international hotels in Asia, congee is kept piping hot in a cauldron and surrounded by many accompaniments.

Western travellers may give their attention to fruit platters, cereal, bacon and eggs, toast or pancakes; but Asians seem to gravitate to this most basic comfort food and usually start the day with rice congee.

Among the tasty side dishes offered with the congee will be such pungent items as salted radish, sliced green onions, fried shallots, fried garlic and chilli, crisply fried salted fish, fermented black beans, chicken cooked in soy sauce, fried peanuts, soy sauce and oriental sesame oil. Accompaniments are added in very modest amounts, since congee is the main event and anything else is simply a seasoning.

Congee

Makes 2 meal-sized portions, or 4 breakfast bowls.

3 tablespoons short or medium grain rice
1 litre/2 pints/4 cups water

Put rice and water into a saucepan, bring quickly to the boil.

Stir, then reduce heat but allow rice to remain at a brisk simmer. Place lid on pan, leaving it slightly open so the congee doesn't bubble up and spill over. In 45–50 minutes the congee should be ready.

A popular addition is thin slices of fresh white fish, which are dropped into individual bowls just before the boiling congee is ladled in. Small bowls of sliced spring onions, fresh chillies and chopped fresh coriander are also offered.

Note: A quick way to make congee is to use leftover cooked white rice, add water or stock to cover and simmer about 15 minutes or until it is a gruel.

Conpoy

Pinyin for gan bei, the Chinese name for a type of scallop. These very expensive molluscs are cut from a type of sea scallop, dried and sold in Chinese herbal shops. They require long soaking and steaming before they are ready to be eaten. A humble congee is elevated by adding 2–3 dried 'scallops' which improves the flavour no end.

Purchasing and storing: The large ones have better flavour. Purchase from a shop which has good turnover. They will keep indefinitely in an airtight glass jar, but you don't want to buy any which are too ancient.

Preparation: Soak 4 dried scallops in enough warm water to cover and steam 30 minutes or until soft. Pull apart into shreds, add to 2 cups cooked rice and 4 cups chicken stock together with the soaking liquid, and simmer with 4 slices fresh ginger until the rice becomes a porridge. Discard ginger. Stir in a few drops of sesame oil, season congee with salt and white pepper, and serve hot, sprinkled with chopped spring onions (scallions). Serves 4.

Coriander Herb

(*Coriandrum sativum*) SEE ILLUSTRATION. Also known as cilantro.

If ever there was an essential herb (in its fresh green state) and an omnipresent spice (when the seeds are dried and ground) this is it. Indigenous to the Mediterranean and southern Europe, it has been used for a very long time by the Egyptians and the Israelites before the Exodus.

All parts of the plant are used, even the roots which are an essential in Thai cooking. Pounded with garlic and peppercorns, they give Thai food its typical flavour. In red curry pastes, it is the coriander root which contributes its flavour without adding an undesirable green colour to the mixture. In Indian cooking the fresh herb is thrown liberally into and onto almost every dish. Strangely enough, it is not very popular in Sri Lanka. Some good cooks of Sri Lanka turn up their noses at it, saying it smells like garden bugs. (In fact, its name comes from the Greek koris, meaning 'bug'.) It is used throughout Asia.

Purchasing and storing: Buy coriander herb fresh. Dried, bottled or frozen coriander herb is not as good. If storing it, place the roots in no more than 1 cm (½in) of water in a container of suitable size. Put a supermarket carry bag over the bunch, tie the handles together around the container to create a little greenhouse, and store it in the refrigerator. Do not wash coriander before putting it away and it will keep for two weeks at least.

Preparation: To use, remove only just what you will need, and store the rest. Wash the coriander herb shortly before using and if there are more roots than you need for one recipe, they may be frozen for making Thai curry pastes. Do not chop coriander too finely as it will darken and lose its fresh colour.

Medicinal uses: Its use was recorded around 1550 BC for medicinal as well as culinary purposes, as a tonic, cough medicine and stomachic.

Burma: *nannambin*
China: *yuen sai*
India: *dhania pattar, hara dhania*
Indonesia: *daun ketumbar*
Malaysia: *daun ketumbar*
Philipinnes: *ketumbar*
Sri Lanka: *kothamalli kolle*
Thailand: *pak chee*
Vietnam: *ngo*

Coriander Seed

Coriander seed, with its clean, lemony flavour, is the major component of almost every 'curry powder' or spice mixture used in Indian, Sri Lankan, Indonesian and Malaysian, as well as other curries. The flavour of freshly ground coriander is a world apart from that of ground coriander which has lost its fragrance.

Purchasing and storing: Coriander seed is usually sold in plastic packets. Buy only what you will use in a reasonable time, since storing it for too long may result in weevil attack. If it looks dirty wash it in a few changes of water, drain well, then spread on a baking sheet and dry out in the sun or in a slow oven until quite dry. Transfer to airtight jars in a cupboard until required. See also SPICE BLENDS.

Preparation: To bring out the flavour coriander seeds should be gently dry-roasted before grinding, and it is best to grind it in small quantities so it is always fresh.

Medicinal uses: The seed is considered a mild sedative, is also supposed to aid digestion, reduce flatulence and ease migraines. I know for a fact that it is used to help the stuffiness of colds. Many's the time I have bent over a pot of coriander, a towel draped over my head to ensure the steam did not escape, while mother or aunt exhorted me to breathe deeply of the vapours. Cups of Coriander and Ginger Brew, sweetened with sugar, are given to cold and flu sufferers (see recipe below).

Burma: *nannamzee*
India: *dhania*
Indonesia: *ketumbar*
Malaysia: *ketumbar*
Sri Lanka: *kothamalli*
Thailand: *luk pak chee*

Coriander and Ginger Brew

You won't need all this coriander at once, but it saves time if a quantity is well washed, drained and completely dried, either in the sun or in a low oven. Cool and store in an airtight container.

250 g/4 oz coriander seeds
5 cm/2in piece fresh ginger root

Roast 3 tablespoons of the cleaned coriander seeds in a dry saucepan, stirring until the seeds smell fragrant. Add 2 cups water. Peel and slice the ginger, add to pan, cover and simmer for 15 minutes. Strain into a cup, sweeten to taste and drink while very hot. Ideally, one should then go to bed all rugged up and sweat it out.

Coriander Cold Relief

For relieving nasal stuffiness, the steam from boiling coriander seeds is used as an inhalation. Turn off the heat, lean over the pan (not too close) and drape a towel over both head and pan to funnel the steam in the right direction. Breath the vapours for a couple of minutes.

Thai Pepper-Coriander Paste

Very useful to have on hand if you like Thai cooking, because it combines the most basic of Thai flavours: coriander, pepper and garlic. It will keep well in a glass jar in the refrigerator providing a clean dry spoon is used each time.

2 bunches fresh coriander
2 tablespoons chopped garlic
1 tablespoon salt
3 tablespoons whole black peppercorns
4 tablespoons lemon juice

Wash coriander in several changes of cold water, swishing it around until all the soil has been dislodged. Scrub the roots well with a small brush and shake off as much moisture as possible, then pat dry in a tea towel. Chop coarsely and measure 2 cups firmly packed coriander, including the roots. Finely chop the measured coriander, or pound with a mortar and pestle. Crush garlic with salt to a smooth paste. Roast the peppercorns in a dry pan for 1–2 minutes, then coarsely crush using a mortar and pestle. Mix all the ingredients together.

Another method is to use an electric blender, but in this case reduce peppercorns by half, as they deliver more heat when finely ground. Store the paste in an airtight glass jar in the refrigerator.

Coriander Chicken

Rub 3 tablespoons pepper-coriander paste (recipe above) liberally over a jointed chicken, cover and leave for 1 hour. Heat 2 tablespoons oil in a pan and lightly cook the chicken, turning over with tongs. Add 375 ml (13 fl oz) coconut milk and simmer until chicken is tender. Add extra 30 g (1 oz) of finely chopped fresh coriander and, if liked, a finely chopped seeded green chilli just before serving.

Corn

(*Zea mays*) Also known as maize. Native to the New World but now grown throughout the world.

In India it is used as a cereal, ground into fine flour which is incorporated in flat breads or rotis which are the staple food when rice is not. They are usually made from wheat, but occasionally cornmeal is used. See recipe for Cornmeal Roti (page 52).

In South East Asia corn is rarely used ground, but ears of sweet corn are boiled in salted water and sold as a snack. Or the kernels are popped and sold, also as a snack. In Japan, dainty little snacks are made from it, akin to corn chips but crisper in texture and sweeter. Kernels of mature sweet corn are used in sweet snacks in Vietnam and Thailand. A well-known Chinese corn recipe is Crab and Sweet Corn Soup (recipe below).

In Korea, corn kernels are roasted and sold in packets, to be infused and drunk like tea.

Purchasing and storing: When purchasing corn on the cob, make sure it is young and fresh. The kernels should be plump and shiny, their skins stretched taut. If they look dull and shrunken, leave them on the shelf. While they will keep in the refrigerator for a day or two, the fresher the better, as time turns the natural sugar to starch.

Crab and Sweet Corn Soup

Serves 6

3 ears fresh tender corn
 or 400 g/14 oz can cream style corn
1.5 litres/3 pints/6 cups chicken stock
2 tablespoons cornflour (cornstarch)
250 g/8 oz crab meat, fresh or frozen
3 tablespoons Chinese wine or dry sherry
1 tablespoon oyster sauce or light soy sauce
salt and white pepper
1 tablespoon finely chopped spring onions
 (scallions)
2 tablespoons chopped fresh coriander

With a sharp knife, slice off the tops of the corn niblets and use a spoon to scrape out the creamy, sweet juice from the kernels. Combine corn with the chicken stock and simmer for 10 minutes. Mix cornflour with a little cold water and stir into the stock until it boils and thickens. Meanwhile flake the crab meat, discarding any bits of bony tissue. Add to soup with wine, soy sauce, seasonings, spring onions and chopped coriander and heat through. Cover pan, leave for 2 minutes, then serve.

Spinach and Corn Bhaji

1 bunch spinach
2 ears tender sweet corn
1 tablespoon ghee
1 tablespoon oil
1 clove garlic, finely chopped
1 teaspoons finely chopped fresh ginger
1 teaspoon cumin seeds
1 teaspoon black mustard seeds
½ teaspoon nigella seeds
1 teaspoon salt or to taste

Wash spinach well, discard stems and steam the leaves for about 7 minutes. (1 small bunch English spinach will yield about 200 g [7 oz] cooked spinach.) Drain and chop the spinach. Slice niblets from the ears of corn, and scrape the milky portion from the cob.

In a wok or karhai heat the ghee and oil and gently fry garlic and ginger till golden. Add the various seeds and fry until they crackle and pop, then add spinach and corn, salt to taste and cook, covered, for 3 or 4 minutes. Serve with chapatis or cornmeal rotis.

Corn, Miniature

(*Zea mays* var. *rugosa*) Tiny ears of corn just about the size of a finger, are becoming available fresh in Western greengrocer shops or markets. They live up to their name, being tender and sweet, though lacking the corn flavour of larger varieties. Canned mini-corn (baby corn) is a popular ingredient in stir-fried or braised dishes. If using canned corn, simply drain the liquid and add corn during last moments of cooking. If using fresh mini-corn, they will need a few extra minutes cooking.

Purchasing and storing: Miniature corn cobs are usually packed in small plastic trays and covered with plastic wrap. They should be a pale creamy yellow, not brown or withered. If they must be kept for a day or two, store them, still in their covered tray, in the vegetable bin of the refrigerator.

Preparation: Since they are usually sold with husks and silk removed, there is not much preparation needed. Simply rinse the cobs and cut into bite-sized pieces for adding to simmered dishes, or leave them whole to use as the base for little appetisers. I use them as an edible skewer, moulding a small amount of seasoned pork or prawn paste around each and steaming for 10 minutes.

Cornstarch

See FLOURS & STARCHES (Cornflour).

Cowpea

See LEGUMES & PULSES (Yard-long bean).

Crabs

(*Portunidae* spp.) There are many types of crab eaten and enjoyed throughout Asia and the Pacific, and I enjoyed all those I tasted, except for the tiny pickled black crabs which may be included in som

tam (Thai green papaya salad) unless one specifically asks that they be omitted.

A delicate and rich crab is the coconut crab of the Pacific. On the tiny island of Santos I met Lulu, a French woman who ran a restaurant and whose fame had spread to the bigger islands. She invited me to taste not only the crab, but what she called 'crab delice', the fatty material the creature collected in its stomach, which tastes very like rich coconut cream since coconuts are its main food. It seems that it can climb the tall palms and collect its dinner, and even the hard shell of the coconut is no barrier to the powerful pincer claws.

Crabs are plentiful in the waterways of many Asian lands, and are treated quite casually as a food source unless they are the large and expensive varieties. Many of them are of the family Portunidae, including the blue swimmer (*Portunida pelagicus*) and spotted crabs (*P. sanguinolentus*) and the mangrove crab or serrated crab, commonly known as mud crab (*Scylla serrata*), arguably the most prized, expensive and delicious of all. The female crabs were highly regarded because they carry a rich orange-coloured roe. Conservation consciousness has now caused the females to be protected in some places, only until their eggs are ripe, while in others their capture at any time is illegal.

One of our family favourites is crab curry made in the Sri Lankan manner and I have memories of partaking of meals where the crabs were almost the size of dinner plates, and it was a special occasion treat. Only plain white rice was served with the hot crab curry, to better appreciate the rich yet delicate flavour. No side dishes, no distractions. We needed to concentrate on extracting the sweet flesh from claws and body. On these occasions, in addition to the large dinner plates, spoons and forks with which the table was laid, there was something extra — a heavy wooden board and business-like hammer placed at the end of the table. These were passed around to each person in turn to crack open the thick-shelled claws.

As this operation proceeded, everyone else at the table who might be in the line of fire held up their large damask serviettes as a screen — for even a drop of flying crab curry could do terrible damage if it landed in someone's eye, the chilli content being considerable. A crab curry meal was relaxed, informal and quite a hilarious occasion. Even the youngest member of the family (and that was me) was excused from being prim and proper. There was much laughter as we sheltered behind the table linen and noisy enjoyment as we ate the sweet, fresh crab meat swimming in its flavoursome, fiery, coconut milk sauce and sucked recalcitrant bits of meat from legs and claws.

I have eaten Dungeness crabs in Vancouver, cooked Singapore style. They are excellent and would lend themselves to any of the recipes featured below. So, I am sure, would the crabs of the Pacific region, whether coconut crabs, spanner crabs or the common blue swimmer crabs.

Prepare the curry gravy as directed, then cook the crabs in the spicy sauce for 20–25 minutes.

Purchasing and preparing crabs: The best varieties to use are large and heavy mud crabs or Dungeness crabs. Blue swimmers or other smaller crabs may be used too, but there is less flesh when the crabs are small. Choose them alive and lively, and heavy for their size which means they are full-fleshed. Watch out for those nippers: they mean business, though they are usually immobilised with small wooden wedges.

Dispatch the crabs with all possible speed, as freshness is the key. But first do the humane thing by putting the paper-wrapped crabs in the freezer where they go off to a cold-induced sleep in about an hour. Then prepare them for the recipe. In Asian cooking this means removing the carapace, removing and discarding the feathery tissue known as 'dead men's fingers' then, with a chopper, cutting the body in two, leaving legs and large claws attached to each half. Sometimes, the cold makes the crabs throw off their large claws. If the shell is mossy, scrub with a brush. Cracking the shells of the claws before cooking allows more flavour to penetrate.

The alternative is to put the crustacean into cold salted water and gradually raise the temperature to boiling, the theory being that it gradually loses consciousness. This method, however, at least partially cooks the crab, and in some recipes it is necessary to start with raw crabs for best flavour.

Burma: *lamu-ga-nan*
China: *chang haai*
Indonesia: *kepiting*
Malaysia: *kepiting* (blue swimmer),
  ketam batu (mangrove or mud crab)
Philippines: *alimangong, alimasag*
Sri Lanka: *kakuluwo*
Thailand: *thaleh*
Vietnam: *con cua lu*a

Sri Lankan Crab Curry

Serves 4

2 mud crabs
  or 4 blue swimmer or spanner crabs
3 tablespoons oil
2 large onions, finely chopped
2 tablespoons finely chopped garlic
1 tablespoon finely grated ginger
sprig of fresh curry leaves
½ teaspoon fenugreek seeds
1 stick cinnamon
2 teaspoons chilli powder or to taste
1 teaspoon ground turmeric
3 teaspoons salt
2 × 400 ml/14 fl oz cans coconut milk
2 cups drumstick leaves (optional)
3 tablespoons grated coconut
  or desiccated coconut
1 tablespoon ground rice
lime juice to taste

Clean crabs according to first method described above. Divide each large crab into four portions, or smaller crabs into 2. Leave legs attached to body.

In a large saucepan heat oil and gently fry onions, stirring from time to time, until it is soft and transparent. Add garlic, ginger, curry leaves and fry for a few minutes longer, stirring. Add, all at once, the fenugreek seeds, cinnamon, chilli, turmeric, salt and 1 can of coconut milk made up to 1 litre (2 pints) with water. Stir while bringing to a simmer. Cover and simmer gently for 30 minutes. Add crabs and drumstick leaves and cook for a further 20 minutes. Stir from time to time to ensure all the pieces of crab get a turn at cooking submerged in sauce.

In a dry frying pan toast the coconut until golden brown, stirring constantly. Turn out on a plate to cool. Roast the ground rice too in the same way until pale golden. Put both into an electric blender. Add half the second can of coconut milk and blend on high speed for 1 minute. Stir into simmering curry. Wash out blender with remaining coconut milk, add to pan and simmer uncovered for 10 minutes. Turn off heat, stir in lime juice and serve with boiled white rice.

Singapore Chilli Crab

Serves 2–4

2 medium-sized raw crabs
125 ml/4 fl oz/½ cup peanut oil
2 teaspoons finely grated fresh ginger
1 teaspoon finely chopped garlic
3 fresh red chillies, seeded and chopped
3 tablespoons tomato ketchup
3 tablespoons hot chilli sauce
1 tablespoon sugar
1 tablespoon light soy sauce
1 teaspoon salt

Scrub away any mossy patches on the crabs. Remove hard top shell, stomach bag and fibrous tissue. Chop each crab in 2 or 4, depending on size.

Heat a wok and add oil. When hot fry the crab pieces until they change colour, turning them so they cook on all sides. Remove to a plate. Turn heat low and fry the ginger, garlic and chillies, stirring constantly, until they are soft and smell fragrant but do not let them brown. Add the tomato ketchup, chilli sauce, sugar, soy sauce and salt. Bring to the boil, then return crabs to the wok and simmer in the sauce for 3 minutes. If sauce reduces too much add a very little water. Serve with rice.

Crab in Black Bean Sauce

Serves 2

1 large mud crab
  or 2 smaller crabs
1 tablespoon canned salted black beans
1 teaspoon crushed garlic
1 teaspoon sugar
1 tablespoon light soy sauce
4 tablespoons peanut oil
2 cloves garlic, halved
4 slices fresh ginger
185 ml/6 fl oz/¾ cup hot water
3 teaspoons cornflour (cornstarch)
2 tablespoons cold water
2 spring onions (scallions), finely chopped
1 egg, slightly beaten

Clean the raw crabs as described above. Chop body of crab into 4 or 6 pieces, leaving legs attached. Separate large claws from body and crack shells to allow sauce to penetrate.

Rinse black beans in cold water, drain and mash. Mix with garlic crushed with sugar, and the soy sauce.

Heat oil in a wok and fry the halved garlic cloves and slices of ginger until they start to brown. Remove from pan. Over high heat fry the pieces of crab, turning them over in the hot oil for 5 minutes or until shells are bright red. Remove crab pieces from pan. Add black bean mixture to the oil, fry for 1 minute, then pour in hot water and crab pieces. Stir well, cover pan and cook for 3 minutes. Mix cornflour with a little cold water and stir into sauce until it boils and thickens. Add spring onions and dribble in the egg until egg sets. Serve at once with steamed white rice.

Steamed Crab with Ginger

Serves 2

1 large mud crab
  or 2 smaller crabs
3 tablespoons peanut oil
1 teaspoon finely chopped garlic
2 tablespoons fine shreds of fresh ginger
2 tablespoons light soy sauce
2 tablespoons Chinese wine or dry sherry
3 tablespoons water
2 spring onions (scallions), finely sliced

Prepare crabs as described above. Cut in halves or quarters, leaving legs attached to body. Heat oil in a wok and on low heat fry the garlic and ginger for a minute. Add crab pieces and stir-fry for 3 or 4 minutes. Add all the liquid at once, cover wok with lid and allow to steam for 10 minutes or until the crabs are cooked and turn red. Scatter spring onions over and serve with rice.

Pepper and Salt Crab

Serves 2

1 large or 2 medium crabs
60 g/2 oz/½ cup plain (all-purpose) flour
1½ teaspoons salt
1½ teaspoons freshly ground black pepper
2 teaspoons caster sugar (superfine sugar)
oil for deep frying

Prepare crabs as described above, cutting each into 2 pieces. Combine flour with salt, pepper and sugar, and roll each piece of crab in the mixture, then dust off excess. Heat oil until very hot, drop crab pieces in and fry until the crab turns red and is cooked, about 8 minutes. Drain and serve. Eat with fingers for best enjoyment.

Crab and Egg Soup

Serves 4

1 large or 2 medium crabs, cooked
1 litre/2 pints/4 cups chicken stock
salt and white pepper to taste
3 eggs
2 tablespoons cornflour (cornstarch)
4 spring onions (scallions), finely sliced
1 teaspoon oriental sesame oil

Pick out meat from crabs, discarding any bony or fibrous tissue. Bring stock to the boil, season with salt and pepper. Beat eggs slightly and dribble slowly into soup. Stir very slowly so that egg sets in large shreds. Mix cornflour with about 3 tablespoons cold water and stir into soup until clear and thickened. Stir in crab meat and spring onions and heat through. Add sesame oil and serve immediately.

Malaccan Black-Pepper Crab

Unusual in an Asian recipe, the butter reflects the Portuguese influence in Malacca. Serves 4.

2 large, fresh mud crabs
peanut oil for deep frying
4 spring onions (scallions), sliced
1 tablespoon fine shreds of fresh ginger
2 teaspoons finely chopped garlic
sprig of fresh curry leaves
2 tablespoons coarsely cracked black peppercorns
2 tablespoons canned, salted black beans rinsed, drained and chopped
2 tablespoons kecap manis (sweet black soy sauce)
2 teaspoons sugar
3 tablespoons boiling water
2 tablespoons butter
1 or 2 hot chillies, sliced (optional)

Clean the raw crabs and prepare as described on page 109. With a heavy chopper, cut each crab body in two. Detach the large claws and crack them to allow flavours to penetrate.

Heat peanut oil in a wok and when very hot add the crabs and fry, turning them in the oil, until the shells turn red and the crabs are half cooked. Lift out on a slotted spoon and set aside in a dish. Pour away all but about 3 tablespoons of oil and return wok to heat. Fry the spring onions, ginger, garlic and curry leaves, stirring, over gentle heat, taking care the garlic does not burn. Add the black pepper and stir-fry for only a few seconds, then quickly add the black beans, soy sauce, sugar and boiling water, return crabs to the wok, stir to coat with the mixture, and cover with lid. Allow to steam for 10–15 minutes, checking to ensure that sauce does not burn and adding a little water if necessary.

Just before serving, add the butter and chillies if used, toss to distribute melted butter over the crabs, and serve accompanied only by bowls of steaming hot white rice.

South Pacific Crabs with Mayonnaise

Serve the boiled crabs at room temperature or chilled, accompanied by a good mayonnaise and with claw crackers and slender pointed crab forks to enable diners to extract every bit of meat from the shells. This is then dipped in the mayonnaise or after a small pile of crab meat has been extracted, it is mixed with the dressing. Simplicity itself, and the sweet flavour of the crabs is given pride of place, especially if they happen to be coconut crabs.

Cream

In most Asian countries, cream is not an item encountered in the local food. If used at all it comes out of a can. The exception is India, where milk and milk products are widely used and provide nourishment and protein for a largely vegetarian population.

Malai (Indian cream) is quite different to separated cream sold in the West. The nearest thing to it is clotted cream usually associated with Devon in England, or the similar product known as ashtar in Lebanon. (I mention this so that if you have a delicatessen near you selling clotted cream, or a Lebanese pastry shop willing to part with some of their precious ashtar, you can save yourself time and effort.)

Indian Cream (Malai)

Combine 300 ml (10 fl oz) cream and 500 ml (1 pint) milk. In a large, shallow pan stir over medium heat until almost to boiling point, then reduce heat to a slow simmer, stop stirring and allow a fan to play on the surface of the milk to hasten formation of a thick layer of cream. When cool, carefully remove cream to a saucer and repeat the process until the last of the milk is a thick layer in the bottom of the pan. This may be scraped up and added to the rest. This clotted cream is used in sweetmeats and the famous ice cream, Kulfi (see recipe, page 182).

Cucumber

(*Cucumis sativus*) There are many different types, shapes and sizes of cucumber, mostly interchangeable in recipes, bearing in mind some common-sense rules. If they have well-developed seeds and thick skin, these should be removed. If the skin is thin and seeds barely there at all, use the whole fruit. This applies to most cucumber recipes which are salad type accompaniments.

In Japan, the cucumbers are more like Middle Eastern varieties, thin skinned, almost seedless, small — about 2.5 cm (1 in) in diameter.

In China tough cucumber skins are cut into long, fine shreds and preserved in ginger-flavoured syrup. These are sometimes added to savoury dishes for flavour contrast and garnish.

China: *huang-kwa*
India: *khira, kakri*
Indonesia: *ketimun*
Japan: *kyuuri, morokyu*
Malaysia: *timun*
Philippines: *pepino*
Sri Lanka: *pipinya*
Thailand: *taeng-kwa*

Cucumber Sambal

1 large or 2 small seedless cucumbers
1 teaspoon salt
125 ml/4 fl oz/½ cup thick coconut milk
1 fresh red chilli
1 fresh green chilli
1 small red onion, sliced paper thin
2 tablespoons lime or lemon juice

Peel cucumber if skin is thick, otherwise wash and dry the cucumber and slice very thinly. Put into a bowl, sprinkle with salt and leave for 15 minutes. Press out all the liquid and rinse once with cold water. Drain well. Mix with remaining ingredients and serve as a side dish with a curry meal.

Cucumber Raita

Whether made with natural yoghurt only, or a mixture of yoghurt and sour cream, this is a cooling accompaniment to a curry meal.

2 green seedless cucumbers
1 teaspoon salt
2 spring onions (scallions), finely chopped
375 ml/12 fl oz/1½ cups thick natural yoghurt
lime or lemon juice to taste
1½ teaspoons cumin seeds
2 tablespoons chopped fresh coriander or mint

Peel the cucumbers, or run the tines of a fork down the length of them to give a decorative effect on the skin. Cut into small dice, sprinkle with salt and leave for 15 minutes then drain away liquid and rinse the cucumbers quickly in cold water. Drain well. Combine with onion, yoghurt, lime juice and check whether more salt is required. Roast the cumin seeds in a dry pan until brown. Bruise or crush seeds and sprinkle over yoghurt. Serve chilled.

Burmese Cucumber Relish

2 large green cucumbers
125 ml/4 fl oz/½ cup malt vinegar
500 ml/1 pint/2 cups water
1 teaspoon salt
3 tablespoons peanut oil
2 tablespoons oriental sesame oil
2 teaspoons instant minced garlic,
   or 2 tablespoons sliced garlic
1 onion, finely sliced
   or 2 tablespoons crisp fried shallots
2 tablespoons sesame seeds

Peel cucumbers, halve lengthways and scoop out any seeds. Cut the cucumbers into thick strips, then cut strips into 5 cm (2 in) pieces. Bring vinegar, water and salt to the boil in a non-aluminium saucepan and drop in the cucumbers to cook briefly, keeping them crisp.

Drain and leave to cool.

Heat peanut and sesame oils and fry the garlic on low heat until pale golden. Drain. Fry onion until golden brown if using raw onion. Roast the sesame seeds in a dry frying pan, stirring constantly, until they are evenly golden brown. Turn onto a plate to cool. When the oil is cold, dress the cucumbers with 3 table-spoons of the oil, mixing well. Put into a small dish and top with the onion, garlic and sesame seeds.

Cumin

(*Cuminum cyminum*) SEE ILLUSTRATION. Whether spelled cumin or cummin, it is always pronounced with the 'u' as it 'hut'. Every dictionary I ever consulted says so, yet one hears it pronounced with the 'u' as in 'put' or even as in 'cube'. (A bit of a pedant I may be, but let's get it straight once and for all.)

Cumin is one of the most important spice seeds in Indian cooking, indeed it is used throughout Asia in the spice blends which are sprinkled over savouries, or cooked in the sauces called curries. Not to be confused with caraway, which looks similar, but has quite a different flavour. Cumin is used in almost every spice mixture in ground form except in panch phora where the whole seeds are used. In addition, there are some recipes where it is the predominant flavour. For example, zeera pani (or jeera pani), a refreshing drink served as an appetiser or as a digestive. See recipe for Cumin and Tamarind Refresher below.

Besides the pale brown seeds which are so familiar, there are several other kinds of cumin. There is a light green, more acutely curved seed known as Lucknow cumin and the fine, slender seed of shah zeera or royal cumin is darker in colour and therefore also referred to as black cumin or kala zeera. (More information on this vexed subject may be found in the entry for CUMIN, BLACK.)

Roasting cumin brings out different nuances of flavour and it is worth having a separate jar of roasted cumin to be crushed coarsely and sprinkled over a variety of dishes for extra flavour. One of the simplest yet most effective ways of using roasted cumin is to crush it just before sprinkling over banana slices in yoghurt to serve as an accompaniment.

Medicinal uses: Cumin is a digestive and carminative, two good reasons to keep this fragrant spice well represented in everyday food.

China: *ma-ch'in*
India: *jeera, zeera, safed zeera*
Indonesia: *jinten*
Japan: *kumin*
Malaysia: *jintan puteh*
Sri Lanka: *sududuru*
Thailand: *yeera*

Cumin and Tamarind Refresher

The Indian name for this drink, zeera pani, translates as 'cumin water'.

125 g/4 oz/½ cup dried tamarind pulp
500 ml/1 pint/2 cups hot water
3 teaspoons finely grated fresh ginger
3 teaspoons ground cumin
pinch chilli powder (optional)
½ teaspoon garam masala (recipe page 354)
1 tablespoon sugar or to taste
salt to taste
iced water
crushed ice
mint sprigs
lime slices

Soak tamarind pulp in the hot water and leave until cold. Squeeze to dissolve the pulp and separate the seeds. Strain through a nylon sieve. Add remaining ingredients, stir well, then strain again through fine sieve or muslin. Chill. At serving time dilute with iced water, and pour over crushed ice. Decorate each glass with a sprig of mint and slice of lime.

Cumin, Black

SEE ILLUSTRATION. There are two totally different spices which share the name. True black cumin is Umbelliferae, as is cumin. Because its seeds are smaller and darker in appearance than the more commonly encountered safed zeera (white cumin), it has been called shah zeera (royal cumin) and kala zeera (black cumin) even though it is not, strictly speaking, black but rather a rich coffee brown. But then, so-called white cumin is fawny brown.

Then comes the pretender to the throne, *Nigella sativa*, also known as kala zeera (black cumin) or kalonji. Admittedly, its dull seeds, shaped like tiny, angular sesame seeds, are truly jet black; but as for resembling cumin — not by any stretch. Even the flavour is quite unrelated. For more detail on both contenders see CUMIN and NIGELLA.

Curry

There are so many misconceptions about curry that I don't quite know where to start to set the record straight. First of all we should establish what it is not. Curry is not a single spice, not even a blend of various spices, though the word is used loosely to describe spice blends used to flavour many different dishes.

In the strictest sense, the word implies a dish with a fairly liquid consistency since 'curry' comes from the Tamil word karhi meaning 'sauce'.

Curry is not necessarily hot, in fact there are curries which use no pungent flavours at all. And every spiced dish is not a curry.

There are many spicy dishes which are loosely referred to as 'dry curries', 'fried curries', 'Moslem curries', 'white curries' or 'Thai curries' which would be more correctly named bhaji, badung, korma, sayur or gaeng. These terms change according to the language spoken in each country. To the Western curry enthusiast, however, they are all curries because they are flavoured with spices.

Recipes for curries appear under their main ingredient and are listed in the Index of Recipes.

See SPICE BLENDS for formulae to make curry powders or masalas from different countries. See also CURRY PASTES.

Buttermilk Sauce (Karhi)

Here is a recipe for Indian karhi for flavouring and moistening the staple food, rice.

600 ml/20 fl oz/2½ cups buttermilk
1 teaspoon ground turmeric
1 teaspoon sugar
1 teaspoon salt
30 g/1 oz/½ cup chopped fresh coriander
2 finely chopped green chillies, seeds removed
2 tablespoons besan (chick pea flour)
125 ml/4 fl oz/½ cup cold water
1 tablespoon ghee or oil
1 teaspoon cumin seeds
1 teaspoon black mustard seeds
2 dried red chillies
½ teaspoon powdered asafoetida (optional)

In a saucepan heat buttermilk with turmeric, sugar, salt, coriander and chillies, stirring now and then.

Mix the besan with cold water until smooth, stir into the buttermilk and cook for 5 minutes, stirring constantly. Mixture will thicken.

In a small pan heat ghee or oil. Fry the cumin and mustard seeds and the dried chillies broken into pieces with seeds shaken out. When the mustard seeds start to pop, add the asafoetida and stir quickly into the buttermilk. Serve with rice, or as a soup.

Curry Leaf

(*Murraya koenigii*) SEE ILLUSTRATION. Curry leaves are as important to Asian food as bay leaves are to European food, but never try to substitute one for the other. Curry leaves, either fresh or dried, are usually the first ingredient added to the small amount of oil in which a dish is to be cooked, and the fragrance and flavour are unmistakable.

A number of small, shiny, pointed leaflets grow closely along a central stem, and it is customary to toss the whole stem in. A word of warning. When added to hot oil, fresh curry leaves cause much hissing and spattering, so stand back. Dried curry leaves are more sedate, not causing the oil to erupt, but be ready with the next addition to the pan, as they burn easily. While the flavour of dried leaves is not as strong, they still make a contribution and are probably easier to find in Western countries.

Mostly used in South India, Sri Lanka, Malaysia and Fiji, where Indian migrants have taken the plant. The tree is native to the sub-tropical forests of Asia, but we have successfully grown our own supply of curry leaves in a temperate zone garden and so have many others. Look for young plants in pots in some Asian stores, especially those which specialise in Indian ingredients. If you attempt to buy a curry plant in a Western plant nursery, you will probably end up with the herb which goes by the name of 'curry plant' (*Helichrysum italicum*) but which does not taste even remotely like *Murraya koenigii*.

If fresh curry leaves are pulverised in a blender, they make an outstanding contribution to a coconut chatni (see recipe for Coconut Chatni, page 73). Chopped tender leaves are delicious in an omelette or scrambled eggs.

Purchasing and Storing: Fresh curry leaves are usually found in Indian shops, in plastic bags in the refrigerator. They keep very well, but if not using the whole amount within a couple of weeks, dry them gently in a very low oven or in a dehydrator. Dried curry leaves keep indefinitely in an airtight container, but the fresher they are, the better the flavour will be. Dried curry leaves are pulverised and added to certain spice mixtures. See SPICE BLENDS (recipes for Milagai Podi and Indian Curry Powder).

Burma: *pyi-naw-thein*
India: *meetha neem, karipattar, karuvepillay*
Malaysia: *daun kari, karupillay*
Sri Lanka: *karapincha*

Curry Pastes

If you want to know exactly what goes into your cooking, or you just appreciate the superior flavour of home-made curry pastes over their commercial counterparts, you can make a batch of pastes you use frequently and store them in the refrigerator. It saves so much time not to have to make the curry paste each time you cook.

Use very clean, dry jars to store the pastes (coffee jars with glass stoppers are ideal) and use only a clean, dry spoon each time you take some out. With careful handling they keep perfectly well in the refrigerator for up to 4 months.

In Thailand, like many other Asian countries, the colour of the curry is indicative of the flavour which may be expected, though opinions are divided on whether a yellow curry (the colour comes mainly from turmeric) should be mild or hot.

Depending on the type of chillies used for a paste, it may not always be possible to predict the outcome. The smallest chillies are the hottest, so use discretion and err on the side of caution.

Thai Yellow Curry Paste

8 cm/3 in fresh turmeric root
1 large onion or 5 shallots, finely chopped
3 tablespoons chopped galangal
3 tablespoons chopped fresh coriander roots
3 tablespoons chopped garlic
3 tablespoons sliced lemon grass
3 tablespoons chopped fresh yellow or red chillies or 12 dried red chillies, soaked in hot water for 10 minutes
3 tablespoons lime juice
1 tablespoon ground coriander
3 teaspoons ground cumin
½ teaspoon black peppercorns
2 teaspoons dried shrimp paste
2 teaspoons salt
125 ml/4 fl oz/½ cup peanut oil

Scrape any tough skin off the turmeric root and chop it roughly. There should be about 4 tablespoons. Put into blender container with onion, galangal, coriander roots (well washed), garlic and lemon grass.

Adjust number of chillies according to how hot they are and the desired result. Using gloves, discard seeds and central membrane for less heat and roughly chop the chillies.

Add chillies, and if dried chillies are used, some of the water in which they soaked. Add lime juice and blend to a purée. Add coriander, cumin, peppercorns, shrimp paste and salt to blended mixture.

Heat oil in a wok and on low heat fry the paste, stirring constantly, for 5 minutes or until fragrant. Allow to cool. Bottle and store in the refrigerator.

Thai Red Curry Paste

6 large dried red chillies
2 small brown onions, chopped
2 tablespoons washed and chopped coriander root
1 tablespoon chopped garlic
1 tablespoon chopped galangal in brine
1 tablespoon ground coriander
2 teaspoons ground cumin
2 teaspoons dried shrimp paste
2 teaspoons paprika
1 teaspoon salt
1 teaspoon black peppercorns
1 teaspoon turmeric
1 stem lemon grass, finely sliced or 2 teaspoons chopped lemon rind

Remove stems of chillies and shake out the seeds if you don't want the curry paste to be too hot. Soak chillies in enough hot water to cover for 10 minutes, then place in an electric blender with remaining ingredients. Putting the chillies and onions in first will facilitate blending. Puree, stopping frequently to push ingredients down with a spatula. Add a little extra water if necessary to assist with blending.

Thai Green Curry Paste

Depending on the variety of chilli used, this paste can range from mild to mind-blowing.

8 fresh green chillies
2 medium onions, chopped
6 tablespoons chopped fresh coriander roots, stems and leaves
3 tablespoons finely sliced lemon grass
1 tablespoon chopped garlic
1 tablespoon chopped galangal in brine
2 teaspoons ground coriander
1 teaspoon ground cumin
1 teaspoon black peppercorns
1 teaspoon ground turmeric
1 teaspoon dried shrimp paste

Roughly chop chillies and put into an electric blender with remaining ingredients. Process until puréed, adding a little water if necessary.

Thai Masaman Curry Paste

10 large dried red chillies
2 tablespoons oil
2 small brown onions, chopped
1 tablespoon chopped garlic
2 teaspoons dried shrimp paste
2 tablespoons washed and chopped coriander root
1 tablespoon chopped galangal in brine
1 tablespoon chopped krachai in brine
2 stems lemon grass, finely sliced or 3 teaspoons chopped lemon rind
2 tablespoons ground coriander
1 tablespoon ground cumin
2 teaspoons ground fennel
1 teaspoon ground cinnamon
1 teaspoon ground cardamom
1 teaspoon ground mace or nutmeg
½ teaspoon ground cloves
1 teaspoon salt

Snip off chilli stems and shake out seeds if not too much heat is required. Soak the chillies in hot water for 15 minutes. Heat oil and on low heat fry the onions and garlic until pale golden. Add shrimp paste and fry a little longer. Allow to cool.

In an electric blender purée fried mixture with soaked chillies and a little of the soaking water. Also the coriander root, galangal, krachai and lemon grass. Add ground spices, mix well, bottle when cool and refrigerate.

Madras Curry Paste

90 g/3 oz/¾ cup ground coriander
4½ tablespoons ground cumin
1 tablespoon ground black pepper
1 tablespoon ground turmeric
1 tablespoon chilli powder
3 tablespoons salt
1 tablespoon black mustard seed
4 tablespoons vinegar
5 tablespoons peeled, chopped garlic
2 tablespoons peeled grated ginger
200 ml/7 fl oz/¾ cup vegetable oil

Combine ground spices and salt. Soak black mustard seed in vinegar and blend on high speed in an electric blender. Add garlic and ginger and blend until puréed. Mix with the ground spices. Heat oil in a pan and add the mixture, stirring constantly until cooked and fragrant. Cool and store in a clean glass jar. Use a rounded tablespoon of this paste for each 500 g (1 lb) of main ingredient.

Indian Green Masala Paste

1 teaspoon fenugreek seeds
3 teaspoons chopped garlic
2 tablespoons finely chopped fresh ginger
60 g/2 oz mint leaves
60 g/2 oz coriander leaves
125 ml/4 fl oz/½ cup vinegar
3 teaspoons salt
2 teaspoons ground turmeric
½ teaspoon ground cloves
1 teaspoon ground cardamom
125 ml/4 fl oz/½ cup vegetable oil
3 tablespoons oriental sesame oil

Soak fenugreek seeds in water overnight. They will develop a jelly-like coating. Put all ingredients except oils into a powerful electric blender and blend on high speed until very smooth. Heat oils until very hot, then add blended mixture. Bring to boil, turn off heat, cool and bottle. Oil should cover the top of the paste.

Sri Lankan Dark Roasted Curry Paste

10 tablespoons coriander seeds
3 tablespoons cumin seeds
3 teaspoons fennel seeds
2 teaspoons fenugreek seeds
2 tablespoons ground rice
2 tablespoons desiccated coconut
12 large dried red chillies, stems removed
2 cinnamon sticks, broken into pieces
2 teaspoons cardamom seeds
2 teaspoons whole cloves
2 tablespoons chopped garlic
1 tablespoon chopped fresh ginger
vinegar and water for blending
16 dried curry leaves
3 dried pandan leaves
   cut into 2.5 cm/1 in lengths

In a dry frying pan over medium heat roast each of the spice seeds separately, stirring constantly, until each one smells fragrant and turns dark brown. Turn onto plate to cool. Roast ground rice and coconut separately until golden brown. Turn onto plate and when cool place all the ingredients in an electric blender. Add chillies broken into pieces, cinnamon, cardamom, cloves, garlic and ginger. Blend at high speed adding equal amounts of vinegar and water to assist blending. Scrape down sides of jar from time to time until a smooth purée is formed.

Remove from container, stir in curry leaves and pandan leaves and store in a glass jar in refrigerator. Use 2 or 3 tablespoons paste for each 500 g (1 lb) of meat.

Curry Powder

See SPICE BLENDS.

Custard Apple

(*Annona reticulata*) SEE ILLUSTRATION. Under the common name of custard apple are numerous members of the Annona family. Another widely used name for *A. reticulata* is bullock's heart.

The Annona tribe were originally from South America but they are now grown in places as diverse as South East Asia, Spain, Israel, Australia and New Zealand, and islands of the Pacific.

They're all rather similar under the skin, sweet and delicious when ripe, but in some the pulp is softer and smoother while in others it is slightly granular. All feature creamy-white pulp in neat segments, some of which enclose hard, shiny black or brown seeds. Segments radiate from the central core which is attached to the stem.

Some varieties have more seeds than others, and some have pronounced segmented skin while in others the markings are like joined scales rather than segments. The colour of the skin ranges from green to yellowy-green to bronze. Which is which? Not even the experts agree about their characteristics and common names, but at least we can track them down through their botanical names.

Cherimoya (*A. cherimola*) is smoother though the scales are still clearly marked.

Sweetsop (*A. squamosa*) is also known as sugar apple, scaly custard apple, custard apple of India or sharifa. Characterised by more pronounced segments which give it a lumpy, bumpy, green to light green skin.

Atemoya is a cross between *A. squamosa* and *A. cherimola*.

Purchasing and storing: Buy firm but not rock-hard fruit, and avoid those which show signs of turning black. Wrap and store at room temperature until they yield to gentle pressure. Until the fruit is soft and ripe, the flavour is unremarkable, but once ripe they are very sweet, with an elusive, subtly tropical flavour. Eat at room temperature or chilled, spooning segments from the shell. The seeds are large and smooth enough to allow separating them from the pulp within the mouth.

The sweet flesh may also be made into sherbets or ice creams, first scooping it from the shell and removing the seeds. Accentuate with a squeeze of lime or lemon juice, add sugar to taste, but do not drown the delicate flavour in cream. Makes a delicious drink, puréed in a blender with ice and milk.

Burma: *awzathi*
Fiji: *apeli, uto ni bulumakau*
India: *sitaphul, andoos*
Indonesia: *bua nona, srikaya*
Malaysa: *nona kapri, nona serikaya*
Philippines: *anonas, atis*
Sri Lanka: *anoda*
Thailand: *noi-na, noi-nong*

Cuttlefish

(*Sepia pharaonis*) Purchased fresh, one of the most economical seafoods, the low price perhaps an inducement to compensate for the amount of effort needed to clean and prepare them for eating. Cuttlefish have much the same chewy texture and delicate flavour as octopus and squid. Clean as for squid, and use in any of the recipes given for that cephalopod.

In Asian shops dried cuttlefish is sold as a snack. Finely shredded and the colour of chamois, dried slivers are marketed in clear, sturdy plastic packets. In yet another form the body sac has been cut into strips, pressed out extremely thinly and dried in wide ribbons which are reddish brown in colour and seasoned with salt and sugar. The odour is powerful, but the product is popular with those not put off by the smell.

Burma: *kha-wel, kim-mun-leit*
Cambodia: *muk snauk*
China: *mak mo*
Indonesia: *biekutak*
Malaysia: *sotong karang*
Philippines: *bagolan*
Sri Lanka: *dhallo*
Thailand: *muk kla dong*
Vietnam: *ca muc*

Deep Fried Cuttlefish Balls

90 g/3 oz very tiny bread cubes
500 g/1 lb fresh cuttlefish or squid, cleaned
1 teaspoon salt
1 teaspoon sugar
1 teaspoon oriental sesame oil
peanut oil for deep frying

To prepare the bread cubes, cut very thin slices (about 5 mm/¼ in thick) of day-old bread. Trim off crusts and cut the bread into thin strips, then into tiny dice.

Wash cuttlefish well, removing any of the fine membrane that may still be clinging to the flesh. Chop cuttlefish finely or mince in a food processor using steel chopping blade. Transfer to a bowl and mix in the salt, sugar and sesame oil. Take teaspoons of the mixture and roll into small balls about 2.5 cm (1 in) across. Spread diced bread on a sheet of paper and roll the cuttlefish balls in them until they are covered.

Heat oil and deep fry the balls, a few at a time, until golden. Do not overcook. Drain on paper towels and serve warm.

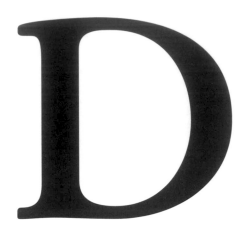

Daikon

See RADISH, WHITE.

Dashi

A mainstay of Japanese cuisine, dashi is a stock base made from kombu (also spelled konbu) which is dried kelp, and flakes of dried bonito (katsuobushi). Instant dashi (various types are sold under the general name of dashi-no-moto) is in concentrated form, requiring only to be dissolved in water. Follow instructions for amount of concentrate needed which will vary from brand to brand.

To make dashi does not take long, even the traditional way. Ichiban dashi (primary dashi) is used for clear soups. It is very delicately flavoured. Niban dashi (secondary dashi) is cooked longer and recommended as the stock to use for thick soups and simmered dishes.

Ichiban Dashi (Primary Dashi)

Not every home has a scale which measures small amounts accurately, so I have included some size and volume equivalents for the seaweed and bonito flakes.

1 litre/2 pints/4 cups cold water
5 cm/2 in square of dried kelp (kombu)
3 tablespoons dried bonito flakes

Put water and dried kelp into a saucepan and bring slowly to a simmer. Remove kelp just before water comes to the boil. (Reserve kelp to make Niban Dashi.)

Add bonito flakes, bring water to the boil and immediately take pan off the heat. Allow flakes to settle for 1 minute, then pour through a sieve lined with muslin and reserve the flakes for the secondary dashi.

Niban Dashi (Secondary Dashi)

1.5 litres/3 pints/6 cups cold water
kelp and bonito reserved from previous recipe
extra 3 tablespoons dried bonito flakes

Put water into a saucepan with reserved kelp and bonito and bring slowly to the boil. Lower heat and simmer uncovered about 20 minutes. Add the extra bonito flakes and immediately remove pan from heat. When flakes have settled, pour through a muslin-lined sieve. This stock is not as delicate as primary dashi.

Day Lily

(*Hemerocallis fulva*) These beautiful yellow flowers are picked at the bud stage and the crop mainly dried so they are available out of season.

Dried lily buds are sold in packets and called golden needles in Chinese cuisine, a bit of poetic licence because when they are dried they are more brown than golden. They must be soaked for 30 minutes or so before adding to a dish. Because they are long and awkward to eat, it is recommended that after soaking they be tied in a knot or cut in halves crossways.

In season they are available fresh. They need very short cooking and their bright colour makes them a decorative addition to any savoury stir-fry. See LILY BUD for recipes.

China: *chin cheng tsai*
Japan: *kanzou*
Thailand: *dok mai cheen*

Desserts

In Asian meals, desserts are not the big feature they are in Western meals. The sweets of South East Asia are usually between-meal snacks made from sticky rice; or cool refreshers of shaved ice sweetened with syrup and bits of fruit or beans cooked in sugar.

The sweets of India may be dry or syrupy, and almost always the main ingredients are reduced milk, ground almonds, lentil flour, ghee and sugar. Indian sweet dishes are just as likely to be served at the start of the meal 'to sweeten the mouth' as at the end.

Colonised countries commonly adopt the customs of the conqueror. Thus we have custards such as vattalappam (recipe below) in Sri Lanka (a baked or steamed custard with a spicy difference), kheer in India (made from creamed almonds or rice), and in Hawaii there is haupia (recipe below), a deliciously creamy pudding made with coconut milk. In the Philippines, the Spanish influence is obvious in leche flan (steamed or baked custard). In Thailand, a small bowl of cool, light syrup and coconut milk with interesting items such as tapioca, tender young coconut and basil seeds may be followed by luk chup ('small magic'), miniature fruit moulded from sweetened mung bean paste — smaller and prettier than any marzipan fruits from the confectioners of Europe. These are served as though they are petits fours (see recipe page 120).

China, Japan and Korea would traditionally offer fresh fruits, sometimes cut decoratively into intriguing shapes, but often bow to Western preference and offer custard desserts or jellies based on seaweed.

Many Asians really enjoy a custard which has become too firm by classic French standards but which is perfectly acceptable in Asian countries. The dissolved palm sugar fills the numerous little holes caused by overbeating the eggs and overheating the oven. So if you are served such a custard by your Asian hosts, they haven't ruined the dish — it is simply that expectations are different.

Haupia

In Hawaii and other Pacific islands, this simple blancmange based on fresh coconut milk is very popular. For convenience I have suggested canned coconut milk, but if you have access to fresh coconuts and extract the milk as described under COCONUT MILK, so much the better.

400 ml/14 fl oz can coconut milk
5 tablespoons white sugar
¼ teaspoon salt
4 tablespoons cornflour (cornstarch)
or arrowroot

If the brand of canned coconut milk is very thick and rich, dilute before it is measured with an equal amount of water, or only 1 cup water if it is not very thick. Combine coconut milk, water, sugar and salt in a saucepan and stir over medium heat until sugar dissolves and simmering point is reached. Mix cornflour or arrowroot smoothly with a little cold water and stir into the hot milk. Stir constantly until it boils and thickens. Pour into a 20 cm (8 in) square glass dish and chill until firm. Cut into squares or diamond shapes. Serve each piece on a strip of banana leaf if liked.

Spicy Coconut Custard (Vattalappam)

Serves 6

250 g/8 oz dark palm sugar (jaggery) or brown sugar
6 eggs
250 ml/8 fl oz/1 cup canned coconut milk
375 ml/12 fl oz can evaporated milk
1 teaspoon ground cardamom
1 teaspoon freshly grated nutmeg
¼ teaspoon ground cloves
2 tablespoons rose water
or ¼ teaspoon rose essence

Chop palm sugar into small pieces and put into a small heavy saucepan with 200 ml (7 fl oz) water. Dissolve over low heat, allow to cool. Beat eggs until well mixed but not frothy, add palm sugar and coconut milk diluted with 125 ml (4 fl oz) water. Strain this mixture through a fine strainer into a large jug. Stir in evaporated milk, spices and rose water or essence.

Pour into individual custard cups placed in a baking dish. Add hot water to come half way up sides of cups and bake at 120°C (260°F) until set, about 1¼ hours. Cool and chill.

Note: Instead of individual servings, the custard may be cooked in one large dish, allowing extra baking time, but do not be tempted to raise heat to more than moderately slow, as this will cause the custard to curdle.

Toast of the Shah

Serves 6

6 slices firm bread,
  cut thick as for toasting
4–6 tablespoons ghee
300 ml/10 fl oz milk
250 ml/8 fl oz cream
¼ teaspoon saffron strands
250 g/8 oz/1 cup sugar
¼ teaspoon ground cardamom
1 tablespoon rose water
1 tablespoon each slivered blanched pistachios
  and almonds

Trim crusts off the bread and if slices are large, cut in halves. Heat ghee in a large, heavy frying pan and fry the bread until golden on both sides. It may be necessary to add more ghee. Remove slices of fried bread to a plate.

Reserve 2 tablespoons milk and add remaining milk and cream to the pan in which the bread was fried. Bring to the boil and add the sugar. Toast saffron strands in a dry pan for about 1 minute over gentle heat, taking care not to scorch them. Tip onto a saucer to cool and become crisp, then crush with the back of a spoon. Heat reserved milk and dissolve the saffron in it. Add to simmering milk in pan and boil hard, stirring constantly, for 10 minutes.

Put in the slices of fried bread in one layer and simmer over low heat until milk is absorbed, carefully turning slices once.

Transfer bread to a heated serving dish, sprinkle with cardamom and rose water and decorate with slivered nuts. Serve hot.

Miniature Moulded Fruits (Luk Chup)

This is for when you have time for making life-like masterpieces of Lilliputian proportions which may be described as therapy by some and absolute waste of time by others. They create a sensation when served.

250 g/8 oz split yellow mung beans
250 g/8 oz white sugar
125 ml/4 fl oz thick coconut milk
few drops of jasmine or rose essence
food colouring

GLAZE AND DECORATION

3 teaspoons agar-agar powder
500 ml/1 pint water
calyxes and stems from fresh chillies and
  strawberries
sprigs of small, non-toxic leaves
  such as Murraya spp.

Buy mung beans which have been husked and split, and are therefore yellow instead of green. Wash several times in cold water, then soak for 1 hour. Drain and rinse, put into a saucepan with cold water to cover. Bring to the boil, then cover and simmer until the beans are soft and mash easily when pressed between finger and thumb, adding extra water if needed.

Drain off any remaining water and mash the beans until smooth. Put into a heavy saucepan with sugar and coconut milk and cook over medium heat, stirring constantly, until mixture becomes dry and of moulding consistency, about 30 minutes. Keep the spoon moving all over bottom of pan to prevent scorching. Remove from heat and when cool enough to handle knead in the flavouring essence. (In Thailand the moulded fruit is usually stored overnight in an airtight container with jasmine blossoms or a scented candle to absorb a faint perfume.)

Take half-teaspoons of the mixture (yes, that's how small the fruits should be) and roll into smooth balls. Mould each one into the likeness of a fruit or vegetable. Insert a fine toothpick in the end of each fruit and paint with food colouring. Stick the other end of the toothpick into a block of polystyrene foam to let the fruit dry without touching painted surface.

To prepare the glaze, sprinkle agar-agar powder over the water in a saucepan and bring to the boil, making sure it is completely dissolved. Cool slightly before dipping the fruit, but remember agar-agar sets at room temperature so it will be necessary to reheat the glaze gently from time to time to keep it liquid.

Dip each model fruit and vegetable into the glaze which will not only make them look luscious, but also prevent the paste from drying out. Once again, leave to dry on the toothpicks. When all have been dipped, start with those which were done first and give each one a second coat of glaze for a very smooth, shiny finish.

In a short time they will be quite dry and no longer sticky to the touch. Now put the finishing touches to your masterpiece — remove the toothpicks and insert tiny stems and leaves (they may be trimmed to size with embroidery scissors) or press in calyxes from strawberries or chilli stems to give a life-like appearance. Serve as the finale to a Thai meal.

Devil's Tongue

(*Amorphophallus konjack*) A perennial plant that has been used in China and Japan for over 2,000 years. The starchy tuber, a member of the yam family, is not unlike taro, hence its Chinese name mo yu, which means 'devil's taro'. In Japan it is known as 'devil's tongue' or konnyaku. Through a complicated process similar to the making of tofu, the large brown roots are peeled, boiled, mashed and then mixed with dissolved limestone to coagulate. The resultant mass is formed into rectangular blocks — strangely gelatinous and a speckled grey colour. It should be parboiled to remove excess lime and to make the texture chewier before including in a recipe. Konnyaku is used primarily as a texture ingredient, with not much flavour but a uniquely chewy, gelatinous texture.

In China there is a darker coloured version of konnyaku, already seasoned, sold as 'black bean curd'. Cut into strips then boiled briefly to remove excess lime, it is added to a number of Szechwan dishes. 'Snowed' black bean curd simply means it has been frozen, which changes the texture, making it chewier and porous, like frozen tofu.

In Japan, konnyaku comes both in a 'black' and a 'white' form. The 'black' is the natural state; 'white' (which is really more a pale grey) has been filtered and bleached. Sold as small rectangular slabs, it will keep for a while. It is popular in soups, stews and, cut in large triangles, in oden and one-pot cookery.

Starch from the same plant is refined to make the Japanese noodles known as shirataki, literally 'white waterfall'. This is an apt description as the cooked noodles are transparent and white. The thicker version of konnyaku noodle, called ito, literally 'string' konnyaku, is available both in natural and refined (white) forms. Sometimes a dozen strands of konnyaku are wound around the fingers into a little bundle and tied in the middle with a single strand. This adds texture as well as an attractive garnish to a bowl of broth. Sometimes fresh konnyaku or konnyaku noodles are available, packed in water, like fresh bean curd. Because of its unusual texture, devil's tongue, in any form, can be an acquired taste.

Dhal

Dhal refers to dried legumes (pulses) of all kinds. The word dhal indicates that the pulses have been husked and split. The most frequently used dhals are: channa dhal – Bengal gram, husked; mattar dhal – split peas, both yellow and green; masoor dhal – red lentils; moong dhal – green gram (yellow when husked); toor dhal – red gram dhal; urad dhal – black gram dhal (white when husked).

The word dhal also commonly applies to the prepared dish of lentil puree which accompanies most Indian meals.

Dill

(*Anethum graveolens*) This herb has won favour in cuisines as diverse as Mediterranean, Scandinavian, Russian and Iranian, both the seeds and feathery leaves being used. Although it originated in Asia, its use in Asian cooking is not widespread. It is used in certain dishes in Sri Lanka, Laos, Vietnam, and Thailand. One instance that comes to mind in which the flavour of the fresh herb is essential, is the Dutch-influenced frikkadel which has become part of the tradition of Sri Lankan cuisine, and the fresh dill-flavoured scrambled egg, courtesy of one-time conquerors, the Portugese and the Dutch. For recipe, see EGGS.

No doubt the Dutch also bequeathed the herb to some Indonesian dishes, for it is known there. In Laos the herb is used in fish dishes. The Thai name translates as 'Laotian coriander'. The seeds, curiously enough, are not used in Asia (and I am curious because fennel seeds, closely related, are widely used).

India: *anithi*
Indonesia: *adas manis*
Laos: *phak si*
Sri Lanka: *enduru*
Thailand: *phak chee lao*

Dim Sum

Literally, this means 'dot heart' or 'touch the heart'. It takes in all the small, tempting, steamed or fried mouthfuls served with numerous cups of steaming hot tea at those long brunches called yum cha ('drink tea') which Chinese people have made a way of life. For recipes, see YUM CHA.

Domburi

This is a heavy earthenware lidded bowl much used in Japan, and also refers to the food cooked or served in it.

Drinks & Beverages

In tropical countries, fluid intake is as important as nutrition and there are many hot and cold drinks which expatriates and visitors alike remember with great fondness. They may be based on buttermilk or coconut water, fruit juice or purée, scented syrups or fruit cordials and, of course, ice.

There are countless hot drinks served for refreshment and hospitality. See TEA for more about these. Most of the drinks served are not merely an indulgence: they have a specific effect, such as 'cooling the system', 'purifying the blood' or 'helping the digestion'.

Some well-known drinks you may encounter in Asian travels or upon inspection of the refrigerator section of your local Asian grocer include:

Avocado sherbet (sinh to bo): A filling and soothing drink which only needs half an avocado per serve, and is a popular drink from Vietnam to Indonesia. Blended with ice, sugar syrup and a little condensed milk, the result is smooth and so thick you nearly need to spoon it from the glass. If you've only ever tasted avocados in a savoury context, try them this way at least once.

Chrysanthemum tea: Sold in cans, this sweetened beverage is an acquired taste.

Coconut juice: A cooling drink sold in cans or frozen in plastic tube containers. The canned drink usually has a lot of sugar added. The flavour of frozen coconut juice is superior and the pieces of coconut flesh floating in it younger and sweeter. If you're lucky, you'll find one with soft, jelly-like pieces of young coconut meat inside. This light and refreshing drink is made from the clean-tasting 'water' inside a fresh coconut.

Durian sherbet: Made with fresh, frozen or canned durian, the forthright flavour of the fruit is somewhat muted by puréeing with ice, sugar syrup and condensed milk. Probably a good entry level for those who have never tried durian before. See also DURIAN.

Falooda: An exotic Indian milk-based drink flavoured with rose syrup (sharbat gulab) and named for the strands of cornflour (cornstarch) vermicelli that float in it. The vermicelli are not easy to make at home. An acceptable substitute is agar-agar jelly, flavoured with rose and coloured green or red. See also FALOODA.

Ginger tea (salabat): A traditional Filipino hot beverage brewed with fresh ginger, brown sugar and water (see recipe page 123).

Grass jelly drink: A sweet, almost malty tasting beverage that looks like flat cola. Some brands include soft jelly-like bits made by thickening the grass liquor with cornflour (cornstarch) (see recipe page 123).

Jakfruit sherbet (sinh to mit): Fresh is best, but canned jackfruit is not bad in this drink. Made with ice and sugar syrup, and a little condensed milk which rounds out the flavour. See also JAKFRUIT.

Kyauk kyaw: The main ingredients of this popular drink are canned grass jelly cut into thin slivers and a syrup sweetened with palm or slab sugar, flavoured with a dash of rose essence. Served in a glass filled with crushed ice, it is truly cooling on a hot day. Agar-agar jelly may be substituted for grass jelly.

Lassi: There are sweet and salty versions of this Indian drink based on soured milk. Made with buttermilk or yoghurt diluted with iced water, it can be plain; savoury, seasoned simply with salt, pepper and roasted cumin; or sweet, flavoured with rose water, cardamom, pistachio nuts and even mango.

Lime juice: A refreshing 'limeade' is made in Asia. Called soda chanh in Vietnam and nimboo pani (literally lime water) in India, it is simply made with fresh lime juice, sugar or sugar syrup, soda (or water) and ice cubes. If you prefer a frappe, process briefly in an electric blender.

Mattha: A buttermilk or yogurt-based drink flavoured with mint and roasted, ground cumin.

Moh-let-saung: A cooling Burmese beverage of iced coconut milk and sago sweetened with palm sugar. In these days of calorie counting and cholesterol consciousness, it makes sense to dilute the coconut milk with water or use a low-fat cow's milk and only flavour it with a small quantity of coconut milk. (See also TAPIOCA.)

Panchamrita: A nectar made with yoghurt, cardamom and honey.

Pennywort drink (rau ma): A bold green, frothy beverage served at Vietnamese food stalls or cafés made from fresh pennywort leaves, sugar syrup, water and ice liquefied in a blender. (In cans, it is a bitter disappointment, literally.) It is said to have the added advantage of relieving the pain of arthritis. See also PENNYWORT.

Persimmon tea (soo jeung kwa): A traditional Korean drink made from dried persimmon, ginger root, cinnamon, sugar and water. Served ice cold.

Soursop sherbet (sinh to mang cau): A number of Vietnamese eateries make this and other delectable fruit-based smoothies, which are both refreshing and thirst-quenching. The main ingredients are fruit pulp (fresh, canned or frozen) and ice with a slurp of condensed milk to sweeten.

Soy drink: Numerous sweetened soy milk drinks are available, mostly in cartons, from your Asian food stockist.

Tea: General term for a hot, brewed beverage which may not necessarily use the 'two leaves and a bud' of *Camelia sinensis*. See main entry for TEA.

Thandai: A popular, refreshing summer drink based on ground almonds, sunflower or pumpkin seeds (optional), sugar, spices and water or milk. (See recipe below.) See also ALMONDS.

Ginger Tea (Salabat)

500 g/1 lb sliced fresh root ginger
185 g/6 oz/1 cup brown sugar
1.25 litres/2½ pints/5 cups water

Boil all ingredients for 30 minutes. Add more water if taste is too strong. Strain. Drink hot.

Thandai

150 g/5 oz natural almonds
5 peppercorns
¼ teaspoon ground cardamom
500 ml/2 pints/4 cups boiling water
2 tablespoons sugar or honey, or to taste
1 tablespoon rose water

Put almonds, peppercorns and cardamom into a large glass or ceramic bowl and cover with boiling water. Allow to steep for 1 hour. Transfer to a blender and process until nuts and spices are finely ground. Add sweetener and blend to combine. Line a nylon sieve with a double thickness of clean muslin and strain the nut milk, squeezing out as much liquid as possible. Stir in rose water, chill and serve over ice.

Grass Jelly Drink

On street corners throughout Asian cities, you will see stalls dispensing cool, thirst-quenching drinks of different kinds, lined up in tall glass containers rather like home aquariums, their straight edges butted together for best use of space. The drinks vary in colour: pale green (pandan flavoured); yellow (chrysanthemum); milky white (soy milk); and invariably there is one which looks quite sinister — clear, deep brown with strands or cubes of translucent blackish jelly in it. This is a very popular choice, because grass jelly is considered a tonic. It has a slight iodine flavour. The fine dark strands float in a lightly sweetened syrup and somehow it is very refreshing and easy to drink. Grass jelly is sold in cans at Asian supermarkets. Grate into fine long strands or cut into mouth-sized cubes and put a couple of spoonfuls into each glass, then add rock sugar syrup and fill up with cold water (not soda or mineral water). This drink should be as cool and dark and still as a deep forest pool. Ice? Of course.

Drumstick

(*Moringa pterygosperma*, *M. oleifera*) SEE ILLUSTRATION. Sometimes referred to as a bean, this long, rigid pod grows on a tree rather than a vine. Its hard, green outer covering is rigid enough to earn its common name of drumstick. Both pods and leaves are relished.

The tree is known as the horseradish tree (since the roots have a similar pungent taste, they are used by Europeans in tropical lands as a substitute for true horseradish) and ben tree (mature seeds yield oil of ben which is used by watchmakers and also in cosmetics and perfumes).

In Asian cooking it is the half-ripe pods and compound leaves made up of many small, tender rounded leaflets, which are most used in a culinary context. Native to India, it now grows wild in the West Indies and some southern parts of North

America. The flavour of the pods has been compared with asparagus and the texture with marrow. They are a popular ingredient in vegetable curries, from southern India to Sri Lanka and Malaysia.

These long, slender pods are tricky for those not brought up to eat them. The only portion consumed is the soft, almost jelly-like interior in which the seeds are embedded. The seeds, too, are nice to eat if the beans are young, but a drumstick is never young enough to eat the outer skin. Simmered in lightly salted water for 7–10 minutes they make good eating — but discard the outer skin after scooping out the pulp.

Delicious cut into finger lengths and cooked in a spicy gravy. At a formal meal, the shell of a piece of drumstick is split open with spoon and fork, and the spoon used to scrape out the succulent interior with all its delicious flavour. During family meals the preferred method is to pick up the section of drumstick with the fingers and, in the manner of eating the fleshy base of an artichoke petal, scrape away the soft centre with the teeth. The woody exterior is also chewed to extract flavour, then discarded on the side of the plate. Much effort yields very little edible vegetable, but it is undeniably popular in many tropical countries.

Drumstick leaves are used not only for their tangy flavour but also because they have a reputation of neutralising any 'poison', especially when cooking crabs. I would not put any faith in that, however. Make sure the crabs are fresh and clean them in the way described (see CRABS), then the leaves of the horseradish tree will not be necessary as a safeguard, though they do add a pleasant sour taste.

If picked at a sufficiently early stage, the leaves may be blanched, dipped in nam prik and eaten as they are in Thailand. Mature leaves are sold in bundles in markets. If the bunch weighs around 375 g (12 oz) you will probably end up with 250 g (8 oz) of edible leaves. The stems and even the smaller stalks are usually too tough to eat. In the Philippines, it is only the leaves which are eaten as a vegetable, being very high in vitamin and mineral content and containing 7–10 per cent protein.

Purchasing and storing: Look for smooth, greenish (rather than brownish) skin on the pods. While most drumsticks have slight bumps indicating where the seeds are, avoid those which have pronounced bumps and attenuated spaces in between. These have reached an age and a stage where the flavour will be strong and rather bitter, and the seeds, instead of being pleasantly crunchy and tender, will be hard and dry. Pods may be stored, wrapped in paper, in the crisper drawer of the refrigerator for a day or two, but like most vegetables, the sooner they are consumed the better they will taste.

Preparation: Wash pods and with a vegetable peeler scrape lightly along the skin, removing any dry looking patches. You cannot remove all the tough outer skin which is cooked along with the edible parts, rather like an artichoke. Be prepared to work a little for the soft, flavoursome, jelly-like pulp inside.

Leaves require a good wash in cold water, and a vigorous shaking. If they are to be fried, pat them in a tea towel and leave for a while to dry or they will spatter furiously when added to hot oil.

Medicinal uses: Sanskrit writings mention the tree as a medicinal plant. The roots are a disinfectant; the bark and leaves are used to cure wounds and stop bleeding; and the seeds, roasted and ground, are said to be effective when applied to painful joints.

India: *muruggai, sahijan, sekta-ni-sing*
Indonesia: *kelor*
Malaysia: *kelor*
Japan: *wasabi no-ki-no-ha*
Philippines: *malunggay talbos*
Samoa: *lopa*
Sri Lanka: *murunga* (bean),
  murunga kolle (leaves)
Thailand: *ma-rum* (bean), *phak ma-rum* (leaves)

Spiced Drumstick Leaves

1 small onion, finely chopped
1 teaspoon ground turmeric
1 teaspoon salt
juice of 1 lime
4 tablespoons grated coconut
  or desiccated coconut
125 g/4 oz drumstick leaves,
  washed, shaken dry and stripped off the stems

Put all ingredients except leaves into a saucepan with 3 tablespoons water, cover and simmer until onion is soft. Add leaves and toss. Cook uncovered, to preserve their green colour, for about 10 minutes or until most of the liquid has evaporated.

White Drumstick Curry

6 fresh drumsticks
  or 250 g/8 oz frozen
400 ml/14 fl oz can coconut milk
1 teaspoon ground turmeric
1 onion, thinly sliced
1 teaspoon finely chopped garlic
1 teaspoon finely grated fresh ginger
½ teaspoon fenugreek seeds
2 sprigs curry leaves
2 strips pandan leaves
3 fresh green chillies, optional
salt to taste
squeeze of lime juice

Wash and prepare the drumsticks as described on page 124. Put 1 cup coconut milk diluted with 1½ cups water into a saucepan with all the ingredients and simmer, uncovered, for 20–25 minutes. Stir in remaining coconut milk, taste and adjust seasoning. Serve with rice.

Duck

This fowl is popular in Asia for both its gamey flesh and its eggs. In China, where no edible part of an animal ever goes to waste, you may encounter salted duck eggs (see EGGS), duck hearts, duck livers and duck webs (which have been deboned and softened). In China, a duck is roasted complete with head, as the brains and tongue are considered delicacies. The only part which is not used is the tail, especially the two oil glands on either side of the tail which are blamed for the strong flavour sometimes detected in the flesh.

Duck is prized for its fatty skin which turns crisp when cooked in the manner called Peking Duck. This is something best left to the experts in a kitchen equipped for the many and varied procedures which must be followed. In the Hong Kong kitchen of a restaurant specialising in northern Chinese food, I was given a demonstration by a master chef of how it is prepared. Ever since, I have thought of it as 'blowing up a duck', because air is forced between the skin and the flesh by blowing forcefully, rather like inflating a party balloon. Before starting, the duck is massaged all over by rubbing the skin back and forth to loosen it from the meat, taking care not to puncture it anywhere. A string is looped over the neck, but not pulled tight. A large plastic straw or tube is inserted in a small slit made in the skin of the

duck's neck about 5 cm (2 in) above the part where the neck joins the breast. The tube is then extended a short way to the breast area so when air is blown in, it separates skin from flesh. The skin has to be taut, the duck looking more like a balloon than a bird. The even distribution of air is achieved by pressing and rubbing during the procedure. When skin and flesh are separated, the tube is gently extracted and the string tightened and knotted so the air does not escape. A hook is then inserted above the string and through the neck to hang the duck.

Now it is evident why duck for this dish has to be prepared in a particular way: with the head left on, the vent as small as practical to allow for the duck to be drawn, and the skin not punctured in any way, for that would make the whole exercise as futile as trying to blow up a balloon with a hole in it. If you are determined to attempt this yourself, my advice is to ask a Chinese butcher to prepare the bird and to remove both the fat from the cavity and the oil glands from the tail. When you get it home, rinse the duck inside and out and drain it, then proceed as described above.

That done, suspend the duck by the hook above a deep pot of boiling water and dip it in and out, ladling water over the skin, for about 5 minutes or until the skin is white. Hang the duck to dry for 6–8 hours in a well-ventilated spot with a large bowl underneath to catch drips.

Next, the duck is brushed all over with a solution of malt sugar syrup (maltose) or honey dissolved in a cup of boiling water, and dried again for 6 hours or until very dry. (Now we know why some restaurants ask for 24-hours notice when patrons order Peking Duck. Others, which specialise in Peking cuisine, have them at various stages of readiness all the time.)

Finally, the duck is roasted until brown, for which special barrel-shaped ovens are used. In a domestic oven, all shelves are removed except the top shelf and the duck or ducks hung from the top shelf by the hook. A large tray covered with foil is placed at the bottom of the oven. After 15 minutes at 220°C (425°F), lower the heat to moderate, 180°C (350°F), and continue roasting for a further 1¼–1½ hours. When done, the duck should be the colour of mahogany — a deep, rich reddish brown.

Cut off legs and wings. With a very sharp knife slice the skin off breast and back with a thin layer of meat attached into pieces roughly 5 cm (2 in) square.

Slice the rest of the meat and arrange separately. Serve with spring onion (scallion) brushes (see page 168), hoi sin sauce and the Mandarin Pancakes (see page 266) which you will have had plenty of time to make while the duck was hanging around drying! Steam the pancakes gently to heat through just before serving.

A whole ritual has sprung up around the serving of Peking Duck in restaurants. The duck is brought to the table by a waiter wearing white gloves. The skin is sliced off with surgical exactitude, and each diner places a piece of skin on a pancake, brushes it with sauce, encloses everything (including the spring onion brush) in the pancake and eats it.

The second course is a stir-fry which includes the rest of the duck meat, and the third offering is duck soup made from the carcass. By necessity, the soup is made from the carcass of a different duck which has done time in the stock pot, but this does not seem to matter. Every part of this duck meal is highly regarded and enjoyed.

Peking Duck, Home Style

Here is a recipe which imitates closely the results, but cuts out much of the effort. I have never attempted to inflate a duck, and am not about to start now. Another advantage of this version is that it can be done with a duck that doesn't have its head attached. Serves 4–6.

1 × 2.5–3 kg/5–6 lb roasting duck
3 teaspoons salt
125 ml/4 fl oz/½ cup vodka
4 tablespoons honey or maltose
500 ml/1 pint/2 cups hot water

Remove fat from inside cavity of duck and carefully slice off the tail and the oil glands on either side of the tail bone. Rinse the duck inside and out, dry with paper towels. Rub inside cavity with salt. Put duck on a large plate and spoon vodka over, rubbing all over the duck. Leave for 4 hours, turning duck from time to time so all the skin comes in contact with vodka.

Dissolve honey or maltose in hot water, brush over the duck, making sure no spot is missed. Place duck on a rack to dry for 4–6 hours in front of a window or with a fan blowing on it to speed things up a bit.

Meanwhile, make Mandarin Pancakes (see page 266) and prepare spring onion (scallion) brushes (see page 168) and small sauce dishes of hoi sin sauce.

Preheat oven to 200°C (400°F). Place duck on a rack which sits well above the roasting pan. Line roasting pan with foil to produce more reflected heat, and pour in about 2 cm (1 in) water. Cook for 30 minutes then turn heat to 180°C (350°F) and cook for a further 1½ hours or until skin is deep golden brown. If wing tips brown too quickly, protect them with foil. Carve and serve with the traditional accompaniments, and no one will mind that your haven't served your apprenticeship in a Peking kitchen.

Quick and Easy Roast Duck

This recipe makes use of a modern innovation, the oven bag. The difference it makes in cooking time is worth the departure from tradition.
Serves 4.

1 roasting duck, about 1.75 kg/3½ lb
1 tablespoon honey
2 tablespoons hoi sin sauce
2 tablespoons light soy sauce
1 teaspoon crushed garlic
1 teaspoon finely grated ginger
2 teaspoons sesame paste
1 teaspoon salt
**½ teaspoon crushed Szechwan pepper
  or black pepper**

Wash duck inside and out and dry on paper towels. Discard tail and oil glands as described in previous recipe. Combine all remaining ingredients and heat in a small pan until honey melts and a smooth, thick paste results. If too thick for spreading add a spoonful of water. Rub 1–2 tablespoons of this marinade inside and outside the duck, reserving the rest to serve as a sauce. If sesame paste is not convenient, substitute smooth peanut butter mixed with 1 teaspoon oriental sesame oil.

Put duck into an oven bag and follow manufacturer's directions about making a few small holes in the bag near the tie. Leave duck to marinate for 1 hour.

Preheat oven to 190°C (375°F) and place duck in roasting pan breast-side down. Cook for 45 minutes, then turn duck breast upwards and continue to roast for 1 hour. Remove from bag, carve thinly and serve hot with sauce, spring onions and Mandarin Pancakes (see page 266). If liked, plum or chilli sauce may be served as well as the reserved marinade.

Braised Duck with Chestnuts

Serves 5

125 g/4 oz dried chestnuts
1 roasting duckling, about 2 kg/4 lb
1 teaspoon crushed garlic
1 teaspoon finely grated fresh ginger
2 tablespoons light soy sauce
1 tablespoon Chinese rose wine or sherry
3 tablespoons peanut oil
3 tablespoons red bean curd
2 teaspoons sugar

Pour boiling water over dried chestnuts and soak for 30 minutes. Drain, replace with more boiling water and soak for a further 30 minutes or until ready to add to dish, when they should be drained again.

Rinse duck well and blot dry. Cut off and discard tail. Combine garlic, ginger, soy and wine, rub all over duck inside and out and leave aside while chestnuts are soaking.

Heat oil in a wok and brown the duck all over, turning to ensure even browning. Transfer duck to a dish. Pour off oil in wok, leaving only about a tablespoon. Return duck to wok. Add bean curd mashed with the sugar and pour in enough boiling water to reach half way up the duck. Add the chestnuts, making sure they are immersed in the liquid. Cover and simmer until duck is tender, about 1½ hours. Turn duck once or twice during cooking, adding a little more boiling water if necessary. Lift duck onto a wooden board and cut Chinese style, first in half lengthways, then turning cut side down and chopping through the bones with a sharp cleaver. Arrange pieces on serving plate and spoon the sauce and chestnuts over them. Garnish with spring onion (scallion) flowers (short lengths stripped with a long pin and dropped into iced water so they curl). If liked, slices of sweet potato may be added during the last 15 minutes of cooking. This also helps to absorb some of the richness. Serve with steamed rice.

Boned Duck with Plum Sauce

Serves 4–6.

1 × 2 kg/4 lb duck
2 teaspoons salt
1 tablespoon light soy sauce
2 teaspoons Chinese wine
1 teaspoon five spice powder
oil for deep frying

MASTER SAUCE
375 ml/12 fl oz dark soy sauce
375 ml/12 fl oz water
125 ml/4 fl oz Chinese wine or dry sherry
3 whole star anise
3 whole cloves
2 sticks cinnamon
1 teaspoon fennel seeds
1 teaspoon Szechwan peppercorns
6 slices fresh ginger
1 tablespoon sugar

BATTER
1 cup plain (all-purpose) flour
¼ teaspoon salt
½ teaspoon bicarbonate of soda (baking soda)
cold water to mix

DIPPING SAUCE
3 tablespoons plum sauce
3 tablespoons chilli sauce
2 teaspoons ginger juice
½ teaspoon crushed garlic

Chop tail off duck, wash and drain the bird and dry it with paper towels. Rub over with salt, soy sauce, wine and five-spice powder and leave for 30 minutes.

Combine ingredients for master sauce in a pan just large enough to hold the duck. If liked, the smaller spices (fennel seeds, Szechwan peppercorns and cloves) may be tied in a knot of muslin for easy removal. Bring to simmering point.

Heat oil in a wok for deep frying, and fry the duck until evenly browned all over, turning it carefully when done on one side. Drain duck from the oil (reserve oil for later use) and put it into the master sauce, cover and simmer for 1 hour or until duck is very tender. Lift out of sauce and drain in a colander until cool.

Combine flour, bicarbonate of soda, salt and enough water to make a coating batter. Set aside while boning the duck.

With a sharp knife make a cut through the skin of the duck from neck downwards. Part the flesh to expose the breast bone, below the neck. Wiggle it out, spreading the skin and flesh away from the bones, and lift out the whole bony framework. Turn duck over and make slits in the legs and wings. Loosen the bones and twist them free at the joints. Remove thigh bones in the same way.

Cut duck in half lengthways and chop the now boneless duck across into strips about 2.5 cm (1 in) wide. Dip each piece in batter before dropping into the hot oil and frying until golden brown. Do not fry too many pieces at a time or the heat of the oil will be diminished and an oily batter will result. Lift out on a slotted spoon and drain on paper towels. When all the pieces are fried, arrange on a platter.

Prepare the sauce by combining all ingredients and dividing among individual sauce dishes. Serve with dipping sauce and steamed rice, or bread.

Thai Green Curry of Duck

Serves 4–5

1 × 1.5 kg/3 lb roasting duck
400 ml/14 fl oz can coconut milk
3 tablespoons Thai green curry paste
3 kaffir lime leaves
2 tablespoons fish sauce
2 teaspoons palm sugar or brown sugar
3 tablespoons chopped green chillies
3 tablespoons chopped fresh basil
  or coriander leaves

Rinse and dry duck. Discard tail, and cut the duck into joints, chopping across the breast to make smaller pieces. Take ½ cup of the thick coconut cream from the top of the can and combine with the curry paste in a heavy pan or wok, stirring over low heat, until it smells fragrant. Put in the pieces of duck and cook, turning them in the spice mixture until coated. Add the rest of the coconut milk mixed with an equal amount of water, the lime leaves, fish sauce and sugar. Stir while bringing to the boil, and simmer until duck is tender. If necessary add more water or coconut milk to keep a fairly liquid consistency. Just before serving sprinkle the chillies and fresh herbs over.

Durian

(*Durio zibethinus*) SEE ILLUSTRATION. This infamous tropical fruit is indigenous to Malaysia, Indonesia, Thailand and the southern Philippines. The reputation of this fruit has gone before it as surely as its aroma trails after it. A good durian is sweet and has the texture of smooth, rich custard and the flavour, while quite unlike anything else, hints at banana, mango, pineapple, pawpaw (all somewhat over-ripe) and vanilla. Some call it the king of fruits, regard it as an aphrodisiac and break hotel rules by sneaking it into their rooms. Others hate it with a vengeance.

So what is it that provokes such passionate reactions? Unless you have smelled ripe durian, it is hard to imagine an odour as invasive.

The most forbidding aspect of this fruit is its spiky skin. Roughly the size of a soccerball, heavy for its size, and coming to a point at one end, the skin of the durian is thick, covered in sharp, sturdy spines of dull green which yellow as the fruit ripens. A fruit is ripe and ready to eat when it splits along its 'seamline'. It may need a little help and, if the spikes are yellow, a sharp thump on a hard surface (a concrete driveway works well) should achieve the same result. Another way, if it doesn't split of its own accord, is to use the point of a knife at the end away from the stem and lever one of the segments of skin upwards. Then prise the shell open, segment by segment, with well-protected hands. I use thick gardening gloves.

Inside, the fruit is divided into sections and within the smooth white walls of each section are three or four large, glossy, cream-beige seeds, each one enclosed in a custard-like covering which can be pale cream to bright yellow in colour (depending on the variety of durian rather than its stage of ripeness). The texture of the flesh that encases the large seeds is dense and creamy, the taste highly praised by all brave enough to venture past the smell. Durian is considered 'heating' to the body and for this reason, a feast of durian is followed with 'cooling' mangosteens.

In some areas durians are never picked, but left to ripen and fall — ensuring they are perfectly ripe. A common saying is 'a durian has eyes and can see where it is falling'. This is because (so the saying goes) the fruit never fall during daylight hours when people may be hurt by their size, vicious

spines and the velocity gathered as they hurtle to earth, but rather in the wee hours when honest citizens certainly would not be prowling under durian trees.

Durians are used to make preserves, ice cream and candy. Commercial durian ice cream sold in Asia is flavoured with artificial durian essence and I don't recommend it. Unless you have tried durian ice cream made with the fruit and a classic crcme Anglaise (a cross-culture recipe if ever there was one, and I am quite unrepentant about creating it), you cannot say you have tried it at its best. Pupils in my cookery classes have tried a timid teaspoonful and without exception have come back for more, demanding a full serving. However, I can't see Baskin Robbins adding this one to their range. Delicious though it is, durian remains an acquired taste.

Australia grows the fruit in its tropical north and air freights it to England when it is out of season in Asia. It is also possible to buy, in firmly sealed plastic boxes, frozen segments of durian.

Bali: *duren*
Burma: *duyin*
Malaysia: *durian*
Indonesia: *ambetan, durian*
Philippines: *duryan*
Sri Lanka: *durian*
Thailand: *tu-lian, tu-rian*

Durian Ice Cream

Serves 6

4 or 5 segments fresh or frozen durian
250 ml/8 fl oz/1 cup milk
250 ml/8 fl oz/1 cup cream
2 egg yolks
125 g/4 oz/½ cup sugar

If using frozen durian, thaw completely. Remove seeds and press flesh through a nylon sieve to eliminate the fine fibres.

Heat milk and cream in a heavy enamel or other non-aluminium pan, stirring until almost boiling. Whisk egg yolks with sugar until light, stir in a ladleful of the hot milk mixture and return to saucepan. Stir over very low heat until custard thickens, taking care not to let it boil or it will curdle. Cool the custard and chill it well, then add a little at a time to the durian pulp, combining it thoroughly before adding more custard. This keeps the texture even.

Freeze in a churn or in a shallow glass dish. If using still-freezing method, stir 2 or 3 times during freezing to enhance smoothness. Or, after it has frozen, break into pieces and purée in food processor until smooth but not melted. Return to freezer until firm. Press freezer wrap directly on surface of ice cream to prevent ice crystals forming. It is advisable to store durian ice cream in a freezer container with a well-fitting lid.

Eel

(*Anguilla anguilla, A. rostrata, A. japonica, A. australis*) In spite of the many classifications, there are two basic types of eel; one freshwater and the other saltwater. Although known in the cuisines of China, Thailand, Malaysia and the Philippines, they are probably most integral to the diet of the Japanese in the form of a topping for sushi or as a braised dish. Freshwater eel is called unagi and marine eel is called anago, and unlike other sushi toppings are never served raw, but are grilled.

There is a tradition in Japan that on a certain day (known as the Day of the Cow) everyone eats eel as this guarantees good health all year. So convinced are the Japanese that in a 24-hour period almost 900 tonnes of eel are consumed. For this special day small pieces of eel are dipped in a sauce, skewered and charcoal grilled.

Eggplant

(*Solanum melongena*) SEE ILLUSTRATION. Originating in Asia, eggplant (known in Europe as aubergine) belongs to the nightshade family (along with tomatoes, chillies and potatoes). It comes in a number of shapes, sizes and colours with a surprising variation in flavour. Originating in India, its name derives from a variety common there which is the colour, shape and size of hen eggs.

In Thailand, a popular variety called pea eggplant (*Solanum torvum*) grows as clusters of tiny green spheres which, in spite of being tough-skinned and somewhat bitter, are used whole in curries or eaten raw with nam prik. These are known in Thailand as makhua puang and in the Seychelles and West Indies as susumber or gully bean. A wild variety, *S. trilobatum*, grows in Thailand. It resembles the pea eggplant, has a bitter taste and similar sized fruit, varying from white streaked with green through to shades of red as it ripens. They are borne on a thorny, climbing herb upon individual stems (rather than in clusters like pea eggplant). This variety is eaten raw with nam prik kapi and is also considered valuable medicinally.

Garden eggplant (*S. melongena*) vary considerably in shape, size and colour: from smallish spheres of white, pale green, white streaked with purple, mauve and shades of yellow to a rich, deep purple fruit which may weigh around 1 kg (2 lb). The Thai name for these is makhua khun. More common in Western countries is the long or teardrop shape, which may be sold as baby eggplant or allowed to grow into larger specimens. In Thailand these are known as makhua yao. Another variety (*S. stramonifolium*), called ma-uk in Thailand, is small, round, orange and hairy. Used to flavour nam prik, it must first be scraped to remove the fuzz. Any sour fruit may be substituted.

Eggplant is a popular vegetable in China, Japan, India, Indonesia, Malaysia, Philippines, Sri Lanka and Thailand. It is often pickled.

Purchasing and storing: Whatever variety of eggplants you buy, they should be firm and smooth. Look them over carefully for small worm holes, brown spots (these are hard to see on dark purple eggplants so be eagle-eyed), or signs of shrivelling which indicate they are older than they should be and consequently may be bitter. Stems are usually present on eggplants and these are a good indication of freshness if they are green and not withered. Eggplants in good condition when purchased will keep for a few days in the vegetable bin of a refrigerator, but don't push your luck — use them fairly soon and they will be more enjoyable.

Preparation: Always use a stainless steel knife for cutting eggplants, or the surface will turn a most unappetising shade of grey or black. Most recipes use the eggplants unpeeled, so simply wash and dry them, cut off the stem ends and then cut into the sizes and shapes called for in the recipe.

It is not always necessary to salt and degorge eggplants, although most European recipes make this a preliminary step in preparation. If the eggplants are fresh and firm they are almost never salted and degorged for Asian food.

The exception is when they are intended for a pickle as the less liquid left in the vegetable, the better the keeping qualities of the pickle.

Medicinal uses: Its roots are expectorant, diuretic and demulcent; the unripe fruit is tonic and expectorant; and the ripe fruit also is expectorant, demulcent and anti-diabetic.

> **China:** *ngai gwa, chieh tse*
> **Japan:** *nasu*
> **India:** *brinjal, baigan, badan jan*
> **Indonesia:** *terong*
> **Malaysia:** *terung*
> **Philippines:** *talong*
> **Sri Lanka:** *vambotu*
> **Thailand:** *makhua terung, makhua yeo*

Sri Lankan Eggplant Pickle

1 kg/2 lb eggplants (aubergines)
2 teaspoons salt
2 teaspoons ground turmeric
oil for frying
1 tablespoon black mustard seeds
125 ml/4 fl oz/½ cup vinegar
1 medium onion, finely chopped
4 cloves garlic, finely chopped
1 tablespoon finely chopped ginger
1 tablespoon ground coriander
2 teaspoons ground cumin
1 teaspoon ground fennel
125 ml/4 fl oz/½ cup tamarind pulp
250 ml/8 fl oz/1 cup hot water
3 fresh green chillies, seeded and sliced
8 cm/3 in cinnamon stick
1 teaspoon chilli powder (optional)
2 teaspoons sugar
extra salt to taste

Wash, dry but do not peel eggplants. Slice eggplants thinly, rub with salt and turmeric, put in a bowl and leave for at least 1 hour. Drain off liquid and blot eggplants dry on paper towels. Heat about 2.5 cm (1 in) oil in a frying pan and fry eggplant slices quite slowly until brown on both sides. Lift out with slotted spoon and put in a dry bowl. Reserve oil.

Put mustard seeds and vinegar in a blender container, cover and blend on high speed until mustard is ground. Add onion, garlic and ginger, cover and blend again until a smooth paste. Set aside.

Put coriander, cumin and fennel in a small dry pan and heat gently, shaking pan or stirring, until medium brown in colour. If preferred, substitute 1½ tablespoons Ceylon curry powder (see page 356).

Squeeze tamarind pulp in hot water, strain and discard seeds, reserve liquid.

Heat ½ cup reserved oil and fry blended mixture for 5 minutes. Add toasted spices or Ceylon curry powder, chillies, cinnamon, chilli powder if used and tamarind liquid. Add fried eggplant and any oil that has collected in the bowl, stir well, cover and simmer for 15 minutes. Remove from heat, stir in sugar. Add extra salt if necessary. Cool thoroughly and store in clean dry jars.

Szechwan Eggplant

Serves 6

2 eggplants (aubergines) about 500 g/1 lb each,
  or 1 kg/2 lb smaller eggplants
500 ml/1 pint/2 cups peanut oil
1 teaspoon finely grated ginger
1 teaspoon finely chopped garlic

SAUCE
4 tablespoons dark soy sauce
2 tablespoons Chinese wine or dry sherry
2 tablespoons sugar
1 teaspoon oriental sesame oil
1 teaspoon chilli oil (optional)
1–2 teaspoons sweet chilli sauce

Slice off and discard the stalk end of the eggplants, but do not peel them. Cut in half lengthways, then into wedges lengthways each about 2.5 cm (1 in) thick. Cut the wedges into 5 cm (2 in) lengths.

Heat the peanut oil in a wok or frying pan, and fry half of the pieces of eggplant at a time on high heat, turning the pieces so that they are evenly browned. Let them cook to a dark golden brown, then lift them out with a slotted spoon and drain on paper towels. When all the eggplant pieces have been fried, set them aside to cool. The oil that remains may be strained and used again.

Combine the sauce ingredients and stir until sugar dissolves.

Pour off all but 1 tablespoon of oil remaining in the pan. Heat, then add the ginger and garlic and stir quickly over medium heat until they turn golden.

Add the sauce mixture, bring to the boil, then return the eggplant and cook over high heat, turning the eggplant pieces over until most of the sauce is absorbed. Transfer to a serving dish as soon as cooking is completed (don't leave eggplant in the wok or a metallic taste will develop). Serve warm or cold.

Thai Stir-Fried Eggplant

Serves 4 as an accompaniment to steamed rice and other dishes.

300 g/10 oz slender eggplants (aubergines)
4 tablespoons oil
1 tablespoon Thai pepper-coriander paste
  (recipe page 105)
2 tablespoons fish sauce
1 teaspoon palm sugar or brown sugar
1 tablespoon lime juice
1 fresh red chilli, sliced

Wash and dry the eggplants and cut into small dice. Heat oil and fry the pepper-coriander paste, stirring, until fragrant. Add the diced eggplant and fry until golden brown. Stir in fish sauce, sugar and lime juice and remove from heat. Serve sprinkled with chilli slices.

Eggs

Since hens and ducks are easy to raise even on the crowded, small plots of land on which most of Asia lives; and since they provide eggs until the moment they become dinner themselves, there are many standard dishes which feature eggs. They are hardly ever used as they are in traditional Western cooking — the yolks to thicken sauces or custards, the whites whipped into mountains of froth to lighten soufflés or cakes or make meringues. When I was growing up in Sri Lanka, the egg seller would come door-to-door with a big basket of eggs. The household cook would bring a large bowl of water into which the eggs were put one by one. Any that bobbed about or floated were discarded and only those that lay on the bottom were accepted. This is a reliable test, because as eggs get older the air sac at the broad end becomes larger and enables them to float.

Purchasing and storing: Unless you raise your own chickens or live close to a farm which sells eggs, you must just resign yourself to eggs which, while not bad, are really not as fresh as one would like them to be. 'Farm fresh eggs' has a nice ring to it, but it is usually quite some time since they left the farm. However, once you get them home remember that they should be refrigerated, because eggs can deteriorate as much in a day at room temperature as they would in the refrigerator over five days. Leaving them in their cartons in the refrigerator (narrow end downwards) is a better idea than taking them out and placing them unprotected in egg racks where they are more likely to absorb other refrigerator odours, such as cheese and fish, through their porous shells.

Eggs are strictly no-nonsense nutrition in India and South East Asia, while in the Philippines and China they appear in strange guises such as balut and thousand year eggs, which aren't really that old.

Hen eggs: White, brown or speckled, the colour of the shell makes no difference to the food value, though the colour of the yolk and the flavour of the egg is ruled by what the hen eats. Eggs laid by battery hens are generally considered to be inferior in colour, flavour and nutrition to those produced by free-range hens.

The shell of any egg is porous, the purpose being to allow air to enter for the developing embryo, and this means that odours can penetrate, so don't store eggs next to strong cheese in the refrigerator. In addition to odours, this porosity allows micro-organisms to enter, especially when the shells are wet, so if eggs need washing they should be used immediately.

The recipes which follow are based on hen eggs, though duck eggs may be substituted if you have a good source.

Duck eggs: The shells are bluish white and in Asia many people prefer them to hen eggs because they are larger, more highly flavoured and the albumen is stronger, making for lighter cakes. However, ducks are not the most particular of creatures when it comes to where they lay their eggs. It is important to be very sure of freshness when using duck eggs, because they can carry dangerous bacteria when stale. The bacteria is destroyed by 10 minutes boiling, or by baking in a cake for not less than an hour.

Duck eggs are much used in making the steamed sponge cakes popular in Asia. They are also used for salted eggs and century eggs. Yolks of salted duck eggs are used in the fillings of moon cakes made for the moon festival, and look like a large golden harvest moon in the centre of the sweet filling of lotus nut paste which is much paler in colour.

Salted eggs are sold at Chinese stores and should be kept in the refrigerator, where they will hold for months. Once opened the yolks will keep for one or two days, covered and refrigerated. They are boiled for 10 minutes before eating as a condiment.

Thousand year eggs: Thousand year eggs (century eggs) are duck eggs which have been coated with salt, wood ash and lime mixed to a paste with water, rolled in chaff so they don't stick to each other, then packed in an earthenware jar with a lid. Every 3 days they have to be turned over so those at the bottom are placed at the top. After 15 days the jar is sealed and left for a month, during which time the eggs turn greenish black. Thousand year eggs are usually served at the start of a meal, quartered and garnished with lime and fresh ginger.

I am indebted to Tom Stobart and his wonderful volume, *The Cook's Encyclopaedia*, for this information on thousand year eggs. I cannot put it better, so here is his advice on the subject: 'They can be bought at shops which specialize in Chinese foods, but it is probably better to be introduced to them by Chinese friends who know what a good bad egg should taste like.'

Emu eggs: A single emu egg is equal to 10 hen eggs and is said to make excellent, light textured omelettes. Whether they will become as fashionable and available as emu meat has become in Australia in recent years, is yet to be seen.

Turtle eggs: While I have never come across these used in recipes, a freshly uncovered clutch of these round, soft-shelled eggs still wearing a dusting of fine golden sea sand, was highly prized. They were a rare treat, looking somewhat similar to ping-pong balls, except that the white shells dent because they are flexible. I cannot tell from personal experience what the flavour of a turtle egg is like. There are enough interesting foods in the world without making survival even more precarious for an already endangered species.

Pigeon eggs: These small eggs are usually served hard-boiled in Chinese cuisine, included in a main dish with other ingredients, not as a featured ingredient on their own.

Quail eggs: I don't know whether there is any truth in the rumour that quail eggs are higher in cholesterol than other eggs. They are considered a delicacy in Asia and certainly their dainty size means they can be used on hors d'oeuvres, usually hard-boiled. I think the most unusual dessert I have been offered was a bowl of cold syrup with hard-boiled quail eggs floating in it, together with sweet beans. This was in Malaysia, where it ranked along with ice kacang as a refreshing snack, but was sometimes served to finish a meal.

Balut: A speciality in the Philippines, these fertilised duck eggs are believed to be beneficial to pregnant women and men whose libido needs bolstering. Balut are eaten when the chick has formed. More than that I don't know, and have no intention of finding out.

The many and varied ways of preparing eggs across Asia certainly makes Western boiled, poached or fried eggs look staid. Not all are spicy and complex, however. Something as simple as beaten eggs dribbled into simmering broth results in the well-known Egg Flower Soup, versions of which appear in more than one Far Eastern country. For garnish and added food value, thin omelettes are cooked flat, cut into narrow ribbons and tossed with fried rice. In Korea, egg yolks and egg whites are cooked separately in flat omelettes, carefully avoiding browning, then cut into fine shreds.

SCRAMBLED EGGS

A favourite way of cooking eggs in Asia as it is so easy to add flavours with fresh herbs and a sprinkling of spices, transforming a nursery dish to something exotic.

Sri Lankan Style Scrambled Eggs

Serves 6

8 eggs
2 tablespoons cold water
2 teaspoons finely chopped fresh dill
1 teaspoon salt
½ teaspoon ground black pepper
2 tablespoons butter or oil
6 shallots or spring onions (scallions),
  finely sliced
2 sprigs fresh curry leaves

Beat eggs to mix yolks and whites, but do not overbeat to the point of frothiness.

Stir in water, dill, salt and pepper. Heat butter or oil in a large frying pan and fry the sliced shallots, stirring, until they are golden. Strip curry leaves off the stem and fry them along with the spring onions. Pour in the egg mixture and stir constantly over medium-low heat, until eggs begin to set. The finished result should be moist and creamy, so stop cooking before the eggs set hard and dry. This is traditionally served with stringhoppers (see recipe page 314) but are just as good on freshly made toast.

Parsi Style Spicy Scrambled Eggs (Akoori)

Serves 4

6 large eggs
4 tablespoons milk
¾ teaspoon salt
¼ teaspoon ground black pepper
½ teaspoon ground cumin
2 tablespoons ghee
6 spring onions (scallions), finely chopped
2 fresh chillies, seeded and chopped
1 teaspoon finely grated fresh ginger
⅛ teaspoon ground turmeric
2 tablespoons chopped fresh coriander leaves
1 small ripe tomato, diced (optional)
coriander sprigs to garnish

Beat eggs until mixed. Add milk, salt, pepper and cumin. Heat ghee in a frying pan and cook the spring onions, chillies and ginger until soft. Add turmeric, coriander leaves and tomato and fry for a minute or two longer, then stir in the egg mixture. Cook over low heat, stirring

and lifting the eggs as they begin to set on the base of the pan. Cook until eggs are creamy, transfer to a serving plate and serve with chapatis or parathas.

OMELETTES

Omelettes take on the flavour of many countries, filled with herbs, zingy with sliced fresh chillies, or delicately seasoned in the Japanese style.

Fresh Chilli Omelette

Serves 2 or 3

4 eggs
1 tablespoon cold water
salt and black pepper to taste
1 tablespoon ghee or oil
3 tablespoons sliced fresh chillies, red or green
3 tablespoons sliced shallots
1 teaspoon chopped fresh dill

Beat eggs slightly, adding cold water, salt and pepper. Heat half the ghee in a small pan and on low heat cook the chillies and shallots until soft. Cool cooked mixture slightly, then stir into the eggs together with the dill. Heat an omelette pan, put in remaining ghee to coat base of pan, and pour in the eggs. As eggs set around edge of pan draw to the centre, tilting pan so uncooked egg mixture runs to the edges. Fold in three and serve hot.

Spring Onion (Scallion) Omelette

This omelette is cooked thin and flat. It is either cut into strips for garnishing fried rice or noodles, or used whole for wrapping a serving of fried rice.

2 eggs
½ teaspoon salt
pinch white pepper
2 tablespoons finely chopped spring onions
  (scallions)
2 teaspoons peanut or sesame oil

Beat eggs, stir in salt, pepper and spring onions. Heat an omelette pan, grease lightly with oil and pour in just sufficient of the beaten egg to make a thin layer. Cook until firm, turn out onto a plate. Repeat with remaining egg mixture.

To make strips, stack omelettes, roll together and cut into slices of the required thickness.

Japanese Omelette

Serves 2

3 eggs
¼ teaspoon salt
¼ teaspoon sugar
2 tablespoons dashi or water
1 teaspoon mirin or sherry
1 teaspoon Japanese soy sauce
2 teaspoons oil
2 tablespoons cooked green peas
2 tablespoons finely diced cooked carrot
2 tablespoons grated white radish
few slices Japanese pickled ginger

Beat eggs lightly till well mixed but not frothy. Stir in salt, sugar, dashi, mirin and soy sauce.

A Japanese omelette pan is rectangular, but a round pan may be used and the omelette trimmed after it has been cooked and rolled. Heat the pan, rub with paper towels dipped in oil and pour in enough beaten egg to coat the pan. The pan should not be hot enough to brown the egg — Japanese omelettes are pale.

Scatter in some peas and diced carrot as soon as the egg is set. Start rolling the omelette in a neat cylinder. Pour in more egg and when set, roll around the first omelette. Remove from pan, press firmly to shape. A bamboo sushi mat is useful for this. Allow to cool, then slice thickly with a sharp knife.

Make a mound with the radish, place the ginger on top and serve alongside the omelette.

Chinese Omelettes (Eggs Foo Yong)

Serves 4–6

250 g/8 oz cooked prawns (shrimp)
6 eggs
½ teaspoon salt
¼ teaspoon ground black pepper
6 spring onions (scallions), finely chopped
peanut oil for frying
2 tablespoons chopped coriander leaves
** for garnish**

SAUCE
1 tablespoon light soy sauce
4 tablespoons dry sherry
2 tablespoons rice vinegar or white wine vinegar
2 tablespoons white sugar
1 tablespoon cornflour (cornstarch)
1 tablespoon shredded red ginger

Shell, devein and roughly chop prawns. Beat eggs with salt and pepper. Mix in prawns and spring onions. Heat wok, add 2 teaspoons oil and swirl to coat centre. Pour in 2 tablespoons egg mixture. When browned on underside, turn and cook other side. Transfer to a plate and keep warm. Repeat until remaining mixture is used up. Wipe out wok with paper towels. Combine soy sauce, sherry, vinegar, sugar and ¾ cup water in wok and stir over medium heat until sugar dissolves. Bring to the boil. Blend cornflour with 2 tablespoons cold water, stir into sauce and cook, stirring constantly until thickened and clear. Add red ginger and mix through. Serve omelettes with sauce and a sprinkling of coriander leaves.

Omelette Curry

6 eggs
1 teaspoon salt
¼ teaspoon ground black pepper
2 teaspoons finely chopped fresh dill
1 tablespoon ghee or oil
2 fresh chillies, chopped
2 spring onions (scallions), finely sliced

SAUCE
375 ml/12 fl oz/1½ cups coconut milk
1 small onion, sliced
1 teaspoon finely chopped garlic
½ teaspoon finely grated ginger
2 fresh green chillies, split
½ teaspoon ground turmeric
small piece cinnamon
sprig of curry leaves
strip of pandan leaf

Beat eggs and mix in the salt, pepper and dill. Heat ghee or oil and gently fry the chillies and onion until soft and fragrant. Pour in eggs and with the flat of a fork keep drawing the outer edges to the centre. When egg starts to set fold one side over to the centre, then tilt the pan so that the omelette is folded in thirds. Turn omelette over to cook top side. Remove to a plate and cut across into 4 pieces.

Make sauce by simmering the ingredients, uncovered, for about 10 minutes, adding a little water if it becomes too thick. Slide in the omelette slices for the last 2 minutes of cooking. Serve with rice.

BOILED EGGS

Hard-boiled eggs are just the starting point for many well-known Asian dishes, and very seldom are they left simply as hard-boiled eggs, except when they are marbled and used as decoration.

Marbling is easy to do: after cooking the eggs for just long enough to firm the egg white (about 7 minutes), the eggs are cooled and the egg shells lightly cracked all over. The eggs are then returned to the pan to cook longer, and left in the water for a further hour or more. Chinese style marbled eggs have tea leaves, salt, soy sauce, star anise or cassia added to the water to flavour and colour the eggs. The patterns made by the cracked shells are like the tracing of spider webs. Serve quartered with a dipping sauce.

Indonesian marbled eggs are treated in a similar fashion, but food colouring is added to the water during a second boiling of 5 minutes. The eggs are left to stand in the coloured water for 2 hours. When the shells are removed there are vividly coloured patterns on the white.

Hard-boiled eggs, halved or quartered, are used as garnish for platters of pilau rice.

In some instances the boiled eggs are given a spicy crust by rubbing over with turmeric and salt and then frying them in shallow oil until golden brown. Piercing the hard-boiled egg with a very fine skewer or a toothpick is advisable, to keep them from bursting during frying.

In India, hard-boiled eggs are enclosed in minced lamb and spices for the famous Nargisi Kofta — a name which evokes the yellow and white narcissus of spring time. They are then fried until the meat around them is cooked.

Throughout Asia hard-boiled eggs are made into curries or sambal, used as a garnish, stuffed with spicy pork or crab, or sliced thinly in big bowls of Korean cool noodle soup. It seems they are never eaten simply as boiled eggs.

Marbled Tea Eggs

Serves 12–18 as part of a selection of hors d'oeuvres.

6 eggs
1 litre/2 pints/4 cups water
3 tablespoons tea leaves
1 tablespoon salt
1 tablespoon five spice powder

Put eggs in a saucepan, cover with cold water and bring slowly to the boil, stirring gently (this helps to centre the yolks). Simmer gently for 7 minutes. Cool eggs thoroughly in cold water. Lightly crack each egg shell by rolling on a hard surface. Shell should be cracked all over, but do not remove.

Bring 4 cups water to the boil. Add tea leaves, salt and five spice powder. Add cracked eggs. Simmer, covered, for approximately 30 minutes or until shells turn brown. Let eggs stand in covered pan for 30 minutes longer (overnight if possible). Drain, cool and shell. The whites of eggs will have a marbled pattern on them. Cut into quarters and serve with a dipping sauce.

Indonesian Egg Sambal

Serves 4–6

4 eggs
3 tablespoons peanut oil
1 onion, finely chopped
1 teaspoon crushed garlic
½ teaspoon dried shrimp paste
1 tablespoon sambal ulek
  or chopped red chillies
1 teaspoon finely chopped galangal,
  fresh or bottled
6 candle nuts or macadamia nuts,
  finely grated or pounded
2 teaspoons palm sugar or brown sugar
125 ml/4 fl oz/½ cup coconut milk
salt to taste
2 tablespoons lime or lemon juice

Have eggs at room temperature or gently warm them in tepid water before cooking them.

Stir for the first few minutes so yolks are centred, then simmer for 8 minutes. Cool in a bowl of cold water. Shell eggs and halve lengthways.

Heat oil and fry onion and garlic until onion

is soft and golden. Add shrimp paste, sambal, galangal and nuts and fry, stirring, until fragrant. Add palm sugar, coconut milk, salt and lime juice and simmer, stirring frequently, until oil shines on surface. Put in eggs, spooning sauce over.

Eggs in Soy and Chilli (Son-in-Law Eggs)

A Thai recipe which has its counterpart in mother-in-law eggs. I have not been able to ascertain the reason behind these curious names. Serves 6.

6 eggs
3 tablespoons oil
1 medium onion, sliced thinly
2 fresh chillies, sliced
2 tablespoons palm sugar or brown sugar
3 tablespoons water
2 teaspoons instant tamarind pulp
1 tablespoon fish sauce
coriander leaves

Bring the eggs to the boil, stirring gently to centre the yolks. Simmer for 8 minutes, then run cold water into the pot until they are quite cold. Shell the eggs and wipe dry on paper towels. Pierce each one 2–3 times with a very fine toothpick.

Heat the oil in a wok and fry the eggs until golden and crisp. Drain on paper towels. Pour off all but a tablespoon of the oil. Heat it again and stir-fry the onion and chillies until the onion is golden and slightly crisp. Drain.

Mix the palm sugar, water, tamarind and fish sauce. Stir over low heat for 5 minutes or until slightly thick. Pour the sauce over the eggs, sprinkle the fried onion and chillies over, and garnish with coriander leaves and a chilli 'flower' (see page 167). Serve with rice.

STEAMED EGGS

There aren't many Asian recipes for eggs cooked in this delicate way, unless you take into account steamed custards based on eggs, coconut milk and palm sugar (see DESSERTS). However, in Japan a favourite is Chawan Mushi, beaten and seasoned eggs steamed in a special cup and eaten with a spoon.

Japanese Savoury Custard (Chawan Mushi)

Serves 4

4 dried shiitake mushrooms
2 tablespoons Japanese soy sauce
1 tablespoon sugar
4 small prawns (shrimp) or 8 slices kamaboko (fish cake)
4 fresh oysters or 4 small slices fresh tuna

CUSTARD
4 eggs
625 ml/1¼ pints/2½ cups dashi
salt to taste
1 tablespoon Japanese soy sauce
2 tablespoons sake, mirin or dry sherry

Soak mushrooms in hot water for 30 minutes, cut off and discard stems and simmer the caps in a small saucepan with 1 tablespoon of soy, a little of the soaking water and the sugar for 8–10 minutes. Shell and devein prawns. If tuna is used, marinate for a few minutes in remaining tablespoon of soy sauce.

Into each chawan mushi cup (custard cup or ramekin) put a mushroom; a prawn or 2 slices of kamaboko; and an oyster or a slice of tuna. Fill cups with custard mixture and put in a saucepan with hot water to come half way up the sides of the cups. If chawan mushi cups with lids are not available, cover the top of each cup with foil, pressing it close to the outside of the cup. Cover saucepan with a folded tea towel and then with the lid and bring water to the boil. Lower heat and simmer for 15 minutes or until set. Serve hot. In summer these custard soups may be served cold. They are the only Japanese soups that are eaten with a spoon. Etiquette for liquid soups is to lift the bowl to the lips with both hands.

If more convenient the chawan mushi may be baked in a moderate oven, standing them in a baking pan with hot water to come half way up the cups. An electric frypan is also a convenient method of steaming chawan mushi, with the cups standing in water.

Custard: Beat eggs, then mix in all other ingredients. When mixture has been poured into cups, carefully skim off the bubbles on the top of the mixture.

Note: If preferred, substitute thinly sliced chicken breast for the seafood.

Steamed Eggs with Mushrooms

4 dried shiitake mushrooms
½ cup soaked cellophane (bean starch) noodles
125 g/4 oz crab or prawn (shrimp) meat
125 g/4 oz cooked pork
5 eggs
2 spring onions (scallions), finely chopped
1 tablespoon finely chopped fresh coriander
   leaves
½ teaspoon salt
⅛ teaspoon black pepper

Soak mushrooms in hot water for 30 minutes. Discard stems, squeeze excess water from caps and slice finely. Soak a small amount of cellophane noodles in hot water for about 10 minutes, then measure ½ cup. Flake crab meat and discard any bony bits, or chop the shelled and deveined prawns into small pieces. Chop pork finely.

Beat eggs until yolks and whites are well mixed but not frothy. Stir in the spring onions, coriander, salt and pepper and the prepared mushrooms, noodles, seafood and pork. Pour into a heatproof dish and steam until firm, exact time depending on the depth of the mixture in the dish. Serve with rice and nuoc cham.

EGG COMBINATIONS

Eggs are so highly regarded as nourishment, they are often added to other dishes which are quite complete in themselves.

Eggs on Spinach

Serves 4

1 bunch spinach
1 tablespoon ghee or butter
1 small onion, finely chopped
1 teaspoon finely chopped garlic
1 teaspoon finely chopped ginger
½ teaspoon cumin seeds
pinch chilli powder (optional)
salt and ground black pepper to taste
6 eggs

Wash the spinach thoroughly, discard any tough stems and cook the leaves in very little water in a covered pan for 10–12 minutes or until soft. Drain and chop the spinach.

In a frying pan heat the ghee or butter and fry the onion, garlic, ginger and cumin until onion is soft and turning golden. Mix in the chopped spinach. Add the chilli powder (if used) and salt and pepper to taste.

Beat the eggs in a bowl and season to taste with salt and pepper. Pour over the spinach mixture in the pan, cover and cook on low heat until eggs set. Serve hot.

Eggs with Savoury Mince

Serves 4

2 tablespoons ghee or oil
1 large onion, finely chopped
2 fresh green chillies, seeded and chopped
2 teaspoons finely chopped garlic
1 teaspoon finely chopped ginger
2 teaspoons ground coriander
1 teaspoon ground cumin
1 teaspoon chilli powder (optional)
1 teaspoon ground turmeric
750 g/1½ lb minced (ground) lamb or beef
1 ripe tomato peeled and chopped
1½ teaspoons salt
pinch of sugar (optional)
1 teaspoon garam masala (recipe page 354)
4 tablespoons finely chopped fresh coriander
4 eggs
salt and ground black pepper to taste

Heat ghee or oil and fry the onion, chillies, garlic and ginger until onion is golden. Add ground spices, stir and fry for 1 minute, then add the meat and fry, stirring, until it changes colour. Add tomato, salt and ½ cup water. Some cooks like to add a pinch of sugar. Cover and cook until meat is tender and liquid almost absorbed. Mix in the garam masala and half the fresh coriander. Spread meat in a buttered ovenproof dish, make 4 depressions with the back of a spoon and break an egg into each one. Season eggs with pepper and salt.

Bake in a moderately hot oven 190°C (375°F) until the eggs are set. Sprinkle with remaining fresh coriander and serve quickly, before eggs get overcooked. Serve with parathas or naan.

Note: A variation on this dish is to beat the egg whites stiffly, mix in the yolks and season with salt and pepper, then to spread this mixture over the meat and bake until the eggs are set.

EGGS AS WRAPPERS

There are many ingenious ways in which omelettes are used as wrappers. Here are two examples.

Shanghai Egg Pouch Soup

Serves 6–8

125 g/4 oz bean thread vermicelli
6 dried shiitake mushrooms
half a Chinese cabbage (wong nga bak)
2 litres/4 pints/8 cups chicken stock

EGG POUCHES
125 g/4 oz minced (ground) pork
1 spring onion (scallion), finely chopped
¼ teaspoon finely grated fresh ginger
½ teaspoon salt
1 teaspoon cornflour (cornstarch)
3 eggs
pinch of salt

Soak the noodles in hot water for 20 minutes, then drain. Soak the mushrooms in hot water for 30 minutes, drain, discard the stems and cut caps into quarters. Wash the cabbage and cut it into thick slices.

To make the pouches: Combine the pork with spring onion, ginger, salt and cornflour; mix well. In a separate bowl, beat the eggs with 1 teaspoon of cold water and a pinch of salt.

Lightly oil a ladle and heat over a low gas flame. Pour in about 3 tablespoons of the beaten egg, swirl to give an even, thick coating of egg and pour excess egg back into the bowl. Put a teaspoon of the pork mixture on one side of the egg and fold the other side over, sealing the edge if necessary with a little of the uncooked egg. The pouches can be made in a heavy frying pan but the shape will not be as good. Place on a plate when made.

Cooking the soup: Heat the stock in a clay pot or flame-proof casserole, and season with salt if necessary. Add noodles, return to the boil and simmer for 5 minutes. Arrange the egg pouches in the pot and simmer for a further 5 minutes. In the centre place the sliced cabbage and the mushrooms, and give the soup a final simmering for 5 minutes.

Note: This dish can be prepared beforehand, to the stage where the noodles have been cooked in the soup. Have the egg pouches, cabbage and mushrooms ready in the refrigerator. About 20 minutes before serving, reheat the soup and continue with the recipe.

Steamed Egg Roll with Pork

Serves 8

FILLING
185 g/6 oz raw lean pork
½ teaspoon salt
2 teaspoons light soy sauce
½ teaspoon oriental sesame oil
1 teaspoon cornflour (cornstarch)
1 tablespoon finely chopped coriander
1 tablespoon finely chopped spring onions (scallions)

WRAPPERS
3 eggs
½ teaspoon salt
1 tablespoon peanut oil
1 teaspoon oriental sesame oil

Filling: Cut pork into pieces and put into food processor with salt, soy sauce and sesame oil. Process until smooth. Scrape mixture into a bowl and mix in the other ingredients, combining well. Alternatively, chop everything very, very finely with a sharp chopper until it has the consistency of a paste.

Wrappers: Beat the eggs well with salt. Reserve 1 tablespoon of beaten egg for sealing the egg rolls.

Heat a small omelette pan. Measure the peanut and sesame oils into a saucer. Dip a paper towel in the oil and grease the pan. Pour 2–3 tablespoons of egg mixture into the pan and make a thin omelette, cooking it on one side only. Turn it onto a plate. Repeat with remaining egg mixture, greasing the pan each time. There will be 4 or 5 omelettes, depending on the size of your pan.

Divide the filling into the same number of portions as there are omelettes. Place each omelette on a board, cooked side up, and spread the filling almost to the edges using an oiled spatula or back of a spoon. Roll up like a Swiss roll and seal the edges with reserved beaten egg

Lightly oil a plate with the mixed oils and

place the rolls on it. Set the plate in a steamer (or on a rack in a saucepan of boiling water), cover and steam for 15 minutes. (The plate should be slightly smaller than the steamer to allow steam to circulate.) Remove from the steamer, allow to cool a little, then cut into slices diagonally. Serve hot or cold.

Elephant Apple

See WOODAPPLE.

Emu

One of the fashionable environmentally friendly meats being farmed commercially in Australia and appearing on menus of top restaurants and on first-class menus of Australia's national airline, Qantas.

The large birds with their soft-padded feet are kinder to the soil than traditional hard-hoofed farm animals, and can successfully be raised on poor soil that would not sustain cattle or sheep.

Mostly they are slaughtered when about a year old or at a live weight of about 45 kg (90 lb). The dressed weight is less than half the live weight, and once boxed the weight is half that again, around 12 kg (24 lb). Sold in shrink packs, it is recommended that after opening the bag the meat should be drained and left in the refrigerator for at least 1 hour prior to cooking.

Emu meat is deep red in colour, tender, has a slightly gamey flavour and delicate texture, and is low in fat. Farm-bred birds yield tender cuts from the fore saddle, hind saddle and drum, which comprises small muscles from the leg, thigh and back. Unlike most birds bred for the table, there is no breast or forequarter on an emu. The meat is suitable for roasting, grilling or may be diced for kebabs. It is best served rare to medium-rare. My own experience of tasting emu was in a terrine with native Australian herbs, well done and well flavoured.

Enokitake

See MUSHROOMS & FUNGI.

Eryngo

(*Eryngium foetidum*) SEE ILLUSTRATION. This herb which is sometimes called foreign coriander, culantro and saw tooth herb, is used in Vietnam, Laos, Cambodia and Thailand. While it may be served raw as a flavour accent, it is more often used to flavour cooked dishes. Its strong flavour is a good foil for offal.

> **Malaysia:** *ketumbar jawa*
> **Thailand:** *pak chee farang*
> **Vietnam:** *ngo gai*

Essences

Scan the shelves of a large Asian store and you will see flavourings you never dreamed existed. Some of them are very convincing, but others do not come up to the standard of the fruit, flower or leaf which they are supposed to represent. Results vary with brands too. Where possible, buy natural flavour essences in preference to imitation.

Almond essence: A flavouring essence reminiscent of bitter almonds, which are toxic in their raw state. Almost identical in flavour are the kernels from apricot and peach stones, which also must be heat treated (boiled or roasted) to make them safe for consumption. As a flavour, popular in some Chinese sweets like almond tea and almond jelly (also called almond tofu).

Banana flavour: Also known as amyl essence. Not guaranteed to appeal to all tastes.

Cardamom extract: There are two distinct grades of cardamom flavour: extract and essence. Extract is the more expensive and has truer flavour. Both enable flavour to be added without the black specks which result if ground seeds are used. In most cases the look of ground cardamom is quite accceptable.

Jasmine essence: In Thailand, jasmine is a favourite flavour. Use this essence with restraint. In times gone by it was the custom to soak jasmine blossoms in water overnight, then use that water to impart flavour. Now it comes out of a bottle and is concentrated.

Kewra essence: The flavouring derived from a variety of pandan, *Pandanus fascicularis*. Used in India, it is also called kevda essence and is from the male inflorescence of the plant. It is strongly floral.

Use an eye-dropper to add a drop at a time in case too much goes in and ruins the dish. (I keep a small eye-dropper attached to each bottle of strong essence with a rubber band. Then a precise measuring device is always at hand.)

Khus essence: Sometimes spelled khas, this flavouring essence is extracted from the aromatic rhizomes of vetiver (*Vetiveria zizanioides*), a tropical grass. Used to flavour sweet syrups and beverages in India, it is particularly popular in Bengal. The oil is a constituent of some of the world's most expensive perfumes. In tropical Asia the roots are also used to make screens, mats and fans which, when damped down, release again their unique fragrance.

Pandan essence: May be either thick and deep green, or thin and clear. The flavour duplicates that which is derived from the leaves of the *Pandanus latifolius* or screwpine which is as popular in Malaysia, Indonesia, Thailand and Singapore as vanilla is in the West. Cakes, jellies, desserts and drinks may be flavoured with the light, pleasant perfume. Even some brands of coconut juice in cans hold a hint of pandan flavour.

Rose water or rose essence: The light, sweet scent of roses may be imparted by using rose water which is more delicate than rose essence. It scents sweets and drinks of all kinds in India. If using rose essence, a much smaller amount is needed.

Sandalwood: A musky, exotic perfume which is not to everyone's liking but can be tantalising if used with discretion. The problem is that most people have been conditioned to accept this fragrance in bath soap, but not in a sherbet.

Ylang Ylang: An essence made from fragrant flowers which was once a vital export to 19th century European perfumeries. The flowers (*Cananga odorata*) are used today to perfume some sweets.

Fagara

See SZECHWAN PEPPER.

Falooda

One of those words which is used not only by the local population, but also by English-speaking people in India and Pakistan when they wish to order the long, cold, sweet drink which takes the place of a milk shake or ice-cream soda in these countries. Very refreshing during the heat of the day. Often served instead of wine and beer during festive meals, especially among the Moslems whose religion forbids alcoholic beverages. The sweet, milky drink goes very well with spicy foods, helping to soothe tongues not accustomed to pungent chillies.

Falooda

1 teaspoon basil seeds
rooh afza syrup or rose syrup
iced water or cold milk
2 tablespoons psyllium husks*
crushed ice
agar-agar jelly (optional)

Soak basil seeds in 1 cup warm water for 10 minutes until they develop a slippery coating.

For each tall glass pour in 2 or 3 tablespoons of syrup, almost fill the glass with water or milk and sprinkle with a teaspoon of psyllium husks. Stir in a teaspoon of the soaked basil seeds and add crushed ice. If liked, small dice of agar-agar jelly may also be added.

* Available at health food outlets.

Syrup for Falooda

The scented syrup is available in Asian shops, but is easy enough to make. Cool and store in a bottle in the refrigerator.

1 kg/2 lb/4 cups white sugar
750 ml/1½ pints/3cups water
30 drops essence of rose
15 drops essence of kewra
red food colouring

Put sugar and water into a heavy pan and dissolve sugar over gentle heat. Cool, then add flavouring and enough red food colouring to give a strong colour as it will be diluted with many times its volume of milk or water.

Falooda Seed

See PSYLLIUM.

Fava Bean

See LEGUMES & PULSES (Broad bean).

Feijoa

(*Feijoa sellowiana*) At the very start, let's establish that this fragrant fruit is not a guava (*Psidium guajava*), whether or not it is given the qualifying description of 'pineapple guava' as it often is. Originating in South America, feijoa are now mainly grown in New Zealand. It is fragrant, but with a perfume more like quince. It is more slender and oval in shape and the skin which is green even when the feijoa is ripe, has a dull appearance, unlike the shiny skin of guavas. The flesh is creamy white and slightly granular, and there is a central arrangement of small edible seeds.

When fully ripe the fruit is scooped from the shell with a spoon and enjoyed just as is. They may be halved and poached, and are spectacularly successful as a glacéed fruit if you have the time and the patience for that sort of thing.

To enjoy feijoas for longer than their brief

season I can recommend the conserve and the jelly. For more immediate consumption simply peel them thinly, poach them in a sugar syrup and serve with cream. Fully ripe and with their thin, astringent skin removed, they may also be used raw as an addition to fruit salad.

Feijoa Conserve

Makes about 6 cups

1.5 kg/3 lb feijoas
1 litre/2 pints/4 cups water
1.5 kg/3 lb/6 cups sugar
juice of 1 lemon, strained

Wash feijoas and trim off stem and blossom ends. Do not peel the fruit, but cut into halves. Put into a heavy preserving pan with the water, bring to the boil and simmer until skins are tender, about 1 hour. Add sugar and lemon juice, stir until sugar dissolves and boil steadily for 20–30 minutes, stirring now and then until jam sets when tested on a cold saucer. Heat clean dry jars in the oven while jam is cooking. Bottle and either seal while hot or leave to become completely cold before covering.

Feni

A clear spirit, very high in alcohol, distilled from the cashew apple (the swollen stem of the cashew). It is the local drink in Goa on the west coast of India. While it is drunk neat by seasoned imbibers, a tamer version is made by mixing a small amount of feni with the liquid inside a fresh coconut and adding flavoured sugar syrup and crushed ice for a thirst-quenching but still potent drink.

Fennel

(*Foeniculum vulgare*) Native to southern Europe and Asia, fennel is used as a vegetable and herb in Europe but in Asia only the seeds are used. The flavour is distinctly aniseed, and the seed is like a larger, paler version of cumin seed. There is a variety known as Lucknow fennel in which the seeds are about half the length of common fennel and olive green compared with the yellowish-green of the larger variety.

The seeds of fennel are sometimes referred to as 'sweet cumin', perhaps because of their similar appearance — certainly not for any flavour similarity.

Whole fennel seeds are part of Bengali panch phora, a mixture of five aromatic seeds (see page 355). It is used in far smaller amounts than are cumin and coriander. In some dishes its sweet aroma is a distinguishing factor and the toasted and ground seeds are given a more prominent role.

The cooks of Malaysia, Indonesia and Sri Lanka use fennel as one of the spices which go to make their complex curries.

In India, the seeds are included in the after-dinner chew of betel leaf as a digestive as well as a breath sweetener. Sometimes the seeds are offered as a breath freshener on their own or sugar-coated and coloured.

In China, fennel may be used in place of aniseed in five-spice powder.

Medicinal uses: Fennel was relied on more heavily in times gone by. The renowned herbalist Culpeper wrote that the seeds were used in medicines to relieve wheezing and shortness of breath. The seeds are chewed or a tea brewed from them as an aid to cure stomach ache and constipation, regulate menstruation and increase breast milk. They are combined with root extract for a diuretic aid to slimming. Research seems to indicate that fennel can help in cases of liver damage as a result of excessive alcohol consumption. As an aid to cleansing the skin, gentle steaming over water in which fennel seeds and leaves have been boiled is said to be effective.

Burma: *samouk-saba*
India: *saunf, sonf*
Indonesia: *adas*
Malaysia: *jintan manis*
Sri Lanka: *maduru*
Thailand: *yira*

Fenugreek

(*Trigonella foenum-graecum*) SEE ILLUSTRATION. Native to both Europe and Asia. Both the seeds and tender sprouted leaves are eaten. The seeds, which are flat, oblong, mustard brownish and about 3 mm (1/8 in) long with a deep furrow along their length, are an important component of Indian curry powders, but should not be used with too much enthusiasm as they have a bitter flavour. In

Sri Lanka a few fenugreek seeds are used whole in certain dishes, in particular fish and seafood curries. When soaked overnight the seed coat becomes soft and jelly-like, and in this state is one of the chief ingredients of a paste of bitter herbs called halba or hilbe, popular with people of Middle Eastern origin. The other ingredients are fresh coriander herb, garlic, salt and lemon juice and a small hot chilli if liked. Once ground in a blender the vivid green, viscous mass is used as a dip for flat loaves. A recipe for this is included below, since many Sephardic Jews settled in India and Burma, taking halba to those countries.

The young plants are used as a vegetable, being harvested when about 20 cm (8 in) high and tied in bundles like mint or parsley. The stems can be quite tough so only the tender top portion is used. It is recommended that home gardeners grow the seeds themselves and harvest them when about half the size of the commercial plants in order to enjoy them when tender. Cooked with potatoes or spinach they add a pleasantly bitter tang. Raw, they make a flavoursome addition to salads but should be picked at the two-leaf stage. Some commercial sprout mixtures include fenugreek sprouts, and there is no mistaking their pungent flavour.

Indian shops usually sell dried fenugreek herb, good for flavouring spinach and other vegetables. It is advisable to strip the leaves from the thicker stalks as these will not become tender even with long cooking. Use sparingly, as a little dried fenugreek goes a long way.

Medicinal uses: An ancient medicinal herb, prescribed in India and the Middle East for a range of conditions from constipation to sore throats, and in particular for tuberculosis and bronchitis. In European herbal medicine, it is a powerful expectorant and used as an infusion, tincture or extract to break up respiratory congestion. The seed is a carminative (taken to relieve flatulence). Like many bitter-tasting foods, it is used as a treatment for diabetes.

The mucilaginous texture of the soaked seeds makes them a very effective demulcent. For inflamed conditions of the stomach and intestines, a decoction of 30 g (1 oz) of seeds in 500 ml (1 pint) of water is administered.

Modern research provides increasing evidence that fenugreek lowers blood cholesterol and blood sugar. It may be taken in the form of an infusion or included in cooked food. The problem with fenugreek is that it makes its presence evident in the smell of the breath, sweat and urine, but there are probably worse things one could smell of than curry!

Externally, the seeds are used as a poultice for abscesses, boils and carbuncles. Also recommended in old herbal books as a wash for the scalp, 'for it taketh away the scurfe, scales, nits, and all other suchlike imperfections'.

India: *methi, ventayam* (seeds)
  methi bhaji (plants)
Malaysia: *alba* (seeds)
Sri Lanka: *uluhaal* (seeds)

Halba

2 tablespoons fenugreek seeds
4 large cloves garlic
1 bunch fresh coriander herb
1 hot green chilli (optional)
lemon juice to taste
salt to taste

Rinse fenugreek seeds and soak overnight in water to cover. They will soften after a few hours and develop a jelly-like coating. Combine in a blender jar with the peeled garlic, coriander (washed and roughly chopped) and the seeded chilli if desired. Add lemon juice and some of the soaking water to assist in blending the mixture to a purée. Blend on high speed, adding more lemon juice or water as necessary. Consistency should be that of mayonnaise. Add salt to taste. Serve as a dip with flat bread or chapatis.

Fern, Fiddlehead

(*Athyrium esculentum*) There are some who would insist all ferns are toxic. Even the fiddlehead fern (a stage of the development — be it ostrich, bracken or osmund fern and not a variety itself), which is considered a delicacy in parts of the world as diverse as Canada, north east America, Japan and Korea, is poisonous once it starts to turn purple and mature. In the Philippines, Thailand and Japan the partly opened leaflets and tender tips of pako fern are snapped into short lengths, blanched and eaten as salad or cooked vegetable. The flavour is mild and texture should still be crisp.

In the countries where fiddleheads are a seasonal delicacy, the tender, jade green, immature curling

heads are sold at market. Their flavour is said to be a cross between artichoke and asparagus, although it is for their unique texture that they are most prized. If the fiddleheads are a variety that are covered in a brown, downy fuzz, rub briskly between the palms to remove and rinse thoroughly before cooking. Some experts strongly advise against the eating of any ferns, bracken fern (*Pteridium aquilinum*) in particular, as they are highly carcinogenic; but opinion is still divided.

Before you go gathering bits and pieces out of the garden to dip in your nam prik, please have the plant identified by an expert.

Japan: *pako shida; zenmai*
Korea: *koh sah li*
Philippines: *pako*
Thailand: *phak kuut*

Fiji

The food of Fiji, like that of most Pacific islands, is influenced by traditional home-grown produce. It has also been influenced by migration from Asia (India in particular).

Books dealing with local produce seem intent on demonstrating how rou-rou (taro leaves), can feature in casseroles, quiche lorraine and soufflés. This is understandable, since local recipes alone would fill a very slim volume indeed.

Reef fish and crustacea, abundant in the islands, are cooked with little seasoning. The native style of cooking features food which is totally innocent of added flavours. Pork, fish, yams and other vegetables are carefully wrapped in banana leaves or breadfruit leaves before being cooked in the earth oven called a lovo which is heated by large rocks lowered into a large hole in the ground. The hole is then covered and all the food steams for hours.

Some favourites which grace the table at a traditional meal include: breadfruit; cooking banana (vudi); taro (dalo) sweet potato (kumala); and yams of various colours, the most startling being bright purple. All of these are simply boiled, baked or steamed.

Kava, also called yang-gona, a ceremonial brew said to be mildly intoxicating, is offered to all tourists and, like the equivalent drink in Hawaii, once tasted is never forgotten.

What most impresses visitors to Fiji is the tropical fruit which is allowed to ripen on the trees,

developing full flavour and sweetness. For export it has to be picked half-ripe, marketing taking precedence over excellence of flavour.

The food is made more interesting by the use of rich coconut milk (lolo).

One interesting Fijian dish is kokoda, a raw fish salad, which probably owes the addition of sliced fresh chilli and onion to the Indian presence.

To make the Fijian version of a dish encountered in many Pacific island countries, use fillets of firm white fish such as Parrot fish (kalia), Spanish mackerel (walu), trevally (saga), or snapper (kabati). Cut into small cubes or fine slices and marinate in lime or lemon juice to cover for 2 or 3 hours in the refrigerator. (Do not use metal utensils.) Meanwhile, mix the grated flesh of a mature coconut with a sliced onion, a chopped chilli and a teaspoon of salt. After kneading with a little water, the seasoned coconut cream is strained and used as a dressing on the fish after pouring off the lime juice. It is served cold but not chilled, since coconut cream becomes granular at low temperatures.

Fish

There are quite a number of species of sea life that are unique to the waters of the Pacific and Indian oceans. While some have no equivalent, others may be substituted with regional variants. For more specific information on seafood of the region, see Alan Davidson's *Seafood of South East Asia*.

It is important to have an understanding of how different seafood works with Asian flavourings. A delicate, white-fleshed fish would not stand up to strong flavours like a vindaloo curry or pungent herbs. A dark-fleshed, oily fish would overwhelm delicate treatment such as marinating in lime juice and dressing in coconut milk. A meaty fish will give a different result to a soft-fleshed fish. Some kinds of fish are better for fillets and others make better cutlets.

A common error made when cooking seafood, in the cuisines of both East and West, is overcooking it. All seafood needs to be cooked only until it turns opaque. Obviously, whole fish and large crustacea in their shells take a little longer, but it is always preferable to under-cook, rather than over-cook it.

Probably the single most common misapprehension about fish is that they are full of bones. The second reason more people don't eat fish is that they think all fish taste fishy, which is also an unfair generalisation. If you haven't enjoyed bony or 'fishy' fish in the past, don't give them a wide berth until you've tried a hot mackerel curry or piquant curry of tuna or bonito. The strong spicing of the first dish and the tangy acidity of the second does much to mute the oily fish flavour.

Arguably the largest number of fish in all the world's oceans belong to the order Clupeiformes. It includes all herring-like fish, regardless of size. These are characterised by a single, non-spiny dorsal fin, an elongated shape and scales which are often deciduous (that is to say they shed readily when handled). It includes species of sardine, herring and larger species with romantic names such as milkfish (in spite of a plethora of long, fine bones, it is a commonly eaten fish whose skin is a delicacy in the Philippines) and ladyfish (variously called banana fish and bonefish).

Selecting and buying fish: There are several ways of telling when fish are fresh, no matter what part of the world you are in or how unfamiliar the variety of fish.

• The flesh of whole fish should always be firm to the touch. If your finger leaves a depression, the fish is not fresh enough to eat. It is not as easy to ascertain the freshness of fillets or cutlets as these are often behind counters. A good fishmonger won't mind filleting or cutting a fish into cutlets after you pick it out. Sometimes this just isn't possible, but make sure the colour is good and the cut surface of the flesh looks succulent and not at all powdery.

• Look into your fish's eyes. They should be clear, bright and shiny, not dull or sunken.

• Try to get a sniff of the fish. A strong fishy odour is not a good sign. Fresh fish and seafood should smell of the sea.

Having purchased fresh fish, it is important to get it home in good condition. As fish is one of the most perishable foods it should be kept as cold as possible. Take an insulated container with a few frozen ice packs when you go to buy fish. Refrigerate immediately, cook and eat within a day or two for best flavour and food value. If it is to be frozen, this must be done within 24 hours of the fish being caught.

In the coastal areas of Asia and the Pacific, people rely on fish for a major part of their diet. People living far from the coast or a fish market rely on frozen fish, or buy fresh fish and freeze it until the next shopping day. If there is a fisherman in the family, a month's supply of fish may arrive all at once and have to be processed, dried or preserved.

On rare occasions, even the freshest fish from warm ocean waters may be potential carriers of ciguatera poisoning. While not common, it occurs sporadically and unpredictably, mainly in reef areas and Pacific atolls. It can affect species such as coral trout, Spanish mackerel, reef cod, grouper, barracuda, emperor, trevally and kingfish, with smaller fish less likely to be carriers. The toxin is not destroyed by cooking, and it is best to avoid locally implicated species should an outbreak occur.

Symptoms include tingling and numbness in fingers, toes and mouth, and a burning sensation on contact with cold water as well as signs of food poisoning. Experts in the field advise that no more than 125 g (4 oz) of these kinds of fish should be eaten at a first sitting, so that even if they are affected, only slight discomfort is experienced.

Cleaning and scaling: Whole fish must be cleaned and gutted before freezing. A sharp knife and gloves make this messy job easier. Remove gills, blood and lining of the stomach. One way to ensure the fish is clean is to dip damp paper towels in coarse salt and scrub the cavity until all blood has been removed, then rinse away the salt.

Scales left on help retain flavour and moisture, but scaling just before cooking the fish is not always convenient. Scaling should be done in a large sink of cold water to prevent scales flying everywhere and turning up in unlikely places for days afterwards. Use a fish scaler or sharp knife and scrape from the tail towards the head. Rinse under a cold tap to remove loose scales, then scrape again until every last scale has been dislodged. Better still, ask the fishmonger to do it.

Filleting: A filleting knife makes this task easier. Keep the knife as close to the centre bone as possible, and use the bones for making stock which can be frozen until required. Fish stock should not be boiled for a long time, as meat stock is. Twenty minutes is sufficient, with just enough water to cover the bones and flavourings.

Skinning: Place fillets on a board with the skin against the board. Hold the tail end firmly with fingers dipped in salt to give a good grip. Slide a sharp knife between the flesh and the skin, starting at the tail. Work away from you, keeping a firm hold of the skin.

Freezing: Freeze fish as you wish to use it, (whole, fillets or cutlets) so that it can be cooked from the frozen state, allowing a little extra time.

Lean fish: If freezing lean fish, immerse for 1 minute in a brine solution of 4 tablespoons salt to 1 litre (2 pints) cold water. This preserves texture and flavour. May be kept frozen for 4–6 months.

Oily fish: If freezing oily fish, immerse for 5 minutes in a solution of 6 tablespoons lemon juice to 500 ml (1 pint) cold water. The fish may be enclosed in a freezer bag or it may first be glazed with layers of ice to form a protective insulation. Optimum storage time is 2–4 months. Glazing is recommended when freezing whole fish. To do this, place the fish, unwrapped, on a tray and fast freeze. When solid, dip it in clean cold water so a thin layer of ice forms on the frozen fish. Place fish on a rack over the tray and return to the freezer. When ice is hard repeat the dipping and freezing until there is a layer of ice about 6 mm (¼ in) thick all over the fish. Enclose in a freezer bag.

Fillets and cutlets may be frozen in the same way. The aim is to exclude air which causes dehydration. Place freezer wrap between slices for easy separation. Mark and date all items before freezing.

Chinese banquets usually include a whole fish, the fish being steamed, deep fried or quick boiled. Delicate fish with large, moist flakes are preferred.

Some Asian countries prefer a stronger flavoured fish since it will most likely be cooked with chillies and other spices. The fish may be cleaned, scaled, scored and spiced, wrapped in whole banana leaves and cooked over coals. Or it may be sliced across into cutlets or 'steaks'.

Cutlets are popular for curries and frying. The tail of a middle-sized to large fish is usually left whole, ideal for grilling in one piece. Large fish heads are much sought after for curries.

Smaller fish are rubbed with spices and grilled over coals, curried, or fried in oil so hot that even the bones become crisp and edible.

While strong-flavoured oily fish such as mullet are not regarded with favour in Western cooking, they stand up to the spicing and sour flavours with which fish is usually cooked in Asia.

The names by which fish are called in various countries can vary widely for the same fish — even in the English language. A name like coral cod or rock cod can mean one species in one country and quite another fish elsewhere. The information that follows is intended as a general guide.

In recipes only the type of fish is specified, e.g. 'delicate white' or 'dark oily', as any fish answering to the description may be used.

Some popular fish in Asia and the Pacific islands are listed below under their common names.

See also SEAFOOD.

Grouper: Firm, white flesh. Bake, steam, shallow fry, grill.

Burma: *nga tauk tu*
China: *lo sue baan*
Cambodia: *trey tukke korm*
Indonesia: *kerapu*
Malaysia: *kerapu*
Philippines: *garopa, kolapo*
Thailand: *pla karang*
Vietnam: *ca mu heo*

Mackerel: Firm, oily fish. Fry, grill, barbecue, curry. Or marinate and serve raw.

Burma: *pa la tu*
Cambodia: *pla lung*
Indonesia: *kembung lelaki*
Hawaii: *opelu palahu*
Japan: *saba*
Malaysia: *kembong*
Sri Lanka: *kumbalava*
Thailand: *pla thu*
Vietnam: *ca bac ma*

Spanish mackerel: Firm flesh, good flavour, and a favourite in South East Asia. Fry, curry, grill, or marinate and serve raw.

Burma: *nga kyi kan*
Cambodia: *trey beka inti*
China: *kau yue*
Fiji: *walu*
Indonesia: *tenggiri*
Malaysia: *tenggiri batang*
Philippines: *tangigi*
Sri Lanka: *thora malu, anjeela*
Thailand: *pla ai bang*
Vietnam: *ca thu dai*

Shark: There is more than one kind of shark and they are often sold as rock salmon, flake or 'boneless fillets' in Western countries. A firm, moist, generally mild-flavoured fish, the great advantage is that there are no bones. Curry, fry, steam, boil.

Burma: *nga man*
Cambodia: *trey chlam*
China: *tsim bay tsai*
Fiji: *nagio*
India: *mussi*

147

Indonesia: *cucut pisang*
Malaysia: *yu pasir*
Philippines: *pating*
Sri Lanka: *mora*
Thailand: *pla chalam*
Vietnam: *ca nham*

Trevally: White flesh, little fat. Steam, fry or simmer in coconut milk.

Burma: *nga dama*
Cambodia: *trey chen chah*
China: *paak so kung*
Fiji: *saqa*
Indonesia: *kuweh rombeh, loang*
Malaysia: *chermin, sagai*
Philippines: *damis lawin*
Sri Lanka: *parau*
Thailand: *pla chom ngam*
Vietnam: *ca lao nhot*

Tuna: Flesh may be red, pale pink or almost white, according to variety, but is always firm. Inclined to be dry if cooked too long. Stands up well to acid flavours. Very popular raw as sashimi. A small variety, Bluefin Tuna (about 1 m/3 ft long), is better known in South East Asia than the larger varieties.

Burma: *nga kyi kan*
Cambodia: *trey chheam khieu*
China: *doe chung*
Fiji: *yatu*
Hawaii: *ahi*
Indonesia: *tuna, tongkol*
Japan: *maguro*
Malaysia: *tongkol*
Philippines: *tulingan*
Sri Lanka: *kelawalla*
Thailand: *pla o maw*
Vietnam: *ca bo*

The following recipes have been grouped according to cooking method. I have made mention of the countries they are most strongly identified with to indicate which flavours to expect.

Fish Kofta Curry (Burma)

Serves 6

KOFTAS

1 kg/2 lb firm white fish fillets
(jewfish, cod or gemfish)
1 medium onion, very finely chopped
1 teaspoon crushed garlic
1½ teaspoons finely grated fresh ginger
2 tablespoons lime or lemon juice
1 tablespoon finely chopped fresh coriander
or dill
2 slices white bread, soaked in hot water
and squeezed dry
1 teaspoon anchovy paste or sauce (optional)
2½ teaspoons salt
½ teaspoon pepper

CURRY

¼ cup gingelly oil or peanut oil
mixed with 1 tablespoon oriental sesame oil
3 medium onions, finely chopped
1 tablespoon finely chopped garlic
1 tablespoon finely chopped fresh ginger
1 teaspoon ground turmeric
1–2 teaspoons chilli powder
1 teaspoon paprika (optional)
2 tomatoes, peeled and chopped
1½ teaspoons salt
1 teaspoon dried shrimp paste
375 ml/12 fl oz/1½ cups hot water
2 tablespoons chopped fresh coriander leaves
2 tablespoons lime or lemon juice

If the fillets have not been skinned, with a sharp knife remove skin from fish. Finely mince fish, taking care to remove bones. (To do this without a mincer, cut fillets into thin slices lengthways, then chop finely across.) Put minced fish in a large bowl, add remaining ingredients. Mix thoroughly with the hands. Shape the mixture into walnut-size balls (koftas). Makes approximately 24 balls.

Curry: Heat oil in a large saucepan and fry onions, garlic and ginger until soft and golden. Add turmeric, chilli powder and paprika, tomatoes and salt. (Paprika is not traditionally used in Burma, but it does give a good red colour without adding excessive heat.)

Wrap dried shrimp paste in aluminium foil and cook under hot griller for a few minutes on each side. Unwrap, dissolve in 1½ cups hot water and add to pan. Cook, covered, until tomato is soft and pulpy. If gravy seems too reduced, add a little hot water. There should be enough gravy to almost cover the fish koftas. Carefully put the koftas in the gravy and simmer over a moderate heat until they are cooked, about 20 minutes. Shake pan gently from time to time. Do not stir until fish has cooked and is firm, or the koftas might break. Gently stir in coriander leaves and lime juice and serve with rice.

Sour Curry of Fish (Sri Lanka)

A very acid curry like this one is the best way to use oily, strong-flavoured fish. Serves 6.

750 g/1½ lb oily fish (tuna or bonito)
1 rounded tablespoon tamarind pulp
  or 4 pieces dried gamboge
3 tablespoons vinegar
1 medium onion, finely chopped
2 teaspoons garlic, finely chopped
1 teaspoon finely grated fresh ginger
1 teaspoon salt
sprig of fresh curry leaves
  or 12 dried curry leaves
1 stalk lemon grass or 2 strips lemon rind
1 cinnamon stick
¼ teaspoon fenugreek seeds
¼ teaspoon ground black pepper
½ teaspoon chilli powder (optional)
2 tablespoons oil

Wash and dry fish, cut into serving pieces. Soak the tamarind in the vinegar and ½ cup boiling water until it is soft. Squeeze tamarind in the liquid to dissolve pulp, strain through a fine nylon sieve and discard seeds and fibres. If using gamboge, soak until soft. Put all ingredients into a non-aluminium saucepan and bring to the boil. Reduce heat and simmer uncovered until fish is cooked and gravy is thick. Shake pan or turn fish pieces carefully once or twice during cooking. Serve with rice.

Fish Curry with Tomato (Sri Lanka)

Serves 6

750 g/1½ lb thick steaks of firm fish
  (Spanish mackerel or jewfish)
1 teaspoon ground turmeric
1 teaspoon salt
oil for frying
1 large onion, roughly chopped
2 teaspoons finely chopped garlic
2 teaspoons finely chopped fresh ginger
1 large ripe tomato, chopped
2 tablespoons oil
1 tablespoon Ceylon curry powder
1 teaspoon chilli powder
salt to taste
500 ml/1 pint/2 cups coconut milk

Wash and dry fish and rub with turmeric and salt. Cut each steak into serving pieces. Heat oil in a frying pan for shallow frying, and fry the fish until golden brown on both sides. Drain.

Put onion, garlic, ginger and tomato in an electric blender and blend to a smooth paste. Heat oil in a saucepan and fry the blended ingredients until oil starts to separate from mixture. Add the curry powder and chilli powder, about a teaspoonful of salt, and the coconut milk. Bring to the boil, stirring. Simmer for 5 minutes, then add the fish and simmer for 10 minutes. Serve with rice and accompaniments.

Fish Curry with Coconut (Goa)

Serves 6

750 g/1½ lb fish steaks
lemon juice
pepper
6 large dried red chillies
  preferably Goan or Kashmiri type
2 tablespoons desiccated coconut
1 tablespoon coriander seeds
2 teaspoons cumin seeds
¼ teaspoon fenugreek seeds
4 teaspoons finely chopped garlic
1 teaspoon finely chopped fresh ginger
1 tablespoon tamarind pulp
2 tablespoons ghee or oil
1 large onion, finely chopped
375 ml/12 fl oz/1½ cups coconut milk
1½ teaspoons salt

Wash fish, rub over with lemon juice, salt and pepper and set aside. Soak the chillies in hot water for 10 minutes.

In a dry pan roast the coconut, stirring constantly, until brown. Remove coconut and dry roast the coriander, cumin and fenugreek seeds, shaking pan or stirring, until brown. Put soaked chillies, coconut, spices, garlic and ginger into electric blender and blend to a smooth paste, adding a little water if necessary. Soak tamarind pulp in ½ cup hot water, squeeze to dissolve pulp, strain.

Heat ghee or oil in a heavy saucepan and fry the onion until soft. Add the blended mixture and fry on medium heat, stirring until it darkens in colour and smells cooked. Add the coconut milk, salt, tamarind liquid and bring slowly to simmering point, stirring to prevent curdling. Add the fish and simmer, uncovered, until fish is cooked. Serve with rice.

Note: Ground coriander, cumin and fenugreek may be used instead of whole seeds, but first roast them on low heat to intensify the flavours, stirring constantly and taking care that they do not burn.

Braised Fish with Saffron and Yoghurt (Punjab)

Serves 4–6

750 g/1½ lb thick fish fillets
lemon juice
1 teaspoon salt
1 teaspoon ground black pepper
1 teaspoon ground turmeric
oil for frying
1 large onion, finely sliced
1 medium onion, roughly chopped
1 teaspoon chopped garlic
1 tablespoon chopped fresh ginger
2 or 3 fresh red chillies, seeded
2 tablespoons blanched almonds
1 tablespoon white poppy seeds (optional)
2 teaspoons ground cumin
2 teaspoons ground cardamom
¼ teaspoon ground cinnamon
small pinch ground cloves
¼ teaspoon saffron strands
125 ml/4 fl oz/½ cup yoghurt
salt to taste
2 tablespoons chopped fresh coriander

Wash and dry fish, cut into large serving pieces and rub with lemon juice, salt, pepper and turmeric. Heat oil in a frying pan for shallow frying and on high heat brown the fish quickly on both sides. Lift out onto a plate. In the same oil fry finely sliced onion until golden brown, remove and set aside. Put roughly chopped onion, garlic, ginger, chillies, almonds and poppy seeds into an electric blender and purée. Add a little water if needed to facilitate blending. Add ground spices and blend once again, briefly.

Pour off all but about 2 tablespoons oil from pan and fry the blended mixture until it changes colour and gives out a pleasing aroma. Stir constantly so that the mixture does not stick to pan and burn. Add ¼ cup water to blender container and swirl out any remaining spice mixture. Add to pan.

Toast saffron strands in a dry pan for a minute, turn onto a saucer and crush with the back of a spoon. Dissolve in 2 tablespoons boiling water and add to pan. Add yoghurt, stir and simmer gently for a few minutes, then add fish pieces, turning them carefully in the sauce. Add salt to taste. Simmer for 10 minutes, sprinkle with coriander and serve hot with rice.

Barbecued Fish (Northern India)

Serves 4

1 whole fish, about 1 kg/2 lb
coarse salt
2 teaspoons crushed garlic
2 teaspoons finely grated fresh ginger
1½ teaspoons salt
1 teaspoon ground cumin
1 teaspoon chilli powder
1 teaspoon ground turmeric
2 teaspoons paprika
2 tablespoons lemon juice
3 tablespoons melted ghee
2 teaspoons garam masala (recipe page 354)

Buy fish cleaned and scaled with head removed. Scrub the cavity of the fish with several pieces of damp paper towels dipped in coarse salt. Wash the fish well under cold running water, then blot dry with paper towels.

With a sharp knife cut slashes on each side of the fish, almost to the bone.

Combine the garlic, ginger, salt, cumin, chilli powder, turmeric and paprika. Add enough lemon juice to form a thick paste. Rub the marinade all over the fish, inside and out. Pass a long metal skewer through the fish from head to tail and cook over glowing coals or under a preheated griller, brushing with the melted ghee. It should take 6 or 7 minutes cooking for each side. When fish is almost done sprinkle with garam masala. Serve with naan, parathas or chapatis.

Singapore Style Fish Cakes (Otak-Otak)

These highly spiced slivers of fish grilled over coals will win even the most determined non-fish-eater. Serves 4.

500 g/1 lb well-flavoured, firm fish
  (Spanish mackerel)
3 dried red chillies
2 stems lemon grass, sliced finely
  or 2 strips lemon rind
1 medium onion, peeled and chopped roughly
1 teaspoon chopped garlic
½ teaspoon ground turmeric
1 teaspoon salt
¼ teaspoon pepper
2 teaspoons ground coriander
3 tablespoons thick coconut milk
4 candle nuts or macadamia nuts (optional)
4 tablespoons chopped Vietnamese mint
  or fresh coriander
2 fresh red chillies, chopped finely

Remove the skin and bones from fillets and purée in a food processor. Discard stems and seeds of chillies and soak in hot water for 10 minutes. Put chillies, lemon grass, onion, garlic, turmeric, salt, pepper, coriander, coconut milk and nuts into blender and blend to a purée. Mix well with fish, adding mint and chillies.

Put 1 tablespoon quantities of mixture onto squares of banana leaf or squares of heavy-duty foil. Shape into flat parcels, fold foil over to seal edges and cook over a barbecue or under a preheated grill for 5 minutes each side. Serve warm or cold as an appetiser.

Note: If using banana leaves, first wash, dry and heat over low flame to make them pliable before making the parcels. Fasten with toothpicks.

Steamed Red Emperor with Ham

A delicately seasoned dish fit for a Chinese banquet. Serves 4–6.

500 g/1 lb skinless fillets red emperor
salt
½ teaspoon sugar
pinch white pepper
1 teaspoon oriental sesame oil
4 teaspoons cornflour (cornstarch)
6 dried shiitake mushrooms
small leaves of Chinese cabbage
  (choy sum or bok choy)
125 g/4 oz cooked ham, sliced thinly
190 ml/6 fl oz/¾ cup chicken stock

Wash fish and cut into thin slices. Sprinkle with ½ teaspoon salt, sugar, pepper, ½ teaspoon of the sesame oil and 2 teaspoons of the cornflour and mix well. Chill for 30 minutes.

Cover mushrooms with very hot water and leave to soak for 30 minutes, then cut off stems and slice caps. Trim small leaves of Chinese cabbage and take as many curved tips as there are pieces of fish. Arrange in a single layer on a heatproof serving dish lightly brushed with sesame oil, each leaf topped with a slice of fish, a slice of ham cut a little smaller than the fish, and a slice of mushroom.

Steam over boiling water for 8 minutes or until fish has become opaque. While fish steams, bring chicken stock to the boil and stir in remaining 2 teaspoons cornflour mixed with a tablespoon of cold water. When sauce boils and thickens remove from heat and stir in remaining ½ teaspoon sesame oil. Season to taste with salt and white pepper. Pour over fish and serve immediately.

Parsi Steamed Fish

One of the most famous Parsi dishes, delicate fish thickly covered with fresh chatni, wrapped in banana leaves and steamed. Serves 4.

4 whole fish or 750 g/1½ lb white fish fillets
salt
1 large lemon
2 medium onions
1 teaspoon finely chopped fresh ginger
1 teaspoon finely chopped garlic
2 large fresh green chillies, seeded and chopped
30 g/1 oz/½ cup chopped fresh coriander leaves
1 teaspoon ground cumin
½ teaspoon ground fenugreek (optional)
4 tablespoons fresh grated or desiccated
   coconut
2 tablespoons ghee or oil
2 teaspoons salt
1 teaspoon garam masala (recipe page 354)
banana leaves or foil

Wash the fish, dry with paper towels and rub with salt. Leave while preparing masala.

Peel the lemon, removing all the white pith. Cut lemon in pieces and discard all seeds. Put into container of an electric blender with one onion, roughly chopped, ginger, garlic, chillies, fresh coriander, cumin and fenugreek. Blend on high speed until puréed, then add coconut and blend again.

Heat oil and fry remaining onion, finely chopped, until soft and golden. Add blended mixture and fry, stirring, until fragrant. Remove from heat. Add salt and garam masala. Coat each fish or fillet with the mixture, wrap securely in banana leaves or foil and steam over gently simmering water for 30 minutes, turning parcels once. Serve in the leaf parcels.

Quick Boiled Fish, Chinese Style

For this dish it is best to choose a fish with delicate flavour since there are no strong spices to stand up to an oily, strong-flavoured fish. Serves 6–8.

1 whole fish, about 1 kg/2 lb
   (red emperor, snapper, coral trout)
1 onion, sliced
8 slices fresh ginger
few sprigs celery leaves
½ teaspoon whole black peppercorns
1 tablespoon chicken stock powder
3 tablespoons peanut oil
½ teaspoon crushed garlic
2 teaspoons finely shredded ginger
2 tablespoons soy sauce
1 tablespoon oriental sesame oil

Have fish cleaned and scaled, but it is usually necessary to scrub cavity with damp paper towels dipped in coarse salt to remove all traces of blood.

Run enough water into a wok to cover the fish, but do not put fish in yet. Add the onion, ginger, celery, peppercorns and stock powder and bring to the boil, then simmer for about 8 minutes to let liquid develop flavour. Gently slide fish into the water and return water to the boil. Lower heat, cover the wok and poach gently for 8–10 minutes or until flesh is opaque when tested. Lift out fish on a large wire spoon, let liquid drain away and carefully place fish on a large platter.

While fish is cooking, heat peanut oil in a small pan and on low heat cook the garlic and ginger for a minute, stirring. Remove from heat, add soy sauce and sesame oil and pour sizzling over the fish. Serve immediately.

Simmered Fish Hotpot

A one-dish meal typical of Japanese home cooking. Serves 6.

500 g/1 lb snapper or bream fillets
1 lobster tail
1 cup cooked cellophane (beanstarch) noodles
1 litre/2 pints/4 cups dashi
2 tender carrots, sliced
small piece kombu (optional)
soy sauce to taste
few young spinach leaves
6 fresh mushrooms, sliced
6 spring onions (scallions), cut in bite-sized
   lengths

Wash fish fillets and cut into 2.5 cm (1 in) pieces. With a sharp cleaver cut lobster tail into slices, then cut each of the larger slices into halves. Drain cellophane noodles and cut into short lengths, put into a saucepan with the dashi and bring to the boil. Reduce heat and simmer for 5 minutes before adding carrots, kombu and soy sauce. Simmer a further 2 minutes, then add fish and lobster, spinach, mushrooms and spring onions and continue to cook for 5 minutes or until everything is just done. Serve in soup bowls accompanied by small dishes of dipping sauces.

Fried Mountain Trout with Ginger (China)

Serves 4

4 single serving size trout,
** about 200 g/7 oz each**
salt and five-spice powder mixed together
4 tablespoons cornflour (cornstarch)
3 spring onions (scallions)
8 tablespoons peanut oil
2 tablespoons fine shreds fresh ginger*

SAUCE

2 tablespoons Chinese red vinegar
** or wine vinegar**
2 tablespoons Chinese wine or sherry
4 tablespoons light soy sauce
2 teaspoons sugar
2 teaspoons oriental sesame oil
2 tablespoons chopped fresh coriander

Clean the cavity of the trout with damp paper towels dipped in salt. Make shallow diagonal cuts on either side of the fish and rub in salt and five-spice powder. Roll fish in cornflour to coat then dust off excess.

Cut the spring onion into bite-sized pieces. Combine the sauce ingredients.

Heat a wok, add peanut oil and when very hot, fry the ginger and spring onions for a few seconds until spring onions are soft but not brown. Remove on a frying spoon and set aside on a plate. Slip fish into the oil and fry until golden brown underneath, then turn them over, lower heat and fry until the other side is browned and the fish are cooked through. Remove to serving dish.

Pour off oil, add sauce mixture to wok with ginger and spring onion. Cook for 1 minute on high heat or until the sauce boils. Spoon sauce over the trout and serve garnished with coriander.

* Young tender ginger, which has translucent skin and pink tips, is best for this dish. If this is not in season, reduce the quantity of ginger by half.

Deep Fried Fish with Sweet-Sour Sauce (China)

Serves 4

500 g/1 lb firm white fish fillets
½ teaspoon salt
½ teaspoon finely grated fresh ginger
1 egg white, very slightly beaten
oil for frying
cornflour (cornstarch) for dusting

SAUCE

1 fresh red chilli
1 fresh green chilli
125 ml/4 fl oz/½ cup canned Chinese pickles
125 ml/4 fl oz/½ cup pickle juice from can
125 ml/4 fl oz/½ cup water
1 tablespoon sugar
½ teaspoon salt
1 tablespoon cornflour (cornstarch)

Remove all skin and bone from fish and cut into short finger lengths. Sprinkle with salt and rub with fresh ginger. Coat fish with egg white. Let stand while making sauce.

Heat about a cup of oil in a wok. Toss pieces of fish in cornflour a few times, until lightly but completely coated. Fry a few pieces at a time over medium heat for a few minutes, until just done. Do not overcook the fish. Drain on paper towels, pour sauce over and serve immediately with rice.

Sauce: Seed and finely slice chillies, shred pickles into fine strips. Heat pickle juice, water, sugar and salt in a small saucepan and when boiling stir in cornflour mixed with cold water and stir until thickened and clear. Stir in pickles and chillies.

Fried Fish Indian Style

Serves 4

500 g/1 lb firm white fish fillets
3 tablespoons plain (all-purpose) flour
3 tablespoons besan (chick pea flour)
1½ teaspoons salt
1 teaspoon garam masala (recipe page 354)
½ teaspoon ground turmeric
oil for frying
1 egg, well beaten

Wash and dry fish fillets. Mix flour, besan, salt, garam masala and turmeric together. Heat oil in wok or karhai (deep frying pan) until smoking hot. Dip fish fillets into beaten egg then lightly coat with flour mixture. Fry quickly until golden brown on both sides. Drain on paper towels and serve immediately with boiled rice and accompaniments.

Grilled Fish, Indonesian Style

Since servings of highly spiced dishes do not have to be large, this will serve 8 people comfortably, with the fish steaks cut into quarters along the natural divisions.

**2 steaks Spanish mackerel
  or other firm white fish
salt and freshly ground black pepper
12 peeled shallots or 2 small onions
2 cloves garlic, peeled
2 teaspoons finely grated fresh ginger
2 teaspoons finely chopped fresh galangal
2 teaspoons finely chopped fresh chilli
1 tablespoon finely chopped lemon grass
  or 1 teaspoon finely grated lemon rind
oil for shallow frying
2 tablespoons tamarind liquid
2 tablespoons dark soy sauce
2 teaspoons palm sugar or brown sugar**

Season the fish steaks with salt and pepper and set aside while preparing the spice mixture.

Pound in mortar and pestle, or grind in electric blender the shallots, garlic, ginger, galangal, chilli and lemon grass. Add a little water if necessary to facilitate blending.

Heat a heavy frying pan with sufficient oil to cover base of pan. Fry the fish steaks until golden brown on both sides. Remove to a dish, divide each one into quarters and discard the bones.

Pour off oil, leaving about 2 tablespoons. Add the ground mixture and fry, stirring, until the fragrance mellows and oil shimmers on top. Add tamarind liquid, soy sauce and palm sugar. Stir and simmer until sauce is thick, then return fish pieces to pan and coat with the piquant sauce. Serve warm or at room temperature.

Fish Cake

Fish cake can be made at home or purchased refrigerated or frozen. This saves time and labour, though it is not clear sometimes just how much fish goes into the fish and starch mixture. Ready-cooked fish cake is available fried, steamed or baked.

Japanese fish cake, kamaboko (sometimes called fish paste), is generally delicate in flavour and smooth and soft in texture, sometimes with a swirl of colour so it doubles as a garnish. Another type of Japanese fish cake is the baked chikuwa, cylindrical, brown on the outside, and with a hollow space in the centre where it has been, presumably, moulded around a stick.

Chinese fish cake comes in a variety of shapes, most often round patties, rectangular slabs, or balls a little smaller than a walnut, sometimes slightly pointed at the ends. It is more chewily textured and highly seasoned than Japanese fish cake.

The fish cake most used in Korean cooking is either Japanese (baked, fried or steamed varieties) or Korean fish cake, which may be shaped in rectangular slabs, balls, sausage shapes or small, thin, banknote-sized sheets.

Vietnamese fish cake is more in the style of Chinese fish cake.

All fish cake should be thinly sliced and, since it is already cooked, added to a dish at the end, just long enough to heat through.

Korean Fish Cake with Chilli Paste

This is served as a kim chi (relish). In South East Asian countries this would be called a sambal. Something to liven up the rice.

**100 g/3½ oz fish cake
3 tablespoons oil
1 large onion, thinly sliced
1 teaspoon crushed garlic
2 teaspoons chilli paste with fermented
  soy beans
2 teaspoons Korean chilli bean paste
  (gochujang)
½ teaspoon sugar
squeeze of lime juice (optional)**

Slice the fish cake thinly into bite-sized strips. Heat oil and over gentle heat fry the onion, stirring, until tender but still slightly crisp. Add garlic and stir until golden, then stir in the two kinds of chilli paste. Add fish cake and heat through, sprinkle with sugar and lime juice and serve as an accompaniment to steamed rice.

Fish, Dried

Fish of all sizes are salted and sun dried, or simply dried and used in many ways, even when the fresh equivalent is available. Whitebait (very small, only 2–3 cm [¾–1 in] in length), or the slightly larger sprats or anchovies up to 6 cm (2½ in) long are usually deep fried and served as a crisp accompaniment to rice. Whitebait can be fried whole, but ideally the larger fish should be picked over to remove heads and intestines before use if this has not been done prior to drying.

If they are to be fried for the delicious crisp snack so popular in South East Asia, make sure they are completely dry, as humidity during storage can make them tough and leathery when fried instead of meltingly crisp, the way they should be. Fry a few as a test first and if they are not crisp when cool, dry the unfried fish in the oven at 150°C (300°F) for 10 minutes and allow to cool. Put them into a wire sieve and shake over a sink to loosen and get rid of any small particles as these will burn when the fish are fried.

Drop by handfuls into hot oil, fry for a few minutes and drain on paper towels. For a slightly more elaborate version, combine them with roasted, salted peanuts, a sprinkling of chilli powder and sugar, and a couple of tablespoons of crisply fried shallots. Serve with pre-dinner drinks, or as a snack at any time.

Large fish are also salted and dried, and these are used as the main ingredient in curries and sambals and added to vegetables both for protein value and for the pungent flavour which lifts a dish from blandness, a cardinal sin in Asian cooking.

See also ANCHOVY, BOMBAY DUCK, MALDIVE FISH, BONITO.

Burma: *nga chauk*
India: *nethali*
Indonesia: *ikan teri*
Malaysia: *ikan bilis*
Philippines: *dilis*
Sri Lanka: *haal masso, karavadu*
Thailand: *plasroi*

Dried Fish and Eggplant Curry

This dish was served regularly by our household cook in Sri Lanka. Serves 6.

250 g/8 oz salted dried fish
500 g/1 lb eggplants (aubergines)
1 teaspoon ground turmeric
1 teaspoon salt
oil for frying
12 banana capsicums (peppers)
12 large cloves garlic, peeled
2 medium onions, finely sliced
3 tablespoons Ceylon curry powder
400 ml/14 fl oz can coconut milk
1 small cinnamon stick
1 tablespoon tamarind pulp
3 tablespoons vinegar
1 tablespoon palm sugar or brown sugar

Cut dried fish into large pieces, about 5 cm (2 in) across. Slice eggplants thickly, rub each slice with turmeric and salt and set aside for 20 minutes, then blot dry with paper towels. (It is wise to wear disposable gloves when doing this, as turmeric stains the hands.)

Heat 1 cup oil in a wok and fry the dried fish. Remove to a plate and fry the capsicums on high heat until the skin blisters. Remove with a slotted spoon. Fry the garlic cloves on medium heat, just until golden. Remove. Fry the eggplant, not crowding pan and replenishing oil if necessary. When brown, remove and put with the other fried items. Finally, in about 2 tablespoons of oil, fry the onions until soft and golden. Add curry powder and fry for 1 minute.

Add coconut milk mixed with an equal amount of water and stir as it comes to the boil. Add cinnamon and the fried ingredients and allow to simmer uncovered, stirring occasionally. Meanwhile, soak the tamarind in ½ cup hot water, knead to dissolve the pulp, and strain. When curry is reduced and thick, stir in the tamarind pulp, vinegar and sugar. Serve with rice.

Fish Head

No one who has visited Singapore with an interest in local food could have escaped being told about restaurants specialising in fish head curry. It is regarded as an important dish. Its origins are in

Fish Maw

India, but as usually happens there has been a little culinary crossover, resulting in a very interesting and spicy dish. The large pieces of flesh within the head are boneless and very sweet, and the lips and eyes are said to be the best parts.

Fish Head Curry

Serves 6

1 or 2 large fish heads 1.5–2.5 kg/3–5 lb
  (snapper, grouper, kingfish)
250 g/8 oz tender okra
2 slender eggplants (aubergines)
2 tablespoons tamarind pulp
4 tablespoons coriander seeds
2 tablespoons cumin seeds
2 teaspoons fennel seeds
4 tablespoons peanut oil
½ teaspoon fenugreek seeds
1 teaspoon black mustard seeds
6 green chillies, halved lengthways
2 sprigs fresh curry leaves, or 20 dried leaves
2 large onions, finely chopped
2 teaspoons chopped garlic
2 teaspoons chopped ginger
1 teaspoon ground turmeric
½ teaspoon ground pepper
2 tablespoons tomato paste
2 firm, ripe tomatoes, quartered
250 ml/8 fl oz/1 cup coconut milk
salt to taste

Clean and scale fish head. Cut okra and eggplants into 5 cm (2 in) lengths. Soak tamarind in 2 cups hot water for 10 minutes, squeeze to dissolve pulp, strain. In a dry pan roast the coriander, cumin and fennel seeds separately until fragrant and slightly darkened in colour. Grind in spice grinder or pound using a mortar and pestle to a fine powder.

  Heat oil and fry eggplant and okra about 3 minutes, remove from oil. Add fenugreek and mustard seeds, fry until mustard seeds pop. Add chillies, curry leaves, onion, garlic and ginger and lower heat. Fry until soft and golden. Add ground spices and fry, stirring, for 1 minute. Stir in tamarind liquid, tomato paste and tomatoes. Bring to the boil, add coconut milk and salt. Add fish head and vegetables and simmer uncovered until cooked.

  Serve with steamed white rice.

Fish Maw

The dried stomach lining of large fish. The term refers to the air bladder (also called swim bladder) that is found in all fish except sharks and rays. The maw we buy is usually from the conger pike and its role is to add texture to a dish. It might sound off-putting but it has no fishy taste. The cleaned maw is dried and then deep fried to make it puff and expand. In this state it will keep indefinitely.

Before it can be eaten, it must first be soaked in water for a few hours, weighted down by a plate. Smaller after soaking, the maw is wrung out and then washed in vinegared water to remove any trace of fishiness. Once again squeezed dry, the maw is cut into fine strips, ready to add to a dish. The maw in itself is a texture ingredient only, and is used with other strongly flavoured ingredients to make it interesting. It usually requires only a couple of minutes cooking to absorb the flavours in the pot.

China: *Yu to*

Fish Paste

In some Chinese stores it is possible to buy raw fish paste by weight. You can then add your chosen seasonings, form it into whatever shape you wish and cook in the required method. 'Fish paste' is also a term applied to Japanese fish cakes which are already cooked. See FISH CAKE.

Fish Roe

Strictly speaking, only the roe of sturgeon qualifies as caviar but in common usage we hear of salmon caviar, lumpfish caviar and rarely but deliciously, flying fish caviar. The caviar of flying fish (tobiko) are tiny, but the most textured of all; they crunch and pop as they are bitten into. In Japan tobiko is popular on sushi, although salmon caviar (ikura) is most often used on sushi, its glistening, bright orange globules making an attractive topping within the encircling band of nori. See SUSHI.

Fish Sauce

Although salt is an important ingredient in Asian cuisine, there are instances where a more complex flavour ingredient takes its place, and this is one. Completely natural, it is the clear, amber-coloured liquor that runs off when small fish are packed in wooden barrels with salt and fermented for a few months.

For those not brought up with this ingredient, the smell may take a little getting used to but if you have eaten and enjoyed the food of Thailand and Vietnam it is certain that you have survived a close encounter with the pungent seasoning. There are a few dashes of fish sauce in most dishes.

In addition to flavour, fish sauce provides protein and vitamin B in diets that are not traditionally rich in these nutrients, being based chiefly on rice.

There are different grades of fish sauce, the Thai version being paler and milder than the Vietnamese. Cheaper fish sauce is used in cooking, and the more expensive first yield is reserved for adding to dipping sauces. It will keep indefinitely without refrigeration.

On some bottles, especially those that originate in China, Hong Kong and the Philippines, the name may be 'fish gravy', but it is essentially the same as fish sauce.

Burma: *ngan-pya-ye*
Cambodia: *tuk trey*
Laos: *nam pa*
Philippines: *patis*
Thailand: *nam pla*
Vietnam: *nuoc nam*

Garlic, Chilli and Fish Sauce (Nuoc Cham)

Fish sauce is not just added to cooked foods. Together with sweet and sour and hot flavours, it is an important ingredient in dipping sauces. This one is a Vietnamese favourite.

2 ripe red chillies
1 clove garlic
1 teaspoon sugar
1 lemon
1 tablespoon vinegar
1 tablespoon water
4 tablespoons fish sauce

Cut off stalks from chillies, split down the centre and remove seeds and centre membrane. Cut into pieces, and pound using a mortar and pestle* together with peeled garlic. Add sugar. Peel lemon, removing all the white pith. Slice and remove seeds. Add a small piece at a time to the chillies and pound to a pulp. Stir in the vinegar, water and fish sauce. Serve in a small bowl and use in small quantities.

* A blender may be used instead of a mortar and pestle, but this aerates the sauce.

Five-Spice Powder

A traditional Chinese spice blend. It seems there are as many opinions on exactly what makes up five-spice powder as there are on what should be in garam masala. One thing is apparent: there are very often more than five flavour ingredients. The blend always includes at least one component to lend a licorice or aniseed flavour. Spices commonly used are anise, cinnamon, cloves and Szechwan pepper, and sometimes fennel, ground ginger and licorice root.

Flavouring Essences

See ESSENCES.

Flours & Starches

In addition to being the principal ingredient in breads, noodles and pastries, flours and starches are used for texture and thickening in Asian cuisines. But not flour as we know it, i.e., white or wholemeal, plain (all-purpose) or self-raising. Wheat flour is used in Asia, but there are also a large number of flours and fine starches from an array of grains, pulses, seeds, roots and tubers. The source of the flour or starch largely determines its properties.

Starch from roots and tubers (e.g. arrowroot, potato starch and tapioca starch) has large grains with a low amylase content which means they will absorb water more readily, thicken at lower temperatures and remain fluid, though viscous. Grain starches (e.g. rice, wheat and maize) have small grains with a high amylase content which are not as willing to absorb water, require higher temperatures to thicken, and solidify somewhat when cooled.

Purchasing and storing: All flours and starches should be stored airtight in a cool, dry place. If they are being kept for long periods and the climate is warm and humid, refrigeration is advisable to prevent weevil infestation.

Some flours and starches used throughout Asia include:

Acorn starch: (*Castanopsis cuspidata, Lithocarpus corneus*) A fine, beige-coloured starch derived from some non-bitter species of acorn. Acorn flour is made into bread in some parts of the world. In Korea, the silky starch, mook, is mixed with water (not as simple as it sounds) and cooked into a 'blancmange' that looks like caramel fudge. It sets into a gelatinous brown slab not tasting of much except, perhaps, green tea. This is cut into pieces and mixed with a dressing of flavoursome ingredients before serving.

Arrowroot: (*Maranta arundinacea*) A fine, white powder with a starch content of 80 per cent. It is extracted from a tropical plant by pulverising the rhizomes and washing them in water to obtain a milky liquid which, after further washing and drying, yields the fine grains of starch.

It is used as a thickener, and often added to rice flour in Thai dessert dishes. It is also used in China to make a variety of clear noodle, slightly tinged with yellow, with a rectangular shape (as distinct from the fine round strands or flat ribbon shapes of bean starch noodles) and a unique texture.

As a thickener, arrowroot starch is considered superior to cornflour in clarity and viscosity, and has no taste of its own, although overcooking will cause the starch to break down and the sauce to separate.

An ingredient long known to the West for its easy digestibility (hence its suitability for infants and invalids), arrowroot jelly is taken to stop diarrhoea.

China: *chuk shway*
India: *tikhor*
Indonesia: *angkrik*
Japan: *kuzu ukon*
Malaysia: *ararut*
Philippines: *aroro*
Sri Lanka: *hulankiriya*
Thailand: *saakhu, pang tao yai mom*

Arrowroot Jelly

2 teaspoons arrowroot powder
250 ml/8 fl oz/1 cup water
honey or sugar to taste
1 teaspoon lime juice
  or few drops vanilla
1 drop red food colouring (optional)

Mix the arrowroot with a tablespoon of cold water to a smooth cream. Bring measured water to the boil in a small pan, stir in honey or sugar and when it has dissolved stir in the arrowroot until it becomes thick and clear. Add lime juice or vanilla and colour a delicate pink, then pour into a glass dish or mould and leave to set.

Atta: (*Triticum vulgare, T. aestivum*) Fine wholemeal flour made from low-gluten, soft-textured wheat, used to make Indian flat breads and also known as chapati flour. It is sold in Indian stores and may be labelled 80/20 or 60/40, the higher figure referring to the proportion of wholemeal to white flour. It is not interchangeable with supermarket wholemeal flour which has a higher gluten content and makes heavier, coarser chapatis. Atta's texture is finer and softer. Being low in gluten, it is easier to knead and roll. If you are unable to get atta, substitute the fine, slightly granular flour sold as 'continental flour', similar to roti flour.

Other flours bearing the name atta are bajra atta (millet flour) or jowar atta (sorghum flour). However, atta usually refers to wheat flour.

Banana flour: (*Musa paradisiaca*) Also known as plantain meal and pisang starch. Made from cooking varieties, it is used as invalid food, since it is strengthening and filling as well as easily digested.

Barley flour: See **Malt flour**.

Besan: (*Cicer arietinum*) Sometimes called besan, patani or channa powder, this pale yellow flour is made from a small, yellow or brown-skinned variety of chick pea. The chick pea has the nuttiest flavour of all dried legumes and is India's most important legume. The variety of chick pea used for besan flour (deshi or kala gram) is smaller and darker than the *C. mediterraneum* and *C. eurasiaticum* varieties. The larger, paler seeds come from a variety called kabuli gram.

A passable substitute is ground roasted yellow split peas, but it lacks the nutty flavour. (Don't try grinding dried chick peas in a domestic blender and expect it to survive the ordeal as they are incredibly hard.)

Besan is used variously as a thickener, as a flavouring, in batter for pakoras (fried savoury morsels) as well as in the meltingly crisp Indian sweetmeat, Mysore pak. Toasted, it is a popular accompaniment in Burma, sprinkled over Moh Hin Gha (see page 23) and Burmese Egg Noodles with Curry (see page 251).

Buckwheat flour: (*Fagopyrum esculenta*) Derived from the seeds of a plant belonging to the same family as sorrel, rhubarb and dock. The flour is used in Japan to make soba, the traditional Edo noodles, long, thin and grey-brown in colour. Dough from flours such as buckwheat, corn and millet are not as elastic as wheat flour and harder to roll (one reason why soba-making is such a skill). Buckwheat, in various degrees of refinement, is the main ingredient in soba noodles. Pure buckwheat noodles, that is to say without wheat flour added to the dough, are known as tachi soba or 'silk cut noodles' after the special cutting action required, reminiscent of the shearing motion used on high-quality silks by the kimono-makers of old.

The darkest buckwheat flour, inakako (least refined), is used to make the dark, sweet noodles known as yabu soba. A medium-grade flour, seiro, is more yellow-green in colour. The most highly refined buckwheat flour (sarashina flour) is also the most expensive. From the endosperm of the kernel, it is pure white, as is the soba it makes, gozen soba, (gozen meaning 'to be served before nobles'). White flour lends itself best to flavouring and colouring, and there are a number of popular variations. These include yuzu rind (fragrant citrus rind that flavours and tints the soba a vivid yellow for kawari soba) and green tea (for cha soba). Other additions include red ginger, green shiso leaves, black sesame seeds and even cherry blossoms.

In Indian cookery buckwheat flour is often blended with other flours such as besan or wheat flour or with cooked, mashed green banana or potato for easier handling. Buckwheat flour is used during the nine-day Navratra fast in spring and autumn, when grains are to be avoided.

See also NOODLES.

Cassava flour: (*Manihot esculenta, M. dulcis*) Cassava flour is made from cassava pulp in the Pacific islands. Cassava tubers must be processed fairly immediately because they begin to ferment within a few hours of being gathered. The flour is used quite widely in Raratonga and the northern atolls, where it is known as pia. A cash crop in the Cook Islands and in French Oceania, with Papeete a large buyer.

Chick pea flour: See **Besan.**

Cornflour: (*Zea mays*) Also known as cornstarch or maize flour (maize being derived from the botanical nomenclature for corn). In a process similar to that used to make arrowroot, cornflour is derived from the starch of corn kernels (with the exception of wheaten cornflour, a misnomer which refers to the fine starch extracted from wheat). The resulting powder is almost pure starch and contains no gluten, hence its lump-free thickening properties. A small amount is mixed with a little cold water to make a smooth paste. It should be stirred again immediately prior to adding it to the cooking pot as it does not stay in suspension long.

Unlike arrowroot, unless a liquid thickened with cornflour is allowed to boil it will have an unpleasantly raw, powdery quality. Used extensively in Chinese cuisine as a thickener.

China: *gandian fen, cheng fen*
Malaysia: *tepung jagung*
Thailand: *pang khao phod*

Cornstarch: See **Cornflour.**

Devil's tongue starch: The starch of the devil's tongue or devil's taro (*Amorphophallus konjac*) is used to make the transparent noodles called shirataki ('white waterfall' in Japanese). Used in the traditional Japanese dish, sukiyaki. Also processed into the greyish, speckled slab with a jellyish consistency called konnyaku. Sold packed in water by Asian food suppliers. Added to Japanese white salads, braised dishes, stews and soups, it is notable for its texture rather than flavour.

Kuzu: (*Pueraria thunbergiana*) Also called kudzu, this tuberous crop was a staple cultivated throughout South East Asia until the arrival of root crops superior in nutrition and taste, such as sweet potato. Related to jicama (yam bean), its flesh is white and sweet but, unlike the yam bean, cannot be eaten raw. Added to Chinese stews and soups, in Japan it is made into a starch and used as a thickener. Claimed to be excellent for digestion and a cure for gastric inflammation. An unattractive, lumpy looking powder, it makes shiny, translucent sauces. Sift before mixing with water to thicken sauces, using half as much as you would arrowroot. Also used to coat foods for deep frying when a very crisp and crunchy crust is desired. One of the more expensive thickeners.

Lotus root starch: Made from the rhizomes of water lilies (*Nelumbo nucifera*). The Chinese use this powder as they would cornflour (cornstarch). It is expensive and similar in appearance to water chestnut starch.

Malt flour: One of the earliest grains to be cultivated, barley is among the hardiest cereal plants (*Hordeum vulgare*). Used today for animal fodder as well as brewing, most of us know the grain from soups or soothing barley water drink. In Korea, the flour is soaked in water and the resulting liquid mixed with red pepper (chilli) powder, wheat flour and soy bean flour to make hot bean paste.

Mung bean starch: Also known as mung bean flour and green pea flour, misnomers for the fine white starch of the green mung bean. Although in no way related to green garden peas, in many parts of Asia the tiny bean with olive green skin (*Phaseolus aureus, Vigna radiata*) is referred to as green pea, hence the confusion and ambiguity for Westerners.

The starch is available in its natural (white) state or tinted pink or green, the colour only showing when water is added. If unavailable, arrowroot or cornflour (cornstarch) is an adequate substitute. This starch is used to make transparent bean thread vermicelli, variously called cellophane noodles, jelly noodles, glass noodles and, even more poetically, spring rain noodles (a literal translation of their Japanese name, harusame). It is also used to produce bean starch sheets (see BEAN STARCH SHEETS).

China: *lue dau fen*
Malaysia: *tepung hoen kwe*
Indonesia: *tepung hoen kwe*
Thailand: *pang tua*
Vietnam: *bot dau xanh*

Potato starch: Obtained from white or sweet potatoes (*Solanum tuberosum*), potato starch used as a thickener, produces thick, clear sauces and soups. Only use if to be eaten that day, as it exudes water. It is stronger than cornflour (cornstarch) by about 50 per cent, so use only two-thirds the amount you would of cornflour. Useful for those with gluten intolerance. Sometimes substituted for kuzu flour.

China: *sheng fen, sung fen*
Japan: *katakuriko*

Rice flour: (*Oryza sativa*) Non-glutinous rice flour is used as the basis of a variety of noodles, pastries and sweets. It is used also as a binder and thickener.

As a coating for frying and roasting it adds crunch. Sold in fine, medium or coarse grades for different uses. Coarse rice flour is also called 'ground rice' or 'cream of rice'. See main entry for RICE FLOUR.

Burma: *hsan hmoung*
China: *pang khao*
India: *chawal-ka-atta*
Indonesia: *tepong beras*
Japan: *joshinko*
Malaysia: *tepong beras*
Thailand: *pang khao chao*
Vietnam: *bot gao*

Rice flour, glutinous: Also labelled 'sweet rice flour', glutinous rice flour is used to make sweets and cakes, most famously the Chinese New Year doughnuts known as jin doi, round balls of chewy dough filled with sweet bean paste, thickly covered with sesame seeds and deep fried. They have a resilient, chewy texture and are so popular that they are sold in Asian shops all year round. Many South East Asian cakes based on this sticky rice flour are coloured, steamed and rolled in freshly grated coconut. Japanese mochi, glutinous rice balls, may be plain or filled with sweet pastes.

Burma: *khao nee hmoung*
China: *nor mei fun*
India: *pottoo arshi*
Indonesia: *tepung pulot*
Japan: *shiratamako*
Malaysia: *tepung pulot*
Sri Lanka: *haal pitti*
Thailand: *pang khao niew*
Vietnam: *bot nep, gao nep*

Roti flour: (*Triticum vulgare*) Not a wholemeal flour like atta, this flour is creamy in colour and slightly granular in texture. Ideal for all unleavened breads. You can find it in Western delicatessens labelled 'continental flour' or at Asian grocery stores as roti flour or 'sharps', the grade to which it is milled.

Semolina: A wheat product, this is the hard endosperm sifted out of wheat during milling. Sold as farina and breakfast delight. Semolina is granular and is available fine, medium or coarse ground. See main entry for SEMOLINA.

Sharps flour: See Roti flour.

Soy flour: A high protein, low starch flour made from soy beans (*Glycine max*) and used mostly in

Japan and China. In Korea, roasted soy bean flour and fermented soy bean flour are used to make a variety of bean pastes.

Tapioca starch: Also known as tapioca flour, this makes a fine thickener, although it is mainly used in combination with other flours and starches to improve the silkiness and pliability of a dough. Extracted from the pulverised cassava root (*Manihot esculenta*) in a process akin to that for arrowroot. The starch grains, once released from the strained pulp, are dried to a paste which is heated on an iron plate to form the balls, pearls and flakes of tapioca that we know, or ground to make flour.

> **China:** *ling fun*
> **India:** *tikhoor*
> **Indonesia:** *katera pohon*
> **Japan:** *tapioka*
> **Malaysia:** *tepung ubi kayu*
> **Thailand:** *pang mun, khanom chaun* (a mixture of tapioca and glutinous rice flours)

Water chestnut starch: Sometimes labelled chestnut powder, or flour. Extracted from water chestnut (*Eleocharis dulcis*), this greyish powder is expensive but gives a beautiful sheen to the liquids it thickens and a crisp, crunchy texture to foods coated in it and then deep fried. It doesn't disperse in water as easily as cornflour (cornstarch).

Wheat starch: A starch derived from wheat. Also known as non-glutinous flour and wheaten cornflour, wheat starch is the by-product when gluten (derived from wheat protein) is made. Although a suitable substitute for cornflour (cornstarch) when thickening, it really comes to the fore in the tender pouches of translucent, pleated dough that enclose tiny, tasty steamed morsels of Chinese dim sum. Don't be confused by the packaging: wheaten cornflour is not a feat of genetic engineering, but merely a misnomer. It is actually a fine wheat starch.

> **China:** *Cheng mein, ngun jump fun, dung mien fun*

Flowering Chives

See CHIVES, CHINESE.

Foil

See GOLD LEAF and SILVER LEAF.

Food Colourings

There are a number of natural substances from which food colour may be derived. Here are some of those most widely used.

Anjan: A vivid cobalt-blue pea flower native to tropical regions, which yields a blue dye when crushed in water. Used to colour sweets and cakes in Malaysia, Singapore and Thailand. Particularly spectacular are the blue tapioca and rice flour, pork-filled dumplings from Thailand called chor lada, sometimes shaped like flowers by pinching up the dough with a tiny pair of tongs to make decorative, ridged petals.

Annatto: Small, angular, dark brick-red seeds used in Filipino cookery. They are also used to colour cheeses and smoked fish a vibrant shade of orange, and to give white butter a yellow colour. The dye from the seeds is fat-soluble and is released when they are fried in oil. Also called achuete.

Chilli: Red chillies give curries a red colour, but also raise the burn factor. If you want to boost the colour without increasing the heat, use paprika.

Pandanus: The leaves of the screwpine give not only an intriguing flavour but are also pounded to yield green colour. The flavour is integral to both savoury and sweet dishes throughout South East Asia. (Spinach, seaweed and green tea are other colorants used to make food green.) See also PANDANUS LEAF.

Paprika: Ground, dried, sweet red capsicum (peppers) with varying intensity of colour and flavour is used to achieve a red colour in a dish when the heat of chillies is not desired or required.

Saffron: The hand-picked, dried stigmas of the autumn crocus yield the minutest quantities of this king of spices, hence its high price tag. Not only do the deep orange threads impart a golden colour, but also a heady perfume. Beware of cheap saffron; it is most likely safflower (bastard saffron). It will colour your food, but that's about all. See SAFFRON.

Soy sauce: The dark, salty liquor that runs off when fermented soy beans are mixed with roasted grain and injected with a yeast mould, comes in two basic strengths. Dark soy has a thicker viscosity and imparts a stronger colour than light soy which, in spite of its clearer colour, tastes saltier. Dark soy, the colour of which is enhanced by caramel, is a colouring agent in many oriental dishes, such as red-cooked chicken. See also SOY SAUCE.

Turmeric: Fresh turmeric is preferred in Asia as it has a distinctive fragrance and many recipes call for a 'thumb-sized piece of turmeric'. More often turmeric is added in the form of a bright yellow powder derived from boiling, drying and grinding the rhizome of the turmeric plant (*Curcuma domestica*). The equivalent of 1 teaspoon of ground turmeric powder is 2 cm (¾ in) of fresh turmeric. See main entry for TURMERIC.

Fox Nut

Seeing a packet labelled 'fox nuts', my curiosity was aroused and I bought it, intending to find out more about how it is used. All the shopkeeper could tell me was that it is used in soup. I bit one but found it chalky and inedible. My friend and counsellor on things Chinese, William Lai, who has a lively curiosity plus the connections to find answers to questions, has given me the following information.

The 'soup' referred to is actually a herbal brew which older generations of Chinese prepare for the family about once a week. The parents of today's young adults complain that no longer is this preventive measure taken as seriously as it used to be. If prepared at all, it is much less frequently. The purpose is to cleanse and tone the system, the Chinese school of medicine believing strongly that prevention is better than cure.

Medicinal uses: Chinese grocery stores sell various mixtures known as ching bo leung (meaning a formula which will clear the system, pamper and enrich). Among the ingredients of the herbal mix are fox nuts (chieh shek).

Fox nuts are used to strengthen the kidneys and enhance sperm production. They are prescribed to vitalise the appetite, relieve hip and knee pain with swelling, and prevent premature ejaculation.

Frikkadel

Traditional Dutch forcemeat balls, essential in the traditional Sri Lankan festive dish, lampries, which combines rice, curry and tasty accompaniments in a single banana leaf wrapped parcel. For recipe see page 204.

Frog

(*Rana esculenta*) Many cultures enjoy what I am told is tender white meat, tasting like chicken. Indonesia and Japan have industries breeding frogs and exporting frog's legs, mostly frozen. Frogs also feature in Chinese cuisine, where they are sometimes called 'mountain chicken'. Tom Stobart's wide-ranging *The Cook's Encyclopaedia* mentions frog farms in Florida and Louisiana. A Taiwanese dish of the day at a cooking class attended by one of my friends was a soup of frog and winter melon, flavoured with dried scallops, Chinese wine and dried tangerine peel. The frog was chopped into small pieces just as a raw chicken is chopped Chinese style, and the cooking took about an hour, the teacher testing every now and then to see if the meat was tender enough.

Most cookbooks are reticent about mentioning frogs and how to prepare them. Books I have seen which give advice on how to cook them are French (fry gently in butter for 5 minutes) and Chinese (braise or stir-fry with strong flavourings like garlic, ginger, chilli and hot bean sauce).

Fruit Bat

Also known as flying fox, these are a delicacy in the Pacific islands. Once, in a French restaurant in Port Vila, I sat next to an intrepid gourmet who ordered fruit bat braised in wine sauce. From my vantage point I could see that the creature had what seemed like hundreds of small bones and the diner had to work very hard for the little meat there was.

Fugu

Each year in Japan there are reports of tragic fatalities, usually as a result of underqualified home cooks or fishermen deciding to prepare and eat fugu. The fearsome reputation of fugu is well earned and no exaggeration — it can cause severe poisoning and even death depending on what part of its anatomy is consumed, one large fish purportedly containing sufficient poison to kill over 30 humans. The most potent concentration of poison is in the ovaries and liver. The toxin will spread rapidly through the rest of the fish unless these organs are promptly removed in the initial stage of cleaning.

The danger of poisoning is elevated if one consumes the male fish's testes (they are believed to enhance virility and as such are highly prized and, accordingly, highly priced). Since, to the untrained eye, they don't look too different to the liver, I would never recommend trying it — even prepared by a restaurant that proudly displays its chef's photo licence. What point is there in being virile and dead? I'm inclined to agree with the Japanese saying '*fugu wa kuitashii, inochi wa oshishii*' ('I would like to eat fugu, but I would like to live').

In flagrant disregard of all precautions, some people maintain that, if a fugu is perfectly executed, the liver (a delicacy) is quite safe to eat. In fact, it was after insisting that a fugu restaurant serve him kimo (fish entrails) that the Kabuki actor Mitsugoro Bando met his death. Nearly 10 years later, in 1984, for the protection of perverse but insistent thrill-seekers, it became illegal to serve kimo.

Although the popularity of fugu could be largely attributed to the excitement that goes hand in hand with playing a form of culinary Russian roulette (or should that read 'Japanese'?), the connoisseur will attest to a unique quality in the flesh of raw fugu that is emphasised by the spicy ponzu sauce with which it is served. When they speak of a numbness of lips and tongue experienced after eating fugu it is no figment of the imagination; tiny traces of poison found in the fish are responsible. To the fugu aficionado, this is a desirable side effect and for that reason the fins, spines and skin (where the concentration of poison is slightly higher) are toasted and served in warmed sake as hirezake, an important part of the entire fugu experience.

From hirezake and the starter of fugusashi (transparently thin slices of fugu sashimi arranged on a platter to resemble a chrysanthemum, peony or crane) to fuguchiri (a hearty stew of fugu and vegetables) to the final course of rice gruel flavoured with leftover fugu stew, eating fugu is a complete dining expedition — one you will pay dearly for (not too dearly, one always hopes), and (if you survive it) one that you will always remember. I don't mean to alarm — only inform. In fact, the unfortunate Japanese actor was the only fatality in a fugu restaurant in nearly half a century. There are stringent requirements to be fulfilled before anyone can receive the licence needed to prepare fugu, (at least two years learning how to surgically dissect it so as to avoid the tetrodoxin venom in its liver and ovaries) which means the chefs are experts in fugu anatomy.

In spite of this, each year in Japan there are one or two deaths from ingesting those parts of fugu which should not be ingested. Also known as globe fish, it is a repulsively ugly fish which puffs itself up into a spiky ball when angry, earning it the names of porcupine fish or swellfish.

For some unfathomable reason, Japanese continue to pay breathtaking amounts for a fugu dinner. Since records were kept in 1886, fugu fish have been responsible for 6,925 deaths in Japan.

For an informative and entertaining dissertation on fugu, read Donald Richie's chapter in *A Taste of Japan*. His description of the 'chopstick-dropping' prankster in a fugu restaurant is wickedly humorous.

Fungi

See MUSHROOMS & FUNGI.

Fuzzy Melon

See GOURDS.

G

Gai Choy

See CABBAGE.

Galangal, Greater

(*Alpinia galanga*) SEE ILLUSTRATION. Native to Java and Malaysia, galangal belongs to the Zingiberaceae family, the most famous member of which is ginger (*Zingiber officinale*).

The rhizome of greater galangal resembles ginger in appearance, and is sometimes called Thai ginger or Siamese ginger, but its flavour is different, with an aroma reminiscent of camphor. The fresh root is much denser than ginger and if at all mature, cutting it requires a sharp cleaver and considerable effort.

Purchasing and storing: Galangal may be purchased sliced and bottled in brine. This is more tender and less fibrous than any fresh galangal I have been able to buy, or even the rhizomes I dig from my own garden. Bottled galangal is also kinder to the electric blender when making spice pastes. After opening, store the bottle in the refrigerator and it will keep for months.

Galangal is used in Indonesian, Malaysian and Nonya cooking and also in Thai food where it takes the predominant place ginger has in the cooking of almost every other Asian country. For examples of recipes which rely on galangal for their distinctive flavour, see Chicken and Galangal soup (Tom Kha Gai) below, and the Thai curry pastes under CURRY PASTES.

Preparation: If using galangal slices in brine, simply chop it roughly before pounding or blending into curry paste. If tender fresh galangal is available, wash the rhizomes and scrape away any woody parts before chopping.

Galangal is also sold dried, in slices. This is fine for simmering in a soup or curry (soak in very hot water for at least 30 minutes first) but it should not be ground in a food processor or blender. Also available in powdered form, but the flavour is more muted than the brined slices. As with all dried herbs and spices, store in an airtight container.

Medicinal uses: Fresh rhizomes are used in the treatment of diarrhoea, vomitting, flatulence and intestinal worms.

Burma: *pa-de-gaw-gyi*
Cambodia: *romdeng*
China: *gao liang jiang, lam kieu, lam keong*
India: *kulanjan, kosht-kulinjan, pera-rattai*
Indonesia: *laos*
Malaysia: *lengkuas*
Thailand: *kha*

Chicken and Galangal Soup

Tom Kha Gai is the Thai name for this favourite soup found on the menu of most Thai restaurants. Serves 6.

1 roasting chicken
10 slices fresh, frozen, dried or brined galangal
400 ml/14 fl oz can coconut milk
4 coriander plants with roots
12 black peppercorns, pounded
2 stems lemon grass, thinly sliced
4 fresh green chillies
1 teaspoon salt or to taste
6 fresh or frozen kaffir lime leaves
1 tablespoon fish sauce
lime juice to taste

Cut the chicken into joints, then chop the joints into small serving pieces. If using dried galangal, soak it in hot water to cover for 30 minutes. Put chicken and galangal into a saucepan. Set aside half the can of coconut milk for adding later, and dilute the rest with water to make 750 ml (1½ pints) thin coconut milk. Add thin milk to the pan with the chicken, add the well-washed and crushed coriander roots, pepper, lemon grass, whole chillies, salt and lime leaves. Bring to the boil over low heat. Simmer, uncovered, until the chicken is tender.

Add the thick coconut milk, stirring constantly until heated through. Remove from heat and stir in fish sauce and sufficient lime juice to give a piquant flavour. Serve sprinkled with chopped coriander leaves and with steamed rice served separately.

Galangal, Lesser

(*Alpinia officinarum*) There are numerous plants belonging to the same botanical family that have been called lesser galangal. It is easy to be misled because common names are practically interchangeable. No great harm will be done by using one rhizome instead of the other since none of them are noxious. However, the flavour will be different. Among the plants that are sometimes mistaken for lesser galangal are *Kaempferia galanga* (see GINGER, AROMATIC) and *Boesenbergia pandurata* (see KRACHAI).

Lesser galangal was used in Europe in mediaeval times, and mentioned in the writings of Arabic physicians Rhazes and Avicenna. It was first recorded by Ibn Khurdadbah in 869, who listed it as an article of trade from the Far East. It was commonly used as a culinary spice together with cloves, nutmeg and ginger, but the plant itself was not described until 1870, when it was named for Prosper Alpinus.

True lesser galangal is native to the island of Hainan, and the south-eastern coast of China. It is not a culinary spice, but used in Chinese medicine.

Purchasing and storing: The Chinese name for lesser galangal is san bai. It is sold at Chinese herbal shops, mainly in the form of small round slices of the dried rhizome. It will last almost indefinitely kept airtight.

Preparation: Simmered in the cleansing, toning and healing soups which are part of the traditional Chinese kitchen, a soup to serve 4–6 people could include 1 tablespoon of dried lesser galangal slices.

Medicinal uses: The classic Potter's *New Cyclopaedia of Botanical Drugs and Preparations* by R. C. Wren and R. W. Wren, yielded useful information: 'Carminative, stimulant is specially useful in dyspepsia, preventing fermentation and removing flatulence. The decoction of 1 oz in 1 pint of boiling water may be taken in tablespoonful to wineglassful doses.'

Chicken Soup with Healing Herbs

1 small roasting chicken
1 tablespoon dried lesser galangal slices
5 slices fresh ginger
5 pieces dried tangerine peel
1 teaspoon salt
1 teaspoon whole peppercorns
2 tablespoons wolfberries (optional)

Cut off the tail of the chicken, taking care to cut high enough so that the two glands on either side are also eliminated. Remove fat from body cavity, and all the skin (except on the wings). Cut chicken into pieces through the bone, Chinese style (see page 77).

Put chicken and all the other ingredients into a Yunnan pot or other heatproof earthenware dish. If a Yunnan pot with its steam-conducting funnel is not available, add about 1 cup of water. (The Yunnan pot will not need any water.) The wolfberries, if used, produce a faint sweet flavour and added benefits.

Place pot on a trivet in a large boiler so it is above the level of water. Cover boiler with a well-fitting lid and cook on medium heat, keeping the water boiling and adding more from time to time as required, for 1½ hours. Serve in the pot.

Gamboge

(*Garcinia cambogia*) An acid fruit commonly used in Sri Lanka and southern India. In its fresh state it is bright orange-yellow and the size of a small orange. It has 6–8 vertical furrows, dividing the fruit into segments. The succulent segments or lobes are cut into sections and spread out on woven mats to dry in the sun. When dry, they are almost black. Largely used for preserving fish, in India it is sometimes known as 'fish tamarind'. It is also used when washing fish to remove fishy odours.

The dried segments are sold by weight in local markets or in packets when exported. They must be rinsed and soaked before being added to curried or pickled fish, popular in Sri Lanka and southern India. They may also be made into a brine with salt. Used as a substitute for tamarind and limes as the acid ingredient in certain dishes, there are also dishes in which the preferred acid ingredient is gamboge, such as the refreshingly sour and hot fish preparation of Sri Lanka known as ambul thial. See recipe for Sour Curry of Fish (page 149).

India: *korrakkai-pulli, kodampoli*
Sri Lanka: *goraka*

Garam Masala

See SPICE BLENDS.

Garlic

(*Allium sativum*) While garlic is a key ingredient in the food of most Asian countries, it is conspicuously absent from two that come to mind — Japanese food and the Brahman food of India, the former for aesthetic reasons (they are working on developing an odourless garlic) and the latter because they believe garlic and onions inflame the baser passions, and both are taboo. Peruse the indexes of books dealing with these cuisines and nowhere is there a mention of garlic, although spring onions (scallions) are used in Japanese food. One exception in Japanese cuisine is beef sushi, as the paper-thin slice of beef is rubbed with crushed raw garlic (instead of wasabi) and then placed on the rice.

Apart from these notable exceptions, garlic is used in almost every cuisine. As a flavouring and a health food, its use has been recorded since biblical times. It was a regular item of diet in Egypt, and perhaps its antibiotic properties were the reason for its being part of the ration of the Hebrew slaves.

Garlic is a biennial herb and the bulb is a compound one, formed from a number of small bulbs or bulbils called cloves. The tough papery skin of each clove is actually a protective leaf, in the axil of which the clove forms. They fit together neatly in the familiar dome shape and are surrounded by thin sheaths of white, mauve or pink. Some kinds of garlic peel easily, while the papery sheaths of others cling tenaciously. Size of the cloves is not indicative of flavour, though in general very large cloves are milder than small ones.

Since garlic cloves come in all sizes, ranging from very tiny to very large, I prefer to give indications of the amount of garlic in a recipe by measured spoonfuls rather than the number of cloves. Where it is not critical or if a generous amount of garlic appeals to you, feel free to adjust the recommended quantity. But do be guided by the way it is treated.

The strength of garlic diminishes as it is cooked. Raw or lightly cooked, garlic lingers on the breath. But if cooked long and gently, becoming sweet and mild in the process, even whole heads of garlic may safely be indulged in.

In some Indian curries where garlic has been long cooked, a little extra crushed raw garlic is added right at the end of cooking, to step up the flavour.

It is used more generously in some cuisines than others, with Burmese, Thai and Korean food relying on it most heavily. Sometimes I catch a whiff of frying garlic and in a trice am transported back to childhood days in Rangoon, Burma. What a long memory the olfactory sense possesses! Fried garlic, crisp and golden, is one of the delights of Burmese food, offered as an accompaniment to sprinkle over food or mixed into a deep-fried relish like balachaung (see DRIED SHRIMP).

Thai food uses garlic generously in its curry pastes and when a curry paste is not part of the dish, slices of whole pickled garlic heads are used as a garnish and flavour accent, as in the famous mee grob (crisp fried rice noodles). This pickled garlic is sold in jars, slightly sweet and quite mild.

Korean style pickled garlic, also served as a relish or accompaniment, is sold sliced and frozen in vacuum-packed plastic sachets. It is used raw and lightly cooked too. Korean food is usually redolent of garlic.

While Chinese food uses garlic in almost every dish, it is not always obvious.

In southern India and Sri Lanka, garlic is used as a vegetable, with whole peeled cloves cooked in a curry until they are soft and gently flavoured.

Purchasing and storing: Press the heads of garlic with your fingers to ensure they are firm. When the skin feels somewhat empty, you may be sure the garlic is old and shrivelled beneath its papery skin. Avoid garlic which is sprouting because the green shoots are slightly bitter. Store in an open basket to avoid mildew.

Preparation: To peel garlic without too much effort, place the clove on a wooden board, cover with the flat of a knife blade and give it a sharp blow with the heel of the hand. The skin splits and can be easily lifted off. To crush garlic, continue to use the flat of the knife blade, first sprinkling the board with some salt or sugar to keep the garlic from slipping and to absorb the juice. Push the blade of the knife down and away from you, putting weight on it with the heel of the hand. The garlic should soon be a smooth purée. Garlic crushers are wasteful and the garlic comes through too chunky.

Medicinal uses: Garlic is considered very beneficial to health, reducing cholesterol and blood pressure and clotting, relieving catarrh, bronchitis and colds. It is also used in the treatment of tuberculosis and whooping cough. It is mildly antibiotic, and tests confirm activity against a range of disease-producing bacteria. It is used as an antiseptic, diaphoretic, diuretic and expectorant and has recently been tested in the treatment of lead poisoning, diabetes and certain carcinomas. Garlic juice mixed with honey or sugar is used to treat coughs, colds and asthma.

Burma: *chyet-thon-phew*
Cambodia: *kthem*
China: *da suan, suen tau.*
India: *lasan*
Indonesia: *bawang putih*
Japan: *nin-niku*
Korea: *ma nl*
Malaysia: *bawang puteh*
Philippines: *bawang*
Sri Lanka: *sudu lunu*
Thailand: *kratiem*
Vietnam: *toi*

Garlic Curry

In this dish whole cloves of garlic are cooked until mild and sweet. Serves 4.

250 g/8 oz large garlic cloves
8 shallots, purple or golden
8 large, mild chillies or banana peppers
2 tablespoons vegetable oil
½ teaspoon fenugreek seeds
½ teaspoon chilli powder
½ teaspoon ground turmeric
250 ml/8 fl oz/1 cup coconut milk
½ teaspoon salt or to taste
walnut-sized piece of tamarind pulp

Choose the largest cloves of garlic for cooking as a vegetable. Peel them but leave them whole. (For this recipe, don't try the quick method of peeling by splitting the skin with pressure, as this causes the garlic clove to split also, and it is better they be kept whole. If the garlic is particularly tight-skinned, place in a bowl and cover with boiling water. Allow to stand for 2 minutes, then drain. Skins will then come away more easily.) Peel shallots and leave them whole. Discard chilli stalks.

Heat oil in a saucepan and fry the garlic, shallots and peppers over medium-low heat until they start to caramelise. Remove from pan with a slotted spoon. Add fenugreek seeds and fry gently until golden brown. Add chilli powder and turmeric, stir for a few seconds. Add coconut milk mixed with ½ cup water and stir while bringing to a simmer. Return the garlic, shallots and peppers to the pan, add salt to taste and simmer uncovered for 30 minutes or until garlic and shallots are soft.

Soak tamarind in ⅓ cup hot water until soft, dissolve tamarind in the water and strain into the curry, stirring gently, during the last 10 minutes of cooking. Serve with steamed rice.

Garlic Chives

See CHIVES, CHINESE.

Garnishes

Carrot flowers: Peel a straight carrot and slice off the narrow end. With a sharp knife make five V-shaped cuts the length of the carrot at regular intervals. Cut across into slices.

Chilli flowers: Choose fresh red chillies which are nice and straight, and not too thick-fleshed. Using a small, sharp knife or pair of straight, small scissors, make five or six slits in the chilli from just below the stem, meeting at the tip. If the chilli is too long, cut a bit off the tip and shape four or five petals around the central membrane covered with seeds. Try not to damage it, as it will make a pretty stamen for the flower. Drop into a bowl of iced water and refrigerate for an hour or two, until the 'petals' curl back. It is wise to wear disposable gloves when handling chillies.

Cucumber leaves: Cut lengthwise slices 10 cm (4 in) long, 5 cm (2 in) wide and 6 mm (¼ in) thick off a green cucumber, leaving skin attached, and shape them at both ends. With a small, pointed knife mark leaf rib and veins in the skin, with shallow cuts running close to each other and meeting in a V shape. Lift out the strips of cucumber skin, and the markings will stand out in white against the green.

Onion flowers: Peel a medium-sized white onion, keeping both ends intact and especially not slicing off the tapered top. If it is sprouting a small green shoot, all the better. With the point of a small knife draw even-sized V shapes around the middle of the onion. Go back to the starting point and insert the knife through to the centre along the lines you have marked. Gently wiggle the two halves of the onion apart, using the knife if some layers have not been completely separated. Each half onion will have the shape of a water lily. Drop into iced water with a few drops of food colouring dispersed through and leave the onions to soak until they have absorbed enough colour and the layers open like petals.

Spring onion (scallion) brushes: These are the traditional accompaniment to Peking Duck, and they have a practical use as well as a decorative one — they are used to brush hoi sin sauce onto Mandarin Pancakes in which slices of duck are wrapped, together with the brushes themselves. Wash the spring onions (scallions) and cut them into finger lengths. With a small, sharp knife make a number of fine cuts a little more than half way down the length of each piece. Drop into iced water and soak until ends spread slightly. Drain on paper towels.

Spring onion (scallion) flowers: Easiest of all, these curly ruffs are made cutting finger lengths of the green portion, and fringing both ends by drawing a pin several times through the leaf. Drop into a bowl of iced water and in a few minutes the ends will have curled attractively.

Tomato rose: With a small, sharp knife peel a firm red tomato in one long spiral strip, as you would an apple. Starting from one end, wind the tomato peeling into a rosette, skin side inwards. With a little practice, a tomato can be turned into a quite credible rose.

Turnip chrysanthemum: Peel a round turnip and take a small slice off one end to make a flat base. Sit it on a wooden board with a wooden chopstick either side to prevent turnip being cut through. With a very sharp, thin-bladed chopper make closely-spaced, parallel cuts straight down at right angles to the chopsticks. Turn the turnip 90 degrees and repeat, so turnip has a fine grid of cuts. Soak turnip in cold salted water and add food colouring if a coloured 'chrysanthemum' is desired. The fine 'petals' will soften and spread. Drain and use for decoration.

White radish flower: For a simple flower garnish cut paper-thin slices across the radish and soak them in salt water (1 tablespoon salt to 1 cup water) for 20 minutes. This makes the radish soft and pliable. Cut each slice from edge to centre, overlap edges and curve to form a cone. Do this with 7 slices. Curve the edge of the circle back to resemble the petal of a flower. Place petals one within the other.

Gelatine, Japanese

See AGAR-AGAR.

Gelugor

(*Garcinia atroviridis*) Known as asam gelugor in Malaysia, this acid fruit is sliced and dried, and sometimes used to give acidity to cooked dishes in place of tamarind. What is confusing is that the dried slices are labelled 'tamarind slices' though they are in no way related.

Ghee

Ghee is clarified butter or pure butter fat. Its main advantage is that it can be heated to a high temperature without burning. Clarifying involves melting butter in a heavy pan either on top of the stove or in the oven, letting all the moisture evaporate and then continuing the heating process until the milk solids have browned on the bottom of the pan.

To make ghee at home, put 250–500 g (½–1 lb) unsalted or cultured butter into a heavy enamelled pan, cutting it into small pieces first. Melt over low heat, then simmer for 10 minutes or so, during which time it will crackle as moisture is driven off. When it stops crackling the thin crust on the surface may be lifted off. The ghee should then be stirred and the cooking continued until the solids on the bottom of the pan have turned nut brown. Let it cool sufficiently to handle, then pour the clarified butter off into a lidded jar. Ghee prepared in this way will keep for months under refrigeration, and for shorter times without refrigeration.

In India, ghee made from butter is called usli ghee, meaning real or genuine ghee. Most people use a much cheaper vegetable ghee called vanaspati. This is made from saturated vegetable oils which, in order to give them a solid consistency, are hydrogenated. From a health point of view, this is probably worse than using real ghee, but more affordable. The processing gives this product a very similar smell and taste to the real thing.

Gingelly Oil

See OILS.

Ginger

(*Zingiber officinale*) In Western cuisine there is ginger as in gingerbread, ginger beer, candied ginger and chocolate ginger. Delicious. But in Asia this fleshy rhizome is used for more serious food. It is mostly always fresh, sometimes brined, occasionally preserved in sugar syrup, seldom dried or ground and never crystallised.

In Asia, fresh ginger is an ingredient basic to many cuisines. Although galangal is preferred in Thailand, young ginger is served thinly sliced and raw as an accompaniment to Thai sausages.

Ginger is used in Chinese cooking to neutralise excessively strong fishy flavours and to add its own aroma to more delicate seafoods. In Burma, fine shreds of ginger are soaked in lime juice (which turns them pink) and served as a digestive, or just as a tasty ending to a meal. For this, the ginger should be so young that the tips are still pink-tinged, the texture soft and non-fibrous, the skin thin enough to be rubbed off between finger and thumb. The flavour of young ginger is comparatively gentle.

If a recipe calls for strips of fresh ginger to be included, try to get tender ginger if it is in season. If you are using mature ginger it may be wise to reduce the quantity because of its stronger flavour. The experienced cook knows instinctively whether to use less or more ginger to flavour the dish, and the inexperienced cook soon learns.

Apart from fresh ginger, there are various forms of preserved ginger that are indispensable in particular cuisines, such as Japan's pickled ginger, of which there is more than one variety: beni shoga, thinly sliced, salmon-pink in colour, pickled in sweetened vinegar is an essential accompaniment to sashimi; and gari, which is yellow and is used with sushi. Other parts of the plant are used. Slender ginger shoots (hajikami shoga), naturally a deep pinkish red, are pickled and sold in jars, packed in like spears of asparagus. Used as a garnish, especially for grilled foods.

China's preserved ginger shreds in heavy syrup with a touch of saltiness, coloured deep red are called hong su jiang and are used to add colour and flavour contrast to savoury dishes. Knobs of preserved ginger in heavy syrup come from Canton in handsome jars with classic Chinese motifs on them. Another contender for the ginger market is a place called Buderim in Queensland, Australia, which processes a superior quality glacé ginger as well as other ginger products. In fact, Australia meets 40 per cent of the world market's processed ginger needs, including Japanese-style pickled ginger.

Ginger tea is popular and refreshing. There are different ways of preparing it. In India, slices of fresh ginger are put into the pot in which tea is being brewed, and the strong tea poured out and served with milk and sugar. In the Philippines, ginger and sugar are simmered in water for 30 minutes and served hot. In almost any Asian store it is also possible to buy packets of ginger tea: granules of dried ginger and sugar which, dissolved in hot water, give a sweet and pungent tea.

Ginger is cooked with soy beans, soy bean sprouts or bean curd dishes, to generate digestive heat and act as an antidote to the negative effects of beans.

Purchasing and storing: When buying ginger, be aware that young, tender ginger is easy to use being non-fibrous and having a thin skin that is easily rubbed off. It sometimes has pink tips. Older ginger has a tougher skin but this may be scraped off with little extra effort once the rhizome is broken into pieces. Mature ginger has more flavour and heat than young ginger. Avoid ginger that has started to look wrinkled or has discoloured or mouldy ends — it will be fibrous and on the dry side. Store ginger in a paper bag in the vegetable crisper of the refrigerator. It will keep quite well for weeks, but if you need to keep it longer still, divide ginger into knobs, peel, drop into a wide-mouthed bottle and fill the bottle with dry sherry. Refrigerate. For convenience, chop the ginger very finely or blend with just enough dry sherry to facilitate the action of the blender. Store in a glass jar. A little citric acid dissolved in water and added to the jar increases its keeping qualities.

Preparation: Keep ginger dry and whole until it is required, then break off as much as is needed and peel only if necessary. To make fine shreds, cut thin diagonal slices off the rhizome. Stack 3 or 4 slices together and cut into slivers. The Japanese style ginger grater, ceramic or metal, does a superb job. The fibres remain caught in the rows of tiny, pyramid-shaped teeth while grated ginger and juice fall free.

The surface of the grater to use with ginger is not the cheese-grating type, but the surface with small, one-directional holes. This has the advantage of keeping the fibres on the outside while all the ginger that is on the inside is free of fibres and ready to use.

Ginger juice is obtained by grating ginger, then gathering it up and pressing with the back of a spoon through a small strainer such as a tea strainer.

Medicinal uses: Ginger helps digestion, relieves stomach aches and reduces excess wind and mucus. It is used in small doses for preventing morning sickness and motion sickness. It is also said to have a calming effect. In Eastern medicine, slices of fresh ginger are simmered with dry-roasted coriander seeds and served as a hot tea to alleviate the symptoms of the common cold. In Western herbal medicine a cold and flu cure is based on a teaspoon each of ground dried ginger and honey, juice and grated zest of a lemon, a bruised clove of garlic and a pinch of cayenne all combined in a mug and boiling water poured over. Drink it last thing at night then rug up and go to bed. The ginger promotes perspiration.

Burma: *gin*
Cambodia: *knei*
China: *jeung*
India: *adrak* (fresh), *sonth* (dried)
Indonesia: *jahe*
Japan: *shoga*
Malaysia: *halia*
Philippines: *luya*
Sri Lanka: *inguru*
Thailand: *khing*
Vietnam: *gung*

Ginger Mix (Gin Thoke)

Popular as a digestive snack after meals in Burma, this is offered in very small bowls, and eaten with the fingers.

125 g/4 oz very tender fresh ginger
6 tablespoons lime or lemon juice
2 tablespoons peanut oil
1 tablespoon oriental sesame oil
12 cloves garlic, sliced
3 tablespoons white sesame seeds
salt to taste

The ginger should be very young with pink tips and almost transparent skin. If more mature, select the small knobs which grow off the main stem.

Scrape skin off ginger and cut ginger into very thin slices. Stack and cut into fine slivers, pour lime or lemon juice over and leave for at least an hour. The action of the acid turns the ginger pink.

Heat both kinds of oil in a small pan and over low heat fry the sliced garlic slowly until pale golden. Remove from heat as soon as it reaches this stage. Do not let it brown or it will taste bitter. Cool on paper towels to drain and crisp. Toast sesame seeds in a dry frying pan over moderate heat until golden brown, shaking pan or stirring to keep them from burning. Turn immediately onto a plate to cool. Just before serving drain ginger and put into a bowl. Add salt to taste and sprinkle with garlic and sesame seeds.

Ginger Tea

2½ cups water
8–10 thin slices fresh ginger
2 teaspoons tea
sugar to taste

Bring the water to the boil with the ginger. Meanwhile, heat teapot and put the tea into it. After water has boiled for a couple of minutes, pour it in with the tea, cover and leave it to stand for 5 minutes. Strain into two cups and sweeten if desired. In India, milk and sugar are added as a matter of course.

Real Ginger Beer

This is the favourite soft drink at young people's parties in tropical Asia. Since it has to be consumed before it builds up too much fizziness and sprays the ceiling (I speak from personal experience), it is best to make it for an occasion when you know there will be a number of people around to help finish it off. Makes about 18 glasses.

**300 g/10 oz ginger root,
   preferably tender and young
2 or 3 stems lemon grass
   or finely peeled zest of 1 lemon
5 litres/10 pints water
1 kg/2 lb sugar
1 whole nutmeg, broken into pieces
few blades of mace (optional)
5 cm/2 in cinnamon stick
whites and shells of 2 eggs
2 limes or 1 lemon, sliced and seeds removed
juice of 3 limes or 2 lemons
1 teaspoon active dry yeast
2 tablespoons sultanas (golden raisins)**

Wash ginger well and scrape away any tough skin. Cut into thin slices. Discard tough outer layers of lemon grass and the green leaves. Use only the tender white lower stem, cut across into thin slices. Soak ginger and lemon grass overnight in the measured water. Next day bring to the boil in a large pan, add sugar and spices and bring to simmering point. Cover and simmer for 1 hour. Add the crushed egg shells and the whites which have been beaten until frothy but not stiff. Whisk and simmer for 15 minutes. Remove from heat, add slices and juice of limes or lemons and leave until cold. Strain through muslin.

Dissolve yeast in a little of the liquid and stir in. Have clean bottles ready, preferably those with clip-on tops. Put a few sultanas into each bottle and, using a funnel, three-quarters fill the bottles with the ginger mixture. If using bottles with corks, tie the corks securely with string. Leave at room temperature for 24 hours, by which time the ginger beer will have a nice fizz and be ready to drink. Chill well and if ginger flavour is too strong, dilute with iced soda water when serving. Serve within 36–48 hours.

Ginger, Aromatic

(*Kaempferia galanga*) In spite of its name and the fact that it is a member of the ginger family, it does not taste at all like ginger, but has a distinctive flavour of its own. *Kaempferia galanga* is sometimes mistakenly called lesser galangal, which is also a rhizome of the Zingiberaceae family. The leaves grow thickly to about 15 cm (6 in) in height under the right conditions. It bears small, fragile, orchid-like flowers, white with purple labellum, fragrant but very short-lived, virtually 'dissolving' in a few hours.

The rhizome of this plant looks something like a small, wizened version of ginger. It has reddish brown skin, the whole rhizome is generally 3–6 cm long (1–2½ in) and is marked at short intervals with raised rings which are the scars of leaf bases.

While it is not an everyday ingredient, where it is traditionally used its flavour is so distinctive that no substitution can be made.

In Sri Lanka, the source of its English name, aromatic ginger is used dried and powdered only for a few special dishes, among them the famous Festive Biriani (see recipe page 172). In Sri Lankan cuisine it is occasionally used roasted and powdered as a flavouring in pork curries. It is also mixed with cinnamon, cardamom and cloves to make spiced tea, and is included in a chew of betel as a masticatory.

In Chinese cuisine, its name is saa jiang ('sandy ginger'). It is pounded, mixed with salt and oil, and served with baked chicken dishes.

Cekur (its Malay name) is used in comparatively few Malaysian dishes. It is, however, an important medicinal herb. Tender leaves are used in nasi ulam, a combination of steamed white rice and many fresh herbs, finely shredded.

In Thailand the young leaves and storage roots are used in fish curries and the tender leaves, gathered during the wet season, are served as a raw vegetable with a hot, shrimp-flavoured curry.

Purchasing and storing: Unless you have access to freshly dug rhizomes you will have to purchase aromatic ginger in dried form, probably in small round slices. It must be powdered using a mortar and pestle or an electric blender before use. (I usually powder the slices and store the powder in a screwtop glass jar, ready for use.) It is also available already ground. Buy small quantities and store airtight. Since such minute amounts are used in cooking, it will last a long time.

Medicinal uses: In South East Asia, the rhizome of *Kaempferia galanga* is considered a stimulant and is combined with pepper, cinnamon and honey as a treatment for colds. During the first 44 days of a baby's life the root is mixed with other herbs, wrapped in a cloth, heated and used to warm the baby's body after his morning bath. This is believed to prevent wind and colic.

In Indonesia the rhizome is given for food poisoning, tetanus, mouth ulcers, coughs and colds. If chewed and swallowed it is said to be a hallucinogen with no recorded ill effects.

In India, a perfume used in hair washes, powders and other cosmetics is made from rhizomes and leaves and worn by women for fragrance and also used for protecting clothes against insects.

In Malaysia, the rhizome is used for chills in elephants. (How does one administer it, I cannot help but wonder.)

The juice of the plant is an ingredient in some tonics used in the preparation of gargles, and administered with honey as a remedy for coughs and bronchial infections.

The leaves are used in lotions, as well as poultices for sore eyes, sore throat, swellings, rheumatism and fevers.

In the Philippines, a decoction of the rhizomes is used for dyspepsia, headache and malaria. It is also used as a wash for dandruff, and for relieving irritation produced by stinging caterpillars.

In Thailand, crushed roots are mixed with whisky and applied to the head as a cure for headaches.

China: *saa jiang, sa leung geung, sha geung fun*
India: *chandramula, kachri, kechulu-kalangu, kacholam*
Indonesia: *kencur, kentjoer*
Malaysia: *cekur, cekuh, kecil galanga*
Sri Lanka: *ingurupiyali, hingurupiyali*
Thailand: *proh hom, hom proh, waan teendin, waan hom*

Chicken with Aromatic Ginger

Serves 6

750 g/1½ lb chicken joints
  or drumstick or thigh fillets
30 g/1 oz fresh aromatic ginger
  or 2 teaspoons ground dried
30 g/1 oz fresh ginger
10 purple or golden shallots, peeled
3 tablespoons peanut oil
125 ml/4 fl oz/½ cup coconut milk
1½ teaspoons salt
2 teaspoons sugar

Cut chicken into curry pieces, chopping large joints in two through the bone. If using fillets, cut into 2.5 cm (1 in) squares.

Scrub fresh aromatic ginger and ginger, cut into slices and pound using a mortar and pestle or grate finely. If using dried aromatic ginger which usually comes in slices, pound to powder and measure carefully (too much will dominate other flavours). Combine with the ginger and shallots and grind to a purée in an electric blender, adding a little water to facilitate blending.

Heat oil in a wok and on low heat fry the ground ingredients, stirring, until fragrant and oil shines on the surface. Add chicken and turn all the pieces in the spice mixture, then pour in the coconut milk mixed with half its volume of water. Stir in salt and sugar. Simmer until chicken is tender, adding a little water if liquid dries up, but remember this is supposed to be a 'dry' dish with only a small amount of concentrated gravy. Taste and adjust seasoning, and serve hot with steamed rice.

Festive Biriani

A one-dish banquet with layers of savoury chicken or lamb. The unique, exotic flavour of this rice pilau owes much to the inclusion of powdered aromatic ginger. Serves 12.

CHICKEN SAVOURY

2 × 1.5 kg/3 lb roasting chickens
185 ml/6 fl oz/¾ cup ghee
  or mixture of ghee and oil
4 tablespoons blanched almonds
4 tablespoons sultanas (golden raisins)
8 small new potatoes, peeled and halved
2 large onions finely chopped
2 tablespoons finely chopped garlic
2 tablespoons finely chopped fresh ginger
1–2 teaspoons chilli powder
1 teaspoon ground white pepper
1 teaspoon ground turmeric
1 tablespoon ground cumin
3 teaspoons salt
2 cups peeled and chopped tomatoes
125 ml/4 fl oz/½ cup natural yoghurt
30 g/1 oz/½ cup chopped fresh mint
2 teaspoons ground cardamom
2 small cinnamon sticks

SPICED RICE

1 kg/2 lb/5 cups basmati or Dehra Dun rice
4 tablespoons ghee
2 large onions, finely sliced
10 green cardamom pods, bruised
5 whole cloves
1 cinnamon stick
2 teaspoons powdered aromatic ginger
½ teaspoon saffron strands
3 tablespoons rose water
or 10 drops rose essence
3 teaspoons salt
2 litres/4 pints/8 cups chicken stock

GARNISH

6 hard-boiled eggs
1 cup blanched pistachios or cooked green peas

Chicken Savoury: Cut chickens into serving pieces. Use backs, necks and wing tips to make stock for cooking the rice.

Heat half the ghee (or ghee and oil) in a small frying pan and fry the almonds over medium heat until they are golden. Drain on slotted spoon and set aside. Fry sultanas for a few seconds, drain and put aside with the almonds. (These are for garnishing the dish later on.) Fry peeled and halved new potatoes until well browned on all sides. Drain.

Pour ghee remaining in frying pan into a large, heavy saucepan, add remaining ghee or oil and heat. Fry the chopped onion, garlic and ginger until onion is soft and golden. Add chilli powder, pepper, turmeric, cumin and fry, stirring, for 2 minutes. Add salt, tomato, yoghurt, mint, cardamom and cinnamon sticks. Cover and cook over a low heat, stirring occasionally, until tomato is pulpy, adding a little water if mixture becomes too dry and starts to stick to pan. When mixture is thick, add chicken pieces and stir well to coat them with spice mixture. Cover pan and cook over very low heat until chicken is tender, about 35 minutes. There should be only a small amount of thick gravy when chicken is cooked. If necessary, remove chicken and cook gravy uncovered for a few minutes until thick enough to mound in the spoon. Return chicken to pan and set aside.

Spiced Rice: Wash rice well and drain in colander for at least 30 minutes. Heat ghee and fry onion until soft and golden. Add cardamom pods, cloves, cinnamon stick, aromatic ginger and rice. Fry, stirring, for about 3 minutes or until rice is coated with the ghee.

Toast saffron strands in a dry pan for 1 minute, shaking pan or stirring so they do not burn. Turn onto a saucer and with the back of a spoon, crush to powder. Pour 2 tablespoons hot water or stock onto saffron powder and stir to dissolve. Stir into the measured stock, together with rose water and salt, and pour over the rice, stirring well. Add chicken savoury and fried potatoes and mix gently.

Cover saucepan tightly, turn heat very low and steam for 20 minutes without lifting lid or stirring. Turn off heat and leave for 10 minutes. With a large metal spoon transfer biriani onto a large warm dish, garnish with almonds and sultanas, halved eggs and cooked peas and serve at once. Accompaniments are Cucumber Raita (page 111) and hot pickles.

Ginger Flower

(*Etlingera elatior*, syn. *Nicolaia elatior*, formerly *Phaeomeria speciosa*) SEE ILLUSTRATION. Also known as torch ginger. The showy pink flowers of a tall perennial look almost too pretty to eat but their flavour is an essential ingredient in some dishes. Difficult to procure outside Asia at present, they will probably soon be grown and sold the way other Asian herbs are in large Western cities.

Vietnamese mint has a remarkably similar fragrance and pungency and may be substituted. Some of the popular laksa soups feature a sprinkling of finely shredded ginger bud, while others use laksa leaf. The Malaysian name for ginger flower is bunga kantan or bunga siantan. In Thailand, young shoots and flowers are served raw with nam prik.

Malaysia: *bunga kantan*
Thailand: *kaalaa*

Ginger, Mioga

(*Zingiber mioga*) A type of ginger flower only used in Japan. The plant is cultivated for its flowers which appear in late summer and are harvested young, before they open. Young leaves are blanched by covering with straw. Both buds and leaves are used in flavouring soups and other dishes. Unlike common ginger, the rhizome is not edible.

China: *xiang he*
Japan: *myohga*

Ginkgo Nut

(*Ginkgo biloba*) The ginkgo nut is the hard-shelled kernel of the fruit of the maidenhair tree, one of the earth's most ancient plants and particularly beautiful when the leaves turn golden yellow in autumn. It is thought to bring good fortune, which may explain why ginkgo nuts are offered at weddings — the shells dyed a vivid red for the occasion.

In China, ginkgo nuts are used in both sweet and savoury dishes. They are sometimes used as an alternative to lotus seeds in 'eight treasure' dishes. They are also a popular snack in Japan and Korea, threaded on pine needles, grilled and salted. They keep well unshelled, but once removed from shells will keep only a short while, even with refrigeration. Soak the kernels in hot water to loosen the skins. Cooked, they turn a delicate shade of green.

Medicinal uses: Leaves and seeds are used in Chinese herbal medicine for lung problems. An extract of *G. biloba* in tablet or liquid form is used to improve the memory. It is also valued as a tonic for the urinary system.

Ginseng

(*Aralia quinquifolia, Panax quinquefolium*) The Chinese ascribe such medicinal power to this spindle-shaped root, that it was given the botanical name 'Panax' meaning all-healing, as in panacea. There are many grades of ginseng, some astronomically expensive and others, not so highly regarded, at a fraction of that price. The Manchurian Imperial is regarded as the best quality, with Korean ginseng, or red ginseng rating second. North America produces a variety which is ranked third or fourth in value, while Japanese ginseng is considered the least valuable. The root with its divisions looks rather like the human form. It is prepared by steaming for 4 hours in wicker baskets over boiling water before drying and packing.

Ginseng extracts have become popular among those receptive to alternative therapies.

Purchasing and storing: In Asia the dried roots of ginseng are sold in Chinese herbal shops. The package is left unopened until ready to use. It is generally made into a soup with chicken.

Preparation: As with other dried ingredients, slow simmering for at least an hour is required.

Medicinal uses: Due to its reputation as a tonic and stimulant which even makes old people young, the best quality ginseng is sold for what has been described as '250 to 500 times its weight in silver'.

Chicken and Ginseng Soup

Make as for Chicken Soup with Wolfberries (see WOLFBERRY) and add 30 g (1 oz) best ginseng before simmering.

Gizzard

See OFFAL.

Globe-Fish

See FUGU.

Gnemon

(*Gnetum gnemon*) Young leaves, shoots, inflorescences and immature seeds are boiled and served with coconut milk as a vegetable, or in soup. However, it is the dried and flattened seeds which are most widely known, exported as emping melinjo or krupuk emping. These are thin, dry discs which, deep fried in hot oil, spread and become pale gold in just a few seconds. Lift out on a slotted spoon and drain on paper towels. Add a fine sprinkling of salt and serve them as a snack or accompaniment to drinks.

See also MELINJO NUT.

Go

See SOY BEAN PRODUCTS.

Goat

See MUTTON.

Gold Leaf

Real gold, beaten into incredibly thin sheets, is a special occasion decoration in Indian cooking. Used with restraint it can be rather elegant, but just a touch will do. It is mainly used on the handmade sweets which are a feature of classic Indian festive food. See also SILVER LEAF.

Golden Apple

See AMBARELLA.

Golden Mountain Sauce

As popular in Thailand as Worcestershire sauce is in England. The short, square brown bottle looks familiar as does the yellow and red label. In any large Asian supermarket, browse among the sauces and you will find more than one brand name in the same type of bottle and with very similar labels.

My guess is that these are clever copies of a long-established Swiss-made sauce based on hydrolysed vegetable protein which gives a lift to any dish. Reading the labels tells me that the Asian product contains MSG and the Swiss product contains no chemical additives, so I opt for the latter, sold as Maggi seasoning.

Gooseberry, Cape

(*Physalis edulis, P. peruviana*) Marketed as golden berry and ground cherry. This delicious member of the Physalis genus is much prized by English and French confectioners, being dipped in fondant and served as petits fours in paper cases, or used to decorate cakes. The lacy, lantern-shaped husk or calyx which protects the small round fruit is pulled back and up, like gauzy dragonfly wings, adding to the decorative effect.

The fruit is grown in New Zealand and Australia, but mostly in South Africa where it takes its name from the Cape of Good Hope. In Hawaii it is called poha. In places where it is plentiful it is used to make jam which makes a proud appearance at the breakfast table.

The fruit is nice to eat ripe and raw — sweet-sour, full of small, soft seeds which slip down without any effort — and it makes a lovely addition to salads; either fruit salads or tossed in with assorted leaves.

Gotu Kola

See PENNYWORT.

Gourds

Gourds are members of the Cucurbitaceae family. While shapes and sizes vary wildly, they all grow on trailing or climbing plants, usually in a warm climate, with a tendency to be vulnerable to frost. They include cucumbers, marrows, squash, pumpkins, melons, zucchini or courgettes, all familiar items in Western countries.

There are also some close relatives which are named gourd, with a qualifying descriptive word preceding, such as bitter gourd, wax gourd, ridged gourd, snake gourd. Since these are not so well known in the West, and are the varieties popular in Asian cooking, they have been grouped below.

Most are delicately flavoured and high in moisture, so the best way to use them is in soups, or simmered in gently spiced coconut milk until tender. There is a notable exception to the 'delicately flavoured' description — the bitter gourd. Since this is treated in ways which makes the most of its aggressive flavour, it has an entry of its own. See BITTER GOURD.

Ash gourd: (*Benincasa hispida*) Also known as wax gourd, winter melon and preserving melon. It is used mainly to make a delicious crystallised sweet called petha in India and puhul dosi in Sri Lanka. Its name in Sinhalese (alu puhul) translates as 'ash pumpkin', and indeed it has a powdery coating on its skin which looks as though the gourd has been rolled in ash. It is round or oblong in shape.

Bitter gourd: See main entry for BITTER GOURD.

Bottle gourd: (*Lagenaria siceraria*) Only the young, tender fruit is used in cooking. Prepare it as any other gourd, peeling it thinly and discarding spongy centre and seeds. When mature it develops a hard, woody shell which renders it ideal for making bottles, bowls and musical instruments.

China: *kwa-kwa*
India: *lauki*
Indonesia: *labu air*
Japan: *yuugao*
Malaysia: *labu air*
Philippines: *upo*
Sri Lanka: *diya labu*
Thailand: *naam tao*

Fuzzy melon: (*Benincasa hispida*) SEE ILLUSTRATION. A species of wax gourd, also known as hairy melon and Chinese vegetable marrow, they are either shaped like a squat eggplant or elongated, like an overgrown zucchini. Amazingly, they share the same botanical identification as that much larger wax gourd, the winter melon. Winter melons mature to enormous proportions. Coloured and shaped like large, round watermelons, they are named for the whitish blotches on the skin which are said to resemble patches of snow.

Fuzzy melons, on the other hand, are harvested and eaten immature, at which stage they have a covering of fuzz that disappears if the melon is allowed to grow past its peak to maturity.

Purchasing and storing: Choose the smallest, youngest specimens, which will be firmer. Expect the skin to have a mottled green appearance with a covering of fine, short white hairs. Use within a few days as, like most gourds, they lose their firm texture with keeping.

Preparation: Fuzzy melon needs to be peeled or scrubbed well to remove all trace of hairs before it can be eaten. It may be cut into chunks and steamed, scooped out and filled then steamed, stir-fried with oyster sauce or stir-fried with meat.

China: *mao gwa, tseet gwa*
Japan: *heari meron*
Malaysia: *timum balu*
Thailand: *faeng*
Vietnam: *bi*

Ridged gourd: (*Luffa acutangula*) SEE ILLUSTRATION. Also known as silk gourd or angled luffa, this vegetable can be found in varying sizes. It is distinguishable by 10 equidistant ridges which run from stem to tip. They must be removed with a vegetable peeler, but in tender young gourds the rest of the green skin is left on and is edible. Sweet and mild in flavour, it is a favourite vegetable in most Asian countries, being used in mild coconut milk curries or stir-fried with meat or other vegetables. A close relative of the smooth loofah (*Luffa cylindrica*), variously known as the sponge gourd, vegetable sponge and towel gourd ever since its usefulness as a bathtime scrubber (loofah) was discovered. The ridged gourd, being more difficult to strip of skin and flesh than its smooth cousin, does not have commercial value as a loofah, in spite of a very similar internal structure. As far as table use goes, the ridged gourd has the subtler flavour.

Purchasing and storing: Buy deep green, smooth skinned gourds with ridges which do not have a shrivelled look, indicating they have been picked a while ago. May be wrapped in paper and stored in a cool place, but not for too many days or they will toughen.

Preparation: Wash the gourd and with a vegetable peeler remove the edge of the ridges. Do not peel, as the skin is soft and edible if the gourd is young.

China: *sze gwa (ling chiao shyr kwa)*
India: *torai, kali, jhingli.*
Indonesia: *hoyong*
Japan: *tokado-hechim*a
Malaysia: *petola-sagi*
Philippines: *patolang*
Sri Lanka: *vatakolu*
Thailand: *boap liam*
Vietnam: *murop kai*

Silk gourd: See **Ridged gourd.**

Snake gourd: (*Trichosanthes anguina, T. cucumerina*) This bright green, thin-skinned gourd sometimes grows to a formidable length of about 2 m (6 ft). It is a common sight to see them growing with rocks tied to their ends so they don't curl into a French horn shape, as they are naturally inclined to do. They are usually cultivated on a frame head-high to the average person, which gives the appearance of a small house with rafters from which the gourds hang.

This gourd does not have much flavour and is popular stuffed with spicy minced meat. It can be used in much the same way that any other delicately flavoured vegetable is used: simmered in a coconut milk broth with spices and herbs.

China: *sze gwa*
India: *chichinda, chirchira*
Indonesia: *pare-belut*
Japan: *hebi-uri*
Malaysia: *petola-ular*
Philippines: *pakupis*
Sri Lanka: *pathola*
Thailand: *boap nguu*

Sponge gourd: (*Luffa cylindrica*) Many of us have used this vegetable in the bath or shower without a clue of its origins. The ripe fruits of the sponge gourd are stripped of skin and flesh to leave a stiff, net-like skeleton, which most people know as a back scrubber or loofah. Japan is a large producer. However, before the fruit reaches maturity, it is an edible vegetable popular throughout Asia. Substitute young sponge gourd in recipes for ridged gourd and snake gourd.

Gourds are not the only part of the plant that is edible. In Thailand the young shoots are blanched and served with nam prik or added to kaeng som or kaeng liang. The flowers also may be blanched and eaten with nam prik. The immature gourds, tender and sweet, are used for soup, fried with pork or shrimp, or boiled to be eaten with a hot sauce.

China: *sze kwa*
India: *meethi-torai*
Indonesia: *belustru*
Japan: *hechima*
Malaysia: *petola manis*
Philippines: *patola*
Sri Lanka: *vatakolu*
Thailand: *boap hom*
Vietnam: *muop huong*

Wax gourd: (*Benincasa hispida*) Also known as ash gourd or winter melon, this is arguably the largest edible gourd. It is not uncommon for the round or oblong specimens to weigh in at 10 kg (20 lb). Thought to have originated in Japan, it has long been used in China and is widely known throughout Asia. Picked before it matures, it is used for the famous dish Winter Melon Pond featuring a hollowed out, intricately cut melon as both the cooking and serving vessel for that flavoursome soup.

China: *tung kwa*
India: *petha, petha-kaddu*
Indonesia: *bligo*
Japan: *tougan*
Malaysia: *kundur*
Philippines: *kundol*
Thailand: *fak-kib*
Sri Lanka: *alu-puhul*

Grains of Paradise

(*Amomum melegueta, Aframomum melegueta*) Other common names for these small seeds are Melegueta pepper and Guinea pepper, as they come from the coastal regions of West Africa. They are beige in colour, dull rather than shiny. Their shape may be described as a sphere with irregular planes, not too dissimilar in appearance to cardamom

seeds. The flavour is pungent (though not as pungent as pepper), with a hint of cardamom and camphor. They are hardly used these days except in West and North Africa. I mention them because these seeds are sometimes passed off as the more expensive and fragrant cardamom seeds. In 1460 a Portuguese squadron brought a large shipment of them to Lisbon, selling them as Mclegueta pepper, and causing what amounted to a stock market crash and a sudden decline in the lucrative pepper trade. The plant, however, is not related to the pepper vine but is a member of the ginger family of which cardamom is also a member.

Grass Jelly

A brown-black jelly made from a type of grass. It is known as leong foon in Malaysia and greatly prized as a healthful addition to the cooling drinks taken often during the heat of the day. It is sold in cans. See recipe for Grass Jelly Drink (page 123).

Green Gram

See LEGUMES & PULSES (Mung bean).

Green Onion

See SPRING ONION.

Green Pea

See LEGUMES & PULSES.

Guava

SEE ILLUSTRATION. There are many varieties of guava. The small, round, deep-red cherry guava, also called strawberry guava (*Psidium littorale*), grows on trees with small, glossy, sturdy, dark green leaves. There is also the more common middle-sized, slightly pear-shaped guava with yellowy-green skin and salmon-pink flesh which grows on trees with larger, lighter coloured, more pliable leaves with prominent parallel veins which are more typical. There is also a dark-green skinned, oval-shaped variety with watermelon-pink flesh. My favourite eating guava is round, almost baseball-sized, with palest green skin and soft white flesh.

One thing they all have in common is a central ball of small, edible but quite hard seeds. In the middle of the ball is the sweetest, softest pulp found in the guava, very smooth compared to the slightly granular texture of the flesh outside the seeds. Guavas have a distinctive fragrance and if there is a bowl of guavas in a room, you cannot enter without noticing it. The skin of guavas of whatever variety is thin and the fruit needs only washing, not peeling.

Ripe guavas are good to eat, but in most Asian countries they are preferred under-ripe: sour, firm and dipped in chilli powder and salt, or fish sauce, or one of the fiery nam priks of Thailand.

In countries which have been colonised, the descendants of Dutch and British traders and rulers have a tradition of serving desserts after their meals. Home cooks like to collect guavas from their gardens and make something akin to poached pears which they serve as dessert. They also use the seasonal bounty to make preserves. Pantries are filled with jars of jelly and jam.

Medicinal uses: Ripe fruit are mildly laxative, and have ten times as much vitamin C as an orange. They also have a high iron content. The leaves and bark are brewed as a treatment for diarrhoea and indigestion. Pacific islanders chew the leaves as a treatment for sore throats.

Guava Jelly

Remember to include some half-ripe fruit to help the jelly set, as fully ripe fruit is low in pectin. I used to stubbornly refuse to add pectin to fruit jellies, preferring to cook them the old-fashioned way my grandmother did. Now I realise that there is fresher flavour and a considerable saving in time if I add pectin; and less evaporation means more jars of jelly which are not as sweet as when they are cooked longer.

3 kg/6 lb guavas
water
sugar
lime or lemon juice
commercial pectin

Wash the guavas and put them into a large stainless steel saucepan. Add water until it just shows beneath the top layer of fruit. Bring to the boil and simmer for about an hour or until the fruit is soft. Cool slightly, then pour into a muslin cloth or jelly bag which has been wrung out in water. (If the cloth is dry, it absorbs too

much of the precious fruit juice.) Place the wet cloth across a deep bowl and pour the fruit into the centre. Bring the corners of the cloth together and tie firmly with string. Allow to hang over the bowl of juice and drip slowly, preferably overnight. (The pulp can be used for making guava butter or guava cheese.)

Measure the liquid and allow ¾ cup white sugar to each cup of liquid. Cook no more than 5 cups of juice at a time, as the secret of fresh flavour and bright colour is quick cooking. Bring to the boil, add sugar and strained juice of 1 lime or lemon. Stir until sugar dissolves. Boil for 5–10 minutes. Draw pan away from heat and add pectin, sprinkling it over the surface if it is in powdered form. For even distribution, mix the dry powder with a few tablespoons of sugar.

Once more, bring to the boil and boil hard, stirring, for 10 minutes or until jelly drops from side of spoon in two or three slow drops, joined by a 'sheet' or 'flake' of the transparent liquid. This is an indication that a good set will be obtained. Do not skim the surface while cooking, or much of the pectin will be lost.

Have ready clean, hot jars. (They may be heated in the oven on a baking tray.) Pour the jelly into a heatproof glass jug and skim any froth off the surface just before pouring jelly slowly and carefully into the jars. (Take the jars from the oven a minute or two before filling them, as if they are too hot the jelly will bubble up in the jars and spill over the rim. Seal with lids and leave to cool.)

Guava Butter

Guava butter is a thick, sweet spread full of the flavour of the fruit and worth making if your family and friends like home-made jam. Strain the fruit through a sieve. Discard the seeds. Measure the strained pulp left over from making guava jelly and allow ¾ cup sugar to each cup of pulp. Cook no more than 4 cups at a time. Add a heaped teaspoon of butter and the juice of a lime or lemon and cook in a heavy-based pan, stirring constantly, until mixture is thick. Fill hot jars and seal. Better still, cook in a large bowl in the microwave oven to avoid constant stirring.

Guava Cheese

Guava cheese is simply guava butter taken a step further and cooked until it is firm enough to cut in slices and serve as a sweetmeat. The problem with making this delicacy the old-fashioned way is that as it thickens, the mixture sputters and plops like lava in a volcano. If you want to try making it, be sure you have a heavy pan, a long-handled spoon and wear long sleeves to protect your arms.

The modern, safe way is to put the pulp and sugar mixture into a large, microwave-proof bowl and cook in the microwave oven, uncovered, for 10 minutes, then stir and continue cooking for 5 minutes at a time, testing until it is thick enough to set when a little is left on a cold plate. Pour into a lightly buttered dish and smooth the top with the back of a buttered spoon. When quite cold, cut into squares or diamond shapes and roll in caster (superfine) sugar. Place in paper confectionery cases for serving.

Guinea Pepper

See GRAINS OF PARADISE.

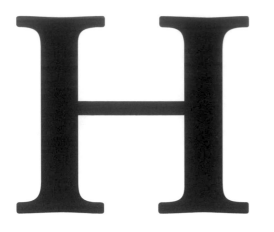

Hawaii

Hawaii enjoys an eclectic population and a cuisine to match. All the same, there is a central core of traditional fare which unites it with many of its Pacific island neighbours. In addition to favourite foods adopted from the various cultures who have made Hawaii their new home there are dishes whose contents and preparation have remained largely unchanged over the centuries. Here are some of the traditional foods you may encounter.

Awa: Ceremonial beverage, pretty unpalatable to all but the natives, made from pepper bush root with an anaesthetising effect on lips and tongue.

Haupia: Sweet pudding made with coconut milk and cornflour (cornstarch).

Kalua pig: Whole pig, filled with hot stones and then roasted underground for hours until the meat is so tender it literally falls off the bone.

Kulolo: Taro pudding.

Laulau: Fresh pork belly and salted salmon wrapped in taro leaves with an outer wrapping of ti leaves and steam-baked in an imu (I use the term steam-baked because, although the imu is an oven, when foods are enclosed in leaves, they steam-cook inside the parcel).

Limu: Seaweeds.

Loli, okole emiemi: Sea cucumber.

Lomi-lomi: A dish of salted (raw) salmon served with green onions and tomatoes.

Luau: A feast for special occasions cooked in an underground 'earth oven' or imu of white hot stones with foods wrapped in leaves (banana or ti).

Okolehao: Ti root liquor.

Poi: Dish of slightly fermented, cooked, mashed taro root.

Wana, haukeuke, ina: Sea urchin.

See also PACIFIC REGION.

Hibiscus

(*Hibiscus rosa sinesis*) The single red hibiscus is one of those flowers used in food and drink. It is probably not the flavour but the curative properties which are sought.

The bright red hibiscus bloom is made into cooling drinks or battered and fried in Sri Lanka where it is called 'shoe flower' and other South East Asian countries.

Pick just before using, since hibiscus flowers cannot be kept fresh in or out of water and, once gathered, will furl their petals in a short time.

Another member of the Hibiscus family is *H. sabdariffa*. See ROSELLE.

Preparation: Wash and shake dry, remove calyx and stamen, using only the petals. Use the flowers in the same way as sesbania blossoms. See recipe under SESBANIA (page 340).

Medicinal uses: Said to be a good blood purifier, especially when the fresh petals are infused in boiling water, usually served sweetened and flavoured with a squeeze of lime juice. Also fried in ghee and used as a medication for excessive menstruation.

> **China:** *fu shong hua*
> **India:** *fasut jasum, vadamal*
> **Indonesia:** *woro wari*
> **Japan:** *bussouge*
> **Malaysia:** *bunga raya*
> **Philippines:** *gumamela bulaklak*
> **Sri Lanka:** *watha wal, sapattu mal*

Hibiscus Drink

30–40 single red hibiscus blooms
1 litre/2 pints/4 cups boiling water
freshly squeezed lime juice
sugar to taste

Take about 30 freshly picked single red hibiscus flowers, preferably from your own garden so you know they are not contaminated by chemical sprays. Remove the calyx and the centre pistil and put only the petals into a heatproof bowl. Pour 4–6 cups of boiling water over the petals, cover and leave to cool. Strain and discard the petals — the liquid will be a pretty, clear pink. Add strained lime juice and sugar to taste and serve as a refreshing beverage. Said to have blood purifying properties. It may also be served as a hot drink after a shorter steeping time.

Hoi Sin Sauce

See BEAN SAUCES.

Honewort

See MITZUBA.

Honeydew Melon

See MELONS, SWEET.

Honey

The first sweetener, it was once used to preserve foods such as kumquat peel, ginger, bamboo shoots and olives. Diluted in water, it is believed to be a beneficial drink for the complexion. Thought to be tonic and good for colds, a range of honeys is available from China. Honey was gradually replaced after the second century following the introduction of sugar, which was also called 'stone honey' — for it was thought of as solid honey; also because it was moulded into stone-like loaves and figurines. One of the ingredients in rock sugar (see SUGAR, ROCK).

Hopper

A crisp pancake made from a batter of rice flour and coconut milk, fermented with toddy or yeast. The word itself is a corruption of the Sri Lankan 'appe' or the Indian 'appam', names by which this traditional breakfast dish is called. For recipe and more information see PANCAKES.

Horseradish Tree

See DRUMSTICK.

Horseradish, Japanese

See WASABI.

Hyacinth Bean

See LEGUMES & PULSES (Lablab bean).

Ice

Ice is one of the most refreshing and most essential items in the heat of a tropical country. For travellers, in particular, it is wise to be sure of the source of water used to make the ice.

Ice Cream

While most Asian frozen confections are based on shaved ice sweetened with syrups, you will also find ice cream in the most exotic flavours. Some, like durian, mango or woodapple, are only variations based on a creme anglaise, whilst India's kulfi (koulfi) ice cream has a personality all its own, redolent of saffron, kewra or cardamon with little lumps of clotted cream and pieces of pistachio punctuating the sweet, scented milk ice. Unlike Western ice cream, which is thickened by egg yolks, kulfi gets its creamy texture from cooked-down milk and a small amount of cornflour (cornstarch). Traditional kulfi is frozen in a metal cone set in ice and salt, unmoulded onto a plate and served with rose flavoured syrup drizzled over it and bits of cornflour jelly pressed through a mould.

If you manage to get yourself a set of the tapering, cone-shaped aluminium screw-topped containers, you can enjoy kulfi as it would be served in India. A handy tip when it comes to filling and freezing the moulds is to tape an empty cardboard egg carton closed or secure it with some rubber bands. Turn it upside down and, with a serrated knife, cut the ends off the egg 'cups'. This will now support the kulfi moulds while you pour in the mixture. Don't worry if you can't get moulds; even fresh from the churn, it is guaranteed to be the talking point of any meal. I simply finish it with a sprinkling of chopped pistachios. Unlike Western ice cream, which is served creamy enough to put a spoon into without too much effort, kulfi is served as firm as possible.

Kulfi (Indian Ice Cream)

For this recipe I thank my friend Aislynn Moses who showed me how to depart from tradition and get a great result with less effort.
Serves 12.

1 litre/2 pints/4 cups full cream milk
400 ml/14 oz can full cream evaporated milk
400 ml/14 oz can sweetened condensed milk
300 ml/10 fl oz dairy cream
1 small can reduced cream (optional)
2 tablespoons sugar
5 bruised cardamom pods
¼ cup pistachio kernels
1 tablespoon cornflour (cornstarch)
4 drops kewra essence
few drops green food colouring (optional)

In an enamel or stainless steel saucepan with a heavy base put the milk, evaporated milk, condensed milk, cream, cardamom pods and sugar. Stir constantly over medium heat until the milk mixture comes to the boil, moving the spoon all over the base of the pan to prevent the milk solids sticking and scorching. Once it has reached boiling point, reduce the heat to its lowest point and simmer gently, without covering pan, for 20–30 minutes so milk reduces in volume. It is not necessary to stir during this time, as the milk will not scorch if the initial stirring has been done.

Blanch the pistachio kernels for 1 minute in boiling water, drain and run cold water over them, then slip off the skins and chop the pistachios finely. Mix cornflour with 2 tablespoons cold water and stir into the simmering milk, raise heat slightly and bring to the boil to cook the cornflour and thicken the milk.

Remove pan from heat and allow to cool,

stirring occasionally. A skin will form on the surface, but simply stir this into the milk — it adds texture. Add the kewra essence and colour a pale green with food colouring if liked. If using an ice-cream churn, chill the mixture well before starting to churn.

If a churn is not available it may be still-frozen, then broken into chunks and puréed in a food processor until smooth but not melted. Stir in the pistachios at this stage, return to trays and freeze. Soften at room temperature for 10–15 minutes before serving. Sprinkle with extra blanched pistachios.

If cone-shaped moulds are available, stir the mixture well before filling each mould so the nuts are evenly distributed. Freeze until firm. Unmould by dipping the mould in slightly warm water just long enough to allow the kulfi to slip onto a plate.

Saffron Kulfi

Omit kewra and green colouring and add ½ teaspoon saffron strands, crushed and dissolved in hot milk.

Mango Kulfi

Prepare half quantity of basic kulfi. When cool, stir in an equal quantity of puréed ripe mangoes, sweetened to taste, since freezing diminishes sweetness. The addition of 3 or 4 drops of cardamom extract adds an exotic touch, not sufficient to drown out the mango flavour, but just enough to complement it. Freeze as before.

Ice Kacang

In Malaysia, Singapore and Indonesia the combination of these two words is music to the ears of those who know the refreshing cooler sold in every little roadside stall, and in grand hotels as well. Sweetened dried beans, small dried fruit, strips of jelly and little droplets of starch in bright colours, preserved sugar palm fruit and seeds, chunks or long slivers of grass jelly are mixed with shaved ice, sugar syrup and sometimes evaporated milk. Nothing is quite as refreshing when the temperature and humidity are high.

In the Philippines, there is a variation on the theme, known as halo-halo. This is served in tall glasses, layers of many coloured beans and white macapuno coconut, pineapple jelly and coconut jelly (all these items may be purchased in jars) making a rich mixture with the shaved ice. On top is sprinkled pinipig (crisply popped rice grains) and one is given a long spoon to mix it all together, halo-halo literally meaning 'mix-mix'.

In the Pacific, roadside stalls sell what is simply a huge cone of crushed ice, drizzled with coloured and fruit-flavoured syrups. No bits and pieces in this, just ice and syrup.

'Three bean drink', served in some Vietnamese restaurants, features a sweetened, yellow paste of cooked mung beans, whole azuki beans, and fine shreds of clear agar-agar jelly covered with shaved ice, with a generous splash of coconut milk poured over.

One of the pleasant surprises I found under a mini-mountain of shaved ice in my ice kacang from a stall in Singapore was a few small, salty-sweet dried Chinese plums. Another time in Penang, I was not so lucky. Out of character were cannned diced peaches and pears, instead of the exotic bits of jakfruit, palm sugar and grass jelly I was expecting. This came with a gratuitous scoop of ice cream. Western convenience foods have infiltrated even this most Asian of delights.

In Thailand, this refresher is called ruam mit, which translates as 'friendship' or 'get together' because of the many items to be found in it, including lotus seeds, sweetened tapioca root, sugar palm fruit and sweet potato. In addition, there are soaked basil seeds (affectionately called 'frog's eggs'), the tiny black seed in the centre of a weird translucent coat that materialises out of nowhere on contact with water, and tasting of nothing at all; but they contribute a different texture plus the health benefits of their soft and slippery coats (see BASIL SEED). Also offered is a translucent golden brown mass which turns out to be a soaked fruit called poontalai, with no flavour but a spongy, jelly-like texture. The whole lot is surmounted with shaved or crushed ice, over which is poured coconut milk sweetened with palm sugar and with a pinch of salt added to heighten the flavour. Sago or tapioca pearls, vividly coloured bits of jelly, and sombre black shreds of grass jelly are also options.

Almost everything you need to create your own

mix is sold in cans or jars at Asian stores. In addition, cooked mung beans, red beans, diced sweet potato or yam, and bananas cooked in syrup would not be out of place.

Idli

Idli are small, round, spongy, light-textured urad dhal and rice-based steamed dumplings popular in southern India. Making them is difficult because it is one of those recipes where nothing quite makes up for years of experience.

Many take-away places selling southern Indian food offer idli, and they are certainly easier to buy than to make. They freeze well, and may be reconstituted over simmering water or by a few seconds in a microwave oven on half power.

Idli

The basic idli is two parts rice to one part urad dhal, both soaked separately, drained, then ground separately. The urad dhal must be very smooth, the rice should be slightly gritty, like coarse semolina. The fermentation process (which can take from 12 to 30 hours depending on weather conditions) is what makes the batter light and foamy.

250 g/8 oz rice
125 g/4 oz urad dhal
½ teaspoon salt
¼ teaspoon baking powder

Soak rice and dhal separately in cold water to cover for 6–8 hours. Rinse both twice, then grind each one separately to a smooth, thick paste. Combine, mix in salt, cover and allow to stand overnight or as long as necessary to form small bubbles and develop a nice sourdough smell. Stir in just enough warm water to give the consistency of a batter thick enough to hold its shape in the spoon.

If you have the special idli steamer (four rounded depressions in each layer of the tiered arrangement) place wet muslin on them, then put a generous tablespoon of batter on each depression and steam over boiling water for 12–15 minutes. Peel off muslin and serve hot, with Coconut Chatni (see page 73) or Milagai Podi (see page 355).

India

Land of contrasts. Unimaginable wealth and abject poverty; unbearable heat and lashing blizzards; killer cyclones and devastating droughts; arid desert and dazzling palm-fringed beaches; serene countryside and crowded, bustling cities. The country's cuisine is equally diverse, from simple meals of chapati and lentils to the most lavish banquets. As well, India has a vegetarian cuisine that is imaginative, varied and nutritionally complete.

In spite of its diversity from north to south, from province to province and within its many religious sects, there is a thread that ties the whole together. Food is recognised as one of life's necessities, and the care and respect which goes into its preparation is as life-sustaining as the food itself.

While rice is the staple, breads, both leavened and unleavened, are daily fare in northern and central regions, though they bear little resemblance to Western loaves. They are not breads for slicing — each flat loaf is an individual serving size, and is usually broken into pieces which are used to scoop up the spicy accompaniments. Besides rice and wheat, millet is a widely used grain, both mixed with wheat flour to make flat breads; or coarse milled and cooked as pilau. Corn is also used, ground into a fine, silky cornmeal which is sometimes added to a pakora batter or combined with wheat flour and made into corn rotis, India's answer to the tortilla.

India's rich and varied cuisine did not develop in isolation. It is the direct result of centuries of cultural and religious influences.

The Aryans who came to India in the second millennium BC brought their own cattle but these were not as well suited to the climate as the native breed which eventually replaced them. As the indigenous inhabitants were introduced to dairy products, demand very rapidly outweighed supply. Over the next thousand years religious laws evolved to protect the cattle, stating first that only barren cows be used for food then, eventually, not even a barren cow. The barren cows were given to Brahman priests for sacrificial use. Over the next few hundred years, as the laws relaxed, cow slaughter began to put an enormous drain on the farmers who relied on cattle, if not as a source of milk, at least as draught animals.

As a backlash against this new wave of wanton killing there arose two new religious sects. Their founders, Buddha and Mahavira, opposed the Aryan divisions of caste and the violence perpetuated by the Brahmans with their ritual cow sacrifice. Buddha discouraged the common practice of honouring a guest by killing an animal while the disciples of Mahavira, the Jains, were forbidden to eat even fruit or vegetable if it contained an insect. Today the most orthodox Jains refuse to breathe the air without a mask lest they inhale some hapless creature, eat tomato because of its blood-red colour or a root vegetable because in uprooting it a grub may be injured. Their diet consists of leafy green vegetables, lentils and rice. This strong swing to vegetarianism, for reasons both virtuous and practical, caused even the most orthodox vedic Brahmans to follow suit. By the first century BC their rituals no longer included animal sacrifice and for a long time the greatest part of India's population followed a predominantly vegetarian diet, with the occasional chicken or goat (or seafood in coastal areas) being the exception, and then only if religion permitted.

The Moslem invasion in the Middle Ages introduced lamb, which is still popular in the north where Moslem customs forbid the eating of pork. Since beef is sacred to the Brahmans it is not bred commercially, and therefore of poor eating quality. However, both Moslems and Syrian Christians, for whom it is an acceptable food, have devised clever ways to prepare it, mincing, cubing and marinating it to disguise the toughness.

Other religions have contributed to the complexity of today's Indian cuisine. Vaishnavas, worshippers of Lord Krishna, are not only vegetarian, they also abstain from onions and garlic, yet theirs is a richly varied and flavoursome cuisine. Brahmans today range from strict vegetarian to those who eat fish and lamb but not chicken or eggs. There are also countless non-Brahmans all over India whose diet is strictly vegetarian, either by choice or financial necessity.

Sikhs, reputedly the best farmers in India, whose preparations often include corn, milk and sugar, make lavish use of ghee. The Persian background of the Parsees is most likely the reason that goat and eggs were introduced into the cuisine of India. Many years of British rule evolved an independent cuisine that is neither British nor Indian, yet brings together features of both (see BRITISH–INDIAN CUISINE).

As a result of the cattle introduced to India by the Aryans, cream and yoghurt are still used to enrich food in the north. In the south, coconut milk is preferred.

A common Western misconception is that a curry, to be authentic, must be searingly hot. While the majority of curries from the south are chilli hot and robustly flavoured, in the north they are subtle, characterised by the use of fragrant spices, saffron, ghee and the perfumed flower essences of the Moghul empire. In coastal regions the abundance of the ocean has inspired many a seafood delicacy. Goa, which was colonised by the Portuguese, has contributed some outstanding seafood specialities as well as spicy pork and liver sausages, the most famed of all being chourisam. Goa is also known for its piquant and pungently spiced vindaloos.

Only in India will you find the tradition of decorating food with edible gold and silver leaf (varak). But such excesses are not unusual; on important occasions, such as weddings, no expense is spared. The not-so-well-to-do take out loans to put on a lavish banquet.

Few cuisines have taken the repertoire of the snack or the sweetmeat to such an extreme. In this realm, milk and milk products have inspired a vast array of cooked sweets and desserts.

At the core of Indian cuisine is its subtle and, sometimes, not so subtle use of a myriad intriguing spices in a limitless variety of combinations, turning even the humblest vegetarian offering into a feast.

Indonesia

An archipelago of more than 17,000 islands strung between South East Asia and Australia, only half of which are large enough to have names and less than a thousand of those inhabited. It includes some of the world's largest islands and is home to over 187 million people, the fifth largest population in the world. The climate is steamy and hot, which accounts for the lushness of its vegetation and the impression of perpetual greenness.

Indonesia has, at different times, embraced animism, Buddhism, Hinduism and Islam and been influenced or conquered by the Chinese, the Indians, the Dutch, the Portuguese and the English.

Indonesia's rich and varied history, its many traditions and languages, have produced a cuisine that is similarly rich and varied, with much to offer the adventurous eater. Not every dish is hot or pungent, and there is an intriguing balance of sweet, sour and salty tastes, from gentle coconut milk sauces fragrant with lemon grass and herbs to fiery sambals intended to be tasted in tiny quantities.

Whatever else is served, rice is always the cornerstone of an Indonesian meal. Cooked by the absorption method, the pearly grains are full of flavour and just the right texture. With the rice it is customary to serve fish and poultry or meat, either curried or spiced and fried, if not both. This is usually accompanied by two or more vegetable dishes, one with lots of gravy and the other either stir-fried, boiled or raw as a salad.

Accompaniments such as krupuk and fresh chilli condiments are an integral part of the meal, as are sambals. This term refers not only to the fiery condiments which are concentrated pastes of sea-soned ground chilli used judiciously as a relish, but also to spicy main dishes, sambals of prawn (shrimp), chicken or beef. Condiment sambals are available in bottles and, in most cases, these versions of the classic sambals, bajak, ulek and petis, are an acceptable alternative to home-made sambals.

To serve an Indonesian meal, place all dishes on the table at once, except sweets or fruit. Rice is taken first, surrounded by small tastes of the strong flavoured dishes. A bowl of clear soup often accompanies the meal, sipped as a palate cleanser between mouthfuls, rather than as a separate course. The correct cutlery is dessertspoon and fork, although it is traditional to eat with one's fingers. Only the tips of the fingers of the right hand should come in contact with the food and a fingerbowl of hot water (with a halved lime) is brought to the table afterwards.

J

Jaggery

Dark, unprocessed sugar derived from various palms or from sugar cane. The dark brown mass is sold in cylindrical shapes or crudely shaped into balls of varying size, from marbles to coconuts. It has a heady aroma and delicious flavour somewhere between brown sugar and molasses with a hint of fermentation. Used to flavour hot milk and many vegetarian curries. It is also served at breakfast (shaved into crumbly flakes or chopped into small pieces) with freshly grated coconut to accompany hoppers (see PANCAKES), or a porridge of unpolished rice.

It sweetens and flavours that rich coconut milk and tapioca drink from Burma, moh let saung, Sri Lanka's famous Vattalappam (recipe page 119), and many local snacks. In Thailand it is used not just for confections but also to add the necessary touch of sweetness to hot curries. See also PALM SUGAR.

Burma: *jaggery*
India: *gur, jaggery*
Sri Lanka: *hakuru, jaggery*
Thailand: *nam taan oi*

Jakfruit

(*Artocarpus integrifolia, A. heterophyllus*) SEE ILLUSTRATION. Also spelled jackfruit. A fast-growing, evergreen tree, native to India's Western Ghats mountain range, it bears the world's largest fruit. A single specimen may grow as large as 1 m (3 ft) and weigh as much as 45 kg (100 lb). The trees, common throughout tropical regions, vary from 7 to 20 m (20–65 ft) in height and have shiny, deep green foliage. The fruit is eaten both immature and ripe. Immature, it is a starchy vegetable which has to be cooked. When ripe, it is sweet and strongly flavoured and eaten raw or canned in desserts and sweet drinks.

The skin of the fruit is light green, deepening to yellow-brown when ripe, and covered in hard, knobbly spines. Inside, the fruit is divided into numerous segments (pericarps) which are encased in stringy, white tissue of inferior quality known as 'rags'. Each pericarp surrounds a large seed. Ripe fruit is sweet and yellow to pink in colour, depending on variety.

The ripe fruit develops a heady aroma which, in tandem with the yellowing of its spiny skin, is a sure sign of readiness. But one seldom has to guess — the size of the mature fruit being such that practically no one buys a whole fruit — they are cut open and sold in sections.

When available in Western countries, segments of ripe jakfruit are sold removed from the skin, arranged neatly in small polystyrene trays and covered with cling wrap. Eat the segments out of hand, or slice and include in a fruit salad of other tropical fruits with flavours which can stand up to the sometimes aggressive fragrance of jak. I've seen jakfruit for sale in supermarkets that stock exotic produce, but they are almost without exception uncut and unripe. Strictly cooking material.

Unripe jakfruit is a staple starch source in many Asian and South Pacific countries, fried, roasted or boiled. When unripe the seeds are immature and easily sliced through. There is a lot of inedible fibrous tissue (like strips of sticky white plastic) that surrounds the edible pockets of fruit, but in the immature fruit this too can be sliced up and cooked.

The seeds of ripe jakfruit are considered a delicacy in some countries. The edible segments enclose large, oval, pale seeds which are also cooked and eaten as a snack, boiled or roasted.

They are notorious for causing intestinal wind, but as with chestnuts, many are willing to risk the after-effects.

A favourite way of cooking jakfruit seeds is to roast them in the coals of a wood fire. The thin but tough covering on the seeds protects them during roasting, and is removed after the seeds are cooked. They are also cooked in curries, often together with potatoes, beans or other vegetables. In this case the celluloid-like covering of the seed must be removed first. They need long boiling in order to become soft enough to eat. When fully cooked they have a soft, mealy texture.

There are two main varieties of jakfruit: one with flesh that is soft and stringy when ripe, and the other with flesh which remains firm and crisp. It is the crisp variety which is canned in sugar syrup, the pericarps sliced into bite-sized pieces. This is an example of a tropical fruit that does not suffer unduly from being canned. Serve with ice cream or custard, or mix into fruit salad.

Fiji: *uto ni idia*
India: *katahal, kathal ke beej*
Indonesia: *nangka*
Malaysia: *nangka*
Philippines: *langka*
Samoa: *moe ulu initia*
Sri Lanka: *polos* (immature), *kos* (mature but unripe), *varaka* (ripe)
Thailand: *kanoon, kha-nun, med-kha-nun*
Vietnam: *mit*

Jakfruit Curry

For cooking, jakfruit should not be ripe with yellow and fragrant flesh, but at the stage when the pericarps (fleshy sacs which cover the large seeds) are pale. Slices of this large fruit are cut like wedges of watermelon and sold by weight at markets. Experienced cooks rub their hands with oil before handling the fruit as it oozes a sticky latex which is hard to remove, and the oil gives protection.

500 g/1 lb unripe jakfruit (pericarps and seeds)
sprig of curry leaves
2 strips pandan leaves
1 medium onion, finely chopped
3 cloves garlic, sliced
1 or 2 fresh green chillies
½ teaspoon turmeric

½ teaspoon chilli powder
1 teaspoon ground coriander
1 teaspoon ground cumin
1 teaspoon ground fennel
250 ml/8 fl oz/1 cup canned coconut milk
    diluted with equal amount of water
1 teaspoon salt or to taste
125 ml/4 fl oz/½ cup undiluted coconut milk

Peel and clean the jakfruit. Remove fine, plastic-like strips which lie close to pericarps, and the celluloid-like skin of the seed. Slice the pericarps into bite-sized pieces. Put all the ingredients into a pan, except for the undiluted coconut milk. Bring to boil and cook until jakfruit and seeds are tender. Add the reserved coconut milk, simmer for a few minutes and serve with rice.

Jakfruit Mallung

Mallung or mallum is a Sinhalese word which means 'mix-up' and is usually applied to the leafy green preparations with everything chopped finely and mixed over heat. This dish is an accompaniment to rice, and is always without a sauce — the liquid that comes out of the leaves or other ingredients is evaporated. This version is made with very tender jakfruit shredded finely and cooked with chillies and other spices.

500 g/1 lb young jakfruit
4 fresh green chillies, sliced
2 teaspoons salt
1 large onion, finely chopped
1 teaspoon turmeric
375 ml/12 fl oz/1½ cups water
125 g/4 oz grated fresh coconut
    or desiccated coconut
2 teaspoons prepared wholegrain mustard
¼ teaspoon ground black pepper
2 teaspoons crushed garlic

Shred the tender jakfruit finely and put it into a pan with the chillies, salt, onion, turmeric and water. Bring to the boil, cover and cook on low heat until jakfruit is tender and water is evaporated. Mix in the coconut, mustard, pepper and crushed garlic, toss and mix well over heat for a few minutes. Serve with rice.

Guinatan with Jakfruit

A popular sweet throughout Asia, this is known as guinatan in the Philippines and bubor cha-cha in Malaysia. The ingredients change according to seasonal availability and the starch component varies from glutinous rice to tapioca to sago. Fresh coconut milk is best, but a good quality, smooth, canned coconut milk may be used. Serves 8.

8 ripe jakfruit pericarps
 or 1 can jakfruit in syrup
3 tablespoons tapioca or sago
250 g/8 oz/1 cup sugar
500 ml/1 pint/2 cups water
500 g/1 lb diced sweet potato, taro or purple yam
3 ripe cooking bananas, sliced
400 ml/14 fl oz can coconut milk
250 ml/8 fl oz/1 cup coconut cream

Cut the jakfruit into dice, and remove the seeds for another use. Or drain the canned jakfruit and reserve the syrup. Cook tapioca or sago in plenty of water until the grains are clear. Rinse in cold water. Drain.

Make a syrup of the sugar and water, add the coconut milk and bring to the boil, then add the diced sweet potato, taro or yam (or a mixture) and boil until tender but still holding their shape. Add bananas and tapioca, and the jakfruit. Remove from heat and stir in coconut cream, or serve in bowls and pass coconut cream for adding to individual servings. Serve warm or at room temperature.

Jambu

(*Syzygium malaccense, S. aqueum, Eugenia javanicum, E. uniflorum*) Many fruits share the name of jambu and also share a thirst-quenching juiciness. While they may be related, the varieties look quite different and taste different too. The one with the most flavour is the large (about the size of a small apple), oval, white variety which develops a pink blush on one side when ripe. The flesh is pure white and slightly sweet. Also known as Malay apple.

A more common bright red variety is known as wax jambu or water roseapple. These very attractive fruits range from white faintly streaked with pink to an overall deep pinkish-red colour that one sees on jelly beans. The thin skin is so shiny that it is obvious why it is called wax jambu. It is pear shaped, small — about 2–3 cm (¾–1 in) long and 4–5 cm (1½–2 in) across — and with a prominent, fleshy calyx on the broad end. As a contrast to its attractive colour, the slightly acid flavour is a big disappointment. Children are attracted to them for their colour and shine, but most people don't bother eating them except that they are a good thirst-quencher. Even for jam making, were it not for a copious dose of lime juice they would not convey much flavour at all. In Thailand, the young leaves of *Eugenia cymosa* are used raw with spicy dips.

Medicinal uses: In Malaysia the dried, powdered leaves are used for treating a cracked tongue, the roots to relieve itch. In Indonesia the bark is made into a mouthwash to treat thrush. In Indochina the seeds and fruits are used to make a cooling drink, administered for fevers.

Malaysia: *jambu ayer, jambu bol*
Sri Lanka: *pini jambu*
Thailand: *daeng khlong*

Japan

Distinct from the cuisine of every other Asian country is the gastronomy of Japan. It is impossible to separate cuisine from culture and the prevailing sensitivity to nature that permeates all things Japanese. Their cookery is as much the embodiment of their respect for nature as is their art, and a sense of the aesthetic is as evident in the presentation of a meal as it is in a silk painting or ceramic form.

The beauty of Japanese cuisine, of all Japanese artistic tradition in fact, is the subtle art of balance. The essence of the Japanese aesthetic can be summed up in two words: simplicity and elegance. What this means in Japanese cuisine is that food looks and tastes as natural as possible. Ingredients are always of premium quality, at their peak of freshness and, of course, in season.

Unlike Westerners who try to outwit the seasonal nature of produce, the Japanese yield to the ebb and flow of climate and how it affects the availability of produce. Where is the thrill of the first ripe strawberry of the season if, by trickery or technology, that fruit is available year round? Regional produce is the fingerprint of regional cookery. Because of the insistence on freshness, this means that regional delicacies are usually only available in their region of origin with an emphasis on freshly gathered seasonal ingredients.

Rice is the cornerstone of a Japanese meal and the Japanese word for boiled rice, gohan, is the same as the word for 'meal'. The variety used is either short or medium grain, and it is always steamed to perfection by absorption. Convenient for this are the electric rice cookers which always do a reliable job. While the earth yields rice and other food crops, the turbulent cross currents of warm and cold waters are rich in marine minerals which cannot settle to the sea floor, providing an excellent feeding ground and resulting in some of the best tasting and most nutritious sea produce in the world.

Besides the many seaweeds rich in iron and iodine, the ocean literally teems with life and the harvest of the deep, added to the bounty of rivers, yield some one thousand varieties of fish and shellfish, the basis of a healthy and nutrient-rich diet. From land and sea come the key flavour ingredients of Japanese cooking: the basic stock, dashi, made from bonito and seaweed, and sake, the sacred drink brewed from rice.

Of all other crops grown, second to rice in importance must be the soy bean, from which is derived a soy sauce without equal, shoyu; the all-important vegetable protein, tofu; and the concentrated flavour base, miso. These give Japanese food its characteristic flavour.

One of the aims of Japanese cookery is to protect food from overcooking and to preserve its natural flavour. Japanese food, though often intricate in presentation, is some of the least 'fiddled with' food in the world, without the guise of complicated sauces and cooking techniques. The Japanese words assari (subtle) and sapari (satisfying) are often applied to food. They illustrate the Japanese need to combine rich and delicate ingredients to achieve that elusive balance of flavour and texture. Food that tastes delicious yet isn't overpowering or obvious; that is satisfying yet light.

Japanese cuisine goes far beyond food: it is the whole cycle from harvest to table with no aspect taken for granted. In the very serious business of the tea ritual, for instance, there is as much notice taken of the dimensions of the room and its decoration, the objects of the tea service and the conversation as of the considerable skills of the tea master in producing the frothy, green brew ceremoniously prepared for each guest and offered in uniquely shaped ceramic cups.

The passing seasons are celebrated in every aspect and this is reflected in a Japanese meal, from ingredients to the choice of serving dish and garnish. A creative presentation will evoke a season or a scene as deftly as a three-line haiku or a few well-chosen brush strokes. Maple leaves, pine needles, and bamboo leaves are just some of the garnishes used to achieve the desired effect. Simple rules of presentation such as round-shaped foods served in dishes with straight sides and square foods in rounded dishes reflect an unerring sense of balance.

The seven basic techniques of Japanese cookery are raw fish preparation, soup-making, grilling, steaming, simmering, deep-frying and 'saucing' (dressings for salads).

The following terms will help you find your way through a Japanese menu.

Aemono: Japanese mixed or dressed salads. These usually have more complex dressings (than vinegared salads) based on miso or tofu and are often flavoured with sesame seeds.

Agemono: Japanese for deep frying. Tempura is probably the best known example. Other examples are the crumbed pork cutlet tonkatsu or a marinated whole fish, dredged in cornflour (cornstarch). Little is done to flavour the food prior to cooking and a dipping sauce, tonkatsu sauce or stronger flavoured condiments such as momiji-oroshi (grated radish and red pepper) or shichimi-togarashi provide the necessary flavour balance.

Mushimono: Japanese steamed dishes. Although steamed at a high temperature, mushimono are traditionally served at room temperature. Chawan mushi is a well-loved, simple yet tasty dish of savoury egg custard which may include ingredients such as ginkgo nuts, prawn (shrimp) and chicken. See recipe for Japanese Savoury Custard (page 137).

Nabemono: Literally 'one pot dish', this is do-it-yourself Japanese cuisine. Raw or previously fried ingredients are arranged on a platter within easy reach of all guests. Picked up with chopsticks a piece at a time, the ingredients are either swirled through simmering stock in a hotpot or briefly seared in an oiled frypan. Each guest has individual bowls of dipping sauce and condiments to season their food to taste. In a formal banquet, this course may replace the quartet of grilled, steamed, simmered and deep-fried dishes.

Nimono: In Japanese cuisine, this term encompasses all simmered dishes. They may include a number of mixed ingredients or only one, the cooking time just long enough to allow the flavours of the simmering liquid to penetrate.

Teppan yaki: Teppan, a post-war addition to Japanese cooking techniques, has become as popular with Japanese palates as the Western tastebuds it was created to please. Literally 'mixed grill', the Japanese sensitivity to texture ensures that everything (beef, chicken, fish or shellfish) is cooked to succulent perfection. There are establishments dedicated to teppan cooking where customers sit around tabletop-sized griddle plates to watch the chef perform something of a floor show. Traditionally oil or suet was used to grease the griddle, but these days chefs in teppan restaurants, more often than not, use butter. Foods are usually accompanied by several dipping sauces for meat and seafood.

Tsukemono: Japanese pickles, served with boiled or steamed white rice (gohan) and soup (clear or miso) are part of the final stages of a banquet, as well as components of a very simple meal in Japan. In addition to their palate cleansing and digestive properties, pickles are also used as a garnish to complement the appearance and flavour of a dish.

Pickles may be made by a variety of methods: salting produces shio-zuke; rice bran makes nuka-zuke; sake lees is used for kasu-zuke; and miso makes miso-zuke. There is a multitude of permutations on these basic themes. Some of the popular tsukemono ingredients include ginger, turnip, radish, cucumber and hakusai, more often referred to as Chinese cabbage.

Perhaps the best known tsukemono is takuan, the crunchy, pungent, yellow pickled radish (daikon) popular since the 17th century. The pickle of salted 'plum' umeboshi derives its colour from the red leaved shiso (beefsteak plant or perilla), adding not only colour but also medicinal value. Umeboshi is an effective preservative, containing a high level of salt and citric acid, and as such is a feature of the pickled plum rice ball (umeboshi no onigiri). A well-known appetite stimulant, usually taken at the start of a meal, it is also used to make a popular bedtime tonic drink.

Yakimono: Traditional Japanese grilled foods, usually served at the second main stage of a banquet.

Grilling is done over a hot charcoal fire or on skewers set above a gas flame. Foods for grilling include fish and seafood, chicken, meat and vegetables. The seasoning is minimal and, as with all Japanese cuisine, freshness of produce is premium.

Jasmine

(*Jasminum sambac*) Also known as Arabian jasmine or biblical jasmine. The flowers are pure white, small and have many more rounded petals than the common *J. polyanthum* with its single layer of petals. Their corolla tube is green. These are the flowers which are used in traditional Thai cuisine to scent sweets. The flowers are steeped in a covered container of water overnight. The strained water is used to extract coconut milk from freshly grated coconuts, or to cook tapioca flour and sugar for small, jelly-like sweets. These days the jasmine flavour comes out of a bottle of essence, but if you have jasmine growing profusely, why not enjoy the experience. *J. polyanthum* may be used. In all cases of using flowers, make sure they have not been in contact with chemical sprays.

Thailand: *mali*

Java Almond

(*Canarium commune*) A towering tree native to Malaysia which attains a height of up to 30 m (100 ft).

The kernels, which are known as kenari in Indonesia and pili nut in the Philippines, are said to be perfectly delicious, resembling sweet almonds. They are eaten fried and salted. They are also used in confectionery in the Philippines and a Moluccan candy similar to halva is made from them.

A lemon-scented pale yellow resin is collected from incisions made in the bark. This is used in incense and an oil distilled from it is an ingredient in in perfume and cosmetics.

Indonesia: *kanari, kenari*
Malaysia: *kanari, kenari*
Papua: *keanee*
Philippines: *pili*
Sri Lanka: *rata kekuna*

Jellyfish

(*Rhopilema esculenta*) This is, of course, the edible jellyfish — not the dangerous type which frequent tropical waters during certain times of the year and can kill unwary swimmers with their poison. The tentacles are removed before the large round upper portion or canopy (as much as 30 cm (12 in) in diameter) is dried. It becomes translucent and yellow, like old parchment. It is usually sold in plastic packets, heavily salted, and needs to be soaked for some hours in several changes of cold water. It is also available already soaked and shredded.

Jellyfish is something to be savoured in small amounts so don't buy or prepare too much. Shred finely (or buy it ready shredded) and marinate in a mixture of rice wine or dry sherry, ginger juice, 2 sliced spring onions (scallions) and lukewarm water to cover. Leave for 15 minutes, then drain. Jellyfish has no flavour to speak of, but the crunchy resilience is a perfect example of the importance Chinese gourmets place on texture ingredients. Because of its texture and appearance, it is jocularly referred to as 'rubber bands'.

Sliced into fine strips and dressed with a mixture of vinegar, light soy sauce and sesame oil, jellyfish is served as one of the appetisers in a cold assortment, or presented as a salad with shredded crisp vegetables. Make a dressing by mixing equal parts of oriental sesame oil and soy sauce, and half the amount of Chinese red vinegar and sugar. Serve cold.

China: *hoi chit*
Japan: *kurage*
Vietnam: *sua*

Jicama

See YAM BEAN.

Jujube

(*Ziziphus jujuba*) Also known as Chinese date and red date, this hardy deciduous tree has been cultivated in northern China for 4,000 years. The olive-shaped fruit have a thin but tough red-brown skin and mucilaginous, sweet white flesh. They may be dried, candied or eaten fresh. After partial drying, the flesh becomes crisp.

Medicinal uses: It is taken to calm nerves, improve blood quality and cure insomnia — hence its title, 'food of harmony'. High in vitamin C.

China: *hung jo, hung zao*
Sri Lanka: *masan*

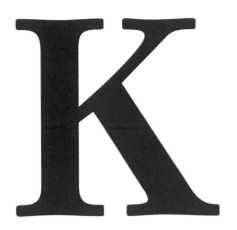

Kaffir Lime

(*Citrus hystrix, C. papedia*) SEE ILLUSTRATIONS. Also *C. amblycarpa* (leprous lime). The fragrant leaves and dark green rind of kaffir limes are used in Thailand and other South East Asian countries to give incomparable flavour to certain dishes. The tree is not large — about 3–5 m (9–18 ft) tall. The fruit is dark green and round, with a distinct nipple on the stem end. It has a thick rind, bumpy and wrinkled, and one of its common names is 'porcupine orange'. As the fruit becomes older, the colour fades to a lighter, yellowish green.

Thanks to the wonderful cultural cross-pollination that has taken place in recent years, many hitherto unobtainable ingredients have become readily available. I remember a time not so very long ago when in a Western city you could as likely find kaffir limes or leaves as moon rocks. Then, as demand grew, first dry leaves were imported, then fresh-frozen leaves and now, in many Asian and even mainstream greengrocers, fresh leaves are brought in every week, and also fruits during the brief season.

The leaves and rind have a perfume unlike any other citrus and are indispensable in the wonderfully tangy soups, salads and curries of Thailand, and even if only for these, are worth seeking out. Some plant nurseries are starting to sell the trees, and they will flourish even in temperate climates and add a wonderful dimension to your cooking.

Kaffir lime is sold bottled in brine; use a teaspoon to scrape away any white pith (which, like all citrus pith, has a bitter flavour) from the inner surface of the skin. The rind is also sold dried, but being in fine strips, it is difficult to separate pith from rind. If this is all you can find, use in small quantities. If unavailable, substitute the zest of fresh Tahitian or West Indian limes.

Purchasing and storing: The leaves may be recognised by their distinctive two sections. For simmering in soups or curries the leaves are used whole. Frozen or dried leaves may be used for simmering if fresh leaves are not available.

The finely grated rind of the lumpy-skinned fruit has its own special fragrance. If you can obtain fresh kaffir limes, they freeze well enclosed in freezer bags and will keep indefinitely in that state. Just grate a little rind off the frozen lime and replace lime in freezer until next required. The leaves freeze well too.

Preparation: Salads or garnishes require fresh leaves. Dried leaves cannot be substituted. The leaves, when young and tender, are finely shredded and added to salads and sprinkled over curries for a burst of flavour. Being rather thick, they must be cut very fine, like threads, and the thick mid-rib excised; all done easily with a small, really sharp knife. Some cooks recommend rolling the leaves tightly from tip to stem, then slicing finely from either end, leaving the tough mid-rib to be discarded. If fresh kaffir lime leaves are not available, use the tender new leaves of lime, lemon or grapefruit. They won't have the same fragrance but are preferable to using dried kaffir lime leaves. Do not use kumquat leaves.

Medicinal uses: In South East Asia, the fruit is boiled until very soft, and the resulting pulp rubbed into the hair and scalp as a remedy for lice and dandruff. It is left on from 30 minutes to 2 hours, then washed off.

Burma: *shauk-nu, shauk-waing*
Cambodia: *krauch soeuch*
China: *fatt-fung-kam*
Malaysia: *limau purut*
Indonesia: *jeruk purut, jeruk sambal*
Philippines: *swangi*
Sri Lanka: *kahpiri dehi, odu dehi, kudala-dehi*
Thailand: *makrut, som makrut*

Kalamansi

(*Citrus microcarpa, C. mitis*) Described as a sour lime, no one would argue with the description after one tongue-curling taste of the juice. The fruit is only 2–3 cm (½–1 in) in diameter, green or green-yellow. Small and round with slightly flattened ends, they can be picked green or ripe but the juice stays sour. It is halved and placed alongside dishes of mixed fried noodles and similar one-dish meals in Malaysia and Singapore, and squeezed over individual servings for a piquant flavour. In the Polynesian islands, the fruit is added to bland fruits such as papayas to make jam. In the Philippines the juice is squeezed from the fruit and used in a cordial concentrate which is diluted to make a refreshing cold drink.

Kalonji

See NIGELLA.

Kamaboko

See FISH CAKES.

Kampyo

Thinly shaved, dried strips of gourd used in Japan as one of the fillings for norimaki (sushi rice rolled in nori seaweed). First it is well soaked in warm, salted water. Reconstituted, it is a pliable, edible, decorative tie for securing daintily wrapped food presentations.

Kangaroo

The first kangaroo eaten by Europeans did not get a very enthusiastic reception, the botanist Joseph Banks dubbing it 'the most insipid meat I did eat'. But another kangaroo dined off within a day or two was, apparently, much better.

In 1862 there was a dinner in Great Britain with an Australian theme, at which Kangaroo Steamer and Kangaroo Ham were served. From accounts, the former was kangaroo and fatty pork seasoned and sealed in a crock which was cooked very slowly for at least 4 hours. A good move, probably planned so the lean kangaroo meat was made rich by the fat of the pork. In the 1960s, boned kangaroo meat was regularly exported to West Germany, together with wild boar.

Australia now exports kangaroo meat to many countries, and it is considered a healthy meat because of its extreme leanness. It can be used much as lean beef is used, and responds well to quick stir-frying in the Asian manner.

Kangaroo with Chilli-Bean Sauce

Serves 4

375 g/12 oz kangaroo fillet
½ teaspoon chopped garlic
½ teaspoon sugar
1 teaspoon finely grated fresh ginger
2 tablespoons light soy sauce
3 tablespoons peanut oil
1 red capsicum (bell pepper), diced

SAUCE
1 tablespoon bean sauce
1 scant teaspoon chilli bean sauce
2 teaspoons sugar
125 ml/4 fl oz/½ cup stock or water
2 teaspoons cornflour (cornstarch)
1 teaspoon oriental sesame oil

Freeze kangaroo fillet until firm so it is easier to slice paper thin. Crush garlic with sugar until smooth, combine with ginger and soy sauce and mix well into the meat. Cover and leave for 15 minutes.

Heat 1 tablespoon peanut oil in a wok and when very hot stir-fry the capsicum for 1 minute. Remove to a plate, heat remaining oil and stir-fry the marinated kangaroo slices for 2 minutes. Remove and put with the capsicum. Add the sauce ingredients mixed together and stir until boiled and thickened. Remove from heat, stir in capsicum and kangaroo and serve at once with steamed rice.

Kanten

See AGAR-AGAR.

Kebab

Marinated meat threaded onto metal or wooden skewers. In India any meat which has been tenderised by marinating may be called 'kebab', whether it be minced (ground), cut into cubes, or a whole joint. Cooked by grilling, roasting in an oven or barbecuing over coals.

Kecap

See SOY SAUCE.

Kedgeree

Anglicised spelling of the Indian dish kitchri or khichari. A nutritious vegetarian dish combining lentils and rice with a tantalising blend of spices. If gently seasoned and moist, it is called geeli khichari, while the denser, more substantial version which might include nuts, vegetables and raisins or currants is called sookha khichari. See recipe for Red Lentil and Rice Kitchri, page 215. The British adaptation is a hearty breakfast dish of rice mixed with smoked fish and hard-boiled eggs.

Kemiri Nut

See CANDLE NUT.

Kencur

See GINGER, AROMATIC.

Kephir

The camel's milk version of kumiss. See also KUMISS.

Kewra

(*Pandanus fascicularis*) A strongly scented flavouring essence favoured in festive dishes, both sweet and savoury, of north India. It is used to flavour beverages, desserts and to add an exotic, flowery fragrance to biriani dishes. Clear and pale yellow, it is distilled from the highly perfumed male flowers of a particular variety of pandanus.

Not to be confused with pandan paste (deep green) or pandan essence (clear pale green), which are made from the leaves of another member of this plant family (see PANDANUS LEAF).

See also ESSENCES.

India: *kewra, talai*
Sri Lanka: *mudu kekiya*

Khoa

See MILK.

Khus

See VETIVER.

Kid

See MUTTON.

Kim Chi

A pungent Korean relish. A testimony to the chilli-eating capacity of Koreans, kim chi is not for the faint-hearted, boldly seasoned as it is with chilli and garlic. Expect to see it on the table at every meal. It's a strong constitution indeed that can face these flavours first thing in the morning! There are two versions of this national relish: winter kim chi and summer kim chi.

Winter kim chi is made with lots of salt, chilli and garlic and has a main ingredient of Chinese cabbage. It is tightly packed into earthenware pots, weighted, and allowed to ferment and mellow. It replaces vegetables through the cold winter months. Variations on this theme may contain tiny, salted shrimp or ground fish. Summer kim chi uses white radish, cucumber, bean sprouts or other available greens and is less salty, often slightly sweet and lightly vinegared. It is eaten fresh and is not fermented.

See recipe page 57.

King Coconut

A distinct cultivar, popular in Sri Lanka where it is said to have originated and where it is called thambili. Most valuable at the immature stage, when the juice inside is sweet and the albumen tender. The colour is an attractive orange-yellow, and large bunches of these nuts are a common sight in every market and roadside stall.

Kiwi Fruit

(*Actinidia chinensis, A. deliciosa*) A good example of what public relations can do for a fruit. Originally a native of southern China, until 1940 it was known as Chinese gooseberry (though not related to gooseberries). Then New Zealand started to produce the fruit in commercial quantities and gave it the name by which it is most widely known around the world today.

It is a berry, brown and furry on the outside,

bright green inside and with a pattern of small black or brown seeds radiating from a round or oval white core.

Purchasing and storing: Often kiwi fruit are sold under-ripe and extremely hard. They will ripen eventually, and to hasten the day should be stored in a bag with an apple or banana. For immediate use feel the fruit gently. Those that are slightly yielding to the touch are the ones to choose.

Preparation: Its furry skin is best peeled with a sharp knife before the fruit is cut into slices. Though some say it needs only to have the hairs rubbed off, the skin itself is thin but very tough — like plastic. Delicious in fruit salads, but do not attempt to add it to fruits which are to be set in jelly. Like pineapple, kiwi fruit contains an enzyme which digests protein and the jelly will not set.

The best way to enjoy them is to cut fully ripe fruit in halves crossways and scoop out the delicately perfumed, acid-sweet flesh with a teaspoon. High in vitamin C.

Kohlrabi

(*Brassica oleracea*, var. *gongylodes*) This is a showy vegetable if ever there was one: purple or green, and sometimes both. It is round with a tapering root end, sprouting leaves on stems from its surface. The flavour is somewhat like a turnip, makes a good flavour accent in vegetable soups and lends itself to being simmered in a light coconut milk sauce with spices. May also be used in Chinese stir-fries or braised dishes.

China: *chou ching gom larn*
Japan: *loorabi*
Philippines: *kohlrabi*
Sri Lanka: *knol kohl*
Thailand: *kalam pom*

Kombu

See SEAWEED.

Konnyaku

See DEVIL'S TONGUE.

Korea

A country with high mountains, coniferous forests, deep valleys, river flats, and a climate embracing the harshest extremes of monsoonal rains, hot summers and freezing winters. The main crops are barley, maize, millet, rice, soy bean, sweet potato and wheat as well as fruit and ginseng.

Home to the Yi dynasty, one of the longest in history — with a succession of twenty-six kings — and a number of religious philosophies including Confucianism, Buddhism and Catholicism, Korea's cuisine has evolved accordingly. A humble yet hearty peasant fare contrasts with the more refined cuisine of nobility with its extended vocabulary of spices. There are a number of ingredients common to Japanese and Chinese cuisine that are also crucial to Korean cooking. Notably the use of soy sauce (Japanese style), toasted sesame oil, seaweed, fish (fresh and dried) and the staple grain, rice. One main difference is the liberal use of red chilli, fresh, dried and powdered, and the traditional Korean chilli paste gochujang.

In spite of the similarity in many basic ingredients, Korean food is distinct from the food of either Japan or China. For example, sesame seeds are almost always toasted before being used, to emphasise their nutty flavour. The basic flavours of Korea include garlic, ginger, black pepper, spring onions (scallions), soy sauce, sesame oil, bean paste, toasted sesame seeds and red chilli, plus the judicious use of sugar and rice vinegar.

Famed for its pickles, none more so than kim chi, boldly flavoured with chilli and garlic and served at every meal. As well as cold pickles, there are a number of cooked relishes, each using a seasonal ingredient lightly cooked in oil flavoured with garlic, onion, spring onion (scallion) or ginger and sprinkled with sesame seeds.

In addition to these, there are a few unique ingredients. Nowhere else have I encountered noodles made from sweet potato known in Korea as dang myun.

There are, courtesy of Japan, other popular varieties of noodle including udon and the famous buckwheat (soba) noodles, naeng myun in Korean.

In contrast with most Asian cuisines, there is great emphasis upon meat, beef in particular, although pork and chicken also play an important role. Lean cuts of pork and beef sliced paper thin may be seen in the freezer of your Korean supplier along with small frozen chickens and assorted seafood. Processed fish in the form of fish cakes is extruded into a variety of shapes from logs to 'lobster tails' to wormlike strands of varying thickness.

A variety of sweet and savoury rice cakes are also available, both fresh and frozen.

Except for those special dishes which require charcoal grilling, Koreans cook mainly by steaming, stir-frying, deep or shallow frying and boiling. Baking is not traditional.

Meat for the famous Korean barbecue Bulgogi (see recipe page 32) is sliced paper thin and marinated in soy, sugar, toasted sesame seeds, ginger and spring onions (scallions), before being cooked on a heated brass dome variously called a Mongolian or Korean barbecue. The finishing touch is a dipping sauce made from soy sauce, sesame oil, bean paste, rice wine, toasted sesame seeds, chilli sauce, spring onion, garlic and sugar.

Steamed rice is always on the table accompanied by some kind of seasoned dipping sauce, as well as a number of tasty raw and cooked relishes. As in all Asian cuisines, there is an acute awareness of balancing the key flavour components of salt, sweet, hot, sour and bitter. Salt is provided by soy sauce, salt or salty bean paste; sweet by honey or sugar; hot by pepper, fresh, dried or powdered chilli, chilli sauce or mustard; sour by vinegar; and bitter by ginger. Korean bean paste, dhwen jang, is considered more flavoursome than the Japanese red bean paste equivalent and the Korean chilli paste, gochujang, is quite unique.

Beverages include the local rice wine, yakju, Korean beer, spiced persimmon punch and various pale-hued teas brewed from roasted grains including corn and barley. Green tea is also popular.

Korma

Also spelled kurmah or quorma, this indicates a braised dish, usually of mutton, long cooked in order to tenderise what is generally very tough meat. While rich and fragrant with spices, a korma is not hot and would be quite authentic without even a touch of chilli. Originally a Moghul-influenced dish, it has become popular throughout India, especially on festive occasions when it is combined with rice pilau, layered in a large pot, the lid sealed with flour and water paste, and the whole thing gently steamed to create a biriani.

For a party dish to serve 12, cook Lamb with Spices and Yoghurt (Korma), page 202 and a double quantity of Saffron Rice Pilau, page 320 Arrange in layers. Moisten top layer of rice with about 8 tablespoons of pouring cream, cover tightly and steam over gentle heat or cover and bake in a low oven for 45 minutes. Garnish with blanched pistachios or toasted almonds, sultanas (golden raisins) fried in ghee, and thinly sliced onions slowly fried until brown. For really special occasions, gild the lily — literally. Decorate with touches of pure gold or silver (see GOLD LEAF and SILVER LEAF). Explain to your guests that you have not absent-mindedly left traces of foil on the food, the precious metal is meant to be eaten. This elaborate dish bears the title of Shahjahani Biriani, in honour of Shah Jahan, the Moghul emperor who caused to be built the most famous love tribute in history, the magnificent Taj Mahal.

Krachai

(*Boesenbergia pandurata*, *B. rotunda*, *Kaempferia pandurata*) SEE ILLUSTRATION. Also spelled kachai. This rhizome is widely cultivated, especially in Thailand, as it gives a subtle, spicy flavour to many popular dishes and is particularly good with seafood. The underground portion of the plant consists of a tuberous rhizome from which protrude fleshy rootlets bearing small oblong or rounded tubers. It looks like a bunch of baby carrots, but is dull beige in colour. The growth habit suggests the large bunch of keys which some Chinese carry on their belts, thus its English name, 'Chinese keys', though it is probably referred to more often by its Thai name, krachai.

It is often mistakenly called lesser galangal, but is different in flavour, appearance and application, its only connection being that both belong to the Zingiberaceae family.

Purchasing and storing: Buy smooth, firm, unwrinkled rhizomes and store them in a paper bag in the refrigerator where they will keep for a few weeks. Use them before they wither. If not available fresh, it is best to buy it in jars, preserved in brine, either whole or cut into strips labelled krachai, kachai or galangal. After opening the jar store it in the refrigerator and it will keep well. Also available dried in fine strips, but better fresh or bottled.

Medicinal uses: The tubers are widely used as a local application for tumours, swellings and wounds. They are given for gastric complaints such as the treatment of diarrhoea and worms and are said to reduce flatulence. They are also used to remove blood clots.

India: *bhuichampa, bhuchampakamu, kondakalava*
Malaysia: *temoo kuntji*
Thailand: *krachai, kachai, chee-puu, poh-see*

Green Curry of Fish with Krachai

Serves 4

500 g/1 lb fillets of firm white fish
2 tablespoons oil
**2 tablespoons Thai green curry paste
   (recipe page 115)**
2 tablespoons fish sauce
4 kaffir lime leaves
**3 tablespoons thin strips of krachai,
   fresh or brined**
250 ml/8 fl oz/1 cup coconut milk
2 sprigs fresh coriander

Cut fish into serving portions — thick fillets are ideal.

Heat oil and on low heat fry the curry paste for 3 minutes, stirring. Add fish sauce, lime leaves, krachai and coconut milk and stir while it comes to the boil. Slip fish pieces into the sauce and cook uncovered for 10 minutes or until fish is done. Garnish with coriander and serve with steamed rice.

Steamed Fish Curry

Serves 4

500 g fillets of delicate white fish
375 ml/12 fl oz/1½ cups thick coconut milk
**2 tablespoons Thai red curry paste
   (recipe page 114)**
2 eggs
1 teaspoon salt
**1 tablespoon thin strips of krachai,
   fresh or brined**
20 basil leaves
1 tablespoon rice flour
2 fresh kaffir lime leaves, finely shredded
2 red chillies, seeded and finely sliced

Rinse the fish fillets and wipe with paper towels, making sure no trace of skin, bones or scales remain. Cut fish into thin slices, put into a bowl and mix in half the coconut milk, the red curry paste, beaten eggs, salt and krachai. Knead to mix evenly. Scatter basil leaves over the base of a heatproof dish. Spread fish mixture in it. Combine remaining coconut milk with rice flour and pour over the fish. Scatter shredded lime leaves and chilli slices on top. Steam over boiling water for 15–20 minutes, depending on the depth of the dish.
Serve with rice.

Jungle Curry of Pork

Serves 6

750 g/1½ lb pork
2 tablespoons oil
**4 tablespoons Thai green curry paste
   (recipe page 115)**
**2 tablespoons green peppercorns,
   fresh or brined**
10 small whole bird's eye chillies
**2 tablespoons fine strips of krachai,
   fresh or brined**
375 ml/12 fl oz/1½ cups coconut milk
2 tablespoons fish sauce
1 tablespoon palm sugar or brown sugar
6 kaffir lime leaves
fresh basil leaves

Cut the pork into large dice. Heat the oil and on low heat fry the curry paste, stirring, until it is fragrant and the oil shines on the surface. Add pork and stir until coated with the paste. Add green peppercorns, chillies, krachai, coconut milk, fish sauce, palm sugar and lime leaves. Bring to simmering point and cook on low heat until pork is tender, adding a little water if necessary from time to time. Scatter the basil leaves over and serve with steamed rice.

Krupuk

A large, elongated prawn (shrimp) cracker popular in Indonesia and Malaysia. Bought in dried form, they are made from tapioca flour, prawns, salt and sugar. When deep fried they swell and become crisp. If unavailable, Chinese prawn crackers may be substituted although the flavour and texture are not as robust or substantial as krupuk. See also PRAWN CRACKERS.

Kulfi

See ICE CREAM.

Kumiss

Mongolian name for the fermented beverage made from mare's milk by Asian nomads.

Kumquat

(*Fortunella* spp.) Though they are related and were considered citrus until 1915, these little fruits are not in fact citrus and have a genus of their own. Instead of the 8–15 sections found in citrus fruits, kumquats have only 3–6 sections. Another difference is that the skin is thin and sweet and edible, while the flesh is sour — the opposite is the case for citrus.

When purchasing make sure they are ripe but firm. Wash well as with any fruit which may have been sprayed. Dry them, and if not using the fruit whole, remove seeds after slicing or halving. May be purchased in jars, preserved in syrup.

While Western cooks add sugar to make marmalade and brandied kumquats, it is more likely that oriental cooks will use the flavour to brighten savoury dishes.

Chicken with Kumquats

Serves 6

1 × 1.5 kg/3 lb roasting chicken
1 teaspoon salt
1 teaspoon five-spice powder
½ teaspoon white pepper
4 tablespoons peanut oil
5 spring onions (scallions),
  cut into bite-sized lengths
3 tablespoons Chinese rose wine
3 tablespoons light soy sauce
2 teaspoons ginger juice
  (squeezed from finely grated fresh ginger)
12 kumquats in syrup
2 teaspoons cornflour (cornstarch)

Cut chicken into joints, then chop through the bones to halve the joints, Chinese style (see page 77). Wipe with damp paper towel to remove any splinters of bone. Sprinkle chicken with salt, five-spice powder and pepper mixed together. Leave for 20 minutes.

Heat oil in a wok and fry chicken in batches until pale golden, removing each batch to a bowl with a slotted spoon. Pour off all but a tablespoon of the oil and fry the spring onions for a few seconds. Return chicken to the wok, pour over the combined liquid ingredients and the kumquats. Cover and simmer until chicken is tender, adding a little stock or water if necessary. Thicken sauce with the cornflour mixed smoothly with a tablespoon of cold water and stirred into the simmering liquid until it boils and becomes clear. Spoon over chicken and serve with rice.

Kyringa

A central Asian sour milk drink, slightly gaseous and alcoholic, made from cow's milk.

Lablab Bean

See LEGUMES & PULSES.

Ladies' Fingers

A small, curved, very sweet variety of banana (see BANANA). Also the common name for okra, a pod vegetable used in Indian and South East Asian as well as African and Creole cooking.
See also OKRA.

Laksa

There is more than one version of spicy soup which comes under this heading, but the best known is one made with prawns (shrimp) and featuring rice noodles and a broth enriched with coconut milk. This is known as Singapore laksa or laksa lemak. Then there is Penang laksa, a thin, fragrant, sour fish soup without coconut milk, flavoured with tamarind and shreds of the pink bud of torch ginger. Johore laksa is different in that the fish is puréed, the soup rich with coconut milk. Each has its adherents.

The noodles used in this soupy concoction are traditionally fresh laksa noodles — a soft, white noodle, round as opposed to flat. Rice vermicelli, briefly cooked, is an acceptable substitute.

Prawn (Shrimp) Laksa Lemak

Every time I visit Singapore, my first stop for refuelling is for a bowl of laksa, rich with coconut milk, hot with sambal, pungent with shredded laksa leaf. Now we have the leaf growing in our garden, a jar of prepared spices in the refrigerator and it is a quick, home-cooked meal. I use less coconut milk than would be used in a restaurant version.
Serves 6.

750 g/1½ lb raw prawns (shrimp)
1 tablespoon peanut oil
salt to taste
750 g/1½ lb fresh laksa noodles
    or 375 g/12 oz rice vermicelli
250 g/8 oz fresh bean sprouts
2 small, seedless green cucumbers
small bunch fresh laksa leaves

SPICES AND SOUP

6 large, dried red chillies
4 tablespoons dried shrimp
2 teaspoons dried shrimp paste
2 medium onions, roughly chopped
1 tablespoon chopped galangal in brine
2 stems lemon grass, finely sliced
4 tablespoons peanut oil
1 teaspoon ground turmeric
1 tablespoon ground coriander
400 ml/14 fl oz can coconut milk
sambal ulek and fresh limes

Wash prawns and shell them, reserving heads and shells for stock. Devein the prawns.

Heat 1 tablespoon oil in a large saucepan, add prawn shells and heads. Fry, stirring, until they turn red. Add 2 litres (4 pints/8 cups) water and simmer, covered, for 30 minutes. Strain stock and season to taste with salt. Discard shells and heads.

Pour hot water through fresh noodles or soak rice vermicelli in very hot water for 10 minutes, then drain. Pinch straggly tails off bean sprouts, wash and drain. Wash cucumbers but do not peel. Cut into matchstick strips. Shred laksa leaves finely.

Spices and soup: Remove stems from dry chillies and shake out seeds. Soak chillies in hot water for 10 minutes. In a blender process dried shrimp to a floss. Add chillies and a little soaking water, the shrimp paste, onions, galangal, lemon grass and blend to a purée.

Heat 3 tablespoons of the oil in a heavy pan and fry purée, stirring constantly, until fragrant and browned. Add turmeric and coriander and stir for 1 minute longer. Add strained stock and simmer for 10 minutes. Stir in coconut milk mixed with an equal amount of water. Add salt to taste.

Just before serving, heat remaining tablespoon of oil in a wok and stir-fry prawns over high heat until they become pink and opaque. Sprinkle with salt to taste.

Put a large handful of noodles into each bowl and top with bean sprouts, cucumber strips and a few prawns. Ladle hot soup over, and garnish with shreds of laksa leaf. Offer sambal ulek and wedges of lime.

Penang Laksa

Serves 6

1 kg/2 lb firm whole white fish, including head
2 rounded tablespoons dried tamarind
6–8 large dried red chillies
2 stems lemon grass
2.5 cm/1 in slice fresh turmeric
   or 1 teaspoon ground turmeric
1 tablespoon chopped galangal in brine
2 onions, peeled and roughly chopped
1 teaspoon dried shrimp paste
2 tablespoons oil
2 teaspoons palm or brown sugar (optional)
1 teaspoon salt or to taste
750 g/1½ lb fresh rice noodles
   or 250 g/8 oz dried rice vermicelli
1 onion, sliced thinly
6 slices half-ripe pineapple
1 seedless cucumber cut in strips
good handful fresh laksa leaves
2 torch ginger flower buds

Clean and scale fish and simmer in 1 litre (2 pints) lightly salted water for 15 minutes or until fish is cooked. Strain, reserving stock.

Discard head and remove flesh from bones, discarding skin. Keep half of the fish in large pieces and flake the other half.

Soak tamarind in 3 cups hot water, kneading it in the water to dissolve as much of the pulp as possible. Strain, discarding seeds and fibres. Break off stems of chillies and discard. Shake out and discard seeds and soak chillies in 1 cup hot water.

Slice lemon grass finely. If using fresh turmeric, scrape off skin and chop roughly. In a blender combine lemon grass, turmeric, galangal, onions, soaked chillies and shrimp paste. Add some of the water in which chillies soaked to facilitate blending to a purée.

Heat oil in a saucepan and fry purée over low heat, stirring, until cooked and fragrant, about 5 minutes. Add tamarind liquid, bring to simmering point and let it cook for 5 minutes. Stir in sugar, salt and fish stock and simmer for 10 minutes. Stir in flaked fish and fish pieces.

Pour boiling water over fresh rice noodles in a colander, or cook dried rice vermicelli in boiling water for 3 minutes or until tender. Drain well. Divide noodles among individual bowls, top with sliced onion, pieces of pineapple and cucumber, pour on simmering soup and sprinkle with shredded laksa leaves and finely sliced ginger flowers.

Laksa Leaf

See VIETNAMESE MINT.

Lamb

Traditional fare for the Australian Sunday lunch as well as the meat New Zealand is famous for, its Canterbury lamb being a much sought-after export. The term 'lamb' is hardly ever used in Asia, except in Mongolian dishes from China. Everywhere else, even when the meat qualifies as lamb, it is called 'mutton'. There is no denying that some of the most superb dishes from India are based on the flesh of young sheep, yet will be called mutton. Not every country in Asia uses this meat as many palates find it too overwhelming a flavour. Even in China, where it has limited acceptance, it is first washed and soaked to remove its strong flavour and odour — that taste for which most Western people have developed such a liking.

Milk lamb (the meat of unweaned lambs, a seasonal delicacy) is the mildest flavoured sheep meat, soft and loose-textured. Most lamb is slaughtered between three months and a year, its flesh being tender enough for roasting and grilling. Mutton, technically speaking lamb older than one year, has more flavour and a firmer texture, though it is not necessarily tough. To be on the safe side, for grills, barbecues and recipes that require brief cooking time, or if you like to eat your lamb 'pink', be advised to buy lamb — the younger, the better. For curries, stews and other slow-cooked dishes, mutton can stand longer cooking and its greater depth of flavour complements heavy spicing.

In India, the stronger flavour of mutton is enjoyed and sheep are allowed to fatten for longer than in Western countries, where the quick turnaround makes better commercial sense to lamb growers. In addition, the extra pressure put on farmers in times of drought in recent years has seen the supply of older sheep dwindle, and no longer does every butcher shop offer the choice of hogget (yearling sheep) or 'two-tooth lamb' (two-year old lamb).

Recipes which rely on the tender, sweet flesh of lamb are in this section. For recipes using older sheep, or goat, see MUTTON.

Lamb Kebabs

Wonderful for barbecues and parties, but equally good for family meals. The marinated lamb, covered and refrigerated, continues to improve for up to 4 days. Serves 6–8.

1.5 kg/3 lb lean boneless lamb
1 teaspoon finely chopped garlic
2 teaspoons salt
1½ teaspoons finely grated fresh ginger
1 teaspoon freshly ground black pepper
1 teaspoon ground turmeric
1 teaspoon ground coriander
1 teaspoon ground cumin
1 teaspoon crushed dried curry leaves
1 tablespoon sesame oil
2 tablespoons peanut oil
1 tablespoon lemon juice
  or Worcestershire sauce

Cut lamb into 2.5 cm (1 in) cubes and put into a large bowl. Crush garlic with salt to a smooth purée and combine with remaining ingredients, mixing well. Pour over lamb and stir, making sure each piece of meat is covered with the spice mixture. Cover bowl and refrigerate for at least 3 hours, or up to 4 days.

Thread 4–5 pieces of meat on each skewer and cook under a hot grill, allowing about 5 minutes on each side. When nicely brown, serve hot with boiled rice or parathas, accompanied by onion sambal and mint chatni.

Note: This marinade is also effective as a boned, butterflied leg as well as racks of lamb.

Lamb with Spices and Yoghurt (Korma)

Serves 6

1 kg/2 lb boneless lamb
2 large onions
1 tablespoon chopped fresh ginger
2 teaspoons finely chopped garlic
2 tablespoons blanched almonds
3 or 4 large dried chillies, seeded
2 teaspoons ground coriander
1 teaspoon ground cumin
½ teaspoon ground cinnamon
½ teaspoon ground cardamom
¼ teaspoon ground cloves
½ teaspoon saffron strands
1 tablespoon ghee
2 tablespoons oil
2 teaspoons salt
125 ml/4 fl oz/½ cup natural yoghurt
2 tablespoons chopped fresh coriander leaves

Cut lamb into large cubes. Peel onions, slice one finely and set aside. Chop other onion roughly and put into the container of an electric blender with ginger, garlic, almonds and chillies. Add ½ cup water to blender, cover and blend on high speed for a minute or until all ingredients are ground smoothly. Add ground spices and blend for a few seconds longer.

Toast saffron strands over low heat for 1 minute, then turn onto a saucer to cool. Crush to powder with the back of a spoon, and dissolve in a tablespoon of boiling water.

Heat ghee and oil in a large saucepan and fry the sliced onion, stirring frequently, until soft and golden. Add the blended mixture and continue to fry, stirring constantly until the spices are well cooked and the oil starts to separate from the mixture. Wash out blender container with an extra ¼ cup water, add to pan together with salt and continue to stir and fry until liquid dries up once more. Add the meat and stir over medium heat until each piece is coated with spices. Add dissolved saffron to the yoghurt and stir into lamb. Reduce heat to low, cover and cook at a gentle simmer until meat is tender and gravy thick. Stir occasionally, taking care that the spice mixture does not stick to base of pan. When lamb is cooked, sprinkle with fresh coriander leaves and serve hot with rice.

Mongolian Lamb

In order to reduce the strength of the lamb flavour, the meat is sliced thinly and soaked in cold water. The strong-flavoured sauce ensures acceptance even by those who do not like lamb. Serves 4.

500 g/1 lb lamb tenderloin
2 teaspoons sugar
1 teaspoon salt
2 tablespoons dark soy sauce
1 small egg, beaten
½ teaspoon bicarbonate of soda (baking soda)
2 teaspoons cornflour (cornstarch)
5 tablespoons peanut oil
1 large onion cut into wedges lengthways
1 spring onion (scallion), finely sliced
1 teaspoon finely chopped garlic

SAUCE
½ teaspoon five-spice powder
1 tablespoon hoi sin sauce
1 tablespoon ground bean sauce (mor sze jeung)
1 teaspoon chilli bean sauce
1 tablespoon Chinese wine or dry sherry

Freeze lamb just long enough to make it firm, then slice paper thin. Soak in cold water for 30 minutes. Rinse under a cold tap until water runs clear, then drain well and squeeze out excess water.

Combine sugar, salt, soy sauce, egg, bicarbonate of soda and cornflour. Add the meat and mix well. Add 1 tablespoon of the peanut oil and mix again. Leave to marinate for 2 hours.

Heat a wok, add 1 tablespoon of the peanut oil and, on medium-high heat, stir-fry the onion wedges and spring onion for 1 minute. Remove from the wok.

Add the remaining 3 tablespoons of peanut oil to the wok, heat the oil and swirl to coat cooking surface. Fry garlic for 5 seconds. Then add the lamb and stir-fry on high heat, tossing the meat constantly until it is brown. Add sauce ingredients except the wine, and toss again. Return the onion and spring onion to the wok. Add the wine, pouring it around the side of the wok so it sizzles. Mix, and serve at once with rice.

Note: Mongolian lamb is usually cooked on a flat griddle but can be done in a wok.

Lamb with Apricots

A recipe I learned from the talented cooks of the Parsi community in Bombay. Serves 6–8.

250 g/8 oz whole dried apricots with seeds
  or 185 g/6 oz dried apricot halves
1 kg/2 lb lean lamb
10 large dried red chillies
1 tablespoon finely chopped fresh ginger
1 tablespoon chopped garlic
1 tablespoon ground cumin
3 tablespoons ghee or oil
1 medium onion, finely chopped
1 teaspoon ground cinnamon
½ teaspoon ground cloves
½ teaspoon ground black pepper
½ teaspoon ground cardamom
500 g/1 lb ripe tomatoes
2 teaspoons salt or to taste
1 tablespoon jaggery or brown sugar
2 tablespoons malt vinegar
3 tablespoons chopped fresh coriander
125 g/4 oz potato straws

If apricots are very dry, pour hot water over and soak for 1 hour. Cut lamb into cubes, trimming away excess fat. Break off stems of chillies and shake out seeds, then soak the chillies in hot water to cover for 10 minutes. In an electric blender grind chillies with ginger, garlic and cumin, using a little of the soaking water to facilitate blending to a purée. Pour half the purée over the cubed lamb, mix well and leave to marinate for 1 hour.

In a heavy pot heat the ghee or oil (or mixture of both) and fry onion on low heat until soft and golden brown. This takes some time. Be patient and stir occasionally so onion caramelises and develops good flavour.

Add remaining half of the spice purée and the dry ground spices and fry on low heat, stirring, until fragrant. Add marinated lamb and fry until browned, then add tomatoes and salt, and if you are able to get the whole dried apricots which need long cooking, add them now. Cover and cook on low heat for about 1 hour, until meat is almost tender, adding a little water if necessary. Add the jaggery, vinegar and soft dried apricot halves if used and simmer on very low heat for 15 minutes. Garnish with chopped coriander and sprinkle potato straws over just before serving with a lightly spiced pilau.

Lampries

A corruption of the Dutch word, lomprijst. It is a combination of ghee rice, curries, sambals and frikkadels (a mini rijstaffel, one might say). Neatly wrapped in banana leaf and baked, it is the ultimate in festive Sri Lankan meals. The parcels are brought to the table on a platter, and each guest takes one and unwraps it, savouring the aroma of spices combined with the gentle fragrance of fresh banana leaf.

Banana leaves are stripped from the centre rib, cut into pieces about 30–38 cm (12–15 in), washed, dried and made pliable by holding over a gas flame for a few seconds so they may be folded without splitting. If banana leaves are not available, make parcels from 38 cm (15 in) squares of heavy-duty cooking foil — not as authentic, but very convenient.

This is not a quick and easy meal to prepare, but once the parcels are made they may be refrigerated for a day or two, or frozen for a month or two. The do-ahead possibilities are great, best tackled by a team of at least two people or the whole thing becomes an ordeal.

Make the relishes, sambals and frikkadels the first day and refrigerate; cook the curry the second day and refrigerate; on the third day cook the rice and make the parcels. This way, it is possible to prepare a fantastic meal without wearing yourself out doing it.

Lampries

Makes 20 lampries

3 quantities ghee rice (recipe page 309)
1 quantity lampries curry (recipe below)
3 quantities mild green plantain curry
  (recipe page 284)
1 quantity Sri Lankan dried shrimp sambal
  (recipe page 343)
1 quantity Sri Lankan eggplant (aubergine)
  pickle
1 quantity frikkadels (recipe below)
1 quantity Sri Lankan fried chilli sambal
  (recipe page 92)

To assemble: On each square of leaf or foil put 1 cup firmly packed ghee rice. Arrange around the rice 1 tablespoon of Lampries curry, 1 tablespoon green plantain curry, 1 teaspoon dried shrimp sambal, 2 teaspoons eggplant pickle, 2 frikkadels and 2 teaspoons fried chilli sambal. Pour over a tablespoon of coconut milk, bring edges of leaf or foil together and fold over, turning ends in so parcel is secure. If using leaf wrapping, fasten with wooden toothpicks. If the leaves available are too small to make a decent parcel, simply line the foil with a piece of banana leaf, or double wrap so the leaf is enclosed with foil — a good precaution in case the leaf splits while heating or serving. Heat lampries in a moderate oven for 25 minutes before serving.

Serve Cucumber Sambal (page 111) as an accompaniment.

Frikkadels

500 g/1 lb finely minced (ground) beef
3 slices white bread, crumbed
30 g/1 oz butter
1 tablespoon oil
1 large onion, very finely chopped
1 teaspoon chopped garlic
1½ teaspoons salt
1 teaspoon finely grated fresh ginger
½ teaspoon ground black pepper
¼ teaspoon ground cinnamon
¼ teaspoon ground cloves
3 teaspoons chopped fresh dill
2 teaspoons Worcestershire sauce
1 egg, beaten
dry breadcrumbs for coating
oil or ghee for deep frying

Put beef and breadcrumbs in a large bowl. Heat butter and oil in a small pan and on low heat fry onion until soft and starting to turn golden. Add to bowl. Crush garlic with salt to a smooth paste. In a small bowl combine garlic, ginger, ground spices, dill and Worcestershire sauce. Pour over the beef, breadcrumbs and onion and mix well with the hand to distribute all the seasonings evenly. Shape into small balls about 2.5 cm (1 in) in diameter. Dip in beaten egg and coat with dry breadcrumbs. Deep fry in hot oil until golden brown. Drain on paper towels.

Lampries Curry

This unusual curry combines four different meats. This quantity makes sufficient for 20 lampries.

500 g/1 lb lean stewing beef
500 g/1 lb boneless mutton or lamb
5 teaspoons salt
10 cardamom pods, bruised
1 teaspoon whole black peppercorns
500 g/1 lb chicken thighs and drumsticks
500 g/1 lb pork belly (not too lean, not too fatty)
1 tablespoon ghee
2 tablespoons oil
4 large onions, finely chopped
1 tablespoon finely chopped garlic
1 tablespoon finely chopped fresh ginger
3 sprigs fresh curry leaves
¼ teaspoon fenugreek seeds
4 tablespoons Ceylon curry powder
   (recipe page 356)
1 teaspoon ground turmeric
2 teaspoons chilli powder
1 cinnamon stick
1 teaspoon ground cardamom
6 strips pandan leaf, fresh or dried
2 stems lemon grass
   or 4 strips lemon rind
2 tablespoons lemon juice
2 × 400 ml/14 fl oz cans coconut milk

Put beef and mutton in a large saucepan with cold water to cover. Add 2 teaspoons of the salt, cardamom pods and black peppercorns. Bring to the boil, cover pan and simmer slowly for half an hour. Add chicken and simmer a further 15 minutes. Remove from heat, cool slightly, then strain and reserve stock for boiling the rice. When cool enough to handle, cut the parboiled meats into very small dice. Cut pork also into small dice.

In a large, heavy-based saucepan heat ghee and oil and gently fry onion, garlic, ginger and curry leaves until onion is soft and golden. Add fenugreek seeds and fry for 1 minute, then add curry powder, turmeric, chilli powder, cinnamon stick, cardamom, pandan leaf and lemon grass or rind. Add remaining 3 teaspoons salt, lemon juice and diced pork.

Dilute one can of coconut milk with an equal amount of water and add to pan, stirring. Cover and cook on low heat for 30 minutes, stirring now and then, until pork is half tender. Add parboiled meats and half the second can of coconut milk, and simmer uncovered for about an hour or until meat is tender and gravy very thick. (Reserve remaining coconut milk for spooning over the parcels of rice and curry.)

Laos

This land-locked country shares borders with Vietnam, Cambodia, Thailand, Burma and China. It depends on its rice fields and the Mekong River for the basic foods of rice and fish. What is different about Laos is that while other Asian countries eat glutinous (sticky) rice as sweet snacks, in Laos it is the most important item at breakfast, lunch and dinner.

The Laotian kitchen could not operate without three indispensable items — mortar and pestle, wok (khatak), and rice steamer which consists of a flexible, cone-shaped bamboo basket (hua nung khao) which sits on top of a metal pan (maw nung khao). The pan is wide at the base so it holds plenty of water, and narrow at the neck to keep the basket well above the level of the water.

Glutinous long grain rice is soaked overnight, then drained and steamed until soft. No light, fluffy, separate grains here; instead, shiny, sticky grains which retain their shape and are chewy and firm. Sometimes sticky rice is steamed in individual serving baskets.

Laotian people prefer new crop rice since it is more sticky than old crop (in contrast to some countries where old rice is valued for its quality of producing separate, fluffy grains).

At breakfast, sticky rice is usually served with sun-dried beef flavoured with salt and sugar; small pieces of fried pork, chicken or fish; a chilli and fish paste called jao mak len, similar to nam prik; or padek, strong-smelling salted fish fermented in a jar which is a staple of every Laotian household. Other choices to eat with rice are mangoes, in season; grated coconut; ripe tamarind; and perhaps a fried egg. A common beverage is lemon grass tea, a light, refreshing beverage made by infusing a bruised or sliced stem of lemon grass in boiling water.

Main meals usually include soup and vegetables, steamed or fried fish, meat or chicken, and a chilli-based condiment. Fresh vegetables are the mainstay of meals, most houses having a patch of garden and neighbours being willing to share what grows on their patch of ground.

Spiced dishes are not doused in coconut milk. This rich ingredient is reserved for sweet dishes in Laos. Just as a Western table is set with a cruet containing salt, pepper and mustard, the tables in this part of the world offer fried garlic and the oil in which it was fried; crushed dried chilli toasted and

Laos

blended with other flavours; and nam padek (fish sauce).

For many years I have known Leng, a Laotian woman who is a superb cook. She runs a small restaurant in Sydney offering Asian foods, not only from Laos. She makes as good a Singapore laksa as I have tasted in Singapore, and a Thai som tam which loses nothing in the translation. When asked which of the dishes on her menu was a truly representative Laotian dish, she directed me to a beef salad called larp, and explained how she prepared it. For her, no short cuts such as buying roasted ground rice which does not provide the full flavour which freshly roasted and ground rice offers. Festive occasions, Sundays and celebrations call for larp, which may feature beef or venison, served raw or lightly cooked. Since 'larp' also means 'luck', the dish is traditionally served at weddings and other auspicious occasions.

What makes this dish a favourite are the fresh flavours added to the meat: fine shreds of fresh rhizomes of galangal; finely sliced shallots; three kinds of mint; glutinous rice which is roasted to a golden brown, then pounded finely in mortar and pestle; dried red chillies, fried and ground; and fish sauce and lime juice to 'sharpen the taste'. Without any one of these strongly individual flavours, it would not qualify as a proper larp. Larp (or larb) is also a favourite dish in northern Thailand.

The indispensable flavours of Laotian food are: garlic (phak thiem), chilli (makpet), shallots (hua phak boua), galangal (kha), lemon grass (hwa see kai, bai mak nao), kaffir lime leaves (bai khi hout), tamarind (mak kham), fresh coriander herb (phak hom pom), eryngo (phak hom thet), the varieties of basil used in Thailand; mint (phak hom ho); and fresh dill (phak si).

Laos

See GALANGAL, GREATER.

Lassi

See DRINKS & BEVERAGES.

Leek

(*Allium ramosum, A. porrum, A. ampeloprasum*) Asian leeks are smaller and more slender than the European variety (*A. ampeloprasum*). While it is mainly the white portion which is cooked and eaten, in some countries very good use is made of the long, dark green leaves. Because of their tendency to toughness they are sliced very finely crossways then fried with spices and dried shrimp or Maldive fish, covered and simmered until soft. Like any leek, they need much washing to rid them of sand.

China: *jiu tsung, dai suan, tai chung*
Japan: *poro negi*
Malaysia: *kucai*
Indonesia: *kucai*
Philippines: *kutsay*
Thailand: *krathiam tom*

Leek, Chinese

See CHIVES, CHINESE.

Legumes & Pulses

To this very large botanical group, Leguminosae, belong peas, beans, lentils, peanuts, clovers, vetches, alfalfa, lucerne, tamarind, acacia, mimosa and wattle. In fact there are 12,000 known species of plant that bear seeds in a pod. 'Pulse' is a general term applied to all dried, edible legume seeds.

Legumes are an important crop, not only for human nourishment but also for the nourishment they give the soil as the bacteria in root nodules converts gaseous nitrogen from the air into soil-enriching nitrogen compounds.

A major source of protein for people as well as livestock, legumes provide two widely used oils: soya and peanut. The leaves and sprouts of some varieties of legume are eaten as a vegetable (e.g. broad bean, fenugreek, mung bean, snow pea, soy bean).

Legumes have received a lot of bad press for causing intestinal gas. This is the normal reaction resulting from the metabolism of oligosaccharides (comprising sugar molecules linked together in such a way that normal digestive enzymes cannot process them) by bacteria in the lower intestine, the by-product being a number of gases including carbon dioxide. Research has found the worst offenders on this count to be lima and navy beans. Because oligosaccharides only form in the later stages of seed development, legumes do not seem to cause this problem when eaten fresh or immature (as opposed to dried). Sprouting the seeds reduces the amount of oligosaccharides contained in legumes.

Due to the presence of complex protein structures (trypsin inhibitors and lectins), which interfere with digestion and the body's absorption of nutrients, all legumes should be well cooked. In the case of lima beans (and kidney beans to a lesser extent), depending on where they are grown, there may be a slight health risk due to naturally occurring cyanogens (sugar–cyanide complexes) which in water become metabolised by a special enzyme, forming the gas hydrogen cyanide, a very powerful respiratory inhibitor.

In Western strains of lima bean, the levels of cyanogens are very much lower than in Asia and a negligible risk. Lima beans from Burma and Java, however, contain up to 30 times the level of cyanogens permitted in the West. The best way to destroy cyanogens is to boil the beans in an uncovered pot to allow the toxic gas to escape. Even sprouts (usually served raw in salads and sandwiches) will benefit, nutritionally, from cooking. This does not apply to bean curd which has undergone heat treatment in production.

Purchasing and Storing: Buy dried legumes from shops where the turnover is brisk. They have excellent shelf life, but the older they are the longer they will take to cook, and the more risk there is of weevil infestation. Buy those which look smooth and unwrinkled. This cannot apply to some varieties such as chick peas (garbanzos) which have a wrinkled look right from the start. Store in airtight containers.

Preparation: To cook dried legumes, soak first for at least 4 hours in cold water or, if more convenient, soak overnight. This will help to shorten the cooking time. If you have forgotten to soak in advance, a quick soak can be achieved by washing legumes, covering with triple their volume of water and boiling for 5 minutes. Turn off heat, tightly cover, and leave for 2 hours. Drain and rinse. Cook as for beans soaked overnight. The addition of an alkaliser, such as bicarbonate of soda (baking soda), will also speed the process, but at the sacrifice of nutrients. A quarter teaspoon may be added to the cooking water without too much detriment.

Cooking soaked, dried legumes in a copious amount of water will not make them cook any faster and will contribute to loss of nutrients through leaching, so add enough water to keep them just submerged while boiling. Most of the plumping should have occurred during soaking.

Once legumes are in an acid medium, they will not get any softer, no matter how long they are cooked. So make sure they are as tender as required before adding lemon juice, vinegar, tomato or any other acidulator. This is useful to remember if you need to reheat a legume dish but do not wish the legumes to turn to mush.

Adzuki bean: (*Vigna angularis*) Also called aduki, azuki or red beans. These are a popular bean in China and Japan for festive occasions because of their colour which represents good fortune. They are to Japanese cooking what mung beans are to South East Asian cooking: a staple in the preparation of sweets.

Believed to have originated in China, India or Japan and now grown in many countries including North and South America, India and New Zealand. It is an important food source, as it contains about 25 per cent protein.

Boiled, mashed and sweetened, they are the sweet bean paste known in Japan as an, used as the filling in various rice cakes and are an ingredient in many Japanese desserts (see BEAN PASTE, SWEET). They are also cooked, steeped in sugar syrup and served in a number of shaved ice sweets such as halo-halo in the Philippines and ice kacang in Singapore and Malaysia.

In Japan, adzuki beans are also boiled with rice to make 'red rice', used in soups, or ground into flour. One advantage is that they contain few of the oligosaccharides which cause intestinal gas.

Vietnamese restaurants serve drinks which combine boiled, sweetened adzuki beans, sweetened mashed mung beans, and resilient sheets of extra firm agar-agar jelly, all mixed with sweetened coconut milk and piled high with shaved ice.

Medicinal uses: A broth made from adzuki beans has been used for centuries in Japan as a treatment for kidney complaints.

Asparagus bean: See **Winged bean.**

Asparagus pea: (*Tetragonolobus purpureus*, previously *Lotus tetragonolobus*) Supposed native of southern Europe, the edible pods of this plant are like a miniature version of the winged bean (*Psophocarpus tetragonolobus*), recognisable by the attractive frills adorning the four-angled pod. Let them grow no longer than 2.5 cm (1 in), or they will be stringy and unappetising. Exactly how they acquired the name 'asparagus pea' is a mystery, as they bear as little resemblance to that vegetable in flavour as they do in shape. The mature seeds are brown and smooth and roughly the size of mung beans. The pea flowers are a striking brick red and may be as much a reason for growing this annual as the modest peas. Cook as you would any other tender green beans. The term asparagus pea is sometimes used interchangeably with the many names accumulated by the yard-long bean (cowpea).

See **Yard-long bean** and **Winged bean**.

Black-eyed pea: A variety of cowpea (*Vigna unguiculata,* var. *sinensis*). Also known as black-eyed bean (see **Yard-long bean**, which is its fresh source). Although synonymous with the 'soul food' of America's deep south, they have been grown and eaten in Asia for centuries. Resembling small, cream-coloured kidney beans, they have a distinctive black spot or 'eye' around their hilum (attachment point). In India, they are known as lobia and are cooked whole as a dish, with other vegetables, or hulled and split as chowla dhal. Also ground into flour and used for savoury pancakes. In other parts of Asia they are also cooked with rice. Soaking in warm water for 1 hour reduces the effect of flatulence-producing oligosaccharides.

Black gram: (*Phaseolus mungo*) Black gram or urad, a pulse slightly smaller than a mung bean (green gram), is named for its black seed coat. While the mung bean is yellow beneath its green skin, the black gram without its husk is creamy white. It is sometimes referred to as white gram in its peeled state. An ingredient used in southern India's idli (steamed dumplings) and dosai (lacy pancakes) for its fermenting action, it is soaked before being ground into a paste, then left for a few hours to allow its natural fermenting action to lighten the mixture. Also a popular ingredient for vegetarian curries and pappadams.

Blue pea: (*Pisum sativum*) This is the name given to whole dried peas which started life as garden peas (green peas). They are also known as field peas or, with the skin removed and split in half, as green split peas. On being grown to maturity and dried whole they develop a dull, blue-green colour and some batches may look slightly wrinkled. They should be soaked overnight before cooking.

Broad bean: (*Vicia faba*) SEE ILLUSTRATION. Like a larger, stronger-tasting lima bean, they are some-times known as fava beans. In Shanghai, Beijing and the north of China (they don't grow in the southern regions) broad beans are used fresh and as sprouts. Fresh broad beans are popular cooked with minced ham. When preparing broad beans, after shelling them remove the thick skin around each seed for maximum enjoyment. 'Double peeling', someone has called it, and insists it is worth the trouble. I agree.

Dried beans are soaked and boiled before cooking in soy sauce and sugar. Deep fried and salted, they are a popular snack.

There are two possible dangers associated with eating broad beans. Favism, which is a rare inherited type of anaemia, mainly found in people of Mediterranean origin, can be triggered by eating broad beans or inhaling pollen from the flowers. Also, broad beans can be fatal if eaten in conjunction with monoamine inhibitors, present in some anti-depressant drugs.

China: *tsaam dou*
India: *bakla*
Japan: *sora mame*
Thailand: *thua yang*

Butter bean: See **Lima bean**.

Chick pea: (*Cicer arietinum, C. asiaticum, C. orientale*) Also called garbanzo bean. Roughly spherical peas with a peak at one end and a cleft at the other. The chick pea has the nuttiest flavour of all the dried legumes. India's most important legume, the variety of chick pea (deshi or kala gram) used for besan flour is smaller and darker than the *C. mediterraneum* and *C. eurasiaticum* varieties. The variety called kabuli gram, has larger, paler seeds.

Chick peas provide fibre, complex carbohydrates, protein, trace elements, vitamins, lecithin and linoleic acid. Another factor in their favour is that they do not have the high oligosaccharide content which has earned for pulses the reputation of being difficult to digest and causing flatulence.

Since they also taste good, it is not surprising they are the basis of so many traditional vegetarian dishes. Soak overnight if time permits. The alternative is to quick soak. Bring to the boil in water to cover, turn off heat and allow to soak for 2 hours. Change the water and proceed with recipe.

Cowpea: See **Yard-long bean**.

Fenugreek: SEE ILLUSTRATION. Officially a legume, but since it has such a strong identity as a

flavour ingredient, more people think of it as a spice than a legume. See main entry for FENUGREEK.

Green bean: (*Phaseolus vulgaris*) Also known as French bean, runner bean, climbing bean, snap bean, string bean, stringless bean and wax bean. There are also purple, scarlet or yellow podded varieties, but by and large, the most common bean is green. If the beans are young and tender, the colour does not make a difference to the way they taste.

Few vegetables are as versatile, or as popular in all parts of the world. They originated in central and South America, and are used in the cuisines of just about every country and adapt to the flavours of Asia as though they belong there.

Purchasing and storing: Choose slender beans in which the seeds are not prominent. This is a sure sign of over-maturity. Store for a day or two in a polythene bag in the crisper section of the refrigerator, but use before they develop soft spots.

Preparation: If beans need stringing, do so because strings can be tough. Stringless beans are a time saver. Top, tail and cut as required for the particular recipe, and cook as soon as possible after cutting. To maintain a fresh colour, drop beans into boiling water and cook uncovered until tender but still crisp. Then, if not to be served immediately, drain and drop into iced water to refresh them and set the colour.

> **China:** *tsai dou*
> **India:** *rajama*
> **Indonesia:** *kacang buncis*
> **Japan:** *ingen mame*
> **Malaysia:** *kacang buncis*
> **Philippines:** *habi chuelas*
> **Sri Lanka:** *bonchi*
> **Thailand:** *thua khaek*

Green pea: (*Pisum sativum* var. *sativum*) Also called garden pea. Sweet to eat raw or cooked, peas are one of the oldest known vegetables and may have originated in the Near East. Used green in a variety of dishes through Asia and particularly popular in India, where they are cooked with rice, with savoury meat dishes, and as a vegetable on their own.

The pods are also used as a curry vegetable, and are quite delicious once the tough, clear membrane lining the inside of the pod is peeled away. New varieties of succulent, 'mange tout' peas (sugar snap peas) make all that fiddly work unnecessary, although it is good to know there is a use for the pods after you have shelled garden peas.

Purchasing and storing: Look for unblemished, fresh, smooth pods with stems that are still green. Use as soon as possible after podding. Peas may be stored a day or two in a plastic bag in the refrigerator. Frozen peas are a boon for busy people.

Preparation: Press lightly on the side seams and the pod should open and allow the peas to be scooped into a bowl.

If the pods are as fresh and crisp as they should be, and time permits, remove the tough translucent lining as described here. After removing the peas, separate halves of the pods. Hold each half with the inside facing you, bend ends towards you so that the fleshy outer wall of the pod cracks. Pull downwards, and the thin, tough lining should come away from the fleshy pod. Discard the linings. The pods are now ready to be cooked.

> **China:** *wan dou*
> **India:** *mattar*
> **Indonesia:** *ercis*
> **Japan:** *endou mame*
> **Malaysia:** *kacang manis*
> **Philippines:** *sitsaro*
> **Sri Lanka:** *amu bola kadala*
> **Thailand:** *thua lantao*

Hyacinth bean: See **Lablab bean.**

Lablab bean: (*Lablab purpureus, Dolichos lablab*) Called by many names including hyacinth, Egyptian, bonavista, tonka or wall beans, these are eaten both as a fresh and dried bean. There are a number of varieties, varying somewhat in shape and size. Some are used only for their peas while others, with thicker pods, are used as a green vegetable in curries. The pods of the fresh beans may be green or purple in colour. The best known are papri or popetti (large pea-shaped pods, grown for their attractive dried, brown peas with a white stripe); siem, a flattish pea with a fleshier pod like a pea-length version of the flat, undulating ribbon-shaped continental green beans; and val (valour) which looks more like a green runner bean, bulging with overdeveloped seeds. The last two are eaten fresh, topped and tailed then cut up and added to curries and vegetable dishes.

Lentil: (*Lens culinari, L. esculenta*) One of the most ancient of food crops, their botanical name derives from their semblance in shape to the lens of the eye. They are among the most easily digested of pulses due to a low content of flatulence-producing sugars. Although soaking is not strictly necessary, soaking in warm water for an hour before cooking makes them even easier to digest. There are two basic subgroups within the lentil genus: macrosperma, which have large, flattened seeds and microsperma, with small to medium-sized seeds. Of the small varieties, Persian red and Chinese green are the most popular.

Red lentils lose their colour and shape when cooked with plenty of liquid to a purée for that famous staple of Indian cuisine known simply as dhal. But when combined with rice in that other famous Indian dish, kitchri (after which the kedgeree of Britain is named), they keep their shape if not their bright colour. Green lentils turn light brown when cooked. Grey lentils, a much sought-after variety, are more of a khaki colour. Yellow lentils belong to the large-seeded group. All lentils are annuals bearing flowers of red, pink, purple or white, and carrying pods which contain two seeds. When pods turn golden they are ripe for harvesting. Thought to have originated in the Middle East, they are widespread throughout Asia and will grow in any warm climate.

One good rule to follow with lentils, is to spread the required amount in a large pan and sort through them, keeping a sharp look out for stones and foreign seeds. Some processing plants export very clean lentils while others let slip bits of stone which can be really nasty to bite down on. It does not take long to sort through a cup or two of lentils.

> **Burma:** *pe ni*
> **China:** *sai min dou*
> **India:** *kursam bulle pullie, bagali*
> **Indonesia:** *kacang koro*
> **Japan:** *aoi mame*
> **Malaysia:** *kacang serinding*
> **Philippines:** *patani*
> **Sri Lanka:** *pothundhambala*
> **Thailand:** *thua raatcha maat*

Lima bean: (*Phaseolus lunatus*) Sometimes known as butter beans, Burma beans or sieva beans, these flattish white beans may be either large or small. Rangoon bean is the British name for a red variety of lima bean. Baby lima beans (also called sieva beans) are popular in the United States where they are eaten green (look for tightly-closed, dark green pods bulging with beans, cut along the thin edge, open and remove beans). The large ones are more widely recognised as dried lima beans.

The lima bean is one of the legumes to contain a trypsin inhibitor which can be inactivated by soaking and thorough cooking. Of more concern is the fact that lima beans contain cyanogens that can only driven off by boiling, uncovered, forming the gaseous compound hydrogen cyanide, a respiratory depressant. In water, the cyanogens form the poison hydrocyanic acid. This should not be a major concern if you use commercially grown beans. However, some wild varieties that grow in the West Indies contain very high concentrations of cyanogens which may be lethal.

Long bean: See **Yard-long bean.**

Moong bean: See **Mung bean.**

Moth bean: (*Vigna acontifolia*) Also known as muth, mot, mat, haricot, papillon or dew bean. A very small bean ranging from pale beige to reddish brown in colour, with a flavour similar to that of mung beans. Mainly grown and used in India and only exported when there is sufficient after the home market is supplied. Thailand, on the other hand, grows them for export to Japan. Northern Indian cooking simmers these miniature beans with other vegetables, and all over India the split, soaked and fried muth bean appears as part of the spicy snack known as sev.

Mung bean: Also spelled moong bean (*Vigna radiata, Phaseolus aureus, P. radiatus*) A small bean with olive-green seed coat and yellow interior. This popular dried bean has a number of names. It is also known as green gram or golden gram. Special larger varieties are used for bean sprouts, which sell more widely in Western countries than the dried bean.

There are 2,000 varieties of mung bean, among them yellow, gold and black mung beans. Black mung beans are also called black gram in India and are highly prized and therefore are not an export crop. Black mung beans are not to be confused with urad or urid dhal (*Vigna mungo* or *Phaseolus mungo*) because while the skins of both are black, the inside of urad is very white. More importantly, the flavour is different and they are used in different dishes in Indian cuisine.

Mung beans are easily digested, containing very few oligosaccharides which cause flatulence, and therefore are suitable for children or those with delicate digestive systems. They contain between 19–25 per cent protein, 60 per cent carbohydrate and 4 per cent fibre. They are also rich in lysine and offer appreciable amounts of potassium, calcium, magnesium, iron and traces of thiamin, riboflavin and niacin.

Mung beans are available either as the whole bean (mung saboot), split with skins left on (chilke mung dhal) or split and skins removed (mung dhal). Besides being used for soups and porridge or as a spicy accompaniment to rice, they are versatile enough to provide a base for sweet making.

In Malaysia a sweet porridge served warm has mung beans as its base, then palm sugar and coconut milk are added.

In Sri Lanka, mung beans are roasted and ground, mixed with palm sugar (or brown sugar), spread out thinly and cut into squares or diamond shapes. Thin slabs of it are dipped in rice flour batter and fried to make 'mung kavum', a favourite sweet snack.

In Thailand, husked and split mung beans are cooked until soft, then mashed, mixed with white sugar and rich coconut cream. The resulting pliable paste is formed into the most exquisite tiny fruits called 'luk chup' or 'small magic'. See DESSERTS.

In China, the dried bean, split and hulled, is cooked to a paste and sweetened to make a filling for some popular sweets: steamed buns and jin doi, deep-fried, sesame covered 'doughnuts'.

In Vietnam, the sweetened paste is featured in sweet drinks as well as in soft and chewy rice flour cakes.

The starch from mung beans is used to make delightfully textured vermicelli, also known as bean thread noodles, cellophane noodles and spring rain noodles. (For more information see **Mung bean starch** under FLOURS & STARCHES). Mung beans are the beans most commonly sold as sprouts. For instructions on growing your own mung bean sprouts, see BEAN SPROUTS.

Parkia: (*Parkia speciosa*) This legume, native to Malaysia, has a unique flavour politely described as sharp, bitter and lemony. Bottled in brine, it has a distinctly unfriendly smell to the uninitiated nose. Although many sing its praises, I think it fair to say it's an acquired taste. Also known as peteh (Indonesia). See main entry for PARKIA.

Peanut: (*Arachis hypogaea*) Also called ground nut and guber, peanuts are the seeds inside the under-ground fruit capsules of a bushy leguminous herb and therefore not, technically speaking, a nut. Roasted, it is a favourite in the West as a salted snack or ground into a paste widely marketed as peanut butter. Also the basis of many tasty satay sauces in Indonesia and Malaysia and, crushed, sprinkled over noodle dishes and salads in Thailand and Vietnam. Ground to a powder, sweetened peanut is made into a delicious, crisp, compressed Chinese peanut 'cake'. A delicious snack food from Japan encases peanuts in a 'shell' of slightly sweet, crisp coating. Also used in the cooking of India and the Philippines. Boiled peanuts are a popular snack food across Asia. See main entry for PEANUT.

Pigeon pea: (*Cajanus cajan*) Native to Africa or India, but used more in India, it has been a source of food for mankind for over 4,000 years. In India, where it is known as red gram, it is next to the chick pea in importance. The colour of the peas can vary from white to red, black, brown and mottled. Claimed to be slightly narcotic. Split and husked, it is used as dhal and sold in Indian shops as arhar dhal or toovar or toor dhal. These are a staple in southern India as they are used in sambhar — a spicy lentil and vegetable soup served at almost every meal.

Red bean: See **Adzuki bean**.

Red kidney bean: (*Phaseolus vulgaris*) Popularly known as rajma in India, these members of the haricot bean family have so many close relatives that to attempt classification is a thankless task. The main ones are kidney beans (which can be white, red, pink, mottled, brown or black); navy beans/Boston beans/pea bean (small, round, white and most often the variety used for canned baked beans); haricot (the elongated, slender pale green seeds of a variety of common runner bean); and white haricot (large, broad, creamy-white variety of haricot).

Rice bean: (*Phaseolus calcaratus*, *Vigna umbellata*) A small, slender oblong bean with a raised, white hilum that grows in Malaysia, Nepal and Assam. Native to South East Asia, they are popular in China, India and the Philippines. Resistant to pest attacks, it is edible in both its green and dried forms. However, the fragility of the dried pod makes for difficult harvesting, even by hand, explaining why so little reaches the market. The seeds of the bean vary in colour from pale to deep yellow, green, brown, maroon, black and mottled and, although not suitable for dhal, they are often mixed with rice or eaten as a rice substitute. They have the highest calcium content of all dried beans, containing up to twice the calcium of kidney beans.

Sataw bean: See PARKIA.

Snow pea: (*Pisum sativum* var. *macrocarpon*) SEE ILLUSTRATION. A delectable, tender, flat-podded, small-seeded pea which is known by the descriptive French name mange tout ('eat it all'). They are not the only fully edible pea. The sugar snap pea with its full, fleshy pod and developed seeds has more crunch per munch — but nothing rivals snow peas for elegance. Only used in its fresh state.

The tender, twisting tendrils sold as 'pea shoots', which are the growing tips and top set of leaves on a pea plant, are an oriental delicacy. Expensive and extravagant, they may be eaten as a salad with a little squeeze of lime or lemon juice or tossed ever-so-quickly in hot oil with a little ginger, sugar and wine for a different stir-fried vegetable.

Soy bean: (*Glycine max*) SEE ILLUSTRATION. Also known as soya bean. An ancient food crop native to China. The cultivation of soy beans was recorded in 2,800 BC. Known as the 'meat without a bone', soy beans provide cheap protein to millions in China, Japan and Korea, where they are cultivated and processed in many ways. See SOY BEAN, FRESH.

Sugar snap pea: (*Pisum sativum* var. *macrocarpon*) The botanical name is the same as that given to green peas because they are first cousins, the other parent being snow peas or mange tout.

The similarity between sugar snap peas and small pregnant garden peas is that, like the snow pea, the entire pod can be eaten. They are crisp, crunchy, sweet and succulent. Perhaps their best feature is that they don't have strings as snow peas do, neither do they have the tough, inedible lining of green pea pods. So what do we have? An offspring which possesses the best qualities of each parent, a pea pod which really does answer to the descriptive name, mange tout (eat it all), a leguminous plant used only in its fresh state, a custom-designed vegetable for the cook in a hurry.

Tamarind: (*Tamarindus indica*) While it does answer to the dictionary definition of a legume, i.e. 'the edible pod of a leguminous plant', tamarind is used primarily as a souring agent and not as a staple food crop. See main entry for TAMARIND.

White gram: See **Black gram**.

Winged bean: (*Psophocarpus tetragonolobus*) SEE ILLUSTRATION. Called by many names including asparagus bean, asparagus pea, four-angled bean, frilly bean, manilla bean, Goa bean, Mauritius bean and princess pea. Grown in the Philippines as a decorative plant, it twines and twirls its way over dwellings. Depending on the variety, the flowers may be white, lavender or vibrant blue. The miniature winged bean grown by gardeners in the Northern Hemisphere as 'asparagus pea', has tiny, deep red flowers.

The pods of the winged bean are very decorative with four serrated edges and tiny seeds contained inside a central 'rib'. They are mostly green, but may also be pink, purple or red. Try to make sure they are not much more than finger length, or they will be tough. How the winged bean came to be called 'asparagus' anything is beyond me, as it neither looks nor tastes like asparagus, but it is sometimes briefly steamed or boiled, then dipped in butter or sauce, the way asparagus is. In Asia, they are more likely to be sliced crossways and stir-fried, either alone or with other ingredients.

Very popular in Thailand, served as a salad, lightly cooked, or to dip into one of Thailand's famous nam prik sauces.

Even at their prime they are perishable, so use within a day or two, the sooner the better.

China: *su-ling dou*
India: *Goa bean*
Indonesia: *kecipir*
Japan: *shikakumame*
Malaysia: *kacang botor*
Philippines: *sigarilyas*
Sri Lanka: *dara-dhambala*
Thailand: *thua pu*

Yard-long bean: (*Vigna unguiculata*, *V. sesquipedalis*, *V. sinensis*, *V. cylindrica*) SEE ILLUSTRATION. Known by a host of names including asparagus bean, pea bean, cowpea, catjang, China pea and snake bean, this is the fresh bean from which the black-eyed pea/bean (dried) is derived.

The young pods have a delicate flavour which is alluded to by the name asparagus bean. (These names can be confusing as asparagus bean is a term often used when what is meant is asparagus pea, the smaller relative of the winged bean, Tetragonolobus or Lotus.) Yard-long beans are worth trying for their tenderness and flavour.

Purchasing: Look for firm, deep green beans

without a trace of sponginess or yellowing. Use them as soon as possible, because they lose texture if kept too long.

Preparation: Snip off the stem ends, cut into bite-sized lengths. They don't have strings which must be removed, so are easy to prepare.

China: *tseng dou*
India: *lobia*
Indonesia: *kacang panjang*
Japan: *juuroku-sasage*
Malaysia: *kacang panjang*
Philippines: *sitaw*
Sri Lanka: *makaraal*
Thailand: *thua chin*

Adzuki Bean Soup

Serves 4

250 g/8 oz/1 cup adzuki beans
2 tablespoons oil
2 medium onions, finely chopped
1 teaspoon finely chopped garlic
1 carrot, finely diced
1 stick celery, diced
1 tablespoon Japanese soy sauce
1 tablespoon miso

Wash the beans and soak overnight. Drain, rinse and put into a pan with 1.5 litres/3 pints/ 6 cups fresh water and bring to the boil. Cover and simmer for about 1 hour or until tender.

In another pan heat oil and cook the onions, garlic, carrot and celery over low heat for 10 minutes, covered. Add the beans and extra boiling water if liquid has reduced too much. Add the soy sauce. In a small bowl thin the miso with some of the hot liquid, then stir in.

Savoury Black-Eyed Peas

Serves 4–6

375 g/12 oz/1½ cups black-eyed peas
2 cassia leaves (tej pattar)
3 cardamom pods, bruised
2 whole cloves garlic, unpeeled
½ teaspoon ground turmeric
2 tablespoons ghee or oil
1 medium onion, finely chopped
2 teaspoons finely chopped garlic
2 teaspoons finely grated fresh ginger

2 fresh red chillies
  or 1 teaspoon chilli powder
1 teaspoon ground cumin
1 teaspoon salt
125 ml/4 fl oz/½ cup natural yoghurt
2 teaspoons rice flour
1 teaspoon garam masala
3 tablespoons chopped fresh coriander

Rinse the peas and soak overnight in cold water, or bring to the boil, turn off heat, cover and soak for 2 hours. Drain, cover with fresh water and add the cassia leaves, cardamom pods, garlic cloves and turmeric. Bring to the boil, then simmer for 35 minutes or until almost tender. Drain, reserving liquid.

Heat ghee and on low heat cook the onion, garlic, ginger and chillies until onions are soft and start to turn golden. Add the cumin and salt, the drained peas and 1 cup of the cooking liquid, and simmer for 15 minutes or until the peas are quite tender and the sauce thick. Mix the yoghurt and rice flour with about 3 tablespoons of remaining soaking liquid, stir into the peas and simmer for a further 2 minutes. Stir in the garam masala and sprinkle with the fresh coriander. Serve with chapatis, parathas or rice.

Broad Beans with Ham

This is one of those seasonal treats which can only be enjoyed while fresh broad beans are available. Serves 4.

250 g/8 oz fresh broad beans, pods removed
90 g/3 oz sliced leg ham
1 tablespoon oil
1 teaspoon finely chopped garlic
125 ml/4 fl oz/½ cup hot water
1 teaspoon sugar
¼ teaspoon salt
125 ml/4 fl oz/½ cup light chicken stock
1 teaspoon cornflour (cornstarch)
½ teaspoon oriental sesame oil

Slit the skins of the broad beans with a small sharp knife and remove them. Cut the ham slices into small squares, about half the size of the beans.

In a wok or heavy frying pan heat the oil and on low heat fry the garlic for a few seconds, stirring and not letting it brown. Toss in the beans and stir-fry for 2 minutes. Add water, sugar and salt, bring to the boil, cover and simmer for 3 or 4 minutes over medium heat. The water should be almost all evaporated and the beans a bright green. Add ham and chicken stock and when it comes to the boil stir in the cornflour mixed with a tablespoon of cold water. Stir until it boils and thickens, then turn off heat and stir in the sesame oil. Serve immediately.

Broad Beans with Mushrooms

Serves 4

250 g/8 oz fresh broad beans, pods removed
250 g/8 oz fresh mushrooms
** (enoki, shiitake or other)**
2 tablespoons oil
1 tablespoon Japanese soy sauce
1 teaspoon sugar
½ teaspoon hoi sin sauce
125 ml/4 fl oz/½ cup water or light stock
1 teaspoon oriental sesame oil

Slit the skins of the broad beans with a small sharp knife and remove them. Wipe over the mushrooms and trim stems if necessary. If large, cut in halves.

Heat oil in a wok and when hot add beans and mushrooms and stir-fry over medium-high heat for 1 minute. Add soy sauce, sugar, hoi sin sauce and water or stock mixed together. Bring to the boil, cover and simmer for 5 minutes. Uncover, add sesame oil and toss the beans and mushrooms around in the small amount of liquid left to distribute the seasonings.

Green Bean Sambal

250 g/8 oz tender green beans
1 clove garlic
½ teaspoon salt
2 tablespoons peanut oil
1 fresh red chilli, seeded and chopped
3 shallots or 1 small white onion, finely sliced

Top, tail and string beans if necessary. With a sharp knife, cut into fine diagonal slices. Crush garlic with salt to a smooth puree. Heat oil in a wok and on high heat stir-fry the sliced beans for 2 minutes. Lower heat, add the garlic and

chilli, and fry for a minute or so longer until beans are tender but still crisp. Remove from heat, add sliced shallots or onion and toss together. Serve with rice and other spiced dishes.

Peas with Fresh Cheese

One of the classic vegetarian dishes of India. It is made with home-made cheese and fresh peas, but a short-cut is to use baked ricotta and convenient frozen peas. Serves 4–6.

1 quantity panir (recipe page 74)
** or 500 g/1 lb baked ricotta, diced**
2 tablespoons oil or ghee
1 medium onion, finely chopped
2 teaspoons finely chopped garlic
2 teaspoons finely chopped fresh ginger
1 tablespoon ground coriander
2 teaspoons ground cumin
1 teaspoon ground turmeric
½ teaspoon chilli powder (optional)
3 ripe tomatoes peeled, seeded and chopped
500 g/1 lb fresh or frozen peas
1 teaspoon salt or to taste
1½ teaspoons garam masala (recipe page 354)
3 tablespoons chopped fresh mint or coriander

Heat oil or ghee in a heavy saucepan and fry onion, garlic and ginger over medium-low heat, stirring occasionally, until translucent and starting to turn golden. Sprinkle in ground spices and stir for 2 minutes or until spices smell fragrant and darken slightly.

Add tomatoes, fresh peas, salt and garam masala, cover and simmer until tomatoes are pulpy and peas are cooked. If using frozen peas, add them after tomatoes are soft. Add diced cheese, spoon the sauce over and simmer for 10 minutes. Sprinkle with fresh herbs and serve with rice or Indian bread.

Spiced Chick Peas, Indian Style

Serves 6

250 g/8 oz dried chick peas, soaked overnight
** and drained**
2 cassia leaves (tej pattar) (optional)
½ teaspoon ground turmeric
1 teaspoon salt or to taste
2 tablespoons ghee or oil

1 medium onion, finely chopped
2 teaspoons finely chopped garlic
2 teaspoons finely chopped fresh ginger
2 ripe tomatoes, peeled and diced
1 teaspoon garam masala (recipe page 354)
3 tablespoons chopped fresh mint or coriander
lemon juice to taste
1 or 2 fresh chillies (optional)

Put the soaked chick peas and cassia leaves in a saucepan with fresh water to cover. Bring to the boil and boil hard with lid off the pan for 30 minutes. Add turmeric, cover and simmer until almost tender. Add salt and continue cooking until chick peas are soft but holding their shape. Depending on the age and variety of the chick peas, cooking time could take up to 2 hours. Drain over a large bowl and reserve the cooking liquid.

In a heavy pan heat ghee or oil and gently fry the onion, garlic and ginger until onion is soft and golden, stirring frequently. Add chick peas and tomatoes and half the reserved cooking liquid. Cover and cook until tender, adding more liquid if necessary. Sprinkle with garam masala and chopped herbs, add lemon juice to taste and, if liked, sliced chillies. Serve with chapatis or puris.

Black Gram Pancakes

Called dosa or dosai in India, these are one of the most popular of snacks or light meals, especially the variety known as 'paper dosa' which is at least 40 cm (16 in) in diameter, as fine and crisp as a wafer, and encloses a spicy potato filling. You need to be a professional dosa chef to achieve those, but here is the home-style version. Makes 18.

300 g/10 oz/1½ cups uncooked rice
150 g/5 oz/¾ cup black gram (urad dhal)
2 teaspoons salt
1½ teaspoons sugar
2 teaspoons ghee or oil
½ teaspoon black mustard seeds
1 small onion, finely chopped
1 fresh green chilli, seeded and chopped
extra ghee or oil for cooking

Wash rice and dhal separately and soak each in cold water to cover for at least 8 hours. Drain rice and grind in an electric blender, adding just enough water to facilitate blending.

Strain through a fine sieve and discard any rough residue. Rinse blender and grind the dhal, adding a little cold water if necessary. This should not need straining as the dhal blends more easily than rice. Combine dhal and rice and mix well, adding salt and sugar. Cover and leave to ferment in a warm place for about 3 hours.

Heat ghee in a small saucepan and fry mustard seeds until they begin to pop. Add onion and chilli and fry over low heat, stirring now and then, until onions are soft and start to colour. Remove from heat. When cool, stir onion mixture into the batter, which should be of a thick pouring consistency. Thin it down if necessary with a little cold water.

Heat a heavy frying pan or crepe pan and grease with a very little ghee or oil. Pour in about ⅓ cup batter, or just enough to cover the base of the pan thinly. The trick for making successful dosai is to spread the batter very quickly with the back of the ladle or metal cup used for pouring. Cook on low heat until the bottom is well browned. Turn over and cook other side. Serve with coconut chatni and dry potato curry.

Red Lentil and Rice Kitchri

Similar to a pilau, rice and red lentils prepared in this way are the standby of every Indian cook. Serves 4 as a main dish.

200 g/7 oz/1 cup long grain rice, preferably
    basmati
200 g/7 oz/1 cup red lentils
2 tablespoons ghee or oil
5 cardamom pods, bruised
4 whole cloves
1 stick cinnamon
2 medium onions, finely sliced
750 ml/1½ pints/3 cups hot water
2 teaspoons salt

Wash rice and drain well. Sort, wash and drain the lentils. Both should be washed at least 30 minutes beforehand and allowed to drain completely.

Heat ghee or oil in a saucepan with a heavy base and well-fitting lid. Fry the spices and onions until onions are golden brown. Take half the onions from the pan and set aside. Add rice and lentils and fry, stirring, for 3 or

4 minutes. Add hot water and salt, bring to the boil, then turn heat as low as possible, cover tightly and cook without lifting lid for 20 minutes. Turn off heat and leave covered for a further 5 minutes. Serve garnished with the reserved fried onion and accompanied by natural yoghurt and some fruit chutney.

Note: For invalids, this dish is adapted to a kind of porridge, by increasing the water.

Red Lentils in Coconut Milk

There are many versions of dhal, or lentil purée. This one has South East Asian flavours. Serves 6 with rice.

400 g/14 oz/2 cups red lentils
1 tablespoon oil or ghee
sprig of fresh curry leaves
2 onions, thinly sliced
2 strips pandan leaves
1 teaspoon ground turmeric
2 dried red chillies (optional)
1 stem lemon grass, bruised
250 ml/8 fl oz/1 cup canned coconut milk
salt to taste

Sort through the lentils, discarding any small stones and stalks. Wash the lentils and drain.

Heat oil or ghee (or a mixture of both) in a saucepan and fry the curry leaves, onions and pandan leaves until onions start to brown. Add turmeric and stir, then put in the lentils, chillies, lemon grass and half the coconut milk mixed with 1½ cups of water. Cover and simmer until the lentils are soft and runny, adding a little more water if necessary. Add salt to taste, then stir in remaining ½ cup coconut milk. Heat and serve with rice.

Lentil and Vegetable Soup (Sambhar)

Pigeon peas (arhar dhal, toor dhal) is the preferred legume for this sour and spicy soup, but split peas or red lentils may be substituted. It is served with rice, and also traditionally with lentil pancakes . Serves 6.

200 g/7 oz/1 cup toor dhal
1.5 litres/3 pints/6 cups water
walnut-sized piece dried tamarind
2 tablespoons oil

1 tablespoon ground coriander
2 teaspoons ground cumin
½ teaspoon ground black pepper
½ teaspoon ground turmeric
375 g/12 oz mixed diced vegetables in season
    (pumpkin, eggplants (aubergines), beans,
    potatoes)
2 ripe tomatoes, diced
2 fresh chillies
2 teaspoons salt or to taste
1 teaspoon black mustard seeds
1 small onion, finely sliced
¼ teaspoon ground asafoetida

Pick over the dhal thoroughly for any foreign seeds or impurities. Wash in several changes of water, then soak in cold water to cover overnight or for 3 hours. Drain, put into a saucepan with the measured water and simmer, covered, until soft. Meanwhile, put tamarind pulp in a bowl and pour over it 1 cup of hot water. Leave until cool enough to handle, then knead and squeeze the pulp to dissolve. Strain through a nylon or stainless steel sieve. If there is still pulp left on the seeds, add an extra ½ cup of water and repeat the procedure. Discard all seeds and fibres.

Heat 1 tablespoon oil in another saucepan and fry ground spices for a minute, stirring. Add lentils and tamarind and bring to the boil. Add vegetables, tomatoes, chillies and salt and simmer until vegetables are very tender.

In a small pan heat remaining tablespoon of oil and fry the mustard seeds and sliced onion until seeds pop and onion is deep brown. Add asafoetida and immediately pour a ladle of the soup into the pan. Pour back into the soup, simmer a few minutes longer and serve with rice or lentil pancakes.

Lentils and Vegetables with Meat

This recipe is a perfect example of how many different kinds of lentils may be used together, and even combined with meat which can be omitted for the vegetarian version. An example of Parsi cooking, the recipe has many parts, but is not a difficult one. Serves 10–12.

LENTILS AND VEGETABLES
250 g/8 oz toor, toovar or arhar dhal
125 g/4 oz chick peas
125 g/4 oz mung dhal

125 g/4 oz red lentils
2 slender eggplants (aubergines), thickly sliced
1 slice butternut or other firm squash, peeled
1 large potato, peeled and halved
1 onion, peeled and quartered

OPTIONAL MEAT OR POULTRY

1 kg/2 lb boneless lamb, cubed
  or 1 roasting chicken, jointed

WET SEASONINGS

10 large dry red chillies, soaked
5 fresh green chillies, seeded
10 large cloves garlic, peeled
1 tablespoon chopped fresh ginger
1 onion, peeled and roughly chopped

DRY SEASONINGS

2 tablespoons ground coriander
1 tablespoon ground cumin
2 teaspoons ground turmeric
1 teaspoon black mustard seeds
½ teaspoon ground black pepper
½ teaspoon ground cinnamon
½ teaspoon ground cardamom
¼ teaspoon ground cloves

FOR FINISHING

4 tablespoons ghee or oil
3 large onions, finely sliced

Wash the lentils well, combine in a bowl and soak overnight in water to cover. Drain and replace water with fresh cold water. In a large pan put the lentils, water, meat or chicken (if not making a vegetarian version) and simmer until lentils and meat are tender. Remove meat or chicken and set aside. Purée lentils and vegetables in a food processor.

Purée wet seasonings in an electric blender until a smooth purée, adding a little water if necessary.

Combine ingredients for dry seasonings in a small bowl.

Heat ghee or oil in a large heavy pan and when hot fry the onions, stirring frequently, until the onions are deep brown. Remove from pan and reserve. Fry blended mixture in the same pan, stirring constantly. Add dry seasonings and stir until fragrant. Return half the browned onions to the pan, add the meat or chicken and the lentils and vegetables. Bring to the boil, add salt to taste and simmer for 30 minutes longer. Serve garnished with remaining fried onions and accompanied by brown rice and an onion salad.

Moth Beans with Seasonal Vegetables

Serves 6

100 g/3½ oz/½ cup dried moth beans
220 g/7 oz cauliflower sprigs
220 g/7 oz tender green beans
125 g/4 oz carrot or potato
1½ teaspoons salt

FOR SEASONING

1 tablespoon ghee
1 teaspoon black mustard seeds
1 teaspoon fennel seeds
¼ teaspoon ajowan seeds
½ teaspoon asafoetida powder
½ teaspoon garam masala (recipe page 354)

Soak the beans overnight or for at least 5 hours. Drain, put into a saucepan with 2 cups water, bring to boil, cover and simmer for 25 minutes or until tender but still holding their shape. Add the salt and cauliflower sprigs, the green beans cut into bite-sized pieces and carrot or potato, diced. Cover and simmer for 10 minutes or until all the vegetables are tender.

Prepare seasoning by heating ghee in a small pan. Add the seeds and cover pan to keep mustard seeds from spattering over the cooktop. When seeds have stopped popping add the asafoetida to the hot ghee, stir, and pour a ladle of the cooking liquid from vegetables into the seasoning. Return seasoning to the saucepan, stir well, and finally sprinkle with garam masala. Serve with rice, natural yoghurt and sweet or hot chutney.

Sweet Mung Bean Porridge

Serves 6

300 g/10 oz green mung beans
500 ml/1 pint/2 cups water
2 slices ginger or 2 strips pandan leaf
½ teaspoon salt
400 ml/14 fl oz can coconut milk
125 g/4 oz palm sugar or brown sugar

Pick over the beans for any stones. Wash well and drain. Put beans into a saucepan with the measured water, ginger or pandan, and salt. Bring to the boil, cover and simmer until water has been absorbed. Mix 1 cup of the canned coconut milk with an equal amount of water and add to pan. Bring to the boil once more, add palm sugar and stir over low heat until sugar dissolves. Continue cooking until mung beans are very soft, adding more hot water if necessary. The consistency should be that of a thin porridge. Taste and add more sugar if needed. Combine remaining undiluted coconut milk with a pinch of salt. Serve porridge warm or at room temperature, and top each bowl with a little of the thick coconut milk.

Stir-Fried Long Beans, Chinese Style

Serves 4

1 bunch long beans
1 tablespoon oil
4 slices fresh ginger
1 clove garlic, bruised
1 tablespoon light soy sauce
2 tablespoons water
½ teaspoon sugar
few drops oriental sesame oil

Wash the beans, dry them and snip off stem ends. Cut into bite-sized pieces. Heat oil in a wok and fry the ginger and unpeeled garlic clove for 1 minute. Add the beans and stir-fry for 2 minutes on high heat. Add soy sauce, water and sugar, toss to mix, then cover and simmer for 2 minutes. Sprinkle sesame oil over and serve at once while they are still crisp.

Stir-Fried Long Beans, Indian Style

Serves 4

1 bunch long beans, cut in bite-sized pieces
2 tablespoons oil
2 teaspoons black mustard seeds
2 teaspoons dried fenugreek leaves
1 teaspoon ground turmeric
1 teaspoon finely chopped garlic
½ teaspoon salt or to taste
½ cup stock or water

Heat a wok, add oil and stir in the mustard seeds. Cover to prevent seeds jumping out of wok. When seeds start to pop add fenugreek leaves, turmeric, garlic and salt. Add beans and stir-fry for 1 minute on medium-high heat.

Add water or stock, cover and simmer for 5 minutes. Uncover and stir-fry until almost all the liquid is evaporated. Serve with rice.

Lemon

(*Citrus limon*) Thought to have come to Europe from the East after the time of Christ, there is speculation as to its country of origin. Some would say India, but in that country, as in most of Asia, it runs a poor second to the lime, which grows more readily. Sour fruits used in preference to lemons include tamarind, tomato, green (unripe) mango, gelugor, gamboge and green pineapple.

Lemon Grass

(*Cymbopogon citratus*) SEE ILLUSTRATION. When giving a master class in the United States, I asked for lemon grass as one of the ingredients and was presented with just the leaves! This experience convinced me it is worth mentioning that the business end of the plant, for culinary purposes, is the lower stem.

A tall lemon-scented grass which multiplies into clumps as it grows. The leaves are narrow and sharp-edged, with a central rib. Easy to propagate in most warm climates with a little water and minimum care. It even grows in temperate zones, given enough sun.

One of the most popular herbs of South East Asia, mainly because lemons do not grow easily in the tropics. Used to flavour curries and soups, and a vital flavour in Thai curry pastes. If lemon grass is not available, it is quite acceptable to substitute 2 or 3 strips of thinly peeled lemon zest (no pith) for a stalk of lemon grass.

If using lemon grass, the outer, tougher layers should be peeled away and only the pale lower portion of the stem used. Since it is a very fibrous plant, slice it very thinly crossways so that there are no long fibres to spoil the finished dish.

Lemon grass purchased from markets is usually devoid of leaves. Make sure the stem is firm and smooth. Avoid those stems which look dry and wrinkled.

If you grow lemon grass yourself or someone offers you some from their clump, take care when handling as the edges of the leaves are razor sharp and even brushing past can cause almost invisible lacerations to exposed areas of skin. With a sharp knife, cut a stem close to the ground and trim off the grassy top section. The bulbous lower stem, creamy white to pale green, is the part to use.

The leaves may be used for infusions like tea, but are not used much in cooking. Sometimes the whole stem, bruised first so it imparts its fragrance readily, is simmered in a soup or sauce and discarded before serving. For this, leave it long enough to tie the bruised stem and leaves into a loose knot for ease of lifting from the finished dish.

Purchasing and storing: Lemon grass is usually sold in bunches of 3 or 4 stems, held together with a rubber band. Usually the stems are about 40 cm (17 in) in length of which only the lower half is used.

They will keep for weeks in a plastic bag in the refrigerator and can be kept frozen for up to 6 months, well wrapped.

Preparation: To simmer in a dish, bruise the stem by pounding with a pestle or mallet. Tie it in a loose knot so it is not awkwardly long, and drop it into the dish to cook, removing it before serving. If it is to be pounded or ground in a curry paste, first remove the outer layer (or two if necessary) and slice off the hard root, then cut in very thin crossways slices before putting it into an electric blender.

If preparing lemon grass for a salad, peel off outer layers and use only tender, white portion, very finely sliced. The slicing is easily done in a food processor with fine slicing blade attached. This is a procedure recommended even when grinding lemon grass with other ingredients into a paste, because unless sliced crossways the fine, strong fibres will survive blending and make their undesirable presence felt in the finished dish. See CURRY PASTES.

Medicinal uses: In Chinese medicine a decoction made from the plant is used to treat coughs, colds and blood in the sputum. The roots induce sweating and act as a diuretic. In Asian countries, the leaves in water are used in a bath to reduce swelling, remove body odour, improve blood circulation and to treat cuts and wounds.

In Western herbal medicine a tea made from the leaves is used for stomach ache, diarrhoea, headaches, fevers and flu. The antiseptic oil is a treatment for athlete's foot and acne, and is sprayed to reduce airborne infections. In aromatherapy, the oil is said to improve circulation and muscle tone.

Burma: *zabalin*
China: *heung masu tso*
India: *sera, ghanda*
Indonesia: *sere*
Japan: *remon-sou*
Malaysia: *serai*
Philippines: *tanglad*
Sri Lanka: *sera*
Thailand: *takrai*
Vietnam: *xa*

Lentil

See LEGUMES & PULSES.

Lily Bud

(*Hemerocallis*) The unopened flower buds of orange and yellow day lillies. At certain times of year, you may find fresh lily buds in Asian produce markets, with bright golden petals tightly folded above an emerald green calyx. They are delicious stir-fried with minced (ground) pork and flavoured with garlic, black pepper and fish sauce. Lily buds are known as 'golden needles' because of their original colour, though once dried they fade to a pale brown. Popular with Buddhists and other vegetarians, they add a distinctive, earthy flavour to a dish.

The long, slender dried buds of the day lily are sold in packets and will keep well if stored airtight. Look for buds pale in colour and still flexible, not dark brown and brittle which indicates they are old. Store in a jar with a tight-fitting lid, away from the light. Before adding to a dish, soak in warm water for 20–30 minutes. Trim soaked buds of hard stem tips then either tie each in a knot, shred by tearing, or cut across in halves.

China: *kim chiam, chin cheng tsai*
Japan: *kanzou*
Korea: *pet kup julgi*
Thailand: *dok mai chin*
Vietnam: *kim cham*

Thai Soup with Lily Buds

Serves 4

60 g/2 oz bean thread vermicelli
20 dried lily buds
6 dried shiitake mushrooms
300 g/10 oz raw prawns (shrimp)
2 tablespoons peanut oil
1 onion, thinly sliced
2 tablespoons Thai pepper-coriander paste
  (recipe page 105)
2 tablespoons fish sauce
1 teaspoon sugar
1 egg, slightly beaten
2 spring onions (scallions), sliced

Drop vermicelli into boiling water and boil for 10 minutes. Drain. Soak lily buds and mushrooms in hot water for 30 minutes. Cut off and discard mushroom stems and hard ends of lily buds. Tie the buds in a knot, or cut in half so they are bite-sized.

Cut noodles into short lengths.

Shell and devein prawns. Rinse heads and shells, drain, and use for making stock. Heat 1 tablespoon oil in a pan, when very hot add the shells and fry on high heat until they have turned red. Add 1 litre (2 pints) hot water, cover and boil for 20 minutes. Strain stock, discard shells.

Heat remaining tablespoon of oil and fry the onion until soft. Add pepper and coriander paste and stir over gentle heat for 2 minutes. Add prawns and fry, stirring, until they change colour. Add stock, lily buds, mushrooms and vermicelli and bring soup to the boil. Simmer 5 minutes, stir in fish sauce and sugar. Taste and add more salt if necessary. Pour egg slowly into the boiling soup, stirring so it forms shreds. Sprinkle with spring onions and serve.

Stir-Fried Lily Buds with Pork

Serves 2

200 g/7 oz fresh lily buds
1 tablespoon peanut oil
1 teaspoon finely chopped garlic
3 tablespoons chopped coriander including root
125 g/4 oz minced (ground) pork
½ teaspoon ground black pepper
1 tablespoon fish sauce
1 teaspoon palm or brown sugar
2 tablespoons roasted, crushed peanuts

Wash lily buds and remove the green calyx from each. Heat peanut oil in a wok and fry the garlic and coriander root on low heat, stirring, until fragrant. Add pork, raise heat and stir-fry until no longer pink. Add lily buds and continue to toss and fry for 2 minutes. Add pepper, fish sauce, sugar and a splash of water, cover and simmer for 3 minutes. Sprinkle with crushed peanuts and serve with steamed rice.

Lily Bulb

(*Lilium tigrinum*) The starchy bulbs of a variety of lily are eaten fresh in China, Korea and Japan. The segments of the bulb resemble flattened garlic cloves and are also dried for cooking. Fresh bulbs require parboiling to remove bitterness before adding to dishes.

Lily, Day

See DAY LILY.

Lime

(*Citrus aurantifolia*, *C. latifolia*, *C. limon*, *C. limetta*, *C. hystrix*, *C. amblycarpa*, *C. microcarpa*) It is thought the plant originated in the tropical parts of Asia, probably in the East Indies. Merchants and seafarers took it to other lands, and it is now grown extensively in other tropical countries, notably Tahiti, Florida (key limes) and the West Indies. Limes flourish in tropical climates unlike lemons which prefer colder growing conditions.

Indian limes, nimboo, are relished as the flavouring in a drink of lime juice and water or sparkling mineral water. Sweetened with sugar, a pinch of salt intensifies the flavour. Its acidity is most refreshing, and the British in India could hardly have survived without their frequent drinks of nimboo pani.

The Philippine kalamansi (*C. microcarpa*) is used in a similar manner. Both are also served cut in halves to be squeezed over food as a flavour accent. This practice is also observed in Malaysia, where the small kalamansi is called limau kesturi. In Thailand, the leaves, fruit and rind of kaffir limes (*C. hystrix*, *C. amblycarpa*), which they call makrut is indispensable in curry pastes. See KAFFIR LIME.

The Tahitian or Persian lime (*C. latifolia*) which grows in temperate climates, is a perfectly round fruit with thin, smooth skin. The skin remains bright green when ripe. It is 3–4 cm (1–1½ in) in diameter with seedless green pulp. This lime is used for its grated or finely chopped zest in cakes, and for its refreshing juice in drinks. Also used in dressings, to add acid flavour to curries, and sometimes wedges of lime are put on the table to squeeze over food for extra piquantcy. See recipes for Savoury Semolina (page 336) and Burmese Egg Noodles with Curry (page 251).

See also KALAMANSI; LIME, SWEET.

India: *nimboo*
Malaysia: *limau nipis*
Philippines: *dayap*
Sri Lanka: *dehi*
Thailand: *ma nao*

Salted Limes

Any kind of lime may be used to make this useful pickle. When limes are scarce, use thin-skinned lemons. Time is the chief ingredient in softening the texture and mellowing the flavour of these fruits. They are ready to use after 4–6 months, when they have turned brown and the juices have become a solid amber-coloured jelly. Salted limes will keep indefinitely, ready to add piquant flavour to curries and chutney, or chopped and combined with sliced chillies and shallots in a fresh relish.

2.5 kg/5 lb limes or thin-skinned lemons
500g/1 lb coarse salt

Wash and dry the fruit well. With a sharp stainless steel knife slit each fruit in quarters, leaving them attached at the stem end. Open the slits and press about a tablespoon of salt into each fruit. Put into clean, dry glass jars, pressing the limes down and sprinkling with more salt between layers and on top. Cover jars with stoppers, not metal lids. Cover tightly and leave jars in the sun every day for three weeks, weather permitting. Store in a cellar or cupboard for 6 months or longer. For good keeping qualities, use at least 15 per cent by weight of salt.

Lime Leaf

See KAFFIR LIME.

Lime, Sweet

(*Citrus × nobilis, C. limettioides*) More the size and shape of a small orange, this fruit retains a green skin even when ripe, but the flesh is bright orange, juicy and sweet. It is the nearest thing to an orange which grows in tropical climes and is used in the same way that oranges are used in temperate zones.

India: *naran-kai*
Malaysia: *limau manis*
Sri Lanka: *pani dodan*
Thailand: *som khiew wan, som kleang*

Liver

This largest of the body's organs inspires enthusiasm in some people, loathing in others. For many years upheld as the best treatment for anaemia, but now, along with all organ meats, supposed to contribute to cholesterol. Liver contains at least twice the amount of cholesterol as muscle meats, but it also provides iron, zinc and niacin, is a source of vitamin A and a rich source of vitamin B12. It is worth keeping in mind that organ meats store residues of hormones and chemicals ingested by the animal.

For recipes, see OFFAL.

Lobster

There are many kinds of lobster, varying in size and shape, with shells of orange, red, brown, green, blue or black which may be spiny or relatively smooth. It is largely a matter of using what is available in your region, and buying it live and fresh. The Chinese name for this crustacean translates as 'dragon prawn' (shrimp) and it is a dish served at banquets. It may be presented with delicate flavours such as ginger and spring onions (scallions), or it may be bathed in a pungent black bean sauce. The best restaurants let you choose your lobster live and rampant in its tank. It is then taken to the kitchen and the next time you see it is on the platter. This is undoubtedly the best way to enjoy lobster.

In Western countries lobster is often sold cooked. The reason could be the squeamishness of many home cooks at having to despatch the creature (I cannot pretend I like the job myself) or the uncertainty of how to deal with it once it has been killed. For the lobster enthusiast who would like to try some classic Asian lobster dishes, here is the latest information on humane methods of killing, followed by recipes.

A very primitive creature, a lobster does not have a brain, and therefore cannot be killed instantly with a knife thrust as has been believed for some time. After much research it has been decided that boiling water kills it much more quickly (about 15 seconds based on experimental evidence) than putting it into cold water and slowly bringing to the boil, a method previously advocated. Cold-induced anaesthesia (place it, wrapped in paper, in the freezer for an hour or two) renders it senseless and immobile and, hopefully, it will neither know nor care what happens to it in the pot.

Steamed Lobster with Ginger

Serves 2

1 uncooked lobster tail
1 teaspoon finely chopped garlic
1 teaspoon finely chopped ginger
2 teaspoons canned salted black beans, rinsed
1 tablespoon light soy sauce
1 tablespoon oriental sesame oil
2 spring onions (scallions), sliced
1 tablespoon peanut oil

Cut tail in half lengthways and chop into sections. Put in a heatproof plate, place in a steamer or on a trivet above water level. Mix garlic, ginger, black beans, soy sauce and sesame oil and pour over the lobster pieces. Cover and steam over boiling water for 10 minutes. Remove from heat and scatter spring onion slices over. Heat peanut oil in a small pan until very hot and pour over lobster so it sizzles. Serve at once.

Thai Lobster Salad

1 cooked lobster
juice of 2 limes
1 teaspoon sugar
1 shallot, sliced very fine
2 red chillies, seeded and sliced
1 teaspoon rice flour
250 ml/8 fl oz/1 cup canned coconut milk
1 tablespoon fish sauce
2 fresh kaffir lime leaves, slivered

Cut through membrane on underside of lobster tail, and remove meat from tail. Cut across into rounds. Reserve claws and legs. Place lobster meat in a bowl. Stir together lime juice and sugar and pour over lobster. Scatter with a few slices of shallot and half the chillies. Mix gently.

Mix rice flour with a tablespoon of coconut milk. Heat remaining coconut milk in a small saucepan. Stir in rice flour mixture and cook until slightly thickened. Pour into a bowl to cool. Drain liquid from lobster and stir liquid into coconut milk. Add fish sauce. Pour coconut milk dressing over base of serving dish. Arrange lobster slices on top. Garnish with remaining shallot and chilli slices and thread-fine slivers of kaffir leaf. Lobster claws and legs may be placed around the meat. Serve cold.

Longan

(*Nephelium longana*, *Euphorbia longana*) SEE ILLUSTRATION. Native to South East Asia, the longan is now cultivated as a commercial crop in Australia. A comparison with lychees is unavoidable as they are closely related and appear similar after peeling. Instead of the bright pinkish red, rough skin of the lychee, the longan's skin is smoother, more brittle and pale brown, but its flesh, not as white as that of the lychee, is every bit as luscious and, in my opinion, sweeter and more fragrant. The Chinese name of loong narn translates as 'dragon's eye'. Smaller than a lychee, it is also rounder in shape and as the shiny black seed shows through the translucent aril, one understands the aptness of the Chinese description.

A fruit as delicately fragrant as this should really be eaten on its own — not messed about, cut up, mixed into fruit salads or otherwise compromised. The skin is thin and easily removed. The seeds are not attached to the fleshy aril which yields to gentle pressure of teeth and tongue. In my temperate zone garden we have optimistically planted both lychee and longan trees, and they have both fruited, modestly. They may never produce the crops they would if grown in a more tropical climate, but I appreciate them for the beauty of their shiny leaves, the canopy shape, and the few exquisite fruit they offer.

Dried longan: Longans and lychees are both sold dried. Their skin, even more brittle when dried, surrounds a shrunken fruit which is dark, sweet and slightly smoky in flavour and resembles a round raisin. Sometimes sold minus the seeds, compressed into a cake, in small, expensive packets.

Dried longans are simmered with black sticky rice in a Nonya version of rice pudding, or eaten as a snack like any dried fruit. They are boiled in water to make cool drinks, floating in lightly sweetened liquid together with finely shredded agar-agar jelly, barley, white fungus, water chestnuts, Chinese red dates and crushed ice.

Purchasing and storing: When purchasing longans, try to buy those still attached to stems. They are usually sold in twiggy bunches. When the fruit fall off after a few days they are gathered into bags or sold by weight, and by this stage are not as fresh as they once were, but can still be very nice if they are sound. Make sure the skins are not cracked and that they have no moist spots on them. They should be stored in a cool place and eaten within a day or two.

Out of season, purchase longans in cans. They are one of the few tropical fruits that tolerate canning without losing too much of their flavour and texture. In this form they are delicious with almond jelly, or as part of a fruit medley served in a small watermelon shell offering balls of honeydew, watermelon and longans. Do not include rockmelon (cantaloupe), which would be too strong-flavoured and drown out the rest.

China: *loong narn*
Sri Lanka: *mora*
Thailand: *lam-yai*

Loquat

(*Eriobotrya japonica*) These small, pear-shaped fruit, pale to golden-yellow in colour, are native to southern China and Japan. They grow in temperate climates and in the tropics prefer cooler elevations. The crisp, sweet-sour flesh is wonderfully refreshing, but most of the centre is taken up by large seeds which are quite beautiful, especially when the fruit is freshly opened, as they have a silvery sheen to them. The tree is very attractive, the large leaves having furry white undersides. When ripe the slightly velvety skin is easily peeled off the fruit. Eat fresh or poach in light sugar syrup. The canned version is quite acceptable and makes a good addition to oriental fruit salad.

Lotus

(*Nelumbo nucifera*) SEE ILLUSTRATION. This graceful flowering water plant, grown since ancient times, has a place of honour in the history of three great civilisations: Egypt, China and India. Images of the flower appear in the art of all three cultures and to this day it is a symbol of purity, perfection and beauty. On the culinary side, every part of the plant is used in cuisines of cultures as diverse as China, Japan and India. The beautiful, multi-petalled pink lotus flower, sacred to Hindus and Buddhists, is only half the story. The stamens of the flowers infused with water make a fragrant tea (India), while the seeds, off-white and crisp-textured, are removed from flower pods (that look like some life form from another planet), peeled of their downy skins and eaten raw, or dried and puffed like popcorn (India).

Fresh seeds, both mature and immature, can be eaten raw. Dried seeds, sometimes called 'lotus nuts' must be boiled until soft. Crystallised with sugar as part of Chinese New Year sweet offerings; cooked into a sweet soup; and made into sweetened lotus nut paste which is mostly sold in cans and used as a filling for Chinese moon cakes.

My husband, who grew up in Burma, waxes lyrical when he recalls school days, buying 'gamal-gatta' as the lotus seeds were called, tearing open the velvety green seed pod to find the nutty tasting, tender, creamy white seeds with a thin, pale green coat. As they mature they become crunchy, developing a bitter green core which must be removed.

In Thailand, young tender leaves are eaten with a savoury sauce and the petals can be dipped in nam prik. Dried mature leaves are softened first by soaking in boiling water, then drained and used to wrap sticky-rice parcels and other foods to be steamed. During the steaming process, they impart a delicate musty flavour.

Enfolding a chicken in lotus leaves, then encasing it in pond mud or clay before cooking it, is the famous Beggar's Chicken which has now become an esteemed restaurant dish, with various refinements such as filling the cavity of the chicken with soaked dried mushrooms, soy and wine. Dried lotus leaves are easily obtainable in Chinese food stores.

Apart from those parts which can be seen, beneath the surface of the lakes and ponds in which they grow are edible rhizomes. This grey-brown lotus 'root' is the part most often eaten. With swellings along its length, it resembles links of sweet potatoes, growing in strings up to a metre (3ft) long. Young specimens are peeled and eaten fresh in salads (Thailand). More mature roots are stir-fried, stuffed and deep fried or simmered in soup (China, Japan).

Chinese food features this starchy vegetable in savoury dishes where it not only adds bulk but also has the property of absorbing richness when cooked with fatty meats. Besides the subtle flavour and crunchy texture, in cross-section the root reveals a beautiful, lacy pattern. Appealing to the artistic Japanese chefs, lotus root often finds its way into bento boxes and nimono.

In India, the rhizome is boiled and mashed and included in some vegetarian kofta mixtures which are simmered in a spicy sauce. The rhizomes (usually labelled 'lotus root') may be bought sliced and frozen in plastic packets; canned, either in brine or in a sweet syrup; or among the dried goods, where they are sold sliced in packets. Occasionally one finds the fresh rhizome, even in Western countries. Canned lotus root is ready to use. Dried lotus root needs to be soaked for at least 20 minutes in hot water before cooking. The dried rhizome is also powdered into a fine-textured starch. See FLOURS & STARCHES.

Purchasing: If buying fresh rhizomes ensure there are no decayed spots or perforations.

Preparation: Wash thoroughly, and remove the thin skin by scraping. Since the rhizome discolours easily when cut, treat it as you would apple or pear — as soon as it is peeled and sliced, drop it into water which has been acidulated with lemon juice or citric acid. Slice off and discard the points between sections. The air spaces which run through the cylindrical shape are a decorative bonus.

Medicinal uses: If you manage to obtain fresh, tender lotus roots, peel the thin skin away, slice crossways and marinate in a dressing. They may be eaten raw and enjoyed for their crunchy texture which is said to cool the blood. After cooking for a couple of hours it is credited with stimulating the appetite. Stalks of flowers and leaves counter diarrhoea and the stamens of the lotus flowers are a diuretic.

These names refer to lotus root:

China: *ngau*
India: *kamal-kakri*

Indonesia: *teratai*
Japan: *renkon*
Malaysia: *seroja*
Philippines: *baino*
Sri Lanka: *nelun-ala*
Thailand: *bua-luang*

Beef with Lotus Root

Serves 2–3

375 g/12 oz fillet of beef
½ teaspoon chopped garlic
½ teaspoon salt
½ teaspoon sugar
½ teaspoon ginger juice
2 teaspoons soy sauce
3 tablespoons peanut oil
12 thin slices lotus root, fresh, frozen or canned
125 ml/4 fl oz/½ cup beef stock
2 teaspoons cornflour (cornstarch)

Cut beef into very thin slices. Crush garlic with salt and sugar to a smooth paste. Mix with ginger juice and soy sauce and mix well into the beef. Leave for 10 minutes.

Heat half the oil in a wok and when very hot add beef and toss over high heat until colour changes. Remove to a plate. Add remaining oil and stir-fry the lotus root for 2 minutes. Add stock and bring to the boil. Mix cornflour with a tablespoon of cold water and stir into sauce until it boils and thickens. Return beef and heat through. Serve with rice.

Lychee

(*Litchi chinensis*) SEE ILLUSTRATION. A luxuriously leafy, evergreen tree native to sub-tropical south-east China. The spherical, pinkish-red, thin-shelled fruit are about 4 cm (1½in) in diameter. Firm, translucent white flesh encloses an elongated, dark glossy seed. The smaller the seed, the more luscious flesh there is to enjoy. Easiest to peel starting at the stem end and the bumpy shell belies the smooth, tart flesh it conceals.

The flavour of a fresh lychee is sweet and clean with the slightest hint of acidity. The texture is juicy and springy. Canned lychees are an acceptable substitute when fresh lychees are not in season.

Dried lychees (incorrectly called 'lychee nuts')

are sold in boxes. When completely dry the skin, dull brown and more like a brittle shell, readily cracks open to reveal dark, chewy pulp shrunk to half its original volume, but offering a concentrated, sweet flavour.

Purchasing and storing: Look for fresh lychees during the summer months. The fruit grows on thin, twiggy stems in loose clusters and is ripe when the bumpy skin turns rosy. There should be no discoloured or damp spots. Store in a plastic bag in the refrigerator for a few days, but these are fragile fruits and should be enjoyed as fresh as possible.

Preparation: Simply peel and eat fresh. In China and Thailand, fresh lychees are often added to savoury dishes. Not cooked for long, they are added during the last few minutes.

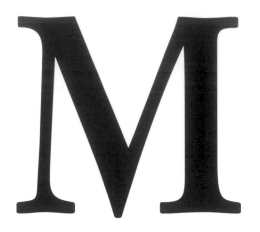

M

Macadamia

(*Macadamia ternifolia*, *M. integrifolia*) SEE ILLUSTRATION. Also named the Queensland nut, since it is native to the forests of coastal Queensland and New South Wales in Australia. One would never think so, since thanks to American business acumen, it has become almost synonymous with Hawaii. You don't have to go further than Honolulu airport to be surrounded by tins of macadamias, boxes of macadamias coated with chocolate, macadamias roasted, salted, sugared, vacuum packed, gift packed. Since their value as a food was recognised by settlers, they are being cultivated in southern United States, the Caribbean, South Africa, the Mediterranean and Hawaii, where it is a flourishing export industry.

Macadamia shells are notoriously hard to crack, the only drawback to the excellent packaging job nature has done. Although it is not traditionally used in Asian cuisine its oily texture makes it an acceptable substitute for the candle nut, not always in plentiful supply outside Malaysia and Indonesia.

In Australia, macadamia nuts are proudly added to cookies and ice cream and make crunchy, delicately flavoured fillings for sweet pastries. Toasted, lightly salted and chopped, macadamias are a tasty addition to salads, and macadamia oil is being hailed as a healthy, mono-unsaturated oil for salad dressings.

Mace

(*Myristica fragrans*) This is the vivid scarlet membrane (aril) that forms a lacy web over the seed of the nutmeg fruit. The fruit, which resembles a plump apricot, splits open when ripe to reveal a shiny, oval, dark brown, brittle-shelled seed draped with a brilliant vermilion, net-like mantle. Enclosed inside this seed is the ridged, brown oily kernel we know as nutmeg. The web of mace is removed for drying, whereupon its colour fades to a dull orange. Mace is a more expensive spice than nutmeg and has a separate, subtler flavour. Used in spice mixes in India, Sri Lanka, Indonesia and Malaysia, it flavours both savoury and sweet foods.

Medicinal uses: A few blades of mace are infused in boiling water for 10 minutes and the liquid sipped as a cure for nausea.

Maize

See CORN.

Makapuno

The name used in the Philippines for a freak type of coconut. Instead of water, the nut contains a soft, white jelly-like mass which is considered a delicacy. Makapuno is preserved in heavy sugar syrup, either as small balls or long shreds, and bottled in the Philippines for export. Often part of a halo-halo mix.

Malaysia

Malaysia is fortunate to be conspicuously devoid of equatorial calamities such as floods, monsoons, typhoons and active volcanoes. The country still enjoys all the earmarks of its tropical situation — lush greenery, dense jungle, cool highlands, fertile deltas, swampy mangroves and golden beaches. The natives of the peninsula, Orang Asli, comprise 20 tribes and today number less than 100,000. The ancestors of the majority of Malays came from Yunnan province of south China some 4,000 years ago. Traders arrived from the West, first Africa and then India, and their religion of Islam was practised by the 15th century sultan of Malacca, as the kingdom was known in those times. The predominantly Moslem population was to experience a shift (both in its religious persuasion and accompanying dietary habits) as the result of an influx of Chinese and Indian labourers brought in by the British in the 1900s.

In 1963, the Federation of Malaysia merged the Borneo states of Sabah and Sarawak with the peninsula. While the Chinese, Indians and Malays perpetuate their own culinary traditions, their presence has resulted in the emergence of a distinctly Malaysian cuisine. In this culinary arena shines a star player, a distinctive and innovative blend of Malay and Chinese called Nonya cuisine, the cooking of Straits-born Chinese (see NONYA).

Maldive Fish

A staple of Sri Lankan cooking. The abundant sea harvest of the Indian Ocean and the South China Sea yields much bonito (*Sarda orientalis*), also known as skipjack) which is processed on the Maldive Islands. This cured fish is the main source of income of the Maldivians. On a good night, given a large shoal of bonito, the fishermen, using simple bamboo poles, catch about 600–1,000 fish in two to three hours, an average of one a minute. The fish is cured by a complex process of boiling, smoking and sun-drying until it resembles bars of mahogany. Similar methods are used in Japan for drying bonito into katsuobushi.

Being dried until hard as timber enables the fish to be kept indefinitely without refrigeration, an important consideration in countries where only a privileged minority have access to refrigerators and freezers.

Purchasing and storing: In the old days Maldive fish used to be sold in the piece — a whole fillet as hard as a block of wood. It was pounded with a huge mortar and pestle (standard kitchen equipment) until it was in fine splinters. These days it is purchased in small plastic packets, already pounded or crushed. Maldive fish is used almost universally in Sri Lankan dishes, sometimes carrying the dish on its strong flavour, sometimes in such small quantities that the flavour is undetectable though it does add a certain indefinable character to the food. It is the Sri Lankan answer to the shrimp pastes and fish sauces of South East Asia. It keeps indefinitely stored in an airtight jar.

Most Sri Lankan dishes, especially vegetable curries, include Maldive fish which acts as a thickening, flavouring and protein component. There are also certain recipes in which it is the main ingredient.

Sri Lanka: *umbalakade*

Chilli Sambal

500 g/1 lb onions, finely sliced
250 ml/8 fl oz/1 cup oil
250 g/8 oz pounded Maldive fish
1 strip pandanus leaf
2 tablespoons finely chopped garlic
2 tablespoons finely chopped fresh ginger
60 g/2 oz dry red chillies, pounded
½ teaspoon ground cloves
1 teaspoon ground cardamom
1 teaspoon ground cinnamon
2 tablespoons lime juice
salt to taste

Fry onions in half the oil until golden and set aside. Heat remaining oil and fry the Maldive fish for a few minutes, stirring. Add pandanus leaf, garlic, ginger and chillies. Stir and fry until fragrant. Add ground spices and onions, cover and cook for 10 minutes, adding a little water if necessary. Stir in lime juice and salt and bootle when cool. Serve in small quantities as an accompaniment.

Maldive Fish Sambal with Onion and Chillies

This simple, uncooked sambal is basic to the food of Sri Lanka, where it is called lunu miris. It is served with rice cooked in coconut milk, boiled yams or breadfruit, steamed rice cakes (pittu), with bland grains such as boiled mung beans, or with rotis (see BREADS) and Hoppers (see PANCAKES). It is one of those preparations which needs a mortar and pestle to achieve the right consistency: an electric blender would require too much liquid to purée the ingredients.

60 g/2 oz dry red chillies
  or 3 tablespoons sambal ulek
15 g/½ oz pounded Maldive fish,
60 g/2 oz shallots or onions, peeled and chopped
lime juice
salt

Soak the chillies in water for 10 minutes, first removing their stems and seeds. Combine with Maldive fish and onions and pound with a mortar and pestle to a coarse paste. Add lime juice and salt to taste. Form into a patty and serve as an accompaniment to be taken in very small amounts.

Maltose

Also called malt sugar, this syrup, which has been produced in China since the second century BC, is the Chinese equivalent of corn syrup or liquid glucose. The raw ingredient is cereal starch which is converted to sugar by the process of malting.

The starch may be from wheat, rice, barley or other grains. The container in my pantry lists its contents as rice, malt and water. It is very thick, sticky and difficult to spoon out, so use a sturdy metal spoon.

Less sweet than sugar, it is traditionally used (diluted) to brush on the skin of Peking Duck before roasting. Also used to sweeten beverages, it is considered to have tonic properties. Available in tins or plastic tubs.

See recipes for Fried Sweet Walnuts (page 401) and Home Style Peking Duck (page 126).

Mandarin

(*Citrus reticulata*) Originating in China and Japan, these loose-skinned oranges came to Europe in the 19th century and took hold in the Mediterranean area.

The colloquial term for these easily-peeled fruit in Burma is 'loose jackets'. There are three distinct categories in the mandarin group: satsumas, tangerines and true mandarins. Then there are also crosses involving grapefruit and oranges. Any loose-skinned, easy-to-peel fruit, whether it has seeds or not, whether it is sweet or not, may be described in Asia as a mandarin. They are eaten out of hand or used in desserts. The loose skin lends itself to decoration, being cut into delicate points and one skin placed inside another to emulate a many-petalled flower.

Burma: *leing maw thee*
India: *nagpur suntra*
Indonesia: *jeruk keprak*
Japan: *satsuma, mikan*
Korea: *kyul*
Sri Lanka: *jamanarang*
Thailand: *som khiew wan*

Mandarin Peel

See TANGERINE PEEL.

Mango

(*Mangifera indica*) Although many of the fruits grown and distributed from tropical Asia came originally from tropical South America, the mango is a true native of India and Malaysia. Now grown in many countries. It is exported from central America, Mexico, Florida, Israel, South Africa and Australia. Selective breeding has produced fruit which are sweet and almost free of fibre.

This queen of tropical fruits, at its best, has bright orange flesh and a fragrance which carries through to a superb flavour. Many varieties of mango have a deservedly high reputation. But there are also some decidedly unroyal relatives with fibrous flesh and a distinctly turpentine flavour.

The thick, protective skin is sometimes green but often wears a blush. Fruit are carried singly on long stems and are usually prolific on high, spreading trees if conditions are right and it does not rain while the tree is in flower. There is one large, flat, fibre-coated seed.

Mangoes vary in size and shape from little round mangoes not much larger than a duck's egg to mangoes so large and rounded they are called 'coconut mangoes'. Some mangoes are long and slender and always green-skinned, even when fully ripe, sweet and orange-fleshed within. There are others which have the long slender shape and a brilliant blush even before they are ripe.

There are some mangoes which are referred to contemptuously as turpentine mangoes, because that is exactly what they smell and taste like. They are not usually sold in markets, so if you find a tree by the roadside laden with fruit that nobody seems to want, there is usually a good reason.

The alphonso mango is greatly prized in India. Large, with a thick skin, it has a sweet flesh that carries only a hint of the turpentine flavour.

There is a particular variety of mango which is small and fibrous. Not the most expensive variety, it is popular because the juice is sweet as honey, with a pervasive fragrance which fills the house. In Sri Lanka they are called dumpara. When these mangoes are in season, families sit down to enjoy a peculiar ritual. The fruit, washed well, are placed in a big bowl. One after another, those partaking in the mango fest choose a mango and start kneading and massaging the fruit. This must not be too vigorous, because the skin of this variety is thin and may split. When the whole mango is pliable and squashy, a small bite is taken from the skin of the mango away from the stem end. The sweet pulp is then sucked through this hole until it seems no more remains. Then the skin is torn away to reveal pulp still clinging to the fibres around the seed.

Purchasing and storing: Colour is not always the best indication of flavour and sweetness. A ripe, sweet mango can be green, yellow, orange, green with red blush, or an overall bronze or purplish hue. Be guided by fragrance. A yellow mango which has been picked while green and then forced to ripen may not have much fragrance or flavour.

If the mangoes are ripe, fragrant and yield to gentle pressure, they are ready to enjoy. A few black spots on a firm-skinned fruit are nothing to worry about. If the spots are soft and the skin pitted they are probably past their eating prime, but don't discount them for a mango purée. Mango purée is used for coulis, drinks, sorbets and kulfi ice cream (see recipe for Mango Kulfi, page 183).

Even when picked slightly under-ripe, mangoes ripen well at room temperature, though it may take up to a couple of weeks. Wrapping them in newspaper speeds the process.

Firm ripe mangoes may be stored for a day or two in the vegetable bin of a refrigerator, but should be left to reach room temperature before eating to allow maximum appreciation of flavour and sweetness.

Preparation: The sap of the mango, concentrated at the stem end, can be fiercely irritating to sensitive throats. Take the precaution of cutting a small slice off the stem end to remove the stem and about 8 mm (⅓ in) of surrounding skin and flesh before cutting the mango.

There are more ways than one to cut and eat a mango, but the most popular is to slice off the cheeks on either side of the flat seed. Score the flesh in each curved cheek, and it is easy to scoop out with a spoon in regular-sized pieces. For more informal eating, hold the scored slice in the hands and press upwards from the skin. Little cubes of mango pop up practically begging, 'eat me!' No spoon required, inevitably one ends up with mango juice all around one's mouth — but it's still most people's favourite way to eat a mango.

Serving suggestions: During the mango season in Asian countries (usually the hottest months of the year) mangoes are enjoyed au naturel or combined with other ingredients to make delicious sweets such as Mangoes with Sticky Rice (recipe page 230) or cooling drinks like mango lassi.

Half-ripe mangoes are invaluable for mango chutney because they hold their shape during cooking. Mangoes which are very immature also have their uses. They are cut into halves or quarters through the seed (which at this stage is tender), and made into the very popular Hot Mango Pickle (see recipe, page 230).

Mature but under-ripe mangoes are used in salads in Thailand, yam mamuang, and the tart fruit is eaten as a snack dipped in chilli powder, sugar and salt by children and adults alike wherever mangoes grow. People in hot, humid climates seem to have a need for pungent, salty tastes and in Burma unripe mangoes are peeled and sliced, dipped in a strong-smelling and salty fish sauce, ngan pya ye, and eaten as a snack.

In India green mangoes are dried and powdered to make amchur, a tart powder used in dishes where acidity is required. In particular, it is used for sprinkling over crisply roasted or fried lentil snacks. Amchur is used to add tartness without moisture. Substitute lime or lemon juice or tamarind pulp where the addition of a wet acid ingredient does not jeopardise the consistency of a dish.

In Thailand tender mango leaves are eaten raw, usually with a fiery nam prik or in salad.

Medicinal uses: The bark of the mango tree is used to treat dysentery, and dried leaves are used to treat diarrhoea. The dried flowers are infused and used as a diuretic. Mangoes are extremely rich in vitamin A, containing about 20 times as much as an orange of similar size.

India: *aam*
Indonesia: *mangga*
Malaysia: *mangga*
Sri Lanka: *amba*
Thailand: *mamuan*

Mangoes, Moghul Style

Serves 4–6

2–3 firm ripe mangoes
125 g/4 oz/½ cup white sugar
125 g/4 oz/½ cup water
3 green cardamom pods, bruised
   or few drops cardamom extract
1 tablespoon pistachio kernels

Cut a small slice from stem ends of mangoes and discard. With a sharp knife peel away the skin, then cut either side off the flat sides of the seed to give two thick slices. Two narrower slices are obtained by cutting the flesh away from the edge of the seed as well. Dice the mango.

Make a heavy syrup by boiling the sugar and water with the bruised cardamom pods for 10 minutes. Add diced mango and simmer gently for a further 10 minutes. Turn off heat and leave the mango in the syrup to cool. If using cardamom essence add a drop at a time, taking care not to overwhelm the flavour of mango with the cardamom. There should be just a suggestion. Meanwhile, blanch pistachio kernels in boiling water for 30 seconds, run cold water over them and slip off the skins. Drop the bright green nuts into the syrup. Serve chilled with either Rabri (see page 370) or pouring cream.

Thai Mango Salad

2 firm, half-ripe mangoes
½ teaspoon salt
125 g/4 oz pork fillet (tenderloin)
   or lean pork mince (ground)
1 tablespoon peanut oil
3 tablespoons shrimp floss*
1 tablespoon fish sauce
juice of 1 lime
1 teaspoon palm sugar or brown sugar
2 teaspoons fried garlic
2 tablespoons crisp fried shallots
2 tablespoons roasted peanuts, crushed
1 red chilli, finely sliced

With a sharp knife cut a small slice off stem ends of mangoes and discard. Peel the mangoes. Cut flesh either side of the seed into 2 or 3 slices, then cut the slices into julienne strips. Sprinkle with salt and toss gently.

Chop pork very finely or use lean pork mince instead. Heat the oil in a wok and stir-fry the pork until brown. Add shrimp floss, fish sauce, lime juice and sugar, mixing well. Add fried garlic and shallots, both of which may be purchased already fried. Otherwise heat 2 tablespoons oil and fry on low heat 2 teaspoons of dried garlic flakes. Lift out on a metal strainer before they brown, then drain on paper towels. Fry ½ cup thinly sliced shallots on moderately low heat in the same oil until golden brown. Drain and leave to become cool

and crisp. Toss with the pork mixture. Shortly before serving, combine the cooked mixture with the mangoes, toss lightly and serve sprinkled with peanuts and chilli slices. Serves 4 as a relish with rice and other dishes.

* Process 2 tablespoons dried shrimp in a food processor to obtain shrimp floss.

Mangoes with Sticky Rice

Serves 6

250 g/8 oz/1¼ cups white glutinous rice
250 ml/8 fl oz/1 cup canned coconut cream
pinch of salt
2 tablespoons white sugar
few drops pandan essence
   or strip fresh pandan leaf
2 or 3 ripe mangoes
extra thick coconut milk (optional)
2 tablespoons toasted sesame seeds (optional)

Wash the rice, place in a bowl with water to cover and soak overnight. Drain off water and put rice in a heatproof bowl. Stir in the coconut cream and salt, sugar and pandan essence or strip of pandan leaf. Place bowl on a trivet in a pressure cooker with 5 cm (2 in) water in the pan. Bring to pressure and cook at half pressure for 30 minutes. Alternatively, steam the rice over boiling water for 1 hour or until rice is very tender and all the coconut milk absorbed. Leave to cool to room temperature.

Use an ice-cream scoop to make balls of the rice. Or press spoonfuls of rice into lightly oiled moulds, then unmould with a sharp tap on a hard surface. Arrange on serving plates. Use a sharp stainless steel knife to remove and discard a small slice from stem end of mango. Peel the fruit, then cut slices and place them alongside the sticky rice. Serve at room temperature. A tablespoon of thick coconut milk may be poured over the rice and a few toasted sesame seeds sprinkled over.

Hot Mango Pickle

This is an oil pickle, made with mangoes so unripe the seeds are easy to cut through.

12 green mangoes
50 fresh chillies, green or ripe
coarse salt
750 ml/1½ pints/3 cups malt vinegar

2 teaspoons fenugreek seeds

25 garlic cloves, peeled

125 g/4 oz fresh ginger root, sliced

60 g/2 oz ground cumin

60 g/2 oz ground coriander

1.25 litres/2½ pints/5 cups mustard oil
    or other vegetable oil

2 tablespoons black mustard seeds

2 tablespoons fresh curry leaves

2 tablespoons fennel seeds

1 tablespoon nigella seeds

1 tablespoon ground turmeric

1 tablespoon chilli powder, or to taste

salt to taste

Wash and dry mangoes well. Cut each lengthways into 6 or 8 sections, through the seed. Split chillies in half lengthways. Sprinkle mangoes and chillies with salt, spread out on a large, flat basket and leave to dry for 3 days in the sun (or use a cool oven or dehydrator).

Soak fenugreek seeds in a little vinegar overnight, then combine with garlic, ginger, cumin and coriander in an electric blender. Blend to a smooth puree, adding just enough vinegar to facilitate blending.

Heat the oil in a non-aluminium pan. Add mustard seeds, curry leaves, fennel seeds and nigella seeds. When mustard seeds stop popping stir in the turmeric, chilli powder and blended mixture. Fry, stirring constantly, for 2–3 minutes. Add salted mangoes, chillies and remaining vinegar. Bring to the boil, reduce heat and simmer, uncovered for about 30 minutes or until the oil rises to the top and the spices smell fragrant. Add salt to taste, cool and bottle in sterile jars. There should be sufficient oil to cover the top of the pickle. Add more if necessary.

Cover with non-metallic lids and always use a dry spoon when taking pickle from the jar.

Note: Use 500 g (1 lb) dried mango instead of the fresh mangoes in this recipe and bypass the salting and drying process.

Mango Ginger

(*Curcuma mangga*) A member of the ginger family with a rhizome which smells of unripe mangoes. Young shoots and tender rhizomes are eaten raw in salads or cooked in coconut milk.

India: *manga injee*

Mangosteen

(*Garcinia mangostana*) SEE ILLUSTRATION. A small, slow-growing tree native to Malaysia which bears round fruit with four prominent sepals around the stem. The thick, dark purple shell protects small white segments which are thirst quenching, sweet with a hint of sourness, and delicious.

A curious fact about mangosteens is that if you look at the blossom end there is always a scar in the shape of a flower. You can predict with certainty that there will be the same number of segments in the mangosteen as there are petals on the 'flower'. There are usually 5, 7 or 9, fruit with even numbers being quite rare. One or two of the segments will be twice the size of the others, and these contain soft seeds.

What to do with mangosteens? I have heard of mangosteen sorbet, even mangosteen jam, but what luxury that the fruit should become so plentiful that one has to cast around for ways to use them. The undoubted best way of all is fresh and raw. They are sold canned in syrup, but please wait until you can taste a fresh mangosteen before forming an opinion as this fruit does not translate well to canning.

Purchasing and storing: Look for shiny, undamaged fruit of deep purple colour with no trace of the yellow latex which indicates bruising. Store at room temperature and eat within a few days. Don't attempt to freeze mangosteens, it completely destroys them. Just eat and enjoy!

Preparation: Opening a mangosteen is an acquired skill, the best way being to place it (stem upwards) between the palms, fingers clasped over the fruit, and exert gentle pressure until the shell cracks open. If serving them at the table it may be better to use a sharp knife and cut only through the shell around the middle of the fruit, leaving the segments whole. Never cut through the segments. Lift off the top and offer the fruit in its own reddish-purple half-shell, for best effect. Once the segments are taken from the shell they don't look quite as attractive.

Burma: *mingut thi*
Indonesia: *manggis*
Sri Lanka: *mangus, mangus kai*
Thailand: *mangkut*

Manioc

See CASSAVA.

Marron

An Australian freshwater crustacean resembling crayfish, rather larger than yabbies and smaller than crayfish or rock lobster. When fresh they are a beautiful blue colour, unfortunately as attractive to marauding birds as to gourmets. Farmed in Western Australia, the large holding and breeding tanks must be protected with nets if wild birds are not to eat into the profits. Cook briefly just until the shells turn red. They may be added to Asian salads, or simply eaten dipped in lightly salted coconut cream.

Marrow & Pumpkin

The family Cucurbitaceae embraces a large number of vegetables and sweet melons which have certain common characteristics: all enjoy a warm climate, all grow on vines and all have fruits which are watery and mild. The term 'melon' as applied to bitter gourd and winter melon is interchangeable with 'gourd' — both referring to hard-shelled fruit of the Cucurbitaceae family. Throughout history, man has put the gourd to good use. Scooped out and dried over a fire, the shell becomes a useful container for water, and many cultures have discovered their beauty as musical percussion instruments. Large melons are still a vehicle for intricate carvings and Asians make a delicious snack from roasted pumpkin and melon seeds as well as candied rind (wintermelon). See also GOURDS, SQUASH, ZUCCHINI.

Masala

Spice blends, either dry (powder) or wet (pastes). See SPICE BLENDS, CURRY PASTES.

Master Sauce

Also known as 'flavour pot' or lu, this sauce has a base of soy sauce, water, sugar and Chinese wine or sherry with a few variable additions which may include star anise, dried tangerine peel, cinnamon and fennel seeds. The sauce will colour as well as flavour any ingredient cooked in it and, while the sauce may not be quite as dark, salty or unctuous as a 'red' sauce, the method is similar to 'red-cooking'.

Meats done this way are usually blanched first to remove the scum, then slow cooked and allowed to cool in the sauce and brushed with sesame oil before serving. Strain left-over cooking sauce and store in refrigerator or freezer. With regular use (cooking in the sauce once a week and topping it up as it evaporates), the sauce will last indefinitely.

Matsutake

See MUSHROOMS & FUNGI.

Melegueta Pepper

See GRAINS OF PARADISE.

Melinjo Nut

(*Gnetum gnemon*) The small oval fruits of the gnemon tree, which are both red and green, contain a seed which is used to make tantalising, deep-fried crisps known as melinjo nut crackers. In Indonesia they are called emping melinjo or belinjo. They may be labelled 'melinjo wafers', 'dried bitter nuts' or 'bitter nut crackers'. Some brands list the ingredients as melinjo nuts and tapioca starch. Others simply state that they are melinjo nuts, and indeed they look like nuts which have been rolled out thinly. One source states: 'The fruit consists of little more than the skin and a hard pip. The whole fruit is boiled, dried and then flattened...' Another source says the seed is ground into flour, then pressed into a thin wafer and dried in the sun. Whatever the method, the crackers are parchment coloured, thin circles 2.5–3.5 cm (1– 1½ in) in diameter, with somewhat jagged edges.

Deep fry them in oil hot enough to puff them but not brown them. Only cook a few at a time.

Some varieties come with a coating of sugar which browns when the crackers are fried. The texture is not as light and crisp as unsugared melinjo wafers. Some are already fried, ready to eat. The plain wafers are best and most typical.

If stored airtight, dried melinjo wafers keep for extended periods. Once they are fried it is best to serve them right away. If they must be fried ahead of time, cool completely and store in an airtight container, then sprinkle with salt before serving. With their intriguing, slightly bitter flavour, they make a great nibble pre-dinner or anytime.

They are also used to garnish Indonesian dishes,

although they lose their crispness and charm if placed on hot food.

Melons, Sweet

(*Cucumis melo*) Grown since ancient times, these trailing vines yield fruit high in water and, despite their sweetness, quite low in calories. A popular finish to the meal, they are sold at roadside stalls (chilled and behind glass) as a thirst quenching snack. The main varieties are described below.

Honeydew melon: Sought after in Japan, their fragrance is mimicked by an internationally famous green liquor. Honeydew melon is also an ingredient in a popular Singaporean dessert which includes finely diced melon, coconut milk and sago. If honeydew melon is not available, use another green-fleshed melon such as galia or ogen.

Musk melon: Closely related to the cantaloupe or rockmelon. So highly prized were they by the wealthy in India that they were brought in from Samarkand. The Japanese also enjoy this fragrant and sweetly perfumed melon. It may be identified by the cream-coloured, ropey netting overlaying a skin shaded green to apricot, with or without vertical indentations marking it into segments. The orange flesh is sweetly succulent. Sometimes called netted melon or nutmeg melon, presumably because the netting resembles the lacy shroud of mace that veils the nutmeg seed.

Rockmelon: Also known as cantaloupe and musk melon. Although more common than the true musk melon, a good rockmelon can be ambrosial. When choosing a melon, look for one that is not bruised and is free of mould at the stem end. Hold the fruit to your nose and inhale. If it is sweetly perfumed, there is a good chance it will be sweet tasting. Unfortunately, with melons more than most other fruit, there are no guarantees. If you are unlucky enough to get one with little flavour, remove the seeds, peel off the skin and dice the flesh. Sprinkle with ¼ cup caster (superfine) sugar and, if liked, fine slices of glacé ginger. Allow to macerate at least an hour. Toss and serve, on its own or with ice cream.

Watermelon: (*Citrullus vulgaris, C. lanatus*) The largest of all the sweet melons, its fruit are round or oval with an all-over light green skin, or a pale green skin with dark green veining or stripes. Believed to have originated in Africa, it would appear to have been long cultivated in India, as there is a Sanskrit name for it. What better vehicle for talented Thai and Chinese artists who hollow it out and turn it into a decorative as well as functional centrepiece. The green skin contrasts vividly with the white rind and shows off to best effect their intricate carvings. The decorated vessel is then used to serve sweet soup or fruit.

Once picked, a watermelon will not get sweeter but will, in fact, begin to slowly deteriorate and its flesh become softer. Fresh, ripe watermelon flesh should be firm and a deep shade of pink and the mature seeds black or brown, though there are varieties bred with white seeds and some with yellow flesh (sometimes called champagne melons). Choose a melon with a matt skin, rather than a shiny one.

Wherever possible, buy whole fruit, especially when travelling.

Once cut, refrigerate and consume watermelon within a few days. Once the flesh takes on a red colour and a shiny look it is not worth eating, nor is it once it has absorbed refrigerator odours. The white rind of watermelon may be pickled or, like that of winter melon, candied.

Burma: *hpage thi*
China: *sai gwa*
India: *tarbuz, kalinger*
Indonesia: *semargka*
Malaysia: *semargka*
Sri Lanka: *pani komadu*

Milk

This staple of Western diets is not relied on in Asia, perhaps because most areas cannot support dairy herds and also because many Asian people have a lactose intolerance. The exception is India where milk and milk products take on great importance nutritionally, especially in vegetarian diets (about 85 per cent of India's population is vegetarian). Perhaps the most commonly used milk product is yoghurt, called dahi. It is present in almost every meal — either as an accompaniment, simply seasoned or mixed with vegetables. See YOGHURT.

Another form of milk is khoa — unsweetened condensed milk, made at home by cooking milk until the water content is almost totally evaporated. This is used in Indian sweets and needs only patience to make (see recipe page 234).

Millet

Malai is clotted cream, not separated cream. See CREAM for details on how to make it and what to substitute for it. Another concentrated milk product is rabri, a delicious dessert on its own or incorporated into another famous sweet, ras malai. For recipes, see SWEETMEATS, INDIAN.

See also GHEE.

Khoa

Pour 1.25 litres/2½ pints/5 cups milk into a large, heavy non-stick pan. The larger the pan, the more surface evaporation takes place, speeding the process. Bring milk to a full boil, stirring constantly, and keep stirring and boiling for 15 minutes, until the milk is like thickened cream. Reduce heat to moderate and continue cooling and stirring until the consistency of uncooked pastry. This quantity of milk yields about 220 g (7 oz) khoa and requires 30 minutes cooking.

Millet

Various kinds of millet are raised as grain crops in drier regions of India and Sri Lanka. Millet is called bajra in northern India and ragi in southern India and follows rice and wheat in importance as a food crop. The two main types are bulrush or pearl millet (*Pennisetum typhoideum*) and finger millet (*Eleusine coracana*).

Bulrush millet has a cylindrical ear resembling a bulrush. It is an important crop in the driest areas of India and Pakistan. In northern India millet flour is mixed with atta for breads, or hulled whole grains are cooked as a pilau. It provides vitamin B, iron, phosphorus and lecithin and is higher in protein than rice, oats and corn.

Finger millet, called kurakkan in the Sinhalese language, is carried on an erect sedge about 1 m (3 ft) in height. It bears its seeds on 5 spikes which radiate from a central point. It produces round, reddish grains. Commonly cultivated in Sri Lanka, India (especially in Mysore) and Malaysia, where it is called ragi.

The grain is considered a healthy addition to local diets and is purchased in the form of a reddish-brown flour which is mixed with rice flour to make Pittu (see recipe page 313).

Storing: With grains and flours which are not in everyday use, it is a good idea to store them in the refrigerator, especially during summer to prevent weevil infestation.

Purchasing: Indian grocers usually have a choice of hulled millet grains, millet meal, or a mixture of millet and atta flour. The Western health food store version of millet meal is usually a much coarser grind than that offered at Indian shops and will make a rougher, drier chapati.

> **Bengal:** *nacnhi*
> **India:** *ragi, nacher, kel-varagu, bajra*
> **Malaysia:** *ragi, nacher, kel-varagu*
> **Sri Lanka:** *kurakkan*

Millet Pilau

1 small onion, finely chopped
2 tablespoons ghee
3 green cardamom pods, bruised
1 small stick cinnamon
270 g/9 oz hulled millet
750 ml/1½ pints/3 cups water
1 teaspoon salt

In a saucepan, cook onion in ghee over medium heat until golden. Add cardamom pods and cinnamon stick and the millet and fry for 3 minutes, stirring. Add hot water and salt, stir while bringing to the boil, then cover pan tightly, turn heat very low and steam for 30 minutes. Serve instead of rice pilau.

Note: If liked, ¼ cup each finely diced carrots and fresh green peas may be added just before covering and steaming the grain.

Mint

(*Mentha piperita*) This popular herb of the Labiatae family has many varieties. Peppermint and spearmint are the two most widely used. They grow readily in most soils, and are indispensable to Asian cooking. They are used interchangeably with fresh coriander in cooked dishes, but probably the most popular accompaniment made with mint is one which is so simple that most Indian cooks make it without referring to a recipe. Called podina chatni, it is served as a dip with appetisers, an accompaniment with rice and a filling for savoury lentil pancakes. In Thailand, mint leaves are used in salads, as flavour accents with other ingredients as in the northern Thai dish called larb.

Medicinal uses: Peppermint is used as a stimulant, carminative and stomachic. Peppermint tea is used to treat nausea, flatulence, sickness and vomiting.

China: *yang po ho, paoh-ho*
India: *podina*
Indonesia: *janggat*
Japan: *hakuka*
Malaysia: *pohok*
Philippines: *yerba buena*
Sri Lanka: *meenchi*
Thailand: *bai saranae*
Vietnam: *rau huong lui*

Mirin

See WINES & SPIRITS.

Miso

See SOY BEAN PRODUCTS.

Mitsuba

(*Cryptotaenia japonica*) Also known as trefoil and honewort. Used in Japanese food, it is related to parsley and coriander and to my taste resembles both these in flavour, though some opinions tend more toward sorrel and celery. Look for it in Japanese stores (usually found in plastic bags in refrigerator sections) or more adventurous green-grocer shops. Mitsuba, as it is called in Japan, is added to soups, nabemono (simmered) dishes, salads and the delicate steamed custard called chawan mushi. It may be blanched briefly first, but is added at the last moment and never cooked long enough to lose its fresh fragrance. Its stalks are tied in a knot, dipped in batter and deep-fried for tempura.

Mizuna

(*Brassica rapa* var. *nipposinica*) As with Mitsuba, this pretty cut-leaf annual is known by its Japanese name, even in Western countries. The leaf stalks are white and succulent, the leaves only slightly mustardy. Use in salads or as a garnish on Japanese food.

Moghul Food

This is the legacy of the emperors who ruled India for two centuries and gave their names to some of the most splendid dishes. The influence of Persia was strong, since they considered Persia the epitome of elegance. It is still apparent in the architecture of palaces, temples, forts and tombs such as the Taj Mahal. It is also discernible in certain foods, especially those garnished with real silver and gold, perfumed with rose petals, or which include expensive ingredients such as saffron and pistachios.

See Festive Biriani (page 172), Koftas in Saffron Sauce (page 318) and Toast of the Shah (page 120).

Monosodium Glutamate

A flavour enhancing substance which occurs naturally in some foods such as mushrooms, tomatoes, kelp and soy sauce. It is also made from wheat or from glutamic acid recovered from sugar beet molasses. While it has very little taste of its own, when added to foods it acts as a catalyst to bring out other flavours by stimulating taste buds and increasing saliva in the mouth.

In Japan it is known as aji-no-moto, in China as ve-tsin, and in America it is sold as 'ac-cent'. Ten years ago it was impossible to buy stock cubes or packet soups which did not include it in the ingredients. It is not always mentioned by name, and often listed as 'flavour enhancer 621' or simply '621'.

In many Chinese and Japanese restaurants and also those with strong Chinese influence such as the Nonya cooking of Singapore, the addition of MSG, as it is familiarly called, is normal procedure. However, some people react badly to it. Ever since this was discovered, much has been made of MSG not being used. This seems only fair, since symptoms of 'Chinese restaurant syndrome', as it has been dubbed, can include chest pains, asthma attacks, loss of balance, flushing, headache, numbness, dizziness, heart palpitations and a raging thirst.

Baby food manufacturers were forced to omit MSG from their formulae on the grounds that it was suspected of causing brain damage in infants. Just in case someone you are cooking for is allergic to it, I would strongly recommend omitting it. With fresh ingredients and adequate seasoning, it is quite unnecessary.

Moon Cakes

The August Moon Festival (which may fall in September without altering the name) marks the Moon's birthday and is believed to be the only night of the year when the Moon appears perfectly round.

At the time of the Moon Festival, special moon-viewing parties are held with much wine and feasting, and poems composed to the moon. Moon cakes are generally packaged in boxes of four cakes, and are a traditional gift from one family to another.

The reason why moon cakes are so meaningful goes back to the 14th century when China was overrun by Mongol invaders who ruled the country in a cruel and oppressive fashion. The women of the households devised a clever way to organise an uprising. They inserted messages in the filling of the cakes given and received during the Moon Festival, conveying secret instructions to patriots who could be depended on to join in the struggle that ended in war and liberation.

Moon cakes are not easy to make, as special, elaborately carved wooden moulds have to be used to shape them. Most Westerners find the filling made from solid lotus seed paste unpalatable, especially with the salted egg yolk in its centre. If possible try to find mooncakes with a filling of preserved melon and melon seeds. For anyone with a sweet tooth this is irresistible, especially when cut into thin wedges and nibbled while drinking clear, perfumed tea.

It is the packaging of moon cakes that makes them tempting, usually square red and gold tins with Chinese characters and motifs printed on them, and containing four individually wrapped cakes. For the determined cook, the pastry should be very rich and preferably made with at least a proportion of lard. Some popular fillings are candied fruits or sweetened lotus seed paste.

Moth Bean

See LEGUMES & PULSES.

MSG

See MONOSODIUM GLUTAMATE.

Mulligatawny

A word which, in spite of its Indian origins, is now part of the English language. The direct translation from the Tamil (a language of southern India) is 'pepper water' (molagu meaning pepper and thanni meaning water).

The version so popular in Western countries is a hybrid between the rich, meaty soup suited to the tastes of the colonising British, and the spicy, thin, piquantly flavoured digestive soup of Indian cooks. This culinary mixture works brilliantly, enriched with coconut milk, flavoured with curry leaves and tamarind, and carrying the fragrance of many spices in its rich stock which may be based on meat or chicken.

The British served this soup with a mound of steamed white rice in the centre of the plate. I suggest omitting the rice if serving the soup as a first course, to be followed by other substantial dishes. On the other hand, if the soup is to be a one-dish meal, the addition of rice makes it more satisfying.

Mulligatawny

Serves 8–10

**1.5 kg/3 lb chicken backs or wings,
   or soup bones and gravy beef
   or neck of mutton
1 onion stuck with 4 whole cloves
3 cloves garlic, peeled and left whole
2 teaspoons whole black peppercorns
5 cardamom pods, bruised
2 tablespoons ground coriander
1 tablespoon ground cumin
2 teaspoons salt
1 tablespoon ghee or oil
1 onion, sliced very thinly
10 curry leaves
2 teaspoons Madras curry paste (recipe page 115)
400 ml/14 fl oz can coconut milk
lemon juice to taste**

Put chicken and/or meat into a large saucepan with plenty of cold water to cover and add the onion, garlic, peppercorns, cardamom pods, coriander, cumin and salt. Bring slowly to the boil, cover and simmer for 2½ hours. Cool to lukewarm, remove the bones and cut meat into small pieces and set aside. Strain stock. There should be about 6 cups.

Heat oil or ghee and fry the sliced onion, stirring, until evenly browned. Add curry leaves and if a strong curry flavour is desired, add the curry paste. Pour hot stock into pan and simmer for 5 minutes.

Stir in coconut milk diluted with enough water to make 3 cups. Add reserved meat and heat but do not boil. Season with salt to taste and stir in the lemon juice once the soup has been removed from the heat. Serve hot, with a mound of steamed rice in the centre of the plate for a one-dish meal.

Mung Bean

See LEGUMES & PULSES.

Mushrooms & Fungi

SEE ILLUSTRATIONS. When gathering wild fungi, take special care. Either go picking with an experienced, qualified guide or check with local authorities or accurately illustrated identification books. Unfortunately, there are some species which look very much alike and while one may taste delicious, a look-alike could make you very ill or dead.

Many kinds of edible fungi are used in Asian cooking. Those most widely used are black fungus and white fungus, both available in dried form. The advantage of having them on your pantry shelf is that they keep indefinitely and add texture and exotic interest to any dish you prepare. They are, in fact, a great standby for those times when it is too late to go shopping and you wonder what to cook that doesn't take too long and depends on dried and canned ingredients from your pantry.

Black fungus: (*Auricularia polytricha*) SEE ILLUSTRATION. Also known as cloud ear, tree ear, wood fungus, mouse ear, and jelly mushroom. It grows rapidly on a variety of woods including mango and kapok and is very similar to another fungus called Jew's ear (*A. auricula*). Some say the smaller cloud ear or mouse ear has a more delicate flavour than the larger wood ear.

It is mostly sold dried but is also available fresh. In its fresh form (or after the dried fungus has been reconstituted by soaking in water) it is easy to see how it derives its rather fanciful names. The frilly, brownish clumps of translucent tissue with a little imagination resemble the delicate curls of the human ear or billowing clouds. In the case of tiny mouse ear fungus, the rounded shapes which result when it is soaked are amusingly similar to those observed on the heads of Mickey Mouse and his Mouseketeers!

Wood fungus is prized in Chinese cuisine for its crunchy texture and therefore added to dishes only for the last few minutes of cooking. Delightful in salads, soups and stir-fries, it has no flavour of its own, but absorbs the seasonings it is cooked with.

Purchasing and storing: In its dried form there is a choice between the small variety which looks like flakes of greyish-black paper, or the larger variety which, even in its dried state, measures about 5–8 cm (2–3 in) across and is black on one side, grey or beige on the other. After soaking, these need to be sliced into strips. All dried fungi keep well if stored airtight.

Preparation: Fungus must be soaked in warm water prior to use (15 minutes for small, 30 minutes for large). It swells to many times its size. After soaking, the fungus is rinsed thoroughly and trimmed of the tough, gritty part where it was attached to the wood. Then, particularly if using the large variety, it is cut into pieces of a suitable size and shape before adding to a dish.

Medicinal uses: Black fungus has a reputation in Chinese herbal medicine for increasing the fluidity of the blood and improving circulation. It is given to patients who suffer from atherosclerosis. Western medicine is now investigating centuries-old claims made by Eastern sages and finding them surprisingly accurate.

Burma: *kyet neywet*
China: *mo-er, wun yee*
Indonesia: *kuping jamu*
Japan: *kikurage*
Malaysia: *kuping tikus, cendawan telinga kera*
Thailand: *hed hunu*

Braised Bean Curd, Cloud Ear and Vegetables

Serves 4

**30 g/1 oz dried black fungus
or 100 g fresh fungus
6 dried shiitake mushrooms
or 100 g fresh shiitake mushrooms
250 g/8 oz pressed bean curd
2 tablespoons peanut oil
1 teaspoon finely chopped garlic
1 teaspoon finely chopped fresh ginger
2 tablespoons light soy sauce
2 teaspoons sugar
250 g/8 oz sliced green beans
or asparagus
150 g/5 oz matchstick strips of carrot
1 teaspoon cornflour (cornstarch)
1 teaspoon sesame oil**

Soak dried fungus and dried mushrooms in separate bowls of hot water for 30 minutes. Save soaking water after squeezing excess water from mushrooms. Discard mushroom stems and cut caps into slices. Trim any tough gritty portions off cloud ear fungus and cut into bite-sized pieces. Cut bean curd into small dice, drop into a pan of boiling water and simmer for a few minutes until bean curd is heated through. Drain in a colander.

Heat a wok, pour in the oil and fry garlic and ginger for 30 seconds. Add mushrooms and stir-fry for a few minutes, then add soy sauce, sugar and 1 cup of the mushroom soaking liquid. Stir, cover and simmer for 10 minutes. Add prepared vegetables, cover and simmer a further 5 minutes. Add fungus and cook for a minute or two longer. Stir in cornflour mixed with a tablespoon of cold water. When sauce boils and thickens, add the sesame oil, toss through and serve at once with steamed rice.

Cepe: (*Boletus edulis*) Sometimes called edible boletus, these are king of the edible toadstools sold dried in Western delicatessens as funghi porcini. These fungi have tubes rather than gills on the underside of their caps. With an undersized gold to dark brown umbrella cap, this species is distinguished by its large, bulbous stalk, swollen at the base. Eaten blanched in Thai salads and in a northern Thai soup with acacia leaves and bamboo shoots.

Thailand: *hed tab tao*

Chanterelle: (*Cantharellus cibarius*) Easy to identify by their vivid deep yellow colour and funnel-shaped cap (sunken in the middle and wavy at the edges), this mushroom grows on rotting logs and mossy ground under leafy trees. What appear to be gills on the underside of the cap are actually forked ridges that extend down to the stem. The flesh is yellow and the fresh fungus smells of apricot, which helps differentiate it from the false chanterelle (*Hygrophoropsis aurantiacus*). Prized in Europe as well as Thailand.

Thailand: *hed man poo yai*

Enokitake: (*Flammulina velutipes*) SEE ILLUSTRATION. A dainty, slender-stemmed mushroom with a tiny white to pale gold, rounded cap. Traditionally used in Japan for soups or one-pot dishes. Now grown commercially, their wild habitat is the stumps of the Chinese hackberry (enoki) tree. Also a vegetable ingredient in China, where it may be referred to as 'golden needle mushroom' (not to be confused with golden needles, the dried buds of day lilies). Previously only available in cans and jars, more and more greengrocers and supermarkets are stocking them fresh as growing public awareness creates a demand.

The long, thin stalk, which is the main body of the mushroom, is crisp in texture. It has a yeasty or fruity flavour when fresh. This mushroom is prized for its texture and visual appeal. Trim the matted roots off the stalks (they will be tough and, occasionally, mouldy), rinse briefly and dry before using.

Japan: *enokitake, enokidake, enoki*

Matsutake: (*Armillaria edodes, A. matsutake, Tricholoma matsutake*) A seasonal delicacy in Japan, its appearance in September heralds the coming of autumn. The gathering of these fungi from the red pine forests around Osaka and Kyoto is a gastronomic as well as social ritual taken very seriously by its participants who carry sake, rice and cooking pots into the woods so they can savour the matsutake at their just-picked best. The choicest specimens are those which have not yet opened and have somewhat pointed caps. The stems of these mushrooms are long and thick. Matsutake are only available fresh, and Japan cannot even produce sufficient for its own requirements, relying on mushrooms grown in Kunming, a southern city in China's Yunnan province which shares borders with Burma, Laos and Vietnam.

Because these mushrooms can only be harvested in the red pine forests that are their natural habitat, they are difficult to obtain. Some exclusive Japanese restaurants have them flown in, packed in sawdust. If some do come your way, wipe the mushrooms clean with a damp paper towel and cook simply: grill, bake in foil or sauté briefly. Also considered a delicacy in Korea.

Nameko: (*Pholiota nameko*) A Japanese mushroom more often available canned or bottled due to limited cultivation and a short shelf-life. Some adventurous growers in Western countries have been selling them to the larger supermarket chains, but for most shoppers they are a bit of a mystery. Easily identifiable, they have a distinctive, slippery coating on their small, rounded, honey-coloured caps and long, thick, paler curved stems. Add to miso soups and simmered dishes or mix with daikon and season with vinegar, sugar and soy as a topping for the chilled tofu dish nameko-doufu.

Oyster mushroom: (*Pleurotus ostreatus*) SEE ILLUSTRATION. Also known as tree oyster mushroom and abalone mushroom, this white to grey to salmon pink coloured, fan-shaped fungus is claimed to taste faintly of the sea, hence its name. Some might argue that the name has more to do with appearance than taste or, perhaps, to suggest that they would be even nicer prepared with oyster sauce. Grown, like the shiitake mushroom, on dead trees. In my experience, pale salmon-pink oyster mushrooms don't keep as well as the common grey or white ones.

Thailand: *hed nang rom Bhutan*

Shiitake: (*Lentinus edodes*) SEE ILLUSTRATION. Also referred to as fragrant mushrooms, golden oak mushrooms and Chinese black mushrooms, these earthy-smelling fungi have gold to deep-brown caps with a slight bloom and creamy gills. Shiitake mushrooms are now available fresh in many places. However, because they are not well known, they may sit on the shelf a little longer than they should. Make sure they are plump and not shrivelled, sunken, pitted, mouldy, slimy or wet-looking. The stems of dried shiitake mushrooms are usually discarded or used to flavour stock because they are too tough to eat. Often fresh shiitake stems are quite edible. If your knife has difficulty cutting the stems, so will your teeth, so use that as an indication.

Dried shiitake, readily available from Asian stockists, vary in colour, size, quality and price. Mushrooms with thick black caps and deep white creases are most prized and are referred to as 'flower mushrooms' because of the patterned caps. Those with thin caps are called 'love letters'. Dried shiitake are preferred by most Asian cooks because their flavour is more pronounced than when fresh, the best specimens being cultivated solely for drying. They reconstitute well by soaking in hot water for 20 minutes or longer (up to an hour if you've purchased the thicker, more expensive grade). Squeeze gently to remove excess moisture, trim and discard stems, but save them and the soaking water to add to stock. Shiitake mushrooms are a vital flavour ingredient in siew mai and a multitude of other Chinese, Japanese and South East Asian dishes.

Burma: *hmo chauk*
China: *doong gwoo, leong goo*
Japan: *shiitake*
Malaysia: *cendawan*
Thailand: *hed hom*

Braised Soy Mushrooms

Serves 6–8

125 g/4 oz dried shiitake mushrooms
750 ml/1½ pints/3 cups hot water
2 tablespoons dark soy sauce
2 tablespoons sugar
1 tablespoon sesame oil
3 tablespoons peanut oil

Wash mushrooms well in cold water. Put in a bowl, pour hot water over and soak for 30 minutes. With a sharp knife, cut off stems. Squeeze water from caps, and reserve. To the reserved liquid, add some of the water in which the mushrooms were soaked, enough to make 2 cups. Add soy sauce, sugar, sesame oil and stir to dissolve sugar.

Heat peanut oil in a wok and fry mushrooms over a high heat, stirring and turning, pressing them against the wok with the frying spoon, until the undersides are browned. Add liquid mixture, reduce heat, cover and simmer for approximately 30 minutes or until all the liquid is absorbed and the mushrooms take on a shiny appearance. Stir occcasionally towards end of cooking time. Serve hot or cold. Store in refrigerator for up to a week.

Shimeji: (*Tricholoma conglobatum*) SEE ILLUSTRATION. Usually sold fresh, these small mushrooms have an appealing dimple in their concave cap as if someone has pushed down on that point to attach it to its stem. Light grey to fawn in colour, they are rarely more than 4 cm (1½ in) in diameter. A delicate texture and flavour.

Straw mushroom: (*Volvaria esculenta, Volvariella volvacea*) SEE ILLUSTRATION. Also known as 'paddy straw mushrooms' after their most common growing environment. They also grow on dried water hyacinth stems, dried legume leaves and chopped, dried banana stems. Cultivated in China, Taiwan, Hong Kong, Malaysia, Java, Thailand and the Philippines. Asia's most important fresh mushroom, they are very high in protein. Usually available canned or dried outside their country of origin, though sometimes found fresh.

Judging from the photograph in the excellent identification book by Christiane Jacquat, *Plants from the Markets of Thailand*, it would appear that in Thailand these mushrooms are allowed to mature beyond their familiar 'embryonic' stage, and are picked after they break through the volva (veil) that encapsulates them. Once they are open they tend to be tough, so if you are lucky enough to see them fresh, choose immature specimens.

Be very wary of picking and eating what you think may be straw mushrooms because the species amanita, of which many are poisonous and a few deadly, look similar.

Burma: *hmo*
China: *chao gwoo*
Japan: *nameko*
Malaysia: *cendawan jerami padi*
Thailand: *hed fang, hed bua, hed nun*

White fungus: (*Tremella fuciformis*) SEE ILLUSTRATION. In spite of its description it may more accurately be described as having an ivory colour. Closely related to black cloud ear fungus, it is sometimes sold dried and gift-boxed. Varying in size, the larger being more expensive, it resembles crinkled, pale-gold sea sponges. Slightly rarer than black fungus, hence the slightly higher price tag, white fungus is used in much the same way, except that it is also used in sweet soups.

To prepare dried white fungus for cooking, soak in warm water for up to half an hour and then trim off the thick, yellowish base. It needs longer soaking than black fungus because, instead of being flat, the frilly cluster forms a rounded shape like a natural sponge. Like black fungus, it absorbs the flavours it is cooked with. In its dried state, it will keep indefinitely in an airtight container. It has several aliases, among them white tree fungus, silver ear and silver fungus, as well as white wood ears and white jelly fungus. (Not to be confused with 'dried snow fungus', an ingredient in Chinese medicine derived from the dried reproductive glands of the Beijing snow frog.)

Medicinal uses: Regarded as beneficial for the complexion and during pregnancy.

China: *seet gnee*
Japan: *shiro kikurage*
Malaysia: *cendawan jelly puteh*

Asian Mushrooms with Asparagus

Serves 4–6

2 pieces dried white fungus
2 tablespoons dried small black fungus
   or 2 pieces dried large black fungus
12 dried shiitake mushrooms
250 g/8 oz fresh button mushrooms
   or oyster mushrooms
2 tablespoons peanut oil or light olive oil
2 cloves garlic, finely chopped
2 teaspoons grated fresh ginger
3 tablespoons Japanese soy sauce
1 teaspoon sugar
60 g/2 oz butter
250 g/8 oz fresh green asparagus
   cut in bite-sized lengths
1 teaspoon cornflour (cornstarch), optional

Soak the dried fungus and mushrooms in separate bowls of hot water for 20–30 minutes, depending on the thickness of the mushrooms. The thick, top-quality mushrooms require longer soaking than those with thin caps. Squeeze out and save mushroom soaking water, trim off stems and cut caps into halves or quarters. Rinse fungus and cut into bite-sized pieces, discarding any tough gritty bits. Thickly slice or halve the button mushrooms or oyster mushrooms.

Heat a wok, add oil and swirl to coat surface. Fry the shiitake mushrooms for a few minutes, then add garlic and ginger, stir-frying until golden. Add 2 cups of the mushroom soaking liquid mixed with soy sauce and sugar, cover and simmer for 20 minutes. Add all remaining fungus and fresh mushrooms, stir well, cover and simmer for 10 minutes. Stir in butter.

Add asparagus and toss over high heat. If liquid has reduced, add ½ cup hot water or mushroom water, cover and cook for 2 minutes or until asparagus is just tender. If liked, thicken sauce by stirring in 1 teaspoon cornflour mixed with a tablespoon of cold water until it boils and becomes clear. Serve at once.

Mussels

There are different varieties and sizes of mussels, but all of them should be live and tightly shut when purchased. Before cooking, they should be kept cool and damp. Soak in fresh water for 1 hour to encourage them to disgorge any sand. Use a stiff brush to remove moss and barnacles from the shells, and beard them (that is, firmly tug the small brown hairy tuft which protrudes from the shell, or cut it off with a sharp knife). They may be cooked in spicy broth, or steamed until they open and then turned into savoury finger foods or used in spicy curries. Discard mussels which do not open when cooked.

Thai Style Steamed Mussels

500 g/1 lb mussels
125 g/4 oz white fish fillets
125 g/4 oz raw prawns (shrimp)
½ teaspoon chopped garlic
½ teaspoon sugar
½ teaspoon ground black pepper
2 teaspoons finely chopped fresh coriander
¼ teaspoon finely grated kaffir lime rind
  or lemon rind
1 tablespoon finely chopped spring onions
  (scallions)
2 teaspoons fish sauce
2 teaspoons cornflour (cornstarch)
1 egg white

Scrub mussels and beard them as described above, discarding any which are not tightly closed. Steam in a pan with very little water until they open. Discard any that do not open. Remove the top shells and discard.

Finely chop the fish and prawns, either by hand or in a food processor. Crush the garlic with the sugar and combine with all the other ingredients. Mix into the fish, and cover each mussel with a teaspoon of the mixture, moulding it over the mussel. If liked, top each with a slice or two of red chilli. Steam over boiling water for 8–10 minutes or until the fish and prawn paste is cooked. Serve warm or at room temperature.

Spicy Clams or Mussels, Indian Style

Serves 4

1.5 kg/3 lb fresh clams or mussels
3 tablespoons oil
2 medium onions, finely chopped
1 tablespoon finely chopped garlic
1 tablespoon finely grated fresh ginger
3 fresh red chillies, finely chopped
1 tablespoon ground coriander
1 teaspoon ground turmeric
½ teaspoon salt or to taste
150 g/5 oz/2 cups grated fresh coconut
3 tablespoons freshly chopped coriander leaves
juice of 1 lime or lemon

If using mussels, they will probably need more attention than clams. Scrub the shells of any mossy patches, and pull the 'beard' off each mussel. Discard any that are not firmly closed.

Heat oil in a deep pan and on low heat fry the onion, garlic, ginger and chillies until onions are transparent, soft and starting to turn golden. Add coriander, turmeric and salt and stir for a minute or so, then add the clams or mussels and cover the pan with a well-fitting lid. Continue to cook on low heat for about 7 minutes or until they open. Shake the pan from time to time. Discard any that do not open.

Put all the clams or mussels as well as the spicy mixture and their juices into a deep bowl and sprinkle over the coconut, chopped coriander and lime juice. Start eating immediately.

Mustard

Black mustard seed (*Brassica nigra*) is hottest of all, while white mustard (*B. alba*), which is actually dull yellow, is least hot. *B. juncea*, an important oil crop which has brown or reddish-brown seeds, is the variety common in India.

The white variety is not generally used in Asia, with the exception of China, where a mustard similar to English mustard is served as a pungent dipping sauce with certain rich meats. The powder is mixed with sufficient cold water to form a thin paste and left for 1 hour to mellow and develop its pungency. It may be stored in the refrigerator for weeks.

The dark brown or black seeds, used in Indian

and Sri Lankan cooking, are fried in a small amount of oil until they sputter and turn grey, before other ingredients are added. The mustard flavours the oil and the seeds are rendered mild and nutty by the heat. They do not have the characteristic pungency of English mustard. This is because mustard contains an essential oil which is activated by an enzyme upon mixing with cold water. It develops its full strength after being allowed to stand for at least 10 minutes, preferably longer.

In Asia, black mustard is always soaked in vinegar before grinding, and vinegar inhibits the enzyme, so it is never as hot as when mixed with water, English style. Ground mustard seeds, used in Asian pickles, are mixed with grated fresh ginger, garlic and sugar to make a vehicle for lightly cooked, well-drained vegetables. This type of mustard pickle is popular in India, Malaysia and Sri Lanka.

Mustard is a vital component in the Indian blend of five whole spice seeds called panch phora (see recipe page 355).

There are a few recipes, mainly from eastern parts of India, in which mustard is used as the seasoning Western palates know. These are the vegetable stews labra (laphra) and shukta, and the bite of mustard is surprisingly pleasant combined with the natural sweetness of vegetables.

India: *rai, sarson, kimcea*
Indonesia: *biji sawi*
Malaysia: *biji sawi*
Sri Lanka: *abba*

Country Mustard

6 tablespoons black or brown mustard seeds
vinegar
3 cloves garlic (optional)
1 tablespoon chopped fresh ginger
sugar and salt to taste

In a non-metal bowl soak mustard seeds overnight in just enough vinegar to cover. Puree all ingredients in an electric blender, adding sugar and salt to taste. Store in a glass jar with non-metal lid.

Mustard Pickle

90 g/3 oz/½ cup mustard seed
750 ml/1½ pints/3 cups vinegar
2 teaspoons salt
1 teaspoon turmeric
6 cloves garlic
1 tablespoon chopped fresh ginger
1 tablespoon brown sugar
250 g/8 oz dates, stoned and cut in quarters
1 cup peeled shallots or small red onions
1 cup stringless green beans, sliced
1 cup small cauliflower sprigs
1 cup carrot strips
few fresh red or green chillies

Soak the mustard seeds overnight in just enough vinegar to cover. Bring remaining vinegar to boil with salt and turmeric in a non-aluminium saucepan. Briefly cook each of the vegetables (about 2 minutes after coming to the boil) and put into a non-metallic strainer to drain. Put a mixture of vegetables and sliced dates into clean, dry jars with non-metallic lids.

Blend mustard with vinegar remaining in pan and the garlic, ginger and sugar. Pour over vegetables and seal with cork or put a double thickness of greaseproof paper between a metal lid and the pickle. Store in refrigerator where it will keep for months.

Mixed Vegetable Stew with Mustard

A hearty vegetable stew featuring vegetables in season. Make a selection of 4 or 5 varieties and if any need longer cooking than the others, blanch them briefly in a little water first and use the cooking water for the liquid in this dish. Serve with rice. Serves 4.

1 tablespoon black or brown mustard seeds
250 ml/8 fl oz water or vegetable stock
2 tablespoons ghee or oil
2 green chillies, split
2 teaspoons chopped fresh ginger
1 teaspoon cumin seeds
½ teaspoon nigella seeds
¼ teaspoon fennel seeds
½ teaspoon turmeric
3 teaspoons ground coriander
1½ cups peeled and cubed firm yellow pumpkin
1½ cups green beans, cut in 5 cm/2 in lengths
1½ cups cauliflower sprigs

1 cup thinly sliced carrot
1 potato or sweet potato, peeled and diced
2 teaspoons salt
1 cassia leaf (tej pattar), optional
3 teaspoons brown sugar
good grinding of black pepper
3 tablespoons freshly chopped coriander leaves
lime wedges for serving

Soak the mustard seeds in the water for at least an hour, then grind in an electric blender. Alternatively, stir a tablespoon of prepared whole grain mustard into a cup of cold water.

Heat ghee or oil in a heavy pan or wok and fry the chillies, ginger, cumin, nigella and fennel seeds until they are fragrant. Stir in turmeric and ground coriander and fry for a few seconds, then add all the prepared vegetables and stir over low heat for 5 minutes. Pour in mustard blended with water. Add salt, cassia leaf and sugar, mix gently, cover and cook for 15 minutes or until vegetables are tender. If necessary, add a little more stock or water. Stir in pepper and sprinkle with chopped coriander leaves. Serve with steamed rice and wedges of lime for squeezing over.

Mustard Oil

See OILS.

Mutton

In Asia mutton can mean lamb or its more elderly counterpart, hogget (yearling sheep) or mutton; it can also mean the flesh of kids or goats. Goat meat is usually leaner than that of sheep or lambs.

This is not deliberate deception, it is simply that in India and among Indian populations in Malaysia, Fiji and Sri Lanka, it is considered quite legitimate to refer to meat from both sheep and goats as 'mutton'. The animals are closely related, their meat tastes similar and there is more likely to be a difference due to age rather than breed.

In some instances, the older meat is actually better as it stands up to long cooking. The following recipes may be used with lamb, but reduce cooking time so the meat doesn't fall to pieces.

See also LAMB.

Malaysian Mutton Curry (Gulai Kambing)

Serves 6

750 g/1½ lb mutton
4 tablespoons desiccated coconut
125 ml/4 fl oz/½ cup tamarind liquid
2 large onions, roughly chopped
1 tablespoon chopped garlic
1 tablespoon chopped fresh ginger
2 teaspoons ground coriander
1 teaspoon each ground cumin and turmeric
½ teaspoon each ground cinnamon, fennel,
   nutmeg and black pepper
¼ teaspoon each ground cloves and cardamom
4 candle nuts or macadamia nuts
4–8 dried large red chillies or to taste
1 stalk lemon grass
   or 1 teaspoon finely chopped lemon rind
2 tablespoons peanut oil
2 ripe tomatoes, chopped
300 ml/10 fl oz/1¼ cups coconut milk
1½ teaspoons salt

Cut mutton into small cubes. Brown the coconut in a dry frying pan, stirring constantly over medium-low heat for 4 or 5 minutes or until it is a rich golden brown colour. Turn onto a plate and set aside. Pour ½ cup very hot water over a walnut-sized piece of dried tamarind pulp and leave for 5 minutes. Squeeze the tamarind in the water to dissolve. Strain.

In the container of an electric blender put the tamarind liquid and onions and blend to a smooth, thick liquid. Add garlic and ginger and blend again. Add the spices, candle nuts, dried chillies and, last of all, the toasted coconut. Blend until smooth and well combined. If lemon rind is being used it can be blended too, but if lemon grass is available add it later on.

Heat the oil in a large saucepan and fry the blended mixture for 5 minutes, stirring frequently at the beginning and constantly at the end. Add meat and fry, stirring well so that each piece is coated with spices. Add tomato and fry for a further 4 minutes. Add coconut milk, salt and lemon grass and bring slowly to the boil. Reduce heat to very low and simmer, uncovered, until meat is tender, stirring now and then and adding extra water if necessary. This may take from 1½ to 2 hours. Serve with white rice.

Mutton with Onions

The Indian name of this dish, doh piaza, translates literally as 'two onions'. It has never quite been settled whether this means the onions are added in two forms, or at two different stages of cooking, or that the dish has twice as much onion as most other preparations of this type. Serves 8–10.

1.5 kg/3 lb shoulder of lamb or mutton
1 kg/2 lb onions
1 tablespoon chopped garlic
2 teaspoons finely grated fresh ginger
3 tablespoons yoghurt
1–2 teaspoons chilli powder or to taste
1 teaspoon paprika
3 tablespoons chopped fresh coriander leaves
2 tablespoons ground coriander
2 teaspoons nigella seeds
3 tablespoons ghee
3 tablespoons oil
8 cardamom pods
1 teaspoon garam masala (recipe page 354)

Cut meat into large cubes. Slice half the onions finely and chop the rest. Put the chopped onions into the container of an electric blender with garlic, ginger, yoghurt, chilli powder, paprika, coriander leaves, ground coriander and nigella seeds. Blend until smooth.

Heat ghee and oil in a large heavy pan and fry the sliced onions, stirring frequently, until evenly browned. Remove from pan. Add cubed meat to pan, not too many pieces at one time, and fry on high heat until browned on all sides. Remove each batch as it is browned and add more. When all the meat has been removed from pan, add a little more ghee or oil if necessary and fry the blended mixture over medium heat, stirring constantly until it is cooked and smells aromatic. Oil should appear around the edges of mixture. Return meat to pan, add cardamom pods, stir well, cover and cook on low heat until meat is almost tender. Stir occasionally. It might be necessary to add a little water, but usually the juices given out by the meat are sufficient. When meat is tender and liquid almost absorbed add garam masala and reserved fried onions, replace lid of pan and leave on very low heat for a further 15 minutes. Serve with rice or Indian breads.

Mutton Curry

Serves 6–8

1.5 kg/3 lb boned shoulder of mutton
2 tablespoons ghee or oil
2 large onions, chopped
1 tablespoon chopped garlic
1 tablespoon finely chopped fresh ginger
2 tablespoons Indian curry powder
  (recipe page 356)
3 teaspoons salt
2 tablespoons vinegar or lemon juice
3 large tomatoes, chopped
2 fresh chillies, split lengthways
2 tablespoons chopped fresh mint leaves
1 teaspoon garam masala (recipe page 354)
fresh coriander or mint leaves for garnish

Cut mutton into cubes. Heat ghee in a heavy pan and fry onion, garlic and ginger on low heat until soft and golden. Add curry powder, salt, and vinegar. Stir thoroughly. Add mutton and cook, stirring constantly, until mutton is coated with the spice mixture. Add tomato, chillies and mint. Cover and cook over low heat until mutton is tender, stirring occasionally. The tomatoes should provide enough liquid, but if necessary add a little hot water to prevent meat sticking to pan. Add garam masala and chopped coriander leaves for the last 5 minutes of cooking time.

Mutton, Kashmiri Style

Serves 6

1 kg/2 lb lean, boned lamb
125 ml/4 fl oz/½ cup yoghurt
2 tablespoons melted ghee
peppercorn-sized piece of asafoetida
  or ½ teaspoon asafoetida powder (optional)
2 teaspoons salt
1 teaspoon ground dried ginger
1 teaspoon chilli powder or to taste
1 tablespoon finely grated fresh ginger
2 teaspoons Kashmiri garam masala
  (recipe page 355)
2 tablespoons chopped fresh coriander leaves

Use a large, heavy-based saucepan for this recipe as a lightweight pan will not do. Trim excess fat from lamb and cut meat into large cubes. Combine the yoghurt, ghee, asafoetida dissolved in about a tablespoon of hot water, salt and dried ginger. Mix with the lamb in the heavy saucepan, cover and cook, stirring occasionally. The juices given out by the lamb will evaporate and the spice mixture will start to stick to base of pan. Add ½ cup hot water, the chilli powder and grated fresh ginger and stir well with a wooden spoon, scraping the dried mixture from base of pan. Continue to cook, covered until the liquid evaporates again and mixture sticks to pan. Add ½ cup more hot water and repeat first process. Do this until meat is very tender, adding no more than ½ cup water at a time. When liquid evaporates again, sprinkle with Kashmiri garam masala and fresh coriander. Replace lid and leave on very low heat for 10 minutes longer. Serve hot with rice, chapatis or parathas.

Naan

See BREADS.

Nam-Nam

(*Cynometra cauliflora*) Native of India and Malaysia, also found in Sri Lanka. This fruit is borne on a many-branched tree of the Leguminosae family. The fruit is a semi-circular pod with a wrinkled appearance, rough skin and green-yellow colour and grows straight out of the trunk, mostly at the base of the tree. It is refreshingly sweet-sour and when ripe can be very pleasant despite its unappealing appearance. In the unripe state nam-nam is a candidate for the pickle jar, or for stewing with sugar.

> **Malaysia:** *nam-nam*
> **Sri Lanka:** *nam-nam*
> **Thailand:** *amphawa, nam-nam,*
>   *naang aai, buuraanam, hee maa*

Nam Prik

There are many kinds of nam prik, best described as sauces or dips, though they can also be used as an accompaniment. Always pungent and hot, though the heat is usually balanced with a good deal of sweetness.

There are cooked and uncooked varieties of nam prik. The most popular cooked nam prik, nam prik pao, is sold in bottles: a hot, oily blend of chilli and shrimp — a delicious accompaniment to rice — sometimes referred to as chilli jam. See SAUCES.

Nashi

(*Pyrus pyrifolia*) Also known as Japanese pear, Korean pear, Asian pear and apple pear, this sweet, crisp-fleshed fruit is growing in popularity in Western countries. Round and roughly apple-sized, I have also seen them much larger, about the size of a grapefruit. The skin is thin and there are greenish-yellow varieties and bronze skinned varieties. One of the best is the nijisseiki, also known as 'Twentieth Century'. It is pale green. Of the bronze-skinned varieties, hosui and kosui are those grown in Australia and popular because of their sweet, full flavour.

Japanese and Koreans are the chief users of this fruit, and they are for the most part enjoyed raw, peeled and thinly sliced crossways in perfect circles.

In Korea, the fruit may be sliced thinly and floated on a bowl of cold noodles in clear soup for a favourite summer meal.

Purchasing and storing: When buying nashi ensure they are firm. They should not be bruised or have spots which feel spongy when touched. Nashi will keep well in the refrigerator provided they are in good condition.

Preparation: Wash, peel if preferred, slice thinly and add to fruit platters or salads for flavour and delightful crunch. Rub over with a cut lime or lemon, or drop into acidulated water to keep cut fruit from going brown.

They may also be poached like apples and pears, in light sugar syrup. A stick of cinnamon, a few cardamom pods, cloves, or a segment of star anise may be added to the syrup if liked.

Nata

Nata is a chewy, fruit-derived gel based on pineapple or coconut, made in the Philippines by a long and involved process. In the final stages the gel is removed from its host and boiled until transparent, then cut into small blocks and preserved in heavy syrup. It is sold in jars labelled 'nata de pina' or 'nata de coco', exported from the Philippines.

Natto

See SOY BEAN PRODUCTS.

New Zealand

Fresh produce from unpolluted waters and rolling green hills is the proud boast of the 'Land of the Long White Cloud'. Justly famous for its tender, sweet Canterbury lamb which is exported far and wide; kiwi fruit; farmed cervena (venison); whitebait; Tasman salmon; ocean trout; green lip mussels; and recently, from the South Island, black truffles.

There are also delights available only to those who seek them locally, and scarce even then. Lake trout which is never sold in a fish shop, but brings game fishermen from all over the world to obtain a licence to fish in the cold, clear streams and lakes during the season; toheroas (shellfish) may only be dug at the water's edge for a two-week period each year; bluff oysters for a short season of 6–8 weeks; tui-tui, clams, pippies and sea urchins; the delights and denials of seasonal availability are alive and well in these islands.

Probably the best known New Zealand dish is the disputed dessert Pavlova, named for the famous ballerina. Both Australia and New Zealand lay claim to it. Agreement will probably never be reached on who invented it, but it is agreed by those who have lived in both countries that there are essential differences. The Australian pavlova has more of the soft, marshmallowy centre; the New Zealand version has more of the crisp crust, being rather flatter. Both are topped with whipped cream. While the Australian version usually has a topping of passionfruit pulp, sliced strawberries, sliced bananas and peeled, sliced kiwi fruit, the New Zealand version is more austere, with only whipped cream and passionfruit pulp, and perhaps some kiwifruit slices. Controversy reigns! Under PASSIONFRUIT which is the predominant flavour, I have included a recipe you can adapt to either school of thought, and attribute to whichever country you wish.

Ngapi Nut

(*Pithecellobium lobatum*) The seed of the Jungle tree is called ngapi nut because its pungent smell is reminiscent of the fermented prawn (shrimp) paste which is known by that name in Burma. It is a round seed measuring about 2.5 cm (1 in) in diameter. Sold in Asian stores bottled in brine.

In Burma it is used brined or cooked. A relish is made by thinly slicing the nuts and combining with fried garlic, toasted sesame seeds and sesame oil. This tasty snack is sometimes served as an accompaniment to steamed rice, with chillies fried along with the garlic.

In Indonesia it is boiled or fried and used as a vegetable, but always in small quantities since large amounts of this pungent seed are said to be toxic. Emping (crackers) are made by pounding it flat, sun-drying, then deep frying in coconut oil.

Medicinal uses: The seeds are boiled and the liquid drunk as part of the treatment for diabetes.

Burma: *dhinyindi*
Indonesia: *jengkol*

Nigella

(*Nigella sativa*) SEE ILLUSTRATION. The small, peaked, jet-black *Nigella sativa* seed is hard to mistake for any other spice, yet there is considerable confusion because of the colloquial name given it in Hindi. In India it is known both as kalonji (which is the Hindi name for nigella), and kala zeera. Although 'kala zeera' translates as 'black cumin', there is another spice which more justly bears that name since it is a member of the botanical family to which cumin belongs. Nigella is sometimes wrongly called wild onion seed, black onion seed or, simply, onion seed.

Nigella is an essential ingredient in the Bengal mix of five whole spice seeds known as panch phora or panch puran (see recipe page 355). Added to cooking oil, the seeds impart a distinctive flavour.

Nigella is also used for sprinkling over the popular bread, naan, and in rice pilaus and some curries.

Nonya

Perhaps it should be spelled 'Nyonya', because that is the correct pronunciation, but 'Nonya' has become the accepted spelling. It is used in reference to a cuisine peculiar to Malaysia and Singapore, a unique style of cooking resulting, literally, from the marriage of Malay and Chinese gastronomy in the last century, with the influx of Chinese who settled in the Straits area (Penang, Malacca and Singapore) to trade and work. These men took Malay brides, and so was born a new style of eating, a blend of Malaysian spices and Chinese ingredients.

The women became known as 'Nonyas' and the men as 'Babas'. Collectively, they were referred to as 'Peranakan'. Unlike other Malays who, because they are Moslem, refuse to eat pork, Nonyas cook and eat it as enthusiastically as their Chinese forebears. Nonya recipes are hot and spicy, often based on a rempah (a paste of various spices including blacan, chilli, lemon grass, lengkuas (galangal), turmeric, shallots and candle nuts pounded together using a mortar and pestle).

The spicy coconut milk soup, laksa, is a Nonya specialty. A Nonya meal may comprise rice or noodles, sambal, curries, soup and vegetable dishes and is traditionally eaten on a dinner plate with the fingers at family meals, although Western cutlery is gaining popularity on more formal occasions.

See recipes for Chicken in Tamarind Gravy (page 373), Prawn Sambal (page 300) and Singapore Style Fish Cakes (page 151).

Noodles

With the advent of grain mills around the first century BC came noodles, and China has long been given credit for their invention. According to Reay Tannahill in her fascinating volume, *Food in History*, the common story that Marco Polo discovered noodles on his travels to China and brought the idea back to Italy may not be accurate at all. Depending on your interpretation of the account, what may actually have occurred is that Marco Polo found they also had noodles in China. There is no doubt that few foods are as widely enjoyed the world over.

There are a multitude of noodle varieties. Not only are there differences in shape, but flavour and texture, the result of different starch bases. Throughout Asia there are egg noodles and wheat noodles, closest in flavour and texture to pasta. Also common to many countries are the shiny, transparent bean thread noodles. Rice noodles are almost as widespread, used both dried and fresh.

Arrowroot noodles: A translucent, whitish noodle eaten in China for medicinal reasons. Arrowroot is believed to be an effective purgative and has been used by villagers in this way for centuries. Noodles used in soup or sweet dessert soup, they are primarily eaten by the lower classes.

Bean starch noodles: These are made from mung bean flour extruded either as thin vermicelli or flatter 'tagliatelli'-shaped noodles. They are tough and difficult to cut or break in their dried state, so unless using a large quantity, buy a brand that packages them as a number of individual bundles. Used in the cuisines of countries as diverse as Japan (harusame), Thailand (woon sen), Burma (kyazan), Vietnam (mien), China (bi fun, ning fun, sai fun, fun see), Malaysia (sohoon, tunghoon), Philippines (sotanghon) and Indonesia (sotanghoon), they are variously called cellophane noodles, glass noodles and, even more poetically, spring rain noodles (a literal translation of their Japanese name, harusame). They may be soaked before boiling, and after soaking they are easier to cut into shorter lengths with scissors. For deep frying do not soak. Drop small amounts into very hot oil. They will puff instantly. Remove immediately with a slotted spoon and drain on paper towels.

Buckwheat noodles: See Soba under **Japanese noodles.**

Devil's tongue noodles: Made from the starch of the devil's tongue or devil's taro (*Amorphophallus konjac*). Shirataki, as they are known, are a feature of the traditional Japanese dish, sukiyaki. The starch is also made into a greyish, speckled slab with a jellyish consistency called konnyaku. It is sold, not unlike bean curd, in tubs of water by Asian food suppliers. Added to braised dishes and soups, it is noted as a texture rather than a flavour ingredient.

Egg noodles: Like pasta, made from a paste of wheat flour, water and egg. They are extruded into shapes like fine vermicelli or flat ribbon noodles of varying widths. Most typically identified with Chinese cuisine (mien), they are also used in Japan (tamago somen), Philippines (miki), Vietnam (mi), Thailand (mee, ba mee), Malaysia and Singapore (hokkien mee), Indonesia (mee) and Burma (kyet oo kaukswe). Egg noodles are most often available dried, but fresh egg noodles, like fresh pasta, are a special treat. Do not overcook, remembering that, after boiling, the recipe may call for a further cooking step, e.g. stir-frying.

Hokkien noodles: A round, medium-thick yellow egg noodle. Available fresh in the refrigerator section of Asian grocery stores.

Japanese noodles: The most popular noodle (menrui) in Japan is, ironically, the Chinese style noodle, ramen. This is the instant noodle variety most often found in packets of Asian instant soup sold in supermarkets.

Worthy of mention is the fact that while all other Japanese food is expected to be consumed in silence, the eating of noodles should be accompanied by much slurping and smacking of lips if it is to be done correctly. One explanation is that the procedure helps cool the hot noodles, but since it is correct etiquette to eat cold noodles in identical manner, this does not seem too convincing an excuse. Yet another theory is that noodles, peasant in origin, have always been consumed in that manner by the lower classes. Whatever the origins of the tradition, it is a fact that even in the most prestigious establishments serving soba and udon, unless an appropriate level of noise accompanies the consumption of those foods, it is considered that adequate appreciation is not being shown.

Soba: A specialty of northern Japan, soba are slender noodles made from buckwheat flour: either unadulterated 'silk cut noodles' (tachi soba) or mixed in varying ratios with wheat flour. They are available both dried and frozen. There are few foods as refreshing or fortifying on a hot day as a bowl of cold soup and soba noodles.

The darkest, least refined milling is used to make yabu soba (dark, sweet noodles made from the whole buckwheat grain), while the whitest, most highly refined sarashina flour, from the kernel of the grain, is used to make gozen soba, or 'soba to be served before nobles'. This white flour is also required for flavoured soba, and a number of natural flavouring and colouring agents (green tea, yuzu rind, shiso leaves, black sesame seeds) are employed.

In Korea, buckwheat noodles are very popular and are called naeng myun. During the heat of the summer they are served chilled, in big bowls of clear soup.

As well as being a valuable source of dietary fibre, soba is high in protein, vitamins B1 and B2, vitamin P, rutin (a bioflavinoid for lowering blood pressure), calcium and iron.

Somen: Extremely thin noodles made from wheat. The variety which is made with egg yolk is known as tamago somen. Not much thicker than threads, somen are sometimes available fresh but, more commonly, dried.

Udon: Wheat noodles which may be round, square or flat, udon come in a wide variety of lengths and thicknesses and are usually available fresh in the refrigerators of Japanese ingredient stockists. One variety, hiyamugi, round and slender (though not quite as slender as somen), is served cold.

Rice noodles: These are available dried or fresh and in widths from the finest vermicelli to sheets of fresh dough. Fresh rice noodles are ready-cooked and need only to be swished through hot or boiling water to loosen them up, then drained before combining with other ingredients. Wide, ribbon-like fresh rice noodles make the traditional Malaysian dish char kway teow. Fresh rice noodles will not keep for very long. If not using on the day of purchase, refrigerate. This will make them go hard, but they revert to a soft state when heated.

Dried rice vermicelli or rice sticks come in a variety of thicknesses, from the flattened ribbons resembling fettucini, commonly used in Vietnam, to the thread-like rice sticks called bihoon (bihon) in the Philippines. Dried rice noodles are cooked in boiling water (1–2 minutes for vermicelli, longer for the flatter, thicker noodles). Product labelling can cause confusion. For example, 'rice sticks' made in Hong Kong can be thread-like, while 'rice sticks' made in Thailand can be flat and more than 6 mm (¼ in) wide. Use your discretion, and test a few strands at intervals, making sure they don't become soft and mushy.

Sweet potato noodles: Some of the most delicious and intriguing noodles I have tasted are the Korean specialty dang myun. They feature in chap chae, a dish served at festive meals and special occasions. An unexciting shade of grey in their dried state, they cook to beige transparency with a resilience that surpasses even bean starch noodles. Virtually tasteless, they are ideal for carrying the flavours of whatever they are cooked with. A word of caution. They possess a springy texture which requires thorough chewing. Not a food to be eaten in haste!

Chilled Buckwheat Noodles

In Japan, cold noodles are served with dipping sauce and seasonings. Serves 4.

300 g/10 oz buckwheat noodles
4 small fish cakes (chikuwa)
1 tablespoon finely grated ginger
3 spring onions (scallions), finely sliced

DIPPING SAUCE

500 ml/1 pint/2 cups dashi (recipe page 118)
4 tablespoons Japanese soy sauce
4 tablespoons mirin or sherry

Bring a large saucepan of water to the boil and add noodles. When water returns to the boil add 1 cup cold water. Bring to the boil again and cook until noodles are just tender, testing at 1-minute intervals. Stop cooking as soon as they are tender to the bite. Run cold water into the pan and drain in a large colander. Rinse under cold water two or three times, until they are completely cold. Drain well and put on 4 plates.

Dipping Sauce: To make the dipping sauce, bring ingredients to the boil in a small pan, allow to cool.

Cut fish cakes into thin slices and place on noodles. Combine ginger and spring onions. Pour some of the cooled sauce into small sauce dishes beside each serving, with some of the ginger and onion mixed in. Noodles are dipped into the sauce before eating.

Korean Cold Noodles in Soup

This recipe should be started a day ahead, as the soup has to be chilled in order to remove all traces of fat. It would be a good idea to make more than is immediately needed and freeze the stock for future use. Serves 4.

SOUP

500 g/1 lb shin beef or brisket in one piece
1 beef knuckle or soup bones (beef ribs)
30 g/1 oz fresh ginger, sliced
3 cloves garlic, peeled
4 spring onions (scallions)
2 tablespoons Korean soy sauce
20 whole black peppercorns
1 tablespoon vinegar

FOR SERVING

300 g/10 oz buckwheat noodles
2 hard-boiled eggs, halved
8 thin slices nashi fruit or firm pear
12 thin slices chilled cooked beef
thin slices of pickled white radish
hot mustard (optional)

Put all the soup ingredients into a large pan, add 3 litres (6 pints) water and bring quickly to the boil. Lower heat, partially cover with lid and simmer for 3 hours, skimming top frequently. Pour through a fine sieve and chill until surface fat is firm enough to remove. Taste and adjust seasoning. Chill the beef.

To serve: Cook buckwheat noodles as described in previous recipe. Arrange noodles in four large, deep bowls. Korean bowls are straight-sided and hold quite a lot of soup. Pour chilled soup over the cold noodles, and garnish with hard-boiled eggs, nashi or firm pear, sliced beef and pickled radish. Mustard may be offered as a relish.

Bean Thread Vermicelli Fried with Chicken (Burma)

Serves 6–8

500 g/1 lb bean thread vermicelli
500 g/1 lb chicken fillets,
    preferably drumstick or thigh
2 chicken livers
2 chicken gizzards
3 tablespoons peanut oil
4 medium onions, finely sliced
2 tablespoons garlic, sliced
3 tablespoons light soy sauce or fish sauce
quarter white cabbage, shredded
2 stalks celery, sliced
6 fresh shiitake mushrooms, sliced
    or 6 dried shiitake, mushrooms soaked
    for 30 minutes
6 spring onions (scallions), finely sliced
3 eggs, beaten and seasoned with pepper and
    salt

Boil bean thread vermicelli in lightly salted boiling water for 8–10 minutes or until just tender. Drain. Cut chicken meat into bite-sized pieces. Parboil chicken liver and gizzards, and when liver is firm and gizzard half-tender, slice them thinly.

Heat oil in a wok and fry onion and garlic

until soft. Add chicken, livers and gizzards and toss for 3 minutes. Add soy sauce, cover and simmer until chicken is tender. Add cabbage, celery, mushrooms and spring onions and toss until tender. Add vermicelli and heat through, taste and season with more soy sauce or fish sauce if preferred. Remove from wok. Add a little oil to the wok and cook the eggs, breaking them into pieces as they set. Place the noodles on a serving dish, and top with the eggs. Serve warm.

Burmese Egg Noodles with Curry (Panthe Kaukswe)

A favourite Burmese one-dish meal based on egg noodles. Known as ono kaukswe if it has a lot of coconut milk gravy, while panthe kaukswe features a spicier, drier curry. Serves 6.

1 × 1.5kg/3 lb roasting chicken
2 tablespoons chopped garlic
2 tablespoons chopped fresh ginger
2 large onions, chopped
2 teaspoons dried shrimp paste (ngapi)
3 tablespoons peanut oil
1 tablespoon oriental sesame oil
1 teaspoon ground turmeric
1–2 teaspoons chilli powder
2 teaspoons salt
500 ml/1 pint/2 cups thin coconut milk
500 ml/1 pint/2 cups thick coconut milk
2 tablespoons chick pea flour
500 g/1 lb egg noodles

Joint chicken and remove any excess fat. Cut joints into smaller pieces so flavours will penetrate. Purée garlic, ginger, onion and shrimp paste on high speed in an electric blender, adding a spoonful of peanut oil if necessary to facilitate blending.

Heat the remaining oils together in a large, heavy pan and fry blended ingredients, stirring, for 5 minutes. Add chicken and continue to fry, turning chicken pieces until they are no longer pink. Add turmeric, chilli powder, salt and thin coconut milk. Simmer until chicken is tender, adding a little hot water if it dries up.

Stir in thick coconut milk and stir constantly while it comes to simmering point. Mix chick pea flour with a little cold water, add to gravy and stir until it thickens.

Cook noodles in a large saucepan of lightly salted boiling water until done. Pour cold water into the pan to stop noodles cooking, drain in a colander and serve at once with curry and a selection of accompaniments. These are intended for each person to add according to taste and include fried garlic flakes, crisp fried shallots, crisp noodles, fried dried chillies, chilli powder, roasted chick pea powder, lemon wedges, chopped fresh coriander, finely sliced spring onions and fish sauce.

Fresh Rice Noodles, Fried

This is the famous char kway teow that hawker stalls in Malaysia and Singapore make for customers in minutes. Most of the ingredients may be bought ready to use. Serves 6–8.

1 kg/2 lb fresh rice noodles
250 g/8 oz barbecued pork
250 g/8 oz small prawns (shrimp)
2 lap cheong (Chinese sausage)
125 g/4 oz fresh bean sprouts
3 tablespoons oil
2 teaspoons finely chopped garlic
3 shallots, finely sliced
3–4 fresh red chillies, sliced
3 tablespoons soy sauce
1 tablespoon oyster sauce
2 eggs, beaten
4 spring onions (scallions), chopped
salt and pepper to taste

Pour boiling water over noodles to soften and separate them. Drain in a colander. Slice pork finely. Shell and devein prawns. Steam sausages for 5 minutes, and when plump and soft, cut into thin diagonal slices. Rinse bean sprouts and pick off tails.

Heat half the oil and fry garlic, shallots and chillies until soft. Add pork, prawns and sausage. Stir-fry for 2 minutes or until prawns change colour. Add bean sprouts and toss for 30 seconds. Turn mixture out of wok, heat remaining oil and stir-fry the noodles to heat through. Add soy sauce and oyster sauce and mix. Push noodles to side of wok, pour eggs and spring onions into the centre and stir till set. Return fried mixture and toss with the noodles. Season with salt and pepper. Serve hot.

Hokkien Noodles, Fried

A favourite Singapore Chinese recipe using fresh yellow Hokkien noodles. Serves 4.

500 g/1 lb fresh Hokkien noodles
250 g/8 oz fresh small prawns (shrimp)
250 g/8 oz roasted or boiled belly pork
250 g/8 oz bean sprouts
6 cloves garlic
3 shallots
2 tablespoons canned salted black beans
1 bunch garlic chives
3 tablespoons oil
2 stems Chinese celery (optional)
2 red chillies, sliced
4 tablespoons fried shallots for finishing

Run hot water over the noodles, leave for 2 minutes then drain in a colander. Shell prawns, reserving heads and shells to make stock. Devein the prawns and if large, cut in two. Cut pork into small, thin slices. Pinch straggly tails off bean sprouts.

Put unpeeled garlic cloves on a wooden board and smash them with the flat of a knife to split the skins. Lift off skins and bruise the garlic. Finely chop shallots. Mash salted beans. Cut garlic chives in short lengths. Chop celery finely.

Fry prawn heads and shells in 1 tablespoon oil on high heat, tossing until they turn red. Add 1 cup of water and bring to the boil. Cover pan, simmer for 5 minutes, then strain stock. Drop prawns into the simmering stock just until they change colour. Strain again, reserving stock.

Heat remaining 2 tablespoons oil in a wok and on gentle heat fry the garlic and shallots until golden. Add mashed salted beans and pork, celery and chives. Stir-fry for 1 minute. Add stock, prawns and bean sprouts and when boiling add the noodles and stir until heated through. Serve garnished with chillies and fried shallots.

Crisp Fried Rice Vermicelli

This is a dish usually known by its Thai name (mee grob or mee krob) and one by which many a Thai restaurant stands or falls. Done properly it is delightful, but for maximum enjoyment it should be eaten as soon as it is ready, on its own rather than as part of a menu. Serves 4–6.

250 g/8 oz rice vermicelli
185 g/6 oz chicken or pork fillet
250 g/8 oz raw prawns (shrimp)
1 cake yellow bean curd
3 tablespoons white sugar
3 tablespoons fish sauce
3 tablespoons white vinegar
750 ml/1½ pints/3 cups peanut oil for frying
3 eggs, beaten
2 whole heads pickled garlic, finely sliced
2 red chillies, sliced
small bunch fresh coriander, chopped

Dip vermicelli quickly in a bowl of cold water, shake off as much water as possible, and leave it near a window to dry for 30 minutes or more. While it is drying, prepare the other ingredients.

Finely chop the meat until it is almost minced (ground). Finely chop the prawns. Cut bean curd into small dice. Combine sugar, fish sauce and vinegar, stirring to dissolve the sugar.

Separate rice vermicelli into small handfuls. In a wok heat oil and when a haze rises from the surface, test the heat with a few strands of noodles. They should puff and swell immediately. If not, let the oil get a bit hotter, or the noodles will be tough instead of crisp. Have ready large sheets of paper towels to drain them on, as they increase greatly in volume. A large frying spoon also helps. Fry in small handfuls, and as soon as they puff and become white, scoop them out onto the paper. Continue until all are fried. Allow to cool completely. This may be done ahead of time, and the cold noodles stored in an airtight container or plastic bag for a few hours.

Drain oil into a heatproof bowl, but leave a couple of spoonfuls in the wok. Heat the oil again until very hot, and stir-fry the meat on high heat, tossing until it is no longer pink. Add prawns and fry a minute longer. Add bean curd and fry until hot. Add the vinegar, sugar and fish sauce and when mixture boils add the beaten eggs and stir constantly until the egg is set and firm and almost dry. Toss in the crisp noodles and quickly scoop together with the fried mixture. Sprinkle pickled garlic, chilli slices and chopped coriander leaves over and serve at once.

Mock-Stringhopper Pilau

Serves 8

500 g/1 lb rice vermicelli
60 g/2 oz ghee or butter
2 tablespoons oil
3 large onions, finely sliced
sprig of fresh curry leaves
½ teaspoon saffron strands
1 teaspoon ground turmeric
1½ teaspoons ground cardamom
1½ teaspoons salt or to taste
1 teaspoon freshly ground black pepper
4 eggs, hard-boiled peeled, quartered
90 g/3 oz raw cashews, fried until golden
1 cup cooked and drained peas

If rice vermicelli is very fine it may need only to have boiling water poured over to cover, and left to soak for 3 minutes or until a strand, bitten, is soft. Drain. Or cook in a large amount of lightly salted boiling water for 1 or 2 minutes only before draining.

In a large saucepan heat ghee and oil. Fry the sliced onions and the curry leaves, stirring now and then, until onion is deep golden. Meanwhile, toast saffron strands in a dry pan for less than a minute, turn onto a saucer and when cool and crisp, crush with the back of a spoon and dissolve in a tablespoon of hot water. Add saffron, turmeric, cardamom, salt and pepper to the onions and stir well. Add rice vermicelli and toss together with a metal spoon until the vermicelli is evenly coloured yellow. Taste and check seasoning.

Serve on a large dish, surround with quarters of hard-boiled egg and scatter cashews and peas over. Serve hot. Delicious with chicken or beef curry, or spicy roast chicken.

Korean Sweet Potato Noodles

These noodles are sold in quite large packets, each packet holding 3 hanks of noodles, each one held by a paper band. This makes it convenient to cook sufficient noodles for 6 people by using one of the hanks. This is a simple version of chap chae devised on the lines of the version served at a favourite Korean restaurant.

250 g/8 oz sweet potato starch noodles (dang myun)
2 medium carrots
1 red capsicum (bell pepper), sliced finely
1 leek or 6 spring onions (scallions), finely sliced
3 tablespoons peanut oil
3 teaspoons finely chopped garlic
250 g/8 oz lean rump or fillet, sliced paper-thin
2 tablespoons Korean chilli bean paste
3 tablespoons Korean or Japanese soy sauce
2 teaspoons oriental sesame oil

In a large pot of lightly salted, fast boiling water, cook the noodles allowing 7 or 8 minutes rather than the 5 or 6 recommended on the packet instructions. Drain in a colander, run cold water through and leave to drain again.

Shred the carrots very finely. Japanese graters do this without much effort. Have all the vegetables ready before starting to cook.

Heat oil and on low heat fry the garlic until soft. Add beef and stir-fry until colour changes. Add vegetables and stir-fry until half tender, then stir in the chilli bean paste, soy sauce and sesame oil and add the noodles, tossing until they are well combined with the rest. Taste and add more soy sauce if necessary. Serve hot.

Nutmeg

(*Myristica fragrans*) SEE ILLUSTRATION. The seed of the yellow nutmeg fruit, from which is also derived that other popular spice, mace. The nutmeg is encased in a shiny, brittle, dark brown shell around which the scarlet aril (mace) furls like a wisp of torn lace. The aril is removed and dries, fading to become the ochre blades of mace as we know it. The shell of the nutmeg is glossy when released from its fruit and fragrant oils are apparent in the dried and slightly shrivelled nutmeg seed. For superior flavour, grate nutmeg only as you need it.

Although nutmeg was known to Europe as long ago as the 12th century, it was not until the Portuguese discovery of the Spice Islands (Moluccas) that nutmeg came into general use, and abuse. Control of the spice became a licence to print money and the Dutch drove out the Portuguese after less than a hundred years of occupation. They themselves were ousted by the British, but not before a stranglehold of nearly two centuries on production and marketing of the spice. During the time of Dutch occupation, the production of nutmeg was restricted and they systematically destroyed all nutmeg trees growing anywhere but on the islands of Banda and Amboina. Their plans were thwarted by fruit pigeons who swallowed nutmeg seeds and dropped them on nearby islands.

The British introduced nutmeg trees to Penang and, later, Singapore. The largest producers of nutmeg are Indonesia, Grenada (in the West Indies) and Sri Lanka.

For those who thought nutmeg was a flavour restricted to the Western pastrycook's armoury of spices, it is interesting to note that it is one of the fragrant spices vital to spice blends across India (garam masala), and curries generally (Indonesia, Malaysia and India). Interestingly, although Sri Lanka is a major grower of the spice, it does not feature much in that cuisine, except in traditional Dutch sweets.

In Malaysia and Indonesia, the thick outer shell of the yellow fruit which looks rather like an apricot, is sliced finely, cooked and crystallised to make a fragrant candy called manisan pala. This is some-times served with cups of clear tea at the end of the meal.

Purchasing and storing: Buy whole nutmegs if possible. Nutmegs are almost round and about 3 cm (1¼ in) long and very slightly more in diameter.

Some nutmegs are sold still in their thin shells which must be cracked to reveal the fragrant kernel within. Stored in an airtight jar they will keep indefinitely, but once grated or crushed, the volatile oils and accompanying fragrance quickly dissipate.

Preparation: Grate finely, ideally just before use.

Medicinal uses: Nutmeg taken in very large doses is said to cause hallucinations or drowsiness. It is alleged to increase the intoxicating effects of alcohol, which perhaps would explain its presence in recipes for eggnog. There are also claims that it is an aphrodisiac. In Malaysia, nutmeg oil and nutmeg balm (important commercial products) are used externally for muscular aches and pains, sprains, bruises and insect bites. Internally (and the dose must be carefully regulated) they are useful for relieving flatulence, nausea and vomiting. They are also said to cure palpitation of the heart and prevent swooning. Self-treatment is not recommended. Nutmeg contains the hallucinogen myristicin.

Burma: *zalipho thi*
China: *tau kau*
India: *jaiphal*
Indonesia: *pala*
Malaysia: *buah pala*
Samoa: *atong-ula*
Sri Lanka: *sadikka*

Octopus

There are several species of octopus which inhabit the waters of the Indian and Pacific oceans. The domain of *Octopus aegina Gray* extends from the Red Sea to the western Pacific. This species is brown on its body and arms with a double row of suckers on the underside of each arm. A slightly inferior species, *Octopus macropus Risso* (even more widespread), is distinguished by single rows of suckers and longer, thinner arms. The Chinese call it sui gwai or 'water ghost'.

The major commercial octopus in the Asian market is *Cistopus indicus* which is brown or grey in colour and identifiable by an iridescent green on the underside of its mantle.

Purchasing and storing: Usually sold whole, so it is easy to judge size and state of freshness. Buy small octopus if possible, with firm flesh and no discernible smell except of the sea. Plan to use within a day or two, and store in a plastic bag in the refrigerator after cleaning.

Preparation: Tentacles and body sac are the edible parts. To prepare an octopus for eating, first remove beak, eyes and internal organs. With a sharp knife cut off head below the eyes. The 'beak' (which is the mouth) will be in the centre of the tentacles. Push upwards with finger placed underneath, remove and discard. If octopus is big,

tenderise by beating with a mallet, or hanging (tentacles down) overnight. Some fish vendors do the work for the customer by giving octopus a good going over in a cement mixer so it is already tenderised when purchased. Cut into pieces or leave whole if tiny. Slow cooking is needed, except in the case of baby octopus.

Octopus may be used in place of other seafood in recipes for curries, soups and salads. In curries they will receive the long slow cooking they need. For soups and salads they should be cleaned, put into cold, lightly salted water and brought slowly to the boil, simmering for 1 hour, then left to cool to room temperature in the liquid. The tentacles and body sac are then cut into bite-sized pieces and added to soup or salad. For barbecued octopus, pre-cooking is not necessary. Purchase small specimens which should be very tender, marinate in soy sauce with garlic and pepper or other flavours of choice. Cooking time should be very short, just until the flesh becomes opaque.

Offal

In much the same way as kidneys, liver, brains, sweetbreads, oxtail, tongue, trotters and tripe have found their way onto Western dinner tables, so an Asian meal might include intestines, stomachs, giblets, udders, bladders, lips, eyes and feet of beast, fowl or fish.

There are many tasty dishes made from parts of the animal that Western cooks would throw out and an equal number using the more traditional organ meats. For those without hangups, here are a few recipes.

Chicken Gizzard Curry

Some people are very partial to the firm, bouncy texture of this muscular second stomach where food is broken down. In some Asian countries, cooks have to skin and clean the gizzards before cooking as they generally come complete with grain. In Western countries all the work is done and they are purchased cleaned and ready to cook. They do require long cooking, so allow plenty of time to tenderise. If preferred, the gizzards can be parboiled first, then added to the spicy sauce for the second half of cooking.

500 g/1 lb chicken gizzards (giblets)
2 tablespoons oil or ghee
2 large onions, finely chopped
1 tablespoon finely chopped garlic
1 tablespoon finely chopped fresh ginger
1 tablespoon ground coriander
2 teaspoons ground cumin
1 teaspoon chilli powder
½ teaspoon ground turmeric
¼ teaspoon ground fenugreek (optional)
1 teaspoon salt or to taste
2 ripe tomatoes, chopped

Wash and clean gizzards. In a heavy-based saucepan heat the oil or ghee (or mixture of both) and on gentle heat fry the onions, garlic and ginger until soft, stirring occasionally. While they are cooking, dry-roast the coriander and cumin in a small pan, stirring constantly, until coffee-brown and fragrant. When onions are golden add the spices and cook, stirring, for 1 minute. Add salt, tomatoes and gizzards. Add boiling water to just cover, place lid on pan and simmer for 1 hour or until gizzards are tender. Serve with steamed rice.

Devilled Tongue

Serves 6

1 fresh ox tongue
1 teaspoon finely chopped garlic
1 teaspoon salt
1 teaspoon finely chopped fresh ginger
1 tablespoon vinegar
1 tablespoon Worcestershire sauce
1 tablespoon chilli sauce
2 tablespoons arrack or whisky
2 teaspoons prepared grain mustard
   or hot English mustard
2 teaspoons sugar
1 teaspoon freshly ground pepper
2 tablespoons ghee or oil
2 sprigs fresh curry leaves
about 10 cm/4 in pandan leaf
2 large onions, thickly sliced
1 stick cinnamon
5 whole cloves
500 ml/1 pint/2 cups chicken or beef stock

Put the ox tongue into a pan of salted water and parboil. Drain, run cold water over and leave until cool enough to handle. Remove skin and cut into thick slices or large cubes.

   Crush garlic with salt and mix with the ginger, vinegar, Worcestershire sauce, chilli sauce, arrack, mustard, sugar and pepper. Pour over the tongue, mix well and leave to marinate for at least 1 hour.

   In a heavy-based saucepan heat ghee or oil and fry curry leaves, pandan leaf and onions until onions are nicely browned. Add marinated tongue, whole spices and stock. Cover and simmer until tongue is very tender. Taste and adjust seasoning, adding some hot English mustard if you like it more devilish. Serve with boiled or fried potatoes.

Sliced Beans with Chicken Livers, Chinese Style

A simple dish where much depends on the thin slicing of both beans and chicken livers. There will be almost twice the volume of beans, and these proportions too are important to offset the richness of the livers. Serves 2–3.

150 g/5 oz fresh green beans
125 g/4 oz chicken livers
1 tablespoon oil
4 thin slices fresh ginger
1 large clove garlic, thinly sliced
2 tablespoons light soy sauce
½ teaspoon sugar
1 teaspoon sesame oil
125 ml/4 fl oz/½ cup stock or water
1 teaspoon cornflour (cornstarch)

Top and tail the beans and cut them in thin diagonal slices. They should measure about 2 cups in volume. Put the chicken livers in a small saucepan with just enough salted water to cover. Bring to the boil and simmer gently for 5 minutes. Cool for a few minutes, then drain and slice just as thinly as the beans — about 6 mm (¼ in).

   In a wok heat the oil and on low heat fry sliced ginger and garlic for a minute or so, then add beans and toss in the oil. Add soy sauce, sugar, sesame oil and stock. Cover and cook for about 4 minutes. Add sliced chicken livers, pushing them down into the liquid. Cover and simmer a further 2 or 3 minutes or until beans are tender but still crisp. Meanwhile, mix cornflour with a tablespoon of cold water. Push beans and liver slices to side of wok and stir cornflour mixture into the liquid until it boils and thickens. Serve with steamed rice.

Liver Curry

In the cuisines of Asia, it would be rare to find liver cooked pink. In this traditional curry it may seem the liver is overcooked, but the firm, small dice in their spicy gravy seem just right to serve with rice. Serves 4.

500 g/1 lb calf's liver
1 tablespoon ghee or oil
1 onion, finely chopped
2 teaspoons chopped garlic
1 teaspoon finely chopped ginger
10 whole black peppercorns
1 teaspoon salt
1 stem lemon grass
pinch of ground cloves, pepper and cinnamon
sprig of fresh curry leaves
2 tablespoons vinegar
250 ml/8 fl oz/1 cup coconut milk
1 tablespoon chopped fresh dill

Cook liver in lightly salted water until firm, about 15 minutes. When cool enough to handle, dice it very small. Heat ghee and fry onion, garlic and ginger until soft. Add all ingredients including liver and cook uncovered until gravy is thick.

Kidneys in Hot Sour Sauce (Szechwan Style)

250 g/8 oz pork kidneys
¾ teaspoon salt
1 tablespoon Chinese wine or dry sherry
2 teaspoons cornflour (cornstarch)
125 ml/4 fl oz/½ cup peanut oil
2 dried red chillies
1 teaspoon finely chopped fresh ginger
1 teaspoon finely chopped garlic
2 spring onions (scallions), finely chopped

SAUCE

2 tablespoons light soy sauce
2 tablespoons vinegar
1 tablespoon sugar
1 teaspoon ground Szechwan pepper
125 ml/4 fl oz/½ cup stock or water
2 teaspoons cornflour (cornstarch)

Cut kidneys in halves lengthwise and remove the central core and any fat. Turn them cut sides down on the board and with a sharp knife score the outside surface first one way and then another, holding the knife at a 45 degree angle. Cut into pieces along the natural divisions of the kidneys. Soak in salted water for 10 minutes, then drain and marinate in the salt, wine, cornflour and 2 teaspoons of the oil for 30 minutes. Combine sauce ingredients and have ready.

Heat oil and fry the dried chillies for 1 minute or until they turn black. Drain on paper towels and when cool and crisp break into small pieces. Deep fry the kidneys on high heat for 2 minutes. Lift out on a slotted spoon, pour off all but about a tablespoon of oil and stir-fry the ginger, garlic and spring onions for 30 seconds. Return kidney to the wok. Add the sauce mixture and crumble the dried chillies in, stirring until sauce boils and thickens. Serve with steamed rice.

Tripe Curry

750 g/1½ lb tripe, preferably honeycomb tripe
1 tablespoon coriander seeds
2 teaspoons cumin seeds
1–2 teaspoons chilli powder
½ teaspoon ground turmeric
½ teaspoon ground aromatic ginger
2 sprigs fresh curry leaves
** or 20 dried curry leaves**
1 strip pandan leaf
1 stem lemon grass, bruised
6 cardamom pods
3 whole cloves
1 small stick cinnamon
1 medium onion, finely chopped
2 teaspoons finely chopped garlic
2 teaspoons finely chopped ginger
1 teaspoon salt
400 ml/14 fl oz can coconut milk
lime juice to taste

Wash tripe and cut into 5 cm (2 in) squares. In a dry pan roast coriander seeds, shaking pan or stirring constantly, until they are fragrant and darker in colour. Turn out onto a plate and dry roast the cumin seeds in the same way. Pound using a mortar and pestle or grind to powder in an electric grinder. Put all ingredients (except half the coconut milk) into a large, heavy-based saucepan, adding 250 m/8 fl oz/1 cup water. Stir well, bring to the boil, cover and simmer until tripe is tender and gravy thick. Stir in reserved coconut milk and simmer uncovered for a few minutes longer. Serve with rice or pittu.

Oils

Oils are produced from a wide variety of seeds and nuts. Each has its own, distinctive flavour. Sometimes this is emphasised by heating. I find safflower and soy bean oils unsuitable for frying because, to my nose at least, they acquire a 'fishy' smell upon heating.

Another consideration which makes some oils more suitable than others, especially for frying, is the temperature they can be heated to before burning (e.g., the burning point for olive oil is 140°C/275°F, while for peanut oil it is 260°C/500°F).

Without doubt, there are certain oils which will never be appropriate for Asian food due to their distinctive taste. Hazelnut oil, walnut oil and extra virgin olive oil are all delicious in their own right, but have too distinctive a flavour.

Oils vary in health value (from mono-unsaturated and poly-unsaturated to highly saturated). In countries where coconuts are a major trading crop the air is heavy with the smell of copra from which coconut oil is pressed. The smell is not so obvious once the oil is refined but it remains a highly saturated oil, as is palm oil.

In the light of modern research and discoveries about the effects certain oils have on health and how beneficial some oils are, I have been doing some serious thinking about how to combine oils to provide a cooking medium that will not only do the average person no harm, but actually do a great deal of good.

My solution is to mix the flavoured oils which are required for some cuisines with pure olive oil to have the taste of one and the health benefits of the other. (Not extra virgin olive oil, but simply a good quality, moderately priced, pure olive oil.) It is hard to ignore the findings of food scientists that the fruit of the olive offers protection from heart disease, lowering levels of bad cholesterol while leaving the good cholesterol intact. In addition to that, it contains a number of antioxidants. The informed reader will recognise them as those components of food which prevent the effects of ageing and afford a degree of protection against disease.

While the thought of cooking Asian food in olive oil is totally unorthodox, in my kitchen I use either olive oil or a mixture of equal parts of unrefined peanut oil (mono-unsaturated) with olive oil. The resulting blend is most pleasant.

I use another blend if cooking northern Indian food. The flavour of ghee is essential to the dish so I use half ghee, half olive oil. In savoury dishes the flavour can hardly be detected. In a sweet dish, my solution is to use half ghee and half extra light olive oil or any other flavourless oil, such as grapeseed or canola oil.

Below is a summary of the oils most used for Asian cooking.

Coconut oil: This heavily saturated oil is liquid at tropical temperatures but below 20°C (70°F) is a white solid. Extracted from the dried flesh of mature coconuts (copra). Because of its high burning point, it is often used for deep frying. However, many people find it difficult to digest. It is a favoured cooking medium in southern India, Sri Lanka and the Philippines. Even preparing a Thai dish in which coconut milk needs to be cooked down to fry the curry paste, coconut oil will separate out. As coconuts are highly saturated, health conscious people would do better to substitute another oil, such as peanut oil.

Gingelly oil: Spelled this way on labels of bottles and in common usage in Indian cookbooks, though English dictionaries spell it 'gingili'. See **Sesame oil.**

Mustard oil: A pungent oil pressed from the seeds of the Indian mustard plant *Brassica juncea*, used both as a cooking medium and a hair beautifying treatment in India. Mustard oil, called sarson ka tel in India, has good preserving qualities, so is used for pickles as well as curries. The mustard oil produced in the West is generally milder than the pungent Indian version.

Palm oil: An oil pressed from the oil-rich pericarp of the palm fruit (the fibrous layer just under the skin). In its unrefined form it is orange-yellow and very high in carotene (vitamin A). Used more in Africa than Asia.

Palm kernel oil: Pressed from the kernel of the 'nut' or seed inside the palm fruit, this white or pale yellow oil is used for margarine making. Another oil from a vegetable source that contains saturated, mono-unsaturated and poly-unsaturated fatty acids. The first two predominate.

Peanut oil: The peanut oil used in Asia is not the highly refined, flavourless oil we get in the West but an unrefined version of the same thing, full of peanutty flavour. If this is too strong for your palate, try diluting it with a flavourless oil (grapeseed, maize, refined peanut, olive, sunflower). For deep frying, peanut oil is ideal as it may be taken to high temperatures without burning and absorbs very little taste or odour, making it suitable to strain and re-use. Good for stir-frying also. The flavour is especially appropriate for Chinese, Japanese and Korean cooking, usually flavoured with a small proportion of oriental sesame oil.

Perilla oil: A golden oil used mostly in Korea and, from what I can tell, more in a medicinal than gastronomic capacity. A strong-flavoured oil, it is pressed from perilla seeds.

Sesame oil: Also known as gingelly oil and til oil. Sesame oil is a very ancient ingredient. The Assyrians, more than 600 years BC, used it as a vegetable oil. It was expensive, however, and a hundred years later it is recorded as being used only by the rich as food, ointment and medicine during the reign of King Cyrus of Persia (559–529 BC).

Still used as a medicine in India, oil pressed from the raw seed is used as a massage oil in Ayurvedic medicine.

In Burma and some parts of India, sesame oil has long been the universal cooking medium and is what gives the typical flavour to foods of those regions, although fairly tasteless in itself. It may be a clear or golden colour compared to the darker, more aromatic oriental sesame oil used in China, Japan and Korea, which is pressed from toasted sesame seeds.

If gingelly oil or til oil is unavailable, use the cold-pressed sesame oil from health food shops mixed with 20 per cent oriental (toasted) sesame oil or use one part oriental sesame oil to 3 parts other flavourless vegetable oil such as corn oil, grapeseed oil or light olive oil. This is a reasonable substitute for the til oil or gingelly oil called for in recipes from India and Burma.

Oriental sesame oil derives its dark amber colour and nutty flavour from hulled sesame seeds, toasted prior to pressing. It is used in Chinese and Korean cuisine, not as a cooking medium but generally added at the end of cooking in small quantities as a flavour highlight.

There are quite dramatic colour variations in sesame oil, depending on its source. Cold-pressed sesame oil is almost colourless; sesame oil from an Indian store (probably labelled gingelly or til oil) is golden; and sesame oil from a Chinese shop is dark, almost red-brown. Cold pressed sesame oil, however healthy, has none of the flavour of oriental sesame oil since it is pressed from raw, not roasted seeds, and will therefore not produce an authentic result if used in an Asian recipe.

Dark sesame oil, one of the intriguing flavours of the orient, is the one to use when a recipe from China, Japan or Korea calls for sesame oil. Oriental sesame oil is popular in Japan as a flavouring oil for tempura (deep frying) blended with peanut, rapeseed (canola) or soybean oil in a ratio which varies according to personal taste.

Burma: *hnan zi*
China: *ma yau*
India: *gingelly, til ka tel*
Japan: *goma abura*
Korea: *chan keh room*
Malaysia: *minyak bijan*
Sri Lanka: *thala thel*
Vietnam: *dau me*

Okara

See SOY BEAN PRODUCTS.

Okra

(*Hibiscus esculentus*) SEE ILLUSTRATION. One of those vegetables which people either love or hate. The slender, tapering pods are mostly emerald green, although there is a pink variety. They are 7–20 cm (3–8 in) long, contain small, round white seeds, have a slightly furry exterior and distinctive ridges which run from stalk to the tip.

The main characteristic of this vegetable, a native of Africa, is its mucilaginous quality. It is used in the gumbos of Creole cooking in the United States, and also in Caribbean cooking. Okra is also used in Asian countries, particularly India where it is stuffed with spices and deep fried; pickled in spices and oil; curried with coconut milk, much as any other vegetable; and stir-fried in a dry style of dish. In Sri Lanka it is also used as a salad, lightly boiled and topped with finely sliced shallots and a vinegar-pepper dressing.

Purchasing and storing: Avoid okra which are thick and on the large side, with prominent seeds showing under the skin. They will be fibrous, stringy and almost inedible. Choose smaller pods which are no thicker in the middle than at the stem end. Bend the tip of the pod. If it snaps off about a centimetre (⅓ in) from the tip, it indicates tenderness. Keeps for a few days in a plastic bag in the refrigerator.

Preparation: Most recipes call for the pods to be simply washed and used whole, if they are small enough. Larger pods are cut crossways into bite-sized rounds.

Medicinal uses: Okra, simply boiled in salted water, is eaten as a cure for heartburn, in particular the heartburn of late pregnancy.

India: *bhindi, bamia*
Indonesia: *okra*
Japan: *okura*
Malaysia: *bendi*
Philippines: *okra*
Sri Lanka: *bandakka*
Thailand: *krachiap*

Spicy Stir-Fried Okra (Bhindi Bhaji)

500 g/1 lb okra
2 tablespoons ghee or oil
1 teaspoon panch phora (recipe page 355)
2 medium onions, finely chopped
2 teaspoons ground coriander
1 teaspoon ground cumin
½ teaspoon ground turmeric
½ teaspoon chilli powder or to taste
½ teaspoon salt or to taste
½ teaspoon garam masala (recipe page 354)
1 tablespoon lime or lemon juice
   or 1 teaspoon amchur (dried green mango
   powder)

Wash okra, discard stem ends and slice across into bite-sized chunks. Heat ghee or oil and fry the panch phora until mustard seeds pop. Add onion and fry, stirring, until onion is soft and starting to colour. Add coriander, cumin, turmeric, chilli and salt. Add okra, toss with the spices, cover and cook on low heat, stirring now and then, until okra is tender but still crisp. Sprinkle with garam masala and lime juice or amchur and serve with chapatis or rice.

Olive Nut

(*Canarium album*) Kernel of a fruit called white Chinese olive. The olive nut is delicately flavoured, flaky-textured and cream in colour. Although sometimes known as pine kernels, the olive nut is a distinctly different nut, with a flattened, tapering oval shape. It is about the size of pumpkin seed and composed of spiral-wrapped layers. An expensive nut, it is to be expected that stocks don't move very fast, so make sure they do not have a dark colour or oily appearance because that would indicate staleness and a rancid flavour.

If cooking olive nuts, do not have the oil very hot because the fragile nuts would burn in seconds. Fry briefly over medium-low heat, lift out of the oil onto paper towels, and scatter over the dish just before serving. The traditional garnish for the popular Chinese dish 'fried milk'. Pine nuts can be used as a substitute.

China: *Larm yin*

Onion

The genus Allium includes several varieties of onion as well as chives, spring onions (scallions), leeks, shallots and garlic. The smaller members of the family have a more distinctive flavour and pungency. Often classified as belonging to either the daffodil (Amaryllidaceae) or lily (Liliaceae) family, onions are bulbs of multi-layered, crisp, odoriferous flesh.

The cuisine of almost every Asian country revolves around the onion and its cousins. The main exceptions are Japanese cuisine (whose only concession may be the odd slender leek or spring onion[scallion]); Kashmiri Brahmans (for whom garlic and onion belong to the category of forbidden, strong-flavoured foods) and India's Vaishnava (Hindu) vegetarian cuisine, arguably the most ancient of all the world's cuisines still in practice. In certain cuisines the pungent bulb and related plants, especially garlic, are forbidden because of their strong flavour and a belief that they inflame the baser emotions. Kashmiri Brahmans eschew onions for this reason, as do some Chinese Buddhists.

My instinct was that food prepared without these 'essential' ingredients could never measure up in flavour, but on trying some recipes, I found Vaishnava cookery exceptionally tasty. Any disbelievers should seek out Yamuna Devi's excellent book, *The Art of Indian Vegetarian Cooking*, and try a few recipes to prove the point.

The onion is basic to curries in which it gives flavour and cooks down to thicken the spicy gravy.

Large white, brown and purple onions are used in Asian cooking but for the most part small red onions (*Allium cepa*) or purple shallots (*A. ascalonicum*) are preferred by local cooks. The former grow singly and are round in shape, while the latter grow in clusters like garlic, but without the several layers of thin skin which bind garlic cloves into a compact head. They are pointed and curved like cloves of garlic, requiring more time to peel and slice than a single large onion, but their distinctive flavour means that not so many are needed. See SHALLOT.

On the Hawaiian island of Maui grows an onion said to be so sweet, mild and juicy it can be eaten like an apple. Apparently this is a hybrid which, when grown in the soil and weather conditions prevailing on Maui, results in an unusually sweet onion. Pale in colour and rather flat in shape, it does not keep well as the moisture content is high. Good in salads and sandwiches.

See also CHIVES, CHINESE; GARLIC; LEEK; SHALLOT; SPRING ONION.

China: *tsung-tau*
Japan: *tama-negi*
India: *piaz*
Indonesia: *bawang Bombay*
Malaysia: *bawang besar*
Philippines: *sibuyas*
Thailand: *hom yao*
Sri Lanka: *rata lunu*

Oyster

Two types of oysters are found in Asia, one a very large type (*Crassostrea* sp.) which is cooked, sundried or used in making oyster sauce. The smaller variety, *Saccostrea cucullata*, are eaten raw with just a squeeze of lime juice, or added to certain dishes such as Singapore's famous oyster omelette, and the hawker specialty of any South East Asian country, deep-fried oysters.

Penang Oyster Omelette

A favourite hawker food on the streets of Malaysia and Singapore, usually made to serve 2–3 people.

3 tablespoons rice flour or cornflour (cornstarch)
300 ml/10 fl oz cold water
4 tablespoons oil
3 large eggs, beaten
salt and pepper to taste
250 ml/8 fl oz/1 cup raw oysters, preferably small
2 teaspoons oyster sauce
1 fresh red chilli, sliced
2 tablespoons chopped fresh spring onions (scallions)
2 tablespoons chopped fresh coriander

Mix cornflour and water together. Heat a large, flat frying pan and add half the oil, swirling to coat base of pan. Pour in the flour and water and cook until browned on bottom. Pour in the eggs seasoned with salt and pepper. When set, turn and brown other side, adding remaining oil gradually as required. When omelette is golden on both sides, use a wok chan or other frying spatula to cut roughly into pieces. Add the oysters mixed with the oyster sauce and stir-fry for only 30 seconds. Sprinkle with chilli, spring onions and coriander and serve at once.

Oyster Sauce

A thick, salty, oyster-flavoured sauce called ho yau in Cantonese and mostly sold in bottles, sometimes in cans. Cornflour (cornstarch) gives it a smooth, heavy texture and caramel contributes a rich brown colour. Once opened, it should be stored in the refrigerator and if purchased in a can, transferred to a glass jar. Use in small amounts to add flavour to many dishes. It goes equally well with meats and vegetables. Originally it was made from oysters, salt and water and had a grey, unappealing appearance, but it has been improved. There are different price ranges and it is false economy to purchase the cheapest. Hong Kong is known as the best producer of oyster sauce.

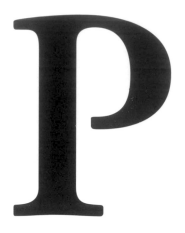

Pacific Region

This covers a lot of territory, most of it ocean. The islands in this region include Hawaii; Micronesia (literally 'little islands'), which comprises the main groups of the Marshalls, the Carolines and the Marianas; French Polynesia which embraces the Marquesas and Society Islands (of which Tahiti is the best known destination); the Solomon Islands; the Cook Islands; Samoa; Tonga; Fiji; and Vanuatu. These islands are home to the Polynesian, Micronesian and Melanesian peoples.

The people of the Pacific islands accept nature's bounty gratefully and live mostly on yams, coconut and seafood with the occasional feast at which a whole pig is cooked in an earth oven for hours until the meat is so tender it falls off the bone.

Foods that form a staple part of the South Pacific diet include cassava; banana, ripe and green; coconut; sweet potato and its leaves; pandanus drupes, heart and seeds; arrowroot; sago; taro and its leaves. The diet is supplemented with protein from sources such as pig, fish, sea cucumber, sea urchin, some crustacea and, in some places, seaweed. Fruit bat is considered a delicacy.

Leaves eaten include taro, water-spinach, Ceylon (creeping) spinach and amaranth. Ti leaves, banana leaves and breadfruit leaves provide eating plates as well as wrappers for food to be cooked.

Missionaries, as well as bringing religion and social customs, introduced foods from the West. One which caught on with a fervour is canned corned beef, served to honoured guests at special feasts.

Spices and seasonings are practically unknown except among migrant populations such as the Indians in Fiji, the Chinese, Japanese, Koreans and Filipinos who settled in Hawaii, and in the French influenced food of New Caledonia and French Polynesia.

It is interesting to look at the countries which surround the Pacific on a map of the world. North of the equator, on one side there is Japan, Korea, and the Philippines, which are part of Asia. In the Southern Hemisphere are Australia and New Zealand. On the opposite side of the Pacific Rim are the west coasts of Canada, North America, Mexico, central America and South America.

While their native cuisines are quite different to those on the other side of the ocean, there are certain similarities caused by connections which were made in centuries gone by. The seafaring Spaniards and Portuguese were responsible for much transoceanic cultural exchange. Foods and flavours made their way across the world and merged almost imperceptibly with cuisines of lands a long way off.

Coriander, indigenous to the Mediterranean region, is better known and more widely used in Asia and Mexico. Chillies (or chiles as they are called on the other side) are native to Mexico but just as strongly identified with the food of Asia. Food plants from the New World are now grown and distributed throughout Asia. Many exotic fruits believed to be natives of South East Asia, in fact had their genesis in the tropics of South America. And many spices of the Moluccas are now grown as commercial crops in the Western tropics.

In recent years there has been a noticeable change of attitude towards food in the European-settled countries of the Pacific Rim. In restaurants in North America, Canada, Australia and New Zealand there has been an explosion of 'East meets West' cuisine. This 'fusion cuisine' as it has been called, introduces flavours such as lemon grass, chillies and fresh coriander, and uses noodles, seaweed and soy sauce. Hawaii also provides a good example of a hybrid cuisine.

Influences of the Asia-Pacific region have brought the innovative thinking of Western-trained chefs to heights of inspiration. A marvellous hybrid cuisine is emerging.

Paddy Bird

Even smaller than sparrows, these birds live in rice fields and feed on paddy (rice grains in husks). Caught by flinging nets over them, the birds are plucked, cleaned, marinated, threaded on long slivers of bamboo and sold to be deep fried or grilled.

Palm, Heart of

(*Cocos nucifera* and other palms) The tender core of different kinds of palm. The queen of them all is the heart of a coconut palm, firm and crunchy and slightly sweet. In order to enjoy this luxury the tree has to die. In many countries it is becoming increasingly rare with the realisation that it is better to let the tree live and bear fruit. However, under some circumstances a tree has to be sacrificed for very good reasons, and then the heart of palm may be enjoyed without guilt.

I grew up in a house with a large garden in which were many coconut palms, and while these were valued for the nuts they provided for everyday cooking, sometimes a tall palm leaned dangerously close to the house and had to be felled before the season of the monsoon winds. It was then that I learned how delicious the heart of this particular palm could be.

Called ubod in the Philippines, it is added to the filling of a very special variety of lumpia (fresh spring rolls), lumpiang ubod. There are special sacrificial enclosures of coconut trees barely a foot apart, all meant to be cut down when very young to make lumpiang ubod.

Other types of palm such as Sabal palmetto yield smaller hearts, which are canned and sold for quite high prices but are a poor substitute for the fresh item.

> **Indonesia:** *kalada*
> **Japan:** *paam haato*
> **Malaysia:** *nyur*
> **Philippines:** *ubod*
> **Sri Lanka:** *pol bada*
> **Thailand:** *kaoteran*

Palm Honey

This is a form of palm sugar mostly labelled treacle, its source also indicated, e.g. kitul treacle, coconut treacle.

In Sri Lanka this luxurious syrup is smoked after being boiled until thick, which gives it a delicious, unusual flavour. The syrup is greatly prized for the national treat called simply 'curds and honey', the curds being rich, firm yoghurt made from buffalo milk with a thick layer of yellow cream on top. See PALM SUGAR.

Palm Oil

See OILS.

Palm Sugar

More than one kind of palm yields sugar, among them the toddy or kitul palm (*Caryota urens*); palmyra palm (*Borassus flabellifer*); coconut palm (*Cocos nucifera*); sugar palm of India (*Phoenix sylvestris*); sugar palm of Java and Malaya (*Arenga saccharifera*). Those most prized are the palmyra and kitul sugars, and it is usually these which are bottled as thick palm honey of pouring consistency. See PALM HONEY.

When boiled down further, the sap of the palm tree is concentrated into heavy, moist palm sugar such as that used in Thai cooking, and sold in wide-mouthed jars from which it is spooned. The sugar ranges from almost white to pale honey-gold to deep, dark brown in colour with variable consistency.

When the palms are from 15 to 20 years old they commence flowering and it is only then that they yield the sweet sap from which palm sugar is made.

Toddy tappers have to be extremely agile to shin up palm trees with only a circle of rope around their ankles for support. The sap flows when the inflorescence is tapped but first it must be beaten (gently) with a mallet for a couple of days. A small slice is taken off the end and a receptacle (usually an earthenware pot or gourd) hung close to the cut to collect the sap each night. The sap is known as 'sweet toddy' and for those lucky enough to be around when this is brought in, has a taste of ambrosia. The fresh sweet toddy is boiled down shortly after collection to make palm syrup and palm sugar. If this is not done, within a few hours the 'sweet toddy' ferments into a sour, potent brew called toddy, a very intoxicating drink. It is the 'cheap grog' of tropical lands and is not fit to drink the next day.

Palm Vinegar

To concentrate the nectar into solid sugar, the fresh juice is boiled down and evaporated before being poured into bamboo sections to form cylindrical shapes, or into coconut shells so they emerge as large shallow hemispheres, or into small baskets woven of palm leaves. In this form, the sugar has to be scraped or chipped from the rather hard block. This gur as it is called in India, or jaggery as it is known in Sri Lanka and Burma, gula melaka in Malaysia or gula jawa in Indonesia, is used on a daily basis in these countries as a sweetener. Be aware, though, that unrefined cane sugar is also sold in these shapes. Read the label carefully to make sure you get palm sugar.

There is no identical Western counterpart, but there are substitutes which give a reasonable flavour likeness. If the recipe calls for a quantity of palm sugar, use a mixture of equal parts maple syrup and either soft brown sugar or black sugar (depending whether you desire a lighter or darker-coloured result).

Palm sugar is sold in rounded cakes, cylinders, blocks or large plastic or glass jars. The jars are easiest for spoon measurement but use a sturdy metal spoon because this sugar, even when soft, can be extremely dense and very sticky.

Sometimes the surface of the sugar is sealed with a fine layer of wax. Scrape the top before digging in so you'll know whether you need to lift off the wax first.

See also JAGGERY.

Burma: *jaggery, tanyet*
India: *jaggery* (raw cane sugar),
  gur (date palm sugar)
Indonesia: *gula jawa, gula aren*
Malaysia: *gula melaka*
Sri Lanka: *jaggery, kitul-hakuru, tal-hakuru,*
  pol pani
Thailand: *nam taan pep, nam taan bik,*
  nam taan mapraow

Palm Vinegar

See VINEGAR.

Pancakes

This may seem an incongruous entry in an Asian food book, but certain snacks answer to the description of pancake better than to any other. They do have specific names in their country of origin, but it is reasonable for the newcomer to Asian food to think of them as pancakes and look for them here.

Hoppers: Known as hoppers (ah-pay) in Sri Lanka, appam in southern India, these bowl-shaped, rice flour pancakes are served at breakfast, sometimes with an egg broken into the centre, which is perfectly poached in the time it takes the pancake to cook. The batter of rice flour and coconut milk traditionally has toddy added for the typical sourish flavour and, more importantly, the fermentation which makes the centres full of little holes like crumpets. If toddy is not available, the same action is duplicated by using yeast, either fresh or dry. After leaving to rise, the batter is swirled in a hemispherical pan, rather like a small, more acutely curved wok. Even without the traditional hopper-pan, it is possible to enjoy the unique texture and flavour using a small omelette pan. Crisp and delicate, this pancake has a dual function. While it is an everyday breakfast food either made at home or purchased from a food shop, it also appears as a late-night snack, the traditional treat for revellers who visit specialist 'hopper boutiques' before they go home to bed.

Hoppers

Makes about 20

**15 g/½ oz fresh compressed yeast
  or 1 teaspoon dried yeast
125 ml/4 fl oz/½ cup warm water
1½ teaspoons sugar
185 g/6 oz/1½ cups medium-coarse ground rice
185 g/6 oz/1½ cups fine rice flour
  or plain (all-purpose) white flour
2 teaspoons salt
400 ml/14 fl oz can coconut milk
500 ml/1 pint/2 cups water**

Sprinkle yeast over warm water, stir to dissolve, add sugar and leave for 10 minutes or so. If yeast starts to froth it is active and you can proceed with the recipe. If it has no reaction, start again with a fresh batch of yeast.

Put ground rice, rice flour and salt into a large bowl. Combine 300 ml (10 fl oz) canned coconut milk with measured water and add yeast mixture. Stir into dry ingredients to form a smooth, thick batter. Allow to stand overnight, or put in a warm (turned off) oven for 1 hour until the mixture rises and froths. The batter should be of a thick pouring consistency, but thin enough to cover the sides of the pan with an almost transparent coating when the batter is swirled. It will probably be necessary to add extra water. A little practice will tell you when you have achieved the perfect consistency, and so much depends on the absorbency of the flour (which is variable) that it is not possible to give an accurate measurement.

Heat the pan over low heat until very hot, rub the inside surface with a piece of folded paper towels dipped in oil, or spray with one of the light oil or non-stick lecithin-based sprays and pour in a small ladle of the batter. Immediately pick up the pan by both handles, using potholders, and swirl it around so that the batter coats the pan for two-thirds of the way up. Cover pan (any saucepan cover that fits just inside the top edge will do) and cook on very low heat for about 5 minutes. Lift lid and peep. When the upper edges begin to turn a pale toasty colour, the hopper is ready. Where the batter has run down the sides to the centre there will be a little circle of spongy mixture, rather like a crumpet, while the curved edge is very thin, crisp and wafer-like. With a curved slotted utensil or flexible metal spatula, loosen edges and slip the hopper from the pan on to a wire rack. Wipe pan again with oiled paper and repeat. Serve the hoppers warm, accompanied by a hot chilli, Maldive fish and onion sambal or any kind of meat, fish or chicken curry.

Note: The remaining undiluted coconut milk, with a pinch of salt and teaspoon of sugar added, is usually spooned into the centre of the last few hoppers which are made. This is a special treat, known as miti kiri appe or coconut cream hoppers and may be served with shavings of jaggery (or brown sugar).

Egg Hoppers

Have ready an egg broken into a cup. As soon as the batter has been swirled to coat the pan, gently slip the egg into the centre of the hopper. Cover and cook as in previous recipe, and the egg will be done to perfection by the time the hopper is cooked. Serve with pepper and salt for grinding over the egg. This type of hopper is generally served with a knife and fork, and a plain hopper which can be rolled up and dipped into the egg.

Coconut Pancakes

Do not use desiccated or shredded dried coconut for this recipe. It needs the moist, delicate texture of grated fresh coconut to be a success. Serves 4.

2 eggs
125 ml/4 fl oz/½ cup milk
125 ml/4 fl oz/½ cup water
pinch salt
1 tablespoon melted butter
125 g/4 oz/1 cup plain (all-purpose) flour, sifted
butter or ghee for frying

FILLING
1 coconut, freshly grated
125 g/4 oz jaggery or brown sugar

In a large bowl, beat the eggs just until yolks and whites are combined. Add milk, water, salt and melted butter, then add all the flour and beat with a wooden spoon or rotary beater until smooth. Leave batter for 1 hour at least before cooking.

To make a filling, combine coconut with the jaggery which has been finely scraped with a knife or on a grater, or broken into pieces and pounded using a mortar and pestle.

Grease a heavy pancake pan with butter or ghee, using just enough to give a thin film. Pour in a small ladle of the batter and swirl the pan to coat the base thinly. Cook over medium heat until golden brown on the underside. Turn pancake over and cook the other side for a few seconds. Turn onto a plate. Cook all the batter in this way, then fill each pancake with 2 tablespoons of the coconut filling and roll up. If liked, sprinkle with roughly chopped raw cashews.

Mandarin Pancakes

This traditional accompaniment to Peking Duck is also useful for wrapping other savoury mixtures. Serves 4–5.

250 g/8 oz/2 cups plain (all-purpose) flour
185 ml/6 fl oz/¾ cup boiling water,
  plus 1 tablespoon extra
1 tablespoon oriental sesame oil

Measure unsifted flour into a bowl. Bring water to the boil and pour at once onto the flour, stirring with chopsticks or the handle of a wooden spoon for a few minutes. As soon as it is cool enough to handle, knead for 10 minutes until the mixture is a soft, smooth dough. Form into a ball, wrap closely in plastic and let it stand for at least 30 minutes.

Roll the dough into a cylindrical shape and cut it into 10 slices of equal width. Cover with plastic wrap to prevent drying out.

Take one slice at a time and cut into 2 equal pieces. Form each one into a smooth ball, then roll out on a lightly floured board to circles about 8 cm (3 in) in diameter. Brush one circle lightly with sesame oil, taking it right to the edges. Put the second circle on top of the first one and roll again, both circles together this time, until the pancakes are 15–18 cm (6–7 in) across. They must be very thin. Cover each pancake with plastic as it is made.

When all are rolled out, heat a heavy frying pan or griddle and cook pancakes one at a time on the ungreased surface. Cook over low heat until the pancake develops small bubbles. Turn it frequently so that it cooks on both sides. A few golden spots will appear.

Remove from pan and gently pull the 2 circles apart. The sesame oil they were brushed with makes this quite easy. Pile cooked pancakes on a plate, and cover tightly or they will dry out. Pancakes should be soft and pliable, not brittle.

To re-heat, arrange the pancakes in a steamer lined with a clean towel, cover and put over simmering water for 1–2 minutes. To serve, fold each pancake into quarters.

Serve with Quick and Easy Roast Duck (see page 126). They can also be used to enclose a variety of fillings such as shredded pork or chicken.

Spring Onion (Scallion) Pancakes

These are crisp and brown on the outside, flavoured with salt and spring onions. Serve as a savoury hors d'oeuvre, or to accompany rice porridge. Traditionally they might be made with melted lard, but I prefer to use a light vegetable oil mixed with oriental sesame oil with its wonderful toasted sesame flavour.

250 g/8 oz/2 cups all-purpose flour
190 ml/6 fl oz/¾ cup boiling water,
  plus 1 tablespoon extra
3 tablespoons vegetable oil
1 tablespoon oriental sesame oil
salt to taste
4 spring onions (scallions), finely chopped
oil for shallow frying

Place flour in a bowl. Measure the boiling water and pour over flour, stir with a spoon to moisten all the flour and, as soon as cool enough to handle, knead hard for 10 minutes until smooth. Form a ball, wrap in plastic and let dough rest for at least 30 minutes.

Form dough into a roll and divide into 6 equal portions. Roll each portion on a lightly floured surface into thin pancakes about 25 cm (10 in) in diameter. Combine both kinds of oil, and brush some on top of pancake. Sprinkle with ¼ teaspoon salt and 2 teaspoons chopped spring onions. Roll pancake like a Swiss roll, press ends to seal and coil up the roll like a snail. Tuck the end into the middle. Flatten with the hand, then roll once again on a lightly floured surface to a smaller pancake than the first, about 12 cm (5 in) in diameter and 6 mm (¼ in) thick. Repeat until all the pancakes are rolled.

Heat a heavy frying pan and add a tablespoon of oil. When hot add 1 pancake, turn heat low and cover pan with lid. Cook for 2 minutes, then turn pancake over and cover for a further 2 minutes or until pancake is golden brown on both sides. Do not have heat too high or the pancakes will brown before the centre is cooked. Pressing centre of pancake with a frying spatula helps it to brown evenly. Cut pancakes into 6 triangular pieces. Serve warm. Makes 6 round pancakes which cut into 36 serving pieces.

Singapore Style Filled Pancakes (Poh Pia)

A great informal meal, as each person fills his or her own pancake and adds extras to suit their own taste. This is a version of fresh spring roll which is sold at every open-air eating centre in Singapore. Makes about 25 rolls.

EGG ROLL WRAPPERS

5 eggs
375 ml/12 fl oz/1½ cups cold water
½ teaspoon salt
2 tablespoons oil
125 g/4 oz/1 cup plain (all-purpose) flour

FILLING

4 tablespoons oil
2 cakes yellow bean curd, cut into strips
500 g/1 lb belly pork, boiled and diced
1 tablespoon finely chopped garlic
3 tablespoons salted soy beans, mashed
 or bean sauce
250 g/8 oz raw prawns (shrimp)
800 g/1¾ lb can bamboo shoot
 drained and cut into matchstick strips
250 g/8 oz Chinese sweet turnip (see YAM BEAN),
 peeled and cut into matchstick strips
½ teaspoon salt or to taste

GARNISHES

1 large crisp lettuce
185 g/6 oz canned or frozen crab meat
250 g/8 oz bean sprouts
1 small cucumber
6 lap cheong (Chinese sausage)
3 eggs
5 tablespoons finely chopped garlic
small bunch fresh coriander leaves
chilli sauce
dark soy sauce, sweetened, or kecap manis

Egg roll wrappers: Beat eggs and water together until well mixed but not frothy. Add salt, oil and flour and beat until smooth. Allow to rest for 30 minutes while preparing filling. Lightly oil a heavy frying pan or pancake pan with a piece of paper towels dipped in oil and rubbed over the heated pan. Pour in a small ladle of batter, swirl the pan quickly to make a very thin coating and pour any excess back into the container of batter. Cook over low heat until underside is cooked and pale golden. Turn and cook other side for a few seconds only. These wrappers should not be allowed to brown. Pile one on top of the other on a flat plate as they are cooked.

Note: Batter may be made in an electric blender, putting in the liquid ingredients first, then the flour. Blend for just a few seconds, stop motor and scrape down sides of blender container, then blend for a further few seconds. This batter must be allowed to rest for a longer time. If there is still froth on top when ready to cook the wrappers, spoon it off before starting to cook.

Filling: Heat oil in a wok and fry the strips of bean curd until golden brown. Drain on paper towels. Cut into small dice.

Pour off all but 1 tablespoon of oil from the wok, add the diced pork and fry, until the fat begins to run. Add the garlic and mashed soy beans and fry, stirring, until the garlic begins to smell cooked. Add the shelled, deveined and chopped raw prawns and toss until the prawns change colour. Add the bamboo shoot and sweet turnip and fry, stirring and tossing, until cooked but still crisp, then add the bean curd. Sprinkle with salt and mix. Simmer uncovered in the wok until filling is almost dry. Taste and add more salt if necessary. Invert a small bowl inside a larger bowl and put the filling on this so that any liquid or oil can drain away under the small bowl.

Garnishes: Wash lettuce well, separating the leaves. With a stainless steel knife remove the thick leaf rib and cut each leaf into 2 or 3 pieces lengthways. Blot lettuce gently on paper towels and pile leaves on a plate. Flake the crab meat, removing any bits of bony tissue. Put into a small bowl. Pinch straggly 'tails' off bean sprouts, wash well, scald by pouring boiling water over, and refresh in a bowl of iced water. Drain well, pile into a bowl. Peel and seed cucumber, then cut into strips.

Steam the lap cheong in a colander for 10 minutes, then cut into thin slices. Put into a bowl and keep warm. Beat the eggs, season with salt and pepper, and fry in a lightly oiled frying pan to make 4 or 5 very thin omelettes. Do not fold. Turn onto a plate as they are done. When cool, roll up and cut into thin strips. Put into a bowl.

To make crisp fried garlic which is one of the

important additions, finely chop garlic, or bruise using a mortar and pestle. Rinse garlic in cold water, drain well in fine sieve, then wrap in paper towels and squeeze gently to remove as much moisture as possible. Heat about 4 tablespoons oil in a small pan and fry the garlic over low heat, stirring constantly, until it starts to turn golden. Remove pan from heat at once, before it starts to brown. Garlic will finish cooking in the stored heat of the oil. When cool remove from oil and drain on paper towels. Put into a small bowl.

Wash fresh coriander leaves very well, dry on paper towels, then chop fairly fine. Put into a small bowl. Put chilli sauce into a small bowl. In another bowl mix dark soy sauce with a little sugar to sweeten.

Have all the garnishes ready before starting to cook the egg roll wrappers and the filling.

To serve: Assembling the poh pia is half the fun and adds greatly to the enjoyment of eating this snack. Each person puts an egg roll wrapper on his or her plate. On this goes a piece of lettuce leaf, which is spread with chilli sauce or sprinkled with the sweetened soy. A spoonful of cooked filling is put on the leaf and garnishes as desired are added. Roll up the egg wrapper, turning in the sides so that the filling is completely enclosed. Poh pia should be eaten immediately they are filled or the wrapper will become soggy.

Thai Rice and Coconut Pancakes (Khanom Krok)

These creamy rice cakes are baked in a clay pan with small round indentations, placed over glowing coals. The size and shape of the indentations are similar to the iron pan used for gem scones, or an aebelskiver pan which Danish cooks use and which is probably more common in Europe and the United States. The heavy iron pans may be placed over a gas flame or electric hotplate. A convenient modern appliance is an electric doughnut cooker which offers the small round shapes and does the job perfectly. Makes about 24.

200 g/7 oz/1 cup uncooked rice
4 tablespoons cooked rice

90 g/3 oz/1 cup freshly grated coconut
pinch of salt
1 tablespoon sugar
750 ml/1½ pints/3 cups boiling water
oil

TOPPING
125 ml/4 fl oz thick coconut milk
2 tablespoons sugar
¼ teaspoon salt
1 spring onion (scallion), chopped
2 tablespoons corn kernels
2 tablespoons pounded dried shrimp

Put first 6 ingredients into a bowl, pour the boiling water over and leave to get cold. Blend at high speed in an electric blender until very finely ground. Mix the coconut milk, sugar and salt together and reserve.

Heat the indented pan and brush with oil. With a ladle, pour rice mixture into each hollow, to almost fill. Cook over low heat or in a hot oven, 220°C (425°F), until firm. Top each with 1 teaspoon of the coconut milk mixture. Add a sprinkling of chopped spring onion, a few corn kernels, or some dried shrimp powder and finish by cooking for a further 1–2 minutes. Run a small spatula between the pan and each cake to loosen, and if the outside is well browned and crisp, remove to a wire rack. Serve warm.

Panch Phora

See SPICE BLENDS.

Pandanus

The species of pandanus (*P. odoratissimus, P. tectorius*) known as Nicobar breadfruit is a valuable food source in islands of the South Pacific. The fleshy base of the single-seeded fruit (drupe), which vaguely resembles a pineapple, is eaten when ripe, sweet-scented and reddish-orange; or cooked, mashed and mixed to a paste with coconut milk. It is formed into flat, thin cakes, which are further cooked; wrapped in leaves ready to eat or added to other dishes, or sun-dried and crushed to a powder to be stored, later mixed to a thick paste with palm syrup; and diluted with water as a drink. The single seed of the fruit, pleasant tasting and oil-rich, is dried and smoked to preserve it. In times of famine, the heart of the pandanus is eaten after thorough washing in salt water to remove oxalate crystals. The inflorescence bracts are used to scent coconut oil.

Micronesia: *kaina*
Polynesia: *hala, ara, fa*

Pandanus Flower

(*Pandanus fascicularis*) This variety yields a floral essence (ruh kewra) which is popular in northern Indian food. Extracted from the male spadices of the plant, it is best described as a mixture of intense rose and jasmine, with undertones of sandalwood and musk. Used to scent shreds of betel nut (areca nut) sold in small packets, ready to use in the Indian digestive chew of paan (wrapped in a betel leaf with spices).

Indispensable in the scented syrups which go into sweet drinks such as falooda and sherbet, more unusual is the use of this essence in savoury foods — meat dishes and biriani. This is typical in festive Kashmiri dishes.

Kewra is a powerful perfume and a few drops only are needed. The effect should be so subtle as to be just a hint of fragrance at the back of the nose, not strong enough to be detected on the tongue. See recipe for Spiced Lamb Slices (page 319).

India: *kewra, talai*
Sri Lanka: *mudu kekiya*

Pandanus Leaf

(*Pandanus latifolius, P. amaryllifolius*) SEE ILLUSTRATION. Also known as pandan leaf. Almost every kitchen garden in Sri Lanka, Malaysia, Indonesia and Thailand boasts a pandanus plant, the leaves of which are used in both savoury and sweet dishes. A strip of leaf about 10 cm (4 in) long is dropped into the pot each time rice is cooked, to perfume it. Two or three strips are simmered with curry.

In Thailand, pieces of marinated chicken are enclosed in a clever wrapping of bai toey (the local name for pandan leaf) and grilled or deep fried, their subtle flavour being imparted to the chicken. In Malaysia, Indonesia, Singapore and Thailand, the leaves are pounded and strained (or blended with a little water) to yield flavour and colour for cakes and sweets. The flavour is delicate, and as important to Asians as vanilla is to Westerners.

Pandan leaves used to be available in Western countries only in dried form. Gradually, enterprising shopkeepers offered them fresh frozen. It is a sign of the times that for the past few years fresh pandan leaves have been available in at least some large Western cities. Surplus fresh leaves may be frozen in plastic bags.

In South East Asia the leaves are used to make containers for sweets. Cooks are adept at folding them so they make perfect boxes hardly 2 cm (¾ in) each way, just right for holding little jellies or puddings.

Indonesia: *daun pandan*
Malaysia: *daun pandan*
Sri Lanka: *rampe*
Thailand: *bai toey*
Vietnam: *la dua*

Chicken in Pandan Leaves

Little bundles of marinated chicken wrapped in pandan leaves and deep fried are very popular as an hors d'oeuvre but I have found it easier, less oily and just as delicious if the bundles are grilled or barbecued.

500 g/1 lb chicken thigh fillets
1 tablespoon Thai pepper-coriander paste (recipe page 105)
1 teaspoon finely grated fresh ginger
1 tablespoon finely chopped shallot
2 tablespoons fish sauce
2 tablespoons coconut milk
1 teaspoon palm sugar or brown sugar
pandan leaves, fresh or frozen

Trim any visible fat from chicken, and cut meat into bite-sized pieces. Combine the remaining ingredients in a bowl, add the chicken and mix well. Leave to marinate for 30 minutes. Put 2 pieces of chicken on each strip of pandan leaf, cut long enough to allow the chicken to be wrapped in it. Fasten with toothpicks. When all are made, place about 15 cm (6 in) from source of heat and cook over barbecue or under a preheated griller for about 8 minutes, turning after 4 minutes.

Let guests unwrap them and enjoy the aroma and flavour.

Pandan Flavoured Sticky Rice

185 g/6 oz/1 cup white sticky rice (glutinous rice)
185 ml/6 fl oz/¾ cup thick coconut milk
¼ teaspoon salt
1 tablespoon white sugar
pandan leaves or pandan flavouring

Wash rice and soak overnight in water to cover. Drain, place rice in a heatproof dish or bowl, stir in coconut milk, salt, sugar and pandan flavouring. Place bowl in a steamer or pressure cooker. Cover and cook over boiling water. If steaming, allow 1 hour or until rice has become very tender and absorbed all the coconut milk. A pressure cooker at half pressure will take 30 minutes.

Serve with sliced ripe mangoes, toasted sesame seeds, or shavings of palm sugar.

Papaya

(*Carica papaya*) This fruit can range from very small to very large and is eaten green or ripe. There is much discussion about the differences (if any) between 'papaya' and 'pawpaw' and 'papaw'. In spite of what a vendor in the market insists is true (that those with red flesh are papaya and those with orange flesh are pawpaws), it just depends which country you are in. I know for a fact that if I spoke of pawpaw instead of papaw in Sri Lanka, people would snigger behind their hands and think it utterly affected. Papaya is accepted, but never pawpaw.

Red, orange or yellow flesh, they are all sisters under the skin and if allowed to mature and ripen on the tree, are beautifully sweet. If not, the flavour is not as good. Rich in vitamin A, papaya have a musky-sweet, refreshing flavour that may be enhanced by a squeeze of lime. A ripe papaya should be soft enough to hold an impression from gentle thumb or finger pressure.

While they may be native to central and South America, they are very popular in Asia, thriving in the tropical zones. The flowers, leaves and young stems are cooked and eaten. The seeds are used as a somewhat peppery spice. The tenderising enzyme papain is obtained by tapping the skin of an unripe fruit. In Indonesia, a salad may contain very small new leaves of papaya to be dipped in the hot, sour dressing. For cooking a tough old hen, it is custom-ary to first wrap the plucked and de-feathered bird in large papaya leaves to tenderise it, and to drop a piece of unripe fruit in the pot as it simmers. Papain is the base of many meat tenderisers.

Throughout the tropics it is possible to breakfast on the sweetest of ripe fruit, served simply with a wedge of fresh lime for squeezing over it. But in Thailand the most popular way of eating the papaya is in a salad while still unripe and hard, the skin a dark green and the flesh white. They are peeled, cut into fine, long shreds and given a rough pounding using a mortar and pestle with garlic, hot chillies, dried shrimp and sometimes tiny black crabs which have been pickled. Be warned, som tam, as this salad is called, might require chilli tolerance.

Medicinal uses: The leaves and seeds of papaya are a very effective vermifuge, destroying worms and intestinal parasites that settle in the large or small intestines. Papaya leaf, extremely high in beta carotene, is also claimed to prevent infection. Papayasan, made from the leaves and juice of unripe fruits, is said to be a great boost to the pancreas and is prescribed for diabetics. Also, it is recommended as a precaution against amoebic dysentery when travelling.

India: *pappali*
Indonesia: *pepaya*
Malaysia: *kepaya, ketela*
Pacific languages: *maoli, oleti*
Sri Lanka: *gaslabu, pepol*
Thailand: *ma-la-ko*
Vietnam: *du du*

Green Papaya Salad

For this salad, the papaya must be hard and very under-ripe, the flesh almost white with no trace of orange colour. In Thailand it is so popular that there are food stalls devoted just to this one salad. It is always made by hand, the pawpaw shredded incredibly finely with a sharp chopper, the ingredients pounded together using a mortar and pestle, each order executed separately. If you have a Japanese daikon grater, long, even shreds can be easily achieved. Serves 4.

300 g/10 oz/2 cups finely grated green papaya
1 handful tender green beans

2 tablespoons dried shrimp
2 tablespoons crushed roasted peanuts
1 clove garlic
2 shallots or small purple onions
2 or 3 fresh bird's eye chillies
1 tablespoon fish sauce
1 tablespoon palm sugar or brown sugar
lime juice to taste
dried chilli flakes (optional)

Peel papaya and shred the flesh or grate into fine, long strands. Cut beans into short lengths. In a blender process the dried shrimp to a floss. Combine with the crushed peanuts and set aside. Use a mortar and pestle to pound the garlic, shallots and chillies to a paste. Add fish sauce and sugar, then the beans and pound gently so the beans don't lose their shape. Add papaya shreds and pound lightly. Turn out into a bowl, add lime juice and toss. Sprinkle with dried shrimp and peanuts, and if liked, some dried chilli flakes.

Papaya Drink with Lime

Cut a ripe papaya into quarters, scoop out and discard seeds, and with a sharp knife remove the skin. Roughly cube and drop into an electric blender. Add the juice of a lime, a tablespoon of sugar, 2 or 3 ice cubes and a little soda water. Blend until smooth and serve right away.

Pappadam

Also spelled poppadum, paparh, papad. Lentil wafers with varying degrees of spiciness, sold dried in packets. They have to be deep fried for a few seconds before serving. The oil should be hot enough so they more than double in size immediately and become crisp and light, not leathery and oil sodden. Some varieties with a smooth or shiny surface cook successfully in the microwave oven or under the grill. If the pappadams are covered in a fine flour they need to be deep fried or at least brushed with oil before grilling.

Paratha

See BREADS.

Parkia

(*Parkia speciosa*) SEE ILLUSTRATION. The common names are twisted cluster bean and stink bean. A long, flat bean with bright green seeds the size and shape of plump almonds which have a rather peculiar smell. They are an acquired taste, but are popular in southern Thailand, Burma, Malaysia and Indonesia and are sold in bunches, still in the pod, or the seeds are sold in plastic bags. They are exported in jars or cans, pickled in brine. Depending on the country of origin they may be labelled peteh, petai or sataw (sometimes spelled sator). Best when combined with other strong flavoured foods such as garlic, chillies, dried shrimp, or added to a Thai curry such as Thai Green Curry of Duck (see page 128).

When young the pods are flat because the seeds have not yet developed, and they hang like a bunch of slightly twisted ribbons, pale green, almost translucent. At this stage they may be eaten raw, fried or pickled.

In Burma, there is a related seed, dhinyindi, which is larger and even more strongly flavoured. See NGAPI NUT.

Indonesia: *peteh*
Japan: *nejire-fusamame*
Malaysia: *petai*
Thailand: *sataw, sator*

Fried Sataw with Shrimp

3 tablespoons peanut oil
3 tablespoons finely sliced purple shallots
3 red chillies, sliced
2 tablespoons fish sauce
2 teaspoons dried shrimp paste (blacan)
3 tablespoons stock or water
10–15 fresh raw shrimp, shelled and deveined
90 g/3 oz sataw seeds
125 ml/4 fl oz/½ cup thick coconut milk
2 teaspoons palm sugar or brown sugar

Heat oil in a wok and fry shallots and chillies until fragrant. Add fish sauce and shrimp paste and press against side of wok. Add stock and stir to dissolve shrimp paste. Add shrimp and sataw seeds and stir-fry over high heat for 4–5 minutes. Add coconut milk and stir while bringing to the boil. Taste and if more saltiness is required add more fish sauce. Stir in the palm sugar and serve with steamed white rice.

Fresh Petai Sambal

Seeing piles of fresh petai in the markets in Kuantan, Malaysia, was exciting. I usually make do with bottled or canned ones. The market stalls offered both the twisted whole beans and the bright green seeds removed from the pods. I bought the latter and created a sambal which featured those flavours (Indian, Chinese, Nonya) which come together so harmoniously in the food of Malaysia. Serve as an accompaniment to rice and other dishes. Serves 6–8.

3 tablespoons peanut oil
1 sprig fresh curry leaves
2 tablespoons chopped garlic
1 tablespoon chopped fresh ginger
12 sliced hot chillies
1 teaspoon dried shrimp paste (blacan)
1 tablespoon finely grated ginger
1 tablespoon mild chilli paste
3 tablespoons salted yellow beans
4 tablespoons dark roasted coconut,
   finely ground
500 g/1 lb fresh petai seeds or canned petai,
   drained
1 tablespoon palm sugar or brown sugar
1 torch ginger bud, very finely sliced
   or 4 tablespoons chopped Vietnamese mint

Heat oil and toss in curry leaves. After 30 seconds add chopped garlic and ginger and sliced chillies and stir-fry for 1 minute. Add blacan and fry, crushing it against the wok with back of frying spoon.

Add grated ginger and chilli paste, salted yellow beans and roasted coconut. Add the petai and ½ cup water, stir into the spice mixture, cover and simmer for about 10 minutes or until petai are tender. Stir in sugar. Serve sprinkled with sliced ginger bud.

Thai Curry of Chicken with Sataw

Serves 4–6

500 g/1 lb chicken thigh fillets
2 teaspoons chopped garlic
¼ teaspoon whole black peppercorns
6 tablespoons chopped coriander,
   (roots, stems and leaves)
small piece fresh turmeric root
   or ½ teaspoon ground turmeric
3 tablespoons finely sliced lemon grass
1 teaspoon shrimp paste
2 teaspoons chopped fresh chillies
2 tablespoons peanut oil
1 small can petai or sataw, drained
1 tablespoon fish sauce
375 ml/12 fl oz/1½ cups coconut milk
sweet basil leaves and coriander leaves

Trim any excess fat from the chicken and cut into thin slices. Using a mortar and pestle pound the garlic, peppercorns, coriander, turmeric and lemon grass to a paste (or blend with a small amount of water). Combine with shrimp paste and chopped chillies. Marinate chicken in this spice mix for 1 hour.

Heat a wok, add oil and swirl to coat the wok. Add the chicken and stir-fry on high heat until chicken is no longer pink. Add sataw, fish sauce and coconut milk, stir until it comes to a simmer. Simmer for 5 minutes, uncovered. Turn off heat, sprinkle with basil or coriander leaves and serve with steamed jasmine rice.

Parsi

The word indicates a community of people from Persia (now Iran), Zoroastrians, who went to India as refugees from religious persecution 13 centuries ago. Welcomed by the Indian rulers, they stayed to make a significant contribution to the land of their adoption, not only in business, the arts and sciences, but in their distinctive cuisine.

They are proud of the rich dishes which are their heritage, and also proud of the way they have improved them in the land of their adoption, borrowing some of the spiciness of Indian food, particularly that of the states of Maharashtra and Gujarat, where many of them settled.

Their food retains many of the characteristics of Persian cuisine, yet is blended with the ingredients used in their new homeland to create a hybrid cuisine.

For recipes demonstrating Parsi cuisine see: Parsi Style Spicy Scrambled Eggs (page 134), Eggs with Savoury Mince (page 138), Carrot and Dried Fruit Chutney (page 66), Parsi Steamed Fish (page 152), Lentils and Vegetables with Meat (page 216).

Passionfruit

(*Passiflora edulis*) SEE ILLUSTRATION. Another native of the new world which has ventured further afield than its native Brazil and is quite at home in Asia and the Pacific. It is just about the most popular flavour in cordials and aerated bottled drinks.

The fruit is so named because of its curious flower. While the colour changes according to variety, they all have, in the centre, features which to the faithful, denote the symbols of Christ's Passion: the crown of thorns, nails, wounds and apostles.

There are many kinds of passionfruit. Purple passionfruit, about the size of a lime and either round or slightly oval, has a distinctive flavour, unique aroma and can be quite acid; it is hardy enough to thrive in temperate and Mediterranean climates.

Yellow passionfruit (*P. edulis* var. *flavicarpa*), has a firm, round, shiny shell. It is sometimes called sweet granadilla and is more common on Pacific islands since it will grow only in the tropics or subtropics. It is lower in acid, so that it may be eaten straight from the shell, whereas most purple passionfruit, for all their fragrance and flavour, cry out for a little touch of sugar.

Not only the fruit are for eating. The tender leaves were gathered by my mother, who would shred them and toss them briefly over gentle heat with spices and shredded coconut, bringing out their piquant flavour, a similar treatment to any edible greens. See AMARANTH.

A different kind of yellow passionfruit (*P. mollissima*) is known as banana passionfruit because it resembles a fat yellow banana; the skin is velvety rather than glossy and is not hard but quite leathery and must be cut through, revealing large, musky-flavoured, tightly packed juice sacs of orange-yellow, each with its shiny black seed enclosed within a thin membrane. The seeds and juice sacs look like other passionfruit but lack the aroma and flavour. However, their flowers are beautiful, like upside-down pink water lilies hanging from the vine and worth growing for decoration alone.

There is also what is labelled 'Panama passionfruit', larger and with a smoother shell which, when ripe, is mauve and speckled, sometimes tinged with yellow or green. This variety is sweet even before its skin wrinkles, which is generally the sign of ripeness in round-shelled types of passionfruit.

Purchasing and storing: Never mind the lusciously smooth, more recently picked specimens which are more expensive. Look at the back of the display or the box off to the side where older fruit sit, neglected, their skins sagging and wrinkled, certainly not very pretty; but the connoisseur knows that these are at their prime, and that inside they will be sweeter and more juicy than smoother ones.

Even bought in this condition, passionfruit have good keeping qualities and need not be refrigerated if you intend to use them in a week or 10 days. If you wish to keep them longer, cut open, with a teaspoon scoop the juicy pulp into a bowl, add sugar equal to half the weight of the pulp, and either refrigerate or, for longer storage, freeze. It will keep for a year in the freezer.

Australians and New Zealanders have adopted this Brazilian fruit with fervour, and most would be surprised to hear that it is an import. One of the glories of Australian country cooking is the fabled Passionfruit Sponge (see recipe page 274) — light as a feather, its layers sandwiched together with sweetened whipped cream and frosted with passionfruit icing — a picture in white and gold.

Passionfruit is also a feature of that other classic dessert, the Pavlova (see recipe page 274), laid claim to by both Australia and New Zealand. The snowy white meringue, the red of strawberries, the brilliant green of kiwi fruit, the golden slices of ripe banana are all very well, but it is the passionfruit with its perfume and piquant flavour which ties the whole together. If not for the sharpness of passionfruit pulp to tone down the sweetness of meringue and richness of whipped cream, it would surely have faded into obscurity long ago.

The flavour of passionfruit is so powerfully pervasive that a small amount of pulp can flavour a hot soufflé, a Bavarian cream, or Passionfruit Flummery (see recipe page 274), a particularly useful recipe since it requires no whipped cream to make it light and fluffy.

Medicinal uses: In herbal medicine, the plant and leaves are used for a liquid extract which is antispasmodic, sedative and narcotic. It is prescribed for neuralgic pains, debility, nervous headache, hysteria, spasms and convulsions.

Indonesia: *markisa*
Malaysia: *buah susu*
Thailand: *linmangkon* (purple),
  sawarot (yellow)

Passionfruit Flummery

1 tablespoon unflavoured gelatine
500 ml/1 pint/2 cups water
250 g/8 oz/1 cup sugar
1 level tablespoon all-purpose flour
125 ml/4 fl oz/½ cup orange juice
3 tablespoons lemon juice
125 ml/4 fl oz/½ cup passionfruit pulp

Sprinkle gelatine over ½ cup cold water and leave for 5 minutes to soften. Put remaining water and sugar into a pan and bring to the boil. Add flour mixed smoothly with 2 tablespoons cold water. Stir until it boils and cook for 5 minutes. Remove from heat, stir in the softened gelatine until dissolved, and allow to cool to room temperature, then stir in the orange and lemon juice. Cool completely, pour into the bowl of an electric mixer and whisk until light and frothy, about 15 minutes. Beat in passionfruit pulp, pour into a glass bowl and chill. Serve with cream or ice cream, or to accompany a fruit salad.

Australian Passionfruit Sponge

Australian cooks are rightly proud of their feather-light sponge cakes. None is more typical than passionfruit sponge.

4 eggs at room temperature
185 g/6 oz/¾ cup caster sugar (superfine sugar)
½ teaspoon vanilla essence
125 g/4 oz/1 cup self-raising flour
1 tablespoon cornflour (cornstarch)
90 ml/3 fl oz very hot water
15 g/½ oz butter
whipped cream
2 passionfruit
caster sugar (superfine sugar)
150 g/5 oz/1 cup icing sugar (confectioner's sugar), sifted

Brush two 20 cm (8 in) layer cake tins with melted butter and line bases with non-stick baking paper. Preheat oven to moderately hot, 190°C (375°F).

In electric mixer whip eggs until light, add sugar gradually while beating. Add vanilla and continue beating for about 10 minutes or until mixture is light and thick. Sift flour and cornflour together twice, then gradually fold into egg mixture, using a large metal spoon.

Pour hot water onto butter, stir into mixture and divide batter between the prepared pans. Bake for 20–25 minutes, or until cakes shrink slightly and spring back when lightly touched. Remove to a wire rack to cool. Sandwich together with whipped cream and spread with half the passionfruit pulp sweetened with caster sugar.

Mix remaining passionfruit pulp with icing sugar in a bowl, beat until smooth and with a palette knife dipped in hot water, spread over top of sponge.

ANZ Pavlova

Being careful not to attribute this famous dessert to one country or the other. For the softer, higher Australian pavlova, pile the meringue thickly, about 6 cm (2½ in) high. For the slightly flatter but crisper New Zealand version, spread it out a bit more thinly into a larger circle. Serves 8.

whites of 4 large fresh eggs
¼ teaspoon salt
¼ teaspoon cream of tartar
1 teaspoon vanilla essence
250 g/8 oz/1 cup caster sugar (superfine sugar)
1 teaspoon vinegar
1 tablespoon cornflour (cornstarch)
300 ml/10 fl oz whipping cream
125 ml/4 fl oz passionfruit pulp, sweetened
3 ripe bananas, sliced
2 kiwi fruit, peeled and sliced
ripe red strawberries, halved lengthways

Preheat oven to 220°C (450°F). Line a baking tray with non-stick paper and mark a circle about 18 cm (7 in) in diameter. Put egg whites into large, very clean bowl (the slightest hint of grease and they will not whip up as they should). Whisk egg whites, salt, cream of tartar and vanilla essence with an electric mixer until stiff, add sugar by tablespoons while beating and when all the sugar is added and the meringue is glossy and thick, stir in the vinegar and cornflour. Pile onto the baking tray and smooth the top. Turn oven to 150°C (300°F) before putting meringue in and bake for 1 hour 20 minutes or until outside is firm but not browned. Remove from oven and allow to cool before topping with whipped cream, passionfruit pulp and any or all of the fruit.

Pastry

Pastries unique to Asia include the transparent pastry used in prawn (shrimp) dumplings, the coconut milk pastry used for curry puffs, paper-thin wonton pastry, thicker gow jee pastry, and gyoza wrappers. Many of these are available in sealed packets from the refrigerator section of Asian stores. For those who do not have such a store within reach, they are within the capability of a keen home cook and I am including some recipes here.

See also SPRING ROLL PASTRY and YUM CHA.

Transparent Steamed Dumpling Pastry

125 g/4 oz/1 cup Chinese wheat flour
3 tablespoons cornflour (cornstarch)
210 ml/7 fl oz water
1 tablespoon lard

Mix wheat flour and cornflour together in a bowl. Put measured water and lard into a small saucepan and bring to a boil. Turn off heat and cool for exactly 20 seconds, then pour all at once onto the flour. Mix with chopsticks or a wooden spoon. As soon as cool enough to handle, knead to a smooth, pliable dough. Shape into cylinder and wrap in plastic film to prevent drying out. See recipe for Steamed Prawn (Shrimp) Dumplings, page 416.

Curry Puff Pastry

Makes about 25

250 g/8 oz/2 cups plain (all purpose) flour
½ teaspoon salt
60 g/2 oz butter
3 tablespoons canned coconut milk

Sift flour and salt, rub in butter and add sufficient coconut milk to make a fairly firm dough. Knead lightly, form into a ball, wrap in plastic and chill for at least 30 minutes before rolling out thinly on lightly floured surface, to a thickness of 3 mm (⅛ in). Cut circles 8 cm (3 in) in diameter with a pastry cutter.

To make curry puffs, fill with a teaspoon of curried meat or chicken and seal pastry edges, pressing firmly together. Deep fry shortly before serving.

Won Ton Pastry

250 g/8 oz/2 cups plain (all purpose) flour
½ teaspoon salt
1 egg
125 ml/4 fl oz/½ cup cold water
cornflour (cornstarch)

Sift flour and salt into a large bowl. Beat egg with water. Make a well in the centre of the flour, pour in the egg mixture gradually and work into flour until it is all moistened. Knead on a floured surface at least 5 minutes, until smooth. Cover with a damp cloth and allow dough to rest for 30 minutes. Divide dough into 4 equal portions. Roll out one portion at a time on floured surface until very thin. With a ruler, cut dough into 8 cm (3 in) squares. Stack the squares, dusting generously with cornflour to prevent sticking. Wrap each stack in plastic and refrigerate until required. Will keep for about a week. See recipes for Steamed Pork Dumplings and Fried Wontons (pages 415 and 416).

Pawpaw

See PAPAYA.

Pea

See LEGUMES & PULSES.

Pea Flower

See SESBANIA.

Peanut

(*Arachis hypogaea*) These nuts, which are in fact a legume, grow underground, which is why they are also known as ground nuts. The 'nuts' are the seeds within the pod, each pod containing only 2 or 3. The bushy herb, which is a native of South America, pushes its pods into the earth and they are dug up like potatoes. Peanuts are an important source of oil, and if not refined and deodorised so that it loses all character, this mono-unsaturated oil gives a delightful nutty flavour to food cooked in it. It is capable of being heated to high temperatures without burning, which is why it is specified in Chinese cooking, particularly stir-frying where strong heat and quick cooking are essential for successful results. In France it is known as huile d'arachide and is widely used as a cooking medium.

A popular snack food in Western countries, these tasty nuts are sold in attractive, hermetically sealed foil packets with many variations — dry roasted, honey roasted, chilli fried, salted and salt-free.

Not everyone likes peanuts roasted and crunchy. In Vietnam, Thailand and other South East Asian countries they are boiled in the shell in very salty water, resulting in dark and soggy looking shells. They are sold in twists of paper. The shell is discarded and the mealy-textured nuts eaten as a snack.

Another instance of peanuts cooked until soft is the famous Thai Masaman Beef Curry (see recipe page 37), in which peanuts and potatoes are added to beef cooked slowly in flavours which are a pleasing combination of Thai and Indian spices.

Peanuts are also a mainstay of satay sauces, so much a part of Malaysian and Indonesian cuisine. Satays have become popular in Western countries and various satay sauces are available. For the best peanut sauce of all, however, try the recipe below. It can be kept for months in the refrigerator, and doubles as a tasty spread for crackers, toast, sandwiches and, for real addicts, is eaten by the spoonful. For use as a sauce, the base is thinned with coconut milk or water and spooned over gado-gado or served as a sauce for satays, those universally popular spicy morsels of skewered and barbecued meats.

Ground peanuts are also used as a base for cakes and candies, most of which are commercially made.

Medicinal uses: In a street market near Penang in Malaysia, I got into conversation with a young couple purchasing strange looking plants, mostly roots with lumps on them. They were peanut roots. They must be well cleaned and boiled in a strong chicken soup. I was told that boys, when they reach puberty, are given this soup three or four times in as many months. Presumably the pair were the parents of a teenage lad. They said they had no proof that it did any good, but were doing it just the same.

China: *fa-sang*
India: *mung-phali*
Indonesia: *kacang tana*
Japan: *rakkasei*
Malaysia: *kacang tanah*
Philippines: *mani*
Sri Lanka: *rata caju*
Thailand: *thua lisong*
Vietnam: *dau phong*

Peanut Sauce

This recipe makes the base for peanut sauce which, stored in a screw-top glass jar in the refrigerator, will keep for months. It makes a delicious spread, or relish with grilled meats. When required as a sauce, simply spoon out a quantity and mix in sufficient coconut milk or water to give a thick, pouring consistency.

125 ml/4 fl oz/½ cup peanut oil
4 tablespoons finely sliced shallots
1 tablespoon finely chopped garlic
2–3 large dried chillies
1 teaspoon dried shrimp paste (blacan)
2 tablespoons dark soy sauce
1 tablespoon lime or lemon juice
250 g/8 oz peanut butter
3 tablespoons coarse raw or demerara sugar or brown sugar
125 g/4 oz roasted peanuts, coarsely crushed

Heat oil and fry the sliced shallots on low heat, stirring constantly, until they are golden brown. Lift out on perforated spoon and drain on paper towels. In the same oil fry the garlic on low heat, lift out on a fine wire strainer before they brown. Fry chillies until puffed and almost black, about 1 minute. Lift out and allow to cool, then break off and discard their stems and crush or chop the chillies into small pieces. Reserve shallots, garlic and chillies to add later.

In the same oil fry the dried shrimp paste on low heat, crushing it with frying spoon. Remove from heat and stir in the soy sauce, lime juice and peanut butter and sugar until well blended. Cool the mixture before mixing in the fried shallots, garlic, chillies, sugar, and the roasted, crushed peanuts. Bottle and refrigerate.

Note: If preferred, use ready-fried shallots and garlic which are sold at Asian stores. Or purchase dried onion flakes and dried garlic slices and fry them for a short time on low heat as they burn easily.

Peanut Oil

See OILS.

Pear, Asian

See NASHI.

Pennywort

SEE ILLUSTRATION. (*Hydrocotyle* or *Centella asiatica*) small variety; (*Hydrocotyle* or *Centella javanica*) large variety. The common English name for this leaf is not widely known (except among gardeners and plant nurseries), but say the words 'gotu kola' (which are from the Sinhalese language) and a Western health shop assistant will immediately know what you're talking about.

The larger leaf variety is sold in Vietnamese areas. They have a slight bitter tang and are good to eat combined with shallots and lightly seasoned.

Another way this leaf is taken is as a sweetened beverage. Look in the refrigerator section of large Asian grocery stores and there, among the canned soft drinks featuring tropical fruit juices, you will also find pennywort drink. The canned version does not appeal much in colour or flavour, but the drink made with fresh pennywort leaves is entirely different and very refreshing. Frothy and bright green, its piquant herb flavour sweetened by the addition of sugar syrup and poured over crushed ice, it quenches thirst and does you good at the same time. In Vietnamese areas, certain shops make it to order. If you have a supply of leaves, it is easy enough to make at home (see recipe below).

Medicinal uses: Pennywort is used for purifying the blood and curing nervous conditions and is said to be 'good for the eyes'. It is also one of the herbs used in tonics to improve the memory. Eating 2 leaves each day is said to relieve the pain of arthritis and it is sold in plant nurseries as 'the arthritis herb'.

Burma: *myin-kwa-ywet*
China: *hang kor chow*
Indonesia: *pegagan*
Japan: *tsubo-kusa*
Malaysia: *daun pegaga*
Philippines: *takip-kohol*
Sri Lanka: *gotu kola, heen gotu kola*
Thailand: *bai bobo, bua-bok*
Vietnam: *nuoc rau ma*

Fresh Pennywort Drink

Wash the leaves well, pinch off stems and, for each handful of leaves, add 2½ cups cold water and ½ cup simple syrup made with equal parts of sugar and water. (Boil to dissolve sugar, allow to cool and store in a bottle.) Add 3 or 4 ice cubes and blend at high speed. Blend the drink just before serving or it will lose its bright colour.

Pennywort (Gotu-Kola) Salad

Shredding these small leaves is much easier if the entire amount is rolled tightly within a larger leaf such as lettuce. Then it is a simple matter of slicing thinly through the bundle. This is how Asian cooks do it, without the aid of food processors. Serves 4.

2 bunches gotu-kola
or about 250 g/8 oz/2 cups leaves
without stems
3 shallots or 1 small onion, finely chopped
good squeeze lime or lemon juice
1 sliced chilli (optional)
75 g/2½ oz/1 cup fresh grated coconut
salt to taste
½ teaspoon sugar

Wash well and strip leaves from stems. Shred finely with a sharp knife, combine with other ingredients and serve immediately. The flavour is slightly sour, slightly bitter.

Some people prefer this salad to be lightly cooked, if so bring a tablespoon of water and ½ teaspoon salt to the boil in a wok or pan, add all ingredients and toss over heat briefly, stopping before leaves lose their green colour.

Peperomia

(*Peperomia pellucida*) The glossy, heart-shaped green leaves and succulent stems of peperomia look like a decorative house plant, almost too pretty to eat. They are a favourite in Vietnam and Thailand, and are eaten raw or briefly blanched. My guess is that this may be an acquired taste for newcomers, and I have not been able to overcome the fact that they smell almost fishy. No doubt to some their odour is not off-putting, otherwise this leaf would not be on sale.

Indonesia: *rangu-rangu*
Japan: *suna-kosho*
Malaysia: *ketumpangan ayer*
Philippines: *olasiman ihalas*
Thailand: *pak krasang*
Vietnam: *cang cua*

Pepper

(*Piper nigrum*) SEE ILLUSTRATION. Perhaps the best known and most universally used spice. Small, round berries growing in trailing clusters, deep green turning red as they ripen, are borne on a vine with dark green heart-shaped leaves. This is true pepper.

There are other spices which, because they have a pungency reminiscent of pepper, have been given the name: chilli pepper (Capsicum family), Szechwan pepper (*Zanthoxylum piperitum*), and Jamaica pepper (*Pimenta dioica* or allspice). However, they are unrelated botanically.

The word pepper comes from the Sanskrit pippali, referring to *Piper longum* or long pepper — of the same botanical family as *P. nigrum* but somewhat milder in flavour and, instead of round berries, bearing fruit about 2.5 cm (1 in) long and about 6 mm (¼ in) wide. This was the pepper, more likely than not, used as currency in Roman times and said to be 4 times more valuable than black pepper. It seems not to be specified in today's recipes. However, the fact that I did find some in a supermarket in Switzerland implies that someone, somewhere, is using it. It is always used whole, as a pickling spice.

It is difficult to believe that black pepper was what provided the heat in Asian foods until the sea voyages of Columbus and others brought back chillies from the New World, but it is indeed so. Even today, black pepper together with fresh coriander and garlic provides the basic flavouring of Thai food. Black pepper is also prominent in some Portuguese-influenced dishes of Goa and Spanish-influenced dishes of the Philippines.

Black pepper: (*Pepper nigrum*) Obtained by drying the green berries in the sun, making the outer skin turn black and take on the familiar shrivelled appearance.

> **Burma:** *nga-youk-kaun*
> **China:** *hu-chiao*
> **India:** *kali mirich*
> **Indonesia:** *merica hitam*
> **Japan:** *kosho*
> **Laos:** *phik noi*
> **Malaysia:** *lada hitam*
> **Philippines:** *paminta*
> **Sri Lanka:** *gammiris*
> **Thailand:** *prik thai*

Green peppercorns: The immature berries of the *Piper nigrum* species which are sold fresh, brined or dried. Popular in certain Thai dishes such as Jungle Curry. Also used in Western style patés and terrines.

White pepper: From the *Piper nigrum* berries left to become ripe, packed into sacks and soaked in slow-flowing water for around 8 days, after which the softened outer coating is rubbed off. The inner portion is then dried in the sun for several days until the grey colour becomes creamy white. They are somewhat hotter than black peppercorns and not as fragrant, but are useful for white sauces or other dishes where the speckling of black would spoil the appearance of a dish.

Cubeb pepper: (*P. cubeba*) A member of the pepper family. It looks rather like a black peppercorn with a stalk and is hardly ever found these days, though they were valued as a medicine and as a spice up to the 17th century. The king of Portugal forbade their sale, thus hoping to promote the universal use of black pepper grown in the colonies he ruled. It seems he was spectacularly successful. If cubebs are found at all today, it will probably be in the pharmacopoeia of a herbalist.

Jamaica pepper: (*Pimenta doica*) Aromatic berries of a tree of the myrtle family. The dried berries are sold as allspice.

Pink peppercorns: (*Schinus molle*, or *S. terebinthifolius*) Enjoyed immense popularity in Western cooking a few years ago, but are not pepper at all. They don't grow on a vine but on a feathery-leaved ornamental tree, commonly known as mastic tree. All parts of the tree are fragrant, and the bright pink berries of both varieties of Schinus are used in fancy pepper mixes, or pickled in brine and sold as pink peppercorns. While they are decorative and have a distinctive aroma, the fibrous outer shell is not easy to eat. They are not used in Asian food.

Pepper, Szechwan

See SZECHWAN PEPPER.

Pepper-Coriander Paste

See CORIANDER.

Perilla

(*Perilla frutescens*, *P. crispa*) SEE ILLUSTRATION. This herb, which the Japanese call shiso, is a relative of basil and mint, but with a stronger flavour reminiscent of anise. It is also known as beefsteak plant. There are red as well as green-leaved varieties.

More than a thousand years ago the Chinese used perilla as a vegetable and extracted cooking oil from its seeds. This herb is now rarely used in modern Chinese cooking, but they did introduce it to the Japanese who use both the small green variety (ao-shiso) and the large red-leaved variety (aka-shiso, shiso noha). The latter has earned the plant its common name of beefsteak plant. Leaves of both varieties are fried as tempura. Stalks with buds and flowers (mejiso, hojiso) are used as a garnish. Perilla is also sometimes included in sushi. Red shiso leaves are sold packed in brine, to be added when pickling plums. In Vietnamese cuisine they are served raw as part of the salad, or wrapped around grilled meats.

Purchasing and storing: In Japanese stores one may come upon the green variety sold fresh in plastic envelopes of just a few leaves at a rather high price. Store for a day or two, keeping them in their plastic package to prevent drying out.

Medicinal uses: Fresh leaves are said to be antibiotic and guard against fish poisoning. Dried leaves are used to treat flu, coughs and nausea.

Japan: *shiso*
Vietnam: *la tia to*

Perilla Oil

See OILS.

Perilla Seed

(*Perilla frutescens*, *P. crispa*) These small, rounded, beige-coloured seeds are sold in Korean grocery stores. They are popular added to meat marinades and, ground, are added to soups. In Japan they are a popular seasoning used fresh or in miso pickles. I was warned that over-indulgence may result in diarrhoea.

Japan: *shisonomi*
Korea: *deul gge*

Persimmon

(*Diospyros kaki*) Native to northern China, this fruiting tree is one of the few temperate relatives of the primarily tropical ebony species. Bearing globular yellow or orange fruit which become translucent when ripe, they are unpleasantly astringent if consumed much before their pulp turns almost to purée. The astringency is due to the high levels of tannin in the fruit.

A persimmon tree, laden with ripe fruit, is a sight to behold — bereft of leaves, with eye-catching fruit like glowing lanterns contrasting with dark, bare branches. In Japan, where persimmons are very popular as fruit or made into sherbets and dried sweet treats, non-astringent varieties have been cultivated, designed to be eaten while hard, like an apple. The variety known as fuyu or fuji fruit is often flatter and squatter in appearance (but not always) than the persimmon and ready to eat even though it exhibits all the signs of unripe fruit: a pale, undeveloped colour and extreme hardness. They are, however, actually ready to eat, sweet and curiously 'crunchy'.

You can try an experiment to remove the astringency from unripe persimmons. Wrap a fruit in a few layers of cling film (plastic wrap) and leave in a warm spot for 3–4 days. If successful, the fruit will remain firmer than if it had air-ripened and have developed a more pronounced flavour without being astringent. Alternatively, place a few fruit in a large freezer bag (heavy duty), remove the oxygen (by pump or mouth), exhale some carbon dioxide into the bag and knot securely. As the fruit ripen over a few days, they will exude gases of their own, further inflating the bag. The de-astringency theory is based on the exclusion of oxygen.

It is inadvisable to over-indulge in persimmons, especially to the exclusion of all else, as they are the most common cause of bezoars, a kind of gastric blockage that results from an excessively high intake of tannin. I have made ripe persimmons into a very refreshing drink, blended together with half as much lime juice, caster sugar to taste, some ice cubes and water. It was a thick, sweet but tangy drink. It is also a suitable ingredient for sorbet.

Dried persimmons are available from Asian stockists and they are either eaten as they are after washing off the white powder that coats them, or steamed for 15 minutes before eating. A favourite sweet, tea-coloured drink in Korea (soo jeong gwa)

Petai

is made from dried persimmon boiled in water with cinnamon, sugar and ginger.

Also related to the persimmon is the mabolo or velvet apple (*D. discolor*).

Petai

See PARKIA.

Philippines

The cuisine of the Philippines demonstrates unmistakably that the islands have been, over the years, visited by traders and colonisers from both East and West. The most lasting impact was made by the Spanish, and on formal occasions the menu will reflect that influence. On the other hand, when families get together their favourite food will be those dishes which owe little, if anything, to outside influences. Even if they were originally borrowed they have been 're-composed', adding new flavours and generally acquiring a new personality.

It was not only the Spanish who left their stamp on Filipino food. There were the Malays, Chinese and Indonesians and, more recently, the Americans.

While important meals may sound more Spanish than anything else, a day in the Philippines is broken up by as much snacking as goes on in Malaysia, Singapore or Indonesia. Breakfast is followed mid-morning by sweet rolls (see BREADS) with hot chocolate or coffee; lunch, however substantial, is not expected to sustain anyone until the very late dinner hour, so in the afternoon there is the typical merienda.

Rice belongs to the main meals, lunch and dinner. Merienda food is served purely for enjoyment and hospitality. Among the items served there may be dishes as substantial as fried noodles with mixed meats, pancit guisado, and noodle soups, pancit luglug; fresh or fried spring rolls, lumpia; and always some sweet treats such as rice cakes, puto and bibingka, a cake very similar in taste and texture to a Western teacake.

Traditional Filipino food takes in dishes such as sinigang (a sour soup); guinatan (fish, meat, vegetables or yams cooked in coconut milk); adobo (a piquant preparation of chicken or pork cooked with vinegar, garlic and black pepper); kari-kari (a stew which features oxtail, stewing beef, or sometimes tripe as well as eggplants (aubergines) and other vegetables simmered in a sauce made

bright with the addition of annatto); lechon (a whole roast pig served with a special sauce which includes liver pate); dinuguan (pork meat and organ meats with spices stewed in fresh pork blood). Another popular local food is lumpiang ubod, a delicious spring roll which has as part of its filling the fresh heart of a coconut palm.

While wealthy Filipinos can afford kitchens equipped with modern appliances, it is in country kitchens or those of very particular cooks (who say that modern utensils and methods don't give quite the right result) that the heritage of Filipino cooking is preserved. Here the stone mortar and pestle, round-bottomed earthen pots (carajay) and heavy cast-iron kuwali (shaped like a small wok) are considered the best utensils which give the best results. To the traditional way of thinking stainless steel and aluminium may be convenient but simply cannot compete. The table setting always includes spoons, forks and knives, the spoon being used for eating rice.

Pickles

Home made pickles are popular in Asian cuisine, and may be vinegar, brine or oil based. They are a way of preserving food in times of plenty, to be used throughout the months when supplies may not be as bountiful. Some of the most popular Indian pickles feature seasonal fruit and vegetables such as mangoes, limes and eggplant and tomatoes. See recipes for Hot Mango Pickle (page 230), Sri Lankan Eggplant Pickle (page 131) and Tomato Oil Pickle (page 389). Also see Index of Recipes.

There are also mild pickles purchased ready made, such as pickled garlic, one of the key ingredients of Mee Grob, the famous Thai dish of crisply fried rice noodles. There are other pickles to be found, in cans and jars, that add piquancy to many a dish.

Salted vegetables such as radish and cabbage are not simply a tantalising taste, they are important sustenance and are eaten every day of the year (see recipe for Kim Chi, page 57).

Pigeon Pea

See LEGUMES & PULSES.

Pilau

Pilaf, pulao and pullao, are some of the names by which you may encounter a spiced rice dish in India. The word comes from the Persian word for cooked rice, polo. The original dish dates back to Moghul times, with a strong Persian influence since the Moghul emperors admired and emulated Persian culture.

A pilau may simply be rice fried in ghee with whole spices and cooked in stock, always by the absorption method; it may also incorporate vegetables or chicken or seafood or lamb, lentils or cubes of cheese. The variations are endless, but rice is always the main component.

When spiced rice and savoury meats are combined in layers and finished by steaming or baking, the dish is elevated to the status of biriani (see Festive Biriani, page 172). For some examples of pilaus, see Ghee Rice (page 309), Saffron Rice Pilau (page 320), and Cauliflower Pilau (page 70).

Pine Nut

(*Pinus pinea*) SEE ILLUSTRATION. There are about 80 varieties of pine which yield edible nuts of varying quality. The main variety used in Asia is *Pinus koraiensis* which grows in Korea, northern Japan and Manchuria. Compared to its Mediterranean counterpart, the long, slender kernels of the stone pine, Asia's pine nuts are short and squat. Pine nuts are often used in place of olive nuts, which are harder to come by and more expensive. Pine nuts are the kernels or seeds of the pine cone which are released as the cone matures and opens. White or cream-coloured, their delicate flavour is enhanced by light roasting or frying, but be watchful as they burn easily.

They are used in Korean cuisine as a garnish on special dishes or cooked into a porridge with ground rice and dried jujubes (red dates). This is considered a special treat and served as a restorative.

China also grows pine nuts, not as slender and creamy white as the Mediterranean variety, but more affordable. These small kernels are ivory in colour and soft textured. Their flavour is slightly resinous.

Korea: *jaht*

Pineapple

(*Ananas comosus*) This native of central America is now well known and widely cultivated wherever a tropical or sub-tropical climate permits.

It is actually a false fruit, made up of a hundred or more seedless true fruits, which are the regular shaped segments on the outside and the 'eyes' which are revealed when the coloured skin is sliced away. The 'eyes' consist of round holes arranged in rows, in the centres of which are stiff, short brown hairs, remnants of the hundred or more flowers which crowded the woody spike.

There are many varieties of pineapple, small, large, round, oval, green, orange, yellow, shiny or matt surfaced. The flesh is pale to bright yellow with variable sweetness and fibre. Those with a matt orange or yellow-coloured skin might not look as attractive as those with shiny skin but this, teamed with a short crown of spiky-edged leaves, usually indicates a very sweet variety of pineapples commonly called 'roughies'.

While it is a delicious fruit to eat ripe and sweet for breakfast, lunch or dessert, in Asia the pineapple is used in many other ways. For instance, half-ripe pineapples are used in Vietnamese and Cambodian sour soups and Malaysian or Indonesian curries.

Pineapple contains an enzyme called bromeline which digests protein, which is why fresh pineapple will not allow gelatine to set and should not be included in a fruit jelly. On the other hand, this property is used to good effect to tenderise tough cuts of meat by rubbing it over the meat before cooking.

Purchasing and storage: If you wish to buy a fully ripe pineapple, be guided by the scent of the fruit. A ripe pineapple will smell deliciously fragrant. Tug at one of the smallest outer leaves in the crown. If really ripe, the leaf will detach itself without too much effort, though this is not always the case, depending on variety. Some part with their leaves easily, others don't. If the thin skin which half covers each segment has brown tips, it indicates the pineapple is fully ripe.

If you want to select a half-ripe pineapple which is firm and right for cooking, make sure it is hard to the touch. Colour is not a good indication of how ripe a fruit is, and even a deep green pineapple may be ripe and sweet. Firm ripe or half-ripe pineapples are best for Thai salads which combine fruit, seafood, beef or chicken with a salty, sour dressing.

Pineapples can be left at room temperature for a few days and will stay firm and continue to ripen. To hasten ripening, put the fruit in a polythene bag with a ripe banana, close the bag and leave at room temperature.

Preparation: Too much of a pineapple gets wasted because many people think the only way to remove all traces of the 'eyes' is to slice off a thick layer of flesh with the skin. There is a better way to do this, decorative and much less wasteful.

For a start, use a good, sharp stainless steel knife as the fruit reacts with carbon steel. Cut a small slice off the top, removing the crown of leaves. Cut another slice from the bottom of the fruit so it will stand flat and firm on the chopping board. Then, beginning at the top, thinly slice off the coloured skin in strips. Never mind if the eyes are left. Notice how they are arranged in beautifully regular spiral rows around the fruit. Lay the fruit on its side and make a series of angled, V-shaped cuts, following the rows and excising 3 eyes at a time. Place the next cut where the last one ended. When you have gone all the way around the fruit following that row, start on the next one. This not only saves wasting much of the fruit, but gives a most decorative effect for serving the fruit whole or cut into crosswise rounds or lengthwise spears.

To cut pieces for including in soups or curries, after the pineapple has had the skin and eyes removed as described above, slice lengthways into 6 or 8 sections, depending on the size of the fruit. Then lay the pieces on the board and cut off the core. The wedges of fruit can then be sliced across into neat, entirely edible pieces.

There is no denying that there is a lot wasted in a pineapple. Wash the fruit well before peeling it and use the peel, core and trimmings from removing the 'eyes' to make a refreshing thirst-quenching cordial, boiled with water and sugar.

Even the leaves can be put to good use. Cut off the leafy crown attached to a thick slice of the fruit, plant it in a warm sunny spot and it will, given a couple of years, grow into another pineapple plant.

Fiji: *vadra*
India: *ananas*
Indonesia: *nanas*
Malaysia: *nanas*
Philippines: *pina*
Sri Lanka: *annasi*
Thailand: *supparot*

Pineapple Coconut Curry

This spicy curry from South East Asia is a surprising setting for fruit. Serves 4.

half a large firm pineapple
1 medium onion, finely chopped
2 teaspoons finely chopped garlic
2 tablespoons oil
1 tablespoon ground coriander
2 teaspoons ground cumin
1 teaspoon chilli powder
   or 1 fresh red chilli, sliced
250 ml/8 fl oz/1 cup thick coconut milk
3 cardamom pods, bruised
3 whole cloves
1 small stick cinnamon
1 teaspoon salt or to taste
1 teaspoon palm sugar or brown sugar

Peel and trim pineapple as described above. Cut in 2 or 3 lengthwise wedges depending on the size of the pineapple. Remove core and cut the fruit into crossways slices. On low heat fry onion and garlic in the oil until soft and starting to turn golden. Add coriander, cumin and chilli, stir and fry for a couple of minutes longer, then add pineapple and stir well. Stir in coconut milk, whole spices, salt and sugar. Do not stop stirring until coconut milk reaches simmering point, then simmer for a few minutes, uncovered, until pineapple is just tender. Serve with rice and other accompaniments.

Vietnamese Sour Soup with Pineapple

This refreshing soup is made with fresh pineapple, preferably half-ripe and tart. It may be made with chicken or beef, thinly sliced, instead of the prawns (shrimp). Serves 2.

250 g/8 oz raw prawns (shrimp)
4 spring onions (scallions), sliced
2 tablespoons oil
750 ml/1½ pints/3 cups water
   or light chicken stock
2 tablespoons fish sauce
salt and pepper to taste
¼ small pineapple, peeled and cored

Shell and devein the prawns and chop them coarsely. Mix spring onions with the prawns, heat oil and stir-fry until they change colour. Add water or stock, fish sauce, salt and pepper, and the pineapple either sliced thinly or crushed. Bring to a boil, simmer for 2 minutes and serve.

Pistachio Nut

(*Pistacia vera*) SEE ILLUSTRATION. These mild-flavoured, vivid green nuts are highly prized, and are used mostly in rich, extravagant Moghul dishes. Native to the mountains of central Asia and cultivated from the Eastern Mediterranean to South West Asia, pistachios are now grown in California, Texas and Arizona in the United States, as well as in Australia. Iran is also a major producer of pistachios, used in the rich, expensive sweet pastries identified with Middle Eastern countries.

Pistachios are mostly sold roasted and salted in their shells, but shops which sell Middle Eastern and Indian ingredients also sell pistachio kernels which have been dried but not roasted, toasted or salted. These are the ones to purchase for any of the recipes in this book. They still need to be blanched and the thin purplish skin slipped off, and are deep green within, unlike the roasted nuts which have lost their colour. The greener the kernel, the better the quality.

It is also possible to buy, in their brief season, fresh pistachio nuts. At their freshest and best, they are beautiful to behold, with each shell encased in a soft skin tinged with magenta. The shell of the nut is creamy white. Inside it is the nut with its purplish skin (blanch in boiling water for 30 seconds, drop into cold water) which comes off to reveal a more vividly green kernel than any dried pistachios can offer. In my freezer is a small packet of blanched fresh pistachios, ready to be used in very special dishes.

See recipe for Shrikhand (page 415) and Pistachio Barfi (page 370).

India: *pista*

Plantain

There is more than one claimant to the common name plantain: firstly members of the family Plantaginaceae, not generally used for food, with the exception of *Plantago ovata* and *P. psyllium* which have tiny seeds capable of absorbing 25 times their weight in water. See PSYLLIUM.

The word 'plantain' in a food context also refers to a cooking banana (*Musa sapientum*) or any banana which is green and unripe, and cooked as a vegetable. However, this appellation is not standardised, for in some countries any banana, even a sweet and ripe dessert banana, is called a plantain.

In the Pacific, the plantain is usually cooked in its thick skin and peeled after it is soft. The skin is removed before serving. It can also be peeled using a knife (although the skin is not as easily peeled off unripe fruit) and the starchy fruit can be cut in slices and fried, as potatoes are. In South East Asia, where spicier flavours are preferred, green plantains are relished as a vegetable, cooked in coconut milk with fresh flavours such as green chillies, lemon grass and fresh curry leaves. They may also be peeled, sliced and fried, the slices rubbed first with turmeric and salt, making the end result more savoury. The thick skin is not wasted either, being the starting point for a tasty accompaniment to rice.

Perhaps this is the spot to include recipes for unripe green bananas. These are usually sold in shops where Pacific peoples are catered for, or in Asian areas.

Green Plantain Skin Temperado

Serves 2

3 or 4 plantains or 2 if very large
250 ml/8 fl oz/1 cup water
¼ teaspoon ground turmeric
1 scant teaspoon salt
2 tablespoons dried prawns (shrimp)
½–1 teaspoon chilli powder

FOR FINISHING
1 tablespoon oil
1 small onion, finely chopped
2 sprigs fresh curry leaves

With a sharp paring knife cut off and discard the stem end of each plantain. (It helps to smear the hands lightly with oil before preparing plantains to protect against sticky sap.) When removing the skin, first make a shallow scraping cut and pull away and discard any long fibres in the outer layer, as you would with celery.

Slice off the skin with a small sharp knife, as if peeling a potato thickly. Because the skin will discolour very quickly, shred it crossways into thin shreds and put it straight into a small saucepan with the cup of water and the next 4 ingredients. Cover and simmer for 20 minutes or until skins are soft.

Meanwhile, cut the peeled plantains into thick slices, rub both sides of each slice with ground turmeric and salt and set aside.

When dried prawns and plantain skins are soft and water almost evaporated, in another pan (preferably a wok which requires very little oil) heat the oil and fry the onions and curry leaves on medium high heat, stirring frequently, until the onions are brown. Add contents of the first pan to the oil and continue to toss mixture over heat until almost no liquid remains. Serve as an accompaniment to rice.

Mild Green Plantain Curry

Serves 4

sliced plantain from previous recipe
1 teaspoon ground turmeric
1 teaspoon salt or to taste
oil for frying
2 fresh green chillies (optional)
sprig of curry leaves
1 medium onion, finely chopped
375 ml/12 fl oz/1½ cups thin coconut milk
125 ml/4 fl oz/½ cup thick coconut milk

Heat about ½ cup oil in a wok and fry the plantain slices which have been rubbed with turmeric and salt, not too many at a time, until golden brown. Lift out on slotted spoon and drain on paper towels.

Put the rest of the ingredients except thick coconut milk into a saucepan and simmer uncovered for about 10 minutes. Add the fried plantain slices and simmer for a further 5–8 minutes, then stir in the thick coconut milk. Taste and correct seasoning if necessary. Serve with rice.

Spicy Plantain Curry

Serves 4

500 g/1 lb green plantains
1 teaspoon ground turmeric
½ teaspoon salt
oil for frying
sprig of fresh curry leaves
small stick cinnamon
2 cardamom pods, bruised

small strip pandan leaf
¼ teaspoon fenugreek seeds
1 medium onion, finely chopped
1 or 2 fresh chillies, seeded and sliced
1 tablespoon Ceylon curry powder
  or 2 teaspoons ground coriander, 1 teaspoon
  ground cumin and ½ teaspoon ground fennel
500 ml/1 pint/2 cups coconut milk
1 teaspoon salt
1 teaspoon chilli powder (optional)
squeeze of lime juice

Prepare the plantains as described in previous recipes, rubbing the slices with turmeric and salt and setting aside for 15–20 minutes. Deep fry a few slices at a time until golden. Pour off the oil, leaving about 2 tablespoons. Heat oil and fry curry leaves, cinnamon, cardamom, pandan leaf and fenugreek seeds for 1–2 minutes. Add onion and chillies and fry a minute longer, then add the curry powder or individual spices, coconut milk, salt and chilli powder. Simmer uncovered for 10–15 minutes. Add lime juice to taste and serve with rice.

Plantains with Coconut and Chilli

2 green plantains
90 g/3 oz/1 cup freshly grated coconut
3 tablespoons finely sliced purple shallots
1 or 2 fresh green chillies, seeded and sliced
1 tablespoon thick coconut cream
salt to taste
squeeze of lime juice

Peel the plantains and boil them in lightly salted water until soft. Drain and mash, adding the coconut, shallots, chillies and coconut cream. Add salt to taste and a good squeeze of lime juice to sharpen the flavour. Serve with rice.

Pomegranate

(*Punica granatum*) A large, berry-like fruit with thick, leathery, brightly coloured skin, originating in Persia, western or southern Asia. The juice is the basis of the red cordial, grenadine. There are a number of varieties, but a good pomegranate contains a mass of ruby-coloured seed sacs that are tangy-sweet and juice filled. Although now more associated with the Middle East than Asia, the seeds are used in Indian cookery.

The pink or red sparkling juice sacs which look like rubies are nice to eat, if rather time-consuming. In the centre of each sac is a small white seed which is edible (if you don't mind the astringency) but hard enough to make most people spit them out.

The seeds of a variety of wild pomegranate, daru (native to the Himalayan foothills of Kashmir and Jammu), are dried and used in some northern Indian dishes. Anardhana, as they are called, are used most often in the fillings of pastry snacks or stuffed breads. They contribute a sour flavour. They are also used on meat dishes in Middle Eastern cooking.

Purchasing and storing: Israel, Italy, South Africa, Spain and California grow and export top quality pomegranates which look beautiful while they are fresh and the leathery skin is red and shiny. Long lasting, the fruit will adorn a fruit bowl for weeks and may be kept in cold storage for months. They turn brown and dull as they age, but the fruit inside remains juicy and edible, protected by the thickness of the skin.

Preparation: Use a sharp stainless steel knife to cut through the skin lengthways 3 or 4 times from stem to calyx, dividing the skin into segments, then peel skin back from the juice sacs. The seeds of fresh pomegranates are used for garnishing dishes, but first they must be picked out and separated from the creamy white inedible membrane which divides them into 6 segments.

Pomelo

(*Citrus grandis, C. maxima*) (Also spelled pummelo). SEE ILLUSTRATION. Native to South East Asia, this largest of the citrus fruits can weigh up to 10 kg (22 lb). It looks like a grapefruit with a slightly pointed stem end. The flesh is sweeter than grapefruit, although somewhat drier. There are two varieties, pink (sometimes quite deep red) and white (which, to be accurate, is a pale greenish yellow). Often eaten in a savoury context, with meat or shellfish and seasoned with salt, lime juice and chilli.

A good specimen is delicious, sweet and juicy. A poor specimen can have bitter, fibrous pulp. It is said to be a cross between the shaddock and the grapefruit. A favourite in South East Asia and now being grown in other countries. Pick one which is heavy for its size. Until you gain sufficient experience to judge whether your surprise package is going to be worth the trouble of removing its very thick skin, ask guidance from the seller.

In Thailand there is a charming saying that the fruit must have time to forget the tree. Freshly picked fruit can be tart, while those that have been kept a few weeks are much sweeter. Usually eaten as a snack and thirst-quencher, but occasionally the large juice sacs are teased apart, tossed with a salty and fiery chilli dressing, and used in salads. To serve whole segments, first peel off the thick, white membrane which encases them.

Malaysia: *pomelo, limau besar*
Philippines: *naranja*
Sri Lanka: *jumbola*
Thailand: *som-or*
Vietnam: *buoi*

Pomelo Salad

Use pomelos, pink or white grapefruit or golden-fleshed ugli fruit. Mandarins or oranges do not have quite enough acidity to contrast with the strong flavours, except early in their season when they are tart. Serves 2–3.

2 cups peeled pomelo segments
1 cup cooked and shredded pork or chicken
3 tablespoons coconut milk
2 tablespoons nam prik pao*
2 tablespoons lime juice
1½ tablespoons sugar
1–2 tablespoons fish sauce
2 tablespoons ground roasted peanuts
1 tablespoon chopped fresh chillies
2 tablespoons crisp fried shallots
1 tablespoon crisp fried garlic

Remove the membrane enclosing the segments of fruit, discard seeds and break the fruit into bite-sized pieces.

Cut chicken or pork into fine shreds.

Heat coconut milk in a wok and add nam prik pao, stirring until it is thick. Stir in the shredded pork or chicken. Add lime juice, sugar and fish sauce, using 1 or 2 tablespoons depending on how salty the particular brand of fish sauce is. Remove from heat and cool the mixture slightly, then toss everything together in a bowl and serve.

*Nam prik pao is a thick, chilli and shrimp Thai relish sold in jars in Asian shops. I have included a recipe for a similar relish, Thai Chilli and Shrimp Sauce, on page 332.

Candied Pomelo Rind

The thick skin of pomelo is ideal for candied rind which turns out beautifully soft and luscious.

pomelo rind
sugar
water

First wash the fruit well, scrubbing at any patches of stubborn soil on the skin. Peeling a pomelo is not as effortless as peeling a mandarin or orange; the thick pith requires a special technique as it is firmly attached to the large segments. With the point of a sharp knife cut lines from stem end downwards, the lines meeting at top and bottom of the fruit but about 5 cm (2 in) apart around the middle. Prise one section of rind loose and it will then be somewhat easier to remove the remaining sections.

Cut into thick strips and drop into a pan of boiling water. Bring to the boil, simmer for 5 minutes and drain. Repeat with fresh water 3 times to get rid of excess bitterness. (If using the pink variety of pomelo, do not be surprised if the pith which is white when raw, develops a pink colour when it is cooked.) Allow the rind to cool and squeeze out as much water as possible.

Measure the peel and for each cup allow ½ cup sugar and ¼ cup water. Don't attempt to cook more than about 3 cups of peel at one time. In a heavy pan dissolve sugar in water to make a thick syrup. Add the peel, and simmer until the peel is soft and translucent and all the syrup absorbed. Stir from time to time, ensuring that all the pieces have a turn at being immersed in the syrup and that the sugar does not caramelise.

Allow to cool and for better keeping quality place on a wire rack and dry in a cool oven, 90°C (190°F), and preferably fan-forced, for 40 minutes. This should make the pieces of peel drier. Avoid leaving them in the oven too long or on too high a temperature or the outer skin will become tough and leathery. Allow them to retain sufficient moisture to hold a coating of sugar and roll the pieces in caster (superfine) sugar. Can be stored airtight for 2–3 weeks.

Pomfret

(*Pampus argenteus, Stromateus argentus* and *Formio niger, Parastromateus niger*) One of the most highly regarded fish with firm white flesh and delicate flavour.

There are two main varieties of this fish eaten in Asia. The first is the silver or white pomfret. Suitable for all methods of cooking, the cooked flesh of the fish falls away from the bones for easy eating. Those familiar with the fish eat the lower fin and tail which are considered too tasty to waste. Smoked pomfret is a delicacy in Hong Kong and southern China.

The black or brown pomfret, grey-brown with blue reflections, is more prevalent in the waters of Indonesia and the Philippines. Not regarded quite as highly as the white pomfret, it is still considered an excellent fish. Also available salted and dried.

Two dishes featuring pomfret have survived years of being filed away in my taste memory, crowded though those files are. One was served in a leading restaurant in Bombay, stuffed with a fresh chutney and fried to perfection — the flesh moist, the fins and tail meltingly crisp; the other, in a seafood restaurant in Singapore, offered the fish steamed with subtle Chinese flavours.

Burma: *ngamotephyu*
Cambodia: *trey chap sar, trey pek chhieu*
China: *pa chong*
India: *chamna*
Indonesia: *bawal putih*
Malaysia: *bawal puteh*
Philippines: *duhay*
Vietnam: *ca chim trang*

Pan Fried Pomfret with Fresh Chutney

Serves 2

1 pomfret, about 750 g/1½ lb
1 lime or lemon
1 teaspoon salt
½ teaspoon ground turmeric
½ teaspoon chilli powder
flour or cornflour (cornstarch) for dusting
oil for shallow frying

MIXTURE FOR STUFFING

1 tablespoon ghee
1 tablespoon slivered almonds

3 tablespoons finely chopped spring onions
   (scallions)
4 tablespoons cooked and mashed green peas
2 tablespoons chopped fresh mint
2 tablespoons chopped fresh coriander
½ teaspoon garam masala (recipe page 354)
½ teaspoon finely grated fresh ginger
2 green chillies, finely chopped
finely grated rind of 1 lime

Clean the fish, leaving it whole. Scrub the cavity with coarse salt, rinse well and dry with paper towels. Score the flesh at its thickest point. Finely grate the rind of the lime and set aside for the stuffing. Squeeze the juice of half the lime over the fish and inside the cavity, rub salt, turmeric and chilli powder both inside and outside the fish and leave while preparing stuffing.

Heat ghee in a small pan and fry the slivered almonds until golden. Lift out and cool. Fry the spring onion until soft, add to the mashed green peas with the chopped fresh herbs, garam masala, ginger, chillies, grated lime rind and the almonds, coarsely chopped. Add salt to taste.

Fill the cavity of the fish and, if necessary, tie once or twice with string. Dip the fish in flour or cornflour, dusting off excess.

Heat oil in a heavy frying pan and when very hot put in the fish and fry until crisp and brown all over, turning once. Remove string and serve immediately with wedges of lime if desired.

Deep Fried Pomfret with Spicy Sauce

Coat the whole fish with seasoned flour and deep fry until golden brown. Have ready fresh chillies pounded with garlic, shallots and shrimp paste so the sauce may be quickly cooked and poured over the fish while it is still warm. Serves 4.

2 whole pomfret, cleaned
2 tablespoons plain (all-purpose) flour
1 teaspoon salt
¼ teaspoon pepper
oil for deep frying

SAUCE
2 tablespoons chopped fresh red chillies
1 tablespoon chopped garlic
2 tablespoons sliced purple shallots
2 teaspoons shrimp paste
2 teaspoons fish sauce

Clean fish, score flesh and coat with flour mixed with salt and pepper. Dust off excess flour. Have sauce ingredients pounded to a paste (or blended in an electric blender) before starting to fry fish. Heat oil for deep frying and fry the fish until golden brown. Drain on paper towels. Pour off all but 3 tablespoons oil and fry the sauce ingredients, stirring constantly, until fragrant and oily, about 4–5 minutes. Spoon over the fried fish and serve at once, with steamed rice.

Steamed Pomfret, Chinese Style

Serves 2

1 large pomfret, about 500 g/1 lb
1 teaspoon salt
¼ teaspoon white pepper
4 dried shiitake mushrooms
2 tablespoons tender fresh ginger, finely
   shredded
4 tablespoons finely chopped spring onions
   (scallions)
1 tablespoon peanut oil
1 teaspoon oyster sauce
pinches of sugar, salt and white pepper to taste
1 teaspoon oriental sesame oil
½ teaspoon cornflour (cornstarch)
sprigs of coriander and red chilli slices
   to garnish

Clean fish, scrubbing cavity with paper towels dipped in coarse salt. Rinse and blot dry, then score flesh with diagonal cuts on both sides and rub with measured salt and pepper. Soak dried mushrooms in very hot water for 25 minutes, discard stems and cut caps into strips. Scatter half the ginger on a heatproof dish, place the fish on it and sprinkle with mushrooms, spring onions, the remaining ginger and ½ tablespoon of peanut oil. Cover dish with foil, place over boiling water and steam for 10 minutes or until fish is opaque when tested at thickest part.

Pour off and reserve the liquid from the fish, replace foil to keep fish warm and add a little water or light chicken stock if necessary to make about 1 cup of liquid. Heat remaining

Ponzu

½ tablespoon oil in a small pan, add liquid and oyster sauce, sugar, salt, pepper and sesame oil. Bring to the boil and stir in the small amount of cornflour mixed with a little cold water if a slightly thickened sauce is liked, but it must in no way be thick enough to coat the fish. Serve hot, garnished with coriander and chillies.

Ponzu

Japanese sauce of equal parts shoyu (Japanese soy sauce) and lemon or lime juice.

Poontalai

Olive-sized dried fruit exported from Thailand. Its name in Hokkien is similar (pong tai hai) and there is no English name for it that I can trace. It has an enormous capacity for absorbing water and expands like a sponge when left to soak. The Malay name, buah kembang sa mangkok, which translates as 'the fruit that becomes a bowl', proves the point. It is used in ice kacang for its interesting texture. See ICE KACANG.

Poppy Seed

(*Papaver somniferum*) The poppy seeds used in Indian cooking are not the blue-black seeds used in European cakes and sweets, but smaller, creamy white poppy seeds, used mostly as a thickener for gravies. They are rich in oil and protein and are best stored in the freezer to prevent rancidity. The flavour is developed by lightly roasting the seeds which are then ground into spice combinations for various regional dishes. They may be used instead of ground almonds in northern Indian kormas (see recipe for Braised Fish with Saffron and Yoghurt, page 150) and in Goan curries known as Xacuti or Shaguti (see recipe for Crab Xacuti, page 412).

India: *khas khas, posta*

Pork

Pork is a meat favoured by many Asian and Pacific peoples, though perhaps nowhere has the cooking of it reached the high art it is in China. Prepared in the traditional way, even fatty pork is cooked to translucent, melting perfection. It epitomises the care and finesse that has made Chinese cuisine legendary.

Whole roast pig is a feature of Pacific Island feasts.

Pork is not eaten for religious reasons by Jewish and Moslem people, but even in Moslem countries there are Hindu or Christian communities where pork is not against the rules. Examples are Bali in Indonesia and Goa in India.

Balinese Style Pork

Serves 4

500 g/1 lb pork neck
2 tablespoons oil
4 shallots or 1 small onion, finely chopped
1 teaspoon finely grated garlic
2 teaspoons finely grated ginger
6 thin slices ginger root
2 tablespoons sweet soy sauce (kecap manis)
1 tablespoon light soy sauce
¼ teaspoon ground black pepper
2 fresh hot chillies, sliced
125 ml/4 fl oz/½ cup hot water

Cut pork into thin slices, then into small dice.

Heat oil and cook onion and garlic over low heat, stirring occasionally, until soft and golden. Add ginger and pork and stir-fry over high heat until pork is no longer pink.

Add sauces, pepper, chillies and hot water. Cover and simmer for 10 minutes, then uncover and cook until sauce is reduced. Serve with rice.

Lion's Head

Tender and meltingly soft, these large meatballs are full of exotic flavours.
Serves 5.

MEATBALLS
2 rose-leaf sized pieces dried tangerine peel
500 g/1 lb minced (ground) pork
1 teaspoon finely grated fresh ginger
1 teaspoon salt
½ teaspoon sugar
3 tablespoons finely chopped spring onions, green leaves included
1 tablespoon cornflour (cornstarch) mixed with 2 tablespoons cold water
1 egg white, stiffly beaten

SAUCE AND VEGETABLES

**3 or 4 bunches Shanghai bok choy
(3 in each bunch)**
2 tablespoons peanut oil
4 thin slices fresh ginger
½ teaspoon salt
500 ml/1 pint/2 cups chicken stock or hot water
3 tablespoons warm Chinese wine or dry sherry
2 teaspoons cornflour (cornstarch)

Soak tangerine peel in 3 tablespoons warm water until softened, then chop very finely and return to the soaking liquid. Mix all ingredients for meat balls together well, folding in egg white last. Cover and chill for 30 minutes or longer, then form into 5 large meatballs.

Slit bok choy down the centre, wash well, and soak in salt water for 20 minutes. Drain well and shake dry.

Heat wok, add 1 tablespoon oil and when oil is hot fry the ginger for a few seconds, then add the bok choy and stir-fry for 2 or 3 minutes. Remove from wok. Add remaining tablespoon oil and lightly brown the meatballs. Put half the bok choy in a flameproof casserole or a sandy pot. Arrange meatballs on the layer of vegetable and cover with the rest. Add salt, hot stock and wine, cover and simmer gently until meatballs are well cooked, about 35 minutes.

Before serving, thicken liquid with cornflour mixed with a little cold water. Serve hot.

Spicy Spareribs

The spareribs to buy for this dish are not the thick, meaty ones with layers of fat and lean, but small spareribs in racks which are sold as American (as distinct from Chinese) spareribs. Serves 6.

1.5 kg/3 lb pork spareribs
2 teaspoons chopped garlic
1½ teaspoons salt
½ teaspoon ground black pepper
½ teaspoon five-spice powder
1 tablespoon honey
1 tablespoon oriental sesame oil
3 tablespoons soy sauce

Separate spareribs into lengths which will fit into roasting pan. Sprinkle garlic with salt and crush to a paste with flat of a knife. Combine

with pepper, five-spice powder, honey, sesame oil and soy sauce. Rub well all over the spareribs and leave to marinate for 20 minutes. Preheat oven to 200°C (400°F). Place spareribs into roasting pan and cook in a hot oven for 20 minutes. Turn spareribs, add ½ cup hot water to pan and continue roasting for a further 20 minutes.

Alternatively, heat 2 tablespoons peanut oil in a large, heavy frying pan and brown spareribs. Add ½ cup water, cover and simmer until tender. Serve hot.

Chinese Barbecued Pork

Special barrel-shaped ovens are used to cook this popular item in those shops which specialise in Chinese roasts. This recipe suggests two ways to get almost the same effect at home.

750 g/1½ lb lean, boneless pork
1 teaspoon finely chopped garlic
1 teaspoon salt
1 teaspoon finely grated fresh ginger
2 tablespoons dark soy sauce
2 tablespoons honey
1 tablespoon Chinese wine or dry sherry
½ teaspoon five-spice powder
1 tablespoon hoi sin sauce

Cut the pork lengthways into 3 or 4 strips. Sprinkle garlic with salt on a wooden board and crush to a purée with the flat of a knife. Combine with all the remaining ingredients in a large bowl. Add pork strips and mix well together so the meat is covered on all sides with the mixture. Allow it to marinate for at least 15 minutes.

Method 1: Remove all racks from oven except the top one. Hang the pork in strips from the top rack. Put a roasting pan with a little water in it on the bottom shelf. Use hooks made from lengths of wire 10 cm (4 in) long from wire coat-hangers. Curve each end into a hook. The top hook which fits over the oven rack should be smaller than the hook at the bottom which holds the pork.

Preheat oven to 200°C (400°F). Insert wide end of metal hook in the end of each strip of pork and hang from the rack. Roast for

15 minutes in the hot oven, then reduce the temperature to 190°C (375°F), brush pork with marinade and continue roasting for a further 30 minutes or until pork is cooked. Remove from oven, allow to cool for at least 10 minutes, then cut into thin slices against the grain.

Method 2: Half-fill a roasting pan with hot water and rest a wire rack across the top. Place the strips of pork on the rack (reserving the marinade) and roast in an oven preheated to 200°C (400°F) for 15 minutes, then turn the pork, brush with marinade and continue roasting for 15 minutes. Turn the meat again and baste it, and roast for another 15 minutes or until the pork is tender and well glazed.

Barbecued pork may be served hot or cold as an hors d'oeuvre or part of a meal, or the meat can be used in other dishes such as fried rice. Stir-fried with snow peas or fresh green beans, it makes a quick, light meal. On its own, serve with plum sauce and steamed bread.

Steamed Five-Flower Pork

Serves 6

1 kg/2 lb lean belly pork
4 tablespoons dark soy sauce
2 tablespoons Chinese wine or dry sherry
½ teaspoon five-spice powder (optional)
1 teaspoon crushed garlic
220 g/7 oz/1 cup uncooked rice

Ask butcher to remove pork skin. Cut pork into large squares and marinate in a mixture of soy sauce, wine, five-spice powder and garlic for at least an hour, preferably longer.

Roast uncooked rice in a heavy frying pan over medium-low heat, stirring constantly, for 15 minutes or until the grains are golden in colour. Put into the container of an electric blender and blend on high speed until ground to powder. If blender is not available, pound a little at a time using a mortar and pestle. (See RICE, ROASTED AND GROUND.)

Roll pieces of pork, one at a time, in the rice powder and put them into a heatproof dish. Steam over rapidly boiling water for 2 hours or until the pork is so tender it can easily be broken with chopsticks. Replenish water as it boils away with more boiling water. Serve hot, accompanied by steamed white rice.

Japanese Pork Cutlet (Tonkatsu)

Originally a foreign dish, it has become one of the most popular fast foods in Japan. 'Ton' is Japanese for pork, 'katsu' is the Japanese pronunciation of 'cutlet'. Serves 4.

4 × 2 cm/¾ in thick slices pork fillet
salt
pinch of sansho or ground black pepper
flour for dredging
1 egg, beaten
Japanese dried breadcrumbs
oil for deep frying
shreds of pickled ginger (beni shoga)

Season pork with salt and pepper, dip in flour and shake off excess, then dip pork in egg. Coat with breadcrumbs, pressing them on firmly.

Heat oil in a deep pan and fry crumbed slices over medium heat until golden brown all over, about 7 minutes. Drain on paper towels, cut each one in slices and assemble in original shape.

Serve with white rice and garnish with pickled ginger. Or serve with shredded white cabbage (hakusai) and a dipping sauce made up of tomato ketchup, Japanese soy sauce, Worcestershire sauce, mustard and sake. The proportions vary according to personal taste. Plain hot mustard may also be served separately.

Vietnamese Pork on Skewers

So popular is this dish that in some Vietnamese butcher shops the lean pork paste mixed with pieces of pork fat is sold by weight, making it easier for the home cook. In some shops, it is already seasoned. Serves 6.

500 g/1 lb lean boneless pork
1 teaspoon chopped garlic
1 teaspoon salt
1 teaspoon sugar
3 teaspoons rice wine or dry sherry
90 g/3 oz pork fat
1 tablespoon melted lard
1 tablespoon roasted ground rice
2 teaspoons fish sauce

SAUCE

2 hot red chillies
1 clove of garlic
1 teaspoon sugar
1 lemon
4 tablespoons fish sauce
1 tablespoon vinegar
1 tablespoon water
shreds of carrot (optional)

FOR SERVING

500 g/1 lb fresh rice noodles
   or 125 g/4 oz dried rice noodles
1 lettuce
sprigs of fresh coriander or mint
garlic, chilli and fish sauce (nuoc cham)

Cut the pork fillet into small dice. Crush garlic with salt and sugar to a smooth paste, mix with wine or sherry, pour over the pork and mix well. Set aside for 30 minutes.

In a food processor pulse the meat to a smooth paste. Remove to a bowl. Cut pork fat into thin slices, then into small squares. Mix in pork fat, lard, ground rice and fish sauce. Knead mixture well, form small balls or sausage shapes and mould them onto bamboo skewers, squeezing them on very firmly. Barbecue over coals or under a griller, at a good distance from the source of heat so they are well done before the outside is browned. Turn the skewers every few minutes to ensure the meat cooks on all sides.

To make the sauce, pound chillies with a small clove of garlic, a teaspoon of sugar and a peeled lemon. Add all other ingredients. Mix well and if liked add a few fine shreds of carrot.

Slice fresh rice noodles and steam them, or cook dried rice noodles in boiling water until tender. Do not overcook. Drain. Serve skewers of pork with well-washed and dried lettuce separated into leaves, the noodles, and a small bunch of fresh coriander or mint.

Each person assembles his own snack. A leaf of lettuce is topped with a few rice noodles, some of the barbecued pork, a sprig of fresh coriander or mint and rolled up to form a neat roll. Serve the sauce for dipping rolls before eating.

Burmese Pork Curry

Serves 8–10

2 kg/4 lb boneless pork, not completely lean
4 medium onions, roughly chopped
20 cloves garlic
150 g/5 oz/1 cup peeled and roughly chopped
   ginger
2 teaspoons salt
2 tablespoons vinegar
2 teaspoons chilli powder
185 ml/6 fl oz/¾ cup peanut oil
3 tablespoons oriental sesame oil
1 teaspoon ground turmeric

Cut pork into 2.5 cm (1 in) cubes. In food processor or blender finely chop onions, garlic and ginger. Turn into a strainer set over a bowl and push with spoon to extract as much liquid as possible. Pour this liquid into a large saucepan, add the pork, salt, vinegar, chilli powder and half the peanut oil. Bring to the boil, cover and simmer over low heat for 1½ hours or until pork is almost tender.

In another large pan with heavy base heat remaining peanut oil and the sesame oil. Add the garlic, onion and ginger solids left in the strainer. Add turmeric, stir and cook over low heat. Cover pan and simmer the mixture, lifting lid frequently to stir, and scrape base of pan with a wooden spoon. This initial frying takes at least 15 minutes. If mixture fries too rapidly and begins to stick before the smell has mellowed and the onions become transparent, add a small quantity of water from time to time and stir well. When the water content of the onions has evaporated and the ingredients turn a rich brown colour with oil showing round the edge of the mass, the first stage of cooking, and the most important one, is complete. Because of the large quantity it takes almost 25 minutes to reach the right stage. Half way through cooking the onion mixture, spoon off some of the oil that has risen to the top of the pork mixture and add it to the onions.

When mixture is a reddish-brown add the contents of the first pan and cook, uncovered, until the oil separates again and the liquid is almost evaporated. Stir frequently during this stage to ensure it does not stick and burn at base of pan. Serve with white rice and accompaniments.

Sri Lankan Fried Pork Curry

Very lean pork is not suitable for this particular dish, as it needs to be fried in the fat of the pork after it has simmered to tenderness. It is customary to leave the skin on, so choose a cut such as pork belly or loin. Serves 6–8.

1 kg/2 lb pork including some fat
3 tablespoons oil
sprig of fresh curry leaves
  or spoonful of dried curry leaves
½ teaspoon fenugreek seeds (optional)
2 medium onions, finely chopped
1 tablespoon finely chopped garlic
2 teaspoons finely grated fresh ginger
3 tablespoons Ceylon curry powder (recipe page 356)
2 teaspoons chilli powder
2 teaspoons salt
1 tablespoon vinegar
1 tablespoon tamarind pulp
5 cm/2 in cinnamon stick
4 cardamom pods
1 teaspoon ground aromatic ginger (optional)
1 cup thick coconut milk

Cut pork into large cubes. Heat oil in a large saucepan and fry curry leaves and fenugreek, if used, until they start to brown. Add onion and garlic and fry over a low heat until onion is soft and golden. Add ginger, curry powder, chilli powder, salt, vinegar and pork. Stir and fry until meat is well coated with the spices. Soak tamarind pulp in 1½ cups hot water, knead to dissolve pulp, strain and discard seeds. Add tamarind liquid, cinnamon, cardamom and aromatic ginger. Cover and cook on low heat until pork is tender, about 1 hour. Add coconut milk and cook for 10 minutes or more, uncovered.

Pour gravy into another saucepan, return pork to heat and allow to fry in its own fat. (If pork is not fat enough, add 1 tablespoon of ghee or oil to pan.) When pork is nicely brown, return gravy to pan and cook, uncovered, until gravy is thick. Serve with boiled rice.

Pork Vindaloo

Serves 6–8

1 kg/2 lb pork
6–8 large dried red chillies
250 ml/8 fl oz/1 cup coconut vinegar
2 teaspoons chopped fresh ginger
1 tablespoon chopped garlic
2 teaspoons ground cumin
½ teaspoon ground black pepper
½ teaspoon ground cinnamon
½ teaspoon ground cardamom
¼ teaspoon ground cloves
¼ teaspoon ground nutmeg
2 teaspoons salt
2–3 tablespoons ghee or oil
2 medium onions, finely chopped
1 tablespoon brown sugar

Cut pork into large cubes. Soak chillies in vinegar for 10 minutes. If coconut vinegar which is quite mild is not available any kind of vinegar may be substituted, diluting it if very strong. Put chillies and vinegar, ginger, garlic, all the ground spices and salt into an electric blender and blend to a purée. Pour over the pork in an earthenware bowl, cover and marinate for 2 hours.

Heat enough ghee or oil to cover base of an enamel or stainless steel saucepan. (Because of its acid content this dish is cooked in earthenware pots in India.) Fry the onions on low heat until soft and golden, stirring frequently. Drain pork from the marinade and fry on medium high heat, stirring, until it changes colour. Pour in marinade, cover pan and simmer on low heat until pork is tender. Stir in sugar. Serve with plain boiled rice.

Goan Sorpotel

Serves 6–8

1 kg/2 lb pork from leg or shoulder
250 g/8 oz pork or calves liver
10–15 dried large red chillies
250 ml/8 fl oz/1 cup coconut vinegar
  or other mild vinegar
2 or 3 fresh green chillies
2 tablespoons chopped ginger
2 tablespoons chopped garlic
½ teaspoon ground black pepper
2 teaspoons ground coriander
2 teaspoons ground cumin
1 teaspoon ground turmeric
1 teaspoon ground cinnamon
½ teaspoon ground cloves
2 teaspoons salt
1 tablespoon tamarind pulp
1 teaspoon sugar

Put the pork into a saucepan with just enough lightly salted water to cover, bring to the boil and simmer for 5 minutes. Cook the liver separately in the same way. Discard stock from the liver, allow liver to cool and cut it into very tiny dice. Reserve the pork stock and cut the pork, together with its skin and fat, into larger dice.

Discard stalks of the dried chillies. If a milder curry is preferred discard the seeds as well. Soak the dried chillies in the vinegar for about 10 minutes. Put dried chillies, vinegar, roughly chopped green chillies, ginger and garlic into an electric blender and blend to a purée. Add the ground spices and salt. Put pork, pork stock, diced liver and the blended spices into an enamel or stainless steel saucepan and simmer, covered, until pork is tender, about 1 hour. Meanwhile soak tamarind pulp in ½ cup hot water, squeeze to dissolve the pulp and strain through a fine sieve. Discard seeds and fibres. Stir in tamarind liquid and sugar. Cook, uncovered, until gravy is thick and dark. Serve with rice.

Pork Adobo

This method of cooking with plenty of garlic, pepper and vinegar is popular in the Philippines. Serves 6.

1 kg/2 lb pork loin or leg chops
8–10 cloves garlic
250 ml/8 fl oz/1 cup white vinegar
250 ml/8 fl oz/1 cup water
1½ teaspoons salt
2 bay leaves
½–1 teaspoon ground black pepper
lard or oil for frying

Cut skin from pork and discard. If chops are large, cut into serving pieces. Put pork and all other ingredients except lard or oil into a heavy non-aluminium saucepan and marinate for 1 hour. Bring to the boil, then reduce heat and simmer for 40 minutes or until pork is tender. Remove pork from pan, boil liquid over high heat until reduced and thickened. Strain into a small bowl. When fat rises to the top, spoon it into a frying pan. Add lard or oil to cover base of pan with 6 mm (¼ in) fat and fry the pork until brown and crisp on both sides. Transfer to a heated serving plate and pour the sauce over. Serve hot accompanied by white rice.

Potato

(*Solanum tuberosum*) The humble potato, grown as a food crop worldwide, originated in the Andes of South America. In Asia it never takes the place of rice as the staple carbohydrate food but is cooked with spices and served in curry or as a dry, spicy dish, a popular accompaniment to chapatis, lentil pancakes and rice. It is also popular in Indian snacks, being a neutral carrier for spicy flavours.

I have tasted potatoes made into a chilli-hot accompaniment in Korean food, but China and Japan seem to stand aloof from this tuber. If used at all, Chinese chefs may grate long strands and deep fry them between two curved wire frying ladles to make the banquet presentation called phoenix nest. This may also be done with other tubers, and taro is the one most likely to be used. The 'nest' itself is not eaten.

Snubbed though it may be as a vegetable in the Far East, the potato as used in spice cultures is enough to surprise those who have not encountered it other than boiled, baked, steamed, mashed or fried. In the recipes which follow the potato is chief ingredient. Potatoes also appear as subsidiary but intrinsic parts in dishes such as Thai Masaman Beef Curry (see recipe page 37) and the Parsi dish, Lamb with Apricots (see recipe page 203).

Starch from the potato (potato starch) is used as a thickener. See FLOURS & STARCHES.

Potato Dry Curry

Serves 4–6

750 g/1½ lb potatoes
2 tablespoons ghee or oil
1 teaspoon panch phora
1 large onion, finely chopped
1 teaspoon ground turmeric
2 teaspoons ground cumin
½ teaspoon chilli powder or to taste
1 teaspoon salt or to taste
3 tablespoons chopped fresh mint or coriander
1½ teaspoons garam masala
squeeze of lime or lemon juice

Peel and dice potatoes. In a heavy-based saucepan with well-fitting lid melt ghee and add panch phora. When mustard seeds pop, add onion and stir occasionally over low heat until soft and starting to turn golden. Add ground spices and salt and stir. Add potatoes, mix well and sprinkle with ¼ cup water.

Cover pan tightly, cook on very low heat for 20 minutes without lifting lid. Shake pan occasionally to keep potatoes from sticking. Scatter chopped herbs, garam masala and lemon juice over, and a tablespoon more water if necessary. Cover pan again and cook a further 10 minutes or until potatoes are soft and a slight crust has formed on base of pan. Serve with chapatis or rice. Serve the crust too. It is a prized part of the dish.

Indian Sweet-Sour Potatoes

Serves 4–6

750 g/1½ lb potatoes
2 tablespoons ghee or oil
1 teaspoon black mustard seeds
2 fresh chillies, sliced
2 teaspoons ground coriander
1 teaspoon ground cumin
½ teaspoon ground turmeric
½ teaspoon salt or to taste
½ teaspoon chilli powder or to taste
1 tablespoon dried tamarind pulp
2 teaspoons palm sugar or brown sugar

Peel and dice potatoes. In a heavy saucepan heat ghee or oil and fry mustard seeds until they pop. Add chillies and ground spices and stir for 30 seconds or until fragrant. Add potatoes, sprinkle with salt and about ¼ cup water, cover pan tightly and cook on very low heat for 15 minutes.

Meanwhile, soak tamarind pulp in ½ cup hot water and squeeze to dissolve pulp. Strain out seeds and fibres. Dissolve sugar in tamarind liquid. Add to potatoes, stir gently, cover and cook for a further 10 minutes or until potatoes are tender.

Herbed Mashed Potatoes

Serves 4

500 g/1 lb potatoes
2 tablespoons melted ghee or butter
3 tablespoons boiling milk
3 tablespoons lime or lemon juice
½ teaspoon salt or to taste
6 tablespoons finely chopped fresh mint leaves
3 tablespoons finely chopped spring onions (scallions)
mint sprigs for garnish

Boil potatoes until tender, drain in a colander, peel and mash while still hot. Add melted ghee and boiling milk and mix to a creamy, fluffy consistency. Add remaining ingredients and mix well. Pile into a bowl or pat into a flat cake and garnish with mint sprigs.

Savoury Fried Potatoes

Serves 4

500 g/1 lb potatoes
1 tablespoon ghee or oil
½ teaspoon black mustard seeds
2 medium onions, finely chopped
½ teaspoon ground turmeric
½ teaspoon chilli powder
1 teaspoon salt

Boil, peel and dice the potatoes. Heat ghee or oil and fry the mustard seeds until they pop. Add onions and continue frying on low heat until they are soft and golden brown. Add turmeric and chilli powder and stir, then add potatoes, sprinkle salt over and turn gently to distribute flavours. Serve hot or cold.

Potato and Cashew Nut Fudge (Potato Alluwa)

This sublime candy depends on the humble potato for its texture and flavour and is a favourite in Sri Lanka.

375 g/12 oz/1½ cups sugar
375 ml/12 fl oz/1½ cups milk
400 g/14 oz can sweetened condensed milk
125 g/4 oz ghee or butter
1 cup cooked, smoothly mashed potato
185 g/6 oz finely chopped raw cashew nuts
2 tablespoons rose water
** or 1 teaspoon vanilla essence**
1 teaspoon ground cardamom (optional)

Put sugar, milk, condensed milk and ghee into a large heavy saucepan (a non-stick pan is excellent for this). Cook over medium heat, stirring constantly, until mixture reaches softball stage or 116°C (240°F) on a candy thermometer. (To test for softball stage without a thermometer, drop a little into a cup of ice-cold water. If it firms enough to be moulded into a soft ball, it has reached the required temperature.)

Remove from heat, add smoothly mashed potato and beat with a wire whisk or rotary beater until all lumps are beaten out. If using a pan with non-stick lining, pour mixture into a bowl before doing this or the metal beaters will scratch the non-stick surface. Return to heat and cook again to softball stage or 116°C (240°F). Remove from heat, stir in nuts, flavouring and cardamom and mix well. Pour into a well-buttered shallow dish or baking tin. Press lightly with a piece of buttered banana leaf or aluminium foil to smooth and flatten the surface. Allow to cool and set, then cut into diamond shapes.

Potato, Sweet

(*Ipomoea batatas*) Native to South America, sweet potatoes in many colours, shapes and sizes are now grown all over the world.

Sweet potato is the only edible tuber of more than 400 varieties of morning glory. Perhaps the best known is the white-fleshed sweet potato which has either a thin, purplish-red skin or a pale beige skin.

An orange-fleshed variety with a brownish-pink skin is known in Japan as satsuma imo and to the Western world by its Pacific and New Zealand name, kumara. It is popular in tempura (sliced and deep fried in thin, crisp batter) and yakimo (roasted, unpeeled, on hot stones, a wintertime treat sold from street carts). Also used in a Japanese New Year confection in the shape of chestnuts.

Another variety is a purple sweet potato with pale brown skin, the flesh pale-purple and creamy-white in concentric rings.

The skin on all sweet potatoes is thin and smooth and the colour patchy. The leaves also vary in shape, size and colour. In Asia, the leaves and tendrils of some varieties are eaten as a vegetable, a delicacy in Korea and Hawaii, either in soups, stir-fried or simmered in coconut milk until soft. Dried sweet potato stems are also available from some Japanese and Korean stockists.

The tubers themselves are mainly boiled or steamed, or in some instances sliced finely and fried as for potato crisps.

Purchasing and storing: Choose unblemished specimens of relatively even shape to make peeling easier. Store them in the dark alongside your other potatoes in a wire basket, with air circulating around them. They will keep well for a couple of weeks.

Preparation: Scrub them and cook whole or cut into chunks, peeling either before cooking or after cooking. (After cooking is easier.) Cut sweet potato discolours readily if exposed to air, so put it into water or the cooking pot as quickly as possible.

China: *tiem shee, faan shu*
Fiji: *kumala*
India: *shakar-kandi*
Indonesia: *ubi-jalar*
Japan: *satsuma imo*
Malaysia: *keledek*
New Zealand: *kumara*
Philippines: *kamote*
Sri Lanka: *bath-ala*
Thailand: *man-thet*

Prawn (Shrimp) Crackers

Large, crisp, deep-fried crackers popular in Indonesia and Malaysia, where they are called krupuk udang and Vietnam, banh phong tom. Sold in packets in dried form, they are made from starch (usually tapioca flour), salt and sugar, together with varying amounts of prawn (shrimp) or fish. They are sun dried and keep very well.

To eat them, they must be deep fried. It is important that the crackers are dry and the oil hot enough. If either of these conditions is not met, the crackers, instead of being crunchy, crisp and airy, will be tough and chewy, which no self-respecting cracker should be. This can happen, if they are not stored airtight or if the weather has been humid. To test the condition of the crackers is simple.

Heat oil until very hot and drop in a crisp. It should puff and swell to about 3 times its size within a minute. If it doesn't, perhaps the oil was not hot enough. Try another one. If it seems that you have the temperature of the oil correct but the crackers are not puffing as they should, the crackers may be damp. The solution is to spread the crackers on an oven tray and dry them out in a very slow oven. Once cool, store in an airtight container. Fry as required, though it is possible to fry them in advance, cool completely, then store airtight for a day or two.

The best prawn crackers are usually large, pale cream in colour, Indonesian in origin and quite a bit more expensive because they contain more prawn.

Prawns

If unavailable, Chinese prawn (shrimp) crackers may be substituted although they are mostly decorative, being made in an assortment of colours. These are quite vivid but become paler and prettier when they are deep fried and expand in the hot oil. However, the flavour is not as pronounced and the texture not as substantial as Indonesia's krupuk udang.

Use the crackers either as garnish around a dish, or as a crisp accompaniment to a meal of fried rice or fried noodles, or other similar dry dishes. Otherwise serve them separately, as contact with sauce or other liquids will destroy their delightful crispness which is the reason people eat prawn crackers.

Prawns

Also called shrimp. One and the same creature, the only distinction being one of size, and even that depends on which continent you are on. North Americans call them all shrimp, but in Britain and its colonies the name 'shrimp' is reserved for those of small size, while larger specimens are called 'prawns'.

Small or large, they are one of the most popular crustaceans in Asia, valued for their sweet meat and enticing flavour. They may be caught in salt water, fresh water, rivers, dams, and increasingly they are being farmed. It is better to buy them fresh and raw rather than cooked, as more flavour is retained. In some inland areas, though, only cooked prawns are available. In this case, add them to the dish at the last stage of cooking, only to heat through. Overcooking is to be avoided as this makes prawns tough.

Purchasing and storing: When buying prawns, look for glossy, undamaged shells; legs and tails which show no signs of becoming dark or discoloured; and plump, shiny black eyes, not shrunken or missing — a sure sign that they have been frozen. If they are in poor condition, the shells take on a dull, mushy appearance, legs and eyes come adrift and they get an ammonia odour. Cooked or raw, they should smell fresh and of the sea. Refrigerate very soon after purchase.

Cooked prawns may be stored in a plastic bag in the refrigerator until needed, and shelled just prior to eating to keep them moist. Raw prawns are better immersed in iced water in the refrigerator (no more than 2 or 3 days) until needed. This prevents oxidation.

To freeze prawns, divide into quantities required for a meal or recipe. Place in a shallow dish and just cover with water. Freeze uncovered, and when solid transfer to a freezer bag. Seal and label with date. Raw prawns may be kept in optimum condition for 2 months when frozen in ice. Cooked prawns do not benefit from being frozen.

Preparation: Some recipes require prawns to be whole and in their shells, but it is still possible to draw out the intestinal vein without dismembering the prawn. Since their shells are segmented, bend the shell just above tail fin. Make a small incision in each prawn just above tail segment and snip the dark vein. Bend head to expose flesh. From just below the head find other end of vein and carefully draw out whole length. Sometimes this is not easily achieved, and in that case use pointed scissors to snip the shell open the whole curve of the prawn's back. With a small sharp knife make a shallow slit in the flesh and lift out the vein. Some recipes require prawns to be shelled, but even so, retaining the last segment of shell and the tail fins gives a more decorative appearance to the finished dish, as the fins turn red when cooked.

When prawns have to be shelled save the shells and heads for making stock. Simply fry them on high heat in a tablespoon of oil, add hot water to barely cover, and boil for 10–15 minutes. Strain, discard shells and freeze the stock if not immediately required.

Singapore Prawns (Shrimp) in Shell

Serves 4

500 g/1 lb large, raw tiger prawns (jumbo shrimp)
3 tablespoons peanut oil
2 spring onions (scallions), cut in short lengths
2 red chillies, sliced
1 tablespoon shredded fresh ginger
2 teaspoons finely chopped garlic
2 tablespoons dry sherry
2 tablespoons light soy sauce
1 tablespoon sugar
2 teaspoons oriental sesame oil

Make a small incision in each prawn just above tail segment and snip dark vein. From just below the head find other end of vein and carefully draw out whole length. Rinse prawns, leaving entire shell on. Blot dry with paper towels.

Heat wok, then add peanut oil. When oil is very hot, add prawns and stir-fry on high heat until they change colour. Add spring onions, chillies, ginger and garlic and fry for 30 seconds. Add remaining ingredients, and turn prawns in the sauce constantly for 1 minute. Serve at once.

Butter Prawns (Shrimp)

The Portuguese influence apparent in Malacca has also spread to other parts of Malaysia, as evidenced by the use of butter in certain dishes. It was in Kuala Lumpur that I watched this dish being prepared by a Chinese chef using flavours that are unmistakably Indian. Serves 3–4.

375 g/12 oz fresh prawns (shrimp)
125 ml/4 fl oz/½ cup peanut oil for deep frying
1 tablespoon ghee or butter
sprig of fresh curry leaves, stripped from stem
2 hot green chillies, sliced
1 teaspoon finely chopped garlic
1 teaspoon white sugar
1 teaspoon coarsely cracked black pepper
½ teaspoon salt
60 ml/2 fl oz evaporated milk or pouring cream

Remove and discard hard shell from heads of prawns. Split shell down the back with scissors and lift out vein. Wash the prawns and roll in paper towels to dry exceedingly well or they will spatter when fried.

Heat oil in a wok until almost smoking and deep fry the prawns very quickly for only 1 minute. Pour prawns and oil into a sieve over a metal bowl.

Return wok to heat, add ghee and a tablespoon of the oil in which the prawns were fried and sizzle the curry leaves, green chillies and garlic for a few seconds. Return prawns, sprinkle over them the sugar, pepper and salt and stir-fry for 1 minute. Stir in the evaporated milk or cream and serve at once, with steamed rice.

Sri Lankan Prawn (Shrimp) Curry

Serves 6

750 g/1½ lb raw prawns (shrimp)
1 medium onion, finely chopped
2 teaspoons finely chopped garlic
2 teaspoons finely grated ginger
1 small stick cinnamon

½ teaspoon fenugreek seeds
sprig of fresh curry leaves
 or 12 dried curry leaves
1 stem fresh lemon grass, bruised
 or 2 strips lemon rind
1 strip pandan leaf, fresh, frozen or dried
½ teaspoon ground turmeric
1–2 teaspoons chilli powder
2 teaspoons paprika
1 teaspoon salt or to taste
400 ml/14 fl oz can coconut milk
lime or lemon juice to taste

Wash prawns and remove heads, but leave rest of shells intact. Carefully draw out vein (see Singapore Prawns in Shell recipe, page 296). Put all ingredients, except prawns and lime juice into a saucepan. Stir in 1 cup water and bring slowly to simmering point. Simmer, uncovered for 10 minutes. Add prawns and lime juice and stir. Simmer for a further 10 minutes. Add more salt and lime juice if necessary. Serve with boiled rice.

Burmese Prawn (Shrimp) Curry

Serves 4

500 g/1 lb raw prawns (shrimp)
1 large onion, chopped roughly
2 teaspoons finely chopped garlic
1 teaspoon finely grated fresh ginger
½ teaspoon ground turmeric
½ teaspoon chilli powder
3 tablespoons gingelly oil*
salt to taste
2 tablespoons chopped fresh coriander leaves
2 tablespoons chopped spring onions (scallions)

Shell and devein prawns. Place onion, garlic and ginger in a blender and grind to a purée. Mix in turmeric and chilli powder.

Heat oil in a saucepan until very hot. Carefully add puréed ingredients. Be careful because the oil will spatter violently. Lower heat and stir ingredients. Cover pan and simmer for 15–20 minutes, lifting lid frequently to stir and scrape base of pan with a wooden spoon. If mixture fries too rapidly add a little water as necessary and stir well. When ready, the onion mixture will have a rich red-brown colour and mellow aroma, and oil will show around edge of mass.

Add prawns and stir well. Add salt to taste.

Sprinkle with fresh coriander leaves, then cover pan and cook for 10 minutes or until prawns are done. Remove from heat and stir in spring onions. Serve hot with rice.

* If gingelly oil is not easy to find, use 2 tablespoons corn or peanut oil and add 1 tablespoon oriental sesame oil for flavour.

Thai Chilli Prawns (Shrimp) with Lime

Serves 4–6

30 medium-sized raw prawns (shrimp)
2 teaspoons finely chopped fresh ginger
1 tablespoon fish sauce
2 teaspoons palm sugar or brown sugar
4 spring onions (scallions), sliced diagonally
4 fresh red chillies
2 teaspoons finely chopped galangal
1 teaspoon Thai pepper-coriander paste
2 tablespoons peanut oil
3 tablespoons canned coconut milk
1 teaspoon rice flour
salt to taste
2 fresh kaffir lime leaves
   or lime rind
sliced red chillies for garnish

Shell prawns, but leave tail segment intact. Carefully devein and use a sharp knife to slit each prawn lengthways from the top, for about a third of its length. Place in a bowl and mix in ginger, fish sauce, sugar and spring onions. Marinate for 10 minutes.

Split chillies and discard seeds for less heat. Puree in a blender with galangal, lemon grass, onion and pepper-and-coriander paste, scraping down sides of blender as necessary.

Heat oil in a wok or frying pan, add paste mixture and stir-fry until fragrant. Add prawns with their marinade and cook, turning constantly for about 3 minutes or until they change colour. Remove pan from heat.

Mix coconut milk with rice flour and heat in a small saucepan, stirring as it comes to the boil and thickens. Add salt to taste and pour immediately into the centre of a serving plate or bowl. Place prawns on sauce and sprinkle with thread-fine strips of kaffir lime leaves or rind and fresh chilli.

Thai Hot Sour Prawn (Shrimp) Soup

This is the famous Tom Yum Goong which anyone who knows and appreciates Thai food has experienced. Serves 6.

1 kg/2 lb medium or small raw prawns (shrimp)
1 tablespoon oil
2 litres/4 pints/8 cups prawn (shrimp) stock (see below)
salt to taste
2 stalks lemon grass, bruised
   or 4 strips thinly peeled lemon rind
4 kaffir lime leaves
4 fresh red chillies
2 tablespoons fish sauce
lime or lemon juice to taste
2 tablespoons chopped coriander leaves
4 spring onions (scallions), including green tops, chopped

Shell and devein prawns, reserving heads and shells. Heat oil in a saucepan and fry heads and shells until they turn pink. Add 2 litres (4 pints) hot water, salt, lemon grass or rind, kaffir lime leaves and 3 of the chillies left whole. Bring to the boil, cover and simmer for 20 minutes. Strain stock, return to pan and bring to the boil. Add prawns and simmer for 3 minutes, or just until prawns are cooked. Stir in fish sauce and lime or lemon juice to taste, making it nicely piquant. Serve sprinkled with remaining chilli finely chopped, coriander leaves and spring onions.

Crystal Prawns (Shrimp) with Asparagus Tips

Like many Chinese recipes, there are two steps and two methods of cooking combined which makes this an ideal dish for preparing ahead, requiring only final stir-frying just before serving.Serves 4–6.

500 g/1 lb medium to large raw prawns (jumbo shrimp)
salt
1 egg white
1 tablespoon cornflour (cornstarch)
1 tablespoon oil
½ teaspoon chopped garlic
pinch of sugar
1 teaspoon finely grated fresh ginger

oil for deep frying
1 bunch fresh asparagus*

SAUCE

125 ml/4 fl oz/½ cup chicken stock
1 tablespoon oyster sauce
1 tablespoon Chinese wine or dry sherry
1 teaspoon oriental sesame oil
2 teaspoons cornflour (cornstarch)

Shell and devein prawns. Slit them half way through along the outer curve. Put the prawns in a large bowl, sprinkle with 1 teaspoon of salt and stir the prawns briskly for 1 minute.

Transfer prawns to a colander and rinse under cold water for 1 minute, turning them over and over. Drain, return them to the bowl and sprinkle with another teaspoon of salt. Repeat the procedure, stirring vigorously for 1 minute, then rinse as before. Drain and repeat a third time. (This treatment removes the slippery feel and makes the flesh crisp.)

Dry the prawns on paper towels and marinate in a 'velveting' mixture of egg white, cornflour and oil which gives them a protective coating and keeps them moist. Sprinkle the prawns with ½ teaspoon salt. Beat egg white only enough to break it up, and pour it over the prawns. Sprinkle tablespoon of cornflour over and mix well. Add tablespoon of oil and mix again. Cover and chill for 30 minutes or longer.

Crush the garlic with sugar. Mix all sauce ingredients together.

In a wok, heat 3–4 cups oil until moderately hot. Turn heat to medium, drop in the prawns and stir to keep them separate. They will turn white in less than a minute. Lift them immediately from the oil.

Pour oil into a metal bowl. (It can be strained and re-used, frying a few slices of ginger in it first.) Wipe the wok with paper towels and place it over high heat. When very hot, add 1 tablespoon of oil and swirl to coat the surface. Add the garlic and ginger, stir for 10 seconds, then add the asparagus tips and stir-fry over high heat until they turn brilliant green (about 1 minute). Add 2 tablespoons water, cover wok and allow asparagus to steam for 2 minutes.

Stir the sauce mixture to ensure cornflour is smoothly mixed. Pour it into the wok and stir constantly until it boils and thickens. Return the prawns, mixing them through the sauce and serve immediately with rice.

* This dish needs only the most tender asparagus tips. No need to waste the lower portion. Use it for soup that can be puréed and strained to remove tough fibres.

Thai Red Curry of Prawns (Shrimp)

Serves 6

750 g/1½ lb large raw prawns (jumbo shrimp)
400 ml/14 fl oz can coconut milk
2–3 tablespoons Thai red curry paste
   (recipe page 114)
4 kaffir lime leaves
½ teaspoon finely grated lime rind
2 tablespoons fish sauce
2 teaspoons palm sugar or brown sugar

For the best flavour, cook and serve the prawns in their shells. If the shell is split down the back it will be easy to remove the shell with spoon and fork.

With kitchen scissors trim any long feelers and cut open the shell down the curve of the back without removing it. With a sharp, pointed knife slit the flesh to expose the vein and lift it out.

In a wok or frying pan, heat half the coconut milk until bubbling, add the red curry paste and cook, stirring, until oil shines on the surface and it smells fragrant. Dilute remaining coconut milk with an equal amount of water and add, together with lime leaves and rind, fish sauce and palm sugar. Simmer uncovered, stirring now and then, for 5 minutes. Add prawns and continue to cook uncovered for 10 minutes or until prawns are cooked and the sauce has slightly reduced and thickened. Serve with rice.

Prawn (Shrimp) Sambal

Serves 6

500 g/1 lb shelled raw prawns (shrimp)
walnut-sized piece of dried tamarind*
2 tablespoons peanut oil
1 onion, finely chopped
3 cloves garlic, finely chopped
½ teaspoon finely grated fresh ginger
1 tablespoon sambal ulek (recipe page 91)
   or 8 fresh red chillies
2 teaspoons chopped galangal
2 stems lemon grass, bruised
   or 2 strips thinly peeled lemon rind
1 teaspoon palm sugar or brown sugar

Chop prawns into pieces the size of a peanut. Soak tamarind in ½ cup hot water, squeeze to dissolve pulp and strain out the seeds and fibres.

Heat oil in a frying pan and fry onion, garlic and ginger until soft and starting to turn golden. Add sambal ulek, galangal and lemon grass or rind, then add chopped prawns and fry, stirring constantly, until prawns change colour.

Add tamarind liquid to prawns and simmer on low heat until gravy is thick and oil starts to separate. Remove lemon grass or rind. Stir in salt and sugar. Taste and correct seasoning if necessary. Serve as a side dish with rice and curries.

* If more convenient, use tamarind purée or tamarind concentrate, available in plastic jars and about the consistency of tomato paste. Do not confuse with instant tamarind which is almost solid and sold in small containers.

Prawns, Dried

See SHRIMP, DRIED.

Psyllium

The epidermis and collapsed adjacent layers of the seeds of *Plantago ovata*. Known as blond psyllium, Indian plantago seed, flea seed and falooda seed. These small, pale buff, translucent husks are hydrophilic, meaning they have an affinity for water and absorb it readily. Widely used as a natural dietary fibre supplement, and if you're in the habit of reading labels you will recognise the words as the essential ingredient in pharmaceutical products which act as natural laxatives by providing bulk.

The recommended daily intake is 5–10 g (1–2 teaspoons) and it is stressed that psyllium must be taken with sufficient liquid to prevent compaction in the gastro-intestinal tract. Why are you reading about psyllium husks in a book about Asian food? Because they are widely used in the long, cool drinks based on syrups and cordials, and you may have come across them and wondered about the identity of the small particles. In the amounts used in beverages they are perfectly safe, indeed beneficial. Some of the husks stay in suspension while others float on the surface or sink to the bottom. They have no flavour of their own, but absorb flavour from the rose or fruit scented drinks and, in the mouth, feel like minuscule pieces of jelly.

Medicinal uses: It is said to be 'cooling', and its mucilaginous quality soothing to the stomach. Used in the management of constipation, diarrhoea and irritable bowel syndrome. There is also evidence it lowers cholestrol. Available in health food stores as psyllium husks and in Indian grocery stores as sat isabgol. Add a teaspoonful to each glass of falooda or sherbet a few minutes before drinking. If left soaking in liquid too long it tends to become a large mass.

India: *sat isabgol*
Common names: *flea seed, falooda seed.*

Pulasan

(*Nephelium mutabile*) Native to Malaysia, and described as a cross between a rambutan and a lychee, this delicious fruit, also known as meritam, is a member of the same family and has a similar translucent flesh, sweet and juicy. The skin, rough and segmented, is thicker than that of a rambutan, and devoid of the hairs which distinguish its better-known cousin. Starting off a deep red, the colour of the skin darkens unattractively within a few days and the flesh loses its crisp texture, so enjoy them quickly. The seeds are said to be edible raw or cooked.

Pulses

See LEGUMES & PULSES.

Pumpkin

See MARROW & PUMPKIN.

Purslane

(*Portulaca oleracea*, *P. quadrifida*) SEE ILLUSTRATION. The succulent stems and small fleshy leaves with a slightly mucilaginous quality are eaten raw, served with a salty dip of fish sauce, or cooked and eaten as a vegetable. There are two varieties, one called wild purslane or yellow portulaca which has stems tinged with pink and small yellow flowers and is more or less prostrate in growth, reaching only 15 cm (6 in). It is native from Greece to China and has been used as a food in India and the Middle East long before it was cultivated in Europe in the Middle Ages. In tropical countries it is eaten as a vegetable.

Another variety is garden purslane, green purslane or winter purslane, *Montia perfoliata*, which has a more upright growth habit to 50 cm (20 in), thicker stems and bright green, succulent, spatulate leaves. It is not used as a medicine and is mainly eaten cooked. It is sometimes sparingly used in salads. The sharp flavour makes it suitable for pickling for winter use.

Purchasing and storing: Buy fresh, unwilted bunches and try not to store it for more than a day, as it is prone to wilt rather quickly. The most successful way of keeping it fresh is to cut off the roots and stand the bunch in a stainless steel bowl with the stems in about 2.5 cm (1 in) of cold water.

Preparation: Trim away roots, wash and shake dry. Cut into bite-sized lengths just before cooking.

Medicinal uses: In Indonesia, purslane is traditionally prescribed for cardiac weakness. The latest research in Western medicine reveals that it is one of the few vegetable sources of omega 3s, essential fatty acids present in fish oils which have an anti-inflammatory effect. It has a high iron and vitamin C content, hence its use in the prevention and treatment of scurvy, especially by Australian Aborigines, who call it munyeroo and eat it raw and cooked. They also grind the nutritious seeds into flour. Purslane also has diuretic properties.

China: *kwa-tsz-tsai*
India: *kulfa*
Indonesia: *krokot*
Japan: *suberi-hiyu*
Malaysia: *gelang pasir*
Philippines: *olasiman*
Sri Lanka: *genda-kola*
Thailand: *phak bia-yai*

Stir-Fried Purslane, Chinese Style

Serves 4

1 or 2 bunches purslane
1 tablespoon oil
1 teaspoon finely chopped garlic
1 tablespoon light soy sauce
½ teaspoon sugar
½ teaspoon oriental sesame oil

Wash the purslane, shake dry and trim off the roots and tough lower ends of stems. Cut into bite-sized pieces.

Heat oil and fry garlic on low heat until fragrant. Toss in the purslane and stir-fry for 1 minute, add soy sauce, sugar, sesame oil and mix quickly.

Spicy Purslane, Sri Lankan Style

A dish that demonstrates how tasty a wild weed can be. Serves 4 as an accompaniment to rice.

1 bunch purslane
1 small leek
2 tablespoons oil
1 teaspoon crushed garlic
2 teaspoons pounded Maldive fish
½ teaspoon salt
½ teaspoon chilli powder
4 tablespoons water
squeeze of lime juice

Trim off and discard roots, wash the purslane and shake off excess water. Wash leek thoroughly, slice finely. Heat oil in a wok or saucepan and gently fry the leek and garlic, stirring from time to time, until soft and fragrant. Cut purslane into short lengths and stir-fry for 1 minute. Add the Maldive fish, salt and chilli powder, fry a few seconds longer and add water. Cover and simmer for 10 minutes. Sprinkle lime juice over, mix, taste and adjust seasoning.

Qabargah

A Kashmiri recipe for lamb chops simmered in milk and spices, then fried in batter. Also known as kamargah.

Qahwah

See TEA.

Quail

(*Coturnix coturnix*) A popular game bird bred in Japan for its eggs as much as for its flesh. All the more popular because the birds need a relatively small area for breeding (they will breed in small cages), are economical eaters and begin laying an egg a day from 6 weeks of age. Hard-boiled quail eggs are a delicacy in Japan, skewered and fried. Quail eggs are also widespread in Thailand and Vietnam. Not much different in flavour to chicken eggs, their appeal is due to their dainty size and attractive shells, covered with chocolate-brown speckles and a delicate shade of blue inside.

Vietnamese Style Quails

Serves 6

6 quails
2 tablespoons fish sauce
2 tablespoons rice wine or dry sherry
1 tablespoon light soy sauce
1 teaspoon crushed garlic
1 teaspoon finely grated fresh ginger
½ teaspoon freshly ground black pepper
½ teaspoon five-spice powder
1 teaspoon hoi sin sauce

Cut each quail in half lengthwise and wipe out the body cavity with paper towels. If the quails have been frozen, dry them well after defrosting.

Combine the fish sauce, wine, soy sauce, garlic, ginger, pepper, five-spice powder and hoi sin sauce in a shallow bowl. Marinate the quails in the mixture, turning them a few times, or cover with plastic and refrigerate overnight.

Barbecue the quails on a well-oiled grill, skin side upwards, and cook until done on one side. Brush skin with vegetable oil, turn the pieces over with tongs and cook other side, not too close to the heat. When skin is brown and crisp transfer to a warm dish and serve with a salad or rice.

Quails with Indian Spices

Serves 4

4 quails
1 teaspoon chopped garlic
1 teaspoon salt
1 teaspoon finely grated fresh ginger
1 tablespoon oil
3 tablespoons natural yoghurt
3 teaspoons ground coriander
2 teaspoons ground rice
1 teaspoon ground cumin
1 teaspoon garam masala (recipe page 354)
½ teaspoon ground turmeric
½ teaspoon white pepper
½ teaspoon chilli powder

Split the quails down the back with poultry shears and open out flat. Rinse and clean cavity and dry thoroughly with paper towels. Crush garlic with the salt until very smooth. Mix with the ginger and all other ingredients and rub mixture on both sides of each quail. Cover and marinate at room temperature for 1 hour or refrigerate if longer marinating time is more convenient. Two skewers may be used to keep the birds flat during cooking.

Place under a preheated grill or barbecue, turning and brushing the quails twice with the remaining marinade. If marinade is too thick to brush on, add a tablespoon each of oil and water. Cook until the quails are brown and crisp (ground rice gives a crunchy coating) and serve with spiced rice and a salad of sliced cucumbers with yoghurt.

Deep-Fried Quails

To achieve a crisp skin, the quails are left to dry after immersing in a honey or maltose mixture.

1.5 litres/3 pints/6 cups water
2 teaspoons five-spice powder
1 tablespoon salt
2 tablespoons maltose or honey
4 quails
4 cups oil for deep frying

Bring water to the boil with the five-spice powder, salt and maltose. When the maltose has dissolved, immerse the quails in the liquid and let it return to the boil. Turn off heat, cover and leave for 10 minutes then lift out the quails, turning each bird so any liquid drains from the cavity. Place on a rack in front of an open window or electric fan and let the birds dry for about 3 hours. Check that there is no liquid inside the birds or the oil will spatter when they are fried.

Heat oil and fry quails until brown all over, ladling oil over them and turning so they cook evenly. Drain and serve with spiced salt for each person to sprinkle over their portion. This is a mixture of ½ teaspoon five-spice powder and 1 tablespoon salt.

Quandong

(*Sandalum acuminatum, Eucariya acuminata*) Also called native peach. Red and shiny fruit, with a thin layer of acid flesh and large, hard seed. Eaten raw when ripe, especially by the Aborigines of central Australia, which is its natural habitat. Good for pie fillings and jam.

Quandong, Blue

(*Elaeocarpus grandis*) An amazing, bright turquoise-blue fruit with a thin layer of fruit pulp which is eaten raw. Native to Australia and Fiji.

Queen of the Night

(*Epiphyllum strictus*) An ornamental cactus which only blooms around midnight and wilts before dawn. The large, many-petalled flowers are gathered after their short blooming period and the petals boiled and eaten with dressing, or deep fried as tempura.

China: *tan hua*
Japan: *gekka-no-bijin*

Quince

(*Cydonia vulgaris*) Related to the pear and the apple, this handsome fruit of downy golden hue and sweet perfume does not yield easily to the knife. There is some uncertainty as to whether it hails from western or central Asia, but it was most certainly embraced by the ancient civilisations of Greece and Rome. There it acquired various appellations (including the golden apples of Hesperides) and was dedicated to both Venus and Aphrodite. In so far as Asian cuisine is concerned, my only experience of quince was in a Sri Lankan sambal where the grated raw fruit was used as a substitute for unripe woodapple, an exotic and often hard-to-find native of the tropics.

Quince Sambal

1 large quince
salt and chilli powder to taste
1 tablespoon finely chopped shallot (optional)

Peel the quince and grate the flesh finely on a stainless steel grater. Sprinkle with ½ teaspoon salt and 1 teaspoon chilli powder, mix lightly with the fingers, then taste and adjust seasoning. Because it is not eaten in large quantities, the sambal should be quite strongly flavoured — hot with chilli, salty, and sour. The quince should provide the sour flavour but if you like to emphasise it, add a good squeeze of lime or lemon juice. Mix in shallot just before serving.

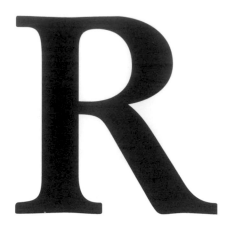

Radish, White

(*Raphanus sativus*) SEE ILLUSTRATION. Well known by its Japanese name, daikon, this white radish is often big enough to warrant its description of 'giant' in the species which offers a large range of sizes and colours. In Japan daikon is cooked in stewed dishes, used as a garnish and made into relishes and pickles.

In the skilled hands of those trained in vegetable carving, daikon can be transformed into roses, chrysanthemums, carnations, white swans and other birds. Even in simpler ways, daikon makes an impressive garnish.

Fresh radish, finely grated and mixed with finely chopped fresh hot chillies is used as a relish with Japanese food. A Japanese cook showed me how fresh red chillies (perhaps 3 or 4) are inserted in a section of white radish and the radish then grated very, very finely. The result is a rosy purée which has a definite bite. It is called momiji oroshi, which translates as 'maple leaf in autumn' because of its colour. Served with seafood or as a dip with seafood nabemono.

It contains the enzyme diastase (now made into a commercial anti-indigestion pill), paesin and vitamin C. The sweetest part of the radish is the top end (just below the leaves). However, the root is not the only part which is eaten. The leaves, rich in iron, calcium and vitamin C, may be sautéed or eaten raw in salad. The seed pods are crunchy, with a mild or hot radish flavour, depending on the variety. Much

favoured as an addition to salads. Some varieties are from 4–7 cm (1½–3 in) long and others can be as much as 30 cm (12 in) in length. The seed pods may also be lightly pickled in the same way as mustard cabbage. See recipe for Mustard Cabbage Relish (page 60).

When using radish, grate just before serving for maximum nutritional value. A special kind of grater is available for grating the fresh root into long, fine shreds (daikon-oroshi). A good vegetable for pickling (takuan, miso-zuke) or shredding then drying (kiriboshi). In Korea, white radish is used to make a pickle similar to kim chi, called kaktugge.

China: *loh-bak*
India: *mooli*
Indonesia: *lobak*
Japan: *daikon*
Korea: *moo*
Malaysia: *lobak*
Philippines: *labanos*
Sri Lanka: *rabu*
Thailand: *phakkat-hua*
Vietnam: *cu cai trang*

Raita

Cooling yoghurt-based accompaniments to Indian meals. The type of yoghurt used in India is rather thicker and richer than that available in a western supermarket, but natural yoghurt is an acceptable substitute so long as it is not the non-fat variety. Skim milk yoghurts are too tart, tangy and thin to give a good result. See YOGHURT for how to make the next best thing to Indian style buffalo milk yoghurt. Or, if time does not permit, stir an equal amount of cultured sour cream into commercial yoghurt. Season with fried black mustard seeds, toasted and crushed cumin seeds, pinch each of salt and sugar. Mix in boiled, diced potatoes or beetroot, sliced ripe bananas, diced cucumber, diced and fried eggplant, or simply stir in fresh herbs like mint or coriander, roughly chopped.

Ragi

See MILLET.

Rambutan

(*Nephelium lappaceum*) SEE ILLUSTRATION. In the months of July and August, fruit stalls and door-to-door vendors in many South East Asian cities present an extra colourful picture. The reason is the bunches of a strange looking oval fruit with bright crimson or yellow skin covered with short fleshy hairs — rambutan — is in season, and plentiful. The word comes from the Malay, 'rambut' meaning hair. Inside is a narrow sced covered with semi-transparent flesh which is crisp and mainly sweet. A lot depends on the variety, but it is obvious that the best varieties have been chosen for propagation and export.

During the rambutan season, fruits are displayed in great heaps in roadside stalls called boutiques. This is the local term for small shops that sell vegetables, fruit and some of the necessities of life. At this time of year, itinerant vendors who carry their 'shop' on the pingo or flexible pole which is slung over one shoulder with a basket on either end, start carrying a different kind of basket. Not open baskets which display their wares, but large, egg-shaped baskets a bit wider at the bottom than at the top, woven from tender green coconut leaves. Every child knows without having to look inside that these baskets hold rambutans; and every child will run to ask the adult in the home to buy some of the fruit which is so popular.

Since rambutans are now being exported and distributed widely in areas where they have not been available before, I thought it wise to write a brief guide to eating a rambutan. Never cut the fruit in half right through the seed. Make a cut with a sharp paring knife, as if you were going to slice the fruit in half, but only cut through the skin. Then lift off half the skin, leaving the rest as a decorative holder, especially when presenting rambutans as part of a fruit platter. This half shell is disposed of before starting to eat the translucent flesh. Hold the rambutan with the fingers.

Be careful not to bite too deeply or the flesh will come away complete with the tough, papery skin of the seed attached, and that is not rambutan at its best. Nibble daintily and detach only the succulent flesh. Then you are enjoying rambutan as seasoned veterans do. Rambutans make a lovely addition to a selection of dessert fruit. Leave some whole for guests to admire. Slit the skins and lift off half the shells of the rest; or make 4 equally spaced longitudinal slits three-quarters of the length of the fruit to the stem end. Spread the sections like petals, making the flesh accessible and giving those who have not encountered the fruit before a hint of what lies within. It is a shame to do anything to this fruit other than eat it raw. Don't even think of cooking it!

Red Kidney Bean

See LEGUMES & PULSES.

Red-Cooking

See TECHNIQUES.

Red Date

See JUJUBE.

Relishes

Whether called achar, atjar, sambal, sambol, chatni, pachchadi, kasaundi or any of the other names denoting accompaniments served in small amounts, relishes are ever-present at the Asian table. Colloquially they are known as 'rice pullers', used to enliven its neutral flavour. They can range from very hot to very mild. While many are bought ready made, there are some which may be made by the home cook. See CHATNI, CHUTNEY, SAMBAL. My favourite relish relies on salted limes or lemons (see LIME) which will keep for years in the pantry. All that is necessary is to chop a salted lime which is at least 6 months old (this makes it soft, and no longer bitter). Add 2 or 3 finely sliced shallots (or small purple onions), 2 fresh chillies, sliced, and a big pinch of sugar. Mix together and serve with rice and curries. No nicely aged salted limes? Here are some ideas which don't need as much pre-planning. Relishes made in minutes include:

Firm diced tomatoes, chopped spring onions (scallions), sliced hot chillies and chopped fresh coriander or mint, seasoned to taste with salt and lime or lemon juice.

Half-ripe pineapple, peeled, cored and chopped, mixed with finely diced cucumber and sliced shallots, a splash of white vinegar and pinch of salt.

Thinly sliced salad onions sprinkled with salt and sugar, mixed and left for 10 minutes, then rinsed and drained, seasoned with chilli powder. If the onions are preferred crisp and strongly flavoured, don't leave them for 10 minutes and rinse them, but serve immediately.

Rice

(*Oryza sativa*) Eaten by the richest and poorest of families on the humblest and most auspicious of occasions, rice is the foundation of an Asian meal. Be it gruel, cake, roll, cracker, paper, pilau, pudding, noodle or dessert, rice forms the staple diet of 60 per cent of the world's population. In the populous lands of Asia, rice means the difference between life and death and as such is treated with utmost respect.

In China it is considered bad luck to upset a rice bowl, and the worst insult imaginable is to pick up someone's bowl of rice and tip it onto the floor. To quit your job translates as 'breaking your rice bowl' and in Asia you are asked whether you've had a meal by 'have you eaten rice?'

Rice as a crop was being cultivated around the Ganges delta as early as 2000 BC and within the next millennium found itself established in China, Indochina, Malaysia, Indonesia, the Philippines and Thailand. Between 300 BC and 200 AD it made its way to the Middle East and Japan. Rice is now a major crop in every Asian country. Some are self-sufficient and some have to supplement their crops with imported rice.

Throughout Asia, polished (white) rice is considered superior to unpolished, the latter being purchased for household servants, the lowly classes enjoying superior nutrition but the moneyed employers insisting on snowy white grains. In some poorer areas, any kind of rice would be welcome and when people cannot afford it they supplement their diet with maize and cassava.

Rice is a grass and, in this respect, related to the cereals barley, oats and wheat. *O. sativa* is the species cultivated today, and there are three identifiable groups:

Indica, characterised by long grains and a non-sticky result when cooked;

Japonica, with short grains and some degree of stickiness;

Javanica, with long grains and a tendency to be sticky.

Basically there are two types of rice. There are the long grain types such as basmati and jasmine rice (which by the way are not brand names but varieties). The best basmati is called Dehraduni basmati and is grown in the northern Indian state of Uttar Pradesh in the Himalayan foothills. Patna rice is a variety of basmati. The grains have a fragrance particularly suited to Indian food. Thai jasmine rice is lightly perfumed and goes well with all kinds of Asian food.

The other category is medium or short grain which cooks to a softer consistency. The grains, instead of being fluffy and separate, cling together. This makes it much easier to eat with chopsticks, which explains why it is preferred by Chinese, Japanese and Koreans, though in some Chinese restaurants there is a trend toward serving long grain rice (not basmati, which would be inappropriate because of its distinctive flavour) but jasmine or Carolina-type rice.

In Western cuisines where rice is mainly considered a mere accompaniment to main dishes, it is difficult to comprehend the subtleties that Asians take into account when choosing rice. Not just the length of the grain, but the aroma, flavour, firmness, stickiness, and that all-important 'mouth feel'.

I was amazed, when travelling in North America, to find that every time I had rice on my plate, it was 'converted' or 'pre-cooked' rice. This kind of rice is easier to cook in that it is almost impossible to get a sticky result, but flavour and texture are sacrificed. Please do not use this rice for Asian meals. You will get a wrong impression of how an authentic meal should taste.

For Indian, Sri Lankan and Malaysian meals rice is usually cooked with salt added and, because the desired result is fluffy, separate grains, long grain rice is preferred. In India, where patna and basmati (scented long grain) are favoured, the result will be dry and separate grains. This is more so in the case of pilau, where the raw rice is first cooked in a little ghee or oil to coat each grain before the cooking liquid is added.

In Vietnam, rice is either sticky or, in some instances, very dry and fluffy. In order to achieve the latter, 'pot roast' 500 g (1 lb/2½ cups) long grain rice in a heavy saucepan in 3 tablespoons oil, butter or pork fat for 10–15 minutes, stirring constantly until grains first turn opaque, then start to brown. Add 750 ml (1½ pints/3 cups) hot water, cover pan with well-fitting lid and cook over low heat for 15–20 minutes so all the water is absorbed.

In China and Japan short, pearly grains are preferred. These cling together and can be picked up with chopsticks or eaten with the bowl held close to the mouth. Indonesians and Filipinos like it somewhere in between. The Thais mostly eat jasmine rice, except in the north and north-east of the country where sticky (glutinous) rice is favoured. Sticky rice requires overnight soaking, then draining before it is steamed.

In India and Sri Lanka forgetting to add salt to the rice would be an unpardonable oversight for which the cook would surely be rebuked, but in Indonesia, Malaysia, Thailand, Burma, China, Japan and Korea salt is considered to mask the flavour of a good rice.

The variety of rice you use will, to a large degree, dictate the result. For instance, even with a minimum of water, it is almost impossible to turn short grain rice into anything other than grains that cling together, though there are exceptions.

In Sri Lanka both long and short grain rice are eaten. A preference for separate grains led to the introduction of muttu samba, a very short and pearly grained variety that has been parboiled. As well as keeping the grains distinct, parboiling gives a curious flavour to the rice, one that not everyone will care for. Muttu samba is traditionally used for lampries, although in wealthier households basmati rice may be preferred. There are instances, though, when firm and separate grains are not ideal, as in rice congee or milk rice. Broken rice (known as kakulu-haal) is sold especially for these preparations. It may be 'red' (unpolished) or white (polished) rice. The small bits of broken grains are the by-product of pounding, husking and winnowing. It cooks more quickly and is very soft.

The practice of parboiling rice originated in India some 2,000 years ago and it is still the preference of many northern Indians.

Although parboiling techniques vary, the process basically involves soaking the unhusked grains for several hours, steaming for a short time (about 10 minutes), then allowing to dry before polishing. Coincidentally, this gives parboiled rice superior nutritional value to regular polished rice because in the steaming process some additional goodness from the bran is forced into the grain. Parboiled grains are harder than untreated rice, which would explain why it is easier to mill, more resistant to breaking and requires slightly longer cooking time.

There are as many opinions on how rice should be cooked as there are cooks, but here are the two main schools of thought:

1 Rice should be boiled in plenty of water. Wash the rice in several changes of water and drain well. Bring water measuring 6 times the quantity of the rice to a rolling boil. Add rice and cook uncovered for 8 minutes. Lower heat and with lid slightly ajar cook for a further 3 minutes. Test that grains are no longer chalky in the centre then drain in a colander, place rice in a serving dish, cover with foil and keep warm in 120°C (250°F) oven for up to 1 hour.

2 Rice should be cooked by steaming (the absorption method). Wash the rice thoroughly and drain well. Place in a cooking pot and add water until it comes up to the first joint of your finger, with your fingertip resting on the surface of the rice. Bring to a rolling boil, cover with a well-fitting lid, turn heat low and simmer for 15 minutes. Turn off heat and allow to stand a further 5 minutes without lifting the lid. Even left for 30 minutes with the cover on, it will continue to hold steam. As you can imagine, this method leads to varying results depending on the size of the pot or length of fingers. To eliminate these variations, use the following formula.

For recipe purposes I prefer to measure rice in a cup. Even if you don't use standard measuring cups, simply use the same size cup for measuring rice and water, and the results will be successful.

For 1 cup of short grain rice, allow 1½ cups of water. For each additional cup of rice thereafter, 1 cup of water. If using long grain rice, allow 2 cups of water to the first cup of rice, then 1½ cups water for every additional cup of rice. If you still don't trust your ability to cook rice, rice cookers make perfect rice with a minimum of effort — just follow the manufacturer's instructions. Unless I'm making an exceptionally large quantity of biriani or pilau, I'm quite happy to use the electric rice cooker.

The best rice has usually been aged by storing and cooks drier and fluffier than new rice. It is also more expensive since the cost of storage is added. But it all depends on the needs of the consumer. It seems that people with large families (and extended families in Asia usually include old folk and young children) prefer new rice, because it gives a softer result when cooked, more suited to both the elderly and very young.

Unpolished rice (brown rice or 'red rice') is rice which retains the bran layer after husking. It requires the same amount of water as long grain rice, but longer cooking. It may be pale or reddish brown depending on the rice variety. In Japan brown rice is called gen mai. It is not popular in Asian countries, white rice being preferred, but those who cannot afford white rice buy red rice with most of the reddish brown bran left on the grains. Each has its merits.

Sticky rice (also known as glutinous rice and sweet rice) may be either white or black in colour, short or long grain. Chinese and Japanese prefer the short grain variety while in Thailand, long grain glutinous rice is preferred. White sticky rice is used primarily in sweet dishes throughout Asia, with the exception being the mountain areas of northern Thailand, Cambodia, Laos and parts of Vietnam, where long grain white sticky rice is the staple.

Black sticky rice owes its colour to the layer of bran left intact and in spite of its name there is a small percentage of grains which are brown and a few which are creamy coloured. Under the black coat the grain is white, but because the colour runs when it is cooked, the entire mass becomes black. Popular in Burma, Thailand and the Philippines, it is usually served as a sweet. It may be cooked by the absorption method, but I prefer to soak it overnight, drain it and steam it over boiling water for 45 minutes to 1 hour, or in a pressure cooker (at half pressure) for 30 minutes. The Chinese believe eating it improves the colour of the blood and keeps hair black. See RICE, BLACK GLUTINOUS.

Sweet rice is a name given to short grain sticky rice in Japan. It is used mostly to make mochi or rice cakes in Japan, and in China for the savoury parcels of rice which are combined with pork and salted eggs, wrapped in lotus leaves or bamboo leaves and steamed. These are a favourite snack offered at dim sum.

Wild rice (*Zizania aquatica*, *Zizania palustris*) is also a grass. Closely related to oryza, it grows wild in the shallows of only a few North American lakes. Not used in Asian cuisine, though it is grown in China primarily for the solid base of the stem. See WILD RICE SHOOTS.

Medicinal uses: Rice is completely non-allergenic. It is the grain for people with digestive problems. Rice gruel is the first food given to Asian babies and the first semi-solid food for those recovering from an illness. Rice is the perfect food for those with a gluten intolerance as no rice contains gluten. When the term 'glutinous' is used in regard to sticky rice, it simply means having the quality of glue (i.e. stickiness). Cooked rice should not be left at room temperature for more than a day, as it harbours all kinds of unfriendly organisms.

There are different words for cooked and uncooked rice in Asian countries, and for types of rice as well. Here are some of the most useful.

Cooked Non-sticky rice
Burma: *htamin*
China: *fan*
India: *namkin chawal*
Indonesia: *nasi*
Japan: *gohan*
Korea: *bahb*
Malaysia: *nasi*
Sri Lanka: *buth*
Thailand: *khao*
Vietnam: *com*

Cooked sticky rice
Burma: *khaonee* (white), *nga cheik* (black)
China: *nawmai*
Japan: *mochigome*
Malaysia: *beras pulot, pulot hitam*
Philippines: *malagkit*
Thailand: *khao niew*
Vietnam: *xoi*

Plain Steamed Rice

Serves 4

2 cups basmati or other long grain rice
3 cups water
1½ level teaspoons salt or to taste

Basmati rice needs picking over, as it may contain paddy grains, small stones and other foreign matter. It is not difficult and takes very little time if the rice is spread out on a baking sheet and sorting started at one corner, removing any impurities and separating the sorted rice from the rest. The rice should then be washed several times in cold water until the water looks clean. Drain in a large colander or sieve and leave to dry about for 30 minutes.

Put rice and water into a heavy-based saucepan with salt, bring quickly to the boil, then turn heat down very low and cover pot with a well-fitting lid. This is essential, since it is the steam which cooks rice when using the absorption method. Cook on low heat for 15 minutes, turn off heat and leave without uncovering for a further 5 minutes. Uncover and allow steam to escape for a few minutes, still not disturbing the rice. Fluff with long fork or use a thin metal spoon. Wooden or other heavy spoons crush the rice grains and spoil its appearance and texture.

Ghee Rice

This rice dish also uses the absorption method. After washing and draining the rice and leaving it to dry, it is fried in ghee with spices. The liquid used is flavourful stock. Many elaborate dishes such as biriani or pilau are based on layering rice with spiced meat, poultry or seafood. Serves 4–5.

500 g/1 lb/2½ cups basmati rice
2 tablespoons ghee
1 large onion, finely sliced
5 green cardamom pods, bruised
3 whole cloves
1 cinnamon stick
2 teaspoons salt
1 litre/2 pints/4 cups stock

Pick over the rice, wash, drain and dry as described in previous recipe. In a heavy saucepan heat ghee or oil and fry the onion until golden. Add spices and rice and fry for about 3 minutes, stirring with a metal spoon in order not to crush the grains. Add stock and salt, bring to the boil, then lower heat, cover and cook for 15 minutes, not lifting lid. Turn off heat and let rice continue to steam for a further 5 minutes. Uncover and after steam has escaped for a further 5 minutes, fluff rice gently with fork, remove spices and serve out with a metal spoon.

When doubling or trebling rice recipes, remember not to increase liquid in the same proportion. Three times the amount of rice for this recipe will be 1.5 kg (3 lb) (7½ cups). The liquid required, however, is only 2.75 litres (5½ pints) (11 cups).

Yellow Rice

A favourite festive dish in more than one South East Asian country. The flavourings and spices may vary but the end result is rich and delicious. It may be served wrapped in individual packets, or moulded into the cone shape favoured for special occasions in Indonesia. Serves 8–10.

1 kg/2 lb/5 cups long grain rice
5 tablespoons ghee or oil
2 large onions, finely sliced
1 teaspoon whole black peppercorns
15 green cardamom pods, bruised
10 whole cloves
2 teaspoons ground turmeric
4 teaspoons salt
2 sprigs fresh curry leaves
2 stems lemon grass, bruised
2 fresh, frozen or dried pandan leaves
2 × 400 ml/14 fl oz cans coconut milk
1 litre/2 pints/4 cups hot water

Wash and drain the rice, leave to dry for at least 30 minutes. Heat ghee in a large, heavy saucepan and fry the onion until golden. Add whole spices, ground turmeric, salt, curry leaves, lemon grass and pandan leaves. Stir over heat for 30 seconds. Add rice and fry, stirring with a metal spoon, until rice is coated with ghee and turmeric.

In a large jug dilute coconut milk with measured hot water and stir to disperse any lumps of coconut cream. Add to pan and stir while it comes to the boil. Reduce heat to very low, cover with a well-fitting lid and cook for 20 minutes without lifting lid. Turn off heat, leave for a further 5 minutes, then uncover and pick out spices which will be resting on top of the rice. Fluff rice lightly with a fork. Serve hot with curries and sambals.

Rice in Coconut Milk

This may mean the dish of Malay origin — long-grain rice steamed in coconut milk known as nasi lemak; or it could be short-grain rice boiled in coconut milk until soft, then pressed into a flat cake and served cut in large diamond-shaped pieces. This is known in Sri Lanka as kiri bath, Sinhalese for 'milk rice'. It is served on New Year's Day, to augur prosperity for the coming year. In many homes it is also served at breakfast on the first day of each month, usually with an accompaniment of coconut sambal or shaved palm sugar for those who prefer it sweet. Serves 6.

500 g/1 lb/2½ cups short grain or broken rice
1 litre/2 pints/4 cups water
400 ml/14 fl oz can coconut milk
2 teaspoons salt
1 stick cinnamon (optional)

In a heavy-based saucepan bring rice and water to a boil. Cover and cook on low heat 15 minutes. Dilute coconut milk with sufficient water to make 500 ml (1 pint) and heat gently almost to boiling point, stirring. Add to rice with salt and cinnamon stick, stirring well with the handle of a wooden spoon. Replace lid of pan and continue to cook over low heat for a further 15 minutes or until all the milk is absorbed. Remove cinnamon stick, and turn rice onto a flat dish. Smooth top with a piece of banana leaf or oiled foil. Mark in large diamond shapes. Serve with accompaniments.

Sushi Rice

This is the slightly sweet, slightly sour rice which forms the basis of all sushi.

500 g/1 lb/2½ cups short grain white rice
600 ml/20 fl oz/2½ cups water
5 cm/2 in piece dried kelp (optional)

SEASONING

4 tablespoons rice vinegar
3 tablespoons sugar
2½ teaspoons salt
2 tablespoons mirin

Wash rice several times in cold water and drain well for 1 hour, then put into a saucepan with the measured water. If using kelp, wipe over with a slightly damp cloth and add it to the pan. Bring to the boil, turn heat very low, cover and steam for 15 minutes without lifting lid. Remove pan from heat and leave it covered for 10 minutes longer. Discard kelp and turn rice into a large bowl.

Mix seasoning ingredients together until sugar is completely dissolved, heating it slightly, but cool completely before adding to rice. Spread rice on a large dish. Pour cooled dressing over the rice and mix gently but thoroughly through. Fan the rice to cool it quickly to room temperature.

To make mounds of rice for nigiri-zushi, moisten hands with cold water mixed with an equal amount of mild vinegar. Take a rounded tablespoon of sushi rice and form into a neat oval shape a little smaller than the slices of fish used for topping. Fish should completely cover top of the rice mound. Lightly smear one side of fish with wasabi and place it, wasabi downwards, on the rice. Garnish with a strip of nori or pickled ginger. Moisten hands again before starting on next mound of rice to prevent rice sticking.

For recipes see SUSHI.

Sticky Rice with Coconut

Sticky (glutinous) rice is the ubiquitous ingredient for many of the sweet snacks enjoyed in Asia. The method of cooking it is markedly different to those used for rice which is not sticky. Serves 4.

250 g/8 oz long grain glutinous rice, white or black
200 ml/7 fl oz coconut milk
1 tablespoon white sugar
¼ teaspoon salt
grated fresh coconut

Soak rice for 6–8 hours in water to cover. Drain in a colander or sieve, put rice into a heatproof dish and stir in coconut milk, sugar and salt. Steam over boiling water for 1 hour or pressure cook at half pressure for 30 minutes. When cool enough to handle take small spoonfuls of rice and form even-sized balls. Roll in fresh coconut and serve on the same day as they do not improve with being refrigerated. If liked, serve with a sprinkle of toasted and roughly ground sesame seeds mixed with a good pinch of sea salt.

Fried Rice

Leftover cold rice is one of the most useful items to have in the kitchen, as it can be turned into a meal or snack with the flavours of any Asian country. Cooked rice should not be left unrefrigerated.

If rice is being cooked specifically to make fried rice, one can ensure a good result by using slightly less water when steaming it. Turn it out of the pan as soon as it is cooked, spread out on a large baking tray or other suitable surface to cool, and hasten the cooling process by placing it near an open window or in the refrigerator. The longer it cools and firms, the better the results will be when it is fried. One of the simplest recipes for fried rice follows. Serves 2.

3 tablespoons peanut oil
4 cups cold cooked rice
2 tablespoons light soy sauce
6 spring onions (scallions), sliced diagonally

Heat a wok until very hot. Add oil and swirl to coat surface, then add the rice, toss and fry until grains are separate. Sprinkle with soy sauce and keep tossing to distribute evenly. Add sliced spring onions and keep tossing for a minute or two.

Vary the recipe by frying the following ingredients before adding rice:

For Chinese flavour: diced barbecued pork, roast pork, barbecued duck or lap cheong (Chinese sausage).

For Korean flavour: finely chopped garlic, thinly sliced beef. Add bean paste, black pepper, Korean soy sauce.

For Indonesian flavour: chopped raw prawns (shrimp), chopped garlic and onion, small piece dried shrimp paste wrapped in foil and roasted. Garnish with cucumber and a fried egg. Serve with sweet chilli sauce.

For Thai flavour: Thai red curry paste, garlic, small prawns (shrimp), flaked cooked crab meat, use fish sauce instead of soy and add sliced hot chillies and a splash of sweet chilli sauce.

See Index of Recipes for listing of rice recipes.

Rice Bean

See LEGUMES & PULSES.

Rice, Black Glutinous

While unknown in some Asian countries, this sticky rice is very popular in others, among them Burma, Thailand, Malaysia, Singapore and Indonesia. White glutinous rice is more widely used, but the glistening, long, black grains have an earthy appeal all their own — firstly because of their unusual appearance, and secondly because of their ability to combine with sugar and a few simple flavours such as toasted sesame seeds, and be transformed into a sweet snack or delicious dessert.

My maternal grandmother, who taught me about Burmese food, used to make a delicious tea-time treat of steamed sticky black rice (khao nieo, she called it) which she put before me with freshly grated coconut, some scrapings of palm sugar for sweetness, and sprinkled with sesame seeds toasted until brown then roughly pounded using a mortar and pestle with a pinch of sea salt. This final addition focused the flavours in an incredible way.

Burma: *khao nieo*

Indonesia: *pulot hitam*
Malaysia: *pulot hitam*
Thailand: *khao niew*

Black Rice Porridge

In Singapore and Malaysia, you'll find this under the name of pulot hitam, a slightly sweet, comforting porridge served with coconut milk. Serves 6.

220 g/7 oz/1 cup black glutinous rice
1.5 litres/3 pints/16 cups water
60 g/2 oz palm sugar or brown sugar
2 tablespoons granulated sugar
2 strips pandan leaf
6 dried longans
250 ml/8 fl oz/1 cup coconut cream
¼ teaspoon salt

Wash rice in several changes of water and drain. Put into a heavy saucepan with the measured water and bring to the boil. Cover and simmer for 30–40 minutes, stirring occasionally to make sure the rice doesn't stick to the bottom of the pan. Add palm sugar and granulated sugar, pandan leaf and dried longans. (If the longans are still in their shells, discard the shells.) If the porridge becomes too thick, add more hot water. Continue cooking until the rice grains have become very soft. Serve warm, with coconut cream to which the salt has been added.

Black Sticky Rice with Sesame Seeds

Serves 4

200 g/7 oz/1 cup black glutinous rice
sea salt
1½ cups freshly grated coconut
3 tablespoons sesame seeds, toasted
jaggery or dark brown sugar

Wash the rice well, put it in a bowl and soak overnight or for at least 3 hours in cold water to cover. Drain the rice, saving the water. Place rice in a heatproof bowl and add ¾ cup of the soaking water and ¼ teaspoon salt. Place the bowl on a trivet in a large pan with well-fitting lid and steam over boiling water for 45 minutes to 1 hour, or until rice is tender and water absorbed. Add more boiling water to the pan as necessary.

If a pressure cooker is available it takes half the time. Place bowl on a trivet with about 5 cm (2 in) water in the cooker, and cook at half pressure for 25–30 minutes. Serve with coconut, a sprinkling of toasted sesame seeds lightly bruised with ½ teaspoon salt, and jaggery either shaved with a sharp knife or cut into small pieces with a chopper.

Rice Cakes

Also known as rice crackers. In the cuisines of Thailand and China the crust of rice which sometimes sticks at the base of the pan is not wasted, indeed it is prized. It is dried in the sun (or in a very low oven) and stored airtight. In these days of foolproof rice cookers and non-stick pans, we can quite deliberately make a rice crust which is rice pressed flat and oven dried. To serve, break into bite-sized pieces and fry in hot oil. The oil must be hot enough to make the rice crust puff and swell. A few seconds is all that is needed. Lift out with a slotted spoon, drain on paper towels, and when quite cool, transfer to an airtight container. Will keep for a day or two. However, it is better to store the dried rice crust and fry it shortly before serving with dips such as Thai nam prik or Malaysian peanut sauce.

In Chinese cuisine, freshly fried rice crackers are taken to the table, where they are topped with a savoury dish of prawns (shrimp) or chicken in sauce. The sound which ensues when the sauce is poured over the hot rice results in the names 'singing rice' or 'sizzling rice'. The secret is to have both the rice and the sauce very hot, requiring considerably more organisation than it takes for the simple rice crackers served in Thailand. A dish like this should be eaten on its own, immediately it is served and before the rice has lost its crispness.

To make Rice Crackers

Put 1 cup raw white rice, preferably short grain, into a large saucepan and add 1½ cups water. Bring to a boil and cook uncovered on medium-low heat until all the water is absorbed. Cover with lid and leave the pan on very low heat for 15 minutes longer. Allow to cool. Lift the rice out of the pan using a spatula. Put it on a non-stick or foil-covered oven tray and press with the heel of the hand to compress and flatten as much as possible. Bake at 150°C (300°F), for 1 hour or until the rice is completely dried out. Cool, then break into pieces of roughly equal size. Store airtight and it will keep for months, provided it is completely dry.

To serve, heat oil for deep frying and fry just 1 or 2 pieces at a time. They will puff and swell as soon as they are dropped into the oil if the oil is the right temperature. They should be done in a few seconds, and the colour should not be more than the palest gold, especially if serving them the Chinese way. For Thai rice crackers, they may be fried a little longer so that they achieve not only a golden brown colour but a slightly stronger flavour.

Sizzling Rice Crackers with Sweet Chilli Prawns (Shrimp)

Serves 4

375 g/12 oz medium sized raw prawns (shrimp)
3 tablespoons peanut oil
1 teaspoon crushed garlic
1 teaspoon finely grated fresh ginger
3 spring onions (scallions),
  cut into 2.5 cm/1 in pieces
1 small red capsicum (bell pepper), diced
250 ml/8 fl oz/1 cup chicken stock
3 tablespoons tomato ketchup
2 tablespoons sweet chilli sauce
1 tablespoon cornflour (cornstarch)

FOR THE CRACKERS
rice prepared as above, dried out but not fried until required
oil for deep frying

Shell and devein the prawns. Heat 3 tablespoons peanut oil and stir-fry the prawns on high heat just until they turn pink and curl. Lift out on slotted spoon. Lower heat and in oil remaining in wok, stir-fry the garlic, ginger, spring onion and capsicums until slightly softened. Add stock, ketchup and chilli sauce and bring to the boil. Mix cornflour with about 3 tablespoons cold water and stir into the sauce until it boils and thickens. Return prawns to the wok and set aside.

Heat oil for deep frying and fry the rice crackers as described on page 312. Lift out on a slotted spoon and drain for a minute on paper towels. Reheat prawns, but do not overcook. Serve rice crackers and prawns in separate dishes and ladle the prawn mixture over the rice crackers. Serve immediately.

Rice Flakes

Not a breakfast cereal as the name might suggest, but rice grains which have been parboiled, flattened by heavy rollers, then dried. It is called poha or powva in India and habalapethi in Sri Lanka. Used as an ingredient in either savoury snacks such as chiura or cooked in milk as a pudding. Thai or Vietnamese shops sell a pale green version of flaked rice, kao mao, which is used to make a sweet with coconut cream and sugar.

Indian shops also sell a puffed poha, light and dry as rice cereal but not sweetened, and white instead of golden. It may be used in either savoury or sweet snacks. Immature rice grains, roasted and pounded, are called pinipig in the Philippines and are used as a sprinkle on desserts such as ice cream or the famous halo-halo.

Rice Flour

Sold in large packets (1 kg/2.2 lbs) and slightly roasted, the flour is a pale, creamy colour. It is used for southern Indian and Sri Lankan preparations such as pittu (also called puttu), which may be described as a steamed dumpling (though lighter and more crumbly than any Western style dumpling).

Roasted rice flour is not to be confused with dark-roasted rice powder, which is golden brown and coarser in texture and generally sold in smaller amounts.

The famous southern Indian and Sri Lankan specialty, stringhoppers, are made from a paste of rice flour and water (see recipe page 314).

A popular use for leftover or broken stringhoppers is stringhopper pilau. This can be easily made substituting dried rice vermicelli for broken stringhoppers (see recipe page 253).

Pittu

Pittu (or Puttu) is steamed in narrow cylindrical moulds with a loose, perforated base. These are sold in shops specialising in Indian and Sri Lankan ingredients. Improvise by using a narrow tin about 12 cm (5 in) long and 6 cm (2¼ in) wide, with a press-on lid. A Dutch cocoa can is the perfect size and shape. Cut away base of can and invert so the lid is now the base. Drill small holes in the lid so steam can penetrate. After steaming, remove lid and push the steamed rice cake through the wider opening.

150 g/5 oz/¾ cup roasted rice flour
150 g/5 oz/2 cups fresh grated coconut
½ teaspoon salt or to taste
about 3 tablespoons cold water

In a large bowl combine rice flour, grated coconut and salt. Add a few drops of water at a time and lightly mix the flour and coconut together until moistened, but under no circumstances should the mixture be wet or lumpy. Lightly fill cylinders, not compacting the mixture. Place on a trivet in a deep pan, cover and steam over boiling water for 15 minutes. Allow to cool slightly, then unmould onto a plate and cut each cylinder in 2 or 3 pieces. Serve pittu with coconut milk and a hot sambal or curry. Tripe Curry (see page 257) is a traditional accompaniment.

If preferred, serve pittu with coconut milk and sugar or jaggery.

Note: Millet flour, sold as kurakkan flour, may be substituted for half the rice flour.

Stringhoppers: Small mats of fine, white, fresh rice noodles. Since the local name of stringhoppers is iddi-ah-pay and they look as though made with fine white string, I suppose it was natural enough that they came to be described as stringhoppers.

At breakfast, stringhoppers are served with coconut sambal and a thin coconut milk soup. They are light but satisfying, with a texture that is fluffy and dry. On festive occasions stringhoppers may take the place of rice at a main meal. They are piled on a large oval dish in heaps of 6 or 8 and served with mulligatawny, scrambled eggs, poultry and meat curries, frikkadels and chilli sambal.

To make these you will need a stringhopper press mould and steaming racks. Not so for Mock Stringhopper Pilau which is within the scope of anybody (see page 253).

Stringhoppers

Makes about 30

**250 g/8 oz/2 cups Chinese rice flour
(not glutinous) or
Sri Lankan lightly roasted rice flour
400 ml/14 fl oz/1¾ cups water
2 level teaspoons salt**

If more convenient, plain (all-purpose) wheat flour may be used, but it must be steamed beforehand. Put an unopened 1 kg (2 lb) packet of flour into a steamer and steam over boiling water for 1 hour. Turn onto a fine sieve and, while still fairly hot, rub through the sieve. The flour will have become a hard lump through steaming and a large wire sieve is best. When cool, this flour can be stored in an airtight container for future use in making stringhoppers.

Measure the water into a small pan with the salt and bring to the boil. Turn off the heat and allow 40 seconds off the boil, then pour all at once onto the flour, stirring with the handle of a wooden spoon until the flour is moistened. When cool enough, gather it together with the hand and ensure there are no pockets of dry flour by kneading lightly. Put some of the dough into a stringhopper mould, of which there are various types, some much easier to use than others. Line up 6 to 8 small bamboo steaming racks on kitchen bench. If they are new, wash and dry them and rub the surface lightly with a piece of cloth or a paper towel dipped in oil so that they don't stick to the dough. Now comes the tricky part. Squeeze dough through the fine holes in the mould, at the same time moving the mould over each steaming rack so that the fine strings fall in two circles. (In some moulds which are fixed to the work table, the rack is moved in a circular fashion under the disc extruding the strands, which is rather easier.) When all the racks have been used, carefully position them one over the other and place the pile in a steamer. Cover and steam over fast boiling water for 8–10 minutes. Remove from steamer, allow to cool slightly, then gently peel the stringhoppers off the bamboo mats, put them on a plate, and start the procedure over again until the dough is used up. Stringhoppers should be fine and lacy, and the texture moist yet light and fluffy. Serve as described on page 313.

Rice, Ground

The term used for coarser ground non-glutinous rice, marketed in Western supermarkets for use as an ingredient in Scottish shortbread. It is also used in India to make the delicately rose-scented rice blancmange called Firni.

Firni

Serves 4

**750 ml/1½ pints/3 cups milk
3 tablespoons ground rice
3 tablespoons white sugar
pinch ground cardamom (optional)
1 tablespoon rose water
or 3 drops rose essence
pink food colouring
2 tablespoons pistachio kernels**

Put milk into an enamel or stainless steel saucepan. Reserve a little and mix with ground rice to make a smooth cream. Heat milk and sugar, stirring constantly so milk solids don't scorch on bottom of pan. When milk is almost at boiling point move pan off the heat and stir in the ground rice. Return pan to heat and stir constantly until mixture boils and thickens. Simmer, stirring, for 3 minutes. Remove from heat, add cardamom if used and rose flavouring. Stir in a drop of food colour or just enough to achieve a very delicate rose pink. Pour into individual dessert dishes and allow to set.

Drop pistachio kernels into a small pan of boiling water, boil for 30 seconds, then pour into a strainer and run cold water over to cool them. Slip off the skins and chop the bright green pistachios finely. Scatter a little over each serving. Serve chilled.

Rice, Iced

The Royal House of Thailand in the days of King Chulalongkorn, would import ice by ship from freezing works in Singapore. During the hottest months of the year, one of the palace dishes was 'iced rice': cooked fragrant rice in iced water scented with jasmine and rose petals, served with highly spiced foods to tempt the monarch's heat-jaded appetite. This was a creation of the ladies of King Chulalongkorn's court. Ladies-in-waiting to the king's wives were often chosen for their culinary skills. Each house had its own kitchen and the better the food the more often His Majesty would visit! These days, iced rice (khao chae) is sold in fast food centres and the common folk can enjoy it also.

Rice Noodles

See NOODLES.

Rice Paddy Herb

(*Hydrophyllum* spp.) SEE ILLUSTRATION. A pale green, small-leafed herb on soft stems called ngo om in Vietnamese, used to flavour soups and curries. It is similar to a wild aquatic herb which grows in rice paddies and ponds and is known to Thais as phak khayaeng or phak phaa (*Limnophila aromatica*). Also added to curries or eaten with nam prik, a pungent fish and chilli sauce.

Rice Paper

Rice paper as used in Asian cuisine, called bahn tran in Vietnamese, are the thin sheets of basket-weave textured rice and water paste stamped into perfect rounds. Bought in sealed packets, they will keep indefinitely in their dried state, although they are brittle and may shatter if dropped. When moistened with water they become the flexible wrappers for Vietnamese fried spring rolls (cha gio) or fresh spring rolls (goi cuon) and the fresh spring rolls of Thailand (poh pia).

The attractive woven pattern on the wrappers is the imprint of bamboo mats on which the thin circles of dough are dried. To render them flexible, first moisten lightly with either a brush dipped in water or by immersing individual sheets in water for just a few seconds. This will enable a filling to be enclosed in the 'skin' without it splitting. If the wrapper starts to disintegrate, it got too wet. Trial and error is the best teacher.

The fine, wafer-like 'rice' paper which is used in confectionery making is misleadingly named, as it is not made from rice. It is an edible paper made from various plants: *Tetrapana × papyriferus* (rice paper plant), *Edgeworthia tomentosa* (nakai) and *Wikstroemia canescens* (maisin).

Rice, Roasted and Ground

The special flavour and texture of this roasted and pounded rice is very important in Thailand, Laos, Vietnam and China. Rice grains are stirred constantly in a dry pan over low heat until golden brown, then pounded or ground in a blender and any large bits sifted out.

In Chinese cooking, ground roasted rice is used to coat meats before steaming. In Thai and Vietnamese cooking it is sprinkled over a dish shortly before serving, both for its unique toasty flavour and as a texture ingredient. Roasted rice powder is available in small packets in Asian grocery shops, or you can make it yourself.

Thailand: *khao kua*
Vietnam: *thinh*

Rice Sticks

See NOODLES.

Rice Vermicelli

See NOODLES.

Rice Wrapper

See RICE PAPER.

Ridged Gourd

See GOURDS.

Rijstaffel

A Dutch word which means 'rice table'. Though it is a relic of Dutch colonial times, it still survives today, mainly in the five-star hotels of Asia. Gourmet tourists are keen to experience the meal which can have as many as thirty different dishes, all eaten with steamed white rice. Some are hot, some are mild, some are dry and others are liquid. While it used to be the custom for a procession of servers to bring in each dish (and it still happens in some grand hotels), it is far more common for the food to be presented buffet style, clay pots holding richly spiced food bubbling over small table burners.

In addition to made-up dishes, accompaniments include sliced fresh fruit such as pineapple and bananas; grated fresh coconut; fried bananas; fried peanuts and coconut; crisply fried krupuk (crackers) made of starch flavoured with dried shrimp, or pressed and dried melinjo nuts. There is usually at least one kind of satay served with peanut sauce, and more than one kind of sambal — the fiery accent which sets an Indonesian meal apart. The foundation of the meal is always fluffy white rice.

There are many recipes in this book which would be appropriate for a rijstaffel, especially those which are from Indonesia or Malaysia such as Indonesian Egg Sambal, Indonesian Braised Chicken, Beef Rendang, Satay (one or more kinds); Prawn Sambal; Balinese Style Pork; Bean Sambal; a soupy dish (such as Coconut and Vegetable Curry), but substitute dried shrimp paste for Maldive fish in the recipe); and Grilled Fish, Indonesian Style.

Rose Apple

(*Eugenia jambos*, *Syzygium jambos*) Native to India and Malaysia, and probably introduced to Sri Lanka by the Portuguese. The fruit is small, about 4 cm (1½ in) in diameter, and pale greenish-white changing to yellow tinged with pink. It is eaten in South East Asia dipped in soy or fish sauce, or added to Thai savoury salads. While the faintly rose-scented flesh is intriguing for the reason that it smells like a rose, it has very little to commend it apart from this, for it can be woolly and rather dry. To make use of an abundance of these fruit, they are best used in conserves with perhaps a little rose water added after cooking to accentuate the flavour and help it live up to its name. See also JAMBU.

India: *veli jambu*
Sri Lanka: *seeni jambu*

Roselle

(*Hibiscus sabdariffa*) The common names of this plant are Indian sorrel and Jamaican sorrel, and one can understand why, for the leaves have the same refreshingly sour tang as European sorrel leaves. It grows up to 2 m (6 ft) in height and has an erect, branched form. The stems are purplish and the flowers look like miniature single hibiscus. The fleshy sepals which make up the calyx are a beautiful crimson colour and are cooked into jams and jellies and infused to make a refreshing drink. The leaves are eaten as a vegetable.

The leaves are featured in the Burmese sour soup

known as chin ye hin. In Thailand, young leaves are blanched and eaten with nam prik, and also used in hot sour soup, as they are in the sinigang of the Philippines. Sorrel may be substituted.

The colourful, succulent calyxes which one sees in crimson heaps in Western markets and greengrocers, are used to make jam, jelly, juice and wine. They also provide a food colouring and a purple dye.

Medicinal uses: The dried corollas are a diuretic, and are used to treat fevers and tapeworm. They are said to reduce fat levels in the blood and heal internal stomach wounds.

Burma: *chinbaung ywet*
India: *pulincha kira*
Sri Lanka: *rata bilincha*
Thailand: *krachiap*

Sour Soup

Serves 4

1 chicken thigh and drumstick
1 lean pork chop
2 tablespoons dried shrimp
1 onion, sliced
1 cup roselle leaves
fish sauce and pepper to taste

Cook chicken and pork in 1 litre (2 pints) water with salt to taste. Cool and shred into small pieces. In the same liquid simmer the shrimp, onion and roselle leaves for 10 minutes. Add fish sauce and pepper to taste, return chicken and pork and serve hot.

Rose Water

Often called for in recipes for Indian sweets, and not the same as rose essence. Rose water is a 1 in 40 dilution and instead of looking for it in grocery stores (unless they are Indian grocery stores), you should perhaps ask your chemist. Rose water is the diluted essence extracted from rose petals by steam distillation. If you substitute rose essence or concentrate, be careful to use only a drop or two, as compared with the tablespoon or so of rose water that can safely be added. Rose water is called gulab jal and rose essence is called ruh gulab.

Roti

See BREADS.

the thread-like stigmas of true saffron, safflower petals are shorter, straighter and thicker. Native to India, and grown in the Philippines to a limited extent, the seeds of safflower are a valuable source of polyunsaturated vegetable oil.

Saffron

(*Crocus sativus*) SEE ILLUSTRATION. It takes approximately 70,000 flowers of the saffron crocus to obtain half a kilogram of saffron; little wonder it is the world's most expensive spice. Thankfully, a mere ¼ teaspoon of loosely packed strands can flavour and colour a dish to serve 6 people. The spiky, grass-like leaves and small, fragile mauve flowers grow low on the earth, up to 23 cm (9 in). All harvesting is by hand. The flowers are picked and the three hair-like stigmas removed and dried, losing about 80 per cent of their weight in the drying.

Saffron is mentioned in a Theban medical papyrus from 1552 BC. It is also mentioned in the Old Testament. The ancient Romans used it lavishly, indeed wastefully (an emperor in AD 220 liked to bathe in saffron-scented water), and probably introduced it to Britain and northern Europe.

In ancient times it was credited with reviving the spirits and making one optimistic, and a 16th century English saying was that a cheerful, jovial person must have 'slept in a bagge of saffron'. Research of that period also revealed that saffron tea was put in canaries' drinking water if they'd run out of song. (I've tried this and it works!)

By the eighth century, Arabs had taken saffron corms to Spain where it is cultivated to this day. It is also grown in Turkey, Iran and Kashmir. In the 16th century it was extensively cultivated in Essex in Britain; the nearby town of Saffron Walden was so named because saffron was produced in the area for over 400 years.

Not everything with 'saffron' on the label is the real thing or has even a remote connection with it. Sometimes it is merely a matter of terminology, and many who use the word loosely do it not to deceive, but because they simply do not know the difference. Turmeric is called 'saffron', or 'Indian saffron' by cooks throughout southern India and Sri Lanka and, as a consequence, wherever people from these parts have settled. When the mistake is made by those who package and sell the spice, however, it may be assumed that they are not as ignorant or

Sabah Vegetable

(*Sauropus albicans*, *S. androgynus*) The common English name arises from the fact that a vegetable grower in Sabah, Malaysia, discovered a method of cultivation resulting in quick growth and tender stems. While a plant that grows wild in many South East Asian countries, this version is superior and regarded as the local equivalent of asparagus, though the stems are darker green and more slender. The vegetable and its leaves may be steamed, boiled or stir-fried with a variety of seasonings.

China: *so-kun-mu*
Indonesia: *katuk*
Japan: *ruridama no ki*
Malaysia: *cekur manis*
Philippines: *malunggay hapon*
Thailand: *phak waan*
Vietnam: *rau nyot*

Safflower

(*Carthamus tinctorius*) The dried edible petals of safflower are used in the Philippines (where they are called casubha or kasubha) for colouring dishes such as arroz caldo and paella, in the way that saffron would be used in the original Spanish version.

Although it does not contribute the exquisite fragrance and flavour that saffron does, it is often substituted by less reputable merchants and restaurants. Also known as bastard saffron. Compared to innocent. 'Saffron powder' and even, in some instances, 'crocus powder' is sometimes printed on labels when the contents are nothing but ground turmeric. There are also packets of bright orange powder labelled 'saffron colour' which are neither saffron nor turmeric. These are best avoided.

There is no such thing as cheap saffron; it is most likely dried edible petals of marigold (*Calendula officinalis*) or safflower (*Carthamus tinctorius*), known as bastard or false saffron. These will add colour but not flavour.

Saffron may be used with equal impact in savoury and sweet dishes, as illustrated by the recipes which follow. An intrinsic flavour in many regional dishes the world over, including paella (Spain), bouillabaise (France), Scandinavian breads and numerous exotic northern Indian dishes including curry, pilau, and ice cream.

Kashmir, where saffron is grown, boasts many recipes in which it is used in the lavish cooking known as Moghul style. The Moghul emperors considered Kashmir their summer playground, away from the heat of central India and the capital city. Dishes from this era are still served on festive occasions.

Saffron is used in samovars of Qahwah, Kashmiri tea. I visited Kashmir during November and it was cold enough to make the tea doubly welcome — warming my hands as I cupped them around the bowl and sipped the clear liquid perfumed with cardamom, saffron and lotus honey.

Purchasing and storing: Buy saffron from a reputable supplier, preferably in small glass jars or sealed plastic containers. Saffron lasts well, but may be kept in the freezer if preferred.

Preparation: There are two ways to use saffron. Either soak the whole strands in hot milk or water for about 15 minutes and add to the dish; or toast strands lightly in a dry pan over low heat, just to make them crisp enough to crush with the back of a spoon, and not long enough for their glorious colour to darken. To measure saffron, drop loosely into the half or quarter teaspoon measure, do not pack it down. Be careful not to use too much saffron in a dish because it can impart a medicinal flavour. See recipes below, also Shrikhand (page 415) and Saffron Kulfi (page 183).

Medicinal uses: This ancient spice is used in homeopathic medicine. It is said to be an effective stimulant, and is used to treat hyperthermia during winter in the snow-clad Himalayas. In books on herbal medicine it is recommended for the treatment of fevers, menstrual problems and hysteria. It is used to calm nerves, promote perspiration, and as an aphrodisiac, although too much can be narcotic. Externally it is applied for bruises, rheumatism and neuralgia.

India: *zaffran, kesari*
Malaysia: *koma-koma*

Koftas in Saffron Sauce

In Kashmir these are invariably part of the Kashmiri wazwan or feast of many courses. Four to six people eat from the same tray, but always from their own corner of it, with hands which have been ceremoniously washed before the meal begins. Serves 6.

1 kg/2 lb lamb tenderloin
½ teaspoon ground cardamom
1 teaspoon Kashmiri garam masala
  (recipe page 355)
2 teaspoons salt
3 tablespoons arrowroot or cornflour
  (cornstarch)
1 teaspoon ground turmeric
2 teaspoons chilli powder or to taste
2 tablespoons ghee
2 tablespoons oil
125 g/4 oz/½ cup finely sliced shallots or brown
  onions
2 teaspoons finely chopped fresh ginger
4 brown cardamoms
  or 6 small green cardamoms, bruised
4 whole cloves
1 small stick cinnamon
2 teaspoons paprika
2 teaspoons tomato paste
¼ teaspoon saffron strands
2 tablespoons chopped fresh coriander

Trim fat from lamb and cube the meat. Divide into 4 portions. Process one portion at a time in a food processor, using steel chopping blade, until it is a smooth, thick paste. Mix in the ground cardamom, garam masala and salt. Combine arrowroot or cornflour with 2 tablespoons cold water and add to meat, mixing well. Form into koftas (large balls). Bring to the boil in a saucepan just enough salted water to simmer the koftas. Add half the turmeric and chilli powder to the water and parboil koftas for 10 minutes.

In another saucepan with heavy base heat the ghee and oil and on low heat fry shallots, ginger and whole spices until onions are soft and fragrant. Add remaining turmeric, chilli powder, paprika and tomato paste. Add the koftas and liquid they were cooked in. Toast saffron strands in a dry pan for 1 minute, shaking the pan and taking care they don't scorch. Turn onto a saucer and when cool and crisp, crush with the back of a spoon. Dissolve in a tablespoon of boiling water and add to pan. Cover and simmer until tender. Sprinkle with coriander and serve hot with pilau or steamed basmati rice.

Spiced Lamb Slices

This dish is perfumed with two exotic flowers — saffron and kewra (from a variety of pandanus). Serves 4.

750 g/1½ lb lean lamb tenderloin or boned leg
3 teaspoons finely chopped garlic
2 teaspoons finely grated fresh ginger
1 medium onion, chopped
1 teaspoon fennel seed
1 teaspoon salt
125 ml/4 fl oz/½ cup yoghurt
1 teaspoon chilli powder
2 teaspoons ground coriander
¼ teaspoon saffron strands
2 or 3 drops kewra essence
2 tablespoons ghee
2 tablespoons oil
1 tablespoon boiling water
125 ml/4 fl oz/½ cup hot water
1 teaspoon Kashmiri garam masala
  (recipe page 355)
125 ml/4 fl oz/½ cup finely chopped fresh
  coriander

Beat lamb with a meat mallet to flatten and cut into serving-sized pieces.

Grind garlic, ginger, onion, fennel seeds and salt in an electric blender until smooth. Mix with the yoghurt, chilli powder, garam masala, coriander and rub over the lamb slices. Marinate for at least 2 hours.

Toast saffron strands in a dry pan over low heat for 1 minute, taking care they do not scorch. Turn onto a saucer to cool, then crush with back of a spoon. Dissolve in a tablespoon

of boiling water and mix in the kewra essence. Set aside.

Heat ghee and oil in a heavy frying pan and fry the pieces of meat over fairly high heat, turning them frequently. Add about 3 tablespoons hot water to pan, cover and cook until the liquid evaporates. Stir to release meat and spice marinade from base of pan. Add another 3 tablespoons water and repeat. When this has evaporated, sprinkle with garam masala, saffron and kewra liquid, cover and simmer a few minutes then serve garnished with fresh coriander. Serve with rice or naan and a salad of sliced onions, tomatoes and chillies.

Roast Leg of Lamb

The traditional roast dinner takes on overtones of splendour with flavours that graced the tables of emperors. Serves 8.

1 × 2.5 kg/5 lb leg of lamb
1 tablespoon finely grated fresh ginger
2 teaspoons crushed garlic
3 teaspoons salt
1 teaspoon ground cumin
1 teaspoon ground turmeric
½ teaspoon ground black pepper
½ teaspoon ground cinnamon
½ teaspoon ground cardamom
¼ teaspoon ground cloves
½ teaspoon chilli powder (optional)
2 tablespoons lemon juice
250 ml/8 fl oz/1 cup natural yoghurt
2 tablespoons blanched almonds
½ teaspoon saffron strands
3 teaspoons honey

With a sharp knife remove skin and excess fat from lamb. Using point of knife make deep slits all over the lamb. Combine ginger, garlic, salt, ground spices and lemon juice. If mixture is too dry to spread, add very little oil. Rub spice mixture well over the lamb, pressing it into each slit.

Put yoghurt and almonds into a blender container. Toast saffron strands in a dry pan over low heat for 1 minute, taking care they don't scorch. Turn onto a saucer to cool and crisp, crush with back of spoon and dissolve in 2 tablespoons hot water. Add to almonds and yoghurt, then blend together until smooth.

Spoon the purée over the lamb, drizzle honey over, cover and allow lamb to marinate for 2 days in the refrigerator, or at least overnight.

Allow 1 hour per kilogram (½ hour per pound) cooking time. Preheat oven to 230°C (450°F), and roast lamb in a covered baking dish for 30 minutes. Reduce heat to moderate, 170°C (350°F) and cook for a further 1½ hours or until lamb is cooked through. Uncover lamb and cool to room temperature. Serve with steamed basmati rice or a light pilau.

Saffron Chicken

Simple, yet with superb flavour. No wonder this recipe becomes a favourite with all who try it. Serves 4–6.

½ teaspoon saffron strands
1.5 kg/3 lb chicken pieces or roasting chicken
3 tablespoons ghee
1 large onion, finely chopped
2 teaspoons finely chopped garlic
1½ teaspoons finely grated fresh ginger
3 fresh red chillies, seeded and sliced
½ teaspoon ground cardamom
1½ teaspoons salt

Toast saffron strands in a dry pan over low heat for 1 minute without scorching them. Turn onto a saucer to become cool and crisp, then crush with the back of a spoon. Dissolve in a tablespoon of very hot water.

If using a whole roasting chicken cut into small serving pieces, dividing breast into quarters, separating thigh from drumstick and jointing wings.

Heat ghee in a heavy saucepan and gently fry onion, garlic, ginger and chillies until onion is soft and starts to turn golden. Stir frequently. Add dissolved saffron to pan with cardamom and stir well, then add chicken. Increase heat and turn chicken pieces in the mixture until each piece of chicken is golden. Add salt, cover and cook over moderate heat for 10 minutes or until chicken is tender. Uncover pan and continue cooking, turning pieces of chicken often, until almost all the liquid evaporates. Serve with parathas or pilau.

Fresh Cheese in Saffron Sauce

Serves 4

375 g/12 oz panir (recipe page 74)
   or 1 block ricotta cheese
2 tablespoons ghee
2 tablespoons oil
1 medium onion, finely chopped
500 g/1 lb ripe tomatoes, peeled and chopped
1 teaspoon ground turmeric
1 teaspoon chilli powder
3 whole cloves
3 cardamom pods, bruised
1 teaspoon sugar or to taste
¼ teaspoon saffron strands

Cut panir in slices about 1 cm (½ in) thick and cut each slice in half to make serving-sized pieces. Fry in half of the ghee and oil until golden. Put on a plate and set aside. If using ricotta cheese (it must be in a block, not in a tub) it should be baked to make it firm as panir. Cut block into 3 or 4 thick slices. Place on a baking tray lined with non-stick paper and bake in a moderate oven (350°F) for 30–35 minutes until slices are golden.

Heat remaining oil and ghee in a saucepan. Fry onion until golden brown. Add tomatoes, spices, salt and sugar and simmer until gravy is thick. Add the slices of cheese and allow them to simmer in the gravy. Toast saffron in a dry pan over low heat for about 1 minute. Crush with the back of a spoon and dissolve in a tablespoon of hot water. Stir in about 5 minutes before end of cooking. Serve with rice or chapatis.

Saffron Rice Pilau

Serve this lightly perfumed rice with any meat, poultry or vegetable dish. Serves 4–5.

500 g/1 lb basmati rice
1 onion, thinly sliced
2 tablespoons ghee
2 teaspoons salt
1 litre/2 pints/4 cups hot water or stock
¼ teaspoon saffron strands
2 tablespoons sultanas (golden raisins) (optional)

Wash basmati rice well in several changes of water, and leave to drain and dry for at least 30 minutes. In a heavy-based saucepan with a

well-fitting lid cook the onion in ghee very slowly until it starts to turn golden brown. Add the rice and fry for a few minutes until all the grains are coated with ghee. Add salt and hot water. Toast saffron strands on low heat in a dry pan for 1 minute, turn onto a saucer to become cool and crisp, and crush with the back of a spoon. Dissolve in a tablespoon of hot water and stir into the pan of rice together with sultanas. Bring to the boil, then turn heat very low, cover tightly and cook on low heat for 15 minutes without lifting lid or stirring. Uncover, allow steam to escape for a few minutes, then transfer to serving dish with a slotted metal spoon, not a wooden spoon which will crush the grains. Serve with other dishes.

Sago

(*Metroxylon sagu*) A pure starch foodstuff extracted from the sago palm or other palms which develop a starchy pith. The palm flowers only once in its life, and not until it has about 15 years growth. Just before this, it builds up a large reserve of starch in the pith. The tree is felled, the pith scooped out and ground. The starch is washed with water, allowed to settle and the water poured away from the top. If the remaining starch is dried at this stage it becomes sago flour. For preparing pearl sago the wet starch is pressed through a sieve and dried on a hot surface, resulting in the familiar white pellets which turn transparent when cooked. In Asia these are used in ways rather different from the nursery puddings of the West.

In southern India the starch is used to make wafers which are dried in the sun before being stored in airtight containers. Just before serving they are deep fried to make them puff and become crisp. In Thailand a popular savoury is a dainty bite-sized snack, saku sai moo, which has a cooked filling of pork, coriander, garlic, peanuts, fish sauce and palm sugar inside a sago covering which steams to glistening translucency.

Probably the best known use of sago is in the Asian dessert, gula melaka, which is sago pudding served with fresh coconut milk and palm sugar. It is the traditional finish to legendary curry tiffins or rijstaffel, served in many grand hotels in Asia.

Sago Pudding (Gula Melaka)

This is the famous pudding which has changed many people's feelings about the dreaded sago. Serves 6–8.

2.5 litres/5 pints/10 cups water
300 g/10 oz/2 cups sago
2 tablespoons fresh milk or coconut milk
pinch of salt

FOR SERVING
250 g/8 oz palm sugar (gula melaka) or brown sugar
125 ml/4 fl oz/½ cup water
2 strips pandan leaves
300 ml/10 fl oz/1¼ cups coconut milk
pinch salt

Bring water to a fast boil and slowly dribble in the sago. Let it boil fast for 5–7 minutes. Turn off heat, cover the pan with a well-fitting lid and leave for 10 minutes. The sago will finish cooking in the stored heat and the grains will become clear. Run cold water into the pan, stir, then pour contents of pan into a sieve, shaking the sieve so the water runs off.

Put sago into a bowl, stir in milk and add salt. This quantity of milk is just enough to give it a pearly white appearance. Divide between individual dessert dishes or moulds, or pour into one larger mould and chill.

To make the syrup, chop palm sugar into small pieces. Put into a small saucepan with the water and pandan leaves and heat gently until melted. Strain through a fine sieve or tea strainer to remove any small impurities.

Either extract coconut milk from grated fresh coconut or use a good brand of canned coconut milk. Canned coconut milk may need diluting with a little water if very thick or lumpy. Stir in a good pinch of salt as this accentuates the flavour. Coconut milk should be served at room temperature, as chilling will solidify the fat.

Serve the sago accompanied by palm sugar syrup and coconut milk in separate jugs.

Pork-Filled Sago Balls

In Thailand, sago is used for more than puddings. It makes shells for savoury mixtures, steamed until the chalky white sago turns glistening and clear. Makes 50–60.

250 g/8 oz/1½ cups sago
185 ml/6 fl oz/¾ cup hot water
¼ teaspoon salt
tapioca flour

FILLING

2 tablespoons oil
1 medium onion, finely chopped
1 tablespoon Thai pepper-coriander paste
  (recipe page 105)
250 g/8 oz lean minced (ground) pork
1 tablespoon palm sugar or brown sugar
2 tablespoons fish sauce
2 teaspoons finely chopped fresh hot chillies
3 tablespoons crushed roasted peanuts

GARNISH

2 teaspoons crushed fried garlic flakes
  or extra crushed roasted peanuts
sliced red chillies (optional)

Rinse sago in a fine strainer, drain and transfer to a bowl. Dissolve salt in hot water and gradually add to the sago, mixing well. Cover and leave for 1 hour.

Filling: Heat the oil in a wok or frying pan and cook the onion over low heat until soft. Add the pepper-coriander paste, and cook, stirring, until the mixture is fragrant.

Add the pork, increase heat and fry, breaking up lumps to keep it crumbly. Cook until browned. Reduce heat to medium, stir in palm sugar and fish sauce. Cover and cook on low heat until pork is tender and liquid is absorbed. As it becomes drier stir frequently to ensure the mixture doesn't stick and burn. Remove from heat, mix in the chilli and crushed peanuts and cool to room temperature. Taste and add more salt or chilli. The filling must be strongly seasoned to stand up to the coating of bland sago.

To shape the balls: Using a wet spoon take equal amounts of sago and roll into balls with damp hands. Cover with a damp cloth. Wash and dry your hands and dust them with tapioca flour. Press thumb or finger into each ball to form a cup shape. Put in a teaspoon of pork mixture and seal the sago over the filling. Mould into balls again and cover with damp cloth until ready to cook. (If all are not required immediately, pack some in a freezer container and freeze, ready to steam when needed.)

Place the balls on oiled or non-stick paper strips in a steamer, leaving some space between as they increase slightly in size. Steam over fast-boiling water until the sago is quite clear, about 20 minutes. Remove the steamer from the heat and leave for 5 minutes for the balls to dry slightly before transferring to a serving dish. Sprinkle with crushed fried garlic or crushed roasted peanuts and garnish with chilli slices. Serve at room temperature.

Sake

This fermented rice wine is the national drink of Japan. There is sweet sake and dry sake, the former considered to be superior. Store it in a cool dark place. Once the bottle is opened it is better to use it up quite soon. Do not confuse sweet sake with mirin which is a heavily sweetened rice wine used only in cooking.

Sake is almost always served warm, in small cups holding hardly a couple of tablespoons. It is served from a narrow-necked porcelain flask.

Sake should not be allowed to become too hot. Place the filled flask in a pan of warm water and heat very gently until sake is a little warmer than blood temperature. Dry the flask before taking it to the table.

There is a ritual to be observed in the pouring and drinking of sake. Lift your cup to the person pouring the sake, placing it on the left hand and steadying it with the right hand. Japanese etiquette forbids filling your own sake cup. The gesture of topping up another guest's sake might prompt the refilling of your own cup. Sake is supposed to be drunk in one swallow, but perhaps this is only for practised sake drinkers.

In summer, sake may be served cold, often in small square wooden boxes instead of cups. Tilt the box and drink from a corner. Sometimes salt is sprinkled on the edge of the box. Sake is also used in cooking, as a marinade and added to dishes to tenderise, add flavour and counteract fishy odours.

Salads

Asian salads are a far cry from the green salads on Western menus. They may be more like a relish or salsa, piquant and used as an accent; or they can be an entire meal, combining raw and lightly cooked vegetables, fried bean curd, slivers of cooked meats and a dressing or sauce which ties the ingredients together, as in Indonesia's gado-gado with its celebrated peanut sauce; or urap, steamed vegetables dressed with fresh grated coconut, dried shrimp paste and lemon juice.

In all of the Pacific countries, there is a raw fish salad by one name or another, the fish marinated in lime juice until it turns white and opaque, then dressed with fresh coconut milk and raw onions.

China has its cold platters with thinly sliced cooked meats, but these are banquet platters, not usually part of an everyday menu.

Korean cuisine includes namul and saingchai, two categories of dishes which can be said to resemble salads since they combine fruits and vegetables, which are sometimes raw, and use a dressing of crushed toasted sesame seeds, soy, vinegar, sesame oil, pepper, sugar, salt and sometimes chilli and garlic.

Japan offers aemono (mixed things) and sunomono (vinegared things) with cold sauces which could be described as salad-type dishes. They are served in tiny portions as an appetiser before the meal. They may include fish or shellfish, seaweed, sliced or shredded raw vegetables, or lightly steamed vegetables. Dressings are made from mild rice vinegar, crushed sesame seeds, tofu or a thick, oil-free dressing which looks like mayonnaise. The portions are never the serving size of a Western salad.

In Malaysia a traditional dish which might fit the description of a rice salad is simply steamed rice mixed with many different kinds of finely shredded fragrant herbs including such exotics as leaves of aromatic ginger, turmeric, kaffir lime, basil, Vietnamese mint, stem of lemon grass, bulb of shallot, and bud of torch ginger. This is usually served with a relish and dry curry.

It is in Thai cuisine that salads (yam) are given most prominence, combining fruits both ripe and unripe, vegetables, seafood, meat, leaves and flowers — lotus and rose petals, no less. The dressing will always be piquant with lime, hot with chilli, and salty with fish sauce.

Raw, tender leaf-tips gathered from hedges and trees by those who know their species, are an important part of the meal, and are a vital source of vitamins and minerals in Asian diets. They may be tossed with flavoured oil, toasted sesame seeds, fried garlic, fish sauce and a good squeeze of lime juice. Or they may be dipped into a pungent sauce such as the various nam priks of Thailand.

Indian salads may include small portions of fresh tomatoes, onions and chillies, seasoned with salt and lime juice, and used as a fresh relish. Yoghurt 'salads' known as raitas can include fried lentil drops, diced boiled potato and beetroot, sprouted mung beans, sliced ripe banana, cooked spinach or okra, fried eggplant (aubergine), sliced or diced raw cucumber or a mixture of any vegetables in season. The yoghurt itself is the dressing, seasoned with fried mustard seeds, crushed toasted cumin seeds, salt, sugar, chilli powder and garam masala.

Salads in Asia may be called rojak or yam or mallun or ahthoke depending on which country you are in. One thing they have in common is that they are fresh-tasting, perhaps a little more fiery than one expects of a dish in the category of salad, and feature unexpected combinations of ingredients.

Pacific Islands Raw Fish Salad

Kokoda in Fiji, poisson cru in Tahiti, oka or ota in Samoa and Tonga. There may be minor variations but all refer to the popular salad of marinated fish. Serves 4–6.

750g/1½ lb fillets of delicate white fish
juice of 4 limes or lemons
4 shallots, peeled and finely sliced
½ teaspoon salt
3 firm ripe tomatoes, diced
2 small green seedless cucumbers
1 small red capsicum (bell pepper), diced
1 small green capsicum (bell pepper), diced
2 sliced fresh chillies (optional)
washed and chilled salad greens

DRESSING
400 ml/14 oz can coconut cream
1 clove garlic, crushed
1 teaspoon finely grated fresh ginger
½ teaspoon ground turmeric
**   or 2.5 cm/1 in slice fresh turmeric**

Remove all skin and any remaining bones from fish fillets. Cut into thin slices and put into a glass or pottery bowl. Pour lime or lemon juice over, add sliced shallots and salt and mix with a wooden spoon. Cover and leave to marinate for 6 hours in the refrigerator, stirring 2 or 3 times with a non-metallic spoon.

Shortly before serving drain away the lemon juice. Combine dressing ingredients. If using fresh turmeric, pound to a paste and mix with some of the coconut cream. Pour over fish and diced vegetables and mix gently. Arrange leaves on serving plate and pile fish salad in the centre. Serve chilled.

Indonesian Vegetable Salad (Gado-Gado)

Serves 4

3 medium potatoes, boiled
3 small carrots, thinly sliced
half a small cabbage, thickly sliced
125 g/4 oz tender green beans
125 g/4 oz fresh bean sprouts
125 g/4 oz fried bean curd
2 small green cucumbers
small bunch watercress
3 eggs, hard-boiled, shelled and quartered
peanut sauce (recipe page 276)

Peel and slice the potatoes. Blanch the carrot slices in a little boiling water until tender but still crisp. Do the same with the cabbage and beans. Put the bean sprouts in a colander and pour boiling water over them. Slice the bean curd and cucumbers and break watercress into small sprigs. Arrange all the blanched vegetables on a platter, surround with slices of cucumber and sprigs of watercress, and garnish with wedges of egg and slices of bean curd. Serve at room temperature, accompanied by a bowl of peanut sauce to spoon over individual servings.

Cambodian Lobster and Orange Salad

A generous Cambodian restaurateur shared this recipe with me. Lobster is a luxury ideal for special occasions. Serves 4–6.

1 large cooked lobster
2 cups finely shredded Chinese cabbage
    (wong nga bak)

2 seedless cucumbers, finely sliced
60 g/2 oz bean thread vermicelli
1 tablespoon dried wood fungus,
    soaked for 10 minutes
2 tablespoons peanut oil
2 teaspoons finely chopped garlic
125 g/4 oz minced (ground) pork
1 tablespoon minced (ground) dried shrimp
    (optional)
5 tablespoons fish sauce
3 tablespoons sugar
3 tablespoons lime juice
3 tablespoons desiccated coconut
3 tablespoons crushed, roasted peanuts
2 tablespoons shredded mint leaves
3 oranges, peeled and segmented
mint sprigs for garnish
3 whole heads pickled garlic, thinly sliced

Divide lobster where head and body join. Reserve head and claws, whole, for garnishing salad. Remove meat from the body and shred with fingers. Reserve shell. Combine shredded lobster meat, cabbage and cucumber.

Boil noodles for 10 minutes or until soft. Drain, then cut into short lengths. Trim any gritty parts off wood fungus and divide into small pieces. Add to the lobster, cabbage and noodles.

Heat oil in a wok and fry the garlic, stirring over low heat without browning, then raise heat, add the minced pork and minced dried shrimp and stir-fry until well cooked and brown. Add 1 tablespoon each of the fish sauce and sugar, stir and cook until liquid evaporates, remove from wok and cool.

Combine remaining fish sauce and sugar with lime juice, stirring to dissolve sugar. Pour over the lobster mixture and toss well.

Toast the coconut in a dry pan over medium heat, stirring constantly, until evenly golden brown. Turn out on to a plate at once to cool.

Make a bed of crisp salad greens on an oval platter, pile the lobster mixture in the centre and place orange segments around. Sprinkle with the pork and shrimp mixture, toasted coconut, crushed peanuts and shredded mint. Place head and tail of lobster at opposite ends of the pile of lobster meat. Garnish with sprigs of mint and slices of pickled garlic.

Rose Petal Salad

Serves 8

6–8 sweet-scented roses
1 cooked chicken breast
500 g/1 lb cooked prawns (shrimp)
500 g/1 lb lean pork
6 tablespoons fish sauce
2 tablespoons sugar
2 green limes
90 g/3 oz/½ cup crushed, roasted peanuts
1 tablespoon dried garlic slices or chips
4 tablespoons sliced crisp-fried shallots
  (available ready-fried)
watercress or other salad greens (optional)
3 fresh red chillies, seeded and finely sliced
fresh coriander leaves for garnish

Use roses that are home grown and unsprayed with pesticides. Wash thoroughly under a gentle spray of cold water, then shake off as much water as possible, trying not to bruise the petals. Place on paper towels to dry.

Remove bones of chicken breast and cut flesh and skin into fine strips. Shell and devein the prawns and chop into small pieces.

Put the pork into a saucepan with 2 tablespoons of the fish sauce and 1 tablespoon of the sugar. Add 2 cups water, bring to the boil, cover pan and cook until pork is well done. Cool, then cut into small dice.

Peel the limes very thinly and cut the rind into threads. Combine rind, strained juice of the limes and the remaining fish sauce and sugar, stirring until sugar dissolves. Add pork, chicken, prawns and peanuts and toss well with the dressing.

Fry dried garlic on low heat until pale golden. Do not brown or it will become bitter. Drain on paper towels and when cool, crush into small pieces. Salad may be prepared ahead up to this point.

Add garlic, fried shallots, half the rose petals and chilli slices to the mixture and toss gently. Pile into bowl or plate lined with greens and scatter with reserved rose petals, chillies and coriander leaves. Serve at once.

Water Chestnut Salad

Serves 4–6

2 small cans sliced water chestnuts
5 tablespoons fish sauce
5 tablespoons lime juice
2 tablespoons sugar
250 g/8 oz small cooked prawns (shrimp)
  peeled and deveined
250 g/8 oz cooked crab meat, flaked
30 g/1 oz/½ cup chopped fresh coriander
6 fresh kaffir lime leaves, shredded finely
2 or 3 fresh red chillies, seeded and chopped
3 tablespoons fried shallots
1 tablespoon fried garlic

If possible, buy sliced water chestnuts in cans. Otherwise, drain whole water chestnuts from liquid and cut into circular slices. Combine fish sauce, lime juice and sugar. Combine prawns, crab meat and water chestnuts, pour over the fish sauce mixture and leave for 15 minutes, or prepare ahead. Toss together with the coriander, lime leaves, chillies, shallots and garlic, reserving some coriander and chillies for sprinkling over the top. Garnish with a chilli flower, made by slitting a chilli from the point almost to the stem and soaking overnight in cold water for petals to curl.

Chiang Mai Salad (Larb)

The flavours of this dish from northern Thailand are fresh, piquant and mouth-filling. It can feature chicken or beef, but what matters is the toasty aroma of the rice grains, the sharp, refreshing taste of mint and the sting of fresh chillies. Serves 4.

1 cooked whole chicken breast
  or 500 g/1 lb lean minced (ground) beef
90 ml/3 fl oz lime juice
60 ml/2 fl oz fish sauce
3 tablespoons finely sliced shallots
2 fresh red chillies, seeded and sliced
2 stems lemon grass
30 g/1 oz/½ cup roughly chopped fresh mint
3 tablespoons roasted rice powder*
lettuce leaves, mint sprigs and lime wedges
  for garnish

Remove skin and bones from chicken breast and dice the flesh finely. If using minced beef, poach it in a small amount of boiling water for a minute or two, just until colour changes. Leave to cool, drain liquid. Put beef or chicken into a bowl, pour over the lime juice and fish sauce and mix. Mix in the sliced shallots and chillies. Slice very finely only the tender white portion (lower stems) of lemon grass and add together with the chopped mint and roasted rice powder. Toss together lightly. Serve on lettuce leaves, garnished with small sprigs of mint and lime wedges.

* Roasted rice powder is sold in small packets in Asian stores, but may also be made at home quite easily (see RICE, GROUND AND ROASTED).

See Index of Recipes for listing of salad recipes.

Salak

(*Salacca edulis*) From Indonesia and Malaysia come the exotic looking, sweet-sour fruits of this relatively short, intimidatingly thorny palm. The scaly, light brown-skinned fruits grow in clusters close to the base of the plant among the thorn-studded leaves, just above the ground.

Unripe, they are made into pickles and ripe they are eaten as is or preserved in sugar syrup. The skin, which is leathery and looks like brown, shiny snakeskin, is not eaten.

Salam Leaf

(*Eugenia polyantha*) SEE ILLUSTRATION. The aromatic young leaves which contain volatile oils are used, a few fresh leaves being simmered whole in Indonesian curries to impart a unique flavour. Sold dried outside the region. If not available substitute curry leaves, which are somewhat similar in flavour, but certainly not bay leaves.

Indonesia: *daun salam*
Malaysia: *daun salam*

Salmon

A cold water fish found in the southern waters of the Pacific Ocean as well as north of Japan's main island, Honshu. It is an oily fish, good for grilling, steaming, smoking, or for curing with sugar or salt. Curiously, although Japanese sushi bars serve salmon, it is not served raw but cured or briefly grilled. In the West raw salmon is as popular as raw tuna for sashimi.

Atlantic salmon is known in Australia as Tasmanian salmon, where it is farmed in salt water ponds. These fish are every bit as tasty as their Northern Hemisphere counterparts although they do not grow as large. Even more beautiful than the salmon pink flesh of this fish is its roe: large, limpid, glistening eggs. The colour should be a vibrant pinky-orange and the skin of each egg taut yet soft. If they are not as plump as they should be and have begun to wrinkle or toughen due to exposure to air they can be revived by soaking in a little sake then draining before use. Fresh salmon roe (ikura) is a popular topping for sushi and equally delicious on a blini topped with sour cream.

Salt

(Sodium chloride) What has always been a natural seasoning in food has come to be regarded with a great deal of suspicion, mainly because prepared foods are often overloaded with salt. Since first-world countries have become addicted to salty snacks such as potato crisps, corn chips and peanuts, salt has earned a reputation for causing high blood pressure and heart disease, which seemingly go hand in hand with 'the good life'.

Yet lack of salt can cause heat exhaustion and if one sweats profusely because of climatic conditions or exercise, both water and salt must be replaced either in food or dietary supplement (salt tablets). When cold climate dwellers were stationed in the tropics during wartime, salt tablets were a regular part of their rations.

Food without a moderate amount of salt is at best bland and, at worst, singularly unappetising. The sea is the source of salt and even primitive people found that adding sea water to their food made it taste better.

In addition to flavouring food, it is used for preservation in pickling and drying, not only in Asia but throughout the world. In Asia it is necessary in making those indispensable and universal ingredients soy sauce (shoyu), fish sauce (nam pla) and shrimp paste (blachan), not to mention the many varieties of salted dried fish which can be stored unrefrigerated for long periods without deteriorating, so great is the proportion of salt that is added.

Salt mixed with spice is served as a sprinkle or dip with many famous Chinese dishes, for instance the roasted salt and Szechwan pepper seasoning that is served with Crisp Skin Chicken.

In Chinese cuisine, salt is used to roast with dry heat, much as a Western cook would use an oven. Since most Chinese households do not have an oven, roasting is done by heating 2–3 kg (4–6 lb) of coarse salt in a wok on the fireplace or stovetop and burying food to be roasted in it. A wrapping of muslin or lotus leaf prevents the salt making the food inedible.

Chinese chefs also use salt to change the texture of ingredients. The best example of this is salt-whipped shrimp, involving a treatment during which the shrimp or prawns lose their slippery feel and become clean. When cooked, their texture becomes crisp. See recipe for Crystal Prawns with Asparagus Tips (page 298).

In Japan, salt is used not only to preserve food but also for protection during cooking, as in the case of grilled whole fish, the fins and tail coated with salt to prevent burning.

In India, in addition to common salt, there is a particular type of salt used to flavour certain dishes. It is called kala namak which translates as 'black salt', and is available either in lump form or ground. Its colour is really not black once it is ground, but greyish pink due to the presence of trace minerals and iron. It cannot be substituted for salt in recipes because it has a distinct 'rotten egg' type of sulphuric odour and flavour. It is the distinctive flavour in jal jeera and chat masala. My first encounter with it was in Kashmir, where it had been sprinkled on a glass of salty lassi, and the initial reaction was 'Wow! Gunpowder!' I cannot pretend it has become a personal favourite, but it certainly won a fan in my husband who sprinkles it on every kind of snack food, over the protests of family members.

Chat Masala

Chat masala is a dry spice mix specifically to sprinkle over snacks, especially crisp ones such as bhel puri or chiura, and on simple foods such as sliced boiled potatoes or sliced fruit, served as a snack. Try it also as a seasoning on steamed vegetables.

2 tablespoons cumin seeds
1 tablespoon fennel seeds
1 tablespoon amchur (dried mango powder)
** or 1 teaspoon powdered citric acid**
1 tablespoon black salt
2 teaspoons garam masala (recipe page 354)
1 teaspoon hot or mild chilli powder
½ teaspoon asafoetida powder
** (mixed with ground rice)***

Roast cumin and fennel seeds in a dry pan, stirring constantly over low heat until fragrant and slightly darker in colour. Grind finely in blender or spice grinder. Mix with other ingredients and store airtight.

* See ASAFOETIDA.

Roasted Pepper and Salt

Roast 2 tablespoons whole black peppercorns in a dry pan over medium heat, stirring, about 5 minutes or till pepper smells fragrant. Allow pepper to cool slightly, then pound using a mortar and pestle and mix with 3 tablespoons salt. Store in an airtight bottle. Sprinkle on roast duck or chicken. (See also SZECHWAN PEPPER.)

Sambal

A fresh or cooked relish served in small amounts to add zest to a meal. The word indicates that it contains more than a little chilli. Sambal or sambol (the latter is the Sri Lankan spelling and pronunciation) is to be eaten with rice, not on its own. In Malaysia and Indonesia sambal can also mean a hot curry.

Sambal bajak (badjak): One of the most popular Indonesian sambals, based on red chilli, onion, garlic, prawn (shrimp) paste, tamarind, galangal and palm sugar. For recipe see page 91.

Sambal bawang: A delicious sambal with main ingredients of shallot, chilli, garlic and dried shrimp paste. For recipe see page 340.

Sambal kecap: Based on the sweet soy sauce unique to Indonesia, fresh chilli and onion or shallots add zest to this popular dipping sauce.

Sambal trasi: Chillies and dried shrimp paste are the flavour key to this pungent relish.

Sambal ulek (oelek): A hot sambal made from pounded chillies, salt and vinegar or tamarind. In a traditional ulek, the chillies are not seeded. For recipe see page 91.

Samoa

One of my nicest holidays was spent in Apia, Western Samoa. The food, prepared without spices, was abundant and fresh and the markets are situated so close to the sea that some of the fish are sold alive.

Samoans live mainly on taro, yams, fruits, vegetables and seafood of all kinds. For special feasts, a whole pig is cooked in an underground oven (umu) along with everything else. It is cooked until it is so tender it falls to pieces.

Alcoholic beverages are made by fermenting fruit and sugar, or from baked and mashed ti roots, or else the fermented sap of coconut palms. The everyday drink which is consumed by everyone, including tourists, is the juice of young coconuts.

Coconut milk and coconut is used extensively in day-to-day cooking. The skill required to grate the coconut meat and extract the milk is something learned early in life and never forgotten. The task has to be performed every day since coconut milk does not keep and must be freshly made. The grater used for scraping the mature meat out of the shell is a primitive object — a stout low stool fitted with an iron disk with sharp serrations over which the halved nut is passed again and again. The grated meat is wrapped in fibre from the husk, and the fibre is twisted to wring out the milky juice. The first extract, the cream, is the richest and subsequent extractions with water added get thinner and less rich with each pressing. Coconut milk or cream goes into or onto most kinds of food.

Samosas

These triangular pockets of pastry filled with curried minced (ground) meat or spicy vegetables are popular Indian snacks. They can be made substantial enough to constitute a light meal, or dainty enough to serve as a cocktail savoury. Also known as singaras when filled with vegetables.

Samosas

Makes about 20 large or 36 small samosas.

PASTRY

**185 g/6 oz/1½ cups roti flour
  or plain (all purpose) flour
3 tablespoons fine semolina
½ teaspoon salt
60 g/2 oz ghee or butter
approx 90 ml/3 fl oz iced water
oil for deep frying**

POTATO FILLING

**750 g/1½ lb potatoes
1 tablespoon ghee or oil
2 teaspoons panch phora (recipe page 355)
½ teaspoon ground turmeric
½ teaspoon chilli powder
1 teaspoon salt
2 fresh green chillies, sliced
3 tablespoons chopped fresh mint or coriander
lime or lemon juice to taste**

MEAT FILLING

**2 tablespoons ghee or oil
2 large onions, finely chopped
1 teaspoon crushed garlic
1 teaspoon finely chopped ginger
2 teaspoons ground coriander
2 teaspoons ground cumin
1 teaspoon chilli powder (or to taste)
1 teaspoon ground turmeric
1 teaspoon salt or to taste
lemon juice to taste
500 g/1 lb minced (ground) lamb
1 teaspoon garam masala (recipe page 354)
1 medium potato, peeled and diced
2 teaspoons extra chopped ginger
3 tablespoons chopped fresh mint or coriander
2 fresh red or green chillies, chopped (optional)**

Pastry: Sift flour, semolina and salt into a bowl and rub in the softened ghee or butter. Add iced water to form a firm dough and knead for 8–10 minutes until it is smooth and elastic. Cover and set aside for 30 minutes or longer while making filling.

For large samosas, roll pastry thinly and cut into 15 cm (6 in) rounds, then cut each circle in half. Place a generous tablespoon of filling on the half circle of pastry, damp edges with cold water and seal firmly to form a triangle; or moisten one straight edge, pick up the half circle and form a cone shape, overlapping straight edges 6 mm (¼ in) and pressing firmly to seal the seam. Fill cone two-thirds with filling, fold top edge over and crimp, roll or simply press together to make a secure join. Place each one as it is made on a tray, cover with clean cloth and fry just before serving.

Deep fry in hot oil. Do not add too many at one time or the temperature of the oil will drop, resulting in the pastry becoming greasy. Drain on absorbent paper towels and serve warm, with Mint Chatni or Tamarind Chatni.

Potato filling: Boil potatoes until almost tender. Peel and cut into fairly small dice. Heat ghee or oil and fry the panch phora until mustard seeds pop, covering pan to prevent them jumping out. Add turmeric and chilli powder and fry for a few seconds. Add salt, sliced chillies and the potatoes. Toss to mix, remove from heat and sprinkle with herbs and lime juice to taste.

Meat filling: Heat ghee or oil and fry half of the chopped onion until soft and transparent. Add garlic and ginger and fry, stirring, until golden. Add ground spices and stir for a few seconds, add salt, lemon juice, minced lamb and stir-fry until lamb is no longer pink. Add diced potato and about 4 tablespoons hot water, cover and simmer until lamb and potato are tender. Sprinkle with garam masala and remove from heat.

When lukewarm, stir in reserved onion and extra ginger, chopped herbs and chillies. (The half-cooked ginger, onion and chillies contribute a fresh flavour to the samosas). Serve warm or at room temperature.

Note: For dainty, party-size samosas or singaras, use ready-made spring roll pastry. (See instructions under SPRING ROLL PASTRY.)

Sansho

(*Zanthoxylum* spp.) The pod of the prickly ash, dried and ground, gives a slightly hot flavour to certain Japanese foods, especially rich foods like eel. It is used to counter fatty tastes. Sansho is only available ground.

Sprigs of young leaves of the same plant, called kinome, are used as a garnish in Japanese cuisine. The plant, a shrubby tree, is closely related to Szechwan pepper.

Sapodilla

(*Achras sapote, Manilkara zapota, M. zapotilla*) SEE ILLUSTRATION. Though indigenous to central and South America, members of the Sapotaceae family were introduced to Asia's tropical regions in the 16th century. Probably the most popular is sapodilla, which varies in appearance. Some are round, some are oval and slightly more pointed at one end. The thin skin is brown and slightly rough, the flesh slightly granular in texture and pale beige to reddish-brown in colour. The fruit has flat black seeds.

When ripe, it is very sweet and has a gentle fragrance. It should be completely ripe before eating, and even then there are traces of the chicle or rubbery latex which is a feature of these fruits. The latex from one variety is used commercially in chewing gum. If you have eaten well but not too wisely and your mouth and lips are sticky, slowly dissolve a square of chocolate in your mouth. The fat content neutralises the chicle. For lips, smear a little butter over them and wipe off with a tissue.

While the fruit may be peeled and cut into pieces, it is probably better to halve it with a knife, then scoop flesh from the skin with a teaspoon. In Thailand it is presented halved and carved to resemble a flower, all with a few clever strokes of a small, sharp knife. While not a huge commercial crop, sapodillas are grown in India, Sri Lanka, Thailand, Indonesia, Malaysia and the Philippines as well as in its countries of origin. In the West Indies it is known as naseberry.

India: *chikoo*
Indonesia: *sawu*
Malaysia: *chikoo*
Philippines: *sapote*
Sri Lanka: *sapodilla, rata-mi*
Thailand: *lamoot*

Sapote, Black

(*Diospyros digyna*) Known also as black persimmon, this fruit is native to Mexico. The thin green skin conceals a rich, purplish-brown pulp which, when ripe, resembles chocolate pudding (hence one of its names, the chocolate pudding fruit). Chocolate lovers, beware: do not expect the flavour to mimic your favourite food. Best described as sweet, the pulp can be processed to a shiny, rich, dark chocolate brown purée which, when flavoured with a little vanilla or lime juice, makes a perfectly delicious dessert, without the need for added sugar. As a bonus, a single fruit contains at least four times the vitamin C of an orange, as well as being a good source of phosphorus and calcium. Like persimmon, there are varieties with and without seeds. I suggest 'feeling' the pulp (with well-washed hands, of course) before blending to eliminate the seeds, hard pieces of which would not enhance the silky smooth texture of the dessert.

Sapote, Mamey

(*Pouteria sapota, Calocarpum sapota*) A member of the Sapotaceae family, this fruit is prized for its striking flesh which varies in colour from pink to burnt orange. The fruit is oval with a rough, brown skin and between one and four large, brown seeds. In its native Mexico it is popular eaten au naturel as well as made into ice cream, sorbets, milkshakes and preserves.

Sapote, White

(*Casimiroa edulis*) Not actually a member of the sapote family, in spite of its common name and some superficial similarity. A native of central America and Mexico, it will grow in most sub-tropical climates. A pale green, thin-skinned fruit, roughly spherical or a slightly flattened sphere in shape, the size of a large apple. The fruit should yield readily to pressure when ripe. The pulp varies from white to cream to orange in colour and has a creamy-smooth, almost buttery texture not unlike ripe avocado, and a sweet and slightly tangy flavour. Contains between one and five large, creamy-white seeds. Eat when ripe or use to flavour smoothies, milkshakes, desserts and ice cream.

Sashimi

Although the literal translation means raw fillets of fish eaten alone, some other seafoods have come under this umbrella and these include crustacea, molluscs and shellfish. Most formal Japanese meals include sashimi which, served with sake, is the first course in a sushi bar. For non-seafood fanciers, there are a couple of variations based on raw beef: au naturel (niku-no-sashimi) or marinated (niku-no-tataki).

With the exception of tuna (maguro) — arguably Japan's most popular sashimi — which is usually served in neat little oblong blocks, a large part of the spectacle of sashimi is the transparent thinness of the slices of raw fish and their artistic arrangement. The fattier, belly tuna (toro — ranging in fat content from chutoro or moderately fatty cut to otoro, the fattiest, palest pink, most tender cut) is often cut into thin slices which are arranged in the form of a rose (maguro no bara). Some other popular sashimi fish, particularly suited to being thinly sliced, are sea bream (tai, madai), sea bass (suzuki), halibut (hirame), carp, jewfish, bonito (katsua), mackerel (saba), kingfish, trout (masu) and, though not usually eaten raw in Japan, a popular sashimi fish in the West is salmon (sake). Add to this a selection of other sea creatures including squid (ika), octopus (tako), horseneck clam or geoduck (mirugai) and abalone (awi).

There are several basic cutting techniques used for sashimi. Thick-sliced sashimi (hira zukuri) is suitable for any fish, especially those with soft or fragile flesh. Thin-sliced sashimi (usu zukuri) works best with firm, pale-fleshed fish. Thread-cut sashimi (ito zukuri) suits squid and other thin-sliced muscle meats. Cube-cut sashimi (kaku zukuri) suits tuna or thick-filleted, soft-fleshed fish.

Sashimi is traditionally served with wasabi (Japanese green horseradish) and a dipping sauce of soy (with a little of the wasabi mixed in) for dipping tuna or, for white fish, ponzu. Quality and freshness of fish is paramount.

Pollution in oceans and rivers necessitates that you be sure about the source of fish for sashimi. Even freshwater fish from a clean river can be risky as freshwater fish sometimes carry parasites that cannot exist in salt water. This would not normally pose a health risk in Western cuisine as bacteria and parasites are killed by cooking.

Eating sashimi is most hazardous when the sashimi is fugu (blowfish, globefish, pufferfish). See FUGU.

Sataw Bean

See PARKIA.

Satay

Small pieces of meat or poultry are marinated in a spicy mixture, threaded on bamboo skewers and grilled over charcoal. By association, the accompanying peanut-based sauce is called 'satay sauce'. Satay is such a favourite in South East Asia that in Singapore there used to be an institution known as the Satay Club which has given way to development. Satay lives on, however, in every food centre. Beef, chicken or pork may feature, and these are served with compressed rice in little woven baskets of coconut leaflets called ketupat. Satays can be eaten as light snacks or an entire meal. They are wonderful for barbecues, where guests can make their choice and then cook their own. The hosts provide peanut sauce, rice, fresh raw cucumbers and onions to go with the satays, and can relax and enjoy the party while everyone has the fun of grilling their own meal.

Satay should be cut into quite small pieces. It is traditionally well cooked, not pink or rare.

Soak the bamboo skewers in water for at least an hour before threading the meat cubes. This will prevent the skewers from burning before the meat is cooked. Have ready bowls of satay sauce, squares of compressed steamed rice and bowls or platters of onion and cucumber wedges.

Satay

This recipe uses a marinade which suits any kind of meat. Serves 6.

**750 g/1½ lb rump steak, pork fillet
  or chicken fillets
1 stem lemon grass or 3 strips lemon zest
4 shallots, chopped
1 teaspoon chopped garlic
2 teaspoons finely grated ginger
3 teaspoons ground coriander
2 teaspoons ground cumin
1 teaspoon ground fennel
1 teaspoon ground turmeric
2 teaspoons brown sugar
1½ teaspoons salt
2 tablespoons light soy sauce
2 tablespoons tamarind liquid
  or 1 tablespoon bottled tamarind purée
2 tablespoons peanut oil**

Cut meat into small squares and put aside. Slice tender white portion of lemon grass finely across, combine with shallots, garlic and ginger and pound using a mortar and pestle. Transfer to a bowl and mix in the remaining ingredients. Pour over the meat, mixing well. Cover and leave aside for at least 2 hours, overnight if possible. Thread 6 or 7 pieces on each soaked bamboo skewer, leaving half the skewer free. Grill over coals or under a preheated griller until brown and serve immediately with peanut sauce and steamed rice.

Sauces

In Asian food, sauces are usually served separately for dipping. There are some quite famous sauces such as nam prik of Thailand, nuoc cham of Vietnam (see page 157), ponzu of Japan, and Tamarind Sauce of India (see page 373), Peanut Sauce of Indonesia and Malaysia (see page 276), ngan pla ye chet of Burma, lu, the master sauce of China, as well as bottled, cooked and fresh chilli sauces. Another famous sauce is the sesame sauce served with Shabu-shabu (see recipe page 338). There are also bottled sauces used in cooking. See SOY SAUCE; FISH SAUCE; GOLDEN MOUNTAIN SAUCE; OYSTER SAUCE; HOI SIN SAUCE; BEAN SAUCES. For home-made chilli sauce, see CHILLI.

Thai Shrimp Sauce (Nam Prik)

Nam prik is essentially a flavouring sauce or dip and should be thick enough to coat food dipped into it. Look for dried shrimp which are salmon pink and yield slightly when pressed through the packet, indicating freshness.

**3 tablespoons small dried shrimp
1 teaspoon chopped garlic
2 shallots or small red onions
2 fresh red chillies
2 tablespoons lime juice
2 teaspoons palm sugar or brown sugar
2 tablespoons fish sauce
2 tablespoons water**

Wash the dried shrimp and put in a shallow dish. Soak in just enough hot water to cover for about 10 minutes. This softens the shrimp and any sandy veins can be removed. Put shrimp into a mortar with the garlic, shallots and chillies, all chopped. Pound steadily for a few minutes until mashed to a paste. Gradually stir in the lime juice, palm sugar, fish sauce and water. If preferred, pulverise in an electric blender, though a little extra water may be needed. Serve in a small bowl with a selection of vegetables in season to be dipped in the nam prik and eaten as an appetiser.

Thai Chilli and Shrimp Sauce

This relish (sometimes called chilli jam and similar to bottled nam prik pao) keeps well if stored in a clean glass jar in the refrigerator and is delicious with rice, as a dip, or a rather fiery sauce. Makes about 500 ml (2 cups).

10 large dried red chillies
1 rounded tablespoon dried tamarind
185 g/6 oz/1½ cups dried shrimp
375 g/12 oz shallots, peeled and sliced
   or 3 large onions, finely chopped
4 tablespoons chopped garlic
250 ml/8 fl oz/1 cup peanut oil
125 g/4 oz palm sugar or brown sugar
2 tablespoons fish sauce
2 teaspoons lime juice

Break stems off chillies and shake out seeds. Pour boiling water over the chillies and leave to soak for 15 minutes. In another bowl soak dried tamarind in ½ cup boiling water. When cool enough, squeeze to dissolve pulp, then strain. Repeat with a little more water if there is still pulp to be dissolved.

In an electric blender blend shrimp on high speed until reduced to a floss. Empty into a bowl and without washing the blender put in the drained chillies, shallots, garlic and peanut oil. Blend on high speed until puréed. Pour into a shallow pan and fry on medium heat, stirring constantly, until the oil comes to the surface. Add palm sugar, tamarind liquid and shrimp floss and simmer for 5 minutes, or until sauce reaches a thick dipping consistency. Add the fish sauce and simmer for 2–3 minutes. Transfer to a bowl. When cool stir in the lime juice.

Sweet Dipping Sauce

Makes nearly 1 cup

4 tablespoons caster sugar (superfine sugar)
125 ml/4 fl oz cold water
2 tablespoons fish sauce
finely sliced red and green chilli
1 tablespoon lime juice or vinegar

Stir the sugar with the cold water until the sugar dissolves, then add the remaining ingredients.

Thai Eggplant Dipping Sauce

Serves 6

375 g/12 oz eggplant (aubergine)
2 limes
2 small purple shallots, sliced
   or 2 tablespoons chopped spring onions
   (scallions)
½ teaspoon crushed garlic
½ teaspoon salt or to taste
1 teaspoon palm sugar or brown sugar
1 or 2 fresh red chillies, seeded and sliced

In a stainless steel saucepan bring to the boil 1 litre (2 pints) of lightly salted boiling water. Using a stainless steel knife peel eggplant and dice it. Drop dice into the boiling water, cover and cook for about 8 minutes or until tender, pour into a colander at once to drain.

Finely grate lime rind, then halve the limes and juice them. Mash eggplant with fork or potato masher and mix in lime rind and juice, sliced shallots, garlic, salt, sugar and chillies. Taste and adjust seasoning. Serve in a small bowl, surrounded by vegetables for dipping.

Sausages

Sausages do not belong solely to the West. There are some quite famous sausages found in Asia. Some specialty sausages are delicious and worth the trouble needed to make them. They contain no bread or other fillers. They are filled with lean and fat pork, pork and beef, chicken, or a mixture of meat and seafood.

China has its lap cheong — a kind of sweet and salty salami which keeps for weeks without refrigeration. The most popular one is made with pork, but alongside them hang the darker sausages (gum gun yuen) which contain liver.

In the north of Thailand there are many kinds of sausage (sai klok), each distinctly different in flavour and appearance. In Goa, on the west coast of India, where the Portuguese ruled for some time and left influences which are undeniably Portuguese to this day, there are spicy sausages called chourisam. Nonya sausage (lor bak, lobah), is made from strips of pork seasoned with five-spice powder, rolled in bean curd skin and deep fried, but modern versions include prawns (shrimp), crab meat and water chestnuts. Sri Lanka has its lingus — peppery, vinegary and strongly spiced with cloves.

Sri Lankan Sausages

sausage casings from butcher
750 g/1½ lb lean pork
250 g/8 oz fat pork
3 teaspoons coriander seeds,
  toasted and ground
1 teaspoon ground cinnamon
½ teaspoon ground cloves
1 teaspoon coarsely ground black pepper
half a nutmeg, finely grated
2 teaspoons salt
3 tablespoons vinegar or sufficient to moisten

Run cold water through the sausage casings, checking for any holes. Trim the lean pork and chop it finely or mince (grind) coarsely. Cut the fat pork into small pieces and mix with the lean pork. Add ground spices, nutmeg and salt. Knead well together and moisten with a little vinegar. Fill prepared skins and twist at intervals of 10–12.5 cm (4–5 in) to form small sausages. Smoke the sausages for a few hours.

To smoke sausages: Have the temperature of the smoker or covered barbecue no more than 85°F (30°C). If using a covered barbecue, place two or three barbecue briquettes to one side and let them reach the proper temperature. Add mesquite or hickory chips, soaked in water for at least 30 minutes. Place sausages as far away from the heat as possible, cover and smoke for 3 hours. Do not open lid more than necessary. Each time you do, add 15 minutes extra smoking time.

To cook sausages: Put sausages into a frying pan with enough water to cover base of pan and just a dash of vinegar. Let them cook slowly for 10 minutes or until the vinegar and water evaporate. Prick the sausages with a fine poultry skewer to prevent them from bursting, and fry them in a little oil. Keep turning them so they brown on all sides.

Lobah

Serves 6 as an entree

375 g/12 oz pork neck or other lean pork
125 g/4 oz belly pork
125 g/4 oz raw prawns (shrimp)
90 g/3 oz cooked crab meat (optional)
3 tablespoons finely chopped water chestnuts
2 spring onions (scallions), finely chopped
½ teaspoon salt
¼ teaspoon pepper
¼ teaspoon five-spice powder
1 teaspoon cornflour (cornstarch)
1 small egg, beaten
dried bean curd skin
peanut oil for deep frying

Dice both kinds of pork very finely. Shell, devein and chop prawns almost to a paste. Mix the pork, prawns, crab, water chestnuts, spring onions, seasoning, five-spice powder and cornflour together, using the egg to bind the mixture.

Dampen and soften the bean curd sheet by wiping over with hand dipped in warm water. Cut into squares measuring about 15–18 cm (6–7 in). Place a small amount of the mixture on each square, shape it into a neat roll, then enclose by rolling it in the bean curd wrapper, turning in the ends. The rolls should be no thicker than a thumb. When all are ready, fry in hot oil over medium heat until golden brown, 3–4 minutes. Drain on paper towels. Cut into diagonal slices and serve with chilli sauce and sliced cucumbers.

Saw Tooth Herb

See ERYNGO.

Scallion

See SPRING ONION.

Scallops

These delicately flavoured bivalves are found in cold waters, and are looked upon as a luxury in whatever cuisine they appear. It is best to buy those which are still on the half-shell, as they lend themselves to more elegant presentation and also have better flavour, not having been washed or soaked in water. Over-fishing has rendered them in short supply and therefore expensive.

An ingredient sold as dried scallops is actually conpoy. It is not found fresh, but sold at great price in Chinese stores, and used sparingly for flavouring special dishes. See CONPOY.

China: *gong yew chew*

Steamed Scallops in Shells

Serves 6 as an entree

18 scallops on the half-shell
¼ teaspoon grated fresh ginger
1 teaspoon oyster sauce
1 tablespoon Chinese wine or dry sherry
½ teaspoon sugar
1 spring onion (scallion)

Remove dark veins from scallops. Leave red roe attached. Combine the ginger, oyster sauce, wine and sugar. Spoon this over the scallops in shells. Cover and chill for 30 minutes. Cut the spring onion into fine shreds and sprinkle over the scallops. Place the scallops in a steamer over boiling water.

Cover steamer and cook over a moderately high heat for 5 minutes. Serve immediately.

Garlic Scallops

Serves 4

375 g/12 oz scallop meat
half a small capsicum (bell pepper)
1 teaspoon finely chopped garlic
1 tablespoon light soy sauce
1 tablespoon oyster sauce
1 tablespoon dry sherry
1 teaspoon cornflour (cornstarch)
1 tablespoon cold water
2 tablespoons peanut oil
1 teaspoon sesame oil
shredded lettuce for garnish

Remove any dark streaks on the scallops. Dice the capsicum. Crush or finely chop the garlic. Mix together the soy sauce, oyster sauce and sherry. Mix cornflour with cold water in a separate container and have all the ingredients assembled before starting to cook.

Heat wok, add peanut oil and heat again for 30 seconds, then swirl to spread oil. On low heat fry garlic for a few seconds, stirring. Do not let it brown or it will taste bitter. Increase heat, add capsicum and stir-fry for 1 minute. Add scallops and stir-fry for 30 seconds. Do not over-cook scallops or they will shrink and toughen. Pour in the mixed seasonings, stir in the cornflour mixture and continue stirring until the sauce boils and thickens slightly. Sprinkle sesame oil over, garnish and serve at once with rice.

Sea Cucumber

(*Holothuria* spp.) Also known as sea slug, sea rat or, in French, béche de mer. Shaped like a cucumber, it is sold dried and requires many days of soaking and repeated scrubbing to clean out its digestive system. There are varying sizes and qualities, the black variety being inferior and cheaper.

To give you some idea of the preparation involved, here is a quote from Alan Davidson's *Seafood of South East Asia*:

The first step is to slit them open along the belly, wash well and boil. They must then be immersed in sand for two nights, after which a stiff brush is used to remove the sand, bringing the rough skin with it. Next, boiling water is poured over them, after which they are held over the fire to dry. They still have to be soaked to soften them and make them swell before they are finally ready to be made into soup or otherwise cooked. The preparation of these creatures for consumption is so arduous that it certainly seems necessary to postulate some special reason for taking the trouble.

The Chinese name, hai-shen, translates as 'sea ginseng' because of its supposed aphrodisiac qualities. This accounts for the centuries of enthusiastic harvesting of this unattractive sea creature. After days of soaking and cleaning and repeated boiling, draining and rinsing, it contributes no flavour, only a gelatinous texture. It is usually cooked with other ingredients which give it some flavour.

Burma: *pin le hmyaw*
China: *hai shen, hoy sum*
Indonesia: *teripang*
Malaysia: *trepang*

Seafood

See ABALONE; ANCHOVY; BOMBAY DUCK; CLAMS; CONPOY; CRABS; CUTTLEFISH; EEL; FISH; FISH CAKE; FISH HEAD; FISH MAW; FISH PASTE; FISH ROE; FISH SAUCE; FISH, DRIED; FUGU; KEDGEREE; LOBSTER; MALDIVE FISH; MARRON; MUSSEL; OCTOPUS; OYSTER; POMFRET; PRAWNS; SASHIMI; SEA CUCUMBER; SEA URCHIN; SHARK'S FIN; SHRIMP, DRIED; SQUID; SHRIMP PASTE, DRIED; WHITEBAIT; YABBIES.

Sea Urchin

If you've only ever seen the pinhole-patterned, dried-out skeletons of these creatures you'd be forgiven for not recognising a live sea urchin. Often seen huddled in seaside rock pools, they are a veritable pincushion of spines. The roe of the sea urchin is considered a delicacy in certain cuisines, and is said to be at its best eaten fresh (live), spooned straight from the half shell. To serve, collect the urchin, rinse, taking care to avoid the spines, slice in half crosswise and scoop out the roe (which is arranged in the form of a five-pointed star). The colour is usually dark yellow or orange. In Japan, it is used as a sushi topping. Like oysters, they have the taste of the sea, while the texture is smooth and buttery.

Seaweed

Sea vegetables provide much nutrition to Asian diets. In Japanese cuisine, especially, there are a number of seaweeds which are basic to Japanese food. Kombu, nori and wakame are three of them.

Agar-agar: Sometimes referred to as vegetable gelatine as well as by its Japanese name, kanten, it is derived from a number of different kinds of seaweed. See AGAR-AGAR.

Hijiki: (*Cystophyllum fusiforme*) Sold dried, looking like short lengths of black wire. Soaked before use, it swells to about three times its original size. This takes about 20 minutes. Simmer in stock until tender but still crunchy and combine with vegetables and rice for a delicious and healthy meal.

Kombu (konbu): (*Laminaria japonica*) Also called kelp or seatangle, it is boiled with dried bonito (katsuobushi) to make dashi, the slightly salty stock fundamental to Japanese cuisine. The fine, salty mould covering its surface is desirable and is the key to its flavour. Cut off as large a piece as you need and wipe over with a dry cloth before using. Do not rinse or wash it, or the flavour will be lost. Kombu is also sold pickled in packets. The slightly sweet, slightly sour strips (sukombu) look like shiny black licorice and have a crunchy texture. There is also a variety known as golden kelp.

Mozuku: A very fine seaweed, it is sold in plastic tubs, packed either in water or tosa (seasoned vinegar).

Nori (laver): (*Pophyra tenera, P. umbilicalis*) Classified as marine algae and mainly used for wrapping sushi, hence the name norimaki-zushi. It is sold in tissue-thin sheets, often lightly oiled, salted and toasted (yaki-nori) and eaten as a snack or crumbled over a bowl of rice. It is easy enough to crisp-toast plain sheets of laver, and is probably a good idea as the pre-seasoned varieties vary greatly in quality. I've tried some excellent ones and some that were absolutely inedible, smelling overpoweringly of rancid oil. In Korea, nori is known as keem. It is brushed with sesame oil and grilled, then crumbled over food. Store nori airtight or in the freezer and before using toast on one side under a grill or in the oven. It will become greenish (as opposed to black) in colour, crisp and develop a better flavour. Nori is also sold in flaked form, in small bottles.

Wakame: (*Undaria pinnatifida*) A member of the brown algae family, it is cultivated in the warm Pacific waters off Honshu and Kyushu. Between spring and early summer the green, ribbon-like tresses are sold fresh. Wakame is also sold dried or moist and salted. More usually, however, it is found in dried form. If dry, it needs up to 2 hours soaking. Washed, vinegared and chilled, it makes sunomono (a light, refreshing salad) and aemono (more substantial dressed salads).

Dried, it resembles pale brown tresses with a whitish bloom. Premium wakame should have a rich, green-black hue. Moist wakame must be soaked in warm water for 10–15 minutes and the tough mid-rib sections cut away before use. It is used in soups, added a couple of minutes before serving. Its texture is crunchy and the flavour very much the essence of the ocean. A valuable source of nutrients, it is particularly rich in calcium, niacin and protein and is virtually calorie free.

In Chinese cuisine, especially around the Chinese New Year, a different 'seaweed' attains prominence — the black, hair-like sea vegetable *Gracilaria verrucosa*. Also called black moss, sea hair and hair seaweed, it is moderately expensive. See BLACK MOSS.

Semolina

(*Triticum durum*) The hard endosperm sifted out of durum wheat (hard wheat) during milling is used only for making pasta. When milled from wheat which is not durum wheat (*T. vulgare*) it is labelled, variously, farina and breakfast delight. Semolina is granular and available milled fine, medium or coarse. It is used in India to make a pudding (sooji halva) flavoured with cardamom and saffron. In southern India it is lightly cooked with spices and vegetables into a fluffy savoury breakfast dish called uppuma.

Biscuits known as naan khatai (Indian short-bread) are made from medium-fine semolina, ghee, sugar and cardamom. If stored airtight (and kept well hidden) they will last for a week or more.

Some Indian breads use a proportion of semolina in the dough, and when fried they seem to puff and stay puffed better than those made with flour.

Semolina is also used in cakes in Sri Lanka, Malaysia and Singapore.

Savoury Semolina (Uppuma)

There are many versions of this favourite dish. Some are simply semolina and spices without the addition of vegetables. Serves 6.

2 tablespoons vegetable oil
1 tablespoon ghee
400 g/14 oz/2 cups coarse semolina
1 tablespoon urad dhal
1 tablespoon channa dhal
1 teaspoon black mustard seeds
2 fresh chillies, sliced
2 teaspoons finely chopped ginger
1 medium onion, finely chopped
1 cup diced vegetables
  (cauliflower, carrots, capsicum [bell pepper])
500 ml/1 pint/2 cups hot water
1½ teaspoons salt
3 tablespoons chopped fresh coriander
wedge of lime or lemon

Heat half the oil and half the ghee in a heavy saucepan and fry the semolina, stirring constantly, over medium-low heat until it is golden. Turn it into a bowl and wipe out the pan with a paper towel.

Heat remaining oil and ghee and fry the dhals until they are golden. Add the mustard seeds, chillies, ginger, onion and vegetables and stir for about 5 minutes or until they smell fragrant. Add hot water and salt, bring to the boil, then add semolina and stir until it boils. Cover pan with well-fitting lid and cook on low heat for about 8 minutes until semolina is cooked through. Sprinkle with coriander and serve with a wedge of lime or lemon.

Note: A variation on this recipe is to use 1 cup diced eggplant instead of the other vegetables, and add an extra tablespoon of oil when frying it with the onion, chillies, and ginger.

Cardamom Scented Semolina Shortbreads (Naan Khatai)

This biscuit, rich with ghee, is a glorified version of shortbread. It does not have quite the same quality when made with butter or margarine. Makes 2 dozen.

125 g/4 oz ghee
125 g/4 oz/½ cup caster sugar (superfine sugar)
200 g/7 oz/1 cup fine semolina
3 tablespoons plain (all-purpose) flour
1½ teaspoons ground cardamom

Cream ghee and sugar together until light. Sift semolina, flour and cardamom together, stir into creamed mixture and mix well. Chill slightly or in cool weather leave to stand for 30 minutes. Take scant tablespoons of the mixture, roll into balls and flatten slightly. Place them slightly apart on an ungreased baking tray. Bake in a preheated oven at 150°C (300°F) for about 30 minutes or until pale golden and firm. Cool on a wire rack and store in an airtight container.

Semolina Pudding

Serves 6

185 g/6 oz/¾ cup sugar
300 ml/10 fl oz water
60 ml/2 fl oz milk
¼ teaspoon saffron strands
125 g/4 oz ghee
90 g/3 oz/½ cup medium semolina
2 tablespoons sultanas (golden raisins)
2 tablespoons slivered almonds
1 teaspoon ground cardamom

Bring first 4 ingredients to the boil in a saucepan, stirring until sugar dissolves. Set aside. In a heavy-based pan melt the ghee and fry the semolina over low heat, stirring all the time, until golden. Add the syrup, sultanas, almonds and cardamom and stir over medium heat until mixture thickens and leaves sides of pan. Pour into a shallow dish. Serve warm or cold, with or without cream. This pudding is

usually served with a disc of deep-fried bread, puri, which has itself been fried in ghee. It may be served at the beginning of a meal instead of at the end. The pudding can also be served cold cut into diamond shapes.

Burmese Semolina Cake

2–3 tablespoons sesame seeds
400 ml/14 fl oz can coconut cream
185 g/6 oz/1 cup medium or fine semolina
250 g/8 oz/1 cup sugar
125 g/4 oz ghee or butter
pinch of salt
½ teaspoon ground cardamom
3 eggs, separated

Toast the sesame seeds in a dry pan over medium heat, stirring constantly, until they are golden. Turn out onto a plate to cool, or they will become too dark.

Dilute coconut cream with equal amount of water. Put semolina in a large, heavy saucepan and stir in the diluted coconut milk gradually, keeping the mixture free from lumps. Add the sugar, put over medium heat and stir while bringing to the boil. When the mixture boils and thickens add a small amount of ghee or butter at a time and continue cooking until mixture becomes very thick and leaves the sides of the pan. Add salt and ground cardamom and mix well.

Remove from heat and beat in egg yolks. Stiffly beat egg whites and fold in. Turn mixture into a buttered 22 cm (9 in) square cake pan or ovenproof dish and smooth the top. Sprinkle toasted sesame seeds liberally over semolina mixture. Bake at 160°C (325°F) for 45 minutes to 1 hour or until well risen and golden brown. Cool in the dish, then cut into large diamond-shaped pieces. Serve as a sweet snack or dessert.

Sesame Oil

See OILS.

Sesame Paste

In Far Eastern cooking, sesame paste is made from toasted sesame seeds. Thick and brown, it resembles peanut butter. This sesame paste is not to be confused with the pale Middle Eastern paste called tahini which is made from untoasted or only lightly toasted sesame seeds and has a different flavour.

Because sesame seeds contain about 50 per cent oil, sesame paste will separate into an oil layer over an almost solid paste layer at the bottom of the jar or tin. Be warned, many a spoon has been bent trying to prise the paste from the jar. Smooth peanut butter may be substituted although, obviously, the flavour won't be the same. See recipe for Quick and Easy Roast Duck (page 126).

Sesame Seed

(*Sesamum indicum*) Sesame is an annual herb yielding small, flat, teardrop-shaped seeds, ranging from cream to black in colour. Unhulled 'white' sesame seeds are beige rather than white and extremely high in calcium. Except for some Japanese, Korean and a few Chinese dishes, it is invariably white, hulled sesame seeds which are used in Asia. Indian vegetarian cookery uses sesame seeds in combination with lentils, milk and rice to maximise protein content. Hulled, toasted sesame seeds are indispensable in certain Japanese and Korean sauces and marinades.

In Sri Lanka, one of the most popular confections is a sticky mixture of hulled white sesame seeds and palm sugar pounded together, shaped into bite-sized balls and wrapped in either cellophane or greaseproof paper. These are sold by roadside vendors and known as thala-guli (sesame pills).

Toasting hulled white sesame seeds gives them a wonderful nutty flavour and attractive deep golden colour. It is from toasted seeds that we get oriental sesame oil — rich golden brown and strongly flavoured. See OILS.

Black sesame seeds have an earthy taste in their raw state and are not suitable for toasting as they become bitter. They are used in the Japanese condiment, gomashio (sesame salt) and indispensable when making the famous showpiece Chinese dessert, toffee bananas — battered and deep-fried fruit dipped in clear caramel with black sesame seeds stirred through. The caramel-coated pieces of fried fruit are dropped into a bowl of ice and water to harden the caramel, then quickly transferred to a lightly oiled serving dish and eaten without delay. Slices of apple or sweet yam may be used instead of bananas. See recipe for Chinese Toffee Bananas (page 20).

Burma: *hnan si*
China: *chih mah* (white), *hak chih mah* (black)
India: *til, gingelly*
Indonesia: *wijen*
Japan: *muki goma* (white), *kuro gomah* (black)
Korea: *keh*
Malaysia: *bijan*
Philippines: *linga*
Sri Lanka: *thala*
Thailand: *nga dee la*
Vietnam: *me*

Simmered Steak and Vegetables (Shabu-Shabu)

Serves 6–8

1 kg/2 lb fillet steak
1 small white Chinese cabbage
12 spring onions (scallions)
2 tender young carrots
500 g/1 lb button mushrooms
2 litres/4 pints/8 cups chicken stock

SESAME SEED SAUCE

4 tablespoons sesame seeds
2 tablespoons mild white vinegar
8 tablespoons Japanese soy sauce
3 tablespoons finely chopped spring onions (scallions)
2 teaspoons finely grated fresh ginger

Cut steak into paper-thin slices. (It is easier to do this if the meat is partially frozen.) Cut cabbage into short lengths. Cut spring onions into bite-sized lengths. Cut carrots into round slices, parboil and drain. Wipe mushrooms with damp paper towels, trim ends of stalks and cut in halves unless mushrooms are very small. Arrange food on serving platter, cover and refrigerate.

At serving time, pour stock into shabu-shabu cooker, cover with lid and fill chimney with glowing coals, or use a tabletop electric pan. Heat and place in the centre of the table within easy reach of everyone. Keep stock simmering throughout the meal, adding more as necessary.

Set each place with a bowl, chopsticks and individual bowl for sauce. Also set a large bowl of hot white rice on the table so guests can help themselves.

Ingredients are picked up with chopsticks and held in the boiling stock until just done, then transferred to individual bowls, dipped in sauce and eaten with rice. Care should be taken not to overcook the food. Steak should be pale pink when cooked and vegetables tender but still crisp.

When all the meat and vegetables are eaten the stock is served as a soup. The bowls should be lifted to the lips and the soup sipped from the bowl Japanese fashion, rather than with a spoon.

Sesame seed sauce: Lightly brown sesame seeds in a dry pan over moderate heat, stirring constantly with a spoon or shaking the pan. Turn on to a plate to cool, then crush using suribachi (see UTENSILS) or a mortar and pestle. Combine with remaining ingredients. Alternatively, put ingredients in container of an electric blender and blend on high speed for a few seconds.

Korean Marinade with Sesame Seeds

One of my favourite marinades, this is sufficient for about 500 g (1 lb) beef.

1 teaspoon finely grated fresh ginger
2 teaspoons finely chopped or crushed garlic
2 teaspoons finely chopped spring onions (scallions)
2 teaspoons sesame oil
1 tablespoon toasted, crushed sesame seeds
2 tablespoons light soy sauce
2 teaspoons honey or sugar
¼ teaspoon ground black pepper

Combine all the ingredients. Pour over finely sliced beef, ribs or steaks, and leave for about 30 minutes or longer before stir-frying, grilling or barbecuing.

Sesame Seed and Palm Sugar Balls

2 cups sesame seeds
500 g/1 lb palm sugar (jaggery) or brown sugar
generous pinch of salt

Using a mortar and pestle, pound the sesame a little at a time until the seeds are crushed and oily. As each batch is done, turn it into a bowl. Grate the palm sugar and add to the crushed sesame with the salt. Mix well with hands. The heat of the hands and vigorous kneading slightly melts the palm sugar, and after a while the mixture will hold together. Make balls the size of a large marble. Wrap in rectangular pieces of wax or greaseproof paper fringed at the ends. Twist the paper on either side of the balls so each looks like a miniature Christmas cracker. Serve at the end of a curry meal, or as a between-meals treat.

Sesbania

(*Sesbania grandiflora*) This small tree (sometimes called West Indian pea tree) belongs to the Leguminosae family. It is cultivated as an ornamental and bears feathery compound leaves, handsome flowers and pods, all of which are used as food. The flowers, known as pea flowers, 2–3 in (5–7 cm) in length, are creamy white or a brilliant red, depending on the variety. The young leaves of both varieties are stripped from the stalks and served as a cooked vegetable. The white flowers are used to make tempura in Japan, curries in Sri Lanka and Malaysia, soup in the Philippines, or eaten raw or lightly cooked in more than one Asian country.

In Asian markets you will see them in big bunches, quite beautiful and perhaps more appropriate in a floral arrangement. However, they are edible.

The calyx, stamens and pistils are bitter and should be removed, and in some flowers even the petals are bitter. The bitterness can be reduced by parboiling, but this slightly bitter flavour is accepted, even prized, by well-trained tastebuds in the belief that bitter foods are beneficial to health.

Purchasing and preparation: Buy fresh leaves and white flowers for cooking. The red flowers are considered too bitter to eat and grown only for their ornamental value. Even the white flowers should have their bitter stamens and green calyx removed. The leaflets of either variety must be stripped from the tough stems and shredded finely. Because of their small size some cooks prefer to wrap the pile of leaves in a large leaf such as lettuce and press into a firm bundle, making handling and shredding easier.

Medicinal uses: In Malaysia the crushed leaves are applied to relieve sprains and bruises, and the bark used as a purgative. It is also used to treat scabies. In Indochina the bark is considered a tonic and used to prevent fever and to treat colic, diarrhoea and dysentery. In the Philippines the bark is used to treat spitting or coughing of blood.

China: *ta-hua, tien-tsing*
India: *agust*
Indonesia: *daun turi, turi*
Japan: *shiro-gochou*
Malaysia: *daun turi, turi*
Philippines: *katuray*
Sri Lanka: *katurumurunga kolle* (leaves), *katurumurunga mala* (flowers)
Thailand: *dok khae baan*

Sesbania Leaf Stir-Fry

Serves 6–8

250 g/8 oz sesbania leaves
1 onion or 3 shallots, finely chopped
3 fresh chillies, seeded and sliced
75 g/2½ oz/1 cup freshly grated coconut
½ teaspoon ground turmeric
3 tablespoons water
1 teaspoon salt or to taste

Wash the leaves while still on their stems, and shake well to get rid of the water. Strip leaves from tougher stems and compress into a bundle, then shred finely. Mix with shallots, chillies, coconut and turmeric in a pan, add water, cover and cook on low heat for 5 minutes or until leaves are soft. Add salt to taste and serve as an accompaniment to rice and curry.

Note: Another method is to heat about two teaspoons of oil, and fry the onions and chillies first. Add turmeric, coconut, shredded leaves and water and cook, stirring, until leaves are soft and liquid evaporated.

Sesbania Blossoms, Fried and Curried

Serves 4

CURRY SAUCE

1 tablespoon oil
6 shallots, finely chopped
3 fresh chillies, chopped
½ teaspoon ground turmeric
1 tablespoon pounded Maldive fish or dried shrimp
small stick cinnamon
1 teaspoon salt
125 g/4 fl oz/½ cup canned coconut milk
squeeze of lime juice

FLOWER FRITTERS

16 white sesbania blossoms
6 level tablespoons plain (all-purpose) flour
6 level tablespoons rice flour
1 egg, beaten
185 ml/6 fl oz/¾ cup water
½ teaspoon salt
oil for frying

Make curry sauce first and have it ready. Heat the oil and fry shallots and chillies until soft. Add remaining ingredients and simmer for 10 minutes or until slightly thick.

To make the fritters, remove green bases, calyxes and stamens of flowers. Put flour and salt into a bowl. Combine egg and water, add to flour and mix to a smooth batter. Heat oil for deep frying. Dip flowers into the batter one at a time and drop into the hot oil, not too many at once. Drain on paper towels. Serve while warm and crisp, with curry sauce for dipping.

Note: Taste a petal raw, and if it is too bitter, blanch the flowers in boiling water to remove some of the bitterness before using.

Shallot

(*Allium ascalonicum*) SEE ILLUSTRATION. Purplish-red or brown-gold in colour, these members of the onion family grow like garlic, with a number of single bulbs clustered together at the root. (If you are looking for long, slender, green and white onions, see SPRING ONION.)

Shallots have a more intense flavour than onions, and are widely used in South East Asia. In Malaysia and Singapore shallots are used in the spicy pounded base known as rempah.

Because the layers are so much finer than the layers of large onions, they are ideal for slicing and scattering over salads, or for slow, deep frying to make a crisp and tasty garnish. For salads, I prefer to use golden shallots which are sweeter and not as pungent as purple shallots. It is possible to buy shallots already fried, packed in tubs or plastic bags. Store these in the freezer to prevent the oil turning rancid. They are used to sprinkle over noodles, rice, soups and just about any dish that needs a flavour boost. Crisply fried shallots are wonderful for adding to peanut sauce (Malaysia, Indonesia) and substituted for onions and garlic in a short-cut version of balachaung, a Burmese relish. Although using ready-fried shallots cuts preparation time dramatically, it doesn't yield the bonus of shallot oil — delicious for flavouring vegetables or noodles.

A more unusual use of fried shallots is in some Asian sweet biscuits. A specialty pastry shop in Penang makes biscuits with a filling made from sweetened mung bean paste with fried shallots mixed through. This sweet-salty combination is very popular and supply can hardly keep up with demand, but the first bite sends conflicting signals to unwary taste buds.

Burma: *kyet-thun-ni*
Cambodia: *khtim kraham*
China: *kon tsung-tau*
India: *chota piaz*
Indonesia: *bawang merah*
Japan: *aka wakegi*
Malaysia: *bawang merah*
Philippines: *sibuyas*
Sri Lanka: *rathu-lunu*
Thailand: *hom daeng*
Vietnam: *hanh huong*

Sambal Bawang

250 ml/8 fl oz/1 cup peanut oil
250 g/8 oz shallots, peeled and sliced
8–10 fresh hot red chillies, finely sliced
1 tablespoon dried shrimp paste
½ teaspoon salt
1 tablespoon lime juice

Heat oil and gently fry shallots until soft. Add chillies, shrimp paste and salt and cook, crushing the shrimp paste against the side of the pan with the back of a spoon. Fry for a few minutes more, then remove from heat. When cooled, stir in lime juice. Store in refrigerator.

Crisp Fried Shallots and Shallot Oil

This is a tedious business, but the advantages are many. The peeling and slicing of shallots and slow frying in oil result not only in a crisp-textured garnish which adds fresh flavour to many dishes, but also produces shallot oil which, drizzled over steamed vegetables, makes a world of difference to their flavour. To store crisp-fried shallots, first cool thoroughly then pack into airtight containers and freeze.

500 g/1 lb shallots
1 litre/2 pints/4 cups peanut oil

Peel the shallots and slice as evenly as possible so that all the slices take the same time to cook. Heat the oil and add all the shallots at once, cooking on fairly low heat so they cook through. Stir with a slotted spoon during the frying, and be prepared to let them cook slowly. When shallots turn golden brown pour entire contents of pan through a wire strainer over a metal bowl. Turn shallots onto paper towels and leave to cool. Those not used immediately may be packed into plastic containers and stored in the refrigerator or freezer.

Bottle the oil when cool. Use for flavouring noodles, rice and vegetables.

Shark's Fin

Included in banquet menus to impress or honour a guest, this most extravagant ingredient was not widely known or used until the Sung Dynasty of 960–1279 AD. It is, in fact, shark's fin, the dorsal (preferred) or ventral (second choice) fins of a variety of shark that inhabits Asia's waters.

Only sold dried, it undergoes 4 days of preparation before it reaches the Chinese grocer or herbalist. It is skinned, simmered and scraped clean of mucilage, but this is nothing compared to the further preparation required by the cook. The process is long and involved and justifies the cost of the dish. It is regarded as a general tonic and, specifically, an appetite stimulant. For this last reason, a shark's fin dish may be served at the start or climax of a banquet. Only if you wish to insult the chef in the worst possible way should you allow your shark's fin soup bowl to be returned to the kitchen in any state other than empty. Perhaps we should all take the trouble to make it once to fully appreciate why.

The needle-like projections making up the fin's framework are the part of the fin that is eaten, their unique texture only arrived at after a tedious process of soaking, simmering, washing and steaming. The fins must be completely free of any fishy odour by the time they reach the table. Served in a rich stock, the flavour of the amber-coloured strands of shark's fin should have the faintest suggestion of the sea. The longest, unbroken strands signify the highest quality shark's fin. The smaller fins with shorter strands are cheaper.

Shark's fin is used to flavour scrambled egg, stuffed inside duck before it is steamed, and sometimes served in delicately pleated dumplings at dim sum restaurants. You'll find restaurants in Hong Kong that specialise in shark's fin dishes, with a small bowl of food featuring the exotic ingredient sometimes costing hundreds of dollars.

Although the preparation process is a protracted one, don't yield to the temptation of purchasing the softened shark's fin in the freezer of an Asian store. I'm told it falls far short of the results achieved by making it from scratch. Buy dried fins, hunting down the palest, cleanest specimens you can find, free of specks of dried skin or dirt.

China: *yu chee*

Shark's Fin Preparation

500 g/1 lb refined shark's fin
3 tablespoons oil
1 tablespoon finely sliced fresh ginger
8 spring onions (scallions), cut in short lengths
2 tablespoons rice wine
500 ml/1 pint/2 cups chicken or duck stock

Soak the dried fin in a large pot of cold water for 1 day, changing the water 4 times. Scrub with a brush. Add to a wok filled with cold water and slowly bring to the boil. Remove and plunge into cold water. When cool, rinse and place in a heatproof dish that will fit a steamer. Heat oil and stir-fry the ginger and spring onions, adding wine and stock. Bring to the boil. Pour stock onto the fin and steam for 3 hours. Remove fin (discarding stock) and wash in hot water, changing the water 3 times. The shark's fin is now ready to use.

Shark's Fin And Crab Meat Soup

Serves 6

prepared shark's fin (see preceding recipe)
250 g/8 oz fresh or frozen crab meat
1 leek, shredded
8 slices fresh root ginger
1 litre/2 pints/4 cups chicken stock
2–3 tablespoons light soy sauce
60 ml/2 fl oz/¼ cup Chinese wine
2 teaspoons sugar
salt to taste
2½ tablespoons cornflour (cornstarch)
3 tablespoons finely shredded Yunnan ham
  or double smoked ham

Cover prepared shark's fin with cold water. Add ginger slices and scatter with shredded leek. Bring to the boil, then simmer for 30 minutes. Drain shark's fin and rinse in cold water. Flake crab, removing any bony tissue. Heat stock and, when boiling, add shark's fin and flaked crab. Cook for another 30 minutes. Add soy sauce, wine, sugar and salt. Blend cornflour with 2 tablespoons cold water. Add to soup, stirring constantly, until it boils and thickens. Transfer to a soup dish, mounding ham in centre.

Shichimi

Also known as shichimi-togarashi. A Japanese spice blend that translates literally as 'seven flavours'. Traditionally it includes dried red chilli flakes, sansho, dried tangerine or mandarin peel, sesame seeds, black sesame seeds, white poppy seeds and flakes of the dried sea vegetable, nori. I have seen ground, dried Japanese pepper (sansho) leaf, or even black pepper included as alternatives to sansho; some blends include rape, hemp or mustard seeds in place of black sesame; others omit the nori.

Like spice blends from other parts of Asia, a given region or even a family may have its own interpretation of the blend and include a few secret ingredients. The basic ingredients are chilli, some form of pepper, sesame seeds and the dried peel of an orange coloured, loose-skinned citrus fruit. These are always included, no matter what other components are added.

Whatever its seven secret herbs and spices, it is an undeniably popular condiment, for cooking and table, often sprinkled over udon noodles. Some manufacturers make a container with seven discrete compartments to keep each ingredient separate, while a rotating lid makes it possible to 'dial a flavour' for your own personalised blend. Others are sold ready-mixed in versions ranging from mild to hot, to cater for all palates.

Shiso

See PERILLA.

Shoyu

See SOY SAUCE.

Shrimp

See PRAWNS.

Shrimp, Dried

Dried shrimp are usually sold in plastic packets either whole or shredded (labelled powder or floss). I prefer to buy packets of whole shrimp because it is easier to judge the quality. They should be deep salmon pink and yield only slightly to the touch. Don't buy them if the prawns are hard like chips of wood or smell strongly of ammonia. Kept refrigerated, they should last for months. If they develop a strong smell, rinse in warm water and leave to dry. If they become powdery, or start to disintegrate, discard them. Used in Asian cuisine both as a flavouring agent (added to vegetable stir-fries, seafood and soups) and main ingredient. See recipes below and recipe for Thai Chilli and Shrimp Sauce (page 332).

China: *hay bee*
Indonesia: *eibei*
Japan: *ebi*
Malaysia: *udang kering*
Thailand: *goong haeng*
Vietnam: *tom kho*

Burmese Dried Shrimp Relish (Balachaung)

Mention balachaung to someone from Burma and watch them get misty-eyed over this popular accompaniment. It is served with rice, and even used as a sandwich filling by those who succumb to its charms. It may be crisp and dry, or it may be oily. I prefer the drier version.

250 g/8 oz/2 cups dried shrimp
20 cloves garlic, peeled and sliced
  or 3 tablespoons dried garlic flakes
185 g/6 oz/1 cup thinly sliced shallots,
  or 60 g/2 oz/1 cup crisp-fried sliced shallots
375 ml/12 fl oz/1½ cups peanut oil
125 ml/4 fl oz/½ cup sesame oil
ground dried chillies to taste
2 teaspoons salt
2 cm/1 in square of dried shrimp paste
½ cup vinegar

Put the dried shrimp into a food processor and process with steel blade to a floss. If using fresh garlic and shallots, fry them separately in heated peanut and sesame oil, not hurrying the process, until golden. They will become crisp as they cool. The best balachaung I have tasted was made by my mother and grandmother who did it the old-fashioned way, peeling and slicing shallots and garlic cloves. For ease one may use dried garlic flakes, but take care to keep the heat low and lift them out in a wire strainer before they darken, otherwise they will become bitter. Drain on paper towels. Pour off 1 cup of oil if you prefer a relish that is not too oily. (Bottle and use as flavouring.)

Reheat remaining oil and fry the prawn floss for 5 minutes, stirring constantly. Add chillies mixed with the vinegar, salt and shrimp paste. Fry until crisp, stirring constantly. Allow to cool completely before mixing in the fried onion and garlic, stirring to distribute evenly. Store in an airtight jar and it will keep for months.

Sri Lankan Dried Shrimp Sambal

125 g/4 oz/1 cup dried shrimp
90 g/3 oz/1 cup desiccated coconut
3 teaspoons chopped red chillies
  or sambal ulek (recipe page 91)
2 medium onions, chopped
2 tablespoons chopped garlic
185 ml/6 fl oz/¾ cup lime or lemon juice
1 teaspoon salt or to taste

Floss prawns in a blender or food processor.
Put desiccated coconut in a dry frying pan and

toast, stirring constantly, until a rich brown colour. Immediately turn out onto a plate to cool.

Blend chillies, onion, garlic, lime juice and salt to a smooth purée in a blender, add coconut and blend again, adding a little water if necessary to produce a smooth paste. Add shrimp floss and blend again, scraping down sides of goblet with a spatula. Serve as a relish with rice and curries.

Shrimp Paste, Dried

A pungent paste made from fermented prawn (shrimp). There is hardly a South East Asian kitchen where dried shrimp paste of one kind or another is not essential. Sold in cans, jars, slabs and cakes, it keeps indefinitely without refrigeration. Once opened, store in a tightly closed jar. Some shrimp pastes (blacan, trasi, ngapi) are in firm blocks and must be cut into cubes or slices. There are other kinds which come as a soft, thick paste and may be spooned from jars (see SHRIMP SAUCE). All are used not just to add flavour, but also to provide protein.

Its odour may be very off-putting on first acquaintance, but the magic it works when added to a dish is known to all good cooks. Its use is not confined to seafood dishes. Many beef, pork, poultry or vegetable dishes also owe something to the addition of shrimp paste. It is sometimes just a subtle hint, while at other times it is knock-you-down powerful, for instance in the Burmese sambal known as ngapi htaung.

Dried shrimp paste is always cooked before eating, and since it is usually part of the rempah (spice base), it does get fried as a preliminary step to preparing a dish. However, if the other ingredients are to be eaten fresh and raw, the shrimp paste is usually grilled or roasted. The best way to achieve this without smelling out the entire house is to wrap a small square in foil, folding in the edges to enclose it completely. Grill it for 2 or 3 minutes. Turn and repeat. If the slice cut off the block is thin, about 6 mm (¼ in), a couple of minutes on each side under a preheated grill is plenty.

Burma: *ngapi*
Indonesia: *trasi*
Malaysia: *blacan, blachan*
Thailand: *kapi*
Vietnam: *mam tom*

Roasted Shrimp Paste Relish (Ngapi Htaung)

A favourite in Burma, this is served in small quantities with rice.

60 g/2 oz dried shrimp paste
2 medium onions
4 whole large cloves garlic, unpeeled
2 tablespoons dried shrimp floss
2 teaspoons chilli powder
1 teaspoon salt
2 tablespoons lime or lemon juice

Press the shrimp paste into a flat cake, wrap in aluminium foil, folding in the edges to seal, and grill under a preheated griller for 10 minutes, turning to cook both sides. Wrap onions and garlic in foil and put under the griller with the shrimp paste. When cool, remove and discard skin of onion and garlic. These ingredients are pulverised using a large mortar and pestle or in an electric blender until very smooth, and the remaining ingredients are then mixed in.

Rojak

More subtly used than in the previous recipe, a dressing flavoured with shrimp paste is what turns a salad into rojak. The dressing may be made more spicy by adding, to taste, ground chillies, ground peanuts, and thick black shrimp sauce called hay koh. Serves 6.

1 pomelo or 2 mandarins
1 seedless cucumber
1 small half-ripe pineapple
1 half-ripe mango
2 tablespoons finely sliced chillies
1 small yam bean
1 square firm bean curd

DRESSING

3 tablespoons Chinese red vinegar
   or tamarind liquid
3 tablespoons lime juice
2 tablespoons palm sugar or brown sugar
1 tablespoon kecap manis (sweet soy sauce)
1 teaspoon dried shrimp paste,
   wrapped in foil and roasted under grill
4 tablespoons crushed, roasted peanuts
salt to taste

Peel and segment the citrus fruit and remove the covering membrane. Cut cucumber into halves, then into fine strips. Remove skin and 'eyes' of pineapple as described in the entry for PINEAPPLE. Cut in quarters lengthwise and remove core, then dice the flesh. Peel mango and cut in thin strips. Peel yam bean and cut into fine strips. Slice bean curd. Put all into a bowl. Combine the ingredients for the dressing, stir well, and pour over. Cover and chill.

Shrimp Paste, Fresh

Fresh shrimp paste is not a pungent seasoning like dried shrimp paste, but a minced (ground) shrimp mixture which is made and used on the same day, preferably within hours. Peeled, deveined, raw shrimp is pounded or blended with a small amount of pork fat (about one-sixth its weight), seasoned with salt and pepper and sugar, perhaps a touch of pounded shallot or crushed garlic, and a little egg white mixed in. The paste is used to make fillings for steamed dumplings, small balls for soup, patties for grilling or frying or is moulded onto slender sticks of fresh sugar cane and grilled over coals — the famous Vietnamese snack chao tom.

Shrimp Sauce

There is more than one kind of shrimp sauce. In an Asian supermarket, bottles of many shapes and sizes bear the label of shrimp sauce. They have one thing in common —a frighteningly strong smell. To the aficionado they each have their own characteristics and uses.

Shrimp sauce usually denotes a product which is served as an accompaniment, rather than as an ingredient which must be cooked. Yet, with the perversity of labelling which seems to observe no rules, some shrimp sauces should be cooked.

Read the labels. Most tell you only what the ingredients are. If one of the ingredients is oil, chances are the mixture in the bottle has been cooked. Even those which contain only 'fermented shrimp, salt and water' may be diluted and used as a condiment, though cautious cooks advise heating first to sterilise the sauce.

Shrimp sauce: A product of Hong Kong where it is known as hom ha. A soft paste usually greyish pink in colour and of an easily spoonable consistency. Labelled 'fine shrimp sauce' or 'fine shrimp paste' or 'sauce de crevette raffinee'. Used as a seasoning when stir-frying leafy greens such as water spinach.

Chinese cooks might add it to marinades for chicken which is to be deep fried or pork which is to be steamed.

As a condiment, it is dissolved in water with lime juice, finely sliced onion and chillies. Popular as a dip with stir-fried octopus or cuttlefish.

In Vietnam, where it is known as mam ruoc, it is sometimes a flavouring in rice noodle soups.

Bagoong alamang: Product of the Philippines. Basically a salty, pungent sauce of pouring consistency made from tiny shrimps and salt, used as an accompaniment. It looks like anchovy sauce and the shrimps do not retain their shape to the same extent as they do in Malaysian cincalok. Some varieties are called 'sauteed shrimp sauce', the bagoong having been cooked with onions, garlic and chillies.

There are various types. The word is used also to describe a thick fish sauce of pouring consistency (bagoong balayan).

Cincalok: Product of Malaysia. Minute pink shrimps complete with shells, each no larger than a fingernail paring, with eyes like black pin points. These are fermented in brine and sold in glass jars. Used as a dipping sauce, just as is, or mixed with lime or kalamansi juice and finely chopped shallots. In Singapore and Malaysia cincalok (pronounced chin-cha-lo) enlivens the flavours of steamed eggplant, okra and long beans.

A Nonya recipe for belly pork uses a marinade of cincalok with finely ground garlic, onion, lemon grass, fresh chilli and gelugor. The pork is then steamed until tender. A Hainanese variation is to stir-fry thinly sliced pork with garlic and cincalok.

Petis udang, hay koh: Product of Malaysia. Also spelled heiko. In Nonya cooking, this black shrimp sauce which looks like molasses is made from shrimp, salt, sugar, flour and water. Dissolved in a little water it is served as a condiment and added at the diner's discretion. It is commonly added to Penang laksa, a fish soup which is sour with tamarind and uses no coconut milk; but never added to Singapore laksa with its rich coconut milk soup. Thinned down, hay koh is also served as an accompaniment to rojak, a type of salad, or may be included as part of the dressing.

Petis udang should not be confused with patis (Philippines), the latter being a clear, salty fish sauce almost identical to nam pla and nuoc mam.

> **China:** *hom ha, hay koh*
> **Malaysia:** *petis*
> **Vietnam:** *mam ruoc*

Silver Leaf

Edible silver leaf, finer than tissue paper, is used in Indian cuisine to garnish special festive dishes on grand occasions. It can be purchased at Indian specialty food shops and some art suppliers. It is made from pure silver, small blocks of which are interleaved with paper, wrapped in leather and then beaten with a constant, drumming action (which effectively puts a stop to conversation if one is anywhere near the shops which make it) until uniformly thin. In India silver leaf is known as varak. Even more expensive is beaten gold leaf. Besides being very decorative it is reputed to have an aphrodisiac effect.

Singapore

The Lion City, as the name 'Singa Pura' translates, only came into its own as a vital sea port and exporter of rare and exotic foodstuffs in the 19th century. Sago, tea, sugar, cloves, coriander, cassia, nutmeg and that most sought-after spice, black pepper, were the precious cargo.

By the start of the 20th century, Singapore was the cosmopolitan hub of Asia, trading in commodities such as ebony, ivory, gold, silk and cotton.

The original melting pot, the culture that is now so distinctively Singaporean is the result of a mingling of many ethnic backgrounds and their time-honoured traditions. Moslems and Buddhists live side by side, Indians and Chinese cook side by side, and as a result there has been an inexorable blurring of the edges.

A fusion food culture is nowhere more clearly illustrated than in the emergence of Nonya cuisine. The cuisine of the Straits-born Chinese reflects their mixed Malay and Chinese heritage (see NONYA).

Singapore is a haven for the professional as well as amateur gastronome. Cuisines as diverse as Indian, Japanese and Chinese are represented by establishments fit for royalty. But the spirit of Singapore is captured best in its open-air eating places and street stalls. The Orchard Road car park of old, a car park by day where by night itinerant food hawkers once strutted their stuff under a canopy of stars has been replaced by modern, air-conditioned food courts or, as the Singaporeans like to call them, hawker centres. Don't be fooled into thinking that price reflects quality. The food at hawker centres can be even tastier than at the most prestigious and expensive restaurants.

Some of Singapore's most famous dishes, laksa lemak, chilli crab, satays, char kway teow (tasty stir-fried rice noodles) and otak-otak (spicy char-grilled fish cakes) bear testament to the island nation's love of chilli and spices.

Snake

Among traditional Chinese, late autumn is the time of year to partake of snake soup to prevent winter chills. When a Chinese friend told me this, I asked, half unbelieving, 'What kind of snake and where would you buy it?' The answer is that five kinds of snake are supposed to make up the packets of frozen snake meat imported from China. He says snake tastes somewhat like chicken. It is combined in strong chicken stock with white meat of chicken or pork, fish maw, ham, dried mushrooms and bamboo shoot, flavoured with fresh ginger and dried tangerine peel, and the traditional garnishes are fresh white chrysanthemum petals, finely shredded lemon leaves and crisp-fried strips of wonton pastry.

It is a restaurant dish rather than something one whips up for a family meal at home. Snake soup, with its capacity to get one's metabolism into top gear, is priced to appeal to well-heeled diners.

Snake Bean

See YARD-LONG BEAN.

Snake Gourd

See GOURDS.

Snow Pea

See LEGUMES & PULSES.

Soba

See NOODLES.

Sorrel

The soft-leaved French sorrel is, to the best of my knowledge, not used in Asia. Perhaps the climate is too severe for it to grow, otherwise I'm sure it would find favour along with the many other sour-tasting leaves which are common fare. It may be used as a substitute for tamarind leaves and roselle leaves in Burmese, Thai or Philippine sour soups or to dip in nam prik. More widespread in Asia is Jamaican or Indian sorrel. See ROSELLE.

Soup

Unlike the soup course in a Western meal, soup in Asia is seldom served as a course on its own but more often alongside rice to moisten and flavour, occasionally sipped from the bowl or spoon.

There are, of course, exceptions. For example, at Chinese banquets the soup may be the high point of the meal, especially if the main ingredient is shark's fin or bird's nest.

In Japan, clear soups are served at the start of a meal and miso soup at the end of a meal. Neither are mixed with food. Soup is sipped from the bowl held in both hands. No spoon is used.

Soup in Asia and the Pacific, served as part of a meal or as a one-dish meal, is as diverse as the races of this region.

There are the hot, piquant, thin soups of Thailand (tom yum); clear, piquant soups of Cambodia (chhrook); the gently flavoured one-dish meal of Vietnam (pho); the t'ang of China, ranging from rich and unctuous to light and palate cleansing; the Tamil mulligatawny (pepper-water) of India; and the simple but elegant miso soups of Japan. Some soups have gained such acclaim that they have acquired the status of national dishes, such as the spicy laksa of Singapore and Malaysia or Burma's famous banana trunk soup, Moh Hin Gha. Korea's kaleidescope of soups, kuk and tang, run the gamut from delicate dumpling broth to hearty gruel. An array of fish, meat, vegetable and legume soups hail from the Philippines and vegetable soups using local ingredients like green papaya, sweet potato vines and taro leaves together with many varieties of seafood chowder are popular throughout the Pacific islands.

Vietnamese Pho

Serves 4–6

SOUP

2 kg/4 lb beef bones
500 g/1 lb shin (gravy) beef
1 whole onion, peeled
6 cloves
1 teaspoon whole black peppercorns
1 knob of ginger, sliced
1 stick cinnamon
3 star anise
5 cardamom pods
2 carrots
1 sprig celery leaves
2 tablespoons fish sauce

TO SERVE

500 g/1 lb fresh rice noodles
250 g/8 oz fresh mung bean sprouts,
  roots removed
500 g/1 lb beef fillet, thinly sliced
2 white onions, thinly sliced
mint sprigs
chopped coriander
sliced chillies

Put bones and beef, onion stuck with cloves, whole spices and all the other soup ingredients into a large stockpot and add cold water to cover, about 5 litres (10 pints). Bring to the boil, skimming top several times. Turn heat very low, cover and simmer for 6 hours. Add salt to taste. Remove beef and cut into thin slices. Set aside. Strain stock, return to pan and keep on the simmer.

Pour boiling water over rice noodles, drain. Put a serving of noodles in each bowl and top with a handful of bean sprouts. In a large ladle put some slices of beef and onions. Dip ladle into boiling soup until beef is pale pink. Pour over noodles, and add more soup to each bowl. Serve immediately, with a plate of mint, coriander and chillies, to be added as wished. Lime or lemon wedges and fish sauce are passed separately.

Szechwan Hot and Sour Soup

Having strong stock on hand is a great time-saver. Freeze it in meal-sized portions. Serves 6.

1.5 litres/3 pints/6 cups pork or chicken stock
60 g/2 oz bean thread vermicelli, cooked

200 g/7 oz/1 cup finely chopped cooked pork or
  chicken
4 dried Chinese mushrooms,
  soaked and chopped
1 small can bamboo shoot, chopped
1 teaspoon finely grated fresh ginger
1 tablespoon cornflour (cornstarch)
1 egg, slightly beaten
1–2 tablespoons tomato sauce
½ teaspoon salt or to taste
1 tablespoon Chinkiang or cider vinegar
ground black pepper to taste
2 teaspoons oriental sesame oil
2 spring onions (scallions), finely chopped
1 teaspoon chilli oil, or to taste

Strain stock, chill and remove fat from surface. Bring to the boil in a large pan and add noodles cut in short lengths, pork or chicken, mushrooms, bamboo shoot and ginger. Mix cornflour smoothly with 3 tablespoons cold water and add to simmering soup, stirring constantly until it boils and clears. Pour beaten egg into soup in a fine stream, stirring rapidly with chopsticks or fork so it sets in fine shreds. Remove soup from heat, add remaining ingredients and mix well, adjust seasoning to taste. The taste should be quite sour and hot.

Spicy Chicken Soup

This is a Malaysian version of a one-pot meal, substantial and spicy. Serves 4.

1.5 kg/3 lb roasting chicken
  or chicken drumsticks and thighs
2 litres/4 pints/8 cups cold water
3 teaspoons salt
½ teaspoon whole black peppercorns
few celery tops
1 large brown onion, sliced
2 tablespoons peanut oil
2 salam leaves or 6 curry leaves
1 teaspoon finely chopped garlic
1 teaspoon finely grated fresh ginger
½ teaspoon dried shrimp paste (blacan)
½ teaspoon ground turmeric
3 teaspoons ground coriander
1 teaspoon ground cumin
4 candle nuts, finely grated
250 g/8 oz rice vermicelli
3 large potatoes, cooked and halved
lemon juice to taste

GARNISH

8 spring onions (scallions), finely sliced
3 hard-boiled eggs, quartered
crisply fried shallots

Cut chicken into joints and put into a large saucepan with enough cold water to cover the chicken. Add salt, peppercorns, celery tops and half the onion. Bring quickly to the boil, then lower heat, cover and simmer for 30 minutes or until chicken is tender. Cool to lukewarm, leaving chicken immersed in the liquid. Strain stock into a bowl, remove skin and bones from chicken and with a sharp knife cut flesh into dice or strips. Set aside.

Heat peanut oil in the saucepan and fry salam or curry leaves and the rest of the onion until onion is golden brown. Add garlic, ginger, shrimp paste and stir over medium heat, crushing the shrimp paste with back of spoon. Add the turmeric, coriander, cumin and candle nuts and fry, stirring, for a few seconds longer. Add stock and bring to the boil, then reduce heat, cover and simmer for 10 minutes. Meanwhile cook rice vermicelli in boiling water for 3 minutes, drain and cut into short lengths. Add it to the simmering soup, return to the boil and cook for 1 minute. Add chicken meat, potatoes and lemon juice and heat through. Pour into a large soup tureen or individual soup plates and garnish with spring onions, egg and fried shallots.

Korean Dumpling Soup

Serves 4–6

2 litres/4 pints/8 cups beef stock
2 tablespoons light soy sauce
salt to taste
omelette strips to garnish
toasted, crumbled nori to garnish

DUMPLINGS

125 g/4 oz pork mince (ground pork)
125 g/4 oz lean beef mince (ground beef)
3 spring onions (scallions), finely chopped
1 tablespoon toasted, crushed sesame seeds
1 teaspoon chopped garlic
½ teaspoon salt
¼ teaspoon ground black pepper
125 g/4 oz wonton pastry squares

Prepare and de-fat beef stock. Add soy sauce and salt. Have garnishes ready. Prepare dumplings as described below, cover with plastic wrap and have ready. They may be made a few hours ahead and put on a lightly floured dish, not touching each other. Bring stock to the boil and drop in the dumplings a few at a time, taking care they do not stick together. If necessary cook them in batches. Simmer for 10 minutes or until dumplings come to the surface and are cooked. Serve immediately in small bowls.

Dumplings: Mix all ingredients together. Put a teaspoonful of the filling in the centre of each square of pastry, dampen edges with water and press together to form a triangle. Cover so they do not dry out before cooking.

See Index of Recipes for listing of soup recipes.

Soursop

(*Annona muricata*) SEE ILLUSTRATION. Elongated heart-shaped fruit with deep green to yellow-green skin dotted at intervals with short, soft, fleshy hooks. Sometimes called prickly custard apple. The largest of the Annona family (see CUSTARD APPLE), the soursop can weigh up to 3 kg (6 lb).

Possibly the member of the Annona family most heartily embraced by the Asian palate, it is made into a refreshingly sour drink sold in single-serving cans.

The white interior is sweet yet tangy and often inedibly fibrous, requiring straining. The pulp is ideal for making into juice, smoothies, sorbets and ice cream and takes on a thick, creamy consistency blended with water alone. The strained pulp is blended with ice and condensed milk (or sugar and milk) to make a delicious drink.

Like other members of the Annona family (custard apple and cherimoya), it has large, hard, shiny black or brown seeds which need to be removed prior to pulping. The seeds are said to be toxic.

Fiji: *seremaia*
India: *seetha*
Indonesia: *sirsak*
Malaysia: *durian belanda, duran maki*
Philippines: *guayabano*
Sri Lanka: *katu-anoda*
Thailand: *thurian thet, thurian khaek, ma thurian*
Vietnam: *mang cua*

Soy Bean, Dried

(*Glycine max*) Also known as soya bean. The richest natural vegetable food, the soy bean is the only pulse which contains protein (20–35 per cent, depending on country of origin), complex carbohydrate, vitamin A, niacin, thiamin and riboflavin from the B group, potassium, calcium, magnesium and iron, making it the richest of all vegetable foods.

Soy beans are among the hardest beans dried, and need at least 15 hours soaking time and long cooking before they are edible. They contain a trypsin inhibitor which must be destroyed through long soaking and cooking before the protein is available to the body. This may explain why, in the orient, they are processed into readily digestible products: bean curd, soy milk, and fermented products such as Japanese miso, Chinese salted black beans, Indonesian tempeh and soy sauce.

There are many varieties of soy beans apart from the familiar dried yellow beans we see in health food shops. Growing on an annual plant, the seeds may be green, yellow, grey, brown or black.

Yellow soy beans are used for soy bean curd, soy milk, soy flour, soy grits and soy sauce. These are also the pale yellow beans sold in health food stores. They need long soaking (preferably overnight) and long cooking, changing the water half way through. It is important that they should be boiled vigorously for 20 minutes.

Black soy beans are easier to cook, needing less time. They are used for making fermented black beans so popular in Chinese cooking, and are also the basis of black bean paste, both salty (dow see) and sweet (dow sah), and black bean sauce.

> **China:** *wong dau, mao dau,*
> *hak dau, tai dau*
> **Indonesia:** *kacang kedalai*
> **Japan:** *daizu, eda mame*
> **Korea:** *jaa jang*
> **Malaysia:** *kedalai*
> **Philippines:** *utaw*
> **Thailand:** *thua lueang*

Soy Bean, Fresh

SEE ILLUSTRATION. Better known in their dried state, soy beans are also popular in some countries cooked fresh. Green seeded soy beans are grown for using fresh as they are the most tender and well flavoured. They are enclosed in small furry pods with from 2 to 6 seeds in each pod. The pods grow on an erect, bushy plant up to 2 m (6 ft) high with short, brownish hairs covering its stems and leaves.

Soy beans are fiddly to shell while raw, so the best method is to drop the whole pods into lightly salted boiling water. Very young, tender beans need just to be brought back to the boil for 2 or 3 minutes. Peel one, taste and decide whether it is cooked sufficiently. If necessary cook them for a little longer. Drain, refresh under cold water and peel. Discard the pods.

The beans can be added to salads, tossed with pasta, or served as a vegetable accompaniment. They are a very popular snack with beer in Japan and Taiwan. Recently, in some top Western restaurants, fresh soy beans have begun appearing on menus.

Because soy beans contain a trypsin inhibitor, it is inadvisable to eat them raw.

> **China:** *da dau*
> **Indonesia:** *kacang soja*
> **Japan:** *daizu, endamame*
> **Malaysia:** *kacang soja*

Fresh Soy Beans with Bean Curd

Serves 4

250 g/8 oz fresh or frozen soy beans
2 tablespoons peanut oil
5 thin round slices ginger
1 clove garlic, bruised
1 small red capsicum (bell pepper), diced
2 cups chopped gai larn or choy sum,
cut into bite-sized lengths
125 ml/4 fl oz/½ cup light stock
2 tablespoons light soy sauce
½ teaspoon sugar
2 teaspoons cornflour (cornstarch)
250 g/8 oz firm tofu, diced
½ teaspoon oriental sesame oil

Blanch and peel the soy beans as described above. Heat peanut oil in a wok and fry the ginger and garlic until golden. Add capsicum, soy beans and gai larn and stir-fry for 2 minutes. Add stock, soy sauce and sugar and when it comes to the boil stir in the cornflour mixed smoothly with a tablespoon of cold water. When it boils and thickens turn heat down, slip in the diced bean curd and gently heat through. Sprinkle with sesame oil and serve.

Soy Bean Products

Miso: Japan's famous bean paste made from cooked, mashed, salted, fermented soy beans. It varies in colour, texture and saltiness and is used for flavouring soups, salad dressings and pickles. In the Philippines, a similar preparation called misi, which is saltier than miso, is made from cooked, salted, fermented soy beans.

Miso Soup

Serves 4

5 cups dashi
2 tablespoons aka miso (red bean paste)
4 cubes tofu (bean curd)
2 spring onions (scallions), sliced diagonally
2 sliced mushrooms

Bring dashi to the boil, then mix some of the hot liquid with the bean paste in a small bowl, stirring until smooth. Pour mixture back into saucepan, stir well, add bean curd and spring onions and return to the boil. Simmer for a few seconds only.

Ladle into bowls, garnish each with a slice or two of mushroom and serve hot.

Natto: The Japanese preparation of fermented soy beans which renders them dark brown, strong-smelling and tasting, and sticky-slimy in texture. Normally hard to digest because of their carbo-hydrate/protein composition, the fermented beans are easily digested due to the breakdown of protein in the fermentation process.

Soy bean paste: Dried soy beans are soaked in water and ground to a paste which, in Japan, is known as 'go'. This is used to make soy milk and bean curd. It is vital to use the paste in a very fresh state.

Soy milk: A popular drink in many Asian countries and increasingly in Western countries. It is sold fresh (refrigerated), in long-life cartons, or canned. It has many health-giving properties and is believed to be beneficial for conditions including anaemia (it is rich in iron), diabetes (it is low in starch), heart disease, high blood pressure and hardening of the arteries (it is low in saturated fats and high in lecithin and linoleic acid — lowering harmful LDL cholesterol levels and raising levels of protective HDL cholesterol).

It has been credited with softening corns, strengthening the digestive system, alkalising the bloodstream, stemming chronic nosebleed, healing persistent bruises and restoring colour to black hair. In Japan the thickest soy milk — used to make kinugoshi (the rich, smooth custard-like soft tofu) is considered the most delicious. A thinner soy milk, used for making tofu, is the preferred beverage in other parts of Asia.

To make soy milk, add go to a pan of water and bring to a foaming boil, stirring with a wooden spatula to prevent sticking. Strain and squeeze mixture through muslin to separate liquid from solids. Return liquid to pan and cook for 10 minutes longer. This resulting soy milk may be flavoured and drunk as a beverage or further processed to make bean curd (tofu).

The residue of solids, a by-product of making soy milk and tofu, is called okara. The okara, a protein rich source of dietary plant fibre, may be added to soups, salads, burgers and croquettes, soufflés, scrambled eggs and omelettes. It is used in baking (muffins, breads and cookies) and gives much lighter results than flour alone.

In Indonesia, fermented soy beans are the basis for tasty little protein-packed cakes called tempeh (see TEMPEH).

Tahuri: A fermented soy bean product made in the Philippines by packing cakes of firm moulded bean curd with salt. No alcohol or brine is used in the process. Matured for several months, it turns a brownish-yellow and acquires a complex salty flavour.

Tokwa (tokwan): A very firm, square tofu with slightly enhanced handling and keeping qualities. All the same, it needs refrigeration and should be used within a few days. Mashed and mixed with meat to extend the protein and increase the nutrition, it may also be sliced and deep fried, then used like age (see BEAN CURD).

Soy Bean Sprouts

Soy bean sprouts are larger than mung bean sprouts, and can be recognised by their colour (deep yellow instead of white) and their seed head, the size of a peanut. While not as readily available nor as universally popular as mung bean sprouts, these large, long bean sprouts are nutritious and supply a level of protein unusual in a vegetable. To store them, rinse, drain and cover with water and refrigerate for a few days, changing water daily.

Soy bean sprouts contain less calories per gram of protein than any other vegetable food and are a traditional ingredient in Korean soups and salads.

While mung bean sprouts may be eaten raw, soy bean sprouts must be cooked, because they contain a trypsin inhibitor which impedes action of the enzyme trypsin, secreted by the pancreas for the digestion of protein and maintenance of normal growth.

William Shurtleff and Akiko Aoyagi, experts on soy products and authors of *The Book of Tofu* and *The Book of Tempeh* recommend that soy bean sprouts, even for a salad, be parboiled for a minimum of 4 minutes to inactivate the trypsin inhibitor.

Unlike mung bean sprouts, the white sprouted 'stalk' of a soy bean sprout tends to be stringy — chewy at best, tough at worst. The bean end is definitely the best part, so when trimming the root ends off the tails, don't be too timid. Because soy beans are thought to be 'cooling', ginger is sometimes cooked with them to generate digestive 'heat'.

See also BEAN SPROUTS.

China: *dai dau nga choi*
India: *bhat*
Indonesia: *kacang kedele, taugeh*
Japan: *daizu, daizu no moyashi*
Korea: *kong namul*
Malaysia: *kacang soja, taugeh*
Philippines: *utaw*
Thailand: *thua-lueang*

Soy Bean Sprout Salad

250 g/8 oz soy bean sprouts
1 tablespoon oriental sesame oil
2 tablespoons peanut oil
2 tablespoons toasted sesame seeds, crushed
3 tablespoons Korean soy sauce
2 teaspoons ginger juice pressed from
 grated ginger
2 spring onions (scallions), finely chopped

Trim roots off bean sprouts and discard. If sprouts are long cut into convenient lengths. Drop into a pan of lightly salted boiling water and boil until just tender. Drain, drop into iced water and drain again. Combine all other ingredients and toss with sprouts. Serve chilled.

Soy Sauce

Soy sauce was invented by the Chinese and introduced to Japan about a thousand years ago. Devised as a means of preserving food, the first soys were in all probability liquid bean sauces.

Soy sauce is a naturally fermented product made from ground soy beans, roasted wheat (or other grain) and mould starter. After fermentation has begun, salt equal to the original weight of the soy beans is added, together with *Lactobacillus* (the starter used for yoghurt) and yeast. The resultant mash is allowed to age. When sufficiently mellow, it is strained and bottled. Beware of imitation soy sauce, produced synthetically from hydrolysed vegetable protein and coloured with corn syrup or caramel.

Only two products can be relied upon to be pure soy sauces: shoyu and tamari. Shoyu, which contains a higher percentage of roasted cracked wheat than its Chinese 'dark soy' sauce counterpart, is not as salty. Tamari should contain no wheat, although true tamari is rare, even in Japan. A dark, rich soy sauce is also brewed with rice (the original method learned from the Chinese), making it safe for people with a wheat allergy. Some Japanese shoyu is produced with less salt, and labelled as such for those who need to watch their intake of sodium.

There are many different kinds of soy sauce, but the majority fit into two main categories: light and dark. Light soy sauce is thinner, saltier and more appropriate when it is desirable not to change the colour of an ingredient. In Vietnam, for instance, light soy sauce is used for dipping and sauces while dark soy sauce is used for cooking. Dark soy sauce is thicker and darker in colour due to longer brewing and the addition of molasses. It is used to add a rich, dark-brown colour to the appearance of a dish, as in red-cooking. It is also not quite as salty as light soy sauce.

Chinese soy sauces

Dark soy sauce: Used for colour and flavour. Suitable for red meat and chicken, red-cooking and 'master sauce' (also called 'flavour pot' or lu). The only soy sauce used in northern China.

Light soy sauce: Usually labelled 'superior soy', it is saltier and will not darken food. Ideal for soups, seafood, vegetables and dipping sauces. Since most labelling does not state which type of soy the bottle contains, to distinguish between dark and light soy, tip the bottle and look at the neck. If it is only lightly tinged with colour (a pale gold) it is light. If the glass is stained with a rich brown and takes a while to clear, it is dark.

Mushroom soy sauce: Dark soy sauce that has been flavoured by straw mushrooms. It has a full, rich flavour and may be used in place of dark soy.

Japanese soy sauces

Koikuchi shoyu (regular shoyu): This is the most widely used Japanese soy sauce, less salty and lighter in colour than Chinese soy sauce. Made with cooked soy beans, wheat which has been roasted and crushed, and brine.

Tamari: Made with soy beans and rice or a much smaller amount of wheat (ideally none). It has a rich colour and flavour.

Usukuchi shoyu: Light in colour but saltier than regular shoyu.

Korean soy sauce

About the same colour value as Chinese light soy sauce, but not as fiercely salty and with a sweet, malted aroma.

Thick and flavoured soy sauces

Thick soy sauces are not interchangeable with any of the above mentioned soys in a recipe, owing to their very pronounced sweetness. Conversely, when a recipe calls for some of these regional soys, any of the above soys wouldn't really fit the bill, even with sugar added.

Kecap asin: A dark, salty soy sauce, from Indonesia, a little thicker than the dark soy of China.

Kecap manis: Because Java is one of the few South East Asian countries with a climate conducive to the growing of soy beans, the salty seasoning sauce here is soy rather than fish based. Kecap manis is a thick, sweet soy sauce.

Kicap cair: The Malaysian equivalent of light soy sauce.

Kicap pekat: The Malaysian equivalent of dark soy sauce, though thicker than the Chinese version, but not as thick as kecap manis.

Ponzu shoyu: A lemon flavoured soy sauce used in Japan.

Toyo mansi: A soy sauce used in the Philippines soured with kalamansi juice. This is used in addition to, not instead of, Chinese style soy sauce.

Spices

Who knows how different world history might have been if not for the value placed upon these products: seeds, berries, bark, flower buds, roots and rhizomes of a variety of plants. They provide the flavours which Europe demanded with sufficient gusto to send Portuguese, Spanish, Dutch and British seafarers across uncharted oceans to wrest the spice trade from the Arabs.

Until the sea routes were found and established, Arab traders had a monopoly on the lucrative spice trade. In time the land routes, including the famous Silk Road from China to the Mediterranean via India, were supplemented (and eventually supplanted) by sea routes, the first detailed records of which were made by an unknown Greek sea captain in the first century AD.

The Roman Empire began to trade directly with India, and when the Goths laid siege to Rome in AD 408, gold and pepper were included in the ransom demands. No doubt this pepper was in the form of whole pepper, not ground pepper, as it was the practice to adulterate precious spices — an offence punishable by death. It was probably long pepper they demanded, as the historian Pliny recorded that long pepper was worth four times as much as black peppercorns.

Constantinople (Istanbul) was built by the Roman emperor Constantine where ancient Byzantium used to be, and became the capital of the Eastern Roman or Byzantine Empire. Land and sea routes developed around this city, and for the first time cloves and nutmeg became known in the West, brought by seafarers from the Moluccas to India, China and Ceylon and from there to the spice routes dominated by Arabs and Romans.

After the fall of the Roman Empire its spice

trade diminished. Between 641 and 1096 AD, Arab conquests, including the takeover of Alexandria, ensured that they once again controlled the powerful commodities of gold, silk and spices.

It is not widely known that the Prophet Mohammed (570–632 AD), leader of Islam, was a spice merchant. When he was young, he worked with Meccan spice traders and eventually became a partner in a shop in Mecca, trading, among other things, in perfumes and oriental spices. He established a lucrative spice trade before he established the religion which bears his name. Four hundred years after his death, his followers were spreading the Moslem religion in India, Ceylon (Sri Lanka) and Java (Indonesia), conquering first by the sword and then by trade.

It was not until the Crusades, 1096–1204, that the pendulum swung again to give Europe, via Italian ports such as Venice, Genoa and Pisa, access to luxurious imports from the Holy Land. These included, apart from the almonds, figs, raisins, and dates which grew in the area, oriental spices such as cardamom, cloves, pepper and nutmeg, brought to the Near East (now known as the Middle East) by spice traders.

In 1180, a pepperers' guild of wholesale merchants (later to be incorporated in a spicers' guild) was established in London, still later (1429) to become the Grocers' Company. In the 16th century, the price of pepper in Antwerp served as a barometer for European business, much as the price of gold governs the market today.

When Constantinople fell to the Turks in 1453 and the spread of the Ottoman Empire made land routes unsafe, it became a priority to find a sea route to the Orient. Spanish and Portuguese navigators were to make their mark in doing so, and the names of Christopher Columbus, Vasco de Gama, Pedro Alvarez Cabral and Ferdinand Magellan, intrepid explorers of the 15th and 16th centuries, still illuminate the pages of history.

While Columbus's claim to fame is that he discovered the Americas, he was really searching for India and its fabled wealth and spices. Colombus died in 1506, still convinced that he had almost reached the eastern country he had sought to find by sailing west. (Which is why the natives of the lands that he did reach were referred to as 'Indians' though later with prefixes such as Mexican, North American, etc., to establish that these were not the people of the Indian subcontinent.)

Where Columbus failed others succeeded, paying a high price in lives lost through sickness and shipwreck. De Gama's voyage from Lisbon to Calicut around the Cape of Good Hope and across the Arabian Sea was most significant to the spice trade. It took just over 12 months, and after a stay of 6 months on the Malabar Coast, he returned to Portugal in 1499 bearing not only rare jewels and precious spices, but also an approach from the Hindu king, the zamorin of Calicut, to trade with the King of Portugal. He offered those items in which his country was rich — cinnamon, cloves, ginger, pepper and precious stones in exchange for gold, silver, corals and scarlet cloth.

Elated, King Manuel I of Portugal sent Pedro Alvarez Cabral back in March 1500 with a fleet of 13 caravels. It is not known to this day why he sailed west, crossed the South Atlantic and claimed Brazil for Portugal. He lost four ships off the Cape of Good Hope but, with what was left of the fleet, he reached Calicut in September the same year and traded with the king. On his return to Lisbon with cargoes of spices and gems, the centres of trade abruptly shifted from Venice and Alexandria to Lisbon.

By 1511 the Portuguese had gained control of the major spice-producing areas — the Malabar Coast in India, Ceylon, Java, Sumatra and Malacca. Later they took the Spice Islands. Their reign was a cruel one, full of violence, oppression, plunder and outright murder. In 1612, the Portuguese taxed the citizens of Ceylon on their land holdings and insisted the taxes be paid in pepper and currency.

Meanwhile, the British had established the British East India Company in 1600, and the Dutch East India Company was established in 1602. The arrival in the Indian Ocean of the more powerful fighting ships and well-trained soldiers of the Dutch was the beginning of the end for the Portuguese.

The Dutch ousted the Portuguese from the Spice Islands between 1605 and 1621, and took Ceylon in 1636. But this was no boon to the natives, for the Dutch exacted from them a stipulated amount of cinnamon bark and if the quota could not be met the punishment was severe — torture or death for men, severe whipping for the women. Thus it was that the Dutch established a monopoly over nutmeg, mace, cloves, pepper, ginger, turmeric and true cinnamon (native to Ceylon, as against cassia or bastard cinnamon which is native to China).

To break this monopoly, the French administrator of Mauritius, Pierre Poivre (a singularly appropriate name) managed to smuggle spice plants out of the Spice Islands and establish plantations in Reunion, the Seychelles and other French colonies. By 1796 the British had taken over all Dutch possessions in the East Indies, and Holland no longer was in control except in Java and Sumatra, which they held until World War II.

Near the end of the 18th century the United States entered the spice trade, bartering salmon, cod, tobacco, flour, soap, candles, cheese, butter and beef (salt beef is still a prized delicacy in Asia) for textiles, tea, coffee, pepper, cassia, cloves, cinnamon and ginger. There were fortunes made by entrepreneurs who financed the voyages of trading ships.

It says something about British taste buds that spices played a comparatively unimportant part in the economy of the British Empire — tea, sugar and other products were the leading commodities. In spite of being ousted by the British as the ruling sea power, the Dutch continued to lead in spice processing and production up to the early 20th century and many spice products which are Indonesian in origin are produced by Dutch firms and sold all over the world.

In the late 20th century, there are no longer monopolies. By a quirk of fate, the very spices native to Asia which Columbus was in search of when he stumbled upon America, are now being grown in the tropical parts of South America. Brazil grows black pepper, Guatemala grows cardamom, Granada grows nutmeg. Even more curious is that the spices found in the New World — especially chillies, became a staple flavouring of the food of Asia.

Spice Blends

Known as masalas in India, there are many different kinds. The nearest equivalent is curry powder, but no self-respecting Indian cook would use a commercial curry powder. The advantage of making masala is that the spices are freshly ground as required and can give each dish the individuality it demands. Making spice blends in small quantities ensures optimum flavour every time. However, it is often convenient to make a larger quantity. Stored correctly, it will last well. Store dry masalas in air-

tight glass jars in a cupboard protected from heat and sunlight. Store wet masalas or pastes in tightly stoppered glass jars in the refrigerator and use a clean dry spoon each time. Both dry and wet mixtures will keep perfectly for 6 months or more.

Dry spice blends are covered below. Pastes are discussed further under CURRY PASTES.

One of the best known spice blends is garam masala. There are as many versions as there are cooks. The recipes which follow are those I use. Feel free to modify them to create your own.

Use a heavy pan to roast the spices on very low heat. Roasting brings out the flavour, but keep stirring and remove from pan as soon as they are fragrant as scorching turns them bitter.

Roast cardamom in its pods. Large brown cardamom are then split by pounding roughly using a mortar and pestle or with the handle of a stout knife, to make it easier to remove the seeds. Discard the thick shells. Small green cardamom may be ground, pods and all, as the pods are thin enough to disintegrate. If you have the time and patience and decide to use only the seeds, the flavour will be more intense. This is decorticated cardamom.

Garam Masala

4 tablespoons coriander seeds
2 tablespoons cumin seeds
1 tablespoon whole black peppercorns
2 teaspoons cardamom seeds
  (measured after roasting and removing pods)
4 cinnamon quills
1 teaspoon whole cloves
1 whole nutmeg

In a dry wok or heavy frying pan roast individually the coriander seeds, cumin seeds, peppercorns, cardamom pods, cinnamon quills (roughly broken) and cloves. They need to be roasted individually because of varying sizes and moisture content. As each one starts to smell fragrant turn onto a plate to cool. After roasting, peel the cardamoms, discard pods and use only the seeds. Put all into an electric blender or spice grinder and grind to a fine powder. Finely grate the nutmeg and mix in. Store in a glass jar with an airtight lid.

Note: For convenience, the blend may be made using ground spices, roasting them over lowest heat as ground spices burn more readily. When fragrant, turn onto a plate to cool. Mix and store airtight.

Kashmiri Garam Masala

1 tablespoon small green cardamom pods
2 teaspoons black cumin
1 teaspoon nigella seeds
1 teaspoon whole black peppercorns
2 cinnamon quills
½ teaspoon whole cloves
1½ teaspoons freshly grated nutmeg
   (half a nutmeg)

Roast each spice (except nutmeg) separately, breaking cinnamon quill into pieces and separating the fine layers. Grind together to a fine powder. Add grated nutmeg and store airtight.

Kashmiri Garam Masala (2)

30 g/1 oz cumin seeds
30 g/1 oz large brown cardamom pods
30 g/1 oz fennel seeds
15 g/½ oz green cardamom pods
2 cinnamon quills
3 cassia leaves, optional
   (do not substitute bay leaves)
1 teaspoon ground cloves
2 teaspoons ground mace
1 whole nutmeg, finely grated

In a heavy pan roast separately the cumin seeds, brown cardamom pods, fennel seeds, green cardamom pods, cinnamon quills (broken into pieces) and cassia leaves until they are fragrant and slightly darker in colour. As each one is ready, turn onto a plate to cool.

Give the brown cardamom pods a few good thumps with a rolling pin, or in a mortar and pestle, just enough to break open the pods. Remove and discard the pods, reserve the seeds. (Pods of green cardamom have thin shells and may be ground together with the seeds.)

Grind the roasted spices to a fine powder. Sift out any large pieces, combine with the ground cloves, mace and nutmeg and store the powder airtight.

Panch Phora

A blend of five spice seeds which are added whole to the oil in the first stage of cooking.

2 tablespoons brown or black mustard seeds
2 tablespoons cumin seeds
2 tablespoons nigella (kalonji) seeds
1 tablespoon fenugreek seeds
1 tablespoon fennel seeds

Combine in a glass jar. Shake before use to ensure seeds are evenly mixed as the heavier seeds tend to gravitate to the bottom.

Milagai Podi

Also called idli podi, paruppu podi, dhal powder or 'gun powder'. A southern Indian blend of toasted pulses and spices which is ground to a powder and stored in an airtight jar. When required, a spoonful or two may be mixed with melted ghee and used like a chatni.

It is possible to buy milagai podi in a packet, but I have found it to be too hot and harsh, nothing like the blend which my southern Indian friends make at home to serve with idli or dosa (see recipe for Black Gram Pancakes, page 215). This crunchy spice mixture can be sprinkled on bread and butter, either crusty Western style loaves or flat Middle-Eastern bread.

3 tablespoons urad dhal
3 tablespoons channa dhal
3 tablespoons coriander seeds
   (or ground coriander)
6 tablespoons white sesame seeds
3 tablespoons ground rice
1 teaspoon black pepper or chilli powder
1 teaspoon asafoetida powder
2 teaspoons salt

In a dry pan roast each kind of dhal separately over medium-low heat until deep golden brown. The larger channa dhal will take longer than urad dhal. Roast coriander seeds until fragrant, stirring constantly. Using ground coriander will save time, but roasting the seeds and grinding it fresh makes for better flavour. Roast sesame seeds until golden brown, stirring so they are all evenly browned. Turn them out of the pan immediately they are done.

After roasting all the seeds and the ground

rice, combine and leave to cool on a baking tray. Pound to powder using a mortar and pestle, an electric blender or powerful coffee grinder reserved for spices. The ingredients should be powdered finely, but there will be crunchy bits of dhal which give it texture. Mix with the ground pepper or chilli powder, asafoetida and salt and store in an airtight jar.

To prepare the milagai podi for serving, melt 2 teaspoons of ghee, add 1 tablespoon oil, and stir in 3 tablespoons powder or sufficient to make a thick paste. This is served with idli or dosai. It can also be sprinkled on in powder form. Try it on fresh bread and butter or steamed potatoes.

Milagai Podi with Chillies

1 tablespoon oil
2½ tablespoons urad dhal
6 tablespoons channa dhal
5 large dried red chillies
3 tablespoons coriander seeds
2 teaspoons whole black peppercorns
2 tablespoons very finely sliced ginger
6 large cloves garlic, peeled and finely sliced
handful of dried curry leaves
3 teaspoons salt

Heat oil in a heavy pan or a wok and on low heat roast all ingredients together, except the curry leaves and salt, stirring constantly, for 10 minutes or until they are brown and smell fragrant. The curry leaves will burn if subjected to this roasting, so leave them out until the roasting is done and mix through. Spread on a tray and leave until cool, then grind to powder in an electric blender. Mix in salt and store in a jar.

Ceylon (Sri Lanka) Curry Powder

75 g/2½ oz/1 cup coriander seeds
60 g/2 oz/½ cup cumin seeds
1 tablespoon fennel seeds
1 teaspoon fenugreek seeds
1 cinnamon stick
1 teaspoon whole cloves
1 teaspoon cardamom seeds
2 tablespoons dried curry leaves
2 teaspoons chilli powder (optional)
2 tablespoons ground rice (optional)

In a dry pan over low heat, roast separately the coriander, cumin, fennel and fenugreek, stirring constantly until each one becomes fairly dark brown. Do not let them burn. Put into a blender container together with cinnamon stick broken in pieces, cloves, cardamom and curry leaves. Blend on high speed until finely powdered. Combine with chilli powder and ground rice if used. Store in an airtight jar.

Indian Curry Powder

While most Indian home cooks blend spices for individual dishes, it is very convenient to have on hand an all-purpose curry powder. If it is kept airtight and out of direct sunlight, it should retain its fragrance for a few months.

10 tablespoons coriander seeds
5 tablespoons cumin seeds
3 tablespoons fennel seeds
1 tablespoon whole black peppercorns
2 teaspoons fenugreek seeds
1 small stick cinnamon
15 small green cardamom pods
10 whole cloves
10 dried red chillies
50 freshly dried curry leaves
1 tablespoon ground turmeric

Dry roast each whole spice separately over medium heat until fragrant, but not long enough to darken the colour as required for Ceylon curry powder. Turn out onto a plate to cool. Grind finely in coffee grinder or electric blender, or pound using a mortar and pestle. Sift through a fine sieve, pound coarse residue and sift again. Stir through the curry leaves and ground turmeric and bottle airtight.

Spinach

(*Spinacea oleracea*) True spinach is the annual belonging to the Chenopodiaceae family with soft arrow-shaped leaves, hollow stems and slightly pinkish roots, commonly called English spinach. But the word is loosely applied to leafy greens of various families including Basellaceae (Ceylon spinach, Indian spinach), Convolvulaceae (water spinach or kangkung), Amaranthus (Chinese spinach or een choy) *Beta vulgaris* (spinach beet, silverbeet, seakale beet or chard), and Tetragonia spp. (New Zealand or Botany Bay spinach or

Warrigal greens). Each has a distinctly individual leaf, shape, colour and size. (SEE ILLUSTRATIONS of Ceylon spinach, Warrigal greens and water spinach.)

What they have in common is a high protein and vitamin A content, and more iron and calcium than many other green vegetables. They also have a high oxalic acid content, which when combined with the calcium and iron forms insoluble oxalates, preventing the digestive system benefiting from the minerals.

The soft green leaves are very popular, especially when cooked in a creamy sauce and subtly seasoned.

See also AMARANTH.

Purchasing and storing: Make sure the leaves are not wilted. Avoid crushing them in the shopping bag or basket. They can be kept for a day or two, wrapped loosely and stored in the vegetable bin of the refrigerator.

Preparation: Wash very well in several changes of cold water to get rid of any sand. Half fill a deep bowl or sink, shake leaves and stems vigorously, then lift out the spinach rather than pour the water past them. The sand will have settled on the bottom. Trim off roots and tough stems, cut into short lengths. Use as soon as possible.

Cooking: Steam in a tightly covered stainless steel pan with just the water that remains on the leaves after washing. Drain, roughly chop and season to taste.

Medicinal uses: Oxalic acid, contained in spinach, is not recommended for those with rheumatic problems. A little bit now and then will probably not have an effect unless one is in the middle of an acute episode.

Spiced Spinach and Potatoes

1 bunch spinach
250 g/8 oz new potatoes
2 teaspoons ghee
2 tablespoons oil
2 teaspoons brown mustard seeds
1 teaspoon cumin seeds
1 teaspoon ground coriander
½ teaspoon ground cumin
½ teaspoon ground turmeric
1 teaspoon salt or to taste
½ teaspoon grated nutmeg

Wash spinach well, put into a large non-aluminium saucepan and cook, covered, for 10 minutes. Scrub the potatoes and cut into quarters or eighths according to size.

In a wok heat ghee and oil and fry mustard and cumin seeds, covering wok with a frying screen, until mustard seeds have finished popping. Add ground spices and potatoes and fry for a minute, then add salt and ½ cup water, cover and cook for 10 minutes. Add spinach, cover and cook for 10 minutes longer. Sprinkle with nutmeg and serve with rice.

Spinach with Yoghurt

1 bunch spinach
2 teaspoons ghee or oil
1 teaspoon black mustard seeds
1 teaspoon cumin seeds
1 teaspoon ground cumin
pinch chilli powder (optional)
salt to taste
500 ml/1 pint/2 cups natural yoghurt

Wash spinach very well in several changes of water. Discard tough stems and steam leaves in a pan with very little water about 7 minutes or until spinach is tender. Drain spinach in colander and chop finely. Heat ghee or oil in a small pan, add mustard seeds and cover pan to prevent spattering. When mustard seeds have stopped popping add the cumin seeds and ground cumin. Stir for a few seconds. Remove from heat, stir in chilli powder and salt to taste, then stir the spices and spinach into the yoghurt. Serve at room temperature as a side dish with rice and curry.

Sponge Gourd

See GOURDS.

Spring Onion (Scallion)

(*Allium fistulosum*) SEE ILLUSTRATION. Also known as scallion. Sometimes what is sold as spring onions have a bulbous white base and these are most probably *Allium cepa* or common onions harvested young. Spring onions can also be found without the bulb, slender throughout their length and these are called bunching green onions or scallions in the United States, but in Australia were once mistakenly labelled shallots and, unfortunately, the name stuck. Both the white and green portions are used.

Spring Rain Noodles

Purchasing and storing: Buy slender specimens with plump, erect, deep-green leaves. They will keep in the crisper section of the refrigerator for a few days. To keep them fresh long term and have them on hand whenever needed, plant them in a pot and watch them flourish.

China: *da cong, tai tsung*
India: *hari piaz*
Indonesia: *daun bawang*
Japan: *negi*
Malaysia: *daun bawang*
Philippines: *sibuyas na mura*
Sri Lanka: *lunu kolle*
Thailand: *ton hom*
Vietnam: *hanh la*

Spring Rain Noodles

See NOODLES.

Spring Roll Pastry

Spring roll pastry is suitable for wrapping foods for deep frying, such as spring rolls, cha gio, lumpia (fried) and samosas. The light, pliable pastry is available frozen and comes in three sizes, 250 mm (10 in) square; 215 mm (8½ in) square; 125 mm (5 in) square. It is sometimes labelled 'egg roll wrappers', although it contains no egg at all. Allow a packet to thaw until pliable to facilitate separating without tearing the delicate layers. Peel off as many as required, reseal the packet and return the unused portion to the freezer.

As an alternative wrapper for samosas and singaras, spring roll pastry is a great time saver. Simply cut the large (25 cm/10 in square) sheet into three even strips. Place a teaspoon of cooked filling in the bottom corner and fold up in neat triangles, lining up the corners with the edge of the strip until you reach the end of the strip. Seal with water or flour and water mixed to a paste. Keep the remaining sheets covered with a clean tea towel as you work so they do not dry out before you get to them. Freeze until required or use immediately. Deep fry until golden brown or, if making ahead, pack airtight in freezer bags. The advantage of using spring roll pastry is that the samosas will not stick together.

Spring Rolls

Authentic spring rolls are delicate, delicious bite-sized morsels while often their Western namesake, grossly oversized, can be quite off-putting. Even among totally authentic spring rolls there are types that you may not immediately recognise as spring rolls if you've been accustomed only to the deep-fried variety. When next you visit a Vietnamese or Thai restaurant, try a serve of uncooked spring rolls. A transparent, fragile rice paper wrapper envelops the surprise package of cooked pork, prawns (shrimp), bean sprouts and rice vermicelli with a zesty hit of fresh mint or basil.

Fresh Spring Rolls

Makes 8

60 g/2 oz/½ cup dried shrimp
1 cup soaked rice vermicelli
1 or 2 chillies, finely sliced
3 teaspoons fish sauce
1 teaspoon lime juice
1 teaspoon sugar
1 tablespoon shredded salted radish
8 rice paper sheets
16 small cooked prawns (shrimp),
  shelled and deveined
about 48 mint or basil leaves
lettuce leaves
shredded carrot and white radish

CLEAR SAUCE
4 tablespoons sugar
125 ml/4 fl oz/½ cup cold water
2 tablespoons fish sauce
finely sliced red and green chilli
1 tablespoon lime juice or vinegar

Soak the dried shrimp in hot water for 10 minutes, drain and chop. Measure out the rice noodles after soaking them in hot water for 10 minutes. Drain well and chop into short lengths. Mix shrimp and noodles with chillies, fish sauce, lime juice and sugar. Simmer the shredded radish in water for a few minutes to remove excess salt. Drain and mix with noodles.

Dip a sheet of rice paper in warm water and lay on a flat surface until it softens. Place 2 prawns to one side of the rice paper and then a heaped tablespoon of the noodle mixture. Cover with about 6 basil leaves and a small piece of lettuce. Bring the ends of the rice paper together and roll up, enclosing the filling firmly, then arrange on lettuce leaves with the prawns showing through on top and the seam underneath.

Garnish with fine shreds of carrot and giant white radish, and serve with a clear sauce made by stirring all the ingredients together until sugar dissolves.

Note: Salted radish is sold in plastic packets. It has a reddish brown colour because it is partially dried.

Vietnamese Fried Spring Rolls

Makes about 24

½ cup soaked bean thread vermicelli
2 shallots, finely chopped
6 spring onions (scallions), finely chopped
250 g/8 oz minced (ground) pork
185 g/6 oz crab meat, frozen or canned
½ teaspoon salt
1 tablespoon fish sauce
¼ teaspoon ground black pepper
12 Chinese spring roll wrappers
  or 24 rice paper sheets
oil for deep frying
lettuce leaves
fresh mint, Vietnamese mint
  or coriander leaves
strips of cucumber
nuoc cham (see recipe page 157)

Soak a small skein (approx. 50 g) of bean thread vermicelli in hot water for 10 minutes, then drain and measure. Cut noodles into 2.5 cm (1 in) lengths. Put into a bowl with the shallots, spring onions, pork, flaked crab meat, salt, fish sauce and pepper. Mix well.

If using small sheets, 125 mm (5 in) square, use 1 sheet per roll. If using large sheets, 250 mm (10 in) square, cut in half. Put 2 teaspoons of filling at one end. Roll up tightly, folding in the sides so the filling is completely enclosed. Moisten edge of wrapper with a little water or egg white to help it stick. If using rice paper, brush sheets with lukewarm water in which a teaspoon of sugar has been dissolved. Besides making the sheets pliable, the sugar helps the rolls to brown.

When all the rolls are made, heat oil in a wok and fry a few at a time on medium heat until golden. Oil should not be too hot or the filling will not cook through. Drain on paper towels.

To serve: Wrap each roll in a lettuce leaf including a small sprig of Vietnamese mint, coriander or parsley and a strip of cucumber. Dip in nuoc cham and eat immediately.

Cambodian Style Spring Rolls

Makes about 20

250 g/8 oz finely minced (ground) pork
250 g/8 oz fresh mung bean sprouts
1 cup soaked bean thread vermicelli
6 dried Chinese mushrooms
1 small onion, finely chopped
1 tablespoon sugar
1 tablespoon soy sauce
1 tablespoon fish sauce
1 packet frozen spring roll pastry
oil for deep frying

SAUCE

2 cloves garlic
1½ tablespoons sugar
1 hot red chilli, seeded and chopped
5 tablespoons fish sauce
3 tablespoons boiling water
2 tablespoons lemon juice
1 tablespoon vinegar
3 tablespoons roasted crushed peanuts

Put the pork and the washed, drained bean sprouts into a bowl. Cut soaked vermicelli into 5 cm (2 in) lengths. Soak dried mushrooms in hot water for 25 minutes, discard stems and slice caps finely. Combine all these ingredients with the onion, sugar, soy sauce and fish sauce, mixing thoroughly.

If using small sheets, 125 mm (5 in) square, use one sheet per roll. If using large sheets 250 mm (10 in) square, cut in half. Take 2 teaspoons of the mixture and shape into a neat roll. Place at one end of the pastry square and roll up, turning ends in so the filling is completely enclosed. Deep fry in hot oil over medium heat, cooking the rolls for at least 2 minutes on each side so the filling is thoroughly cooked. Drain on paper towels and serve warm, accompanied by the dipping sauce.

Sauce: Crush the garlic with some of the sugar. Combine with the chilli and fish sauce, leave for 10 minutes. Add the boiling water, lemon juice and vinegar and leave in a warm place for 30 minutes for flavours to mellow. Stir in the peanuts just before serving.

Squash

(*Cucurbita maxima* and *C. moschata* species) What is called squash in the United States is known elsewhere as pumpkin. What is called pumpkin in the United States is the over-sized, watery member of the Cucurbita family used for stock feed and Jack o' Lanterns at Halloween. That famous American dessert called Pumpkin Pie, uses calabaza squash, also known as gramma pumpkin. This or any other firm, sweet, bright orange-fleshed member of the gourd family may be used in Asian cooking in a number of ways, both savoury and sweet.

A popular squash is kabocha, decorative because of its flattened spherical shape and patterned skin, deep green with pale markings. Because of its shape, it is also called turban squash. The flesh is firm, sweet and rather drier than the soft gramma. Butternut squash and similar firm varieties would be equally suitable.

The sweet dumpling squash (*C. pepo*) is not as well known as some of the Cucurbita. This dainty squash has a most attractive exterior. Deep mottled green stripes outline the indentations of the vertical furrows against a pale, cream-coloured background, sometimes splashed with orange. Cut across, the squash reveals a scalloped flower shape. The flesh is pale orange to yellow, close textured and sweet with a flavour vaguely reminiscent of corn. Suitable for steaming or baking, wash well or remove the skin if you wish.

Purchasing and storing: When choosing squash make sure the skin has no soft spots and is not pitted. The stem should be intact. Whole squash keeps well in a cool, airy place. Or buy in the piece so some of the hard work of cutting into it is already done. You can then see whether the squash is as bright as you want it to be and you can also examine the texture and make sure it is close and firm.

Preparation: If cutting a large squash, make sure the knife or chopper is large enough and sharp enough. Place the knife off centre so it doesn't come up against the hard, woody stem. Hit the blunt edge of the knife with a wooden mallet until the squash is cut open. With a spoon, scoop out and discard the seeds and fibres.

Most squash does not need to be skinned. Some have a tender rind which is nice to eat and others, especially when cooking a whole squash the oriental way, utilise the skin as a place on which to carve a decoration.

Thai Pumpkin Soup with Shrimp

Serves 6

500 g/1 lb butternut pumpkin (squash), peeled and cubed
2 tablespoons lime or lemon juice
1 rounded teaspoon dried tamarind
60 g/2 oz/½ cup dried shrimp
6 shallots or 1 onion, finely chopped
3 hot red chillies, chopped
1 stem lemon grass, finely sliced
½ teaspoon dried shrimp paste
1 × 400 ml/14 fl oz can coconut milk
1 tablespoon fish sauce
250 ml/8 fl oz chicken stock
about 30 small basil leaves

Sprinkle squash with the lime juice. Put tamarind in a bowl and soak in ½ cup (4 fl oz) hot water. When water is cool squeeze to dissolve pulp, strain and discard seeds. Soak dried shrimp in just enough hot water to cover, leave for 10 minutes, then drain.

Put soaked shrimp, shallots, chillies, lemon grass and shrimp paste into an electric blender and blend to a paste, adding a little water if necessary to facilitate blending. Put paste into a saucepan, rinse out blender with 1 cup hot water and add to pan. Add half the coconut milk and the chicken stock, stir while bringing to the boil. Add squash and tamarind liquid, stir and simmer for 10 minutes or until squash is tender. Stir in remaining coconut milk and bring back to the boil. Sprinkle with basil leaves and serve.

Custard Steamed in Squash

Use a sweet, dry-fleshed, small squash and allow one for every two servings. Or choose a larger squash and cut it into wedges to serve. Serves 4.

1 medium-sized turban squash
or 2 sweet dumpling or golden nugget squash
300 ml/10 fl oz canned coconut cream

4 eggs, beaten
220 g/7 oz palm sugar or brown sugar
4 tablespoons water
rose or jasmine essence (optional)
⅛ teaspoon salt

Cut top off squash neatly to enable seeds and membrane to be scooped out with a spoon. Combine coconut cream and eggs. Dissolve palm sugar with water over gentle heat, cool to room temperature and mix with the coconut cream, stir in flavouring essence and salt, and strain the custard into a jug.

Place squash in a steamer, or on a rack in a large pan of hot water. Pour custard into the hollow centre of the squash and place the top beside it to cook along with the squash. Cover pot and steam for 30–40 minutes or until custard is firm and a knife inserted in the centre comes out clean. Allow to cool. Remove squash from steamer and refrigerate before serving.

Squash Flower

Male flowers of pumpkin, squash and summer squash are sold in bundles at market. Zucchini flowers are also very popular. After removing the stamen and calyx, they may be added to soup or boiled and eaten as salad (ohitashi). Cut in half, lengthwise, they are battered in tempura or made into pakoras.

Squid

(*Loligo edulis*) Squid comes in varying sizes, ranging from tiny specimens hardly the size of a child's thumb, to those which are 30 cm (12 in) or more in length. They may also be purchased as cleaned tubes, or may be complete with all the bits and pieces which may be quite daunting to the cook who has not confronted one before.

Purchasing: Buy fresh squid and prepare as soon as possible. As with any seafood freshness is of paramount importance.

Preparation: Hold down the head of the squid with the blunt edge of a knife and pull the body. The head and contents of the body sac will come away. Cut off the tentacles and reserve, discarding everything else including the small, sharp 'beak' situated in the centre of the tentacles.

Slit body of the squid lengthways and rinse well,

unless you intend to stuff the body sac, in which case it will require a little more effort to rinse the sand out without slitting the squid. This is best done under cold running water. Scrub off spotted skin.

If stuffing squid, do not fill the sac too full, or it will burst when cooked.

For a dish in which the squid is cut into pieces, cut the body sac open and lay on the chopping board with the inner surface upwards. Make a series of diagonal cuts parallel to each other, about 6 mm (¼ in) apart with a sharp knife, holding knife at a 45 degree angle and taking care not to cut through the squid. Make another series of cuts across the first lines, to form a pattern of small diamonds. Divide squid into bite-sized pieces, about 5 cm × 2.5 cm (2 in × 1 in). When dropped into hot oil or water, the squid will curl and turn white in a matter of seconds. This is when it must be lifted out because if it is overcooked it will be tough and rubbery.

Burma: *kin-mun-yet-phout*
Cambodia: *muk bampoung*
China: *chin sui yau yue*
Indonesia: *cumi-cumi, sotong*
Malaysia: *sotong*
Philippines: *pusit, calmar*
Sri Lanka: *dhallo*
Thailand: *muk kluay*

Szechwan Style Squid

Larger sized squid tubes with thick walls are best suited to this dish. Serves 6.

500 g/1 lb squid
½ teaspoon salt
1 egg white, slightly beaten
1 tablespoon peanut oil
2 tablespoons cornflour (cornstarch)
1 red capsicum (bell pepper)
4 spring onions (scallions)
peanut oil for deep-frying
1 teaspoon finely chopped garlic
1 teaspoon finely chopped ginger
1 tablespoon bottled chilli radish
6 tablespoons chicken stock
½ teaspoon oriental sesame oil

Prepare squid as described above, scoring the flesh and cutting into pieces. Season with salt, pour over the egg white, oil and 1½ tablespoons of the cornflour and mix well.

Cover and chill for about 30 minutes. Cut capsicum and spring onions into bite-sized strips.

Heat peanut oil and when moderately hot drop in the squid, stirring to keep pieces separate. In less than a minute they will curl and become white. Either scoop out the squid with a large wire spoon, or pour contents of wok through a metal strainer over a metal bowl. Return wok to heat and in the film of oil that remains stir fry garlic, ginger, capsicum and spring onions for 1 minute. Add chilli radish and toss, then add stock and bring to the boil. Thicken with remaining cornflour mixed with 2 tablespoons cold water. Stir in squid and sesame oil, toss well and serve immediately with steamed rice.

Squid with Pork Stuffing

Serves 6

500 g/1 lb large squid tubes
6 dried shiitake mushrooms
10 dried lily buds
60 g/2 oz bean thread vermicelli
250 g/8 oz minced (ground) pork
2 cloves garlic, crushed
1 teaspoon finely grated fresh ginger
3 spring onions (scallions), finely chopped
salt to taste
1 tablespoon fish sauce
¼ teaspoon ground black pepper
peanut oil for frying

Clean squid, leaving tubes whole. Tentacles may be reserved for chopping and adding to filling. Soak mushrooms and lily buds in very hot water for 30 minutes. Soak bean thread vermicelli separately for 20 minutes. Discard mushroom stems and finely chop the caps. Chop lily buds also, and mix both with pork. Add garlic, ginger, spring onions, salt, fish sauce and pepper and combine thoroughly.

Lightly pack pork mixture into sac and fasten with toothpicks. Heat oil and fry the squid about 5 minutes on medium heat. Turn squid over and cook over low heat for a further 10 minutes or so. Allow to cool, then cut into slices crossways and arrange on a plate, on crisp salad greens.

Squid Sambal

This is a hot sambal, popular in Malaysia and Indonesia. Its heat can be adjusted by adding more sambal ulek or chilli powder (or less, for timid tastebuds). Since it is eaten in small amounts, it will serve 6–8.

500 g/1 lb small squid
2 onions, roughly chopped
3 cloves garlic
½ teaspoon dried shrimp paste
1 stem lemon grass, finely sliced
2 tablespoons sambal ulek
  or 1 tablespoon hot chilli powder
3 tablespoons tamarind puree
3 tablespoons peanut oil
2 teaspoons brown sugar
1 teaspoon paprika, optional

Prepare squid as described above. Slice body across into rings.

In an electric blender or food processor grind onions, garlic, shrimp paste, lemon grass, sambal ulek and tamarind to a purée.

Heat oil in a wok or frying pan and fry the blended mixture, stirring, until it is thick and oil appears around edges. Add sugar and, if a redder colour is required, the paprika. Stir in squid and cook uncovered until squid is tender, adding a little water if necessary. Cook until gravy thickens again.

Serve as an accompaniment with rice and other dishes.

Sri Lanka

Formerly Ceylon, this little island situated at the southernmost tip of the Indian sub-continent has a wonderfully varied cuisine, reflecting not only the traditions of the indigenous people, the Sinhalese, but also the different nations which either colonised the island or came to trade and stayed for many generations.

While the cuisine is rice based and spice orientated, there are many flavours which arrived with the Portuguese, Dutch and British.

Various sweetmeats are a legacy of the Portuguese. Go to a birthday celebration in Sri Lanka and many of the delicious cakes and pastries you will be served are directly traceable to the seafaring and conquering Portuguese. Some introduced dishes which Sri Lanka made its own are: lampries (from the Dutch lomprijst), a popular party meal especially when there is a large number to be catered for. Love cake (Portuguese), a rich confection of sugar, eggs, semolina and cashew nuts, is the traditional birthday cake in Sri Lanka. Foguete (Portuguese), tubes of pastry fried and stuffed with preserved fruit, then dipped in heavy sugar syrup to crystallise, are a favourite sweetmeat. Bolo folhado (Portuguese), a many-layered pastry with finely chopped nuts and sugar between each layer, is a test of a patience and skill. Rich cake (Dutch) is a fruit cake served at weddings and Christmas. It uses no flour and is moist, sweet and full of brandy-soaked fruit.

Apart from these occasional and festive foods, the main meals eaten by the population are based on rice accompanied by fish, meat and vegetable curries and sambals based on coconut and chillies or other strong-flavoured ingredients such as dried and salted fish. Everything is brought to the table at once and there are no separate courses as in a Western style meal. It is perfectly correct to take a little of everything and taste it against the neutral rice. There will probably be a 'dry curry', that is, with a rich thick gravy which is cooked for hours until concentrated flavour clings around the main ingredient. Another will be a soupy curry with coconut milk gravy to moisten the rice. Midway between these two are curries which have a moderate amount of fairly spicy gravy and are not to be taken with the same abandon as the mild, soupy type. Sri Lankan food is incendiary — an average 'red' curry to serve 6–8 people will use around 30 hot red chillies! (See recipes for Sri Lankan curries and accompaniments under heading of main ingredient, e.g. BEEF, CHICKEN, FISH.)

Sri Lankan curries are classified by colour, and the aficionado then knows what flavour to expect as well. Red curries are hot and spicy. White curries are mild but still flavoursome and, depending on the potency of the green chillies (used whole, to flavour the gravy), could also be a bit fiery. If avoiding hot flavours simply don't eat the chillies floating in the milky sauce. 'Black' curries are not actually black but a rich coffee colour, achieved by roasting the curry spices until really dark brown. This roasting changes the flavour in a way which is unimaginable until you've tried it, and a Sri Lankan black curry is well worth trying. A black curry usually has enough chilli to make it exciting, but because of the complex and intense flavour of the roasted spices the chilli may be omitted or greatly reduced. These curries

are most typical of Sri Lankan cooking, so purchase Sri Lankan curry powder or make your own.

Sri Lanka's most popular staple foods apart from rice are preparations made from rice flour which are usually served for breakfast. There are crisp, bowl-shaped rice flour pancakes called 'hoppers' or 'appe'; cylinders of coconut and flour known as 'pittu', which get their shape from being steamed in a hollow section of bamboo; small lacy, circles of rice flour paste pressed through an incredibly fine mould, then steamed on bamboo mats, which are called 'stringhoppers' or 'iddi appe'. Each of these also have their traditional accompaniments. They are never served as accompaniments to rice but replace rice in the meal.

On festive occasions these special foods may be served at a meal other than breakfast, and then the usual accompaniments are changed. The coconut sambal which is a constant partner to stringhoppers at breakfast time is supplemented by mulligatawny, chicken curry, frikkadels, seeni sambal and a herbed scrambled egg dish known as ogu ruloung or ovo roering (other reminders of Portuguese and Dutch times).

Desserts are an imported notion, but small sweetmeats are popular for snacking on between meals. Typical are sesame balls and potato alluwa.

Being one of the world's producers of top quality tea, a lot of tea is drunk, almost always with sugar and milk. Every day begins and every meal ends with a cup of tea.

Throughout the country, cooking is done in shallow, round-bottomed clay pots called chatties placed on rough, soot-blackened brick hearths in which wood fires burn. Even in modern city homes, most of which boast a gas or electric cooker, the day to day meals of breakfast, lunch and dinner are cooked with time-honoured methods, clay pots and wood fires.

Cooking spoons are made from coconut shells polished smooth and with wooden handles attached. Spices are ground early each morning for the day's needs. Implements used for this task are a large oblong stone on which another stone shaped like a bolster is held in both hands and rubbed back and forth, a few drops of water being sprinkled over the spices from time to time until a smooth paste results. A powerful electric blender does almost (but not quite) as good a job in a Western kitchen, requiring less time and muscle power but more liquid in order to facilitate blending.

Star Anise

(*Illicium verum*) SEE ILLUSTRATION. The dried, eight-pointed star-shaped seed pod of a tree belonging to the Magnolia family. In spite of its intense licorice flavour it is not related botanically to aniseed.

Star anise is one of the ingredients of Chinese five-spice powder, and is also used either whole or in segments to give flavour to long-simmered meats and poultry, which is why a master sauce will always be redolent of the sweet fragrance it imparts. Without star anise, the traditional Vietnamese soup, pho, would be sadly lacking.

It is also ground and used in smoking mixtures when its flavour is desired to accent a smoked dish. Not widely used in Thailand, except in stewed pork dishes which originated among the Chinese community.

China: *baht gok*
India: *badian*
Indonesia: *bunga lawang*
Malaysia: *bunga lawang*
Thailand: *poy kak bua*
Vietnam: *hoi*

Star Apple

(*Chrysophyllum cainito*) SEE ILLUSTRATION. Native of the West Indies and central America, this attractive fruit grows well in Australia. Spherical with a smooth, shiny purple skin (sometimes green, yellow flushed with rose or coppery toned) which encloses a white pulp with 8 translucent segments each containing a hard, dark-brown, shiny seed. Sliced in half, laterally (the seeds will stay in one of the halves — they're too hard to cut), the star-shaped pattern of the segments reveals how the fruit acquired its name. Do not attempt to eat star apple until it yields slightly to the touch — the texture will be too hard, and the sweetness not fully developed. Worst of all, the under-ripe fruit yields a sticky sap that will give new meaning to the phrase 'my lips are sealed'. In some countries the tree is grown as an ornamental because of the gold undersides of its leaves.

Star Fruit

(*Averrhoa carambola*) SEE ILLUSTRATION. Sometimes known as 'five corners', star fruit is the common name of this thirst-quenching pale green or yellow fruit. With reason — in cross-section the slice is a definite five-pointed star. Lovely as a garnish. A recent hybrid, 'Honey Starfruit', is bright yellow and very sweet.

Native to China, India and Indonesia. The preferred way of eating them in tropical countries is half-ripe, dipped into or lightly sprinkled with salt. Apart from appealing to the taste buds, this propensity for eating half-ripe fruit with salt is not just to satisfy a craving for snacks, but to replace body fluids which are constantly lost through perspiration in very hot climates.

Purchasing and storing: For eating ripe, choose those that are deep yellow or almost yellow. The skin is very thin and shiny, and the fruit needs only to be washed, not peeled. They are not sweet as some fruits are, but neither are they acid (as they are when unripe and green).

For cooking (when they act as souring agents) or eating as a salted snack, buy green fruit. As they become riper, they make a thirst-quenching drink.

Medicinal uses: It is claimed eating the fruit reduces blood sugar levels in diabetics. In Chinese medicine, they are used as a diuretic.

India: *kamrakh*
Indonesia: *belimbing*
Malaysia: *belimbing batu*
Philippines: *belimbing*
Sri Lanka: *kamaranga*
Thailand: *ma fueang, fuang*

Stringhoppers

See RICE FLOUR.

Sugar Apple

See CUSTARD APPLE.

Sugar Cane

(*Saccharum officinarum*) A tall, coarse, perennial grass that grows with a thick, dense stem. A native of Asia, it needs a tropical or sub-tropical climate to do well. It was known in India so long ago that the word we use today, sugar, comes from the Sanskrit.

Sugar cane is the primary source of most of the world's refined (white) sugar, its major producers being Cuba, Brazil and India. Australia has a flourishing sugar cane industry in north-east Queensland.

Crushed between steel rollers, the juice of fresh sugar cane is sweet and very refreshing. It is enjoyed throughout the tropics at roadside stalls and open-air markets as well as more ostentatious establishments. To taste it at its best, have it freshly pressed and still frothy. The canned version sold in some Asian groceries bears no resemblance.

The cane itself may be split lengthwise to form skewers for grilling, around which are formed a tube of finely minced green prawns (shrimp), as in the Vietnamese snack, chao tom. Sticks of peeled sugar cane are sold in tall cans for this purpose.

Although palm sugar is still dominant in the cuisines of South East Asia, cane sugar is now widely used for preserving and to sweeten snacks, cakes, drinks and sweetmeats.

Sugar Cane Flower

Sugar cane flowers are the blossoms of a variety of sugar cane with abnormal inflorescence which is cultivated specially for its flowers. These swell but never break through the sheath. Harvested and sold in bunches, they are peeled and eaten raw, steamed or cooked, on their own, dipped in sauces, added to soups and stews or included in stuffing. If you can get the inflorescences of regular sugar cane before they open, they can be eaten in a similar manner.

China: *kon-tse hua*
Indonesia: *tebao-endog*
Japan: *satoukibi-no-hana*
Malaysia: *tebu-telur*
Philippines: *tubo bulaklak*
Thailand: *dok-oi*

Sugar Palm

(*Caryota urens, Arenga saccharifera, A. pinnata, Borassus flabellifer, Cocos nucifera*) There are many types of palm from which the sap of the young inflorescence is extracted. It may be drunk fresh, fermented to make toddy or tuwak, distilled into arrack, boiled down to a syrup or further evaporated to make palm sugar. See PALM SUGAR.

Each palm provides a sugar of distinctive flavour and while the discerning palate has its favourites, most of the sugars are pleasant and one is readily substituted for another.

Tender inflorescences are eaten raw or cooked, and the pith of most varieties provides a sago-like starch. The fruits of *B. flabellifer*, the palmyra palm, are much sought after for their sweet, jelly-like seeds which are eaten raw or exported in cans or jars. The orange-coloured pulp of ripe palmyrah fruits is eaten fresh, or sun-dried and pressed into a sticky cake called punatoo. This is not palm sugar but has a flavour and sweetness which makes it a popular snack.

Sugar Palm Seed

(*Borassus flabellifer, Arenga pinnata*) When unripe, sugar palm seeds may be added to Thai soups. White, jelly-like and semi-transparent, the immature seeds are preserved in heavy sugar syrup and exported in cans or jars. Probably too sweet for most tastes, it is a popular item of the sweet assortment which goes into the famous halo-halo of the Philippines or the equally famous and well-loved ice kacang of Malaysia. When mixed with ice the sweetness is not overwhelming, and the restorative powers of one of these mixed refreshers is unquestionable. See ICE KACANG.

Asian stores usually stock jars labelled 'halo-halo mix', or 'sweet mixture', giving an assorment of at least six different varieties including sugar palm seeds.

Indonesia: *kolang kaling*
Malaysia: *attap*
Philippines: *kaong*
Thailand: *taan*

Sugar, Rock

Known also as lump sugar, yellow rock sugar or rock candy, this is a solidified mixture of honey, refined and unrefined sugar. Traditionally used in braised 'red-cooked' dishes, soups, sweet soups and beverages, it is also considered a tonic.

Sugar, Slab

Also called brown sugar and brown sugar candy (in pieces), this sweetener is sold in thin, caramel-coloured layers in packets or in bulk from Asian food stores.

Sugar Snap Pea

See LEGUMES & PULSES.

Sushi

If you've never tried freshly prepared sushi, you are missing out on a treat that is intriguing both visually, texturally and tastewise. To see a sushi master at work one cannot help but be impressed by the speed and precision. The hand-formed, bite-sized morsels can be prepared at home and, with a little practice, a newcomer can make this deliciously different entree or dinner party hors d'oeuvre, light lunch or healthy snack. The main component of nigiri-sushi is vinegared rice which is moulded into bite-sized, mounded pads then overlaid with a thin slice of raw fish, cuttlefish, eel, abalone, lightly cooked prawn (shrimp), sea urchin roe or any number of delicacies from the deep. Only the freshest fish and seafood should be used.

Rolled up in a sheet of toasted, dried nori (seaweed), the flavour and texture contrast to the vinegared rice is provided by a central core of 'gu'— a selection of pickled radish, dried gourd, pickled lotus root, seasoned carrot, cucumber, omelette, grated ginger and wasabi in any number of combinations, with or without the addition of seafood. This sushi is known under the broad category of nori-maki or maki-zushi. Cut in slices, it looks impressive and with a little practice, isn't hard to make (see recipe page 368). Included in this category are the cone shaped, hand-rolled sushi, temaki-sushi.

Some vegetarian examples of sushi are kappa-maki (nori-maki rolled around thin slivers of cucumber); oshinkomaki (nori-maki filled with the tangy, yellow pickled daikon); inari-zushi (flavoured rice in pouches of deep-fried tofu); date-maki-zushi (sushi rice rolled with various vegetable fillings inside an omelette); and fukusa-zushi (rice, vegetable and crumbled nori wrapped in a fragile omelette parcel).

Among the other varieties of sushi you might come across are chirashi-zushi (literally 'scattered sushi'), which is rice in a bowl or box strewn with nine different fish and vegetable toppings (see recipe page 368); chakin-zushi sushi (named after the small piece of cloth used in the Japanese tea ceremony), a small mound of sushi rice enclosed in a thin square of omelette, tied with a couple of strands of wilted mitsuba to resemble a drawstring purse; and mushi-zushi (steamed sushi served hot).

If you go to a sushi bar, don't expect to be offered anything but sashimi and sushi. Perusing the menu, even limiting yourself to nigiri-zushi, you may be confronted with an intimidating number of unfamiliar terms referring to the different dane or tane (toppings for the pad of sushi rice). There are five main categories: aka-mi (red-meat), shiro-mi (white meat), hikari-mono (shining tane), nimono (cooked tane) and a last category including shrimp, shellfish and squid. However, the distinction is not always apparent on a menu.

The following list should help demystify the selection.

Aji: Horse mackerel, a shining tane, treated with salt and vinegar. Also served raw with minced (ground) green onions and grated ginger.

Akagai: Red clam. Quite toxic if not fresh. In the cold months the colour is reddest and in summer it is almost white. Formerly eaten vinegar-dipped, now au naturel is the preference.

Anago: Conger eel. A traditional nimono-dane, it is also the key flavour in the intensely flavoured, reduced broth called nitsume.

Aoyagi, kobashira: Japanese red clam/skimmer. The adductor muscles are said to have a flavour better than the clam itself. The adductor muscle (kobashira) is a pale peach tint while the meat is a vivid orange-salmon colour. The meat must always be partially cooked. The timing is critical, so leave it to the experts.

Awabi, mushi-awabi: Abalone. An aristocratic sushi-dane, its price alone makes it a delicacy. Killed just prior to serving if eaten raw, it is otherwise boiled (mushi-awabi) and topped with nitsume (a reduced broth of conger eel).

Buri, hamachi: Yellowtail and young yellowtail. Tastes best in the colder months. Although white-fleshed fish, they are quite oily and so are sometimes substituted for the richer cuts of tuna (toro).

Ebi: Shrimp. Uses freshly killed ebi. Its taste, attractive shape and colour have made shrimp a prized sushi-dane.

Hamaguri: Clam. A popular nimono-dane.

Hirami: A flat fish with both eyes on top of its body, the side with the darkest colouring, the underside, being white. Best eaten in winter. One of the fish traditionally sliced paper thin for sashimi, halibut (flounder) is also a favourite sushi, with its delicate flavour and translucent, pink flesh.

Hokkigai: Surf clam. Its distinctive feature is a striking purplish-black 'foot'. Mostly served raw.

Hotategai: Scallop. The large adductor muscle is the only part used. In the areas it is caught, sushi shops serve it raw, otherwise it is served as nimono-dane, spread with nitsume. Also served raw as sashimi.

Ika: Cuttlefish and squid are both classified as ika and while traditionally nimono-dane, they are served raw as well as cooked. The practice of scoring the surface of the flesh (like the ribbon cutting of ika sashimi) is not purely decorative. As well as giving the dipping sauce something to cling to, it severs the strong muscle fibres and renders it chewable.

Iwashi: Sardine. Not traditionally highly regarded, it is now quite a popular sushi tane. The variety favoured in Japan is ma-iwashi, and is categorised according to its three stages of growth. Served raw after filleting, salting and soaking in vinegar.

Kajiki: Swordfish. Sometimes served as a substitute for tuna.

Kanpachi: A kind of yellowtail, this fish is best eaten before it is three years old and not in the autumn (after the spawning season), as at this time it can have a bad smell. A white meat tane.

Kasugo: Young sea bream, one of the three most popular shining tane, along with kisu (sillago) and sayori (halfbeak). Served salted and vinegared.

Katsuo: Bonito (a type of mackerel). Seasonal and regional, the deep-red flesh is richly flavoured and highly prized.

Kisu: Sillago, a long, slender fish with a golden sheen, is a favoured shining tane. Not a fatty fish, its flavour deteriorates rapidly, so eat very fresh. Usually served after a brief soaking in vinegar.

Kohada: Gizzard shad. This fish, categorised as shining tane, is related to herring and mackerel. Seasoned with salt, soaked in vinegar, then allowed to drain for half a day before serving.

Maguro: The cut of tuna most associated with sashimi and sushi, deep red and soft.

Mirugai: Horse-neck clam or geoduck (pronounced gooey-duck). Its siphon, peeled of its black skin, turns a startling shade of crimson after being subjected to a special hot and cold water treatment. Colour may vary from red to pale peach. It is cut thin and scored to tenderise.

Saba: Mackerel. Though paler in colour than tuna, its flavour is less subtle. Kyoto is famous for its saba-zushi. The dark and light flesh are an indication that this is an oily fish. Usually salted and marinated a few days before being served as nigiri-zushi. Don't order it unless you're a fan of strong-flavoured fish. Said to be most flavoursome in autumn.

Sake: Salmon. Spelled like the Japanese word for rice wine, but pronounced with a short final syllable ('sah-keh' for fish as opposed to 'sah-kay' for wine). Interestingly, salmon isn't served raw in Japanese sushi bars — it is either cured in sugar and salt for a few days or else it is lightly smoked. Treated this way, the flesh is still red and soft, thinly sliced and draped or folded over the finger of rice. Sometimes the chef will grill it lightly, its colour fading to peach and its flavour even more delicate.

Sayori: Halfbeak has a jutting, red, swordlike protrusion from its lower jaw. The brighter the colour, the fresher the fish. Although white fleshed, its silver skin makes it a shining tane and it is traditionally salted and vinegared.

Shako: Mantis shrimp. This odd-looking crustacean is said to taste midway between shrimp and crab. Cooked as soon as it is landed, it is only available cooked. Served with either nitsume or wasabi.

Shima-aji: Yellowjack. A highly regarded white meat tane, it is claimed to be tastiest in June, just before spawning, with the smaller specimens having a superior flavour.

Suzuki: Sea bass. A delicately flavoured fish with white, large-flaked meat. Also popular sliced paper-thin as sashimi.

Tai: Includes a number of varieties of which madai is considered the best. It has a distinctly different flavour but is only available in Japan. Red Snapper and porgy are acceptable substitutes for tai.

Tairagai: The large adductor muscle of this shellfish are used for sushi.

Tako: Octopus. Only in the last 50 years has tako or 'devil-fish' ceased to be in the lowest class of sushi-dane.

Torigai: Cockle. Enjoyed for its colour, flavour and texture, this tane is eaten mainly raw, sometimes dipped in diluted sweetened vinegar after blanching in boiling water.

Toro: Also tuna, this refers to a particular cut from the pink-coloured, fatty belly of the fish. Further distinguished as chu-toro (medium fatty) or o-toro (most fatty) — the higher the fat content, the more tender and buttery the texture. At its best during winter months, it is considered unparalleled among tane.

Other toppings for sushi include various kinds of roe and caviar: salmon (ikura), flying fish (tobi-uonoko, tobiko), capelin (masago), sea urchin (uni), herring roe (kazunoko). See FISH ROE.

The traditional vegetarian sushi is tamago (sweetened omelette) and a fairly thick slice of this is laid over the rice pad, served with a 'belt' of nori.

Tossed Sushi (Chirashi-Zushi)

1 quantity sushi rice (recipe page 310)
4 dried shiitake mushrooms
1 tablespoon Japanese soy sauce
1 teaspoon sugar
125 g/4 oz crab meat or cooked, shelled prawns (shrimp)
2 eggs, beaten
salt to taste
6 tablespoons finely shredded bamboo shoot
6 tablespoons cooked green peas
12 thin slices lotus root
1 tablespoon pickled kombu (kelp), thinly sliced
1 tablespoon pickled radish, thinly sliced
slices of gari or beni shoga (pickled ginger) to garnish

Prepare and cool sushi rice. Soak mushrooms in very hot water. Squeeze out and reserve water, discard stems and slice caps thinly. Simmer for 10–15 minutes in some of the soaking water with soy sauce and sugar. Flake crab meat or slice prawns lengthways in halves. Beat eggs slightly, season with salt and cook in a non-stick or lightly oiled frying pan to make a thin omelette, taking care not to let it brown. Cool, then cut in thin strips. Toss rice gently with all the ingredients, reserving some for garnish. Serve cold.

Sushi Wrapped in Omelette (Fukusa-Zushi)

A variation on the above, this is the same mixture wrapped in omelette. Press chirashi-zushi into a square oven dish, press down firmly, place non-stick paper on top and weight down while preparing omelettes.

Make thin omelettes using 4 eggs instead of 2, and use a small frying pan in order to get about 8 very thin omelettes. Cook on low heat so omelettes do not brown. Cut pressed sushi into pieces about 5 cm (2 in) square. Place a square in the centre of each omelette and wrap, envelope fashion, so rice is completely enclosed. Wrap a thin strip of nori around the parcel or tie with a green onion leaf dipped in boiling water to make it pliable. Place on serving plate with joins underneath. Serve cold.

Sushi Wrapped in Seaweed (Norimake-Zushi)

Braised mushrooms can be kept in the refrigerator or freezer to save time. The raw fish is not mandatory — a totally vegetarian sushi is also delicious. Makes about 36 pieces.

1 quantity sushi rice (recipe page 310)
6–8 braised shiitake mushrooms (see recipe for tossed sushi)
2 eggs
¼ teaspoon sugar
¼ teaspoon salt
½ teaspoon sesame oil
1 green cucumber
1 small piece pickled radish
125 g/4 oz raw tuna, bonito or kingfish (optional)
1 teaspoon prepared wasabi
6 sheets nori (dried laver seaweed)

Prepare sushi rice. Slice braised mushrooms into strips.

Beat eggs with salt and sugar, cook in lightly oiled pan like a flat omelette. Cool, then cut in thin strips. Peel cucumber thinly, leaving a trace of green. Cut lengthways in strips the size of a pencil. Drain the pickled radish and cut in thin strips. If using fish, remove skin and bones, cut the fish in pencil strips and smear with wasabi. Toast sheets of nori to crisp them by passing back and forth over a gas flame or electric hotplate a few times.

Put a sheet of nori on a sudare (bamboo mat), or on a clean napkin. Divide the rice into 6 equal portions and spread one portion evenly over two-thirds of the sheet of nori, starting at the end nearest you. In neat lines across the middle of the rice stack a combination of ingredients.

Roll up the sushi in the mat, keeping firm pressure on the filling so that a neatly packed cylinder results. Let the rolls rest for 10 minutes before cutting into about 6 pieces. Arrange, cut side up, on a tray decorated with leaves.

Sweeteners

See HONEY; MALTOSE; PALM SUGAR; SUGAR CANE; SUGAR, ROCK; SUGAR, SLAB.

Sweetmeats, Indian

Indian confections have won so many tastebuds that, around the world, you will find Indian shops selling a large variety of sweets. These fall into different categories: there are dry sweetmeats which may be held in the fingers and nibbled like a piece of fudge; syrupy sweetmeats which are probably best eaten with a spoon, though they are often sold on a square of greaseproof paper; fried sweetmeats which coat one's fingers with ghee; sticky, starch-based halvas like extremely rich and chewy Turkish delight; crisp sweets made on chick pea flour with texture reminiscent of butterscotch brittle; and creamy milk puddings with rice, vermicelli or fried bread, all of which must be served on a plate.

Bengal is famous for syrupy sweets such as rasgullas. In Agra, India, there is an industry making petha, which is crystallised white melon. An entire street is devoted to preparing this sweet which starts out as great wedges of melon and ends up days later as translucent pieces of glacé fruit with a wonderfully crisp texture.

Fruit and vegetables are used as a base for certain sweets, and the fragrance of rose or cardamom, depending on the skill of the sweet maker, lifts the mundane to heights of delight.

Indian sweetmeats and sweet makers are a world unto themselves, a world that draws anyone who has a very sweet tooth into a spiral of temptation, the trick being to satisfy one's curiosity about the different types of sweets without overdoing the tasting. They are not only sweet, but also rich. If one is able to find a halvai (confectioner) who makes really good Indian sweets and is willing to pay the price (in money and gained weight), it is easier to settle for the bought product. But for those who enjoy tracking down a recipe that works, perfecting it and actually making the sweets themselves, it can be a long, sticky road to success.

Because sweet making is usually a family business handed down from one generation to the next, halvais are understandably reluctant to pass on their recipes and the tricks that make them work, so finding the perfect recipe requires luck and persistence. Then, as in all branches of confectionery making, it requires not only the ability to follow a recipe, but practice and observation of how the mixture behaves at every stage of preparation so that the end result is worth the time and effort invested.

Here are some of the favourite sweetmeats of India, not necessarily eaten as dessert at the end of a meal, but as indulgences any time energy needs a boost or life needs sweetening.

Rose-Flavoured Milk Balls in Syrup (Gulab Jamun)

Makes about 20

8 tablespoons full-cream milk powder
3 tablespoons self-raising flour
¼ teaspoon bicarbonate of soda (baking soda)
¼ teaspoon ground cardamom
1 tablespoon soft butter or ghee
approximately 3 tablespoons water
ghee or oil for frying

SYRUP
2 cups white sugar
4 cups water
5 bruised cardamom pods
2 tablespoons rose water or few drops rose essence

Sift milk powder, flour, bicarbonate of soda and cardamom into a large bowl. Rub in butter or ghee, then add enough water to give a firm but pliable dough which can be moulded into balls the size of large marbles, or into small sausage shapes.

Fry slowly in hot ghee (or oil flavoured with ghee) until they turn golden brown. The frying must be done over gentle heat. Drain on paper towels.

Have ready the syrup, made by combining sugar, water and cardamom pods and heating until sugar is dissolved. Put the fried gulab jamun into the syrup and soak until they are almost double in size, soft and spongy. Add rose water when they have cooled slightly. Allow to cool completely and serve at room temperature or slightly chilled.

Condensed Milk Fudge (Perhas)

Not half as sweet as Western style fudge, but rich and satisfying. Makes 10–12.

1.25 litres/2½ pints/5 cups milk
1 teaspoon ghee
4 tablespoons white sugar
½ teaspoon ground cardamom or grated nutmeg
few slivered almonds or pistachios (optional)
gold or silver leaf

Put the milk into a large, heavy, non-stick pan and make Khoa which is unsweetened condensed milk (see page 234). This will yield approximately 220 g (7 oz) of khoa.

Combine with ghee, sugar and cardamom and cook, stirring, until it forms a thick mass and leaves the side of the pan. This only takes a few minutes. Turn onto a plate and leave until cool enough to handle.

Lightly grease hands with ghee and shape mixture into small balls by rolling between palms, then flatten the balls slightly. Put on a buttered dish to cool and firm. The perhas will not get hard, and are not supposed to. A soft, fudge-like texture is correct. If liked, decorate each with half a blanched pistachio or a small piece of gold or silver leaf.

Pistachio Barfi

In Indian and Middle Eastern shops, pistachio kernels are sold which are not the usual roasted, salted pistachios in shells. It is these softer kernels which are used whenever pistachios are called for in recipes.

125 g/4 oz raw pistachio kernels
1 litre/2 pints/4 cups full-cream milk
220 g/7 oz caster sugar (superfine sugar)
pinch of ground cardamom (optional)
gold or silver leaf (optional)

Drop the pistachio kernels into a small pan of boiling water and boil for 1 minute. Tip into a strainer and run cold water over to set the colour. Slip off the skins and pound the nuts or pass them through a nut mill.

Grease a flat plate and back of a large spoon with ghee and have ready for when the mixture has been cooked.

In a medium to large pan with heavy base boil the milk over high heat, stirring constantly,

until it is very thick. Add sugar, lower heat and stir for 10 minutes. Add ground pistachios and continue to cook, stirring, until the mixture comes away from the sides and base of pan in one mass. Remove from heat, sprinkle cardamom over and mix well. Turn onto the greased plate and smooth top with back of spoon. Cool slightly, mark in squares or diamond shapes with back of a knife. Decorate with halved pistachio nuts and small pieces of silver leaf if liked. Before it is quite firm, use a sharp knife to cut along the markings, but leave until cold before separating pieces. May be wrapped and stored airtight for up to two weeks.

Ras Malai

Considered the queen of Indian sweets, it is a combination of fresh cheese balls (Rasgullas) (recipe page 75) and Rabri, (recipe below), both of which may be served independent of the other. For Ras Malai the cheese balls are cooked in syrup as described, then immersed in 1.5 litres (6 cups) milk. When cool, they are removed from the milk and the milk used to make rabri as described in the next recipe. However, instead of reducing it to a third of its original volume, reduce it to half so it is not very thick. Remove from heat, stir in sugar and a few drops of rose or kewra essence and return cheese balls to the mixture. Cover and refrigerate. Serve sprinkled with finely chopped pistachio nuts.

Reduced Milk Pudding (Rabri)

Serves 4

1.5 litres/3 pints/6 cups fresh milk
4 tablespoons sugar
2 drops kewra essence or rose essence
1 tablespoon slivered blanched almonds
1 tablespoon slivered blanched pistachios*

Put milk into a heavy-based saucepan and stir constantly while bringing to the boil. Cook steadily and continue stirring until reduced to about 2 cups. Lower heat, add sugar and stir until sugar dissolves. Remove pan from heat. Add flavouring when it is lukewarm and scrape in milk crusts from side of pan. Pour into a pretty bowl and sprinkle with nuts. Chill before serving.

*Use unsalted, untoasted pistachios and boil them for 1 minute to bring out their green colour and make it easy to slip off their skins.

See Index of Recipes for listing of sweetmeat recipes.

Sweet Potato

See POTATO, SWEET.

Sweetsop

See CUSTARD APPLE.

Szechwan Pepper

(*Zanthoxylum piperitum*, *Z. simulans*) SEE ILLUSTRATION. Two closely related plants. Also known as Sichuan pepper, anise pepper, Chinese pepper, fagara, wild pepper and sansho. In China it is called faah jiu and hua chiao and is native to Szechwan province. It is one of the ingredients of five-spice powder. In spite of its many alternative names which include the word 'pepper', it is not related to true pepper. Szechwan peppercorns are small, reddish-brown berries which grow on a shrubby tree, not on a vine as pepper does. The berries are dried and sold either whole or with the shiny black seed removed. It is best to buy the seeded variety as the seeds are gritty when crushed. The reddish-brown husks or 'fruit' are the part used for their distinctive fragrance and flavour and curious numbing effect on the tongue; quite different from the pungent bite of pepper or the sting and burn of chilli.

Dry roasting in a pan brings out the flavour and makes them easy to grind using a mortar and pestle.

This may be done ahead and the ground spice stored in a bottle. Szechwan pepper is also roasted and ground with salt and used as a dip with dishes such as Crisp Skin Chicken (see recipe page 81), mainly to counter the richness of the crisp skin which is so seductive that even the most diet-conscious person could not resist. Also used to make Szechwan pepper oil, useful to have on hand as it gives flavour to stir-fried dishes or when drizzled over plain steamed vegetables. Add to dips served with plain steamed or boiled fish, poultry or meat.

Stored in an airtight bottle, Szechwan pepper will keep well. The oil should not be stored for too long, but will keep for a few weeks.

Salt and Szechwan Pepper Mix

2 tablespoons salt
1 tablespoon Szechwan peppercorns (without seeds)
1 teaspoon white peppercorns

In a small, heavy pan toast salt and peppercorns over medium heat, shaking the pan or stirring constantly, until they are smoking hot and smell fragrant. Remove from heat and grind to powder using a spice grinder or mortar and pestle.

Szechwan Pepper Oil

1 tablespoon Szechwan peppercorns
250 ml/8 fl oz/1 cup peanut oil

Roast the Szechwan pepper in a clean, dry pan until fragrant. Add oil and cook on low heat about 10 minutes, stirring now and then. Allow to cool. Strain and store in a glass jar in a cool, dark cupboard.

Tamarind

(*Tamarindus indica*) SEE ILLUSTRATIONS. Native to tropical America, this plant of the Leguminosae family is so widely used throughout Asia that it has acquired the common name asam, meaning, simply, 'acid'. In their English translations, other acid fruits have assumed the name 'tamarind', for example 'fish tamarind' (see GAMBOGE) and 'tamarind slices' (see GELUGOR), simply because they too are used as acid flavours.

The tall, spreading trees with compound leaves are planted for shade as well as for the long bean pods with brittle brown shells. When unripe, the shell is greenish brown and closely attached to the pale flesh. It is in this unripe state that tamarind is used in sinigang, a category of sour soupy dishes popular in the Philippines.

When ripe, the shell is reddish brown and more easily separated from the pulp, which becomes rich brown and sweeter, though still acid. The pulp surrounds large, shiny brown seeds and a few strong fibres run the length of the pod between the pulp and the shell.

In southern India and the northern part of Sri Lanka, tamarind is made into a brine for preserving fish. In many Asian countries it is cooked with sugar to make a cordial base. With the addition of ice and water or carbonated water, it is a refreshing drink.

Tamarind may also be used as a base for delicious raw or cooked chutneys, its fruity acidity combining well with sugar, chilli and other flavours.

In Asian shops, look for sweetmeats made from sugared tamarind, the pulp and seed being semi-dried and rolled in crystal sugar and sometimes a touch of chilli powder.

There is a variety of tamarind called 'sweet tamarind' in which the pulp is distinctly sweeter, though still nicely tart. It looks identical before the pod is opened, but the pulp is shiny and darker in colour. In Thailand it is called makham wan and is eaten fresh as a snack. In Vietnam it is called me ngot.

Purchasing and storing: Green tamarind is sold in jars, pickled in brine. Ripe tamarind, in some instances, is dried on the seeds, only the shell being removed. In other instances the seeds and fibres are removed and the flesh dried and compressed into flat cakes. Dried tamarind is sold in packets. Malaysian tamarind tends to have salt added, while tamarind produced in India or Thailand is unsalted. Read the label to find out whether you are buying a salty tamarind. The unsalted variety gives more flexibility, as it can be used for a sweet cordial or chutney if you wish. Both kinds keep indefinitely without refrigeration.

Sometimes the seeds and fibres are strained out and the thick pulp sold as tamarind purée or tamarind concentrate which needs only to be spooned from the jar. There is also tamarind powder and instant tamarind, the former being self-explanatory and the latter anything but instant since it has been concentrated into a stiff paste which takes longer to dissolve than the dried pulp.

Preparation: In curries and other cooked dishes it does not seem to matter which form is used, but if making something in which tamarind is the predominant flavour such as the refreshing zeera pani (cumin water), it is best to use tamarind which has been processed as little as possible, and that is the dried variety. The truest tamarind flavour is obtained by soaking tamarind, fresh or dried, in hot water for a few minutes to soften, squeezing and kneading the pulp to disperse it in the water, then straining it before use. Repeat with a little more hot water if there is still plenty of pulp left undissolved. To save time, I prepare a quantity larger than my immediate needs and freeze the strained liquid in ice cube trays. Each cube equals roughly a tablespoon and the cubes store well in freezer containers, needing only to be gently heated or left to thaw.

Medicinal uses: Tamarind is said to cool the system and cleanse the blood. The pulp, rich in vitamins and minerals, is used in Chinese medicine. The bark treats asthma, and a paste made from the leaves or the seeds is used to treat boils. The flowers are said to reduce blood pressure.

See recipe for Cumin and Tamarind Refresher (page 112).

Burma: *ma-gyi-thi*
Cambodia: *ampil tum* (ripe), *ampil kheei* (green)
India: *imli*
Indonesia: *asam, asam jawa*
Laos: *mak kham*
Malaysia: *asam*
Philippines: *sampalok*
Sri Lanka: *siyambala*
Thailand: *som ma kham*
Vietnam: *me*

Tamarind Sauce

Serve with samosas, pakoras, or lentil pancakes. Makes 1 cup.

1 rounded tablespoon dried tamarind pulp
250 ml/8 fl oz/1 cup hot water
1 teaspoon ground cumin
1 teaspoon finely chopped ginger
1–2 tablespoons brown sugar
½ teaspoon salt
pinch of chilli powder (optional)

Soak tamarind in hot water until soft and cool enough to rub with the fingers to dissolve pulp in the water. Strain through a fine sieve, and if necessary add a few tablespoons more water to dissolve any remaining pulp. Discard seeds and fibres. Stir the other ingredients into the tamarind and serve as a dipping sauce or to spoon over savoury snacks just before eating.

Chicken in Tamarind Gravy

A favourite recipe in Malaysia and Singapore over the period of Chinese New Year, when household staff go on holiday and shops and markets are closed. The acidity of tamarind preserves the poultry for a few days even without refrigeration. This Nonya recipe for chicken is called ayam siyoh. Serves 6.

1 × 1.5 kg/3 lb roasting chicken
185 g/6 oz dried tamarind pulp
500 ml/1 pint/2 cups hot water
3 tablespoons ground coriander
2 tablespoons dark soy sauce
5 tablespoons sugar
2 teaspoons salt
4 tablespoons peanut oil

Cut the chicken into quarters. Soak tamarind in half the hot water and when cool enough to handle, squeeze to dissolve pulp in the water. Strain through a fine sieve and if there is more pulp on the seeds, add remaining hot water and continue rubbing pulp between the fingers to dissolve. Strain and discard the seeds and fibres. Roast coriander in a dry pan over low heat, stirring constantly, until it becomes fragrant and darkens in colour. Combine with the tamarind. Add soy sauce, sugar and salt and stir well. Pour over the chicken in a bowl just large enough to hold the chicken and marinade. Leave for 6–8 hours, turning chicken pieces over at least twice.

In a non-aluminium pan simmer chicken in the marinade on low heat, uncovered, until tender, about 40 minutes. Lift chicken pieces from gravy and drain thoroughly. Continue to simmer sauce until very thick and reduced. Cut chicken into smaller pieces, heat oil and fry until brown. Place chicken on a serving dish, ladle the tamarind gravy over and serve with steamed rice.

Tamarind Slices

A misnomer, these are dried slices of another acid fruit used in like manner. See GELUGOR.

Tandoori

The tandoor or clay oven used in India has given its name to certain dishes which are cooked in it and gain an incomparable smoky flavour from the charcoal.

To conserve heat, it is usually sunk in the ground at least half way, but if built above ground is heavily insulated with mud, cement or plaster. The fire must be lit about 2 hours before cooking commences so that there is fierce heat from the base to the half-way point. There is still enough heat above that to cook the delicious breads that are pressed directly against the inner walls of the tandoor, where they cook to perfection in minutes.

Marinated meats, fish and chicken are pierced with long skewers and cooked in the hottest part of the oven.

The word 'tandoori' may also mean 'tandoori style', indicating the marinade which is used on food cooked in a tandoor, even though cooking may take place on a barbecue, or in a Western-style oven or grill. A popular dish within India, tandoori chicken is now served in restaurants around the world, often cooked in a gas tandoor. Although gas is cleaner and easier, there is a sacrifice in flavour. But using the traditional marinade with its gentle spicing, a reasonable result can be achieved (see recipe for Tandoori Style Chicken, page 84).

When choosing a tandoori restaurant, try to find out if they have a coal-fuelled or gas tandoor. There is a marked difference in flavour.

Tangerine Peel, Dried

Chinese shops sell this rather expensive ingredient for flavouring. However, it is something that anyone can make during the citrus season — the peels of oranges, mandarins, tangerines or tangelos can be dried out in a very slow oven or in a dehydrator, or left to dry naturally, then stored airtight. Do not remove the white pith, as it contains bio-flavonoids and is good for you. The Chinese believe that the older the peel, the better the flavour and the more effective its curative powers. One or two pieces may be added when braising or simmering long-cooked dishes such as duck and pork. Or the peel may be soaked in a little hot water until soft, pounded or chopped and incorporated in mixtures such as meat balls.

Simmered in braised dishes or soups, it adds a zesty flavour. Mixed with finely minced (ground) beef in those delicious, springy beef balls offered at dim sum, the flavour is intriguingly heady and fragrant. Pounded and mixed with sugar and sometimes tea leaves (dry) in a smoking mix, it imparts a delicate aroma to food which is steamed and then smoked.

Purchasing and storing: Either buy in packets from a Chinese grocer, or make your own. Store airtight and leave at least six months to age and mellow.

Preparation: Soak in a little warm water to soften before adding to the dish. The peel may be pounded or shredded for best effect. In some instances, after simmering the whole pieces with a dish, they are discarded. See recipes for Tangerine Chicken (page 82), Chinese Clay Pot Beef (page 34), and Beef Balls with Tangerine Peel (see page 35).

Medicinal uses: It is considered effective in fevers, coughs, acne, and is said to be an antidote to fish and shellfish poison.

China: *gom pei, chin pei*

Tapioca

(*Manihot esculenta*) A refined starch food made from peeled and grated cassava root. The juice is extracted and the pulp soaked in water and kneaded to release the starch grains. Fibres are strained out and the residue heated until it forms the typical balls or pearls of tapioca. Tapioca starch (flour) is a staple in some Asian cuisines, particularly in the making of sweets (see FLOURS & STARCHES). The translucent balls of cooked tapioca are also floated in the sweet drinks and liquid desserts beloved of South East Asians. See also CASSAVA.

Burmese Tapioca Refresher (Moh Let Saung)

185 g/6 oz/1 cup tapioca pearls
1.5 litres/3 pints/6 cups boiling water
250 g/8 oz chopped palm sugar or brown sugar
ice cubes
coconut milk
salt

Wash and soak tapioca in cold water for 1 hour. Drain, drop into a large pan of boiling water and simmer over medium heat until the tapioca grains are clear. Cool and chill. Put palm sugar into a small pan with 1 cup of water and dissolve over low heat. Cool and strain the syrup. (Or buy palm sugar syrup from an Asian grocery.)

For each serving, put 3 or 4 tablespoons of chilled tapioca into a tall glass, add the same amount of syrup and mix well. Add 2 tablespoons crushed ice or 2 ice cubes and fill the glass with coconut milk which has been diluted with water if very thick and rich. Add a pinch of salt, stir and serve.

Taro

(*Colocasia esculenta, C. antiquorum*) SEE ILLUS-TRATION. Taro is to the Pacific what potatoes are to Ireland — a staple food. The corms are the starchy staple and are the basis for the much-talked-about poi of Hawaii, cooked, mashed and fermented, and described as 'one-finger poi', 'two-finger poi' and 'three-finger poi', depending on its thickness. One-finger poi is the thickest, presumably solid enough to be scooped up and eaten on one finger. The leaves are also eaten, cooked like spinach.

My first experience of taro was not a happy one. In a Pacific island market I was trying typical local fare and enjoying the rich creaminess of palusami — taro leaves and coconut cream wrapped in banana leaves and breadfruit leaves and steamed in an underground oven. Delicious! I said I would have another little parcel, and that's when trouble struck. I felt a sensation of a hundred red hot needles in my throat. Panicked, I stopped eating immediately and tried to wash away the irritation by drinking fresh coconut juice, but it was hours before my throat felt normal again. Later, I was told that I was extremely lucky, because some people end up in hospital! There seemed to be two theories — either the taro leaves were not sufficiently young, or else had not been sufficiently cooked. Years later, reading Katherine Bazore's book, *Hawaiian and Pacific Foods*, I found the answer.

'*The green leaves of taro served as their [Pacific islanders'] favourite green vegetable. But even they may have lost some of their nutritive properties since the leaves, like any and all taro products, have to be cooked for* at least *45 minutes to destroy an irritating substance.*'

The substance is tiny crystals of calcium oxalate, exceedingly sharp, which puncture delicate membranes of mouth and tongue and cause intense irritation. One publication says 'some varieties have higher acidity but most of the cultivated varieties are free from it'.

The late Jane Grigson, in her excellent book, *Cooking with Exotic Fruits and Vegetables* relates an experience after she and her daughter had cooked and tasted taro leaf stalks, runners and shoots.

'*Our throats began to ache in a strange way, as if they were swelling up. We feared we were soon going to be unable to breathe. After a lot of water the sensation vanished.*

…I resent the lack of frankness about this in many of the cookery books that I possess. Even botanists do not quite come clean, sternly observing that you should be quite all right if the vegetable is 'properly cooked'. By which they mean boiling for an hour. Now this may be all right for tubers, but it is plain ridiculous for greenery because young shoots and leaves are ruined by such treatment.'

Ruined they may be, but as established by her experience and mine, it would be unwise to try them short-cooked.

Spinach or silverbeet leaves may be substituted for taro leaves and then the cooking time may be shortened.

Pursuing the subject with Dr Alistair Hay of the Botanic Gardens in Sydney, Australia, he had this to say:

'*The irritant factors in Aroids including* Colocasia esculenta *are much more complicated than just calcium oxalate… there is a cocktail of crystals and other irritating substances, and the range of irritation found in different cultivars and the different cooking times required probably reflects variation in amounts of the different substances, some of which are more quickly destroyed by heat than others.*'

Most books say very little about the care needed when cooking and eating taro. After my experience in Samoa (which proves that even Pacific island cooks who know the plant well are not infallible), I want to prevent anyone else having a similar episode, though my editor sighs and says, 'You do go on about it'.

There are many kinds of taro, and one member of the Colocasia family, *Colocasia gigantea*, produces no tuber, neither is the leaf eaten, but the leaf stalks are sliced and used in Cambodian and Vietnamese soups, lightly cooked and still crisp. Their porous structure enables them to hold the flavoursome stock much as a sponge holds water. They have also been discovered by adventurous chefs of other persuasions and are served sliced in salads and other dishes where the delicate flavour and crisp texture find favour. These petioles (leaf stalks) may even be eaten raw, but first make sure they are the right kind — the Japanese call it zuiki; Cambodians and Vietnamese, bac ha. Ask for an English translation and they will tell you 'taro', but it is best to buy it from a shop and not to go foraging yourself unless you are knowledgeable about such matters.

Cambodia: *bac ha* (leaf petioles)
China: *woo tau, yu*
Fiji: *rou rou*
Hawaii: *luau*
India: *arvi, patra*
Indonesia: *talas*
Japan: *sato-imo* (yam), *zuiki* (leaf petioles)
Malaysia: *keladi*
Philippines: *gabi*
Sri Lanka: *kiri ala*
Tahiti: *fafa*
Thailand: *phueak*
Vietnam: *khoai mon*

Taro Leaves in Coconut Cream

This is a favourite in many parts of the Pacific, and is known as palusami or lau me wau niu. Serves 4.

30 taro leaves or spinach leaves
125 ml/4 fl oz/½ cup canned coconut cream
½ teaspoon salt
banana leaves and breadfruit leaves
or aluminium foil for wrapping

Wash taro or spinach well in cold water, remove stems and any tough veins. Blanch spinach leaves briefly just long enough to soften or boil taro leaves for 45 minutes. Drain in a colander.

Wash and dry banana leaves. With a sharp knife remove any portion of thick mid rib that remains and cut the leaves into 20 cm (8 in) squares. Pass each one over a low flame to make them pliable or they will split when folded. On each square of banana leaf place some of the spinach or taro leaves. Spoon some coconut cream seasoned with salt onto the centre, and make a parcel of the leaves, enclosing them in the banana leaf. Finally wrap in breadfruit leaves or large squares of aluminium foil.

Place in a steamer and steam for 1 hour, or bake in a moderate oven. If using spinach, 15 minutes cooking time will be enough.

How to Prepare and Cook Taro Root

Taro tubers should be washed well and peeled deeply. The sticky juice can irritate the skin, so gloves are a good idea. Immerse the tuber in water immediately. This may be done hours before cooking, but once cooked it should be eaten hot as the texture becomes gluey on standing. It is improved by pan frying after it has been boiled, drained and dried on paper towels. Very thin slices of taro may be deep fried without boiling. In Chinese cuisine, the tuber is grated into long strips which are placed between two bowl-shaped frying spoons and deep fried to form the 'bird's nest' presentation which is popular at grand banquets.

Tea

(*Camellia sinensis*) Tea originated as a beverage in south-west China. It was China tea, drunk without milk, which was first introduced to the British by the early traders, and that is how it was drunk until well into the 1900s. The ritual of afternoon tea, practised with religious fervour by the English, was begun by the seventh Duchess of Bedford. The practice of putting the milk in the cup first was simply to protect the fine bone china cracking from the heat of the tea, but the practice has stuck.

The British, wanting to expand the existing tea growing regions, decided that Assam would be a good place to plant more tea and upon arriving there in the early 1900s with seeds and labourers from China were astonished to find lush forests of native tea bushes already well established. Tea plants were taken to Sri Lanka, Indonesia, Africa and a host of other countries with a suitable climate. Tea has since become a universal beverage.

There are shops which specialise in tea and sell teas from everywhere, teas of every kind and every price. Green teas and fermented black teas, teas which taste proudly of nothing but their own fragrant leaves, and teas which carry the aromas of jasmine, bergamot, almond, apricot and strawberry. Boutique teas are combined with dried edible flowers and look quite beautiful. Some teas are best taken black (for my palate those which have strong herbal or floral overtones, as well as green tea and those made from roasted grain).

But there are no hard and fast rules.

Tea should be kept in an airtight, light-proof container, away from heat and strong smelling foods or spices. Don't store the lapsang souchong next to your best flowery orange pekoe or they'll both end up tasting like lapsang souchong. My maiden aunts always stored a vanilla bean in the tea caddy, as they enjoyed the fragrance it imparted (forerunner of today's flavoured teas?).

Green teas are not fermented, black teas are fermented and oolong teas are semi-fermented. There are five distinct grades of leaf, with the distinctions based on shape and age of leaf. Even though it is only the downy terminal bud, also called the pekoe (in Chinese peh ho, which means 'white down') and the top two leaves that are picked, it is generally considered that the younger and smaller the leaf, the better quality the tea. The five grades are as follows:

Flowery orange pekoe: The classification given to the most refined teas using only the terminal bud and first leaf of each branch.

Orange pekoe: Harvested as soon as the terminal buds open into long, pointed leaves.

Pekoe: Shorter leaves, without bud.

Pekoe souchong: Still shorter, older leaves.

Souchong: The coarsest of all, even older leaves rolled into balls.

In China, tea is always drunk plain and very weak, compared to the way it is made in India, Sri Lanka and most Western countries. Whereas the rule for Western tea is 1 teaspoon for each cup and 1 for the pot, Chinese tea calls for a teaspoon of tea leaves for an entire pot (about 4 cups water); and when the first round has been poured, more boiling water is added to dilute the concentrated liquor. In most countries where there is a Chinese influence on food, weak, plain tea is drunk in the Chinese fashion with the meal.

Kashmiris also drink green (unfermented) tea, but sweetened and spiced (those who can afford spices) with cinnamon, cardamom, sometimes clove, ginger and saffron.

There are more teas and traditions of tea drinking in the continent of Asia than I will ever experience, but to help demystify the subject, here are a few of the most common tea terms:

Assam: Full-bodied teas from one of the most prolific growing areas in the world.

Black tea: Sourced from India, Sri Lanka, China and Africa, the basis of most Western blends.

Broken grades: Usually a quality tea such as orange pekoe, may contain tips (likely if 'flowery' appears in the name).

Ceylon: (Former name for Sri Lanka) High-grown Ceylon teas, from altitudes 1,800 metres and higher, have a reputation for quality.

Cloud mist (wun mo): A high-grown green tea from the Kiangsi mountain cliffs. So high grown, legend has it, that it is picked by trained monkeys.

Congou: A black China tea with large leaves.

Darjeeling: Expensive black tea from the foothills of the Himalayas. Often blended with lower quality tea.

Earl Grey: A tea attributed to the second Earl Grey, it is scented with oil of bergamot.

Fragrant petals (heung peen): An unusually fragrant tea.

Gunpowder: Also called 'pearl' or 'pinhead' tea, it is a green tea rolled into balls. A pale brew with a sharp taste.

Ichang: A rare and expensive high grown China tea from Hupeh with a mellow flavour.

Iron goddess of mercy: Traditionally served in small cups, this thin brew is a black tea made from stiff, shiny leaves. Like cloud mist, said to be picked by monkeys on account of the steep cliffs on which it grows.

Jasmine: A green China tea blended with jasmine flowers, steamed and spin-dried.

Keemum: A black tea with delicate flavour and spicy scent grown in the mountain regions of the southern provinces of Anhwei and Kiansi.

Laspang souchong: A black tea from Fukien and Taiwan, its tar-like flavour derives from the smoke fires over which it is dried.

Lung ching, jun jing: Also called dragon's well, this is a flat-leafed green tea with a distinctive taste, making a light, fresh brew. Considered the finest green tea in China. Limited production.

Oolong: Partially fermented tea from China and Taiwan, the best have a taste that hints at peach and have large, jagged leaves, occasionally tipped with white.

Panyong: Similar to keemun, but better quality, it comes from the Fukien province.

Souchong: A large-leafed Chinese tea.

Yunnan: Distinctive flavoured tea named after the Chinese province where it grows.

Long tea: Not a variety but a way of serving sweet, milky tea sold by street vendors in Asia. It is sometimes called 'tea by the yard' and is poured from tumbler to tumbler held about a metre apart, to make it froth and cool down somewhat.

China: In a 3rd century Chinese manuscript there is a reference to tea which reads 'When true tea is drunk, it keeps one awake'. Lu Yu, one of the earliest writers on tea, wrote in the 8th century, 'Tea tempers the spirits, calms and harmonises the mind; it arouses thought and prevents drowsiness, lightens and refreshes the body, and clears the perceptive faculties'. In the Cantonese Amoy dialect, tea is tay, the word first used for it by the English.

The Chinese drink both unfermented (green) and fermented (black, or as they more accurately describe it 'red') tea as well as oolong, a semi-fermented leaf, and teas scented with flowers. Some of the more popular black teas that use blossoms are jasmine (mook lay fa) and gardenia (pouchong). Lychee tea is flavoured with lychee leaves, rose tea (mei kwei) with rose petals, and some green teas are perfumed with narcissus or, more commonly, chrysanthemum (chiu hwa). Taken without milk, tea in China is restorative, tonic and a gesture of hospitality.

India: About the only part of India you'll find green tea drunk for pleasure is Kashmir. Elsewhere it is used as a medicinal drink for colds and indigestion. In Kashmir, the fragrant green tea qahwah is served at the end of a meal. The topaz-coloured liquid, redolent of cinnamon, cardamom and saffron, is brewed in a metal samovar (a jug with a central funnel filled with hot coals) and poured into small bowls from which it is sipped, sweetened with honey or sugar.

The tradition of adding spices to tea is a common practice in the colder parts of India as spices promote heat in the body. In Kashmir, as well as other parts of India, tea is infused in a mixture of water and milk. The liquid is first brought to a boil. As soon as it froths the leaves are added and the vessel covered tightly for 2–5 minutes to steep (until the tea is orange in colour, but not bitter). Some add a pinch of bicarbonate of soda (baking soda) to enhance the colour. Strained and served sweetened, the beverage is known as chai, the addition of spices such as cardamom, cloves, cinnamon or garam masala making it masala chai. Custom dictates that the more important the guest, the milkier the brew.

Japan: Tea is serious business in Japan. Ocha, as the national beverage of green tea is called, has its colour preserved by a process of steaming after it is picked. This destroys an enzyme which would otherwise cause the tea to ferment and turn black. The drinking of leaf tea was a later innovation, the first tea introduced from China being in powder form (matcha).

Just as there are grades of black tea, so are there grades of green. The elite tea of Japan, and most expensive, is gyokuro, which uses only the youngest, most tender buds from the oldest, most highly regarded bushes. Next comes sencha which is still a quality tea drunk for its flavour, rather than to quench thirst. At the bottom of the ladder is bancha, a common tea more yellow than green and slightly astringent. There are two other types of bancha: hoji-cha roasted and smoky tasting, which may be drunk cold; and genmai-cha, a coarse mix of leaves, stems and roasted rice, which has a pleasant, nutty flavour. Other popular brews include mugi-cha (roasted barley) and kobu-cha (kelp).

At any hour of the day, for any reason or none at all, green tea is drunk as a matter of course. Offered to every guest and client, and served, gratis, to coffee shop customers before they are brought their coffee, it is a sign of courtesy and welcome. The Japanese call the green tea served on such occasions nihon-cha, as opposed to kocha, which is the black tea drunk elsewhere in the world.

In May, the highly regarded sincha (first new leaves) are picked and sent to market. This is the leaf of the green tea that is for every-day drinking. Sincha itself can only be enjoyed for a brief period, the month in which it is picked, and it is claimed that the brighter-coloured brew from the fresh leaves has a mellower flavour. The water must not be boiling hot, nor should the tea brew for more than 2 minutes.

So fond are the Japanese of the flavour of green tea that it is even poured over rice to make chazuke which is eaten with chopsticks or, in more informal settings, drunk from the bowl. Some versions of chazuke include grilled, slivered nori, sesame seeds and bonito flakes.

The Japanese tea ceremony, which uses a green tea ground to a fine powder, has a whole cuisine to accompany it called kaiseki ryori (tea cooking). The tea ritual dates back to the practice of Zen Buddhist monks in China who drank the invigorating brew to help them stay alert during long devotions and was refined by Japanese tea masters in the 15th and 16th centuries. Legend has it that the priest, Daruma, not able to stay awake, tore off his eyelids. They took root and became a tea plant which, to this day, bears eyelid-shaped leaves. The rules laid out by the tea masters are still observed today and govern aspects of the ceremony as diverse as the dimensions of the tea room, the number of guests, the choice of plates and utensils and the depth of froth on the green tea whisked in each individual cup.

Korea: Korea has a number of delicious brews which all come under the category of tea, although the only one actually made of tea leaves is green tea. Roasted barley, corn and ginseng are very popular hot beverages brewed in a teapot at the table.

Sri Lanka: Formerly Ceylon, I still see signs of an identity crisis on packets labelled 'Ceylon Tea, Product of Sri Lanka'. Old habits die hard. Sri Lanka probably has the British to thank for its own very particular tea making habits. The water must be boiling and the pot (warmed, by rinsing out with boiling water) taken to the kettle where freshly boiled water is poured over the measured tea leaves. Allowing one teaspoon of tea leaves for each person and one for the pot, leave the tea to steep for a few minutes (longer if you prefer a stronger brew) before stirring and pouring. Always served, if not taken, with milk and sugar. The idea of drinking tea with lemon did not originate in Asia.

Vietnam, Thailand, Laos, Cambodia: Tea is drunk throughout the day in Vietnam. It is not uncommon for the morning pot to still be poured in the afternoon, having been continually topped up with boiling water. Called tra, it is drunk black and unsweetened. The most prized tea grown in Vietnam is from the central highlands and called tra bao loc. Green and black teas are drunk, as well as floral teas.

Tea Leaf Relish

Other people drink tea — in Burma, people also eat it. Made from fermented tea leaves, lephet is a nibble, an appetiser and a digestive. It is also a stimulant, since tea contains caffeine. Young tea leaves are picked before the rainy season, steamed to wilt them, and compressed into bamboo cylinders which are buried or cellared until fermented. Serving lephet is a tradition and special lacquered dishes hold the leaves as well as crisply fried garlic,

toasted sesame seeds, roasted peanuts and dried shrimps. The fermented leaves are dressed with a little oil and salt, each person mixing and kneading them with the fingers, then adding accompaniments to flavour the leaves to personal taste. Having partaken of lephet, I've never quite worked out whether it is the tea leaves or the items which season it that have won such a strong following. Lephet nibbling is something of a national pastime.

Techniques

Methods of preparing, cooking and presenting food vary from country to country. Cutting, squeezing, scoring, grating and garnishing are seldom parallel with Western methods. Various food preparation techniques are described below followed by cooking methods.

Preparation techniques

Crushing: Using a cleaver or broad-bladed knife, it is possible to crush garlic to a smooth paste without the wastage necessitated by a Western garlic press. The process begins by laying the broad side of a knife blade or cleaver on the garlic clove. A sharp blow will loosen the papery skin. After this, trim a thin slice off the hard stem end and proceed to scrape or drag the garlic against the wooden surface of the board. This process is greatly facilitated by the addition of an abrasive. If the recipe calls for an amount of salt or sugar, add it now to make the crushing easier and give a smoother result.

In many South East Asian countries, garlic is crushed in a tall stone mortar (usually granite) with a stone pestle, in an earthenware mortar with a hard wooden pestle (as in Thailand and Malaysia) or in a shallow dish-shaped mortar with stone pestle (as in Indonesia).

In Sri Lanka and India a 'flatbed' grinding stone (actually a pair of stones, one shaped like a bolster and the other like a bed) is used for crushing or grinding larger amounts and wetter pastes.

Cutting: Cutting techniques vary, but familiarity with ways of cutting is particularly important in Chinese cuisine. Once comfortable with these techniques, you will be able to see many applications, regardless of national borders.

Before mastering cutting techniques, you need to learn how to wield a chopper (cleaver) with skill and confidence. Choose the right chopper for the job: a fine-bladed chopper for cutting and slicing vegetables and meat and one with a thicker, heavier blade for chopping through bone. Almost as important is a heavy wooden chopping board. Avoid slick modern surfaces. They are inefficient, even dangerous, when it comes to serious chopping.

Straight chop: Used for cutting through ingredients with soft bones (fish, poultry, spareribs). Never use a sawing motion — it leaves rough edges. Hold the cleaver on the place you wish to cut, raise it up a little and then bring it down with a single, sharp stroke. If you need extra force, don't raise the cleaver. Hold it in position where you wish to make your cut and hit the top (blunt) edge of the cleaver blade with the side of a wooden or rubber mallet. Experienced chefs use the thickest part of their palms but for the inexperienced, there is potential for much pain and bruising. At all times, keep the hand that is holding the food as far from the cleaver as possible. See page 77 for instructions on how to cut up a chicken, Chinese style, through the bones.

Fine chop: I seem to have finely chopped more onions than anything else. It is best to use a chopper or knife with a thin blade so the tear-inducing tissues are not crushed more than necessary. Peel, leaving the root end on. Cut in half lengthways and place cut side down on board. Make close parallel cuts along its length from just near the root to the pointed end. Keeping one hand on the onion, slice parallel to the board from the point to the root. Lastly, make closely spaced downward cuts. Whatever the ingredient which needs fine chopping, the result is better and, eventually, quicker if this method is followed rather than random chopping.

Mincing chop: Used to mince meats and vegetables finely. For meat, first cut roughly and gather into a pile. With a cleaver, or two if you're game, chop finely from one edge of the pile to the other. If using two cleavers, keep them close and parallel, working up to a brisk, alternating rhythm between right and left hand. Flip mass of meat and repeat, rotating it 90 degrees. Repeat until the mince is as fine as required. To mince vegetables, an extremely finely chopped texture can be achieved by first thinly slicing, shredding, then cross-cutting finely.

Tenderising chop: Used on tough meats to break down the fibres, it is particularly effective in tandem with marinating. Use the blunt edge of the cleaver blade to finely cross-hatch the surface of the meat.

Scoring: A cut used on the surface of ingredients for decorative purposes, to tenderise or to help flavours penetrate. If the purpose is simply to facilitate the penetration of flavours, as in a marinade, cut slashes through the skin or surface of the flesh (half way to the bone for maximum flavour) before applying marinade. For a decorative scoring, as in squid scored before stir-frying, hold the cleaver at a 45 degree angle and make deep, evenly spaced parallel cuts into the flesh without cutting completely through. Cut again, keeping the cleaver at the same angle, 90 degrees to the initial cuts. This may take a little practice, but is effective for tenderising as it breaks down long fibres that make the flesh tough and helps it cook quickly.

Dicing: A fine texture square cut, between cubing and mincing. Slice, then cross cut into dice.

Cubing: Cut into large or coarse dice.

Roll cutting: This gives a maximum number of cut surfaces for quicker cooking and better penetration of flavours. Mostly used for long, slender vegetables such as asparagus, carrot and white radish. Place on board and take a diagonal slice from the tip. Roll one quarter turn and cut without changing the angle of the knife. Continue turning and cutting to end. The pieces will have a triangular appearance.

Slicing: A simple cutting action used for meat and vegetables. Always cut across the grain of the meat, for the most tender result. You'll get the finest, paper thin slices by partially freezing the meat. It needs to be firm enough not to 'give' under the pressure of the blade but not so hard that you can't cut into it.

Diagonal slicing: A useful technique to know when the ingredient is thin and you want the slices to look broad. Lay the ingredient flat on the board and make a diagonal cut at the top edge. The flatter you angle the knife or cleaver, the broader the slice will be. Useful for slicing thin cuts of meat, it is also an effective and attractive way to cut asparagus, spring onions (scallions), carrots and cucumbers.

Horizontal slicing: The cleaver is the ideal implement for this task. Particularly suited to round or flat items, from kidneys to abalone to water chestnuts. With the cleaver in one hand, place your free hand flat on ingredient to be cut. Holding cleaver blade parallel to the board, slice through food to be cut, removing each slice as it is completed. If you're unsure of your ability not to cut your hand (or if you're a concert pianist), use the slanting cut technique instead. It is safer.

Shredding: Slice finely, then cut into even julienne strips about matchstick width. To shred in quantity, stack up 3 or 4 thin slices and then, holding firmly, cut into strips.

Grating: There are a number of grating devices and each has a particular use (see UTENSILS). However, grating can achieve an effect from extremely fine shreds to a coarse purée, depending on the food being grated and the grating implement chosen. Grated daikon (giant white radish), for example, requires fine, long shreds while grated ginger should be a fine pulp. Take your cue from the recipe and how the grated ingredient is to be used. For example, grating an ingredient (e.g., onion, zucchini, taro) for fritters does not require too fine a shred, and long bits would make eating awkward, so use a grating surface that would give broad, short shreds. An ingredient that is grated so that it can be mixed into a sauce, marinade or dressing should be fine enough both for the flavour to penetrate it and to be evenly distributed through the liquid.

When the recipe calls for grated citrus rind (zest), it is important to grate (very finely) only the coloured portion as the white pith beneath it is unpleasantly bitter. Sometimes a small knife with very fine serrations will do a better job than a Western style grater, even on the side designed for zest. If you have no option but to use a metal zest grater, try this tip: hold a piece of greaseproof paper over the grater and rub the citrus skin across. With care, the paper won't tear and the zest will lift off easily, rather than be caught in the sharp metal teeth. As the paper gets damp, move to a fresh patch to avoid it disintegrating.

Grinding: Before the blender was invented, curry pastes were prepared by grinding the spices between two stones. In the hands of a skilled operator the two stones, clumsy though they may seem, give infinitely better results than a blender. For small quantities and dry grinding or crushing, a stone mortar and pestle is used with a pounding motion. Wet pastes work best on a flat, oblong stone slab with a cylindrical, bolster-shaped stone pestle using a rolling 'push and pull' rather than pounding action.

Marinating: A process of steeping meat in a wet mixture that both adds flavour and tenderises. Generally, the longer the marinating process, the better the flavour and more tender the texture. The addition of an enzyme like papain or tenderiser such as bicarbonate of soda (baking soda) may be helpful if the cut of meat is exceedingly tough. Don't leave meat unrefrigerated, even in a marinade, for more than a couple of hours, even less if the weather is hot.

Marinades vary from oriental mixtures of soy sauce, wine, oil with sugar, honey or five-spice powder added, to the more pungent marinades of South East Asia which can include various mixtures of ground spices, puréed onion, garlic and ginger and pungent ingredients such as shrimp paste.

Marinating raw fish in lemon or lime juice has a chemical action on the flesh which virtually 'cooks' it. Drain off the soaking juice as this will have a fishy taste, and if the recipe calls for more lime juice in the dressing, add it freshly squeezed. The acidity is often balanced by the addition of coconut milk. Because of the action of acid substances on seafood, it is best not to marinate prawns (shrimp) in marinades containing vinegar, citrus juice or even yoghurt for a long period or the texture will be spoiled, the natural firmness of the flesh becoming floury.

Salt curing: Salt curing is the process whereby large cuts of meat or whole poultry are rubbed with coarse salt and Szechwan pepper which is left to penetrate for a couple of days before simmering or steaming. Intended for cold eating, salt curing brings out the flavour and refines the texture of the flesh. Small items such as unshelled prawns (shrimp), pieces of poultry and organ meats are treated by an abbreviated method called 'salt watering'. The process removes strong flavour from organ meats and gives them a firm texture, without making them dry. Chilling the cooked meat in the cooking brine is the secret of the flavour which improves, except in the case of prawns, over a couple of days. Meats cooked by either of these methods will keep for up to a week in the fridge.

Salt whipping: A technique used to obtain the texture that makes Crystal Prawns such a special dish. Shelled raw prawns (shrimp) are sprinkled with salt and whipped or beaten briskly with a wooden spoon or chopsticks for a full minute, then rinsed under cold water for an equal length of time. Repeated twice, the technique makes the flesh of the prawns crisp.

Squeezing: One of the techniques which is probably unfamiliar to a Western cook is what translates roughly as squeezing. Coconut milk (if being made fresh and not poured out of a can) needs the richness squeezed from grated coconut. Finely shredded Asian salad ingredients such as leaves, finely sliced onions and grated fresh coconut are also squeezed with a simple seasoning of salt and lime juice, and perhaps a sliced fresh chilli or two. The difference this makes to the flavour rather than just tossing or combining, must be tasted to be believed.

Velvet and velveting: While they may sound connected, these two words describing Chinese preparation techniques indicate separate and quite different procedures.

Applied to the ingredient chicken, for example, 'velvet' is a noun denoting finely puréed breast fillets, generally hand chopped using two choppers at once. Chopping in a food processor is acceptable as long as it is not overdone. The purée is made very light by gradually working in a small amount of cold water, then seasoning and some fine starch such as water chestnut flour or cornflour (cornstarch). Finally, egg whites whipped to the soft peak stage are folded into the puréed chicken. The mixture is chilled for 30 minutes before cooking in water or oil. The chicken should remain white with the texture similar to a soft custard.

Velveting is a term used in Chinese cooking to denote that an ingredient is given a protective coating of egg white, cornflour (cornstarch) and peanut oil. A technique widely used in China with delicate meats such as seafood and chicken breast, to prevent them drying out during cooking.

Cooking techniques

Barbecuing: See **Roasting**.

Boiling: To cook in bubbling hot water. Fast boiling is not generally done for prolonged periods. More often, it is called for to bring a dish to a required temperature before lowering heat to a simmer.

Braising: In any cuisine, braising means sealing food by cooking in a little oil or fat, then adding minimal liquid (water, wine or stock), or simply covering and cooking until tender. A technique used globally but known by many names. In China, according to some recipes, red-cooked dishes are braised; in India, all spiced dishes with the name korma undergo the same cooking process, using different flavours, of course; some Filipino beef and chicken specialties are also braised. Many Sri Lankan curries are also based on this technique

which deepens the flavour while still achieving a tender result.

Clear-simmering: A Chinese technique which captures the natural flavours of food by slow cooking in stock until the food is tender and the broth is enriched. Flavours may be extremely simple, e.g. stock, salt and Chinese wine or sherry; or quite complex, e.g. dried mushrooms, shrimp, scallops, pepper, garlic and soy sauce, depending on the meat or fish being cooked. Also used for cooking vegetables and vegetarian products. The method preferred for delicate foods such as shark's fin. Cuts of meat should be sinewy or slightly fatty as they more readily turn the cooking liquid unctuous.

Curry cooking: There are a number of techniques used in the stages of making a curry. First the spices are roasted (see **Dry roasting**) and ground. If it is based on a wet paste, the spices are ground with herbs or other flavour ingredients (see **Grinding**). Some curries begin and others end with a few whole seeds and spices fried in oil or ghee (see **Tempering**). After the initial slow frying of the ground curry paste ingredients (onion, garlic, spices), a good curry cook will know the sign that all the moisture has been evaporated when the mixture exudes oil. Called see byan in Burmese, it translates as 'oil returned' and is the signal to add the main ingredients and proceed with the recipe. In some curries it occurs after hours of cooking, indicating that the curry is ready.

Dry roasting: (Also called dry frying or pan roasting) Altering flavours by roasting is a technique much used in South East Asia with spices and ingredients such as rice, sesame seeds and coconut. There are degrees of roasting which the experienced cook knows will give a certain effect. For instance, a light roasting of spices will barely change their colour but will bring out the flavours. Medium roasting will change the flavours somewhat and really dark roasting will produce a completely different effect in the finished dish. It must be emphasised that the roasting is done over low heat, and the ingredient is constantly stirred and never allowed to burn.

The sweet, fresh taste of grated coconut becomes much richer and more complex when it is roasted until chestnut brown. It is used to flavour and thicken sambals and curries.

Roasted and ground rice gives a very special

flavour and crunch to certain salads, and what is essentially a bland, neutral ingredient takes on quite a distinctive flavour through dry roasting.

Sri Lanka is famous for its 'black' curries, the colour a result of long, slow dry roasting of spices such as fennel, cumin and coriander. The dark roasting brings out nuances of flavour in a subtle way. Although the final colour of the dry roasted spices should be a deep, rich coffee brown, at no time should the heat under the roasting spices be high or the curry will have an undesirable burnt taste.

Flavour potting: A Chinese technique similar to red-cooking, with the flavour pot sauce simmered by itself before any ingredient to be cooked is added to it. Like red-cooking sauce, it may be kept alive in the freezer for months or, if used regularly (weekly), refrigerated between times and topped up with each use. Some of Peking's best restaurants claim their flavour pots are 20 generations old! Often more aromatic than a red-cooked sauce with the addition of spices such as cinnamon, fennel, star anise or licorice root, dried tangerine peel, Szechwan peppercorns and five-spice powder.

Frying: Whether shallow frying, deep frying or stir-frying, the oil should be the right temperature for the result you wish to achieve. A general rule is that the oil should be hot enough to seal the food, or it will absorb oil and be heavy and greasy.

Shallow frying: Best done in a heavy frying pan (skillet). This technique is used when the aim is to seal an ingredient and brown it. A large flat surface is necessary and sufficient oil to cover the base of the frying pan to a depth of about 3 mm (1/8 in).

A well seasoned cast-iron frying pan or other heavy pan in one of the modern, non-stick materials is suitable. Thin metals would scorch and burn. Make sure the pan is very hot before the food is added so a crust forms on the outside, then turn heat to medium so food will cook through without burning.

Ideal for browning meats, for crisping the surface of cooked and drained noodles, and indispensable for those fried and steamed dumplings known as pot stickers (see YUM CHA).

Deep frying: Requires that the oil be deep enough to completely surround the food being cooked. If not using a special deep fryer I recommend using a wok as it needs less oil to achieve the required depth than a straight-sided pan. Because of its curved shape, the same amount of oil will give

at least twice the depth in a wok as it would in a large frying pan. Any pan in which deep frying is done should never be more than half full of oil. The greater depth of a wok also ensures there is less danger of the oil overflowing and igniting. Limit the amount of food added at any one time, as too much will lower the temperature of the oil and will result in greasy food. Always drain fried foods on paper towels to blot excess oil.

After frying, the cooled oil should be passed through a fine strainer. Store in a bottle in a cool, dark place. It may be re-used for frying for up to a month.

Stir-frying: The technique most used in Asian cooking, probably as a result of the need to conserve fuel. The food is cut into small pieces of even size, and ingredients added to the wok with those that take longest to cook going in first. A dish for 4–6 people can be cooked in 3 minutes. It is organising the ingredients and having everything measured and ready which enables this to be done. When stir-frying, remember the golden rule: 'hot wok, warm oil'. In other words, heat the wok first before adding the oil. This stops food sticking to the wok. A minimal amount of oil is heated and swirled around in the wok, then the ingredients quickly cooked in it over high heat, constantly flipping and tossing (stir-frying).

Griddle baking: Cooking on a hot griddle is the technique used to achieve the delicious flat breads of India. The charring and puffing of chapatis and rotis is done by passing the cooked bread over a naked flame. The griddle is vital to the Japanese technique of teppan yaki, in which foods are rapidly cooked on a hot metal plate using a limited number of seasonings and butter for flavour and to prevent sticking.

Grilling: Small pieces of food are marinated, sometimes on skewers, and cooked over glowing coals. A quick cooking process that enhances the flavour of the food and imparts a complex, smoky taste. Used in India, Indonesia, Malaysia, Singapore, Vietnam and Japan.

Pit cooking: The popular Pacific island practice of cooking in an earth oven (in the ground on a bed of heated stones), the food wrapped in leaves (banana or ti leaves), covered with wet sacks or hot stones and left to 'steam' for a few hours.

Techniques

Red-cooking: Sometimes called Chinese stewing, red-stewing or red-braising and similar to the technique called flavour potting. The key ingredients in a red-cooked dish, responsible for both its unique colour and flavour, are dark soy sauce, light soy sauce and salt (optional), star anise or five-spice powder, sherry and sugar. Meats done this way are sometimes blanched first and then slow-cooked in the sauce before being allowed to cool in it, and brushed with sesame oil before serving.

Another method is to sear the main ingredient in oil before adding seasonings and boiling water and simmering until done. Or put the raw meat straight into the pot with the flavour ingredients and cold water. After bringing to the boil, the heat is lowered and the meat left to simmer until tender. It is important, if serving cold, to allow meat to cool in the liquid to retain maximum moisture.

Red-cooked dishes may be dense with meat or contain a variety of meats and vegetables, in that respect not unlike a Western stew. After red-cooking, strain leftover cooking sauce and store in refrigerator or freezer. With regular use (cooking in the sauce once a week and topping it up as it evaporates), the sauce will 'live' indefinitely.

See recipe for Red-cooked Chicken (page 79).

Roasting: Not a technique used in a domestic situation in Asia, due to the absence of Western-style ovens. In China and countries where there is a Chinese population, roast pork, barbecued pork and Peking duck are bought from commercial establishments with large, barrel-shaped ovens. Food is roasted in a vertical position to allow drainage of fat and equal exposure of all surfaces to the heat. In India, shops specialising in tandoori food turn out delicious meats roasted on skewers and breads, slapped directly onto the walls of a huge, coal-fired, clay oven called a tandoor.

Salt grilling: Also known as steam grilling, this is a Japanese method of cooking in which the bottom of an unglazed earthenware casserole is covered with coarse salt to a depth of about 1 cm (½in), sprinkled with a little water and heated for 5–10 minutes until the salt is heated through. Onto the salt bed is spread a fine layer of pine needles and then the food to be cooked (prawns [shrimp], shelled and deveined with tails intact, ginkgo nuts on skewers, chicken, mushrooms and chestnuts). It is covered with a well-fitting lid or foil, and cooked over a medium-high heat for 5–15 minutes (seafood requiring only short cooking, poultry longer).

Salt roasting: A stovetop method of cooking without liquid used in Chinese cuisine. A whole chicken or duck is rubbed with marinade, wrapped in softened, oiled lotus leaves or muslin and buried under a hill of hot salt in a covered pan or wok and cooked until tender.

Scorching: A cooking technique used to give a slightly charred, quite delicious flavour to a dish, this technique is unique to Bengali vegetable dishes and involves a three-step process: boiling, steaming and frying. Quite deliberately the liquid in the pan is allowed to evaporate completely, and the contents allowed to stick slightly to the bottom of the pan. In some instances as soon as the scorching starts a little water is added and cooking continues until the pan is dry again. This is repeated a few times until the correct flavour is achieved. Heavy pans and careful observation are necessary. Don't go away and leave the pan as burning (not the same as scorching) will not improve the dish at all.

Do not stir during cooking, for it would hinder the formation of the 'scorched' crust which is the secret of the flavour. Coarsely cut vegetables placed in a heavy-based pan are briefly boiled in a spiced liquid. Covered with a loose-fitting lid, they are then steamed for about half an hour or till soft. It is important not to let all the liquid evaporate at this stage, as the charring should only take place after the ghee has been added. If it looks dry, add a little more water.

When vegetables are done and the liquid has dried up, add ghee, butter or oil and leave on low heat until a crust forms on the bottom of the pan. Listen for it. A slight sizzling sound will indicate that the crust has formed. Remove from heat and without lifting lid, allow a few minutes for the crust to soften before stirring to mix the brown crust into the vegetables. Serve as a side dish with rice or breads and curries. Also called charchari.

Smoking: A technique used in Chinese cooking more to flavour foods than to cook them. Foods to be smoked are often cured or steamed first, to shorten the smoking period. Although some people advise that you can smoke foods in the oven, the smell of burnt material lingers and might flavour cookies and cakes baked in the oven at a later date.

I use a tall, heavy-based pot with a tight-fitting

lid and line it with a double layer of aluminium foil. There are a number of ingredients which are recommended for smoking fuel and these include tea leaves (dry), sugar, rice, wood shavings (be sure they are not from a toxic tree) and pine needles. I mostly use tea and brown sugar, with delicious results. To boost flavour, try adding some crushed dried tangerine peel, star anise or Szechwan pepper and sprinkle evenly over foil. Arrange food on a wire rack ot trivet, cover pan with lid and place over medium-high heat. Heating these substances causes a build-up of smoke in the pan. Turn heat very low. The smoky flavour permeates the food as well as giving it an appetising colour. Smoking is especially suitable for poultry and seafood.

Steaming: A technique used throughout Asia. Food is placed on a rack or trivet inside a pot with a well-fitting lid and cooked in the captive steam. There is a difference between direct steaming (where food is cooked on a rack above boiling water as in dim sum) and indirect steaming (where the food is placed in a plate which sits on a rack or trivet over boiling water). In the second method, the juices from the steaming food are an important part of the dish.

In India steamed food is called dumned (breathed in). The Asian method of rice cooked by absorption produces 'steamed rice', since a tight-fitting lid holds in the steam.

Steaming can be an entire cooking process, or one of a number of steps in a more complicated recipe. If you don't own a steamer you can easily enough improvise one using a large pot with a well-fitting lid and a trivet or cake rack. See UTENSILS.

Stored heat cooking: For a succulent result, this method is ideal. Bring to the boil sufficient water to cover the meat, fish or poultry. Add onion, celery, slices of ginger, whole peppercorns, salt or whatever flavours you wish to have in the dish. Cover and simmer for 10 minutes to flavour the cooking liquid. Lower the item to be cooked into the pot, bring it back to simmering point, cover and continue simmering for half the time it would normally require. Turn off heat, leave pot covered for 45 minutes, (20 minutes for a whole fish) and it will finish cooking in the stored heat. Lift out of the liquid and serve with dipping sauces and rice.

Tempering: This technique, widely used in India and Sri Lanka, and whichever countries have adopted those cuisines, involves frying certain ingredients in hot oil or ghee to enhance their flavour. This may be done at the start of cooking or the end. If frying a mixture of whole spices, it is best to add them to the oil one at a time, starting with the one that needs longest cooking and ending with those that need least. If using ground spices be watchful: the cooking time will be dramatically reduced as they burn easily.

When mustard seeds are sufficiently tempered they will turn grey and pop, often right out of the pan. Keep a lid or spatter screen handy.

Allow cumin seeds to take on a rich brown colour. Add after the mustard seeds if using both.

Fresh chillies usually blister when fried, at which point they are done. If using dried chillies, fry them before anything else, removing them as they start to darken as they burn easily. Sometimes their crisp texture is required, in which case they are crumbled over the food when it is ready to be eaten.

Many a delicious dish is begun by frying onions. This is a basic tempering ingredient which may be followed by fresh curry leaves, chillies, ginger or garlic. Often a dry spice mix or curry powder may follow, to be tempered before the addition of the main (protein or starch) ingredient. In some cases, after a dish is cooked, a fragrant powdered spice mix (called suwanda kudu in Sri Lanka) is tempered briefly and then sprinkled over the finished dish just before it is served.

In India tempering is known by several names including chaunk, baghar and tadka, and often these descriptions find their way into the name of the dish. The degree of tempering (how long the spices are allowed to fry) is a matter of personal preference — a lightly tempered spice mix resulting in a fairly mild chaunk while long tempering results in an almost charred chaunk with more pungent aroma and taste. Chaunk, containing a liberal amount of ginger (believed to be carminative) is particularly popular with dhal (lentils). Some traditional flavour combinations for dhal include: garlic and red chilli; cumin and onions; asafoetida; onions and cloves.

White-cut cooking: A Chinese technique. A whole chicken or a cut of pork, simmered without soy sauce and served cold, with a sauce poured over it or dipping sauces on the side, is said to be 'white-cut'. The meat or chicken is simmered and steeped in boiling water until just done, then immediately plunged into iced water which tightens the muscle fibres and seals in the moisture, making the meat firm and tasty. Suitable for ham, pork and chicken. See recipe for White-cut Chicken (page 78).

Tempeh

Made from fermented soy beans, this product is popular among vegetarians as it provides protein in a meatless diet. It is quicker to produce than many other soy products. The beans are soaked overnight, hulled, steamed for 30 minutes, soaked overnight again and then inoculated with a pure culture of *Rhizopus oligosporus*. In about 24 hours the soy beans have become the solid product which is sold in the freezer section of Asian stores and health food stores, mostly in 250 g (8 oz) blocks.

It has an attractive appearance, the whole beans visible under a whitish bloom reminiscent of the velvety rind on camembert or brie. The flavour is savoury and the food value includes riboflavin, niacin, thiamin and a vitamin usually only available in animal products, vitamin B12. Tempeh may be steamed, boiled, shallow or deep fried, baked or grilled. It can be blended into a dip or dressing, grated to include in a vegetarian loaf, or cooked like minced (ground) chicken or steak, with flavours which make it quite delicious.

Savoury Tempeh

Serves 4

250 g/8 oz tempeh
3 tablespoons oil
2 medium onions, finely chopped
3 teaspoons finely chopped garlic
2 teaspoons finely chopped fresh chilli
2 teaspoons ground coriander
1 teaspoon ground cumin
1 teaspoon ground turmeric
salt and pepper to taste
2 tablespoons chopped fresh mint
2 tablespoons chopped spring onions (scallions)

Cut cakes of tempeh into 6 mm (¼ in) slices, then stack the slices and cut into tiny dice. Heat oil and fry the tempeh until golden brown and crisp. Remove from pan. In remaining oil (add a little more if necessary) fry the onions and garlic over low heat until soft and golden. Add chilli and ground spices and fry for a minute longer. Add tempeh, salt, mint and spring onions. Serve with rice.

Thai Style Tempeh

Serves 4

250 g/8 oz tempeh
4 tablespoons oil
2 tablespoons Thai red curry paste
  (recipe page 114)
400 ml/14 fl oz can coconut milk
2 teaspoons palm sugar or brown sugar
2 tablespoons fish sauce
2 fresh, frozen or dried kaffir lime leaves
fresh basil leaves or coriander

Cut tempeh into thin slices, about 6 mm (¼ in) and then into bite-sized pieces. Heat oil in a wok and fry tempeh slices until golden. Drain on paper towels. Discard all but 1 tablespoon of the oil, and in it fry the curry paste, stirring, until fragrant. Add coconut milk, stirring. Add palm sugar, fish sauce and lime leaves. Allow to simmer uncovered for 10 minutes before adding the tempeh. Return to simmer for 5 minutes and scatter fresh herbs in just before serving with steamed rice.

Tenderisers

Meat in Asia is not always of premium quality. More often than not, it is extremely tough. Therefore, longer cooking times are essential and sometimes sterner measures resorted to. However, there is a trade-off. It is important that you understand that any chemical tenderiser (including natural substances) must alter the texture of the meat, and this is not always to everyone's liking.

Wrap the meat in bruised papaya leaves, or marinate it using pieces of green papaya. Papaya bark, leaves and fruit, contain papain, an enzyme which breaks down meat protein. Pineapple is another effective tenderiser, its enzyme being bromelin, which also breaks down protein. Contact for too long with such an efficient tenderising agent will literally turn meat to powder (as I discovered with horror when I tried to eat a day-old dish of chicken and green papaya salad).

Rubbing meat with pineapple or marinating it in pineapple juice (fresh, not canned or processed) will also tenderise it. The problem is that the enzymes only work on the surface they come in direct contact with, so in order to allow it to tenderise the meat through and through it must be pricked all over so the enzymes can do their work.

Unfortunately, this causes a loss of juices, resulting in a drier end result. While these methods have been used for hundreds of years, it is probably best to just allow extra cooking time.

Vinegar, lime juice and yoghurt are also used as tenderisers in marinades. The problem, as Harold McGee points out in his book *On Food and Cooking*, is that 'tenderizers do not accomplish much until they reach a temperature of 140–160°F (60–79°C) so there is no point in letting them sit on the meat at room temperature. The enzyme is inactivated when boiling point is reached. Marinades containing wine or vinegar can also tenderize the surface of meat — their acid denatures the surface proteins — but again the result will be drier meat. In general, there are at present no really satisfactory ways of tenderizing meat chemically.'

If cooking in Asia with the local meat or poultry, it seems you'll have to dust off the pressure cooker, or else accept that dinner will take longer to cook than it does in Western lands.

The Chinese method of tenderising is to marinate thinly sliced meat for at least 4 hours in a mixture of ½ teaspoon bicarbonate of soda (baking soda) in 3 tablespoons water for each 500 g (1 lb) of meat. This transforms cheaper, long-cooking cuts into the equivalent of fillet steak which takes just a minute or two of stir-frying, but meat tenderised with it acquires a distinctive flavour and texture. It is a method commonly used in Chinese restaurants and a good thing for home cooks to know when watching the budget.

Beating steaks with a wood or metal mallet fitted with spikes which break up fibres is as good a tenderising treatment as any. Of course, this is only really suitable for treating fairly thin steaks. It has the advantage that spices and flavours can be simultaneously beaten into the meat.

Thailand

My introduction to Thai food could not have been more felicitous. I had the privilege of sitting in the kitchen of one of the best exponents of Thai cuisine and learning, watching, discussing; absorbing not merely recipes and techniques but the essence of how Thai food was regarded by one of the great teachers of this art. On subsequent visits I have been fortunate to meet other skilled and mature women and learn from them. The maturity is important. They belong to the generation which regards the finer points of culinary art as treasure to be entrusted to the next generation, who hopefully will keep the tradition alive. Somehow I cannot see frozen Thai dinners taking hold — though supermarkets now sell instant tom yum soup cubes, some of which are very good.

As in other Asian countries, Thailand offers, along all its busy roads, a stream of eating stalls from which one can compile an entire menu. Go to a market where fresh produce is sold, and there will also be stalls selling prepared food, anything from freshly cooked curry puffs and crisp pancakes to green papaya salad, fiery with chilli. More up-market are the fast food shops taking perhaps an entire floor of a busy shopping centre, or situated in the grounds of a five-star hotel.

As befits a country which has never been conquered or colonised (something which cannot be said of many countries), the food of Thailand is unique. Yet there is obvious cross-pollination when ingredients are deemed worth adopting. For example, Indian spices have been grafted onto already complex flavours to give the world Thai Masaman Curry. Chinese influenced one-dish meals abound too, yet no one would say they are purely Chinese or that the Thais have copied blindly. It has always been a prerogative of creative cooks to pick the best features of neighbouring cuisines; but the Thais create bold combinations of flavours to make the resulting dishes quite individual.

The blending of spices and fresh herbs in Thai curries is more complex and sophisticated than in any other South East Asian cuisine, with the balance of sweet, sour, hot and salty flavours observed in a way that is a treat for the tastebuds.

Thai meals are based on rice, mostly steamed long grain jasmine rice with a delicate natural perfume. It is cooked without salt to balance the salty flavours in accompanying dishes, served steaming hot, and kept at the desired temperature in a covered container or individual woven baskets. Traditionally the complete meal is presented at once. Rice is the most important item, and is served with one or two liquid dishes called kaeng; side dishes which come under the heading of krueng kieng; a soup or kaeng chud; and raw or cooked vegetables served with a hot dip (nam prik).

In modern Thailand, especially in elegant hotels and restaurants, the meal is served in courses starting with tiny, palate-challenging appetisers and followed by the main course of rice accompanied by soup, curries, a steamed dish, a fried dish and salad.

A plate of exquisitely carved fruit is sometimes served after the main dishes are cleared away. Desserts are a western notion, but Thailand's sweets which are normally eaten as between-meal snacks, are sometimes presented at the end of a meal.

Food presentation is all-important. Thai skills in fruit and vegetable carving are legendary. The decorative detail even on bite-sized curry puffs, dumplings and other appetisers is ingrained in Thai cooks. Thai haute cuisine is beautiful to behold. I observed young girl apprentices in a top restaurant carving intricate designs into the skin of pale green gourds hollowed out to hold dipping sauce.

Among an array of small, prettily coloured sweets, mostly based on tapioca starch, glutinous rice, agar-agar jelly, palm sugar and coconut milk, one is dazzled by the miniature painted fruits moulded from sweet bean paste, their form and colour rivalling the marzipan fruits of Europe. Thai cuisine is undoubtedly one of the world's greatest, appealing to all of the senses.

Knowing a few terms will help you negotiate your way through a Thai menu: tom yum (soup), yum (salad), khao (rice), mee (noodles), kaeng phed (hot soup or curry), kaeng chud (mild soup or curry) nam prik (hot dipping sauce), nam oi (sweet sauce), pla (fish), poo (crab), goong (prawns [shrimp]), nuer (beef) and moo (pork).

Tiffin

Even in the heat of the tropics, somewhere between breakfast and the evening meal, hunger demands a stop for refuelling. This meal is referred to as tiffin or curry tiffin. Where the Indian influence does not reach, lunch is the equivalent word.

Tiffin almost always includes a curry or other spiced dish. During the working week, tiffin is, more often than not, prepared in the home kitchen, packed and sent to the office where it arrives, still hot, to nourish the breadwinner. This custom spawned a whole industry — manufacturing tiffin carriers and employing tiffin boys.

Tiffin carriers consist of 2 or 3 straight-sided containers of steel, or enamel-coated metal. Sometimes the enamel is decorated with elaborate designs. The containers are fitted with metal lugs to slip onto the tall metal frame which holds them together.

Tiffin 'boys' are often more mature than the description implies, and ride bicycles fitted with large wooden crates back and front, into which they load more meals than one would believe possible. They collect hundreds of tiffin carriers (or, in some cases, lunches packed in enamel plates tied with a starched white cloth) deliver all these lunches to the correct office, collect them afterwards and return them to the home address.

How do they get the right lunch to the right person? It is a highly organised industry, the tiffin boys arriving from their suburban pick-up points to a central area where lunches are sorted according to which office they are destined for.

Tiffin, to the British in India or elsewhere in Asia, meant a quite substantial meal, especially Sunday Tiffin. This usually included mulligatawny, rice with various curries, and the myriad relishes which made a curry meal special. Guests usually ate themselves to a standstill and retired to sleep off the effects of too much food (and probably too many drinks) in the middle of the day.

In many of the luxury hotels of Asia, this custom still prevails, and the legendary Raffles Hotel in Singapore boasts a magnificent room which has always been called The Tiffin Room.

Not to confuse, but to explain that 'tiffin' has different connotations to different people, in the days when I was growing up in a beautiful and peaceful island called Ceylon, 'tiffin' was afternoon tea — a snack served when children got home from school and needed something to stave off starvation between then and the usually quite late dinner hour.

This would take the form of banana fritters, Bombay toast (you may know it better as French toast) or, during times of wartime shortages of just about everything, bread and tinned butter sprinkled with pepper and salt. It was not until I grew up, moved in more sophisticated circles and got invited to Curry Tiffin at the stately Mount Lavinia Hotel looking out on a golden, palm-fringed beach, that I realised tiffin was something more than a simple snack.

It is, one may safely assume, the British version of Rijstaffel.

Tofu

See BEAN CURD.

Tom Yum Goong

One of the popular and quite famous soups of Thailand featuring chilli and prawns (shrimp). See recipe for Thai Hot Sour Prawn Soup (page 298).

Tomato

(*Lycopersicum esculentum*) Native to South America and cultivated widely in Central America and Mexico. When taken to Europe, the earliest record (1544) is of a yellow-fruited tomato, which led to its Italian name, pomodoro (golden apple). Today, however, red varieties are more numerous.

Tomatoes are used more in India and South East Asia than in the cuisines of the Far East. They are eaten raw in salads, diced to make relishes, and added to curries to cook down and contribute moisture and a red colour to the sauce. They lend themselves to many decorations, notably the tomato rose, simply formed with a long strip of tomato peel (see GARNISHES). They also feature in India's tomato oil pickle, which even Westerners know and embrace as Tamatar Kasaundi (recipe below).

> **China:** *faan kee*
> **India:** *tamatar*
> **Indonesia:** *tomat*
> **Japan:** *tomato*
> **Malaysia:** *tomato*
> **Philippines:** *kamatis*
> **Sri Lanka:** *thakkali*
> **Thailand:** *makheua thet*

Tomato Oil Pickle (Tamatar Kasaundi)

2 tablespoons black mustard seeds
500 ml/1 pint/2 cups malt vinegar
250 g/8 oz fresh ginger
20 large cloves garlic, peeled
30 fresh chillies, red or green
2.5 kg/5 lb firm ripe tomatoes
500 ml/1 pint/2 cups vegetable oil
2 tablespoons ground turmeric
6 tablespoons ground cumin
2 tablespoons chilli powder or to taste
375 g/12 oz/1½ cups sugar
1½ tablespoons salt or to taste

Soak mustard seeds overnight in the vinegar. Grind to a purée using an electric blender. Add roughly chopped ginger and garlic and blend until smooth.

Halve chillies lengthways. Remove seeds if liked. Blanch tomatoes briefly in boiling water, peel, halve and gently squeeze out most of the seeds. Dice the flesh of the tomatoes.

In a large, non-aluminium pan heat the oil until smoking. Remove from heat and allow to cool slightly so dry spices will cook without burning. Stir in ground turmeric, cumin and chilli powder. Add tomatoes, chillies, blended mixture, sugar and salt. Simmer until tomatoes are reduced to a pulp and oil starts to float on top. Taste and add more salt if required. Put into clean, dry bottles heated in the oven to sterilise. Cover with non-metallic lids and allow to mature for a week before using. Keeps well.

Ti Leaf

(*Cordyline terminalis*) These are tough, oblong leaves used throughout the Pacific, particularly in Polynesia, for wrapping food before cooking. They range in size from small to quite large. They keep well in paper or plastic in the refrigerator and are ready to use after rinsing in cold water and drying. They are also sold dried and in this form will keep for years, but will need soaking to make them pliable. In Hawaii they are used as the wrapping for laulau, leaf parcels containing chicken or pork which are cooked in an underground oven as part of the festive luau. In Tahiti they are used to wrap fish for cooking. In fact, they are nature's answer to aluminium foil. In Samoa, they are used only to wrap fish as it is thought the flavour enhances fish, but not other foods.

A spirit distilled from the baked mash of the roots and known as okelehao (abbreviated to oke) is another product of the plant.

Trefoil

See MITZUBA.

Tripe

See OFFAL.

Tropical Almond

(*Terminalia catappa*, *T. kaernbachii*) Various seed kernels are given this rather loose description. Also known as country almond and Indian almond. Grown on spreading trees with very large, leathery, oval leaves which turn red before they fall. The tree has a distinctive shape, its horizontal branches growing in wide spreading circles at different levels on the trunk. Commonly seen in the South Pacific islands, Papua and South East Asia.

The pale green fruit is the size and shape of an almond in its shell. Some varieties become reddish-purple when ripe. Each fruit has a fibrous seed containing a narrow, pointed edible kernel, which has been described as 'beyond comparison, the most delicious nut of any kind India affords'.

An old book says: 'In its native home the nut is much relished by all classes, being eaten raw or cooked and prepared in different ways'.

My personal experience is that the kernels are usually eaten fresh and raw. The fibrous fruit and shell needs to be smashed open with a hammer or pestle, carefully gauging how hard to hit so that the fragile kernel is not destroyed.

In market stalls, the kernels are usually sold in twists of paper. Each kernel has a thin, parchment-like covering easily removed with a fingernail. The covering is quite soft, but has an astringency which spoils the enjoyment of the milky nut, so my advice is to peel away the skin before eating the nut. The nut itself, instead of being in two halves like most kernels, is formed of a thin continuous layer, rolled like a miniature cigar. *T. kaernbachii*, known as okari nut, has a mild almond flavour and may be eaten raw, roasted or salted. See also JAVA ALMOND.

Fiji: *tavola, tavola lato*
Hawaii: *kamani*
India: *kottai*
Malaysia: *ketapang, ketapang lintak*
Philippines: *talisay*
Singapore: *ketapang almond*
Sri Lanka: *kotamba, kotang, kadoru*
Tahiti: *tamanu, autera'a*
Tonga: *fetau*

Tup Tim Grob

This is an instance where foreign words can't be avoided because that is the name by which this delicious, refreshing Thai sweet is known. 'Water chestnut in syrup with coconut milk', would be a brief description. The literal translation is 'crisp rubies', tup tim meaning 'rubies', but at the same time the word for 'pomegranate'. The connection is clear to anyone who has seen glistening red seeds inside a ripe pomegranate. In this Thai sweet, however, the appearance is derived from soaking finely diced water chestnuts in a diluted solution of red food colouring. After 15 minutes they are stained with colour. Then the dice are drained and tossed in tapioca flour to coat. When dropped into boiling water the tapioca flour becomes transparent and the tiny glistening red nuggets take on the appearance of pomegranate seeds or rubies. The word grob or krob means 'crisp'.

Most Westerners meeting this or any other liquid dessert for the first time are doubtful whether they will like it, and may leave most of it in the bowl which is disappointing for the cook. I think it needs to be tried for the first time on a scorching hot day, when anything wet and cold just hits the spot, and it will ever after be regarded with affection. Tup Tim Krob is simple to prepare, but time consuming. I suggest reserving it for occasions when genuine aficionados are present. It could be made up to a day ahead and refrigerated. Any longer and the colour bleeds, leaving it much less attractive. (Don't attempt it for large numbers unless you have many helpers.) See recipe page 404.

Turmeric

(*Curcuma longa*, *C. domestica*) SEE ILLUSTRATION. A rhizome of the ginger family, it has large leaves (sometimes simmered in Nonya dishes for flavour). Young, tender shoots are boiled and used as a vegetable in Thailand, usually served with nam prik. The reason turmeric is cultivated on a commercial scale, however, is for its brilliant orange-yellow rhizome. The rhizome is used fresh in South East Asia, but has more widespread application dried and ground. It is included in almost every commercial curry powder. From a culinary viewpoint, simply be aware that when a southern Indian or Sri Lankan recipe calls for saffron, what is meant, in all likelihood, is turmeric. One should not be substituted for the other as the flavours are totally different; and while the colour of a freshly cut piece of turmeric may be orange, the colour which turmeric gives to food is definitely yellow. Saffron imparts a warm orange tint.

In the cooking of South East Asia, turmeric is invaluable for colouring and flavouring, especially in the yellow rice which is so much part of festive occasions. See recipe for Yellow Rice (page 309).

In Thailand there is another turmeric, khamin kao, which translates as 'turmeric, white'. It is, however, lemon yellow rather than white (I gather it is called white to distinguish it from its bright orange cousin). See ZEDOARY.

Medicinal uses: Seldom used now in medicine though it is known to have carminative and stimulating properties. It was also used to treat skin diseases as it has antiseptic properties. In Lesley Bremness' *Herbs*, we read: 'In Chinese medicine the root stimulates circulation, resolves bruises and clots, and is a Thai treatment for cobra venom. Research shows turmeric strengthens the gall-bladder; inhibits dangerous blood-clotting; reduces some liver toxins and helps it metabolize fats (possibly assisting weight loss); and has an anti-inflammatory, non-steroidal action.'

Burma: *sa-nwin*
Cambodia: *romiet*
China: *wong geung fun, yu-chin, wong-keong, ng-kiew*
India: *haldi, manjal*
Indonesia: *kunyit*
Japan: *ukon*
Malaysia: *kunyit*
Philippines: *dilaw, dilao*
Sri Lanka: *kaha*
Thailand: *khamin*
Vietnam: *nghe*

Ube

See YAM.

Udder

Cow's udder, while not sold in Western butcher shops, is sold in Asian markets. The udder can be made into roasts and curries. In Sri Lanka it is considered a special treat and while it can be chewy if not properly prepared or sufficiently cooked, is delicious when prepared either as a pot roast or what is known as a 'black curry' in which the spices are roasted to the colour of coffee. Instead of the muscle fibres of red meat, udder has a crunchy texture, is pale cream in colour, firm and non fibrous.

Udon

See NOODLES.

Ugli

(*Citrus* sp.) A hybrid resulting from a cross between grapefruit and tangerine. The hybridisation took place, apparently, in Jamaica, which now claims this fruit as its own. Since one of the parents (grapefruit) was originally from East Asia or Polynesia and the other (tangerine) from China or Japan, it has territorial rights to appear in a book concerned with the food of Asia and the Pacific. It makes an excellent substitute for pomelo in Thai style salads and it is likely that North American and European readers have more access to ugli than to pomelo. The flesh is bright yellow and sweeter than grapefruit, juicier than pomelo and more easily peeled. Although common mispronunciation has led to this less than beautiful citrus being branded 'ugly', the correct way to pronounce its name is 'oog-li'.

Utensils & Cooking Equipment

Utensils in Asian kitchens are generally unsophisticated when compared with the standard equipment of Western cooks. While the utensils commonly found in the kitchens of Asia have a romantic and exotic appeal, there is usually something that can do the job almost as well to be found in most Western kitchens. However, you may wish to invest in a few items that just don't have a Western counterpart.

Coconut grater: There is more than one type of coconut grater in South East Asia. Mine has a handle which rotates a serrated blade. A half coconut in the shell is pressed against it until all the white meat is grated. Care should be taken to grate all the white and none of the brown shell. Deluxe models clamp to the kitchen table. Grated fresh coconut is called for in many South East Asian recipes.

Cooking vessels: Many cooking vessels common throughout Asia and the Pacific make use of natural materials. Unglazed earthenware pots or clay cooking pots are used, as are hollow sections of green bamboo in which food is steamed. Rice is by far the most important single item of food which is cooked, and while it may be steamed in special, closely woven baskets (especially sticky rice) the usual way is in a clay or metal pot with a lid to hold in the steam. The most common modern innovation in Asian kitchens is the electric rice cooker, and those cooks who have access to electricity and can afford one, invariably use the rice cooker every day. The Yunnan pot from China, a terracotta or porcelain vessel with a fitting lid, has a tapering central funnel inside. Food to be cooked is placed around the funnel, covered with the lid and the pot placed on a rack over water inside a larger pot to steam. Steam rises up the funnel, hits the lid and fills the vessel. Foods cooked this way are full of flavour.

Earth oven: The Pacific practice of cooking in the ground on a bed of heated stones, the food wrapped in leaves (banana or ti leaves), covered with sacks or more hot stones and left to 'steam' for a few hours. Variously called imu, umu, hangi.

Grinders: It is impossible to make an authentic curry without something with which to grind whole spices to a powder. If you buy ready-ground spices you are settling for second best, unfortunately. What you save in time and effort you sacrifice in taste, for once spices are ground, the volatile oils which are the essence of their flavour are much more readily dissipated. Buy a good electric coffee grinder and reserve it for spices if you do not have time to pound them using a mortar and pestle.

For wet grinding, a blender will often do the job. If there is not a high enough moisture content in the ingredients being blended it may be necessary to add a little water or oil to keep the mixture in motion. Traditionally, wet pastes were ground on a large stone slab with a heavy stone roller. This is time-consuming and hard work, but the resulting paste is much more homogenous.

Ice shaver: A fairly primitive device that combines a fixed blade and a turning handle that rotates the block of ice. An expensive electric machine is also available. The 'snow' made by both is very fine indeed, just what's required for those fascinating desserts like halo halo and ice kacang.

Ovens: Due to the fact that ovens are not a feature in many Asian kitchens, most cakes are either fried or baked in a pan placed on the hearth, the top heat being provided by another pan with some hot coals in it covering the first one. Another version of an oven is a large, clean tin which originally contained coconut oil or some other edible bulk commodity, placed over a kerosene burner. At best, these are primitive. The well-to-do in cities have gas or electric ovens installed. Otherwise, those cakes which require baking are taken to the local bakery to be cooked in the commercial oven.

Steamboat: A metal brazier with a central funnel designed to hold hot coals, sometimes called a fire-pot. Used in Chinese, Korean and Malaysian table-top cooking. Each diner immerses their own thinly sliced meats or vegetables into the simmering broth using chopsticks or small wire spoon. Also useful to keep a dish hot at the table, as in the Korean dish 'stew' sinsollo.

Wok: There are a number of cooking utensils unique to Asia, but if I had to name the single most important, it would have to be the wok. Not only is it the perfect shape for stir-frying, with its large expanse of surface area and gently curved sides to keep in food that is being tossed and flipped, it is also ideal for deep frying as it requires less oil than a straight-sided cooking pot. I've used a wok to make dishes from one side of Asia to another. It is certainly the single most useful cooking pot in my kitchen! Even more useful because mine is enamel-lined; which means no reaction between metal and food.

I don't recommend stainless steel because, on its own, this metal is not a good heat conductor, which defeats the purpose of trying to cook quickly on high heat. Woks with non-stick coatings are not recommended either, because in time they scratch and stick. New non-stick surfaces which are permanent and hard wearing are an option, but very expensive.

There are variations on the wok theme in other countries. In Burma it is the dare-oh; in Malaysia and Singapore it is the kuali; in Indonesia the wadjan; in the Philippines a carajay; and in India, the karhai. No one can dispute the functional shape. It is echoed, although more acutely curved, in Sri Lanka's cheena chatti, the miniature semi-spherical metal pans, mandatory if you wish to make hoppers or egg hoppers and invaluable for deep frying on a small scale. Like the wok, these metal pans need to be seasoned and the surface kept dry and smooth.

Cleaning a new wok: A rolled steel wok (the common, very reasonably priced wok available from Chinese stores), should be cleaned thoroughly to remove any trace of the protective coating designed to prevent rust during shipping and storage, then seasoned before use.

Fill it with hot water, add a few tablespoons of bicarbonate of soda (baking soda) and let it simmer for about 20 minutes. This should soften the coating sufficiently to allow it to be scrubbed off with a scourer. Repeat the process, if necessary, to remove all traces of the coating. The wok is now ready to be seasoned. After this, the wok should never again be scoured. Wash it with soap, but do not use an abrasive. Otherwise it will need to be seasoned again to restore the cooking surface. After each washing, dry thoroughly, not merely with a tea towel, but by putting it back on the heat and making sure every trace of moisture is gone. Store it in a dry, airy spot or wipe it over with a paper towel dipped in oil to prevent rust. A well-used wok will develop a shiny black surface.

Seasoning a wok: 'Seasoning' is the term given to the process of preparing the metal to be cooked on. A wok is seasoned to create a smooth cooking surface that prevents food from sticking, discolouring or imparting a metallic taste. A highly acidic dish (containing lemon or vinegar) will react even with seasoned metal and should be transferred out of the wok immediately to avoid tainting the flavour. This is not necessary with a wok which is coated with enamel or some other non-reactive material.

After thoroughly cleaning your new steel wok, it is ready to be seasoned. Heat the wok and wipe over the entire inner surface with wads of paper towels dipped in peanut oil. The first few wads will turn a rusty brown colour. Repeat with fresh paper and oil until the paper no longer discolours. Allow the wok to cool, rinse with warm water and then repeat the heating process, rubbing once again with oiled paper. The wok is now ready to be used for cooking.

Remember the first rule of stir-frying, let the wok get hot before adding the oil. Make sure the oil is hot before adding food to be cooked and the food should slide easily over the surface of the wok. Use a wok chan or a curved slotted spoon to avoid scratching the seasoned surface.

After use, wash thoroughly and scrub with a dish mop or plastic brush but never with metal cleaning pads or abrasive powders. If someone does this by accident the wok will need to be seasoned again.

Wok accessories: When you buy your wok, it makes good sense to buy a lid at the same time. It needs to fit inside the rim of the wok and have a high enough dome to allow for a whole chicken or duck to fit underneath, sitting on a trivet or steaming rack. Pot holders are useful as the metal handles can get very hot.

There are steaming baskets made of bamboo or metal in various sizes which are very useful. They are stackable, which means more than one layer can be steamed at a time. You can improvise a single layer steamer with a trivet and a round cake rack, provided the food you're steaming is larger than the gaps between the wire of the cake rack. Choose a large, well-fitting lid to contain the steam. A bamboo steamer is ideal for steaming buns as it absorbs

the moisture and avoids condensation dripping onto the buns, spoiling their smooth shiny surface. To get around this problem with a metal steamer, lay a clean tea towel over the top steaming rack before covering with the lid.

Use a wok chan for stir-frying or a slotted frying spoon which is not only useful for stir-frying but also for lifting out small amounts of deep-fried items. For larger items, such as whole fish, a Chinese frying spoon made of twisted brass wire is best. Large and flat, it can support a large item or lift numerous smaller items from oil or liquid in one motion. It also has an extra-long bamboo handle which makes it easier for the cook to avoid oil spatters.

Your wok is only as good as your heat source, so for those whose domestic appliance is not suited to wok cooking, to get the best results a portable gas ring is the answer. They are quite modestly priced, are available with one, two or three concentric rings of gas jets and deliver the kind of heat Chinese chefs use in restaurants. Barbecue specialists and Asian supermarkets do a brisk trade in these. Some gas-fired barbecues feature a special wok burner in addition to grills.

Following are country-by-country descriptions of utensils and cooking equipment.

Burma: As in most Asian countries, a portable charcoal brazier is a convenient and affordable 'stove'. In more affluent households there is a brick fireplace in which charcoal or wood is burnt. The wok in Burma is a heavy, two-handled iron pan called a dare-oh, and is the only cooking vessel Western pots and pans can't replace. Other items found in a Burmese kitchen are a large, flat grinding stone, a mortar and pestle, sieves, colanders, wooden and bamboo spatulas, skewers and ladles, cleavers and knives.

China: For Chinese cooking a wok is essential. Nothing else could handle the job of stir-frying. Not only is it the perfect shape for stir-frying, with its large expanse of surface area and gently curved sides to keep in food that is being tossed and flipped, it is also ideal for deep frying as it requires less oil than a straight-sided cooking pot. Steaming baskets are also useful, or a wok can be used as a steamer with a large, domed lid and a small, round trivet. For both stir-frying and deep frying a curved, slotted stainless steel frying spoon is ideal.

Invest in a ladle with a good sized 'bowl', some bamboo or melamine rice paddles and stainless steel serving spoons. Wire drainers or frying baskets in different sizes and depths are handy for deep frying, and a colander with small holes is indispensable for draining rice and fine noodles.

Chopsticks are not only appropriate for eating, but a long pair can also be used for cooking.

A knife or cleaver does more than slice and chop; it is used for transferring diced or sliced ingredients from chopping board to wok; the flat of it can crush garlic to a paste with salt or sugar; the blunt edge is an effective tenderiser.

An inexpensive but practical as well as aesthetic cooking utensil is the sandy pot or earthenware casserole, ideal for slow simmered dishes and handsome enough to use for serving. The outside is cream to light pink in colour with a hollow, cylindrical handle and a sandy texture; the inside of pot and lid is glazed and smooth. It should not be heated without liquid in it. If ingredients need to be browned first, do that in a wok and then transfer them to the sandy pot for simmering.

Another attractive cooking vessel is the Yunnan pot, a round-bellied unglazed terracotta pot with two decorative, rounded handles, a fitting lid and a narrow central funnel through which steam is forced into the pot. It is meant to sit on a trivet or rack over water inside a larger covered pot to steam food.

The steamboat, or firekettle, cooks food in liquid rather than steam. It is designed around a wide central funnel which, filled with hot coals, keeps the liquid in the moat at a steady simmer throughout the meal. There are electric versions.

India: Cooking pots usually found in an Indian kitchen include the degchi or pateela. These traditionally brass (but now more commonly aluminium) saucepans are of varying sizes with a flat rim and no handles and dhakkan (flat lids) to cover them.

The karhai (kadhai, karai) is a bowl-shaped cookpot with two handles, resembling a heavy wok, with sloping sides and a curved base. It comes in a range of sizes for various uses. Usually made of iron, it must be seasoned before use like a wok.

The tava (tawa) is a flat, iron griddle with a single wooden handle used for cooking bread. A heavy iron frying pan does as well. Chitma are flat, smooth-edged, long tongs used for a variety of purposes including turning flatbreads, picking up live coals and lifting a tava.

A typical Indian kitchen usually has a sil-batta (the sil is a flat stone slab with pitted surface and batta is the grinding stone shaped like a half moon or triangle); a chakki (mill for dry grinding of grains, pulses and spices); a kaddoo-kas (for grating vegetables) and narial kas (coconut grater). The most primitive coconut grater is an iron scraper, shaped like a striking cobra with a serrated 'head' which is fixed to a low wooden stool. The cracked, husked coconuts are dragged across its surface until all the white flesh is grated.

Japan: If you like to cook Japanese food, collect a few serving plates of irregular shape; rectangular and square as well as shallow, curved and footed dishes in ceramic or lacquerware.

There are some Japanese utensils that look unlike anything in a Western kitchen, but with a little creative thinking it is possible to find some quite acceptable substitutes.

Makiyaki-nabe: Nothing in a Western kitchen quite duplicates the results from this rectangular Japanese omelette pan.

Oroshi-gane: An extremely fine-toothed grater made of metal or glazed ceramic. No Western grater could ever do as fine a job as this Japanese version, especially on fresh wasabi or ginger.

Sudare: Bamboo mat used for rolling up nori-maki sushi and Japanese omelette.

Suribachi, surikogi: Mortar and pestle. Not the usual design, this mortar (suribachi) literally means grater. The closely scored inside surface has a grating action on foods pressed against it with the long, hard wooden pestle. Very useful for nuts and seeds.

Korea: A metal brazier sometimes called a Mongolian or Korean barbecue is needed to make authentic bulgogi at the table. Otherwise, cook it on a very hot griddle plate, and take the cooked meat to the table as soon as possible. Also popular in Korean cuisine are the hotpot soups, hearty with vegetables and pieces of seafood or meat, and kept hot at the table in a sinsollo (steamboat).

Another popular Korean cookpot is the tukbaege — a round covered clay pot used to cook stews and soups on the stovetop. Taken directly to the table, it holds the heat well. A flameproof casserole would do the same job.

Malaysia: With its cultural diversity, it is inevitable that Malaysian cuisine feels the influence of its closest neighbours and of its largest ethnic populations, Chinese, Indian and Malay. The Malaysian kitchen uses kuali (the Malay version of the wok) and blangah (clay pots). Tradition calls for onions to be pounded into rempah (spice pastes) with batu lesong (mortar and pestle), and wetter spice mixtures to be ground with batu giling (grinding stone) as in most other South East Asian cuisines, but quite acceptable results may be obtained using a blender or food processor.

A solid wooden chopping board (a cross section of tree trunk) and sharp cutting knives (cleavers are favoured) are necessities. A tawa for Indian flat breads, a four-spouted cup for roti jalah and a steamer for any number of Chinese dishes. As in most kitchens of today, the old makes way for the new innovations of our technological age, and rice cookers are as popular in Malaysia and Singapore as any other country where rice is eaten.

Philippines: The following is a list of some of the more common cooking utensils found in the Philippines.

Palayok: Round, covered clay cooking pot.

Bangas: Clay water jars serve a dual purpose of storage plus keeping the water cool by evaporation.

Gilingan: Stone grinder for grinding rice.

Carajay, kawali: Wok-shaped, native pan.

Tachos: Two-handled copper preserving pan.

Llaneras: Mould for custard.

Cafateras: Coffee pot.

Chocalateras, batidors: Brass or enamel pot used to make frothy hot chocolate.

Kabayo: Coconut grater.

Almirez: Stone mortar and pestle.

Sri Lanka: Some Sri Lankan utensils simply don't have a Western equivalent, but a blender or food processor serves many purposes. The grinding done by hand on my old granite grinding stone — shaped like a large flat slab 'bed' with a cylindrical 'bolster' and is thorough but slow. With time at a premium, it gets little use, but my electric blender works overtime.

Saucepans and frying pans take the place of clay cooking pots, but for hoppers (see page 264) one needs special pans; and for Pittu (see page 313), cylindrical steamers.

For making stringhoppers, Sri Lanka's lacy rice flour specialty, I use a brass cylinder which extrudes dough by down force. The rice flour is pushed through a disc with scores of tiny holes by turning a handle. While extruding the threads of rice noodle, it is necessary to move the whole press in a circle above a woven cane mat to form a lacy noodle 'doily'.

Serving spoons of polished coconut shell with wooden handles are both aesthetic and authentic.

Thailand: To cook Thai food it is important to have a wok, a steamer, a pot with a tight-fitting lid (or a rice cooker), a mortar and pestle or a blender with a powerful motor for grinding hard spices and roots and a food processor or mincer to purée raw fish and meats.

Among my Thai souvenirs are jelly moulds (for making tiny, jewel-coloured agar-agar jellies), a set of fruit and vegetable carving knives, and some fluted cutters for agar-agar jelly (a wavy metal blade set in a wooden handle).

Vanilla

(*Vanilla planifolia*) Native to Mexico, vanilla is produced from a bean which is the seed pod of an orchid. Tahiti has a reputation for producing some of the best vanilla. It is also grown on the Pacific islands of Tonga, Vanuatu and Fiji as well as in Malaysia, Indonesia, Sri Lanka and other Asian countries.

The story of vanilla is a fascinating one. After it had been transported to the other side of the world it did not produce pods in the new lands, though it grew with vigour. The vines flowered, but no fruit ever resulted from the yellow orchids. It was 16 years before the mystery was solved. Without the melipone bees and certain species of hummingbirds to pollinate the flowers, nature could not take its course. Artificial pollination was the solution.

Each flower lasts less than a day, so pollination must take place early in the morning on which the flower opens. Experts can pollinate from 1,000 to 1,500 flowers a day. After fertilising, the pod takes from 4 to 9 months to mature. Then comes the drawn out process of curing or fermenting the pods and drying them. Up to 6 months after picking, curing is complete.

Vanilla is one of the most important flavouring agents for sweet foods in the Western world. In Asia, while it is not a traditional food flavouring in the way that pandan leaves, rose and other flower essences are, vanilla is still used for many sweet-meats. While the sticky rice and tapioca cakes are traditionally coloured and flavoured with pandan leaves, milk fudge is always vanilla flavoured. Cakes, biscuits and frosting are more likely to be redolent of vanilla than anything else.

China: *hsiang-ts'ao*
Japan: *banira*

Vegetarian Meals

Asia has a richly varied vegetarian cuisine based on grains, seeds, legumes and pulses combined with an endless variety of vegetables, fruits and flowers. Each country has its own spectrum of flavours and the results are quite tantalising. In any of the Asian countries one may eat very well without using meat, fish or fowl — though the definition of 'vegetarian' may vary from culture to culture. Among the coastal dwellers in Bengal, India, for instance, fish is described as 'fruit of the sea' and is therefore permitted in many a vegetarian diet. Yoghurt and milk and ghee (clarified butter) are freely used, as well as infertile eggs.

On the other hand, there are vegetarians who will not eat any animal products at all. Jains (members of a sect which is an offshoot of Hinduism) will not even eat vegetables with the 'colour of blood' such as beetroot or tomatoes, or root vegetables which, when harvested, may result in the death of microscopic insects living in the soil. Their diet is mainly rice and other grains, leafy green vegetables and lentils.

Some of the best meals I have enjoyed in my travels through Asia have been vegetarian. Vegetarianism is a way of life in the Indian sub-continent, especially in central and southern India. Indian vegetarian food is delicious. Fragrant spices and herbs and cooking techniques such as scorching give interest and flavour to even the blandest of vegetables.

By far the most important vegetarian food in the Far East, featuring largely in Chinese, Japanese and Korean meals, is bean curd which is known as 'the meat without a bone' because of its high protein content. See BEAN CURD.

For a listing of vegetarian recipes, see Index of Recipes.

Velvet Tamarind

(*Dialium cochinchinense, D. ovoideum*) There is often a confusion of identity between this little fruit and the tamarind plum (*D. indum*). One passes for the other and no harm done, for they are very similar and are used in the same way. Native to Malaysia, Sarawak and Sabah, they both belong to the botanical family Leguminosae-Caesalpiniodea, both grow on tall trees which thrive in evergreen forests, and near rivers. Both bear bunches of small fruit from 1–1.5 cm (½–¾ in) long, but the velvet tamarind is not quite as wide. Both have thin, brittle shells which are easily cracked between the fingers, revealing pale brown pulp with a dry, powdery appearance, surrounding a flat, round, shiny seed.

The descriptive name of 'velvet tamarind' refers to the suede-like surface of the shell. The tamarind plum is generally considered better to eat.

The flavour is sweet-sour and while it can be used for cooking, it is not as acid as tamarind in long pods and takes a lot of shelling to yield sufficient pulp quantity for a recipe.

India: *kallu pullium*
Malaysia: *keranji, kanji*
Sri Lanka: *gal siyambala*
Thailand: *khleng, kaa yee, naang dam, yee*

Vetiver

(*Vetiveria zizanioides*) A perennial aromatic tropical grass known in India for its fragrant oil which is used in khas syrup and khas water to flavour sherbets as well as to perfume soaps and cosmetics. The matted roots are made into fans and a faint, sweet fragrance wafts from them as they are moistened and used to create currents in the still, tropical air.

The Indian term for vetiver is khus-khus (not to be confused with khas-khas, the name for white poppy seeds). Like sandalwood, it is a flavouring which is not to everyone's taste.

Medicinal uses: In Indonesia, used to treat rheumatism. In aroma therapy, used to reduce tension.

Ve-tsin

See MONOSODIUM GLUTAMATE.

Vietnam

The cooking of Vietnam is like — and yet unlike — the cooking of China, with some influence from its other neighbours, Laos and Cambodia. There are also traits which are reminiscent of Thai food. Not the complex spicing of curries nor the richness of coconut milk, but the use of fresh herbs and salad-like ingredients.

Vietnam's national dish, pho, is basically a rice noodle soup, the beef stock strong and flavoursome, simmered for at least 6 hours. In the bowl are fresh bean sprouts, sliced onions and tomatoes and handfuls of fresh mint, bringing to mind Thailand's tom yum. Unlike tom yum, pho is not fiery with chilli but headily redolent of star anise, surprising at first encounter.

The single most important ingredient in Vietnamese food is nuoc mam, fish sauce. It is used to season food the way salt is used in a Western kitchen. Nuoc mam is now available in most Asian stores. When mixed with garlic, chilli, sugar and some lime or lemon juice, it is called nuoc cham and is put on the table to be added to almost everything, starting with the breakfast bowl of noodle soup and continuing through lunch to dinner.

These meals may begin with an entree of fresh or fried rice paper spring rolls, wrapped in a lettuce leaf, with sprigs of fresh coriander or mint, the whole thing dipped in nuoc cham and eaten. Nuoc cham, (or the components which go to make up the salty, hot, sharp and sweet flavours) is also used as a salad dressing — oil free and refreshing. Vietnamese Chicken and Cabbage Salad (page 60) is one of my favourite Vietnamese dishes.

While many of the ingredients used in Vietnam are common to the Chinese kitchen, Vietnamese cooks fry fewer foods than Chinese cooks do, so naturally the food is lighter. Rice is the staple, and fish from the long coastline provides most of the protein. Pork and poultry are more readily available than beef. Beef is considered a luxury meat, which is what makes pho so popular. Paper-thin slices of beef are barely cooked by the heat of the stock. With the generous helping of soft, fresh rice noodles, there is no need to eat large amounts of beef — it is a seasoning rather than a main ingredient. Migration has resulted in restaurants as well as stores selling ingredients such as fresh rice noodles, fruits, vegetables and herbs needed for Vietnamese cooking in many a Western city.

Nearly 100 years of French colonisation has also influenced the cuisine. Most intriguing is the sight of a Vietnamese bread or sandwich shop. Baguettes a French baker would be proud of are filled with thinly sliced cold roast pork and pork sausage, sprigs of fresh coriander, thinly sliced onion or spring onion (scallion), shreds of raw carrot and, of course, nuoc cham sauce. Extra slices of red chilli are offered for the brave. A petit pain with a difference!

Vietnamese may go out for pho and sandwiches, but traditional Vietnamese food as cooked in the home is based on rice served with steamed, stir-fried or braised dishes, soup and salad. A Vietnamese kitchen equipped with the bare essentials would boast a mortar and pestle, woks, saucepans, bamboo or metal steamers and clay pots. The table setting comprises bowls and chopsticks, and small teacups. The custom of drinking plain, weak tea with the meal prevails and all the dishes are brought to the table at once.

If you visit a Vietnamese cafe offering a drink based on soursop, I recommend this refreshing seasonal treat. Jakfruit or durian drinks with their challenging flavours, are for the more adventurous. My particular temptation in a Vietnamese restaurant is a three-bean drink, with its contrasting textures of agar-agar shreds, cooked adzuki beans and sweetened mung bean paste mixed with shaved ice and coconut milk.

Vietnamese Mint

(*Persicaria odorata*, syn. *Polygonum odoratum*) SEE ILLUSTRATION. This pungent herb is not mint but widely known by this common name. It is also known as hot mint, Cambodian mint and laksa leaf. It does not belong to the mint family, and was *Polygonum odoratum* or *P. hydropiper* until recently, when it was re-classified as *Persicaria odorata* (syn. *Polygonum odoratum*).

The narrow, pointed leaves of Vietnamese mint have distinctive dark markings in the centre, but not every leaf bears this marking, even on the same plant.

This herb is such an intrinsic part of the famous Singaporean/Malaysian seafood soup, laksa, that it is known locally as daun laksa (laksa leaf).

In Vietnamese cuisine, it is not normally cooked but used in salads, or eaten as a fresh herb with the popular Vietnamese spring rolls, cha gio. May also

be used in Thai salads alongside mint and coriander leaves.

If buying a plant from a nursery, it is most likely to be identified by one of the botanical names given above. If you cannot find it in a nursery, it is easily propagated from the herb purchased from Asian greengrocers by placing some stems in water and waiting for it to sprout roots. Plant in a sunny spot and keep well watered.

Indonesia: *daun kesom, daun laksa*
Laos: *phak pheo*
Malaysia: *daun kesom, daun laksa*
Singapore: *daun kesom, daun laksa*
Thailand: *phak phai, phrik maa, chan chom, hom chan*
Vietnam: *rau ram*

Vinegar

Besides the vinegars we know made from wine (vin aigre means, literally, sour wine), beer hops (malt vinegar), apple cider (cider vinegar) and grain (spirit or white vinegar), there is a whole other world of vinegars in the Asia–Pacific region.

The acetic acid in vinegar is a tenderiser and preservative. The Chinese were making vinegar from grains (barley, millet and rice), fruits (dates, cherries, grapes and peaches) and honey long before the Japanese borrowed the technique and began making rice vinegar in the 4th or 5th century. Further south and west across Asia, vinegar is less depended upon as a souring agent, with lime juice and tamarind performing this function. There are also a number of acid fruits and leaves which add a piquant bite to dishes from Sri Lanka to Thailand. See ACID FRUIT.

Perhaps the most common vinegar in South East Asia and the Pacific, particularly favoured in the Philippines, is palm vinegar. Made from the sap of palms, the inflorescence of the coconut palm or kitul palm is tapped and the sap collected and stored in wooden barrels. A starter is added and it is left to mature, after which it is strained and distilled.

There are dishes which depend on vinegar for their piquant flavour. For examples of these, see vindaloo, sorpotel and adobo under PORK. In addition, there are various kinds of pickle (achar) which are as necessary to the Indian and South East Asian table as pepper and salt in the West.

The distinctive flavour of sushi, Japan's most

popular finger food, is contributed to by sushi rice, made by sprinkling cooked rice with a 'dressing' of vinegar and sugar. (See RICE.) Japan also makes a sweet vinegar called yamabukusu.

Black vinegar: Made from rice, wheat, millet or sorghum. It varies in quality in the same way that balsamic vinegars vary. One of the best, a vinegar from Zhejiang on China's north coast made from glutinous rice and malt, is Chinkiang Vinegar, definitely worth seeking out. The better black vinegars are well aged and display a complex, smoky depth of flavour. Chefs in the Shanxi region, near Beijing, are so fond of vinegar they add it to just about everything.

Red vinegar: Made from rice and mildly acidic with a hint of sweetness. A favourite dipping sauce for seafood and those delicious dumplings called pot stickers. It is sometimes added to Shark's Fin Soup.

Rice vinegar: Made from fermented rice, this vinegar is popular in China, Japan and Korea. Dilute white wine vinegar or cider vinegar if you can't get the real thing. Remember, Japanese and Chinese white rice vinegar is a milder, sweeter product than the white wine or spirit vinegars on our supermarket shelves. There is no Western equivalent. However, don't assume all rice vinegars are mild. One Korean vinegar, hyunmi sikcho, made from unpolished rice is as aggressive as cider vinegar. It is wise to taste the vinegar you plan to use and dilute if necessary.

Although rice vinegar was originally made from rice cooked with water then treated with yeast to ferment the sugar in the grain, these days it is usually made from rice wine lees and alcohol. Adding sugar also speeds up the process.

Sweet vinegar: Has a distinctive flavour and cannot be used in place of black vinegar. Although it, too, is dark brown in colour and is brewed from rice, it is fragrant with cassia, star anise and sugar and quite lacking in acidity. Featured in the traditional Cantonese dish of pork knuckles, hard-boiled eggs and whole baby ginger, it is frequently used to flavour stock, pork and braised dishes.

White vinegar: Made from glutinous rice. Colourless and quite delicate. Used in sweet and sour sauce.

Medicinal uses: Considered to cleanse the system. Used as an antiseptic both internally and externally.

China: *cho*
India: *seerka*
Korea: *sik cho*
Japan: *su, yone-zu*
Malaysia: *cuka*
Philippines: *suka*
Sri Lanka: *vinakiri*
Thailand: *nam som*

Walnut

(*Juglans regia*) A native of south-east Europe which grows in western and central Asia and China. Much of the carved woodwork for which Kashmir is famous is walnut wood. Walnuts are called akroot or akhrote in India, where the kernels are ground and used to thicken sauces.

Some dishes using walnuts are reminiscent of Persian dishes — just as Moghul cooking reflects the same quality of luxury. Walnuts are exported from China either in their shells or as shelled halves or peeled halves.

Purchasing and storing: To improve their keeping qualities, some walnuts are kiln-dried in their shells. This, combined with the astringency of the thin brown skin of the kernel, can make them taste somewhat bitter.

If you don't have time to shell them, walnuts in vacuum-packed cans are probably the best, but can be expensive. Buying shelled walnuts gives you the chance to taste and ensure they are fresh. Avoid buying nuts in plastic packets if possible. Always taste walnuts just before using them. Old, bitter or rancid walnuts will spoil any dish they are added to.

Storage: If keeping nuts for any length of time, I prefer to store them in the freezer as the best insurance against their high oil content becoming rancid. Protect them from other flavours with thick freezer bags or airtight containers. Better still, buy only what you will use in a short time.

Preparation: Peeled walnuts are good for lightly frying and adding to dishes so the astringency of the thin skin which covers the kernel does not intrude on the flavours of the dish. Usually available in Chinese grocery stores. See instructions below for peeled walnuts. After peeling, if not to be used right away, allow them to dry in the sun or in a very low oven, pack in bags and freeze.

Walnut kernels are also sold in vacuum packed cans, coated with sugar and salt. The most popular Chinese style walnut has a caramel coating of sugar and soy sauce. Serve as hors d'oeuvres. See recipe for Chinese Style Honey-Soy Walnuts (page 402).

Peeled walnuts: Walnut skin has an astringency which turns bitter when fried. This can be avoided by peeling them. Bring water to the boil in a small saucepan, drop in 1 cup walnut halves or large pieces. When water comes back to the boil cover pan, turn off heat and leave for 5 minutes. Drain, then lift the skin with the point of a pin or a pair of tweezers.

The convoluted portion of the walnut is admittedly difficult to peel completely, but the thickest skin is on the comparatively smooth centre surface of the walnut halves. This contributes most of the bitterness and is easier to remove.

Fried walnuts: Allow peeled walnuts to dry thoroughly. Heat 1 cup oil in a wok over high heat, but don't let it get too hot. Add the walnuts, turn heat lower and stir constantly while frying for about 2 minutes. Walnuts burn easily. Immediately strain the walnuts, reserving the oil for future use. Spread the walnuts on paper towels to drain and crisp.

Their colour will darken a little even after they have been removed because nuts absorb hot oil and continue to cook. Frying can be done in advance and when completely cold the nuts may be stored airtight for a few days and used as required.

Fried Sweet Walnuts

125 g/4 oz/1 cup peeled walnut halves
375 ml/12 fl oz/1½ cups water
½ teaspoon salt
250 ml/8 fl oz/1 cup sugar
3 tablespoons maltose
500 ml/1 pint/2 cups peanut oil

If time and patience are in good supply, peel the walnut halves as described above, otherwise simply blanch the walnuts in boiling water for 1 minute and drain.

In a saucepan combine measured water with salt, sugar and maltose. Bring to the boil and simmer for 5 minutes. Add walnuts and bring to the boil again. Remove from heat, leave walnuts in syrup for 3 hours, then pour into a sieve to drain and dry.

Heat oil in a small pan or wok, but do not make it too hot as walnuts burn easily and will become bitter. Fry walnuts for 2 or 3 minutes, stirring and turning constantly with a slotted spoon. Lift out on a wire frying spoon or other slotted spoon, shaking off as much oil as possible. Leave on a metal tray to cool. Do not drain them on paper towels, as they will stick to the paper. When cold store them in an airtight container and serve within a week.

Chinese Style Honey-Soy Walnuts

125 g/4 oz/1 cup walnut halves
3 tablespoons liquid honey
2 teaspoons light soy sauce
4 tablespoons caster sugar (superfine sugar)
oil for frying

Peel the walnut halves as described on page 401 and dry them on paper towels. Combine honey and soy sauce, pour over the walnuts in a bowl and leave for 1 hour, stirring now and then, turning the nuts over in the mixture. Drain walnuts, leave for 15 minutes to dry, then toss in sugar to coat.

Frying method: Heat oil in a wok. Turn heat low, add the walnuts and fry for 2–3 minutes, stirring and turning the walnuts constantly until they are golden brown and the sugar coating forms a glaze. Pour into a wire strainer then spread on a plate to cool, keeping pieces separate. Use within a day or two.

Baking method: The nuts may also be placed on a baking tray lined with non-stick baking paper and roasted in oven at 180°C (350°F) for 10 minutes. If non-stick paper is not available, transfer walnuts to a lightly oiled plate as soon as possible, or the melted honey and sugar, when cold, will harden and stick the nuts to the tray.

Moghlai Lamb with Walnut Sauce

Serves 6–8

1 kg/2 lb boned leg of lamb
1 tablespoon finely grated fresh ginger
2 teaspoons crushed garlic
2 teaspoons salt
1 tablespoon ground coriander
2 teaspoons ground cumin
2 teaspoons Kashmiri garam masala (recipe page 355)
1 tablespoon soft ghee
24 dried apricot halves
375 ml/12 fl oz/1½ cups hot water
pinch of saffron strands

SAUCE
125 g/4 oz/1 cup walnut kernels
3 teaspoons honey

Trim excess fat from the lamb and make a few deep slits in the meat with the point of a sharp knife. Combine ginger and garlic with salt, spices and half the ghee. Press a little of the mixture into each of the slits in the lamb and rub remaining mixture well over the meat.

Soak apricots in hot water to cover while lamb marinates for at least 2 hours, overnight if possible. Toast saffron strands in a dry pan for a minute or less, taking care not to burn them. Turn onto a saucer to cool, then crush to a powder with the back of a spoon. Dissolve saffron powder in 2 tablespoons boiling water.

Heat remaining ghee in a large, heavy pot and on medium heat lightly brown the lamb all over. Add apricot soaking liquid and dissolved saffron, making up to 1½ cups with hot water. Cover and simmer on very low heat for 40 minutes. Add apricots to pan and continue simmering for a further 20 minutes or until fruit is soft and lamb is tender.

To make the sauce, pour off lamb juices and skim off excess fat floating on the surface. Grind walnuts in a blender with lamb juices and honey. Taste and adjust salt if necessary. Slice the lamb and pour walnut sauce over. Serve with pilau rice or naan roti.

Wasabi

(*Wasabia japonica*) Also known as Japanese horseradish, this nose-clearing condiment is the potent little mound of green paste that accompanies sushi and sashimi. Not a true horseradish (it is a different species of the family to which mustard belongs), the name probably derives from the similar effect both condiments have on the nasal passages.

The knobbly green root is indigenous to Japan where it grows beside cold mountain streams. Leaves, flowers, stems and freshly sliced rhizomes are used to make a popular Japanese pickle, wasabi-zuke. The rhizome, which takes a couple of years to mature, is said to be superior in its fresh state, although difficult to obtain.

Preparation: Scrape off the tough outer skin and then grate the green part finely. The other more accessible option is dried, powdered wasabi which, like mustard powder, loses potency once exposed to air. For this reason buy the smallest size tin if you'll only use it infrequently. Mix roughly equal quantities of wasabi powder and room temperature water and allow to stand for about 15 minutes so the flavour can develop. Wasabi is smeared over rice balls for sushi and a little is mixed with soy sauce as a dip for sashimi (raw fish). Also available as a paste in tubes which should be refrigerated once opened to minimise flavour loss. The product in a tube does not usually have as intense a flavour as the powder mixed with water.

China: *shan yu cai*
Japan: *wasabi*

Water Apple

See ROSE APPLE.

Water Chestnut

(*Eleocharis dulcis, E. tuberosa*) SEE ILLUSTRATION. Resembling a chestnut, although its shape is more symmetrical, the water chestnut is the underwater corm of a variety of water grass. A papery skin in shades of brown peels away to reveal a densely textured, white 'nut', slightly sweet and crisp to the tooth.

The greatest appeal is that water chestnuts retain their texture when cooked. Featured in savoury as well as sweet dishes throughout China and South East Asia. Even when canned, the texture is not dramatically altered. Canned water chestnuts are readily available and widely used.

Flour made from dried, ground water chestnuts is more expensive than cornflour (cornstarch) and harder to dissolve, but when used as a thickener gives sauces a clear sheen and when used to coat foods before deep-frying, a delightful crunch.

There are two other water tubers used like water chestnuts, but not to be eaten raw. One is the yellow-husked corm of the swamp plant, arrowhead (*Sagittaria sinensis*) (see ARROWHEAD). The other is the shiny black nut of a floating water plant (*Trapa bicornis*), named for two horn-like protuberances that give it a rather sinister appearance. Probably just as well, since in its raw state it can contain a parasite that is harmful to the digestive system. Safely edible only after an hour's boiling, they also are eaten in China, combined with other ingredients, preserved as sweetmeats or made into a starch, similar to water chestnut starch. This nut is related to the water chestnut known in southern Europe and eastern United States, which is the four-horned nut of *T. natans.*

Preparation: Cut off pointed end and woody base and immerse in cold water immediately the skin is removed to prevent discolouration. Slice or dice and use raw or cooked.

Medicinal uses: Traditionally used as a medicine, it is yin (cooling) and said to sweeten the breath.

Burma: *ye thit eir thee*
China: *ma tai, po-chi*
India: *pani phul*
Indonesia: *tike*
Japan: *kuwai, kurogu-wai*
Philippines: *apulid*
Thailand: *haeo-song krathiem, haeo cheen*
Vietnam: *go nung*

Water Chestnut Salad

The crisp texture of these corms makes them popular though their flavour is not memorable. Simply toss drained canned water chestnut slices with cooked seafood (prawns [shrimp], crab meat) or meats (roast pork, chicken or duck) and dress with a light and tangy dressing of fish sauce, lime juice, sugar and crushed garlic, adding a touch of chilli if preferred.

Tup Tim Krob

In Thailand, this is one of the favourite ways to cool off during a hot day. Also an impressive ending to a fiery Thai meal. Light and refreshing, with glistening 'rubies' swimming in sweetened coconut milk and crushed ice. Serves 4.

220 g/7 oz canned water chestnuts
red food colouring
few drops jasmine or rose essence
185 g/6 oz/¾ cup white sugar
185 ml/6 oz/¾ cup water
4 tablespoons (approx.) tapioca flour
¼ teaspoon salt
250 ml/8 fl oz/1 cup coconut milk
ice

Cut canned water chestnuts into small dice. Put into a bowl and add just enough cold water to cover. Drop food colouring into the water, stirring, until there is a strong red colour. Add a few drops of jasmine or rose essence. Leave water chesnuts to absorb the colour for 15–20 minutes. Meanwhile, dissolve sugar and water in a saucepan to make a syrup and let cool.

When the water chestnuts have absorbed enough colour, drain in a sieve. On a sheet of paper spread the tapioca flour and roll the pieces of water chestnut in the flour until well coated. Bring a saucepan of water to the boil. Put the water chestnuts in a dry sieve and shake off excess flour. Drop into the boiling water and cook until the pieces rise to the surface. Lift out on a slotted spoon and drop immediately into a bowl of iced water. In each serving bowl or glass pour some of the syrup, then spoon in some water chestnuts. Gently pour in some of the coconut milk mixed with the salt, and last of all add a spoonful of crushed ice. Serve at once.

Note: If fresh water chestnuts are used, peel, dice and boil them for 10 minutes and drain before proceeding with recipe. A good precaution for anything that grows in water.

Water Convolvulus

See WATER SPINACH.

Watercress

(*Nasturtium officinale*) Belonging to the Cruciferae family, along with other pungent mustard greens, watercress is an aquatic herb with a vibrant, peppery flavour that is very much muted by cooking. Despite the Asian inclination towards pungent foods and fresh herbs, watercress is not generally used in that capacity. Often added to soups in China, it does wilt to an insipid olive green, but imparts an interesting flavour. Another way to prepare it is to chop finely, macerate with salt to remove excess water, and quickly stir-fry. The addition of a chilli or two adds some sparkle.

Water Lily

(*Nymphaea lotus*) SEE ILLUSTRATION. In Asian markets a circular loop of water lily stems with beautiful blooms still attached is not a flower arrangement — it's dinner! The flowers on offer can be blue-mauve, white or dark pink. They are all large, with 12–14 pointed petals and four fleshy outer segments of deep green. Sweetly fragrant and very handsome, since it is the stem which is eaten, cut off the blooms and use them as decoration before cooking the stems.

An annual aquatic herb cultivated in Thailand and the Philippines, its succulent stems are used in hot sour soup, cooked with fish in a curry, or fried with pork or prawns (shrimp). They may also be eaten raw with nam prik.

Purchasing and storing: Stems are stored in water at the shops selling them. Choose those with firm stems denoting freshness and use within a day or two.

Preparation: Peel the stems just like rhubarb. They have a very thin outer skin which comes off when one end is cut and pulled down the length of the stem. Cut into bite-sized pieces or thick diagonal slices, exposing more surface area. Cook for only a minute or two so their crisp texture is preserved.

Water Lily Curry with Shrimp

Serves 4

3 or 4 water lily stems
500 g/1 lb small raw shrimp
400 ml/14 fl oz can coconut milk

2 tablespoons Thai red curry paste
   (recipe page 114)
1 tablespoon fish sauce
2 teaspoons palm or brown sugar
3 kaffir lime leaves
few fresh basil leaves

Peel the water lily stems and cut in thick diagonal slices. Wash the shrimp and remove only the hard shell on the head. In a wok heat ½ cup coconut milk and when bubbling add the curry paste, stirring, and cook for a few minutes until fragrant. Add shrimp and turn them in the spicy mixture until coated, then gradually stir in the rest of the coconut milk. Stir until it reaches simmering point, then add the fish sauce, sugar, lime leaves and the water lily stems. Simmer uncovered for 5 minutes. Remove from heat and serve scattered with basil leaves and accompanied by steamed rice.

Water Lily Sour Soup

In the Philippines the water from washing rice is used as the cooking liquid. It is the second washing water which is used, the first rinse carrying away dust and impurities. Serves 4.

1 litre/2 pints rice water
4 whole pods green tamarind, fresh or bottled
4 small fish steaks
   or 500 g/1 lb fillets cut in pieces
2 tablespoons fish sauce
1 cup sliced water-lily stems
½ cup sliced spring onions (scallions)
   with green leaves
salt and lime juice to taste

Put the water and tamarind pods into a non-aluminium saucepan and bring to the boil, simmer until tamarind is soft. Add the fish and fish sauce, simmer until fish is cooked, then add water lily and simmer for a few minutes, just until tender. Add spring onions, salt and lime juice to taste. This soup is intended to be nicely sour. If green tamarind is not available, add extra lime juice.

Watermelon

See MELONS, SWEET.

Water Spinach

(*Ipomoea reptans*, *I. aquatica*) SEE ILLUSTRATION. Also known as water convolvulus and swamp cabbage. This leafy vegetable is prolific in many parts of Asia. The leaves are long and pointed and dark green, the stems paler green and hollow.

Preparation: It should be washed thoroughly as it grows in swampy areas. It may be cooked like spinach, stir-fried with various sauces, or added to soups. To keep a bright colour blanch in boiling water for 30 seconds, refresh in cold water and drain. Add to recipe and toss with flavours for a minute or so.

Often, in Asian shops, the stems alone are sold in plastic bags, looking like pale green corkscrew curls. This is because they have been cut into lengths, split into thin shreds and soaked in cold water to make them curl. The swollen stems split readily, making it a decorative effect that could be achieved at home.

China: *ong choy, ung tsai*
India: *kalmua*
Indonesia: *kangkung*
Japan: *kankon*
Malaysia: *kangkung*
Philippines: *kangkong*
Sri Lanka: *kangkung*
Thailand: *pak boong*
Vietnam: *rau muong, rau muong che*

Water Spinach Stir-Fried Thai Style

Serves 4

1 large bunch water spinach
2 tablespoons oil
3 cloves garlic, finely chopped
10 purple shallots, sliced
good grinding of black pepper
2 tablespoons Golden Mountain sauce
   or Maggi seasoning
1 teaspoon chopped fresh chilli

Wash water spinach well, shake dry and break into bite-sized lengths, discarding any tough lower stems. Heat the oil in a wok and on gentle heat soften the garlic and shallots. Add the water spinach, stir-frying until wilted.

Sprinkle with pepper, Golden Mountain sauce and chopped chilli. Serve at once with rice.

Note: Maggi seasoning, a Swiss-formulated sauce of hydrolysed vegetable protein, has much the same flavour as Golden Mountain sauce and no added monosodium glutamate.

Water Spinach with Dried Shrimp, Thai Style

Serves 4

60 g/2 oz/½ cup dried shrimp
large bunch water spinach
1 tablespoon oil
2 cloves garlic, crushed
1 teaspoon sugar
1 tablespoon oyster sauce

Soak the dried shrimp in hot water to cover for about 10 minutes. Drain and pound using a mortar and pestle. Wash water spinach well, shake dry and break into bite-sized lengths.

Heat oil and on gentle heat cook the garlic, stirring, until pale golden. Add shrimp and cook for a minute longer, then add the greens and sugar and stir-fry until wilted. Stir in the oyster sauce and serve with steamed jasmine rice.

Water Spinach Chilli Fry, Sri Lankan Style

Serves 4

500 g/1 lb water spinach
2 tablespoons oil
sprig of fresh curry leaves
1 medium onion, finely chopped
2 teaspoons dry chilli flakes
1 teaspoon salt

Wash water spinach well, shake dry and break into bite-sized pieces, using only the leaves and tender tips of stems for this dish. Heat oil and fry curry leaves and onions until onions are soft and turning brown. Add dried chilli, salt and the prepared water spinach. Toss over medium heat for about 5 minutes. Serve as an accompaniment to rice.

Water Spinach, Malay Style

Serves 4

500 g/1 lb water spinach
250 g/8 oz dried shrimp
½ cup peeled shallots
2 cloves garlic
1 hot red chilli
2 tablespoons oil
salt to taste

Wash the water spinach well, shake dry and cut into short, bite-sized lengths. Soak the shrimp in a little warm water for 10 minutes, drain and chop in a food processor or pound roughly. Pound or blend together the shallots, garlic and chilli.

Heat oil in a wok and fry the pounded mixture and the shrimp, stirring constantly, until it smells cooked. Add water spinach and stir-fry for a minute or two, add salt and mix well. Serve hot with rice and a main dish.

Water Spinach, Chinese Style

Serves 4

500 g/1 lb water spinach
3 tablespoons oil
2 teaspoons shrimp sauce
¼ cup hot water
1 teaspoon sugar

Wash the water spinach well and break into short lengths. Heat the oil and stir-fry the vegetable over high heat until wilted. Add the shrimp sauce mixed with hot water and sugar, toss well to mix, cover and simmer for a few minutes.

Wax Gourd

See GOURDS.

Whitebait

Very small fish, but just how small they have to be to be called whitebait is debatable. They can be the fry of sprats, herrings or anchovies. They can be up to 7 cm (3 in) long and small but perfectly formed; or so tiny that they have been described as looking like a mass of jelly with thousands of pinpoint eyes in it.

New Zealand whitebait is the latter and white-bait 'fritters' are a well-known local speciality. The whitebait is mixed with beaten egg and flour and shallow-fried, resulting in omelette textured patties.

Whitebait Fritters

Serves 4

250 g/8 oz whitebait
1 egg
125 ml/4 fl oz/½ cup milk
60 g/2 oz/½ cup flour
salt and pepper to taste
oil for shallow frying
lemon wedges for serving

Rinse the whitebait in a sieve, running cold water through them. Leave to drain while preparing batter. Beat egg and milk, whisk in flour until smooth, adding salt and pepper. The batter should be of a thin, pouring consistency. When ready to cook, mix in the whitebait. Have the oil heated in a heavy frying pan. Drop tablespoons of fritter mixture into the hot oil, not too many at one time. Cook quickly until undersides are golden, then turn and cook other side. Lift out on slotted spoon onto paper towels and cook in batches until all are done. Serve hot with wedges of lemon.

White Gram Bean

See LEGUMES & PULSES.

White Fungus

See MUSHROOMS & FUNGI.

Wild Rice Shoots

(*Zizania aquatica* or *Z. palustris*) Wild rice is an aquatic grass. Its seeds or grains are slender, long and black but should not be confused with the black glutinous rice used in Asia. Although related to *Oryza*, it is not, as some may misconstrue, a variety of rice, but quite a separate species that grows wild in the shallows of a few North American lakes. Traditionally harvested by native American Chippewa in canoes — it was fought over by Sioux and Chippewas — it is now grown commercially in eastern and central North America in irrigated fields.

Though wild rice grows in Japan, China and Taiwan, it is cultivated as a vegetable rather than as a grain crop. The rice shoot is harvested when attacked by a fungus that swells the shoots and, in advanced stages, causes black dots (spores) in the centre. It is best eaten before the spores are visible.

Purchasing and preparation: The shoots are from 25–35 cm (10–15 in) in length, tapering to a leafy tip from a base about 2.5 cm (1 in) in diameter. Select firm shoots with broad white bases. Only the solid pith of the stem is eaten, so the greater its diameter, the more edible portion there will be in the stalk. Discard leaves on the outside and diagonally slice the inner white shoot. The shoot is then stir-fried with other ingredients. Because these shoots have very little flavour, they are usually cooked with shreds of pork, chicken or beef and absorb flavours from the other ingredients. Canned winter bamboo shoot may be substituted.

Medicinal uses: Considered to be cooling in effect.

China: *gau sun, gao bai shun*
Japan: *makomo-zuno*
Malaysia: *rebong ayer*
Thailand: *normai-nam*

Wines & Spirits

Alcoholic beverages are produced throughout Asia from a variety of grains and plants. Generally speaking, grape wine is a rare commodity. Kashmir, where wine has been produced for over 500 years, is one of Asia's few grape wine regions. Liquors are fermented from sugar cane, honey, jaggery, molasses, breadfruit, rose apple and rice. In Marco Polo's travels to China, 54 different varieties of rice wine were documented. Arrack and toddy were originally made from the sap of palmyra, talipot and coconut palms. Toddy is the sweet, slightly opaque sap which makes a refreshing and not at all alcoholic drink if drunk soon after it has been collected. The term also applies to the sap fermented to become a potent 'cheap grog'. (In the West, 'toddy' also means a hot, sweet drink with some spirits and spices in it.) Toddy is fermented and distilled to produce arrack, but 'arrack' now refers to any strong, clear-coloured spirits made from fermented palm sap or rice.

Arrack, arak: Powerful and rather coarse spirit distilled from grain, rice or sugar cane.

Brom: Potent Balinese rice wine.

Chi: Millet beer from north east India.

Chig-g: Ceremonial spirit from Inner Mongolia distilled from fermented milk.

Feni: Spirit made in Goa from the fruit of the cashew nut.

Kumiss, koumiss: Mongolian beverage made from fermented mare's milk.

Lambanog: Sweet palm wine made in the Philippines from the strong liquor, tuba.

Mei: Potent Tahitian brew made from breadfruit.

Mirin: Sweet rice wine. Used only for cooking except on the four or five days of the New Year holiday, when it is flavoured with pepper and spices and sipped from ceremonial cups. Mixed in equal quantities with soy sauce to make that most versatile of Japanese sauces, teriyaki, which serves as a marinade, a glaze and a dipping sauce. Look for a naturally brewed mirin (hon-mirin) and beware of 'new, improved mirin' (aji-mirin) which contains salt and corn syrup. Sweet sherry may be substituted, but the flavour is not the same.

Miti hue: Tahitian buttermilk-like beverage made from fermented coconut milk.

Rose wine: A Chinese brew which is described on the label as being made from 'kaoliang chiew with the admixture (sic) of distilled fresh rose of a famous variety and granulated sugar. It has a permanent fragrant flavour and a slightly sweet taste'. With an alcohol content of 54 per cent, I would recommend its sparing use. Pour a small quantity of it around the edges of a hot wok towards the end of cooking so the alcohol vaporises, leaving behind only the flavour.

Sake: Brewed and filtered rice liquor of Japan. Traditionally served warm from small, narrow-necked porcelain or glazed ceramic bottles and drunk from miniature ceramic cups. Also known more generally as rice wine. In summer, served cold in a square wooden box. (Shirosake is a weaker, colourless sake, about 5 per cent alcohol.) There are regional Chinese versions with poetic names.

Sam shiu (chiew): A general Chinese term for spirits.

Samchu: A Manchurian beverage made from fermented sorghum.

Schochu: Japanese vodka-like spirit made from sweet potato.

Shao hsing, Shaoxing: A town in the northern Chekiang province of China that for more than 2,000 years has produced China's most famous rice wine of the same name. It is like a fine dry sherry. Blended from glutinous rice, millet, a special yeast and local mineral spring waters, the best shao hsing is aged at least 10 years and is drunk warm. Braised foods use more liberal amounts and 'drunken' dishes require lashings. Also known as huang chiu (yellow wine) because of its amber hue. Shao hsing comes in three varieties: shang niang, which is robust; chu yeh ching (bamboo green), which owes its pale green colour and delicate flavour to young bamboo leaves added during fermentation; and hsiang hsueh (fragrant snow), which is sweet and pale.

Shochu: Japanese spirit distilled from sake.

Toddy: Fermented local brew produced throughout Micronesia and South East Asia from sweet-sapped palms, such as coconut.

Toeak: Balinese beer brewed from palm juice.

Tuba: The Filipino version of toddy.

Wak shee: A highly intoxicating Tibetan spirit.

Yintsieu: Sweet Chinese wine.

Winged Bean

See LEGUMES & PULSES.

Winter Melon

See GOURDS (Ash gourd).

Wok

See UTENSILS.

Wolfberry

(*Lycium chinense*) The fruit of the matrimony vine or Chinese boxthorn sometimes called boxthorn berries. SEE ILLUSTRATION. The soft, slightly bitter leaves are used in soups or cooked with pork. The berries have a pleasant, slightly sweet taste and while not adding strong flavour, blend with other seasonings and add a touch of bright colour. For tonic purposes they are mainly added to soup or congee. Sold dried in packets.

Medicinal uses: In Chinese medicine wolfberries are believed to help both vision and kidney function. Publications dealing with medicinal properties of plants reveal that the berries are indeed rich in carotene so the claim of improving eyesight does have some nutritional basis. They also contain vitamin C and are combined with other herbs to retard ageing and are credited with lifting the spirits.

China: *gau gei jee, kei chi, ji zi* (berries), *gau gei choi* (leaves)

Chicken Soup with Wolfberries

Strong, clear chicken soup is considered as much of a cure-all in Chinese cuisine as the traditional Jewish mother's chicken soup. It is particularly favoured for helping women recover strength after childbirth. Serves 2–3.

1 small roasting chicken
6 slices fresh ginger
2 spring onions (scallions), sliced
2 tablespoons Chinese wine or sherry
1 tablespoon light soy sauce
½ teaspoon salt
2 tablespoons wolfberries
few drops oriental sesame oil

Cut off the tail of the chicken, taking care to cut high enough so that the two glands on either side are also eliminated. Remove fat from body cavity, and all the skin except from the wings. Cut chicken into pieces through the bone, Chinese style (see page 77).

Put the chicken and all the other ingredients except sesame oil into a yunnan pot or other heatproof earthenware dish. If a yunnan pot with its steam-conducting funnel is not available, add about 1 cup of water. (The yunnan pot will not need any water.)

Place pot on a trivet in a large boiler so it is above the level of water. Cover boiler with a well-fitting lid and cook on medium heat, keeping the water boiling and adding more from time to time as required, for 1½ hours. Juices from the chicken will form the soup. Sprinkle sesame oil over and serve in the pot in which it was cooked.

Steamed Chicken and Wolfberries

A quickly prepared dish to serve simply with steamed rice. Children love the gentle flavours. Serves 2–3.

375 g/12 oz chicken thigh or drumstick fillets
1 teaspoon finely chopped fresh ginger
2 teaspoons light soy sauce
2 level teaspoons cornflour (cornstarch)
½ teaspoon salt
½ teaspoon sugar
½ teaspoon oriental sesame oil
1 tablespoon dried wolfberries
2 tablespoons dry sherry

Trim any fat from chicken and cut the meat into bite-sized pieces. Combine with ginger, soy sauce, cornflour, salt, sugar and sesame oil and mix well. Put onto a heatproof plate.

Soak the wolfberries in the sherry and sprinkle over the chicken. Place in a steamer, cover and steam over boiling water for 15–18 minutes. Serve with steamed rice.

Woodapple

(*Feronia elephantum*, *F. lucida*) A native of India and Sri Lanka, this jungle fruit from the wilds of Sri Lanka's tropical forests has gained popularity among urban dwellers. Also found in deciduous forests in central and north-eastern Thailand.

It is called woodapple because the shell is hard and woody. The commonest way of getting to the pulp is by hurling the fruit against a concrete floor. Another fruit with a shell similarly hard and woody (and therefore often confused with woodapple) is the bael fruit (*Aegle marmelos*). The bael fruit has a smooth, pale green shell and pale orange pulp when ripe (see BAEL FRUIT). The shell of the woodapple, on the other hand, is rough and greyish in colour. The fruit is collected under licence as forest produce and often sold in the markets.

Another name for this fruit is elephant apple. While I cannot vouch for the accuracy of the legend, it is said that elephants reach up with their trunks, pick the ripe fruit and swallow them whole. The story is that whole fruit may be found in elephants' droppings, but that the shells are empty. The implication is that somehow the digestive system of the elephant is capable of extracting the pulp of the fruit without the shell being crushed or broken.

Once, in a game sanctuary in the south of Sri Lanka, it may have been possible to check the truth of the story; but the tracker forbade anyone alighting from the vehicle as we had seen a baby elephant, and elephants are very protective of their young.

The pulp of unripe woodapples may be grated, mixed with hot chilli powder and finely chopped red onions, and seasoned with salt and lime juice to make an exceptionally sour sambal, mainly eaten on its own as a snack rather than as an accompaniment to rice as most sambals are. At this stage the pulp is a pale creamy colour. When fully ripe the pulp turns from pale cream to dark chocolate brown, is mealy and pleasantly sour-sweet with numerous, pea-sized, pale seeds.

In Thailand, the young shoots and leaves are eaten raw with larb and sometimes included in sour bamboo shoot salad. Thais use of the fruit is almost incidental. On the other hand, Sri Lankans ignore the shoots and leaves, and make a feature of the fruit.

Purchasing: To judge whether a woodapple is ripe, gently shake the fruit. If it can be felt moving around, loose within the shell, it should be ripe.

Canned, sweetened woodapple pulp (labelled 'woodapple cream') is exported from Sri Lanka. It can be inconsistent in quality, as though some of the fruit which is canned is not ripe enough. The colour of the purée should be a rich, dark brown and not a reddish brown. Fruit which is not fully ripe has a good deal of astringency and a slightly mouth-puckering effect. If, however, you are in a country where the fresh fruit itself is available, there is a better chance of knowing the fruit you buy is really ripe. When opened, the pulp should be the colour of chocolate mousse.

Preparation: At the fully ripe stage the fruit is used for a popular drink known in Sinhalese as dimbul kiri (woodapple milk). The milk is extracted from freshly grated and squeezed coconuts, mixed with woodapple pulp, then strained to eliminate seeds and fibres. Sugar or palm sugar is added to taste. The mixture is strained into a jug with crushed ice. A pinch of salt helps bring out the flavours of both the fruit and the coconut milk. About the consistency of a thick milkshake, this drink is one of the treats one can experience at its best made with fresh fruit. The same mixture can be used to make woodapple ice cream or mousse.

Medicinal uses: The unripe fruit checks diarrhoea. Ripe fruit is used for kidney complaints.

South India : *villa, villati*
Sri Lanka: *dimbul, diwul*
Thailand: *ma sang*

Woodapple and Coconut Drink

**2 fully ripe woodapples
  or canned woodapple pulp
1 litre/2 pints freshly squeezed coconut milk,
  first and second extracts kept separate
sugar to taste
pinch of salt**

Break the shells and scoop out the fruit which should be a rich chocolate colour. In a glass or china bowl mix the pulp with 2 cups of thin coconut milk, squeezing and kneading to dissolve the pulp. Strain through a nylon sieve. Pour more thin milk over the pulp and knead again, dissolving as much pulp as possible. Strain once more. Add ½ cup sugar or jaggery and a good pinch of salt. Stir to dissolve. Taste and add more sugar if necessary. Cover and chill. Just before serving, stir in the first extract (coconut cream) and serve at once.

Note: This can be made using canned woodapple pulp and canned coconut milk. Dilute coconut milk with an equal amount of water or more, if it is very thick and rich. Stir woodapple pulp in the can as it usually settles due to its rather mealy texture. Pour some into a jug, add twice its volume of diluted coconut milk and a pinch of salt. Stir to mix thoroughly. Pour over crushed ice in glasses. If a lighter drink is preferred, woodapple pulp may be mixed with soda water instead of coconut milk. After mixing, pour the drink through a fine strainer into another jug and discard the mealy pulp.

Woodapple Jelly

I remember the woodapple jelly made by my grandmother. Wonderful flavour, and the deep ruby colour of port wine. The last jar was opened 11 years after she died and it was still in perfect condition. Obviously a recipe with good keeping qualities, due no doubt to the meticulous care she took and the extreme cleanliness of utensils used in preparation and every bottle used to store the jellies.

6–8 woodapples
sugar

Half-ripe fruits may be used to help the jelly set. Break the shells, scoop out the pulp with a spoon and weigh it. Allow 500 ml (1 pint) water to each 500 g (1 lb) pulp. Put fruit and water into a heavy pan and bring to the boil, then simmer until liquid is reduced to half its volume.

Strain through a jelly bag or cheesecloth. Do not squeeze the bag or the jelly will not be perfectly clear. Measure the liquid and allow ¾ cup sugar to each cup of liquid. In a clean pan cook the sugar and juice, stirring, until the jelly sheets as it falls from the spoon. It should set when a little is dropped on a cold plate. Pour into hot sterile jars and seal.

Wood Fungus

See MUSHROOMS & FUNGI.

Xacuti

A curry prepared in Goa with quite complex spicing, including white poppy seeds and large dried red chillies.

Crab Xacuti

Pronounced shaguti and sometimes spelled shakootee or shagotti. Roasted and ground coconut is an important flavour in this dish. Serves 4.

2 fresh raw crabs
6 large dried red chillies
1 tablespoon coriander seeds
1 teaspoon cumin seeds
½ teaspoon fenugreek seeds
½ teaspoon whole black peppercorns
4 whole green cardamom pods
4 whole cloves
small piece cinnamon stick
2 tablespoons white poppy seeds
5 tablespoons freshly grated or desiccated coconut

2 medium onions, finely sliced
1 teaspoon ground turmeric
2 tablespoons vegetable oil
1 tablespoon ghee
2 teaspoons chopped garlic
2 teaspoons chopped ginger
1 teaspoon salt or to taste
2 tablespoons tamarind purée or lime juice

Clean the crabs as described under CRAB and cut each into 2 if small, 4 if large.

Remove stems from chillies and soak in a little hot water to cover for 10 minutes. In a dry pan over low heat stir the coriander seeds constantly until fragrant. Turn onto a plate then dry roast the cumin, fenugreek, peppercorns, cardamoms, cloves and cinnamon in the same way, just until fragrant. Turn onto a plate with the roasted coriander. Roast the white poppy seeds, stirring constantly, until golden. Roast the coconut until quite dark brown. Finally dry roast the sliced onion, stirring, until brown. Put all the roasted ingredients into a powerful electric blender with the turmeric, chillies and some of the soaking water. Blend to a smooth paste.

In a heavy pan heat oil and ghee and fry the ground mixture on low heat, stirring constantly, until oil separates from the mass. Add the crab pieces, salt, tamarind and just enough water to cover base of pan and prevent spices sticking. Cover and cook for 10 to 15 minutes, turning crab over in the spice mixture from time to time until crab shells are red. Add a little water if necessary but the gravy should be very thick and dark. Serve with plain steamed rice.

Xanthoxylum spp.

Anise pepper, Chinese pepper, Japanese pepper, fagara, prickly ash, sansho, Szechwan pepper, wild pepper. Sometimes spelled with 'Z' instead of 'X' (it is pronounced as Z). See SZECHWAN PEPPER and SANSHO.

Yabbie

An Australian freshwater crustacean occasionally available in fish markets. Often bred in dams on farming properties, but prone to migrate without notice. If yabbies decide to march, en masse, to the next dam they will, regardless of boundaries. While the flesh is tender and sweet, it is only the tail meat which is worth eating and that is barely a mouthful in size.

Yabbies are caught with cunning and patience, using fresh meat as bait. They are seldom very much larger than 7.5 cm (3 in) in length, so if satisfying hunger is your priority it would be better to opt for a larger crustacean; but if eating them for the experience, they are best tasted simply boiled and served with freshly ground pepper, a good mayonnaise or sprinkled with vinegar. They can also be cooked in a chilli and lime flavoured broth, such as the Thai tom yum which features prawns (shrimp).

Purchasing and preparation: As with any other shellfish, look for bright (not sunken) eyes, undamaged shells and a fresh smell. If they are being freshly caught, the flavour improves if, once fished from their muddy dams, they are soaked in fresh water with a handful of oatmeal added. Drop into lightly salted boiling water and as soon as the shells turn red, they are cooked and ready to eat.

Yam

(*Dioscorea* spp.) In a botanical sense, yams are only those which belong to the *Dioscorea* species, but in general, and especially when shopping in native markets, all kinds of starchy tubers, root crops and even sweet potatoes are referred to as yams. The difference becomes important only when preparing these tubers for cooking. The sweet potato may be scrubbed and cooked in its skin, and the skin may be eaten. The skin of the taro, however, is never eaten as irritating crystals of calcium oxalate present in taro are concentrated under the skin and deep peeling is recommended. See TARO.

These carbohydrate foods are important staples in some countries. While to the uninitiated they may seem insipid and lack appeal, to those who have been brought up on them, they are very important indeed. The people of the Hawaiian islands, for instance, relish poi, the sticky grey substance made from cooked, mashed and fermented taro roots, but the rest of the world cannot understand why. In the Pacific, it would be a rare meal which did not include taro boiled, baked or steamed.

Yams come in a variety of colours, shapes and sizes. The cush-cush yam (*D. trifida*) has sweet, smooth flesh that ranges from white to rich purple. Most varieties are tropical, and they grow as a vine, the stems having a climbing habit. Purple yam is known as ube or ubi in the Philippines, and often made into jam or cakes. The great yam (or asiatic yam) can grow to an enormous size, as much as 45 kg (90 lb). However, it is those of a more moderate size which are preferred for eating.

While yams may not have much flavour in themselves, they are cooked with great ingenuity to make both savoury and sweet dishes. Yams may be used in curries the same way as potatoes. Yams and sweet potatoes also appear in a sweet dish called guinatan in the Philippines but known mainly by its Malay name of bubor cha cha which may sound like a Latin American dance step but is a combination of diced boiled yams in sweetened, freshly extracted coconut milk. See JAKFRUIT.

The foreign names below are first for greater yam (*D. alata*) and second for lesser yam (*D. esculenta*).

China: *taai-shue, siu-chue-shue*
India: *kham, sinna-valli-kelangut*
Indonesia: *ubi-kemali, ubi-arumanis*
Japan: *oo-yama-imo, ama-yama-imo*

Malaysia: *ubi-kemali, ubi-torak*
New Zealand: *uwhi, uwhikaho*
Philippines: *ubi, tugi, buga*
Sri Lanka: *raja-ala, java-ala*
Thailand: *man-sao, man-chuak*

New Zealand yam: (*Oxalis tuberosa*) Belonging to a different botanical family, these attractively coloured and shiny-skinned edible tubers are only about the size of a man's thumb. In New Zealand they are simply called yams, though the Maori name for yams of the Dioscorea species is uwhi-kaho or uwhi.

Yams are thought to have come to New Zealand via Samoa, from their native Peru where they are known as oca. Very popular because of their sweet flavour and versatility, they may be steamed, boiled, baked or eaten raw, or candied like sweet potatoes.

Apparently they do contain calcium oxalate when freshly dug, but this is reduced when the tubers are dried in the sun, becoming wrinkled, floury and sweet. Those I have seen and eaten were certainly not dry and wrinkled, but smooth and shiny. Thankfully, they showed no signs of containing calcium oxalate.

Yam Bean

(*Pachyrhizus erosus, P. angulatus*) SEE ILLUSTRATION. Many plants of the Leguminosae family which produce both tubers and pods are referred to as yam beans. Known as sweet turnip as well as by its Mexican name, jicama (pronounced hee-cama). A native of tropical America, it is also grown in South East Asia.

The variety grown in Asia usually produces single, lobed tubers which are quite decorative in shape. The colour of the skin is pale and brown. The flesh at its best is white, crisp and slightly sweet. It provides mainly carbohydrate and is widely used in Asia as an ingredient in the filling of spring rolls.

Purchasing and storing: Choose tubers of moderate size with smooth, fine skin indicating that they are young and fresh. If the skin is thick and the tubers extra large, it indicates greater maturity than is desirable and the texture will most likely be fibrous and starchy instead of sweet, moist and crunchy. Smaller sizes also minimise waste.

Stored in the crisper of the refrigerator the tubers will keep for several weeks. If you do have to store a cut tuber, wrap it closely with cling wrap (plastic wrap) to prevent it drying out. It will last as long as an uncut yam bean.

Note: The bean pods that grow above ground should only be eaten when very young, as mature pods contain rotenone and can be poisonous.

Preparation: Peel away the skin of the tuber, taking with it any fibrous under-layer. Slice or dice as required and add to salads or stir-fry until tender but still crisp for the spring roll recipe.

While its flavour is delicate, it takes on other flavours cooked with it. In Thailand it is eaten raw in salads, or dipped in a hot, salty dip based on fish sauce and chilli. With its crisp texture, it makes a good addition to mixed salads, either thinly sliced, finely diced or julienned. Also, try peeling and slicing it finely and tossing with a salad such as pomelo salad for crisp texture contrast.

See recipe for Singapore Style Filled Pancakes (page 267).

China: *saa got, dou-su*
India: *sankalu*
Indonesia: *bengkowang*
Japan: *kuzu-imo*
Malaysia: *bangkwang, singkwang*
Philippines: *singkamas*
Thailand: *man kaew*
Vietnam: *cu san*

Yard-Long Bean

See LEGUMES & PULSES.

Yoghurt

Milk and milk products are not commonly used in Asia as oriental digestive systems are, generally speaking, unable to cope with the casein in milk. In India, however, milk products are an important source of protein, especially in vegetarian diets.

Yoghurt in India and Sri Lanka is made mostly from buffalo milk which is much higher in butterfat (over 10 per cent) than cow's milk sold in Western supermarkets (around 4 per cent). The milk in these countries is generally pasteurised but not homogenised. Both of these factors result in a very thick yoghurt with a solid buttery layer of yellow cream on top.

To emulate Indian yoghurt, add one part cream

(35 per cent butterfat) to three parts of whole milk and heat to 96°F then stir in the yoghurt culture or 2 tablespoons commercial yoghurt mixed with a little of the warm milk. Leave undisturbed in a warm place (a vacuum flask works well) for about 6 hours or until firm, then refrigerate.

Yoghurt is used in cooked sauces of both meat and vegetable dishes, to enrich and thicken; mixed with spices and used as a marinade; folded into rice for a south Indian specialty; combined with tamarind chatni or finely chopped herbs and used as a sauce or dip. Its versatility is apparent in the cooling salads known as raitas, where it is gently spiced and seasoned, then folded into diced vegetables or fruit (see Bananas in Yoghurt, page 20 and Cucumber Raita, page 111). Other combinations with yoghurt are cooked and mashed eggplant, diced cooked potatoes, steamed and finely chopped spinach, or diced beetroot (canned beets work well).

Yoghurt (dahi) is served at almost every meal, sometimes as a raita and often as a drink called lassi. This is simply yoghurt mixed until smooth with water or soda. It is either seasoned with salt and cumin or the condiment called jhal jeera which includes black salt.

Lassi may also be sweetened and flavoured with rose water, or have a pinch of cardamom added. It is sometimes combined with mango pulp, thick and delicious like a fruit smoothie.

My favourite recipe using yoghurt is a dessert called Shrikhand (recipe below) which originates in northern India where it is known as the 'honeymoon sweet'. It is very easy to make and needs no cooking, being thick yoghurt flavoured with saffron, cardamom and rosewater, then sprinkled with blanched unsalted pistachio kernels and, for a romantic touch, a few (unsprayed) fragrant rose petals. If you can, obtain fresh pistachios when they are in season, shell, blanch and store them in the freezer for a special dessert like this.

Shrikhand

Serves 4–6

500 ml/1 pint/2 cups thick yoghurt
3–4 tablespoons caster sugar (superfine sugar)
2 drops rose essence
¼ teaspoon ground cardamom or 4 drops
  cardamom extract
¼ teaspoon saffron strands
1 tablespoon pistachio kernels

Put the yoghurt into a bowl with the sugar, flavouring and cardamom and mix together. Lightly toast the saffron strands in a small pan over low heat, making sure they do not burn. Turn out onto a plate to cool. Crush with back of spoon and dissolve in a tablespoon of boiling water. Stir into the yoghurt, turn into a serving bowl or individual dessert dishes, cover and chill.

Blanch the pistachio kernels in boiling water for 30 seconds, drain and remove skins, then chop finely. Sprinkle over the surface before serving.

Yuca

See CASSAVA.

Yum Cha

Literally translated as 'drink tea', yum cha refers to the custom of eating tiny tastes of many different foods while drinking tea.

In any city with a sizeable Chinese population, yum cha is a tradition on Sunday mornings, and whole families gather to talk and eat dim sum and drink pot after pot of Chinese tea. The tea is important, for it is said to help digest the rich foods which may be included in the choice of offerings. Here are some recipes for the simpler dim sum which can be made at home.

Fried Wontons

Makes about 40 wontons

1 quantity dumpling filling (see following recipe)
1 packet wonton pastry squares
peanut oil for deep frying

Take a few squares of wonton pastry from packet and keep remainder covered so they won't dry out. On each square put a scant teaspoonful of filling. Dampen edge of pastry with finger dipped in cold water, and fold over to form a triangle, overlapping points slightly. Press firmly to seal. Bring the lower points of the triangle down to meet below the base, dab with a little filling and press to seal. When all are made, deep fry a few at a time in hot oil over medium heat until golden. Drain on paper towels and serve with a dipping sauce.

Steamed Pork Dumplings

Known as siew mai, these are among the most popular as well as being easy to make. Makes about 25 steamed dumplings.

DUMPLING FILLING

6 dried shiitake mushrooms
250 g/8 oz minced (ground) pork
250 g/8 oz raw prawns (shrimp), shelled and deveined
1 teaspoon finely grated fresh ginger
6 tablespoons finely chopped spring onions (scallions)
6 tablespoons finely chopped canned water chestnuts
½ teaspoon salt or to taste
1 tablespoon light soy sauce
1 teaspoon oriental sesame oil
1 packet wonton pastry squares
25 small school prawns (shrimp) (optional)

Soak mushrooms in very hot water for 30 minutes. Squeeze out excess liquid, discard stems and chop caps finely. Put mushrooms and pork into a bowl with the prawns, finely chopped. Add ginger, spring onions, water chestnuts, salt, soy sauce and sesame oil. Mix thoroughly with hands to combine and distribute seasonings.

Put a heaped teaspoon of filling on a square of pastry and gather pastry around filling, leaving top open like a little drawstring purse. Put a shelled small prawn on top of each if liked, pressing it down firmly on filling. Brush strips of greaseproof paper with sesame oil and place in steamer. Arrange dumplings on the paper and steam over boiling water for 15 minutes. Serve warm with soy or chilli sauce for dipping.

Pot Stickers

1 quantity dumpling filling
250 g/8 oz/2 cups plain (all-purpose) flour
250 ml/8 fl oz/1 cup boiling water
4 tablespoons peanut oil

Prepare filling as described in recipe above, but omit prawns and increase pork to 375 g (12 oz).

Put flour into a large bowl and pour in boiling water, stirring with handle of wooden spoon or chopsticks. When cool enough to handle, knead well until soft and smooth, dusting hands with flour if necessary. Shape dough into a cylinder 2.5 cm (1 in) in diameter and slice into 30 pieces of even size. Cover with plastic or a damp cloth to prevent surface becoming dry.

Roll each piece of dough on a lightly floured board to a circle 10 cm (4 in) in diameter. Pleat half of circle to form a pouch, place a teaspoonful of filling inside and press edges together to seal. If necessary, dampen edges with a little cold water. Place dumplings on a tray not touching each other and keep covered with a damp cloth.

Heat a large, heavy frying pan over medium heat. Add 2 tablespoons peanut oil and tilt pan to coat base and half way up side of pan. (This is important. If pastry touches side of pan that is not oiled, it will stick and tear.) When very hot add half the dumplings in one layer, pleated side up and fry until golden underneath.

Add ½ cup boiling water to pan, using a long-handled ladle as it will hiss and sputter. Cover immediately and cook on low heat for 5 to 8 minutes. Uncover and cook until liquid evaporates and pot stickers become crisp and deep golden brown underneath, lifting occasionally with a spatula to prevent them sticking too firmly.

Remove to a platter, clean the pan and cook remaining pot stickers in the same way. Serve hot, with a dip of chilli sauce or Chinese red vinegar.

Note: Pastry rounds are available in plastic packets from the refrigerator section of most Asian grocers.

Steamed Prawn (Shrimp) Dumplings

1 quantity transparent pastry (recipe page 275)

FILLING

250 g/8 oz raw prawn (shrimp) meat
2 tablespoons finely chopped ham fat
2 tablespoons finely chopped water chestnuts or bamboo shoot
2 tablespoons finely chopped garlic chives
1 teaspoon finely grated fresh ginger
1 teaspoon salt

1 teaspoon sugar
1 teaspoon oriental sesame oil
3 teaspoons cornflour (cornstarch)

Make pastry and set aside while combining the filling ingredients and mixing well.

Divide pastry into 20 slices, and flatten one at a time with the lightly greased blade of a wide Chinese chopper to a circle about 10 cm (4 in) in diameter, pleating the edge on one side. Put teaspoon of filling on pastry, bring edges together and pinch to seal.

Brush lightly with oriental sesame oil and place each one on an oiled square of greaseproof paper. Steam in bamboo steamer over boiling water for 10 minutes. Serve with red vinegar for dipping.

Prawn (Shrimp) Toast

The same mixture used for filling prawn (shrimp) dumplings may be spread thickly on triangles of thinly sliced bread and fried in hot oil, dropping a few pieces at a time into the oil, prawn side downwards. When bread is golden, lift out with slotted spoon and drain on absorbent paper. Serve hot.

Indonesia: *temu putih*
Malaysia: *temu putih*
Thailand: *khamin khao*

Zucchini

(*Cucurbit* spp) Zucchini may not be a name known and used in Asia but there are many similar squashes, gourds, marrows and melons which are used. Indian cooking uses vegetables similar to zucchini (for which zucchini may be substituted). They are either simmered in soups or stir-fried with spices and seasonings, giving a much needed lift to their rather bland flavour.

Always choose young, tender specimens of whichever gourd is in season. They may be diced and added to any mixed vegetable dish, or they may be cooked to a pulp, which is then spicily seasoned by frying a teaspoon each of black mustard seeds and cumin seeds in a tablespoon of ghee with a finely chopped onion and perhaps a fresh sliced chilli or two. Add cooked zucchini pulp, salt and garam masala to taste, and sprinkle with fresh mint or coriander.

Spicy Zucchini Purée

Serves 4

750 g/1½ lb tender zucchini or squash
1 tablespoon ghee or oil
1 teaspoon black mustard seeds
1 teaspoon cumin seeds
2 fresh chillies, sliced
1 large onion, finely chopped
1 ripe tomato, peeled and diced
1 teaspoon salt or to taste
½ teaspoon garam masala
chopped fresh coriander or mint

Wash and dice zucchini or squash. Cook in a covered pan with very little water until soft. Drain away any liquid and roughly mash the vegetable. Heat ghee and fry the mustard and cumin seeds until they pop. Add chillies and onion and cook until onion is golden. Add tomato and salt, cover and cook until tomato is pulpy. Add zucchini, mix well and heat through. Sprinkle with garam masala and chopped herbs and serve with rice or chapatis.

Zedoary

(*Curcuma zedoaria, C. zerumbet*) Browsing in a Thai store one day, I found a box of fresh rhizomes which looked like a slender ginger. I was told it was 'white turmeric' (khamin khao).

The colour was not really white but lemon yellow, but is so named because it is pale in comparison to the vibrant orange-yellow of turmeric. It is not used in curries the way common turmeric is. It is peeled, shredded finely and added to nam prik and salads such as larb. The flavour resembles that of unripe wild mangoes, with more than a hint of turpentine. Use sparingly or it may subjugate other flavours. One source says that only the heart of the young shoots, and sometimes the flowers, are eaten either raw or cooked.

In a book written in Singapore in the early 1950s, I came across a reference to zeodary (sic) in which it is mistakenly identified as kencur, adding yet another element of confusion to the many members of the Zingiberaceae family. Kencur is *Kaempferia galanga* and is different in flavour and application. See GINGER, AROMATIC.

Medicinal uses: Used as a stimulant and carminative for stomach disorders. One source says that because it is rich in starch, it is given to babies and invalids in India, but I cannot imagine any baby being able to cope with the strong flavour.

Bibliography

BACON, Josephine, *Exotic Fruits A–Z*, Xanadu, London, 1988.

BAZORE, Katherine, *Hawaiian and Pacific Foods*, Gramercy, New York.

BREMNESS, Lesley, *Herbs*, D.K. Publishing, New York, 1994.

BRENNAN, Jennifer, *Cuisines of Asia*, Macdonald, London, 1984.

—— *Thai Cooking*, Norman and Hobhouse, London, 1981.

CORDERO-FERNANDO, Gilda, *The Culinary Culture of the Philippines*, GCF Books, Manila, 1976.

COST, Bruce, *Bruce Cost's Asian Ingredients*, William Morrow, New York, 1988.

The Wealth of India. A Dictionary of Indian Raw Materials and Industrial Products, Council of Scientific & Industrial Research, New Delhi, 1959.

CREBER, Ann, *A Multitude of Fishes*, William Heinemann Australia.

DAHLEN, Martha, *A Cook's Guide to Chinese Vegetables*, The Guidebook Company, Hong Kong, 1992.

DASSANAYAKE, M. D. and FOSBERG, F. R., *A Revised Handbook of the Flora of Ceylon*, Ashgate Publishing Co., Brookfield, Vermont, 1988.

DAVIDSON, Alan, *Seafood of South East Asia*, Federal Publications, Singapore, 1977.

—— *Fish and Fish Dishes of Laos*, Davidson, Vientiane, 1974.

DEKURA, Hideo, *The Fine Art of Japanese Cooking*, Bay Books, Sydney, 1984.

DETRICK, Mia, *Sushi*, Chronicle Books, San Francisco, 1981

DEUTROM, Hilda, *The Ceylon Daily News Cookery Book*, Lake House Publishers, Sri Lankas, 1978.

DISSANAYAKE, Chandra, *Ceylon Cookery*, Dissanayake, Ceylon, 1968.

DOWNER, Lesley and MINORU, Yoneda, *Step by Step Japanese Cooking*.

FACCIOLA, Stephen, *Cornucopia. A Source Book of Edible Plants*, Kampong Publications, Vista, California, 1990.

FREEMAN, Meera, *The Vietnamese Cookbook*, Penguin, Melbourne, 1995.

GOODE, John and WILLSON, Carol, *Fruits and Vegetables of the World*, Lothian, Melbourne, 1987.

GRIGSON, Jane and KNOX, Charlotte, *Exotic Fruits and Vegetables*, Henry Holt, New York, 1986.

GRIGSON, Sophie, *Book of Ingredients*, Pyramid Books, Reed, 1991.

HARGREAVES, Dorothy and Bob, *Tropical Trees of the Pacific*, 1970.

HARRISON, S. G., MASEFIELD, G. B. and WALLIS, Michael, *The Illustrated Book of Food Plants*, Peerage, London, 1985.

HUTTON, Wendy, *Singapore Food*, Ure Smith, Sydney, 1979.

JACQUAT, Christiane, *Plants from the Markets of Thailand*, D.K. Book House, Bangkok, 1990.

JOHNS, Leslie and STEVENSON, Violet, *The Complete Book of Fruit*, Angus & Robertson, Sydney, 1979.

JAYAWEERA, D. M. A. *Medicinal Plants (Indigenous and Exotic) Used in Ceylon*, The National Science Council of Sri Lanka, 1982.

JOHARI, HARISH, *The Healing Cuisine. India's Art of Ayurvedic Cooking*, Healing Arts Press, Vermont, 1994.

LIN, Hsiang Ju and LIN, Tsuifeng *The Art of Chinese Cuisine*, Tuttle Publishing, Boston, 1996.

MacMILLAN, H. F. *Tropical Planting and Gardening*, Macmillan, London, 1956.

MALLOS, Tess, *The Bean Cookbook*, Summit Books, Sydney, 1980.

MARTIN, Peter and Joan, *Japanese Cooking*, Bobbs-Merrill, New York, 1970.

MARTINDALE, *The Extra Pharmacopoeia*, Royal Pharmaceutical Society, London, 1993.

McCALLUM, Cass, *Legumes, Grains and Seeds*, Doubleday, Sydney, 1982.

McGEE, Harold, *The Curious Cook*, Harper Collins, London, 1992.

—— *On Food and Cooking*, Harper Collins, London, 1991.

NORMAN, Jill, *The Complete Book of Spices*, Dorling Kindersley and Readers Digest, 1990.

OWEN, Sri, *Indonesian Regional Food and Cookery*, Doubleday, London, 1994.

——*The Rice Book*, 1993.

PASSMORE, Jackie, *The Encyclopedia of Asian Food and Cooking*, Doubleday, Sydney, 1991.

PAYNE, Selma and W. J. A. *Cooking with Exotic Fruit*, Batsford, London, 1979.

PHILLIPS, Roger and Rix, Martyn, *Vegetables*, Macmillan, London, 1995.

PIJPERS, Constant and Jansen, *The Complete Book of Fruit*, Gallery Books, New York, 1986.

Page, P. E. (Ed.) *Tropical Tree Fruits for Australia*, Queensland Department of Primary Industries, Brisbane, 1984.

RICHIE, Donald, *A Taste of Japan*, Kodansha International Ltd, Tokyo, 1985.

ROSENGARTEN, Frederic, *The Book of Spices*, Jove Publications, New York, 1981.

SANTHA RAMA RAU, *The Cooking of India* Time-Life International (Nederland), 1969.

SCHNEIDER, Elizabeth, *Uncommon Fruits & Vegetables, A Commonsense Guide*, Harper & Row, New York.

SHURTLEFF, William and AOYAGI, Akiko, *The Book of Tofu*, Autumn Press, Massachusetts, 1975.

SKINNER, Gwen, *The Cuisine of the South Pacific*, Hodder & Stoughton, 1993.

SOLOMON, Charmaine, *The Complete Asian Cookbook*, Tuttle Publishing, Boston, 1992.

—— *Indian Cooking for Pleasure*, Ure Smith, Sydney, 1978.

———*Thai Cookbook*, Penguin Books, Ringwood, 1991.

SPAYDE, Jon, *Japanese Cookery*, Doubleday, New York, 1984

STOBART, Tom, *The Cook's Encyclopaedia*, Batsford, 1980.

TANAKA, Tyozaburo, *Tanaka's Cyclopedia of Edible Plants of the World*, Keigaku Publishing, Tokyo, 1976.

TANKARD, Glenn, *Tropical Fruit*, Viking O'Neil, Melbourne, 1987.

TANNAHILL, Reay, *Food in History*, Penguin, London, 1973.

UDESKY, James, *The Book of Soba*, Kodansha International, Tokyo, 1988.

WALDO, Myra, *Travel Guide to the Orient and the Pacific*, Macmillan, New York, 1977.

WREN, R. C. and WREN, R. W., *Potter's New Cyclopaedia of Botanical Drugs and Preparations*, Health Science Press, Devon, 1980.

YAMUNA Devi, *The Art of Indian Vegetarian Cooking*, Angus & Robertson, Sydney, 1987.

YOSHIKO Yoshida, *Tropical Cookery (Encyclopedia of Asian Vegetables)*, National Book Store, Quezon City, 1981.

YOSHINO, Masuo, *Sushi*, Gakken, Tokyo, 1986.

Indexes

Illustrated Index of Selected Ingredients

The colour illustrations, listed below in alphabetical order, have been grouped to enable easy reference. The groupings are as follows: Flowers; Fruits; Nuts; Pods and Legumes; Gourds and other Vegetables; Leaf Vegetables; Flavourings; Roots, Tubers and Rhizomes; Water Plants; Mushrooms and Fungi; Spices; and Stems.

The illustrations are in most cases smaller or larger than the real ingredient. To give you an indication of actual sizes, an approximate dimension is given for each illustration.

Ajowan seeds 455
Amaranth 441
Bamboo shoot 456
Banana flower 425
Banana stem 456
Basil leaves 444
Betel (Areca) nuts 433
Betel leaves 444
Bitter gourd 437
Black cumin seeds 455
Black fungus (Cloud ears) 452
Boxthorn leaves and
    wolfberries 441
Breadfruit 428
Broad bean 434
Candle nuts 433
Cardamom pods 454
Cashew fruit and nut 432
Cassava 448
Cassia leaves 447
Ceylon spinach 442
Cha Plu 442
Chilli varieties 440
Chinese cabbage (Wong nga bak) 443
Chinese chard (Bok choy) 443
Chinese chives 445
Chrysanthemum leaves 441
Cinnamon quill 454
Clove flowers 455
Cumin seeds 455
Curry leaves 446
Custard apple 430
Drumstick pod and leaves 436
Durian 429
Eggplant (Aubergine) varieties 439

Enokitake mushrooms 453
Eryngo leaves 447
Fenugreek leaves 446
Fenugreek seeds 455
Flowering chives 445
Fuzzy melon 437
Ginger flower 425
Greater galangal 449
Guava 427
Jakfruit 429
Kaffir lime 431
Kaffir lime leaves 446
Krachai (Chinese keys) 449
Lemon grass 456
Longans 428
Lotus rhizome 451
Lychee 428
Macadamia nut and kernel 433
Mangosteen 427
Mustard cabbage (Gai choy) 443
Nigella seeds 455
Nutmeg 454
Okra 436
Oyster mushrooms 452
Pandanus leaf 446
Parkia 434
Passionfruit 427
Pennywort 442
Pepper 455
Perilla leaves 444
Pine nuts 432
Pistachio nuts 432
Pomelo 431
Purslane 441
Rambutan 428

Rice paddy herb 447
Ridged gourd 438
Rosette bok choy 443
Saffron crocus flower
    and stigma 454
Salam leaves 447
Sapodilla 426
Shallots 445
Shiitake mushrooms
    (fresh and dried) 452
Shimeji mushrooms 453
Snow pea and shoots 435
Soursop 430
Soy bean 435
Sponge gourd 438
Spring onion (Scallion) 445
Star anise 455
Star apple 426
Star fruit 426
Straw mushroom 453
Szechwan pepper 455
Tamarind, sour 431
Tamarind, sweet 431
Taro 448
Turmeric 449
Vietnamese mint leaves 444
Warrigal greens 442
Water chestnuts 451
Water lily 450
Water spinach 451
White fungus 452
White radish (Daikon) 448
Winged beans 434
Yam bean 448
Yard-long bean 435

Flowers

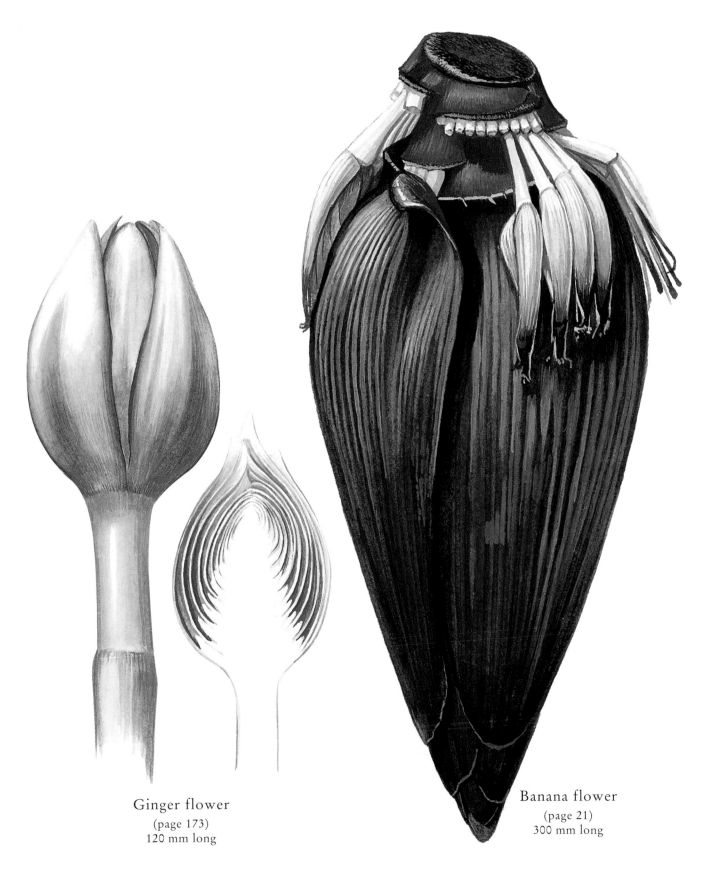

Ginger flower
(page 173)
120 mm long

Banana flower
(page 21)
300 mm long

Fruits

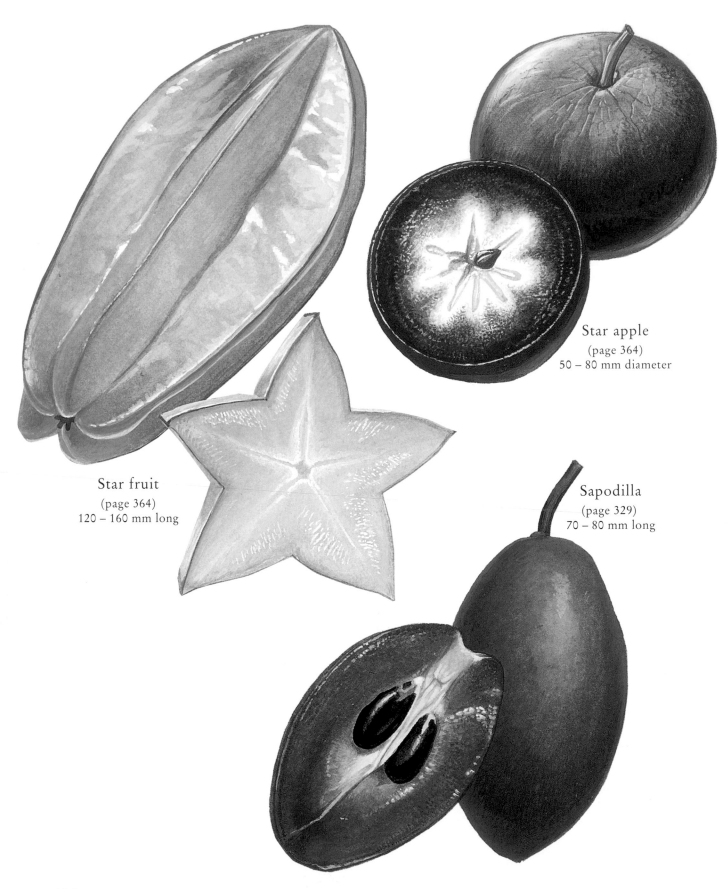

Star apple
(page 364)
50 – 80 mm diameter

Star fruit
(page 364)
120 – 160 mm long

Sapodilla
(page 329)
70 – 80 mm long

Guava
(page 177)
95 mm diameter

Mangosteen
(page 231)
60 – 70 mm diameter

Passionfruit
(page 273)
smaller fruit 50 mm diameter

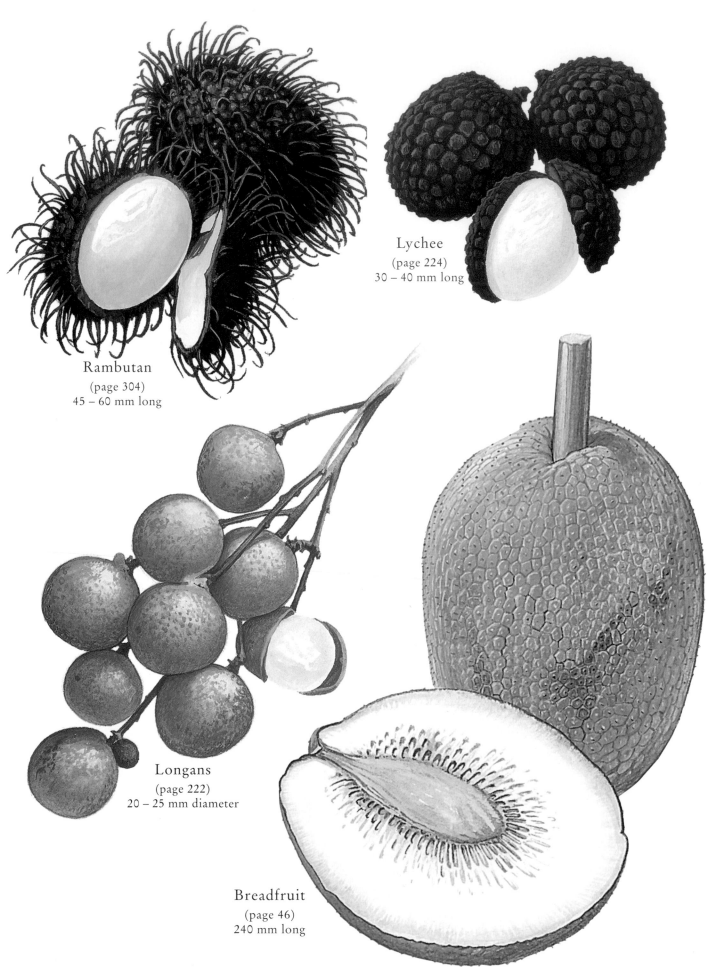

Rambutan

(page 304)

45 – 60 mm long

Lychee

(page 224)

30 – 40 mm long

Longans

(page 222)

20 – 25 mm diameter

Breadfruit

(page 46)

240 mm long

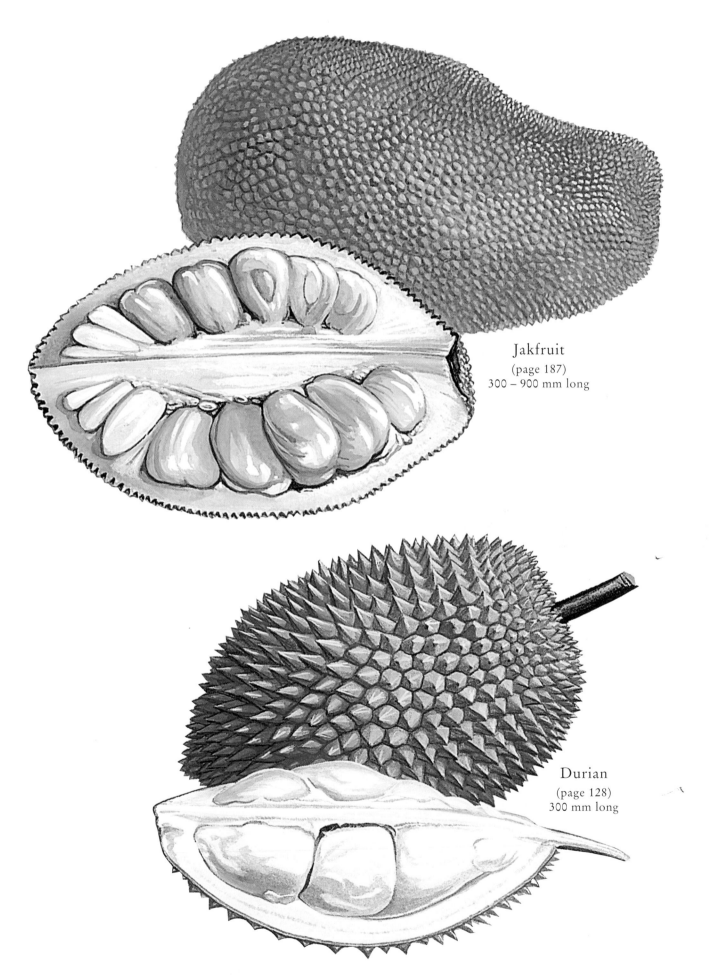

Jakfruit
(page 187)
300 – 900 mm long

Durian
(page 128)
300 mm long

429

Custard apple
(page 116)
100-170 mm long

Soursop
(page 348)
200 – 300 mm long

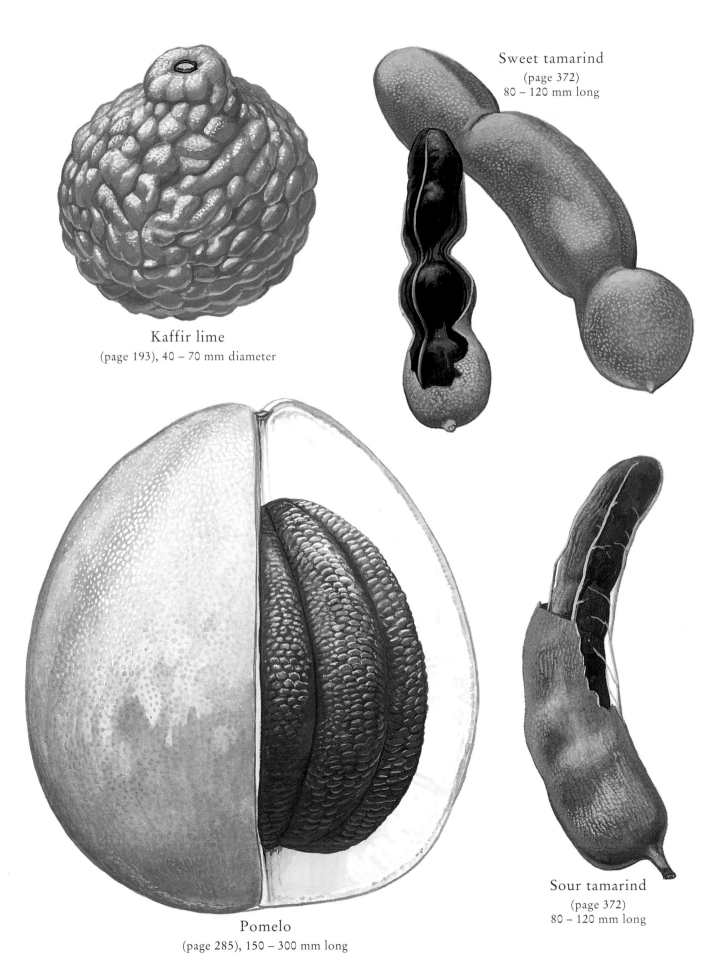

Kaffir lime
(page 193), 40 – 70 mm diameter

Sweet tamarind
(page 372)
80 – 120 mm long

Pomelo
(page 285), 150 – 300 mm long

Sour tamarind
(page 372)
80 – 120 mm long

431

Nuts

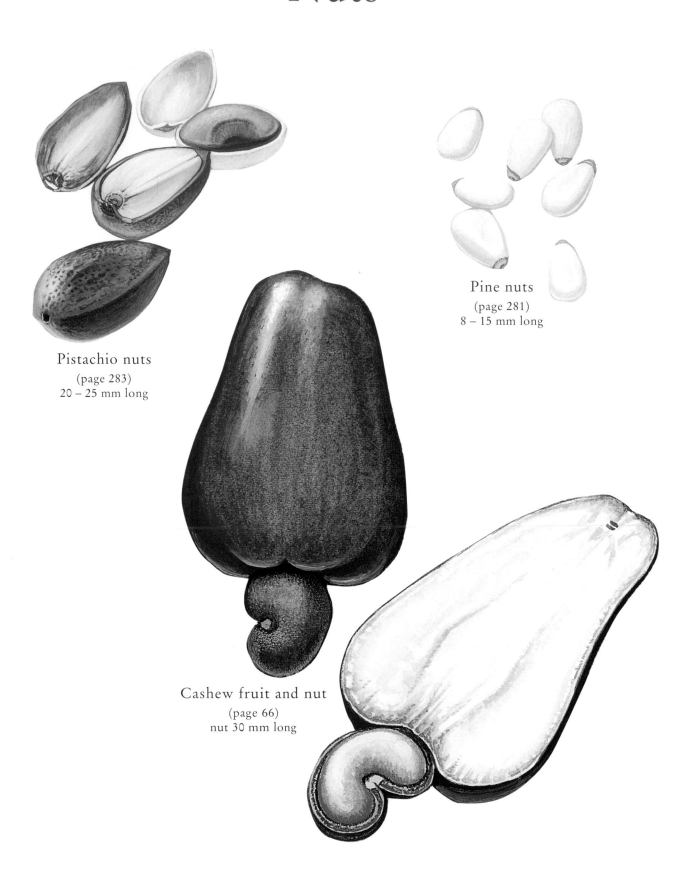

Pistachio nuts

(page 283)

20 – 25 mm long

Pine nuts

(page 281)

8 – 15 mm long

Cashew fruit and nut

(page 66)

nut 30 mm long

Macadamia nut
and kernel
(page 226)
nut 15 – 25 mm diameter

Candle nuts
(page 63)
20 – 25 mm diameter

Betel (Areca) nuts
(page 38)
nut 15 – 25 mm long

433

Pods and Legumes

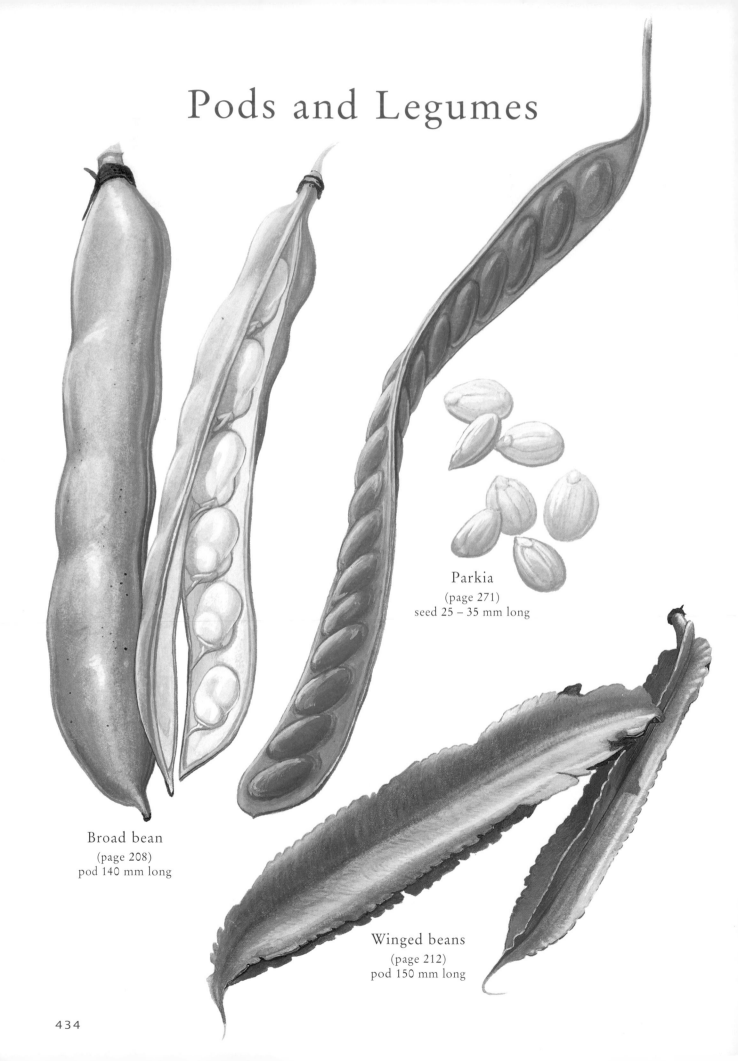

Parkia
(page 271)
seed 25 – 35 mm long

Broad bean
(page 208)
pod 140 mm long

Winged beans
(page 212)
pod 150 mm long

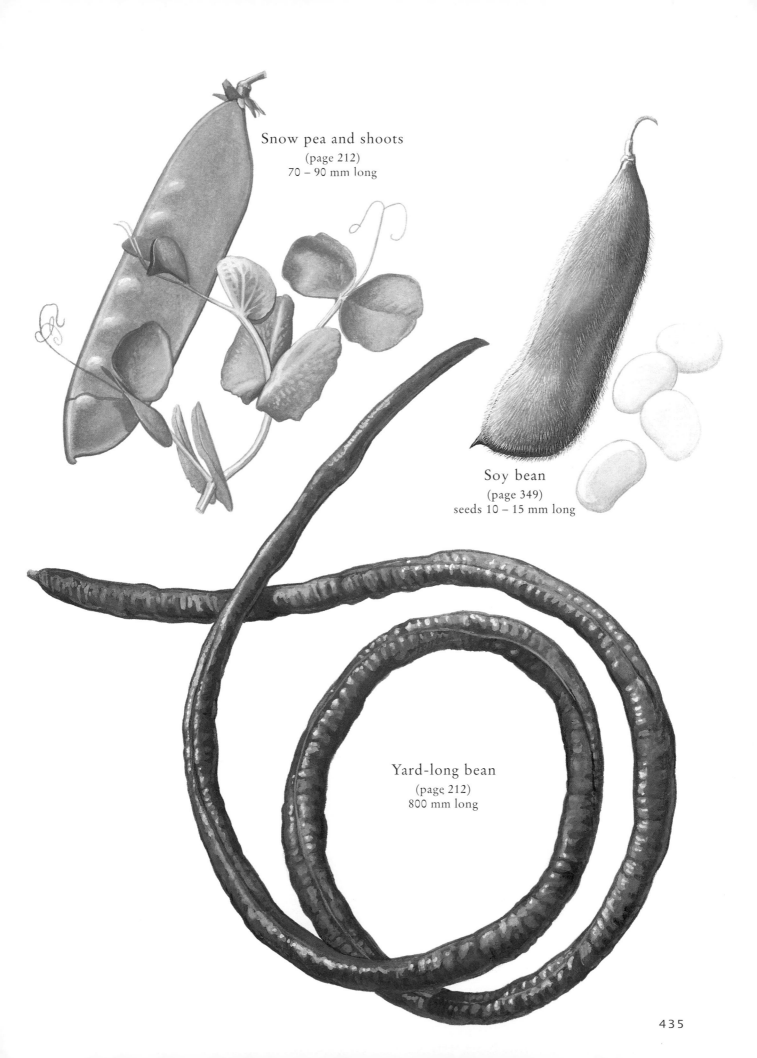

Snow pea and shoots
(page 212)
70 – 90 mm long

Soy bean
(page 349)
seeds 10 – 15 mm long

Yard-long bean
(page 212)
800 mm long

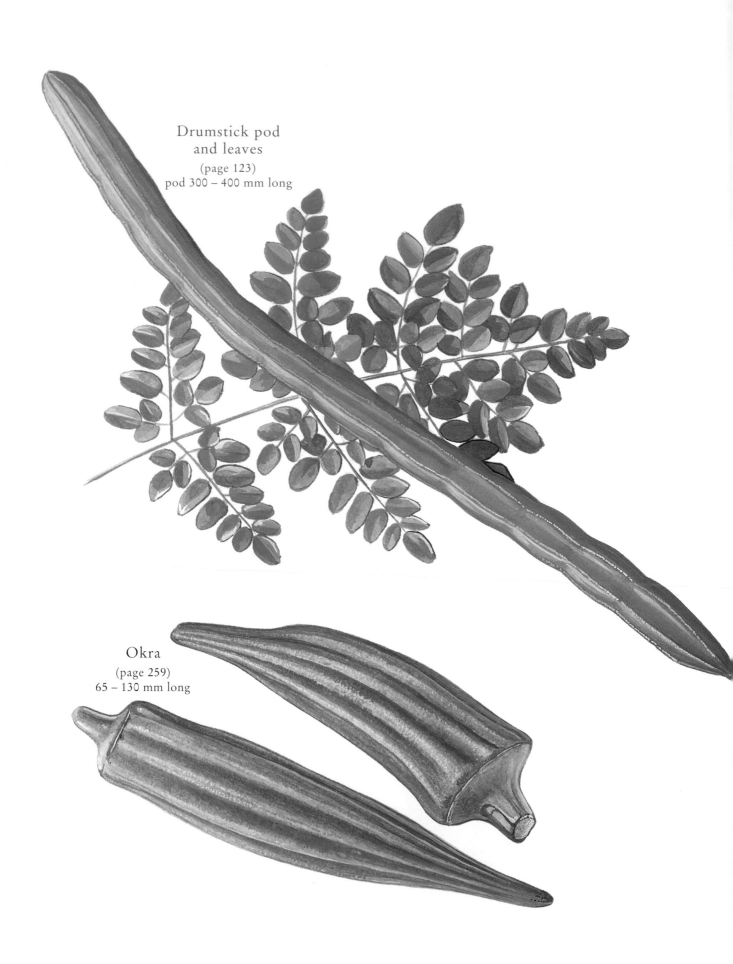

Drumstick pod
and leaves
(page 123)
pod 300 – 400 mm long

Okra
(page 259)
65 – 130 mm long

Gourds and other Vegetables

Bitter gourd
(page 40), 250 mm long

Fuzzy melon
(page 176), 360 mm long

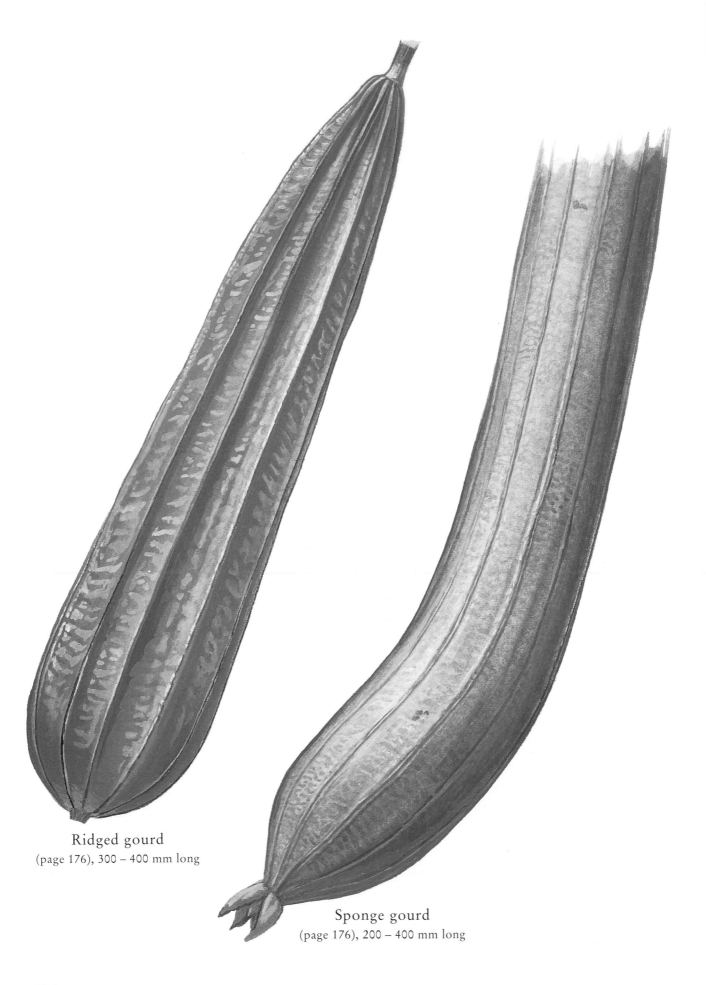

Ridged gourd
(page 176), 300 – 400 mm long

Sponge gourd
(page 176), 200 – 400 mm long

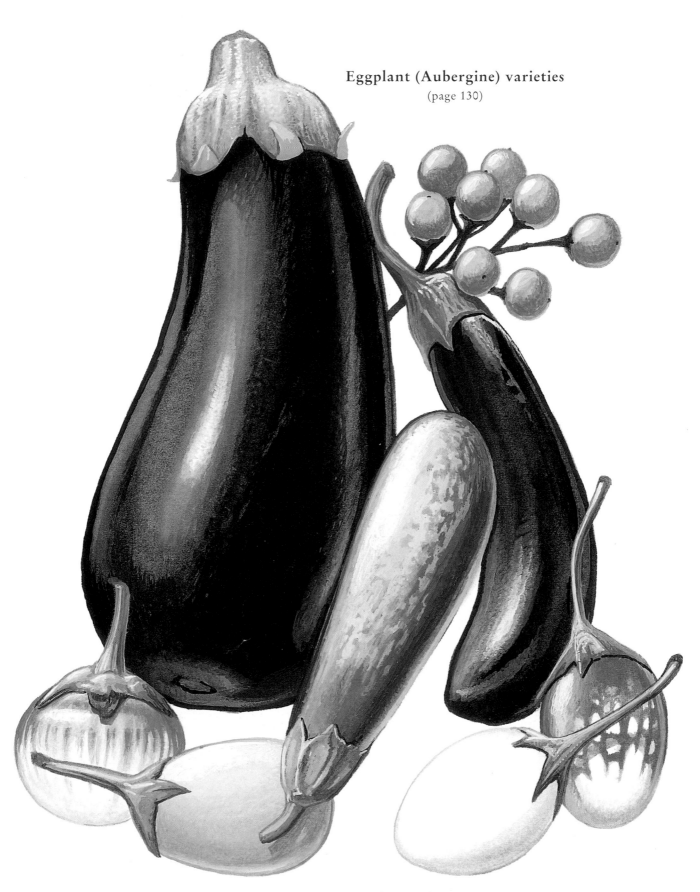

Eggplant (Aubergine) varieties
(page 130)

(Clockwise from top left): Large purple eggplant, 250 mm long;
Pea eggplant, 20 mm diameter; Slender white and purple eggplant,
160 – 180 mm long; Small green and white eggplant, 60 mm diameter.

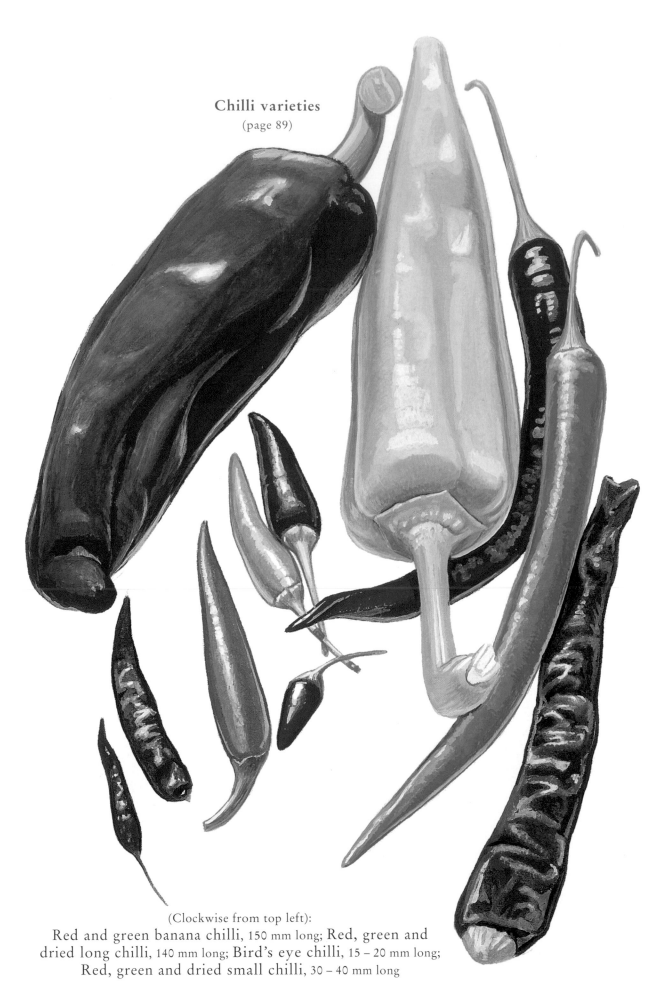

Chilli varieties
(page 89)

(Clockwise from top left):
Red and green banana chilli, 150 mm long; Red, green and
dried long chilli, 140 mm long; Bird's eye chilli, 15 – 20 mm long;
Red, green and dried small chilli, 30 – 40 mm long

Leaf Vegetables

Amaranth
(page 7)
stem and leaves
360 mm long

Boxthorn leaves
and wolfberries
(page 45)
400 mm long

Chrysanthemum
(page 96)
240 mm long

Purslane
(page 301)
200 mm long

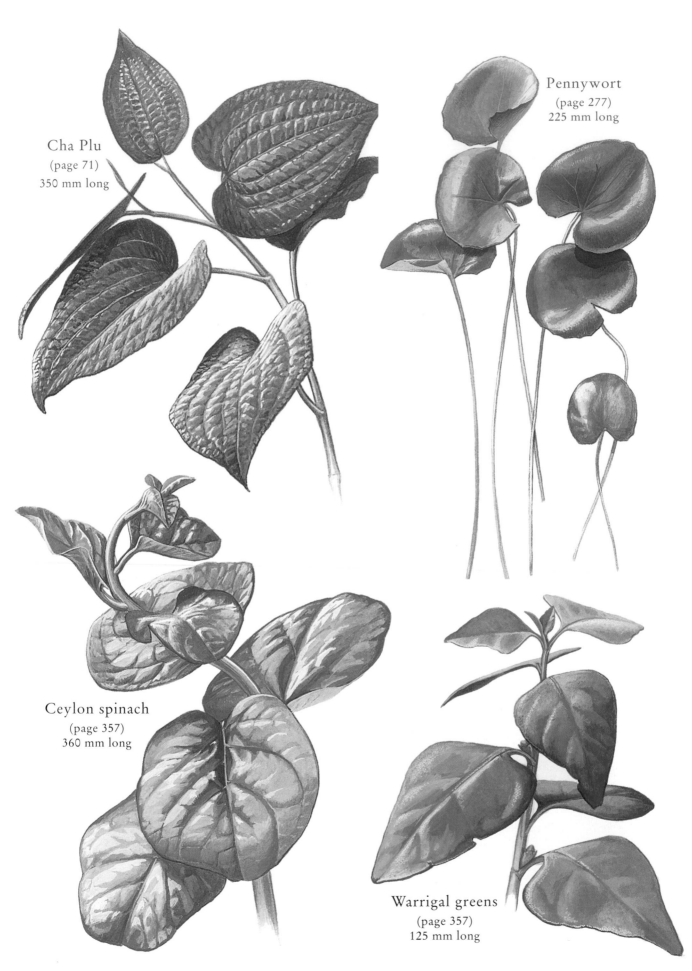

Cha Plu
(page 71)
350 mm long

Pennywort
(page 277)
225 mm long

Ceylon spinach
(page 357)
360 mm long

Warrigal greens
(page 357)
125 mm long

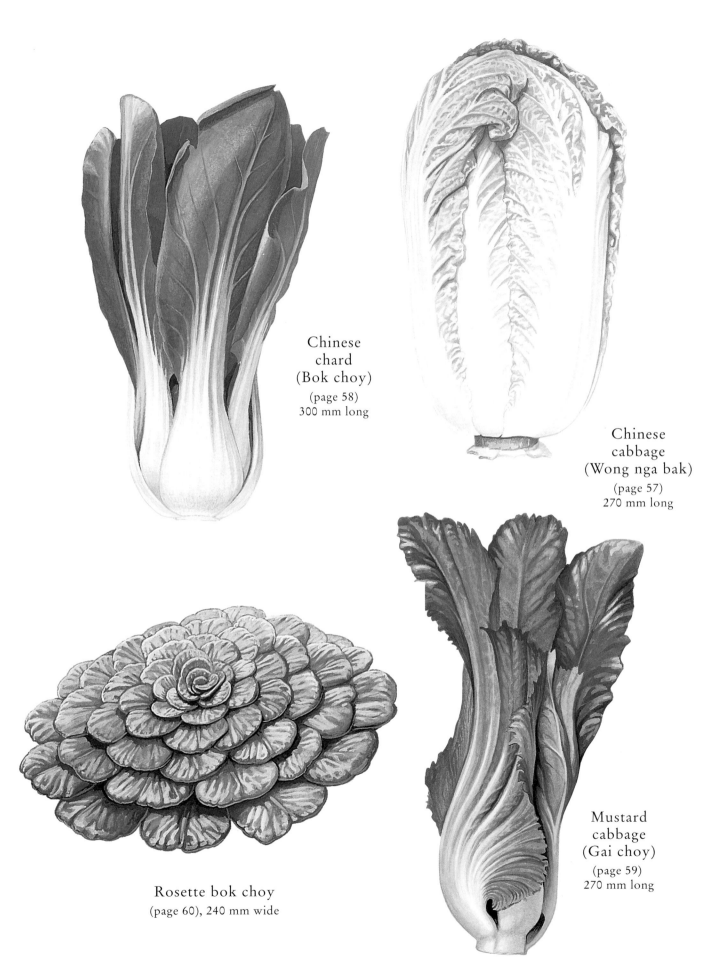

Chinese
chard
(Bok choy)
(page 58)
300 mm long

Chinese
cabbage
(Wong nga bak)
(page 57)
270 mm long

Rosette bok choy
(page 60), 240 mm wide

Mustard
cabbage
(Gai choy)
(page 59)
270 mm long

Flavourings

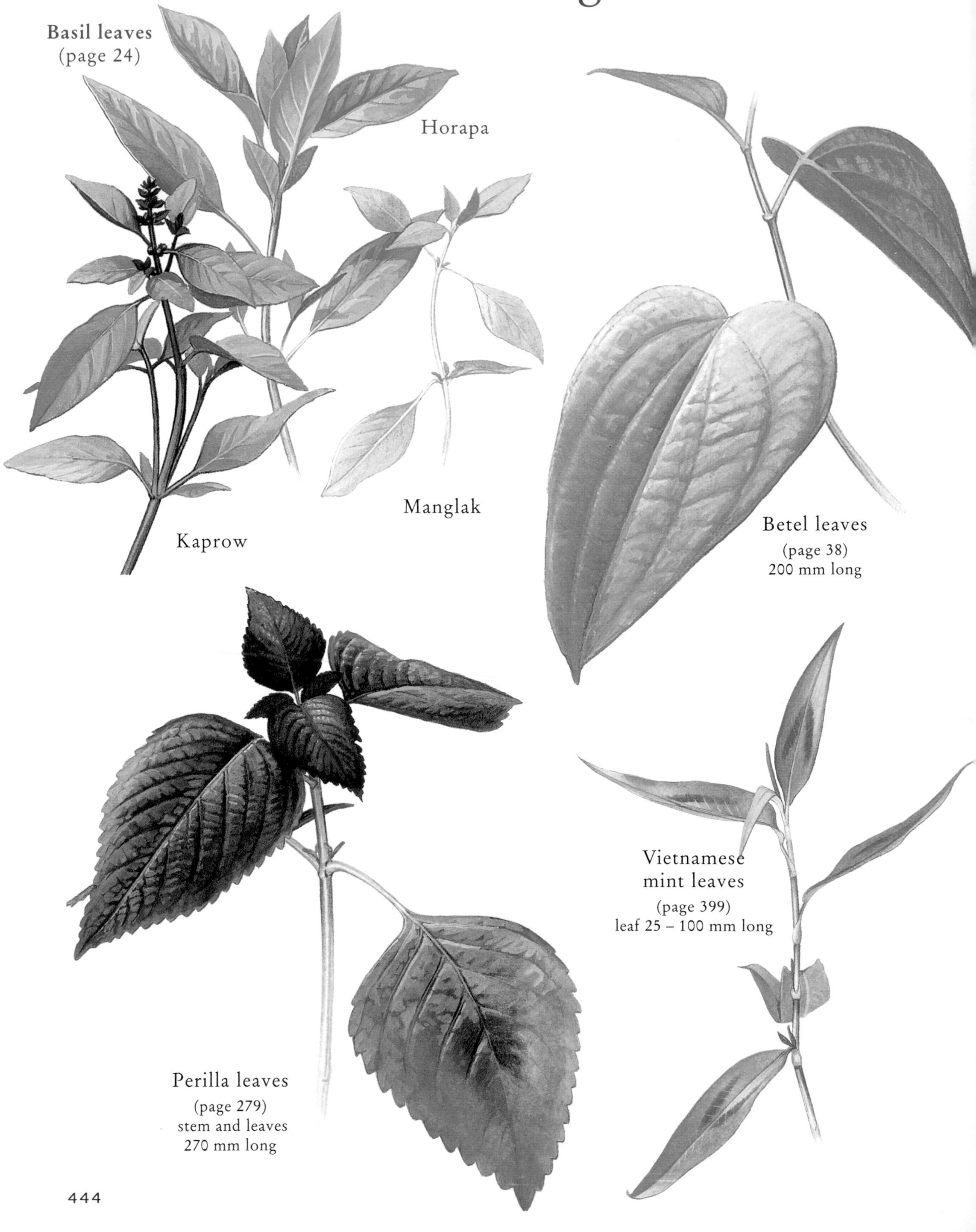

Basil leaves
(page 24)

Horapa

Kaprow

Manglak

Betel leaves
(page 38)
200 mm long

Perilla leaves
(page 279)
stem and leaves
270 mm long

Vietnamese
mint leaves
(page 399)
leaf 25 – 100 mm long

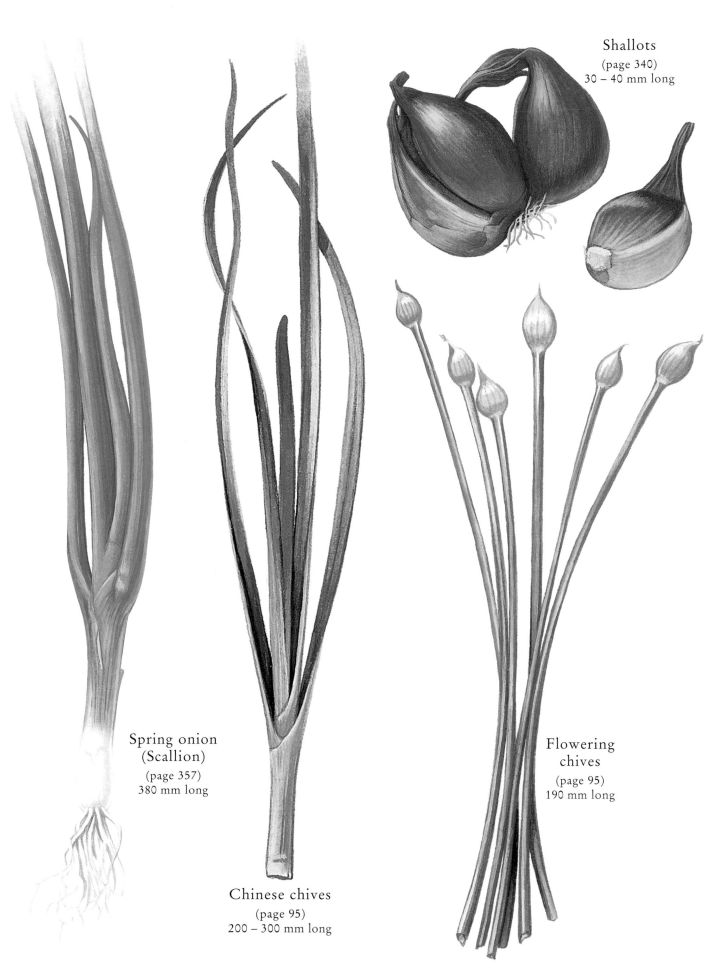

Shallots
(page 340)
30 – 40 mm long

Spring onion
(Scallion)
(page 357)
380 mm long

Chinese chives
(page 95)
200 – 300 mm long

Flowering
chives
(page 95)
190 mm long

Fenugreek leaves
(page 143)
stem and leaves
100 mm long

Pandanus leaf
(page 269)
leaf 60 mm wide

Curry leaves
(page 113)
leaf 35 – 60 mm long

Kaffir lime leaves
(page 193)
double leaf 50 - 110 mm long

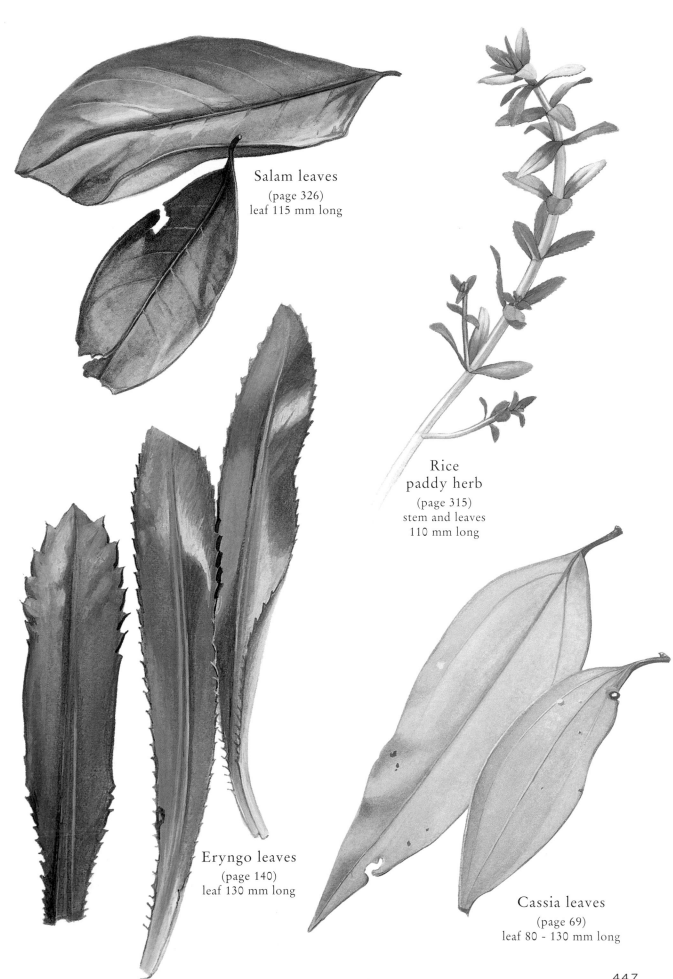

Salam leaves
(page 326)
leaf 115 mm long

Rice
paddy herb
(page 315)
stem and leaves
110 mm long

Eryngo leaves
(page 140)
leaf 130 mm long

Cassia leaves
(page 69)
leaf 80 - 130 mm long

447

Roots, Tubers and Rhizomes

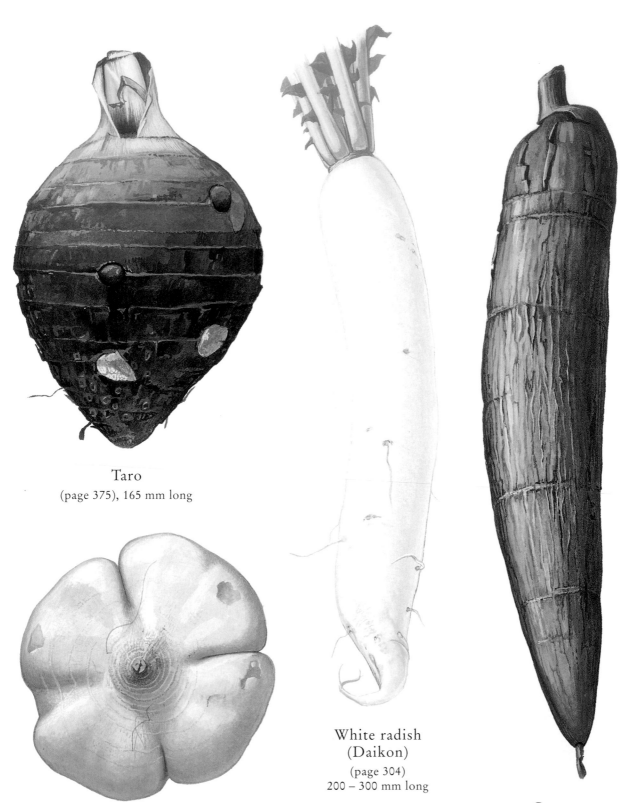

Taro
(page 375), 165 mm long

Yam bean
(page 414), 140 mm diameter

White radish
(Daikon)
(page 304)
200 – 300 mm long

Cassava
(page 67)
400 mm long

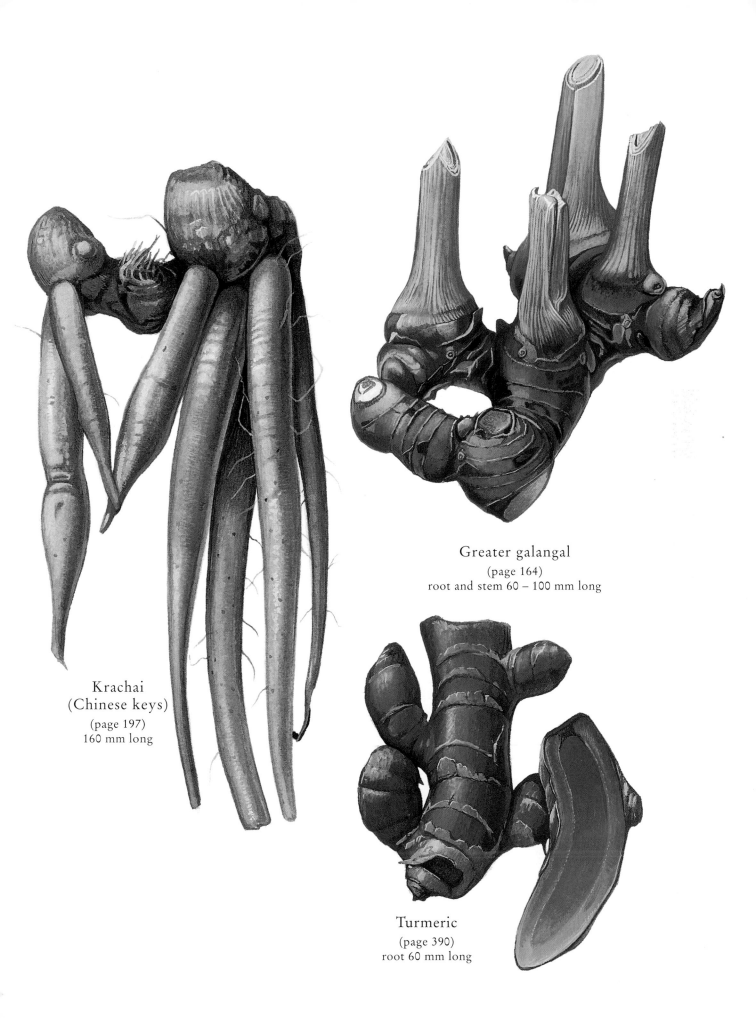

Krachai
(Chinese keys)
(page 197)
160 mm long

Greater galangal
(page 164)
root and stem 60 – 100 mm long

Turmeric
(page 390)
root 60 mm long

449

Water Plants

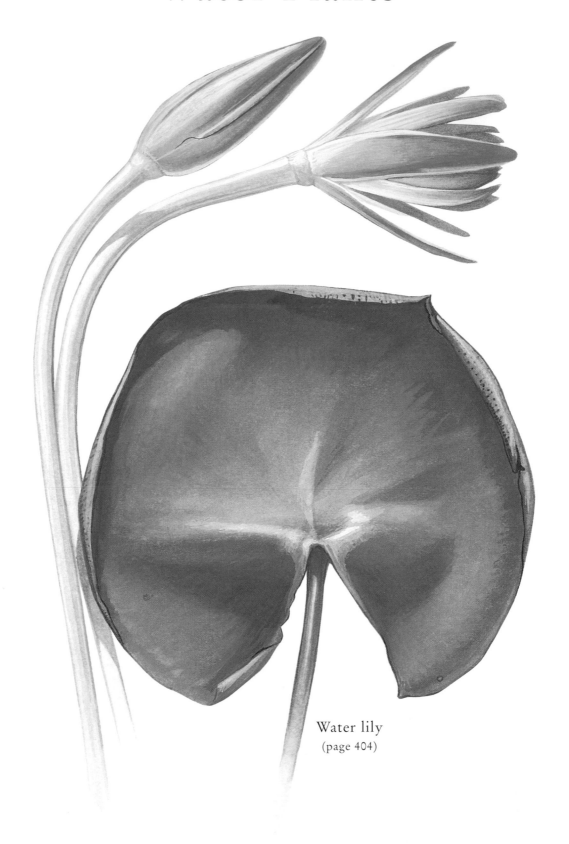

Water lily
(page 404)

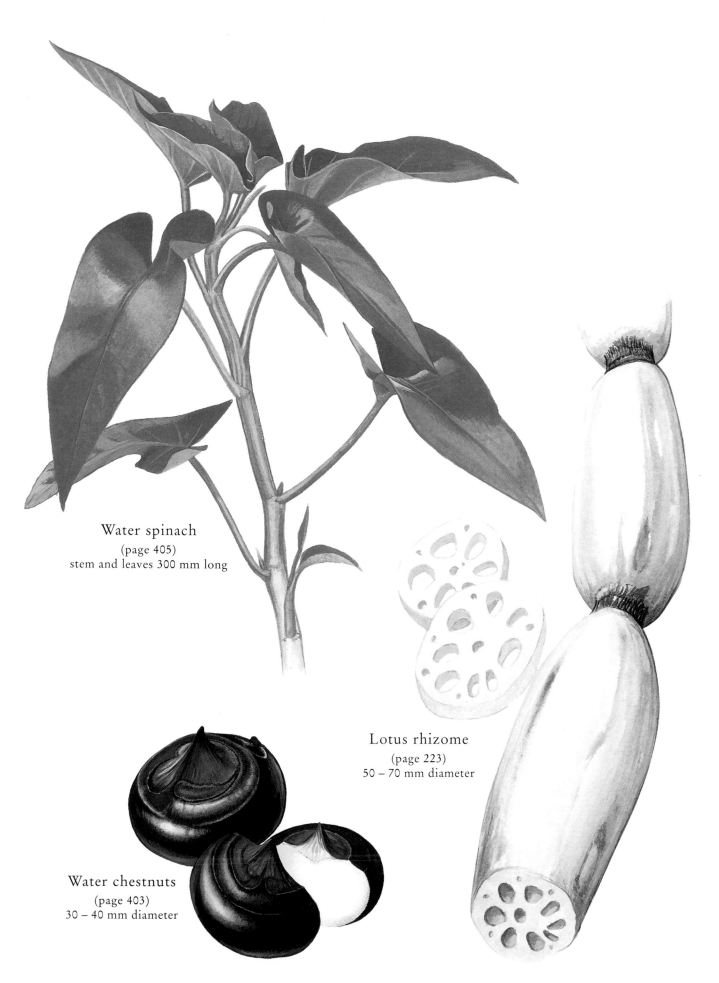

Water spinach
(page 405)
stem and leaves 300 mm long

Lotus rhizome
(page 223)
50 – 70 mm diameter

Water chestnuts
(page 403)
30 – 40 mm diameter

451

Mushrooms and Fungi

Shiitake mushrooms
(fresh and dried)
(page 239), fresh 50 mm diameter

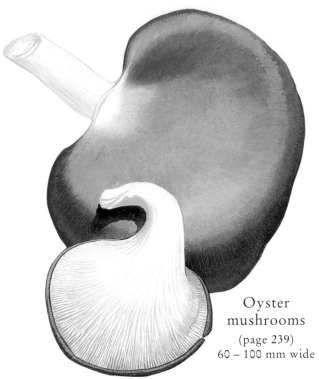

Oyster
mushrooms
(page 239)
60 – 100 mm wide

Black fungus (Cloud ears)
(fresh and dried)
(page 237), fresh 95 mm wide

White fungus
(page 240)

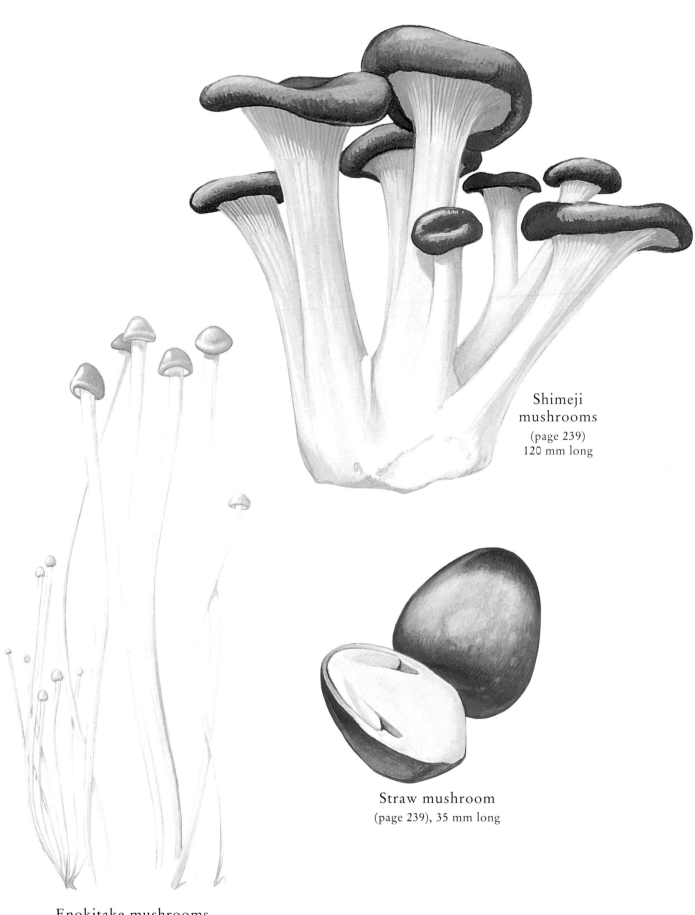

Shimeji
mushrooms
(page 239)
120 mm long

Straw mushroom
(page 239), 35 mm long

Enokitake mushrooms
(page 238), 120 mm long

Spices

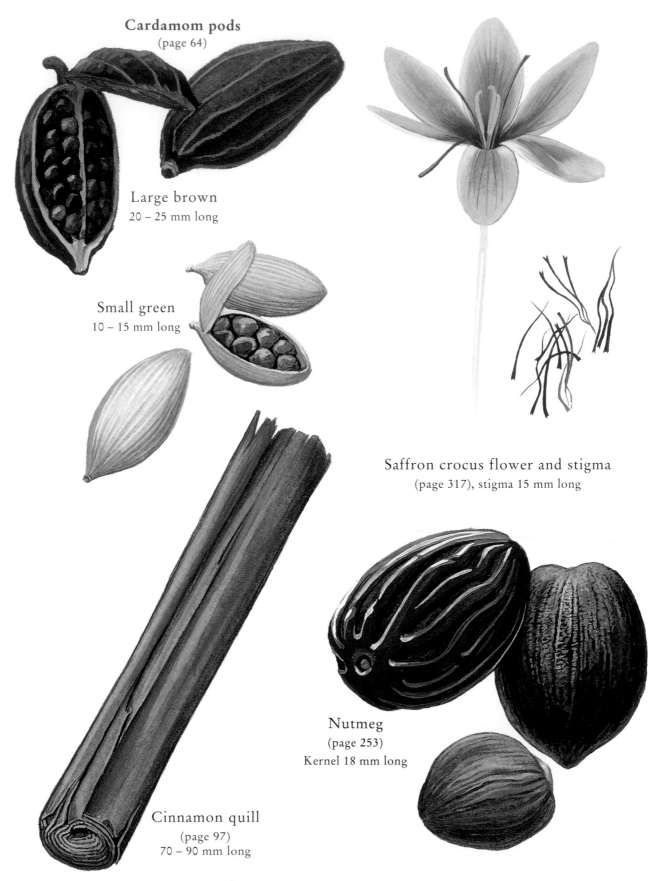

Cardamom pods
(page 64)

Large brown
20 – 25 mm long

Small green
10 – 15 mm long

Saffron crocus flower and stigma
(page 317), stigma 15 mm long

Nutmeg
(page 253)
Kernel 18 mm long

Cinnamon quill
(page 97)
70 – 90 mm long

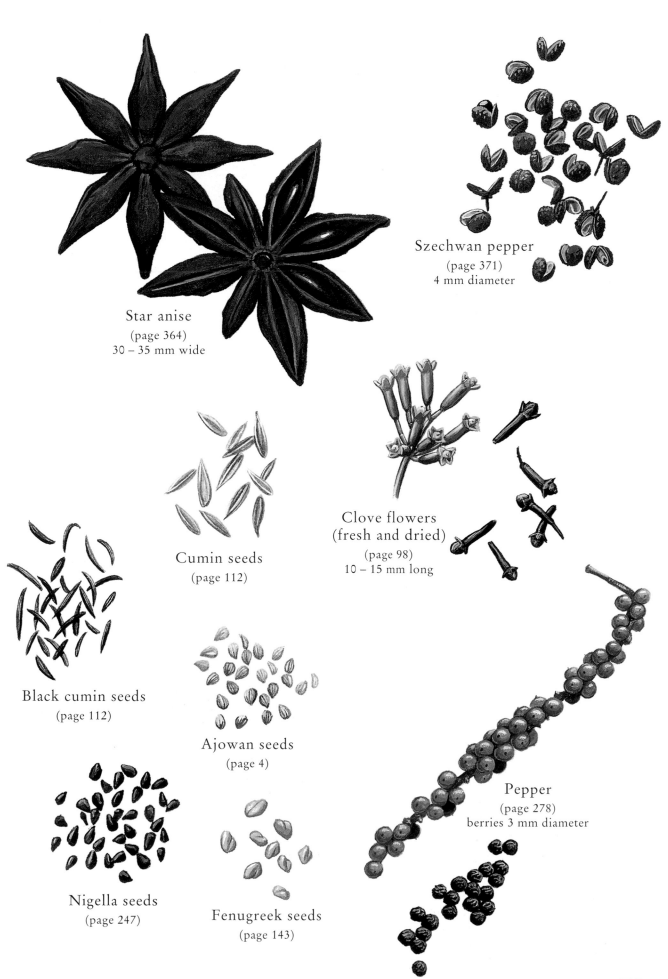

Star anise
(page 364)
30 – 35 mm wide

Szechwan pepper
(page 371)
4 mm diameter

Cumin seeds
(page 112)

Clove flowers
(fresh and dried)
(page 98)
10 – 15 mm long

Black cumin seeds
(page 112)

Ajowan seeds
(page 4)

Pepper
(page 278)
berries 3 mm diameter

Nigella seeds
(page 247)

Fenugreek seeds
(page 143)

Stems

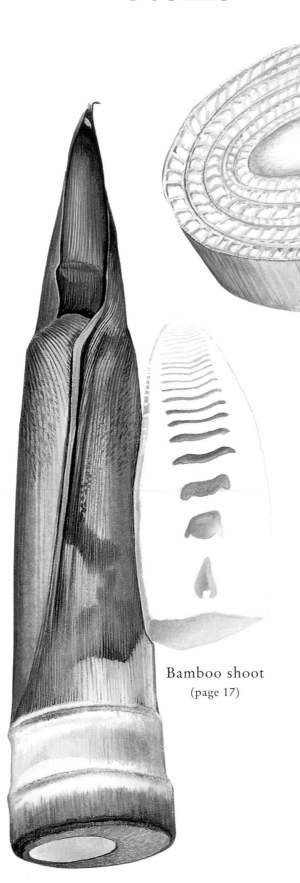

Banana stem
(page 22)
70 – 150 mm diameter
(cross-section)

Bamboo shoot
(page 17)

Lemon grass
(page 218)
300 – 400 mm long

Index of Recipes

abalone
  and shiitake soup 2
  marinated 1
agar-agar
  almond bean curd 3
  coconut jelly 4
  Japanese jelly dessert 3
  salad 4
ajowan
  deep fried crisps 5
akoori 134
almond
  bean curd 3
  beverage 6
  cream fudge 6
  creamed almonds 6
  thandai 6, 123
almonds, Chinese
  almond jelly 94
  Chinese almond tea 95
amaranth
  red, with garlic and oyster sauce 8
  stir-fried green, with coconut 7
  with flowering chives 8
  with red lentils 8
ambarella
  and raisin chutney 9
  conserve 9
an 29
anchovy
  fried anchovies with peanuts 10
  relish, fresh 10
annatto
  chicken with bean thread noodles 11
arrowroot
  jelly 158
asafoetida
  chick peas with vegetables 13
asparagus
  Asian mushrooms with 240
  Chinese style 14
  Thai style 14
  tips, crystal prawns with 298
aubergine *see* **eggplant**
avocado
  fool 16
  sashimi 16
awayuki 3
badam barfi 6
badam kheer 6
balachaung 342
bamboo shoot
  chicken curry with 18
  Thai beef with 18
  yellow curry of chicken and 88
banana flower
  banana blossom guinatan 21

  plantain flower with spices 21
  Thai soup with 22
  with petai 22
banana trunk
  spicy fish soup 23
bananas
  Chinese toffee bananas 20
  fried 21
  fried, Thai style 20
  in yoghurt 20
  see also **plantain**
basil leaves
  deep fried 25
basil seeds
  young coconut and 25
bean curd
  almond 3
  braised, cloud ear and vegetables 237
  fresh soy beans with 349
  Korean braised 28
  rice with fried 27
  with hot sauce 28
  with meat 28
  see also **tempeh**
bean paste
  red 29
bean starch sheets
  with prawns 30
beans
  adzuki bean soup 213
  fermented, bitter gourd with
    pork and 42
  fresh soy beans with bean curd 349
  green bean sambal 214
  moth beans with seasonal vegetables 217
  savoury black-eyed peas 213
  sliced, with chicken livers
    Chinese style 256
  stir-fried long beans, Chinese style 218
  stir-fried long beans, Indian style 218
  see also **broad beans**
beef
  and vegetable rolls 33
  balls with tangerine peel 35
  Chinese clay-pot 34
  Chinese stir-fried 34
  curry, Thai Masaman 37
  Korean barbecued 32
  rendang 36
  salad, Thai 37
  satays, curried 34
  simmered steak and vegetables 338
  stew 36
  sukiyaki 33
  teriyaki steak 32
  Thai, with bamboo shoot 18
  with black bean sauce 35
  with lotus root 224

bhaji
  bhindi 260
  spinach and corn 106
bhel puri *see* **breads**
bibingka especial 69
bilimbi
  curry 39
  pickle 39
biriani, festive 172
bitter gourd
  curry 41
  curry, Bengal style 41
  salad, Burmese 42
  salad, fried 42
  pickle 43
  stuffed with seafood 43
  with pork and fermented beans 42
Bombay duck *see* **fish, dried**
boxthorn
  soup 46
breadfruit
  baked stuffed 47
  boiled 47
  chips 46
  coconut curry 47
  with coconut cream 47
breads
  bhel puri 49
  chapati 48
  chick pea flour 52
  Chinese steamed 53
  cornmeal roti 52
  ensaimada 54
  naan 51
  naan, garlic 51
  paratha 49
  paratha, lentil-filled 50
  paratha with sweet lentil filling 50
  puri 49
  roti with coconut, onion and
    chilli 52
broad beans
  with ham 213
  with mushrooms 214
bulgogi 32
burdock root
  gobo and hijiki with
    brown rice 55
buttermilk sauce 113
cabbage
  braised bok choy 59
  kim chi 57
  mermaid's tresses 58
  mustard cabbage relish 60
  stir-fried choy sum with
    barbecued pork 59
  Vietnamese chicken and, salad 58

cakes
Australian passionfruit sponge 274
bibingka especial 69
Filipino bibingka especial 62
Goan bibingka 62
Indonesian spice layer cake 61
Sri Lankan love cake 61

capsicum
banana peppers in coconut milk 63
stuffed banana peppers, Thai style 64

carrot
and dried fruit chutney 66
halva 66
relish 65

cashews
boiled 67
cashew nut curry 67
devilled 67

cassava
bibingka especial 69
boiled 68
fried 68
savouries 69

cauliflower
braised, Chinese style 70
pilau 70
spiced, Indian style 70

celery
stir-fried, prawns and 71

Ceylon curry powder 356

cha plu
leaf-wrapped snacks 72

chapati see **breads**

chat masala 327

chatni
coconut 73
mint or coriander 73
tamarind 73

chawan mushi 137

cheese
fresh, in saffron sauce 320
guava 179
koftas 74
panir 74
peas with fresh 214
rasgullas 75
spinach and 75

chestnuts
duck braised with 127
Peking dust 77
pork with 76

Chiang Mai salad 325

chick peas
spiced, Indian style 214
with vegetables 13

chicken
and taro leaves, Hawaiian 88
bean thread vermicelli fried with 250
barbecued, Thai style 87
biriani, festive 172
braised, and mushrooms 84
braised, Indonesian 86
braised, with ginger 80
Burmese egg noodles with curry 251
Chiang Mai salad 325
coriander 106
country captain 86
crisp skin 81

curry, Sri Lankan 88
curry of, with sataw, Thai 272
curry with bamboo shoot 18
gizzard curry 255
grilled teriyaki 84
Hainan 82
Hunan 81
in coconut milk, Malay style 87
in pandan leaves 269
in tamarind gravy 373
laulau 89
lentils and vegetables with meat 216
liver curry 257
red-cooked 79
roast, Kashmiri 85
roast, spiced 80
saffron 320
smoked jasmine tea chicken 79
soup, and galangal 164
soup, and ginseng 174
soup, spicy 347
soup with healing herbs 165
soup with wolfberries 409
steamed, and wolfberries 409
steamed, Cantonese 83
stew, Korean 84
stock, Chinese 78
Szechwan 82
tandoori style 84
tangerine 82
tikka 85
velveted, with snow peas 83
Vietnamese chicken and
cabbage salad 58
white-cut 78
wings, glazed 80
wings, Thai, stuffed 87
with aromatic ginger 172
with kumquats 199
with lemon grass, Vietnamese 86
yellow curry of,
and bamboo shoot 88

chilli paste
Korean fish cakes with 154

chilli-bean sauce
kangaroo with 194

chilli
crab, Singapore 109
garlic, and fish sauce 157
Maldive fish sambal with onion and
chillies 287
pickle, Indian 92
plantain with coconut and 284
prawns with lime, Thai 298
sambal 227
sambal bajak 91
sambal, fried 92
sambal ulek 91
sauce, sweet 92
sauce, Thai chilli and shrimp 332
Thai dipping sauce 92

chirashi-zushi 368

chives, Chinese
flowering, amaranth with 8
stir-fried flowering chives 95

chutney
ambarella and raisin 9
carrot and dried fruit 66

fruit 97
mango 97
pan fried pomfret with fresh 286
see also **chatni**

cilantro see **coriander**

clams
Indian style spicy, or mussels 241

coconut
and dried shrimp mallung 102
and vegetable curry 103
banana peppers in coconut milk 63
breadfruit, curry 47
breadfruit with coconut cream 47
chatni 73
chicken in coconut milk, Malay style 87
crab xacuti 412
custard, spicy 119
dark roasted, curry with 101
drink, woodapple and 410
fish curry with 149
jelly 4
milk soup 102
pancakes 265
pancakes, Thai rice and 268
pineapple, curry 282
plantain with, and chilli 284
raw fish salad, Pacific Islands 323
red lentils in coconut milk 216
rice in coconut milk 309
roti with, onion and chilli 52
sambal, red 102
sambal, roasted 102
sticky rice with 310
stir-fried green amaranth with 7
young, and basil seeds 25

congee 104

conserve
ambarella 9
feijoa 143

coriander herb
mint and coriander chatni 73
Thai pepper-coriander paste 105

coriander seeds
coriander and ginger brew 105
coriander chicken 106
coriander cold relief 105

corn
bhaji, spinach and 106
cornmeal roti 52
crab and sweet, soup 106

crab
and egg soup 110
and sweet corn soup 106
curry, Sri Lankan 108
in black bean sauce 109
Malaccan black-pepper 110
pepper and salt 109
shark's fin and crab meat soup 342
Singapore chilli 109
South Pacific, with mayonnaise 110
steamed, with ginger 109
xacuti 412

cream
Indian 111

cucumber
relish, Burmese 111
raita 111
sambal 111

cumin
  and tamarind refresher 112
curry
  bilimbi 39
  bitter gourd 41
  bitter gourd, Bengal style 41
  breadfruit coconut 47
  buttermilk sauce 113
  cashew nut 67
  chicken gizzard 255
  chicken, Sri Lankan 88
  chicken with sataw, Thai curry of 272
  coconut and vegetable 103
  coconut, dark roasted, with 101
  crab, Sri Lankan 108
  crab xacuti 412
  dried fish and eggplant 155
  drumstick, white 125
  duck, Thai green curry of 128
  fish head 156
  fish kofta 148
  fish, steamed 198
  fish, with coconut 149
  fish, green curry of, with krachai 198
  fish, with tomato 149
  garlic 167
  jakfruit 188
  lampries 204
  liver 257
  mutton 244
  mutton, Malaysian 243
  of chicken with sataw, Thai 272
  omelette 135
  pineapple coconut 282
  plantain, mild green 284
  plantain, spicy 284
  pork, Burmese 291
  pork, jungle curry of 198
  pork, Sri Lankan fried 292
  pork vindaloo 292
  potato, dry 293
  prawn, Burmese 297
  prawn, Sri Lankan 297
  prawns, Thai red curry of 299
  sesbania blossoms, fried and curried 340
  sour, of fish 149
  tripe 257
  water lily, with shrimp 404
  yellow, of chicken and bamboo shoot 88
curry paste
  Indian green masala paste 115
  Madras 115
  Sri Lankan dark roasted 116
  Thai green 115
  Thai Masaman 115
  Thai red 114
  Thai yellow 114
custard
  savoury, Japanese 137
  spicy coconut 119
  steamed, in squash 360
cuttlefish
  deep fried, balls 117
dashi
  ichiban (primary dashi) 118
  niban (secondary dashi) 118
desserts
  almond bean curd 3

avocado fool 16
  Chinese almond jelly 94
  coconut jelly 4
  firni 314
  guinatan with jakfruit 189
  haupia 119
  Japanese jelly dessert 3
  kulfi 182
  miniature moulded fruits 120
  passionfruit flummery 274
  pavlova, ANZ 274
  Peking dust 77
  reduced milk pudding 370
  sago puddding 321
  semolina pudding 336
  spicy coconut custard 119
  toast of the shah 120
dhal
  black gram pancakes 215
  red lentils in coconut milk 216
dosai 215
drinks and beverages
  almond beverage 6
  almond tea 95
  coriander and ginger brew 105
  falooda 142
  fresh pennywort drink 277
  ginger tea 170
  grass jelly drink 123
  hibiscus drink 180
  ice kacang 183
  lassi 122
  moh let saung 374
  papaya drink with lime 271
  real ginger beer 170
  thandai 6, 123
  woodapple and coconut drink 410
drumstick
  spiced, leaves 124
  white, curry 125
duck
  boned, with plum sauce 127
  braised, with chestnuts 127
  Peking, home style 126
  quick and easy roast 126
  Thai green curry of 128
durian
  ice cream 129
eggplant
  curry, dried fish and 155
  Sri Lankan, pickle 131
  Szechwan 131
  Thai dipping sauce 332
  Thai stir-fried 132
eggs
  custard, Japanese savoury 137
  foo yong 135
  in soy and chilli 137
  omelette curry 135
  omelette, fresh chilli 134
  omelette, Japanese 135
  omelette, Penang oyster 261
  omelette, spring onion 134
  omelette, sushi wrapped in 368
  omelettes Chinese 135
  on spinach 138
  sambal, Indonesian egg 136
  scrambled, Parsi style spicy 134

scrambled, Sri Lankan style 134
  soup, crab and egg 110
  soup, Shanghai egg pouch 139
  marbled tea 136
  steamed egg roll with pork 139
  steamed, with mushrooms 138
  with savoury mince 138
ensaimada see breads
falooda 142
feijoa
  conserve 143
fenugreek seeds
  halba 144
firni 314
fish
  barbecued 150
  braised, with saffron and yoghurt 150
  curry of, sour 149
  curry with coconut 149
  curry with tomato 149
  curry, steamed 198
  deep fried, with sweet-sour sauce 153
  deep fried pomfret with spicy sauce 287
  fried, Indian style 153
  green curry of, with krachai 198
  grilled, Indonesian style 154
  fried mountain trout with ginger 153
  hotpot, simmered 152
  kofta curry 148
  laksa, Penang 201
  pan fried pomfret with fresh chutney 286
  quick boiled, Chinese style 152
  raw, salad, Pacific islands 323
  soup, spicy 23
  steamed Red Emperor with ham 151
  steamed, Parsi 152
  steamed pomfret, Chinese style 287
fish cakes
  Singapore style 151
  Korean fish cake with chilli paste 154
fish, dried
  and eggplant curry 155
  fried Bombay duck 44
  Bombay duck sambal 45
  chilli sambal 227
  Maldive fish sambal with onion and chillies 227
fish head
  curry 156
fish sauce
  garlic, chilli and 157
frikkadels 204
fukusa-zushi 368
gado-gado 324
gajjar halwa 66
galangal
  chicken and, soup 164
  chicken soup with healing herbs 165
garam masala 354
garlic
  curry 167
  scallops 334
gin thoke 170
ginger
  braised chicken with 80
  brew, coriander and 105
  Burmese pork curry 291

Index of Recipes

crab, steamed with 109
mix 170
real ginger beer 170
tea 170
ginger, aromatic
chicken with 172
festive biriani 172
ginseng
soup, chicken and 174
gotu-kola *see* pennywort
grass jelly
drink 123
guava
butter 178
cheese 179
jelly 178
guinatan
with jakfruit 189
gula melaka 321
gulab jamun 369
gulai kambing 243
halba 144
haupia 119
hibiscus
drink 180
ice kacang 183
ice cream
durian 129
kulfi 182
mango kulfi 183
saffron kulfi 183
idli 184
Indian curry powder 356
jakfruit
curry 188
guinatan with 189
mallung 188
jelly
arrowroot 158
almond bean curd 3
Chinese almond 94
coconut 3
grass jelly drink 123
Japanese jelly dessert 3
woodapple 410
kangaroo
with chilli-bean sauce 194
karhi 113
kari-kari 36
Kashmiri garam masala 355
kebabs
lamb 202
kela raita 20
khanom krok 268
kim chi 57
khoa 234
koftas 318
fish 148
in saffron sauce 318
kokoda 323
korma 202
krachai
green curry of fish with 198
jungle curry of pork 198
steamed fish curry 198
kulfi 182
mango 183
saffron 183

kumquats
chicken with 199
laksa
Penang 201
prawn, lemak 200
lamb
kebabs 202
lentils and vegetables with meat 216
moghlai, with walnut sauce 402
Mongolian 203
roast leg of 319
slices, spiced 319
with apricots 203
with spices and yoghurt 202
see also mutton
lampries 204
curry 204
frikkadels 204
larb 325
lassi 122
laulau 89
lemon grass
Vietnamese chicken with 86
lentil
and vegetable soup 216
filled paratha 50
filling, sweet, paratha with 50
lentils and vegetables with meat 216
red, and rice kitchri 215
red lentils in coconut milk 216
red lentils, amaranth with 8
lily buds
stir-fried, with pork 220
Thai soup with 220
limes
papaya drink with lime 211
salted 221
Thai chilli prawns with lime 298
lobah 333
lobster
Cambodian, and orange salad 324
salad, Thai 222
steamed, with ginger 222
lotus root
beef with 224
luk chup 120
malai 111
Maldive fish *see* fish, dried
mango
chutney 97
kulfi 183
mangoes, Moghul style 229
mangoes with sticky rice 230
pickle, hot 230
salad, Thai 230
mee grob 252
mermaid's tresses 58
milagai podi 355
with chillies 356
milk
khoa 234
millet
pilau 234
mint
chatni 73
miso soup 350
moh hin gha 23
moh let saung 374

mulligatawny 236
mung beans
miniature moulded fruits 120
sweet mung bean porridge 217
murukku 5
mushrooms
abalone and shiitake soup 2
Asian, with asparagus 240
braised bean curd, cloud ear and
vegetables 237
braised chicken with 84
braised soy 239
broad beans with 214
steamed eggs with 138
mussels
spicy clams or, Indian style 241
steamed, Thai style 241
mustard
country 242
mixed vegetable stew with 242
pickle 242
mutton
curry 244
curry, Malaysian 243
Kashmiri style 244
koftas in saffron sauce 318
with onions 244
see also lamb
naan *see* breads
naan khatai 336
nam prik 331
ngapi htaung 344
noodles
bean thread vermicelli fried
with chicken 250
buckwheat, chilled 250
Burmese egg noodles with curry 251
crisp fried rice vermicelli 252
fresh rice, fried 251
Hokkien, fried 252
Korean cold, in soup 250
sweet potato, Korean 253
norimake-zushi 368
nuoc cham 157
offal
chicken gizzard curry 255
devilled tongue 256
kidneys in hot sour sauce 257
liver curry 257
sliced beans with chicken livers,
Chinese style 256
tripe curry 257
okra
spicy, stir-fried 260
omelettes *see* eggs
otak-otak 151
oysters
Penang oyster omelette 261
palm sugar
balls, sesame seed and 339
palusami 376
pancakes
black gram 215
coconut 265
egg hoppers 265
hoppers 264
Mandarin 266
Singapore style filled 267

spring onion (scallion) 266
Thai rice and coconut 268
panch phora 355
pandanus leaves
chicken in pandan leaves 269
pandan flavoured sticky rice 270
panir 74
panthe kaukswe 251
papaya
drink with lime 271
salad, green 270
paratha *see* **breads**
parkia
fresh petai sambal 272
fried sataw with shrimp 271
Thai curry of chicken
with sataw 272
passionfruit
ANZ pavlova 274
flummery 274
sponge, Australian 274
pastry
curry puff 275
transparent steamed dumpling 275
won ton 275
peanuts
fried anchovies with 10
peanut sauce 276
peas
with fresh cheese 214
savoury black-eyed 213
pennywort
drink, fresh 277
(gotu-kola) salad 277
pepper
and salt crab 109
Malaccan black-pepper crab 110
roasted pepper and salt 327
Thai pepper-coriander paste 105
perhas 370
petai
banana flower with 22
pho 347
pickle
bilimbi 39
bitter gourd 43
eggplant, Sri Lankan 131
hot mango 230
Indian chilli 92
kim chi 57
mustard 242
pilau
cauliflower 70
millet pilau 234
mock-stringhopper 253
saffron rice 320
savoury semolina 336
pineapple
coconut curry 282
Vietnamese sour soup with 282
pistachio
barfi 370
pittu 313
plantain
curry, mild green 284
curry, spicy 284
green, skin temperado 283
plantains with coconut and chilli 284
poh pia 267

pomelo
rind, candied 286
salad 285
pomfret
deep fried, with spicy sauce 287
pan fried, with fresh chutney 286
steamed, Chinese style 287
pork
adobo 293
Balinese style 288
barbecued, Chinese 289
barbecued, stir-fried choy
sum with 59
curry, Burmese 291
curry, Sri Lankan fried 292
cutlet, Japanese 290
filled sago balls 322
Goan sorpotel 292
jungle curry of 198
laulau 89
lion's head 288
lobah 333
on skewers, Vietnamese 290
sausages, Sri Lankan 333
spicy spareribs 289
squid with, stuffing 362
steamed egg roll with 139
steamed five-flower 290
stir-fried lily buds with 220
vindaloo 292
with chestnuts 76
potatoes
herbed mashed 294
savoury fried 294
potato and cashew nut fudge 294
potato dry curry 293
sweet-sour, Indian 294
prawns
bean starch sheets with 297
butter 297
chilli, with lime, Thai 298
curry, Burmese 297
curry of, Thai red 299
curry, Sri Lankan 297
crystal, with asparagus tips 298
in shell, Singapore 296
prawn dumplings, steamed 417
prawn laksa lemak 200
prawn sambal 300
prawn toast 417
sizzling rice crackers with
sweet chilli 312
soup, Thai hot sour prawn 298
stir fried, and celery 71
pumpkin
Thai pumpkin soup with shrimp 360
puri *see* **breads**
purslane
spicy, Sri Lankan style 301
stir-fried, Chinese style 301
quails
deep-fried 303
Vietnamese style 302
with Indian spices 302
quince
sambal 303
rabri 370
raisin
chutney, ambarella and 9

raita
bananas in yoghurt 20
cucumber 111
ras malai 370
rasgullas 75
relish
carrot 65
cucumber, Burmese 111
dried shrimp, Burmese 342
fresh anchovy 10
mustard cabbage 60
roasted shrimp paste 344
rendang
beef 36
rice
and coconut pancakes, Thai 268
biriani, festive 172
black, porridge 311
black sticky, with sesame seeds 311
brown, gobo and hijiki with 55
cauliflower pilau 70
congee 104
fried 310
ghee 309
in coconut milk 309
kitchri, red lentil and 215
plain steamed 308
saffron, pilau 320
sticky, mangoes with 230
sticky, pandan flavoured 270
sticky, with coconut 310
sushi 310
with fried bean curd 27
yellow 309
rice cakes
sizzling rice crackers with
sweet chilli prawns 312
to make rice crackers 312
rice, ground
firni 314
rice crackers *see* **rice cakes**
rice flour
pittu 313
stringhoppers 314
rice vermicelli *see* **noodles**
rojak 344
rose petal
salad 325
roselle
sour soup 316
roti *see* **breads**
saffron
braised fish with, and yoghurt 150
chicken 320
rice pilau 320
roast leg of lamb 319
sauce, fresh cheese in 320
sauce, koftas in 318
spiced lamb slices 319
sago
balls, pork-filled 322
pudding 321
salabat 123
salad
agar-agar 4
beef, Thai 37
bitter gourd, fried 42
bitter gourd, Burmese 42
Cambodian lobster and orange 324

Index of Recipes

Chiang Mai 325
chicken and cabbage,
    Vietnamese 58
green papaya 270
Indonesian vegetable 324
lobster, Thai 222
mango, Thai 230
pennywort 277
pomelo 285
raw fish, Pacific Islands 323
rose petal 325
soy bean sprout 351
vegetable, Indonesian 324
water chestnut 325
salt
    chat masala 327
    roasted pepper and salt 327
sambal
    bajak 91
    bawang 340
    Bombay duck 45
    chilli 227
    cucumber 111
    fried chilli 92
    green bean 214
    Indonesian egg 136
    Maldive fish, with onions
        and chillies 227
    prawn 300
    quince 303
    red coconut 102
    roasted coconut 102
    squid 362
    Sri Lankan dried shrimp 343
    ulek 91
sambhar 216
samosas 328
sataw see parkia
satay 331
    curried beef satays 34
sauces
    buttermilk 113
    sweet chilli 92
    peanut 276
    sweet dipping 332
    tamarind 373
    Thai chilli and shrimp 332
    Thai eggplant dipping 332
    Thai shrimp 331
sausages
    lobah 333
    Sri Lankan 333
scallion see spring onion
scallops
    garlic 334
    in shells, steamed 334
seafood
    bitter gourd stuffed with 43
semolina
    cake, Burmese 337
    pudding 336
    savoury 336
    shortbreads, cardamom scented 336
sesame seeds
    Korean marinade with 338
    sesame seed and palm
        sugar balls 339
    simmered steak and vegetables 338

sesbania
    blossoms, fried and curried 340
    leaf stir-fry 339
sev 5
shabu-shabu 338
shallots
    crisp fried, and shallot oil 341
    sambal bawang 340
shark's fin
    and crab meat soup 342
    preparation 341
shrikhand 415
shiitake
    soup, abalone and 2
shrimp
    fried sataw with 271
    Thai pumpkin soup with 360
    water lily curry with 404
    see also prawns
shrimp, dried
    coconut and dried shrimp
        mallung 102
    Burmese, relish 342
    mermaid's tresses 58
    Sri Lankan, sambal 343
    Thai chilli and shrimp sauce 332
    water spinach with, Thai style 406
shrimp paste
    sambal bawang 340
    roasted, relish 344
    rojak 344
snow peas
    velveted chicken with 83
son-in-law eggs 137
soup
    abalone and shiitake 2
    adzuki bean 213
    boxthorn 46
    chicken and galangal 164
    chicken and ginseng 174
    chicken, with healing herbs 165
    chicken, spicy 347
    chicken stock, Chinese 78
    chicken, with wolfberries 409
    coconut milk 102
    cold Korean noodles in soup 250
    crab and egg 110
    crab and sweet corn 106
    fish, spicy 23
    Korean dumpling 348
    lentil and vegetable 216
    miso 350
    mulligatawny 236
    noodles in, Korean cold 250
    Penang laksa 201
    prawn laksa lemak 200
    Shanghai egg pouch soup 139
    shark's fin and crab meat 342
    sour soup 316
    spicy fish 23
    spicy chicken 347
    Szechwan hot and sour 347
    Thai hot sour prawn 298
    Thai pumpkin, with shrimp 360
    Thai, with banana flower 22
    Thai, with lily buds 220
    Vietnamese pho 347
    Vietnamese sour, with pineapple 282
    water lily sour 405

soy beans
    fresh, with bean curd 349
    soy bean sprout salad 351
spice blends
    Ceylon curry powder 356
    garam masala 354
    Indian curry powder 356
    Kashmiri garam masala 355
    milagai podi 355
    milagai podi with chillies 356
    panch phora 355
spinach
    and cheese 75
    and corn bhaji 106
    eggs on 138
    spiced, and potatoes 357
    with yoghurt 357
spring onion (scallion)
    omelette 134
    pancakes 266
spring rolls
    Cambodian style 359
    fresh 358
    Vietnamese fried 359
squash
    custard steamed in 360
    Thai pumpkin soup with
        shrimp 360
squid
    sambal 362
    Szechwan style 361
    with pork stuffing 362
stock
    chicken, Chinese 78
    dashi 118
stringhoppers 314
    stringhopper pilau, mock 253
sukiyaki 33
sushi
    rice 310
    tossed 368
    wrapped in omelette 368
    wrapped in seaweed 368
sweetmeats
    condensed milk fudge 370
    pistachio barfi 370
    ras malai 370
    reduced milk pudding 370
    rose-flavoured milk balls
        in syrup 369
Szechwan pepper
    mix, salt and 371
    oil 371
tamarind
    chatni 73
    gravy, chicken in 373
    refresher, cumin and 112
    sauce 373
tamatar kasaundi 389
tangerine peel
    beef balls with 35
tapioca
    refresher, Burmese 374
taro
    leaves in coconut cream 376
    leaves, Hawaiian chicken and 88
    root, how to prepare and cook 376

tempeh
  savoury 386
  Thai style 386
teriyaki steak 32
thandai 6
tamatar kusundi 389
tofu *see* bean curd
tom kha gai 164
tom yum goong 298
tomato
  pickle 389
tonkatsu 290
tup tim krob 404
uppuma 336
vattalappam 119
vegetarian dishes
  adzuki bean soup 213
  agar-agar salad 4
  Asian mushrooms with asparagus 240
  banana peppers in coconut milk 63
  bean curd with hot sauce 28
  bilimbi curry 39
  bitter gourd curry, Bengal style 41
  bitter gourd curry 41
  black gram pancakes 215
  braised bean curd, cloud ear and
    vegetables 237
  braised cauliflower, Chinese style 70
  braised soy mushrooms 239
  breadfruit coconut curry 47
  broad beans with mushrooms 214
  Burmese bitter gourd salad 42
  buttermilk sauce 113
  cashew nut curry 67
  cauliflower pilau 70
  cheese koftas 74
  chick peas with vegetables 13
  coconut and dried shrimp
    mallung 102
  coconut and vegetable curry 103
  coconut milk soup 102
  eggs on spinach 138
  fresh cheese in saffron sauce 320
  fresh soy beans with bean curd 349
  fried bitter gourd salad 42

gado-gado 324
garlic curry 167
gobo and hijiki with brown rice 55
green bean sambal 214
herbed mashed potatoes 294
Indian sweet-sour potatoes 294
jakfruit curry 188
Korean braised bean curd 28
lentil and vegetable soup 216
lentil-filled paratha 50
mild green plantain curry 284
mixed vegetable stew with
  mustard 242
mock-stringhopper pilau 253
moth beans with seasonal vegetables 217
omelette curry 135
peas with fresh cheese 214
pineapple coconut curry 282
plantains with coconut and chilli 284
potato dry curry 293
red lentil and rice kitchri 215
red lentils in coconut milk 216
saffron rice pilau 320
savoury black-eyed peas 213
savoury fried potatoes 294
savoury tempeh 386
spiced cauliflower, Indian style 70
spiced chick peas, Indian style 214
spiced drumstick leaves 124
spiced spinach and potatoes 357
spicy purslane, Sri Lankan style 301
spicy stir-fried okra 260
spinach and cheese 75
spinach and corn bhaji 106
spinach with yoghurt 357
Sri Lankan eggplant pickle 131
stir-fried long beans, Chinese style 218
stir-fried long beans, Indian style 218
stir-fried purslane, Chinese style 301
stir-fried purslane, Sri Lankan style 301
Szechwan eggplant pickle 131
Thai style asparagus 14
white drumstick curry 125
walnuts
  Chinese style honey-soy 402

fried sweet 401
moghlai lamb with walnut sauce 402
water chestnut
  salad 403
  tup tim krob 404
water lily
  curry with shrimp 404
  sour soup 405
water spinach
  Chinese style 406
  chilli fry, Sri Lankan style 406
  Malay style 406
  stir-fried Thai style 405
  with dried shrimp, Thai style 406
whitebait
  fritters 407
wolfberries
  chicken soup with 409
  steamed chicken and 409
woodapple
  and coconut drink 410
  jelly 410
xacuti
  crab 412
yard-long bean
  stir-fried long beans,
    Chinese style 218
  stir-fried long beans,
    Indian style 218
yoghurt
  bananas in 20
  cucumber raita 111
  lassi 122
  lamb with spices and 202
  shrikhand 415
yum cha
  fried wontons 415
  pot stickers 416
  prawn toast 417
  steamed pork dumplings 416
  steamed prawn dumplings 416
zeera pani 112
zucchini
  purée, spicy 418

Index of Alternative Words and Main Entries

Words in capital letters are head words with an associated entry in the A–Z of Asian Food. Bracketed words are sub-entries.

A

aam *see* MANGO
ABALONE
abalone mushroom *see* MUSHROOMS & FUNGI (Oyster mushroom)
abba *see* MUSTARD
abba kolle *see* CABBAGE (Mustard cabbage)
aburage, abura-age *see* BEAN CURD
ac-cent *see* MONOSODIUM GLUTAMATE
achar, acar, atjar *see* RELISHES
achuete *see* ANNATTO
ACID FRUITS
ACORN
adas *see* FENNEL, DILL
adas manis *see* DILL
adrak *see* GINGER
adzuki bean *see* LEGUMES & PULSES
aemono *see* JAPAN
AGAR-AGAR
age *see* BEAN CURD
agemono *see* JAPAN
agust *see* SESBANIA
aji *see* CHILLI
aji-no-moto *see* MONOSODIUM GLUTAMATE
AJOWAN
ajwain *see* AJOWAN
aka miso *see* BEAN SAUCES
aka-shiso *see* PERILLA
aka wake, aka wakegi *see* SHALLOT
akagai *see* SUSHI
akhrote, akroot *see* WALNUT
alba *see* FENUGREEK
alibangbang *see* BAUHINIA
alimangong *see* CRABS
alimasag *see* CRABS
alligator pear *see* AVOCADO
allspice *see* PEPPER (Jamaica pepper)
almirez *see* UTENSILS
ALMOND
alphonso *see* MANGO
alu puhul *see* GOURDS (Wax gourd)
ama-yama-imo *see* YAM
AMARANTH
amba *see* MANGO
AMBARELLA

ambetan *see* DURIAN
ambul thial *see* GAMBOGE
amchur *see* MANGO
ami-shakushi *see* UTENSILS
amli *see* BAUHINIA
ampalaya *see* BITTER GOURD
amphawa *see* NAM-NAM
ampil kheei *see* TAMARIND
ampil tum *see* TAMARIND
amu bola kadala *see* LEGUMES & PULSES (Green pea)
amu miris *see* CHILLI
amyle *see* ESSENCES (Banana flavour)
an *see* BEAN PASTE, SWEET
anago *see* EEL
ananas *see* PINEAPPLE
anardhana *see* POMEGRANATE
ANCHOVY
andoos *see* CUSTARD APPLE
anjeela *see* FISH (Spanish mackerel)
angkrik *see* FLOURS & STARCHES (Arrowroot)
anise pepper *see* SZECHWAN PEPPER
ANISEED
anithi *see* DILL
anjan *see* BUTTERFLY PEA FLOWER
annasi *see* PINEAPPLE
ANNATTO
anoda *see* CUSTARD APPLE
anonas *see* CUSTARD APPLE
ANTIGONON
ao-shiso *see* PERILLA
aoi mame *see* LEGUMES & PULSES (Lentil)
aoyagi *see* SUSHI
apeli *see* CUSTARD APPLE
appam, appe *see* HOPPER
APRICOT
apricot kernel *see* CHINESE ALMOND
apulid *see* WATER CHESTNUT
ara *see* KEWRA
arak *see* ARRACK
araluk *see* FLOURS & STARCHES
ararut, araroht *see* FLOURS & STARCHES
areca nut *see* BETEL NUT
arhar dhal *see* LEGUMES & PULSES (Pigeon pea)
aril *see* MACE
aromatic ginger *see* GINGER, AROMATIC
aroro *see* FLOURS & STARCHES
ARRACK
ARROWHEAD
arrowroot *see* FLOURS & STARCHES

ARTICHOKE, CHINESE
arvi *see* TARO
ASAFOETIDA
ASAM
asam gelugor *see* ACID FRUITS
asam jawa *see* TAMARIND
ash gourd *see* GOURDS
Asian pear *see* NASHI
ASPARAGUS
asparagus pea *see* LEGUMES & PULSES
asparagus bean *see* LEGUMES & PULSES (Winged bean)
atis *see* CUSTARD APPLE
atjar *see* RELISHES
atong-ula *see* NUTMEG
atsuete *see* ANNATTO
atta *see* FLOURS & STARCHES
attap *see* SUGAR PALM SEED
aubergine *see* EGGPLANT
AUSTRALIA
autera'a *see* TROPICAL ALMOND
AVOCADO
avocado pear *see* AVOCADO
avocado sherbet *see* DRINKS & BEVERAGES
aw za thi *see* SWEETSOP
awabi *see* ABALONE
awayuki *see* AGAR-AGAR
awzathi *see* CUSTARD APPLE
azuki bean *see* ADZUKI BEAN

B

baak choy *see* CABBAGE (Chinese chard)
baby corn *see* CORN, MINIATURE
bac ha *see* TARO
badam *see* ALMOND
badam barfi *see* ALMOND
badam kheer *see* ALMOND
badan jan *see* EGGPLANT
badian *see* STAR ANISE
badung *see* CURRY
BAEL FRUIT
baeli *see* BAEL FRUIT
bagali *see* LEGUMES & PULSES (Lentil)
baghar, boghara *see* TECHNIQUES
bagoong alamang *see* SHRIMP SAUCE
bahb *see* RICE
bahn trang *see* RICE PAPER
baht gok *see* STAR ANISE
bai bobo *see* PENNYWORT
bai cai *see* CABBAGE (Chinese chard)
bai kravan *see* CASSIA LEAF
bai maha *see* BITTER GOURD
bai saranae *see* MINT

bai toey *see* PANDANUS LEAF
baigan *see* EGGPLANT
baino *see* LOTUS
bajra atta *see* FLOURS & STARCHES
    (Atta)
bajra *see* MILLET
bakla *see* LEGUMES & PULSES
    (Broad bean)
BALACHAUNG
balsam pear *see* BITTER GOURD
balut *see* EGGS
BAMBOO
bamia *see* OKRA
BANANA
BANANA FLOWER
BANANA PLANT
banana bell *see* BANANA FLOWER
banana blossom *see* BANANA FLOWER
banana chilli *see* CHILLI
banana flavour *see* ESSENCES
banana heart *see* BANANA FLOWER
banana no tsubomi *see* BANANA
    FLOWER
banana pepper *see* CAPSICUM
bancha *see* TEA
bandakka *see* OKRA
bangkwang *see* YAM BEAN
banh phong tom *see* PRAWN CRACKERS
banira *see* VANILLA
BARBECUE SAUCE
barfi *see* SWEETMEATS, INDIAN
bari mirch *see* CAPSICUM
BARLEY
barra illaichi *see* CARDAMOM
BASIL
BASIL SEED
basmati *see* RICE
bastard saffron *see* SAFFRON
bath-ala *see* POTATO, SWEET
batidor *see* UTENSILS
batta *see* UTENSILS
batu lesong *see* UTENSILS
BAUHINIA
bawal puteh, bawal putih *see* POMFRET
bawang besar *see* ONION
bawang Bombay *see* ONION
bawang *see* GARLIC
bawang merah *see* SHALLOT
bawang puteh, bawang putih *see* GARLIC
BAY LEAF
bayam *see* AMARANTH
bean *see* LEGUMES & PULSES
BEAN CURD
BEAN PASTE, SWEET
BEAN PASTE, YELLOW
BEAN SAUCES
BEAN SPROUTS
bean starch noodles *see* NOODLES
BEAN STARCH SHEETS
bean cake *see* BEAN CURD
bean thread noodles *see* NOODLES
    (Bean starch noodles)
bean thread vermicelli *see* NOODLES
    (Bean starch noodles)
BEANS, SALTED YELLOW
BEEF

beefsteak plant *see* PERILLA
bel fruit *see* BAEL FRUIT
belacan *see* SHRIMP PASTE
belanoi *see* BASIL
BELE
beli fruit *see* BAEL FRUIT
belimbing *see* STAR FRUIT
belimbing asam *see* BILIMBI
belimbing batu *see* STAR FRUIT
belimbing walah, belimbing wuluh *see*
    BILIMBI
belinjo *see* MELINJO NUT
bell pepper *see* CAPSICUM
belustru *see* GOURDS (Sponge gourd)
benculuk *see* BAUHINIA
bendi *see* OKRA
bene, beni *see* SESAME SEED
Bengal gram *see* LEGUMES & PULSES
    (Chick pea)
Bengal quince *see* BAEL FRUIT
bengkowang *see* YAM BEAN
beni shoga *see* GINGER
beras pulot *see* RICE
besan *see* FLOURS & STARCHES
BETEL LEAF
BETEL NUT
bhat *see* SOY BEAN SPROUTS
bhel puri *see* BREADS
bhendi, bhindi *see* OKRA
bhuchampakamu *see* KRACHAI
bhuichampa *see* KRACHAI
bi fun *see* NOODLES (Rice noodles)
bi *see* GOURDS (Fuzzy melon)
bibingka *see* CAKES
bihoon *see* NOODLES (Rice noodles)
bijan *see* SESAME SEED
biji sawi *see* MUSTARD
biju *see* BANANA
BILIMBI
bilimbikai *see* BILIMBI
bilimbing *see* BILIMBI
billing *see* BILIMBI
BIRD'S NEST
bird's eye *see* CHILLI
biriani *see* RICE
bishop's weed *see* AJOWAN
biththara appe *see* HOPPER
bitter almond *see* CHINESE ALMOND
bitter cucumber *see* BITTER GOURD
BITTER GOURD
bitter melon *see* BITTER GOURD
blacan, blachan *see* SHRIMP PASTE,
    DRIED
BLACK BEAN
black cumin *see* CUMIN, BLACK
black-eyed pea *see* LEGUMES & PULSES
black fungus *see* MUSHROOMS &
    FUNGI)
black gram *see* LEGUMES & PULSES
BLACK MOSS
BLACK NUT
blangah *see* UTENSILS
bligo *see* GOURDS (Wax gourd)
BLOOD
bo la lot *see* CHA PLU
boap hom *see* GOURDS (Sponge gourd)

boap liam *see* GOURDS (Ridged gourd)
boap nguu *see* GOURDS (Snake gourd)
bog rhubarb *see* BUTTERBUR
bok choy *see* CABBAGE
BOMBAY DUCK
bonchi *see* LEGUMES & PULSES
    (Green bean)
BONITO
bot gao *see* FLOURS & STARCHES
    (Rice flour)
bot nep *see* FLOURS & STARCHES
    (Glutinous rice flour)
bottle gourd *see* GOURDS
bow yu *see* ABALONE
BOXTHORN
BREADCRUMBS, JAPANESE
BREADFRUIT
BREADS
breakfast delight *see* SEMOLINA
brinjal *see* EGGPLANT
BRITISH–INDIAN CUISINE
broad bean *see* LEGUMES & PULSES
bua-bok *see* PENNYWORT
bua-luang *see* LOTUS
bua nona *see* CUSTARD APPLE
bua susu *see* PASSIONFRUIT
buah keluak *see* BLACK NUT
buah kembang sa mangkok *see*
    POONTALAI
buah keras *see* CANDLE NUT
buah pala *see* NUTMEG
buah pelaga *see* CARDAMOM
Buddha's chicken *see* BEAN CURD
Buddha's ham *see* BEAN CURD
BUFFALO
buga *see* YAM
bulath *see* BETEL LEAF
bulgalbi *see* BEEF
bulgogi *see* BEEF
bummalo *see* BOMBAY DUCK
bunga kantan *see* GINGER FLOWER
bunga kol *see* CAULIFLOWER
bunga lawang *see* STAR ANISE
bunga raya *see* HIBISCUS
bunga siantan *see* GINGER FLOWER
bunga telang *see* BUTTERFLY PEA
    FLOWER
bungah cengkeh *see* CLOVE
buoi *see* POMELO
BURDOCK ROOT
buri *see* SUSHI
BURMA
bussouge *see* HIBISCUS
buth *see* RICE
butter, clarified *see* GHEE
butterbur *see* COLTSFOOT
buuraanam *see* NAM-NAM
BUTTERFLY PEA FLOWER
buyok-buyok *see* BITTER GOURD

C

ca bac ma *see* FISH (Mackerel)
ca bo *see* FISH (Tuna)
ca chim trang *see* POMFRET

ca com, ca cum *see* ANCHOVY
ca lao nhot *see* FISH (Trevally)
ca mu *see* FISH (Grouper)
ca na *see* CEYLON OLIVE
ca nham *see* FISH (Shark)
ca thu dai *see* FISH (Spanish mackerel)
CABBAGE
cabe besar *see* CAPSICUM
cacao *see* COCOA
cadju *see* CASHEW
cafateras *see* UTENSILS
caffier lime, caffir lime *see* KAFFIR LIME
cai xin *see* CABBAGE (Flowering cabbage)
CAKES
calamansi *see* KALAMANSI
CAMBODIA
Cambodian mint *see* VIETNAMESE
    MINT
camel's milk *see* KEPHIR
camias *see* BILIMBI
camote (kamote) *see* POTATO, SWEET
CANDLE NUT
cang cua *see* PEPEROMIA
cantrelle , chanterelle *see* MUSHROOMS
    & FUNGI
Cape gooseberry *see* GOOSEBERRY,
    CAPE
CAPSICUM
carajay *see* UTENSILS
carambola *see* STAR FRUIT
CARAWAY
CARDAMOM
careless weed *see* AMARANTH
CARROT
CASHEW
casoy, casuy *see* CASHEW
CASSAVA
CASSIA BARK
CASSIA LEAF
casuba *see* SAFFLOWER
catjang bean *see* LEGUMES & PULSES
    (Yard-long bean)
CAULIFLOWER
Cavendish *see* BANANA
caviar *see* FISH ROE
cay cuc *see* CHRYSANTHEMUM
ceci *see* LEGUMES & PULSES
    (Chick pea)
cekor, cekuh *see* GINGER, AROMATIC
cekuk manis *see* SABAH VEGETABLE
cekur *see* GINGER, AROMATIC
CELERY
celery cabbage *see* CABBAGE
    (Chinese cabbage)
cendawan jelly puteh *see* MUSHROOMS
    & FUNGI (White fungus)
cendawan jerami padi *see* MUSHROOMS
    & FUNGI (Straw mushroom)
cendawan *see* MUSHROOMS & FUNGI
    (Shiitake)
cendawan telinga kera *see* MUSHROOMS
    & FUNGI (Black fungus)
cep, cepe *see* MUSHROOMS & FUNGI
Ceylon curry powder *see* SPICE BLENDS
CEYLON OLIVE
CHA PLU

cha gio *see* SPRING ROLLS
cha soba *see* FLOURS & STARCHES
    (Buckwheat flour)
chakla *see* UTENSILS
chakoo *see* UTENSILS
chalni *see* UTENSILS
chamna *see* POMFRET
champurado *see* COCOA
chan chom *see* VIETNAMESE MINT
chan keh room *see* OILS (Sesame oil)
chandramula *see* GINGER, AROMATIC
chang haai *see* CRABS
channa dhal *see* LEGUMES & PULSES
    (Chick pea)
channa powder *see* FLOURS &
    STARCHES (Besan)
chanterelle *see* MUSHROOMS & FUNGI
chao gwoo *see* MUSHROOMS & FUNGI
    (Straw mushroom)
chao tom *see* SHRIMP PASTE, FRESH
chap chae *see* NOODLES
    (Sweet potato noodles)
chapati *see* BREADS
CHAR MAGAZ
char kway teow *see* NOODLES
    (Rice noodles)
charchari *see* TECHNIQUES
CHAROLI
chat masala *see* SALT
CHATNI
chaunk *see* TECHNIQUES
chawan mushi *see* EGGS
chawan *see* UTENSILS
cheena chatti *see* UTENSILS
CHEESE
cheng fen *see* FLOURS & STARCHES
    (Cornflour)
cheng mein *see* FLOURS & STARCHES
    (Wheat starch)
chenna *see* CHEESE
cherimoya *see* CUSTARD APPLE
chermin *see* FISH (Trevally)
CHESTNUT
chi *see* WINES & SPIRITS
chiang *see* BEAN CURD
chichinda, chirchira *see* GOURDS
    (Snake gourd)
chick pea *see* LEGUMES & PULSES
chick pea flour *see* FLOURS &
    STARCHES (Besan)
CHICKEN
chieh shek *see* FOX NUT
chieh tse *see* EGGPLANT
chig-ge *see* WINES & SPIRITS
chih mah *see* SESAME SEED
chikoo *see* SAPODILLA
chikuwa *see* FISH CAKE
chilke moong dhal *see* LEGUMES &
    PULSES (Mung bean)
CHILLI
chin cheng tsai *see* LILY BUD
chin pei *see* TANGERINE PEEL
chin sui yau yue *see* SQUID
CHINA
chinbaung ywet *see* ROSELLE
CHINESE ALMOND

Chinese brocolli *see* CABBAGE
Chinese chard *see* CABBAGE
Chinese keys *see* KRACHAI
Chinese artichoke *see* ARTICHOKE,
    CHINESE
Chinese date *see* JUJUBE
Chinese kale *see* CABBAGE
    (Chinese broccoli)
Chinese pepper *see* SZECHWAN PEPPER
Chinese potato *see* ARROWHEAD
Chinese spinach *see* AMARANTH
ching bo leung *see* FOX NUT
ching tsai *see* CABBAGE (Chinese chard)
chinkeh, cingkeh *see* CLOVE
chirashi-zushi *see* SUSHI
chironji *see* CHAROLI
chitma *see* UTENSILS
chiu hwa *see* TEA
CHIVES, CHINESE
chives, garlic *see* CHIVES, CHINESE
chocalatera *see* UTENSILS
chocolate *see* COCOA
chocolate pudding fruit *see* SAPOTE,
    BLACK
CHOKO
chompoo phuang *see* ANTIGONON
chongho *see* CHRYSANTHEMUM
chor lada *see* FOOD COLOURINGS
chorizo, chourisam *see* SAUSAGES
choro-gi *see* ARTICHOKE, CHINESE
chota piaz *see* SHALLOT
chou ching gom larn *see* KOHLRABI
CHOW CHOW PRESERVE
chowla dhal *see* LEGUMES & PULSES
    (Black-eyed pea)
choy sum *see* CABBAGE
    (Flowering cabbage)
christophene *see* CHOKO
CHRYSANTHEMUM
chu-tsao *see* BEAN CURD
chuk shue, chuk shway *see* FLOURS &
    STARCHES
chun chow *see* AGAR-AGAR
chung koo *see* BAUHINIA
chuoi *see* BANANA
churi *see* UTENSILS
CHUTNEY
chutoro *see* SASHIMI
chye sim *see* CABBAGE
    (Flowering cabbage)
chyet-thon-phew *see* GARLIC
cidra, cidran *see* CITRON
cilantro *see* CORIANDER
cili, cili padi *see* CHILLI
cincalok *see* SHRIMP SAUCE
cingkeh *see* CLOVE
CINNAMON
CITRON
CITRUS FRUITS
CLAMS
climbing bean *see* LEGUMES & PULSES
    (Green bean)
cloud ear *see* MUSHROOMS & FUNGI
    (Black fungus)
CLOVES
COCOA

COCONUT
COCONUT APPLE
cocoyam *see* TARO
COFFEE
COLTSFOOT
com *see* RICE
con cua lua *see* CRABS
CONGEE
congou *see* TEA
CONPOY
CORIANDER HERB
CORIANDER SEED
CORN
CORN, MINIATURE
cornstarch *see* FLOURS & STARCHES
    (Cornflour)
country almond *see* TROPICAL
    ALMOND
cowpea *see* LEGUMES & PULSES
    (Yard-long bean)
CRABS
CREAM
cu cai trang *see* RADISH, WHITE
cu san *see* YAM BEAN
cubeb *see* PEPPER
CUCUMBER
cucut pisang *see* FISH (Shark)
culantro *see* ERYNGO
cumi-cumi, sotong *see* SQUID
CUMIN
CUMIN, BLACK
CURRY
CURRY LEAF
CURRY PASTES
curry powder *see* SPICE BLENDS
CUSTARD APPLE
custard marrow *see* CHOKO
CUTTLEFISH

D

da dau *see* SOY BEAN, FRESH
da suan *see* GARLIC
daeng khlong *see* JAMBU
daeng nam teuy *see* CRABS
dahi *see* YOGHURT
dai choy goh *see* AGAR-AGAR
dai dau nga choi *see* BEAN SPROUTS
dai dau *see* SOY BEAN, FRESH
dai gai choy *see* CABBAGE
    (Mustard cabbage)
dai suan *see* LEEK
daikon *see* RADISH, WHITE
daizu no moyashi *see* BEAN SPROUTS
daizu *see* SOY BEAN
dalchini, darchini *see* CINNAMON
dalo *see* TARO
damis lawin *see* FISH (Trevally)
dara-dhambala *see* LEGUMES & PULSES
    (Winged bean)
darchini *see* CINNAMON
dare-o *see* UTENSILS
daru *see* POMEGRANATE
DASHI
dau hu *see* BEAN CURD

dau me *see* OILS (Sesame oil)
dau phong *see* PEANUT
daun kadok *see* CHA PLU
daun kesom *see* VIETNAMESE MINT
daun ketumbar *see* CORIANDER HERB
daun laksa *see* VIETNAMESE MINT
daun pandan *see* PANDANUS LEAF
daun pegaga *see* PENNYWORT
daun salam *see* SALAM LEAF
daun sop *see* CELERY
daun turi *see* SESBANIA
DAY LILY
dayap *see* LIME
degchi *see* UTENSILS
dehi *see* LIME
dehradun *see* RICE
deshi channa *see* LEGUMES & PULSES
    (Chick pea)
deshi gram *see* LEGUMES & PULSES
    (Chick pea)
DESSERTS
DEVIL'S TONGUE
devil's dung *see* ASAFOETIDA
dhakkan *see* UTENSILS
DHAL
dhallo *see* SQUID
dhania *see* CORIANDER SEEDS
dhania pattar *see* CORIANDER HERB
dhel *see* BREADFRUIT
dhinyindi *see* NGAPI NUT
dhwen jang *see* BEAN SAUCES
dilao *see* TURMERIC
dilaw *see* TURMERIC
dilis *see* FISH, DRIED
DILL
DIM SUM
dimbul *see* WOODAPPLE
diwul *see* WOODAPPLE
diya labu *see* GOURDS (Bottle gourd)
do-nabe *see* UTENSILS
doe chung *see* FISH (Tuna)
doeng sun *see* BAMBOO
dok galum *see* CAULIFLOWER
dok khae baan *see* SESBANIA
dok kluai *see* BANANA FLOWER
dok mai cheen *see* DAY LILY
dok-oi *see* SUGAR CANE FLOWER
DOMBURI
doong gwoo *see* MUSHROOMS &
    FUNGI (Shiitake)
dou-su *see* YAM BEAN
doufu, dow foo *see* BEAN CURD
dow sa, dow sah *see* BEAN PASTE,
    SWEET
DRINKS & BEVERAGES
DRUMSTICK
du bu *see* BEAN CURD
du du *see* PAPAYA
dua *see* COCONUT
DUCK
duhay *see* POMFRET
dumned *see* TECHNIQUES
dumpara *see* MANGO
dung mien fun *see* FLOURS &
    STARCHES (Wheat starch)
duran maki *see* SOURSOP

duren *see* DURIAN
DURIAN
durian belanda *see* SOURSOP
duryan *see* DURIAN
duyin *see* DURIAN

E

ebi *see* SHRIMP, DRIED
eda mame *see* SOY BEAN, DRIED
eddo *see* TARO
EEL
een choy *see* AMARANTH
EGGPLANT
EGGS
eibei *see* SHRIMP, DRIED
eintopf *see* SOUP
elaichi *see* CARDAMOM
elephant apple *see* WOODAPPLE
emping *see* MELINJO NUT
emping melinjo *see* GNEMON
EMU
enasal *see* CARDAMOM
endou mame *see* LEGUMES & PULSES
    (Green pea)
enduru *see* DILL
enoki *see* MUSHROOMS & FUNGI
    (Enokitake)
enokitake , enokidake *see* MUSHROOMS
    & FUNGI
ensaimada *see* BREADS
ercis *see* LEGUMES & PULSES
    (Green pea)
ERYNGO
ESSENCES

F

fa *see* KEWRA
fa yeh tsoi *see* CAULIFLOWER
fa'i *see* BANANA
fa-sang *see* PEANUT
faah jiu *see* SZECHWAN PEPPER
faan shu *see* POTATO, SWEET
faba *see* LEGUMES & PULSES
    (Broad bean)
faeng *see* GOURDS (Fuzzy melon)
fafa *see* TARO
fagara *see* SZECHWAN PEPPER
fak-khaao *see* BITTER GOURD
fak-kib *see* GOURDS (Wax gourd)
fak mao, fak meo *see* CHOKO
fak thong *see* SQUASH
FALOODA
falooda seed *see* PSYLLIUM
fan *see* RICE
fan su *see* POTATO, SWEET
farina *see* SEMOLINA
fasut jasum *see* HIBISCUS
fat shau kwa *see* CHOKO
fat tsai *see* BLACK MOSS
fatt-fung-kam *see* KAFFIR LIME
fava bean *see* LEGUMES & PULSES
    (Broad bean)

fei *see* BANANA
FEIJOA
FENI
FENNEL
FENUGREEK
FERN, FIDDLEHEAD
fetau *see* TROPICAL ALMOND
FIJI
finger millet *see* MILLET
firni *see* RICE, GROUND
FISH
FISH CAKE
FISH, DRIED
FISH HEAD
FISH MAW
FISH PASTE
FISH ROE
FISH SAUCE
fish gravy *see* FISH SAUCE
fish tamarind *see* GAMBOGE
five corner fruit *see* STAR FRUIT
FIVE-SPICE POWDER
flavouring essences *see* ESSENCES
fleaseed *see* PSYLLIUM
FLOURS & STARCHES
flowering chives *see* CHIVES, CHINESE
foil *see* GOLD LEAF, SILVER LEAF
foo kwa, foo gwa *see* BITTER GOURD
FOOD COLOURINGS
foreign coriander *see* ERYNGO
foreign cumin *see* CARAWAY
forng tao hu *see* BEAN CURD
FOX NUT
French bean *see* LEGUMES & PULSES
    (Green bean)
FRIKKADEL
FROG
FRUIT BAT
fu gwa *see* BITTER GOURD
fu shong hua *see* HIBISCUS
fuang *see* STAR FRUIT
FUGU
fuguchiri, fugusashi *see* FUGU
fuji fruit *see* PERSIMMON
fuki *see* COLTSFOOT
fun see *see* NOODLES
    (Bean starch noodles)
funa-zushi *see* SUSHI
funan *see* BEAN CURD
fungi *see* MUSHROOMS & FUNGI
furu *see* PERSIMMON
fuyu *see* BEAN CURD
fuzzy melon *see* GOURDS

G

gado-gado *see* salads
gaeng *see* CURRY
gai choy *see* CABBAGE
gai larn *see* CABBAGE (Chinese broccoli)
gajjar *see* CARROT
gajjar halva *see* CARROT
gaju *see* CASHEW
gal siyamabala *see* VELVET TAMARIND
galanga *see* GINGER, AROMATIC

GALANGAL, GREATER
GALANGAL, LESSER
galia *see* MELONS, SWEET
GAMBOGE
gammiris *see* PEPPER
gan bei *see* CONPOY
gan lu zi *see* ARTICHOKE, CHINESE
gandian fen *see* FLOURS & STARCHES
    (Cornflour)
ganmo *see* BEAN CURD
gao bai shun *see* WILD RICE SHOOTS
gao liang jiang *see* GALANGAL,
    GREATER
gao nep *see* FLOURS & STARCHES
    (Glutinous rice flour)
garam masala *see* SPICE BLENDS
garbanzos *see* LEGUMES & PULSES
    (Chick pea)
gari *see* GINGER
GARLIC
garlic chives *see* CHIVES, CHINESE
GARNISHES
garopa *see* FISH (Grouper)
gaslabu *see* PAPAYA
gata *see* COCONUT (Coconut milk)
gau choi *see* CHIVES, CHINESE
gau gei choi *see* BOXTHORN
gau sun *see* WILD RICE SHOOTS
geeli khichari *see* KEDGEREE
gekka-no-bijin *see* QUEEN OF THE
    NIGHT
gelang pasir *see* PURSLANE
gelatine, Japanese *see* AGAR-AGAR
GELUGOR
genda-kola *see* PURSLANE
ghanda *see* LEMON GRASS
ghara *see* UTENSILS
GHEE
gia *see* BEAN SPROUTS
gilingan *see* UTENSILS
gin *see* GINGER
gin thoke *see* GINGER
gingelly *see* SESAME SEED
gingelly oil *see* OILS
GINGER
GINGER, AROMATIC
GINGER FLOWER
GINGER, MIOGA
GINKGO NUT
GINSENG
gizzard *see* OFFAL
gizzard shad *see* FUGU
globe-fish *see* FUGU
GNEMON
go *see* SOY BEAN PRODUCTS
go nung *see* WATER CHESTNUT
goa bean *see* LEGUMES & PULSES
    (Winged bean)
goat *see* MUTTON
gobo *see* BURDOCK ROOT
gochu jang *see* BEAN SAUCES
gohan *see* RICE
goi cuon *see* RICE PAPER
GOLD LEAF
GOLDEN MOUNTAIN SAUCE
golden apple *see* AMBARELLA

golden berry *see* GOOSEBERRY, CAPE
golden needles *see* DAY LILY
gom pei *see* TANGERINE PEEL
goma *see* SESAME SEED
goma abura *see* OILS (Sesame oil)
gomashio *see* SESAME SEED
gong yew chew *see* SCALLOPS
goong haeng *see* SHRIMP, DRIED
goorakathee *see* CHOKO
GOOSEBERRY, CAPE
goraka *see* GAMBOGE
gotu kola *see* PENNYWORT
GOURDS
gozen soba *see* NOODLES
GRAINS OF PARADISE
GRASS JELLY
green gram *see* LEGUMES & PULSES
    (Mung bean)
green onion *see* SPRING ONION
green pea *see* LEGUMES & PULSES
ground cherry *see* GOOSEBERRY, CAPE
ground nut *see* PEANUT
GUAVA
guayabano *see* SOURSOP
guber *see* PEANUT
Guinea pepper *see* GRAINS OF
    PARADISE
Guinea grains *see* CARDAMOM
gula aren *see* PALM SUGAR
gula jawa *see* PALM SUGAR
gula melaka *see* PALM SUGAR
gulab jal *see* ESSENCES (Rose water)
gulab jamun *see* SWEETMEATS, INDIAN
gulal tulsi *see* BASIL
gulaman *see* AGAR-AGAR
gum gun yuen *see* SAUSAGES
gumamela bulaklak *see* HIBISCUS
gung *see* GINGER
gur *see* JAGGERY
gyokuro *see* TEA

H

haal masso *see* ANCHOVY
haba *see* CHILLI
habalapethi *see* RICE FLAKES
habanero *see* CHILLI
habi chuelas *see* LEGUMES & PULSES
    (Green bean)
haeo cheen *see* WATER CHESTNUT
haeo-song krathiem *see* WATER
    CHESTNUT
hai-shen *see* SEA CUCUMBER
hajikami shoga *see* GINGER
hak chih mah *see* SESAME SEED
hak dau *see* SOY BEAN, DRIED
hakuka *see* MINT
hakuru *see* JAGGERY
hakusai *see* CABBAGE
    (Chinese cabbage)
hala *see* PANDANUS LEAF
halba *see* FENUGREEK
haldi *see* TURMERIC
halia *see* GINGER
halo-halo *see* ICE KACANG

halvas *see* SWEETMEATS, INDIAN
hamachi *see* SUSHI
hamaguri *see* SUSHI
han-gawaki *see* BEAN CURD
hana yasai *see* CAULIFLOWER
handai *see* UTENSILS
handies *see* UTENSILS
hang kor chow *see* PENNYWORT
hangi *see* UTENSILS
hanh huong *see* SHALLOT
hara dhania *see* CORIANDER HERB
harp jeung kwa *see* CHOKO
harusame *see* NOODLES
    (Bean starch noodles)
HAWAII
hay bee *see* SHRIMP, DRIED
hay koh *see* SHRIMP SAUCE
hayato-uri *see* CHOKO
he *see* CHIVES, CHINESE
heari meron *see* GOURDS (Fuzzy melon)
hebi-uri *see* GOURDS (Snake gourd)
hechima *see* GOURDS (Sponge gourd)
hed bua *see* MUSHROOMS & FUNGI
    (Straw mushroom)
hed fang *see* MUSHROOMS & FUNGI
    (Straw mushroom)
hed hom *see* MUSHROOMS & FUNGI
    (Shiitake)
hed hoo noo MUSHROOMS & FUNGI
    (Black fungus)
hed hunu *see* MUSHROOMS & FUNGI
    (Black fungus)
hed man poo yai *see* MUSHROOMS &
    FUNGI (Chanterelle)
hed nang rom bhutan *see* MUSHROOMS
    & FUNGI (Oyster mushroom)
hed nun *see* MUSHROOMS & FUNGI
    (Straw mushroom)
hed tab tao *see* MUSHROOMS & FUNGI
    (Cepe)
hee maa *see* NAM-NAM
heen gotu kola *see* PENNYWORT
heung masu tso *see* LEMON GRASS
heung peen *see* TEA
HIBISCUS
hijiki *see* SEAWEED
hilbe *see* FENUGREEK
hing *see* ASAFOETIDA
hingurupiyali *see* GINGER, AROMATIC
hira zukuri *see* SASHIMI
hirame, hirami *see* SASHIMI
hirezake *see* SASHIMI
hiyuna *see* AMARANTH
hmo chauk *see* MUSHROOMS & FUNGI
    (Shiitake)
hmo *see* MUSHROOMS & FUNGI
    (Straw mushroom)
hnan zi, hnan si *see* OILS (Sesame oil)
ho ha *see* SHRIMP SAUCE
hoi sin sauce *see* BEAN SAUCES
hoi chit *see* JELLYFISH
hoi sin jeung *see* BEAN SAUCES
hoi *see* STAR ANISE
hojiso *see* PERILLA
hokkigai *see* SUSHI
hom chan *see* VIETNAMESE MINT

hom daeng *see* SHALLOT
hom ha *see* SHRIMP SAUCE
hom proh *see* GINGER, AROMATIC
hom yao *see* ONION
honewort *see* TREFOIL
HONEY
honeydew melon *see* MELONS,
    SWEET
hong su jiang *see* GINGER
HOPPER
horapa *see* BASIL
horseradish tree *see* DRUMSTICK
horseradish, Japanese *see* WASABE
hosui *see* NASHI
hot dieu mau *see* ANNATTO
hot mint *see* VIETNAMESE MINT
hot pepper *see* CHILLI
hotategai *see* SUSHI
hoyong *see* GOURDS (Ridged gourd)
hsan hmoung *see* FLOURS & STARCHES
    (Rice flour)
hsiang-ts'ao *see* VANILLA
hsien tsai *see* AMARANTH
hu-chiao *see* PEPPER
hua chiao *see* SZECHWAN PEPPER
huang-kwa *see* CUCUMBER
hung jo *see* JUJUBE
hung ngan *see* CHINESE ALMOND
hung yun *see* ALMOND
hung zao *see* JUJUBE
huuraanam *see* NAM-NAM
hyacinth bean *see* LEGUMES & PULSES
hyunmi siksho *see* VINEGAR

I

ICE
ICE CREAM
ICE KACANG
IDLI
ika *see* SUSHI
ikan bilis *see* FISH, DRIED
ikan teri *see* FISH, DRIED
ikura *see* FISH ROE
illaichi *see* CARDAMOM
imli *see* TAMARIND
in-tsai *see* AMARANTH
inakako *see* FLOURS & STARCHES
    (Buckwheat flour)
INDIA
Indian almond *see* TROPICAL
    ALMOND
Indian bael *see* BAEL FRUIT
Indian bay leaf *see* CASSIA LEAF
Indian shortbread *see* SEMOLINA
Indian sorrel *see* ROSELLE
indica *see* RICE
INDONESIA
Indonesian bay leaf *see* SALAM LEAF
ingen mame *see* LEGUMES & PULSES
    (Green bean)
inguru *see* GINGER
ingurupiyali *see* GINGER, AROMATIC
isabgol *see* PSYLLIUM
ito zukuri *see* SASHIMI

J

jaa jang *see* SOY BEAN, DRIED
jackfruit *see* JAKFRUIT
JAGGERY
jahe *see* GINGER
jaiphal *see* NUTMEG
JAKFRUIT
jal jeera *see* SALT
jalebi *see* SWEETMEATS, INDIAN
jallah *see* UTENSILS
Jamaican sorrel *see* ROSELLE
Jamaican plum *see* AMBARELLA
jamanarang *see* MANDARIN
JAMBU
janggat *see* MINT
jantung pisang *see* BANANA FLOWER
JAPAN
Japanese artichoke *see* ARTICHOKE,
    CHINESE
Japanese horseradish *see* WASABE
Japanese pear *see* NASHI
japonica *see* RICE
jardaloo *see* APRICOT
JASMINE
JAVA ALMOND
java-ala *see* YAM
javanica *see* RICE
jeera *see* CUMIN
jeera pani *see* CUMIN
jelly mushroom *see* MUSHROOMS &
    FUNGI (Black fungus)
JELLYFISH
jengkol *see* NGAPI NUT
jeruk bodong *see* CITRON
jeruk keprak *see* MANDARIN
jeruk purut *see* KAFFIR LIME
jeruk sambal *see* KAFFIR LIME
jeung *see* GINGER
Jew's ear fungus *see* MUSHROOMS &
    FUNGI (Black fungus)
jhingli *see* GOURDS (Ridged gourd)
jicama *see* YAM BEAN
jie lan *see* CABBAGE (Chinese broccoli)
jin doi *see* LEGUMES & PULSES
    (Mung bean)
jintan manis *see* FENNEL
jintan puteh *see* CUMIN
jinten *see* CUMIN
jiu tsai *see* CHIVES, CHINESE
jiu tsung *see* LEEK
jook gai choy *see* CABBAGE
    (Mustard cabbage)
jook sun *see* BAMBOO
joshinko *see* FLOURS & STARCHES
    (Rice flour)
jowar atta *see* FLOURS & STARCHES
    (Atta)
JUJUBE
jumbola *see* POMELO
jun jing *see* TEA
jungle tree *see* NGAPI NUT
jungli amba *see* AMBARELLA
juruk bali *see* POMELO
juuroku-sasage *see* LEGUMES & PULSES
    (Yard-long bean)

K

ka-ling-pring *see* BILIMBI
kaa yee *see* VELVET TAMARIND
kaan ploo *see* CLOVE
kabayo *see* UTENSILS
kabocha *see* SQUASH
kabuli channa *see* LEGUMES & PULSES (Chick pea)
kacang botor *see* LEGUMES & PULSES (Winged bean)
kacang buncis *see* LEGUMES & PULSES (Green bean)
kacang *see* ICE KACANG
kacang kedalai *see* SOY BEAN, DRIED
kacang kedele *see* SOY BEAN SPROUTS
kacang koro *see* LEGUMES & PULSES (Lentil)
kacang manis *see* LEGUMES & PULSES (Green pea)
kacang mete *see* CASHEW
kacang panjang *see* LEGUMES & PULSES (Yard-long bean)
kacang serinding *see* LEGUMES & PULSES (Lentil)
kacang soja *see* SOY BEAN SPROUTS
kacang tanah *see* PEANUT
kachai *see* KRACHAI
kacholam *see* GINGER, AROMATIC
kachri *see* GINGER, AROMATIC
kaddoo-kas *see* UTENSILS
kadhai, karai, karahi *see* UTENSILS
KAFFIR LIME
kaha *see* TURMERIC
kahpiri dehi *see* KAFFIR LIME
kailan *see* CABBAGE (Chinese broccoli)
kaina *see* KEWRA
kairan *see* CABBAGE (Chinese broccoli)
kajiki *see* SUSHI
kaju *see* CASHEW
kaki fruit *see* PERSIMMON
kakri *see* CUCUMBER
kakrol *see* BITTER GOURD
kaku zukuri *see* SASHIMI
kakulu-haal *see* RICE
kakuluwo *see* CRABS
kala gova *see* CABBAGE (Chinese cabbage)
kala gram *see* LEGUMES & PULSES (Chick pea)
kala namak *see* SALT
kala zeera *see* CUMIN, BLACK
kalada *see* PALM, HEART OF
kalam pom *see* KOHLRABI
KALAMANSI
kalans *see* UTENSILS
kale *see* CABBAGE
kali *see* GOURD (Ridged gourd)
kali mirich, kali mirch *see* PEPPER
kalmua *see* WATER SPINACH
kalonji *see* NIGELLA
kalu pullium *see* VELVET TAMARIND
kamaboko *see* FISH CAKES
kamal-kakri *see* LOTUS
kamani *see* TROPICAL ALMOND

kamaranga *see* STAR FRUIT
kamargah *see* QABARGH
kamias *see* BILIMBI
kamin khao *see* ZEDOARY
kamote *see* POTATO, SWEET
kamoteng kahoy *see* CASSAVA
KAMPYO
kamrakh *see* STAR FRUIT
kan-shue *see* POTATO, SWEET
kan-ssu *see* BEAN CURD
kan-tsai *see* CELERY
kana-gushi *see* UTENSILS
kanari *see* JAVA ALMOND
KANGAROO
kangkong, kangkung *see* WATER SPINACH
kanji *see* VELVET TAMARIND
kankon *see* WATER SPINACH
kanoon *see* JAKFRUIT
kanpachi *see* SUSHI
kanten *see* AGAR-AGAR
kantola *see* BITTER GOURD
kanzou *see* DAY LILY
kao ko, kao koi *see* ANCHOVY
kao mao *see* RICE FLAKES
kaong *see* SUGAR PALM SEED
kaoteran *see* PALM, HEART OF
kapi *see* SHRIMP PASTE, DRIED
kapiak *see* BREADFRUIT
kaprao, krapao *see* BASIL
kapulaga *see* CARDAMOM
karabu *see* CLOVE
karachi halwa *see* CHAR MAGAZ
karashi-na *see* CABBAGE (Mustard cabbage)
karavadu *see* FISH, DRIED
karavila *see* BITTER GOURD
karchi *see* UTENSILS
karela *see* BITTER GOURD
karhai *see* UTENSILS
karhi *see* CURRY
kari-kari *see* BEEF
kasaundi *see* RELISHES
kasu-zuke *see* TECHNIQUES
kasuba *see* SAFFLOWER
kasugo *see* SUSHI
katae-kae *see* CASHEW
katahal *see* JAKFRUIT
katakuriko *see* FLOURS & STARCHES (Potato starch)
katera pohon *see* FLOURS & STARCHES (Tapioca starch)
kathal ke beej *see* JAKFRUIT
katori *see* UTENSILS
katsua, katsuo *see* SASHIMI
katsuobushi *see* BONITO
katu-anoda *see* SOURSOP
katuk *see* SABAH VEGETABLE
katuray *see* SESBANIA
katurumurunga *see* SESBANIA
kau tue *see* FISH (Spanish mackerel)
kavum *see* CAKES
kawali *see* UTENSILS
kayu manis *see* CINNAMON
kazunoko *see* FISH ROE
keanee *see* JAVA ALMOND

KEBAB
kecap *see* SOY SAUCE
kechulu-kalangu *see* GINGER, AROMATIC
kecil galanga *see* GINGER, AROMATIC
kecipir *see* LEGUMES & PULSES (Winged bean)
kecup pekat *see* SOY SAUCE
kedalai *see* SOY BEAN, DRIED
KEDGEREE
kedondong *see* AMBARELLA
keem *see* SEAWEED
keh *see* SESAME SEED
kehel *see* BANANA
kehel mal *see* BANANA FLOWER
kei chi *see* WOLFBERRY
kekuna *see* CANDLE NUT
kel-varagu *see* MILLET
kela *see* BANANA
keladi *see* TARO
kelapa *see* COCONUT
keledek *see* POTATO, SWEET
kelor *see* DRUMSTICK
kemangi *see* BASIL
kembang sa mangkok *see* POONTALAI
kembong *see* FISH (Mackerel)
kembung lelaki *see* FISH (Mackerel)
kemiri nut *see* CANDLE NUT
kenari, kanari *see* JAVA ALMOND
kencur *see* GINGER, AROMATIC
kentjoer *see* GINGER, AROMATIC
kepaya *see* PAPAYA
KEPHIR
kepiting *see* CRABS
keranji *see* VELVET TAMARIND
kerapu *see* FISH (Grouper)
kere kafool *see* BANANA FLOWER
kesari *see* SAFFRON
ketam batu *see* CRABS
ketapang lintak *see* TROPICAL ALMOND
ketapang *see* TROPICAL ALMOND
ketela *see* PAPAYA
ketimun *see* CUCUMBER
ketjap manis *see* SOY SAUCE
ketjap *see* SOY BEAN PRODUCTS
ketumbar *see* CORIANDER SEED
ketumpangan ayer *see* PEPEROMIA
kevda *see* ESSENCES (Kewra)
KEWRA
kha *see* GALANGAL, GREATER
kha-nun *see* JAKFRUIT
kham *see* YAM
khamin kao, khamin khao *see* TURMERIC
khanom chaun *see* FLOURS & STARCHES (Tapioca starch)
khanom krok *see* PANCAKES
khao chae *see* RICE, ICED
khao nee *see* FLOURS & STARCHES (Glutinous rice flour)
khao nieo, khao niew *see* RICE
khao *see* RICE
khas khas *see* POPPY SEED
khas *see* VETIVER
khasa-khasa *see* BASIL SEED
khee kwai *see* CHRYSANTHEMUM

kheer *see* DESSERTS
khichari *see* KEDGEREE
khing *see* GINGER
khira *see* CUCUMBER
khleng *see* VELVET TAMARIND
kho qua *see* BITTER GOURD
khoa *see* MILK
khoai mon *see* TARO
khtim kraham *see* SHALLOT
khus *see* VETIVER
kichri *see* KEDGEREE
kid *see* MUTTON
kikurage *see* MUSHROOMS & FUNGI
     (Black fungus)
kim cham, kim chiam *see* LILY BUD
kimcea *see* MUSTARD
KIM CHI
kimo *see* SASHIMI
kin chai, kin chye, kinchay *see* CELERY
kin-mun-yet-phout *see* SQUID
KING COCONUT
kinome *see* SANSHO
kintsay *see* CELERY
kinugoshi *see* BEAN CURD
kiri ala *see* TARO
kiri bath *see* RICE
kiri-komaki *see* BEAN CURD
kiriboshi *see* RADISH, WHITE
kisu *see* SUSHI
kitul *see* PALM SUGAR
kitul-hakuru *see* PALM SUGAR
KIWI FRUIT
kiyuba *see* BEAN CURD
kluay *see* BANANA
kluwek *see* BLACK NUT
knhei *see* GINGER
knol kohl *see* KOHLRABI
ko-domburi *see* UTENSILS
kobashira *see* SUSHI
kobis *see* CAULIFLOWER
kobis china *see* CABBAGE
     (Chinese cabbage)
kochchi miris *see* CHILLI
kodampoli *see* GAMBOGE
koe-chiap *see* SOY SAUCE
kohada *see* SUSHI
KOHLRABI
koitha *see* UTENSILS
kokoda *see* SALADS
kolang kaling *see* SUGAR PALM SEED
kolapo *see* FISH (Grouper)
koliplower *see* CAULIFLOWER
koma-koma *see* SAFFRON
komaki *see* BEAN CURD
kombu *see* SEAWEED
kon loh *see* ARTICHOKE, CHINESE
kon tsung-tau *see* SHALLOT
kon-tse hua *see* SUGAR CANE FLOWER
kon-tsung tau *see* SHALLOT
konbu, kombu *see* SEAWEED
kondakalava *see* KRACHAI
konnyaku *see* DEVIL'S TONGUE
koo chye *see* CHIVES, CHINESE
kopi tarek *see* COFFEE
KOREA
korean pear *see* NASHI

KORMA
korrakkai-pulli *see* GAMBOGE
kos *see* JAKFRUIT
kosho *see* PEPPER
kosht-kulinjan *see* GALANGAL,
     GREATER
kosui *see* NASHI
kotamba *see* TROPICAL ALMOND
kotang *see* TROPICAL ALMOND
kothamalli *see* CORIANDER SEED
kothamalli kolle *see* CORIANDER
     HERB
kou-kay-choi *see* BOXTHORN
koulfi *see* KULFI
koumiss *see* WINES & SPIRITS
KRACHAI
krachiap *see* ROSELLE
krapow *see* BASIL
krathiam tom *see* LEEK
kratiem *see* GARLIC
krauch soeuch *see* KAFFIR LIME
kravan *see* CARDAMOM
krokot *see* PURSLANE
krupek *see* KRUPUK
KRUPUK
krupuk emping *see* GNEMON
krupuk udang *see* PRAWN CRACKERS
kthem *see* GARLIC
kuali, kwali *see* UTENSILS
kucai *see* CHIVES, CHINESE
kueh *see* CAKES
kui chaai *see* CHIVES, CHINESE
kuk *see* SOUP
kukui *see* CANDLE NUT
kula *see* BREADFRUIT
kulanjan *see* GALANGAL, GREATER
kulfa *see* PURSLANE
KULFI
kulitis *see* AMARANTH
kumala *see* POTATO, SWEET
kumara *see* POTATO, SWEET
kumin *see* CUMIN
KUMISS
KUMQUAT
kundol *see* GOURDS (Wax gourd)
kundur *see* GOURDS (Wax gourd)
kunyit *see* TURMERIC
kuping jamu *see* MUSHROOMS &
     FUNGI (Black fungus)
kuping tikus *see* MUSHROOMS &
     FUNGI (Black fungus)
kuppamaki *see* SUSHI
kurage *see* JELLYFISH
kurakkan *see* MILLET
kuro gomah *see* SESAME SEED
kuro mame *see* SOY BEAN, DRIED
kurogu-wai *see* WATER CHESTNUT
kursam bulle pullie *see* LEGUMES &
     PULSES (Lentil)
kurundu *see* CINNAMON
kutsay *see* CHIVES, CHINESE
kuwai *see* WATER CHESTNUT
kuweh rombeh *see* FISH (Trevally)
kuzu ukon *see* FLOURS & STARCHES
     (Arrowroot)
kuzu-yuba *see* BEAN CURD

kwa-kwa *see* GOURDS (Bottle gourd)
kwa-tsz-tsai *see* PURSLANE
kyainthee *see* CANDLE NUT
kyauk kyaw *see* AGAR-AGAR
kyet neywet *see* MUSHROOMS &
     FUNGI (Black fungus)
kyet-thun-ni *see* SHALLOT
kyethinkhathee *see* BITTER GOURD
KYRINGA
kyuuri *see* CUCUMBER

L

la chiao *see* CHILLI
la dua *see* PANDANUS LEAF
la tia to *see* PERILLA
labanos *see* RADISH, WHITE
lablab bean *see* LEGUMES & PULSES
labong *see* BAMBOO
labra *see* MUSTARD
labu air *see* GOURDS (Bottle gourd)
labu siam, labu siem *see* CHOKO
lada hitam *see* PEPPER
lada merah *see* CAPSICUM
LADIES' FINGERS
LAKSA
laksa leaf *see* VIETNAMESE MINT
lam keong *see* GALANGAL, GREATER
lam kiu *see* GALANGAL, GREATER
lam-yai *see* LONGAN
lama *see* CANDLE NUT
LAMB
lambanog *see* WINES & SPIRITS
lamoot *see* SAPODILLA
LAMPRIES
lamu-ga-nan *see* CRABS
langka *see* JAKFRUIT
LAOS
laos *see* GALANGAL, GREATER
lap cheong *see* SAUSAGES
laphra *see* MUSTARD
larb *see* SALADS
larm yin *see* OLIVE NUT
lasan, lassan *see* GARLIC
lassi *see* DRINKS & BEVERAGES
lauci *see* CANDLE NUT
lauki *see* GOURDS (Bottle gourd)
laulau *see* TI LEAF
laung *see* CLOVES
laver *see* SEAWEED
leche flan *see* DESSERTS
LEEK
leek, Chinese *see* CHIVES, CHINESE
LEGUMES & PULSES
lemai *see* BREADFRUIT
LEMON
LEMON GRASS
lengkuas *see* GALANGAL, GREATER
lentil *see* LEGUMES & PULSES
leong foon *see* GRASS JELLY
leong goo *see* MUSHROOMS & FUNGI
     (Shiitake)
lephet *see* TEA LEAF RELISH
leprous lime *see* KAFFIR LIME
ley-nyin-bwint *see* CLOVE

LILY BUD
LILY BULB
lily, day *see* DAY LILY
limau besar *see* POMELO
limau kesturi *see* LIME
limau manis *see* LIME, SWEET
limau nipis *see* LIME
limau purut *see* KAFFIR LIME
limau susu *see* CITRON
LIME
lime leaf *see* KAFFIR LIME
lime, caffir *see* LIME, KAFFIR
LIME, SWEET
ling chiao *see* GOURDS (Ridged gourd)
ling fun *see* FLOURS & STARCHES
    (Tapioca starch)
linga *see* SESAME SEED
lingus *see* SAUSAGES
linmangkon *see* PASSIONFRUIT
lintak *see* TROPICAL ALMOND
litchi *see* LYCHEE
LIVER
llaneras *see* UTENSILS
lo sue baan *see* FISH (Grouper)
loang *see* FISH (Trevally)
lobah *see* SAUSAGES
lobak, loh-bak *see* RADISH, WHITE
lobia *see* MUSHROOMS & FUNGI
    (Yard-long bean)
LOBSTER
lolo *see* COCONUT (Coconut milk)
lombok *see* CHILLI
LONGAN
loofah *see* GOURDS (Ridged gourd)
loong narn *see* LONGAN
loong nga *see* BIRD'S NEST
loorabi *see* KOHLRABI
loose jackets *see* MANDARIN
lopa *see* DRUMSTICK
LOQUAT
lor bak, lobak *see* SAUSAGES
LOTUS
lu *see* MASTER SAUCE
luffa *see* GOURDS (Ridged gourd)
luk chup *see* LEGUMES & PULSES
    (Mung bean)
luk kravan *see* CARDAMOM
luk manglak *see* BASIL SEED
luk pak chee *see* CORIANDER SEED
lumbang bato *see* CANDLE NUT
lung ching *see* TEA
lung yue *see* ANCHOVY
lup chew *see* CHILLI
luya *see* GINGER
LYCHEE

M

ma fueang *see* STAR FRUIT
ma nao *see* LIME
ma sang *see* WOODAPPLE
ma tai *see* WATER CHESTNUT
ma thurian *see* SOURSOP
ma yau *see* OILS (Sesame oil)
ma-ch'in *see* CUMIN

ma-gyi-thi *see* TAMARIND
ma-kok farang *see* AMBARELLA
ma-la-ko *see* PAPAYA
ma-rum *see* DRUMSTICK
mabolo *see* PERSIMMON
MACADAMIA
MACE
madai *see* SASHIMI
maduru *see* FENNEL
maduru-tala *see* BASIL
magoro no bara *see* SASHIMI
maguro *see* SASHIMI
mahkua terung *see* EGGPLANT
mahkua yao *see* EGGPLANT
mai tai *see* FENI
mai *see* RICE
mai'a *see* BANANA
maize *see* CORN
MAKAPUNO
makaraal *see* LEGUMES & PULSES
    (Yard-long bean)
makhua puang *see* EGGPLANT
makiyaki-nabe *see* UTENSILS
makomo-zuno *see* WILD RICE SHOOTS
makrood, makrut *see* KAFFIR LIME
mal gova *see* CAULIFLOWER
mal kham *see* TAMARIND
malagkit *see* RICE
malai *see* CREAM
Malay apple *see* JAMBU
MALAYSIA
MALDIVE FISH
mali *see* JASMINE
mallung *see* JAKFRUIT
MALTOSE
malu miris *see* CAPSICUM
malunggay hapon *see* SABAH
    VEGETABLE
malunggay talbos *see* DRUMSTICK
mam ruoc *see* SHRIMP SAUCE
mam tom *see* SHRIMP PASTE, DRIED
mamuan *see* MANGO
mamuang himmaphaan *see* CASHEW
mamul *see* SALADS
man kaew *see* SHRIMP PASTE, DRIED
man-chuak *see* YAM
man-sao *see* YAM
man-thet *see* POTATO, SWEET
manao *see* LIME
MANDARIN
mandarin peel *see* TANGERINE PEEL
mang *see* BAMBOO
mang cua *see* SOURSOP
manga ingee *see* MANGO GINGER
mange tout *see* LEGUMES & PULSES
    (Snow pea)
mangga *see* MANGO
manggis *see* MANGOSTEEN
mangkut *see* MANGOSTEEN
manglak *see* BASIL
MANGO
MANGO GINGER
MANGOSTEEN
mangus, mangus kai *see* MANGOSTEEN
mani *see* PEANUT
manihot *see* CASSAVA

manioc *see* CASSAVA
maniokka *see* CASSAVA
manjal *see* TURMERIC
mao dau *see* SOY BEAN, DRIED
mao gwa *see* GOURDS (Fuzzy melon)
maoli *see* PAPAYA
maprao *see* COCONUT
mara *see* BITTER GOURD
mare's milk *see* KUMISS
markisa *see* PASSIONFRUIT
MARRON
MARROW & PUMPKIN
marsa *see* AMARANTH
masago *see* SUSHI
MASALA
masala chai *see* TEA
masala *see* SPICE BLENDS
MASTER SAUCE
masu *see* SASHIMI
masu-zushi *see* SUSHI
matsutake *see* MUSHROOMS & FUNGI
mattar *see* LEGUMES & PULSES
    (Green pea)
mattha *see* DRINKS & BEVERAGES
mau-dau *see* SOY BEAN, FRESH
Mauritius bean *see* LEGUMES & PULSES
    (Winged bean)
me *see* SESAME SEED
me wai niu *see* COCONUT
    (Coconut milk)
med-kha-nun *see* JAKFRUIT
mee *see* NOODLES (Egg noodles)
meenchi *see* MINT
meethi-torai *see* GOURDS (Sponge gourd)
mei *see* BREADFRUIT
mei kwei *see* TEA
mejiso *see* PERILLA
melagueta pepper *see* GRAINS OF
    PARADISE
MELINJO NUT
MELONS, SWEET
menrui *see* NOODLES
    (Japanese noodles)
merica hitam *see* PEPPER
meritam *see* PULASAN
methi *see* FENUGREEK
Mexican creeper *see* ANTIGONON
mi *see* NOODLES (Egg noodles)
mian-boo-kuo *see* BREADFRUIT
mien *see* NOODLES (Egg noodles)
mikan *see* MANDARIN
miki *see* NOODLES (Egg noodles)
milagai podi *see* SPICE BLENDS
MILK
MILLET
mimi *see* BEAN CURD
min sze jeung *see* BEAN SAUCES
mingut thi *see* MANGOSTEEN
MINT
minyak bijan *see* OILS (Sesame oil)
mioga *see* GINGER FLOWER
mirch *see* CHILLI
mirin *see* WINES & SPIRITS
mirliton *see* CHOKO
mirugai *see* SUSHI
misi *see* SOY BEAN PRODUCTS (Miso)

473

miso-zuke *see* RADISH, WHITE
mit *see* JAKFRUIT
mithai paratha *see* BREADS
miti hue *see* WINES & SPIRITS
miti kiri *see* COCONUT
 (Coconut milk)
MITSUBA
MIZUNA
mo sun *see* BAMBOO
mo yu *see* DEVIL'S TONGUE
mo-er *see* MUSHROOMS & FUNGI
 (Black fungus)
mochigome *see* RICE
moe ulu initia *see* JAKFRUIT
MOGHUL FOOD
moh let saung *see* DRINKS &
 BEVERAGES
mokube-tsushi *see* BITTER GOURD
molagu thani *see* MULLIGATAWNY
momiji oroshi *see* RADISH, WHITE
MONOSODIUM GLUTAMATE
mook lay fa *see* TEA
mooli *see* RADISH, WHITE
MOON CAKES
moong bean *see* MUNG BEAN
mor sze jeung *see* BEAN SAUCES
mora *see* LONGAN
mora *see* FISH (Shark)
moth bean *see* LEGUMES & PULSES
mouse ear *see* MUSHROOMS & FUNGI
 (Black fungus)
moyashi *see* BEAN SPROUTS
mozuku *see* SEAWEED
MSG *see* MONOSODIUM
 GLUTAMATE
mudu kekiya *see* PANDANUS FLOWER
mugi miso *see* BARLEY
muk bampoung *see* SQUID
muk kluay *see* SQUID
muk-shu *see* CASSAVA
muki goma *see* SESAME SEED
MULLIGATAWNY
mulunggay hapon *see* SABAH
 VEGETABLE
mung bean *see* LEGUMES & PULSES
mung-phali *see* PEANUT
murop kai *see* GOURDS (Ridged gourd)
muruggai *see* DRUMSTICK
murunga, murunga kolle *see*
 DRUMSTICK
mushimono *see* JAPAN
MUSHROOMS & FUNGI
MUSSELS
mussi *see* FISH (Shark)
MUSTARD
mustard oil *see* OILS
mustasa *see* CABBAGE
 (Mustard cabbage)
musubi yuba *see* BEAN CURD
MUTTON
muttu samba *see* RICE
myin-kwa-ywet *see* PENNYWORT
myohga *see* GINGER, MIOGA
mysore pak *see* FLOURS & STARCHES
 (Besan)

N

naam tao *see* BITTER GOURD
naan *see* BREADS
naan khatai *see* SEMOLINA
naang aai *see* NAM-NAM
naang dam *see* VELVET TAMARIND
nabemono *see* JAPAN
nacher *see* MILLET
nachni *see* MILLET
naeng myun *see* NOODLES
NAM-NAM
NAM PRIK
nam katee *see* COCONUT (Coconut milk)
nam pa, nam pla *see* FISH SAUCE
nam taan bik *see* PALM SUGAR
nam taan mapraow *see* PALM SUGAR
nam taan pep *see* PALM SUGAR
nama-gawaki *see* BEAN CURD
nameko *see* MUSHROOMS & FUNGI
 (Straw mushroom)
namkin chawal *see* RICE
nanas *see* PINEAPPLE
nangka *see* JAKFRUIT
nannambin *see* CORIANDER HERB
nannamzee *see* CORIANDER SEED
nanru *see* BEAN CURD
nanyu *see* BEAN CURD
napa cabbage *see* CABBAGE
 (Chinese cabbage)
naran-kai *see* LIME, SWEET
naranja *see* POMELO
narial kas *see* UTENSILS
NASHI
nasi *see* RICE
nasu *see* EGGPLANT
NATA
natto *see* SOY BEAN PRODUCTS
naw mai *see* RICE
negi *see* SPRING ONION
nejire-fusamame *see* PARKIA
nelun-ala *see* LOTUS
nethali *see* FISH, DRIED
NEW ZEALAND
ng-kiew *see* TURMERIC
nga chauk *see* FISH, DRIED
nga cheik *see* RICE
nga choi *see* BEAN SPROUTS
nga dama *see* FISH (Trevally)
nga dee la *see* SESAME SEED
nga kyi kan *see* FISH (Tuna)
nga tauk tu *see* FISH (Grouper)
nga-nan-gyaung *see* ANCHOVY
nga-youk-kaun *see* PEPPER
ngai gwa *see* EGGPLANT
ngamotephyu *see* POMFRET
ngan pla ye chet *see* SAUCES
ngan pya ye *see* FISH SAUCE
NGAPI NUT
ngapi, ngapi htaung *see* SHRIMP PASTE,
 DRIED
ngapyaw phoo *see* BANANA FLOWER
ngapyawthee *see* BANANA
ngau *see* LOTUS
nghe *see* TURMERIC

ngo *see* CORIANDER HERB
ngo gai *see* ERYNGO
ngo om *see* RICE PADDY HERB
ngun jump fun *see* FLOURS &
 STARCHES (Wheat starch)
niga-uri *see* BITTER GOURD
NIGELLA
nijisseiki *see* NASHI
niko-no-tataki, niku *see* BEEF
nimboo, nimbu *see* LIME
nimono *see* JAPAN
nin-niku *see* GARLIC
ning fun *see* NOODLES
 (Bean starch noodles)
nira *see* CHIVES, CHINESE
niu *see* COCONUT
no-ki-no-ha *see* DRUMSTICK
noi-na *see* CUSTARD APPLE
noi-nong *see* CUSTARD APPLE
nona kapri *see* CUSTARD APPLE
nona serikaya *see* CUSTARD APPLE
NONYA
NOODLES
nor mai farang *see* ASPARAGUS
nori *see* SEAWEED
nori-maki *see* SUSHI
normai *see* BAMBOO
normai-nam *see* WILD RICE
nuka-zuke *see* TECHNIQUES
nuoc cham *see* SAUCES
nuoc mam *see* FISH SAUCE
nuoc rau ma *see* PENNYWORT
NUTMEG
nyur *see* PALM, HEART OF

O

ob chuey *see* CINNAMON
ocha *see* TEA
OCTOPUS
odu dehi *see* KAFFIR LIME
OFFAL
ogen *see* MELONS, SWEET
oharagi *see* BEAN CURD
ohitashi *see* SQUASH FLOWER
OILS
okara *see* SOY BEAN PRODUCTS
okari nut *see* TROPICAL ALMOND
okolehao *see* TI LEAF
OKRA
okura *see* OKRA
olasiman ihalas *see* PEPEROMIA
olasiman *see* PURSLANE
oleti *see* PAPAYA
OLIVE NUT
omum *see* AJOWAN
ong choy *see* WATER SPINACH
ONION
oo-yama-imo *see* YAM
oolong *see* TEA
oroshi-gane *see* UTENSILS
ot *see* CHILLI
otaheite apple *see* AMBARELLA
otak-otak *see* FISH
otoro *see* SASHIMI

otoshi-buta *see* UTENSILS
OYSTER
OYSTER SAUCE

P

pa chong *see* POMFRET
pa la tu *see* FISH (Mackerel)
pa-de-gaw-gyi *see* GALANGAL, GREATER
paak so kung *see* FISH (Trevally)
paam haato *see* PALM, HEART OF
paan *see* BETEL LEAF
pachchadi *see* RELISHES
PACIFIC REGION
PADDY BIRD
pai-yeh, pai-yeh chieh *see* BEAN CURD
pak boong *see* WATER SPINACH
pak chee *see* CORIANDER HERB
pak chee farang *see* ERYNGO
pak choi *see* CABBAGE (Chinese chard)
pak hom *see* AMARANTH
pak khom hat *see* AMARANTH
pak khom suan *see* AMARANTH
pak krasang *see* PEPEROMIA
pak ku *see* BETEL NUT
pako, pako shida *see* FERN, FIDDLEHEAD
pakupis *see* GOURDS (Snake gourd)
pala *see* NUTMEG
palayok *see* UTENSILS
palita *see* PALM SUGAR
PALM, HEART OF
PALM HONEY
palm oil *see* OILS
PALM SUGAR
palm vinegar *see* VINEGAR
palmyra *see* PALM SUGAR
palusami *see* TARO
paminta *see* PEPPER
pan-no-mi *see* BREADFRUIT
PANCAKES
panch phora *see* SPICE BLENDS
panch puran *see* NIGELLA
panchamrita *see* DRINKS & BEVERAGES
pandan *see* PANDANUS
PANDANUS
PANDANUS FLOWER
PANDANUS LEAF
paneer *see* CHEESE
pang khao chao *see* FLOURS & STARCHES (Rice flour)
pang khao niew *see* FLOURS & STARCHES (Glutinous rice flour)
pang khao phod *see* FLOURS & STARCHES (Cornflour)
pang mun *see* FLOURS & STARCHES (Tapioca starch)
pang tao yai mom *see* FLOURS & STARCHES (Arrowroot)
pani dodan *see* LIME, SWEET
pani phul *see* WATER CHESTNUT
panir *see* CHEESE
panko *see* BREADCRUMBS, JAPANESE

panthe kaukswe *see* NOODLES
panyong *see* TEA
paoh-ho *see* MINT
papad *see* PAPPADAM
paparh *see* PAPAYA
papaw *see* PAPAYA
PAPAYA
papayasan *see* PAPAYA
PAPPADAM
pappali *see* PAPAYA
papri *see* LEGUMES & PULSES (Lablab bean)
paprika pepper *see* CHILLI
paruppu podi *see* SPICE BLENDS
paratha *see* BREADS
parau *see* FISH (Trevally)
pare *see* BITTER GOURD
pare-belut *see* GOURDS (Snake gourd)
PARKIA
PARSI
PASSIONFRUIT
PASTRY
patani *see* LEGUMES & PULSES (Lentil)
pateela *see* UTENSILS
pathola *see* GOURDS (Snake gourd)
pating *see* FISH (Shark)
patis *see* FISH SAUCE
patolang *see* GOURDS (Ridged gourd)
patra *see* TARO LEAF
pau tsai *see* CABBAGE (Chinese chard)
pawpaw *see* PAPAYA
pe' *see* BEAN SPROUTS
pe'epe'e *see* COCONUT (Coconut milk)
pea *see* LEGUMES & PULSES
pea flower *see* SESBIANA
PEANUT
peanut oil *see* OILS
pear, Asian *see* NASHI
pegagan *see* PENNYWORT
Peking cabbage *see* CABBAGE (Chinese cabbage)
Peking dust *see* CHESTNUT
PENNYWORT
pepaya *see* PAPAYA
PEPEROMIA
pepinella *see* CHOKO
pepino *see* CUCUMBER
pepinpauk *see* BEAN SPROUTS
pepol *see* PAPAYA
PEPPER
pepper, Szechwan *see* SZECHWAN PEPPER
pepper-coriander paste *see* CORIANDER
peppercorn *see* PEPPER
perhas *see* SWEETMEATS, INDIAN
peria *see* BITTER GOURD
PERILLA
perilla oil *see* OILS
PERILLA SEED
PERSIMMON
perunkaya *see* ASAFOETIDA
petai *see* PARKIA
peteh *see* PARKIA
petha, petha-kaddu *see* GOURDS (Wax gourd)
petis, patis *see* FISH SAUCE

petis udang *see* SHRIMP SAUCE
petola manis *see* GOURDS (Sponge gourd)
petola-ular *see* GOURDS (Snake gourd)
petsai *see* CABBAGE (Chinese chard, Chinese cabbage)
petsai tsina *see* CABBAGE (Chinese cabbage)
phak bia-yai *see* PURSLANE
phak chee lao *see* DILL
phak i leut *see* CHA PLU
phak khayaeng *see* RICE PADDY HERB
phak kuut *see* FERN, FIDDLEHEAD
phak ma-rum *see* DRUMSTICK
phak phai, phak pheo *see* VIETNAMESE MINT
phak si *see* DILL
phak waan *see* SABAH VEGETABLE
phakkat khaoplee *see* CABBAGE (Chinese cabbage)
phakkat khieo *see* CABBAGE (Mustard cabbage)
phakkat-hua *see* RADISH, WHITE
phakket bai *see* CABBAGE (Chinese chard)
phalazee *see* CARDAMOM
phik noi *see* PEPPER
PHILIPPINES
phluu *see* BETEL LEAF
pho *see* SOUP
phrik maa *see* VIETNAMESE MINT
phueak *see* TARO
phul gobi *see* CAULIFLOWER
pia *see* FLOURS & STARCHES (Cassava flour)
piaz *see* ONION
PICKLES
pig weed *see* AMARANTH
pigeon pea *see* LEGUMES & PULSES
pigeon wings *see* BUTTERFLY PEA FLOWER
piiman *see* CAPSICUM
pilaf *see* PILAU
PILAU
pili *see* JAVA ALMOND
pin kiew *see* FLOURS & STARCHES (Glutinous rice flour)
pin lung *see* BETEL NUT
pina *see* PINEAPPLE
PINE NUT
pine kernels *see* OLIVE NUT
PINEAPPLE
pini jambu *see* JAMBU
pinong *see* BETEL NUT
pinipig *see* RICE FLAKES
pipinya *see* CUCUMBER
pippali *see* PEPPER
pisang *see* BANANA
pista *see* PISTACHIO NUT
PISTACHIO NUT
pittu *see* RICE FLOUR
pla ai bang *see* FISH (Spanish mackerel)
pla chalam *see* FISH (Shark)
pla chom ngam *see* FISH (Trevally)
pla karang *see* FISH (Grouper)
pla lung *see* FISH (Mackerel)
pla o maw *see* FISH (Tuna)

pla thu *see* FISH (Mackerel)
PLANTAIN
plantain flower *see* BANANA FLOWER
plasroi *see* FISH, DRIED
po-chi *see* WATER CHESTNUT
podina *see* MINT
poh pia *see* SPRING ROLLS
poha *see* GOOSEBERRY, CAPE
pohok *see* MINT
pol bada *see* PALM, HEART OF
pol *see* COCONUT
pol pani *see* PALM SUGAR
polo *see* PILAU
polos *see* JAKFRUIT
POMEGRANATE
POMELO
POMFRET
pong tai hai *see* POONTALAI
poo thaleh *see* CRABS
POONTALAI
popadum *see* PAPPADAM
POPPY SEED
porcupine orange *see* KAFFIR LIME
PORK
poro negi *see* LEEK
posta *see* POPPY SEED
POTATO
POTATO, SWEET
pothundhambala *see* LEGUMES &
    PULSES (Lentil)
pottoo arshi *see* FLOURS & STARCHES
    (Glutinous rice flour)
powva *see* RICE FLAKES
PRAWN CRACKERS
PRAWNS
prawns, dried *see* SHRIMP, DRIED
preserving melon *see* GOURDS
    (Ash gourd)
prickly custard apple *see* SOURSOP
prik chee faa *see* CHILLI
prik kee noo *see* CHILLI
prik thai *see* PEPPER
prik yuak *see* CAPSICUM
princess pea *see* LEGUMES & PULSES
    (Winged bean)
proh hom *see* GINGER, AROMATIC
PSYLLIUM
pu thong *see* CRABS
pu'a, lama *see* CANDLE NUT
puhul dosi *see* GOURDS (Ash gourd)
pulao *see* PILAU
PULASAN
pulincha kira *see* ROSELLE
pullao *see* PILAU
pulot hitam *see* RICE, BLACK
    GLUTINOUS
pulses *see* LEGUMES & PULSES
pummelo *see* POMELO
pumpkin *see* MARROW & PUMPKIN
punatoo *see* SUGAR PALM
puri *see* BREADS
PURSLANE
pusit, calmar *see* SQUID
puso *see* BANANA FLOWER
puwak *see* BETEL NUT

Q

QABARGAH
Qahaw *see* TEA
QUAIL
QUANDONG
QUANDONG, BLUE
que *see* CINNAMON
QUEEN OF THE NIGHT
QUINCE

R

rabri *see* SWEETMEATS, INDIAN
rabu *see* RADISH, WHITE
RADISH, WHITE
ragi *see* MILLET
rai *see* MUSTARD
RAITA
raja-ala *see* YAM
rajama *see* LEGUMES & PULSES
    (Green bean)
rajma *see* LEGUMES & PULSES
    (Red kidney bean)
rakkasei *see* PEANUT
RAMBUTAN
ramen *see* NOODLES
rampe *see* PANDANUS LEAF
Rangoon bean *see* LEGUMES & PULSES
    (Lima bean)
rangu-rangu *see* PEPEROMIA
ras malai *see* SWEETMEATS, INDIAN
rasa kavili *see* CAKES
rasgullas *see* CHEESE
rata bilincha *see* ROSELLE
rata caju *see* PEANUT
rata kekuna *see* JAVA ALMOND
rata lunu *see* ONION
rathu lunu *see* SHALLOT
miris *see* CHILLI
rau cai *see* CABBAGE (Mustard cabbage)
rau huong lui *see* MINT
rau ma *see* DRINKS & BEVERAGES
rau muong, rau muong che *see* WATER
    SPINACH
rau que *see* BASIL
rau ram *see* VIETNAMESE MINT
rawa *see* SEMOLINA
rebong ayer *see* WILD RICE SHOOTS
rebong, rebung *see* BAMBOO
red date *see* JUJUBE
red kidney bean *see* LEGUMES &
    PULSES
red bean *see* LEGUMES & PULSES
    (Adzuki bean)
red lentil *see* LEGUMES & PULSES
    (Lentil)
red pepper.CHILLI
red-cooking *see* TECHNIQUES
RELISHES
remon-sou *see* LEMON GRASS
renkon *see* LOTUS
RICE
rice bean *see* LEGUMES & PULSES

RICE, BLACK GLUTINOUS
RICE CAKES
RICE FLAKES
RICE FLOUR
RICE, GROUND
RICE, ICED
rice noodles *see* NOODLES
RICE PADDY HERB
RICE PAPER
RICE POWDER, ROASTED AND
    GROUND
rice sticks *see* NOODLES
rice vermicelli *see* NOODLES
rice wrapper *see* RICE PAPER
ridged gourd *see* GOURDS
RIJSTAFFEL
rimas *see* BREADFRUIT
rock sugar *see* SUGAR
rockmelon *see* MELONS, SWEET
rojak *see* SHRIMP PASTE, DRIED
romdeng *see* GALANGAL, GREATER
romiet *see* TURMERIC
ROSE APPLE
ROSE WATER
ROSELLE
rosette bok choy *see* CABBAGE
roti *see* BREADS
roti jalah *see* BREADS
rou rou *see* TARO
ruam mit *see* ICE KACANG
rufu *see* BEAN CURD
ruh gulab *see* ROSE WATER
runner bean *see* LEGUMES & PULSES
    (Green bean)
ruridama no ki *see* SABAH VEGETABLE

S

sa leung geung *see* GINGER, AROMATIC
sa-nwin *see* TURMERIC
saa geung *see* GINGER, AROMATIC
saa got *see* YAM BEAN
saa jiang *see* GINGER, AROMATIC
saake *see* BREADFRUIT
saakhu *see* FLOURS & STARCHES
    (Arrowroot)
saba *see* FISH (Mackerel)
SABAH VEGETABLE
sabzah *see* BASIL
sadikka *see* NUTMEG
safed zeera *see* CUMIN
SAFFLOWER
SAFFRON
sagai *see* FISH (Trevally)
SAGO
sahijan *see* DRUMSTICK
sai fun *see* NOODLES
    (Bean starch noodles)
sai gwa *see* MELONS, SWEET
sai klok *see* SAUSAGES
sai min dou *see* LEGUMES & PULSES
    (Lentil)
sai-bashi *see* UTENSILS
saingchai *see* SALADS

saishin *see* CABBAGE
   (Flowering cabbage)
SAKE
saku sai moo *see* SAGO
salabat *see* DRINKS & BEVERAGES
SALADS
SALAK
SALAM LEAF
salderi *see* CELERY
SALMON
SALT
sam shiu *see* WINES & SPIRITS
SAMBAL
sambol *see* SAMBAL
SAMOA
SAMOSAS
samouk-saba *see* FENNEL
sampalang *see* CASSAVA
sampalok *see* TAMARIND
san bai *see* GALANGAL, LESSER
sankalu *see* YAM BEAN
SANSHO
santan *see* COCONUT (Coconut milk)
sapattu mal *see* HIBISCUS
SAPODILLA
SAPOTE, BLACK
SAPOTE, MAMEY
SAPOTE, WHITE
saqa *see* FISH (Trevally)
sarashino *see* FLOURS & STARCHES
   (Buckwheat flour)
sarson *see* MUSTARD
SASHIMI
sat isabgol *see* PSYLLIUM
sataw bean *see* PARKIA
SATAY
sato-imo *see* TARO
sator *see* PARKIA
satoukibi-no-hana *see* SUGAR CANE
   FLOWER
satsuma imo *see* POTATO, SWEET
satsuma *see* MANDARIN
SAUCES
saunf *see* FENNEL
SAUSAGES
saw tooth herb *see* ERYNGO
sawi *see* CABBAGE (Flowering cabbage,
   Chinese cabbage)
sawi hijau *see* CABBAGE
   (Mustard cabbage)
sawi puteh *see* CABBAGE (Chinese chard)
sawleaf herb *see* ERYNGO
sawarot *see* PASSIONFRUIT
sawu *see* SAPODILLA
sayori *see* SUSHI
sayote *see* CHOKO
sayur *see* CURRY
scallion *see* SPRING ONION
SCALLOPS
schochu *see* WINES & SPIRITS
SEA CUCUMBER
SEA URCHIN
sea rat *see* SEA CUCUMBER
sea slug *see* SEA CUCUMBER
SEAFOOD
SEAWEED

see keh *see* BETEL LEAF
seeni jambu *see* ROSE APPLE
seet gnee *see* MUSHROOMS & FUNGI
   (White fungus)
seetha *see* SOURSOP
seiro *see* FLOURS & STARCHES
   (Buckwheat flour)
seiro *see* FLOURS & STARCHES
   (Buckwheat flour)
sekta-ni-sing *see* DRUMSTICK
selaseh, selasih *see* BASIL
selderi *see* CELERY
semargka *see* MELONS, SWEET
SEMOLINA
sera, serai, sere *see* LEMON GRASS
seremaia *see* SOURSOP
seroja *see* LOTUS
serori *see* CELERY
SESAME OIL
SESAME PASTE
SESAME SEED
SESBANIA
sha geung fun *see* GINGER, AROMATIC
shabu-shabu *see* BEEF
shaguti *see* XACUTI
shah jeera, shah zeera *see* CUMIN,
   BLACK
shakar-kandi *see* POTATO, SWEET
shako *see* SUSHI
shakushina *see* CABBAGE (Chinese chard)
SHALLOT
shan yu cai *see* WASABI
shang chao fua *see* BANANA FLOWER
Shantung cabbage *see* CABBAGE
   (Chinese cabbage)
shao hsing *see* WINES & SPIRITS
SHARK'S FIN
sharps *see* FLOURS & STARCHES
   (Roti flour)
shauk-nu *see* KAFFIR LIME
shauk-waing *see* KAFFIR LIME
sheingho *see* ASAFOETIDA
sheng fen *see* FLOURS & STARCHES
   (Potato starch)
sherbet *see* DRINKS & BEVERAGES
SHICHIMI
shien *see* AMARANTH
shiitake *see* MUSHROOMS & FUNGI
shikakumame *see* LEGUMES & PULSES
   (Winged bean)
shima-aji *see* SUSHI
shimeji *see* MUSHROOMS & FUNGI
shimofuri niku *see* BEEF
shingiku *see* CHRYSANTHEMUM
shiozuke *see* TECHNIQUES
shirataki *see* FLOURS & STARCHES
   (Devil's tongue)
shiratamako *see* FLOURS & STARCHES
   (Glutinous rice flour)
shiro-gochou *see* SESBANIA
shiro kikurage *see* MUSHROOMS &
   FUNGI (White fungus)
shiso *see* PERILLA
shisonomi *see* PERILLA SEED
shochu *see* WINES & SPIRITS
shoe flower *see* HIBISCUS
shoga *see* GINGER
shoyu *see* SOY SAUCE

shrikhand *see* YOGHURT
shrimp *see* PRAWNS
SHRIMP, DRIED
SHRIMP PASTE, DRIED
SHRIMP PASTE, FRESH
SHRIMP SAUCE
shukta *see* MUSTARD
shungiku *see* CHRYSANTHEMUM
shyr kwa *see* GOURDS (Ridged gourd)
siaine *see* BANANA
Siamese ginger *see* GALANGAL,
   GREATER
sibuyas *see* ONION
siew mai *see* YUM CHA
sigadilas, sigarilyas *see* LEGUMES &
   PULSES (Winged bean)
sil-batta *see* UTENSILS
silgochu *see* CHILLI
sili *see* CHILLI
sili peaman *see* CAPSICUM
siling labuyo *see* CHILLI
siling *see* CHILLI
silk gourd *see* GOURDS (Ridged gourd)
SILVER LEAF
silver sprouts *see* BEAN SPROUTS
sim-sim *see* SESAME SEED
simla mirich *see* CAPSICUM
sincha *see* TEA
SINGAPORE
singaras *see* SPRING ROLL PASTRY
singkamas *see* YAM BEAN
singkwang *see* YAM BEAN
sinh to bo *see* DRINKS & BEVERAGES
sinh to mang cau *see* DRINKS &
   BEVERAGES
sinh to mit *see* DRINKS &
   BEVERAGES
sinna-valli-kelangut *see* YAM
sinsollo *see* UTENSILS
sirsak *see* SOURSOP
sitaphul *see* CUSTARD APPLE
sitaw *see* LEGUMES & PULSES
   (Yard-long bean)
sitsaro *see* LEGUMES & PULSES
   (Green pea)
siu-chue-shue *see* YAM
siyambala *see* TAMARIND
SNAKE
snake bean *see* LEGUMES & PULSES,
   Yard-long bean
snake gourd *see* GOURDS
snap bean *see* LEGUMES & PULSES
   (Green bean)
snow pea *see* LEGUMES & PULSES
so-kun-mu *see* SABAH VEGETABLE
soba *see* NOODLES
som khiew wan *see* LIME, SWEET
som kleang *see* LIME, SWEET
som ma kham *see* TAMARIND
som makrut *see* KAFFIR LIME
som mu *see* CITRON
som saa *see* CITRON
som tam *see* PAPAYA
som-or *see* POMELO
somen *see* NOODLES
sonf *see* FENNEL

sonth *see* GINGER
soo jeung kwa *see* DRINKS &
  BEVERAGES
soojee *see* SEMOLINA
sookha khichari *see* KEDGEREE
soon du bu *see* BEAN CURD
sora mame *see* LEGUMES & PULSES
  (Broad bean)
sorpotel *see* PORK
SORREL
sotanghon *see* NOODLES
  (Bean starch noodles)
sotong *see* SQUID
souchong *see* TEA
SOUP
SOURSOP
soursop sherbet *see* DRINKS &
  BEVERAGES
SOY BEAN, DRIED
SOY BEAN, FRESH
SOY BEAN PRODUCTS
SOY BEAN SPROUTS
SOY SAUCE
SPICE BLENDS
SPICES
SPINACH
sponge gourd *see* GOURDS
SPRING ONION
spring rain noodles *see* NOODLES
SPRING ROLL PASTRY
SPRING ROLLS
SQUASH
SQUASH FLOWER
SQUID
SRI LANKA
srikaya *see* CUSTARD APPLE
STAR ANISE
STAR APPLE
STAR FRUIT
stink bean *see* PARKIA
strawberry guava *see* GUAVA
string bean *see* LEGUMES & PULSES
  (Green bean)
stringhoppers *see* FLOURS &
  STARCHES (Rice flour)
stringless bean *see* LEGUMES & PULSES
  (Green bean)
su *see* VINEGAR
su-chi *see* BEAN CURD
su-ling dou *see* LEGUMES & PULSES
  (Winged bean)
sua *see* JELLYFISH
suberi-hiyu *see* PURSLANE
sudare *see* UTENSILS
sudu lunu *see* GARLIC
sududuru *see* CUMIN
suen tau *see* GARLIC
SUGAR CANE
SUGAR CANE FLOWER
SUGAR PALM
SUGAR PALM SEED
sugar, palm *see* PALM SUGAR
SUGAR, ROCK
SUGAR, SLAB
sugar snap pea *see* LEGUMES & PULSES
suhuo-t'ui *see* BEAN CURD

suk ju *see* BEAN SPROUTS
suka *see* VINEGAR
sukiyaki-nabe *see* UTENSILS
sukun *see* BREADFRUIT
sulasi *see* BASIL
suna-kosho *see* PEPEROMIA
sunomono *see* SEAWEED
supari *see* BETEL NUT
supparot *see* PINEAPPLE
suribachi *see* UTENSILS
surikogi *see* UTENSILS
SUSHI
suwenda-tala *see* BASIL
suzuki *see* SASHIMI
swamp potato *see* ARROWHEAD
swangi *see* KAFFIR LIME
sweet potato *see* POTATO, SWEET
sweet cumin *see* FENNEL
sweet pepper *see* CAPSICUM
sweet turnip *see* YAM BEAN
SWEETENERS
SWEETMEATS, INDIAN
sweetsop *see* CUSTARD APPLE
sze gwa *see* GOURDS (Ridged gourd)
sze kwa *see* GOURDS (Sponge gourd)
SZECHWAN PEPPER

T

tachi soba *see* NOODLES
ta paak tsai *see* CABBAGE
  (Chinese cabbage)
ta-hua *see* SESBANIA
ta-ling-pring *see* BILIMBI
taai-shue *see* YAM
taan *see* SUGAR PALM SEED
tadka *see* TECHNIQUES
taeng-kwa *see* CUCUMBER
Tahitian quince *see* AMBARELLA
tahu *see* BEAN CURD
tahuri *see* SOY BEAN PRODUCTS
tai chung *see* LEEK
tai dau *see* SOY BEAN, DRIED
tai gu choy *see* CABBAGE
  (Rosette bok choy)
tai *see* SASHIMI
tairagai *see* SUSHI
taisai *see* CABBAGE (Chinese chard)
takana *see* CABBAGE (Mustard cabbage)
take-gushi *see* UTENSILS
takenoko *see* BAMBOO
takip-kohol *see* PENNYWORT
tako *see* SUSHI
takrai *see* LEMON GRASS
takuan *see* RADISH, WHITE
tal-hakuru *see* PALM SUGAR
talai *see* PANDANUS FLOWER
talas *see* TARO
talisay *see* TROPICAL ALMOND
talong *see* EGGPLANT
tama-negi *see* ONION
tamago *see* SUSHI
tamanu *see* TROPICAL ALMOND
tamari *see* SOY SAUCE
TAMARIND

TAMARIND SLICES
tan hua *see* QUEEN OF THE NIGHT
TANDOORI
tang *see* SOUP
TANGERINE PEEL, DRIED
tangerine *see* MANDARIN
tangigi *see* FISH (Spanish mackerel)
tanglad *see* LEMON GRASS
tanyet *see* PALM SUGAR
tao hu *see* BEAN CURD
taoge *see* BEAN SPROUTS
TAPIOCA
tapioka *see* FLOURS & STARCHES
  (Tapioca starch)
TARO
tasai *see* CABBAGE (Rosette bok choy)
tau kau *see* NUTMEG
tau ngork *see* BEAN SPROUTS
tau-sa *see* BEAN PASTE, SWEET
taugeh *see* SOY BEAN SPROUTS
taukwa *see* BEAN CURD
tava, tawa *see* UTENSILS
tavola, tavola lato *see* TROPICAL
  ALMOND
TEA
TEA LEAF RELISH
tebao-endog *see* SUGAR CANE
  FLOWER
tebu-telur *see* SUGAR CANE
  FLOWER
TECHNIQUES
tej pattar *see* CASSIA LEAF
tel kekuna *see* CANDLE NUT
TEMPEH
temu putih *see* ZEDOARY
TENDERISERS
tenggiri batang *see* FISH
  (Spanish mackerel)
tenggiri *see* FISH (Spanish mackerel)
tepong beras *see* FLOURS & STARCHES
  (Rice flour)
teppan yaki *see* JAPAN
tepung hoen kwe *see* FLOURS &
  STARCHES (Mung bean starch)
tepung jagung *see* FLOURS &
  STARCHES (Cornflour)
tepung pulot *see* FLOURS & STARCHES
  (Glutinous rice flour)
tepung ubi kayu *see* FLOURS &
  STARCHES (Tapioca starch)
teratai *see* LOTUS
terong *see* EGGPLANT
teruah *see* BITTER GOURD
terung *see* EGGPLANT
Thai ginger *see* GALANAGAL,
  GREATER
Thai olive *see* CEYLON OLIVE
THAILAND
thala *see* SESAME SEED
thala thel *see* OILS (Sesame oil)
thala-guli *see* SESAME SEED
thaleh *see* CRABS
thali *see* UTENSILS
thambili *see* KING COCONUT
thampala *see* AMARANTH
thandai *see* DRINKS & BEVERAGES

thinh *see* FLOURS & STARCHES
(Roasted rice flour)
thit-ja-boh-gauk *see* CINNAMON
thora malu *see* FISH (Spanish mackerel)
thua chin *see* LEGUMES & PULSES
(Yard-long bean)
thua khaek *see* LEGUMES & PULSES
(Green bean)
thua lantao *see* LEGUMES & PULSES
(Green pea)
thua lisong *see* PEANUT
thua lueang *see* SOY BEAN, DRIED
thua raatcha maat *see* LEGUMES &
PULSES (Lentil)
thua yang *see* LEGUMES & PULSES
(Broad bean)
thurian khaek *see* SOURSOP
thurian thet *see* SOURSOP
TI LEAF
tiem shee *see* POTATO, SWEET
tien chiao *see* CAPSICUM
tien-tsing *see* SESBANIA
tientsin cabbage *see* CABBAGE
(Chinese cabbage)
TIFFIN
tike *see* WATER CHESTNUT
tikhoor *see* CASSAVA
tikhor *see* FLOURS & STARCHES
(Arrowroot)
til ka tel *see* OILS (Sesame oil)
til *see* OILS (Sesame oil)
tim mein jeung *see* BEAN SAUCES
timum balu *see* GOURDS (Fuzzy melon)
timun *see* CUCUMBER
tobiko *see* FISH ROE
tobiuonoko *see* SUSHI
toddy *see* PALM SUGAR
toeak *see* WINES & SPIRITS
tofu *see* BEAN CURD
togarashi *see* CHILLI
toi *see* GARLIC
tojo *see* BEAN CURD
tokado-hechima *see* GOURDS
(Ridged gourd)
tokua *see* BEAN CURD
tokwa, tokwan *see* SOY BEAN
PRODUCTS
tom kho *see* SHRIMP, DRIED
TOM YUM GOONG
TOMATO
ton hom *see* SPRING ONION
tong ho choi *see* CHRYSANTHEMUM
tongkol *see* FISH (Tuna)
tonkatsu *see* PORK
tookmuria *see* BASIL SEED
toor dhal, toovar dhal *see* LEGUMES &
PULSES (Pigeon pea)
torai *see* GOURDS (Ridged gourd)
torch ginger *see* GINGER FLOWER
torigai *see* SUSHI
toro *see* SASHIMI
tou-p'i *see* BEAN CURD
tougan *see* GOURDS (Wax gourd)
toyo mansi *see* SOY SAUCE
toyuba *see* BEAN CURD
trasi *see* SHRIMP PASTE, DRIED

tree ear *see* MUSHROOMS & FUNGI
(Black fungus)
trefoil *see* MITZUBA
trey beka inti *see* FISH (Spanish mackerel)
trey chap sar *see* POMFRET
trey chen chah *see* FISH (Trevally)
trey chheam khieu *see* FISH (Tuna)
trey chlam *see* FISH (Shark)
trey pek chhieu *see* POMFRET
trey tukke korm *see* FISH (Grouper)
tripe *see* OFFAL
TROPICAL ALMOND
tsaam dou *see* LEGUMES & PULSES
(Broad bean)
tsai dou *see* LEGUMES & PULSES
(Green bean)
tsampurado *see* COCOA
tsee goo *see* ARROWHEAD
tseet gwa *see* GOURDS (Fuzzy melon)
tseng dou *see* LEGUMES & PULSES
(Yard-long bean)
tsim bay tsai *see* FISH (Shark)
tsubo-kusa *see* PENNYWORT
tsubushi-an *see* BEAN PASTE, SWEET
tsuei *see* CHINA
tsukemono *see* JAPAN
tsumami *see* SASHIMI
tsung-tau *see* ONION
tu-rian, tu-lian *see* DURIAN
tua kwa *see* GOURD
tua pu *see* LEGUMES & PULSES
(Winged bean)
tuba *see* WINES & SPIRITS
tubo bulaklak *see* SUGAR CANE
FLOWER
tubu *see* BEAN CURD
tucmeria *see* BASIL SEED
tugi *see* YAM
tuitui *see* CANDLE NUT
tuk trey *see* FISH SAUCE
tukbaege *see* UTENSILS
tulingan *see* FISH (Tuna)
tulsi *see* BASIL
tumba-karavila *see* BITTER GOURD
tumpeang *see* BAMBOO
tung hoa *see* CHRYSANTHEMUM
tung kwa *see* GOURDS (Wax gourd)
tunghoon *see* NOODLES
(Bean starch noodles)
TUP TIM GROB
turi *see* SESBANIA
TURMERIC
tutui *see* CANDLE NUT
tuwak *see* SUGAR PALM
twisted cluster bean *see* PARKIA

U

ube, ubi *see* YAM
ubi kayu *see* CASSAVA
ubi-arumanis *see* YAM
ubi-jalar *see* POTATO, SWEET
ubi-kemali *see* YAM
ubi-torak *see* YAM
ubod *see* PALM, HEART OF

uchiwa fan *see* UTENSILS
udang kering *see* SHRIMP, DRIED
UDDER
UDON *see* NOODLES
UGLI
ukon *see* TURMERIC
ulam *see* CHA PLU
ulek *see* SAMBAL
ulu *see* BREADFRUIT
uluhaal *see* FENUGREEK
umba-karavila *see* BITTER GOURD
umbalakade *see* MALDIVE FISH
umeboshi *see* TECHNIQUES
umekyu *see* SUSHI
umpiang ubod *see* PALM, HEART OF
unagi *see* EEL
ung tsai *see* WATER SPINACH
uni *see* SUSHI
upo *see* GOURDS (Bottle gourd)
uppuma *see* SEMOLINA
urad dhal *see* LEGUMES & PULSES
(Black gram)
urad *see* LEGUMES & PULSES
(Mung bean)
uru *see* BREADFRUIT
usli ghee *see* GHEE
usu zukuri *see* SASHIMI
usuwaki-yuba *see* BEAN CURD
utaw *see* SOY BEAN, DRIED
UTENSILS & COOKING
EQUIPMENT
uto *see* BREADFRUIT
uto ni bulumakau *see* CUSTARD
APPLE
uto ni idia *see* JAKFRUIT
uwhi *see* YAM
uwhikaho *see* YAM

V

vadamal *see* HIBISCUS
vadra *see* PINEAPPLE
vambotu *see* EGGPLANT
vanaspati *see* GHEE
VANILLA
varak *see* SILVER LEAF
varaka *see* JAKFRUIT
vatakolu *see* GOURDS (Sponge gourd)
vattalappam *see* DESSERTS
ve-tsin *see* MONOSODIUM
GLUTAMATE
vegetable gelatine *see* AGAR-AGAR
vegetable pear *see* CHOKO
vegetable sponge *see* GOURDS
(Sponge gourd)
VEGETARIAN MEALS
veli jambu *see* ROSE APPLE
velvet and velveting *see* TECHNIQUES
VELVET TAMARIND
velvet apple *see* PERSIMMON
velvet, velveting *see* TECHNIQUES
ventayam *see* FENUGREEK
verali pallam *see* CEYLON OLIVE
veralu *see* CEYLON OLIVE
vermicelli *see* NOODLES

VETIVER
VIETNAM
VIETNAMESE MINT
villa *see* WOODAPPLE
villati *see* WOODAPPLE
vilvam *see* BAEL FRUIT
VINEGAR
vudi *see* BANANA

W

waan hom *see* GINGER, AROMATIC
waan teendin *see* GINGER, AROMATIC
wah-bho-khmyit *see* BAMBOO
wakame *see* SEAWEED
WALNUT
walu jepan *see* CHOKO
walu *see* FISH (Spanish mackerel)
wan dou *see* LEGUMES & PULSES
    (Green pea)
wansuy *see* CORIANDER HERB
WASABI
wasabi no-ki-no-ka *see* DRUMSTICK
WATER CHESTNUT
water convolvulus *see* WATER SPINACH
WATER LILY
WATER SPINACH
water chestnut powder *see* FLOURS &
    STARCHES (Water chestnut starch)
WATERCRESS
watermelon *see* MELONS, SWEET
watha wal *see* HIBISCUS
wax gourd *see* GOURDS
wax bean *see* LEGUMES & PULSES
    (Green bean)
wazwan *see* SAFFRON
white fungus *see* MUSHROOMS &
    FUNGI
white gram bean *see* LEGUMES &
    PULSES
white wood ear *see* MUSHROOMS &
    FUNGI (White fungus)
WHITEBAIT
wi *see* AMBARELLA
wi-tree *see* AMBARELLA
wijen *see* SESAME SEED
WILD RICE SHOOTS

wild betel leaf *see* CHA PLU
wild pepper *see* SZECHWAN PEPPER
WINES & SPIRITS
winged bean *see* LEGUMES & PULSES
winter melon *see* GOURDS, Ash gourd
wok *see* UTENSILS
WOLFBERRY
wong bok *see* CABBAGE
wong dau *see* SOY BEAN, DRIED
wong geung fun *see* TURMERIC
wong nga bak *see* CABBAGE
    (Chinese cabbage)
wong-dau *see* LEGUMES & PULSES
    (Soy bean)
wong-keong *see* TURMERIC
woo tau *see* TARO
wood ear *see* MUSHROOMS & FUNGI
    (Black fungus)
wood fungus *see* MUSHROOMS &
    FUNGI
WOODAPPLE
woon *see* AGAR-AGAR
woon sen *see* BEAN STARCH
    NOODLES
woro wari *see* HIBISCUS
wu ta cai *see* CABBAGE
    (Rosette bok choy)
wun mo *see* TEA
wun yee *see* MUSHROOMS & FUNGI
    (Black fungus)

X

xa *see* LEMON GRASS
XACUTI
XANTHOXYLUM SPP.
xian cai *see* AMARANTH
xiang he *see* GINGER, MIOGA
xoi *see* RICE

Y

YABBIE
yabu soba *see* FLOURS & STARCHES
    (Buckwheat flour)
yaki-nori *see* SEAWEED
yakimo *see* POTATO, SWEET

yakimono *see* TECHNIQUES
YAM
YAM BEAN
yam mamuang *see* MANGO
yamabukusu *see* VINEGAR
yan yang *see* AMARANTH
yang po ho *see* MINT
yao dou *see* CASHEW
yard-long bean *see* LEGUMES & PULSES
yatu *see* FISH (Tuna)
ye thit eir thee *see* WATER CHESTNUT
yee *see* VELVET TAMARIND
yeera *see* CUMIN
yellow portulaca *see* PURSLANE
yen wuo *see* BIRD'S NEST
yerba buena *see* MINT
yin choy *see* AMARANTH
yin waw *see* BIRD'S NEST
yintsieu *see* WINES & SPIRITS
yira *see* FENNEL
ylang ylang *see* ESSENCES
YOGHURT
yu chee *see* SHARK'S FIN
yu pasir *see* FISH (Shark)
yu *see* TARO
yu to *see* FISH MAW
yu-chin *see* TURMERIC
yuba *see* BEAN CURD
yuca *see* CASSAVA
yuen sai *see* CORIANDER HERB
YUM CHA
yuugao *see* GOURDS (Bottle gourd)
yuzu *see* CITRON

Z

zabalin *see* LEMON GRASS
zaffran *see* SAFFRON
zalipho thi *see* NUTMEG
zaru *see* UTENSIL
ZEDOARY
zeera *see* CUMIN
zeera pani *see* TAMARIND
zenmai *see* FERN, FIDDLEHEAD
ZUCCHINI
zuiki *see* TARO
zushi *see* SUSHI